THE END OF EMPIRES AND A WORLD REMADE

The End of Empires and a World Remade

A GLOBAL HISTORY OF DECOLONIZATION

Martin Thomas

PRINCETON UNIVERSITY PRESS

PRINCETON & OXFORD

Published by Princeton University Press
41 William Street, Princeton, New Jersey 08540
99 Banbury Road, Oxford OX2 6JX

press.princeton.edu

All Rights Reserved

Library of Congress Cataloging-in-Publication Data

Names: Thomas, Martin, 1964– author.
Title: The end of empires and a world remade : a global history of decolonization / Martin Thomas.
Description: Princeton, New Jersey ; Oxford, United Kingdom : Princeton University Press, [2024] | Includes bibliographical references and index.
Identifiers: LCCN 2023030324 (print) | LCCN 2023030325 (ebook) | ISBN 9780691190921 (hardback : acid-free paper) | ISBN 9780691254449 (e-book)
Subjects: LCSH: Decolonization—History. | Globalization—History. | Wealth—Moral and ethical aspects. | BISAC: HISTORY / World | HISTORY / Modern / 20th Century / General
Classification: LCC JV151 .T563 2024 (print) | LCC JV151 (ebook) | DDC 325/.309—dc23/eng/20230801
LC record available at https://lccn.loc.gov/2023030324
LC ebook record available at https://lccn.loc.gov/2023030325

British Library Cataloging-in-Publication Data is available

Editorial: Priya Nelson and Emma Wagh
Production Editorial: Natalie Baan
Jacket Design: Chris Ferrante
Production: Danielle Amatucci
Publicity: Carmen Jimenez and Alyssa Sanford
Copyeditors: Gráinne O'Shea and Katherine Harper

Jacket image: The first Algerian refugees from Tunisia wait to cross the electrified border in eastern Algeria on May 30, 1962, as they return to their country. Source: Getty Images.

This book has been composed in Miller

Printed in the United States of America

10 9 8 7 6 5 4 3 2 1

CONTENTS

ABBREVIATIONS AND TERMS

AAPSO   Afro-Asian People's Solidarity Organization, founded 1957.

ACKBA   American Committee to Keep Biafra Alive.

AEF   Afrique Equatoriale Française: the federation of French Equatorial Africa, comprising the French Congo, Oubangui-Chari, Gabon, and Chad. The former mandate of French Cameroon, declared a UN trust territory in 1945, was economically tied to AEF.

AFD   Agence française de développement.

AFPFL   Anti-Fascist People's Freedom League (Burma).

ALN   Armée de Libération Nationale, armed wing of the Algerian FLN.

ANZUS   Australia–New Zealand–United States defense treaty, 1951.

AOF   Afrique Occidentale Française: the federation of French West Africa, comprising Senegal, Mauritania, French Soudan, Niger, Ivory Coast (Côte d'Ivoire), Guinea, Dahomey, and, from 1948, Upper Volta (Haute-Volta). Federal authorities in Dakar also retained links with Togo, another former mandate, made a UN trust territory in 1945.

ARC   Asian Relations Conference (India, 1947).

ASSRA   Assistances Sanitaires et Sociétés rurales auxiliaires (in Algeria).

AU   African Union, launched in 2002 as successor to the OAU.

BMEO   British Middle East Office.

BNA   British Nationality Act (1948).

CAF   Central African Federation, established 1953; dissolved 1963.

CAO   Committee of African Organizations (African student group in Britain).

CDC   Commonwealth Development Corporation (British, established 1947).

CGT   Confédération Générale du Travail, French trade union confederation.

CICRC   Commission Internationale Contre le Régime Concentrationnaire (Commission against the Concentration Camp Regime).

COMECON   Council for Mutual Economic Assistance (Soviet-directed).

COREMO   Comité Revolucionário de Moçambique.

CPC   Colonial Policy Committee (of the British government).

CPGB   Communist Party of Great Britain.

CPP   Convention People's Party, founded in the Gold Coast, 1949.

CRIT   Conference (of Asian Countries) on the Relaxation of International Tension, 1955.

CRO   Commonwealth Relations Office.

DGS   Direção-Geral de Segurança (Portuguese security service).

DOMS   Départements d'outre-mer, French overseas departments, post-1946.

DRV   Democratic Republic of Vietnam, established in Hanoi in 1945.

DST   Direction de la Surveillance du Territoire, French internal security service.

ECOWAS   Economic Community of West African States.

EEC   European Economic Community.

EFO   Economic and Financial Organization (of the League of Nations).

EMB   Empire Marketing Board, (British) in existence from 1926 to 1933.

EMSI   Équipes Médico-Sociales Itinérantes (in Algeria).

ENA   Étoile Nord-Africaine: North African Star; Algerian nationalist party, established 1926.

EOKA   Ethniki Organosis Kyprion Agoniston: National Organization of Cypriot Fighters.

FAO   Food and Agriculture Organization (of the United Nations).

FCO   Foreign and Commonwealth Office (British).

FIDES   Fonds d'Investissement pour le Développement Économique et Social: Economic and Social Development Fund, set up in 1946.

FLN   Front de Libération Nationale, Algerian National Liberation Front, founded in 1954.

FRELIMO   Frente de Libertação de Moçambique.

GATT   General Agreement on Tariffs and Trade.

GCO   General Counter-Offensive (in Vietnam).

GIEDC   Groupement internationale d'études pour le développement du Congo.

GPRA   Gouvernment Provisoire de la République Algérienne (Algerian provisional government, established 1958).

G77   Group of 77 (coalition of developing countries).

Haganah   Zionist paramilitary organization.

Histadrut   Federation of Jewish Labor.

IBRD   International Bank for Reconstruction and Development.

ICFTU   International Confederation of Free Trade Unions.

ICP   Indochinese Communist Party, formed in 1930.

ICRC   International Committee of the Red Cross.

ILO   International Labour Organization.

ILRM   International League of the Rights of Man.

IMF   International Monetary Fund.

INA   Indian National Army.

Irgun Tzva'i Le'umi	National Military Organization in the Land of Israel.
ITO	International Trade Organization.
KAU	Kenya African Union.
LAI	League against Imperialism.
Lehi b'Herut b'Yisrael	Fighters for the Freedom of Israel.
LNHO	League of Nations' Health Organization.
LZVN	Liga zur Verteidigung der Negerrasse: 'League for the Defense of the Negro Race'.
Mau Mau	Kenyan anticolonial movement, sometimes translated as 'the ravenous ones'.
MCA	Malayan Chinese Association.
MCF	Movement for Colonial Freedom (British pressure group).
MCP	Malayan Communist Party.
MDP	Masai Development Plan (in Kenya).
MDRM	Mouvement démocratique de la rénovation malgache, Madagascar nationalist party, founded in 1946.
MEO	Military Evacuation Organization (Indian subcontinent), founded September 1947.
MNA	Mouvement National Algérien, rival to the FLN, led by Messali Hadj.
MPAJA	Malayan Peoples Anti-Japanese Army, largely ethnically Chinese guerrilla force in Malaya in the Second World War.
MPS	Minorities' Protection Section (of the League of Nations).
MRLA	Malayan Races' Liberation Army, armed wing of the Malayan Communist Party.
MRP	Mouvement Républicain Populaire, French Christian Democrat Party, founded in 1944.
MSS	Malayan Security Service.

MTLD   Mouvement pour le Triomphe des Libertés démocratiques, Algerian nationalist party, forerunner to the FLN.

NAACP   National Association for the Advancement of Colored People, founded 1909.

NAM   Non-Aligned Movement.

NATO   North Atlantic Treaty Organization, set up in April 1949.

NIEO   New International Economic Order.

OAS   Organisation de l'Armée Secrète, reactionary counterterror group.

OAS   Organization of American States, established in 1948.

OAU   Organization of African Unity, founded 1963.

OS   Organisation Spéciale, pre-FLN paramilitary group linked to the MTLD.

OTC   Overseas Trade Corporation (British, founded 1957).

PAIGC   Partido Africano para a Independência da Guiné e Cabo Verde.

PAVN   People's Army of Vietnam.

PCF   Parti Communiste Français, French Communist Party, established in 1920.

PIDE   Polícia Internacional e de Defesa do Estado (Portuguese).

PLA   People's Liberation Army, national army of the People's Republic of China.

PMC   Permanent Mandates Commission (of the League of Nations).

PMI   Protection Maternelle et Infantile (in French Morocco).

PPA   Parti Populaire Algérien, Algerian Popular Party, founded in 1937.

PSD   Parti social démocrate: [Malagasy] Social Democratic Party.

RAF   Royal Air Force.

RDA   Rassemblement Démocratique Africain, established in 1946.

RENAMO   Resistência Nacional Moçambicana.

RF   Rhodesian Front.

RPF   Rassemblement du Peuple Français, Gaullist movement, launched in 1947.

SAA   Syndicat Agricole Africain: West African planters' association.

SAS   Sections Administratives Spécialisées, army civil affairs specialists in Algeria.

SAU   Sections Administratives Urbaines (urban counterpart to the SAS).

SDECE   Service de Documentation Extérieure et de Contre-Espionnage, French overseas intelligence service, broadly equivalent to Britain's MI6.

SEATO   South East Asia Treaty Organization, established 1955.

SFIO   Section Française de l'Internationale Ouvrière, unified French Socialist Party, founded in 1905.

SIG   Special Investigations Group (of the British Ministry of Defence).

SIP   Sociétés indigènes de prévoyance (French Empire rural credit agencies).

TOMs   Territoires d'outre-mer: French overseas territories, post-1946.

UCTAN   Union Générale des Travailleurs d'Afrique Noire.

UDC   Union of Democratic Control, British pressure group founded in 1914.

UDHR   Universal Declaration of Human Rights (December 1948).

UDI   Unilateral Declaration of Independence (by Southern Rhodesia).

UDMA   Union démocratique de Manifeste algérien, Algerian proto-nationalist group.

UGCC   United Gold Coast Convention, founded in 1947.

UMHK   Union Minière du Haut Katanga.

UMNO   United Malays National Organization.

UNCTAD   United Nations Conference on Trade and Development.

UNESCO   United Nations Educational, Scientific and Cultural Organization.

UNIA   Universal Negro Improvement Association, established 1914.

UNICEF   United Nations International Children's Emergency Fund.

UNITA   União Nacional para a Independência Total de Angola.

UNRWA   United Nations Relief and Works Agency.

UNSCOP   United Nations Special Committee on Palestine.

UPA   Union of Angolan Peoples.

UPC   Union des Populations du Cameroun.

VNQDD   Viet Nam Quoc Dan Dong: Vietnam National Party, founded in 1927.

VWP   Dang Lao Dong Viet Nam: Vietnamese Workers' Party, designation for the Vietnamese Communists from 1951.

WFDY   World Federation of Democratic Youth.

WFTU   World Federation of Trade Unions.

WHO   World Health Organization.

ZANU   Zimbabwe African National Union.

ZAPU   Zimbabwe African People's Union.

ACKNOWLEDGMENTS

THERE'S A LOT of book ahead of us, so I'll keep my acknowledgments short. Although brief, every thank you that follows is heartfelt. Each of the groups and individuals mentioned has been fundamental in getting me over the finishing line of a project that, in many ways, goes back over thirty years. I owe huge debts of gratitude, first to the Leverhulme Trust, which funded Major Research Fellowships and an International Research Network that made the research and writing feasible. Another UK-based scholarly funder, the Independent Social Research Foundation, supported a project on imperialist humanitarianism that brought me into lasting contact with the inspiring community of ISRF fellows in social sciences and the humanities. I've had constant support from colleagues and students at the University of Exeter, whose Centers for Imperial and Global History and for Histories of Violence and Conflict have become terrific forums for the exchange of ideas.

A wonderful 2019 semester at the Netherlands Institute of Advanced Studies in Amsterdam, as part of the 'Comparing the Wars of Decolonization' project team led by Thijs Brocades Zaalberg and Bart Luttikhuis, transformed my thinking about colonial violence. For that, plus their great company, I thank all the team members, including Pierre Asselin, Huw Bennett, Roel Frakking, Brian Linn, Peter Romijn, Stef Scagliola, and Natalya Vince. (And thanks again for the All Bran, Natalya's mom.) Visitors to the project, including David Anderson, Saphia Arezki, Miguel Bandeira Jerónimo, Raphaëlle Branche, Elizabeth Buettner, Rémy Limpach, and Kim Wagner, helped me better understand how to approach decolonization conflicts. An international research network on 'Understanding Insurgencies', co-organized with my Exeter colleague Gareth Curless, provided the platform for seven workshops over three years that, again, proved how much we learn as historians of empire from collaborative research across countries and disciplines: a special thank you to everyone who took part. Closer to home, it's been a pleasure and a privilege getting to know Alex Zhukov and Tanya Zhukova.

Turning ideas into books needs the help of a great press. The team at Princeton has been exemplary: generous with their time, thoughtful with their comments, and patient with their author. To my editor, Priya Nelson, production assistant, Emma Wagh, production editor, Natalie Baan, and

[xv]

copyeditors, Gráinne O'Shea and Katherine Harper, a massive thanks. I'm also indebted to Tarak Barkawi and Nicholas White. Their forensic analysis as press readers was matched by their generosity of spirit in suggesting improvements. I could not have asked for more. I thank Getty Images for awarding image rights. And thank you to my co-authors, Andrew Thompson and Roel Frakking, and to Cambridge University Press, Cornell University Press, and Oxford University Press for allowing me to use elements from chapter contributions I've published with them, credited below.

A last word to Suzy: thanks for everything; you're the one.

Martin Thomas, "The Challenge of an Absent Peace in the French and British Empires after 1919," in *Peacemaking and International Order after the First World War* ed. Peter Jackson, William Mulligan, and Glenda Sluga (Cambridge, UK: Cambridge University Press, 2023), 151–75.

Roel Frakking and Martin Thomas, "Windows onto the Microdynamics of Insurgent and Counterinsurgent Violence: Evidence from Late Colonial Southeast Asia and Africa Compared," in *Empire's Violent End: Comparing Dutch, British, and French Wars of Decolonization, 1945–1962* ed. Thijs Brocades Zaalberg and Bart Luttikhuis (Ithaca, NY: Cornell University Press, 2022), 78–126.

Martin Thomas and Andrew Thompson, "Rethinking Decolonization: A New Research Agenda for the Twenty-First Century," in *The Oxford Handbook of the Ends of Empire* ed. Thomas and Thompson (Oxford: Oxford University Press, 2018), 1–26.

Martin Thomas, "Decolonization and the Civilianization of Violence," in *The Oxford Handbook of Late Colonial Insurgencies and Counter-Insurgencies* ed. Martin Thomas and Gareth Curless (Oxford: Oxford University Press, 2023), 141–60.

ENDING EMPIRES

Ending Empire and Remaking the World

DECEMBER 1963 FOUND BARBARA Castle in Kenya. Labour Party politician, writer, and parliamentary voice of Britain's leading anticolonial pressure group, the Movement for Colonial Freedom, Castle arrived in Nairobi on the 10th. She was there to celebrate. Hours after her arrival, Castle attended a multiracial 'civic ball'. Diary entries record her thrill at what was to come: 'Atmosphere so gay: races mixing equally and naturally—so diff. from the old Kenya! I twisted and jived uninhibitedly and I felt like a 20 yr old'.[1] The next day brought wildlife-watching before another night of celebration. The evening began with drinks on the terrace of the Lord Delamere Bar, once an exclusive settler haunt, now, in Castle's oddly colonialist metaphor, the 'Piccadilly Circus of a world society'.[2] Six hours later, Castle was an honored guest at the Uhuru (Freedom) Stadium for Kenya's independence ceremony. Other British dignitaries included Anglican priest and antiracism campaigner Michael Scott, Oxford anthropologist and Colonial Office adviser Margery Perham, the departing colonial governor Malcolm MacDonald, and Prince Philip, the Duke of Edinburgh. The duke took the salute of a King's African Rifles parade marching to the strains of "Auld Lang Syne." Jarringly inappropriate, the traditional invocation of a freezing Scottish new year was meant to convey the warmth between hosts and visitors. Besides, the regimental band knew it well— they were required to play it often. The music done, MacDonald offered Britain's congratulations to Kenya's first president, Jomo Kenyatta, as the Union Jack was lowered for the last time on the stroke of midnight, December 11, 1963.[3]

The imperial choreography of an end to empire was one thing, but the lived experience, for ordinary Kenyans and honored guests alike, was rather different. Castle arrived late. She got stuck in a traffic jam of cars and minibuses convoying people to the stadium. Anxious not to miss out, she tore her clothes clambering over a fence, to find thousands already celebrating with singing and dances of their own. The band was drowned out. So too was the Duke of Edinburgh's whispered aside to Kenyatta just before that flag came down: 'Want to reconsider? There's still time'.[4]

Ten years earlier, thousands of Nairobi residents had faced beatings, expulsion, and internment, accused of association with Mau Mau in a war against British colonialism. Kenyatta had been locked up for much of it but emerged on the side of the conflict's 'loyalist' winners.[5] Was December 11, 1963, a celebration of victory or the burial of a traumatic, divisive past? Arguably, it was neither. Beyond Kenya, ceremonies of this type were commonplace in the early 1960s.[6] Formal declarations of independence were supposed to mark something definitive, a societal transition from one political condition, colonial dependency, to another, sovereign independence. Liberation from discriminatory foreign rule was meant to enable authentic freedom, both individual and collective.[7] But decolonization was not a single event, once accomplished, forever done. Processes of ending empire and breaking with colonialism were messier, more attenuated and less final than independence ceremonies suggested.

Ending Empire?

Empires, until relatively recently, were everywhere.[8] A minimalist definition of what they were is the foreign enforcement of sovereign political control over another society in a delimited territorial space. But that's not enough. Describing the varieties and degrees of imperial influence, and the lived experience of empire, demands more than such coldly geopolitical terms. Eurocentric or Westphalian notions of sovereign independence tied to statehood and international legal recognition were difficult to translate to colonial spaces, where relational politics, religious loyalties, and kinship obligations suggest more layered, pluralistic attachments to multiple sources of authority.[9] Economic influence, sometimes exercised without 'formal' political dominion, could be crucial. Most importantly, the 'political control' over territorial space fails to capture the fragilities of colonial governance, its unevenness across vast geographical areas whose territorial limits were often porous. Movements of people, goods, money, ideas, and beliefs were impossible to confine within a single colonial polity.[10] The tensions between movement and restriction, between cosmopolitanism and compliance, between private spheres of life beyond colonialism and lives constrained by it, would lend decolonization local variegations that nationalist political schema rarely captured.

For most of those affected by it, opposing empire was more visceral than ideological. The constraint of rights and opportunities was part of something bigger, the restriction of freedoms—to move, to associate, to own certain things, to practice one's culture. These limitations were, and are, what makes colonialism possible. More a pervasive social condition than an exact political relationship, the colonialism of empire describes not just the maintenance of unequal political relations between a controlling imperial power and a dependent society, but the socioeconomic hierarchies, the cultural discriminations, and the racial inequalities such relations entail.[11]

Imperialism, understood as the ideas and practices of empire, lingers on. So do numerous silences and occlusions surrounding it, a consequence of what one analyst has described in a British governmental context as a systematic 'deprioritizing of empire'.[12] Empires may no longer dominate global politics, but multiple colonial legacies endure.[13] Some are so invidious that they cry out for our attention: acute inequalities of global wealth, uneven access to the resources essential to human security, and the persistence of societal racisms. In other ways, searching out colonialism's imprint seems easier. Less than half a century ago, foreign colonial rulers were still geographically widespread. The job is to work out how much changed when they left or were compelled to go. Elsewhere, empire's impact is more oblique but remains imminent even so. From the use of land and the extraction of resources to borders and administrative structures, the language and patterns of global commerce, and the social and cultural identifications that people make, our contemporary world is inflected with recent imperial history.

This is where decolonization comes in. It stands alongside the twentieth century's world wars, the Cold War, and the longer arc of globalization as one of the four great determinants of geopolitical change in living memory.[14] The chapters to come suggest that decolonization was one globally connected process. Their cumulative argument is that we cannot understand decolonization's global impact by examining individual empires or single colonial histories. Decolonization worked as much across nations, empires, and boundaries as within them. It proceeded by forging new global connections that reordered relations between First World, Second World, and Third.[15] Colonialism's devastating impact on the 'Fourth' World of indigenous peoples and first nation communities was replicated in their sublimation within a broader 'Third World' designation. Decolonization, indeed, is why this three worlds construction came to be used in the first place. Usually portrayed as disintegrative, decolonization was anything but. Instead, decolonization is intrinsically connected to globalization, whether that is conceived as a process of increasing global connectivity or as competing ideological visions of how the world might be reconfigured through economic, cultural, and political exchange. The conditions and possibilities of globalization—or rival globalizations—assured the supporters of decolonization greater access to essential resources, to wider networks of influence, and to global audiences. But globalization could also hinder. Its neoliberal variant has reinforced economic inequalities and facilitated imperial forms of influence, making decolonization harder to complete.[16] The first section of this book tries to explain why the deck was so heavily stacked against newly independent nations.

Ending empires occasioned many of the longest wars of the twentieth century, reminding us that decolonization was more than a political contest.[17] It energized different ideas of belonging and transnational connection, of sovereignty and independence and the struggles necessary to achieve them. Late colonial conflicts spurred other connections as the colonized 'weak' built transnational networks of support to overcome the military and economic advantages of 'strong' imperial overseers. Insurgencies spread. The counterinsurgencies that followed triggered rights abuses whose global exposure left empires shamed and morally disarmed. In its violence as in its politics and economics, decolonization reshaped globalization just as globalization conditioned decolonization.[18]

This book is about what brought down European overseas empires, whose constituent territories were separated by oceanic distance but conjoined by global processes of colonialism. The opening three chapters deal with ideas and concepts. The first concentrates on what decolonization means and when it occurred, examining its twentieth-century chronology. The second chapter addresses the relationship between decolonization and globalization. And the third considers alternatives to decolonization, revisiting debates over the rights and wants of people living under colonial rule. Scholars familiar with the panoply of reformist engagement with empire, with proposals for different governing structures and pooled sovereignties, and with diverse viewpoints that were never simply 'anticolonial' remind us that decolonization was not a foregone conclusion.[19] We know that claims to nationhood built on various models of sovereign independence eventually prevailed. But what contexts made these outcomes more likely?

My attempt to answer this question accounts for the transition from part I to part II of this book.

Beginning with chapter 4, my attention shifts toward factors which, it seems to me, were crucial in triggering European colonial collapse. Briefly summarized, they are these:

- issues of political economy;
- the global weight of anticolonial opposition and rights claims;
- the transformative aftereffects of two world wars;
- territorial partitions;
- the violence of those fighting to end empire and those fighting to keep it; and
- the vulnerability of the colonial civilians at the epicenter of decolonization.

The list could be much longer. Questions of identity and culture, gender and ethnicity, ideology and ethics are each central to the factors I've highlighted. So are other, perhaps more familiar matters of geopolitics, international organization, and a globalizing Cold War. It would also be wrong to assume that identifying causes makes prioritizing among them easy. The problem, of course, is that the conventions of historical analysis demand such differentiation. So the dilemma for anyone attempting to compare how and why European empires were brought down is twofold: first, to distinguish between major and minor in teasing out causes, and, second, to avoid the oversimplification of a complex historical process by ascribing too much transformative power to a single factor. This is a difficult line to tread. Decolonization was pluri-continental, supranational, and globally comparable at the same time as it was locally specific and highly contingent.[20] These traits are not contradictory. Its local iterations might defy generalization, but decolonization had distinctive patterns nonetheless. I've tried to strike a balance here. I make frequent use of archival sources to make the case, although the work of other scholars in history and social science figures prominently throughout. My aim in identifying particular triggers and their consequences is to keep those global patterns in view without losing sight of the people caught up in the decolonization process.

Remaking the World?

Placing decolonization within a temporal frame, beginning with the First World War and ending somewhere in the 1970s, makes good sense insofar as the great majority of formal decolonizations occurred at some point within these years.[21] But there are gaps. Colonies still exist. Economic dependencies are real. Attitudinally and emotionally, colonialism is with us still.[22] Twentieth-century decolonization was transformative even so. It lent political coherence to the global South as a transregional bloc united in its rejection of the white racial privilege that for so long underpinned rich-world politics. As applied to Africa, Asia, and Latin America, that shorthand term 'global South' encompassed a wide spectrum of nations and dependencies, from middle-income countries to colonial territories. For all that, the global South was identifiable less by geography than by shared opposition to the colonialist interventions and discriminatory practices of imperial powers. For its constituent territories, ending empire was integral not just to the rights claims or freedom struggles of particular nations, but also to changing the north–south dynamics of rich world and poor. As historian Angela Zimmerman has suggested, by the early 1900s the global South was evident in a 'colonial political economy' at once tied to, but kept distinct from, rich-world capitalist economies by the racial hierarchies of colonialism. Put differently, it was not the equator but rather what W. E. B. Du Bois identified as 'the color line' that separated global South from global North.[23]

In the 120 years or so since Du Bois mapped out the global color line, the collapse of formal colonial control, the end of empires, or, as specialists usually term it, decolonization has reshaped the world's political geography. Its impact on political culture—on the ways regimes, governments, and social movements justify their behavior—has been equally profound. Whatever the arguments about its finality, rejecting colonialism was the necessary precursor to the creation of new nation-states, new ideological attachments, and new political alignments in much of the global South. For some, that rejection did not produce support for decolonization but, rather, for alternate claims to political inclusion, social entitlements, and cultural respect: aspirations thought to be achievable within rather than beyond the structures of empire. For others, anticolonialism demanded a fuller decolonization—of politics, of economies, and of minds. These more radical and rejectionist objectives implied profound social transformations, placing decolonization within a spectrum of revolutionary change.[24]

The historical record lends weight to this revolutionary reading of events. Decolonization fostered bold experiments in social, racial, and gender equality. It changed prevailing ideas about sovereignty, citizenship, and collective and individual rights.[25] Its contestations stimulated new types of social activism, innovative forms of international cooperation between governments, and a global surge in transnational networking

between nonstate actors, activist groups, and those that colonialism otherwise excluded.[26] Some of the ideas involved were locally specific, but many
more were shared, borrowed, or adapted among the peoples caught up in
fights for basic rights, for self-determination, for the dignity of cultural
recognition.[27]

So where are we? If decolonization was once depicted in reductive
terms as the sequence of high-level reforms leading to a definitive constitutional transfer of power, it now risks being freighted with so many
elements that it loses coherence. At one level, this book's purpose is thus
a basic one: to rethink what decolonization is. The end of empires catalyzed new international coalitions and diverse transnational networks
in the second half of the twentieth century. It triggered partitions and
wars. It challenged ideas about individual and collective rights, and which
mattered most. And it shaped the ways in which globalization gathered
momentum. Decolonization, in other words, signifies the biggest reconfiguration of world politics ever seen.

PART I

Globalizing Decolonization

CHAPTER ONE

Decolonization and the End of Empires

THE NUMBERS SEEM to speak for themselves. In the two hundred years since the American Revolution of 1776, more than 160 dependent territories either achieved sovereign independence or were assimilated into larger states and confederations. Stretch back the chronology by another couple of centuries to encompass the initial spread of European imperial dominion in the Americas, Asia, and Africa, and the end of empires becomes the mirror to their beginnings. What sociologist Raewyn Connell describes as 'truly the first world war' spanned four centuries, during which European armies subjugated much of the world's population.[1]

The reversal of this process—the disintegration of European overseas empires and their replacement by a multiplicity of sovereign nation-states— is handily described as decolonization.[2] Jan Jansen and Jürgen Osterhammel suggest that decolonization might even be conceptualized 'as an apparatus for the serial production of sovereignty'.[3] Arguments continue about how 'real' such sovereign independence is.[4] Rightly so: identifying decolonization with a shift from rule by foreigners to government by locals is analytically limiting. Its antecedent, colonization, left imprints in patterns of inequality, in degraded environments, and in systems of belief that could not be undone by a simple handover of political power.[5] Historian of Pacific territories Tracey Banivanua Mar puts it nicely, suggesting that 'uncolonizing' is more gradual, impossible to map onto neat timelines of imperial departure.[6] For indigenous peoples of the 'Fourth World' in particular, claims to decolonization remain substantially unrealized.[7]

But still, those numbers. From a global perspective, the direction of historical travel looks pretty clear—toward a decolonization destination signposted by empire disintegration and the proliferation of nation-states.[8] At its foundation in July 1945, the United Nations boasted a membership of fifty-one states. That figure had climbed to seventy-six a decade later. The year 1955 alone saw a record-breaking addition of sixteen new members.[9] The numbers crept over the one hundred mark in 1961. Disbarred from the United Nations until its eventual admission in October 1971, the People's Republic of China (PRC) still rode the African decolonization wave.[10] Beijing hosted fifty 'official' African delegations in 1959 and ninety-eight a year later. Having lent material support to what it considered the most promising African revolutionary regimes of the late 1950s—Gamal Abdel Nasser's Egypt, Algeria's FLN government-in-exile, and Ahmed Sékou Touré's Guinea—by 1964 Chinese military advisers based in Kwame Nkrumah's Ghana coordinated support to client movements throughout the continent.[11] UN membership, meanwhile, surged again during the 'African decade' of the 1960s, from ninety-nine members in 1960 to 127 in 1970. This rate of growth was exceeded in the 1970s, thanks primarily to the admission of four Arabian Gulf states in 1971, West and East Germany in 1973, and an influx of former Portuguese colonial dependencies in 1975–1976. With the addition of Zimbabwe in 1980, the United Nations housed 154 national delegations. Numbers climbed steadily, although more slowly from the 1980s onward, peaking at 193 with the admission of South Sudan in 2011.[12]

Processes of Decolonization

My argument begins from recognition that decolonization signifies a global historical process. Individual empires decolonized. But we cannot tease out the causes and consequences of decolonization if we limit ourselves to analyzing one empire alone. A solitary example of a colonial path to statehood, no matter how instructive, is unlikely to explain decolonization as a whole, so why should we expect a single empire to exemplify something much bigger? To borrow the language of international relations, whether in terms of an international order of states or an international society in which interactions between national actors followed distinct economic, political, and cultural patterns, decolonization increased the number of players on the field more than it changed the rules.[13]

From the United Nations' hierarchies of power to patterns of neoliberal capitalism and prevailing ideas of international law and governmental legitimacy, international politics and trade retained 'a normative architecture intrinsically tied to European [and, more recently, American] supremacy'.[14] Decolonization changed the world inexorably even so. With the end of empires there were over 150 national players, where barely fifty years earlier there were fewer than half that number.

Most former colonial territories, in achieving independence, asserted the right to national self-determination, commonly understood as a community's legitimate claim to govern itself. Recognized in international law, self-determination has both internal and external aspects: internally, the right of a people to choose a government representative of their wishes, externally, the right to live free of foreign interference.[15] Problems abound. Is self-determination a projection of Western political thinking, born of the liberal internationalism that decolonizers opposed? What makes a community or people into a 'nation', and what confers their right to self-determination? Are its precepts fairly applied within societies internally divided by ethnicity, politics, or religion, let alone by other indexes of gender, sexuality, or class? Does its political form require economic substance to make self-determination meaningful? All of these questions will be tackled in the chapters comprising part II of this book.

The problems in realizing self-determination, from differential rights to persistent inequalities, should not, though, distract us from the fact that, after the Second World War, decolonization as understood in international law signified the concession of national self-determination to sovereign peoples.[16] It remade a world, not just of many more states but of different transnational connections as well. To be sure, the distribution of power, wealth, and opportunities between them was sharply uneven, but the withering of empire signified a profound, multicontinental shift. Social movements and nongovernmental organizations changed their ways of doing things in response to it. Movements of people, goods, and ideas were transformed by it.[17]

These processes are perhaps easier to understand not as waves, which come and go, but as currents, whose intensity might change but whose flows never stop. As we shall see, the strength of these currents gathered over the middle decades of the twentieth century, from the 1920s to the 1960s. Viewed as a process with increasing momentum, it becomes easier to see how and why decolonization changed international politics, altered cultural interactions within and between nations, and provoked several of the defining conflicts of the twentieth century. That this process is not entirely done is confirmed by what decolonization failed to do. The pillars of self-determination, domestic jurisdiction, and territorial integrity have been rocked to their foundations since empires supposedly decolonized, so much so that some scholars insist we live in a new imperial age in which stronger powers violate state sovereignty almost at will.[18] At the other extreme, critics of universal rights point out that their moral cosmopolitanism is also imperialistic, claiming ethical authority for humanitarian interventionism in former colonial spaces.[19]

Similar reservations appear as we move from the realm of sovereignty and international law back to material concerns. As it turned out, the unmaking of empires did not, in and of itself, destroy patterns of unequal trade and economic domination. No matter how revolutionary the takeover of political power, no matter how total the military defeat of an imperial ruler, colonialism was never abruptly turned off. Its aftereffects persisted, registering in debt burdens, externally imposed 'structural adjustments', and the degradation of ecosystems despoiled by extractive industries or poisoned, mined, and deforested during colonial military operations.[20] Another aspect of these aftereffects is what might be described as colonial blowback, the ways in which once-colonized societies have reshaped their former imperial metropoles through migration, changing rights to citizenship and claims to social inclusion.[21]

For all that, the gulf separating the wealthy nations of the industrialized global North from the poorer nations of the global South is still evident decades after 'formal' decolonization occurred. For many in these poorer regions life expectancy and living standards have improved since national independence. It would, though, be confusing correlation with causation to conclude that decolonization ameliorated economic conditions within once-dependent territories. The eclipse of colonial governance created new conditions of possibility, but it did not transform life chances overnight. Decolonization triggered big changes in political affiliation, in the expression of cultural attachments, and in people's claims to rights, dignity, and respect; sometimes, too, in the fabric of relationships and family life, the patterns of land use and work, and the aspirations and opportunities around which human histories cohere. But it did not change the north–south geometry of global capitalism. That being the case, I'll be suggesting that processes of decolonization were less transformative economically than they were politically, culturally, or ecologically.

Ideas of Decolonization

Before grappling with the finality or incompleteness of empire collapse, it's worth thinking about the specialist vocabulary to hand. Specialists may use 'decolonization' as shorthand for the disintegration of modern overseas empires and transitions from colony to statehood. In the public sphere, though, decolonization is more readily identifiable with something else: the crying need for an overhaul of public culture, from place names and statues to museum holdings, media, academic curricula, and political language.[22]

Within countries implicated in empire, slavery, and their legacies of racial discrimination, public calls to decolonize are bound up with the contemporary condition of those societies.[23] Demands for decolonization in this context turn on attitudinal change toward histories that societies, as refracted through their public institutions, laws, and police practices, their museums, monuments, and heritage sectors, find difficult to confront.[24] In shining a spotlight on police brutality and the cultural blindness of some public institutions to structural racism, Black Lives Matter and Rhodes Must Fall have galvanized antiracist opposition to what they decry as colonialist behavior.[25] People striving for 'decoloniality' emphasize the enduring tendency to construct social and societal differences—of ethnicity, of gender, of language and power—according to colonialist standards of modernity.[26] The primary focus is not on what postcolonial scholarship situates as 'historical colonialism' but on hegemonic forms of colonialist thinking that inhibit the achievement of genuine postcolonial freedom.[27] For others, studying empire is resonant because it speaks to the observed reality of persistent inequalities between rich world and poor.[28] Often drawing on Italian philosopher Giorgio Agamben's ideas of biopolitics, in which colonized peoples were denied the freedoms necessary to more than a 'bare life' of subjugation, both perspectives read the imminence of colonialism in terms of contemporary injustice.[29]

Where do imperial and global historians fit in? For imperial historians, decolonization is centrally about empire—its demise, its worldwide ramifications, its persistence in other forms. In part, the imperialism they study connotes the accretion of power by the colonizing minority—settlers, administrators, and business managers—over a subjugated indigenous majority.[30] Decolonization, then, is framed in terms of the loss of that power. That's not enough. The neatly bounded 'colony' beloved of imperial cartographers was at variance with the spatial fluidity of imperial territories and the enduring webs of connection across borders and between empires.[31] Much of the violence of empire disintegration stemmed from colonial interference in longstanding patterns of transnational cultural, religious, and commercial attachment.[32] This is where global history comes in. Its central insight is methodological, rejecting the nation-state as the analytical starting point and focusing instead on colonialism's entanglements of peoples, ideas, and discriminations. Described as a decentered approach, it neither begins with European imperial heartlands nor ends with the ascendancy of new nation-states at the formal 'end of empire'.[33] As defined by two German historians who combine imperial and global perspectives, decolonization has twin axes: 'the disappearance of empire as a political form' and 'the end of racial hierarchy as a widely accepted political ideology and structuring principle of world order'.[34]

In the broadest geopolitical terms, twentieth-century empires were of two types. In the land-based empires, such as Imperial Russia, Qing China, Ottoman Turkey, or the Habsburg Empire, a central authority, often configured around a dominant ethnic group, gradually extended its dominion over contiguous territories to rule a single, geographically connected area. The other form of empire was oceanic. A metropolitan power with naval capacity occupied, claimed, and then administered disparate territories spread over multiple continents. The British and French empires were the largest latter-day examples of such empires but their Portuguese and Dutch cousins, although smaller, were older. And while the modern iteration of oceanic empires was European in origin, by the 1900s other states—most notably Japan and the United States—were building them as well.

It is with the ending of these oceanic empires that this book is concerned. For the most part, the land-based empires of the early 1900s would be pulled apart by the pressures of war, by revolution, and by the claims made by various ethnic groups to nationhood immediately before, during, and after the First World War. For that reason alone, the first global conflict of the twentieth century helped to catalyze a particular form of empire collapse. Still, the more widespread understanding of decolonization, I would suggest, relates less to the disintegration of the land empires than to the more attenuated and globally diffuse contraction of the oceanic empires. To be sure, these agglomerations were rocked by the turbulence of the 1910s and 1920s, but the disintegrative forces within them—and the external pressures pushing in on them—built stronger momentum with the coming of a second global conflict, the post-1945 aftershocks of which would finally bring them down. The story of these collapses is the history of decolonization.

Decolonization and International Relations

The chapters that follow combine imperial and global history. They also draw on social science scholarship, particularly from international relations (IR). Because of this, it's worth considering how IR, the branch of political science devoted to understanding the mechanics of global politics, approaches decolonization.[35] This may seem counterintuitive. Critical

IR theorists have castigated their discipline as 'constitutively blind to the non-Western world'.[36] To be sure, prominent IR thinkers after 1945 recognized the significance of decolonization as colonial pressure for nationhood gathered momentum, but few welcomed it.[37] What was described as a 'revolt against the West' was depicted as destabilizing, a pandemic of authoritarian nationalisms likely to balkanize international society, stirring conflict along disputed borders or between Cold War proxies.[38]

Whatever the opinions of particular IR scholars, the analytical problem is not that IR had little to say about decolonization but that its conceptual tools whittled down empire and imperialism to familiar problems of interstate rivalry and territorial competition. There was a hubbub of discussion, much of it internationalist in inspiration and with women IR thinkers at the fore, about doing international politics differently, whether through heightened public consultation, new legal and bureaucratic instruments, or supranational institutions.[39] But the corrosive effects of cultural stereotypes and enduring racism on international affairs were elided.[40] Several leading scholars in the field acknowledge the usefulness of a more global approach, decentered from the European states' system once regarded as the core of 'international society'.[41] Some argue that this change in perspective marks the start of a bigger task, requiring the deconstruction of Western presumptions about colonized peoples and their freedom struggles as part of any revaluation of decolonization.[42] Others contend more basically that imperialism should be fundamental to international studies.[43] The struggles within empires and not just between them hold significance at a global, systemic level.[44]

Whether we are trying to understand the inner weaknesses of empires or their external interactions with other nations and oppositional networks, it's worth remembering two things. First, empires' ability to accomplish their goals depended on the power and permissiveness of their opponents and friends in an international order. Second, foreign interference in the affairs of others was always a part of the game.[45] From the Manchester Pan-African Congress convened in 1945 through the Bandung Conference ten years later to the consolidation of the G77 and countless statements of anticolonial intent in between, an alternative architecture of global politics was always on offer.[46] Put differently, regional interactions between non-Western actors, plus the proliferation of transnational contacts between those working against empire, had an impact on the international system: decolonization is the proof.[47]

Not surprisingly, in light of IR's intellectual development as a discipline after World Wars I and II, the international politics first of Britain, then

of the United States figured largest among the external actors in IR thinking, as well as in its real-world policy prescriptions.[48] Within early IR
scholarship, as among the Western political actors being studied, it was
but a short leap from Eurocentric and state-centric preoccupations to
an imperial worldview in which power radiated outward from the predominant nations of the day.[49] The result was a sort of intellectual 'color
line'.[50] Insofar as that line ran through IR analyses of empire breakdown,
it emerged in Western-centric treatments that reduced decolonization
to the redistribution of power between imperial states.[51] Bringing these
arguments together, Nicolas Guilhot has suggested that 'realism', a powerful analytical trend in international relations thinking during the early
Cold War, was uncertain how to incorporate the unfolding collapse of
empires within its conceptualization of interstate competition. Realists, he
argues, were thrown off balance by modernization theories developed by
Boston-based academics Walt Rostow and Max Millikin and others who
depicted the emergence of new nations as a triumph of Western models
of nationalism, of the nation-state and, crucially, of a resultant transition
to 'modern' societies that promoted individualism and meritocracy. In this
construction, the West led and the rest were to follow.[52] It was this, rather
than a methodological aversion to studying the non-Western world, that,
in Guilhot's view, accounts for IR's relative silence about decolonization.[53]

The salient point is that leading actors within a field of scholarship
whose disciplinary contours were first defined after 1919 and then reshaped
during the post-1945 years of empire breakdown found it difficult to think
beyond Western models of international politics.[54] In IR, as among the governments to which IR applied itself, 'West and the rest' narratives spoke
loudest, muffling nonstate actors and nonwhite voices in the dramas of
decolonization.[55] From that intellectual position, it was but a short step to
another, an 'imperial realism' that suggested European colonialism lent stability to a postwar international system led by a US hegemon.[56] Early historians of the Cold War also perpetuated a normative distinction between
active 'First' and 'Second' Worlds—the Western powers and the Communist
bloc in bitter ideological competition—and a passive 'Third' World in which
the opposing Cold War actors intervened at will.[57]

Location Problems

Defining decolonization is one thing, locating it another. These location
problems become harder once we accept that 'flag independence' is not
a reliable signifier.[58] Take Iraq. Where should we place it in a history of

Ottoman, British, European, or 'Middle Eastern' decolonization? Subdivided into semiautonomous districts, or *vilayets*, by the Ottoman Empire, Iraqi territory was occupied by British imperial forces between 1915 and 1918.[59] British commanders initially relied on Indian *sepoys* to suppress Iraqi dissent. Later they turned to the bombs of Britain's new service arm: the Royal Air Force (RAF).[60] Imperial bureaucracy in Baghdad carried an Indian flavor. Britons with administrative experience in the Government of India predominated. Middle-ranking clerical positions were packed with Delhi appointees.[61] These placemen lost influence after Iraq was declared a British mandate accountable to the League of Nations in 1920. In the following year Winston Churchill lent political support to RAF claims to administrative primacy in that mandate at a Middle Eastern planning conference in Cairo.[62] Britain's air force, eager to prove itself as more than a coercive instrument, deployed its officers as regional envoys— in the jargon of the day, Special Service Officers.[63] But they could never govern alone. Local appointees were essential, the majority of them urban notables, tribal elders, and former administrators familiar with Ottoman systems of government, revenue collection, and justice. Few identified themselves as 'Iraqi', far more as Arab or Kurdish patriots.[64]

Changes at the top in early mandate Iraq reveal little about what was happening across the country. Permeable frontiers and deep economic connections with Persia and the Indian subcontinent to the east and with Turkish Anatolia, the Syrian Levant, and Saudi Arabia to the north and west confirm that Iraqi 'nationhood' was nascent at best. Iraq's complex ethnoreligious fault-lines were represented at one regional pole by Kurdish separatist sentiment in the northern Mosul vilayet and, at the other, in the southern Basra vilayet, by religious devotion to Shia religious leaders in Iran. These differences underline that, while Arab-led Iraqi independence was a cherished goal for some, it was cultural anathema to others. The regional patchwork of transnational commercial ties, ethnic affiliations, and religious loyalties was matched by Iraq's peculiar status as a League territory under supranational supervision. Governed contingently and 'in trust' by Britain, it was abundantly clear before the mandate was even confirmed that imperial authority was febrile.

Beginning in 1919, rebellions in Kurdish northern Iraq and in Shia southern Iraq were matched by persistent cross-border raiding by Wahabite Ikhwan levies loyal to Saudi Arabia.[65] Add to this the presence of Turkish-sponsored paramilitaries in the far north whose determination to weaken the British presence in Western Asia threatened a more serious insurgency igniting the ethnic irredentism of the Kurds.[66] The Kurdish people had lived for centuries at the nexus of a transregional space connecting southern Anatolia in the west with Persia's northern highlands to the east. Kurdish rejection of the reconfiguration of frontiers, rulers, and political obligations that, in 1919, surrounded them began from the premise that their interests were irreconcilable with the new dispensation of nations and territories in the Middle East.[67]

The Kurds' transregional perspective was far from unique. In the cities of Iraq and Syria, working arrangements among pan-Arabist military officers, local politicians, and an emergent middle class were not easily suborned to the nation-state model of mandate governance in which power was supposed to radiate from a central administration throughout a bounded polity.[68] In Iraq's case, its imperial overseers laid the groundwork for lasting British control of the country's nascent oil industry but, despite this early denial of Iraq's raw-material sovereignty, in other respects the country was never economically integrated into the British Empire before it achieved paper independence under the terms of the Anglo-Iraqi Treaty of Alliance in June 1930.[69] For all that, the first mandate to become a sovereign nation—at least in constitutional form—would remain within a British sphere of imperial influence for another generation.[70] The bargains between elites that made this connection possible were personified by Ja'far Pasha al-Askari, a Baghdadi born in 1885. A graduate of Ottoman and German military academies who was imprisoned by the British in the Cairo Citadel during the First World War, Ja'far Pasha served as governor of Aleppo under Emir Feisal's short-lived Syrian Republic before following Feisal to Iraq. There, he held a succession of ministerial posts until his assassination in May 1936. Senior Iraqi representative at the Lausanne Conference in 1923, Ja'far was lead Iraqi negotiator of the 1930 independence treaty. Alongside his diplomatic day-job, he took examinations in London to become a qualified barrister. An Arabist, an Iraqi patriot, but, in the eyes of his local critics, a British lackey, Ja'far paid with his life for the quasi-imperial relationship he did so much to cement.[71]

Ja'far's successors all lost power in their turn. First came the militaristic regime of Bakr Sidqi, then a pro-British regency government temporarily ousted by Rashid Ali al-Gaylani's pro-Axis coup d'état on April 1, 1941. Turning Iraq's political compass in a defiantly nationalistic direction, al-Gaylani's government lasted barely a month. British and Transjordan imperial forces marched in to overthrow it, an indicator of where real power lay in this part of the world. Iraq's oil supplies and the expanding revenues generated by the Anglo-Iraqi Petroleum Company (later to be absorbed into British Petroleum) became vital to Britain following the decisive 1940s shift away from transatlantic sources of oil toward Middle Eastern ones. And, until the secular modernizers of the Baathist revolution overthrew Iraq's monarchy in July 1958, a conservative Sunni elite had been a model for the pro-Western clientelism upon which—as Ja'far Pasha's example illustrates—the foundations of British regional influence were built.[72] These imperial entanglements are hard enough to digest, but looming over any attempt at historical contextualization is the specter of the 2003 invasion and the sorry legacy of further Western military interventionism, which many insist was imperialist in design if not in intent.[73] So when, if at all, did Iraq decolonize?

Locating decolonization means pinpointing when people in a society began thinking and acting toward a future in which imperial formations would no longer be there.[74] For some, this was an ideational process, a matter of imagining futures differently. For others, the issues were of practical politics and economics, of wanting to regulate their affairs autonomously with political, commercial, ethnic, or religious partners of their own choosing. For most, decolonization was less visible. Only in its latter stages, if at all, was it articulated in binary terms for or against national independence. Prior to that, processes of empire disintegration gathered momentum through gradual shifts in outlook toward a condition in which empire became anachronistic and ultimately intolerable.[75] These attitudinal changes are traceable in the archives and other administrative records, which are the raw ingredients of historical research. But, as a colonial construction, the official archive sometimes replicates or even represents the very colonialism that supporters of decolonization rejected.[76]

The archive of decolonization comes freighted with the baggage of its creators. Quite apart from their colonialist tropes and institutional boundaries, officials kept records selectively. Much went unsaid; more went unsaved. Colonial archives also have their own histories of repatriation, destruction, and concealment.[77] Records seized by incoming anticolonial victors or spirited away by departing bureaucrats reinforced the idea of an abrupt cut-off point or 'transfer of power'.[78] As I've said already, such formal 'transfers' were important, but not in the way their architects presented them—in historian Lydia Walker's telling phrase, 'not a flipped switch, but a set of negotiations with no predetermined end result'.[79] Is it really a surprise that the webs of economic and cultural connection that held empires together did not unravel overnight? Rather than marking a precise imperial end and a postcolonial beginning, formal departures were milestones in a longer process of lending substance to notional freedoms and legal sovereignties.[80] The departure of a colonial power—as for example, from the Pacific Island territories of Fiji, Papua New Guinea, and Vanuatu—did not mean that indigenous cultures were restructured or foreign exploitation of environmental resources and strategic assets ended. In these Pacific territories, authentic decolonization, achieved through the construction of nations sensitive to indigenous requirements and responsive to local need, occurred 'from the inside out' more after formal independence than before it.[81]

It was only relatively late in the story—for most observers, probably somewhere between Vietnamese victory over France in 1954 and 'the year of Africa', 1960, when seventeen colonial pullouts occurred below the Sahara—that empire no longer pervaded languages of global and local politics. The significance of United Nations Resolution 1514, whose wording included the definitive statement that 'inadequacy of political, economic, social or educational preparedness should never serve as a pretext for delaying independence', seemed to be that old 'standards of civilization' were finally being cast aside.[82] Self-determination as a collective right of peoples had taken hold.[83] Institutionally, the United Nations established a Special Committee on Decolonization in 1961.[84] Better known as 'the Committee of 24', this grouping became a bugbear of imperial powers as the 1960s unfolded.[85] Its purpose was to promote 'self-government' and 'independence', terms whose meaning the United Nations considered self-evident.[86] In theory, at least, conditional rich-world judgments about which dependencies could handle independence and poor-world struggles to force the pace were superseded by judicial pronouncement from the world's preeminent supranational authority.[87]

The UN Committee of 24 captured a decolonization zeitgeist that was inspiring new networks of transnational solidarity among women's groups, trade unionists, athletes, artists, and youth activists throughout the global South.[88] Cutting across Cold War divisions and other reductive binaries of language, gender, and ethnicity, these connections signified a form of subaltern internationalism, much of it channeled through the Non-Aligned Movement (NAM) and Third Worldist radicalism.[89] To be sure, the Cold War's regional dynamics in Southeast Asia and the Middle East made neutralism increasingly difficult in the twelve years that separated the NAM's founding conference at Belgrade in September 1961 from its fourth, at Algiers in 1973.[90] But nonalignment remained distinctive because its protagonists refused to be defined by the Cold War's opposing ideologies and strategic positions. For nonaligned states, the essential problem was the poisonous combination of colonial racism and global capitalism, issues that antedated and transcended the competition between superpower blocs. As later chapters will show, decolonization ran deeper and longer, a global framing for the more short-term phenomenon of the Cold War.[91]

Locating Violence

If the normativity of empire and the need for a global, multiempire analysis of it make it harder to locate decolonization's start and end points, so does what might be called the violence problem. Again, viewed globally, it appears obvious that decolonization was a violent business. That proposition looks self-evident whether the focus is on the macro-level (the many wars of decolonization that shaped and disfigured the past century or so) or the micro-level (the workaday violence of exclusions, compulsions, and indignities that made discriminatory imperial rule tangible).[92] Some of that violence was interpersonal and physical. Some of it was psychological, derived from the refusal by some in charge to recognize the shared humanity of those they subordinated. Sometimes described as epistemic violence, this silencing of marginalized people and the effacement of their culture that went with it epitomized the banality of colonial racism.[93] Within South Africa—which, after the formalization of apartheid in 1948, was the most unapologetically racist of all colonialist societies—the depth of white ignorance about the daily hardships of life for township-confined black citizens was revealed by, for instance, the efforts of advertising executives and marketing strategists from the 1950s onward to get 'inside the skin' of black consumers. What did black South Africans eat for breakfast? Which products did they want most, and how did black women's consumption patterns differ from men's? Not until they employed so-called black gurus, male (and only male) researchers sufficiently urbane to be granted access to corporate whites-only meeting rooms, did the advertisers have the slightest clue.[94]

As the everyday presence of discrimination suggests, colonial violence was also structural.[95] It was evident in colonial practices that left environments despoiled, communities evicted, and moral economies disrupted.[96] But even if we accept that empires were violent places, does that take us very far? Plenty of nonimperial spaces and different political systems could be just as violent, often more so. Some inflicted violence systematically, whether to remove opponents, to coerce compliance, or to hasten the social transformations that their governing ideologies demanded. This, of course, takes us into the realm of ontology, of trying to establish what, if anything, set colonial violence apart and gave it meaning. Leaving this issue to one side for now (we'll return to it in chapter 12), the challenge

I'd like to tackle here is how we might configure violence as a dynamic of decolonization: was it the motor or simply one among many types of fuel? Did violence propel change or merely alter its rate of advance, either slowing things down, usually through repressive crackdowns, or speeding things up, as, for example, through the adverse local and global reactions such clampdowns provoked?

The place of violence in decolonization is another marker that shapes our understanding of how, when, and why empires ended. If, for example, we prioritize arguments over individual and social rights, from access to citizenship to improvements in basic welfare and workplace treatment, the end of empires coheres around essentially sociopolitical struggles. If, on the other hand, we focus on the part played by organized violence in ending empire, we risk losing sight of the many nonviolent debates, nonviolent discussions, and at least relatively nonviolent spaces that were part of the global decolonization story.[97] More basically still, both approaches risk a presumption of politicization, a prior assumption that most people were actively engaged in something called decolonization, whether violently, discursively, or otherwise.

Conclusion

It was well into the 1950s before the idea of decolonization gathered momentum as part of a wider reevaluation of Europe's overseas fortunes. As the term became common currency, few people considered its conceptual origins or identified in any way with the term's German originator, Moritz Bonn. His certainty in the aftermath of the Versailles settlement that Germany's loss of global status prefigured a wider European decline underlined what Stuart Ward describes as the European provenance of the idea of decolonization.[98] In decolonization, Bonn saw not just a global pivot toward the nation-state, but a disaggregation of economic blocs as countries aimed for independence in all realms of national activity. He recognized, though, that economic dependency might continue despite the achievement of national sovereignty. Indeed, the League of Nations nurtured new ideas and, with them, new institutions of international economic governance, from its own Economic and Financial Organization to the Bank of International Settlements, whose presumptive power 'to meddle' in financial affairs seemed at odds with ideas of sovereign independence.[99] Evidence from as far afield as China and Austria pointed to the continuation of informal imperial control, as in the former case, or supranational oversight, as in the latter.[100] Political decolonization and the concomitant creation of new national frontiers, in other words, might be less definitive than they appeared.[101] The persistence of imperial influence, and of economic imperialism especially, suggested that decolonization would unfold gradually, in discrete political and economic stages.

A number of Bonn's defining characteristics of decolonization, as well as his Eurocentric perspective on the phenomenon, resurfaced when the term came into more common use in the 1950s. One influential example is the work of the eminent French scholar of Africa (and former colonial administrator) Henri Labouret. His study *Colonisation, colonialism, décolonisation* (1952) was the first book in any language to use 'decolonization' in its title. Like Bonn before him, Labouret placed his subject in the context of the 'stages of history', the fifth and final being 'the phase of decolonization' in which the global preeminence of the colonial powers was swept aside by a 'triumphant liberalism'.[102] Swept aside, perhaps, but the unmaking of empires was rarely the victory for individual liberties that Labouret predicted. Instead, historians Todd Shepard and Stuart Ward are closer to the mark in their identification of two countervailing explanations of decolonization to emerge from the violent end of French colonialism in Algeria, one metropolitan, the other colonial. For Shepard, decolonization was articulated to explain a reverse: the abandonment of an integrationist colonialism predicated on the eventual erasure of Algerian difference through legal and cultural assimilation to France. Decolonization, then, was 'invented' almost, but not quite, after the fact of its being. It enabled a French public confronted with imminent national humiliation in Algeria to reimagine the process as something historically rooted and explicable.[103]

Reducing decolonization to a constitutional exercise, a transfer of sovereignty to an independent nation-state in conformity with the spirit of the times, also made it easier to overlook the crises of governance and political legitimacy that had brought France to this point.[104] Within Algeria, the FLN's uncompromising literary advocate, Martinique-born psychologist Frantz Fanon, explained decolonization differently, not as the high-water mark of an irresistible historical tide, but as the beginning of a purge. True decolonization would be registered through not some phased program of incremental reform, but the violent effacement of all traces of the colonial presence from Algerian society. This, Fanon insisted, was necessary to free Algerians as much psychologically as politically. Decolonization was less a state-directed political project than a social revolution, a catharsis requiring the total engagement of its true subjects: the colonized. Only then would an authentic national liberation be achieved as

Algerians, freed of all traits of dependency, at last expressed their authentic cultural identities.[105] It would then be incumbent on Algerians, as it was on all liberated peoples, to work across borders to achieve decolonization elsewhere. National independence, in other words, was only a first step: decolonization was internationalist in intent and global in reach, or it was nothing.[106]

Just as colonialism and colonization were global phenomena, so were their antitheses: anticolonialism and decolonization. Garveyism, negritude, Gandhi's ideals of nonviolent protest, colonial struggles against discrimination and other abuses: all provided ideas and impetus to civil rights movements the world over. Connections between anticolonialism and the African American black freedom struggle were especially powerful and long lasting.[107] What connected them was a global sensibility, a realization, as historian John Munro puts it, 'that decolonization was not a series of singular if parallel conflicts between given colonies and metropoles, but rather an assemblage of interconnected if distinct struggles against the transnational structure of racial capitalism'.[108] Anticolonial insurgencies inspired other, peasant-based revolutionary movements from Latin America to East Asia. These oppositional forces drew on global networks of support and communities of practice that highlight a certain paradox: usually understood in terms of the empires they sought to dismantle, late colonial conflicts were, at the same time, unifying. The organizational forms, the politico-military methods, and the ethical justifications for anticolonial movements were remarkably similar. Before considering these, however, we need to locate decolonization both chronologically and in relation to another transformative process working alongside it: globalization. These challenges are the subject of the next chapter.

CHAPTER TWO

Decolonization and Globalization

> As civilization develops, the intercourse of peoples becomes ever more
> frequent, more intimate, and more various. Ideas are exchanged as well
> as commodities, for traders also are men: interests, social and intellec-
> tual as well as material, are created: the political frontiers are crossed
> by multiplying invisible lines: in a word, a common culture comes into
> existence.

SO SAID HERBERT Hensley Henson, the Bishop of Durham, in a February 1927 lecture on 'The Ethics of Empire' to a college audience in
Newcastle-upon-Tyne.[1] Henson never used the term 'globalization' but, for
him, empire was its instrument. It provided the commercial opportunities,
the communications routes, and the cultural pathways along which the
colonizing power disseminated its values. As Henson was an old-style diffusionist, it is easy to dismiss the civilizational aspect of his argument. It is
harder to disregard his insight about the empire–globalization connection.

Connecting Decolonization and Globalization

This chapter explains connections between two of the most globally
transformative processes of the past century: the end of formal empire
and the acceleration of global integration. It tries to unscramble conflicting perspectives on which of these processes—either decolonization or
globalization—accelerated or even catalyzed the other. The strange thing
is that the contestations over the end of European colonial empires and
the concomitant integration of global markets are not always set alongside

each other, despite the evidence that colonialism's decline presented unprecedented opportunities for market access, transmigration, and new forms of cultural connection.[2] At one level, that omission is explained by a presumption that globalization carried all else before it.[3] Sometimes described as 'globality', conceptualizing the world as a single political arena reflects changes in forms of connectivity, which thickened during the nineteenth century, challenging the sovereignty of nations.[4]

A good example of globality's impact on notions of sovereign independence is the rise of so-called global prohibition regimes in the fields of human trafficking, prostitution, and recreational narcotics. In response to transnational campaigning against prostitution trafficking and opium usage, various international legal restrictions and monitoring regimes were put in place in the first half of the twentieth century, chiefly under League of Nations auspices.[5] The imperialistic and paternalistic flavors of the process are easily discerned. Its impetus came from rich-world anxieties about drug addicts or 'white slaves'; less concern was expressed about the millions of Asians whose drug addiction or sexual exploitation were traceable to the arrival of Western empires.[6] But the ramifications of such prohibitions were global. Moving from illicit to licit activities, similar trends are evident. Spurred by nineteenth-century industrialization, new productive, medical, and military technologies and faster modes of transportation all propelled globalization.[7] As disseminator of these public goods, empire, to quote Tony Hopkins, could be viewed as globalization's enforcer.[8] Undersea cables made the telegraph an instrument of intercontinental connection but also marked out new patterns of colonial exclusion.[9] The telegraph lines snaking across colonial interior spaces met European commercial requirements and settler needs. But electrical communications tended to marginalize indigenous majorities, for whom cutting telegraph posts and wires remained emblematic acts of primary resistance on the eve of decolonization.[10]

None of these dynamics stopped at particular frontiers. Nor have they since.[11] Our world's most existential problems—of climate change and its limitation, of conflict and peace preservation, of human security and chronic poverty—are global, not national.[12] Efforts to tackle economic inequalities and development challenges, environmental destruction and resource scarcity, 'new wars' and other strategic threats have driven governments, NGOs, and supranational agencies to develop partnership arrangements sometimes characterized as 'global governance'.[13] Distinctions between governmental and nongovernmental activities, national interests and transnational working practices have become harder to make.

Decolonization and Globalization after World War I

Without denying globalization's impacts, my purpose here is to cement its place alongside decolonization at the center of world politics in the twentieth century. The end of that century's first global war is a good place to begin.

The nature and outcome of the First World War fostered conflicting ideas about the future of empires and nations, as well as about their relevance in a world in which processes of globalization looked set to intensify. Technological innovations encouraged the standardization of everything from the Fordist production line to the measurement of time and the permissible length of the working week.[14] Improving communications and mass transportation reduced problems of spatial dispersion and geographical distance, facilitating exchange.[15] On the other side of the equation, the First World War destroyed nations' long-term patterns of overseas investment, most obviously with Tsarist Russia and the Ottoman Empire.[16] The disintegration of the three land empires sharpened the sense among Western Europe's imperialists of empires' dualities: as sources of conflict but also of power, as barriers to freedom but also global theaters for reform.[17] Meanwhile another colonial power, the United States, resisted the temptation to grab additional territories, but extended its global reach nonetheless as economic power shifted from old world to new.[18]

Faced with these globalizing pressures, protagonists of neoliberalism talked of a unitary world economy requiring better supranational regulation but otherwise set free. These globalists saw beyond empire but were disappointed in the short term.[19] As the world plunged into economic crisis at the end of the 1920s, empires and nations erected barriers—tariff walls, currency controls, and harsher immigration restrictions that sharpened the global color line.[20] The 1930s saw global integration challenged by 'autarkic' nationalists and sullen protectionists hostile to 'the economic cosmopolitanism of unrestrained capital'.[21] New obstacles to trade suggested that globalization, in the neoliberal sense of an interdependent world economy operating by common rules, had gone into reverse.[22] Some historians warn against misreading Depression-era protectionism as 'deglobalization', missing the continuing relevance of empire and the widening institutional basis of international economic governance.[23] If anything, the imperialist impulse to cling on to empire's dependent markets strengthened. Britain's Empire Marketing Board (EMB), in operation between 1926 and 1933, made the consumption of colonial produce a source of dutiful pride. To quote an EMB advertisement, 'When it is winter with us, the sun somewhere else in the British Empire is reddening apples and putting the juice into oranges': a wholesome image and an expression of Depression-era 'imperial preference'.[24]

Aside from their enthusiasm for autarky, challengers outside the victors' coalition behaved imperially as well. Fascist Italy, the Third Reich, Imperial Japan, and, before this fascistic trio, the Soviet Union, were all convinced that the First World War peace had cheated them of territorial spoils.[25] For post–First World War Japan its marginalization from the Peace Conference flew in the face of the country's breakneck industrialization and its increasing capacity to project regional strategic dominance.[26] For Italy, the revisionist challenge was to restore former glories. For Nazi Germany, empire fulfilled regime imperatives of colonization and racial supremacy.[27] Each of these 'latecomers' rose and fell in pursuit of what Louise Young describes as an 'imperialism after imperialism'.[28]

Whatever their ideological justifications, all were colonizers prepared to remake empires through violent territorial revisionism.[29] The fascist imperialists drove their empire expansionism through highly centralized state or party machines, using aggressive 'hyper-militarism' to crush local opposition.[30] Regime-supporting civil society groups, notably among minority groups such as Muslim communities in China, which fascist imperialists saw as reliably anticommunist and anti-Western, meanwhile spread revisionist thinking transnationally as well.[31] None of the established overseas colonial empires could insulate themselves from these revisionist threats any more than they could ignore changes in global capitalism (although Salazarist Portugal tried at various points to do both).

Moving into the latter half of the twentieth century, the picture looks different. Empire disintegrated at a time of deepening monetary cooperation and renewed efforts among upper-income countries to promote economic integration.[32] The United States led the construction of this post–Second World War apparatus of international economic governance, laying the foundations for American hegemony within Bretton Woods arrangements for currency convertibility and freer trade.[33] The acceleration of mass consumption since the 1950s, the attendant principle that increasing public access to consumer products was a measure of government success, plus the rise of consumer activism as a facet of ethically responsible citizenship, all highlighted inequalities between metropolitan consumers and colonial providers.[34] Changing global trading rules and consumption patterns had profound implications for empires and the nations emerging from them.[35]

Globalization Triumphant?

Scores of new nations that fought, negotiated, or otherwise found their way to sovereign independence might be viewed as intrinsically transformative, making a rapid and geopolitically widespread shift in world politics that, despite the widespread replication of erstwhile colonial borders, changed the meanings and practices of citizenship locally while altering the composition of the international system globally.[36] Yet that 'system' was also an international order—a hierarchy of nations, economic blocs, and ideological groupings. This suggests that we should tread cautiously. Many of the new nations and the peoples comprising them wanted to challenge that hierarchy, but even the most revolutionary adjusted to it. As it turned out, the impact of the end of empires on the international political economy was less pronounced than these multiple struggles for nationhood might imply, something discussed at more length in later chapters. The world remade by decolonization involved considerable elements of continuity.

For some commentators, this flattening of regional difference into a globally dominant capitalist economy was one of empire's greatest achievements. Whatever its discriminations, the institutional structures and educational legacies of empire offered greater possibility for states and peoples to share in the economic benefits of globalization. Imperial infrastructure-building and colonial norms of language and commerce made the supremacy of transnational exchange a reality.[37] The shipment of people and goods once associated with the horror of slavery and the debt bondage of indenture was, by the early twentieth century, more diverse, stimulating the growth of port cities and tying them into global commercial networks.[38] Supply chains thickened thanks to preexisting imperial links. These could be strengthened through corporate investment as multinationals roved a global South of independent nations in search of value and reward.

For other commentators, it was empire that ensured the persistence of global inequalities by reifying ethnic difference and perpetuating unfree labor through indenture and *corvée* obligations (compulsory labor on public works).[39] Imperialist hierarchies of cultural value meanwhile kept the global South at the bottom of the pile. Despite national independence, formerly colonized societies still found themselves consigned to history's 'waiting room', denied access to the same opportunities as their former rich-world rulers because they failed to meet Western expectations.[40]

The resulting catch-22 is this: the decolonized state is expected to meet external standards of governance and economic practice, but doing so circumscribes its independence.[41] Plural and non-Western routes to modernity authentic to local culture become harder to pursue.[42] The original aims of self-declared liberal imperialists who justified empire as an educative process of acculturation to Western norms live on in globalization's patterns of exchange.[43]

Globalization, in this reading, is built on empire's sediments. Globalization promotes interaction, but its economic effects marginalize those living in poorer countries too 'backward' to enjoy its liberating possibilities.[44] Dwelling on the ecological impacts of a globalization that was, for decades, oriented toward satisfying the needs of imperial powers underlines the point. From the eighteenth to the twentieth centuries, the expansion of empires globalized the impact of Europe and North America's industrial capitalism. Spurred by their own industrialization, imperial powers on both continents became 'resource omnivores', extracting their colonies' natural resources to feed a global commodities market, often with the active participation of local elites who enhanced their own power and wealth by joining the 'franchise venture' of imperial capitalism.[45]

Colonialism was, in this sense, globalization's servant, stimulating the unprecedented exploitation of ecological resources alongside changes in land use, dietary patterns, population distribution, and the monetization of commodities.[46] The majority within colonized societies neither shared in the original windfall nor have seen substantial benefits since. For all the advantages of digital technologies, internet availability, cell-phone coverage, and access to markets, the economic convergence promoted by globalization is retarded by legacies of colonialism—the geopolitical interventionism of Western coalitions, the financial preeminence of rich-world corporations and investors, their rules of global trade and economic oversight. Access to the older technologies of nineteenth- and twentieth-century globalization, from bulk-carrying ships, refrigerated goods, and air-conditioning units to prophylactic medicines, remains as important, if not more so, for peoples in low-income countries.[47] Despite the efforts of their supporters, as of yet, decolonization, anticolonialism, and nonalignment have not revolutionized the way global capitalism works. Nor have they reversed the inclination among leading industrial powers to offer capitalist economic models as policy prescriptions in postcolonial nations.[48]

A bigger question is whether 'global capitalism' is really that global after all. Could sub-Saharan Africa be counted as integral to a globalized economy when, during the 1990s, for instance, the entire region counted for barely 1 percent of global trade? Worldwide trade in the Bretton Woods era, plus the deregulated global capitalism that supplanted it from the early 1970s onward, points to a regionalization of international commerce rather than something universal. The first dominant regions within this abstraction were North America and Europe. Beginning in the late 1950s, these two were joined by East Asia and, later still, the commodity-rich BRICS countries (Brazil, Russia, India, China, South Africa). This suggests that large parts of the world were marginal to a globalization in which upper-income nations predominated.[49]

Recognizing these economic imbalances, those who criticized the predominance of national forms at the time and since have tended to equate nationhood with impending dependency and, at the more abstract level of political cultures and ideological change, decolonization with disillusion. Arab politicians offer early examples of such thinking. Jordan's prime minister, Tawfik Abu al-Huda, caught the mood in a January 3, 1953, dinner conversation with Britain's Barbara Castle. Arab communities had hoped for regional confederation after the First World War, he told her. Elites in Amman and other Middle Eastern capitals had worked toward other, less ambitious combinations ever since. What Jordanians achieved instead was a truncated independence. Whatever the dreams of its architects about expanding the country's frontiers, Jordan's future as an independent nation was threatened by the difficulties of supporting hundreds of thousands of displaced Palestinians. For them, decolonization meant not freedom, but war, eviction, statelessness, and loss.[50] Syrian president Adib al-Shishakli made the point more forcefully to her four days later, saying that Western politicians like Castle would tour Middle Eastern capitals saying, 'Let's be friends and defend the Middle East together', conveniently forgetting their earlier colonial divisiveness, the root of the region's human tragedies and interstate disputes.[51] A week later Castle was in conversation with Iraqi opposition leaders in Baghdad. They complained of a police state and detentions without trial, quietly tolerated by Britain, Iraq's external patron. How could Iraqis or other Arabs believe that imperialism was over when the British refused to quit Egypt, the Palestinian refugee problem was ignored, and Iraq's premier, Nuri al-Said, their persecutor-in-chief, virtually lived in the British Embassy?[52]

Their resentment of British imperial actions aside, these Arabs' complaints indicated how difficult it was for societies emerging from colonialism to pursue their political futures alone. 'Independence' signified central control of a bureaucratic apparatus and, notionally at least, the loyal service of the internal security forces that were the legal instruments of violence. Meaningful political authority also demanded oversight of a given territory's natural resources and terms of economic exchange, a gatekeeper function that has been singled out as especially distinctive.[53] Governments sometimes drew legitimacy from democratic elections, more often from their identification with a preceding anticolonial struggle.[54] That struggle, in turn, became a critical marker of national identity.[55] Service to the cause became a benchmark for social inclusion, although women's contributions often went unrecognized.[56] Such, in theory, were some defining features of the postcolonial state. Several nations cleaved politically to favored ideological clients, but few resisted capitalist intrusion entirely. From this perspective we might view decolonization as but part of a longer-term process of globalization: the dissemination of Western capitalistic norms, market influences, and modernizing agendas.[57]

Historian Tony Hopkins pursues this logic to its fullest extent. Decolonization, for him, was the handmaiden of globalization. First, globalization's postwar acceleration drained empires of their economic logic. Bilateral relationships between industrial producers in the imperial heartland and exporters of primary products within the colonies became unsustainable. Tellingly, in the three decades after 1945, several world powers—West Germany, the Scandinavian countries, Japan, and the United States foremost among them—achieved dramatic increases in prosperity without empires. Second, globalization sapped empires of their political rationale. The global connections and informational transparency it promoted were pivotal, exposing colonialism's racial inequality and its authoritarian institutions to relentless, hostile scrutiny. Alongside its integrative economic effects, globalization stimulated innovations in institution-building and supranational cooperation in everything from worldwide vaccination programs to children's welfare. For many, the results were disappointing, but their underlying premise of global applicability highlighted empires' anachronistic quality.[58] Finally, globalization either severed or attenuated the lingering ties between imperial powers and their informal zones of influence—for instance, between Britain and its 'white' Dominions or between Portugal and Brazil.[59] For Britain in particular, this shift was matched by its diminishing influence next to the United States, a transition that British governments chose to exploit rather than to oppose.[60]

Historian Nicholas White adds other dimensions, stressing the conjuncture between the proliferation of new nations in the late 1950s and 1960s and technological innovations identifiable with globalization. Foremost among these was the revolution in global shipping as break-bulk cargoes gave way to containerization. The ability to transport loads in giant boxes by sea, rail, and road transformed the speed and scale of goods trade. Containerization created a more diverse, multicentered maritime system.[61] Some established ports failed to adapt. Others, often in formerly dependent territories, grew rapidly. National shipping lines, much like flagged airlines, proliferated, again leaving some of the European conglomerates, once so dominant in colonial carriage trade, trailing.[62] Indigenous shipping lines, the expansion in flag-of-convenience ship registration from the 1950s and the foreign exchange earnings generated by container traffic all signaled the advent of a postcolonial globalization in international trade.[63]

Meanwhile, the UN Conference on Trade and Development (UNCTAD) worked hard during the 1960s and 1970s to end the dominance of the old shipping cartels. Its efforts were helped by the readiness of the Soviet Union and others to step in as shipping carriers for newly independent states with few vessels of their own.[64] Over the longer term, though, containerization was not quite the triumph of globalization over colonialism that it first appeared. Rich-world shipping conglomerates, such as Japan's Mitsui-OSK or Norway's Hoegh, sustained the capital investment needed to keep their international operations going, outpacing newer competitors in the global South.[65] And while Asian and African seamen predominated below decks, fewer had opportunities to reach the commanding heights of the bridge.

The Case for Globalizing Decolonization

Globalization was a driver of decolonization because its components—cultural, economic, and demographic—could not be confined within a territorialized space, whether that was a nation-state, a colonized region, or an entire empire.[66] Put another way, globalization's impacts on cultural transmission, population movement, economic processes, and environmental change operated beyond the norms and procedures of the international system.[67] Empires, individual governments, and multilateral agreements might affect globalization. But they could not control it.[68]

By extension, taking globalization seriously is at odds with single-nation, single-colony, or single-empire approaches to the study of decolonization. This conclusion sits with the transnational turn in imperial history, which prioritizes the agency of individuals, their patterns of connection, and the resulting social, cultural, and economic networks operating beneath, between, and beyond nation-states or colonial territories.[69] National histories may still be explored within this global story, but the point is that such national—and colonial—histories never unfolded in a vacuum.[70] Globalization's relevance to decolonization is clear, but what about decolonization's impact on globalization? It might seem logical to frame decolonization as a matter of greater urgency for Indians,

Indonesians, and Algerians than for Britons, French, or Dutch. But merely shifting attention from imperial centers to colonial peripheries risks falling into the same analytical trap: an overemphasis on center-periphery dynamics and an underestimation of wider transnational factors. These perspectives suggest that decolonization is better approached as a global phenomenon than as individuated empire-by-empire experiences.[71] Empire-building was shaped by multidirectional flows of ideas, goods, and people. So was empire disintegration.[72]

Back to Nations?

The proliferation of nations through decolonization was the most critical geopolitical element in the remaking of the world after 1945.[73] In place after place, the predominant political form arising from the ashes of imperial fires was the nation-state.[74] Federal interludes and alternatives to decolonization (discussed in the next chapter) notwithstanding, nation-states predominated numerically and ideationally as the organizing form of independence, nationhood, and postcolonial 'freedom'. That is not to dismiss the alternatives on offer, from imperial clientelism to regional confederations and federal mergers—usually bilateral ones—between former colonies. Across the Caribbean, in West Africa, East Africa, and Southern Africa, through the Arab world to Southeast Asia, advocates of federation recognized that national independence might create obstacles to regional cooperation, strategic security, or longer-term prosperity.[75] The commitment to build postcolonial institutional structures that would cement transregional political cultures attracted French West African elites drawn to federalism, as it did Arab regimes sympathetic to Gamal Abdel Nasser's brand of pan-Arabist socialism.

Some federal schemes were designed to mitigate dependency on foreign economic support; others looked to cultural affinities, rejecting ethnic nationalism by thinking beyond the nation-state.[76] It wasn't just opponents of empire who were drawn to federalism. Imperial authorities considered federal power-sharing as a solution in colonies where inter-ethnic tensions threatened to spill over into violence. The British Cabinet Mission, trying to avert the ossification of Muslim and Hindu demands for separate sovereign nation-states to replace Raj India, pushed the idea of federation, in which central government would be constrained by powerful regional autonomy and legal protections for minorities. But this strand of thinking about minority rights proved weaker than another— the enforced 'unmixing of peoples' that India's partition would impose.[77]

Federalism was also discussed in nearby Burma, only to be abandoned in the face of ethnic majority nationalism. The Panglong Agreement, signed in February 1947 between Premier Aung San and leaders of ethnic minorities from the country's Frontier Areas, mapped a federal route to national independence in which the Shans, the Kachins, and the Chins would have enjoyed substantial autonomy from the Burmese central government.[78]

Elsewhere, anticolonial leaders dismissed federalism as colonialism's Trojan horse. Nationalists in the Anglophone Caribbean identified it with constitutional ruses to entrench British influence. Their counterparts in southern Africa read federation as a perpetuation of white settler domination.[79] In a January 1958 letter intended for Britain's Labour Party leadership, Henry Nkumbula and Kenneth Kaunda, president and secretary-general of the African National Congress's (ANC) Northern Rhodesia section, called out the hypocrisy of Britain's Central African Federation (CAF), which cemented the dominance of settler-ruled Southern Rhodesia (Zimbabwe) over Northern Rhodesia (Zambia) and Nyasaland (Malawi). The two men described the CAF as an affront to promises of self-rule for the black majority in all three territories.[80]

Whatever the politics behind them, even federal solutions rarely survived more than a few years, typically between the late 1950s and the mid-1960s. What has been dubbed the 'federal moment' was just that.[81] That is not to say that transnational attachments counted for nothing.[82] After fascism's defeat in 1945, the call for peoples of the global South to unite against Western imperialism retained compelling rhetorical power, as evinced by the symbolic importance of 1955's Bandung Conference and the later refinement of Third Worldist internationalism.[83] Nationalism's core simplicity, next to the more capacious alternatives of pan-Asianism, pan-Islamism, or pan-Africanism, ensured that the narrower vision won out.[84]

For some historians, though, the persistence of national polities after formal decolonization demonstrates the corruptive power of colonialism. From the perpetuation of absurd colonial-era boundaries to the prevalence of international patterns of trade serving rich-world interests, the proliferation of newly independent nation-states, it seems, made little difference. Even anticolonial nationalism bent to these pressures, taking shape, in the words of one trenchant critic, as a 'derivative discourse'.[85] Reviewing decolonization's globalizing of the nation-state model, IR scholar Jennifer Welsh gets to the heart of it: that 'while sovereignty had seemingly triumphed, equality had not'.[86]

Little wonder that leading anticolonial thinkers from Mahatma Gandhi to Frantz Fanon, as well as political figureheads like Kwame Nkrumah and

Nasser, rejected the presumption that the nation-state was decolonization's logical outcome. For Gandhi and others, genuine self-determination
meant a rejection of Western materialist values and political forms. For
Fanon, the predominance of the nation-state confirmed Western imperialism's enduring capacity to undermine those fighting for freedom: 'To the
strategy of Dien Bien Phu, defined by the colonized peoples, the colonialist
replies by a strategy of encirclement—based on the respect of the sovereignty of states'.[87] Real decolonization would be measured in the extent
to which colonized communities rediscovered their cultural identities,
true selves that were stifled as much within the one-party statehood of the
independent nation as they had been under colonial rule. For Nkrumah and
Nasser, the shared experience of colonialism, plus societies' larger ethno-
cultural groupings, whether Africans, Arabs, or Third Worldists, suggested
that governance through confederation was closer to the commonalities of
hope and experience that reconnected communities artificially divided by
imperialists. These views, and their ultimate frustration, point to the same
conclusion: that anticolonial nationalism and its principal organizational
form—the 'national liberation movement'—were playing by their opponents' rules. Boxing themselves into the quest for nationhood, anticolonial
nationalists inadvertently ensured that the international order after formal
decolonization would not redistribute power or resources between north
and south, rich and poor, in any fundamentally different way.[88]

   This pessimistic reading of decolonization as a creature of Western
hegemony typecasts newly independent states as culturally inauthentic,
economically dependent, and politically illegitimate. The prevalence of
authoritarian government in numerous postcolonial countries from the
1960s onward lent weight to this view. From Algeria to Burma, narratives of revolutions betrayed and independence 'stolen' confirm that many
local people felt this way as well. Ironically, efforts by other independent
countries to cultivate democratic accountability have also been criticized
as slavish attempts either to mimic former imperial powers or to satisfy foreign creditors and Western-dominated supranational agencies such as the
International Monetary Fund. No matter if postindependence regimes
restructured society by dismantling colonial and customary institutions
alike, the decolonized nation, it seems, cannot win.[89]

   The territorialization of postindependence states and the styles
of governance within them have thus been used to make two bigger
points. One is that decolonization did not change the hierarchies of
international order. The other is that globalization's inexorable progress
explains why. Following this line of argument, most newly independent

nations missed their chance to organize postcolonial societies differently, whether at the philosophical level of moving beyond nationalism as the primary unifier of peoples or at the constitutional level of regional federations that transcended old imperial boundaries and broke with established trade patterns.[90] In the words of historian of international law Martti Koskenniemi,

> Decolonization effectively universalized the European state as the only form of government that would provide equal status in the organized international community. The first generation of political leaders in the Third World in the 1950s and 1960s may have disagreed about whether to aim for independence by devolution or revolution. But it had thoroughly integrated western ideas about the State form as the only viable shell within which to develop into modernity.[91]

Gandhi's ideas of nonviolence remained integral to the international nonalignment and avowed intercommunalism of India's governing Congress movement but, after 1947, India nonetheless developed as a Hindu-dominated nation-state. From Nkrumah in Anglophone Ghana to Léopold Sédar Senghor in Francophone Senegal, schemes devised by West African statesmen to build regional confederations petered out in the 1960s. After a tense three-year existence, Nasser's United Arab Republic, tying together Egypt with Syria, went the same way in 1961. Are these outcomes entirely reducible to the pull of globalization and the strength of Western influence? Surely not: for many in the decolonizing world, nationhood was something worth fighting for.

Contingency and Alternative Possibilities

Another factor comes into play here: contingency. Herein lies another analytical trap or tautology (circular argument). Decolonization must be about fighting for or negotiating nationhood because nationhood was what was, for the most part, achieved. Put another way, the predominance of nation-states after formal independence risks leading us to think that decolonization is reducible to struggles for self-determination and national sovereignty. The many national liberation movements whose stories have provided foundational accounts of nation-building, especially within the nations they would eventually govern, might distort our historical perspective even more.

Historian Frederick Cooper has been clearest in rejecting this approach as inaccurate, as 'reading history backwards'. Writing in the early twenty-first century, Cooper also questioned the usefulness of globalization as an explanatory tool.[92] As a theory of cultural convergence and economic exchange, globalization is too linear and too dismissive of the specificities of colonialism to convince as a unifying concept. Cooper's plea is to contextualize, to pay attention to the variety of options in late colonial politics.[93] Disputes over social rights and economic entitlements, simple demands for fair treatment, and more ambitious calls for cultural respect and cross-community federation were all aspects of a claims-making politics that either rejected or looked beyond the 'nation-state' as a singular end point.[94] Reminding ourselves that decolonization unfolded globally but contingently avoids the pitfalls of reducing the end of empires to an assemblage of fights for national independence.[95] Todd Shepard, a prominent historian of French imperialism, has amplified these arguments. He, too, has sought to reconcile the variegation in late colonial politics and the multiplicity of sociopolitical outcomes envisaged with the apparent triumph of nation-state models at independence. As we've seen, some anticolonial thought insisted that the nation-state was a Western construction that should not be mapped onto colonized societies. In part, this strand of thinking represented a distinctly anticolonial internationalism, as evinced, for instance, by Nkrumah and Nasser, in which shared experiences of colonial discrimination created deeper affiliation. For others, like Senghor in West Africa or Gandhi in India, nationalism was intrinsically limiting, a pessimistic form of politics that denied the possibility of more meaningful attachments between communities than blood or birthplace. At a more practical level, leading political actors in pre-decolonization negotiations in Africa and Southeast Asia worried that fixating on the goal of sovereign national independence might provoke regional division. The resulting 'balkanization' of integrated colonial regions into smaller territorial units would, they suggested, have damaging economic consequences, causing competition and conflict. These might be avoided by exploring other alternatives: regional mergers, federations, confederations, and schemes to realize pan-African or pan-Asian unity. Shepard's is another call for contextualization, taking seriously the power of ideas. He acknowledges the failure of the many alternatives to national independence, but states that decolonization cannot be solely about tracking paths to nationhood; it must also be about explaining the eclipse of these alternatives—a 'decolonization process' in itself.[96]

In similar vein, historian Cyrus Schayegh has reconceptualized the Middle East region spatially, culturally, and politically in the century or so between the acceleration of Ottoman reformism in the 1840s and the end of the European mandates in *Bilad al-Sham*, broadly speaking, the 'Greater Syria'—for imperialists 'the Levant'—which stretched from Palestinian lands in the south to the margins of southern Anatolia in the north.[97] Schayegh points out that the reconfiguration of economic links, cultural connections, and political influences between Bilad al-Sham's cities and regions was too dynamic to fit either a linear process of globalization or supposedly decisive shifts in central government from Ottomans to Europeans and from Europeans to independent nation-states. The fact that certain cities—Beirut and Haifa, for instance—became stronger poles of economic and cultural attraction in the early twentieth century while other regional ports, such as Tripoli and Tyre, lost ground, was never reducible to some extraneous globalization or which municipalities imperial rulers chose to promote.[98] The relative economic strength and cultural vitality of particular towns, trades, and networks of connection was in flux. All were part of a 'transpatialization' whose dynamics, while affected by changes in imperial governance and the growth of a more Eurocentric world economy, were also driven by more proximate local factors.

Within Bilad al-Sham as a whole, economic activity, cultural connection, and political attachment cohered around cities and their hinterlands. Certain towns and regions drew closer together in the first half of the twentieth century as interior communications and trade between them increased. Others developed stronger cultural and economic links with neighboring territories, most notably Egypt and Kemalist Turkey, meaning that by the time British and French imperial overseers took charge of their new 'mandated territories' of Palestine, Transjordan, Iraq, Syria, and Lebanon, transnational patterns of interurban connection and cosmopolitan networks of trade and sociability were well established.[99] Schayegh's work on the Bilad al-Sham offers two insights especially relevant to us here: the enduring pull of regional cross-border connections and the critical importance of urban centers as trading hubs and cultural foci. Attachments to region and locality emerge as equally significant as those to empire or nation, if not more so.

Security Connections and Supranational Influences

This last section moves from the realms of economic and cultural interaction to those of geopolitics and security. The end of empire did not mean that national armies and police units simply replaced colonial security forces.[100] In practice, the composition, training, and equipment of numerous national security forces reflected past imperial links. In many cases, former colonial military and police commanders remained in place. Some became advisers, helping to forge newly established armies and police cadres. Algeria's fiercely independent Armée Nationale Populaire (ANP), consolidated from within the ranks of the FLN forces that fought for independence from France, was one such hybrid. The ANP relied on a polyglot mixture of military hardware, strategic training, and intelligence cooperation with partners in the Arab world, the Soviet bloc, and, more surprisingly, France.[101] The armies of India and Pakistan, which have fought one another repeatedly since independence in 1947, share similar models of organization and Cold War–era networks of arms supply. Ironically for two such bitter rivals, they also share military traditions fashioned in the colonial era. Few newly independent countries could develop their internal security forces without drawing on support from abroad, whether to equip their cadres, to train them, or, in some cases, to staff senior posts. Strategic connections between security forces and regimes in the global South and their clients overseas reflect relationships cemented during decolonization and the Cold War, but past colonial enmities with former rulers rarely prevent dialogue with them as well.[102]

Similar points might be made about the networks of foreign bases maintained by front-rank military powers in client countries around the world. Numerous base agreements, missile sites, and military transit facilities originate in colonial-era deployments and alliances between Cold War partners.[103] The loss of sovereign control intrinsic to the presence of foreign military forces on home soil points to forms of strategic dependency that, from Japan to Panama, Cyprus to Diego Garcia, were imposed by an occupying power. By the same token, the withdrawal of foreign base rights might be seen as an index of sovereign independence among countries denied the opportunity to voice opposition to such military intrusion in an earlier era of colonial rule.[104]

Military interventions, peacekeeping missions, economic sanctions, and diplomatic mediation have all compromised the sovereignty of former colonies.[105] Anticolonial theorists foresaw this, anxious about the ability of colonized societies to safeguard hard-won independence. As we have seen, some postcolonial leaders were drawn first to internationalism, later to regional supranationalism—the first to deepen cooperation between nations confronting more powerful opponents, the second to establish confederations with common strategic objectives.[106] Whether internationalist or supranationalist, the underlying goal was the same: to ensure that decolonized nations could protect their sovereignty by pooling it. The heyday for regional groupings of such states spanned the late 1950s to the mid-1970s, as we will see in chapter 13. But since that latter tipping point, the Organization of American States (OAS, founded in 1948), the Organization of African Unity (OAU, founded in 1963 and relaunched as the African Union [AU] in 2002) and, more recently, the Economic Community of West African States (ECOWAS) have accepted foreign intervention to ameliorate humanitarian crises or to combat rights violations within fellow member states.[107]

For African countries, a readiness to act against neighboring rogue regimes squares the circle between the ideals of pan-African solidarity and respect for sovereign independence that inspired the original foundation of the OAU.[108] This was one of several supranational groupings across regions of the global South styled after the United Nations. Its establishment in 1963 reflected a sense among its member states that the United Nations did not represent African interests sufficiently. This viewpoint had been evident since the United Nations' inception twenty years earlier. The UN Charter was not an unequivocally anti-imperialist document. It stopped short of condemning colonialism outright. It did not identify empire as incompatible with the new international order it purported to support. Its real significance for decolonization lay elsewhere. In its legal content, as well as its general tone, the Charter presumed the nation-state as the most logical and ethically defensible form of polity. As Sundha Pahuja points out, 'on one hand whilst international law did provide a language in which claims for decolonization could gain a certain audibility, on the other it locked in nation statehood as the only way to claim legal personality'.[109]

Added to this normalization of state sovereignty was another expectation: namely, that a supranational organization claiming global authority to scrutinize international behavior would take an interest in forms of governance as well. The United Nations would be watching the way the world was governed because its core purpose was to promote peace and prosperity. The implications for empires were ominous; in historian Jessica Pearson's words, the UN Charter 'opened a space where—if colonial subjects could not speak on their own behalf—representatives from recently independent nations and other anti-imperial delegations could attempt to speak for them'.[110]

UN supervision of trust territories added to the pressure. Like the mandated territories of the interwar years, trusteeship arrangements organized through the United Nations were subject to supranational oversight.[111] The imperial powers that held them faced mounting opposition from below and hostile scrutiny from without as petitioners inside trust territories and anticolonial advocacy groups beyond them pushed for rapid transitions to independence. Among the former were women's rights groups, whose petitioning for educational access for girls and economic empowerment for women revealed how far the holders of trusteeships still had to go.[112] Foremost among the latter was the International League of the Rights of Man (ILRM), the first human rights nongovernmental organization to secure consultative status at the UN. ILRM leaders were relentless lobbyists, insistent that trusteeship existed to end racial discrimination by promoting individual freedom and national self-determination.[113] This was obviously not happening in trust territories such as French-administered Cameroon. There, the Union des Populations du Cameroun (UPC) led opposition to imperial oversight, only to be met with repression and targeted assassination. Still, the UPC fought on. The confluence between its liberationist insurgency and the radical internationalism of the ILRM exemplified a wider process that made the United Nations a focal point in global pressure for decolonization as a human rights imperative, something explored in the chapters ahead.[114]

Conclusion

Assessing the impact of globalization on the end of empires is difficult in the absence of consensus over which vectors—economic output and trade flows, cultural connections and migratory patterns, or shifts in transregional power—best express its impact.[115] Sticking with vernacular readings of globalization as a capitalistic process, critics suggest that characterizing globalization as something with worldwide relevance misses the significance of its presumptive direction of travel.[116] This, they insist, is always regarded as one-way traffic, the practices and peoples (colonizing settlers especially) of the rich global North inexorably spreading outward in a homogenizing process.[117] Ironically, the same criticism could be leveled at socialist-style globalization, which claimed to be anticolonial and internationalist but was centrally directed from within Communist countries and marred by reflexive racism among some of its practitioners.[118]

For some scholars, these criticisms are precisely the point. What looks like globalization—capitalist or anticapitalist—in the age of empire was actually something unapologetically Eurocentric, a manifestation of imperial powers' efforts to achieve 'planetary hegemony' and the determination of strategic rivals in the Communist 'Second World' to thwart them.[119] For others, a primordial focus on Europe's global reach is distorting. Reciprocal influences, cosmopolitan attachments within the global

South, and migrant movements in Asia and across Africa, plus empire's 'afterlife' in metropolitan social policies, memories, and institutional practices, are underplayed or ignored.[120] Compressing global changes of the past century or so into an explanatory framework in which globalization predominates also diminishes decolonization as a reorganization of the world. This chapter has tried to rebalance things—to unpick interactions between the end of empires and globalization. The two processes were codependent. Together, they shaped the north–south dynamics of global politics.

CHAPTER THREE

Decolonization and Its Alternatives

THE OPENING CHAPTERS indicated that decolonization was never a zero-sum game of transitions from empire to sovereign independence. Imperial connections were too complex to be severed with a surgical cut. To equate political freedom with national independence would be to reduce decolonization to state formation, obscuring the local concerns that animated political engagement in the first place.[1] Defying the timelines of formal decolonization, sovereignty would remain bitterly contested, whether expressed in juridical terms of governmental authority over a territory or as a social construction, the product of people's sense of cultural belonging and economic rights to particular spaces.[2] All of this makes the case for considering alternatives to decolonization, the schemes and worldviews that envisioned futures unbounded from the polar opposites of colonial subjugation and independent nationhood.

Identity Politics and Nationalism

Uncompromising demands for national independence were rare among early opposition movements within colonial territories. 'Integral nationalism' emerged most clearly in the interwar years among Communist groups in Southeast Asia, as well as within Arab political parties, whether locally in the Middle East and North Africa or within communities of Maghreb immigrants in France.[3]

To use French-ruled Vietnam as an example, at the start of the twentieth century leading Vietnamese nationalists such as Phan Bôi Châu were drawn to Japanese-led pan-Asianism and the alternate path to social modernization it promised.[4] Fired by a proliferation of Vietnamese and French-language print journalism before and after the First World War, by the mid-1930s oppositional political culture in Vietnam's major cities diversified.[5] At one end of the ideological spectrum, the VNQDD, a nationalist movement facing ruthless French repression, competed with the newly founded Indochinese Communist Party's promises of socialist redistribution in an independent Vietnamese republic. At the other end, support for closer assimilation to France, largely confined to an urban Vietnamese elite, shaded into a gradualist reformism tolerant of an imperial connection. By 1937 the combination of Japan's aggressive militarism and a brief window of reformist opportunity opened by France's left-leaning Popular Front government generated stronger local interest in electoral participation, Dominion-style autonomy and social rights guaranteed by a written constitution.[6]

In Vietnam, as elsewhere, popular involvement in colonial nationalist schemes began in earnest after the First World War.[7] For students and women's groups active in Vietnam's major cities during the 1920s and 1930s, oppositional engagement was framed as patriotic duty, its target being an end to colonial discrimination.[8] That is not to deny the persistence of cosmopolitan thinking and transnational attachments connecting educated Vietnamese to their counterparts across Southeast Asia.[9] But it is to suggest the consolidation of something new.[10] Before the Second World War, in Vietnam as elsewhere in the colonial world, the politics of contested identities did not catalyze mass support for national independence.[11] Surveying the European overseas empires in the late 1930s, the majority of oppositionists focused on particular community interests, specific local grievances, or the moral indefensibility of colonialism as a social condition.[12] One could go further. Detailed schemes for the distribution of political and economic power, the organization of administrative services and legal systems, and the conduct of international affairs were fashioned as part of 'nation-building' exercises conducted after formal decolonization occurred rather than before it.[13]

International Law and Colonial Visibility

Let's step back further, to the eve of the First World War, to consider why. In 1914 colonial subjects were scarcely recognized, let alone protected in international law. In the words of Martti Koskenniemi, 'Europeans still acted from a position of superiority towards others: capitulation regimes, consular jurisdiction, and brutal colonial wars had become banal aspects of the international everyday'.[14] As discussed in chapter 7, World War I's impact on legal constructions of rights had lasting consequences for empire. Between 1919 and 1922 the Allied powers at the Paris Peace Conference put forward various arguments for instituting war crimes trials, for codifying new instruments of international law to punish acts of wartime violence, and for using international courts to uphold treaty settlements and peace itself. Some commentators interpret these actions as victors' justice, even as retribution. Others see them as politically necessary to justify wartime sacrifices. Still others point to stronger efforts to use law to limit future conflicts or, should such conflicts recur, to constrain their violence.[15]

This ideological contest was most visceral in a band of territory stretching from the southern Balkans in the west through the northern reaches of the Ottoman Empire to the Caucasus. Throughout this part of Eurasia, three land empires, Austro-Hungarian, Ottoman, and Russian, targeted ethnic minorities advancing national claims. The outcomes registered in communal violence, mass expulsions, and genocide.[16] The severity of the war crimes committed against particular communities within the Ottoman Empire, as well as against civilians living under the occupation of the central powers and their clients, left legacies of bitterness and regional instability.[17] The suffering experienced by minority populations catalyzed transnational activism, driving waves of humanitarian interventionism through the interwar years.[18]

The Allied powers responded by punishing selected perpetrators in the short term and by refining mechanisms for the enforcement of international laws in the long term.[19] The consequent judicial process, easily criticized as one-sided, also left its advocates open to accusations of hypocrisy from colonial groups. How could international law be upheld as the embodiment of humanistic values when its protagonists governed empires grounded on racial categorization and differential rights? The reality for the majority of colonial populations remained subject status.[20] Preexisting systems of local justice, community obligation, and religious edicts remained as salient as the colonial laws externally superimposed upon them. Colonial empires were an amalgam of competing laws and obligations, a messy legal pluralism that fed claims to special treatment and to the juridical supremacy of one set of laws over another.[21] In some cases, colonial subjects exploited these contradictory requirements and overlapping jurisdictions to their advantage, seeking judgments from the village council, religious authority, or colonial institution most likely to serve their interest.[22]

In one area—the colonial workplace—the direction of legal travel was clearer.[23] Colonial subjects, as well as the indentured laborers on which numerous colonial export industries relied, became increasingly visible in international law in 1919 and the years that followed. Article 23 of the League of Nations Covenant stipulated that all signatories, including imperial powers, should 'secure and maintain fair and humane conditions of labor for all men, women and children'. And the Treaty of St Germain-en-Laye obliged the League to investigate 'slavery in all its forms' wherever it was found. By 1926 the League was committed to a Forced Labour Convention, the precise drafting of which fell to its affiliate, the International Labour Organization (ILO).[24]

Labor Coercion and the Colonial Workplace

Regulating forced labor did not mean ending it.[25] The League did not oppose empire. The ILO did not dismantle colonial practices of unfree labor.[26] The logic of the Forced Labour Convention as codified in 1930 was that imperialists should police themselves.[27] ILO monitoring was light-touch. League condemnation of known violations was patchy.[28] British representatives, among others, insisted that colonized children in tropical climates 'matured' earlier and actively sought work.[29] An end-of-year report about local workplace legislation, compiled in 1937 by the India Tea Association, the organization representing British estate-owners, typified the elisions encouraged by this 'don't look too closely' approach:

> At present children are sometimes employed in leaf houses attached to tea factories which, by virtue of the provisions of the present rules under the Factories Act [1934] in Bengal and Assam, are not regarded as constituting factories for the purposes of the Act so long as they are effectively separated from the factory proper. Consequently children employed in leaf houses are not affected by Section 50 of the Act, which stipulates that no child under twelve years of age shall be employed in a factory.[30]

In plain language: Assamese tea producers could still use child labor because of where the work was done.

Elsewhere, European imperial governments claimed they had broken the link between debt bondage and indenture in which fixed-term labor contracts promised, but rarely delivered, freedom from debt and a transition to working freely.[31] Indentured Indians and Chinese diaspora communities predominated among those affected. From Fiji in the Pacific through the colonies of Southeast Asia, across Indian Ocean islands to East and Southern Africa, and in Caribbean territories such as Trinidad and Guyana, each encountered workplace discrimination from colonial employers and, sometimes, their local counterparts within the labor force.[32] Indentured labor became less blatant, but the worker indebtedness at its heart endured.[33] In part, this was due to employers' hidden charges such as adding costs for transportation, housing, and upkeep to the laborer's debt burden.[34] In part, indebtedness reflected the failure of ameliorative measures. Colonial cooperative schemes were one such source of disappointment. Their core aim was laudable: to give smallholders loans to buy the fertilizer, tools, and equipment they needed for higher yields.[35] But they made little difference. Colonial employers still prevented their workers from breaking free of debt obligations and workplace attachments.[36]

In larger part, the persistence of coercive labor practices could be put down to the world economic crisis. The Depression of the 1930s spiked imperial government and corporate interest in colonial export production to compensate for declining industrial revenues at home. In certain sectors, colonial tin production for one, the result was to restrict output as a means to reinflate a collapsing commodity price. Complaints from administrators and industry groups focused on the threat to revenue, not the impact on workers and their wages.[37] In other colonial export industries the response to depression was different, but no less damaging to workforces struggling to get by. Falling raw material prices spelled additional burdens for plantation laborers as colonial regimes from British Malaya and Dutch Indonesia to Portuguese Africa depressed wages and intensified production in an effort to cover their losses. Colonial labor inspectorates, more widespread in the wake of the League and ILO reforms, could not reverse things.[38] In the Belgian Congo, for instance, export drives in the rubber, timber, and mining industries followed steep declines in government revenue between 1931 and 1933.[39] In 1933 the Belgian authorities introduced so-called *travaux d'ordre éducatif*—'educational' obligatory works—sending Congolese villagers to work on cash crop production in a thinly veiled forced-labor program still in place at independence in 1960.[40] In the neighboring French equatorial colony of Oubangui-Chari (now the Central African Republic), a notoriously exploitative administration cajoled smallholders into cultivating cotton for export, denying them the opportunity to farm small plots for subsistence. The result by 1936 was famine.[41] French Madagascar's administration also increased forced labor, introducing decree legislation in April 1938 to augment the workforce cultivating Madagascar's most lucrative export crops, vanilla and tobacco.[42] Among the decree provisions were the imposition of ten days' *corvée* for adult males, regulations on the permissible loads pregnant women could carry (twenty kilograms max.) and rules covering forced labor by minors (children of twelve and over could perform hard labor when 'urgently needed').[43]

Falling commodity prices were a trigger, but the toleration of unfree labor also reflected a deeper ideational shift within the League of Nations. Concern for the welfare of all humanity informed the work of specialist League commissions. But the conception of human security that emerged from such thinking suggested that individual well-being was best served by resumption in global economic growth. This assumption created the political space necessary for coerced labor to continue, a 'least said, soonest mended' approach that redounded to the detriment of colonial workers.[44] The Depression as catalyst to imperial production drives also explains the resuscitation after 1929 of dormant post–First World War schemes for colonial development. Infrastructure-building on roads, ports, and power generation, plus relocating rural families to 'model village' settlements, complemented the extraction of more labor by export industries.[45]

Not surprisingly, imperial historians have questioned the International Labour Organization's commitment to tackling colonial abuses. The ILO's Native Affairs Office tried to tighten workplace regulation but did not challenge imperial nations' authority to 'civilize' through the discipline of work.[46] Unfree labor lasted well into the 1940s. In the Portuguese Empire it remained legislatively institutionalized until 1956, despite furious regime assertions to the contrary.[47] Elsewhere, the social conditions that compelled people to submit to forced labor—poverty, gender inequality, and debt—demanded the overhaul of the entire colonial apparatus. ILO representatives discerned this but only confronted these structural conditions in response to demands from their global South representatives.[48]

ILO recognition that colonial laborers needed stronger protections fostered dialogue with a raft of antislavery societies, humanitarian groups, and civil rights activists, including W. E. B. Du Bois, Roger Baldwin, and future national leaders Ho Chi Minh, Mohammed Hatta, and Jawaharlal Nehru. They swapped ideas about workplace rights for subject peoples and how to make them stick. In a similar vein, West African lawyers and other petitioners exploited the mandates system to expose violations of prohibitions on forced labor and conscription. These advocates repeatedly informed the League of Nations' oversight agency, the Permanent Mandates Commission, of abuses. And they used the mandate-holders' obligation to keep an economic 'open door', including free movement into and out of mandated territories, to consolidate connections across West Africa's territorial and linguistic divides. These links anticipated the more organized anticolonialism of later decades.[49]

Indian representatives, meanwhile, focused their petitioning on the League of Nations Secretariat. The only colony granted membership in the League of Nations, partly in recognition of its First World War contributions, partly as an adjunct to the British Dominions that joined as cosignatories of the 1919 Treaty of Versailles, India was never a free agent at Geneva. Its delegates, all of elite background, were answerable to the imperial Government of India (and so, indirectly, to the UK parliament). Nehru surely spoke for many when, in 1936, he dismissed India's League of Nations membership as 'a farce'.[50] Petitioning, though, was no empty gesture. Indian petitioners relentlessly highlighted violations of international law, including cases of police brutality, political imprisonment, and labor coercion.[51] The League Secretariat did little to redress these grievances, but it did make them visible to global audiences. Among them were local stakeholders whose efforts to expose abuses registered in the claims-making about social rights and economic entitlements that spread throughout the colonized world during and after the Second World War.[52] Colonized women, doubly discriminated against, were prominent in this process, demanding advances toward not only racial equality but gender equality as well.[53] Colonial women's groups pushed for gendered social policy action, from educational access and equitable curriculum content to better economic opportunities and primary health care.[54]

Economic and Social Rights after 1945

Looking forward to the postwar world, the ILO, in its landmark May 1944 Philadelphia Conference Declaration, affirmed a global commitment to support the dignity of the individual, building on the Atlantic Charter's earlier stipulations about workers' rights, social security, and workplace standards.[55] There was still friction inside the ILO and cognate agencies such as the United Nations' Committee on the Status of Women (founded in 1946) between Western delegates, who foregrounded political rights to equality, and their global South counterparts, who prioritized economic rights and poverty alleviation.[56] But stronger international interest in universal protections resonated with a postwar world being reshaped by decolonization. Defining international standards for workers regardless of their status as citizens or subjects put the supranational regulation of social rights at odds with imperial powers' insistence on inviolate empire sovereignty. The prospect of other countries, the United States and the Soviet Union included, taking up the cause of colonial workers to advance their own regional interests made economic and social rights a more pressing issue for colonial authorities than the more sporadic controversies over human rights abuses of detainees, protesters, and civilian victims of counterinsurgency operations. The point was being reached where, in public understanding, certain rights attached to each and every individual regardless of their geographical location, their ethnicity, their gender, or their legal status.[57]

Anxious to lend substance to official postwar rhetoric of developmental partnership, colonial governments across British and French Africa tried to minimize the risk of worker radicalization by promoting 'responsible' trade unionism. African workers, particularly in the highly unionized transport sector, had other ideas. Opposition to racially discriminatory pay rates meshed with demands for social rights, safer workplaces, pensions, and other benefits.[58] Moving into the 1950s, the International Confederation of Free Trade Unions (ICFTU), the instrument used by imperial governments to inculcate 'responsible' labor activism, was superseded by its more radical supranational rivals, the Soviet-directed World Federation of Trade Unions (WFTU) and the pan-Africanist Union Générale des Travailleurs d'Afrique Noire (UGTAN). The ideological competition between these confederations was secondary to more imminent concerns as local activists adopted anticolonialist positions.[59] Aware that labor struggles were inflected by markers of difference specific to their colonial situation, trade unionists across imperial territories recognized a common enemy: colonialism itself.[60]

The experience of mineworkers in Northern Rhodesia's (Zambia's) copper belt, the site of recurrent worker protests, is instructive.[61] A Native National Labor Board established in 1947 was meant to introduce legally enforceable social rights, including a minimum wage for industrial workers and entitlement to sick pay. But black workers remained unrecognized as 'employees' under the terms of Northern Rhodesia's Industrial Conciliation Act, making it illegal for them to strike. Mineworkers also faced discrimination outside the workplace, from housing segregation to political surveillance. Supporters of the ANC's Northern Rhodesian wing were blacklisted, dismissed, or detained.[62] A Mobile Police Reserve, on hand to assist the mining companies, sometimes acted without the authorization of British-appointed district commissioners, beating up strike organizers and coercing others back to work.[63] The situation worsened after August 1953 when Northern Rhodesia joined its Southern namesake and Nyasaland in the Central African Federation. Copperbelt policing fell to security force personnel, mostly from Southern Rhodesia, who were determined to enforce the racial hierarchy of white-minority rule.[64]

Discriminatory practices were apparent elsewhere in British Africa. In Kenya, by the 1930s migrant workers figured large in the commercial, mining, and manufacturing sectors, as well as on settler farms. Most colonial employers paid only subsistence wages, expecting the social networks within African 'reserves' to fill the gap. It fell to the inhabitants of the reserves to meet their neighbors' educational, health, and child-support needs, while also providing social protections to returning elderly or sick workers. In historian Sharon Stichter's words, 'the tribal economy became an appendage to the new economy of estate agriculture, subsidizing its low wages'.[65] The pattern of neglect evident in late colonial Kenya was as evident across empires as within them. Until the purpose of empire was rethought during and after the Second World War, colonial governments, corporations, and settler estate-owners in sub-Saharan Africa abdicated responsibility for social security protections for their workers. African families and extended kin networks were left to look after the weakest in society.[66] Colonial authorities justified their inaction with talk of 'respecting tradition', rarely admitting that the status quo benefited the elites on whom local administration relied.

This complicity in local conservatism hit women and girls hardest.[67] It also put colonial authorities on a collision course with supranational agencies wedded to universalist ideals of social rights. Beginning in the 1920s, the League of Nations engaged in a knowledge-gathering exercise, accumulating reports, questionnaires, and data on child marriage and the coercion of young women and girls. The results were analyzed under the rubric of forced labor.[68] The entire process rested on the opinion of 'experts': overwhelmingly male, white Europeans, most of them officials in the colonies under investigation. These 'experts' disagreed on whether practices such as forced genital mutilation and bride-wealth were 'problems' at all.[69] The prevailing tendency was to justify a laissez-faire position as consistent with the tenets of indirect rule.[70] British imperial reluctance to antagonize favored indigenous auxiliaries translated into the toleration of forced marriage as a facet of 'customary' society. This was apparent in well-known criminal cases of the 1930s and 1940s in which African girls forced into marriage in Swaziland and Kenya either resisted or sought sanctuary with sympathetic relatives, missionary educators, or local officials.[71] UN reformers such as French representative Jane Vialle,

FIGURE 3.1. (Male) colonial elites in action: Jules Brévié, Governor-General of French West Africa, salutes the flag, Dakar, 1933. Source: Albert Sarraut papers, Archives départementales de l'Aude.

a Congolese woman of color, were determined to use an updated Anti-Slavery Convention to tackle the subjugation of women and girls, but faced an uphill task.[72]

Nor would Anglophone black Africa replicate social entitlements and worker protections introduced in French West Africa after the industrial unrest of the immediate postwar period. British colonial officials, conscious of the prohibitive cost of rudimentary social welfare measures, insisted that African laborers, male and female, could rely on their extended families to see them through periods of sickness and old age.[73] In Lusophone Africa, a metropolitan dictatorship wedded to the constitutional fiction of a Portuguese empire of freely integrated territories barred the way to workplace reforms for longer still.[74]

Even so, by the early 1950s the scrutiny of the United Nations' specialist multilateral organizations, international trade union federations, and other civil society groups was impossible to shake off.[75] The tenaciousness of external monitoring agencies only intensified as public awareness of racist practices increased, creating a political marketplace in which the remaining imperial powers nurtured relationships with those agencies considered amenable to gradualist reform.[76] The ILO was a case in point. By 1956 Salazar's Portugal treated the organization as an interlocutor and a siphon. It was easier to comply with technical ILO recommendations about the abolition of forced labor and the institution of workplace protections than to bend to hostile UN pressure for rights equivalence between settlers and Africans. And compliance with the ILO's limited technical requirements eased the external pressure for deeper change.[77]

Was the fact that one of colonial Africa's harshest regimes felt compelled to engage with the ILO, finally banning unfree labor practices in 1959, merely sleight of hand? Some grim evidence suggests so. Worker abuses persisted, from coercive labor recruitment in the vast Diamang Mining Company operations in northern Angola to the yawning wage gaps between settlers and Africans working in agriculture throughout Portuguese Africa.[78] Violence against protesting dockworkers at Pidjiguiti in Guinea-Bissau saw scores gunned down by police on August 3, 1959, underlining the regime's contempt for organized dissent. Killings of nationalist demonstrators at Mueda on Mozambique's Makonde plateau in June 1960 and at Baixa de Cassange in northern Angola's cotton-producing Malanje region on January 4, 1961, were pivotal to the outbreak of independence struggles in all three Portuguese territories in mainland Africa.[79]

State Legitimacy and Arguments about Rights

Lusophone Africa could, though, be viewed as an outlier. In other colonial empires after 1945 prospects for staking claims to rights looked brighter than during the preceding years of economic crisis and global war. From the victory of Clement Attlee's Labour Party in July 1945 to Harry Truman's two-term presidency and the resurrection of democratic republics in France and Italy, a welfarism characterized by big government and a preoccupation with living standards took root among imperialist nations. In France, as in Britain, the identifications among state support, social rights minima, and societal cohesion emerged more strongly after the Second World War than the First.[80] This developmental turn, based on the measurement of socioeconomic outcomes, had begun earlier in the twentieth century. It was only after 1945, though, that the money available began to match the rhetoric of empire as socially improving.[81] Within the UN General Assembly, signatories to the UDHR in December 1948 agreed on provisions for economic and social rights alongside the more familiar clauses regarding civil and political liberties.[82] As Jane Burbank and Frederick Cooper put it, 'Development promised to make empires richer and more politically legitimate at the same time'.[83]

Putting together the emergence of new frameworks of human rights with the leftward shift within multiple imperialist countries after 1945, it becomes easier to see why their governments were drawn to colonial development plans and, in the most volatile territories, counterinsurgency strategies that shaded into schemes of coercive social engineering.[84] Colonial state violence was defended as not repression but the adaptation of European welfarist schemes to dependent territories.[85] Counterinsurgency was reinvented, whether at the familial level, as the imposition of improved standards of hygiene and household management, or at the national level, as the prerequisite to modernization.[86]

Practitioners of coercive development argued that it was pointless to concede political freedoms without tangible improvements in the quality of colonial lives. Health centers, maternity clinics, and district hospitals built in the 1940s and 1950s diminished the European tendency to pathologize colonial bodies as disease carriers to be regimented and controlled.[87] Reducing infant mortality, curbing epidemic illness, and extending rural health care: these were the postwar indexes on which imperial administrations expected empires to be judged.[88] The new language of development correlated necessary infrastructures and welfare provision with the statistical measurement of economic output and gross domestic product (GDP). Informed by older ideas of rural poverty reduction, late colonial development professed to be something else: a scientific objectivity responsive to community need.[89]

Supporters of decolonization were constrained by other factors as well. International law was one. This might seem counterintuitive. Hadn't the UDHR claimed a global applicability, embracing those living under colonial rule? Indeed so, but it was independent national governments that were to be held to account for rights violations. Aside from the fact that there were, as yet, few independent national governments across the global South, the problem was that, in making nation-states responsible for upholding human rights, supporters of the Universal Declaration locked anticolonialists into replicating the territories contrived by their imperial rulers.[90] Another constraint was the widespread presumption that the legitimacy of a postindependence regime rested on the people's willingness to hold democratic elections to validate its claim to power. The expectation of quick 'national' elections added to pressures to work within old colonial boundaries, turning what some analysts describe as 'multiple possibilities into a single future'. In the three former British colonial territories of Ghana, Kenya, and Uganda, for instance, the link between decolonization and national elections favored the literate, the educated, and the organized, cementing the dominance of nationalist elites committed to social modernization.[91] Prevailing developmental agendas presupposed that nation-states would be the containers through which improvements in living standards were delivered. Whether invoking international law for sovereignty claims, to secure the legal protections of belligerent status, or to reap the fruits of development, independence struggles were widely articulated as national.[92]

The traffic in ideas was never one-way, of course. By the mid-1950s rich-world advocates of development faced stronger opposition from recipient communities and governments in the global South who insisted on the primacy of social and economic rights within poor societies, not as gifts bestowed by wealthy outsiders but as fundamental human security needs.[93] ILO delegates from South Asia and sub-Saharan Africa took issue with the organization's lingering assumptions that religion, 'tradition' and 'custom' rather than colonialism and economic structures confined women of the global South to household labor, informal employment, and unequal pay.[94] On taking power, some independence movements justified authoritarian government by asserting an ethical imperative to satisfy their people's primordial requirement for basic necessities, not the luxuries of political inclusion on which their rich-world critics fixated.[95]

In recent years, historians of human rights have disputed whether the 1940s or the 1970s marked the definitive arrival of what has been dubbed the global 'human rights imagination' in world politics.[96] The sanctity of individual rights registered in the raft of international law inscribed after the Second World War.[97] Running in parallel to the United Nations' creation, denazification programs and the reconstruction of defeated and occupied states brought opportunities to embed principles of global justice in international politics. But glaring omissions remained. Where were women's rights, children's rights, rights for the segregated, or legal clarity over the rights of colonial subjects?[98] White citizens within empires were bound by different, more lenient legal systems than colonial subjects; women in most dependencies had fewer rights than men; and the colonial distinction between nationality, by which individuals were legally connected to a particular territory, and citizenship, a status conferring civil rights, went largely unchallenged.[99]

Reacting to the wartime displacement of families and the millions of children who lost or were separated from their parents, UDHR articles 12 and 16 identified the family as the 'fundamental unit' of human societies and declared that families should be protected from 'arbitrary interference'. Yet, as with social rights, so with the defense of the nuclear family: purportedly universal standards were differentially applied in dependent territories.[100] Some humanitarian organizations in European imperial countries, such as Britain's Save the Children Fund and France's Red Cross, even became adjuncts of postwar counterinsurgency as they focused their attention on vulnerable colonial subjects—nursing mothers, children, and refugees.[101]

It is also questionable how far human rights concerns swayed the actions of regimes and social movements until a later generation of rights advocacy groups founded in the 1960s harnessed the moral authority of witnessing rights abuses, using newer communications mediums and the power of global condemnation to hold perpetrators to account.[102] Some historians even suggest that making minority rights a humanitarian concern was a trap. Treating oppressed minorities as communities in need of international assistance rather than as peoples with claims to sovereign independence halted decolonization at the point where former colonies escaped European colonial rule. From India's Nagaland to Biafra's putative independence from Nigeria, minorities demanding separation from decolonized states confronted an international community, which treated them at best as charity cases, at worst as destabilizing secessionists, but never as legitimate claimants to national sovereignty.[103]

The Decolonization Factor

Decolonization is bound up with these debates. If human rights could be codified and enforced, they might alter relationships among individuals, those who governed them, and the wider world watching what was done. The limits to state sovereignty would surely change if a higher supranational authority claimed powers to intervene against egregious rights abuses within any territory.[104] The UN Charter's Article 56, described as the 'domestic jurisdiction clause', seemed to preclude UN intervention in a country's internal affairs, but its ambiguous phrasing left the inviolability of empires open to challenge.[105] Decolonization put growing international pressure for human rights protections on 'a collision course with claims to sovereignty'.[106] South African premier Jan Christian Smuts, one of the Charter's many fathers, discovered this to his cost in 1946 when India's UN delegation protested South Africa's discriminatory Asiatic Land Tenure and Indian Representation Act, a plank of its segregationist politics.[107] In this and later cases, the assertion that people are born with basic human rights, plus the granular individualization of inalienable freedoms from broader economic and social rights to welfare, education, and employment, bore directly on colonial subject peoples. Conversely, the presumption that basic rights should be guaranteed in law imposed heavy obligations on newly independent nations whose constitutional settlements and legal codes were still to be written.[108]

A year after Smuts ran into trouble with India's UN representatives, on July 30, 1947, Congress Ministers in New Delhi pressed for General Assembly condemnation of Dutch actions in Indonesia. It was impossible, they insisted, for a people to emerge from decolonization only to acquiesce in the colonial subjugation of others.[109] The presence of millions of ethnic Indians in diaspora communities across southeast Asia and eastern and southern Africa added another human dimension to this cosmopolitanism.[110] Pakistan's leaders were less confrontational but also used their achievement of nationhood to deepen transnational connections with South Asian Muslim diaspora communities overseas and with Muslim majority territories still under imperial control.[111] Nonetheless, different conceptualizations of rights and disagreement about whose rights to defend make it hard to argue that decolonization was the outcome of a struggle between imperial authorities and colonial peoples over individuated human rights.

In some places, these arguments had crystalized earlier in the twentieth century. By 1919 Venustiano Carranza's Constitutionalist government in revolutionary Mexico defended social rights to human security over individual private property rights while pushing for a nonhierarchical League of Nations that respected the equal status of all member states. The unifying message was that imperialism's denial of social and economic rights was the greatest obstacle to justice domestically and globally.[112] Moving into the 1940s, consider for a moment the Malayan Communist Party's 'Nine Point New Democratic Program', laid out at its eighth plenum in January 1946. Points 1 and 2 called for self-determination and universal suffrage—thus ending British rule—but the remaining elements focused on immediate social concerns: an eight-hour working day, the right to strike, reduced taxation, social security legislation, and four months' statutory maternity leave.[113] Familiar in socialist thought, this prioritization of collective rights to satisfy economic needs was more than a challenge to Western rights thinking. Described as 'a counter-ordering of rights', it put colonialism's destruction first.[114]

Anticolonial movements invoked human rights talk instrumentally at the United Nations and elsewhere, without taking the concept of individuated and inalienable human rights that seriously. Exposing colonial rights abuses mobilized support locally and transnationally, while shining a spotlight on colonialism's political crimes made the case for an alternative global order.[115] Social rights were a more pressing concern even so. Numerous governments in decolonizing countries recognized that poverty and ill health among their people left the door ajar to colonialist influence in the guise of foreign lending, developmental initiatives, and other technocratic expertise. So their interest in materializing economic and social rights was as much political as it was ethical. As the practical obstacles to going it alone became more obvious, so former colonies in the Third World insisted that the achievement of economic and social rights without political strings attached was what mattered most.[116]

The prioritization of collective social and economic rights over individual freedoms continued into the 1960s as newly independent regimes enacted modernization programs. Government diktat was justified by the urgency of the social transformations required in the interests of the many, a form of majoritarianism at odds with Western rights thinking. From Southeast Asia to Latin America, authoritarian rulers turned to foreign clients, the United States prominent among them, to provide finance and training for the 'modernization' of internal policing apparatus, opening the way to political clampdowns and the systematic maltreatment of internal oppositionists.[117] Other post-independence regimes were ousted by coups.[118] Twenty-six occurred in Africa alone between 1960 and 1969.

The UN International Conference on Human Rights, which opened in Tehran in May 1968, twenty years after the signing of the UDHR, tightened the global South authoritarians' grip over the UN human rights agenda.[119] Statist modernizers stressed their nations' economic requirements, insisting that improvements in living standards for the poorest counted for more than fixation on legal equality.[120] During the 1970s supporters of the Tehran conference agenda still pushed social rights above all. Foremost were the G77 countries supportive of the New International Economic Order (NIEO), which identified global capitalism as the barrier to human security for the world's poorest.[121]

Conclusion

Spurred by the reformist impulses and new rights thinking that wartime suffering inspired, by the late 1940s governments and publics spanning the geopolitical divisions of decolonization and the Cold War increasingly acknowledged that the satisfaction of basic economic needs and social rights was intrinsic to human security. Disagreement remained about what such rights comprised and what their minima should be. Also unresolved was the relationship between such rights and the regimes under which people lived.[122] Were freedoms sustainable under one-party rule?[123] Were increasing economic rights compatible with the inequalities of free market capitalism? Most crucially, could colonial subjects enjoy social rights while their claims to collective self-determination were denied? Some minority groups, such as the Igbos of Southeastern Nigeria, understood self-determination less in terms of decolonization from European rule than escape from the local dominance of a different ethnoreligious majority.[124]

Paradoxically, arguments about the economic viability of newly independent territories and the potential for conflict between them melded with an anticolonialist rhetoric that identified self-determination for minority communities with imperialistic efforts to undermine decolonization and the unity of colonized peoples.[125] As a result, few transitions out of empire redrew the geopolitical maps demarcating one colony from another. The two instances of African secession that bookended the 1960s, Katanga's breakaway from the Congo in 1960–1961 and the Biafra Republic's disavowal of Nigeria between 1966 and 1970, ended in catastrophic violence and reversal.[126] Biafran suffering failed to persuade the majority of states to accept secessionist self-determination as legitimate. This reluctance reflected a pervasive fear that granting self-determination to aggrieved minorities in multiethnic settings would result in the balkanization of Africa, state fragmentation, and a gradual unraveling of the interstate system. More common was an insistence on the sovereign supremacy of a unitary central authority that occupied the sites and bureaucratic spaces of the old colonial government. Those wedded to other alternatives—federations and pan-Africanism, decentralization, and regional autonomy—were dismissed as ideological dreamers or condemned as self-interested reactionaries, opponents of authentic decolonization.[127]

PART II

Tracing Paths of Empire Destruction

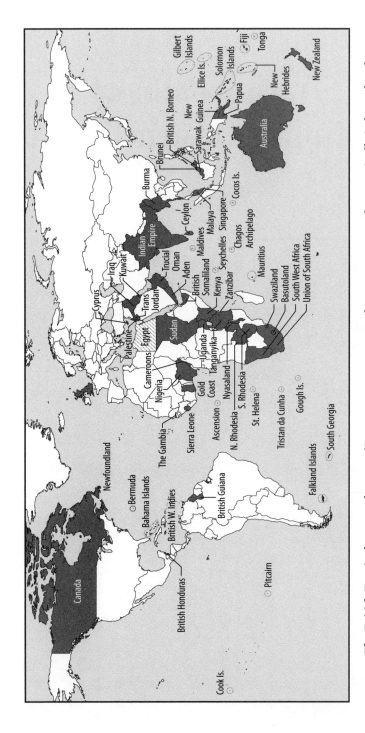

MAP 4.1. The British Empire between the wars. (Egypt was a protectorate from 1914 to 1922, then nominally independent but still under British influence.)

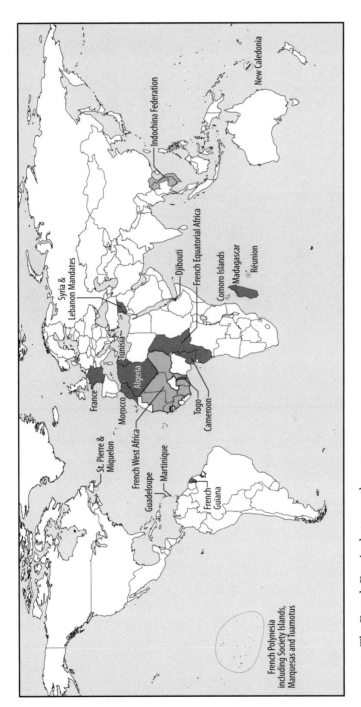

MAP 4.2. The French Empire between the wars.

CHAPTER FOUR

Greater War and Decolonization's First Global Wave

ON JANUARY 3, 1922, the Edinburgh Egyptian Society sent a new year's message of support to Cairo: 'We greet in your noble person the heroic representative of Egyptian womanhood and the devoted mother of the Egyptian people assuring you of the full support of your loyal sons'.[1] The recipient was Madame Zaghloul Pasha, wife of Saad Zaghloul, Egypt's revolutionary leader. Safiya Zaghloul was keeping up the pressure for Egyptian self-rule after Britain's imperial administration deported her husband to the Seychelles. She knew that British sensibilities made her own expulsion unlikely. Her chief antagonist, Field Marshal Lord Allenby, saw the danger. Aside from the astute political organizer she was proving to be, Safiya Zaghloul was a national figurehead and a champion of women's rights. Allenby, though, viewed things in chauvinistic terms. High commissioner in Cairo, he authorized a secret monthly stipend for her of five hundred Egyptian pounds, confident that he could buy the woman's silence.[2] It didn't work. On February 4, 1922, Safiya Zaghloul issued a public appeal. She lambasted the British authorities for deporting Wafd Party leaders prominent in Egypt's 1919 revolution and for interning scores of

* The term 'Greater War' was coined by the American Christian Socialist George D. Herron in a book of the same title published in 1919. Arguing from Wilsonian precepts to support US membership of the League of Nations, Herron insisted that Allied victory in World War I would count for nothing unless the democratic powers sustained peace through internationalist engagement: see George D. Herron, *The Greater War* (New York: Mitchell Kennerley, 1919).

their supporters back home. She ended with a warning. The British, Safiya insisted, fatally underestimated the determination of the Egyptian people to fight for national independence.[3]

These were not empty words. Days later the Cairo Department of Public Security intercepted a letter Safiya had sent her exiled husband. It brimmed with news of incipient revolution. The latest deportations had provoked a three-day strike by state employees. Egypt's mixed courts, the linchpin of the country's judicial system, were crippled by a public boycott. Even the tamer Egyptian political parties still tolerated by the British risked a ban by joining the protests. The ferment culminated at the start of February 1922 with riots in Cairo. Government offices were burned out and tram cars overturned. Police killed eight demonstrators and wounded hundreds more before driving the protesters off the streets.[4]

For a brief moment, Safiya Zaghloul's campaigning helped to unite Egyptians against the British presence. Anxious not to make another martyr to the national cause, the Department of Public Security changed tack. They exploited Saad Zaghlul's poor health to coax his wife out of the country. The first step was to relocate the elderly revolutionary from his Seychelles exile to Gibraltar, a move portrayed as a humanitarian gesture that would allow Saad to convalesce in a climate better suited to his failing lungs. Its ulterior motive became apparent with step two in the British plan: persuading Safiya to join him. Arrangements were put in place over the summer of 1922. On October 9, a party of five left Port Said aboard the SS *Neldera*. The group consisted of Safiya; her son, Said Bey Zaghloul; Safiya's longtime companion, thirty-year-old teacher Fahima Sabet; a nineteen-year-old maid, Sekina, in service to the family since birth; plus Saad's Sudanese manservant, Ibrahim Fadl Mohammed. Crowds of well-wishers, mainly Wafd members, students, and Egyptian Ladies Society activists, accompanied Madame Zaghloul's party on their journey to the coast. With Safiya Zaghloul at their head, Egypt's nationalists identified British persecution of female oppositionists with their country's symbolic violation by European colonialism.[5] Three years after Egypt's putative 1919 revolution, a feminized Zaghloulism retained its power.[6] The prelude to another forty years of Anglo-Egyptian contestation, a nominal declaration of Egypt's independence on February 9, 1922, left British administrators with so-called reserved powers over defense and foreign affairs, among other things. But the de facto expulsion of Safiya Zaghloul and her retainers eight months later underlined how threatened the Cairo High Commission felt by expressions of Egyptian national—and transnational—unity.

The chicanery of the British authorities in Cairo points to a broader conclusion. Egypt epitomized processes unfolding within the British and other European empires because of the First World War. Wartime disruption to Egypt's cotton economy was intensified by conscription and livestock requisitioning. Public support for the independence petition launched by Saad Zaghloul's Wafd Party soon after the November 1918 armistice delegitimized British authority before revolutionary violence broke out in March 1919.[7] Selective repression, limited administrative reforms, and collaboration with favored local elites, for so long the preferred imperial tactics in managing colonial politics, could not neutralize sources of dissent, which now had multiple transnational connections.[8] Like so many others across the colonial world, Wafdists wanted their demands aired at the Paris Peace Conference.

Henri Gaillard, the senior French diplomat in the Egyptian capital, saw things in apocalyptic terms. Cairo was a magnet for political exiles. It sheltered the Syrian Republic's deposed—and bitterly Francophobic—republican government. It introduced revolutionary supporters of pan-Islamism to Wahhabi fundamentalists en route to the hajj. Year by year it turned out cohorts of students drawn to El-Azhar University's Islamic curriculum. They were forever bound into pan-Islamist networks thereafter. And the city played host to Soviet, German, Turkish, and other agents working to destroy the French and British empires.[9] Although Gaillard never used the term, he clearly understood the phenomena he described as transnational—operating below state level, crossing political frontiers, and transcending intangible barriers of cultural difference. Gaillard failed to acknowledge that what lent force to the networks he described was colonialism itself. From the religious activists that so concerned him to the sons and daughters of the best Egyptian families, even in places as remote from Cairo as frosty Edinburgh, all despised the injustice of colonial rule.[10]

Empires and World War I

Beginning the book's second part, focused on causes of empire destruction, this chapter identifies the central paradox of the post–First World War settlement in the racism underpinning it. Colonial territories were excluded from the liberal order that Europe's imperial powers sought to establish.[11] The racial hierarchies intrinsic to imperialism instead condemned dependent territories to the everyday violence of colonialism at the same time as new ideas of sovereignty and self-determination set the

European continent apart from the wider world over which its leading state actors claimed dominion. Viewed from a decentered, non-European perspective, liberal internationalism was a mockery of itself.[12]

In some ways, this wasn't new at all. Anticolonial opposition was as old as colonialism. So was the imperial use of lethal force to suppress it with measures described in terms of internal policing rather than the prosecution of warlike violence against sections of the colonized population.[13] In other ways, the Great War changed the rules of the game. August 1914 began with Germany's invasion of Belgium. This spectacular violation of sovereign neutrality cornered the British government into declaring war. Never a neutral, Britain had profited mightily from neutrality. The largest of the empire states, its maritime supremacy and breakneck colonial expansion rested on keeping out of most big interstate wars after 1815. That all changed with the First World War.[14]

The conflict was a global one, fought over multiple continents by people of many cultures.[15] Empires' troops, military laborers, and war workers were pivotal throughout.[16] The global shipment of colonial bodies to assist imperial war efforts marked the largest spike in the oceanic transportation of subject persons since the end of transatlantic slavery, a parallel that, unsurprisingly, Allied propagandists chose to ignore.[17] Crass miscalculations—about African porters' capacity to survive on starvation diets, about Indian laborers' immunity to African malarial strains—contributed to high mortality rates among colonial subjects forced to work for imperial war efforts.[18] In a bittersweet irony, the war's insatiable appetite for manpower, resources, and capital built transnational networks of connection among the imperial subjects of multiple empires called upon to satisfy these demands.[19] Unsatisfied promises of postwar rewards for wartime services rendered created other bonds of solidarity among colonial subjects.[20] The motivations, experiences, and grievances of colonized war workers, civilian and military, would have lasting ramifications for the politics of the global South.[21] On the front line, as in the munitions factory, racial coding mattered, a poignant daily reminder that the war's principal antagonists were imperialists.[22] They drew on all their global resources in trying to win it.[23] As the editors of a defining work on the subject point out, not only was the war 'fought by empires to determine the fate of those empires', but those who took part 'experienced the war . . . in imperial terms'.[24]

It's questionable, though, whether colonial possessions were as economically vital as their imperial owners presumed. Germany and the United States, latecomers to empire, enjoyed faster economic growth before 1914 than the more established empire states. Of these, the foremost,

Great Britain, certainly milked its largest colony, India, for human and material resources, but the other major centers of wealth within its empire were self-governing Dominions, including Canada, Australia, and South Africa. It was war itself that made empire seem more, not less vital as each side worked globally to sever their enemies' trade, grab their property, and block their capital movements.[25] Take Argentina. Its beef-canning factories provided a protein staple for British soldiers and households, prompting the British government to buy the lease for the country's largest cannery immediately after the war began. Although Argentina was never 'formally' a British dependency, the war nonetheless consolidated its position as the Latin American cornerstone of Britain's global patchwork of 'informal' empire.[26]

Formal and 'informal' empires, even territorially contiguous ones, were hard to defend. There were multiple flanks to attack, numerous ethnicities whose loyalties might be swayed. Rebellions were always likely.[27] Combatant powers tried to hasten victory by offering support to their enemies' colonial subjects, separatists, secessionists, and religious revivalists above all. Most of these strategies failed in the short term.[28] But their consequences lingered. The war mixed together peoples within and between continents.[29] Could they really be 'unmixed' as some hoped? To paraphrase historian Leonard Smith, would boundaries be made to fit peoples, or would peoples be moved to fit boundaries?[30] The resulting disruptions continued for years. In this sense, the war did not end; its disintegrative legacies created additional grievances while deepening others. Its reverberations also connected oppositional voices in new ways, making their claims audible to wider global audiences and the institutional apparatus of supranational oversight created by the peace settlement.

Was this a surprise? By 1917 what historian Georgi Derlugian describes as 'three great revolutionary projects' promised to break the mold of world politics. First, communist revolution in Russia rejected capitalist economics and the belief in national and imperial sovereignties on which it rested. Second, new strains of anticolonial nationalism in China, India, Turkey, Egypt, Korea, and elsewhere posited different ideas of belonging, rejecting the imperial order as a self-serving deceit.[31] Consider Ottoman Beirut, a city flooded with refugees and facing starvation. There, the prominence of women's volunteer associations and other civil society groups in dispensing famine relief delegitimized Turkish authority and amplified Lebanese calls for self-government.[32]

Even liberal internationalism, the third project, held revolutionary potential in its recognition that legitimate aspirations to statehood demanded some reconfiguration of the old imperial order.[33] Other threats were more proximate. Within a few years, fascism's racial ideologies would add a fourth revolutionary challenge to the way international politics had worked before 1914.[34] In Quinn Slobodian's telling comment, 'a new principle of national self-determination was going global, readying an ambush against the old language of empire'.[35] Colonialism was in trouble. Naturally enough, the severity of that trouble touches on the question of decolonization, the unmaking of some empires between 1917 and 1923, and the decline of others that, by outward appearances, still had decades ahead of them.[36]

Decolonization's First Global Wave

Historians of the global aftermath of the First World War ascribe distinct qualities to the political instabilities and social unrest provoked by the conflict. They dwell upon its legacies of competing local and imperial claims to territories and sovereignties, foregrounding the population transfers, paramilitarism, and intrastate violence that ensued.[37] The expulsion and mass killings of the Ottoman Empire's Armenian population displaced upward of three million people and left almost a million dead. The ensuing Turkish–Greek War culminated in a population exchange deal sanctified by international treaty forcibly removing almost two million people, which blurred the line between minority protection and what we might now describe as ethnic cleansing.[38]

Whatever it was, this was hardly peace. There was, though, a different architecture of international order, its globalism expressed in new regulatory agencies affiliated with a supranational body, the League of Nations. Supporters of ethnic self-determination petitioned these agencies for redress. Anti-imperialists used a new vocabulary to do so.[39] Excluded from Peace Conference deliberations in Paris, those pressing for colonial freedoms invoked Woodrow Wilson's identification of 'the self-determining nation-state as the sole legitimate unit of international society' for decades afterward.[40] The simplicity of this message—that self-determination should become an organizing principle of international affairs—lent Wilson's words a universalism he never intended.[41] As for other supranational forms of governing the world, Wilson presupposed that any pooling of sovereignty could only work if governments became accountable to global public opinion. Self-determination was not solely about *who* governs but about *how* they governed and for what purpose.[42] If empire was to survive, it had to meet higher standards of conduct, subject to oversight by a critical world.

Nor was it the Peace Conference alone that defined how global politics would be transacted. Peacemaking in Paris was part of a wider turn to summitry in which social movements and nonsovereign communities were already caught up. Efforts by marginalized groups and diaspora communities to make their voices heard globally through conferences began at the dawn of the twentieth century with the 1900 Pan-African Congress in London. Others followed: the 1911 Universal Races Congress, also in London, and two Pan-African Congresses in Paris in 1919 and 1921.[43] These were followed later in the decade by another pairing, this time of Pan-Asian People's Conferences, one in Nagasaki in 1926, the other in Shanghai in 1927. That same year saw the foundational conference of the League against Imperialism in Brussels, a high-profile meeting attended by many of the anti-imperial figures previously shut out from the Peace Conference in 1919.[44] Delegates personified aspirations to nationhood across Asia, Africa, and Latin America. Nehru, who led the Indian delegation to the conference, insisted that the Brussels Congress signified the convocation of an authentically global 'league' assembly, unlike its European-dominated counterpart in Geneva.[45] His accusations stuck. Admittedly, sixteen Latin American states joined the League of Nations, but this was no protection against infringements of their economic sovereignty and strategic autonomy by richer member states, let alone by the League's foremost absentee, the United States.[46]

For Nehru and others, anger at colonial subordination reconciled tensions between the transnational sentiments of pan-Asianism and pan-Africanism and narrower claims to nationhood.[47] Nehru had written immediately before the Brussels conference began about his sense of alienation from an international society that denied a platform to anticolonial voices.[48] Another of the excluded was W. E. B. Du Bois. He traveled to the French capital in 1919, ostensibly to gather information about the experiences of serving African American troops still in the country for the National Association for the Advancement of Colored People (NAACP), which he had founded with Mary White Ovington and Moorfield Storey in 1909. Unable to get an audience with either the American or Allied delegation to the Peace Conference, Du Bois, an attendee at the inaugural Pan-African Congress in 1900, resolved to organize another. He did so in conjunction with two prominent French colonial politicians, Blaise Diagne from Senegal and Gratien Candace from Guadeloupe.[49] Assimilationists to the core, their elite status and eagerness to work with Georges Clemenceau's government made Diagne and Candace unlikely partners in radical anti-imperialism. Du Bois also faced questioning within the NAACP about aligning the African American freedom struggle with the interests of black Africans living under European colonialism. His answer was to ensure that the Paris Pan-African Congress lived up to its title. Du Bois appealed in humanist terms to the Allied powers picking over the bones of Germany's African colonies to remember the interests of the peoples living within them. By highlighting issues of racial discrimination, labor exploitation, and limited educational opportunity, he ensured that Congress resolutions were as resonant for African colonial subjects as for members of African diaspora communities in North America and the Caribbean.[50]

Other evidence that anti-imperialism was becoming more globally connected emerged from the western hemisphere in the decades bisected by the First World War. That the rhetoric of self-determination originated in President Wilson's Washington made US refusal to permit Central American and Caribbean republics to govern themselves harder to stomach.[51] Resentments were stoked when representatives of Nicaragua, Haiti, and Dominica, territories invaded by US forces between 1913 and 1917, were unable to make their case against American occupation to the Peace Conference. They enjoyed greater success in mobilizing other Latin American governments, as well as the European and US reading publics, to oppose US colonialism in the Caribbean.[52] Political exiles and public intellectuals from Dominica, united in their support for an independent Dominican Republic and an end to the US occupation that began in 1917, consolidated transnational support in the Caribbean, Latin America, and, from 1919, the United States. Lobbyists used their inroads into sympathetic diplomatic missions and anticolonial movements to shine a spotlight onto rights abuses by occupation forces. These networks of the excluded, while themselves elitist, practiced a subversive diplomacy that exposed the coercion intrinsic to the postwar international order.[53] In 1920 and again in 1921, consequent US official inquiries into allegations of summary killings, torture, and other crimes produced equivocal findings but nonetheless increased American public awareness of the realities of colonial occupation.[54]

Political figures from neighboring Haiti, another territory recently brought under US tutelage through a 1916 invasion, found it much harder to work across the racial divides, which still rendered white and Hispanic Dominica an easier sell to other Latin American governments than black and Francophone Haiti. That said, Haiti's racial marginalization, confirmed by the official US characterization of the country as their most backward Caribbean dependency, stirred Marcus Garvey's Universal Negro Improvement Association (UNIA) and the NAACP to take up the

Haitian cause. These connections thickened during the 1920s as Haiti was denied the independence that the Dominican Republic secured in 1924.[55]

Hostility to empire was also expressed in more populist terms. In India especially, some of those angriest at their condition eschewed the elitism of proto-nationalist movements in favor of the raw rejection of foreign domination.[56] Visceral and emotive, this form of protest signified less of a radical ideological departure than the adoption of different strategies of opposition, which exploited the singular advantage enjoyed by colonial populations: their strength in numbers. The power of majoritarianism could be mobilized politically to support claims to self-determination. But its stress on hard facts of colonial demography was also biopolitical, conjuring the image of an overwhelming, irresistible human tide demanding dignity, respect, and rights. In China and Korea, too, anger at the imperialist tenets of the Peace Conference melded with hostility to Japan's regional—and, in Korea's case, colonial—dominance. The resulting 1919 social movements, known by their shorthand appellations, May 4th in China and March 1st in Korea, invoked cultural traditions and overlooked political demands as justification for an assertion of claims to national independence unfettered by imperialist intrusion.[57] The funeral of former Korean emperor Kojong on March 1, 1919, saw popular nostalgia for the precolonial regime escalate into demands for self-determination.[58] Building on demands for national sovereignty made by Korean students studying in Japan, Seoul protesters chanting *Mansei!* (Long Live Korean Independence!) catalyzed the establishment in Shanghai of a Korean provisional government later that year. Japanese repression was swift and severe, even though supporters of Mansei, from Protestant evangelicals to Marxist socialists, appealed to a shared East Asian interest in expelling Western colonialism.[59]

Populist rejection of empire was matched by the evolution of panAsianist thinking in India and Japan. Its advocates concluded from the devastation of the First World War that Western materialism lacked the spiritual depth of Indian cultures or the modernizing vigor of Japanese imperium.[60] The peacemakers' deafness to Indian pleas and Japanese demands also pushed pan-Asianists toward radical revisionism.[61] In Japan's governing circles it seemed that another successful test of arms counted for nothing in Western eyes.[62] Responses in India were more diffuse. The resulting cultural shifts traced an arc from the nonviolence of Gandhi's *swaraj* civil disobedience movement to the revolutionary attacks of Bengal's 'gentlemanly terrorists'.[63] Japan followed a more reactionary path. Its career diplomats committed to engagement with League agencies were swamped by the revisionist intellectual current flowing against them.[64] Leading pan-Asianists retracted their support for closer integration with non-Chinese territories in Asia to embrace an avowedly imperialist position, which would culminate in the embrace of an extended Japanese empire on the Asian mainland, the Co-Prosperity Sphere.[65]

Non-European critics of the racial foundations of the post–First World War order hit upon the imperialist hypocrisy fundamental to liberal internationalism. Tellingly, key architects of the League of Nations, among them Woodrow Wilson and South Africa's Jan Christian Smuts, shaped the League's normative standards by framing self-determination as a prize to be awarded by the industrialized nations of the global North to the most deserving dependent societies.[66] Theoretically measured through standards of governance, the criteria for this prize were actually imagined in terms of proximity to 'Western' cultural values.[67]

Wilson was the outlier here, attaching greater weight to democratic self-government than to national independence for ethnically homogeneous communities.[68] For others, ethnicity, an ascription of identity sometimes conflated with religious affiliation, remained more significant than civic politics.[69] The global vision of racial hierarchy shared by two of the League's founding fathers would be confirmed by the organization's dismissive treatment of its two black African member states, Abyssinia and Liberia.[70] Drawing on these examples, Adom Getachew identifies the League as an instrument of 'imperial counter-revolution' in which respect for the sovereign rights of black peoples was unthinkable.[71]

Minorities and Mandates

We turn our attention now to other vulnerable communities, where peacemaking was accompanied by the discussion of legal protection for ethnic minorities, the prelude to a clearer definition of collective and, later, individual human rights.[72] The First World War shattered preexisting ideas about 'limited' war, the treatment of civilians under occupation, and the coexistence of multiple ethnic groups within a single heterogeneous polity, whether an empire or a nation-state.[73] Among Allied victor powers and, even more so, within those states, societies and political movements represented ethnic groups persecuted in wartime. There was a powerful impulse to elaborate international laws defining war crimes and the means to prosecute their perpetrators. For some groups, this meant building on the foundations of nineteenth- and early twentieth-century international law, the Hague Conventions of 1899 and 1907 above all.[74] Drawing on their wartime experience, Red Cross societies pressed for an international commission to investigate violations of the laws and customs of war by any belligerent. Others favored something more radical: making politicians and military leaders individually liable before a permanent international criminal court for especially heinous acts, crimes against humanity.[75]

Calls for trials of Ottoman leaders as war criminals allegedly complicit in the Armenian genocide were loudest in Britain.[76] American relief agencies, once predominant in the region, would see their local presence fade as the United States withdrew into isolation.[77] But all agreed that wartime violence should be subject to stronger legal sanction, particularly when perpetrators acted beyond the battlefield to advance political rather than strategic objectives by killing defenseless civilians. Formulated in light of wartime events in Europe and the Ottoman Empire, these strands of legal thought were tied together by their focus on the protection of minority groups from political oppressors, foreign and domestic. This 'new justice' had implications for empires as multiethnic agglomerations held together by an occupying imperial power.[78] Extending the temporal and geographical application of these international laws would assist those who insisted that colonialism was criminal.

As it turned out, the new rights thinking conferred few immediate benefits for colonial populations. Minorities' protections as they emerged from the Paris peace settlement had minimal imperial traction beyond mandated territories. Even there, the French and British made sure that they alone held the type A mandates of Syria, Lebanon, Palestine, Transjordan, and Iraq, carved out from the Ottoman Empire's Middle Eastern vilayets.[79] Bizarrely, at the same 'moment' that colonial communities asserted their claims for self-determination as 'nations', imperial powers insisted that empire administration offered the best protection for ethnic minorities otherwise liable to be subsumed—and maltreated—in postcolonial states.[80] The mandate system was one result.

Even inside the mandates, League of Nations' protections for ethnoreligious minority groups, a striking feature of the peace treaties, were more evident in their breach than their application. This was surprising. Protections for minorities were also enshrined within the treaties signed with defeated powers and in the attendant settlements with Europe's new 'successor states'.[81] These protections were devised in the context of different decolonizations—of the contiguous Habsburg, Tsarist, and German land empires—whose collapse prefigured nationhood for Eastern European countries, ethnically mixed and established in the shadow of larger neighbors that had once claimed imperial dominion over them.[82] Minority

groups facing infringements of cultural freedoms, including religious practice and linguistic autonomy, or the abuse of social rights such as access
to schooling and employment, could petition the League for help. Albeit
focused principally on Eastern European minority communities, various
lobby groups, including the International Federation of League of Nations
Societies, the World Alliance for Promoting International Friendship
through the Churches, and the Women's International League for Peace
and Freedom, pushed for action. Each combined evidence-gathering and
grassroots campaigning with face-to-face contacts with the bureaucrats
of the League's Minorities' Protection Section (MPS).[83] A Permanent
Court of International Justice, established in 1922, raised the prospect,
revolutionary at the time, of a persecuted individual seeking redress via
an agency with global authority. Defying their government, subjects might
take claims of maltreatment directly to a supranational legal body.[84] Revolutionary indeed.

So why didn't the mandates' minorities fare better? The League's judicial institutions included a Permanent Commission to oversee protections
within the mandates. Other specialist League agencies that monitored
aspects of human security, from food value and epidemiological data collection to workplace conditions, also took an interest in imperial territories.[85]
Petitioning thus became integral to the language of social protest in the
mandates.[86] Ethnoreligious minorities or, as in the case of the Zionist movement's arguments for a Jewish national home in Palestine, those claiming
rights of residence within a particular mandated territory asserted their
political rights in a supranational forum.[87] What did this signify? People
living under foreign rule claimed legal rights to be heard by a court of opinion that operated, at least nominally, independent of their rulers.[88] This
was not just about high politics. Individuals petitioned for medical support
for family members, a more intimate register of petitioning indicative of a
growing expectation that mandate authorities should 'care' for the communities they governed.[89] The trouble was that it remained unclear whether
such rights, collective or individual, would be enforced.[90]

League monitoring of the mandates was hampered because its oversight agency, the Permanent Mandates Commission (PMC), although
not beholden to the mandate-holders, was conditioned by their requirements.[91] For many, the internationalization of sovereign control between
mandate powers, mandate populations, and the League's protection agencies seemed paradoxical. Mandates facilitated imperialist governance,
but those governing were subject to a form of supranational regulation,
however imperfect and partial it might be.[92] Mandate-holders were

supposedly ruling in the interests of those they governed. Administration was, in theory, not only dispassionate but temporary.[93] The presumption was that, within the type A mandates of the Middle East, sovereign legitimacy rested not on conquest but on educative governance meant to prepare the local population to administer their affairs.[94]

Patronizing as it was, this obligation kept the issue of sovereignty in the minds of the mandate-holders, who could not simply annex the territories they administered. This was a real hindrance. South Africa could not absorb South-West Africa (Namibia), Britain could not add Tanganyika to a projected British East African Federation, and Rwanda and Burundi would remain territorially and politically distinct next to the vast domains of the Belgian Congo at their western edge.[95] Inhabitants of these type B mandates in sub-Saharan Africa recognized the possibilities. The juridical instantiation of sovereignty in the League of Nations nourished a claim-making culture of petitioning the PMC. In Togoland and Cameroon, former German colonies awkwardly partitioned between their new French and British overseers, local lawyers and clerks, already accustomed to highlighting administrative misdeeds, complained of a reinstalled colonialism masquerading as something else.[96]

What did this mean? Empires as organizing political units simply 'did not make sense in the same way' after the mandate system was enacted.[97] Sovereignty had been understood as indivisible, as something either attained or not. But the idea of trusteeship behind the mandate system proposed that sovereign control could be subdivided.[98] Overseen by the PMC, the balance of sovereign control between mandate-holders and local governments would alter as territories edged toward independence. The question was: would sovereignty be shared?[99]

Some thought not. Britain's foreign secretary, Arthur Balfour, pro-Zionist and hostile to Arab claims to self-determination, admitted that the Anglo-French pursuit of strategic and commercial advantage in the Middle East contradicted their responsibilities as mandate-holders over nations-in-the-making. For Balfour, the advantages were sure to trample the responsibilities.[100] His skepticism resonated in some faraway places. For the first generation of international lawyers to emerge from the Soviet Institute of State and Law, the idea that the League, a supranational body designed by Western imperialists, would defend the rights of imperial subjects was laughable. The two preeminent Soviet jurists of the 1920s, Evgeny Korovin and Evgeny Pashukanis, were remorseless critics of the League's legal instruments. Korovin went furthest. He skewered the mandates system, international trade rules, and even treaties of independence, showing that none conceded legal reciprocity to colonized peoples. In a 1927 article, Korovin pinpointed how Britain had inserted itself into Iraq, controlling governmental appointments in Baghdad, while claiming Iraqi 'sovereignty' over Mosul—to the exclusive advantage of Britain's oil industry.[101]

Korovin was onto something. Before returning to the more familiar type A mandates, whose regimes were obliged to promote self-government, consider for a moment two type B mandates in black Africa where the injunction to work toward eventual decolonization was blurry and distant. The two mandates in question were Rwanda and Burundi, East African neighbors placed under Belgian administration after the eviction of their former German rulers. In December 1928, more than eight years after these mandates were conferred, the permanent administrative staff of the two territories numbered seventy-six. Most worked in outlying district offices. A further 132 personnel filled the ranks of technical posts, from the police to public health and veterinary clinics.[102] The PMC expected Belgium as the mandate-holder to take steps—albeit baby ones—toward the indigenization of bureaucracy and eventual power-sharing. But in 1928 Brussels had yet to establish any education service in either Rwanda or Burundi. Nor had it assigned anyone to work on educational matters. Tempting as this makes it to dismiss the type B variant of mandatory governance as a colonial ruse, the administrative paperchain suggests otherwise. Belgian officials in Rwanda and Burundi agonized about their inability to train local personnel. Their argument was about means and ends. Belgium's new African territories might look like colonies, but their rulers insisted they weren't. Administrators wanted to improve things but lacked the institutional apparatus to do so.[103]

The same rhetoric of reform once circumstances allowed was evident in territories where political power was divided between an imperial government and an indigenous regime, usually a monarchy, whose authority the imperialists claimed to 'protect'. French-ruled Morocco was one among many such 'protectorates' in the European overseas empires. Established in the decade before the First World War, the administrative duality of Morocco's protectorate was no barrier to violent conquest and a racially configured distribution of power.[104] Early Moroccan nationalists such as Allal al-Fasi stressed that the protectorate regime held Morocco's people, its Sultanate, and its *salaffiya* Islamic traditions captive.[105] The exercise of 'protecting power' was theoretically circumscribed, typically by treaty arrangements imposed with local dynastic rulers. Cooperation with local elites was intrinsic to the protectorate system, but external scrutiny of the process was not. So the mandate system appeared at once derivative and novel. Meanwhile its oversight arrangements reverberated transnationally. It became harder for protectorate authorities to ignore the power-sharing, legal pluralism, and conflicting political and religious sovereignties that figured in original protectorate arrangements such as Morocco's March 1912 Treaty of Fez. (Wrongly) declaring the containment of political dissent accomplished in 1934, French Morocco's protectorate authorities announced job creation schemes for local personnel in central and local government. Top positions were reserved for French citizens, from the 'civil controllers' who oversaw regional affairs to police commissioners and criminal magistrates.[106] Equally, administrative and judicial roles within the sultan's administration, the *makhzen*, were reserved for Moroccans. But the longer-term survival of this and other protectorates rested on making shared sovereignty real.[107] This was their Achilles's heel.

As long as Moroccans could claim that the protectorate existed to serve French and not Moroccan interests, the entire governmental apparatus looked dishonest and hollow. Infringements of the sultan's juridical authority as an Islamic ruler were especially resented.[108] The bitterest pill was the long-running 1930s crisis over the so-called Berber Dahir, a French attempt to impose ethnic boundaries between Arabs and Berbers in the application of sharia law, which triggered virulent nationalist protest in Morocco's northern cities.[109]

Violence and the Absence of Protection

The same evidence of differential treatment for nonwhite peoples is apparent when it came to suppressive imperial violence. In the British Empire, Winston Churchill argued relentlessly for using chemical weapons against Kurds and Shia Marsh Arabs in Mesopotamia/Iraq during 1919 and 1920.[110] Cabinet colleagues sympathetic to the League of Nations' ban on gas warfare managed to overrule him. Churchill's lobbying nearly succeeded because using military force within empires was not legally conceptualized as 'war' but as the pursuit of internal security or 'pacification'. Regulating repression was a domestic issue. Imperial powers legislated their own emergency powers, martial law, or states of siege. They monitored their own effectiveness in sticking to rules they devised.[111]

Protracted rebellion was rare, but numerous colonies in the early twentieth century remained tense societies in which European hegemony was always contested.[112] Mandates were not thought much different. Police powers, collective punishments, and detention without trial expanded in colonies, protectorates, and mandates alike. Viewed from this colonial perspective, 1919 might be singled out less as a faltering start to the international regulation of imperial spaces and more as a milestone year in the development of colonial 'lawfare'.[113] In the British Empire alone, 1919 saw British India's Anarchical and Revolutionary Crimes legislation of February through April, tough emergency restrictions after the Egyptian revolution, the proscription of Dáil Éireann and a ban on Sinn Féin in September, followed by the defeat and imprisonment of Shaykh Mahmud Barzanji and his Kurdish supporters in Sulaymaniyah at the close of the year.[114] The paradoxical combination of limited reforms alongside tighter repressive measures persisted throughout the interwar decades. In 1919 Britain was peacemaking and persecuting. In 1939 it was war-making and persecuting. Both were done in defense of the same global order. Intervening British plans to widen political participation in East Africa, in India, and in mandate Palestine came with harsher police powers attached.[115] And colonial law was gendered. It was arbitrated by white males, applied by masculine security forces, and constructed in ways that objectified colonized women.[116]

Martial law, meanwhile, was applied ipso facto in military-administered territories of French Africa and Indochina. 1919 saw *états de siège* in force from French Morocco's highland interior in the west to a French-occupied Syria in ferment at the overthrow of its popular republic in the east.[117] Disorder pervaded other parts of the colonial world where peacetime administration was supposedly returning to normality. In the aftermath of the First World War, the Belgian Congo witnessed sustained resistance to taxation. Although mainly localized within districts (termed *chefferies* or 'chiefly areas'), the violence sometimes engulfed entire provinces, requiring intervention by paramilitary units of the Congo's Force Publique. In 1918 and 1919, lethal confrontations attended the annual taxation round in the provinces of Equateur, South Kasai, and Orientale.[118] Chronic poverty and sleeping sickness epidemics in other regions made tax collection either pointless or politically explosive.[119]

In these testing conditions, security specialists calculated that policemen, soldiers, and military aircraft rapidly deployed kept empires intact.[120] This 'repressive consensus' rarely broke down in European colonial territories between the wars. Spectacular instances of such breakdown—as, for example, during the French war in the Moroccan Rif in 1925 or in British quarrels over the recruitment of Jewish police auxiliaries and the use of death squads during the Arab rebellion in Palestine after 1936— were exceptions, not the rule.[121] Clashes were most frequent in empires' borderlands where the colonial aspiration for control was frustrated by the inability to achieve it. These were areas where sovereignty was 'indeterminate', sometimes disputed between rival claimants, at others beyond central government reach.[122] Borderlands were more than frontier zones. They were places where the legitimacy of authority, whether local or imperial, was perennially contested, where nations 'frayed at the edges'.[123]

The 'Great Revolt' of 1925–1927 confirmed that Syria was one such space.[124] Its external frontiers and internal administrative boundaries were disputed.[125] Differing ethnoreligious groups and tribal confederations expressed competing claims and territorial loyalties.[126] Local inhabitants and their cousins in the Syrian diaspora, as well as Sunni Muslims more widely, bridled at the French preference for Maronite Christians in the neighboring Lebanon mandate.[127] Economic attachments also cut across bordered divisions. Syria's commercial centers retained their connections to cities and agricultural hinterlands from Turkey and Iraq to Lebanon and Palestine.[128] With fluid borders that made little sense ethnically, culturally, or agronomically, the lands of Bilad al-Sham, although subdivided into French and British mandates, were never rigidly territorialized. Interurban trade, seasonal livestock movements, and patterns of interior economic migration endured. The region's new imperial rulers were desperate to regulate these exchanges, if not to end them, to make the peoples of the mandates administratively legible and easier to tax.[129]

Conclusions

The collapse of the Russian, Austro-Hungarian, and Ottoman empires amid the fallout from the First World War compelled imperial rhetoricians in Britain and France to wrestle with the contradiction between their reflexive inclination to equate empire with geopolitical strength and cultural vitality and the mounting evidence that their empires might not withstand stronger local pressure for self-rule.[130] The configuration of ethnic minority rights and claims to national self-determination as elements of the Paris Peace Settlement lent a different vocabulary to anticolonial petitioning and stirred transnational demands that racial discrimination and political exclusion be addressed within the crafting of a new international system.[131] These demands were substantially frustrated in the 1920s, but the arguments deployed, particularly through the institutions of the League of Nations Secretariat and its Permanent Mandates Commission, compelled political leaders in Britain, France, and their mandate territories to devise more convincing justifications for empire.[132] They came up short.

The League of Nations mandate system as it emerged between 1919 and 1923 was assuredly imperial in its presumption that better-qualified rulers of empires should offer their benevolent guiding hand to peoples previously mal-administered by the defeated 'bad' colonial powers, Imperial Germany and Ottoman Turkey. The descriptive labels chosen were significant. Governments in London and Paris led a retreat from the Wilsonian language of self-determination, preferring the fuzzier timetables and wider margins for maneuver intrinsic to trusteeship. But President Wilson's self-determination genie was not easily forced back into its bottle. Its implied support for ethnically homogeneous, self-governing polities was widely translated into a political vernacular of national independence.[133] Its legacy lived on in stronger anticolonial claims articulated in a language of sovereign rights and often by means of traveling delegations and erudite petitions: in short, with all the trappings of diplomatic legalism and Western respectability.[134]

In line with their contrasting methodological approaches, imperial and global historians have categorized this colonial fallout as the 'Greater War'. For the former, the years 1918 to 1923 have been viewed top-down in terms of crisis, whether as a geopolitical indicator of failing European imperial power or as preludes to decolonization, imminent in the Irish case, narrowly averted in others.[135] Working outward from local experiences, global historians have asked bigger questions about causation and transimperial connection, drawing fascinating conclusions about worldwide dimensions of Greater War and the persistence of collective demands for self-determination.[136] In this telling, the conceptualization of self-determination as a collective right to statehood owed as much to early Soviet support for anticolonialism as it did to Woodrow Wilson's whites-only liberalism. The Bolsheviks' Congress of Peoples of the East, convened in Baku in September 1920, which asserted the right of colonized societies to fight imperial rule, might thus be set alongside the better-known but abortive efforts of colonial leaders to break into the Paris peace negotiations.[137]

The mandated territories of the Middle East have attracted the most attention from global historians of empire. For some, the underlying issue is one of territorialization, which Cyrus Schayegh defines in the context of Greater Syria as a transpatialization, in which the absence of geopolitical fixity combined with the contingency of the mandates to produce a remarkable political fluidity.[138] For others, the core issues are juridical and normative: about the ways in which the mandate system altered conceptions of political legitimacy and imperial sovereignty, opening empire

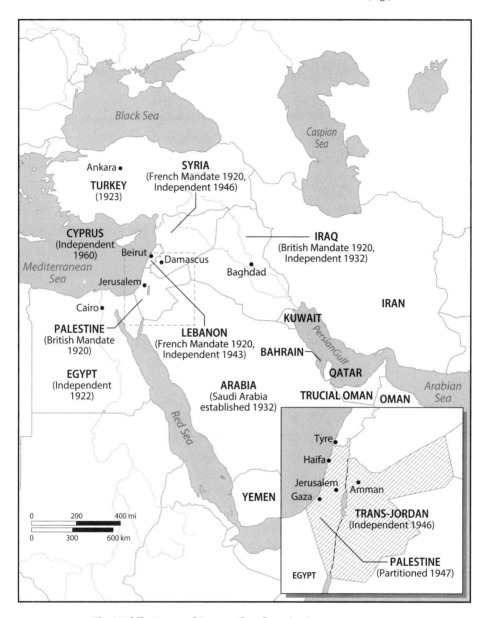

MAP 4.3. The Middle East and its mandated territories.

to unprecedented oversight and challenge at the ideational level of a presumptive rich-world 'right to rule'.[139]

There's a profound concern here for the analytical categories of war,
peace, and enduring political violence, but the working assumption is that
these concepts may be clearly separated and temporally limited. Empirical

observation lends weight to this assessment. The 1923 Treaty of Lausanne, the first interstate accord acknowledging the failure of the preceding peace settlement, capped one intense phase of region-wide disturbance in Western Asia, much as the equally contingent end of civil war in Ireland curbed the first twentieth-century phase of political violence on the island.[140] But demarcating 'wartime' from 'peacetime' and setting the imperial limits of Greater War becomes harder the further we travel from European or Mediterranean shores, particularly so if we fix upon the vulnerabilities of colonial subject status in conditions of social unrest.[141]

Such were the transformative effects of total war that it is easy to miss an underlying continuity. Colonial subjecthood, at once a juridical category that varied colony by colony and a generic measure of cultural difference within and between empires, was substantially unaffected by wider international efforts to define civilian status and noncombatant rights in time of war.[142] After the First World War, colonial subjects, still the overwhelming majority among empire populations, were neither citizen nor 'civilian'. Nor did they inhabit territories with the autonomous capacity to declare war or peace. Many colonial servicemen who had fought in the First World War would find their presumptive connection between war service, citizenship rights, and welfare support in peacetime denied.[143] And, as seen in the examples of forced labor and repressive violence, colonial subject status inhibited local efforts to achieve enforceable protections for women, children, and the elderly, while setting narrow parameters to supranational jurisdiction in cases of empire rebellion or social protest.[144]

The proclivity to excuse forced labor, discriminatory legal regimes, and rights restrictions as necessary, if temporary, administrative tools was underpinned by an imperialist rhetoric that claimed to be saving misguided colonial subjects from themselves and that contrived different cultural standards for the treatment of colonial child workers.[145] According to this worldview, tough working conditions, arbitrary detentions, and even military violence and collective punishments did not transgress ethical standards, nor were they the antithesis of freedom.[146] They were precursors to an orderly society where rights and responsibilities would be codified to the benefit of all. The tendency among imperialist politicians, journalists, and civil society actors in Britain and France to invoke local examples of massacre, population displacement, and other abuses of minority populations as justification for humanitarian, yet still imperial intervention was strongest in the former Ottoman territories bounding the eastern Mediterranean.[147]

Political violence within French mandate Syria makes the case for picking apart the causal links between world wartime change and the outbreak of 'postwar' insurgencies. While anger simmered over the Western rejection of Syrian claims to statehood and self-determination during and after 1919, by 1925 most rebel grievances during Syria's Great Revolt were local.[148] They related to lost communal rights, tax burdens, and regional maladministration. French High Commission staff, the local officials working beneath them, and the nationalists of the Syrian National Bloc meanwhile offered competing definitions, first of the mandate's purpose and second of what Syrian 'national identity' actually meant. The treatment of incoming refugees—Armenian Christians and Kurdish Muslims from Turkey, joined, in the early 1930s, by Assyrians from Iraq—was a case in point.[149] For French officials, refugee settlements offered the pretext for more expansive border demarcation and a bigger administrative presence. Welcoming refugees as permanent residents, at the same time, enabled France to territorialize the mandate, presenting it as a nonsectarian sanctuary, even a moral enterprise.[150] For their local opponents, the refugee presence worked differently, as evidence of Syria's connection with the wider Middle East and proof that Syrian identity was as much civic as it was ethnic.[151] Violence in Syria ebbed and flowed but was consistently present from the wartime years of collapsing Ottoman rule to the supposed 'postwar years' of the early mandate. Legally and experientially, for the majority of people living under variants of colonialism during and after 1919, the varying degrees of coercion and constraint that shaped their daily lives point to an intermediate condition: neither war nor peace, but imminently affected by the proximity of violence.

CHAPTER FIVE

The Economic Side of Empire Decline

THE MONETIZATION OF COLONIAL ECONOMIES, colonial obstacles to wealth accumulation, how property is held and transferred, and workplace discrimination are four factors that make a case for the salience of political economy to decolonization. All were powerful determinants of the ways daily lives were lived and the grievances people felt.[1] For all that, most studies of colonialism dwell on cultural factors of identity and belief, as well as political questions of ideology and allegiance, rather than on the economic dimensions that shaped conditions of possibility for rulers and ruled.[2] This chapter bucks that trend, assessing decolonization's economic causes leading into the Second World War.

Biopolitics and Population

Alongside disputes over the universality of self-determination, the starkest signs of global imperial crisis in 1919 were the prevalence of hunger and the dislocation of ethnic minority groups inside shifting colonial boundaries and jurisdictions.[3] Territories severely hit included Indian Bengal, scene of desperate food riots, and Ottoman Syria, where famine took hold in 1915.[4] Also chronically affected was Africa's Red Sea region, a vast area of recent European colonization stretching from the Anglo-Egyptian Sudan to Italian-ruled Somalia and Eritrea. Wartime disruptions to crop cultivation and grain markets, plus the interruption of maritime trade, exacerbated the chronic insecurity of food supply, leaving millions from Darfur to Djibouti facing malnutrition.[5]

Peacemakers in Paris ignored the magnitude of these human disasters in 1919. Gradually, though, the case made for or against empire began to reflect the interplay between geopolitical rivalries and economic needs.[6] Let's return to the concept of biopolitics to explain why. Biopolitics melded ideas about eugenics, demography, and access to resources to produce distinct hierarchies of ethnicity.[7] It sharpened the sense of a 'shrinking world' where political alignments would be determined by demographic pressure, the consequent movement of peoples, and the claims of settlers versus indigenous peoples.[8] Biopolitical challenges for governments— from improving living standards and reproductive health to alleviating hunger—were conceptualized between the wars as global, rather than national, issues.[9] Which peoples would settle successfully where? Who had defensible claims to do so? What national or supranational organizations should judge? Or were population increases destined to intensify conflict over land and resources?[10]

Interwar demographers from Europe, the Americas, and Asia had different answers, but most thought geopolitically. At the Geneva World Population Conference in August 1927, migratory patterns and population densities caused the most concern.[11] Conference attendees did not consider the First World War peace settlement a 'done' global deal, arguing instead that successful societies would expand, acquiring additional territory as their populations grew. Competition over space and resources was likely to resolve itself into peaceful pathways of migration and assimilation or violent contests between imperialists. Whichever the case, a global 'demopolitical' economy existed, making the settlement of excess populations a central foreign policy objective.[12]

Professional networks linking eugenicists with supporters of population control add other elements to the mix.[13] Global populations, including the still imprecisely measured millions living under colonial rule, were an obvious focal point of interest for demographers, eugenicists, and other race theorists. Immigration officials of the 1920s were also eager to substantiate the view that racial difference could be calibrated as an index of cultural value.[14] Imperial governments were concerned not just with measuring the size of their dependent populations but with regulating their movement as well. The French took an early lead. The mass expulsion of miners, specialist farm laborers, and other skilled North African workers from France between 1922 and 1925 exposed the contradiction at the heart of French 'republican imperialism': when times got tough economically, the Republic dispensed with its 'loyal' colonial brothers.[15]

The number of French government departments and colonial administrations involved in the resultant process of registration, monitoring, and removal of North African immigrant workers exposed another facet of colonialism, this one less distinctively French. Discriminatory acts of government were overlaid with multiple layers of paperwork, from visa requirements and registration documents to employer contracts and police permits.[16] This bureaucracy disguised expulsion as due process, covering it in a veneer of impartiality. The business of letting colonial people in, then shutting them out at government convenience was as scrupulously legal as it was unethical.[17] Not everything was so duplicitous. French authorities felt compelled to erect a complex apparatus of police surveillance, administrative reportage, and judicial restrictions to contend with seditionist threats conjured up in the imagination of the official mind.[18] If there was a kernel of logic in this otherwise grotesque overreaction, it was the unspoken assumption that colonial peoples would, at some stage, try to overthrow foreign rule.[19]

The proliferation of legislative restrictions on nonwhite migration, evident for instance in British colonial India, Malaya, and Burma, was not matched by equal stringency in matters of population control.[20] In the French case, gendered restrictions on colonial economic migration enacted in the 1920s did not stimulate equivalent efforts to regulate local population growth.[21] The strongest advocates of population control operated outside government. Their pressure for policy action and spending initiatives originated in transnational pressure groups and nongovernmental agencies affiliated first with the League of Nations and then its United Nations successor.[22] The irony is that, despite the moral opprobrium heaped upon eugenics and the pseudoscience of race, population control would make a bigger impact in the twentieth century as imperial administrations justified their existence with talk of societal modernization and development 'packages'.[23]

Measuring Change: Food, Nutrition, and Economic Performance

Biopolitical thinking about world politics was also rooted in early twentieth-century breakthroughs in nutritional science, particularly calculations of calorific value as an index of healthy bodies and living standards. The ability to count calories transformed the connection between food and politics. Assuring an adequate supply of food was now subject to statistical analysis, allowing precise comparison between the food regimes—and rates of malnutrition—in different countries and empires.[24] 'Food' could now be measured uniformly—by calorific value—regardless of its particular form. The later calibration of nitrogen content (and thus of food's use as an energy provider) plus a greater understanding of essential vitamins would politicize food even further. Evidence about dietary intake became a way to assess governance scientifically.[25] This 'caloric internationalism' pervaded supranational institutions, which gathered data on colonial malnutrition from the 1920s onward.[26] Imperial agronomists, statisticians, and dieticians, many affiliated with League of Nations agencies, proved that tropical environments were not naturally bountiful. This combination of nutritional science with agronomy and economic geography was politically explosive. The scientific calculation of nutritional needs shaded into criticism of colonial markets and patterns of food production.[27]

Two commonly held presumptions were quickly disproven. One was that 'tropical health' and colonial diets were qualitatively different from those of temperate, noncolonial regions. The other was that colonial hunger was a natural occurrence rather than a consequence of market activity and the relative prices of nutritious foods versus less nutritious staples such as rice.[28] League of Nations scientists joined the dots between colonial disruption to former patterns of land use, increased labor migration, the spread of transmissible diseases, and the devastating dietary impact of debt burdens on peasant households.[29]

Beginning in 1925 the League of Nations Health Organization (LNHO) and the International Labour Organization began producing national nutritional surveys predicated on calorific content. These would be used, in turn, to determine minimum requirements of daily food intake. In 1935 the League publicized a global daily minimum of 2,500 calories for a working adult. This calorific base line was not enforceable in international law. It was, though, cited by imperial governments and their local opponents, either to defend colonialism or to discredit it.[30] British scientists, meanwhile, took the lead in formulating measurable standards of food value and minimum vitamin requirements, working alongside an LNHO subgroup, the Mixed Committee on the Problem of Malnutrition, established in 1935. Applied first to combat child malnutrition in Europe, these statistical standards had major implications for a colonial world whose governments were reluctant to disburse subsidies or enact price caps.[31]

Humanitarian relief agencies in conflict-affected regions shared the League statisticians' conviction that human security, as evinced by the provision of food and shelter, was the best guarantor of peace.[32] These operating principles also shaped interest among imperial administrations in basic health care. Preventive rather than curative, and focused around improved rural housing, sanitation, dietary provision, and midwifery, this 'social medicine' was widely regarded as a key to unlock the potential of peasant populations dogged by epidemic illness, high levels of infant mortality, and other poverty-related conditions.[33]

Equally significant were the connections made between calculable standards of material improvement and perceptions of imperial responsibility or what was still articulated as the 'right' to administer dependent populations. By 1928, for instance, the British Empire alone included fifty separate forestry departments whose management of woodland reserves extended over almost 8 percent of the world's landmass—a vast but measurable responsibility and a formidable reservoir of specialist global knowledge.[34] Numerical indicators were becoming integral to colonialism and anticolonialism alike.[35] To give an example, Belgian, British, French, and American colonial administrations from the Congo to the Philippines proselytized the benefits of formula milk, wrongly convinced that a turn away from breast-feeding would reduce infant mortality, proving the benefits of imperial health care.[36] Tabulating the colonial use of formula milk was, like other instances of 'social medicine' in action, politically transformative. By gauging the 'quality' of imperial governance in terms of public health and infant survival, this statistical turn rendered imperial projects accountable.[37] Something similar could be said about the standards of transparency promoted by the League of Nations.

The League had limited capacity to bring imperial powers to book, but this misses the point about the nature of its global influence. As Susan Pedersen observes, 'Against expectation, the League's own character and practices—its legalism, proceduralism and "publicness"—tended to amplify rather than to abate imperial contestation'.[38] Imperial powers like France were often frustrated by the League's presumption that decades of colonial medical expertise required supranational oversight.[39] More galling was that League monitors, such as its Nutrition Committee, enabled colonial oppositionists to take empires to task over aspects of social policy never questioned in such detail before.[40]

The political weight attached to scientific evidence about governmental performance would only increase as the century progressed. The trend accelerated thanks to the early 1940s innovation of national income accounting, which allowed the comparative—and 'scientific'—measurement of national incomes and, thus, of relative economic performance.[41]

The First Turn to Development

Ideas of development and modernization shared common points of origin. Their advocates in industrialized societies treated their own historical pasts as emblematic. Agricultural societies were depicted as lacking the economic capacity and cultural openness they needed to advance.[42] Their wage workers should be organized under colonial leadership, not by local activists or foreign leftists.[43] The Second World War further stimulated governmental interest in regulating economic activity. The conflict's demands for manpower and materials increased the value attached to colonial labor and to essential foodstuffs, metals, and other strategic raw materials. Britain's wartime innovation of colonial marketing boards was especially significant. Bureaucracies invested with the authority to buy and sell commodities across vast colonial spaces, marketing boards prefigured the statist orientation of postwar development policies. The Colonial Development Corporation launched by Clement Attlee's Labour government in 1948 was typical, directing investment toward infrastructure projects tendered by British contractors. A French equivalent ensured that lucrative government contracts went to French firms eager to build French West African docks, roads, and airports. Early postwar development, in other words, was subordinated to metropolitan reconstruction.[44] After 1945 especially, the potential for colonial markets to absorb the rich world's surplus production capacity of refined products, from steel and aluminum to plastics and canned goods, added to the sense of a World War watershed.[45]

The expansion in global economic activity after 1945 also helps to explain the late twentieth-century 'great acceleration' in environmental damage wrought by human activity in the colonial world.[46] The point is not that this damage was unprecedented, but that existing trends accelerated. Two African examples, south and north of the Sahara, show that fundamental ecological changes were happening already. Beginning in the 1920s colonial governments in tropical Africa resettled rural populations in purpose-built villages as a shortcut to improvements in public health, economic output, and the expansion of export crop production from cotton in Upper Volta and Mozambique to coffee in Angola and Kenya. The disruption of established agricultural practices caused by enforced sedentarization was dismissed as incidental to their developmental potential.[47] North of the Sahara, the French administration in Protectorate Morocco moved quickly to sedentarize pastoralists whose nomadic lifestyle rendered them difficult to track and control. Protectorate officials knew that such interventionism clashed with their declared precepts of government. Associationism was supposed to be everything that sedentarization was not. The policy claimed, among other things, to resist the predation of settlers and corporate agribusiness, instead respecting cultural practices relating to land use and tax payment.[48] Uneasiness among officials was not enough. A 'protectorate' in name, the French administration was still a colonial venture. Land reforms from the 1910s to the 1930s privatized huge areas of pastorage, opening communally farmed land to commercial speculation, a settler influx, and a loss of ecological diversity.[49]

Depression and Radicalization

Sticking with North Africa, this section dwells on the transformative effects of the global Depression in the Arab territories bordering the Mediterranean. Two things justify this case study. First, as in other sub-continental spaces, notably South and Southeast Asia, the crisis had a transregional impact, its effects extending between territories. From the Bay of Bengal to the South China Sea, the Depression confronted millions of migrant laborers and diaspora communities with joblessness, repatriation, or worsening conditions in the mine encampments, plantation settlements, and informal urban economies of Malaya, Burma, Vietnam, and Thailand.[50] So blatant was the wage discrimination against Tamil Indian laborers in Malaya's rubber sector that in 1938 the Government of India prohibited state-assisted economic migration across the Bay of Bengal, a remarkable instance of one British colonial authority imposing sanctions on another.[51] In Arabic-speaking territories, the economic crisis was felt less in enforced population movements than in chronic poverty and hunger. This was evident in catastrophic losses of grazing livestock, critical to pastoralist economies from Morocco to Syria. But depression in the Arab world was also part of a global economic downturn.[52] Beginning in Australasia, then engulfing Southeast Asia and, next, Europe and the Americas, in Arabic-speaking lands the world economic crisis was experienced as not an overnight collapse but a long-term contraction in trade, falling agricultural incomes, and loss of credit liquidity as capital reserves declined and banks collapsed.[53]

The second reason for this regional case study is to illustrate how interlocking global economic connections created a double bind for dependent territories. Their economies were colonially oriented toward commodity exports and therefore dangerously reliant on the creditworthiness and currency stability of their imperial overseers.[54] This proved critical for the

French-ruled Maghreb. France, repelled by the 'Anglo-Saxon' roots of free trade, favored protectionism.[55] Its North African territories were encased within higher tariff walls, their goods prices and capital controls regulated from Paris.[56]

Tighter protectionism heightened the economic dependency of Maghreb territories on trade with France and, in Libya's case, with Italy. Algeria was already reconfigured into a wine-exporting colony and was bound to France through an 1884 customs union, an obvious model to follow.[57] The Depression raised the stakes even so. Access to the French market, guaranteed to Algerian wine producers by the customs union, came under threat as winegrowers in southern France and their political supporters in Paris complained of being undercut. When push came to shove, metropolitan cultivators came first.[58] French protectionism, like British 'free' trade, was colonialist after all. Amid turmoil on global foreign exchange markets, in June 1931 the Paris government and its three North African administrations enacted a French Maghreb customs union. Intended to solidify connections between France and its southern Mediterranean territories, the proposed customs union was consistent with other initiatives, including improved trans-Saharan communications, the alignment of colonial customs tariffs, and measures to increase colonial maritime trade, fishing rights, and cereals supplies; all strengthened an imperial economy.[59]

Other Depression-era initiatives followed the same trend. The North African territories exemplified a wider colonial shift. From the freer passage of goods and livestock between territories to new commercial air routes, telephone services, and underwater cable links between colonies, the impulse was to integrate dependencies, insulating them from global economic pressures.[60] The consequences? Trade increasingly flowed within empires rather than between them.[61] Metropolitan governments and lobby groups set the terms.

Exporters in the Middle East mandates faced a different problem. Their legal obligation to uphold free trade, sanctified under the mandates' 'Open Door' terms, jarred with the global protectionist turn. Mandated territories were left exposed to 'dumping' by foreign exporters desperate to offload unsellable produce. The timing could not have been worse. As cheap foreign goods flooded their domestic markets, protectionist measures elsewhere denied the mandates tariff-free entry to their established overseas markets.[62] Consider the Greater Syria of Bilad al-Sham. Economic disruption caused by the region's subdivision into British- and French-mandated territories was still playing out. Transnational networks of interurban connection did not fit this new imperial territoriality. The national identifiers of Syria, Lebanon, Palestine, and Transjordan crystalized in the 1930s as political attachments were reconfigured around particular national formations.[63] At another level, though, previous commercial integration and cultural interchange across these new borders sustained a different sense of belonging. Mandate authorities even endorsed aspects of this integration despite their impulse to divide territory and demarcate boundaries. A region-wide customs-free zone was maintained. Whether by accident or design, economic policies enacted in French-ruled territory affected trade, prices, and consumption in neighboring British-ruled mandates.[64] 'Cross-border movements of people, animals, goods, and ideas', some of it by motorized transport, forced mandate governments into dialogue on everything from law enforcement to public health.[65]

Producers and merchants throughout Bilad al-Sham also worked hard to sustain their economic connections, not just across mandate frontiers, but northward into Turkey and southward into Egypt, Arabia, and the Persian Gulf. From northern Syria to southern Palestine, towns, cities, and their agricultural hinterlands retained transnational commercial networks whose importance increased as the Depression intensified from 1932 onward. Conversely, the debilitating effects of imperial control over currency rates, monetary policy, and taxation levels stimulated more nationally focused opposition movements—what Cyrus Schayegh dubs *watani* nationalisms—plus the emergence of *qawmiyya* pan-Arabism, determined to end European interference.[66]

Colonial depressions were, in general, longer and deeper than their European counterparts. Export trade picked up in several Asian and African colonial territories during 1936–1937, but the preceding contraction in colonial economies precluded rapid recovery in import capacity. Japanese colonial Korea was fairly typical: there, the imperial regulation of strategic industries, internal markets, and pricing regimes advantaged metropolitan investors, not local producers and consumers. In Korea, as throughout the colonial world, necessities remained unobtainable for many.[67] Moving southward and returning to the French Empire example, desperate socioeconomic conditions stirred fears within France's leftist Popular Front government about political violence and administrative breakdown.

These anxieties were sharpest in Indochina. The federation's economy had been close to crisis before the Depression struck in 1930. Rising population pressure and commercialized rice cultivation made land shortage worse. Food yields declined.[68] Sharecroppers struggled to get by, making malnutrition endemic. By late 1931 rice exports from the Mekong Delta connecting southwestern Vietnam and eastern Cambodia had tumbled by 46 percent from their predepression peak in 1928. Clothing, salt, soap, and other essentials were either unavailable or unaffordable.[69] Severe deflation and stricter protectionism between 1931 and 1935 lowered prices but pushed rice growers into debt and sharecroppers out of work. To the north, hunger stalked the densely populated settlements of the Red River Delta.[70] A 1937 government inspection mission, headed by Lyonnais senator Justin Godard, confirmed the slump's devastation of French Vietnam. But Godard's team rejected investment in industrial diversification as a solution. The danger of expanding a hostile urban proletariat outweighed likely improvements in living standards. To keep Vietnam, they concluded, France could not risk modernizing it.[71]

In the Indochina Federation, poverty was everywhere, but hunger and, eventually, famine were more regionally confined. French North Africa's gradual economic recovery before 1940 also concealed regional differences among Morocco, Algeria, and Tunisia and within the territories themselves. This was partly explained by varying degrees of trade dependence. Between 1924 and 1938 less than half of Moroccan trade was conducted with France; in Algeria and Tunisia, it fluctuated between 70 and 90 percent.[72] During 1937, Algeria, the largest economy of the three, registered export growth in the colony's main staples—wine, iron ore, and phosphates. These surged ahead by 64 percent, 22 percent, and 25 percent respectively.[73] By the late 1930s Algerian citrus fruit production was also taking off, with growers encouraged to switch from cultivating vines because access to France's wine market was so difficult.[74]

The differing economic experiences of the North African territories highlight the danger of generalization about imperial trade recovery on the eve of the Second World War. Some problems were generic. Drought and harvest failure afflicted the entire Maghreb between 1936 and 1938.[75] Unemployment and seasonal underemployment, characteristic of the agricultural and mining sectors, caused spikes in economic migration. But foodstuff shortages and consequent inflationary pressures were severest in Morocco. Local nationalists in the Spanish Moroccan enclave city of Tetouan seized on reformist initiatives launched by Spain's Second Republic between 1931 and 1936 to demand political freedoms and social rights equivalent to those enjoyed by Spanish settlers in the coastal protectorate. Civilianization of the administration and vague promises of intercommunal equality also stirred hopes of improvement but, in a sad irony, impoverishment in the Depression years drove large numbers of young Moroccans in the Spanish zone to enlist in the Francoist military units that proved decisive first in launching and then in safeguarding the fascist rebellion against the Second Republic.[76]

In another, more general trend, desperate people on the move throughout the Maghreb fed the growth of shantytowns in Casablanca, Oujda, Algiers, Tunis, and elsewhere as rural laborers moved northward to coastal cities in search of work.[77] Mayors' offices and native affairs staffs worried that wide disparities between relatively affluent settler districts and viscerally poor shantytowns might provoke urban rioting or worse.[78] Most internal economic migrants were male, meaning that increasing numbers of peasant families relied on womenfolk and children to keep smallholdings and households viable until they received remittances from their absent menfolk.[79] The insecurities of chronic poverty evident in the damage done to family structures must surely count as a long-term contributor to pressure for decolonization.

Money Worries and Decolonization Pressures

In Morocco alone, by November 1935 state-backed Sociétés indigènes de prévoyance (SIP: rural credit agencies) distributed 5 million francs in emergency relief plus 3.5 million francs in stopgap loans in an effort to prevent starvation.[80] Local farmers faced a triple burden: land lost to settlers, the environmental degradation of the remaining plots and pasturage, and collapsing produce prices.[81] Scratching a living on smallholdings and marginal scrubland became impossible.[82] By early 1937 typhus epidemics, malnutrition, and sharp rises in infant mortality were reported across Morocco from Oujda in the east to Casablanca in the west. Infection spread as tens of thousands of Moroccans moved eastward to Algeria in search of work.[83] City authorities struggled meanwhile to limit the growth of the shantytowns at their margins as more families left the starving countryside.[84] Suffering in Morocco was so acute that, in April 1937, the protectorate authorities opened a string of emergency relief centers stretching in a wide arc from the Atlantic coast along the southern rim of the Atlas Mountains to the Algerian border.[85] In the following year, the National Assembly in Paris approved 250 million francs for emergency relief measures to the North African territories, with Morocco again receiving the largest allocation.[86]

Before the French parliament got involved, in November 1935 Algeria's settler-dominated budgetary assembly, the so-called Financial Delegation, allowed struggling European farmers to consolidate their debts into a single loan payable at preferential interest. Algerian agriculturalists, by contrast, relied on two state-controlled agencies, the SIP and the Fonds Commun, which imposed an eight-year limit on loans payable at 5 percent, a prohibitively high figure. Emergency funding was made available to the SIP to tide over Arab smallholders without animals or crops to sell at market.[87] But this was hardly generous. The sums awarded were to be repaid from the territories' budgets as soon as economic conditions improved, and the Paris parliamentarians meanwhile voted through big increases in French North Africa's monetary contribution to France's rearmament effort.[88] The colonial state gave with one hand but took away with the other.

Another restrictive factor was currency. The franc either remained the currency of exchange or, as in Indochina, Morocco, Syria, and Lebanon, the benchmark against which local currencies were valued.[89] France determined three criteria of the money in circulation colonially—as a unit of account, a store of value, and a medium of exchange. Colonial peoples were debilitated by the second and third of these. The real value of their money declined, but they were not free to select a different, more stable currency in which to keep any savings or to conduct day-to-day business. France's three devaluations between 1936 and 1938 meanwhile wiped out the revenue generated by greater volumes of imperial trade. Inflation returned as stronger demand for local staples fed price increases.[90] The real value of their money already cut, France's colonial subjects faced higher costs for food and fuel. Hungry stomachs and unheated homes stoked public anger.

Two examples from 1930s Algeria illustrate how the Depression fired antagonism against symbols of authority, local and colonial. The first is from Aïn-Fakroun, a farming town in the eastern highlands near Constantine. Dr. Mohammed Salah Bendjelloul, at the time Algeria's foremost parliamentary spokesman for the colony's Muslim majority, traveled to Aïn-Fakroun in September 1932 to canvass support. Conversation soon turned to economic problems. Townspeople complained of maltreatment by local officials, tax collectors, gendarmes, and forest guards who denied them access to grazing and firewood. Impressed by the shared grievances of the people of Aïn-Fakroun, Bendjelloul advised them to begin a tax boycott.[91] This call to make tax payment conditional on the colonial provision of human security needs provoked alarm inside the Algiers government. 'Modern' taxation rested on a sense of reciprocity between people and government—money for services. Bendjelloul took this transactional logic a step further, asserting the social rights of a subject population to withhold consent when the colonial power offered nothing.[92]

Telescoping forward to August 1937, the second example relates to Mohamed Ben Hamida Ben Salem. Born into a family of dignitaries in Laghouat, an oasis city in the Atlas Mountains at the northern edge of the Algerian Sahara, Ben Salem was a professional soldier pensioned off from his colonial cavalry regiment after contracting tuberculosis. He drank heavily, embittered by the loss of his career and exasperated by the conservatism of his peers. But politics gave him hope. He gravitated to the French Socialist Party, canvassing for a seat. He began touring Algeria's Saharan territories and, like Bendjelloul before him, advised supporters not to pay their taxes to a corrupt, self-serving colonial government. Matters came to a head at the French Socialist Party Congress in Marseille that summer. There, Ben Salem made an incendiary speech attacking the Algerian administration. A month later, on August 13, 1937, he was hauled before a municipal court in Laghouat on charges of tax avoidance and threatening behavior. Unable to imprison him for more than two months for these offences, Laghouat's Commission Disciplinaire appealed to the French Interior Minister, requesting that Ben Salem be locked up for at least a year because he was 'an exceptionally dangerous political agitator'.[93] Two examples, one message: as the Depression bit harder, taxes of all sorts, from those levied by the state to the money extorted by local officials, were politicized as part of a colonial 'system' becoming intolerable.

That is why the manner in which French colonial relief measures were funded was so significant. Social spending in Depression-era French North Africa was always issued as a state loan. This included expenditure on public works, social housing, rural schooling, and primary health care. Each was ultimately repayable from the North African territories' ordinary budgets and so liable to arouse opposition among settler taxpayers. Colonial governments already taxed their subject populations heavily but typically did so through indirect taxation as well as various forms of head tax. The ability to raise revenue in this way was not just a matter of fiscal policy; it was also a strong indicator that the taxing authorities exerted tangible political control. In theory, taxes were also fundamental to social improvement, making investment in education, public health, and other collective goods sustainable. The problem for colonial authorities between the wars was that dependent populations were, in the great majority, too poor to pay remunerative taxes on income.[94] Algeria's 1936 budget, for example, recorded only 124,756 income tax payers, nearly all of them settlers, in a total population approaching seven million. Not surprisingly, dislike of progressive direct taxation ran deep among Algeria's European community, as among colonial settlers elsewhere. The hostility was as much racial as economic in origin. Paying more taxes meant supporting the needs of a different ethnic group unable to support itself.[95] Settler hostility to reform was male-dominated. But white women, still denied political or legal equality, guarded their status as members of the dominant cultural group. Their domestic and private spaces were also highly politicized because it was here that cultural expectations of complete racial separation were strongest. Their social status bound up with cultural conformity, few European women challenged the racist precepts of Algeria's political economy.[96]

Government in North Africa simply could not function in the teeth of organized settler opposition; indeed, in Algeria especially, it lost its raison d'être.[97] Working through their elected town mayors and a burgeoning extreme right in the cities along Algeria's Mediterranean coast, between 1936 and 1938 the colony's European population mobilized against a plan to enfranchise an additional 21,000 Muslim males, many of them decorated First World War veterans.[98] The centerpiece colonial reform of the Socialist-led Popular Front government, the so-called Blum–Viollette project, never made it to a National Assembly vote.[99] By March 1938, 91 mayors and 101 deputy mayors had resigned in protest at the proposal. Local government came to a standstill.[100] It is no surprise, then, that Algeria's settlers insisted in the 1938 budgetary round that the French Treasury meet the welfare needs of the Muslim majority, leaving settler taxes to fund social spending for their own community alone.[101] Their demands struck home. Outnumbered more than six to one by the Muslim majority, settlers received the lion's share of Algeria's social spending. Putting the injustice of this disbursement to one side, the stark truth was that even in a relatively well-developed colony like Algeria, neither French investment nor locally raised revenue could cope with the social consequences of rapid population growth. Little wonder that problems of underemployment and economic dislocation, labor migration, urban expansion and the emergence of a proletarian underclass dominated the periodic surveys of local economic conditions filed on the eve of war in 1939.[102]

Back to War

Years before the Second World War broke out, French bureaucrats worried about their country's dependence on imports of oil, grain, and other foods.[103] Sure enough, France's food and fuel shortages continued after the war. The same held true in the Netherlands, Belgium, and Britain. There were no such worries about food security across the North Atlantic.

The United States entered the postwar world with the luxury of producing food surpluses. The sharpest contrast was with the Netherlands. There, internal transport and distribution systems between the country's liberated and occupied regions broke down during its 'hunger winter' of 1944–1945.[104] Famine resulted. The Dutch experience was exceptional, but not unique. Supplies of grain, milk, and other foodstuffs comprised over a quarter of the US support disbursed worldwide through the Marshall Plan. Food supplies gave material form to a tenet of US soft power between the late 1940s and the early 1950s: the use of America's food surplus to cement political relationships, to enhance America's image as a well-governed land of plenty, and to burnish US credentials as a supporter of freedom from want, one of the 'four freedoms' identified by Franklin Roosevelt as a foreign policy principle.[105]

America's postwar preeminence as the world's food superpower contrasted with the decline of the British, French, and other empires as self-sufficient food-producing systems. As global trade in foodstuffs accelerated, the need for empires to serve as silos for the production, storage, and delivery of agricultural goods diminished. Colonies never functioned as fair food distributors anyway. Recurrent famines, bread riots, and the unequal distribution of resources between rulers and ruled testified to that. Measured by the League of Nations' 1935 global dietary standard of 2,500 calories per day, empires were already failing.[106]

That failure became still more obvious after the Second World War. Maintaining supply chains, internal markets, and price stability in British India, the largest colonial agglomeration of them all, was never easy. It demanded coordination between the Delhi government and provinces that were administered, farmed, and fed in locally specific ways. Punjab's cereal farmers opposed the price caps that made flour affordable for the urban poor. Gandhian nationalists viewed the centralized economic regulation of foodstuff prices as the infantilization of Indians supposedly unable to manage their own affairs. Nehruvian planners saw price controls and state distribution as integral to postindependence modernization. There may have been no consensus over how to feed India's population, but it was undeniable that wartime conditions put more people at risk of going hungry.[107] British officials in India did not sustain adequate, affordable food for the population they governed, evidenced by the loss of up to four million lives to famine during 1943–1944.[108]

A manmade disaster, the Bengal famine saw rice, kerosene, and other essentials become unaffordable, the prelude to starvation that hit children, the elderly, and women hardest. Meeting kinship obligations became

impossible, something as devastating culturally as hunger was physi-
ologically.[109] By the end of 1943 thousands were dying every day across
the province of Bengal and in the former imperial capital of Calcutta, the
result of a food supply crisis and chronic price inflation worsened by colonial mismanagement. Secretary of State for India Leo Amery's denial of
famine conditions in January 1943 personified these failings, as did his
later, shockingly inaccurate claims that incoming Viceroy Wavell had
ensured sufficient food distribution over the early months of 1944. The fact
that the colonial authorities could not accurately calculate Bengal's death
toll attested to the bankruptcy, moral and economic, of Britain's presence
in India.[110]

As if to underline the point, in August 1943 the British government
withdrew from a 1937 ILO convention banning the employment of Indian
women as underground mineworkers, labor legislation that was originally
drafted on British advice. Withdrawal was an expedient: by that point,
India's railways, armaments factories, and textile industry were short of
coal supplies.[111] But it was also discriminatory and unjust; 72,345 Bengali
and Bihari women were employed under- and aboveground in northeast
India's mines by 1945. They received lower wages than their male counterparts, and most felt compelled to work in the mining industry by the pressures of hunger. Thousands of peasant smallholders had sold off their land
to pay black-market rice prices. Mineworkers were promised restitution
for their land in the long term, as well as regular meals in the short term,
incentives that, in the circumstances, could be read as compulsion.[112]
The outrage in India over such injustices, echoed by trade unionists and
church groups in Britain, confirmed that the colonial government could
not evade its responsibility for famine in Bengal.[113]

What about French Indochina, where another rice famine took hold
across several provinces of Northern Vietnam in late 1944? Estimates
vary, but a death toll of one million seems credible.[114] Was France even
responsible? Vietnam's wartime incorporation into Japan's Co-Prosperity
Sphere was disastrous for the country's peasantry. Some were forced to
grow unfamiliar crops, including maize and sweet potatoes; others faced
punitive requisitioning. The resulting shortages of rice triggered hoarding and price inflation. The pro-Vichy colonial regime was complicit in
the process, having opted to collaborate with Japan's military occupation
of Indochina.[115] But the provisional government in liberated Paris was
powerless to prevent Vietnam's Japanese occupiers from overthrowing
the colonial administration in Hanoi in March 1945. In a way, though,
that was the point. French preoccupation with the struggle for colonial

power in Vietnam shaded into disregard for the suffering of the North Vietnamese. The immediate cause of Vietnamese starvation may have been ruthless Japanese foodstuff requisitioning, but there were longer-term inequalities in the political economy of rice cultivation and Southern Vietnam's domination of the country's internal market, which again pointed to the bankruptcy of imperial power in Asia.[116]

Next to America's happy abundance of food in 1945, the enduring problems of malnourishment in colonial empires, plus the prevalence of rationing systems in postwar Europe, offered fresh proof that empires were not meeting their inhabitants' fundamental needs.[117] If the availability of food and a state's ability to disburse it to those most in need constituted 'food power', then European empires in 1945 looked powerless. Famines in Bengal, in Northern Vietnam, and in Indonesia as well were tragic proof that mid-twentieth-century imperial powers failed the first test of governance: sustaining the life of their populations. A British Foreign Office under-secretary, Hector McNeil, warned that famine might cause more deaths worldwide in 1946–1947 than in any of the war years.[118] In India especially, the decisive change came after independence, not before it.[119] Nehru's ministers requisitioned food supplies and coerced smallholders into 'modern' production techniques, although these clashed with constitutional claims that democratic power flowed from the people.[120]

Conclusion

Explicit in fascist thought and subsumed within imperialist language and the work of League of Nations specialist agencies, interwar biopolitics was framed partly in terms of competition between population groups, partly in terms of food security, living space, and the rightful 'ownership' of territory and resources.[121] Its precepts were evident in colonial phenomena that seemed otherwise unrelated. From fascist settlement schemes in Italian Libya to the rigging of census results in the Lebanon mandate and the racialized basis for wartime rationing in French North Africa, biopolitics was intrinsic to imperial practice around the Mediterranean's non-European rim.[122] Geopolitically, a key objective of such apparently diffuse imperial actions was to codify boundaries, some physical, others cultural, in territories without fixity, whether as dependencies or as nations.

The global economic crisis drove imperial powers to refashion their empires differently again: as subordinate units within closed economic blocs. Colonial governments tried to extract more from their dependent populations while cutting budgetary spending to the core. By 1930 several of the larger European colonies in black Africa, among them the Belgian Congo, Nigeria, and Kenya, spent between 30 and 45 percent of their annual budgets servicing their debts. In these territories, as elsewhere, administrative costs were another major item of recurrent expenditure. Even before the worst of the Depression, there was little money available to help colonial societies' poorest.[123] These limitations were not new, but they were clearer thanks to new methods of calculating economic output and scientific methods of measuring calorific value and malnutrition.

For the peoples of the Mediterranean's southern shores—this chapter's principal regional case study—deflationary orthodoxy hit home in three distinct ways. Declining purchasing power made everything more expensive. With it came a second hardship: bigger debt burdens as people borrowed more to pay for essentials. The logical impulse to move in search of work was curbed by the third phenomenon: tighter restrictions on freedom of movement. These curbs were largely ineffective, simply criminalizing the movers. Travel restrictions or the risk that an unauthorized shantytown dwelling might be torn down meant little to rural families crippled by debt and vulnerable to foodstuff price variations. Thousands sold up and shifted.[124] Agricultural underemployment fostered economic migration, the growth of urban slums (which would later become vital reservoirs of nationalist support), and a remittance culture in which male relatives working in Europe or elsewhere provided for impoverished families back home.[125]

What does all this mean? Simply put, macroeconomic mismanagement made the global economic crisis worse than it might otherwise have been, pushing the poorest in colonial societies deeper into poverty. To offer a different empire example, Portugal's newly established Estado Novo (New State), with dictator and finance minister António de Oliveira Salazar at its helm, introduced deflationary policies at home to combat the impact of the Depression barely two years after an entirely new currency, the angolar, was introduced to Portuguese Angola in 1928. Metropolitan demand for Angola's raw materials collapsed. State loans dried up. Financial backing for agricultural settlement ended. But Angola's new currency remained chained to the Portuguese escudo regardless.[126]

The interwar turn to what its neoliberal critics would term 'economic nationalism' might be identifiable with the fascist autarkies of Europe, but it had parallels in other empires. One after the other, imperial governments from Britain to Japan closed off access to their reserved colonial markets.[127] A short-term fix for metropolitan economies, this colonial protectionism was globally disastrous and locally devastating, expanding poverty gaps in colonial societies. Debilitating for subject populations, in the short term, the global turn toward protectionism made reserved imperial markets lifelines to the struggling metropolitan economies of Britain, France, and the Netherlands.[128] All three countries came off the gold standard: Britain early (in 1931), France and the Netherlands, the pivotal members of a western European 'gold bloc', late (in 1936). Their currency value no longer held artificially high, each erected higher imperial tariff walls to compel dependent territories to trade more exclusively with the 'mother country'.[129] The 'world economy', insofar as it tangibly existed in the 1920s, was a wounded animal by the mid-1930s.[130]

The partial return to free trade and currency alignment, matched by international migration flows, had seemed to draw the world together in the early 1920s. Protectionism and the diminution of freer Most Favored Nation trading arrangements, the gold standard's collapse, and punitive immigration restrictions divided the global economy once more by the early 1930s.[131] Led by Mexico, at the 1933 World Economic Conference in London and for years afterward debtor country advocates of multilateral cooperation, currency stabilization, and international financial support from rich-world creditors highlighted the dependence between lenders and borrowers in any capitalist system. It was illogical and self-defeating, they argued, to let the lenders make all the rules.[132] That logic went unanswered in London, Washington, and elsewhere. Pervasive and protracted, the Depression was an accelerant to decolonization and a sorry prelude to another World War.

CHAPTER SIX

Making Decolonization's Global Cultures

PATHS TO DECOLONIZATION were constantly mediated by global conversation about possible routes out of empire. After a second global conflict left multiple empires intact, discussion of how to achieve the liberation of societies, cultures, and minds from the constrictions of colonialism sharpened. The languages and registers differed, but the precept was the same: empires reified difference, which generated exploitation.[1] Much of this conversation took place in print and over the airwaves, some through artistic representation, popular culture, and sport.[2] Some was stimulated by physical connection as activists traveled to meet like-minded colleagues, to see different parts of the decolonizing world for themselves. or to escape detention and political oppression.[3] Some was more remote, an intersectional blend combining solidarities of race, class, and poverty with shared identification of the colonial roots of social marginalization among communities that would never meet face to face.[4] Crossing diverse spaces of communication, the resulting cultural output was prodigious. And it spread as everyday lives were inflected with talk of alternate political futures. Inseparable from this literary and artistic production were the political transitions, controversies, and debates that impelled people to oppose colonialism.

Patterns of Transnational Opposition

Much as the voices of political leaders and writers figured prominently in decolonization's global cultures, vital impetus came from other, subaltern voices: peace activists, antiracist and women's rights campaigners, trade unionists, students, and countless others who organized to protest.[5] Non-Western and Western students were especially vocal. The pro-communist International Union of Students, founded in 1946, and the anticommunist International Student Conference, established in 1950, although divided along Cold War lines, found common ground in anticolonialism.[6] To describe these people as members of a global civil society of oppositionists is problematic insofar as empire authorities strove to hold the vibrancy of anticolonial associational culture in check.[7] But such repression could backfire. Much as they wished to do so, colonial authorities could neither shut down overseas contacts nor regulate all travel.[8] Finding the gaps in the apparatus of imperial repression was instrumental to the transnational workings of anticolonial activism, making flight, exile, sanctuary, and migration critical determinants of whether networks were sustained.[9]

Often, anticolonial causes brought local members of these constituencies into contact with international affiliate groups, adding impetus to transnational activism within the colonial world.[10] A panoply of underground newspapers, radio stations, and political pamphlets created new lines of south–south and north–south communication as information about particular national struggles circulated among sympathizer networks, assuring an expanding audience for resonant causes.[11] Students, trade unionists, and print journalists sometimes led the way, but across the British East African territories of Kenya, Uganda, and Tanzania, as in other regional colonial clusters, the gathering sense of shared Afro-Asian interest in ending empire fostered additional connections, some tangible, others nurtured by affinity and common purpose.[12] The Soviet-backed Women's International Democratic Federation, largest of the women's movements within the Communist bloc, was, for instance, increasingly directed by organizers and affiliate women's groups from Nigeria, India, Indonesia, Vietnam, and Algeria from the late 1940s onward.[13] By 1950, its Maoist equivalent, Tsai Chang's Chinese Federation of Democratic Women, was making similar inroads among women's sections of various political parties in colonial Africa.[14]

Gradually, the demarcation between 'official' campaigns and a constant hubbub of direct action blurred. Heightened transnational activism transcended the orthodox and limited frameworks previously available to protest empire—appealing to local authority figures, approaching administrative officers face to face, petitioning more distant bureaucracies, giving evidence to inquiries, and seeking other back channels to government. For all the obstacles placed in its way by colonial authorities determined to belittle it, transnational opposition, by its nature dynamic and multinodal, broke the barriers separating state-to-state or even party-to-party communication from the claims made by colonial subjects mobilizing from below.[15] Anticolonial campaigners bridged the gaps, locally and transnationally, between activists and others willing to lend support for particular causes. Just as core elements of colonialism, its racial and gender discriminations, its economic structures and consequent social iniquities, were common across empires, so too, lived experiences of racism, rights denial, and foreign misrule brought marginalized individuals and groups living outside the colonial world into dialogue with fellow sufferers within it.[16] In Nico Slate's apt formulation, the resulting 'colored cosmopolitanism' affirmed the commonalities of antiracist and anticolonial struggles. At the same time, its protagonists asserted political and cultural identities that transcended markers of ethnicity or colonial subject status.[17]

A crucial transatlantic link developed between people of African heritage in the Americas and Africans living under colonialism.[18] Here, too, a distinctive 'race internationalism' emerged. Some of its strongest advocates were women of color, keenly aware of the intersections between racial and gender discrimination. Discerning the equivalences of exclusionary ideologies across empires, the sense of common purpose lent such internationalist opposition an empowering ethical force.[19] Paralleled by connections spanning the Indian and Pacific Oceans between the descendants of indentured laborers and others subjected to coercive colonial migration, these 'diasporas of decolonization' brought together otherwise disparate communities whose working patterns and life chances were still shaped by colonialism.[20] Discrimination echoed globally. Sharing knowledge of its experiential aspects was often the first step in mobilizing transnationally to end it.[21]

Little wonder that imperialism's transcontinental presence lent opposition to empire, whether wholeheartedly anticolonial or not, an equally global character. From African American civil rights workers and other political campaigners within the Black Atlantic to medical humanitarians and civil society networks in the communist 'Second World' and on to refugee groups and student activists from Palestine to Vietnam, opposition to white supremacy, imperialism, and settler colonialism forged connections that gave decolonization a singular aspect as a global fight against the injustice intrinsic to colonialism.[22] To illustrate the point, consider the 322 students from the Gold Coast known to have applied to study in the United States in 1949–1950. Colonial officials in Accra and London warned of damaging political consequences should the students forge contacts with African American civil rights groups. State Department staffers did not want Africans returning home with stories of Jim Crow racism in the

United States. But each recognized that criticisms were bound to multiply unless such exchanges were banned entirely, hardly a positive outcome. Whatever the State Department's misgivings, the Ghanaian students got their study visas, their voices joining the chorus of opposition to American segregation.[23]

It is a difficult task, even for groups of researchers, to map the scale of decolonization's global cultures. The work may be incomplete, but its first findings confirm the breadth and diversity of the global networks, some highly organized and politically influential, others more informal but still culturally unifying, that coalesced in opposition to colonialism. The harder job is to gauge their impact on decolonization, on the disintegration of empires and the remaking of a different world order. These anti-imperial networks appreciated that discrimination manifested in comparable ways, not just within empires but inside other countries and social systems riven by structural inequality. This encouraged an intersectional perspective on colonialism that viewed racism, gender discrimination, cavernous pay gaps, and other systemic denials of opportunity as products of a rich-world capitalism nourished by imperial hegemony and Eurocentric discourses of Western civilizational primacy. It was easy enough to highlight the persistence of a global color line by drawing parallels between Jim Crow and apartheid. But opposing them was a slow grind, requiring courage and stamina.[24] The installation of a more receptive US administration under John F. Kennedy in 1961 only confirmed how hard it was to dismantle America's racialized power structures, let alone those of empire.[25]

The sense of common struggle was strengthened, not just by parallel postwar trajectories of nonviolent civil rights protest, but by the shared celebration of cultural successes in music and sport.[26] It helped that the antiracism and anti-imperialism of the intellectuals drawn together in what John Munro identifies as the postwar 'anticolonial front' was not just egalitarian, but radically internationalist as well.[27] Even so, when judged by the uncompromising standards of its supporters, in narrowly political terms this brand of radical anticolonialism failed. To be sure, most of the colonial world made formal transitions to nationhood somewhere in the thirty years after 1945. But sovereign independence was diluted by various external forces, among them the persistence of unequal patterns of trade, the commercial dependency on foreign capital, and the strategic frailties of newly independent countries situated along Cold War fault lines. At the same time, that same sovereignty was sometimes depreciated by the postcolonial elites who took up the reins of government. Some proved reluctant to share power and wealth. Others insisted that strongman authoritarianism was necessary to keep incumbent regimes from disintegration. Whether because of external interference or internal misrule, the juridical equality between states essential to effective sovereignty within the postwar international system remained elusive.[28]

Hubs and Precedents

Before looking forward to postindependence regimes, let's step back to consider where decolonization's global cultures came from. Marxist ideology and communist political culture anticipated the globalism of anticolonialists hostile to the limitations of national sovereignty within a capitalistic international system.[29] For these anticolonialists, the nation-state was a rich-world construct, a form of political organization at variance with the authentic social structures and cultural practices of colonized communities.[30] For Marxists, the nation was merely a stepping-stone, a transitional stage before the ultimate triumph of communism. For all that imperial security services exaggerated it, there was some basis for ideological convergence between opponents of colonialism and communists.[31] Little wonder that leading anticolonial figures of the twentieth century, from C. L. R. James and Ho Chi Minh to Frantz Fanon and Walter Rodney, approached Marxism as a lens through which empire's exploitative mechanics could be magnified.[32]

Accustomed to working in secret, across borders, and in small groups, the cellular structures of early communist cadres and communist-affiliated trade unions offered an obvious organizational model for anticolonial social movements to follow.[33] By the late 1920s, several Comintern-backed organizations were also intrinsically transnational, claiming a global reach that transcended national or imperial jurisdiction and the specificities of regional competitions for power.[34] On April 4, 1927, in the week before Nationalist leader Chiang Kai-shek ordered a bloody crackdown against Communist Party networks in Shanghai that quickened China's descent into civil war, anticolonial groups in the city received guidance from the military attaché at Shanghai's Soviet legation. He advised them on how to infiltrate Western embassies, working as cleaners or kitchen staff to steal valuable paperwork from desks and garbage bins. This, he assured them, was not petty theft but vanguard intelligence-gathering: part of the global struggle against capitalist imperialism.[35]

Alongside these covert activities went impressively named and highly publicized transnational support groups—International Red Aid, the World Committee against War and Fascism, and International

Workers' Relief. All gave tangible form to the shared interest between anti-imperialism, antiracism, and antifascism.[36] The point should not be taken too far. These agencies and other, similar bodies founded after 1945 were poorly integrated with communist movements inside the European empires. Of the communist parties within the imperial nations of western Europe, only the Parti Communiste Français could claim either a mass membership or strong ties with anticolonial oppositionists, writers, and artists in France's empire. Britain's Communist Party (CPGB) was numerically small, with fewer than 10,000 members for most of the twenty years after its 1920 foundation. It was also solidly metropolitan, even London-centric. Aside from some trade union and literary sympathizers in India, West Africa, and Trinidad, the CPGB never boasted widespread colonial links. Dutch and Belgian communists were active in Indonesian and Congolese affairs, but again, not decisively so. By 1930 all four parties faced criticism from Comintern patrons for their lack of ethnic diversity, their fitful engagement with colonial affairs, and their reluctance to work with Willi Münzenberg's League against Imperialism (LAI), launched at an inaugural conference in Brussels three years earlier.[37]

As these dislocations suggest, despite the organizational and ideological parallels between communist parties and anticolonial movements, what mattered in practice was the cultivation of relationships between individuals and social movements across countries and colonies. Shapurji Shaklatvala, twice elected communist MP for the London constituency of Battersea North in the 1920s, personified this kind of transnational anticolonialism at work. Building on the radical sympathies of Battersea's large Irish immigrant community, Shaklatvala cultivated mutual support networks between communists in India and Britain. Indian merchant seamen transited between them, while the organizers of textile worker protests in both countries orchestrated joint action against the exploitative dynamics of Britain's colonial cotton trade.[38] These grassroots partnerships had greater impact, first in disseminating information about imperial abuses in India, then in pushing the British government in India toward its 1926 legalization of 'moderate' trade union activity in the colony, than Shaklatvala's efforts to animate the CPGB.[39]

Shaklatvala's example indicates something else: that the working methods and transnational connections between the coordinators of anticolonialist social movements were first steps toward popular mobilization and intercolonial protest. British imperial authorities saw the danger and tried to contain it. In 1930, in a widely publicized raid on communist organizers in colonial Singapore, Special Branch officers descended on the home of well-to-do British expatriates at 24 Nassim Road. There, they arrested the leaders of the newly formed Malayan Communist Party. The detainees included activists from Malaya, French Vietnam, Dutch Indonesia, and Siam. Their meeting had been arranged by the homeowners' two Chinese cooks from Hainan. Interrogations revealed additional supporters in Hong Kong and Shanghai. This was excuse enough for the British authorities to introduce tighter legislative restrictions on Asian immigration to Singapore through an Aliens Ordinance promulgated in 1933.[40]

French officials were equally inclined to monitor, to arrest, and to deport troublesome anticolonialists, but this did not diminish the attractions of Paris as a hub of transnational opposition to empire.[41] In the twenty years after 1919, the city was transformed from a grandiose venue for interstate diplomacy into a more subversive terrain: 'the capital of the men without a country', as it was dubbed by American civil rights activist Roger Nash Baldwin.[42] The anticolonial camaraderie he invoked was genuine but gendered. The organizational work and literary expressions of negritude thought of Antillean women in interwar Paris, such as Suzanne Lacascade and sisters Paulette and Jane Nardal, remained underappreciated,[43] but there is no question that the city was a nexus for petitioners, overseas students, revolutionary idealists, and Comintern operatives from Africa, Asia, Latin America, the Caribbean, and Europe.[44] The capital's favored *quartiers*, libraries, and cafés offered the space necessary for activists to share ideas about futures after empire.[45] Their artistic and journalistic output lent momentum to the process. Paris became an interwar epicenter of an enlarging anti-imperial public sphere, whose cultural production guided the political paths trodden by those who sought it.[46] Books and plays, newspaper articles, and a burgeoning specialist press, plus the visual and musical arts, as well as trenchant criticism of the racism of official colonial exhibitions: all strengthened webs of connection between these anticolonial internationalists and colonial immigrants in the French capital.[47]

Interwar Paris was distinctive in bringing together so many groups, but it was not unique.[48] From Cairo to Harlem, London to Mexico City, Brussels to Baku, Singapore to Shanghai, other cities became foci for transregional cooperation in the fight against imperialistic rule.[49] Paris, though, along with Geneva and Berlin, home of the Comintern-backed LAI,[50] was a continental European pole of attraction that exerted a magnetic pull for dissidents.[51] Hostility to imperialism in all its forms—colonial, economic, cultural—was, by the 1920s, a political accelerant.[52] It catalyzed new alignments between political actors otherwise unable to organize as effectively locally or singly. The German capital, for instance, was home to the Liga zur Verteidigung der Negerrasse (LzVN: 'League for the Defense of the Negro Race'), established in 1929 by a group of German-based Cameroonians led by Comintern activist Joseph Bilé.[53] A year later, the group hosted the First International Conference of Negro Workers in Hamburg.[54] As the LzVN confirmed, heightened migration and student exchange were prerequisites to such organizational activity.

Paris as intellectual forum, student city, and industrial center meanwhile threw together youthful idealists and migrant workers with seasoned political exiles in a capital of empire that, paradoxically, became host to defining anti-imperial movements. For several new arrivals from Francophone dependencies, the racial discrimination they suffered as immigrant laborers or university students in their adopted Parisian home cemented their anticolonialism.[55] Marginalization sometimes had the opposite effect, bringing different constituencies together, whether congregating in the same outer suburbs or meeting to share thoughts and ideas outside the societal mainstream.[56] At the same time, French political culture played a more positive role. Anti-imperial sentiments became inflected with the language of republican universality and citizen's rights. French revolutionary ideals blended with Marxist thought and local variants of cultural self-assertion to produce uniquely Francophone strains of anticolonialism.

Turning ideas into action was contingent upon the level of contacts between the differing individuals and groups animated by colonial injustice. Cosmopolitan cities allowed such networks to thrive, facilitating interactions among Chinese, Latin American, North African, Vietnamese, and other anti-imperial activists. In Paris, especially, communist associational culture was also important. The French capital's 'Red Belt', outer communes of the Île-de-France held by the PCF, offered sanctuary and support.[57] Nineteen-twenty-five was a pivotal year. The Rif War in Morocco and the suppression of mandate Syria's 'Great Revolt' triggered protests among students and Maghrebi workers. Across the English Channel in London, officers of Britain's security service MI5 seized a Comintern tract written for French Communist Party readers but circulated in British hard-left circles as well:

> The Communist International is not satisfied with merely denouncing the action of French imperialism in Syria as contrary to the 'right of self-determination'. It calls upon the French proletariat to fight energetically against imperialism—the instigator of wars.[58]

Communist militants within France's breakaway trade union confederation, the CGTU, responded, coordinating antimilitarist demonstrations and dockside boycotts of materials destined for Morocco and Beirut.[59]

Guided by the Comintern, Communist supporters in North Africa and the Levant Mandates meanwhile tried to build contacts with colonial troops in Morocco and Syria, distributing pamphlets and fliers denouncing French repression.[60]

Less than two years later, China's May Thirtieth Movement provided another unifying anticolonial 'moment' in which an individual anti-imperial struggle achieved global resonance.[61] China's revolutionary fervor reverberated through the February 1927 Brussels Conference of the League against Imperialism and Colonial Oppression, the subject of wild anticipation. In the short term, though, the primary focus on China at the Brussels Congress proved misguided. The presence of a large Kuomintang delegation explained the conference's preoccupation with Chinese affairs. But the imminent split between the Kuomintang and the Chinese Communist Party, soon to register in China's eruption into civil war, cast a pall over the Brussels meeting.[62] Ironically, the conference's secondary focus on India was almost as problematic. Again, the problem stemmed from domestic fractures, this time within the Indian National Congress, whose representatives, led by Jawaharlal Nehru, constituted another large Asian delegation to the LAI. After Gandhi abandoned the *swaraj* noncooperation campaign in 1922, schisms opened within the INC between those committed to civil disobedience versus others prepared to engage with British colonial authority by contesting Indian provincial elections.[63]

But dwelling on the high politics of established anticolonialist movements risks misreading the signals. The significance of the Brussels Congress as a decolonization 'moment' lay elsewhere. Fusing anti-imperialist and anticapitalist internationalism, the Congress was a landmark on the road to transregional anticolonial solidarity.[64] Ethiopia's dogged response to Italy's 1935 invasion was another defining interwar case.[65] It brought Africans into dialogue with African Americans, West Indians, Indian nationalist organizers, and other people of color who called out the racist hypocrisy of the League of Nations' failure to halt fascist aggression.[66] Some of the deepest intellectual and organizational roots of decolonization are traceable to the ideas and practices of these activist networks, many of whose organizers figured prominently in the decades ahead.[67]

Anticolonialism Decentered

Internationalist-minded anticolonialists increasingly congregated in non-European cities after 1945. Newer organizational centers emerged as radical Third Worldism made the case for protesting colonialism from within the societies most warped by it. By the early 1960s Havana, Accra, Algiers, Dar es Salaam, Hanoi, and Saigon figured among the most dynamic hubs for transnational activism against imperialist oppression.[68] This southward reorientation was indicative of another long-term shift: as anticolonialism grew more sharply defined, more widely supported, and more stridently articulated, readiness to work within the boundaries, real or imagined, of a Western-centric and imperialistic international order diminished.[69]

In 1919 it made sense for organizers to head for Paris, London, Geneva, or Berlin to make their claims heard. By 1959 it was almost an anticolonialist matter of principle not to do so. It bears emphasizing that the oppositional communities organizing in European capitals after the First World War were not equally visible to the governing authorities under which they lived. Intermediate between their individual points of colonial origin and the more global anticolonialism to come, as some analysts have suggested, these nonstate internationalists coalesced in the interwar years.[70] In some places their subversive potential was studied and often exaggerated, as we've seen, but in others, anticolonial networks did not stand out from the crowd or, worse, were trivialized.[71] In Algiers, the French Empire's premier city, colonial authorities devoted greater resources to monitoring outsiders and white settlers, each presumed to be more skilled in mobilizing revolutionary opposition than the subaltern Muslim majority. The list of French, Algerian, and other transnational seditionist networks monitored by colonial authorities in Algiers in 1929 was a long one. Groups placed under surveillance, usually in response to police informants' reports, included familiar suspects: the local PCF and CGTU branches, plus pacifist movements, women's rights groups, Spanish-directed Anarchist branches and, more bizarrely, an educational charity and the French Empire youth league.[72] To these were added various ultra-rightist 'Leagues' that were especially popular among urban settlers, whose violent street protests helped define the ideological polarization of the Depression years.[73] It is unsurprising that racist precepts shaped security planning within a quintessential settler colony like Algeria, but worth remembering is that the networks monitored were not just a global phenomenon, but an interwar one.[74]

The anticolonial 'moment' of 1919 was distinctive, ending in frustration for most of its participants.[75] But that moment's challenge to empire was more enduring—something characteristic of the times. The First World War ushered in a succession of crises, from the global influenza pandemic of 1918 and the feminist wave of the 1920s to the Depression and the rise of fascism. Each indicated that little in societal hierarchies was secure. Why not build anticolonial internationalism on principles of equality and shared humanity in a world without empire?[76] After all, as India's leading sociologist Benoy Kumar Sarkar had it, seminal changes, from the Bolshevik revolution and radical Chinese republicanism to the clamor for self-determination, pointed to a more egalitarian future.[77]

Marcus Garvey, the Jamaican-born leader of the Harlem-based Universal Negro Improvement Association (UNIA), recognized that the First World War and its aftermath had done little to improve the standing of a worldwide UNIA rank-and-file membership close to a million strong.[78] Most still lived either as colonial subjects or within black diaspora communities facing discriminatory laws in their countries of residence. This global reservoir of pan-Africanist support was unlikely any time soon to achieve self-government, self-determination, or sovereign independence organized along national principles.[79] In a way, that was the point: peoples of African heritage in the Americas shared with their cousins in Africa the same exclusions and racist maltreatment.[80]

Garvey's insight was to see that the UNIA's global network might constitute an alternate basis for political recognition, the 'general will' of its members as people of African heritage legitimizing their claim to juridical recognition as a sovereign pan-African movement. Garvey drew inspiration from the black Jacobinism of the Haitian revolution some 120 years earlier, which melded revolt against slavery with the ideals of a citizens' republic.[81] It was bitterly ironic that, in the aftermath of the First World War, Haiti was chafing under the strain of US occupation. Nor was there much solidarity to be found from its neighboring state, the Dominican Republic, where fears of US imperialism were too inchoate to overcome racial divides sharpened by inequalities of wealth and social status.[82] Haiti's dilemma and Dominicans' reluctance to identify with it exposed the limits of Garveyist mobilization. Although, by the 1920s, the UNIA boasted some eight hundred local chapters worldwide and famously operated the Black Star shipping line to bring together black communities in Africa and the Americas, Garvey's formulation of a global and diasporic pan-African sovereignty made little headway against the grinding realities of empire and segregation.[83]

Garvey's message, and the methods he and his second wife, Amy Jacques Garvey, devised to achieve it, endured in the work of others even so.[84] A hostile rival to Garvey within the United States, W. E. B. Du Bois, historian, writer and tireless civil rights campaigner, proffered an internationalist vision of antiracist struggle against the global color line.[85] Like many of his antiracist comrades, Du Bois broadened his overseas connections as his thinking about the racial tenets of global capitalism pushed him leftward from the 1930s onward.[86] Du Bois's interwar writing, including articles in the journal *Foreign Affairs*, made the case for pan-Africanism as a remedy for aggressive colonialism in West Africa, Ethiopia, and elsewhere.[87] Hubert Harrison, born in the Danish West Indies in 1900 and appointed editor of the UNIA publication *Negro World* in 1920, went further still, insisting that racial discrimination was intrinsic to capitalism rather than its incidental byproduct. Authentic pan-Africanism, Harrison argued, must be as anti-capitalist as it was internationalist.[88] Anticolonialists such as Trinidad-born George Padmore also discerned that decolonization demanded multilayered strategies capable of drawing local oppositional voices into a coherent transnational framework that, by maximizing members' influence, would be more than the sum of its parts. A former communist and head of the Profintern's International Trade Union Committee of Negro Workers, by 1933 Padmore's concerns fixed on the potential of pan-African unity.[89] Under constant police surveillance of his London home on either side of the Second World War, Padmore retained a black internationalist vision, becoming a leading actor in Cold War–era decolonization but thinking beyond both.[90]

From World War to Third World

More immediately, the colonialist paradox of the Second World War, a conflict whose victorious Allies appeared to be fighting one racist ideology only to uphold another, opened the door to another postwar anticolonial 'moment'. An antifascist war triggered by the revisionist powers' seizure of foreign lands placed empire in question. War-induced famines that claimed millions of lives in colonial Bengal, Indonesia, and Northern Vietnam between 1943 and 1945 offered harrowing proof that Allied professions of imperial solidarity rang hollow.[91] On the other side, the Nazi regime's wartime patronage of Indian, Arab, Central Asian, and Caucasus anticolonialist movements confirms that the Third Reich's ultra-nationalism appealed to colonial revolutionaries repelled by the hypocrisy of Western democracies wedded to colonialism. Superficially, the partnerships established between Hitler's regime and numerous 'national' committees of anticolonialist exiles in Berlin were marriages of strategic convenience sustained by the desire to see the British, French, and Soviet empires fall. At another, deeper level, though, these arrangements signified an ideological congruence—what historian David Motadel identifies as a global 'authoritarian moment'—between the violent revisionism of the Axis Powers and the anticolonial revolutionaries' loathing of liberal internationalism.[92]

From the former Indian National Congress leader Subhas Chandra Bose, the Mufti of Jerusalem, Amin Al-Husayni, and Syrian nationalist Fawzi al-Qawuqji to an array of putative national leaders of breakaway Soviet Republics in the North Caucasus and Central Asia, the list of anticolonialist exiles based in wartime Berlin is long. Equally striking was their shared commitment to raising funds, to disseminating nationalist propaganda, to attracting armed recruits, and to advancing plans for postcolonial independence. These schemes were contingent on wider Axis fortunes in the war. But the authoritarian, antiliberal ideas underpinning them would resurface, along with many of the Berlin exiles themselves, in postwar nationalist groups and post-decolonization regimes. The wartime networks developed among these authoritarian anticolonialists in Berlin also subsisted through transnational connections between movements, several of which were represented at the Bandung Conference in 1955.[93]

Bose, commander of the Indian National Army (INA), led the strongest of these anti-imperial insurgencies but was fatally injured in an August 1945 airplane crash. His INA, its political fortunes tied to the Japanese, failed to expel the British from India. But when Bose's lieutenants were later put on trial for treason, Indian publics, Congress supporters included, reacted with dismay. Viewed from a local perspective, INA actions were patriotic, not treasonous.[94] It was crass to condemn anticolonialists for crossing the line from peaceful opposition to violence within an empire that still denied the human equivalence of its component peoples as rights-bearing individuals.

Bose's apologists were right. And they could point to the Allies' own proclamations to prove it. Roosevelt's January 1941 enunciation of Four Freedoms (of speech, of worship, from want, and from fear), the Atlantic Charter ten months later, the promise in 1944–1945 of a new supranational authority, the United Nations—all pledged to couple peace preservation with rights protection. These pronouncements and new supervisory institutions invested antiracism with a geopolitical logic to match its moral authority.[95] The presumption that individuated human rights would become building blocks of a new international order implied that empire would face an existential challenge once that order became institutionalized. But the everyday reality in 1945 and beyond of persistent racial discrimination and entrenched colonialism suggested otherwise. The war brought colonial injustice into sharper relief but did not end it. Instead, the intolerable hypocrisy of the Allied coalition's racially colored fight for

democratic freedoms, of one rule for whites, another for the rest, stimulated a surge in anticolonialist writings and transnational activism.[96]

Among the first fruits of this clear-eyed militancy was the Manchester Pan-African Congress of October 1945, a conference whose attendees
personified the identification between antiracist intellectual production
and anticolonial politics.[97] Manchester was the fifth Pan-African Congress since the first in 1900, but it was different: uniquely animated by
more imminent possibilities of decolonization.[98] The attendance list
was equally arresting. Trinidadian C. L. R. James, author of *The Black
Jacobins* and *A History of Negro Revolt*, defining studies of black liberation struggle, sat alongside his compatriot Padmore, the antisegregation
campaigners W. E. B. Du Bois and Amy Ashwood Garvey, and a quar-
tet of future political leaders, Ghana's Kwame Nkrumah, Kenya's Jomo
Kenyatta, Malawi's Hastings Banda, and Sierra Leone's I. T. A. Wallace-
Johnson, founder of the West African Youth League. Several rubbed
shoulders at The Cosmopolitan, a Manchester restaurant that offered a
welcoming environment for people of color and a venue for anticolonialist politics. The Cosmopolitan's owner, Guyana-born Ras T. Makonnen,
boasted decades of radical activism in the United States and Europe.
His organizational skills as secretary of Padmore's International African
Service Bureau, plus the money his entrepreneurship generated, helped
bring the Manchester Congress to fruition.[99] In part, the agenda reflected
abiding concerns with workplace discrimination and the denial of social
rights to colonial workers. Condemnation of South Africa's color bar was
understandably virulent.[100] But what echoed longest was something more
radical, a message of pan-African solidarity, which identified imperialism
as the overriding structural impediment to black freedom.[101]

Conclusion

The cosmopolitanism of the black internationalist networks in postwar
Britain and France echoed those of the 1920s in their focus on transnational connection, but as the 1950s dawned with Africa still colonized,
their radicalism increased. Stronger alignments emerged between longtime anticolonialists, negritude thinkers, African nationalist politicians
pushing the boundaries of colonial legality, and more violent oppositionists working beyond them. The critiques of colonialism that emerged from
1950s Paris, in particular, whether through the calls to black empowerment in the writings of Richard Wright and James Baldwin, the feminist
philosophy of Simone de Beauvoir or the new leftism of Jean-Paul Sartre,

were more explicitly revolutionary than their interwar antecedents.[102] But a different intellectual evolution, the marriage achieved in negritude thinking between African cultural attachments and nonviolent solutions for the consolidation of postcolonial politics in Francophone West Africa, registered a more immediate impact in decolonization. Negritude's affirmation of blackness was certainly radical, as much at variance with the colonialism that had stifled it as with the newer Western modernization projects threatening to frustrate it once more. But the pragmatism and political experience of its leading exponents placed it within the spectrum of claims-making central to late colonial reformism in the French Empire.[103] Politically, if not culturally, negritude was more reformatory than revolutionary.

More Anglophone in voice and focus, the Manchester Pan-Africanist Congress did not induce imperialist governments to change political course. It was, rather, among the attendees, their readers, and their supporters that profound changes occurred. As a statement of racial discrimination's structural causes, and as a technique for social movements to coordinate their efforts transnationally, Manchester's message was global. No matter its local manifestation, racial injustice was embedded in colonialism, normalized by empire, and facilitated by an international order that denied rights equivalence between people of different cultures and ethnicities. Solidarity between the victims of discrimination was a prerequisite to effective opposition. It was not that locally focused, gradualist campaigns were irrelevant. Quite the reverse. Anticolonialism derived its transformatory power from the shared realization that individual actions and particular causes were part of something larger: fighting imperialism.

A similar message echoed from the Asian Relations Conference (ARC) hosted by Indian National Congress leaders at Delhi's Purana Qila (Old Fort) in March and April of 1947. The conference brought together 193 Asian country delegates, the majority from South and Southeast Asian territories, plus a further fifty-one observers. Hosted by INC President Jawaharlal Nehru, whose thinking about north–south confrontation was still in flux, the ARC shunned polemical anticolonialism.[104] Delegates concentrated instead on a universalist antiracism and its advancement through pacifist internationalism. In some ways a precursor to the strategies of nonalignment famously introduced at the Bandung Conference in Indonesia eight years later in April 1955, other aspects of the Delhi conference agenda were quite distinctive.[105] For one thing, ARC organizers placed women's rights at the heart of the conference, anticipating the Asian focus in ILO policies on women's work in informal economic sectors across the global South.[106] For another, delegates from Burma, Ceylon, and Malaya, like their Indian counterparts, rejected unfettered migration between territories. They were conscious that immigrant communities presented the most visible challenge to ethnically nationalist conceptions of citizenship. With partition violence continuing, they were also painfully aware that migrant minorities were acutely vulnerable.[107] Set against these tensions, the Nehruvian vision of an Asian-led internationalism was predicated less on the formation of a bloc of nonaligned sovereign nations than on a broader pan-Asianism that rejected the replication of colonial boundaries in balkanized postcolonial states. As historian Cindy Ewing points out, the ARC was a clarion call to the global South antedating the more familiar Afro-Asianism of the 1950s and beyond.[108] Nehru's endorsement of independence for a unified Indonesian Republic typified this viewpoint.[109] Paradoxically, confidence in India's modernizing potential and regional primacy lent such statements a whiff of nationalist assertion.[110] If these ideas were inflected with Congress hostility to partition and the creation of Pakistan, they also indicated an aspiration to Indian-led 'region-building' between Asia's colonized peoples.[111] Aware of the revolutionary implications of this appeal to 'Asian-ness' as a source of cultural identification, Indian High Commissioner Terence Shone gave this unified Asia a name: a 'Third World'.[112]

CHAPTER SEVEN

Decolonization in the Greater Second World War

MAY 17, 1940, A WEEK after Germany's western blitzkrieg began. Around 3,000 residents of Aumale (now Sour el-Ghozlane), a market town 120 kilometers southeast of Algiers, gathered to hear appeals from government ministers, city councilors, and a local mufti to help save France, *la mère patrie*. Thousands of laborers were urgently needed across the Mediterranean to maintain roads, railways, and military installations.[1] Authorities in Algeria knew that war work in France had a bad reputation among the colony's Muslim majority. Stories of maltreatment from the First World War were legion, so much so that the pejorative term *convoyeur* was widely used to describe those duped into performing forced labor for the French military. In the next world war additional inducements would be required.[2] It would take some pleading to persuade the people of Aumale. The officials did their best. Some used Arabic, others French. But their promises were much the same: generous accommodation and food and a minimum daily wage of forty-five francs, plus welfare benefits, to help a motherland resisting German 'barbarism'. Those who signed on were promised an immediate two hundred francs, plus exemption from any subsequent army call-up. The meeting ended with an ecumenical prayer for French victory.[3]

Almost five years later, in mid-May 1945, the French-language press in Algiers printed other prayers: graveside tributes at the funerals of 108 settlers slain during an uprising in the east of the country. Lamentations for lives cut short mixed with demands to avenge the Europeans killed in a week of violence centered on the towns of Sétif and Guelma. Local settlers formed vigilante militias whose stylings mimicked resistance groups in metropolitan France. Militia 'tribunals' were soon at work.

Within weeks these tribunals, actually kangaroo courts run by the mayoral administration, tried and then executed close to seven hundred Algerian males, some barely in their teens. These Algerian victims of retributive settler 'justice' were, in the short term, overshadowed by the thousands more cut down by the returning colonial army, by aircraft strafing, even by a naval bombardment of Philippeville, the region's principal coastal town.[4] This was colonial retribution at its most visceral. For many young Algerians who experienced it, the pitiless crackdown played out across the Constantine *département* catalyzed their turn to revolutionary nationalism. Its instrument would be the National Liberation Front (in French, FLN).[5]

The Algerians' Sétif uprising and its ensuing repression by settlers and state security forces over the summer of 1945 represented 'the worst of both worlds'.[6] First came small-scale but lethal insurrectionary violence. Blunt and spontaneously vicious, its political motivation was clouded by the internal schisms in Algerian nationalism.[7] Next followed a colonial reaction brutal enough to kill off vestigial hopes of reformist compromise. If political middle ground existed when that Aumale crowd gathered in May 1940, it was gone five years later. Algeria's radical shift from 1940 to 1945 seems to confirm that the Second World War changed the possibilities of decolonization. Appeals for colonial war workers framed in a language of shared obligation and social rights at the start of the war seemed to be a sick joke as a ruthless counterinsurgency unfolded in the preeminent territory of France's postwar empire.

Framing Decolonization and the Greater Second World War

In light of these Algerian experiences, this chapter's opening proposition might look paradoxical: that the Second World War was not the main driver of decolonization, at least not in straightforward terms of cause and effect. Devastating though it was, this most cataclysmic of global wars did not somehow destroy empires that might otherwise have survived. The logic of the Second World War as decolonization's catalytic agent is flawed because the disintegrative process had begun decades earlier. It would play out for decades more. The most significant aspect of those 1940 appeals was not the pledges of rights and entitlements that came with them but the crowd's understanding of what being a military laborer, or convoyeur, really meant: the replication of colonial subjugation within a European metropole. Five years later the most significant aspect of the Sétif uprising was not the dreadful manner of its suppression but how that was read locally—as proof that Algerians could only secure freedom, dignity, and nationhood through revolutionary dissent. Rather than one marking the point of departure for the other, global war and imperial disintegration were congruent. Each fed off the other. This process of mutual reinforcement lends substance to the idea of a greater Second World War even more protracted and globally transformative than its predecessor.[8] This is what this chapter explores.

My proposition is that wartime cataclysm did not—indeed, could not— 'cause' decolonization after 1945 because there was no clear division between war and postwar. To understand why the attempted reconstruction and actual disintegration of colonial empires were such entangled processes by the 1940s, we need to abandon two long-held historical presumptions. The first is that a global war ending in 1945 was some sort of hinge between an age of imperialism and coming decades of decolonization. The second is that the definitional simplicity and legal clarity of 'war' and 'peace' were universally applicable. Within empires, such distinctions made little sense.

Moving eastward from Algeria to the final months of the Syrian mandate, in purely quantitative terms more Syrians died in clashes with French imperial forces weeks after the nominal end of the Second World War in Europe than during the preceding six years of alternating wartime regimes in Damascus. With these numbers in mind, conceptualizing the last eighteen months of imperial rule before French withdrawal in December 1946 as a liminal condition between war and peace—as a violent peacetime in which security forces deployed the violence of artillery bombardments and martial law—surely makes sense.[9] Even more so when one recalls that the use of such blunt instruments reprised counterinsurgency tactics adopted during the Great Revolt of 1925–1927, another case of big war methods misused to crush insurgency—what two analysts call 'war in peace'.[10] Methodologically speaking, greater attention to insurgent practices also blurs the distinction between the creation of enhanced possibilities for anticolonial insurgency during major interstate wars and the outbreak of such insurgencies in the aftermath of these global conflicts. The broader conclusion this implies is that notions of 'empires at peace' or 'peacetime colonialism' are misleading.[11]

Japan in Southeast Asia: Empire-Building as Anti-Imperialism

Even more than the First, fighting and winning the Greater Second World War imposed global demands for resources, human and material. Many were extracted from dependent territories. Moving these assets around the world while denying them to opponents was integral to the war's globalizing effects. Strategic raw materials were, by definition, essential to combatant powers. But the scale and scope of total war, and the pace of technological advance within it, sparked major revaluations—literal and figurative—of empires' natural resources, their pricing regimes, and their regulatory oversight. Heightened wartime demand for rubber, sugar, rice, and palm oil fed renewed growth in export-oriented colonial plantations, in labor migration, and in the workplace colonialism that sustained them.[12] Prewar calculations of food value were further refined by national and imperial rationing systems kept in place after 1945.[13] Armed with this information but confronted by the strains of wartime need and postwar shortage, government distribution of food within and between empires was, if anything, more racially stratified than before.[14] The value attached to minerals and metallurgical materials was also transformed by escalating 1940s demand. Coal and iron ore remained the core ingredients of industrial production. But other, scarcer resources found primarily in the global South stirred stronger political interest and stiffer commercial competition, among them tin, bauxite, tungsten, copper, and uranium. The imperial authorities claiming ownership of these natural assets forced colonized men and, increasingly, women to extract more of them, justifying the coercive measures enacted in a companionable rhetoric of shared sacrifice. Deferred promises of future reward were made to sweeten the pill of heightened short-term extraction.[15] Cultures of political expectation among colonial people fighting or working for imperial masters changed in response. Frustrated hopes would prove politically explosive.[16]

One commodity symbolized the changing order of global resource priorities and its entanglement with colonialism more than any other: oil.[17] The Allies entered the Second World War with significant oil advantages over Germany and Japan. Secure access to oil and the merchant shipping to move it acquired greater importance as levels of consumption increased. By 1940 a series of agreements among the United States, Britain, France, and the Netherlands excluded the revisionist powers, Germany, Italy, and Japan, from Middle Eastern and Southeast Asian oil reserves.[18] Little wonder that seizing control over this vital energy resource shaped the imperial ambitions of all three revisionists, helping push them together.[19] Those ambitions were evident in the Italian longing for mastery of the Eastern Mediterranean and Red Sea, in the Nazi push toward the Caucasus oil wells, and in the southward drive to Dutch Indonesia's oilfields that determined the geopolitical complexion of Japan's Greater East Asia Co-Prosperity Sphere.[20]

Originally envisaged as an expanded colonial empire to assure Japan's primacy throughout East Asia, by 1943 the Co-Prosperity Sphere took an anticolonial turn, putting Asians' interests before those of their former British, French, Netherlandish, and other imperial rulers.[21] In the words of Foreign Minister Shigemitsu Momuru, Japanese victory would mean liberation for Asia, affirmation of Japan's mission to lead a region-wide march to self-sufficiency.[22] Admittedly, the Greater East Asia Co-Prosperity Sphere retained a push me–pull you quality. Far from promising freedom, the concept is widely remembered as the ideological instrument of a rapacious Japanese imperialism. Self-determination was on offer to selected client states, but only if they remained subservient members of a Japanese-dominated regional order.

Oil may have been key, but Japan's Co-Prosperity Sphere was also the most self-consciously political-economic project among the various rationales for empire advanced by the major combatants in the Second World War. Japan's style of authoritarian imperial control, extending from its colonies of Korea and Chinese Manchukuo in the north to its newly conquered territories of French Indochina, British Malaya, and Dutch Indonesia in the south, sustained a vast web of economic extraction. Along its threads essential strategic commodities were transferred to feed the Japanese war economy.[23] As part of this scheme, on May 6, 1941, Konoe Fumimaro's Tokyo Cabinet coerced the colonial administration in French Vietnam to concede preferential Japanese access to Indochina's minerals, coal, rubber, and rice. Parallel efforts to bully Dutch colonial authorities in Batavia (Jakarta) into allowing equivalent Japanese access to the much larger stocks of crude oil, rubber, tin, and aviation fuel in the Netherlands East Indies ended in failure on June 27, 1941. Remarkably, Dutch negotiators held out, refusing to sign agreements beneficial to the Axis alliance.[24]

Dutch steadfastness was short-lived. Japan's march into Indonesia in early 1942 makes it tempting to view the political economy of the Co-Prosperity Sphere as nothing more than an attempt to take by force what would not be willingly traded.[25] Its Japanese protagonists did not see things that way. Bureaucrats, intellectuals, and political leaders in wartime Japan dwelled on the economic and cultural benefits the Co-Prosperity Sphere would bring to the peoples brought under its umbrella.[26] Promises of economic integration, social modernization, and self-sufficiency for the territories of East Asia elided the forcible extraction that remained intrinsic to imperial control. Even so, in Japanese eyes, a system regulated by and for Asians remained preferable to the capitalist economics and unequal treaty rights intrinsic to the Western-dominated imperialism that preceded it.[27]

The Co-Prosperity Sphere derived lasting significance less from its contradictory rationale than from the geopolitical disruption it caused. An expanded Japanese imperium ultimately worked in contrary fashion, not to cement a new empire but to destroy older ones. The Co-Prosperity Sphere's role as accelerant to Asian decolonization was multivalent. Most obviously, Japanese invaders quickly routed the old imperial regimes of France, Britain, and the Netherlands in Indochina, Malaya, Singapore, and Indonesia. In these colonial conglomerates, as well as in colonial Korea, the resistance movements that fought Japanese occupation were led by communists, nationalist visionaries, or ethnic Chinese minorities, each of which sustained vanguard roles in later insurgencies.[28] Aside from these local struggles for power, the Greater East Asia Co-Prosperity Sphere worked in other, subtler ways to chart new paths to decolonization in East Asia. For one thing, its architecture of subservient political institutions and autarkic economic relations offered an alternative model of imperial hegemony. These arrangements eliminated any lingering doubts that European imperialism was somehow essential to the development of colonial territories around the East Asian rim. For another thing, Japan's colonial aggrandizement in mainland China worked differently than Japanese imperialism as enacted through the Co-Prosperity Sphere in Southeast Asia. The former originated in a Japanese quest to enlarge its colonial domains and dominate the China market, easing domestic economic and demographic pressures.[29] At the same time, Japan's cultural assault on Han Chinese primacy combined ideological, religious, and ethnic appeals to Chinese minority groups, promising them autonomy and new transnational connections that would break the historic grip of the Han majority.[30]

Japanese dominion over Southeast Asia brought material benefits and strategic advantages to the occupiers, but it was imagined as something more: an authentically Asiatic imperial order without European influence.[31] The Japanese ministers, military leaders, and bureaucratic planners who promoted the Greater East Asia Co-Prosperity Sphere thought in spatial terms of concentric groupings of dependent territories. Closest to Japan's home islands geographically and politically, a regional inner core, including the previously colonized territories of Manchukou, Korea, and Taiwan, would remain within an expanded Japanese Empire. For their local populations, economic diversification and wider educational provision came at the cost of dehumanizing racial and gender discrimination and severe punishment for dissent.[32]

The inner core territories fell within what Japanese strategists had termed 'the interest line' (*riekisen*) as colonial buffers protecting Japan's home islands.[33] An outer core of territories, including the Philippines, Burma, and possibly even India, would be led toward national independence with Japan's guidance. How real this independence might have been remains questionable, as the sovereignty of these outer territories would have been constrained by enduring Japanese oversight. For all that, the Co-Prosperity Sphere, particularly in its final iteration between 1943 and Japan's final defeat in August 1945, could be seen as something supranational. Politically, it underpinned Japanese regional hegemony, while culturally, it promoted an Asian future without Western interference. And, despite fundamental differences of political economy between Japanese-occupied China and Southeast Asia, in both spaces Japanese imperialism promised greater recognition, or at least deeper cultural respect, for Islamic observance and the wider Muslim community, or *ummah*.[34] From its administrative architecture to its religious aspects and the promotion of different concepts of beauty and virtue, the Co-Prosperity Sphere marked a radical break with the Western-centric imperialism of old.[35] Little wonder that it found support among pan-Asianists and Muslim anticolonialists in Malaya and Indonesia.[36] Those who favored political union between Malays and Indonesians, whether framing their ideas in terms of shared ethnolinguistic background, common religious affiliation, or congruent geopolitical interest, drew encouragement from Japan's pan-Asian rhetoric.[37] The simple fact that Indonesian Sumatra and Peninsular Malaya came under the single administrative authority of Japan's 25th Army lent substance to thoughts of a 'Greater Indonesia' free of European influence.[38]

Nationalist elites in Burma and the Philippines also seized on the opportunities presented by Japan's ouster of their former British and American colonial rulers to advance their local interests. In these two dependencies, Asia's Second World War played out very differently. The British found themselves powerless in the face of Burmese pressure for independence.[39] Japan's wartime patrimony nurtured anti-British sentiment among the student nationalists of the Thakin movement while fostering a military leadership determined to assert the primacy of Burmese ethnic identity.[40] For these 'patriotic collaborators', working with the Japanese did not compromise their anticolonialism. These were not quislings, but political operators who bargained collaboration for strategic advantage in the longer struggle against empire.[41]

For a while, a similar outcome looked possible in the Philippines. The initial beneficiaries of Japan's defeat were the country's landed and commercial elites. Although some were former compradors of the Japanese occupation authorities, this proved no barrier to their dominance within the Philippines government and Congress during 1945–1946. Entrenched in a Manila still to be rebuilt from near-total wartime destruction, these conservative autocrats focused not on reconstruction, but on excluding the peasant insurgents, leftists, and trade unionists of the Hukbalahap—the coalition front that had resisted the Japanese.[42] The menace of sectarian violence did not interrupt America's concession of formal independence to the Philippines in 1946.[43] But it did determine the conditions imposed by the Truman administration for the disbursement of US military aid to defeat the subsequent Hukbalahap—or 'Huk'—rebellion.[44]

American influence did not register immediately. Instead, independence was followed by two years of security force counterterror against the civilian population of central Luzon, the so-called Huklandia heartland. Only with the redirection of the Philippine government's counterinsurgency toward social provision, tax reform and rural food security from 1950 onward did support erode among peasant cultivators for the now Communist-dominated Hukbalahap rebels.[45] Promises of amnesty and land redistribution to repentant Huk fighters curtailed the insurgents' ability to sustain their operations, which petered out with the surrender of Huk leader Luis Taruc in May 1954. Containing the Hukbalahap rebellion required promises of a more equitable future, setting new terms for Philippine decolonization. Each signified a remarkable turnaround in which the former colonial power, reinvented as a beneficent aid-provider, attached stringent political conditions to its financial and strategic assistance.[46] US threats to withdraw funding were instrumental in bringing the reformist congressman Ramon Magsaysay to power in a November 1953 electoral landslide.[47] But what looked like America's principled departure from the Philippines was anything but. Working with Magsaysay, as with his predecessor Elpidio Quirino, involved trade-offs: with anticommunism came clientelist oligarchy, pork-barrel politics, and 'strong man' authoritarianism. Promised land reforms never materialized. Seen from below, the new bosses looked much like the old.[48] The quick-fire succession of occupiers, elite bargaining for influence, and localized violence folded into the political alignments, insurgent opposition, and American sponsorship of the new regime.

Europe's Empire States and Decolonization Violence

Emerging from fascist occupation, in 1944–1945 western European imperial states—France, Italy, Belgium, and the Netherlands—restored democratic government and enacted legislation both to punish wartime 'collaboration' and to affirm the rectitude of 'patriotic' resistance to the occupier.[49] They showed little interest, for obvious reasons, in making the same concessions to their colonial subjects. This is not to deny that the Second World War changed ideas about imperial legitimacy. Often observed is that European imperialists who lived through Nazi persecution were unsettled by the repression enforced in 'their' empires. Sadly, though, that discomfort did not lead to very much. Only for activist minorities in imperial metropoles did the juxtapositions between oppressors and oppressed, the victims of occupation and its perpetrators, become impossible to stomach in 1945. Some of these doubters, particularly in France, were communists; others were inspired less by ideology and more by ethics.[50] 1950s Britain saw trenchant criticism, in press and parliament and among civil society groups, of vicious counterinsurgency campaigns, official whitewashing of human rights abuses, and casual settler racism. But several factors dulled its impact. Critics were accused of swallowing anticolonialist 'propaganda'. Governmental stonewalling often succeeded, confining informed discussion to highbrow publications such as the *Manchester Guardian*, the *New Statesman*, and *The Listener*, all strong on journalistic inquiry but short on mass circulation.[51] The wider public showed less appetite for reports that 'their' boys had committed atrocities.[52] Securing evidential proof of violent acts kept hidden or flatly denied was difficult. The drip feed of colonial government press briefings, insurgent crime statistics, and casualty figures constrained even the best investigative journalists, who were unable to find verifiable evidence of systemic rights abuses.[53] Only when policemen, camp guards, soldiers, or officials were brought before the courts, as occurred later in the decade over Kenya and Cyprus, did the British governmental mask of cooperative obfuscation slip.[54]

In the French case, colonial juxtapositions between resister and collaborator, torturer and patriot were starker but still left many unmoved. There were exceptions. Reading news of the Indochina War's opening salvos in North Vietnam, for Claude Bourdet, former journalist of the Combat resistance movement, it was the failure of French ministers to condemn the November 1946 killing of thousands of Vietnamese civilians in the port of Haiphong as much as the 'incident' itself that convinced him the roles had been reversed between occupiers and resisters.[55] As Bourdet's conversion suggests, Second World War traumas cast a long shadow: for some, making it imperative to speak out, for others, shutting down discussion of unsettling news.

Recent military innovations, meanwhile, proliferated in the armory of repressive colonial violence. The refinement of aerial bombing techniques and new forms of airborne transport changed the ways and degraded the environments in which decolonization was fought. The development of napalm (a plasticized fuel-gel firebomb) and air-delivered defoliants incinerated villages and laid waste to forests.[56] Troop-carrying helicopters allowed rapid reinforcement, pursuit operations, and occupations of remote settlements, diminishing the inaccessibility of rebel strongholds. Cross-border sanctuary bases and sympathetic frontline states willing to tolerate their presence became pivotal to insurgent strategies as it became harder to sustain 'liberated' territory inside a colony.[57] Borderlands and the frontiers of limitrophe states were repeatedly violated.[58] Despite its technological advances, colonial counterinsurgency still targeted communities, not individuals, using population displacement and resource denial as weapons of war. Thanks to mass-production processes, the plastics revolution, and diverse global supply chains, other innovations would, by the 1960s and 1970s, tip the balance again. The Kalashnikov rifle, Soviet- and Chinese-manufactured antipersonnel mines, the shoulder-mounted rocket launcher capable of downing slow-flying helicopters, and the ubiquitous transistor radio tuned into subversive radio stations: these were the emblematic weapons of anticolonial revolution. With them, the scale of decolonization violence increased.

To summarize, the general observations being proposed here are, first, that the Second World War was part of a longer decolonization process and, second, that the war itself persisted, mutating into other violent anticolonial struggles in which distinctions between 'war' and 'peace' meant little. Although I've focused mainly on Asian examples so far, the phenomenon described was global. From British Burma to the Belgian Congo, promises of recompense made to ethnic minorities, agricultural producers, and industrial laborers for Second World War contributions went unfulfilled, fueling secessionist demands and adding civil war dimensions to decolonization conflicts. Across British and Free French Africa especially, the racially uneven weight of imperial 'war efforts' poisoned Allied messages of common endeavor.[59] The intolerance of oppositional voices cracked the foundations of French and British imperial dominance in North Africa.[60] Those of Italian Libya, Ethiopia, and Somalia collapsed entirely.[61] At the other end of the continent, wartime social divisions worked to the advantage of South Africa's National Party, adding impetus to the ideological consolidation of white-minority rule in Pretoria through the apparatus of apartheid.[62] Meanwhile a litany of wartime repression, ethnic discrimination, social distress, and famine set the parameters for partition in South Asia and Palestine. Elsewhere, the political economy of war and blockade enhanced American financial and commercial power across much of Latin America and the Caribbean, provoking fresh accusations of Yankee imperialism.[63] In Australasia responses to increasing US power were more positive, less concerned with overbearing economic influence than with strategic protection, but the basic calculation was the same: the United States, the new transoceanic giant, was the decisive external partner.[64]

The exception that proves the rule was the Middle Eastern territories subject to supranational regulation as mandates before the Second World War. Notwithstanding their combination of external oversight and quasi-sovereignty, what definitively ended the Middle East mandates was neither supranational disapproval nor longstanding demands for self-determination. Instead, it was the popular pressure for decolonization released by war. Connections between demands for statehood within the Yishuv of Israel/Palestine and the influx of Jewish refugees to coastal Palestine in 1945–1948 need no amplification. To the north, Lebanon slipped from French grasp in November 1943. Syria followed three years later. In each case, street protest was pivotal. Huge demonstrations in Beirut compelled the Free French authorities to release the Lebanese government and parliamentary leaders previously arrested for unilaterally approving an independent constitution.[65] Eighteen months later, in May 1945, a French army takeover in Damascus failed to cow the city's population and was quickly ended by another military intervention, this time by the British, who declared themselves defenders of Syrian independence.[66] The humiliation of one imperial authority by another in Damascus spoke volumes: the mandate idea was bankrupt.[67]

Empire Pathways through the Greater Second World War

Western Europe's five imperial powers—France, Britain, the Netherlands, Belgium, and Portugal—were either members or neutral adjuncts of the Allied coalition that claimed victory in 1945.[68] The routes these imperial nations followed to decolonization violence from the 1940s to the early 1950s raise the question of how far governments and metropolitan publics framed their actions in terms of the wider requirements of the Greater Second World War. For France, Belgium, and the Netherlands, these costs registered primarily in terms of material losses of people, of resources, and of capital. This trio were locked into a Nazi system of colonial extraction only definitively ended with their liberation in 1944–1945.

As a neutral, Portugal escaped such devastation but found itself suborned to the political-economic requirements of the Allied war effort even so.

For Britain, the burden was different again. A combatant beginning in September 1939, the country became a more multiracial place as the conflict unfolded. Refugees fleeing persecution in Europe, imperial and nonimperial servicemen and women from Allied territories (including almost three million Americans), war workers, and prisoners of war confronted Britons with unfamiliar cultures and visceral challenges to colonialist presumptions.[69] It's easy enough to categorize these new arrivals by their geographical origins. It's harder to do so by their lived experiences of British society. For some, ethnicity conflicted with attachment. Black Caribbean women of the Auxiliary Territorial Service faced continuous racial discrimination from white colleagues and superior officers, yet asserted their own Britishness nonetheless.[70] The wartime Britain these women encountered would never be the same. Essential resources, human, material, and financial, were gone. The country's net asset wealth shrank as armaments spending ballooned. By war's end, Britain was in deep financial debt, not just to the United States but to its dominions and colonies as well. Hindsight might suggest that British pretensions to continuing global power were hopelessly unrealistic, but here, another facet of the Greater Second World War phenomenon intervened—an imperialist reflex that led western Europe's governments to mistake empire for a guarantor of revival.[71] Stalking ministry corridors in London and The Hague, this tendency was strongest in Paris.

With democracy restored to metropolitan France in 1944–1945, the country's new political leadership made unlikely imperialists. Most were ideologically left of center. To their right stood the Christian Democrats of the Mouvement Républicain Populaire (MRP). They came a close second in France's October 1945 general election with 25 percent of the public vote, next to the Communist Party's 26. MRP and Communist voters rejected Charles de Gaulle's vision of presidential republicanism. This 'Gaullism' was refined during the general's leadership of Free France, an external resistance movement turned government-in-waiting that based itself in Francophone Africa for much of the war. Spanning the republican left, the Christian Democrat center, and the Gaullist right, this new political elite remade the French state, fashioning the constitutional reforms of what would become the Fourth Republic from the top down.[72] With that came the opportunity to reshape imperial connections, too.

What would they choose? Several leading government figures had been imprisoned for resistance activities. Some, like Marseille mayor Gaston Defferre, built powerful regional political networks, exploiting their personal sacrifices in defying fascism. Other insider groups—Jean Monnet's *dirigiste* planners and Pierre Mendès France's political economists—were technocratic modernizers. Their reformist sympathies translated into a commitment to use state resources to develop colonial economies, improve welfare provision, and raise living standards. Looking further to the left, one might assume that a rejuvenated French Communist Party (PCF), bolstered by its electoral breakthrough, would oppose colonialism's capitalist complexion. Some members did, but many did not. Christoph Kalter, analyzing the PCF's failure to push hard for decolonization, points to its invocation of Marxist internationalism over ethnic nationalism to justify colonialism as the more enlightened choice. To be sure, PCF-aligned trade unions, grassroots activists, and sympathetic literary figures opposed wars in Indochina and Algeria on grounds of antiracism and antimilitarism. Together, they ensured that the PCF remained the largest 'official' anticolonial organization in twentieth-century France. Yet this fell short of a genuine anticolonial front. Communist ministers sat alongside Socialists and Christian Democrats in the three years of tripartite coalition government between July 1944 and May 1947, insisting that French imperialism offered distinct routes to emancipation. This rhetoric clashed with repression in Algeria and war in Vietnam.[73] The Communists eventually quit government, but their claim that liberation movements were potential partners in socialism rang hollow.[74]

What about the social scientists so influential to French thinking about colonized peoples? Some signs were encouraging. Prominent colonial anthropologists aligned with the United Nations Educational, Scientific and Cultural Organization (UNESCO), which, in 1950, condemned scientific racism, dismissing received wisdom about hierarchies of civilization as a pernicious myth.[75] Unfortunately, this humanist affirmation of cultural parity grated with a French republican universalism whose ethnocentrism was exposed by empire reform. Other avowed reformists chose cosmetic change over genuine abandonment of colonialism. The Paris-based International Colonial Institute, most of whose members hailed from Europe and North America, in 1949 renamed their organization the International Institute of Political and Social Science Applied to the Countries of Differing Civilizations. Decolonizing countries, in their formulation, might follow distinct cultural pathways but should not expect the democratic rights enjoyed by their former imperial rulers.[76] Ignoring their support for respect of the individual through the signing of the December 1948 Universal Declaration of Human Rights (UDHR), government ministers, legal advisers, and empire administrators carved out exceptions precluding equivalence under law between metropolitan citizens and colonial subjects. Meanwhile, granular

UN criticism of rights abuses within individual French dependencies intensified.[77] On the ground, any notion that 'Greater France' had repudiated 'scientific colonialism' was repeatedly contradicted by the proscription of anticolonial parties and interference in colonial elections. A Socialist governor of Algeria, Marcel-Edmond Naegelen, took this manipulation furthest, supervising systematic electoral fraud between 1948 and 1951.[78]

To be sure, there were genuine reformers and significant reforms elsewhere. As we saw in chapter 3, politicians, urban workers, and civil society groups in West African territories achieved breakthroughs in social rights, welfare, and workplace protections, preludes to a progressive social interventionism that emulated entitlements in metropolitan France.[79] Alongside colleagues from the French Caribbean, West African activists, writers, women's rights campaigners, and politicians secured an end to the hated *indigénat*, better pay and working conditions for industrial workers, and the prospect of wider entitlement to citizenship, changing ideas about the reformist potential of an empire rebranded the French Union.[80] Surveying that empire as a whole, though, reforms in some regions were matched by repression elsewhere.

Rebellion in Madagascar

The 1947 rebellion on the island of Madagascar reveals how embedded these contradictions were. We might view the rebellion's outbreak in April and May as two histories, macro and micro, running in parallel. One is the better-known account of a nationalist uprising coordinated by a political movement, the Mouvement Démocratique de la Rénovation Malgache (MDRM).[81] In this master narrative, the political marginalization of ethnic groups that formed the backbone of MDRM support inflated expectations of reform, and a police clampdown on the MDRM leadership caused the eruption of a clearly anticolonial insurgency.[82]

The other, locally focused history is subtler. It paints a variegated landscape of overlapping village-level concerns. In this reading, struggling families took precedence over the MDRM's ideological claims. Rising postwar costs of foodstuff staples, including rice, coffee, and flour, caused widespread hardship and, in some regions, even hunger. Meanwhile, provincial administration was restructured during late 1945–1946, with budgetary responsibility devolved to provincial governors. Central to this program was the opening of sixteen regional tax offices. Their revenue inspectors enlisted the local gendarmerie, the Garde indigène, to collect higher poll taxes.[83] Resultant village-level grievances about unaffordable food and an insupportable tax burden went unanswered because the colonial government had no functioning native affairs service. In other colonies it fell to native affairs officers—the bridge between district administrators, or *commandants de cercle*, and the colonial governor's office—to evaluate local opinion and to relay policy proposals back to the people. This was crucial because administrators in the field could be petitioned in person by village, clan, workplace, or other community representatives. In postwar Madagascar, no such connection existed. This peculiarly colonial problem was compounded by the suppression of chieftaincy authorities in areas where cash crop production on settler-owned farms predominated.[84]

These problems came together in the areas of Eastern Madagascar worst affected by the 1947 rebellion. The new tax offices were targeted. Most were forced to close. Beyond the towns, armed rebels and day laborers joined in acts of political violence, burning settler-owned coffee plantations, sabotaging railroad lines, and ambushing vehicles traveling between farmsteads. Crop destruction, transport disruptions, and attacks on farm trucks loaded with produce underscored two things: the local grievances at the heart of the rebellion and the attackers' lack of weapons with which to take on colonial security forces.[85] Peasant violence served political-economic purposes but was also performative: a culturally resonant act that signified the limit to community tolerance.

The tragedy was that the intended audience—the French administration—wasn't listening. The absence of a working native affairs service left the colonial authorities starved of information and dangerously prone to misreading the scale of the uprising and its underlying causes. Only later did it emerge that in the rebellion's opening months between April and August 1947 all commercial traffic in three heavily settled districts on Madagascar's east coast had ceased because of pervasive social unrest. Unable or unwilling to identify peasant support for the rebellion as a form of protest against chronic poverty, the colonial government instead chose a blunt military response. Madagascar's eastern coastal belt was already saturated with army reinforcements, including Foreign Legion and other assault troops that were en route to fight in Vietnam. Their orders were to act fast in order to resume their original itinerary.[86] If the rebellion's economic and cultural dynamics were never wholly understood, they were indirectly acknowledged. The 'restoration of order' was to be measured in the resumption of movements of people and goods from farms to markets, something that for several months required military escort.[87]

The grimly asymmetric violence of the Madagascar rebellion is also instructive as an example of an ostensibly 'postwar' insurgency rooted in the aftereffects of the preceding war. Economic destabilization intersected with a flawed administrative restructuring that closed off opportunities for nonviolent redress.[88] Violence was triggered as much by societal disruption as by anticolonial sentiment. There is nothing particularly original in this insight. Historians commonly identify decisive wartime changes, whether events or processes, to explain the proliferation of anticolonial insurgencies in the late 1940s. What bears emphasizing is the need to approach decolonization's violence as a social practice, as a form of community protest. Recognizing decolonization violence as a discrete *form* of conflict rather than confining ourselves to explaining its *escalation* is surely crucial if we want to make sense of insurgencies and the nature of counterinsurgent responses to them in the violent peacetime aftermath of bigger interstate wars.[89] Standing back to view Madagascar's 1947 insurrection as an explosion of social conflicts worsened by the local impact of a world war is easy enough. But it requires micro-level analysis to explain the nature and meaning of Malagasy violence.[90]

A year after his administration oversaw the suppression of the Madagascar revolt and the crackdown against the MRDM activists they claimed were behind it, High Commissioner Pierre de Chevigné toured South Africa between December 6 and 18, 1948. The South Africans had shut down their Tananarive consulate in reaction to the previous year's uprising, and French public hostility to apartheid suggested that rapprochement might be difficult. Not so for de Chevigné or his Pretoria Foreign Ministry hosts. Each recognized their common interest in stifling black majority rebellion against white-minority rule. De Chevigné came away from a visit to various mining settlements convinced that apartheid South Africa, like French colonial Madagascar, was working to improve black living standards. South African society, he insisted, could no more handle democratization than Madagascar's people could cope with decolonization.[91] De Chevigné's administration, like the South Africans, was ready to impose its preferred sociopolitical order by intimidation, legislative restriction, and force. Political amnesties were eventually issued to some of the thousands of former rebels interned in French Madagascar after the 1947 uprising, but for years afterward the MDRM was banned, its leaders jailed.[92]

The suppression of Madagascar's rebellion marked one end of a spectrum, an extreme iteration of the limits to French reformism, but it was otherwise typical in its state violence conjured from exaggerated fears of oppositional groups. On February 13, 1949, French police raided an address in the Algiers *casbah* frequented by activists of Algeria's Movement for the Triumph of Democratic Liberties (French acronym, MTLD), the restyled version of an outlawed nationalist group, the Parti du Peuple Algérien (PPA). The search team discovered a rudimentary printing press before rifling through a haul of leaflets. A printed sheet of instructions stood out. Thought to have been drawn up in September 1948 by Dr. Mohamed Lamine-Debaghine, an MTLD deputy to the French National Assembly, it listed plans for the distribution of a brochure written by PPA leader Messali Hadj, who detailed police and military violence against his party. Messali's colleague, Lamine-Debaghine, wanted the brochure distributed at the UN Assembly session in October 1948, a move timed to coincide with the opening of an MTLD-PPA Information Bureau in Paris. Aside from publicizing the Algerian nationalist cause, the Bureau distributed Arab League propaganda in France, as well as in other Francophone and Arabophone territories. Lamine-Debaghine came under suspicion because he had traveled to Cairo in both October and November 1948 to set up another office, this one for 'Maghribi Arab affairs', paid for with 200,000 francs from MTLD funds.[93] What alarmed the investigating officers was not that Algerian nationalists liaised with like-minded groups in North Africa—nothing new in itself—but that they were using front organizations, including sporting associations, scouting groups, theater troupes, and private Islamic schools, to spread a message of anticolonial militancy. Banned from peaceful political engagement, the Algerian nationalist movement was parasitizing civil society networks locally and transnationally.

There were echoes of these actions south of the Sahara. French West Africa's foremost nationalist movement, the confederal Rassemblement Démocratique Africain (RDA), had absorbed communist organizational techniques of 'frontism'. The RDA, so intelligence officers claimed, was doing much the same as the MTLD-PPA. Nominally working within the law, each consolidated transregional connections to get round it. To prove their point, the security services cited the RDA as one among many African anticolonial movements supporting a February 1950 'day of struggle against colonialism' sponsored by the Soviet-funded World Federation of Democratic Youth (WFDY).[94] That colonial intelligence services disliked the WFDY was hardly surprising. That they were shocked when mainstream African political parties paid lip service to stock WFDY propaganda was more revealing. Félix Houphouët-Boigny's RDA exemplified the kind of conciliatory stakeholder that imperial governments dreamed of, what French officials called an *interlocuteur valable* ('valid partner') and their British counterparts termed 'constructive nationalists'. Still, it was crass to expect RDA activists to ignore WFDY appeals to anticolonial solidarity. It made sense for Houphouët-Boigny and other RDA leaders from wealthy backgrounds to burnish their antiracist credentials by endorsing the 'day of struggle'. But the gesture was just that; it did not preclude engagement with Paris. The WFDY had been founded with British governmental support in November 1945 to promote peaceful—and equal—cooperation among global youth movements.[95] The fact that it was, by 1950, directed from the Eastern bloc (with headquarters in Budapest) tempted imperial security services to demonize the group as a Cold War operator. But the WFDY's pro-communist tilt did not invalidate its anticolonial message for those living under colonialism.[96]

Conclusion

Throughout the colonial world of the late 1940s protests, insurgencies, and paramilitarism—the substance of violent decolonization—were all facilitated by the preceding World War, and there's no neat demarcation, as I see it, between one and the other. Much as what Soviet historian Mark Edele terms 'the war after the war' continued in East Central Europe's shatter-zones and Transcaucasia throughout the late 1940s, a parallel violence continuum ran through the decolonizing world of the global South.[97] To suggest, for instance, that the foundation of the Democratic Republic of Vietnam (DRV) on September 2, 1945, or the declaration of the Indonesian Republic a couple of weeks earlier were 'postwar' events seems absurd. Japan's defeat did not mean that its empire disappeared overnight.[98] Japanese occupation forces remained throughout Southeast Asia. British imperial and Chinese nationalist forces were about to replace them. The new arrivals were supposed to disarm the Japanese rather than, as it turned out, assist 'recolonization' by weaker European partners.[99]

We know, too, that a Greater Second World War shaped the entire process. Japan began its conquest of China in 1931, fully nine years before Japanese boots marched southward toward Vietnam and Indonesia on the news that France and the Netherlands had surrendered in Europe.[100] Its attack on Pearl Harbor was part of a transregional strategy for war meant to expel not just American but European colonialism from eastern Asia and the western Pacific.[101] Recall the imperial earthquake that was the fall of British Singapore in February 1942. Consider how far the insurgent strategies of communist movements in Northern Vietnam, Peninsula Malaya, and the Philippine island of Luzon were urgently refined amid the tension of wartime occupation.[102] Crossing these bitter interimperial divides, Japanese occupation forces later became adjuncts in counterinsurgency to the Allied units that supplanted them in the fall of 1945.

Overshadowing these developments in Southeast Asia were two others. One was the hugely expanded role of the United States in East Asia as a whole. Its seismic political implications for European empires had yet to be felt even after the bombs fell on Hiroshima and Nagasaki. The other was the combination of civil war and social revolution in China.[103] This was a societal transformation whose aftershocks registered more strongly through colonial empires than the Bolshevik revolution a generation earlier.[104] To add to the complexity, the Soviet imperium was vastly overextended. Expanded by annexations and occupations on its western and southern Eurasian flanks and militarily dominant in Manchuria, Stalin's Soviet Union prioritized gains in Europe, pursuing more flexible, realpolitik tactics elsewhere. Anxious to secure their East Asian perimeter but reluctant to see a powerful Chinese state reoccupy Manchuria, the Soviets did little to douse the fires of civil war, either in China or in Korea.[105] All these events added to the charged atmosphere that characterized the 1945–1946 interlude between wartime and decolonization, eighteen months of violent peacetime that locked otherwise discrete conflicts into the same sociopolitical orbit of a Greater Second World War.

Why were these conflicts so connected? Most significant were the global interactions between people living under colonialism brought about by the demands of war and mobilization. The struggles reshaping Southeast Asia were not so much 'forgotten wars' overshadowed by the better-known confrontations of the Second World War as continuations of that very conflict.[106] As historians Christopher Bayly and Tim Harper have suggested, this 'Great Asian War' was not only longer but also more revolutionary than its European counterpart.[107] Dwell for a moment on the breadth of cultural diversity in a composite, archipelagic territory as vast as Indonesia. There, the singular fact of Japanese occupation lent commonality to people's identification as victims of empire.[108] Chinese Communist intellectuals, writers, and journalists fleeing from Japan's southward advance meanwhile sought to stimulate resistance among Indonesia's Chinese minority and to build solidarity with native Indonesians.[109] At the same time, the differing reactions of Islamists, communists, ethnic minority groups, and developmental modernizers to that occupation hardened the ideological differences between the four principal strands of opinion competing for power in their tributary of the Great Asian War: Indonesia's final defining struggle against the Dutch.[110] These Asian conflicts form the subject of the next chapter.

CHAPTER EIGHT

Revolutionary Decolonization in Southeast Asia?

Vietnam

On August 26, 1945, officers in the French War Ministry discussed how to invade Vietnam.[1] The country was at that point no longer a part of the French Empire at all. The colonial garrison in Hanoi, tolerated by Tokyo for most of the war, was finally overthrown in a March 1945 coup. An 'Empire of Vietnam', actually a Japanese military protectorate that permitted limited Vietnamese autonomy, opened space for civil society mobilization. Vietnam's religious sects, ethnic minorities, Stalinists, Trotskyites, women's groups, and the country's largest political association—an ecumenical Vanguard Youth Movement—embraced the chance to organize.[2] French colonial post-holders faced internment, house arrest, or worse. Surviving members made a fighting retreat northward to Chinese Yunnan.[3] Before crossing China's frontier, the retreating troops slowed their Japanese pursuers on the wide valley floor of Mùong Thanh—farmland irrigated by the Black River, later to become famous in its Vietnamese-language designation: Dien Biên Phu.[4] The symbolism of that location was still unknown, but the overweening influence of Nationalist China provoked resentments from the start. Chiang Kai-shek's Nationalists wanted the final say on French schemes to reenter Vietnam from Nationalist-administered territory.[5] Chiang's forces meanwhile also made use of Mùong Thanh, coercing local farmers to build a longer runway for airborne supplies to support the Nationalists' occupation of Northern Vietnam.[6] If the French were to return, it would have to be by sea and from the south. Everything rested on whether the British and Americans would help or hinder.[7]

In a pattern soon to be repeated, European plans for colonial reconquest were overtaken by events: first, Emperor Hirohito's announcement of Japan's surrender on August 15; second, Vietnam's August Revolution or 'August General Uprising' (tổng khởi nghĩa), launched a day later; and third, Ho Chi Minh's proclamation of an independent Vietnamese Republic on September 2.[8] The illegitimacy of French colonialism was underscored by four years of Japanese extraction and the collapse of Indochina's infrastructure, including the disruption of vital Mekong Delta rice sales to the north. The result was a northern famine that left an estimated one million people dead in five coastal provinces of North Vietnam's Red River Delta and the three adjacent provinces of Thanh Hóa, Nghê An, and Ha Tinh.[9] Malnourished survivors, vulnerable to malaria, cholera, and other sources of infection, had no prospect of medical help. The colonial state offered nothing. There was barely one doctor for every 200,000 Vietnamese.[10] Galloping inflation and extreme weather events during 1943–1944 exacerbated things. But a combination of harsh Japanese requisitioning, the French colonial ban on interprovincial trade used to enforce it, plus the absence of any remedial measures turned desperation into catastrophe. The death of over 8 percent of Tonkin's inhabitants catalyzed a revolutionary anticolonialism.[11] But the Democratic Republic of Vietnam (DRV), established in August by Ho Chi Minh's Communist-led coalition, the Viet Minh, only held sway in north central Vietnam.[12]

When, on September 2, 1945, Ho took to the stage in Hanoi's Ba Dình Square to give his independence speech, the Japanese occupiers sat tight, waiting to be disarmed.[13] Earlier, they had allowed the Vietnamese 'Army of National Liberation' to seize Gia Lam, Hanoi's airstrip, their first objective after Ho left his headquarters at Tan Trao, fifty miles distant from the capital.[14]

A French expeditionary force was meanwhile readying to sail for Saigon. There, the regional Viet Minh leadership under Trần Văn Giàu knew that the August 'Revolution' was a race against time. It was imperative to seize administrative control before local rivals, the French, or other outsiders got in the way. Winning the support of the Vanguard Youth Movement was key.[15] A fight was coming. A week earlier, those French War Ministry planners, seeing an opportunity to restore something of the army's lost élan, ordered their invasion force (they preferred to call it a reoccupation force) to be 'brutal'.[16]

In September 1945 a temporary 'British Military Administration', sent into Southern Vietnam to police the disarmament of surrendered Japanese forces, set about facilitating a French takeover in Saigon. The

FIGURE 8.1. Ho Chi Minh addresses Viet Minh troops at the Tomb of the Hung Kings, north of Hanoi, undated 1946. Source: Getty Images.

new French arrivals would then relieve the British imperial troops temporarily placed in charge of Southern Vietnam in fulfillment of pledges made at the Yalta Conference seven months before. Tellingly, these arrangements were basically the same as those envisaged for Indonesia, where another British interim occupation would hand over to the old colonial masters. These arrangements were hubristic but true to form. In 1919, France and Britain had not only kept their colonial territories but added to them as well. They also pretended that the First World War had not weakened them economically. Each rejoined the gold standard as if their financial power remained intact. In 1945, the biggest act of imperial self-delusion was geopolitical: the expectation that the wartime overthrow of European empire in Southeast Asia could be reversed.[17] As in 1919, so in 1945: the decisive strategic choices presumed that the preceding World War had not happened at all. In fact, in imperial terms especially, it was still going on.

No one in the War Ministry took seriously an obvious but inconvenient fact: Vietnam's revolutionary upheaval was gathering, not losing, momentum. A once-broad-based Viet Minh coalition, ranking Catholics and Buddhist followers of the Hòa Hảo and Cao Dài sects alongside members of the Indochinese Communist Party, was fracturing into sectarian rivalry, assassination campaigns, and reprisal killings.[18] Throwing a casually brutal expeditionary force into this mix compounded the loss of restraint.[19] Score-settling and race hatred, as well as spiritual unease and rumor, fueled cycles of violence as much as did ideology and anticolonialism.[20] Brutalization was also cumulative, 'each unpunished act pushing the threshold of what was permissible further forward'.[21] In the far southwest, the French military drive into the Mekong Delta between November 1945 and December 1947 and their willingness to arm local paramilitaries from ethnic minority and sectarian groups caused toleration among local Vietnamese, Khmer, Chinese, and others to collapse.[22] By spring 1946 racially motivated killings in numerous Delta provinces blurred the lines between political rivalry, cultural denigration, and ethnic cleansing.[23] Historian Jessica Chapman goes further, describing the efforts of General Nguyen Binh, DRV commander in the south, to coerce Southern Vietnam's paramilitaries into line as the trigger for civil war between them.[24]

Closer to Hanoi, the revolutionary social reordering of North and Central Vietnam had barely begun. Predicated on land redistribution, mass mobilization, and class war, this aspect of the Vietnamese revolution peaked in 1951–1954, the final stages of the fight against France.[25] The revolution of 1945–1947 was ideological in intent but, again, closer to civil war in practice: marked by the elimination of opposition to achieve the Communist commitment to Vietnamese unification. Beyond Hanoi, impacts varied between provinces.[26] Trying to slow the revolution's spread through Vietnam's countryside, returning French officials pursued strategies of divide and rule, exempting highland communities from the taxes and foodstuff requisitioning imposed on their lowland neighbors.[27] Authorities in Paris and, later, Saigon meanwhile chose to ignore facts on the ground that jarred with their imperial objectives, dismissing the implications of events in Hanoi—of anticolonial state-making in civil war conditions.[28] These denials set France and, soon, the United States on a road to forty years of ruin in Vietnam.

There were early signs of division even so. Intervention made more sense to Paris defense experts in August 1945 than to the American Joint Chiefs of Staff who, for some years to come, remained unconvinced that France could—or should—win back control of Indochina.[29] The doubts of top US commanders went unheard over the summer of 1945, despite the Big Power summitry of the day. Paradoxically, summit decisions explained why: the Allies assigned Britain strategic purview over Southeast Asia.[30] In the rush to resurrect empire, General Douglas Gracey's occupation force in Saigon worked alongside French residents, freed POWs, and Japanese garrison troops that it hastily rearmed.[31] Each became adjuncts to the French expeditionary force, killing hundreds of civilians in their search for communist sympathizers through the fall of 1945. The spark for this retributive violence was an earlier Vietnamese pogrom against French settlers, Eurasians, and other non-Vietnamese in Saigon's Cité Héraud district between September 23 and 25.[32] Later attacks by expeditionary force units enacted the War Ministry's 'be brutal' directive, aiming to prove that DRV authority counted for nothing in the south.[33]

In Vietnam, as in China and Korea, two visions for a postwar Asia locate these clashes within the wider regional picture of global war and decolonization. The first, supported by communists in all three countries, repudiated a Western-dominated capitalist international order. The second, backed by noncommunist nationalists in each country, favored integrating with international society, but on different terms. Capitalism was tolerable, but the discriminatory practices of imperialism were not. Rejecting colonialism made common ground between these competing worldviews and, whatever their ideology, East Asia's anticolonialists confronted the same obstacle: vulnerability to foreign control.[34] At times, this provoked friction, notably between Maoist China and the DRV regime, caught between its reliance on Chinese material and technical support and its aversion to the strategic dependency this implied.[35] Each, though, remained convinced that dismantling colonialism's societal structures demanded unprecedented mobilization of the peasantry, what they termed 'the united front' to fight for national liberation.[36] History would prove that communists alone were ruthless enough to pursue this.[37] But they did not paint on a blank political canvas. The backing lent by Chinese communities to DRV supporters along Vietnam's northern frontier highlighted grassroots solidarities more organic than imposed.[38]

As in Vietnam, in Indonesia in the fall of 1945 a British occupation force plunged into that revolution's largest pitched battle, in the Javanese port of Surabaya.[39] Anxious to be free of an increasingly risky imperial obligation and warned by India's Congress Party that the Punjabi troops on which the force relied should no longer be put in harm's way, the British occupiers in Dutch Indonesia (and in Saigon) pulled out in 1946.[40] The damage was already done. In Indonesian Java and Southern Vietnam, interim British occupation was politically disastrous.[41]

Admittedly, the British task was significantly harder in Java. The Indonesian revolution, which saw a Republic declared by President Sukarno and Vice-President Mohammad Hatta on August 17, 1945, was stoked by paramilitarism and retributive militia violence, little of which was centrally controlled.[42] Java, like Northern Vietnam, had experienced a devastating wartime famine, which caused the deaths of some 2.4 million Javanese in 1944–1945.[43] Its lethality was assured by Japanese colonial occupation. Punitive rice requisitioning aggravated the aggregate fall in local foodstuff production, provoking calamitous declines in average calorific intake. Agricultural markets, licit and illicit, were closed down as the occupiers imposed economic autarky on individual Indonesian provinces.[44] But the aftereffects of famine and Republican militia killings do not explain British policy choices in 1945–1946. Rather, in Indonesia and Vietnam, British reasoning was the same. Co-imperialism came first. Defying the revolutionary changes unfolding around them, the transitional British military administrations installed in Indonesia and Southern Vietnam knowingly served as Dutch and French proxies. By October 1945 remaining Japanese troops and Indian Army units were at war with Indonesian Republican forces across a wide belt of central Java from Bandung in the west to Surabaya to the east.[45] The counterrevolutionary violence of returning Dutch imperial forces thereafter against the incumbent Republican regime continued what had started before.[46] British-directed suppression served as prelude to more sustained violence by an imperial invasion force, this time comprising mixed Dutch and Dutch-colonial units.[47]

Malaya

British complicity in the colonial reoccupations of Vietnam and Indonesia prefigured the failure of Whitehall plans for a multicultural Malayan Union. Turning a deaf ear to the quickening pace of decolonization in Vietnam and Indonesia was in accord with the authoritarian turn in the Southeast Asian territories of Britain's empire that had also been occupied by the Japanese. That shift occurred in 1948. Prior to that, official thinking was less rigid. Britain's 1942 eviction from Malaya nourished official appetites for reform.[48] With nothing to administer, Colonial Office Malaya

MAP 8.1. British Malaya.

specialists mulled over their return. They promised improvements, thanks to the projected Malayan Union. In theory, the territory's largest ethnic communities, Malay, Chinese, and Indian, would for the first time enjoy equivalent representative rights in an equitable postwar settlement.[49] In practice, this was not so: as historian Sunil Amrith notes, 'The war had unsettled the ways in which sovereignty mapped onto territory, and citizenship onto residence'. Nowhere more so than in Southeast Asia: there, the region's two largest migrant communities, South Indians and ethnic Chinese, faced acute postwar precarity.[50]

A cosmopolitan, multicultural Malayan Union was a pipe dream. It was abandoned in the teeth of opposition from the country's indigenous Malays.[51] Overcoming cultural prejudice and colonial discrimination against the territory's Indian labor force, for the most part Tamils employed in Malaya's rubber plantations, could not be achieved by legislative sleight of hand.[52] Disaffection also grew among poorer segments of the ethnic Chinese population before the consolidation in 1949 of a moderate and solidly capitalistic Malayan Chinese Association (MCA), linchpin of a tripartite alliance between the imperial administration and the nativist conservatives of the United Malays National Organization.[53] Others rejected compromise. Chinese workers in Singapore's dockyard and elsewhere were hard-hit by postwar inflation, while immigrant laborers in Peninsular Malaya's mining and rubber industries faced marginalization and insecurity of status.[54] Many Chinese, having suffered most under Japanese occupation, cleaved to the Malayan Communist Party (MCP) or its subsidiaries, the General Labour Union and the New Democratic Youth League.[55] Some were former guerrillas of the Malayan Peoples Anti-Japanese Army (MPAJA), which had resisted wartime occupation.[56] Although the Malayan Security Service (MSS) monitored these organizations, that surveillance was doubly ineffective: invasive and resented, but inaccurate and misleading. The MSS, like the colony's police force, lacked Chinese-speakers and was understaffed.[57] But it was not so much the gathering communist threat that was misunderstood as the increasingly rural focus of radical opposition.[58]

The MSS was also fighting a jurisdictional battle with other British intelligence agencies, which culminated in its disbandment on July 13, 1948, a month after the MCP announced its uprising by assassinating three European plantation managers on the Elphil estate in Perak state. The MSS gone, recriminations continued over the Malaya administration's failure to predict the thrust of communist insurgency, allowing a directionless campaign of security force counterterror to escalate in

FIGURE 8.2. A Malayan Security Service officer 'interrogates' Chinese laborers while Gurkhas search their possessions, July 1948. Source: Getty Images.

1948–1949.[59] Punctuated by panicky 'shoot on sight' killings of alleged guerrillas, summary executions of unarmed suspects, and other abuses of detainees, this first stage of the Malayan Emergency illustrated how far the British authorities had retreated from the optimistic reformism of the Malayan Union project.[60] Again, there was a gradual transition from violent peacetime to insurgency and its suppression.

In Burma, too, a chasm opened between London's professed support for Burmese democracy and the local irrelevance of metropolitan pronouncements.[61] A government commitment to 'self-government . . . in the British Commonwealth as soon as circumstances permit' was made contingent on what took place during a three-year transitional period of direct rule instituted by Winston Churchill's cabinet on May 1, 1945. In theory, by the time this probationary interlude ended in 1948 Burma's

devastated economy would be back on its feet and negotiations completed with a Burmese Executive Council preparatory to a classic transfer of power.[62] The likely leader, Aung San, head of an Anti-Fascist
People's Freedom League backed by a network of People's Volunteer
Organizations, was willing. Terms just had to be agreed. But Aung San
could no more control events than the British.[63] He was murdered, along
with six members of his Executive Council, at the behest of his political
rival U Saw on July 19, 1947.

From a decentered perspective, it was clear months before these killings that Burma's path to independence depended on three local factors.
One was the strength of the Burmese left and its threat of a hostile, pro-
communist takeover (a partial explanation for U Saw's actions).[64] Another
was the power of ethnic separatism and the possibility that Burma might
disintegrate into ethnically configured substates.[65] The last was what happened in neighboring India. Britain could never control Burma without
Indian soldiers. What looked like a carefully arranged scheme for phased
decolonization was the exact reverse. Cornered into conceding an explicit
timetable for negotiation, the British authorities were already hostage to
fortune in Burma, as in India as well.[66]

Why did the British, frustrated in their plans to enact reformist
schemes devised during the Second World War, nonetheless resist the
internationalization of decolonization? An answer lies in Whitehall mis-
trust of the United Nations' political direction, combined with skepticism
about the multinational organization's regional effectiveness. A phenomenon that we'll encounter in the next chapter, British suspicion of UN
arbitration in colonial disputes, so evident in the final months of the Palestine mandate, resurfaced in early 1949 as the Truman administration
pushed the Security Council to demand Dutch withdrawal from Indonesia.[67] Attlee's government agreed that the Dutch were the authors of their
own destruction in Indonesia, that time was running out to reconcile the
Indonesian Republic with the Western bloc, and that a cease-fire was desperately needed. So the issue for the British was not the United Nations'
hardening anticolonial stance but its inability to follow through on its
internationalism. UN ambitions to play peacemaker clashed with its lack
of peace enforcement capacity. In February 1949 Foreign Secretary Ernest
Bevin summarized the problem: 'It can smooth over difficulties and iron
out disputes, but it cannot govern'.[68] What he did not say was that his
government colleagues, humiliated in Palestine and locked into a Security
Council deadlocked between Cold War rivals, had no wish for the United
Nations to develop any governance capacity.

Malaya Erupts

That curiously British mixture of ostensible cooperation and actual contempt for international interference in colonial affairs bubbled up months later in Malaya. As we saw earlier, efforts to suppress the MCP uprising went badly after a state of emergency was imposed on June 18, 1948. Security force actions were poorly informed, sometimes criminal, and generally counterproductive. The recruitment of Chinese-speakers to the much-maligned MSS was even cut back on the eve of the conflict, not for lack of qualified applicants but because senior Security Service personnel doubted Chinese loyalties.[69] It was not that the MCP won over rural Chinese to its cause. Quite the reverse: communist recruitment was as much the product of coercion as of ideological commitment.[70]

That said, in contrast to their insurgent adversaries, the British lacked the wherewithal to converse in vernacular languages with Malaya's peoples, the Chinese immigrant minority in particular.[71] Technology was not the problem. Printing presses, films, radio broadcasts, loudspeaker vans, and aircraft boomed out pro-government messages with relentless monotony. The problem was the message itself—its content and mode of delivery. In Malaya's multilingual and multidialect society, the stilted official tone of Emergency propaganda was banal and unconvincing. A Public Relations Office, the principal translation service inside the Malayan colonial administration, contained rich linguistic expertise but was swamped with translating each and every government instruction. Printing Emergency restrictions in local languages was not the same as justifying their purpose. Too often and for much too long, the British could barely speak to the population they were trying to administer.[72]

Deaf to what was going on around them, for much of 1949 British security forces persisted with blunt intimidation, notable for mass arrests and the widespread internment of ethnic Chinese laborers.[73] Acts of security force retribution, including the infamous massacre by a Scots Guards platoon of at least twenty-four unarmed villagers at Batang Kali on December 12, 1948, were the awful but predictable result.[74] Wanting to change course, the Attlee government set up an inner cabinet, the 'Malaya Committee', to oversee new policy initiatives. There would be no let-up in colonial violence; instead, there was a determination to coerce with purpose instead of murdering without it.[75] The new strategy hinged on the deportation of Chinese 'undesirables' and a massive plan of forcible resettlement meant to separate Malaya's Chinese civilian population from MCP guerrillas, or 'communist terrorists' as official nomenclature insisted on labeling them.[76] Significantly, the committee's first item of business was to amend its own terms of reference. Its job was not to 'restore' law and order in Malaya, but to 'preserve' it. Stenographers were warned not to make the mistake of identifying Malaya as a colony; it was a 'Federation', a partner in imperial government (to which the colony of Singapore was politically linked).[77]

Three exigencies led Malaya Committee members toward the expansion of forcible resettlement under a unified civil–military command. First was the rising number of Chinese detainees as the security forces conducted sweep operations state by state across Peninsular Malaya. Labour Ministers wanted to deport them to China but knew that Mao's recent seizure of power complicated matters (although only briefly, as it turned out).[78] Second was the conviction that the MCP's Malayan Races Liberation Army (MRLA) guerrillas relied on Chinese squatter settlements for concealment, food, and recruits. Squatter communities, living in sparsely populated, thinly administered districts without freehold title to the land they worked, were vulnerable to coercion by all sides.[79] The British 'solution' was to move these communities wholesale to guarded 'new villages': displacement as securitized modernization. Third were the economic calculations. Malaya's tin industry relied on Chinese labor. The disruption to its crucial export sector was severest here. Restoring it had required large-scale military reinforcement. Tallied alongside British Army commitments in Korea and Egypt, it was unsustainable.[80] Some cheaper means of coercing rural compliance, putting local police and paramilitaries to the fore, seemed especially appealing by late 1950.[81]

Known by its shorthand appellation, 'the Briggs Plan' attracts two constituencies of analytical interest: historians skeptical of its claims to benevolent, if authoritarian, population control, and counterinsurgency theorists drawn to the plan's preoccupation with social engineering through the forced removal of communities.[82] To these might be added a third: environmental historians who recognize that British actions in Malaya's rural interior prefigured the destruction of tropical ecologies through technologized violence. To deny communist guerrillas sanctuary within Malayan forests, the colonial administration sanctioned jungle clearance, chemical defoliation, and, of course, the construction of almost five hundred fortified 'new villages'. Several were carved out of aboriginal homelands and rare wildlife habitats.[83] However else one views it, the Malayan Emergency was an ecological disaster. Most relevant in exploring decolonization is that the Briggs Plan made it harder for local people to navigate a neutral course between compliance with colonial authority and toleration of the MCP.[84] Arguably, this was the plan's core purpose. But it made light of the agonizing choices facing rural communities and the young Chinese men at the center of the insurgency.

November 1953: The Briggs Plan in action saw members of Kuala Lumpur's Psychological Warfare Interrogation Centre analyzing questionnaires completed by 105 alleged MCP guerrillas. Held as Surrendered Enemy Personnel or 'SEPs', the detainees answered multiple-choice questions probing their reasons for joining the insurgency.[85] Each question had only two possible answers, in deference, the interrogators said, to the detainees' limited reasoning skills. With this racist assumption came another. When SEPs suggested that alternative answers were equally valid, as, for instance, when asked whether fear of arrest or fear of MCP punishment drove them to join the rebellion, it was presumed that the prisoner simply could not distinguish between them.[86] Nuanced responses did not fit the interrogators' 'either–or' schema, a profiling technique designed to pinpoint routes to radicalization and those prone to follow them.[87]

Responses were collated by region alongside tabulations of each SEP's ethnicity, age, and depth of ideological commitment. Statistics about the first two were predictable. A large majority were ethnic Chinese. Those recruited after 1950 were significantly younger (age twenty-one on average) than their elder compatriots who discovered the MCP during the Japanese occupation (twenty-five on average in 1948 and 1949). More revealing was that only 24.3 percent of insurgents were sure they were doing the right thing; 26.2 percent said they had doubts; 49.5 percent insisted they were coerced into joining the insurgents. Even allowing for factors that made such answers unreliable, among them the frightening circumstances of interrogation and SEPs' eagerness to mitigate punishments, two traits seem clear. One is the importance of local insecurity in shaping people's choices. The other is that coercion was the key push factor. Communist beliefs or improved chances to acquire food and other goods came a distant second. The interrogations confirmed that life in Malaya's interior was extremely perilous for young Chinese men. Many turned to violence for fear of the penalties if they did not.[88]

Things might have been different. The Malaya government committee appointed under Chief Secretary Sir Alec Newboult in December 1948 to investigate the 'squatter problem' acknowledged the insecurities facing rural Chinese families barely six months after the MCP uprising began. Their report suggested that the drivers to 'squatting' by Chinese agriculturalists on state lands, on privately owned property, along riverbank clearings, and at the margins of mine-works and rubber estates were illegal immigration, rural poverty, and disruption to land registration services caused, first, by Japanese occupation and, latterly, by the insurgency.[89] Squatters, in this sense, were victims of colonial government breakdown:

> [O]wing to the lack of administrative control and their isolated loca-
> tion the squatters are necessarily susceptible to pressure from the ban-
> dits for the provision of food and shelter. This is not to imply that the
> sympathies of the squatters lie on the side of the bandits. In most cases
> in fact they probably have no sympathies either way but necessarily
> succumb to the more immediate and threatening influence—the ter-
> rorist on their doorstep as against the vague and distant authority of
> the Government of which they are hardly aware and which is only rep-
> resented by a small police station some miles distant.[90]

The committee's solution was sensible: to offer legal resettlement, ideally on sites close to those presently occupied by the squatters.[91]

It was not to be. Events overtook the committee's recommendations on the same day they were finalized: January 10, 1949.[92] At the same time as High Commission civil servants pondered land redistribution to ease the 'squatter problem', police and army commanders reached the opposite conclusion. It was by then apparent that most MCP guerrillas concealed themselves within squatter communities and preyed upon those same settlements for recruits and resources. Lacking precise intelligence and facing community silence, Malaya's security forces lobbied for sweep-ing powers. Emergency Regulation 17D, issued two days later, on Janu-ary 12, 1949, was the result. The Malayan High Commission could order that entire communities be detained on security force advice. Anyone held could also be expelled from Malaya.[93] To preserve the element of surprise, detentions could be conducted without warning. A further Emergency Regulation, 17E, passed in May 1949, empowered Malaya's state admin-istrations to issue squatters with eviction notices that required families to report for resettlement within one month. In August, a third regula-tion, 17F, completed the restriction process. It authorized district commis-sioners to confine the movements of individual families within particular areas. The net tightened inexorably. The declared aim of these Emergency Regulations was to resettle 63,000 squatter families, an estimated 300,000 people. Conciliating the squatters gave way to interning, deporting, or otherwise moving them to wherever the colonial authorities saw fit.[94]

In Malaya, as during the Palestine Revolt of 1936–1939, collec-tive punishments—restriction, relocation, and expulsion—came veiled in paper. Ordinances and council decisions gave legal authority and administrative respectability to mass detention. In both places, emergency powers substituted the presumption of innocence with guilt by association and introduced draconian punishments to match.[95] The irony was that the colonial officials directing the process recognized that squatter families, terrified of government crackdowns and MCP reprisals, posed no threat: 'The average squatter family', they concluded, 'is industrious, close-fisted, lacking in civic sense and, just now, deeply bewildered'.[96]

Read 'against the grain', even this colonialist viewpoint affirmed the visceral imminence of insecurity for those forcibly removed. Squatter families were cursed to be the MCP's resource reservoir. Objectified by all sides, entire communities were punished as a result. The ambitious social engineering of Malaya's 'new villages' program lay some distance ahead, but the road to 'screwing down the population' through forced resettlement was taken by January 1949.[97] In revealing asides, Sir Harold Briggs and General Sir Gerald Templer's army command, often credited with ending the Emergency through resettlement and repression, pathologized communism in postwar Malaya as a foreign-borne virus transmitted by ethnic Chinese. Using the new village program to isolate MCP guerrillas from their rural networks of support reduced infectivity but, invoking a favored malaria analogy, Briggs insisted that eradication required the destruction of communist base areas: the viral 'breeding ground'.[98]

Demonizing the MCP also cemented the intercommunal coalition with which the British eventually sealed an independence agreement in 1957. The message of an insurgency alien to Malay culture and inimical to Malaysia's future as an independent nation played to the nativism of the United Malays National Organization. Insisting that the MCP was beholden to outside forces offered reassurance to the moderates of the Malayan Chinese Association that the imperial authorities distinguished between Malaya's authentic—and loyal—Chinese community and its foreign-inspired terrorists.[99] Delegitimizing the insurgency as external to Malaya and dehumanizing its supporters as vectors of transmission lent weight to the conclusion that British counterinsurgency in Malaya was a revolution of a different sort: coercive social engineering, not the conciliation of 'hearts and minds'.[100]

North Vietnam at War, 1949–1954

It was meanwhile in the Indochina Federation that decolonization played out with most violence in the late 1940s. Between 1947 and 1949 the Hanoi regime's ability to keep fighting France's attempted reoccupation of

Vietnam was matched by the Fourth Republic's inability to build domestic or international support for their campaign. Early opinion polling suggests that a majority of the French public veered between a lack of interest and a preference for negotiated withdrawal.[101] Internationally, the decisive British assistance in helping French forces return to Southern Vietnam in 1945–1946 gave way to mounting doubts as slow-burning antiwar sentiment sparked into occasional flame among left-wing and civil society groups in Britain, as well as more widely in Malaya, India, and Ceylon.[102] The Truman administration, the preferred provider of material aid to the French war effort, remained unimpressed by France's limited military advance and unconvinced by the deceit of Vietnamese autonomy inside the French Union.[103]

It took the extraneous pressures of Cold War geopolitics to change matters. Hardening divisions in Europe cemented France's place as a Western bulwark. Impending Communist victory in China lent credibility to French claims that Northern Vietnam was a Cold War levee at risk of breach. As a result, over the winter of 1948–1949, the balance of influence within the White House and the State and Defense Departments tilted decisively toward hard-liners ready to buy the 'Bao Dai solution' being hawked in Paris and Saigon: the promise of a nominally democratic, pro-Western, and independent Vietnam, its former emperor restored as head of state.[104] Touted as a state-building project, imposing the associated state model nationwide was impracticable. But it was not insignificant.[105]

Before Bao Dai's June 1949 return as head of this aspirant 'State of Vietnam', a southern 'Third Force' coalition (Mat Tran Thong Nhut Quoc Gia) coalesced around the sects, militias, and noncommunist nationalist parties hostile to the DRV vision of a centralized communist regime. In deference to the multilateral composition of this southern coalition, French high commissioner Émile Bollaert conceded that rural administration, policing, and limited fiscal control might be ceded to favored local clients. National government, though, retained its Gallic flavor.[106] Military commanders could also undo these limited concessions by imposing a 'state of siege', effectively martial law, on particular towns, provinces, or regions. There was the rub. Between 1944 and 1949 French reform plans promised Vietnamese, Cambodians, and Lao their independence while actually withholding it.[107]

This was why the state of Vietnam mattered. After June 1949 the Bao Dai solution engineered a different composite administration. Civilian government acquired institutional substance. Its legal autonomy and sovereign reach extended into town and countryside but awkwardly so.

Religious organizations, sect groups, Catholic, Chinese, and Khmer
minority militias competed to enforce their authority in provincial pock-
ets of the Mekong Delta, bargaining cooperation with the French military for political influence.[108] The 'outlaw partisans' of the Bình Xuyên,
part Vietnamese nationalists, part criminal enforcers, followed suit, seeking to control commercial flows between Saigon-Cholon and its Mekong
hinterland.[109] Complex and conditional, these arrangements enabled
the French military to retain its arbitral position. The State of Vietnam
government was neither independent nor sovereign.[110] For all that, the
new Vietnamese regime, a 'pastiche of uneven and overlapping authority', was different.[111] Micro-level community concerns played upon the
macro-level policy choices of local combatants and their foreign proxies.
Layers of devolved authority, regional power bases, and militia fiefdoms
within an emergent State of Vietnam inhibited communist efforts to break
through.[112] The fact that the south especially remained to be 'won' provided the pretext for what would turn into three decades of US military
involvement in Indochina.[113] To French (and British) governmental relief,
by June 1949 the older 'Anglo-Saxon' co-imperialist was replaced by the
newer, more powerful one.[114]

Soon afterward, frictions between competing French security agencies
in Indochina hit a new low after the leaking of General Georges Revers'
strategic reflections following a tour of inspection.[115] Viet Minh propagandists made hay with the general's recommendations, fixing on his warning that northernmost garrisons might require evacuation. A media storm
blew up in France, questioning the wisdom of army strategy. A year later,
in October 1950, Revers' gloomy predictions came true. Units of General
Võ Nguyên Giáp's People's Army of Vietnam (PAVN) ambushed French
troops pulling back along Route Coloniale 4 from the northerly garrisons
of Lang Son, Cao Bang, and Dong Khe.[116]

Revers had identified these garrisons as the most vulnerable to attack
by PAVN units reinforced with Chinese weaponry. The inability to predict
the timing or scale of an assault in which 5,987 troops were lost made
intelligence failings in Vietnam seem criminal.[117] Above all, the 'Cao
Bang disaster' indicated that the executive direction of the Indochina war
had to change. It did. Appointed in December 1950, a new civil–military
commander, General Jean de Lattre de Tassigny, arrived in early 1951.[118]
Retrenching in the north, de Lattre focused on easier wins in the far south.
The additional money and men that followed the general's appointment
allowed French forces to launch another offensive in the Mekong Delta.
Basic tactics remained unaltered. Local militias and sector guard posts

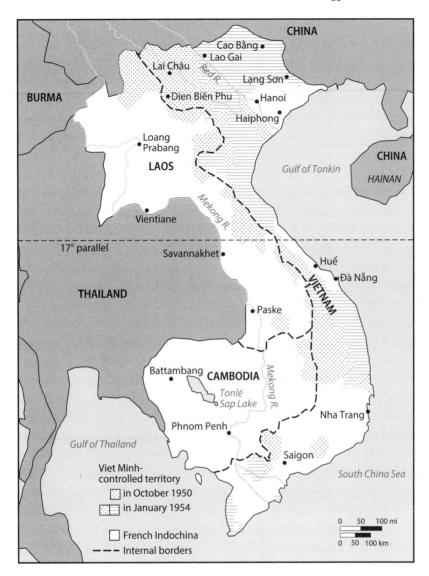

MAP 8.2. Territorial control in French Indochina.

kept a lid on dissent, as did the payments and promises made to cooperative villagers and the collective punishments meted out to those more
hesitant or uncooperative. But now local Viet Minh forces were engaged
in open combat whenever possible. Those who fought on faced economic
blockade and food denial (in violation of international law).[119] De Lattre's
aggressive strategy was not the miracle some claimed. Vietnamization of
the war intensified. Collaboration by minority groups and religious sects

was generously rewarded. But these initiatives only strengthened the conflict's civil war complexion. De Lattre was forced by terminal cancer to return to France in November 1951, and metropolitan support for a distant, unfamiliar war was fading when he died in January 1952.[120]

A different change of partners had taken place on the other side of the Cold War divide. Soviet reaction to communist China's first bid for hegemony over the Asian revolutionary movement was mixed. Outwardly, Moscow supported the Maoist revolutionary prescription—a broad 'united front' against imperialism spearheaded by communist-led peasant armies operating from rural bases. But Politburo chiefs bridled at PRC insistence that Beijing was the epicenter of Asian communism and dismissed 'the theory of Mao Tse-tung' as the fountainhead of revolutionary doctrine. In November 1951 Soviet commentators took the offensive, warning that 'it would be risky to regard the Chinese revolution as some kind of "stereotype" for people's democratic revolution in other countries of Asia'. That verdict stuck. Nearly a decade later, during bitter exchanges at the height of the Sino–Soviet dispute in 1960, the Soviets cited China's support of the Viet Minh as an early indicator of 'sectarianism' in the international Communist movement. Khrushchev made a similar point two years later, mocking Mao's regime over its failure to evict British colonialism from Hong Kong, a territory in China's backyard.[121] So much for revolutionary solidarity.

By contrast, the Hanoi regime in the years 1950–1954 endorsed Beijing's leadership over the Asian revolution and claimed that 'Mao Tse-tung's theory' guided its revolutionary struggle. There were limits even so. Rebranding themselves as the Vietnamese Workers' Party (VWP) in 1951, Hanoi's communist leadership recognized Marxist-Leninism as the taproot of ideological authority in their Lao Dong party statutes of 1952. But the VWP also began a structural reorganization that emulated its Chinese equivalent, embracing Maoist 'rectification' campaigns to purify (i.e., purge) their Party cadres.[122] Nodding to China was nothing new. Ho was an early advocate of Maoist-style insurgency, having encountered the strategy in action during his extended stay in communist-controlled China, initially in Yan'an in the fall of 1938 and later in Guangxi Province in the summer of 1939.[123] But it was Party Secretary Truong Chinh (a name translatable as 'Long March'), who drove the process forward after Hanoi enacted a sweeping conscription law on November 4, 1949. A new People's Army of Vietnam (the PAVN) was expanded to field six conscript divisions, supported by tens of thousands of peasant food producers and civilian porters. Equipped with Chinese weapons and trained by PLA advisers, PAVN troops prepared for a 'General Counter-Offensive' (GCO), the decisive final battle with colonial forces.

The success or failure of the North Vietnamese strategy rested on its micro-level impact on civilian families. The goods, labor, and resilience of North and Central Vietnam's peasantry were crucial to everything, making villagers the GCO's decisive instruments.[124] Their daily resource struggles of agricultural work and food accumulation were complicated by these wartime impositions, storing grievances that reverberated through the DRV for years to come.[125] Equally fundamental was the prevalence of the very young within and alongside North Vietnamese forces. Child soldiering in Vietnam was symptomatic of wider processes of youth politicization, social mobilization, and labor coercion.[126] In Malaya, too, the MCP rethought its insurgent strategy after 1951, placing greater emphasis on youth recruitment as the vanguard of mass mobilization.[127] The DRV went much further, building on Viet Minh precedents from the Second World War. To Ho Chi Minh's 'Child Pioneers' were added shock brigades tasked with diverse support roles; their numbers ran into the hundreds of thousands. According to one calculation, perhaps 8,000 Vietnamese children participated in the battle of Dien Biên Phu.[128]

Corralling teenagers into guerrilla units traversed lines between combatant and civilian already blurred by the Hanoi regime's November 1949 mobilization of all adults aged between eighteen and fifty as 'labor fighters'. Additional legislation in September 1952 compelled able-bodied Vietnamese adults to serve as military porters for the PAVN. Mobilizing civilians to carry weapons and supplies, sometimes over hundreds of miles, was already commonplace. Estimates suggest that the DRV command used 300,000 porters who put in almost three million working days as part of the North Vietnamese campaign to secure the Red River Delta in early 1951.[129] These enormous numbers would be exceeded over each of the next three years. Precise casualty figures are impossible to tally, but fatigue, poor diet, malaria, dysentery, and exposure to aerial bombardment and enemy ground fire imposed terrible human costs.[130]

In the short term, the Hanoi regime used stick and carrot to ensure peasant compliance. Legal punishments for disobeying military and labor drafts became harsher. Politically, tighter VWP control of labor brigades was matched by closer monitoring of the village politics and northern rice economy the porters left behind. Coercive measures were made more tolerable by the promise of land reforms. A 1953 program of rural redistribution became the centerpiece of free Vietnam's social revolution.[131] A village public health scheme, focused on improving peasants' access to primary health care and basic medicines, added credibility to the regime's insistence that material improvements were coming.[132] Maoist-style demands for selfless sacrifice continued in the interim. The extent of Chinese influence was demonstrated graphically in December 1952 when Ho Chi Minh delivered a policy speech in Hanoi, much of which was drafted in Beijing, either by a Maoist official or by one of Ho's writers with Chinese guidance.[133]

The stages on which the war's final dramas played out meanwhile worked in North Vietnam's favor. French aircraft commanded the skies in the months preceding France's defeat at Dien Biên Phu, but PAVN units controlled the land. This spatial division was critical. Lacking secure supply lines, French military plans in the winter of 1953 to link up their forces in Northern Vietnam and Laos fell short.[134] Instead, continued PAVN ability to move people and supplies altered the strategic landscape.[135] Vietnamese victory owed much to this human supply chain, the 260,000 women and men who transported munitions, food, and other supplies on backs and bicycles through miles of punishing terrain.[136] The Hanoi government's Front Supply Council worked through the PAVN's General Supply Department to agree on logistical details. General Giáp, VWP Secretary Truong Chinh, and Supply Department Director Trân Dang Ninh set the targets. Foremost among them was 24,086 tons of rice.[137] The unbroken supply chain ensured that heavy casualties among PAVN infantry besieging the Dien Biên Phu fortress complex did not affect the outcome.[138]

French airborne support to the defending garrison was speedier but more tenuous. Framed against a mountainous background, photogenic airdrops into the valley floor prolonged the battle and added to its symbolism. Here, too, equipment, food, and medicines proved decisive, but differently so. The declining arc of French fortunes matched the ascending curve of the Vietnamese advance. On March 13, 1954, the first major PAVN artillery barrage destroyed Dien Biên Phu's airfield. Images of French materiel dropping by parachute onto vulnerable open ground after the garrison was routed from Dien Biên Phu's outer fortresses was one of many signifiers of a 'last stand' whose outcome would be politically determinate.[139] After the last defenders, principally Moroccan colonial soldiers and French officers, were overrun by a PAVN assault on the evening of May 7, images of over 11,000 French military prisoners heading to captivity confirmed that decolonization's Asian scales had tipped decisively.[140]

Conclusion

Dien Biên Phu, the climax of DRV resistance to an attempted restoration of imperial authority, could be read as an end to Vietnam's Greater Second World War, if not to the country's continuing fight for decolonization. The Vietnamese experience drove home a lesson of the Second World War: the yawning gap between European pretensions to imperial power and their inability to sustain it against hostile challengers. This deficit used to be studied primarily in geopolitical terms, but it is increasingly explained through more intimate registers: everyday encounters and shifting cultural perceptions of empire. But macro-histories of national struggle and the grassroots perspectives of colonial social history might be enriched by rethinking the extent and experience of the Greater Second World War. From the perspective of decolonization, 1945 signified neither an end to fighting nor the beginning of a more peaceful 'postwar'. From colonial Southeast Asia to North Africa the reverse applied: an end to war in Europe made possible the assertion of renewed imperial control through violence.[141]

As for the mechanics of that violence, the heightened threat of collective targeting in this violent peacetime increased the vulnerability of colonial civilians. Their sense of exposure was well justified by changes in the availability and use of violence instruments. A war waged across continents made global supplies of weapons between Allied coalition partners routine, meaning that the use of technological violence against colonial opponents was easier in the late 1940s than, say, in the late 1920s. More locally, the availability of weapons and people's familiarity with them increased thanks to processes of militarization, conscription, and demobilization intrinsic to global war.[142] The same was true in those parts of continental Europe where foreign occupation severed the connection between the legitimacy of state authority and its claimed monopoly on the use of force to preserve order.[143] Put differently, the forms and scale of violence intrinsic to decolonization in the later twentieth century were powerfully affected by the preceding dynamics of a Greater Second World War.[144] The imminence of everyday abuses for colonial subjects was superseded for many by the insecurities resulting from insurgent pressures and counterinsurgent repression. Europe's empires were anything but at peace in the global 'postwar' in which most decolonization conflicts played out. Before that process was completed, the human calamities of violent peacetime were first and most acutely felt in the imperial partitions of the late 1940s.

CHAPTER NINE

Partitions Dissected

Partitions and Decolonization

Partitions complicate decolonization. Their territorial form was a result of seemingly irreconcilable pressures: the schemes of those in charge; what political, religious and civil society actors wanted; and 'facts on the ground' produced locally by the dynamics of demographic pressure, land and property seizures, population displacement, and intercommunal violence.[1] Recent precedents, including the refugee movements and population expulsions of the First World War, plus the division of Ireland soon afterward, normalized what was a deeply traumatic process.[2] During the First World War Ottoman governments mobilized interethnic frictions to justify central imperial control. Ironically, the Ottomans' French and British opponents did something similar. Folded untidily into their empires, the mandates established in former Ottoman lands exploited local claims to nationhood and pleas from minority communities for external protection to justify an imperial oversight, which supposedly respected the demands of particular ethnoreligious groups for separate administration.[3]

Ironically, imperial authorities, seeing no room for compromise between competing community claims, insisted that partition was the only viable option.[4] Dividing up colonial territory became another political instrument within a broader geopolitics of decolonization that included population exchanges, mass resettlement, and minorities' protections within new 'successor states'.[5] Ireland, Palestine, India, Vietnam, Cyprus, and many others since: the list of empire territories subdivided by some subjective combination of ethnicity, religious affiliation, political pressure, and strategic convenience is a long one.[6]

For all that, historians of empire disintegration have sometimes viewed partition as incidental to decolonization. Imperial historians have treated these last-resort responses to irreconcilable differences, a failure of negotiation, or compromise as by-products of withdrawal decisions already made or as improvisations intended to avoid something even worse—civil war or regional conflagration, interethnic killing, and dystopia.[7] At the heart of partition, the story goes, lies a paradox. Sovereign authority is devolved to an identifiable ethno-national population, ostensibly a victory for self-determination. At the same time, territory is contested between local population groups, creating endless grievances over the dividing lines drawn. The unspoken villains here are not so much empires as the intractability of ethnic nationalisms within them. Those who study partitions, their dynamics, their outcomes, and their victims, are less forgiving.[8] They see partition itself as the catalyst to violence, feeding intercommunal frictions, creating claims and counterclaims of dispossession, violation, and murder.

The problem becomes more complex when settlers, their numbers swelled by recent immigration, comprise one of the communities involved. Matters of citizenship aside, the more emotive questions are these: When do settlers become locals with claims on the land, and at whose expense? And what if settlers have other identities as refugees from persecution claiming cultural ties to the region of settlement—as in Palestine? For those in Europe, North America, and the Soviet Union for whom the Holocaust held supreme moral importance as the ultimate evil, Jewish rights to settlement in Palestine seemed self-evident.[9] Arab anticolonialists were less convinced. Algeria's FLN, for instance, insisted that partition could never be a route to self-determination because its operating principle was that minority rights to nationhood supplanted those of the indigenous majority.[10]

Interpretational chasms like these between the analysts of—and actors in—the twentieth century's colonial partitions left only the narrowest bridge in between: a presumption that partition was pursued for want of better options.[11] What, though, if partition was not a last resort but a first? Or what if it were just one of several political alternatives in play during decolonization? To be clear, the partition of colonial territory typically followed administrative efforts to impose some other political settlement, often a federal one, in which different ethnoreligious groups would share power within a larger conglomerate: a postimperial India with autonomous provinces and a weak federal center; a tripartite division of territory in Palestine predicated on Jewish–Arab power-sharing in Jerusalem; a quasi-independent Vietnamese 'associated state' with regional governments in Hanoi and Saigon operating within a larger French Union; a cross-community constitutional settlement in Cyprus in place of union with Greece.[12] Each of these proposals was a unique product of local conditions, but all of them were similar in their top-down imperial design and their ultimate failure. Aside from their common colonial origins and the heterogeneous populations involved, there is something to the sequence of events in imperial partition that pulls these and other examples into the same analytical field. A change of perspective along these lines would suggest that partition was not only central to the decolonization process but directly produced by it.

This chapter explores this proposition in the unmaking of empire. Echoing historians Arie Dubnov and Laura Robson, I see partitions not as something ahistorical and timeless, but as the exact reverse: a contextually specific product of twentieth-century decolonization, the competing ideas of ethnic self-determination and sovereign rights underpinning it and the contest between those trying either to precipitate empire disintegration or to prevent it.[13] Locating ideas and early experiments in partition in the immediate aftermath of the First World War, Dubnov and Robson stress the idea's imperial provenance as a way to force particular communities to fit within political borders demarcated by colonial authority. Partition, they suggest, 'was less a vehicle for national liberation than a novel, sophisticated *dīvide et imperā* tactic that sought to co-opt the new global tilt toward the ethnic nation-state'.[14]

The nature of partition violence and its legacies of displacement and discrimination were both instantiated by colonialism and reproductive of it. Partitions in British India and Palestine were conflict escalators, triggering communal violence, the forced removal of populations, and war immediately afterward. Across South Asia, minority communities residing on the 'wrong side' of partition lines became hostages to the power struggles, border conflicts, and local competitions for legitimacy between the newly configured nations of India and Pakistan.[15] Both states tried to put arrangements for minority protections in place, each responding reciprocally to initiatives formulated by the other.[16] Meanwhile, what historian Taylor Sherman describes as a moral economy of retributive violence emerged. Its targets were victimized to atone for similar crimes allegedly perpetrated against their attackers' coreligionists. The resultant 'symmetry of suffering' replaced calculations of personal guilt or innocence with a simpler arithmetic of equivalent confessional killing.[17]

Sharpened by the bitterness resulting from the Muslim League's reluctance to endorse the Congress-led Quit India movement, wartime terminology of 'fifth columnists', 'collaborators', and 'traitors' was misapplied to entire minority groups, a terrifying development that reduced people's affiliations to their ethnoreligious background. Observing these developments from the Pakistan side of the dividing line, Sir Francis Mudie, soon to be appointed Governor of Sind Province, recognized their significance: the existential power struggle between supporters and opponents of an independent Pakistan was more significant than its precondition, Britain's departure from the Indian subcontinent.[18]

In South Asia and Palestine the speed of intercommunal breakdown, the scale of personal losses, and the regional destabilization that resulted are the connective tissue between the macro-level politics of decolonization and micro-histories of dispossession, separation, and bodily violation. Both partitions were linked, not just by shared experience of British colonialism and of the communal divide and rule practices that came with it but by their global placement in a post–Second World War order in which population displacement and mass violence had become all too familiar.[19] Historical treatments of these events differ between those that consider enforced pullouts the prelude to permissive political violence and those that take a more sympathetic view of the imperial powers' readiness to leave. In some ways, these differing approaches—one decentered and locally oriented, the other politically focused and fixated on governmental decisions—reflect their authors' concerns with different actors: the first with partition's victims, the second with partition's architects.

Several colonial withdrawals immediately after the Second World War facilitated territorial partitions and the forcible removal of peoples. None were accomplished peacefully. India and Palestine top this list, but other, supposedly temporary partition arrangements in Vietnam, Korea, and Libya fomented violence as well. The difference between the first group and the second—an end to British imperial administration in India and Palestine; partition as prelude to the continuation of foreign, colonial-style occupation in Vietnam, Korea, and Libya—should not mask the combination of indigenous decolonizing pressures and endogenous geopolitical interests that place them in the same analytical framework of contested decolonization. Tragic as they were, these experiences were not unprecedented. Similar pressures and equivalent outcomes emerged a generation earlier in the killings and forced population exchanges that accompanied the disintegration of the Austro-Hungarian, Russian, and Ottoman empires. As after the First World War, so amid the fallout from the Second partitions dislocated economic and cultural relationships within and among communities.[20] With more precedents to draw upon and stronger local pressure for decolonization, after the Second World War: 'Once again, partition emerged as a "solution" to ethno-communal divisions in the context of an emerging and unstable international-imperial system built around the rhetorical principle of ethnic nation-statehood'.[21]

Partitions after the Second World War

Before returning to motivations for partition, the following section considers the ways in which the Greater Second World War discussed in previous chapters leached into these early instances of decolonization as partition after 1945.

The 'human rights surge' of the 1940s was predicated on traumatic experiences of wartime violence in Europe, primarily inside societies living under Nazi occupation. Crimes included genocide, collective punishments, mass killings, and rape. These referents underpinned the Genocide Convention and early human rights initiatives within the United Nations, its affiliate agencies, and the committees of jurists who formulated the Universal Declaration of Human Rights. Albeit to a lesser extent than in the whites-only thinking that informed Wilsonian ideas of self-determination, concepts of individual and group rights developed in the immediate postwar years still took European experiences as their referent.[22] The huge numbers of displaced persons, refugees, and, most poignantly, Holocaust survivors spread across the continent after 1945 added urgency to juridical questions of what rights inhered to them as individuals, as members of particular ethnic groups, as political refugees, or as persecuted coreligionists.

Britain was a leading actor in Europe's postwar refugee crisis in its role as governor of the most densely populated of Germany's four zones of occupation. Violent partitions in India and Palestine put the British Empire at the heart of the global refugee crisis as well. At least eighteen million people were displaced in the Indian subcontinent in late 1947. The lived experience of partition was scarring, its scale almost unimaginable.[23] People moved quickly in Punjab, where almost 80 percent of displacements occurred. Some 850,000 moved eastward across the Punjab partition line into India in barely six weeks during August and September. Hundreds of thousands more moved in the opposite direction. Crossing the line of partition from one state to another was no guarantee of safety. Refugee camps proliferated on either side of the frontier in newly partitioned Punjab.[24] They swelled into massive encampments without sanitation or basic medical provision. Cholera, dysentery, and chronic diarrhea became endemic. Without the clean water supplies essential to rehydration and recovery, curable illnesses became life-threatening conditions, particularly for small infants, the elderly, and the malnourished. Within a month of independence, the numbers involved remained a matter of guesswork. But they were clearly vast: over 105,000 in Gurdaspur district, 380,000 in Jullundur (now Jalandhar), 210,000 in Ludhiana, and another quarter of a million each around Simla and Ambala. In several other Punjabi districts, refugee numbers had yet to be estimated, let alone tabulated.[25]

Some of those displaced rejected the label of refugee. To the hundreds of thousands compelled to move across frontiers must be added those members of minority communities who sought protection among coreligionists who lived in larger numbers close by. Experiences of violence during riots and clearances were decisive for many, but others moved because former employment or schooling opportunities were gone.[26] The scale of this internal displacement also remains to be tallied, although evidence of the original clustering of exposed minority groups became apparent in urban ghettos and border settlements.[27]

Mass displacement, if not the levels of violence accompanying it, was foreseeable.[28] Provincial votes were held in the early summer of 1947. They yielded majorities for partition in Punjab and Bengal, as well as support in East Bengal, West Punjab, and Sindh for a Constituent Assembly in a separate state of Pakistan.[29] These votes worsened the crisis of legitimacy for the central Indian government, whose claim to authority over the entire country was no longer self-evident.[30] In the final weeks of pre-partition negotiation between June and August 1947 arguments persisted between Congress, the Muslim League, and the departing British authorities over the relative powers of central and regional government, the legal relationship between putative Indian and Pakistani administrations, the implications of Commonwealth membership after independence, and Britain's residual responsibilities as the colonial power.[31]

What government should do, and on whose behalf, was neither clear nor generally accepted. Rancor about the fates of Kashmir and Hyderabad, princely states large enough to subsist as independent polities, underlined the potential for violent irredentism.[32] Communal violence increased in both places after popular preferences in Kashmir and elaborate schemes for Hyderabad's future within a looser South Asian federation were overruled.[33] An influx of traumatized Sikh and Hindu refugees from Pakistani Punjab into Jammu (part of the larger princely state of Jammu and Kashmir) fed retaliatory violence against local Jammu Muslims.[34] Hyderabad,

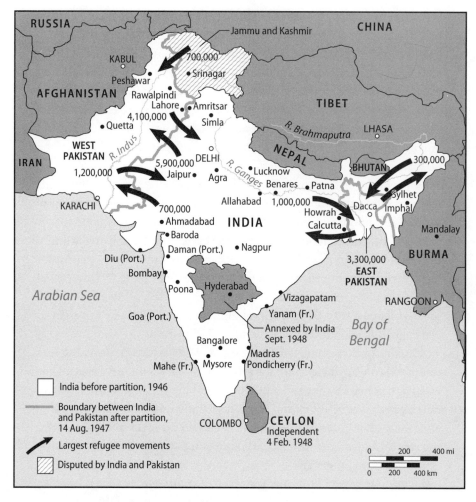

MAP 9.1. Indian partition, 1947.

meanwhile, became a hub for a communist-inspired peasant uprising and the scene of bloody confrontations between Muslim *Razakar* militiamen and the local Hindu majority.[35] The Indian Army intervened in both places but with different results: the first Indo-Pakistan War over Kashmir in October 1947 and Hyderabad's forcible incorporation into India in September 1948.[36] These outcomes left Muslim 'minority citizens' and 'foreign' Muslims of non–South Asian origin acutely vulnerable to discrimination, retribution, and eviction.[37]

Perhaps most striking of all, Punjab's four million Sikhs were to be arbitrarily divided. Their community identity and geographical attachments defied the binary geometry of the India–Pakistan division. Facing forced removal from Pakistani West Punjab, the inclination among some Sikhs to cluster their community together while evicting other religionists from an East Punjabi 'Sikhistan' was but one indication of what was to come.[38] These were not propitious circumstances in which to keep the peace once partition took place.

To write of transitions of power is to miss the point, sanitizing something that was anything but transitory or clean.[39] Power certainly changed hands, but not to those intended. The human consequences of partition were neither anticipated nor administered.[40] Nor did the governments of the princely states prove any more able to cope with cycles of retaliatory communal violence, as indicated by the course of events in Kashmir and Hyderabad, as well as in Rajasthan (formerly Rajputana).[41] It was left to the Indian and Pakistan governments to establish a Military Evacuation Organization (MEO) in September 1947 to oversee the movement of people across the northwestern frontiers.[42] Partition violence had reconfigured social landscapes and built environments by the time the MEO began working in Punjab, Sindh, and Delhi.[43] Violence processes, from intimate traumas of assault to familial experiences of home invasion, arson, and eviction, and the regional movements of people seeking safety, were locally determined, often orchestrated street by street, village by village, district by district. The walled city of Lahore, the administrative hub of a once-unified Punjab, was emptied of some 30,000 non-Muslim residents within a week between August 15 and 21. The High Commission only learned of these and other premeditated urban attacks by one community on another in Lahore and Amritsar days after they occurred.[44]

The imperial authorities in West and East Punjab, overwhelmed by the scale of displacement, laid on special trains and ordered regional police and army commands to let refugee columns pass without personal searches or restrictions on the goods transported.[45] But local practice was far different. Livestock, family valuables, and other precious items were often 'confiscated' by officials or stolen by armed civilians on either side of the partition line. Working in dangerous conditions in West and East Punjab, some police and troops tried to help; others did not.[46] In one dreadful incident, at Sheikhupura in West Punjab, soldiers of the 3rd Baluch Regiment shot down some 3,000 Hindu and Sikh refugees.[47] Nonlethal assertions of coercive power were also devastating. 'Searches', for many women and girls, were preludes to ritual humiliation, sexual violence, and kidnap.[48] Sickening enough, the physical and emotional dislocation of partition was, for many, punctuated by terror—of massacres and lynchings, of exhaustion for the eldest and frailest, of separation for families and children, of abduction and sexual violence for women and girls of all confessions.[49] The inclination to seek safety in numbers by traveling in columns could also backfire. Reprisal attacks were commonplace, their perpetrators increasingly seeking out larger refugee clusters.[50] Trains and lorry convoys made easy and richer targets for armed attackers, sometimes several hundred strong.[51] Male passengers were killed, women and girls violated, abducted, or disappeared.[52]

On September 24, 1947, an Indian Army commander in Amritsar, struggling to comprehend what was taking place, suggested that mass killings of local Muslims in the surrounding towns and villages of East Punjab were falling off simply because there was no one left to attack.[53] As this comment implies, the extent of group violence did not diminish; it shifted. Villages that escaped the initial wave of attacks at the announcement of partition witnessed cycles of retributive violence after rumors and reports of killings circulated to areas outside heavily policed boundary districts.[54] Collective violence also surged once more in urban areas within the Amritsar, Firozpur, and Jullundur districts in September.[55] Eight refugee trains were attacked over four days between September 19 and 22, six in East Punjab and two in West. The death toll in each case ran into the hundreds and, in the worst attack, to over a thousand.[56] An Amritsar refugee train was ransacked on the 23rd. Most of its occupants were reported killed, wounded, or kidnapped. Exact numbers were not even counted.[57] In this, as in other massacres, security forces either dared not intervene, were killed after doing so, or colluded in the original assaults.[58] Whether in its absence, its partiality, or its ineffectiveness, state authority became part of the calamity.[59]

Far to the east, in partitioned Bengal, curfews in Calcutta (Kolkata) and joint governmental statements imploring peaceful acceptance of the newly divided states only underlined how disjointed, how unworkable, and how unjust the eastern partition line actually was.[60] British judge Sir Cyril Radcliffe was assigned the job of frontier delimitation. He chose not to visit the regions he proposed to divide, spending barely six weeks in India.[61] In similar fashion, the judges who worked with Radcliffe's Boundary Commission never developed an observer's 'feel' for the communities they were about to destroy.[62] The regions Radcliffe's pen dissected were left bleeding without the administrative support necessary to staunch multiple wounds. At the micro-level, cultivators were separated from their lands, earners from their employments, family from relatives.[63] In India's northeast, millions found themselves on the 'wrong' side of the line. Among them were large religiously homogeneous communities such as the Hindus of the Chittagong Hill Tracts assigned to East Pakistan. Densely populated areas, including the Darjeeling and Jalpaiguri districts of West Bengal, were scythed apart. For some of the poorest people, especially day laborers and sharecroppers attached to smallholdings, relocation was never a viable option, meaning that East Pakistan would retain especially large numbers of non-Muslims and other minority groups. Even the Muslim majority in East Pakistan found themselves isolated and, on occasion, overlooked by their coreligionists in West Pakistan.[64]

Violence between communities continued in post-partition Bengal, culminating in the Khulna–Barisol riots of February 1950, disturbances that triggered the biggest cross-border migration between East Pakistan and India since 1947.[65] The intersectionality between bodily violence and cultural denigration amplified feelings of personal insecurity. In addition to the physical traumas of assault, refugee victims read the violence they suffered as the nullification of their culture, their religion, and their honor. Upheld as the physical embodiment of these qualities, women faced the greatest risk of abduction and sexual violence.[66] For those caught up in the cyclical routines of intercommunal hostility, the politics of independence was doubly confounding: culturally remote but physically determinant, a paradox that reasserted itself in the refugee exodus that accompanied the foundation of Bangladesh in 1971.[67]

That same contradiction between distance from high political power and proximity to violence was evident in the breakdown between India and Pakistan over the fate of Kashmir, a former princely state with a Hindu-dominated government and a Muslim majority population. The Kashmir dispute threatened an even wider regional conflagration.[68] Indian troops occupied Kashmir's Srinagar Valley in October 1947 in a bid to impose a fait accompli. It failed. The Srinagar occupation instead marked the first of several hostile interventions that would spiral into war between the South Asian states and decades of rumbling insurgency, emergency rule, and rights abuses for Kashmiris.[69] Behind the scenes, old imperial habits died hard. General Douglas Gracey, former head of British occupation forces in South Vietnam and, in October 1947, the Pakistan Army's 'officiating Commander', defied Muhammad Jinnah's instruction to send troops into Kashmir to fight off impending Indian military occupation. Jinnah had ordered a preemptive seizure of Baramula and Srinagar but backed down after Gracey insisted that the action would lead to a war that Pakistan would lose.[70]

In public though, things were different. Official British rejection of responsibility for what had taken place across the subcontinent was rapid, total, and breathtakingly arrogant. The most 'authoritative' account, an untitled memorandum by the Commonwealth Relations Office put before the British Cabinet's India and Burma Committee on September 3, blithely noted that reported killings in the Punjab in the fortnight after independence ranged from 25,000 to 150,000.[71] The longest departmental commentary on this document included the following reflections:

> Indian efforts to accuse the British of responsibility need not be taken seriously. All Indians—certainly all Indian politicians—are conditioned to blame the British for everything, and it will take time for this habit to wear off. All reports emphasize that Britons have been left unharmed in the midst of the most shocking massacres, and the man in the street quite certainly does not blame the British. He blames the other side as being solely responsible, with that pathological and unreasoning hatred which only Indian communalism can breed. . . .
>
> Although the deaths and exoduses have been enormous, they seem much smaller when considered against a background of the Indian peninsula as a whole. A hundred thousand have been killed—but there are five thousand more Indians in the world every month.[72]

Colonialist tropes were tacitly understood, from the presumption that only British officials and Raj security forces had kept the subcontinent from anarchy to the familiar racist stereotypes of Indians' emotional immaturity, their pathological inclination to sexualized violence, and the religious 'frenzy' of ringleaders and their followers.[73] The valedictory report from New Delhi of the departing supreme commander, Field-Marshal Claude Auchinleck, filed on September 28, 1947, rehearsed the familiar script of well-intentioned British efforts to arbitrate derailed by intolerant communalism. Auchinleck said almost nothing about the insecurities created by partition. He dwelled instead on the frustration of his efforts to cement military partnerships with the armed forces of the newly independent states.[74] This was of a piece with the preoccupation in Whitehall, not so much with partition violence as with two other issues. First was the potential for India (and, to a lesser extent, Pakistan) to disrupt Britain's postwar recasting of its empire as a Commonwealth. Should either country refuse to join, the proposition that amicable Commonwealth partnership represented the green uplands of decolonization would collapse. Second was India's financial capacity to undermine Britain's already desperate balance of payments position by calling in the sterling credits it had accumulated as a net lender to the British state. By 1947 British indebtedness to the Indian exchequer was huge, thanks to Britain's unilateral decision to use Delhi's colonial budget to help finance the war effort.

As partition unfolded, the Attlee government, its room for maneuver shrinking as Congress–Muslim League antagonism deepened and imperial authority decayed, congratulated itself on resolving each of these two problems.[75] The South Asian giants joined the Commonwealth, and Delhi was not demanding its money back. To those two preoccupations, one might add a third: the avoidance of a subcontinental civil war, even at a cost of mass dislocation and long-term regional instability.[76] For the imperial power, partition was a lesson in how to misrepresent, to move on, and to deny culpability. Satisfied that its work was done, on October 13, 1947, Prime Minister Attlee abolished the Cabinet's India and Burma Committee entirely.[77]

Palestine: Partition and Loss

For Palestinians, the *nakhba*, or catastrophe, of May 1948 was less about the foundation of the state of Israel and more about the effacement of a national culture through forced population removal and the physical erasure of villages and cultural sites.[78] By July 1949 the first government of Israel had established a Names Committee within the Prime Minister's Office, its express purpose being to designate Hebrew place-names to replace the Arabic titles for settlements and archaeological ruins in newly occupied territories. Palestinians were not just to be removed but also denied their geographical heritage.[79] Such nullification was bound to fail, nourishing popular resentment and, in the longer term, precluding dialogue. An assault on Palestinian identity, partition strengthened a people's identification with the historic Palestine from which they were expelled.

The Palestinian experience was closer to systemic ethnic cleansing than the terrifying mixture of insecurity, collusion, retributive violence, and opportunistic seizures enacted in India.[80] Palestinian displacement connected individual experiences of violence and eviction to the cultural calamity of a people rendered stateless by decolonization.[81] The totality of Palestinian dispossession, the disaggregation—physical, architectural, and cultural—of pre-partition communities, the wide distribution of the Palestinian diaspora, and the presumptive connections made between settler colonialism, Western dominance of Arab world economies, and unrepresentative local rulers forged new links between oppositional voices who found connection in their stronger self-identification as Arab. From North Africa to the Persian Gulf, *al-Nakhba* was a unifier for political movements, civil society groups, and migrant workers. Its injustice catalyzed early transnational associations such as the Movement of Arab

Nationalists, founded by Kuwaiti physician Dr. Ahmad al-Khatib, while ideas of empowerment through citizenship and anticolonial activism nourished support for Nasserist republicanism.[82]

The plight of Palestinian refugees was written in their inability to build 'authoritative national institutions'.[83] Holocaust suffering, meanwhile, nourished militant Zionism, assuring international sympathy for Jewish refugees in Europe, many of them forced to relive their traumas inside postwar Germany's resettlement camps.[84] Palestinian and Arab League representatives, still clinging to historical invocations of the centuries-long Arab presence in Palestine, struggled to evoke equivalent concern for dispossessed Palestinians.[85] In part, this was a Palestinian failure, rooted in the factionalism within the Palestinian national movement after the upsurge in popular protest spiked by the Buraq Revolt/Wailing Wall riots of 1929 and Britain's ensuing repression.[86] In part, it was a matter of competitive disadvantage, a consequence of the cold efficiency with which British security forces neutered Palestinian political networks and repressed Palestinian communities during the Arab Revolt of 1936–1939.[87] Recriminations over the Revolt's failure and divisions among its leading sponsors, the Husaynis and their Nashashibi clan rivals, resurfaced once the Mufti of Jerusalem Hajj Amin Al-Husayni and his cousin Jamal took charge of a reconstituted Arab Higher Committee (the ill-fated Palestinian authority in the earlier rebellion) in early 1946.[88]

Again, contrasts were striking. The marginalization of the Palestinians from the institutional politics of the late mandate was at variance with the British High Commission's readiness to work with Jewish paramilitaries, first in mapping, quantifying, and bureaucratizing Palestine's land and natural resources, and, second, in effacing preexisting Arab claims on these assets.[89] British strangulation of Palestinian political culture would be matched by the ethnocentrism of the victorious Israeli state in 1948 and after.[90]

The United Nations was not about to buck the trend by attaching primacy to Palestinian claims. UN Secretary-General U Thant viewed Palestine as the organization's first great test case. He would not risk compromising the organization's moral authority by taking issue with the right of stateless Holocaust survivors to find refuge in a state of their own. When, in November 1947, the United Nations voted in support of a two-state solution, the population of the envisaged Jewish state comprised 538,000 Jews and a large minority of almost 400,000 Palestinians, that of the corresponding Palestinian state some 804,000 Arabs and barely 10,000 Jews. The UN recommendations were presented as fair, but they were anything but even-handed. The priority attached to the creation of a viable Jew-ish state reflected Washington's preferences, turning previously favorable Arab opinion toward US endorsement of self-determination into abiding suspicion of American designs in the Middle East.[91]

The model of a two-state solution built on the longer-term evolution of British schemes for partition. These were codified by Lord Peel's com-mission of inquiry in 1937 but were distilled over the preceding decade.[92] Rising Jewish immigration, changing patterns of land ownership, and episodic but recurrent violence between communities played their part.[93] So did governmental thinking about 'lessons learned' from other British colonial precedents, particularly in Bengal and Ireland, as well as more prescient warnings of partition's pitfalls coming from nationalist voices in the Indian subcontinent.[94] Some mirrored the changing attitudes of Zionist groups toward partition and its near cousin, cantonization. But too few British officials recognized the shift in Zionist thinking from a colonization scheme in which sharing power with Palestinians might be possible toward a settler colonial project requiring the displacement of the indigenous majority.[95] Nor did London policymakers grasp how far the Jewish Agency, the Federation of Jewish Labor (Histadrut), and their paramilitary force, the Haganah, had gone in creating the institutional basis for an Israeli state.[96]

Violence dispelled the fog. British administrators inside Palestine har-bored few illusions after Menachem Begin's Irgun Tzva'i Le'umi (National Military Organization in the Land of Israel) blew the side off Jerusalem's King David Hotel on July 22, 1946, killing almost one hundred mandate secretariat staff.[97]

The bombing forced British personnel, military and civilian, to retreat into fortified bunkers, so-called Bevingrads, deepening their alienation from the communities surrounding them.[98] As if to prove the point, a directive issued by the Irgun executive on February 10, 1947, identified all Britons in Palestine as legitimate targets.[99] At home, too, Britons were con-fronted with the consequences of imperial breakdown. On March 7, 1947, Robert Misrahi, a Sorbonne student of Jean-Paul Sartre's and a member of another Zionist underground movement, Lehi b'Herut b'Yisrael (Fight-ers for the Freedom of Israel), better known as the Stern Gang, bombed the ex-servicemen's Colonies Club near Trafalgar Square.[100] Five weeks later a more audacious attack was attempted a few hundred meters away in Whitehall. A young woman with a discernable French accent smuggled another device into the Colonial Office. Slipping past an unsuspecting security guard, claiming that she needed to fix a laddered stocking, she

FIGURE 9.1. The search for survivors after the King David Hotel bombing, July 22, 1946. Source: Getty Images.

left behind twenty-four sticks of French-manufactured gelignite concealed in a parcel bomb. The detonator failed. Had it not, the British Empire's administrative center would have gone the same way as the King David.[101]

The quickening rhythm of attacks inside Palestine and beyond encouraged fatalistic thinking in London and New York. The outline of a deal looked deceptively simple: a self-governing Jewish state, a Palestinian Arab territory closely tied to neighboring Transjordan, and, ideally, a third, jointly ruled zone in greater Jerusalem.[102] Arguments began as soon as precise boundaries, forms of governance, and power-sharing arrangements were considered.[103] Little wonder that neither the UN Special Committee on Palestine (UNSCOP) nor the Truman administration that nurtured it expected their proposals to stick unless the United Nations itself was prepared to play a muscular role as their guarantor. Translated into plain language, the United Nations would reject federal power-sharing in preference for the creation of a state of Israel.[104] UNSCOP's terms of reference were mapped out during a UN Special Session on Palestine on April 28, 1947. They spurned any proposals that could be linked to Britain's earlier decision to put the future of Palestine into UN hands in the first place.[105] Crucially, the Jewish Agency was invited to make its case to the UN, confirming the agency's de facto status as an executive-in-waiting. The Palestinian Arab Higher Committee was shut out. UNSCOP's terms also precluded deferral to the wishes of the local majority (bound to favor the Palestinians) or to the requirements of neighboring states (all of them Arab). Whatever UNSCOP decided, its preference for Jewish Agency views was obvious.[106]

Assiduous Jewish Agency lobbying over subsequent weeks, coordinated by Walter Eytan, later to become the first director-general of the Israeli Foreign Ministry, garnered further support among General Assembly members. Britain and the Arab nations were left isolated. With Resolution 181, passed on November 29, 1947, the General Assembly approved the UN Partition Plan. Thirty-three members voted in favor, thirteen against, and ten abstained (including Britain).[107] A decisive victory for the Jewish Agency campaign but lacking any enforcement powers, the Resolution was unlikely to be accepted locally. The previous day the CIA warned of a regional conflagration pitting a Jewish state against an Arab coalition. The agency's analysts correctly predicted short-term Jewish military success but expected a longer war of attrition and blockade, which, they thought, would bring Israel to economic collapse.[108]

These calculations were soon overtaken by the events of 1948. The British government, longing to get out of Palestine, was equally desperate not to let UN inspectors in. Or at least not before May 15, the British date for withdrawal. Knowing that war over Palestine was coming, Attlee's cabinet did not want to get mixed up in it. UN proposals were unwelcome, not just because they were read in London as indirect American pressure, but because they required short-term actions with immediate dangers.[109] Typical in this regard was the suggestion from the UN commission on Palestine in February 1948 that British security forces evacuate Tel Aviv, enabling it to become a free port of entry for Jewish weapons and other supplies.[110] Manifestly biased, this proposal came only weeks before Jewish paramilitaries, Irgun fighters among them, began a systematic clearance of the Arab city of Jaffa, to the horror of watching Arab publics.[111] The latest UN intervention was a step too far for Attlee's ministers. Its partisanship was one thing, but worse, it forced the British off the fence. That the fence was rickety and tugged at from all sides didn't matter; it had only to stay up until midnight, May 14. It did, but only just.

Jerusalem's fragile cease-fire collapsed barely two hours after Sir Alan Cunningham handed over the High Commission to the International Red Cross.[112] Months after Palestine's calamitous but predictable war broke out, London's original concern remained unaltered: limiting its wider consequences for British power. The results were confusing, a curious combination of agreements with favored Arab regimes and actual reluctance to do anything much to help them.[113] Others would be left to erect new fences across Israel/Palestine.

Violent regional competition determined Israel's frontiers. Egypt seized control of the Gaza Strip. Jordan's King Abdullah, rightly suspected by other Arab governments of opportunist expansionism, claimed sovereignty over the West Bank.[114] At least three-quarters of a million Palestinians lost their homes. Some four hundred villages were destroyed. Other settlements were reconfigured, their Arab characteristics erased.[115] Israeli security forces enforced what historian Benny Morris termed 'concerted expulsions' from March 1948 to remove Palestinians as a potential internal threat to rural security.[116] Massacres and sexual violence were much rarer than in the divided Punjab and Bengal. But they occurred. The two most notorious instances, at Dayr Yassin and Ayn al-Zayrun in April and May 1948, turned the most radical Jewish movements, the Irgun Tzva'i Le'umi and its smaller rival, the Lehi b'Herut b'Yisrael, from uncompromising insurgents into murderers of unarmed Palestinian villagers.[117] Larger Palmach military formations, although more restrained, were also implicated in the destruction of villages, the eviction of their occupants, and the killing of their menfolk.[118] When the United Nations Relief and Works Agency for Palestinian Refugees in the Middle East (UNRWA) was established the following year, it focused on welfare provision and not the restorative claims of the 910,000 refugees it registered.[119] If anything, the United Nations' humanitarian interventionism, articulated through the supranational authority of its refugee agencies, entrenched the Palestinians' long-term statelessness.[120]

For the Palestinians in 1948, as for the Bengalis who fled their homes for the new state of (East) Pakistan in 1947, the recurrence of regional

war provoked lasting insecurity. The Palestinians would face repeated displacements: in 1956, 1967, 1973, and 1982, as well as during civil wars in
Lebanon and, more recently, Syria. For Hindu and Muslim Bengalis, as
well as for isolated Bihari communities, there was a single attenuated cataclysm:[121] the violent collapse of East Pakistan and the Indo-Pakistan war
attending the establishment of Bangladesh in 1971.[122] Nor was this an end
to decolonization-derived partition violence on the Indian subcontinent.
Kashmir's disputed status has, at the time of writing, provoked three wars,
continuing refugee flows, rights abuses, and the denial of statehood.[123]

Partitions and Rights Protections

Partitions exposed the lack of enforceable protections in international law
for individuals and communities living in imperial territories. Yet the UN
Convention on Human Rights, although finalized in their aftermath, paid
scant attention to them. Opponents of empire anxious to embed human
rights protections in postcolonial states, meanwhile, faced a dilemma:
Which was more important, protecting threatened minorities or individuals facing abuse? If the global push for decolonization was in any
way linked to a presumption of equal rights for all within democratically
organized nation-states, its logical implication was that voting majorities
should decide how those states should be configured. This was fine as long
as minority groups did not face discrimination or worse as a result. In
many cases, though, they would and did.

India's constitution-makers wrestled with these problems as the violence
of partition unfolded around them. The movement of millions of refugees
into the country and the dispossession of others who had fled partition violence only to find their homes destroyed or seized by others in their absence
created extra complexity.[124] Amid this humanitarian crisis, the challenges
for the architects of the Indian Republic were tough: to design a constitution secure enough to hold a vast, heterogeneous society together and to
enshrine sovereignty in Indian precepts of self-rule (*swaraj*) true to principles of nonviolence (*satyagraha* and *ahimsa*).[125] This was not easy, but the
payoff was immense: securing India's status as the world's preeminent postcolonial democracy. Their Pakistani counterparts set about this constitutional process later. They faced their own dilemmas, whether in relation to
popular inclusion and land redistribution or the tension between secularism
and their country's identity as an Islamic republic. A framework document
put forward in March 1949 went through several changes before Pakistan's
constitution was finally approved on March 23, 1956.[126]

For independent India's democracy to operate, its eligible voters—newly enfranchised citizens aged twenty-one and over—had to be registered on an electoral roll. This was difficult in a country where most voters remained illiterate. Registering incoming refugees presented other complications. One was to determine the refugees' domicile status as former residents of a previously unified colonial India. Another was the tendency among both refugees and local officials to conflate eligibility to vote with rights of citizenship.[127] British pressure on India and Pakistan to legislate citizenship provisions compatible with Britain's 1948 Nationality Act (BNA), which assigned different citizen status to peoples of Commonwealth and colonial territories, made the parameters of Indian and Pakistani citizenship still more contentious.[128] Little wonder that the long document India's constitution-writers eventually produced in January 1950 offset an impressive list of judiciable rights and personal freedoms against a series of legal restrictions giving the state extraordinary powers to clamp down on disorder and criminality.[129] Some marginalized groups, including low-caste communities and peasant sharecroppers, also found their rights curtailed or unrecognized when the terms of Indian citizenship were finalized in 1951–1952.[130] Overseas Indians were meanwhile left with a hybrid citizenship that mirrored the discriminations inbuilt within the BNA.[131]

Post-partition property rights were even more problematic than personal rights. The designation of the hundreds of thousands of homes and farms and personal possessions abandoned amid partition violence as 'evacuee property' was followed by the creation of largely unaccountable bureaucracies in India and Pakistan to resolve questions of rightful ownership and due compensation. Their work continued for decades, creating precedents for state seizures of land and inducements to corruption in the redistribution of evacuee property. Other people displaced from their homes took matters into their own hands, occupying abandoned properties, sometimes with the support of local officials desperate to find housing for refugees in their districts.[132] This form of direct refugee action became widespread in India's eastern states, West Bengal and its capital, Calcutta, where large-scale displacements had occurred during prepartition violence in August 1946. After partition in the following year no state-sponsored population exchanges between West Bengal and East Pakistan took place, a critical difference from divided Punjab. Whether or not prompted by the lack of state action, many refugees in West Bengal and East Pakistan took the initiative, squatting on abandoned private and government-owned property. Improvised settlements mushroomed on fallow land at the margins of the larger cities.[133] Millions of other people stayed close to the Radcliffe Line frontier. These rural refugees often lacked the family connections or job skills that pushed others toward urban centers.[134] Principally smallholders and peasant farmers, in Joya Chatterji's arresting phrase, they 'huddled in the long shadows of the new national borders'.[135] The crying need for civil rights protections for partition refugees, as for those minorities who remained behind, pointed to a deeper problem: in the affected regions, peaceful coexistence remained febrile.[136]

Partitions and the Return of Co-Imperialism?

The human misery of partitions lent poignancy to the sentiments expressed in global strike actions among dockworkers, merchant seamen, colonial troops, and GIs unwilling to become complicit in restoring an imperial order in Asia and elsewhere.[137] Conscious of their growing isolation as colonial powers, the British, the French, and, later, the Belgian governments convened a series of talks in 1946–1947, quickly focusing on West Africa, where labor protests registered the greatest policy impact.[138] The three countries agreed in May 1947 to swap information about welfare policies, development plans, and improving life expectancy, with a view to presenting a common front at the United Nations.[139] Detailed statistics of this type were required if the imperial nations were to meet the challenge presented by Article 73(e) of the UN Charter. This envisioned supranational consideration of internal colonial conditions, requiring that imperial policy be shown to work in the interests of dependent populations.[140] The United Nations' evolving conceptualization of those 'interests' exceeded the limited range of indicators that colonial governments were prepared to discuss.[141] Instead of statistically led discussion regarding live births and living standards, matters about which colonial governments could claim postwar improvements, UN and World Health Organization representatives pressed for information about working conditions, employment opportunities, and social inequalities.[142] These were tougher questions that exposed the chasm separating the rights of rulers and ruled.

More an ethical benchmark than a legal obligation, the precise meaning and legal force of Article 73(e) were hotly contested, particularly within the UN special committee on nongoverning territories, which scrutinized the reports submitted.[143] For one thing, other clauses of the UN Charter affirmed the sovereign totality—and thus the political insularity—of empires. For another, European imperial officials complained of differential UN oversight between self-governing and non-self-governing territories. How could empires be vilified as uniquely inimical to their subjects if poverty levels and rights protections in independent territories were not held to the same standards?[144]

UN jurisdiction might be disputed, but it was clear that pressure for external scrutiny of colonial affairs would increase.[145] Refusal to cooperate, as Salazar's Portugal chose to do, would seem petulant and defensive, handing a propaganda victory to anticolonialists everywhere.[146] As we'll see in later chapters, during the late 1940s and early 1950s, these dilemmas were sharpened by another: European imperial powers facing massive reconstruction costs at home looked to US funding and UN technical assistance programs to support the very development projects they hoped might assuage international criticism of colonial social policies.[147] From the empire working parties within the Organisation for European Economic Cooperation, created in 1948 to oversee the disbursement of the Marshall Plan's European Recovery Program, to the inclusion of the French Maghreb within NATO's defensive perimeter, and the consolidation of the European Economic Community's regional trading arrangements in the 1950s, colonial territories were reimagined as subordinate members of a European-led bloc.[148]

Ironically, although the technical groundwork for closer economic partnership was laid, in 1948 the French Foreign Ministry intervened to take the colonial exchanges in a more political direction.[149] Their approach had a coercive edge, the accent being on intelligence cooperation, including joint surveillance of transnational contacts between anticolonial movements, student groups, and religious associations. French officials wanted to know what the British were doing in the Gold Coast, where Kwame Nkrumah's Convention Peoples' Party (CPP) was identified as the tinder liable to ignite flames of anticolonial protest across West Africa.[150] Lethal police violence during ten days of riots beginning in Accra in February–March 1948 cemented disparate Ghanaian grievances over rural poverty, racial exclusion, and broken promises of reform into a coherent mass movement that the Gold Coast administration could not contain.[151] French negotiators needed reassurance that their plans to reorder French West Africa through social entitlements, citizenship revisions, and electoral reforms would not be slowed by political gridlock in neighboring British territories.

The British were happy enough to comply. They even upped the ante during a further conference round in London in October 1948, moving to the sumptuous surroundings of Lancaster House, pulling in Colonial Secretary Arthur Creech-Jones to supervise talks about West Africa, and wheeling out the chief of the British Armed Forces, Field Marshal Bernard Montgomery, to make frightening noises about the menace of African communism.[152] Over the coming winter the British finally responded to French requests for political dialogue and intelligence liaison across the Arab world.[153] This was a more remarkable shift. In the ill-fated last years of the Syrian and Palestine mandates between 1945 and 1947 the two imperial powers had sustained their on–off covert war against one another in the Middle East.[154] By February 1949 that looked set to change. For their part, the French raised no objections to British military agreements with the Syrian and Lebanese regimes. Nor did they obstruct Britain's efforts to pull Libya, technically under UN Trusteeship, into its sphere of Middle Eastern influence. These were Machiavellian quid pro quos of what was supposed to be a bygone age. Alongside the brave new world of technocratic benevolence in West Africa, old-school imperialism subsisted in the post-partition Middle East.[155]

Social Realities

Imperialist politicking only hardened opinion among the Arab political leaders coming to prominence after 1945. Foremost among them was Hasan al-Banna's Muslim Brotherhood, whose vision of transnational Islamic solidarity melded with anticolonialism, activist support for Palestinian self-rule, and grassroots welfarism.[156] But social realities were more influential in shaping their opinions. In 1947 cholera took hold in Cairo. The epidemic was traceable to the nearby quarantine station for Muslim pilgrims transiting through the Suez Canal en route to *hajj* pilgrimage in Saudi Arabia. All pilgrims were supposed to be inoculated against cholera and bubonic plague before landing at the Red Sea port of Jeddah, from which most then traveled overland to Mecca. Those whose journey required passage through Suez were, in addition, expected to spend five days in the El Tor quarantine facility at Port Said. But these *hajj* public heath requirements were patchily applied, and in 1947 they broke down. A municipal spraying program failed to prevent cholera spreading into the wider community. Cairo's death toll rose fast, hundreds succumbing each day. The Egyptian press accused the British of sloppy procedures and, worse, of refusing to distribute an effective cholera serum. Imperial governance, reports claimed, was more than inadequate; it was malevolent.[157]

An irony here is that the standardization of quarantine procedures to combat cholera was part of what Sunil Amrith identifies as the foundational lineage of 'health internationalism', a co-imperialist project among the European colonial powers in South and Southeast Asia.[158] Postwar international health programs in Asia evolved as they did despite the decolonization unfolding around them.[159] Amrith stresses the paradox intrinsic to the thickening internationalism of public health programs in Asia at a time when most parts of the continent were still under colonial domination. Mid-twentieth-century theorists of international relations got around the paradox by suggesting that public health was a field ripe for 'functional internationalism': depoliticized, technical, and ethically imperative.[160] There was not much evidence of this in Cairo politics in the aftermath of the cholera outbreak. On December 25, 1947 the Egyptian Wafd Party lambasted Britain's divisive actions in Palestine and Western imperialism more generally. The Wafdist manifesto voiced Arab amazement at Western readiness to reassign sovereign control of Muslim holy places and deny self-determination in Muslim majority territories such as Kashmir, while claiming expertise in 'dealing' with Muslim peoples. Just like British platitudes about public health, this was an affront to people's intelligence.[161]

Criticism like this stuck. On January 7, 1953, Adib al-Shishakli, the Syrian Army general, recently installed as president, met Barbara Castle, the British Labour Party politician and longtime anticolonial campaigner, in Damascus. Shishakli began by accusing the Western imperial nations of abusing their powers as mandate-holders. He lambasted France and Britain for comparable policies of divide and rule. Syria, subdivided into five substates, had been so chronically misgoverned that it was left in a worse condition in 1945 than at the start of the French mandate in 1920. As for Britain, its abject failure in Palestine opened the door to the regional calamity of the Arab–Israeli conflict, unending territorial disputes, and a chronic refugee crisis. Only if the Western imperialists engaged equitably with the Arab world would the latter's distrust of Britain and France diminish.[162] Castle got the same message in Baghdad a week later. This time she met not military strongmen, but democratic oppositionists, including Mohammed Haded Jamil, leader of the National Democratic Party. The British, he said, backed their local clients in government, regardless of Iraqi pleas for democratization. Apart from adverse local consequences, such divisive interventionism destabilized the entire region because Arabs 'from Casablanca to Basra' refused to accept it.[163]

Conclusion

Colonial partitions of the 1940s played out against a backdrop in which international law was beginning to accommodate individual rights alongside minority protections. But the United Nations and foreign governments observing partitions in India and Palestine concerned themselves with what was done to people as groups, whether Palestinian Arabs and Jewish settlers or Indian Muslims, Sikhs, and Hindus. Only retrospectively did attention shift to the fate of persons and the culpability of perpetrators for the physical, sexual, or psychological abuse of individuals during partition violence.[164] The high incidence of collective violence during Indian partition has become emblematic of the partition trauma.[165] Attacks on refugee columns and trains were sometimes facilitated by collusion between local security forces and their coreligionists among border communities in the Punjab in the northwest and in Bengal in the northeast. Focusing on large attacks should not, though, obscure the everyday violence, including rapes, abductions of women and girls, forcible conversions, and other assaults on refugee families by hostile residents.[166]

Partition violence illustrated how imminent decolonization fueled tensions between the local majority community and minorities of different ethnicity or religion. Minorities and the displaced faced chronic insecurity, exemplified by bodily violation and loss of assets. If Indian Muslims and Palestinian Arabs offer the starkest evidence of such fears, the ethnic Chinese and Tamil Indian communities of British Malaya, the Kabyle Berbers of French Algeria, the Western Saharans of Morocco, and the religious sects of the Middle East from Syria's Alawites and Druzes to the Assyrians, Yazadis, and Christian communities of Iraq and elsewhere remind us that, for many, the end of empire heightened their vulnerability to discrimination and bodily violence.[167] As part of the decolonization process, partitions were particularly decentered. Even if subjects of attenuated negotiation, partitions were made real by facts on the ground, by local action and seizure, not by the division of territory through agreement.

CHAPTER TEN

Hiding Wars

VIOLENT OPPOSITION TO European empire—from colonized peoples, from their external backers, and from revisionist powers determined to seize territory and assets—spurred two waves of decolonization. The first engulfed South, Southeast, and Western Asia in the late 1940s as part of the Greater Second World War. That first wave affected colonial Africa and the Caribbean as well, but, in these regions, second surges of protest catalyzed colonial withdrawals over roughly twenty years between the mid-1950s and the mid-1970s.[1] Neither wave was strong enough to bring down empire immediately. But they fractured empires' three foundational pillars—of politics and administration, social and economic structure, and the cultural norms intrinsic to racial hierarchy.

First to oust European empires were the Japanese, the new imperial occupiers of the Second World War. Japan's victories were reversed, but their effects lingered. Next to win out were Indonesia's Republicans. Their triumph in 1949 proved more permanent. The UN, the United States, and India, among others, endorsed the Republic's claim to sovereign nationhood. Moving north and westward across Asia, the pattern changed again. Ironically, the territorial rearrangements and movements of people triggered by violent partitions, first in the Indian subcontinent, then in Palestine, soon afterward in Korea, and later in Cyprus, caused lasting political stasis, despite enduring local and global opposition to their outcome. British compulsion to leave South and Western Asia did not originate in violence against them but was nourished by it. Leaving India made keeping Burma or Ceylon impossible. The violent competition for power inside Burma ensured a more total British eviction than occurred in the relative peacefulness of Ceylon. To the west, war and its aftermath spelled an end to the imperial arrangements of Middle Eastern mandates and protectorates, only for these to be replaced by more elastic, but still imperialistic arrangements—treaties sealed with Jordan and Iraq, a British trusteeship in Libya, a renegotiated treaty sought but never achieved with Egypt.[2] Close by, the French were finally ejected from Lebanon in 1943–1945 and from Syria in 1946. The lure of ports and petrochemicals, meanwhile, deepened Anglo-American involvement in the Persian Gulf and Saudi Arabia.

This chapter analyzes the later wave of violent opposition to British and French empire. If the first wave built during a greater Second World War, the second offered stronger evidence of a globalizing decolonization that transcended Cold War alignments. Again, the argument is that violence was fundamental to decolonization outcomes, but rarely so in simple military terms.

Hiding Britain's Decolonization Wars

Colonial security forces repressed opponents, dislocated local populations, and drove out insurgents to cross-border sanctuary bases across the global South. Often, they handed the dirtiest work to local clients, paramilitary police, and militia auxiliaries. These 'loyalists' were the principal violence workers of late colonialism: groups and individuals spurred by particular motives into bargaining their collaboration for advantage or simply for survival.[3] Loyalist partnerships were contingent, deals made to secure enhanced opportunities rather than to defend an ideological position.[4] The 'Home Guard' units organized by British authorities among local Kikuyu, Embu, and Meru communities in colonial Kenya's Central Province in 1953 were typical. Based on village self-defense groups, the Home Guard expanded their focus from static protection to become the sharpest edge of repressive violence, responsible for killings, rapes, and other rights abuses conducted with British indulgence.[5] Beyond the close horizon of their violence work, groups of this kind aligned with government in anticipation that power would be shared among the victors in a postcolonial distribution of land, wealth, and influence.[6]

In part, the alliances made by violence workers, loyalist or otherwise, were logical responses to the pressures of war and the conflict environments it created, what political scientists typically describe in terms of the 'security dilemma' and consequent 'collective action'.[7] In part, paramilitary groups used collective violence to exploit opportunities for advancement opened up by the collapse of established patterns of governance. 'Loyalism', then, was more than a survival strategy. It was a process of negotiating the distribution of political authority, economic resources, and claims for cultural recognition.[8] Here we come closer to discovering why the second wave of decolonization violence, like the first, eventually overwhelmed the territories through which it surged.

Psychologies of Colonialism in Kenya

British colonialism dressed itself in scientific language and social scientific methods to justify occupation. As the pace of decolonization quickened after the Second World War, British colonial Africa presented disturbing evidence of this. Take Kenya. There, Jomo Kenyatta's fledgling Kenya African Union (KAU) gained a stronger foothold in the late 1940s. But Kenyatta's attempt to build an interethnic alliance to plead a constitutionalist case for British redress of Kenyans' dispossession and their impoverishment by colonialism came unstuck.[9] A 1952 ban on the KAU was partly responsible. The KAU also struggled to bridge Kenya's internal divides between propertied and landless, countryside and capital, old and young.[10] In the Central Highlands especially, land loss to settlers, rigid patron–client relationships in villages, and the resultant inability of younger, poorer members of rural communities to navigate a path to the self-mastery represented by economic independence and familial stability, caused social destabilization.

What historian John Lonsdale identifies as the 'competitive market of esteem' ceased to function as a meritocratic moral economy.[11] In Kikuyu society, attaining adult autonomy or what, in the language of African sociology, might be defined as 'personhood' rested on individual ability to fulfill relational obligations to family, kin, and community.[12] Removing the means to do so was devastating. It became harder for many residents, impossible for others, to connect years of rural labor with its eventual reward in the assured possession of land, livestock, and a familial household.[13] Diminishing prospects and people's belief that society was stacked against them, what Lonsdale describes as 'intimate unease'—it was that crippling sense of disempowerment that made fertile ground for violent opposition.[14]

These social pressures opened political space for the KAU's radical offshoot, the Mau Mau (the 'ravenous ones', sometimes translated as the 'greedy eaters' of authority, principally that of elders). Much of Mau Mau's rank and file were young people culturally adrift—economically marginalized and alienated from their rural communities of origin.[15] Their situation played into the hands of colonial officials and the humanitarians of Britain's Save the Children Fund, which constructed disaffected young Kenyans as teenage delinquents, 'maladjusted' adolescents to be reeducated to the benefits of British care.[16] After the 1954 implementation of the Child Protection (Emergency Regulation) Act, unaccompanied children in Nairobi were liable to incorporation into the notorious 'pipeline' system of detention camps while they waited for reassignment by Save the Children staff to reserves or missionary orphanages.[17] No one, it seemed, was outside the purview of counterinsurgency. It bears emphasis, though, that people's choices between supporting Mau Mau and opposing it were difficult, complex, and fluid. Aside from the emotional impact of violence on individuals and families, the critical determinant was the calculation of the optimum route toward self-mastery. In the moral economy of Kenya's decolonization, access to land, to family autonomy, and to social respectability were never Mau Mau's to give. The growth in local opposition to Mau Mau, misleadingly dubbed 'loyalism', from 1954 onward is better understood as a calibration of choices about prospects, long-term security, and social standing.[18]

KAU leaders struggled meanwhile to bridge the cultural and generational divides between their rural supporters in Gikuyuland and the more confrontational trade union activism and youth politics of postwar Nairobi. For all that, what startled the colonial administration about the KAU's emergence was its 'pan-tribal'—for which we might read 'national'—basis of support.[19] What alarmed them about Mau Mau was precisely the reverse: its secretive, sectarian violence.[20] Constructions of the Mau Mau threat coalesced in British official minds around sensationalist reports from field ethnographers employed by the colonial authorities. During the early 1950s accounts flooded into district and central administrative offices of Mau Mau oathing ceremonies in which tens of thousands in Central Kenya pledged support, often in small groups and frequently under duress.[21] Drawing on Kikuyu religious practice, oathing ceremonies were equally effective as instruments of political mobilization and social discipline. They had a backstory. Dramatic increases in the numbers making oaths of allegiance to the KAU were pivotal to the efforts of Nairobi-based militants to usurp the party's established leadership of rural elders typified by Kenyatta and another senior Kikuyu chief, Koinange wa Mbiyu. By 1951 the party had a younger, more militant aspect.[22]

Where previous declarations of support for the KAU were conventionally political and limited in number, Mau Mau oathing was ritualized and conducted on an enormous scale. Vulgarized accounts of these ceremonies became staples of settler conversation and British press accounts. Their exaggerations demonized Mau Mau as backward, deviant, and cruel. Reports from district administrators, ethnographers, and government-appointed psychologists interpreted oathing through the cosmologies of early modern witchcraft. Ceremonies sometimes involved animal sacrifice and the eating of raw goat meat, actions interpreted in sexualized terms as frenzied acts of satanic depravity.[23] New initiates, estimated to number around 90 percent of the population in parts of Kenya's Central Highlands, were thereby represented as having been duped, either coerced into compliance or lulled into a trance-like state in which reason and inhibition were lost.

Not surprisingly, a propaganda war developed over the meaning and validity of Mau Mau oaths and the movement behind them. If, as British official statements insisted, followers of Mau Mau had succumbed to a collective psychosis, corrective treatment rather than colonial reform was what was required.[24] So-called counter-oathing ceremonies became a cornerstone of counterinsurgency strategy. Public recantations were organized in which Mau Mau detainees ceremonially repudiated their earlier vows, sometimes kissing a male goat's foot, spitting, and then spurning Mau Mau allegiance. Theatrical recantation, instrumental to British 'rehabilitation' of their Kenyan captives, perpetuated the idea that Mau Mau was closer to a cult than a political quest for 'land and freedom', the movement's core slogan.[25]

The results were poisonous. Historian Erik Linstrom is surely right in discerning a common colonial pattern: 'Like the French tactics known as *action psychologique* in Algeria and Indochina, British efforts to mobilize psychology did not simply coexist with coercion but rationalized and justified it'.[26] Dismissing insurgent opposition as symptomatic of popular delusion, what analysts characterize as the 'disease theory' of anticolonial dissent, was sufficiently widespread among colonial authorities to constitute a pseudointellectual basis for repression.[27] So crass was the equivalence drawn by government-backed psychological surveys between psychotic disorder and violent anticolonialism in Kenya, Algeria, and other late colonial conflicts that social scientists in Britain, France, and elsewhere ridiculed the methods used and the conclusions reached.[28] But the tendency among 'on the spot' officials to pathologize political opposition as evidence of psychosis was not easily dispelled. The results were starkest in Kenya's collective punishment system, which combined forcible population removal and mass internment in so-called screening camps with the denial of freedoms of movement and assembly to those outside the wire.[29]

MAP 10.1. Kenya and Mau Mau.

Social conditions, not mental disorders, were Mau Mau's surest recruiters. Kenya's racialized system of land ownership was key. Settlers in the 'white highlands' required more agricultural labor as their farmsteads expanded. They refused to allow local Kikuyu to farm independently. Doing so prevented infringements on white-owned land and guaranteed an uninterrupted supply of field-workers. Among the Kikuyu, former cultivators became landless laborers, 'squatters' living on the margins of

FIGURE 10.1. Kikuyu-owned cattle assembled in the Kenyan Central Highlands town of Nyeri in 1953, a prelude to the British-ordered livestock cull. Source: Getty Images.

settler farmsteads. Resentment at eviction, landlessness, and racialized day labor were a combustible mix. This was Mau Mau's 'time bomb'.[30]

The Nairobi administration did nothing to defuse it. Social scientific advice instead doubled down on these Kenyan agricultural communities by reinforcing an unspoken colonial logic of rural modernization deaf to local preferences.[31] Kenya's deteriorating security situation made coercive development easier. The colonial authorities armed themselves with sweeping legislative powers after a state of emergency was declared on October 20, 1952.[32] District officers immediately took aim at Kikuyu economic migration, expelling laborers from farms, evicting them from towns and cities, and confining them on 'native reserves'. As Mau Mau intensified, so did administrative pressure to 'rationalize' farming practices in the worst-affected areas. Pastoralists turned to waged agricultural labor. Itinerant herder communities were forced to sedentarize.[33]

Kenya's 1954 Swynnerton Plan, named after Assistant Director of Agriculture Roger Swynnerton, is known for its psychological reading of Mau

Mau resistance.[34] Also integral to it was the consolidation of subsistence smallholdings and restriction of livestock movements.[35] Ignoring its coercive texture, the Swynnerton Plan was officially portrayed as a rationalization of agriculture to alleviate rural poverty. It had the opposite effect.[36] The Central Highlands labor market was already in trouble. Chronic land shortage was visible in overgrazing, soil exhaustion, crop failures, and hunger. But the Swynnerton Plan was no answer. Livestock culls, ordered by the colonial administration in 1954–1955, made matters worse. Meant to ease pressure on land and soil, the slaughter program was devastating for the remaining Kenyan Highlands farmers.[37] Meanwhile, those already forced off their land, mainly ethnic Kikuyu, Embu, and Meru, were crammed into the native reserves and eight hundred new villages, often with a population density exceeding five hundred per square mile.[38]

1955 saw over 78,000 Kenyans detained in prisons and camps, often on the flimsiest suspicions of association with the rebellion. Kikuyu civilians bore the brunt, not Mau Mau's already decimated forest fighters. Army units continued the hunt for remaining insurgent forces, but between 1954 and the lifting of emergency restrictions in early 1960 the Nairobi administration punished an entire community judged collectively suspect.[39] Over a quarter of adult Kikuyu males were killed or incarcerated by security forces by the time the British declared Mau Mau suppressed in January 1960.[40] Kikuyu women, children, and the elderly remained vulnerable throughout to violence by Home Guard auxiliaries in fortified villages, in detention camps, or during reprisal attacks.[41]

Misunderstanding of local opinion and official refusal to acknowledge Kikuyu grievances would soon be echoed elsewhere in British Africa. Facing an upsurge in local protest against the twin authority of the British Crown and the white Rhodesians who directed the Central African Federation of South Rhodesia (Zimbabwe), Northern Rhodesia (Zambia), and Nyasaland (Malawi), colonial administrators expressed surprise when the people of Nyasaland mobilized against British and white Rhodesian domination in 1959 and after. Why? One reason was the persistence among colonial health professionals, psychologists, magistrates, and police of racist stereotypes about Africans, their mental acuity, and their supposed lack of initiative.[42] Layers of colonialist prejudice about local populations lacking political conviction or the capacity for self-reflection were gradually stripped away by well-organized demonstrations coordinated by Hastings Banda's Nyasaland African Congress. But the pattern remained: social psychology was misused to dismiss political opposition as evidence of mental disorder or the malign influence of 'outsiders'.

The numbers of social psychologists and cultural anthropologists roaming colonial Africa were much smaller than those of other scientifically trained personnel—agronomists, medical specialists, and engineers—who worked with colonial administrations after 1945. But the psychologists and anthropologists were more influential in shaping imperial repertoires of repression.[43] Officials cited anthropological studies of 'tribal custom', local 'folklore', and 'authentic tradition' to justify colonialism as a work of social conservation.[44] No matter that the sheen of academic objectivity legitimized policies that typecast Africans in particular ways, consigning them to a premodern status in which industrialization, advanced education, and gender equality became sources of social disruption best avoided.[45] Present-day historians see even baser motives in this 'politics of retraditionalization'.[46] Stripped of its cultural baggage, 'scientific colonialism' signified a turn toward low-cost, high-extraction administration.[47] At its heart was the 'bargain of collaboration' with local elites: the chiefs, mandarins, village elders, and other subordinate administrators who made the system work. The bargain preserved their titles, plus certain legal and tax-raising powers. The elites upheld rural order and supplied the authorities with revenue, labor, and military recruits in return. Any 'science' was rhetorical, not real.

Mau Mau Ignored

It would be mistaken to think that the British approved security force coercion in Kenya because they cared greatly about keeping hold of it. More discomfiting is that, if anything, the opposite applied. British society tolerated violence against entire Kenyan communities because it neither knew nor cared much about what happened there. On February 26, 1955, French diplomats in London reported that neither Britain's broadsheet press nor its domestic readership seemed concerned by reports published a week earlier confirming that the number of individuals hanged in Kenya for Mau Mau–related offences since 1952 had surpassed eight hundred. British society, it seemed, was unruffled by hundreds of colonial executions, unconcerned about adverse international reaction.[48] Lack of public interest in Kenyan affairs was not at variance with government thinking; it echoed it.[49] Neither group shared the existential concerns of the Nairobi administration and the settlers preoccupied with Mau Mau.

The same settlers who so disrupted Kenyan society had a stranglehold over Governor Sir Evelyn Baring's administration.[50] Jomo Kenyatta's April 1953 show trial, alongside five co-accused KAU organizers, was the final straw. The convictions handed down exposed an administration caving in to settler demands for retribution. Yet Baring's administration was upbeat, insisting that the 'wall of silence' within the Kikuyu community was collapsing. Five thousand 'spontaneous confessions' were allegedly secured in the rebellion's epicenter of Fort Hall district alone.[51] Closer to the mark was that violence was spiraling.[52] General Sir George Erskine and police chief Sir Arthur Young, architects of April 1954's Operation Anvil, a sweep in Nairobi that culminated in the arrest of some 30,000 Kikuyu, recognized that crackdowns achieved little so long as settler privilege determined administration policies. They were right. Attacks on loyalist settlements unleashed a cycle of retributive killings.[53]

Empire Violence Exposed

It took the coincidence in 1959 of two episodes of state-sanctioned violence in British Africa to inflict serious damage on a Westminster government. There was, by then, abundant evidence of systematic brutality in Kenya for those who cared to look.[54] Mass detention, collective punishments, plus an unending procession of judicial killings of Mau Mau convicts, were hardly state secrets. Successive Conservative governments minimized but did not refute them.[55]

What distinguished the murder of at least eleven detainees beaten to death by guards at the Hola internment camp was less the criminality of the original acts than the efforts by ministers and officials in Harold Macmillan's government first to deny the crime, then to shift responsibility for it. This pattern was repeated when a state of emergency was declared on March 15, 1959, in Nyasaland, smallest of the three territories forced into the shotgun marriage of the Central African Federation six years earlier.[56] Did this conjuncture of violence exposures in the spring of 1959 mark a watershed: seminal events pushing the lived experience of colonial repression from the shadows into the light? Not quite. Despite abundant evidence that suspected oppositionists were brutally treated, it seems unlikely that British authorities, metropolitan or colonial, felt compelled to decolonize faster as a result. At the same time as the Hola revelations hit domestic and global headlines, the government in Nairobi deepened cooperation with constituencies of Kenyan 'loyalists' set to take power at independence.[57]

Admittedly, no one in authority cared to highlight these working arrangements or the permissive environment for abuses they fostered. Searching for positive publicity elsewhere, administrators fixated on improvements to Kenya's labor market. As propaganda, the pickings were slim. A protracted national rail strike in November 1959 was the largest of sixty-seven registered trade disputes that year, together causing almost half a million lost man-hours among the colony's waged labor force. Set alongside this, women's involvement in the formal economy actually declined during 1959 to 14 percent of the total. The lack of social protections for the much larger proportion of women working in the informal economy of agricultural day labor remained an embarrassment.[58] The colonial government did find something to celebrate in new wage councils and other workplace arbitration committees within the docks industry in and around Mombasa. But this was cold comfort for a colony supposedly on the cusp of a peaceful transfer of power.[59]

As the decade came to an end, few Britons, in government or outside it, paid close attention to black Africa, its problems, or the abuses of its people.[60] Kanyama Chiume, working from exile in London as publicity secretary for the Nyasaland African Congress and backed by the left-leaning pressure group the Union of Democratic Control (UDC), strove to make Britons aware of the repression conducted in their name during the 1959 crackdown in his homeland. Chiume's pamphlet *Nyasaland Speaks: An Appeal to the British People* presumed that the British public would oppose the injustice of white minority rule once they were made aware of it. Some Labour MPs drew on Chiume's analysis to lambast Emergency Rule in Nyasaland but, as historian Ismay Milford points out, to Chiume's chagrin the British public remained more or less unmoved.[61] Evidence of an ingrained casual racism, this was also a double-edged sword. The white settlers of Kenya, the Central African Federation, and South Africa failed to realize that limited British interest in Africa extended to them as well. The dedicated moralists of the UDC and Fenner Brockway's Movement for Colonial Freedom (MCF) notwithstanding, few Britons were much exercised by hangings in Kenyan jails or brutality in its internment camps. But nor were they particularly bothered about settler interests. The brief furor over the Nyasaland Emergency in March 1959 and the coruscating official inquiry—the Devlin Report—that it generated, were indictments not just of British imperial deceit, but of white Rhodesian racist supremacy as well.[62] The problem was that the furor itself was temporary, more a storm in a colonial teacup than a tempest in metropolitan politics.[63] Settlers were still dominant and might even get away with murder, but they were wrong to assume that British society would back them.[64] Few Britons would go to the wall for empire; fewer still would do so for its settlers.

The cognitive gap between diehard settler colonialism and British public apathy was exemplified less by apartheid South Africa, too independent and too stridently different to satisfy the ritualistic requirements of Commonwealth loyalty, than by Southern Rhodesia, the loyal wannabe Dominion that never was.[65] Acutely conscious of their minority status and what one historian describes as the 'hidden ubiquity' of population politics, the fear of being swamped, Southern Rhodesia's whites were increasingly at odds not just with Britain's government but with its society, too.[66] The ersatz English provincial propriety of some South Rhodesian whites and the disappointments among other, more recent immigrants with a country less prosperous than they had assumed were each in different ways a world apart from 1960s Britain.[67] Admittedly, some Britons, including serving military personnel, were swayed by Rhodesian invocations of shared wartime pasts.[68] Far more were either unmoved by the settlers' appeals for support or were uncertain about what differentiated Rhodesia from South Africa. Fewer still understood the challenges of Rhodesia's rural environment and the 'bushcraft' that meant so much to the white conscripts sent to fight for minority rule.[69]

As for South Africa, British peace activists, MCF stalwarts, Anglican churchmen, and university students were so repelled by the apartheid state's racist oppression that they organized against it.[70] But a large proportion of Britain's voters never got involved at all. Things were changing, but gradually. The fusion of anticolonialism and antiracism into an antiapartheid social movement added a clearer moral complexion to the public discussion of colonial violence. And the mass shooting of unarmed protesters by South African security forces at the Sharpeville Township on March 21, 1960, lent that moral dimension imperative power.[71] A larger, more permanent antiapartheid campaign took shape, its progress marked by new tactics of mass opposition, from public boycotts of South African produce to permanent pickets against South African and Rhodesian diplomatic centers and corporate interests in Britain.[72] Two factors worked in its favor. One was that antiapartheid campaigning had global resonance. It chimed with Third Worldist and civil rights causes the world over. The other was that apartheid's injustice stimulated discussion about structural connections between colonialism, racism, and Britain's overseas trade.[73]

Once a blurry background feature of Britain's imperial landscape, the dissonance between changing British political culture and immoveable settler dominance in Southern Africa came into focus after 1959.[74] The toxic mix there of entrenched white-minority rule and British reforms frustrated by settler opposition had a long history. As long ago as 1923, Britain's long-term schema for Northern Rhodesia (Zambia) included democratization and self-government. These plans were thrown into reverse by the creation of the Central African Federation (CAF) in October 1953, which condemned Northern Rhodesia and Nyasaland (Malawi) to the stewardship of Southern Rhodesia's (Zimbabwe) settler government.[75] From that date forward, African anticolonial opposition in all three territories was conditioned by Britain's bad faith.[76] Central to this sense of betrayal was the conviction that the Colonial Office had floated the CAF on three false premises. First was that the industrial wealth of Northern Rhodesia's copperbelt would benefit the agricultural economies of Southern Rhodesia and Nyasaland; second, that federal governance might dilute the stifling dominance of Southern Rhodesia's whites while blocking any northward advance of South African apartheid.[77] The third premise was that the British state accepted the case for black majority rule. Behind the scenes in Whitehall, more instrumental concerns were in play. The CAF was a cost-cutter and a confidence trick.[78] It satisfied Treasury pressure to be rid of unprofitable commitments to Nyasaland. And it allowed the Colonial Office to depict federation as imaginative, well intentioned, even reformist, not the capitulation to white settlerism it was.[79]

By the time of its collapse in December 1963 the CAF had come to symbolize 'the racialized asymmetries of incorporation into the imperial state'.[80] Worse was to come for the African majority in the CAF's dominant component, Southern Rhodesia. Ian Smith's Rhodesian Front (RF), backed by far-right segregationist parties, won Southern Rhodesia's 1962 election on a platform of unilateral independence as protection against externally enforced democratization. When, during 1964, both Zambia (Northern Rhodesia) and Malawi (Nyasaland) became independent 'frontline' states in Southern Africa's transregional struggle against colonialism, a vigorous RF riposte grew more likely. In November 1965 it came. Responding to British efforts to impose a constrictive state of emergency, Smith's government made their long-threatened unilateral declaration of independence (UDI) in a now separate state of Rhodesia.[81]

The 'independence' in question was odd. The RF government in Salisbury was not constitutionally sovereign.[82] Echoing the UN statement on the matter, Labour Prime Minister Harold Wilson insisted that UDI was an illegal action to defend white-minority rule, not a decolonization representing the will of the majority.[83] Wilson was stating the obvious and preparing the political ground for UN-backed sanctions, but his options were otherwise limited.[84] Among the former 'white' Dominions, Canada went furthest in trying to block UDI.[85] Wilson's government expressed outrage at Rhodesia's actions, as did much of the British press, the broadcast media, and the trade union movement. But few in parliament, the military, or the British public favored the intervention needed to get Smith out.[86] Rhodesia's foreign missions faced closure or years of clamorous demonstrations but, as the country's judges conceded, their renegade home government could issue laws, currency, and passports and lock people up.[87] Rhodesia's African political parties and a broader coalition, the People's Caretaker Council, were already outlawed, their leaders jailed. Successor groups were soon established but operated from exile in the frontline states of Zambia, Tanzania, and, later, Mozambique. Working with Soviet bloc, Chinese, and Organization of African Unity sponsors and drawn to pan-Africanist ideals, they recast themselves as liberation movements: Joshua Nkomo's Zimbabwe African People's Union (ZAPU) and its rival Zimbabwe African National Union (ZANU), headed by Herbert Chitepo, Robert Mugabe, and Reverend Ndabaningi Sithole. Of these men, only Herbert Chitepo avoided the long prison terms that kept Nkomo, Mugabe, and Sithole behind bars for much of the decade following UDI. But Chitepo fell victim to a Lusaka car bomb on March 18, 1975, the prelude to a power struggle from which Mugabe emerged as head of a revitalized ZANU (Patriotic Front) in 1978.[88]

Support for Zimbabwean independence brought together African states, the OAU, and Third Worldists, a transnational unity of purpose that jarred with internecine violence between ZAPU and ZANU. It was years before their armed wings maximized their strategic advantages of sympathetic frontline states, widespread sanctuary bases, foreign arms supply, abundant recruits, and global sympathy.[89] Unwilling to endorse armed liberation, in the late 1960s the United States and other leading industrial nations shifted their attention to the sanctions pushed for by Britain and approved by the UN in late 1966.[90]

The Wilson government made it clear before UDI that it would not use military force to dictate the outcome in Rhodesia. So sanctions became Westminster's weapon of choice.[91] The results were disappointing, sometimes paradoxical, and often farcical. Superficially, prospects looked good for the economic strangulation of a landlocked country reliant on oil imports to keep industry working and with a single hydroelectric dam on its Zambian border to keep the lights on. The Rhodesian Treasury's dependence on export revenues from white-owned tobacco farms suggested the same conclusion. Not so. The British government did not enforce an oil embargo, nor did Lyndon Johnson's administration push it to do so.[92] Exporters in partner countries—West Germany, France, Japan, and others—filled the gaps left by those sanctions that Britain did impose.[93] More important locally, South Africa and Portuguese Africa, each offering arterial road and rail communications to the coast, undermined the entire sanctions apparatus. RF strategists and Rhodesia's industrial producers became adept sanctions-busters. The Salisbury government had moved vital cash reserves out of Britain before sanctions were imposed. Rhodesia's expulsion from the sterling area before Britain's severe 1967 devaluation could even be seen as a lucky escape.[94] Local manufacturers meanwhile worked closely with Smith's government in producing those items considered either politically essential or culturally significant in sustaining white community morale—medicines and processed foods in the former category; cosmetics, hosiery, and swimming pool paints in the latter.[95] Sanctions never determined the outcome of Rhodesia's hidden war. They descended instead into knockabout political theater, with symbolic blows struck for or against the regime.[96]

Hiding France's Decolonization Wars

Do French Empire developments suggest distinctive patterns similar to those in decolonization's wars? On May 15, 1954, dignitaries in Phúc Yên, urban hub of Vietnam's Vĩnh Phúc province in the Red River Delta fifty kilometers upstream from Hanoi, submitted a petition to the colonial garrison. The petitioners wanted an hour's extension, from 9:30 to 10:30 p.m., before the nightly military curfew was imposed. The French sector commander, Lieutenant-Colonel Pierre Huot, rejected their request three days later. His response was polite but firm. It was thanks to the army's night patrols that life in Phúc Yên remained so calm. Viet Minh insurgents were active nearby, and experience proved that most attacks were launched under cover of darkness. Far better that Phúc Yên's townsfolk endure curfew restrictions than risk more numerous Viet Minh incursions.[97] A pragmatic discussion between civilian petitioners and their counterinsurgent 'protectors', at another level this dialogue is strange.

Ten days earlier, 435 kilometers west of Phúc Yên's emptied streets, the People's Army of Vietnam (PAVN) had won a signal victory at the Dien Biên Phu fortress complex. News of Dien Biên Phu's fall had an electrifying effect globally and locally. In a peace conference then in session at Geneva, international negotiations for French withdrawal from Vietnam quickened. Meanwhile, at the heart of Huot's patrol sector, in the towns and settlements outlying Hanoi, desertions from 'home guard'-type units surged from a trickle to a flood.[98] These outcomes were not unforeseen. Aware that Indochina was slipping from their grasp, in October 1953 French high command staff in Saigon established a grandly named 'War Committee'—not so much a strategic planning forum as the improvised stopgap of a bureaucracy unfit for purpose.[99] The war's enormous financial costs—over 70 percent of which were met by the US Treasury—stifled French schemes for inward investment or the provision of administrative services of the type commonly tied to counterinsurgency efforts. In May 1953 René Mayer's Paris government devalued the Vietnamese piaster, reducing its franc exchange rate from seventeen to ten.[100] Financially expedient, the decision slashed the piaster's purchasing power, triggering a realignment of noncommunist nationalists in Southern Vietnam. Towns far to the north were closer to the war's epicenter a year later, but Southern Vietnam's politico-religious groups shared the nationwide disgust at the condition in which France was leaving Vietnam.[101] Phúc Yên was typical: being guarded by a corpse command not developed by a living government. The former 'associated states' of Cambodia and Laos were by then edging closer to self-government.[102] Larger tracts of Northern Vietnam were slipping into Viet Minh hands. Refugees were streaming southward, anticipating a Communist victory.[103] Operationalizing French military plans in these circumstances was impossible.

Throughout these turbulent months the inhabitants of Phúc Yên abided by their curfew. Or did they? Huot's sangfroid in May 1954, patiently advising the disappointed petitioners to be indoors by 9:30 p.m., masked the fact that the town's fringes were already beholden to Viet Minh fighters. Stricter lockdowns in the town center were essential to free up troops to patrol Phúc Yên's unruly outer districts. So the town was not some aberrant oasis of calm but a microcosm of the war. Internecine conflicts—between affluent center and impoverished edges, between communist and noncommunist, between those who had taken sides and those desperate to avoid doing so—were part of its endgame.[104] Exposing the complexities of Phúc Yên's violent decolonization means digging beneath a binary narrative of conflict between the French and their external backers, and the North Vietnamese and theirs.

It might seem obvious that hiding decolonization wars was impossible for France because in its two largest empire breakdowns, in Vietnam and Algeria, violent oppositionists won. But things were not so transparent. French governments, colonial administrations, and their security force adjuncts worked hard to conceal the nature of colonial counterinsurgency and its disastrous outcomes. This is where Phúc Yên's disputed curfew comes into the picture. In May 1954 the Vietnamese communist–nationalist coalition secured another victory for violent decolonization, only to see it snatched away by American intervention. The United Nations hosted a conference to discuss the resolution of wars in Korea and Vietnam, but local representatives were never at the top table.[105] Instead, the organization proved toothless, unable to make the Geneva conference settlement over Vietnam stick, unwilling to challenge America's rejection of it.

Painfully visible to its targets, colonial repression required concealment from metropolitan audiences, from hostile nations, from global publics and the transnational networks among them. The imperial strategies adopted to hide decolonization's wars ranged from assertions of unilateral sovereign control and, therefore, of sole competence over 'internal' colonial security, to flat denials about the violence going on—its perpetrators, its purpose, its prospects—and about its victims and their rights. All these strategies were a subterfuge, a lie that denied violent decolonization was gathering pace. Multiple governments, finding empire politically convenient, tolerated the deceit. Others accepted that terroristic disorders required suppression. Supranational agencies did better, less through summitry or intervention than by paying attention to violence. Perhaps the UN had teeth after all.

Psychologies of Colonialist Denial: From Madagascar to Algeria

Hiding decolonization's wars began by minimizing that violence. French social psychologist Octave Mannoni, an ethnographer in Madagascar's colonial administration, dismissed repression of the Malagasy revolt in 1947 as 'theatrical'. Killings of villagers and novel forms of murder such as dropping detainees from aircraft were demonstrative acts to restore order to the minds of a local population reflexively dependent on the discipline of external authority.[106] Frantz Fanon, the Martinican psychiatrist who championed the emancipatory potential of revolutionary anticolonialism, found Mannoni's views repugnant. In his 1952 work *Black Skin, White Masks*, Fanon excoriated Mannoni, also the author of a best-selling book, *Prospero and Caliban: The Psychology of Colonization*, which purportedly explained the rebels' thinking. According to Mannoni, leaders and followers of Madagascar's anticolonial opposition, the Mouvement Démocratique de la Rénovation Malgache (MDRM), were too immature psychologically to make independence work. Fanon tore at the racial stereotyping in Mannoni's interpretation, ridiculing his inability to admit that Malagasy reacted rationally against decades of cultural denigration. In a discussion about hiding decolonization's wars, the point is that French officials drew on Mannoni's work for years to come, dismissing the Madagascar rebellion as the work of educated extremists who manipulated villagers' cravings for social improvements that, in truth, only France could deliver.[107]

The poisonous combination of racist othering, psychiatric manipulation, and social-scientific modernization strategies culminated not in Madagascar but a decade later in Algeria. After the initial Front de Libération Nationale (FLN) uprising on November 1, 1954, the Algerian conflict grew slowly at first, punctuated by insurgent attacks and consequent rural crackdowns until March 1956. At that point, Guy Mollet's Republican Front coalition in Paris dramatically expanded the war. Martial law applied nationally. Hundreds of thousands of conscripts became liable for service in Algeria, a fate young Frenchmen had avoided throughout the war in Vietnam.[108]

Drilling down to the front line, a strange mix of harsh realism and dislocated unreality characterizes day-to-day correspondence surrounding the war's 1956 transformation. The army intelligence bureau in Paris sifted through reports on Armée de Libération Nationale (ALN) killings, security force sweeps, the state of local opinion, and the administrative difficulties within each sector command. In the first reporting period after Mollet's government introduced its Special Powers program to Algeria on March 15, bureau chief Colonel Jean Dalstein was cautiously optimistic.[109] The Special Powers, an about-turn for a newly elected government that had promised a negotiated end to Algeria's war, were meant to be preemptive.[110] Informants indicated that the quickening rhythm of ALN attacks prefigured a general offensive in which the insurgents would try to seize a major town from which to proclaim a 'free Algerian government'. That threat of an attempted urban occupation, it now seemed, was overblown. There was still no nationwide rebellion, no 'general terrorist uprising' in Dalstein's more loaded words. But ALN violence was increasing in regions of the Algerian interior worst affected by rebel exactions. Public servants faced mounting threats. Their places of work—police stations, government buildings, schools, and post offices—were being systematically destroyed. Weekly markets, another favored target, were forced to close, bringing rural commerce to a standstill. The fabric of French administrative and economic control was being torn away.[111]

Two months later, in May 1956, with emergency restrictions and army reinforcement in full swing, Dalstein mulled over the latest intelligence with greater confidence. Conscript deployment freed up frontline units to hunt insurgents. ALN losses looked unsustainable. Algerians caught in the

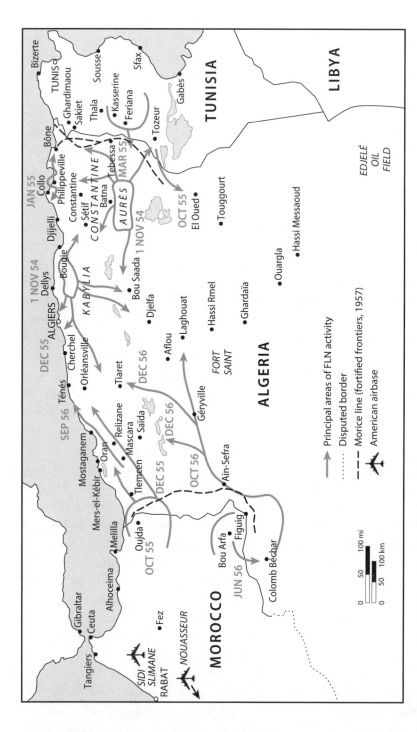

MAP 10.2. The spread of the Algerian rebellion.

crossfire understood that the balance of the war was shifting France's way. Dalstein dwelt on encouraging indications from two regions in particular. Around the eastern market town of Guelma, epicenter of the earlier Algerian uprising in May 1945, locals were requesting army assistance to protect homes and farmland. And south of Algiers in the Soummam Valley, villagers were forming self-defense groups to resist ALN incursions.[112]

Or so it seemed. Reliance on bureaucratized counterinsurgency, statistical analyses of 'kill rates', and other supposed indicators of security force advance flattered to deceive. In July, eight weeks after Dalstein filed his report, ALN commanders and FLN party leaders gathered in that same Soummam Valley to agree to the next stage of the Algerian War. They would sustain rural insurgency (often targeting the loyalists who so impressed Dalstein) while opening a new phase of urban guerrilla warfare and investing in the conflict's internationalization.[113] After Soummam, the FLN-ALN refined their methods of social control, from collecting funds and recruiting informants to enforcing boycotts and punishing 'traitors' to the national cause.[114] The elimination of political rivals intensified in 1957, the principal target being the Mouvement National Algérien (MNA), the only credible challenger to the FLN's hegemonic direction of integral nationalism.[115] Opponents who could not be swayed were coerced or killed. Thousands died in an undeclared civil war between the rival movements across Algeria and cities in mainland France as the FLN, the more aggressive challenger, imposed its vision of nationhood.[116]

As France transitioned to a Gaullist Fifth Republic in late 1958, its response to the insecurities of Algeria's majority population was double-edged: a war of destruction against the ALN and the promise of better living standards through the largest colonial development project of the late 1950s, the Constantine Plan.[117] Launched by President de Gaulle in the eastern provincial capital of Constantine on October 3, 1958, and overseen by his prime minister, Michel Debré, the plan's headline objectives—apartment housing, the rationalization of agriculture, comprehensive educational provision—fitted a social policy agenda focused on the modernization of Algerian domestic spaces, family behaviors, and working practices.[118] The goal was to turn Algerian Muslims into economic actors receptive to integration with France; in the words of Paul Chauvin, president of the Algiers Chamber of Agriculture, to end peasant confinement within their *secteur traditionnel* by giving them opportunities to join settlers and other, more prosperous Algerians in the *secteur évolué*.[119] Again, the coercive dimensions were hidden. The 'Thousand New Villages' Project piloted by Paul Delouvrier, Algeria's final colonial governor, concealed the military strategy driving it.[120] Agricultural cooperatives and rural credit agencies, some of the Constantine Plan's biggest spenders, also facilitated the forcible resettlements that emptied the Algerian countryside between 1957 and 1962.[121]

The Constantine Plan's unspoken military rationale reminds us that it was formulated amid the fallout from the French government's acrimonious closure of the army's Psychological Warfare Bureau following accusations of extremist indoctrination and systematic rights abuses. The bureau's zealous soldier-psychologists, including colonels Michel Goussault and Yves Godard, insisted that the key to defeating the FLN was to outstrip its capacity for social control.[122] But a more recent arrival, David Galula, a colonial infantry captain based in the Berber highlands of Kabylia, exerted more lasting influence over governmental policy.[123] Galula's message was that Algerians remained biddable, their 'allegiance' dependent on deliverable public goods, not intimidation or indoctrination.[124] Mirroring Galula, Constantine Plan director Jean Vibert and his staff avoided using social psychology to describe the change in attitudes sought, stressing material benefits rather than the social engineering behind them.[125]

A Regime Exposed

As mentioned earlier, global decolonization pressures and minimal public identification with Rhodesia's invocation of kith and kin put British society at odds with its African settlers in the nine years separating the Suez humiliation of 1956 and UDI. In each case, the British state was left looking powerless. Over Suez, it was morally discredited as well. British abandonment of an attempted military overthrow of the Egyptian regime followed a joint invasion concocted with France and Israel. American annoyance, UN opposition, and wider global outrage destabilized the British economy, compelling Conservative prime minister Anthony Eden to resign. Nine years later Labour premier Harold Wilson took a more principled stand, this time in opposing Rhodesian white minority rule. Again, though, the limits to British imperial power were exposed.[126] In a favored metaphor of the day, these were transitional years in which history's tide turned against empire before sinking it.[127] At the same time, divisions between France and its African settlers deepened. We need to return to the end of the Second World War to explain why.

The dysfunctional quality of coalition politics in the first decade of the French Fourth Republic can be overplayed. In essence, the country was governed from the center-left in the formative years of 1944–1947 and from the center-right between May 1947 and December 1955. Powerful outsiders sniped from opposing ideological flanks. Neither the Communists nor the supporters of a Charles de Gaulle presidency were reconciled to a parliamentary regime each derided as a self-serving *système*. But the composition of French coalition government made little difference to colonial populations in territories convulsed by decolonization violence in the postwar decade—Vietnam, Madagascar, and Algeria. Political parties, social movements, sects, and religious congregations in these three territories were vigorously repressed.[128] Governing coalitions of differing political stripes in Paris prosecuted war in Indochina despite mounting public opposition to it at home and abroad. Suppression of the Madagascar Revolt was counted a political success at the time. And repression of the Sétif uprising over the summer of 1945 set a postwar course for colonial politics in Algeria in which oppositional voices were silenced, nationalist organizers imprisoned, and elections rigged.[129] Constitutional changes and local government reforms promised within a 1947 enabling law, the Algerian Statute (an awkward afterthought to the previous year's French Union), went unfulfilled.[130] In the Jekyll and Hyde world of Fourth Republic colonialism, these were the destructive counterparts to the postwar flowering of party politics, labor activism, and negritude political culture in French West Africa and stood in contradistinction to it.[131]

Worsening civil–military tensions as the Algerian conflict spiraled out of control made France ungovernable through the mechanisms of the Fourth Republic. Parliamentarians could unseat governments through votes of no confidence. Such votes could be held in check as long as party discipline held and deputies could be persuaded that their electors would punish them for bringing down ministries on a whim. These calculations broke down after 1956 as the Fourth Republic's 'in-groups'—its three main parties of government, the Radicals, the Christian Democrats of the Mouvement Républicain Populaire, and the Socialists—each fell apart.[132]

Antiregime Gaullists reaped the rewards. Clamor for systemic change from France's opposing political extremes was always background noise to Fourth Republic politics, but by 1957 other movements hostile to the Fourth Republic were burning out. On one side, the demi-fascists of Pierre Poujade's Union de défense des commerçants et artisans, raucously sectarian in their defense of small business, were losing grassroots support. On the other side, a French Communist Party massively popular in 1945–1946 looked increasingly irrelevant a decade later. Party grandees finally adopted a firmly anticolonial position at their annual congress in July 1956 and duly opposed collusion against Nasser's Egypt in October.[133] But they squirmed over the Soviet Union's contemporaneous invasion of Hungary, and their blue-collar militancy seemed out of step with a France embracing the high modernism of European integration and consumer choice. In short, extreme right and extreme left were as schismatic as the mainstream parties they detested. The one oppositional movement left to fill the void was Gaullism.[134] An obvious question to ask is why French politics went to war against itself. Structural deficiencies of the Fourth Republic système were there from the regime's inception. It took revolution in Algeria to turn disaffection into political warfare.[135] The stresses of the Algerian conflict undermined the Fourth Republic, but it was the regime itself—the overaccountability of ministers to parliamentary deputies, the unaccountability of governments for abusive security force violence overseas—that was at fault.

Social Dimensions

Security agencies' permissive violence, rights abuses, cover-ups, and collusion with ultra-rightists were echoed in other spheres of policy action, even those whose objectives seemed benevolent. In March 1954 administrative efforts championed by Algiers's reformist mayor, Jacques Chevallier, began to relocate the capital's underclass of shantytown residents to low-cost public housing.[136] The scheme's centerpieces, vast modernist apartment blocks designed by architect Fernand Pouillon, sprang up around the city's margins. Chevallier worked hard to build more, but this final episode in the colonial reconfiguration of the Algerian capital never kept pace with the influx of shantytown dwellers fleeing the insecurities of the countryside.[137] The later construction of *cités de transit*, simpler, temporary housing units terraced along the hillsides flanking the city, conveyed a stark message: moving from shantytown poverty to the relative comfort of public housing was conditional on obedience to French authority.[138]

The 'battle for housing' in Algiers soon emerged as a cultural frontline between the acculturation of Muslim Algerians to European practices of domesticity and popular resistance to the tighter administrative regulation that came with it. Comparable 'battles' over social services and primary health care, additional instruments of colonial assimilation, radiated outward from the coastal cities to the rural settlements at the heart of the shooting war.[139]

Otherwise prescient observers of Algeria's social situation inverted the logic of colonial discrimination to justify a French presence. Sociologist Pierre Bourdieu harbored no illusions about the impact of impoverishment on the rural communities he studied in Algeria's Berber highlands, but his conclusions were bleak: Algeria's social fabrics were so weakened that it was nonsense to imagine a cohesive nation woven together through war. Likewise, social anthropologist Germaine Tillion, a distinguished French resister and survivor of Ravensbrück concentration camp, spoke

FIGURE 10.2. 'Calm Mayor in Violent Algiers': Jacques Chevallier in
conversation with Algiers residents, 1954. Source: author's collection.

out against security force torture of Algerian detainees. Tillion nonetheless calculated that the legacies of economic dispossession among Algeria's peasant majority demanded more colonialism, not less.[140] France had
pauperized rural Algeria, but a de Gaulle presidency could enact the social
policies to rectify matters.[141] Tillion's stance infuriated the FLN leadership, who knew she had the ear of ministers in Paris.[142]

Tillion would get her wish. De Gaulle's return to office on May 29, 1958,
as savior of a new Fifth Republic changed the war but was not the precursor
to peace. As mentioned earlier, his government was quick to dismantle the
army's Fifth Bureau, power base of the protagonists of counterrevolutionary psychological warfare, but this did not signal any let-up in the war's
intensity.[143] From General Maurice Challe's rolling offensives of 1959–
1960 to the last-ditch terrorism of the Organisation de l'Armee Secrète
(OAS) in 1961–1962, Algerians faced greater violence as the Fifth Republic edged toward negotiation and withdrawal.[144] In the eighteen months
after de Gaulle took power in May 1958 the number of civilians forcibly

...Pour le peuple...

*Elle a pris en charge ses besoins,
elle soigne les femmes et les enfants...*

FIGURE 10.3. Healthcare wars—an ALN nursing team at work, no date. IISH, FLN, Fédération de France, AGTA, Bulletin intérieur R1, 'L'Algérie en marche.'

displaced from 'forbidden zones' in the country's rural interior rose from approximately 800,000 to over 1.5 million. Numbers climbed higher still as army offensives continued, eventually reaching 2.5 million, more than a third of Algeria's rural inhabitants.[145]

Housing provision, welfare programs, and medical care for rural Algerians, whether in their communities of origin or within resettlement camps, were meant to surpass FLN efforts to provide anything similar.[146] The FLN tried to establish alternate government structures at regional, or *wilaya*, level through local branches of its Organization of Political Administration.[147] Their efforts built on established village councils, or *djemâas*, and included health clinics, educational facilities, and judicial apparatus.[148]

Rebel governance struggled to put down deep roots because the French were never wholly shut out. Army development workers (in French, the Sections Administratives Spécialisées: SAS) oversaw the process, protected by Algerian auxiliary troops (*moghaznis*) and, once inside the camps, by 'self-defense units' recruited among the residents.[149] SAS-led policies were equally reliant on Algerian personnel, including 7,000 or so Algerian interpreters and ancillary staff of the Assistances Sanitaires et Sociétés rurales auxiliaires (ASSRA), the majority of them women, and the nurses of the mobile health care Équipes Médico-Sociales Itinéran-tes (EMSI). By 1961 SAS and EMSI teams were conducting hundreds of thousands of medical consultations. Although trying to deliver primary social care to every corner of Algerian society, the terms on which they did so provoked suspicion. Derided as *harkiettes* by their local clients, these female auxiliaries would find themselves on the wrong side of the conflict as it reached its climax.[150]

Determined that SAS medical provision should stand alone, the colonial government refused to allow humanitarian workers and medical staff of the Moroccan and Tunisian Red Crescent Societies to treat Algerians suspected of involvement in 'terrorist' violence.[151] For all the colonial effort to frame new settlements, welfare schemes, and medical treatments as proof of Franco-Algerian partnership in social modernization, these programs were tailored to fighting the FLN.[152] Officials and security force commanders still objectified the Algerian population as a blank emotional slate on which French political and sociological solutions could be drawn.[153] The inverse correlation between heightened violence, deeper state intervention, and the imminence of withdrawal was also embedded in a broader decolonization context. As was apparent in Vietnam and Kenya, and as would be repeated in Portuguese Africa, the 'very' late colonial state was the most socially devastating of all.[154]

It took conflict in Algeria, the last of France's major decolonization wars, to demolish the ethical case for empire in French political culture. France, the quintessential 'nation-state', was also an 'empire state' and, by the mid-1950s, finally had the economic wherewithal to pursue ambitious imperial projects. Whether on the new collective measure of gross domestic product or the older indexes of per capita income, French citizens were increasingly prosperous. Long-term economic growth delivered an unprecedented consumer boom, its benefits, from refrigerators to hot-water tanks, apparent in the home. The Treaty of Rome promised bigger markets, stable rural incomes, and European peace. And this more affluent France was the hub of a Francophone world identifiable with the Gaullist promotion of a distinctive *Francafrique* tied to the European Community.[155] Moving across the Mediterranean, there were nearly a million settlers to consider. Some were implicated in Algeria's violence, particularly in coastal cities that were culturally familiar and geographically nearby. Soldiers' letters, pictures, and phone calls home shrank the distance further.[156]

Beginning in July 1956 the French military presence in Algeria never fell below 400,000 for the remainder of the war. Most of those in uniform were conscripts and reservists, not volunteer professionals. Partners and parents saw images, albeit sanitized ones, of what was happening in cinema newsreels and, increasingly, on a living room television. Newspapers, local and national, covered the war extensively.[157] Radio bulletins gave daily casualty figures between light programming, traffic reports, and pop music. Within Algeria, during their May 1958 coup, French army officers of the 'Public Salvation Committee' were quick to air their demands for a Gaullist takeover on a dedicated Radio Algérie.[158] Other radio broadcasts, some sponsored by the FLN, others by Nasser's Egypt, still others by Eastern bloc partners, were equally subversive, broadcasting evidence of colonial misdeeds.[159] Fanon was surely right in arguing that tinny voices from cheap transistor radios cemented Algerians' sense of shared struggle against injustice.[160] Enough French people within and without the state apparatus spoke out against the war to provide incontrovertible proof of human violation, ecological spoliation, military conspiracy, and political corruption. *Algérie française* became a lie to many, a myth others clung onto. At its heart was the idea of a Mediterranean society uniquely forged by European settlement.[161] But if that was Algeria's achievement, why were the indigenous majority so unhappy with the result? Thousands were giving their lives to end it.[162]

Collective sacrifice was powerful, but individual cases of maltreatment were more relatable, their details vivid, visceral, shocking. Those of the 'three Djamilas', Bouhired, Bouazzi and Boupacha, are the best known. Superficially, the three were similar. Aged between nineteen (Bouazzi) and twenty-three (Bouhired) at the time of arrest, they were accused of planting bombs in Algiers, the first two in 1956–1957, Boupacha in 1959.[163] Bouhired was the most ideologically committed, but each defied gender norms. They faced crass stereotyping nonetheless.[164] A fixation in the French media on their European dress and youthful good looks made it easier to misrepresent them as naïve girls led astray by manipulative FLN handlers. Press accounts of their trial hearings, which culminated in death sentences for Bouhired and Bouazzi, were insultingly trivial, sexualizing the defendants by dwelling on the young women's clothing and à la mode hairstyles.[165] FLN propaganda lionized the women but rarely let them speak for themselves.[166] Others were more measured. Djamila

Bouhired's lawyer and future husband, the Franco-Vietnamese lawyer Jacques Vergès, published details of her torture by army interrogators to discredit the verdict against her.[167] Vergès's campaigning exposed the legal system's colonial configuration and institutional bias, adding momentum to international petitions supporting Bouhired from nonaligned and Eastern bloc countries.[168]

Djamila Boupacha's case was more notorious still. She was arrested five months after a bomb was placed in Algiers University's Brasserie des Facultés in September 1959. What happened next was unprecedented, not because its awful details exposed repressive behavior either unusual or unknown, but thanks to the diversity of protest against it. Leftists, anticolonialists, pro-choice women's groups, artists, and civil society petitioners mobilized in support of Franco-Tunisian lawyer Gisèle Halimi's legal challenge against Boupacha's trial within Algeria's criminal justice system.[169] Celebrity involvement, including that of artist Pablo Picasso and writer-philosopher Simone de Beauvoir, was matched by media campaigns across the Arab world and the Communist bloc, plus relentless FLN petitioning at the United Nations and elsewhere. These actions, and the evidence they revealed, lent Djamila Boupacha's experience an emblematic authority. This was not just a test case against army torture; it was an unanswerable argument against colonialism itself.[170]

The emotional intensity of Djamila Boupacha's story exposed colonial power relations by juxtaposing the victim's appalling experiences with the workaday banality of her torturers' cruelty. On the night of February 10, 1960, the twenty-two-year-old was arrested and beaten up in her home, along with her father and brother-in-law. The three were then separated. Djamila Boupacha was detained for thirty-three days, first at the El Biar barracks 'selection center' before her transfer five days later to Hussein-Dey prison, which housed one of several Algiers interrogation centers operated by the army's mobile security group. Her rib, broken during the initial arrest, was left untreated.[171]

But the torture began in earnest at Hussein-Dey. Two French soldiers, three Algerian *harkis*, and a trio of plainclothes policemen took part. Their anonymity stood in mocking contrast to the grotesque intimacy of the pain they were about to inflict. The young woman was stripped. Electrodes were attached with Scotch tape to her breasts and legs. More were taped to her face, her groin, and her vagina. Electric shocks alternated with cigarette burnings, again targeting the most sensitive, private parts of the body. She was later suspended from a rod above a bathtub, submerged, and lifted out just before she lost consciousness. The torturers made jokes, taunting her about imminent sexual violence, much as French soldiers used a convivial patois to euphemize their actions, describing Algerian victims convulsing to shocks delivered from field-radio batteries as *le rock 'n' roll*.[172]

Sometime after, Boupacha, semiconscious and covered in blood, was dragged along a corridor to be paraded before her father, he so grievously injured by repeated beatings that he ended up in the Emergency Room at Algiers's Maillot Hospital.[173] This was counterinsurgency in the Algerian War: casually sadistic, but calculating in its transgression of moral boundaries.

It is easy to point out cause célèbre legal cases in which individual colonial victims, often those tortured in detention or facing capital punishment for alleged involvement in 'terrorist' acts, came to international attention. But it can be misleading. For one thing, countless others never received such scrutiny. For another, neither the abuse of colonial detainees nor governmental toleration of it was new. Feminist writer and investigative journalist Andrée Viollis had denounced the systematic abuses of political prisoners in French Vietnam, which spiked after suppression of the Nghệ Tĩnh soviet movement in 1930–1931.[174] The crackdown decimated Vietnam's leading nationalist force, the VNQDD, and outlawed the newly formed Indochinese Communist Party. Thousands of its rank-and-file supporters were locked up. These measures registered in the radicalization of anticolonial politics.[175] Viollis's resulting book, *Indochine SOS*, first published in 1935, has been held up as the first in a series of literary protests against the habitual use of torture in the French Empire. The book's high-profile reception, including serialization in the national press, makes plain that there was abundant evidence of police and army malpractice decades before the Algerian conflict brought the issue to public attention in France and globally.[176]

So why was there little reaction for so long? A sideways glance at a group determined not to stay silent explains why. From its inception in the late 1940s to its demise at the height of the Algerian War, a French human rights organization, the Commission against the Concentration Camp Regime (Commission Internationale Contre le Régime Concentrationnaire, or CICRC), brought together public intellectuals determined to oppose any recurrence of the Nazi horrors they had experienced.[177] Claiming a universal right to expose internment regimes anywhere, the CICRC fell victim to its internal contradictions. The movement secured unprecedented access to Algeria's prisons, internment camps, and 'triage centers' in 1957, only for its leading French and Belgian members to fall out over how to interpret the illegal mass detention of Algerian civilians, many of whom were also victims of torture.[178]

Some in the CICRC were determined to call out human rights abuses. But others defended France's actions in Algeria in expedient terms of ends justifying means, echoing the excuses advanced by successive governments in Paris. Locking up Algerians in their tens of thousands, subjecting huge numbers to physical, sexual, and psychological torture, and 'disappearing' untold numbers of these victims were actions rationalized through logics of relativity: as understandable responses to FLN killings, as measures that prevented troops from executing detainees on the spot, and as forms of incarceration, which could not be compared to the industrialized murder of the Holocaust. Few CICRC activists were anticolonialists, but it is perverse that, between 1957 and 1959, an organization opposed to political detention found its reports on rights abuses in Algeria cited in the French media, in diplomatic exchanges and at the UN, not to condemn the actions of France's security forces but to expiate them.[179]

This was at a time when counterinsurgency inside Algeria meant mass detentions, free-fire zones, and forcible resettlement, alongside the security forces' campaign against the FLN's urban guerrilla network during the ten-month battle of Algiers.[180] The violence involved left no room for doubt about the loss of Algerians' basic human security, let alone their status as rights-bearing individuals within territory supposedly integrated with France.[181] With Jacques Massu's Algiers army command claiming victory in the battle for control of the city in October 1957, a group of forty-nine attorneys of the Paris Court of Appeals, who defended persons indicted before the Algerian courts, protested against the impossibility of providing normal standards of defense for the accused and the degrading methods of interrogation practiced. Torture of the type meted out to Djamila Boupacha was routine.[182]

The lawyers' evidence was reproduced verbatim in *Le Monde*, but their exposé did not change things.[183] If anything, abuses worsened in the following year. With Charles de Gaulle about to confirm his position as president of a new Fifth Republic in Paris and the United Nations set to go into session in New York, in September 1958 the FLN's provisional government (French acronym: GPRA) suggested there were close to 400,000 civilian victims of aerial bombing, 'collateral damage' in army operations, and mass detentions. Algerian refugee numbers were climbing toward 300,000. And half a million of the 2.35 million rural dwellers eventually herded into resettlement camps were already displaced, their villages burned, their livestock gone.[184]

The collective punishment of Algerian civilians also explained the FLN's decision to act in mainland France. On the night of August 24, 1958, the movement's French Federation sabotaged French oil installations, munitions factories, and railroad signal boxes, evoking the FLN's initial acts in Algeria on November 1, 1954, the first day of the war. The symbolism went deeper. Clearly, the FLN could hit targets in France, but it chose strategic resources, not innocent civilians, to mark its commitment to abide by the Geneva Conventions, rules that France insisted did not apply in this conflict and that its security forces ignored. Blowing up gasoline storage tanks and weapons-making facilities was proof that the Algerian people would resist the extraction of their natural resources in the same way that they opposed their collective repression.[185] Finally, bringing the war to mainland France strengthened the FLN's claim as sole representative and defender of Algerians everywhere.[186]

These were powerful messages, but they jarred with the everyday humiliations experienced by Algerian immigrants. By this point almost half a million Algerian industrial laborers and their families in France lived under restriction.[187] Their unions and civil society groups were outlawed. Their access to social housing was made difficult or denied outright, confining many to shantytowns like those on the western and eastern fringes of Paris in Nanterre and Champigny.[188] Fear of arbitrary arrest and maltreatment in custody were ever-present.[189]

It was not, though, in France, but in Algiers that community protests finally put an end to hiding French decolonization's wars. Algiers exemplified colonial cities that were 'first ports of call' for foreign observers and local people seeking sanctuary from violence in the rural hinterland. It was a 'welfare arena' in which colonial capacity to deliver measurable improvements in living standards was visible to the wider world. The city's urban zoning exposed the hollowness of ameliorative colonial social policies next to severe limits on freedom of movement.[190] The Algiers demonstrations of December 11, 1960 were a case in point. Visually and aurally arresting, the protests proved what was achievable when a community could tolerate humiliation no more. Subject not only to spatial confinement but to OAS violence and the reactionary taunts of the settler-dominated Front for French Algeria, a multigenerational crowd burst out of the ethnically mixed districts of Belcourt and Clos-Salembier.[191]

The protesters chanted nationalist slogans. They waved improvised national flags. They pushed back the police lines trying to contain them. Police, soldiers and administration officials had coerced the capital's Algerian residents since the FLN's urban guerrilla network was broken up in 1957. Settler *ultras* terrorized them with bombs and lynch mobs. But, by December 1960, these instruments of colonial order were divided.[192] Settler support for the Army hard-liners gave license to OAS terror attacks, while police and gendarmes, invested in de Gaulle's emergent policy of negotiated withdrawal, were reluctant to shoot at unarmed demonstrators.[193] On this occasion, the presence of children and ululating women at the front of the protest made the use of live ammunition against them harder. So the December 11 protests got through to a watching world. More than a spontaneous outburst of pent-up frustration at life under colonial restriction, they were a call for the dignity of sovereign rights.[194]

The FLN did not plan them. Party activists were caught off guard, as were the capital's administrative services.[195] This was a community movement, which needed no party direction. The demonstrators' sympathies were abundantly clear anyway. Belcourt and Clos-Salembier were long-standing hubs of nationalist party activity. Overcrowding in these districts, as in the capital's outlying shantytowns, grew worse as rural families fled the violence of the Challe Plan's rolling offensives, undermining the efforts of the SAU (Sections Administratives Urbaines, city counterpart of the rural SAS) to combine welfare provision with political surveillance.[196] Defying the ultras' terror campaign and SAU intrusion, the collective voice of the Algerian street demanded independence now.

The call registered globally. It confirmed the impossibility of any Gaullist 'third way' between colonialism and self-determination. Press commentators, diplomatic observers, and UN delegates agreed that Algeria's authentic majority had spoken. Nationhood was an urgent ethical imperative.[197] Neighborhood activism was no transient phenomenon. Attempts by settler extremists and OAS 'commandos' to stifle it through vigilantism bred deeper defiance.[198] Local chapters of the Algerian women's union built a network of community groups that organized children's play areas, drop-in centers for expectant mothers, food banks, blood drives, homeless shelters, and evening classes. In the Algiers casbah, these initiatives anticipated a comprehensive family registration process, conducted weeks before Algeria's formal independence on July 3, 1962.[199]

Whether or not American observers in Washington or Western delegations to the United Nations in New York viewed these Algerian events through a 'Cold War lens' or superimposed their fears of racial conflict between the white capitalist 'First World' and the Afro-Asian peoples of a radical 'Third World', the result was an unwillingness to align with French colonial interests.[200] Gone forever was the time when an imperial power could hide its violence, claiming a presumptive right to articulate colonial subjects' best interests.[201] Global publics knew better.

Conclusion

This chapter explored conflicts, their scale and practice concealed, whose local complexities and transnational reverberations shaped the forms taken by decolonization. In the imperial rhetoric of decolonization's wars, restoring order meant the resumption of whatever sociopolitical plans, economic projects, or other modernization schemes were interrupted by conflict. The priority was to limit the fallout from the exposure of rights abuses, not to question the actions that produced them as counterinsurgency drives unfolded. The logic of 'order before reform' was trotted out as stock justification for late colonial counterinsurgency until global audiences refused to believe it. But imperial powers felt less need to defend the legal arrangements and security apparatus intrinsic to colonies' violent liminal condition at other times. Instead, the everyday violence of colonialism was just that: a normative standard with supposedly structural causes rather than a massive agglomeration of civilian maltreatment. This is the subject of the next chapter.

CHAPTER ELEVEN

Decolonization and the Civilianization of Violence

LOCAL POPULATIONS BORE the brunt of decolonization's violence.[1] Markers of identity, from the language people spoke and the places they worshipped to the job they performed could prompt accusations of association with colonial authority or insurgent ideology, exposing them to cycles of attack and reprisal.[2] In other communities that were ostensibly multiethnic, multicultural, or multifaith, unarmed colonial subjects from minority or outsider groups faced more violent attacks than did the armed forces or insurgent groups that claimed authority over them. Common throughout was the refusal to acknowledge the 'civilian status' of colonial subjects, something never protected in the pluralities of colonial or international law.

Infants and the extremely old fared worst, particularly so when decolonization pressures triggered famine, the forced removal of resident populations, or hyperinflation and the unaffordability of essential goods. Among colonized women, sexual violence and anxieties about it constrained behavior. Other forms of violence, some clandestine and deniable, some public and demonstrative, targeted alleged supporters of one side or another. All of which raises a question: As analysts, should we approach decolonization through its violence?

Few would disagree that 'everyday violence' was intrinsic to colonialism. Recognizing the purposes of deliberate colonial harm whether physical or psychological, as well as its repetitious banality, is critical to understanding why certain groups among colonial subject populations— women, workers, and the young—were so exposed to it. As this chapter will argue, we need to look for other causal connections as well. One is the linkage between levels of insecurity and the intensity of violence. Another is the tendency for violence actors (those with executive powers) and violence workers (those inflicting the pain) to operate with less restraint over time. Locally, environments of violence differed.[3] A broad generalization may be ventured even so. Although systematized by late colonial authority, decolonization violence was increasingly enacted without precise instruction or concomitant constraint, producing performative cycles of retribution that only embedded colonial violence more deeply still.

Preceding chapters have discussed numerous acts of violence. The structural violence intrinsic to colonialism has also figured large as a social condition, as institutionalized discrimination, as a system of exploitation and rights denial. We've yet to consider something else. Must we identify late colonial violence as something distinct in order to understand decolonization? Discussions among just-war theorists, political scientists, and international lawyers about the ethics of inflicting harm to advance political objectives dwell on questions of intentionality, proportionality, and the status of human targets as combatants or civilians.[4] Comparable discussions about intrastate conflicts and 'irregular wars', in which the legal status of guerrillas and paramilitaries is blurry, often touch on colonial experiences but rarely engage the most basic question of all.[5] That is: What happens when victims of violence are classified not just along axes of combatant and noncombatant, but those of ethnic difference as well?[6]

Did imperial authorities coerce and kill in distinctive, even unique ways? What, if anything, distinguished the violence actors who opposed them as 'colonial' insurgents? After considering these epistemological questions, another task is to disaggregate the most politically decisive aspects of violent decolonization, those that accelerated the end of foreign rule. Politically decisive maybe, but this issue is as much social as it is political because its key component relates not to combatant strategies but to daily lives disrupted for the unarmed local inhabitants facing decolonization's violence.[7] These are the people discussed here. The unifying factor running through this chapter is the unarmed colonial subject: the civilian as victim and agent of decolonization.[8]

Let's first of all reflect on how 'civilians' in decolonization might be described along axes of gender, age, and activity. The tendency to feminize civilian populations can be as limiting as the presumption that acts of political violence were male activity. This is not to deny that colonial violence against civilian populations was highly gendered. It is simply to recall that young men and adolescent boys were peculiarly endangered as civilians, albeit for different reasons than women and girls of similar age.[9] The elderly, as well as the sick and the disabled, were especially vulnerable to population removal, internment, food denial, and other forms of collective punishment.[10] Beyond civilian communities, analyses sometimes characterize insurgencies as male, the involvement of women being treated as unusual whereas men's resorting to political violence is considered a matter of course.[11] This is odd. Women figure in all insurgencies.[12] In insurgent movements from the Viet Minh and Algeria's FLN to the Zimbabwean forces of ZIPRA and ZANLA, plus the PAIGC in Portuguese Guinea, women's participation in party militias, medical teams, and social welfare programs defied cultural mores, sometimes discomfiting patriarchs in the movements they served.[13] A likely underestimate, Algerian government statistics today still record 11,000 women as *moujahidate*, or 'freedom fighters', of whom 18 percent are described as 'military' personnel. In another record that surely conceals untold others, French army statistics list 1,343 Algerian female 'militants' imprisoned and 948 women killed.[14]

During decolonization struggles, women and girls, whether unarmed or armed, faced distinct, often sexual threats and other forms of retribution. But women were not without agency, whether as victims of violence or as individuals resolved to fight back.[15] A different point bears emphasizing here. Insurgent groups in their formative stages relied on their surrounding population not just for resources and other material aid, but for concealment.[16] Withholding information from government representatives about who rebels were and what they were doing was vital to their survival. This responsibility fell disproportionately on female householders tied to their location by family and work responsibilities. Bonds of ethnicity or kinship thickened such veils of secrecy, making it easier for insurgent groups to grow.[17]

Whether focused on issues of gender or not, it is a tautology to assert that high levels of empire violence and their replication between territories confirm the proposition that 'colonial violence' is a species apart. Examples of violence systematically pursued by nations without colonies and, more particularly, within regimes either wedded to purist ideologies or making transitions to democracy give the lie to such reductionist thinking.[18] The unprecedented scale of civilian maltreatment in the Second World War, its racialized character, and its gender imbalances were a dreadful prelude to decolonization's violence.[19] So too the 'violent peacetimes' in the immediate aftermath of the two World Wars, plus the layered violence of civil wars, ranging from the micro-level intimidation and killings within and between communities to the macro-level narratives of conflict between regime forces and their opponents, are now widely recognized as similar to decolonization conflicts that set neighbors against each other.[20]

What singles out late colonial societies are elements of political economy: high levels of male labor migration, gendered agricultural labor in which women fieldworkers played a central role, and the numerical predominance of women within family groups and household industries beyond the gaze of international scrutiny.[21] From these socioeconomic conditions, certain patterns of colonial violence followed. Women, for instance, faced abuse from paramilitaries recruited to police rural communities or resettlement camps where the defense mechanisms of kin networks and gendered living spaces were absent.[22]

Patterns of decolonization violence also inhered in colonial authority structures. Low-level intermediaries, mandarins, *caïds* and mayors, tribal chiefs, and village headmen provided the foundations of local government, tax collection, and legal punishment on which colonial authority was constructed.[23] Take taxes. Most colonial subjects faced levies on their person, property, and livestock, as well as on goods purchased.[1] The point is not that imperial governments were unduly extractive; rather, in delegating tax collection duties to chiefs, village leaders, and other indigenous auxiliaries, colonial administrations left intermediaries with unchecked powers of revenue extraction.[24] Local tax collectors personified the 'decentralized despotism' that Mahmood Mamdani considers characteristic of late colonialism, and they were frequently targeted by insurgent groups.[25]

It was in small towns and villages that violence against civilian officials was harshest. In part, this was a matter of geographical remoteness from police stations or army garrisons. More significant, though, was the poverty prevalent in the rural interior of numerous colonies, where disparities in wealth and social status between those working with the colonial system and those who defied it might be objectively narrow but subjectively critical.

Most local authority figures, whether or not they behaved corruptly, remained relatively poor by European standards. Even so, from Central America to Southeast Asia, these community leaders seemed privileged next to the farmers and laborers who provided the rank and file of so many rural insurgencies. A little more wealth, a whiff of corrupt practice, and accusations of collaboration were enough to condemn countless village officials in the eyes of their neighbors.[26] Discerning a clear line demarcating acts of anticolonial resistance from score-settling between insiders and outsiders to the colonial system is analytically misleading. No such line existed. Outward compliance with foreign rule was not its enthusiastic embrace.[27] Local authority figures performed administrative, juridical, and ceremonial functions in culturally distinctive ways, often subverting them to underline their refusal to identify entirely with the colonial state.[28] During the Arab revolt in mandate Palestine between 1936 and 1939, local authority figures were even held captive by British army units, who used them as highly visible 'human shields' against insurgent attack.[29] There, as elsewhere, post-holders were targeted because their cooperation with colonial authority—and the fruits it bore—caused resentment in others.[30] Resistance to foreign rule meshed with the rivalries intrinsic to the politics of everyday life in settlements, villages, and towns because competing local claims to power and resources mapped onto the wider politics of colonial haves and have-nots.[31]

An Algerian example illustrates the point. The colony's vineyards became a rural front line of the conflict for obvious reasons. Some were capitalized estates, others small farms and cooperatives; most were settler-owned. The majority in the fields were landless rural laborers, descendants of local families evicted from their smallholdings in waves of rural colonization that reserved Algeria's prime farmland for European export producers.[32] Their problems typified what colonialist agriculture had done: displacing farmers, creating a dependent laborer class, and entrenching seasonal patterns of underemployment, poverty, and debt.[33] FLN recruiters saw a reservoir of support in the families of agricultural workers clustered around estates. This, in turn, stimulated French security forces to move such communities into resettlement centers. Forcible relocations achieved a short-term purpose in severing peasant connections with the guerrillas and met the longer-term development goal of restructuring the rural economy.[34] But Algeria's wine industry became more politicized as a result.

Packed with symbolism, pulling up vines and burning farmhouses in the 1950s mirrored the destruction of Algerian settlements, crops, and olive trees during the original colonial occupation a century earlier.[35] Halting wine production struck a blow against the colonial economy. Enforcing FLN boycotts on wine consumption amplified the movement's presence in rural politics. Killing settler farmers and their local 'vineyard guard' auxiliaries underlined the permanence of the revolution and enabled guerrillas to acquire firearms otherwise denied to Algerians. Unsurprisingly, French security forces invested in vineyard protection, anxious to keep the economy running and the settlers in place. Farm outbuildings provided good billets. Huge wine vats offered secure, if airless, containers in which Algerian detainees could be kept out of sight, sometimes fatally so.[36]

The violence in Algeria's vineyards suggests that insurgent groups saw obvious advantage in targeting wealthier landowners, local officials, and their protectors. It removed individuals most likely to feed information to colonial authorities. It diminished opportunities for more socially conservative community members to organize against the insurgency. It made the redistribution of land and other resources easier. It served a radical ideological agenda. And it helped insurgents to persuade local inhabitants to identify with the rebel movement.[37] Another factor connected acts of micro-violence at the village level to the macro-politics of national struggle. Insurgents, unable to strike at central authority in faraway colonial capitals, made surrogate targets of local government agents. Community leaders often hedged their bets in response, either working covertly with rebel groups or cleaving to those loyalist paramilitaries offering better protection. The more that rebels could lay down administrative structures, levy taxes, impose laws, and provide public goods, the greater the likelihood that local officials and the affected population would make a political choice between embracing or opposing what has been described as 'rebelocracy'.[38] Those choices were rarely definitive even so. Anticolonial movements exploited the illegitimacy of colonial institutions to entrench alternate guerrilla states, but life in rebel-held areas remained insecure. In mandate Palestine, for instance, Arab national committees and their local counterparts, backed by youth organizations and, later, a network of rebel courts, built community support. Sometimes they compelled it.[39] For all that, in Palestine, Algeria and other sites of late-colonial conflict, insurgent resources were scarce and economic activity disrupted. The possibility of military intervention or community rejection, meanwhile, pushed insurgent movements toward harsher punishment of dissent.[40] In a pattern still recognizable today, coercion tended to increase in proportion to the level of local insecurity: the stronger the threat against insurgent groups, the greater the probability of collective punishments to compel popular compliance in rebel-held spaces.[41]

Paramilitaries were fundamental to the civilianization of decolonization's wars. Many derived from community self-defense groups trying to remain autonomous actors rather than being folded into the violence work of the conflict's principal combatants. As a result, the microfoundations of violence rarely mapped neatly onto the larger narrative of a single insurgent movement fighting counterinsurgent security forces. As we saw in the previous chapter, a determinant of violence levels was the choices made by local militia forces about community protection, strategies of survival, and settling scores.[42]

Whether working alongside organized military formations or parlaying their own interests between them, paramilitary groups could be decisive. In certain cases, including Indonesia, Kenya, and Bangladesh, militias shaped the outcome of a decolonization conflict and its distributions of power and rewards.[43]

Unarmed colonial subjects were, once again, caught in the middle. Where insurgents such as Vietnam's DRV, Algeria's FLN, or Mozambique's FRELIMO recast civilians as 'the people', the better to assert claims to sovereignty and popular support, their security force and loyalist militia opponents treated civilian inhabitants as raw material for social experimentation in forcible relocation, in counterrevolutionary warfare, in techniques of repression, and as objects of military violence to be physically separated from guerrilla movements acting in their name.[44] There's the rub. Core elements of counterinsurgents' population-centered activity, from identity cards and educational provision to supplying clean water, are also 'tools of control, power projection and monitoring, not simply unproblematic public goods'.[45]

Nor was late colonial rebellion always reducible to an attempt to end empire by force. Sometimes the actions of insurgents and counterinsurgents are better understood as a bargaining process in which those involved tried to secure additional influence over government.[46] Temporary alliances and local deals cut across supposedly binary divides between imperial security forces and insurgents. From Malaya to Algeria, defiance by rebels of a leadership 'line', offers of money to fighters willing to surrender, and even changing sides were sufficiently commonplace to be integrated into security force strategy.[47] Viewed in this light, the job of colonial security forces was not to defeat insurgents outright but to restrict dissent to levels that enabled administration and economic activity to continue.[48]

If the point of colonial repression was not so much to 'win' as to allow imperial economies to function, then one might expect metropolitan governments to reject economic warfare because it undermined the colonial economies they wished to protect.[49] Yet such 'wars of resources' were commonplace.[50] From removing peoples, burning crops, and killing livestock to collapsing agricultural production and creating ecological devastation in conflict zones, various indexes confirm that economic violence was fundamental to decolonization's wars.[51] So was locking people down, regardless of how economically productive they were.[52]

Colonial communities not so directly coerced also faced upheaval. Elaborating on his concept of slow violence, Rob Nixon describes the phenomenon of 'displacement without moving' for communities whose environment and socioeconomic structures are destroyed around them. People might remain in situ only to find their land and resources so denuded that their livelihoods became unsustainable.[53] In this sense, the critical factor was the degradation or repurposing of environmental infrastructure—of the homes, watercourses, and agricultural assets—that assured human security against hard times.[54]

The civilianization of colonial violence cut across racial divides. Security officials, as we have seen, depended on local police and paramilitaries, not just to coerce but to gather information and make sense of it.[55] Rules of colonial difference remained intact because the people directing repression and intelligence collection upheld them.[56] Imperial governments and their security force officers applied solutions based on cultural constructions of subject communities as premodern, emotionally immature, and conspiratorial.[57] This was nothing new. Kim Wagner identifies the late nineteenth-century convergence of racist discourse, the new ballistic technology of the 'Dum Dum' bullet, and medical knowledge of conflict injuries. At that time, racist precepts about fanaticism, sensitivity to pain, and susceptibility to reason supposedly excused the use of weapons outlawed in conflicts between the 'civilized'.[58] The parallel during late twentieth-century decolonization conflicts lies in the triangulation between new technologies of mass violence, notably those delivered by aircraft: high-explosive bombs, chemical defoliants, napalm petroleum jelly, and machine-gun strafing; the prominence of social psychological efforts to manipulate people's behavior; and, finally, the enduring racialized constructions of difference between colonial and noncolonial bodies and minds.[59] Only in October 1957 did Britain's Colonial Office persuade the psychological warfare specialists of the Ministry of Defence to stop referring to dependent territory populations as 'the enemy'.[60]

Restrictions and Punishments

Inflicting violence on civilians was also normalized by the punishment regimes put in place in periods of colonial disorder.[61] Emergency legislation made it possible to wage war inside empires without any prior need to declare it.[62] For members of farming communities whose lives were previously disrupted by land seizures and legal restrictions on freedom of movement, emergency rule or other variants of martial law brought lockdowns of unprecedented duration and intensity. Women, children, and the elderly predominated among the permanent residents worst affected.[63] Their homes were subject to invasion and search. New forms of defensive sociability emerged in response to the threat of sexual violence, especially in camps and new village settlements overseen by loyalist militias.

In Algeria's camps, women minimized their interactions with male guards. Extended families and neighbor networks protected adolescent girls where possible. Within the largest resettlement camps in French North Africa, symmetrically arranged single-story houses of cement blocks were fiercely hot by day, freezing cold at night. Camp housing, whether tented or more permanent, facilitated surveillance, a violation of the privacy of Muslim domestic space that caused profound resentment.[64]

Colonial regimes made access to health care, maternity services, food supplies, and vocational training conditional on the performance of loyalty.[65] In a similar vein, law and policing were the apparatus of 'lawfare', instruments of individual and collective repression, not guarantors of social protection.[66] Colonial Algeria, for example, was thus rendered legally schizoid.[67] After the Algerian Revolution began in November 1954, the territory remained constitutionally part of a French polity still at peace. Yet Algeria was manifestly a society convulsed by war. Once French parliamentarians approved the first of several state of emergency provisions in April 1955, Algeria was simultaneously governed as a hostile space and an integrated colony whose population was there to be won over.[68] Emergency legislation gave legal sanction to increasingly permissive violence meant to isolate insurgents from the surrounding colonial population.[69] Security forces killed civilians and interned more than two million others in punitive actions that supposedly restored order. Yet, even in those regions such as Constantine's rural interior and the Aurès highlands where FLN activity was most intense, administrators recognized that local inhabitants were victims: unable to farm as normal, exhausted by grinding poverty, exasperated by the FLN's exactions and terrified of the army 'clear-ups' that lawfare permitted.[70]

In this topsy-turvy world in which law enabled soldiers to wage peacetime war against the civilians they claimed to be saving, protagonists of repression acknowledged their intellectual debt to their insurgent enemies. Each acknowledged that violence, whether conducted in secret or under a public gaze, was performative, as much about instructing those who feared or witnessed it as about silencing, stopping, or nullifying those who suffered it.[71] Modes of colonial governance also conditioned the way that decolonization's violence unfolded. Empires claimed authority over colonial subjects no matter how thin their administrative presence.[72] So did insurgents laying claim to power. Some, like the North Vietnamese, introduced new currencies and other units of exchange, including salt and essential foodstuffs, changing ideas of monetary value and collective obligation as part of a wider social revolution.[73] Sustaining supply and distribution networks became tests of political credibility for insurgent groups and matters of survival for communities under insurgent control.[74] Again these impositions weighed heaviest on civilian populations.[75]

It follows that we cannot confine discussion of decolonization violence to the encounters between security forces and insurgents. Instead, following the insights of Heonik Kwon into the Korean War, a conflict with staggering levels of civilian killings on all sides, understanding the nature and impact of decolonization's wars is better achieved by focusing on the unarmed. Relational ties of kinship and ethnicity within civilian communities, as well as their physical location within areas identified as hostile to the incumbent regime, made them vulnerable to punitive or retributive violence.[76] Some of this was indiscriminate, but much of it was targeted. All of it was 'social' in the sense that acts of violence affected not just individuals but those with whom they interacted, whether family and kinship groups or neighbors, co-workers, and fellow community members.[77]

The Korean experience portended what was to come elsewhere in the decolonizing world. In the five years from the end of Japan's colonial occupation of Korea in 1945 to the outbreak of the country's civil war in June 1950 at least 100,000 civilians died in acts of political violence in South Korea alone.[78] Such was the determination of the rival Korean regimes to eradicate internal opponents that these killings have been characterized as 'policide': the elimination of anyone considered hostile to the regime's survival.[79] Much like the Korean War experience, colonial regimes and some of their postcolonial successors attached associative guilt to the families and kinship groups of people accused of antiregime activity.[80] 'Loyalty' had to be conspicuously performed.[81]

International Law

The proliferation of restrictions and punishments suggests that international law did little to help colonial subjects despite the human rights 'surge' after the Second World War.[82] A year after the UN General Assembly foregrounded civilian protection through a Convention on the Prevention and Punishment of the Crime of Genocide, in 1949 representatives from sixty-four countries met in Geneva to approve four new conventions previously hammered out at an International Committee of the Red Cross (ICRC) conference in Stockholm. The Geneva Conventions of 1949 mapped out legal protections for three discrete groups: wounded and sick combatants, prisoners of war, and civilians in war zones. Prohibitions included reprisals, hostage-taking, torture and 'degrading treatment', murder, and other collective punishments.[83]

Taking these bans into account, identifying violence against colonial civilians as transgressions of international humanitarian law or the rules of war codified under the 1949 Geneva Conventions seems logical. Abundant evidence indicates that colonial civilians suffered maltreatment that fell within the scope of the above-mentioned prohibitions.[84] In addition, the third article of all four 1949 Geneva Conventions, often described as 'Common Article 3', focused explicitly on civilians caught up in 'armed conflict not of an international character occurring in the territory of one of the High Contracting Parties'.[85] To presume that either the 1949 Conventions in general or Common Article 3 in particular protected civilians against the violence of decolonization would be a mistake even so.[86] The new Conventions were selectively applied at best, completely disregarded at worst. The British government insisted that Common Article 3 was inapplicable in imperial territories where it was legally sovereign and refused to ratify the provision until 1957. Other colonial powers followed suit.[87] But still Common Article 3 mattered because of the link it postulated between international law and violent decolonization.[88]

The weight of evidence about human rights violations against insurgents, detainees, and noncombatants mounted during the 1950s and sapped credibility from the arguments put forward by colonial powers to treat decolonization conflicts as internal disorders—something less than 'armed conflicts not of an international character'—and thus outside the scope of the Geneva Conventions.[89] Global attention on civilian maltreatment fostered public awareness that such claims were self-serving, inhumane, and bogus. For all that, the sorry fact is that rights abuses remained endemic in decolonization conflicts.

The situation after 1949 was different from that at the start of the twentieth century, in which international laws regulating warfare excluded campaigns of colonial conquest and repression.[90] International law by the end of the Second World War had not forgotten colonial wars.[91] Quite the reverse: it was devised to criminalize guerrilla fighters, denying them the protections (particularly as prisoners of war) conferred by belligerent status.[92] Detainees were prosecuted, imprisoned, and even executed for acts defined as criminal. The pattern from French Vietnam in the 1900s to British-ruled Northern Ireland in the 1980s was familiar: rights campaigns, media revelations and prisoner hunger strikes could not persuade metropolitan governments to concede 'political' status to armed opponents.[93]

Emblematic Civilians: Refugees

More than any other group, refugees from decolonization wars became emblematic of civilian maltreatment. Rarely acknowledged primarily as displaced civilians, they were several other things at once: the object of competing transnational relief efforts, pawns in bargaining over humanitarian access to rebel-controlled 'free zones', and powerful symbols in the global war of words about struggles for self-determination.[94] Attempts to shelter them brought together unusual bedfellows whose humanitarian impulse superseded the ideological animosity between them. These working coalitions traversed several invisible divides: between opposing Cold War blocs, between differing ethnoreligious groups, and across national airspaces, territorial waters, and closed colonial frontiers. At the same time, insurgent movements that drew attention to refugees as colonial victims could be ruthless in extracting money, manpower, food, and medical supplies from them.[95] The fate of the decolonization refugee, it seemed, was to be objectified and exploited.[96] This offers some explanation why suicide rates within refugee settlements were, in the French Empire at least, among the highest ever recorded.[97]

Tens of thousands of Algerian refugees living in cross-border encampments in Tunisia and Morocco between 1957 and 1962 were a case in point. In January 1958 French embassy staff in Rabat recorded prevalent 'misère psychologique' among refugee communities in eastern Morocco, a product, they said, of unsanitary conditions, difficulties in accessing emergency relief, and an FLN stranglehold on refugee communities, evident in the extortion of 'taxes' to fund cross-border insurgency.[98] Relations between Moroccan relief agencies and FLN organizers were fraught. The former suspected the latter of pilfering food, medicines, and clothing intended for refugees in Oujda Province for dispersal to ALN fighters.[99]

Refugee settlements in Tunisia and Morocco highlighted the internationalization of the war in neighboring Algeria and the development of a guerrilla state across its frontiers.[100] Morocco's Red Crescent served refugee centers in and around Oujda but came into conflict with an FLN local government apparatus overseeing the 85,000 Algerians encamped in the region.[101] Entrusted in 1959 to distribute 3,750 tons of US wheat flour donated by the American Red Cross, Morocco's relief workers were caught between their international obligations, the refugees' crying need for food, and the FLN's control of the encampments.[102] Refugees thus became a painful reminder to newly independent regimes in Rabat and Tunis of the

Exode vers la Tunisie : ils fuient les « regroupements »

FIGURE 11.1. Algerian refugees make for the Tunisian border to avoid assignment to a resettlement camp, 1959. Source: IISH, COLL00201, 'L'Algérie en marche vers le Socialisme.'

actual limits to their sovereignty.[103] Much as we saw in chapter 9 that partition was fundamental to global decolonization, so were massive displacements of civilians from conflict zones in which final territorial settlements were still to be reached.

France's leading national humanitarian body, the French Red Cross, proved a willing accomplice to counterinsurgency in Algeria, so much so that Léopold Boisser, the Geneva-born president of the ICRC, felt compelled to act on complaints from Jordanian and Syrian Red Crescent representatives who, in late 1957, alleged that French Red Cross workers failed to offer medical assistance to civilians caught in firefights along Algeria's border with Tunisia. Although André François-Poncet, head of the French Red Cross, denied the accusations, the national organization was irredeemably politicized.[104] Individual personnel acted with bravery and compassion.[105] But the charity itself was colonialist. Friction with its parent organization, the ICRC, continued throughout the Algerian War.[106] The UN High Commission for Refugees shared the ICRC's reservations. During 1958 it began circumventing French restrictions, channeling aid to Algerian refugees in Tunisia via other Red Cross societies.[107]

Challenging Rights Abuses

The ICRC's colonial record was blemished, like that of national Red Cross services, Save the Children, Oxfam, and other humanitarian organizations, but this was an inherent risk for agencies that saw political neutrality in the public sphere as a prerequisite to securing access to conflict zones, including those of decolonization's wars.[108] With fewer practical obligations, human rights activists could be more forthright. Free of responsibilities to work with colonial governments in aid distribution or refugee support, they extended the battlefield of insurgencies by shining a light on the grubbiest dimensions of security force repression: the maltreatment of colonial civilians and detainees.[109]

Rights-monitoring groups in colonial dependencies faced official obstruction. In the British Empire, colonial authorities and successive governments in Westminster resisted human rights activists through what historian Brian Drohan identifies as 'cooperative manipulation'.[110] British officials were confronted with revelations of mass detention, torture and even murder thanks to activist groups like the lawyers of the Cyprus Bar Council who defended EOKA detainees in the mid-1950s or the Amnesty International advocates who exposed systematic torture of detainees at the Fort Morbut detention center in 1960s Aden.[111] In each case, though, governments chose damage limitation over engagement with the criticisms made, still less any recantation of human rights abuses that occurred as part of counterinsurgency drives.[112]

Even when agencies were established to put things right, they sometimes did the opposite. A British Defence Ministry Special Investigations Group (SIG), for instance, was set up to investigate claims of maltreatment.[113] Its real purpose was quite different: to find grounds to repudiate torture allegations made by the Greek authorities, the Cyprus Bar Council, the ICRC, and others.[114] The SIG was part of a larger bureaucratic apparatus skilled in obfuscation. Appearing to cooperate with foreign governments, international NGOs, parliamentary missions, and judicial investigators, British officials at the same time denied access to sensitive sites, withheld factual information, and concealed physical evidence of abuses.[115] Reliance on local informants, often 'turned' insurgent fighters or aggrieved relatives of 'traitors' targeted for assassination by EOKA, helps to explain why the impulse within colonial security forces on Cyprus, as elsewhere, was not to reveal their methods, but to cover them up.[116] At best, those ministers and colonial officials 'in the know' tolerated rights abuses as an inevitable by-product of security force intervention; at worst, they colluded in the process with an end-justifies-means logic that excused acts of violence, claiming that order would be more swiftly reimposed. The paradox was obvious: abuses of detainees were explained not as violations of law but as the way to restore it.[117]

As decolonization gathered global momentum, the long-haul 'hearts and minds' strategies so beloved of British and other colonial counterinsurgency theorists lost their rationale. Yet here there was another tragic irony: the greater the imminence of colonial withdrawal, the harsher the punitive strategies employed to sustain imperial control in the short term. This tendency was apparent, for instance, in Indonesia's decolonization war of 1945–1949. There, Dutch troops participated in summary executions of detainees and mass killing of villagers, as at Rawagede in West Java in December 1947, while the collective punishment of civilian communities was delegated to local militias, which acted with minimal colonial oversight.[118] Unable to hide their movements from Republican supporters and chronically short of reliable intelligence themselves, Dutch units took out their frustrations not just on detainees but on the surrounding population.[119] The lethality of the conflict for civilians, often identified with two punitive Dutch military offensives or so-called police actions, in 1947 and 1948, actually peaked in their aftermath as the Indonesian Revolution rolled out across larger swathes of Java and Sumatra in the months preceding the Dutch admission of defeat through an August 1949 armistice.[120]

Returning to the British Empire, to take one lesser known example: the 1964 rules of engagement for British forces fighting the Egyptian-backed Yemeni National Liberation Front designated Aden's entire Radfan region a 'proscribed area' in which 'all movement of any kind in the open [human or animal] should be treated as hostile and engaged'.[121] The declared intention was to make economic life impossible for the Radfan's inhabitants, the Qutaybi people. Systematically uprooted, the Qutaybis became refugees, with neither facilities nor resources, still less compensation offered for a scorched-earth campaign conducted on the precipice of Britain's postimperial age.[122] Even at this last stage in the formal decolonization process, British representatives viewed their role instrumentally, their objective being to contain fallout from the collective punishments, curfews, mass detentions, prisoner killings, and torture of detainees that were the hard edge of British colonial counterinsurgency.

Admittedly, the number of British official inquiries into rights abuses, extrajudicial killings, and massacres piled up over the postwar decades. Nor were all inquiries simply a matter of going through the motions. The first tranche of investigations launched in 1950s Cyprus and 1960s Aden were tame, even willfully blind. Others, though, including later investigations in Cyprus and Aden, were coruscating, their conclusions forcing changes in emergency legislation. But a disquieting fact remains. Neither the findings of exploratory investigations nor the repeal of restrictive ordinances was allowed to interfere with the operational conduct of counterinsurgency, including the mass detention and coercive interrogation practices at its heart.

Cooperative manipulation was a sinister magician's trick, a sleight of hand to disguise continuing repression whatever the criticisms made against it. As late as 1971 in Northern Ireland, British security forces could introduce internment in the expectation that neither Whitehall nor parliament would challenge detention without trial.[123] To the end of empire, the received wisdom that British security forces reflexively followed 'minimum force' doctrine devalued abundant evidence to the contrary.[124] Describing the systematic use of collective punishment, mass detention, and free-fire zones, alongside repeated instances of torture and other rights violations during the Kenya 'Emergency' of the 1950s, historian Huw Bennett gets to the crux of it. Presuming the civilian population to be potentially hostile, 'The international legal environment enabled soldiers to view the use of force against civilians in Kenya as perfectly legal'.[125]

The Northern Ireland conflict eventually changed things. Sustained domestic and international outcry at security forces' treatment of alleged Irish Republican Army detainees as the violence of the 'Troubles' peaked in the early 1970s caused a furor so intense that it could not be brazenly manipulated. Internment and 'interrogation in depth' involving the 'five techniques' to disorient and demoralize prisoners drew on colonial-era precedents.[126] Each was employed as systematically in Northern Ireland as it was in prior wars of decolonization.[127] In other respects, Northern Ireland was different: a (disputed) part of the United Kingdom, its suffering on Irish and British television screens every night. The downfall of cooperative manipulation was gradual even so. Only as the Troubles wore on into the mid-1970s did British authorities' efforts to smother damaging evidence prove counterproductive, undermining claims of impartiality. Prior to that, disarming activist criticism was an essential ingredient of the British 'way' in the counterinsurgencies fought out as part of the British Empire's attenuated twentieth-century decolonization. Humanitarian groups were either kept out of colonial hot spots entirely or, as in the case of ICRC efforts to monitor British suppression of Mau Mau, were only allowed access once the dirtiest work of violence was done.[128]

Significantly, while the ICRC spent three years devising its 1956 'Draft Rules for the Limitation of the Dangers Incurred by the Civilian

Population in Time of War', its prohibitions on particular methods and weapons of war were generally ignored.[129] This, in combination with the omissions and ambiguities of the four 1949 Geneva Conventions regarding civilian protections within colonial wars and insurgents' rights to be treated as combatants with defined protections, left scope to conduct decolonization conflicts not so much outside the rules as substantially without them.

Things might have played out differently. The ICRC found common ground with a superpower, the Soviet Union, during negotiation of the 1949 Geneva Conventions, first in pressing for the extension of protections to insurgents fighting 'unjust' occupation and, second, in according belligerent status to those fighting civil and decolonization wars. This fleeting alignment soon ended. With it went putative recognition that anticolonial insurgents be recognized as combatants entitled to the Conventions' protections.[130] Not until the 1977 Additional Protocols to the Geneva Conventions included insurgencies among conflicts to which protections for combatants and civilian populations should apply did the human rights of colonized peoples figure centrally in international law.[131] National liberation movements knew the score, justifying their recourse to violence on the grounds that legitimate claims to self-determination were denied by their colonial rulers and overlooked by the international community.

There is an alternative perspective, however, one in which transnational activism spearheaded an inexorable shift in popular attitudes locally, nationally, and globally. Gathering certainty that colonialism was indefensible drew heavily on the abuses of human rights that, by the early 1960s, exemplified it.[132] Whereas throughout the global South anticolonialism was bound up with claims to nationhood and demands for equality by nonwhite peoples, among domestic publics in Europe and the United States opposition to empire assumed a more humanitarian form, prioritizing rights abuses. Why it took so long for rich-world publics to recognize the sources of suffering in the global South after the explosions in humanitarian relief efforts during and after the two World Wars is a bigger story bound up with the political economies of decolonization discussed in the next chapter.[133]

Conclusion

Focusing on the experiences of colonial civilian lives makes one thing clear above all. Imperial authorities claiming the right to administer dependent populations did not protect them. Military and police preoccupation with securitization, martial law, punitive restrictions, and other facets of so-called lawfare deepened civilian insecurity as decolonization proceeded, so much so that by 1957 in French Algeria, in British Cyprus, and elsewhere, the ICRC was pressing the French and British governments to permit wider access to cover those subjected to the collective punishments enacted under emergency powers. Colonial subjects could be threatened with violence for defying restrictions or, alternatively, for obeying them. Many adapted as best they could, performing multiple identities to achieve greater security. Public behavior and private lives mirrored these shifts. Sometimes that required outward compliance with authority, at other times a readiness to support anticolonial movements or, varying with circumstance, both. Conversation became more guarded. Trust diminished as loyalties were questioned. Contested decolonization, as a consequence, was experienced as something closer to civil war for many of the rural and urban communities among which it was fought.[134]

Belatedly, the matter of noncombatants targeted by security forces and insurgents was brought into sharper focus by the involvement of international lawyers and transnational disapproval of the ways in which decolonization's wars were being fought. French obstruction of closer UN oversight is well known.[135] Less familiar is the fact that, alongside high-profile cases of rights abuses, another focus of hostile international scrutiny was colonial disregard of civilian status.[136] Criticism of British counterinsurgency was also mounting.[137] To the fury of the Colonial Office in London, the ICRC insisted that unarmed members of local communities detained as a part of collective punishments should be recognized as 'war victims'.[138] As we saw in the previous chapter, the road to hiding decolonization's wars eventually ran out. Still poorly understood, though, is the extent to which colonial populations faced insecurity, fear, dislocation, and violence because their vulnerabilities as civilians counted for so little. Imperial governments preferred to construct dependent populations not as objects of violence but as beneficiaries of modernization. If strategies of development were counterinsurgency's twin, their rationale also reflected the changing political economies in which decolonization took place. So it is to political economy that we now turn.

CHAPTER TWELVE

Political Economies
of Decolonization and
Development

Early Initiatives

As the Second World War drew to a close, governments shifted leftward within most countries with empire attachments. Fascistic regimes in Portugal and Spain became outliers.[1] Elsewhere, interventionist social democracy was on the rise. From the victory of Clement Attlee's Labour Party in July 1945 to Harry Truman's two-term US presidency and the constitutional reordering of democratic republics in France and Italy, imperial powers adopted ambitious social programs meant to raise living standards and prove the benefits of modernizing governance.[2]

This turn toward bigger government, encouraged by the measurement of economic outcomes and social indicators such as infant mortality and literacy rates, was anticipated earlier in the twentieth century.[3] During the late 1930s the two League of Nations–affiliated supranational agencies, the International Labour Organization (ILO) and the Economic and Financial Organization (EFO), worked together in trying to reconcile the interests of workers and capital markets. Each was spurred to action by the global economic crisis. ILO and EFO representatives sat alongside one another on the Depression Delegation. This was a League standing committee, which between 1938 and 1944 sought remedies to the problems of cyclical economic crises worsened by large short-term capital flows.[4] The proposals spawned in this Depression Delegation were of lasting significance. First, in advocating deficit financing to increase consumption and mitigate the impact of trade recessions, the group formed a bridge between the macroeconomic ideas that emerged in the League of Nations' dying days on the eve of the Second World War and the free-trade multilateralism of the Bretton Woods system sanctified at war's end.[5] Second, the Depression Delegation redefined 'living standards' in ways that anticipated the turn to colonial development after 1945.[6]

By the late 1930s the emphasis on living standards among the technocrats of the League was accompanied at national level by a professionalization of colonial specialist services in which applied scientific knowledge was valued over political training. As we've seen, this shift toward the 'technical' echoed what was happening within the League itself, where affiliate health, labor, and economics agencies assumed greater prominence as the League Assembly lost relevance as an actor in regulating international disputes.[7] The League's dilemma was that its commitment to improving the lives of the poorest was matched by the diminishing reach of the agencies involved. League-based practitioners of international economic management, as historian Jamie Martin notes, were better placed to prescribe financial austerity measures than to provide monetary support for economic advancement.[8] The political trajectory of colonial development was different. Only after 1945 did this become central to imperial policy, the political will to pursue it for the first time matching an older rhetoric of empire as socially beneficial.[9] France rolled out a major development scheme, the Fonds d'investissement pour le développement économique (FIDES), in 1946. Across the English Channel, Attlee's Labour government saw in colonial development a parallel to societal reconstruction at home.[10]

Emerging from the war geopolitically weakened and economically needy, the European reflex was to turn outward. Imperial vulnerability generated more, not less colonial interventionism.[11] For some, it marked a resumption of schemes refined in the late 1930s but interrupted by the war. From the social policy initiatives of Lord Hailey's monumental report *An African Survey*, which resonated with the Labour Party's Fabian Colonial Bureau, to the investigations of colonial living conditions sponsored by France's Popular Front in 1936–1938 and dusted off by its left-wing successors in 1945–1946, policymakers in London and Paris shared a taste for reform.[12] Another trend registered in enthusiasm for social psychology among administrators hoping that economic modernization, welfare initiatives, and scientific guidance could divert colonial subjects from radical opposition toward 'constructive nationalism'.[13]

In other respects, though, it was war itself that changed the stakes. Revenues from colonial commodities acquired unprecedented importance owing to European desperation for dollars to fund metropolitan rebuild-ing.[14] For Britain's government especially, empire requirements were subordinated to economic needs at home.[15] Prioritizing reconstruction was often antithetical to colonial economic interests.[16] The sterling area's exchange controls, described more fully below, would be maintained, something beneficial to dollar-starved Britain but damaging to India and other imperial territories with large credit balances.[17] Colonial markets also faced tighter regulation. The production drive, built around increased output of export crops, was king.[18] Britain's stake in Middle Eastern oil would be defended and expanded.[19] Plans to increase agricultural pro-ductivity and to construct better communications links were cast in a new language of 'underdevelopment', described by one historian as an attempt to raise the 'carrying capacity' of the land and the productivity of its ecosystems.[20]

Postwar election victories by left-wing governments in Britain and France cemented the bond between state-led reconstruction at home, the welfare practices of their relief agencies working with millions of dis-placed persons (DPs), and commitment to develop colonial territories.[21] War victims, like colonial subjects, were to be shaped into agents of mod-ernization. So were workers. Both imperial powers lent their backing, for instance, to a World Federation of Trade Unions, established in partner-ship with the Soviet Union and others in 1945, hoping that socialistic labor reforms might provide a new basis for worker internationalism transcend-ing empire divides.[22] The WFTU fractured four years later, partly because of Cold War antagonism but also because of friction between western European trade unionists and the Asian colleagues they hoped to tutor.[23] These ideational divisions were overshadowed by a more tangible obstacle to any transformation of empire: money. Financially, neither Britain nor France had the cash or the creditworthiness to fund metropolitan recovery and colonial development to the extent their governments had dreamed of. Beginning in 1948 Marshall Plan aid and Truman's Point Four program allowed Europe's imperial powers to keep both domestic reconstruction and colonial development in play, but other economic indicators sug-gested that this could not last.[24]

It was longstanding British practice to guarantee the convertibility of colonial currencies at a fixed exchange rate backed by sterling reserves held in London. Colonial monetary systems were thus incorporated into an imperial 'sterling area'. By 1945 India, Egypt, and Canada stood out as net creditors to Britain. Canada could freely renegotiate or write off the sums it was owed. India and Egypt could not.[25] For them, sterling area membership was the financial equivalent of a massive blood transfusion given without consent, their national wealth drained away to finance Britain's war effort. Plainly put, alongside wartime economic extraction went a form of financial extortion set to continue until sterling area operations fundamentally changed. And this was unlikely when UK government priorities were to reduce Britain's national debt and advance domestic reconstruction.[26] Little wonder that Ethiopia, a nation 'freed' by British imperial forces from Italian occupation in 1941, resisted pressure from London for incorporation into the sterling area. Ethiopian leaders, guided by senior financial official Yilma Deressa, opted instead to establish a new currency—the Ethiopian dollar—in July 1945. Ethiopian preference for a US dollar peg over a sterling one underlined the imperialist precepts of Britain's financial policies in Africa and Asia.[27] Behind this imperial reality lay another. The uncomfortable truth for Britain was that its efforts to change the political economy of empire—and country-by-country reactions to it—were conditioned by American money.[28]

Britain duly established a Colonial Development Corporation with a £110 million budget in 1948. In the following year a UN Extended Program for Technical Assistance (EPTA) began channeling Marshall Aid to poorer countries, although in far smaller quantities than the funds channeled to western Europe.[29] More significant than EPTA's money was that ousted colonialists such as the Netherlands could rehabilitate themselves by providing technical support to it.[30] Imperial efforts to sell their 'expertise' were further stimulated by the emergence of an academic subdiscipline: development economics. Its early findings highlighted the prevalence of 'underdevelopment' throughout a colonial world denied the benefits of applied technologies, industrialization, and market diversification.[31] In the words of Jane Burbank and Frederick Cooper, 'Development promised to make empires richer and more politically legitimate at the same time'.[32] Or, to paraphrase environmental historian Gregory Barton, the developmental payoff was minimum resistance to maximum influence.[33]

Interpreting Late-Colonial Development

Only the hardest cynic could interpret Britain's postwar plans to improve colonized peoples' living standards as a by-product of efforts to reduce its dollar deficit. But only the most uncritical imperial apologist could deny the connection between development planning and postwar economic recovery.[34] Selling more colonial commodities on global markets might raise locals' purchasing power but, far from a 'win-win' for all involved, colonial development was intrinsically one-sided. It served metropolitan interests to increase colonial productivity and, with it, export volumes. While less is known about private sector involvement in development initiatives, investment decisions reflected estimations of commercial profit, not community benefit.[35] In state and private sector decision-making alike, attendant improvements in colonial living standards were more than incidental but less than determinant: they were welcome but secondary.

Colonial development oscillated between 'two distinct poles' of enhanced economic performance and poverty reduction.[36] For some recipients, early development initiatives were tainted by their colonial derivation, their underlying purpose being to revalidate imperialism.[37] Analysts, too, have condemned the developmental drive to achieve GNP growth through modernization as inauthentic, a reflection of rich-world trade requirements and investment opportunities underpinned by colonialist attitudes toward 'backward countries'.[38] Unswerving faith among postwar development specialists in the holy trinity of the technocratic expert, the power of statistical data, and the capacity of social-scientific modernizers to make sense of it resulted in vertically implemented projects that grafted rich-world solutions to economic and public health problems onto poor-world societies.[39] Competition with other 'experts' from Socialist countries of the Second World lent a sharper ideological edge to an expanding global market of development assistance. Their ideological differences might be profound but 'First' and 'Second' World developers rarely doubted their own proficiency.[40] A common rationale of external solutions locally imposed gave development encounters, whether colonial and Western or anticolonial and Eastern, their hierarchical quality. Consulting the locals was pointless because, it was assumed, their adhesion to timeless traditions and unhygienic practices were parts of the development 'challenge' to be addressed.[41]

Development could also coerce. French Empire examples show how. In South Vietnam's rice- and rubber-growing areas, colonial disruption of village-based systems of agricultural production led to French-style property legislation, the draining of wetlands, and preferential sales of land to estate-owners, causing lasting resentment among tenant farmers, sharecroppers, and plantation laborers.[42] The 'development' of additional cultivable land was, for them, tied to their impoverishment. Whether under French colonial rule or later American military administration in the 1960s, development experts and counterinsurgent strategists constructed the South Vietnamese as 'unitary objects', elements in a development equation whose outcome could be predicted with the same confidence with which rational choice theorists read economic indicators.[43]

Similar processes of agricultural dispossession justified on specious grounds of better land management were evident in French Algeria, Morocco, and Tunisia. By the time development projects began in both countries during the late 1940s and 1950s, the expulsion of local agriculturalists from their ancestral lands and pasturage was an accomplished fact. Underemployment ebbed and flowed with the rhythm of the harvest. Rural hunger followed the same pattern. Family debts were never cleared. Women labored in fields with no prospect of a living wage or acquiring land.[44] By the early 1950s, Algeria's European settlers, only 3.5 percent of the agricultural population, controlled 38 percent of the most productive farmland. European-owned arable farms ran to ninety hectares on average. Their Algerian-owned equivalents averaged thirteen. Just prior to Morocco's independence in 1956, European settlers, around 4 percent of the country's population of 8.6 million, owned approximately 15 percent of the richest agricultural land. Tunisia's situation was similar: Europeans owned 22 percent of optimum arable land although they constituted under 7 percent of the country's 3.8 million people. Persuading local agriculturalists to buy into development initiatives that left the bulk of decent farmland better irrigated and in settlers' hands was impossible even before decolonization conflicts closed off vast areas of pasturage, killed thousands of head of livestock, and defoliated woodlands with napalm and chemical sprays.[45]

For others, the shift toward technocratic planning characteristic of 'late colonial' development after the Second World War represented the worst of Western diffusionism, its economic transformations unresponsive to community need, its environmental changes at variance with sustainable ecology.[46] A telling example is the Masai Development Plan (MDP), launched in 1951 by colonial administrators in Kenya's Rift Valley. The MDP was meant to increase water supplies, combat tsetse fly infestation, and 'improve' Maasai cattle herding. Partially funded from Britain's Colonial Development and Welfare Act (1940), partially from the taxation of Maasai communities, the scheme was expensive. More problematic was the developers' dismissal of Maasai practices as officials strove to turn herdsmen into ranchers producing cattle for market within narrowly demarcated farmland. Cattle were to be fattened and sold, not conserved for milk or eventual sale in times of chronic hardship.[47]

Sudan, which secured independence from Britain in 1956, illustrated other development challenges. Colonial aftereffects lingered in the unresolved tension between Sudan's limited physical infrastructure, which set limits to what could be achieved, and governmental preference for centrally controlled, capital-intensive development. Ministers in Khartoum fixated on Northern Sudan's cotton production, but the resulting Gezira Scheme worsened Sudan's regional wealth disparities. Sudan's regime adopted the language and tactics of development to coerce Southern Sudanese into meeting the obligations of citizenship within an Arabized regime. The result was a May 1955 mutiny by Southern Sudanese security forces, viewed by some as the beginning of the South's decades-long fight against Northern domination.[48] Moving into the 1960s, Sudan's government justified its Northern-focused economic planning by gathering economic data that vindicated its investment preferences. Southern Sudan's more disparate, but socially vital livestock agriculture was ignored.[49]

Colonial development and its cousin, the exploratory work of industrial conglomerates contemplating new plantations, an oil project, a mine, a hydroelectric dam, or some other transformative construction project, could be criminally neglectful of local environmental concerns.[50] French discovery of offshore oil fields in French-ruled Congo and Cameroon was followed by geological surveys conducted in 1928 by a government-led consortium assisted by the Compagnie Française des Pétroles. No assessments were made of the impact of oil extraction, transportation, and storage on the ecology of affected territories.[51] Government and corporate developers instead mapped their schema as if on a tabula rasa. As elsewhere, the features of this official landscape—administrative implantation, waged employment, investment possibilities, and cost-benefits—dismissed existing patterns of land use as archaic.[52]

Previous strategies of land-extensive farming, appropriate to environments in which human pressure on land was light but soil quality was poor, gave way within colonized territories to intensive land use requiring additional labor. Colonial developers, meanwhile, reframed the declining soil quality as the result of deforestation, particularly the burning of forestland by local cultivators and the cutting of wood for fuel.[53] Yet intensive agriculture sometimes caused the environmental spoliation that land-extensive farming techniques avoided.[54] To generalize very broadly, where once the availability of African land had been sufficient to meet the food security requirements of the resident population, by the mid-twentieth century, local agriculturalists were doubly constrained, first by the colonial subdivision of cultivable lands, which often confined indigenous farmers to 'native reserves', and second by the promotion of waged work on European-owned farms rather than African tenant farming alongside them.[55]

Development Encounters

Development unfolded through encounters, typically between foreign technocrats and local populations, but it was less transactional than this hierarchy of difference implies. Peasant agriculture generated its own knowledge economy, a fund of expertise about appropriate farming practices that went back generations. Often communicated orally and through practical experience, translating this system of knowledge into the development policies of imperial powers demanded respect for local practitioners and readiness to take their advice. Only rarely did this occur. In French Morocco, for instance, a primary health care program, the Protection Maternelle et Infantile (PMI), was rolled out beginning in 1948. Focused on antenatal education, hygiene, and children's well-being, an expanding network of rural PMI clinics worked hard to bring Moroccan mothers into the protectorate's hospital system. A success on its own terms, the proportion of live births occurring in public hospitals and maternity clinics increasing in the final years of imperial rule, these advances were overshadowed by disparities between urban and rural health care and the persistence of water-borne diseases and high levels of child mortality.[56] The toughest challenges for Morocco's infants, in other words, lay not at the point of birth, but afterward, in problems of colonial poverty and water contamination, something their parents knew only too well.

The most capital-intensive postwar development projects—the groundnuts scheme in Tanganyika, a reinvigorated Office du Niger rice-cultivation scheme in French West Africa, the *paysannat* farm program in the Belgian Congo, and the massive rural resettlement in Portuguese Angola and Mozambique—were economic failures. All were tainted by their racial dynamics. Conducted without consulting local farmers about agricultural techniques and soil conservation in particular, they caused lasting environmental damage as well.[57] Even where conservation work, the digging of irrigation ditches, and tree planting to stall soil erosion promised to reverse ecological deterioration, its benefits were sullied by the fact that the necessary labor was forcibly imposed. In a similar vein, there might have been good macroeconomic reasons to turn land in West and Southern Africa over to cotton cultivation, but the impacts were devastating: settled communities uprooted, forced labor generalized.[58] Technocratic faith in new technologies, from tractors to industrial fertilizers and chemical pesticides, ran roughshod over indigenous knowledge, instead compelling people to move, to grow unfamiliar crops, or to farm in unsuitable ecologies.[59]

Alongside issues of insensitivity and coercion, development was some-times just too big. Large-scale infrastructure and agronomic schemes commanded ministerial attention but lower-profile, longer-term inter-ventions were more useful. Vaccination clinics and medical dispensaries in remote settlements, additional primary school places, the association of social rights minima with regular waged employment—these were the grass-roots improvements that altered cultures of expectation about the benefits of development.[60] In this sense, the issue was not whether colonial author-ities were doing enough in different spheres of activity. It was about who should decide.

Some opponents of empire criticized its technocratic authoritarianism but accepted the need for development driven from the political center of independent states. Their aim was to indigenize the process, creating a source of political capital for fledgling regimes.[61] The independent Alge-rian Republic's willingness to resurrect President de Gaulle's Constantine Plan exemplified this transition. A $4 billion development project that had promised one million new houses, education for all, land redistribution, rural credit facilities, and investment in Algeria's vital energy sector, as we saw in chapter 10, it was the modernizing complement to counterin-surgency when it was first elaborated in October 1958.[62] After Algerian independence in July 1962, the plan, although dressed in a new garb of bilateral 'cooperation' with France, was hard to divorce from its colonial past. Other calculations encouraged Ahmed Ben Bella's regime to keep the 'cooperation' variant of the Constantine Plan in play. One was an urgent need for inward investment and technical support for industries and infrastructure projects. Another was that France was now one suitor among many. Competition between aid providers ensured a better deal for Algerians. Most important, Ben Bella's revolutionary regime repurposed late colonial development as something else: the societal transformation of an Algerian Republic.[63]

Algeria was not alone. From India to Guyana and Tanzania, develop-ment became the instrument of nation-building through socialist-style cooperatives and state-led collectivization. There were two sides to this. In the first, development was recast as social engineering in the national interest, its outcomes evident in everything from new infrastructure to goods produced and wealth created.[64] In the second, dutiful citizens within decolonization's 'new' nations met developmental objectives, the modernization of agriculture and landholding systems especially.[65] Com-plaints about individual abuses were countered by reference to enhanced social rights. Postindependence modernizers insisted that economic growth, poverty reduction, and improvements in key indicators from child mortality to life expectancy were what mattered.[66] Development at breakneck speed, in other words, took precedence as Third Worldist nations struggled to free themselves of economic dependence on former rulers and foreign investors.[67]

Development before independence was impossible to dissociate from its political context of imperial authority in long-term decline. Development after independence became identifiable with the authoritarianism of ascendant regimes.[68] Connections between these two tendencies were starkly apparent in the relationship between the European Community's Development Fund and its 'associate' partners in Francophone Africa.[69] Set up through the mechanisms of its foundational Treaty of Rome, European Community development assistance was negotiated, dispensed, and monitored by a French-dominated team of former colonial officials. Many owed their posts to previous experience in running FIDES projects in French black Africa.[70] The risks were obvious. Political clients in Francophone Africa received choice cuts of European Community disbursements from the late 1950s to the mid-1970s. Only later would the receipt of financial aid be tied to standards of governance and observance of human rights.[71]

Hence, the largest irony: colonial development projects so disrupted patterns of settlement, land use, labor migration and livestock farming that they proved a more effective insurgent recruiter than the ideological programs of anticolonial movements.[72] In terms of its consequences for decolonization, the political ecology of development was most significant. From the environmental damage wrought by colonial economic extraction to the forced labor used on conservation projects to alleviate it, the imperial impact on local ecologies stirred opposition.[73] Alongside development efforts to conserve threatened natural resources came tighter regulation of roving pastoralists unaccustomed to colonial frontiers or the security checks and economic controls they entailed. Again, this was immensely resented.[74] Looking forward, the demarcations between winners and losers in the advancement of development agendas after independence often mapped onto patterns of internal conflict and, in the most tragic cases, even civil war and secessionist violence within former colonial states.[75]

Why, then, was development so doggedly pursued? Studies of post–Second World War economic planning remind us that, although rooted in responses to the global Depression of the 1930s, the technocratic state interventionism it implied was, by the late 1940s, a kind of 'political religion'. In postwar Britain and France, adhering to 'the Plan'—for an expanded welfare state, for the nationalization of public utilities, for investment in new export industries—became ideologically charged as the requirements of postwar reconstruction meshed with the strategic competition of the early Cold War.[76] The capacity of scientific, statistically informed planning to improve living standards was oversold, but few questioned the logic that interventionist programs—as well as their colonial cousin, development—were urgently required.[77] The British Middle East Office (BMEO) exemplified this postwar trend. The Foreign Office launched the Cairo-based BMEO in 1945 as a coordinating agency, part political intelligence bureau, part imperial propagandist, but primarily a development mission to the Middle East.[78] The BMEO's core task was political: to gain the ear of the region's rulers as formal structures of imperial control were dismantled. But it achieved more developmentally than politically. Its officers introduced new techniques of forest conservation and ecological management of desert environments, for instance.[79] The tang of neocolonialism, meanwhile, soured the effort to replace imperial government with a regional network of backroom advisers.

So why was it tried? For one thing, money or the lack of it. Advisory support and drip-feed development funding were cheaper than maintaining an imperial bureaucracy in the teeth of local opposition. For another thing, development advice offered a civilian counterpoint to the web of military alliances, airbases, and regional garrisons that tied client states to Britain's Cold War strategy in the Middle East.[80] Perhaps most important was the longer historical perspective. Development was consistent with the ideational precepts of liberal imperialism.[81] Here, though, we come full circle. What would happen if well-qualified technocrats came from nonimperial or anti-imperial countries: the United States, West Germany, the Soviet Union, or Yugoslavia?[82] (They did, and British influence commensurately diminished.) What if technocracy demanded more money than colonial governments could afford? (It did. Only France made up the shortfall, by controlling the lion's share of European Community development spending.)

Bretton Woods and Postwar Political Economy

Late colonial development took shape in a particular macroeconomic context: of an American-led free trade order whose institutional basis derived from arrangements made at the Monetary and Financial Conference in Bretton Woods, New Hampshire, the subject of this section.[83]

The Bretton Woods conference was remarkably productive. It marked the establishment, in July 1944, of the International Monetary Fund (IMF), the World Bank, and its development arm for low-income countries, the International Bank for Reconstruction and Development (IBRD). Supporting this new financial apparatus was an unprecedented availability of American capital. Dollar funding, with political strings attached, sustained the capitalist trade of certain countries while consolidating it in others, what Arne Westad describes as 'Keynesianism used for ideological purposes'.[84] With large capital reserves for emergency loans to nations in financial difficulty, the IMF worked to eradicate the exchange rate fluctuations that pushed countries into economic protectionism in the 1930s. Greater currency convertibility, albeit serving US interests most of the time, was fundamental to the free trade objectives of the 1947 General Agreement on Tariffs and Trade (GATT), the commercial capstone of the Bretton Woods system.[85] The IMF, the World Bank, and the GATT's arrangements for the generalization of tariff-free trade focused initially on economic reconstruction within the industrialized world and Europe especially.[86] Significantly, the GATT was meant to be a provisional arrangement, pending the establishment of a more global International Trade Organization (ITO).[87] But preliminary negotiations for an ITO scheme held in Havana during 1947–1948 were undone by Cold War rancor. Not until the late 1950s did most Bretton Woods institutions become heavily committed in poorer countries, by which point their operating principles were entrenched.[88]

It fell to the IBRD, in the interim, to provide monetary support to the decolonizing world. The sums loaned were small, barely $100 million by 1950 next to the $12 billion already dispersed to western Europe in Marshall Aid.[89] Even so, IBRD loan capital financed essential building blocks for the industrial development favored by America's modernization theorists after the Second World War.[90] Working alongside it was another Bretton Woods agency, the International Essential Raw Material Development Corporation. Its job, in part, was to facilitate reconstruction through global investment in lumber, mineral, and other primary goods production; in part, to keep raw material prices down by ensuring that increasing supplies came to market.[91] This 'resource internationalism' was also consistent with US strategic objectives in the early Cold War. The hope was that commodity producers in South America, Africa, and Asia would come to depend on the new free trade system, their integration into it eased by American capital investment for development, first under the Marshall Plan and then under the Truman administration's 'Point Four' technical assistance program.[92]

From its inception, the global geometry of the Bretton Woods arrangements tied colonial and other economies of the global South to rich-world financial centers, all of them connected to the United States.[93] In a less abstract sense, Bretton Woods changed the terms of pricing and trade, lending and debt in ways advantageous to the system's richest participants.[94] The institutional structures of the new system helped to prevent cyclical extremes of boom and bust, pivotal to the postwar 'super-cycle' of long-term economic growth.[95] But the resulting benefits were unevenly distributed between global North and South.

The new arrangements had few effective challengers. At the close of the Second World War an exhausted Soviet Union, its balance of payments in chronic deficit, did not attack the economic foundations of postwar liberal capitalism and the dollar-dominated Bretton Woods system at its heart.[96] Soviet delegates worked with their Western counterparts at Bretton Woods, and they contributed to the final agreement documents.[97] Rather than confrontation, Soviet trade worked to increase export volumes, to acquire essential manufactures, and to earn much-needed hard currency, policies more redolent of a developing nation than a superpower. With a centralized command economy and uncompetitive heavy industries, the Soviet Union had no realistic prospect of achieving currency convertibility with the dollar, unlike the imperial powers of western Europe, whose improving currency stability underpinned impressive rates of growth in the 1950s.[98] In this sense, decolonizing countries, plus the captive satellite economies of the Eastern bloc came to the rescue, providing vital markets for Soviet export industries.[99]

For all that, the initiative in arranging terms of trade, often in the form of primary products bartered for Soviet manufactured goods, rested with the newly independent countries and not with Soviet envoys. Soviet ability to find new markets across the global South as decolonization quickened was more luck than strategy.[100] Ideological affinity rarely impelled new nations of the global South to look to Moscow. More important was their urgent need for inward investment, plus Soviet readiness to provide the technical expertise necessary to advance major infrastructure projects. To that could be added the lack of political pluralism and strong civil society opposition within numerous decolonized states, which meant that the dominant elite chose its preferred foreign economic partners.[101]

Next to Soviet acquiescence in the consolidation of the Bretton Woods system, opposition from dissentient capitalist economic thinkers was noisier. The institutional apparatus of Bretton Woods jarred with neoliberal visions of a global free market subject to common rules and market discipline and instead provided a global economic framework capable of accommodating political decolonization.[102]

The downside for decolonizing nations was that they remained bound by the dominance of the dollar, the trading strictures of the GATT, and the capital requirements of the IMF. These arrangements were far from a 'done deal', however. For one thing, there was strong right-wing opposition domestically and overseas to a conference agreement condemned as redistributive and internationalist. For another, several European nations integral to the operation of Bretton Woods in general and the IMF in particular took years to achieve the current account convertibility required to play the role assigned to them.[103] But some of the earliest challenges to the Bretton Woods system came from the global South. From the outset, poorer countries from Latin America and the Middle East, later joined by newly independent nations in Asia, Africa, and the Caribbean, objected to rules and institutions whose operations favored rich-world interests.[104] Some, like Mexico, had spent decades arguing for global economic redistribution.[105] Others now joined them. Beginning in 1948, low-income countries pushed for exceptions to global free trade rules to protect their industries from domination by foreign multinationals.[106]

Other criticisms were sterner. Bretton Woods posited a world in which nations, regardless of their relative power, might trade freely as equal partners. Communists, neoliberals, and a broad swathe of anticolonialists dismissed such claims as empty rhetoric.[107] The capacity of partner countries to act independently was constrained by economic inequalities, debt burdens, and the presumption that rich-world creditors would have the last financial word.[108] For these critics, the inclusive language of the Bretton Woods institutions masked the fact that the United States was the world's banker, holding two-thirds of global monetary reserves by 1948. Whatever their frustrations, much of the world—from Europe's imperial powers and the Soviet Union and its satellite states to the world's poorer nations and dependencies—faced the same choice at the end of the Second World War. Should they challenge the new economic order or engage with it?[109]

Bretton Woods was a triumph for the chief US negotiator, Assistant Treasury Secretary Harry Dexter White, for Secretary of State Cordell Hull, and for fellow Southern Democrat New Dealers. But to characterize the resulting 'system' as the cornerstone of an American economic empire ignores the contributions from Latin American, Chinese, Indian, Egyptian, and Ethiopian delegates.[110] Leading figures outside the 'capitalist core' of the northern hemisphere helped sculpt the institutional architecture of Bretton Woods.[111] Some of the ideas and vocabulary of international development had non-Western origins. Chinese nationalist leader

Sun Yat-sen was convinced that state-led industrialization and attendant economic development were essential, both to free East Asia of Western colonialism and to deepen pan-Asian cooperation.[112] Sun's 1920 book *International Development of China* proposed a supranational agency to provide assured credit, investment in industrialization, and balance of payments support for poorer countries. Shunned by delegates to the Paris Peace Conference in 1919, Sun Yat-sen's ideas resurfaced in discussions at New Hampshire twenty-five years later.[113] Kuomintang delegates to Bretton Woods shared their Indian, Egyptian, and South American counterparts' interest in raising living standards through state-led industrialization.[114] Support from Nationalist Chinese diplomats for binding commitments to racial equality in global politics, strongly expressed at the Dumbarton Oaks conference on future international organization between August and October 1944, also resonated with delegates from the decolonizing world.[115]

As it turned out, challenging the predominance of the major combatant powers in the United Nations proved easier than changing the north–south dynamics of global trade. As the Bretton Woods system globalized in the two decades following the Second World War it faced stronger pressure from industrial powers in the global North than from territories in the global South. First among these was the Soviet Union. Its challenge had limited impact even so. Buoyed by strong economic growth in the decade after Stalin's death in 1953, the Soviet economy was still dwarfed by the Western bloc, whose global trade dominance persisted until the oil shock of 1973.[116]

Little wonder that fewer decolonizing nations were drawn to the Soviet command economy model than is sometimes assumed. Admittedly, several of those that were—North Vietnam, North Korea, Cuba, Guinea, Ghana, Algeria, Angola, and, for a time, China—figure prominently in the global decolonization story.[117] Others, like Egypt, short of hard currency and in desperate need of imported grain to feed an expanding population, saw clear advantage in Soviet barter arrangements.[118] For all that, early decolonizers such as India, Indonesia, and Burma typified the more widespread trend. Each followed different but noncommunist paths to economic growth. These and other newly independent countries wanted the industrial hardware and technical expertise that foreign powers offered as new trading partners. But whereas Western countries participated in Bretton Woods institutions, including the World Bank, through which long-term economic arrangements could be mediated, the Communist bloc giants did not.[119]

Soviet preferences were different. Provision was made for support by technical advisers rather than the corporate control that usually accompanied Western-run infrastructure projects in Africa especially. These contrasts cut both ways. On the plus side, the Soviet Union offered long-term loans repayable at low interest in local currencies, a tempting prospect for newly independent states short of dollar earnings. Barter deals were commonplace with member states of the Soviet-controlled Council for Mutual Economic Assistance (COMECON). Again, these came with fewer strings attached than the more complex arrangements favored by Western governments seeking to promote particular corporations and financial conglomerates.[120] The Soviet regime also boasted recent experience in vast agricultural modernization projects, most recently in the 'virgin lands' schemes that produced record 1950s harvests in Western Siberia and the Kazakh Republic.[121] Consistent with this, Soviet-backed development projects promised advisory support to the locals, plus enhanced opportunities for African and Asian students to study in the Soviet Union, appealing prospects for independent governments yet to establish specialist bureaucracies.[122] Decolonizing nations eager to control their industrial development were also drawn to Soviet import substitution schemes offering escape from dependency on rich-world suppliers.[123]

Set against these Soviet selling points, Western-backed projects promised closer involvement of the supranational banking agencies set up under Bretton Woods. Opting for Western backers brought unwelcome financial constraints but represented a 'better the Devil you know' choice. It was difficult for former colonies to cast off commercial ties with former colonial businesses, traders, and investors, let alone the political connections, the army and police trainers, and the development experts whose collective presence ensured basic continuities in public life across the temporal divide of formal decolonization.[124] Even Kwame Nkrumah's Ghana, committed to fighting Western neocolonialism by fast-paced socialist development, proved more cautious in practice. Authorities in Accra stalled repeated offers of Soviet development aid for fear of antagonizing Britain and the United States.[125] Equally, the embrace of Soviet financial, military, and technocratic support by Sékou Touré's Guinea was hardly a choice after the country's acrimonious 1958 rupture with its erstwhile colonizer, France.[126] In each of these West African cases, an initial tilt toward Moscow, limited in the Ghanaian case, pronounced in the Guinean, diminished in the 1960s.[127] In 1961, the Conakry regime even expelled Soviet ambassador Daniel Solod for allegedly supporting a wave of student and teachers' strikes that took aim at Touré's growing authoritarianism.

It took concerted wooing by high-ranking Soviet ministers to repair the damage, an indication that Moscow's influence with its showpiece West African client state rested on shaky foundations.[128]

After a slow start, Soviet efforts to counteract Bretton Woods in the global South were wide-ranging but predictable.[129] British and French responses to an American-led international trade system were subtler. Both countries benefited enormously from dollar support. But neither their political elites nor their voting publics were reconciled to the diminution of global power inherent in dollar-denominated free trade.[130] Each maintained imperial trading zones whose internal transactions were conducted in their metropolitan currency. Postwar indebtedness and the Bretton Woods requirement to maintain currency convertibility only added to the importance of Britain's sterling area and France's franc zone.[131] Indeed, the franc-based currency union expanded, despite the transitions to political independence across West and Equatorial Africa beginning in 1958.[132]

The advantages for metropolitan powers were obvious. Britain and France could buy colonial goods using their own currency and at prices they controlled. Even better, each reduced their chronic dollar deficits by selling colonial products—invoiced in dollars—to outside countries. Few in Britain or France seemed perturbed by the colonialism of these arrangements. To give a couple of well-known examples: The Anglo-Iranian Oil Company (precursor to British Petroleum, BP) guaranteed cheap petroleum for British consumers while skimming the cream off Iran's oil wealth for the British Treasury. After Prime Minister Mohammad Mossadegh of Iran moved to nationalize the company in May 1951, British authorities conspired with the CIA to overthrow him in 1953.[133] On the French side, it bears repeating that the Hanoi regime's efforts to break free of French economic control by creating an independent customs system at the northern port of Haiphong provoked a ferocious response, igniting the Indochina War in late 1946.[134]

Toward Different Partnership Arrangements

In government after the Second World War, most of those inside Britain's Labour Party who thought and wrote about empire were reformists, not anticolonialists. The same could be said of their socialist counterparts in France and Belgium. Anxious to cultivate cooperation with fellow socialists in Asia and Africa, this postwar generation of European reformers defended minority rights, endorsed health and education initiatives, and backed poverty reduction programs, but all within the framework of empire and its postwar cousin, trusteeship.[135] Others, particularly in France, stressed the value of federation. In the late 1940s their discussions centered on the French Union, not as a done constitutional deal to be rolled out across the empire, but as something more elastic: a federal schema capable of accommodating mounting pressure from colonial social movements, and trade unions especially, for parity of treatment with their French equivalents.[136] Constitutional guarantees and voters' rights, citizenship eligibility, and social rights under law were hard-won concessions. The question still outstanding was whether French-ruled colonies in black Africa, Southeast Asia, and the Caribbean should sustain partnership with France as independent nation-states, as satellite territories, or as regional confederations. Matters of cultural authenticity and economic interest figured large in answering it.

Historian Sarah Dunstan points to the liminal status of French African politicians, symbols of French Union progressivism yet open to charges of co-option. The singularity of these Francophone colonial elites rested on two pillars. One was their status as party political representatives, elected to the French National Assembly and operating within the parameters of constitutional politics but voicing African concerns. The other was their prominence as political thinkers, whether in articulating the cultural tenets of African nationalism or in refining schemes for regional integration.[137] They raised fundamental questions in doing so. Was negritude, with its emphasis on shared African cultural heritage, better served by the sublimation of national identity or its assertion? Did colonies need French markets and the backstop protection of Bank of France currency reserves to thrive? For the center-left coalition governments in late 1940s France, the answer was yes. By the mid-1950s longstanding ideas of a *Eurafrique* economic and cultural bloc solidified as French Socialists again took the lead, this time in tying the economies of French West and Equatorial Africa into a privileged trading relationship with the European Economic Community.[138]

From federal schemes to the application of metropolitan workers' rights to colonial territories, dialogue between political elites in Paris and French black Africa about the merits of enduring political connection went furthest.[139] What about the British Empire? For all its talk of a new era of Commonwealth partnership, the probability of federation without independence or of decolonization indefinitely deferred was low. By 1948 the British Empire was already a shadow of its former self, the wartime equivalence drawn between Britishness and the defense of freedom at odds with the millions of British colonial subjects for whom such invocations of democratic inclusivity clashed with the lived experience of colonialism.[140] Compelled to deal with India and Pakistan, first as dominion partners, then as independent republics, the debate between Whitehall and new ruling parties in South Asia followed a different agenda, not of cooperation within an imperial framework but of more equitable arrangements beyond it.[141] Burma, its ties to Britain unraveling after Indian independence, left the fold entirely, authorities in Rangoon having rejected Commonwealth connection before the country descended into civil war.[142]

Enticing South Asian nations toward what looked like a neocolonial confederation with Britain did little to heal the gaping wounds left by partition. Nor could it conceal the conflicting expectations of political leaders in Delhi, Islamabad, and London. The new Indian Republic's January 1950 admission to the Commonwealth thawed some diplomatic frost, but the warmth was fleeting. Shared Commonwealth connections did not ease tensions between India and Pakistan.[143] More useful from the British perspective was the Indian authorities' willingness to accept the precipitous fall in the value of their sterling balances—the outstanding British debts to India held on account in London—after Britain's latest emergency devaluation in 1949. This was remarkable. The British, having extorted war loans from the Indian people, now escaped the obligation to repay the sums borrowed at anything like their real terms value.[144]

Nehru wrote passionately about these unpaid sterling balances, describing them as root causes of 'the hunger, famine, epidemics, emasculation, weakened resistance, stunted growth, and death by starvation and disease of vast numbers of human beings in India'.[145] But the Congress leader chose not to follow through on his criticism, even though Britain's shockingly inadequate response to famine in wartime Bengal was a matter of record. The loss of three million Bengali lives in 1943–1944 perhaps needed no amplification as an indictment of imperial mismanagement. Instead, Indian negotiators accepted a financial settlement on July 9, 1948.[146] Britain promised phased repayments of the sums owed, principally to finance Delhi's massive pension bill for Indian public servants.[147]

The British Nationality Act also passed into law in July 1948. It promised changes to colonial citizenship and rights of immigration to Britain, not least for people from the Indian subcontinent.[148] For all that, as historian Stuart Ward points out, the Act saw a globalist vision of Commonwealth inclusivity clash with the 'disaggregating logic' of colonial difference, meaning that, from its inception, it fractured 'under the weight of its flawed promise'.[149] Behind the rhetoric of Commonwealth inclusivity, in everything from housing and employment to the numbing humiliation of persistent discrimination, the legacies of colonial racism lingered.[150] The cultural backlash against foreign workers and former service personnel who remained in Britain during 1945–1948 suggested that British society was as sensitive to markers of difference after the war as it was before it. 'Loyal' servants of the war effort from the global South—among them Indian soldiers, Jamaican nurses, and loggers from British Honduras (later Belize)—were either expected to leave or, in the most extreme case, that of 1,362 Chinese merchant seamen, were rounded up by police and expelled.[151] The rights to settlement in Britain conferred by the British Nationality Act were hugely significant but not as a definitive breakthrough; from the 1960s onward immigration restrictions proliferated.[152]

Internationally, Anglo-Indian relations were stormy. The generosity shown by the Congress Party leadership over Britain's outstanding debts evaporated when it came to the future direction of decolonization. Nor were the Indians alone. Working through an Asian Socialist Conference established in 1953 as both a partner and a challenger to the European-dominated Socialist International, party political representatives from India, Burma, Indonesia, and elsewhere insisted on the universal right to self-determination.[153] Internationalist solidarity was secondary because logically there must first be nations that could interact.[154] Gradualistic reform, they said, was inescapably colonialist because its operating assumption was that dependent territories should meet rich-world standards before qualifying for nationhood.[155] The Asians were equally dismissive of Labour Party concerns about minority rights: a cover, they insisted, for safeguarding white settler privilege and a convenient means to silence talk of colonial withdrawal.[156] Development, at least as articulated by its European and American advocates, was patronizing and imperialistic, foreign interventionism in disguise. Federal integration would dilute sovereignty and impede real freedom.[157]

Labour's colonial reformers were undeterred.[158] Attlee's government was outwardly respectful of Nehruvian preferences for poverty reduction conducted by independent Asian nations on their own terms. But, rejecting accusations of cultural insensitivity, Attlee's ministers remained convinced that the British Empire could lead the way in improving colonial living standards.[159] The real obstacle, as they saw it, was the shortage of money. Working through the Fabian Colonial Bureau, beginning in 1950 senior Labour politicians honed their ideas for a UN-administered program of coordinated international development. Financial details remained sketchy but, in outline, this proposed rich-world backing for development schemes across the colonial world.[160] The plans coalesced into a policy proposal, 'Towards a World of Plenty', which Labour's annual conference adopted in 1952. Presented as a global poverty reduction scheme running in tandem with vaccination programs and other public health measures, 'Towards a World of Plenty' became the lodestar for Labour's development ideas. James Griffiths, a former Labour colonial secretary, explained the thinking behind it: that the world 'cannot find peace while one-third are rich and two-thirds are poor'.[161]

In the French Empire, too, colonial health care assumed greater prominence in the postwar years as official concern with the national efficiency of the workforce gave way to newer preoccupations with preventive medicine and rural clinics capable of reaching out to colonial populations as a whole.[162] Politicized as they were, health reforms in French Africa at least aspired to the more equitable provision of facilities and treatments.[163] The problem, officials soon realized, was that local populations, and young women in particular, were not the supine citizens-in-the-making that colonial health policy assumed. Often, they spurned clinics or medical inspections, whose infantilizing procedures clashed with the equalization of rights the enhanced health care provision was supposed to embody.[164]

Aid Internationalized

Colonial modernizers read the local suspicions they encountered in particular ways; in Anne Phillips's telling comment, for them, the 'problem' of development was 'a matter of overcoming the obstacles that tradition has set in its path'.[165] Political economy was in the mix as well. Major public health programs could be skewed by the benefits expected to accrue to imperial authorities and supranational agencies such as the United Nations' Food and Agriculture Organization (FAO).[166] The FAO, like its UN cousins the World Health Organization (WHO), UNESCO, and the United Nations Children's Fund (UNICEF), retained humanitarian ideals but found it hard to avoid entanglement in the Cold War politics of rival blocs and the decolonization politics of late colonial development. In 1949, Stalin's Soviet Union withdrew from the WHO, angered by the Truman administration's bid to control UN technical assistance to poorer countries through its Point Four program. Eastern European satellite countries went with it, although they resumed WHO membership in January 1956 in a bid to use technical assistance, trade deals, and medical aid—the central planks of 1950s modernist development—to woo Third World nations and liberation movements toward the Communist camp.[167]

The conflicting pressures facing aid providers were evinced by the worldwide campaigns to eradicate malaria and smallpox.[168] The battle against malaria, officially launched by WHO director Marcelino Candau in 1955, was fought out in regions adjusting to decolonization, the Indian subcontinent, and sub-Saharan Africa above all. Malaria eradication efforts were a classic example of a 'high impact' development project, especially valued for its potential to increase labor productivity, agricultural output, and developing world consumption.[169] The American financing behind it and the DDT chemical spraying that characterized it encountered stiffer political and environmental criticism in the 1960s. Malaria control was also brought into question by the greater success achieved by the WHO's smallpox campaign, an initiative backed by Soviet expertise and a Soviet-developed vaccine.[170] Analyzing the colonialist presumptions of WHO and US-led malaria eradication schemes from the 1940s to the 1960s, historian Randall Packard offers a telling example from British-ruled Rhodesia (Zimbabwe), where

> health officials talked about constructing a protective 'barrier' by spraying the African huts which surrounded white farming areas and by treating migrant workers entering the 'protected zone'. Although this language constructed malaria as the enemy without, Africans, and particularly migrant workers, were clearly the enemy within.[171]

Attitudes among fieldworkers were surely more diverse, but the verticality in global public health programs rolled out from the top down pointed to continuities transcending decolonization's chronologies of national independence. Colonial territories figured among the original fifty-five member states when the WHO constitution was finally approved in 1948 but were only accorded 'associate membership, upon the application of their colonial rulers'.[172] The WHO, in other words, initially upheld the Western-centric paternalism of colonial medicine.[173] Still, this quasi-imperialist picture is easily overdrawn. Independent India, a focus of WHO activity, was never a passive recipient of such support. India's public health programs, practitioner training, and pharmaceutical commerce were more complex and multidirectional than any vertical model of diffusion might imply.[174] The WHO, for its part, recognized the implications of imminent decolonization for the internationalization of public health. As noted above, from 1957 onward, the WHO was subject to stronger influence from the communist 'Second World' as, first, Eastern bloc countries, then the Soviet Union, were readmitted.[175] Distinctively Eastern bloc approaches were soon matched by 'Third World' perspectives as newly sovereign African states joined the organization.[176] Mao's China, and the low-cost mass health care of its 'barefoot doctors', presented a further challenge. During the 1960s and 1970s, the WHO became increasingly receptive to Communist bloc and global South initiatives in response.[177] Less organizationally rigid than its UN parent, the WHO exemplified the emergent supranationalism of a postcolonial age.

Conclusion

The precepts of development thinking, including its presumptions about gender, psychology, and local cultures, tell us a good deal about the persistence of colonialism in new guises. Social scientists were crucial actors in this process, often sharing their ideas about the nature of dependent societies and how best to administer them with counterinsurgency practitioners and development experts.[178] Their ideas have been characterized as a 'transnational cultural code', understood but unspoken.[179] Scientific racism was discarded, but a subtler language of 'good' governance shared its racial binaries.[180] Unsurprisingly, then, many communities encountered development as something unwelcome: as surveillance, as forced population removal, or as the transformation of a familiar environment through different farming practices, the introduction of new industries, or the construction of major infrastructural works. Local responses to development projects were frequently hostile as a result.

Development was also implicit in early humanitarian projects and the internationalization of public health. Transnational networks of philanthropists, charity sector humanitarians, and health care practitioners intersected in colonial territories, where impulses to administer and to mobilize labor might be codified as facets of imperialistic development. Although sometimes predicated on self-help schemes, the better-known showpieces of late colonial development were the antithesis of 'small is beautiful' thinking. Mega-projects framed around power generation, water irrigation, and transformational changes in land use and waged labor were held up as fast tracks to modernity. Their implementation was accelerated by new technologies, from vaccines and insecticides to agrochemicals and cheaper building materials. All facilitated the expansion of colonial primary health care, large-scale agriculture, and so-called model villages. The deepest problem, though, was that some imperialists viewed development as their magic bullet, a way to legitimize colonialism, not to end it.

CHAPTER THIRTEEN

Political Economies
of Decolonization II:
The 1950s and 1960s

Setting the Scene: A New Rights Order?

For the Allied powers, wartime peace planning proceeded on many levels, from the minutiae of occupation tactics to the humanitarianism of relief agencies and the rhetorical flourishes of the Atlantic Charter. Institutionally, the twin conferences on a future international organization, at Dumbarton Oaks from August to October 1944 and at San Francisco between April and June 1945, gave shape to the new supranational body charged with peace preservation: the United Nations. This remapping of international politics was informed by another preoccupation: with the rights of the individual. The caveats surrounding the interwar codification of minority protections were replaced by a simpler vision of shared rights and responsibilities to be upheld by national governments under the United Nations' watchful eye.[1] The authors of the December 1948 Universal Declaration of Human Rights (UDHR) required signatory states to enact its principles, uniting in the UN General Assembly to punish transgressors.[2]

A global human rights regime had huge implications for colonialism. Civilizational hierarchies made no sense in a world in which rights attached equally to every person.[3] But could the new thinking be made to stick? The jurists who formulated the United Nations' early human rights instruments struggled to explain self-determination as a principle inhering in peoples. They disagreed about whether it could be an inalienable human right.[4] In 1952, the emergent coalition of Latin American, Asian, and Arab states within the General Assembly proposed two additional rights instruments, the International Covenant on Civil and Political Rights and the Covenant on Economic, Social and Cultural Rights. In doing so, the sponsoring governments insisted that self-determination, which was missing from the UDHR, was a first right.[5] Sure to be contested by imperial powers, this proposition was accompanied by another: that economic and social rights to housing, health, and other welfare provisions were a primary responsibility of all national governments.[6] Over the next decade or so, imperial governments would turn these arguments on their head by linking the advancement of economic and social rights to the goal of self-determination. They argued that imperial oversight and development programs were the best way to enable colonies to cope with the challenges of self-rule. Self-determination might be cast as a 'first right' but it meant little unless the society in question could provide tangible economic and social rights to its citizens. Imperial rulers were recasting themselves as tutors in development. Decolonization should mark a kind of graduation from dependency to self-rule.

Valuing Empire?

For many historians, the idea of 'managed decolonization' is as analytically ridiculous as it is culturally insensitive because it implies that imperial governments directed the end of empire to the exclusion of other peoples. Less controversial, though, is to suggest some connection between the relative economic decline of imperial powers and their reduction of overseas commitments.[7] Whether such retrenchment was a matter of correlation or causation is problematic, but the underlying point is simple. Lack of funds hastened empire contraction. Sustaining a global empire in the second half of the twentieth century was expensive, possibly prohibitively so.[8] But was decolonization ever a cost-benefit exercise? Historians have tended to think not. Scholars of the British Empire have rarely shown much interest in its balance sheets.[9] To some degree, their inclinations match those of the politicians and peoples they study. If the analytical premise is that empires were brought down by their opponents, political economy looks like a secondary factor. The interaction between economic conditions and political choices is materially salient but not decisive. From street protests to insurgent violence, the case against empire was not primarily made in economic terms, even those of hunger and want. If, however, the analysis concedes that imperial powers to some extent authored their own decolonization, financial preoccupations figure larger.

Sticking with Britain for a moment, money limited development planning. Money shaped the contours of counterinsurgency. Money determined strategic arrangements with client states. And it set the parameters for interventions in—and withdrawals from—Asia in the twenty years after the Suez Crisis of 1956. After Suez, Britain reduced the money allocated to fighting conventional war against the Soviet Union, investing instead in a central strategic reserve, commando assault ships, and long-distance air transports needed for expeditionary operations in a decolonizing Asia and Africa.[10] Whether in the fields of development, decolonization, or defense, money was the stuff of Whitehall argument. It made the British Treasury the foremost office of state and a dominant voice in the high politics of breaking up the British Empire.

Government hummed along to a background noise of monetary concerns. The mood music of financial capacity and political possibility played to a repetitive rhythm in the sixty years after 1919. Its beat of relative economic decline sometimes slowed but never stopped. Its harmonies were more varied. Some were funereal: the contraction of Britain's heavy industries and the regional decline that followed; the lives, money, and material lost in fighting two world wars.[11] Others were jauntier: the ambition of reconstruction, upswings in postwar economic growth, and the expansion of consumer spending. Beginning in the mid-1950s, two other refrains got louder: the importance of trade with Europe and Britain's reliance on the invisible earnings of its finance and service sectors.[12] The City of London, and its arbitrage of a market in 'Eurodollars', became vital in maintaining Britain's economic position. Nowhere in this mood music did empire figure very much, although the expansion of the Eurodollar (and, from the early 1960s, Eurobonds) market was consistent with low levels of state regulation long exploited by companies, merchant banks, and other investors in 'offshore' territories.[13]

To give the metaphor a final squeeze, whereas the harrumph of Victorian government was bombastically imperial, its equivalent by the time Harold Macmillan took office in January 1957 was less self-assured. Yes, dollar earnings from colonial commodities salved Britain's balance of payments deficit in the decade after 1945.[14] Yes, colonies and Commonwealth countries remained important trading partners: after 1955, still second (but an increasingly distant second) to the countries of the European Economic Community. And yes, the global networks of imperial banking, insurance, and other financial services helped sustain London's prominence as a financial center. Offshore tax shelters in the Caribbean and elsewhere also accrued financial importance as political decolonization, business 'money panics', and consequent capital flight from less investor-friendly territories gathered pace.[15] For all that, none of these economic benefits were enough to silence that unremitting beat of Britain's relative economic decline. Nor did they change the economic tune of a country increasingly dependent on European trade and the City of London's earnings. Britain's cultural, emotional, and political attachments to empire, although loosening, were still there in 1960. Its economic ties were unraveling.[16]

The clearest archival evidence to support this proposition are the reports commissioned by Macmillan's government between February and September 1957 to satisfy the new prime minister's wish for an audit of empire.[17] Intended to enumerate the costs and benefits of individual colonies to Britain, the work was assigned to an interdepartmental Colonial Policy Committee (CPC). The Treasury officials at its apex read the committee's task in monetary terms. Their counterparts from the Foreign Office, the Ministry of Defence, the Colonial Office, and the Commonwealth Relations Office insisted that intangible factors of prestige, strategic advantage, political influence, and cultural attachment should somehow figure in any calculations.[18]

Unsurprising in light of these different priorities, the results of this empire audit, laid out in the June 1957 policy paper 'Future Constitutional Development in the Colonies', were a fudge.[19] Even though the CPC sat on the fence, uncomfortable home truths were buried in its procedures and its findings. The fact that senior officials from all branches of government were given the job of saying 'is empire worth it?' indicated a new direction of governmental travel heading toward pullout. And the balance sheet, fudgy though it was, confirmed that colonial commodity producers, particularly Malaya and the Gold Coast (Ghana), brought in the most revenue in proportion to their costs of administration. Ironically, by 1957 this pairing stood on the brink of formal independence. Other territories in sub-Saharan Africa, including oil-producing Nigeria and Mau Mau–riven Kenya, were a tougher financial call. The implication of the CPC's conclusions went unanswered and so, in 1957 at least, remained a bomb that didn't explode: colonial control no longer made sense. Friends in postindependence governments were more valuable and certainly better for Britain's balance of payments than clinging on.[20] The bomb had yet to go off, but senior figures around Macmillan's Cabinet table could see the fuse burning quickly.

The readiness of Conservative Party ministers and policy advisers to apply spreadsheet logic to the future of empire reminds us that another wave of decolonizations was already building and that the British government would try to ride it.[21] In 1957 Macmillan's reconstructed Conservative administration made another signal of what was to come. After years of toying with the idea, the Conservatives finally bowed to pressure from business lobbyists. Tax breaks were offered to British-owned colonial industries that rebranded themselves as 'overseas trade corporations' (OTCs).[22] The point here is not that British businesses were offered favorable terms of colonial trade, but that it took even an avowedly capitalist government six years to offer them much support.[23] The idea that British government and business worked hand in glove to prevent decolonization just doesn't stack up. A Commonwealth Development Corporation (CDC) was established under the Attlee government in 1948 but, while later CDC cooperation in Africa with British-owned conglomerates such as Unilever favored Britain's trade requirements, it did so *after* formal decolonization rather than *before* it.[24] British merchant banks could still expect big profits from colonial lending on infrastructure projects. But their counterparts in British business remained anxious about the threats of trade union militancy, nationalization without compensation, and punitive taxes imposed by postindependence regimes.[25] Not only that, but the OTC scheme was quickly killed off by the incoming Labour government in 1964–1965.[26] From the standpoint of political economy, British decolonization was not a question of thinking the unthinkable but of adjusting to the probable.

Apathy, Pragmatism, and Principle

It's not difficult to pull this line of reasoning apart, not only in the British example but in others as well. What of the extraneous pressures, the hostile opinions, and the insurgent violence that compelled imperial elites to think differently? Macmillan's government only came about in the first place because its predecessor was humiliated in the Suez crisis of 1956. France's Fourth Republic would collapse eighteen months later under the insupportable weight of an Algerian conflict whose sickening human costs, for so long concealed, had become undeniable. Mistakenly, the colony's settlers and the French army in Algeria thought de Gaulle's presidential leadership would help them turn the tide. They realized too late, if at all, that their FLN opponents had put the ethical case for independence before the world and won.[27]

Whether measured in money or reputation, misadventures like Suez and protracted counterinsurgency campaigns like Algeria punched big deficits into imperial balance sheets. UN condemnation, vilification by the

Non-Aligned Movement, and accusations of human rights abuses made the diplomatic huffing and puffing in London or Paris about geopolitics and grandeur seem delusional. Hard evidence of capital flight from colonial territories nearing national independence was closer to the mark. European settlers leaving French North Africa between 1954 and 1962 found low-tax safe havens for their money, first in Tangier, then in Switzerland. Withdrawals of private capital were paralleled by the divestment of specialist banks and businesses from the colonial world, with Switzerland again attracting a large proportion of Francophone funds.[28] Movements of British settler capital (as, for example, from Kenya to tax shelters in the Bahamas), while significant, were generally less abrupt.[29] The relief with which Macmillan's government surrendered unilateral control in Cyprus in 1959 was, in this sense, consistent with its concomitant 'victories' in Malaya and Kenya. In the latter two, friendly clients were lined up to protect British interests after independence. In both places, 'winning' meant handing over to the loyalists who, by doing much of the dirty work of violence, had positioned themselves to profit from it.[30] Meanwhile, making a Cyprus settlement a Greco–Turkish diplomatic problem allowed the British to stop fighting without losing their airbases and listening stations. In all three cases, finding partners to show the way out was more advantageous than trying to stay in. Here, decolonization was something between an optical illusion and a paradox. Being seen to get out was the prerequisite to more stable, and far cheaper, economic and strategic connections.

The trend was similar in France. By 1961 de Gaulle's presidency and a majority of voters in successive referenda on the future of Algeria had channeled their exasperation into a new language of magnanimous decolonization.[31] Militarily on top but morally disarmed, they wanted out. The turn of events south of the Sahara showed an alternate means of escape. In the former federations of French West and Equatorial Africa, France secured enduring strategic influence and economic advantage, working alongside local elites.[32] The Agence française de développement (AFD), effectively a state development bank, led the way. Amid the rash of formal independence settlements in Francophone Africa between 1958 and 1960, the AFD guided the gradual Africanization of banking in Francophone territories, backing the localization of bank ownership. France retained influence over these privatized African banks despite its declining capital interests in the sector.[33] Even Cameroon, by 1958 convulsing from French counterinsurgency against a nationalist *maquis*, joined the subgroup of six former French dependencies tied to France through a Central African franc.[34] *Francafrique*, less than an empire but more than a string of functional partnerships, suggested that French decolonization was anything but final.

Taking all of this into account, it's worth restating that the notion of managed imperial withdrawal, whether in the British Empire case, the French, or any other, remains implausible. Perhaps, though, there's a more prosaic truth in a political economy approach to the politics of decolonization: by the late 1950s European populations weren't willing to pay as much as their forefathers had to keep the empires held in their name. To the pressure from below of colonial communities agitating for social rights or demanding nationhood should be added the reluctance of the relatively privileged: the British, the French and, as we'll see, the Belgian voters unwilling to pay more taxes, still less to give up their lives to protect settler kith and kin or to keep distant flags flying.

This is not to imply that European publics were, by 1960, pushing hard for decolonization. But their indulgence toward empire on the cheap evaporated when larger bills—in lives, money, or reputation—were presented. Again, the British example is telling. Britain's institutions of state—parliament, the armed forces, the monarchy—still bore the trappings of imperial grandeur. But they were mocked relentlessly by new-wave satirists in an assault on deference that helped to define 1960s popular culture.[35] The country's political leadership mirrored this duality. Harold Wilson, Labour Party victor of the October 1964 general election, cultivated his image as a plain-speaking Yorkshireman. Yet he was prone to flourishes of imperial rhetoric. Speaking in New Delhi in 1965, he insisted that Britain's frontiers were on the Himalayas.[36] More seriously, he led Lyndon Johnson a merry dance, invoking other obligations 'east of Suez' as he equivocated over sending British troops into Vietnam without, it seems, ever planning to do so.[37] But when it came to the two most taxing decolonization questions of Wilson's premiership— how to respond to white Rhodesia's illegal Unilateral Declaration of Independence in 1965, and when to cut Britain's unaffordable Southeast Asian garrisons—the Labour Party chose sanctions over force and withdrawal over commitment. It did so safe in the knowledge that Britain's imperial diehards were a shrinking minority.[38] Britain's most definitive break with a loyalist settler population was made easier by the Rhodesians' unapologetic racism. And, by 1967, the argument for pulling back from 'east of Suez' made itself amid Britain's latest devaluation crisis. This was not an agonizing decolonization but a business decision. Like a corporation threatened with bankruptcy, fixed assets were surrendered to assure creditworthiness.

Empire out of Time?

Jibes about an empire in receivership had a ring of truth, but it is questionable whether the British public really cared. Historian Martin Farr evokes the disjuncture between the seeming totality of British imperial decline and the celebratory pop culture of 'swinging London'. From 1963 to 1968, successive colonial withdrawals were punctuated by one Britpop hit after another, the two-minute song providing the soundtrack for this inverse relationship between a fast-shrinking empire and worldwide fascination with the 'fab four' Beatles, the rock-star misbehavior of the Rolling Stones, and the ironic *Sgt. Pepper* militarism of Carnaby Street fashion. Britain's fading global presence, confirmed by Labour's decision to pull out the last garrisons from east of the Suez Canal, was marked by a less familiar statistic: that 1968 was the only year of the twentieth century in which no British service personnel were killed in action overseas.[39]

Britain's balance of payments crisis in 1967 was quickly followed by precipitous falls in sterling against the US dollar. These recurred in 1968. The dislocation between sterling and dollar values seemed to confirm not just Britain's monetary weakness, but the shift in financial power away from the Atlanticist orbit of the Bretton Woods system. The closer integration of global capital markets allowed money to flow faster and in multiple directions. The growing wealth of Arab oil producers pointed to a different global economic future.[40]

That being said, it was too early to write off Britain as a spent economic force. A thought-provoking argument for the persistence of empire through financial rather than political or military power dwells on the high proportion of international loans and monetary deposits made either in the City of London or in British overseas territories—the Cayman Islands and the Channel Islands, for instance—renowned for their tax advantages and limited fiscal regulation. As late as 2009, Britain and its offshore dependencies and linked former imperial territories such as Singapore and Hong Kong accounted for almost 40 percent of outstanding international loans, perhaps the strongest tangible proof of the quasi-colonial configuration of global financial transactions.[41] British or British-administered international financial centers cornered a large share of global financial markets, thanks in large part to their exploitation of interbank trades conducted in foreign currency deposits, the Eurodollar or the Eurobond mentioned earlier.[42] The City of London seized on the potential of the Eurodollar market, which, in the decade following the Suez Crisis of 1956, enabled Britain to accumulate a pool of dollars outside American regulatory restrictions.

As Britain's Westminster elite reeled from its Middle Eastern humiliation by Nasser's Egypt, City of London bankers exploited the tax advantages and limited regulatory oversight in Britain's offshore dependencies to build a massive new financial market in interbank trades. Faced with tighter domestic restrictions introduced in 1957 on the use of sterling in international lending, the City's commercial banks, with encouragement from the Bank of England, chose to use dollars in their international dealings instead.[43] The arrangement suited US banks as well. An emerging Eurodollar market in dollar trading overseas enabled American bankers to conduct international lending beyond the stifling regulatory confines of their country's capital control legislation.[44]

The British Treasury and the Bank of England were surprised by the breakneck expansion of the Eurodollar market. But they allowed its continuation. With decolonization gathering momentum and Britain's relationship with the European Economic Community (EEC) still unresolved, permitting the Eurodollar market to expand was a case of not looking a gift horse in the mouth rather than actively encouraging it to race.[45] The result was crucial. What at first aided the British quest for currency convertibility ultimately 'drowned the Bretton Woods system whole'.[46] The City of London's receptiveness to offshore monetary dealing assured Britain's prominence as a leading financial power regardless of British imperial decline, the contraction of its manufacturing base, and its changing relationship with the EEC/European Union.[47] Put differently, the disintegration of Britain's formal empire proved no barrier to the expansion of the country's role as a global financial hub. Quite the reverse: it catalyzed it.

The Americans Are Coming: The Modernizers

As we saw in the preceding chapter, the emergence of new nation-states in the global South and the shifting contours of the Cold War from the 1950s to the 1970s enhanced the political influence of modernization theorists working within US academia.[48] Many helped to define the priorities of American geopolitics, counterinsurgency strategies, and the development schemes that ran in parallel with them. Southeast Asia predominated in the counsels of leading figures in the field such as Lucian Pye, Clifford Geertz, and Walt Rostow.[49] Rostow's most influential book, *The Stages of Economic Growth: A Non-Communist Manifesto*, evoked Marxist ideas while reversing their proposition that state-led economic development was best accomplished under communism, not capitalism.[50]

The conceptualization of national development as a universal ideal of especial importance to newly independent countries 'transitioning' to modernity was matched by the conviction inside Dwight Eisenhower's administration and redoubled by John F. Kennedy's White House team that targeted economic aid should serve US strategic interests among emerging nations. Economic and military assistance programs were to complement the advancement of America's global presence and its trading partnerships via the IMF, the World Bank, and the UN. Development aid thus became modernization theory's instrument.[51] Protagonists claimed that their ideas had global salience even though the theory itself was diffusionist. It posited that decolonizing societies required Western political guidance and US dollars to wean their peoples from 'traditional' practices, both cultural and economic. Translated into policy prescriptions, modernization theory became a series of vast social engineering projects. Adopting the language of social psychology, its advocates insisted that externally mediated modernization would enable peasant societies to overcome the psychological disorientation that induction into an American-led capitalist system of nation-states provoked.[52] Enacted most famously in the Strategic Hamlet Program imposed in South Vietnam beginning in 1961, modernization theory reoriented US Cold War strategy in the decolonizing world to aggressive counterinsurgency, also known as COIN, and the cultivation of proxy regimes (South Vietnam foremost) and loyal partners (Suharto's Indonesia, for instance) in Southeast Asia and elsewhere.[53]

The American commitment to power projection through applied modernization was part of a larger transition of power in which the United States assumed the role of strongest external actor, a place once occupied by the European imperial powers. In Britain's case, this substitution was more or less consensual.[54] In the case of, first, the Dutch, then the French, in Southeast Asia and northwest Africa, it was not.[55] Modernization theorists were tarnished by their association with new manifestations of American imperial power, evident in heightened interventionism from the 1950s onward.[56] And its anticommunist impulse registered in material support for repressive policing of the kind inculcated by Washington DC's International Police Academy. Significantly, this institution, a training school in coercive techniques whose graduates applied its lessons of political violence and torture against leftist oppositionists in Latin America, Africa, and Asia, was a creation of the Office of Public Safety within the US International Development Agency.[57]

Connections between deterministic ideas of political economy and covert support for repressive apparatus in client states bridged the gap between the late colonial counterinsurgencies pursued by European imperialists and those of the United States. Each assumed that previous military campaigns fell short because they addressed the symptom but not the cause of local grievances that were rooted in poverty, underadministration, and lack of welfare provision.[58] Reflecting the influence of modernization theory, advocates of COIN strategies in the decolonizing world were convinced that insurgents would win out unless security forces delivered lasting improvements in living standards. This thinking reached its apogee under the Kennedy administration, whose 'internal defense' doctrine endorsed intrusive nation-building efforts with client regimes, the most obvious example being Ngô Dình Diệm's South Vietnamese government.[59]

Consistent with these strategic objectives, during the 1960s the Kennedy and Johnson administrations changed the order of priorities governing US food aid. Originally set up through the 1954 Agricultural Trade Development and Assistance Act to reduce the cost of storing American farm surpluses, food aid distribution was harnessed to US foreign policy interests in the 1960s. Spurred by India's requests for food supplies after a shortage of replenishing monsoon rains in 1965, Johnson's 'short tether' policy made monthly releases of food aid conditional on recipients' good behavior. In India's case, this meant cleaving to American wishes after the outbreak of renewed war with Pakistan. The short tether was then used repeatedly, with Egypt, Ghana, and Brazil, among others, its preconditions underlining America's global food power and the geopolitics behind it.[60]

The Decolonizing World Bites Back

The 'short tether' may have been economically effective, but its insensitivity rebounded.[61] Decolonizing nations wove Western pressure of this type into three narratives inimical to Washington and its allies: supporting nonalignment, affirming Third Worldist solidarity, and warning of the perils of neocolonialism. Analyzing the actions of key anticolonial leaders (Tanzania's Julius Nyerere, Ghana's Kwame Nkrumah, and Jamaica's Michael Manley), Adom Getachew traces the ideas of political economy that shaped their arguments for a New International Economic Order (NIEO) between the early 1960s and the late 1970s.[62] Nyerere was the OAU's leading practitioner of frontline state support for Southern Africa's national liberation movements and a pioneer of socialistic self-reliance inside Tanzania. His preference for statist planning and agricultural collectivism drew him toward Communist sponsors alongside more established West German providers of development aid.[63] For Nkrumah, Ghana's core problem was that the global economic order remained imperialistic and unjust. Like other pan-Africanist contemporaries, including Sékou Touré, president of neighboring Guinea, Nkrumah saw remedies in greater political unity among decolonizing societies, backed with regional economic federations to combat neocolonial dependency by creating markets large enough to stimulate rapid economic diversification.[64] As matters stood, terms of trade in the primary goods essential to Ghana's economic development were stacked against the exporter countries of the global South. Commodity prices were determined by rich-world importers and their capital markets and not by African and other Third World producers. Foreign-owned mining concerns and agricultural consortia raked off the profits from commodity production anyway.[65]

Those same processes of imperialist trade and capital accumulation in western Europe and North America were the prelude to environmental spoliation, fossil fuel industrialization, and the climate change crisis of the 'Anthropocene'. This linkage between empire capitalism and ecological damage pervades cross-disciplinary work on problems of global scarcity. As in the age of empire, so in the aftermath of decolonization, shortages of essential resources and consequent insecurity hit the poor hardest, more a reflection of uneven power relations than of there not being enough to go round.[66]

The argument that capitalist intrusion and Western control of global commodity markets perpetuated poverty and inequality in the global South had a long pedigree. Its first regional case study was not Africa, but Latin America. It was there that the underlying problem of economic dependency was first spotlighted in the early years of the Mexican Revolution.[67] Argentine economist Raúl Prebisch subsequently delineated its structural causes. A precocious talent, Prebisch headed the United Nations' Economic Commission for Latin America, for which he wrote a defining 1950 report on Latin America's development challenges.[68] The Non-Aligned Movement endorsed Prebisch's ideas and those of other dependency theorists, among them Brazilian academic and future president Fernando Henrique Cardoso. In the early 1960s this thinking provided philosophical glue to the Group of 77 (G77) developing-country coalition and its UN arm, the United Nations Conference for Trade and Development (UNCTAD).[69]

Nation after nation securing political independence in the decade after Bandung made the call for a new era of postcolonial cooperation, only to find their economic sovereignty compromised by the need for foreign capital and terms of trade, over which they exerted little influence. Disillusionment with the political strings attached to American economic assistance under its Alliance for Progress program, launched in 1961, was also pivotal to Latin American support for UNCTAD.[70] The power of multinational corporations within the domestic markets of Third World countries compounded concerns about neocolonialist influence. The fact that several such corporations originated in trading companies of the colonial era made matters worse. From the Dutch and British East India Companies to the trading companies of British and French Africa, these colonial corporations accrued administrative powers, becoming instrumental in the initial consolidation of imperial control.[71] British governmental anxieties in the early 1900s about capital-intensive investment in oil exploration, for instance, stimulated official interest in working with private-sector consortia willing to assume costs and risks.[72] From Iraq to Nigeria, over later decades oil companies not only advanced British imperial designs but acted as surrogates for government as well.[73] It was easy to cast multinationals, from oil and mining companies to foodstuff and retail conglomerates, in the same light.[74]

That negative image froze more solidly still during the Congo crisis of 1960–1965 thanks to the actions of the Union Minière du Haut Katanga (UMHK). A vast multinational mining corporation whose roots stretched back to the pitiless exploitation of King Leopold's Congo Free State, the UMHK was vilified in Third Worldist circles as a key financial player in the grubby dealings of Western governments, their security agencies, and mercenary surrogates, first in overthrowing Patrice Lumumba's Congolese regime, then in sustaining Katanga's secession from it as the servant of foreign capitalist interests.[75] Other Belgian economic actors were organized into the Groupement internationale d'études pour le développement du Congo (GIEDC), established by the Brussels authorities in May 1960. Preparing for development partnerships after Congolese independence, the GIEDC consortium was reluctant to work with Lumumba's regime in theory and unable to do so in practice.[76] The consequences were soon felt in Third Worldist concepts of international political economy. Dependency theory was nourished by accusations of deliberate underdevelopment and malevolent foreign interference in decolonizing nations. Central to it all were global trading patterns stacked in favor of rich-world manufacturers. By the early 1960s they benefited from falling commodity prices inimical to global South primary producers reliant on transportation systems, bulk carriers, and

La création d'une industrie spécifiquement nationale, permettra enfin à notre économie
de se débarrasser de la dépendance colonialiste.

FIGURE 13.1. Socialist self-sufficiency in action: Algerian textiles factory, early 1963. Source: IISH, COLL00201, 'L'Algérie en marche vers le Socialisme.'

pricing structures outside their control.[77] Meshed together, ideas about these sources of structural economic discrimination gained traction under the moniker of neocolonialism.[78]

Kwame Nkrumah did most to articulate these ideas in his excoriating 1965 book *Neocolonialism: The Last Stage of Imperialism*, but others had been thinking along similar lines for years before. Algeria's GPRA coined the term 'dominated economies', partly to nail economists' preference for more neutral adjectives ('disjointed', 'dualist', and 'unbalanced' were fairly typical) and partly to defend plans to nationalize export production after independence, without necessarily compensating the industrial and agricultural conglomerates involved.[79]

Rarely did such abrupt socializations of economies succeed in either shutting out multinational capitalism or spreading internal wealth more evenly.[80] From early enthusiasts in the 1960s, such as Ghana, Algeria, and Tanzania, to others such as Jamaica, Vietnam, and Angola in the 1970s, a first flush of redistribution eventually gave way either to variants of state capitalism or to chronic indebtedness, appeals to the IMF, and long-term loan adjustments.[81]

All of this suggests that the path to economic sovereignty proved harder to navigate than the route to political independence. 'Enemies' were more varied and harder to pin down. But it was the systemic challenge that was decisive. The world had tilted decisively against the politics of colonialism, a shrinking minority prepared to defend the racist exclusion at its core. The economics of global capitalism was less readily identifiable with a single ethical imperative. That changed in the early 1960s. Where dependency theory led, its cognate, neocolonialism, would follow, making explicit the connection between colonialism and capitalist trade. The frustrations shared by newly independent countries desperate to generate wealth outside the constraints of Bretton Woods–type trading arrangements brought the G77 together.[82] Some frictions remained. National economic priorities sometimes clashed with the internationalist impulses of Third Worldism. Foreign exchange revenues were urgently needed to fund transformational projects at home. These difficulties only confirmed the commonality of economic experience for decolonizing nations unable to reorder patterns of global trade alone. But how should they combine?

Schemes of postcolonial federation between new nations in the Middle East, West Africa, and the West Indies, which Nasser, Nkrumah, Senghor, and others hoped might provide the muscle to match political independence with economic strength, soon fell apart. There was imperialism of a sort here as well. Tensions arose within these federations between the centralizing tendencies of the dominant member state and the national aspirations of its satellite partners. Syrians bridled at political direction from Egypt. Malian interests were bound up with West Africa's Sahel, less with those of Senegambian cultivators in Senegal's fertile interior.[83] Jamaica's bauxite economy and violent party politics might resonate in Trinidad, where oil production was similarly dominant and rival political elites nurtured local client networks. But there were profound regional and cultural differences, too.[84] Nor were all decolonizers agreed that federation made sense. Postcolonial regimes like Ghana's, preoccupied with barriers to independence arising from dependency on rich-world nations, clashed with others, like Nigeria, that were more anxious to promote a unitary state to contain their internal ethnoreligious tensions.[85] Federalism implied a pooling of sovereignty that threatened to empower minority populations to the detriment of central governments and 'national movements' that prioritized their own consolidation of local power. The resultant political frictions broke such unions apart.

If decolonizing countries found it difficult to sustain binding federal arrangements, perhaps they could advance their economic interests by sponsoring fundamental changes in the way global trade was done. Control over domestic natural resources was an acid test of enduring imperial intrusion, something apparent throughout the twentieth century but more sharply felt from the 1950s as decolonization advanced. From Iranian oil in 1951 to the Suez Canal in 1956 and numerous cases before and after, hostile Western reaction to the nationalization of key industries by regimes seeking to curb imperialist influence drew the battle lines for the NIEO's core demand in the early 1970s for global economic redistribution.[86] At issue was the effort to match political independence with economic self-determination.[87] 'Completing decolonization' could only be achieved if new nations united against the structural inequalities of the economic order enshrined at Bretton Woods.[88]

UNCTAD, meanwhile, offered a supranational forum in which to discuss fundamental changes to trade rules, the actions of multinationals, and the redistribution of commercial profits. Challenging the juridical basis of global capitalism required sustained cooperation among UNCTAD commodity producers over a common plan. Central to it was an idealistic vision of an economic order that put people over profit. Global welfarism began with the rejection of an economic system that condemned decolonizing countries to keep supplying the requirements of the rich industrial world. Tanzanian premier Julius Nyerere characterized the UNCTAD response as a 'trade union of the poor'.[89] Two elements were at its heart. One was the assertion of national rights over natural resources and the terms of commerce. The other was a desire to reverse the geometry of international trade law, changing its foremost priority from the protection of private corporations within Third World countries to the defense of developing countries against capitalist predation.[90]

The NIEO was one such initiative. The product of a special session of the UN General Assembly dedicated to global economic problems in May 1974, it marked the most ambitious effort by former colonies and other commodity-exporting countries in the developing world to demolish the precepts of unequal capitalist exchange, placing the interests of primary producers above the requirements of industrialized rich-world importers.[91] Maximizing the weight of its global South members, the General Assembly produced a program of action to make an NIEO stick. It included a moratorium on Third World debts, reduced tariff barriers to developing country exports, arrangements to promote technology transfer to poorer countries, and a UN apparatus to stabilize commodity prices backed by a Common Fund to support them.[92] The Algerian regime was pivotal. The Algerians were key players in OPEC and figured among the Arab oil producers prepared to use the so-called oil weapon of production controls and price rises as foreign policy instruments in the Arab–Israeli conflict. Algeria held the presidency of the Non-Aligned Movement and sought to reorient the NAM toward matters of economic sovereignty and wealth redistribution. And President Houari Boumédiène's regime had already extended state control over its petrochemical sector, justifying its nationalization program as a blow against dependency.[93] Within the countries suffering most from such neocolonialism—commodity producers such as Ghana, Jamaica, and the oil producers reliant on a narrow range of exports to sustain income, liquidity, and currency values—the attractions of a new international economic order were as much ethical as financial.[94]

Others, such as Mexico's President Luis Echeverría, drew on decades of political advocacy for economic sovereignty to make the case for fairer governance of global trade through an NIEO Charter of Economic Rights and Duties of States.[95] Echeverría, rightly confident that the Charter would win UN General Assembly support, focused his negotiation effort on the Nixon administration, National Security Advisor and NIEO critic Henry Kissinger in particular. The Mexican president played on Washington's strategic interests, arguing that rejection of the Charter would be an avoidable error, bound to sharpen ideological polarization between global South nations and their rich-world creditors.[96] Kissinger, though, was unmoved and worked assiduously to undermine the NIEO initiative.[97] Underlying this contextual synopsis is a basic point: by 1964 decolonization's key battleground was a matter of political economy, based on recognition among the leaderships of newly independent nations that their capacity for autonomous decision-making was hamstrung by economic dependence on rich-world trade partners, debt funders, and development agencies.[98]

NIEO-supporting states at the United Nations sought a binding code of conduct to regulate the actions of 'rootless' multinationals, establishing an Intergovernmental Commission on Transnational Corporations to do the job.[99] The aim was to subordinate the commercial priorities of multinational corporations to the development requirements of the commodity producers, in return for which the producing countries would guarantee protections for investor interests.[100] As it transpired, the first objective faded from view as neoliberalism took hold. Aligning multinationals with the development goals of producer states was always improbable. By the 1980s the opposite outcome seemed more likely. Changes in international investment law afforded shareholders in multinational corporations doing business in Third World countries better protection against the expropriation of their capital.[101]

To its defenders, this shift encouraged heightened investment and, with it, trickle-down prosperity. In a move whose financial implications were matched by its powerful symbolism, in January 1976 Michael Manley's Jamaican government hosted a decisive series of IMF meetings in Kingston, the prelude to a severe IMF-imposed devaluation. The resulting Jamaica Accords were not confined to measures affecting the island's economy. They sounded the death knell, not just of the NIEO but of the Bretton Woods system as well. IMF governors ended the dollar–gold standard link pivotal to Bretton Woods trade policy and turned instead to the renegotiation of developing-country balance-of-payments deficits by tying the G77 into programs of long-term structural adjustment.[102] To its critics, the victory of neoliberal commercial practices over the restrictions proposed under the NIEO perpetuated economic injustice, leaching resources from the poor world.[103] Colonial-style extraction continued in exchange-rate differences and unequal terms of trade determined by rich-world importers.[104] In societies where daily resource struggles dominated the lives of the poorest, the structural inequalities of global trade mapped onto local grievances about coercive labor practices and limited access to diverse sources of wealth, from farmland to urban employment.[105]

Conclusion

With the hopes raised by the NIEO project fading as the 1970s wore on, local dissatisfaction with decolonization's limited achievements increased. Patterns of protest in newly independent nations were remarkably similar in the decades after independence, with food riots, demonstrations by excluded ethnic minorities, and demands for the fulfillment of decolonization pledges predominating as causes of social unrest. At a deeper level, the distribution of political power in numerous former colonial dependencies could be characterized as variants of state capitalism. For all the leftist leanings of erstwhile anticolonial movements that took office after the withdrawal of European rulers, few governments in postcolonial nations sustained early commitments to redistribution. Many proved equally unwilling to invest in more social-democratic alternatives of a mixed economy built around a private sector whose growth would be encouraged by selective governmental support. Instead, the Cold War returned to Africa with a vengeance in the 1970s and 1980s, heightened superpower interventionism manifested in proxy wars and deteriorating standards of governance.[106]

Greater effort was invested in ensuring state control over national defense, internal security, and, crucially, the principal sources of export revenue. The resulting shift toward authoritarian politics was thus matched by forms of state capitalism in which ruling parties entrenched themselves in a governing regime by tightening control over their country's natural resources and other sources of wealth. Controlling the commanding heights of the economy, authoritarian governments from the Arab socialist regimes of the Middle East and North Africa to the one-party states prevalent in black Africa proclaimed their commitment to rapid social and economic development. Often, efforts were made to placate the poorest members of these societies, whether rural laborers, workers in the informal sector, or the unemployed, through subsidies guaranteeing affordable foods and fuel and, on occasion, access to cultivatable land. But the tradeoffs involved rarely survived the shift to heavier foreign borrowing, debt restructuring, and other facets of structural adjustment that became increasingly commonplace from the late 1970s onward.[107] If the political economy of decolonization points to a process at worst frustrated, at best incomplete, the international and transnational networks behind it offer a different perspective of political and cultural worlds remade despite—and, at times, because of—the pull of capitalist globalization. This is where the next chapter comes in.

CHAPTER FOURTEEN

Conference Cultures and Third-World Decolonization

SEVERAL FACTORS LENT substance to the idea that global politics was configured into three worlds—first, second, and third—in the thirty years or so after 1945.[1] Cold War confrontation between capitalist West and Communist East rested on ideological rigidities and a geopolitical stasis at variance with the revolutionary ferment and strategic realignments of a decolonizing Third World. This fluidity ensured that from Korea in the early 1950s to Angola, Nicaragua, Afghanistan, and elsewhere from the 1970s onward, it was within territories fighting colonialism that proxy conflicts proliferated as this global Cold War—in reality a series of 'hot war' conflicts in Asia, Africa, and Central America—was fought out.[2]

The rapidity of postwar economic growth in the rich West meanwhile set a more peaceful 'First World' apart from relative stagnation in the Communist East/Second World and enduring poverty and political violence in the global South/Third World. As we've seen, for imperial authorities and Washington administrations infused with vogueish theories of modernization, these contrasts encouraged rescue-like narratives of developmental interventionism. From the colonial world and the Communist powers came rebarbative anti-imperial critiques ridiculing the proposition that global inequality could be tackled within imperialist structures.[3] A Moscow press campaign begun in December 1949 struck back at Western criticisms of the Soviet gulag, characterizing colonial Africa as 'a vast forced labor camp', condemning the affability between the City of London and businesses in apartheid South Africa, and mocking the French Union as a hollow reformist gesture that belied the repression of oppositional movements.[4]

Actions followed ideas. From the teams of Bulgarian physicians staffing field hospitals in North Korea in 1950–1952 to the holistic psychiatric care applied by Yugoslavian medical staff treating mental illness in black Africa, new scientific and medical connections were forged between Second and Third World partners who rejected First World dominance.[5] For Warsaw Pact countries beginning in the 1950s, as for Communist Cuba from the 1960s onward, scientific collaboration, medical humanitarianism, and supplies of affordable pharmaceuticals to low-income societies in the global South affirmed their distinctiveness as socialist nations, cementing internationalist solidarity with a Third World project.[6] What did this project comprise? With social rights and economic needs to the fore, the shift to nonalignment among anticolonialist movements and newly independent nations was a logical outcome of the three worlds construction, while the Third World project was rooted in the recognition that colonized communities shared neither the strategic interests nor the political preoccupations of the opposing Cold War blocs. Nonalignment was more than a geopolitical stance; it asserted a distinctly non-Western politics, a decolonizing republicanism that placed the interests of colonized peoples first.[7]

Nonalignment gestated amid the Cold War but defined itself in opposition to it. Even Cold War giants sometimes bent to the ethical logic of Third World internationalism. Claiming the moral high ground as a proponent of global peace against McCarthyite America, Maoist China hosted an Asian-Pacific Peace Conference in Beijing during October 1952, whose sessions convened beneath a mural by Mexican artist Diego Rivera depicting Asian peoples united in opposition to imperialist persecution and the menace of nuclear annihilation. The emotional power of the Beijing Conference, as historian Rachel Leow suggests, has long been overlooked.[8] The same might be said about the pan-American Continental Congress for World Peace held in Mexico City between September 5 and 10, 1949. Here, too, artistic contributions, from poetry and dance to murals, some of which were, again, designed by Diego Rivera, became central in conveying the primacy of Third World liberation.[9] These meetings and other foundational Third Worldist gatherings mattered, both in defining a distinctly anticolonialist worldview and in framing new ways to make colonized voices heard on a global stage. Consider for a moment the 1947 Asian Relations Conference, whose role in codifying strategies of nonalignment is also underappreciated. The same holds for another Indian-hosted symposium, the Conference of Asian Countries on the Relaxation of International Tension (CRIT), which opened in New Delhi on April 6, 1955. An inclusive gathering open to the public and coordinated by the social worker and Indian women's movement organizer Rameshwari Nehru, CRIT brought together Indian civil society groups, peace activists, and Sino-Indian friendship societies with their colleagues from East and Southeast Asia in particular.[10] Festive in tone, the conference's literary, theatrical, and musical dimensions amplified its political message of anti-imperialist peace activism. The diversity of the associational cultures on display disarmed hostile characterizations of the CRIT gathering as an instrument of the Soviet-directed World Peace Council. If anything, CRIT demonstrated the reverse: that grassroots rejection of colonialism meshed with popular anxieties across Asia about the proliferation of antagonistic Cold War blocs, the latest being the Anglo-American-sponsored Southeast Asia Treaty Organization (SEATO). Hostile camps of nations beholden to the Cold War giants not only heightened the risk of war but threatened to perpetuate imperialistic dominance.[11]

The minimal governmental attention to the CRIT conference underlines the problem that the conference tried to address: how were activist citizens from all walks of life inspired by a shared anti-imperialism to translate cultural protest into material change in the fabric of international relations? Astutely marketed by its host government and mixing scores of 'official' delegations with prominent cultural figures in Asian, African, and black Atlantic anticolonialism, another Asian–African Conference less than a fortnight later promised to break the mold. This meeting, held between April 18 and 24, 1955, in the capital of Indonesia's West Java province, is widely considered so transformative that it is discursively abbreviated to its location: Bandung.[12]

The Panchsheela and Bandung

Before revisiting Bandung, let's travel back twelve months earlier, to April 1954. As North Vietnamese troops neared victory at Dien Biên Phu, India and the People's Republic of China reached a settlement over Chinese-occupied Tibet. At the same time, the two Asian giants elaborated the 'five principles' (*panchsheela*) by which their relations should proceed. Each was to respect the other's territorial integrity. Noninterference in their neighbor's internal affairs would also be upheld. Nonaggression became a formal objective. Relations were to proceed on an equitable basis.[13] The fifth and ultimate goal was summarized as peaceful coexistence. Western observers, inclined to dismiss the five principles as vague and utopian, misunderstood what was happening. According to historian Matthew Jones, the *panchsheela*, perhaps more than any other statement at this time, best represented the philosophical gulf between an 'Asian' perspective on resolving outstanding issues between newly independent states and the fears of a bipolar division of the region into rival military blocs that the Southeast Asia Treaty Organization (SEATO) was helping to excite.[14]

The divide, as much philosophical as ideological, between the Cold War mindsets of the Western and Eastern blocs on the one hand, and the emergent nonalignment of the global South on the other, was underlined eight months later when the five Colombo Powers—Ceylon, Burma, Pakistan, Indonesia, and India—convened their second summit at Bogor, Indonesia, in December 1954. Identified by their inaugural April 1954 meeting in the Ceylonese capital, collectively the Colombo Powers eschewed a militantly anticolonial stance. With the exception of Indonesia, which remained at loggerheads with the Netherlands over control of West Irian (Western Papua), the five were animated by a shared desire to safeguard hard-won national sovereignty rather than continue anticolonial struggle. Indo–Pakistan rivalry over Kashmir caused other frictions within this Southeast Asian neutralist group.[15] But the panchsheela kept them together. The Colombo Powers recoiled from the global 'pactomania' of the Cold War behemoths, convinced that the panchsheela principles offered an alternate basis for sovereign coexistence and wider regional peace. Whether at the geopolitical level of Asian statecraft or the ideational level of loathing for imperialistic interference, the Colombo Powers made panchsheela real.[16] At Bogor they announced a larger conference of Asian and African states for the coming spring.[17] Bandung was the result.

Bandung's symbolic importance outlived its administrative legacies. Both, though, were substantial.[18] In the unfolding history of decolonization, Bandung was everything that the 1919 Peace Conference was not. Where the Paris settlement was unapologetically Eurocentric and imperialistic, Bandung was Afro-Asian and anti-imperial. Its fundamental goal was to topple Western and Soviet bloc presumptions that self-determination could be bargained for political loyalty. Nationhood, it asserted, was a fundamental right, not a gift that foreigners could bestow.[19] In the words of its leading literary observer Richard Wright, Bandung seemed like 'the human race speaking'.[20] In its ethical aspirations as much as in its willingness to blur the boundaries between state actors and liberation movements, the event marked an important step toward norms convergence between nations hostile to colonialism and

FIGURE 14.1. Delegates arrive at the Bandung conference center, May 1955.
Source: Getty Images.

the insurgents and social movements struggling locally to overthrow it. Differences in ideology and strategic priorities among the delegates, from Chinese Foreign Minister Zhou Enlai to Ceylon's anticommunist premier Sir John Kotelawala, did not dilute their unity of purpose in supporting decolonization.[21] Characteristically, these two men got on rather well after some frank exchanges over the communization of Tibet.

Bandung proceeded as the antithesis of formulaic diplomatic stodge. Its Indonesian hosts spruced up the city and its conference venues. Delegates' arrivals, departures, and crowd walkabouts were meticulously choreographed.[22] The attention to spatial design and garlanded promenades matched the harmonious tone of the conference message. From Indonesian President Sukarno's opening address to the longer conference pronouncements by Indian premier Jawaharlal Nehru describing the pull of nonalignment, Bandung was inflected with a moral rhetoric as much spiritual as humanistic.[23]

Tensions occasionally surfaced, apparent, for instance, in the tendency among some Asian delegates to patronize their African colleagues.[24] But by ranging itself against a world of empires, Bandung presented something more united. The five organizing South and Southeast Asian countries were joined by delegations from twenty-four Asian and African territories touched by foreign imperialism. Other invitees included representatives of South Africa's African National Congress, Greek Cypriot nationalists, and Algeria's FLN.[25] A statement of intent from a politicized Third World, Bandung signified the absolute prioritization of global issues of imperialist interference and structural inequality.[26] As the connective tissue between them was colonialism, only drastic surgery—the complete emancipation of peoples living under colonialist influence—could deliver a cure.

The problem confronting attendees was how newly independent states could mobilize against empire at the same time as they strove to improve living standards and 'develop' as integrated economies.[27] Development as discussed at Bandung was less technocratic than ethical, its core purpose being long-term poverty reduction rather than any short-term increase in economic performance.[28] If the paradox of an anticolonialist conference that accepted Western constructions of statehood and modernization went largely unaddressed, awareness of the stark inequalities between rich world and poor pervaded the conference and its extensive final communiqué.[29] In some ways, this was close to dependency theory *avant la lettre*, the articulation of the Third World as both a transregional space scarred by empire and, more optimistically, the vanguard of an equitable global politics.[30]

Bandung's institutional legacies were smaller. The conference did not cement a binding anticolonial alliance of independent and soon-to-be-independent states united around the panchsheela politically and committed to closer cooperation economically. Communist China, the presumptive leader of such a bloc, was left disappointed.[31] In other respects, though, the Chinese broke through. Zhou Enlai was Bandung's star performer, as he had been at Geneva a year earlier. At both conferences Zhou demystified the PRC, clarifying the political benefits of engagement. Building on his invitation to the Egyptian delegation to visit China, on May 30, 1956, Nasser's Egypt became the first African country to establish formal relations with Beijing. Months later, Mao's regime offered to send up to 280,000 'volunteers' to help the Egyptians fight off British, French, and Israeli troops at the height of the Suez Crisis.[32] These cadres proved not to be needed, the Eisenhower administration and not China wielding the hatchet against the Anglo-French-Israeli plot to overthrow Nasser by force, but they pointed to a Third Worldist impetus behind anticolonial rebellion, which would enable numerous insurgencies to last out otherwise asymmetric conflicts.

China's insight was not just to recognize but to accelerate the radicalization of Third World politics. After Bandung, the regional focus of

FIGURE 14.2. Bandung as celebrated by the World Federation of Democratic Youth. Source: IISH archive.

Third Worldism shifted westward toward Africa and Latin America.[33] In tune with the first wave of decolonization, the first decade of nonalignment had been Asian-dominated. Indonesia and, above all, India provided the decisive ideas animating the process. In tune with decolonization's coming second wave, in the decade after 1955, the ratification of a formal 'Non-Aligned Movement' at its inaugural Belgrade conference in September 1961 saw Third Worldism acquire a sharper revolutionary edge in support of the violent overthrow of capitalist colonialism. Cuba epitomized this radical turn on one side of the Atlantic, while Algeria, Ghana, and others did so on the other.[34] But the point should not be overdrawn. Revolutionary Cuba aside, Latin American commitment first to Third Worldism and later to the 'positive neutralism' of the NAM was uneven. Peace activism in Mexico combined leftist support for workers' rights and anticolonialist causes with other ethical concerns for the release of political prisoners and democratic accountability, objectives that prohibited reliance on Soviet or other communist dictatorial sponsors.[35] The resulting March 1961 Latin American Conference for National Sovereignty, National Emancipation, and Peace underlined how testing it would be to pursue authentic 'nonalignment'. Melding anticolonialist concern for popular sovereignty and respect for individual rights of political expression was difficult to reconcile with Third Worldism's identification with revolutionary regimes intolerant of internal opposition.[36] In other Latin American countries where the right, and not the left, was in the ascendancy, there was little sign of a Third Worldist tilt. Strategic ties to the United States, residual anticommunism, and the entrenchment of authoritarian regimes explain this early ambivalence and gave Bandung's opponents hope.[37]

Watching Bandung from a distance, the British feigned calm, predicting that the presence of its Asian alliance partners, Ceylon and Pakistan, would moderate the conference pronouncements. But British diplomats knew that another Commonwealth delegation, India's, would be more vocal and would support China's conference presence as a fellow Asian nation historically fettered by Western colonialism.[38] Foreign Office anxieties about Bandung's transcontinental reach explain the British decision to block Kwame Nkrumah, locked in early-stage talks over Ghanaian independence, from attending. This prohibition reflected the misplaced expectation in London that Bandung, rather than affirming a radical Third Worldism with global valence, might instead seem relatively parochial, speaking purely to Asian concerns.[39] Ironically, the mood in Paris was calmer, despite the adulation for the Vietnamese defeat of French security forces that punctuated the conference proceedings.[40]

To some degree, this official sangfroid was a hangover from the accelerated colonial reformism set in train during the two short-lived governments of Pierre Mendès France. More substantially, it mirrored the combination of relief and readjustment that eviction from Indochina precipitated.[41] Aside from its treaty settlements in India, France was no longer an imperial presence on the Asian mainland. High-profile publicity, transnational sympathy, and implicit recognition for the Algerian National Liberation Front delegates at Bandung caused some in French governmental circles to squirm. But they could hardly profess surprise. The FLN, after all, was at war with the French state.

For most Bandung delegations, the conference was less about military pacts, some attendees being anxious to conceal their countries' existing alliance arrangements with Western powers, and more about attitudinal change.[42] Parallels could be drawn with one of the leading voices of negritude, the journal *Présence Africaine*. Founded in 1947, months after the launch of the French Union, by Senegalese writer and politician Alioune Diop and his wife, Christiane Yandé Diop, the editorial structure of *Présence Africaine* evinced the tension between those who cleaved to French and other European literary cultures and those convinced that cultural decolonization demanded rejection of the language and literatures of the colonists to valorize indigenous forms of thought and expression. Was the language of the colonizer inevitably an instrument of oppression because it silenced authentic local registers? Did real decolonization therefore require the rejection of European literatures if colonized peoples were to be as free culturally as they sought to be politically? Did language and literature express universal ideas, bringing people together across cultures? Or was the very aspiration to universalism an expression of imperialistic intent?[43]

Présence Africaine grappled with these questions from its inception. But, as Sarah Dunstan points out, it was in the weeks after Bandung and, even more so, at the Congress of Black Writers and Artists held in 1956, that *Présence Africaine* decolonized itself. The earlier tensions between assimilationists and separatists were not entirely resolved, but the journal and its literary luminaries from French Africa, the Caribbean, and North America looked with sharper focus toward a postcolonial future in which the language of literature, education, and politics would be a tool of cultural freedom.[44]

As Dunstan's insights suggest, Bandung encouraged those invested in it to see the world differently. It was such a landmark because it identified deeper kindred connections between formerly colonized countries, anticolonial social movements, and guerrilla groups determined to advance the interests, local and regional, of the global South.[45] Nonalignment crystallized as more than a perspective, becoming a rallying point for Asian, African, Latin American, and other neutralist states in international politics and UN agencies over the coming decade. Tracing straight-line connections between Bandung and later iterations of anticolonial internationalism is tempting but misleading even so. Bandung offered inspiration rather than a schematic plan. The Africans took up the baton first, arranging a number of symposia, which climaxed with the July 1958 All-African People's Conference in Accra.[46] Capturing Africa's preeminence in anticolonial struggle, the Accra conference went further than Bandung, welcoming representatives of the continent's national liberation movements as full delegates with a rightful claim to speak for their peoples.[47] Subsequent to that, Bandung echoed through consolidation of the NAM in 1961, the foundation of the Organization of African Unity in 1963, the launch of the United Nations Conference of Trade and Development (UNCTAD) the following year and, later, the creation of the Association of Southeast Asian Nations (1967). The intervening extension of Bandung's globalizing anti-imperial agenda with the 1966 Tricontinental is discussed below.[48] Beyond the formal politics of Third World diplomacy, Bandung's cultural evocations—in literature, in art, in protest movements, in collective memories—were perhaps as influential.[49]

Bandung also called out the timidity of supranational institutions and the insufficiency of international law, challenging the former to make the latter an anti-imperial instrument.[50] Replicated by its successors, the accent at Bandung on sovereignty and noninterference was understandably strong. Ideologically, Bandung linked rights politics and self-determination claims without defining the exact substance of either.[51] Carlos P. Romulo, UN representative from the Philippines, went further than most. Warning against any reversion to narrowly focused nationalism, he reminded delegates of what, in twenty-first century parlance, might be called the realities of globalization: 'We have to strive to become nations in a time when history has already passed from the nation to larger units of economic and social coherence: the region, the continent, the world'.[52] National economies could only thrive if they accepted interdependence. Romolo agreed that self-determination was a prerequisite for all and saw the United Nations as the forum in which to promote it. But this was just a first step toward making it in a globalized world.

Drafted by discrete Economic, Political, and Cultural Committees, among the Ten Bandung Principles of the final conference communiqué was the right of all dependent peoples to 'freedom and independence'.[53] If the legal basis for this claim was not spelled out, in commonsense terms it was clear enough. The Ten Principles were also intrinsically significant insofar as their signatories, the majority representing former colonies, had been denied any influence over either the UN Charter or its subsequent human rights declarations. Here at last were precepts for international order emanating directly from the global South.[54] The communiqué went on to state that Cold War rivalry, and its threat to global peace, made nonalignment the sanest option. But these two equations, the first between decolonization and freedom, the second between peace and nonalignment, identified victory for national liberation movements and the consolidation of an international community of nonaligned nations as end points. The accent on internationalism and moral pressure suggested that the road to these destinations should be peaceful. But the presence of freedom fighters in the conference hall and an ambiance crackling with celebration of North Vietnamese victory over France implied otherwise. And what about after decolonization was won? With the notable exceptions of Nehru and Lebanon's Charles Malik, who had worked on the Universal Declaration of Human Rights, most delegates preferred to say nothing about the rights and freedoms of citizens within newly sovereign, nonaligned countries.[55] Some Bandung attendees equivocated about the universality of human rights and the need for supranational agencies to monitor the actions of abusers within independent states.[56] These blind spots notwithstanding, Bandung had opened Pandora's box: the logic of equal entitlement to freedom would not go away.[57]

The final communiqué was clearer in pledging the raw material–producing nations of this nonaligned world to cooperate in efforts to improve their economic standing. In broader terms of political economy, though, Bandung fell short. Delegates made causal connections among colonialist practices, unfair trade, limited access to lines of credit, and the structural inequalities that resulted, but the conference itself could do little to reverse the patterns of commerce and capital extraction that upheld them.[58] Nor were Bandung's primary sponsors, including Indonesia, India, and Burma, keen to shine a light on yawning poverty gaps in their own societies. Bandung, in other words, dwelt on certain economic ills but neglected others.[59] Nor did the conference reject global capitalism per se. Hostility to colonialism was universally shared, but on other issues of political and economic futures, attendees represented diverse ideological positions. Here, Bandung left a more fractious legacy in which differing economic precepts paralleled splits over the acceptability of revolutionary violence.[60] Incipient in 1955, these divisions lingered. At the founding conference of the Afro-Asian People's Solidarity Organization (AAPSO) held in Cairo over December 1957 and January 1958 Nasser and others invoked a more radical 'people's Bandung', insisting that a dying imperialism could be killed off.[61] Radical anticolonialists keen to develop transnational connections with fellow liberationists and to secure money, weapons, and other material aid for their particular decolonization struggles were increasingly attracted to the Egyptian capital. A regime-backed African Association, plus the Cairo-based Secretariat of the Afro-Asian Solidarity Committee, established after the AAPSO conference, served as intermediaries to sympathetic regional governments, fellow national liberation movements, and Communist bloc suppliers.[62] Their aim was not to reconcile divergent anticolonialist views but to push for direct action: in the first instance, material aid to the independence struggles of Algeria's FLN and Dr. Félix-Roland Moumié's Union of the People of Cameroon.[63]

Nonalignment's Alignments

The PRC and Eastern bloc countries were quick to respond. After endorsing the objectives of the July 1958 All-African People's Conference, Warsaw Pact governments worked with Sékou Touré's newly independent Guinean regime to create a West African bridgehead of diplomatic contacts, trade missions, and technical aid.[64] By 1960 the Communist bloc accounted for 65 percent of Guinea's foreign trade. Eastern European advisers were equally prominent in health and psychiatric care, the army, and the Conakry-based General Union of Black African Workers (UGTAN). Its affiliation to the World Federation of Trade Unions made UGTAN the bogeyman in British and French intelligence assessments of creeping Communist influence in West Africa.[65]

Transnational connections to the Communist Second World were further encouraged by four linked strategies: of civil society connection, of educational exchange, of new media propaganda, and of revolutionary emulation. The first of these centered on cycles of fundraising and delegation visits between Communist 'solidarity' movements, principally youth and workplace groups, and their counterparts in decolonizing territories.[66] The second strategy—of educational exchange—linked offers of degree study in Communist bloc universities to the consolidation of ideological bonds with the political elites of a decolonizing global South. To British consternation, the first Nigerian students arrived in East Germany as early as 1951.[67] As many as 1,500 Kenyans traveled to institutions in eastern and central Europe between 1958 and 1969, some receiving military training.[68] Few, though, would become Cold Warriors in the literal sense. Soviet and Chinese investment in insurgent cadres focused more heavily on Southern African national liberation movements, Angola's MPLA and Mozambique's FRELIMO foremost among them, than on anticolonial activists from the Horn of Africa.[69] As historian Ismay Milford makes plain, for East and Central African students, the Communist designation of Eastern Bloc sponsors and various international student 'front' organizations bore less significance than their support for anticolonialism. Independence for African societies, not Cold War alignment, was what counted above all.[70] That being said, it became harder over time to distinguish between the preoccupation with anticolonialist nonalignment among the participants in educational exchange and the Cold War stance of their host institutions. Plans for the enrollment of 4,000 African, Asian, and Latin American students at Moscow's newly opened People's Friendship University between 1960 and 1964 presented an unprecedented threat to Western predominance in the international market for global South students.[71]

The third strategy—of new media propaganda—exploited the spread of transistor radios and long-wave broadcasting. Following the example of an East German regime desperate to secure diplomatic recognition from independent governments in Africa, between 1958 and 1961

Czechoslovakia, Poland, and Romania began dedicated African radio broadcasts. The East Germans, the Czechs, and the Poles transmitted between three and eleven hours of weekly broadcasts in English and French, while the Romanians offered three and a half hours of Portuguese-language programming.[72] As for the fourth strategy—of revolutionary emulation—the North Vietnamese and Chinese held pride of place as anticolonial revolutionaries whose 'people's war' methods were analyzed by African insurgents, initially from a distance but, after Algerian independence, through study groups, training camps, and informal contacts coordinated by the FLN.[73]

The Algerian Republic also planned to host the summer 1965 sequel to Bandung in Algiers. Eventually the meeting fell foul of Defense Minister Houari Boumédiène's ouster of his longtime FLN rival, Algerian President Ahmed Ben Bella, on June 19.[74] By that point, several other leading lights of the original Bandung and AAPSO, including Sukarno, Moumié, Patrice Lumumba, and Mehdi Ben Barka, had either been overthrown or murdered or were at imminent risk.[75] What the Soviet regime described as postcolonial Africa's 'coup contagion', a reference to the growing political influence of African militaries, threatened to remove some of the defining voices of revolutionary Third Worldism.[76] Sobering as this may be, the 'Bandung spirit' was real enough, particularly when situated historically as part of a continuum. Bandung was another link in an anticolonial chain stretching back to the first Pan-Africanist conferences at the turn of the century, the Brussels conference of the League against Imperialism in 1927, Manchester in 1945, and the ARC and CRIT meetings in Delhi.[77] The last of these, CRIT, had also pointed the way to a fusion between local iterations of popular anti-imperialism and a transregional mobilization of civil-society groups, artistic networks, peace activists, and women's rights movements.[78] An important, if unsung, precursor to AAPSO, CRIT's message of cultural inclusivity and common interest resonated with AAPSO's call for shared investment in anticolonial liberation struggles. The objective of a fairer world meant dismantling empire as a core part of international order. This was bound to be a gradual, attritional process, one in which, as Ahmad Rozky Mardhatillah Umar puts it, Bandung and successor conferences were steps toward 'order transition'.[79] Independence settlements were prerequisites to global systemic change but did not signify its achievement.

Conference cultures of Third World decolonization were, in other ways, iconoclastic.[80] They spurned Cold War strategic imperatives by articulating a global South internationalism grounded in anti-imperialism. They discredited a global order tainted by glaring inequalities. Viewed in this way, it was unsurprising that, barely five years after Bandung, the United Nations made anticolonialism integral to its mission with December 1960's Declaration 1514. Conversely, the longer Bandung's anti-imperialist aspirations went unfulfilled, the more the Bandung spirit was revealed for what it was: a historically contextual vision articulated by elite political actors: the product of a distinct way of anticolonial politics at 'a particular moment' and one supplanted by the more confrontational politics of radical Third Worldism.[81]

The NAM and Third Worldism

Would the global South orientation of radical neutralism be sustained? Yes and no. Yes, nonalignment remained identifiable with a decolonizing world. Although the NAM was formally launched in a European capital, Belgrade, at a founding conference in September 1961, Tito's Yugoslavia, a leftist regime attempting to navigate a path between the Eastern and Western blocs, was the exception that proved the rule.[82] Other European neutrals—Ireland and Sweden, for instance—were denied membership.[83] Still others, such as President Adolfo López Mateos's Mexico, sympathetic to NAM demands for economic sovereignty, stopped short of endorsing the Belgrade agenda to avoid antagonizing John F. Kennedy's new administration.[84] But no, the 'neutralism' of early nonalignment became unsustainable once the radicals—Ghana, Egypt, Algeria, Mali, and others—tied the movement to an anti-Western, anticapitalist agenda.[85]

The Algerians were crucial here. Their delegation to Belgrade included a senior trio from their provisional government (the GPRA), Prime Minister Benyoussef Benkhedda, Foreign Minister Saad Dahlab, and Information Minister M'hammed Yazid, plus GPRA chiefs of mission from various countries, including Lakhdar Brahimi, mission chief in Indonesia (more familiar now as UN special envoy during Syria's civil war), Mohamed Harbi, chief of mission in Guinea (and later a historical authority on the Algerian Revolution), and Abdelkader Chanderli, the US mission chief. Their lobbying registered immediately. Before the conference concluded, Afghanistan, Cambodia, Ghana, and Yugoslavia accorded de jure recognition to the GPRA. And the final conference declaration affirmed the determination of NAM member states 'to extend all possible support and aid to the people of Algeria'.[86] Most important, the Algerian delegation cemented the identification between national liberation and the remaking of global order, shifting the axis of radical transnationalism from one dominated by the Communist world to one driven by the global South's radical anticolonialists. GPRA Premier Benyoussef Benkhedda explained the transition:

> For our people who are at war, for we who are resolutely fighting for liberty and peace and who suffer from the deadly effects of colonial domination, the policy of non-alignment reflects our profound aspirations. We do not conceive that a nation can claim to follow the policy of non-alignment without fully enlisting itself at the sides of those peoples fighting for their independence. Similarly, we do not think that a country can fight for liberation from colonial domination without placing its movement within the independent and dynamic framework of non-alignment. . . .
>
> Non-alignment implies for each people the right to select the form of government it desires, to freely choose its regime, its economic and social system, its way of living—in brief, to act in conformity with its own individuality, free of any external pressure . . . this right, this freedom of choice, is incompatible with any participation in a military coalition.[87]

The quickening pace of decolonization suggested that those mobilizing against imperialist control were the principal drivers of revolutionary change. Between the Cuban revolution of 1959 and the FLN's Algerian victory in 1962 the confluence between anti-imperialism and radical new leftist politics took ideological shape in new-style Third Worldism.[88] Injecting anticolonialism with Marxist internationalism, this brand of Third Worldism was as culturally distinctive as it was historically located.[89] What Ernesto 'Che' Guevara personified, Cuba's medical internationalism, beginning with its deployment of health care workers to hospitals in the Algerian towns of Sétif and Sidi-bel-Abbès in May 1963, made tangible reality.[90] Medical aid from one struggling revolutionary country to another evidenced Third Worldism's claim to universal moral authority in defiance of Cold War bipolarity.[91] Like the international medical support networks that proliferated alongside it, Third Worldism challenged capitalist hegemony and the persistence of imperialistic wars.[92]

There was an academic counterpoint to these real-world changes. Growing receptiveness within governments and the media to the abstractions of social science lent credence to a conceptualization of world politics constructed on distinctive hierarchies of regional power. French demographer Alfred Sauvy exemplified the trend, popularizing the term 'Third World' in 1952.[93] Like Moritz Bonn's invocation of 'decolonization' almost thirty years earlier, Sauvy's identification of a 'Third World' in his August 1952 article 'Three Worlds, One Planet' in the French socialist weekly *L'Observateur* acquired a life of its own. Sauvy's warning that exploited 'Third World' peoples would inevitably demand their rights was prescient. [94] But it was his expertise in economics and population growth that appealed to French ministers and modernization advocates.[95] Their technocratic reading of his terminology missed its wider significance. Beyond government, the generic usage of Sauvy's Third World became a rallying cry for radical anticolonialism and a rich-world vernacular for deprivation and underdevelopment.[96]

Historian Mark Berger disaggregates two distinct Third Worldist 'generations'—a shorthand for particular decolonizing nations and social movements—to explain the changing construction of a 'Third World'. The first generation was bound up with the global South struggle for decolonization through nonalignment. It coalesced at Bandung in 1955, but it acquired a sharper organizational edge with the launch of AAPSO at Nasser's Cairo conference two years later. The second Third Worldist generation was more radical than its predecessor, reacting, in part, to the disappointing incompleteness of decolonizaton, enduring neocolonial influence, and rightist authoritarianism in Latin America especially.[97] Where anti-imperialism led, opposition to neocolonialism and conservative realizations of the nation-state would follow.[98] AAPSO-affiliated groups such as the Jakarta-based Afro-Asian Journalists' Association (AAJA) focused as much on threats to the sovereignty of Third World nations as on the struggles of those still fighting for nationhood.[99] In part, that radicalism widened the 1960s breach within the NAM opened by the rightward shift of two leading nonaligned states—India and Indonesia. In part, it was evidence of the pro-Maoist tilt taken by some nonaligned nations after the Sino–Soviet split worsened following Moscow's 1960 suspension of economic aid to China.[100] In part, it reflected the deeper involvement of Latin American countries. The AAJA illustrated each of these transitions—fleeing Indonesia after the September 1965 coup, taking a stridently Maoist tone during the Cultural Revolution, and lauding the Latin American radical Third Worldism of the 1966 Tricontinental.[101]

Regional Third Worldist clusters figured as well. In West Africa, Guinea and Ghana, joined by Modibo Keita's Mali, were 'vanguard' states while, in the Arab world, Nasser's United Arab Republic and the Algerian provisional government remained the most strident. They insisted, first, that all outstanding anticolonial struggles were part of a larger contest against Western imperialism and, second, that the United Nations' partisan intervention in the Congo crisis underlined the need for Third World solidarity.[102] The Latin Americans' perspective was different again. Their long experience of neocolonial interference drove their engagement with Third Worldist platforms like UNCTAD and the NAM, which were inflected with Latin American thinking about the economic roots of dependency and the statist developmentalism needed to dislodge it.[103] This second generation were also infused with the Fanonian philosophy of personal liberation through revolutionary anticolonialism, sharing Fanon's hostility to the neocolonialist mechanisms that constrained numerous commodity-exporting nations after formal independence in the 1960s and 1970s.[104] For its leading pro-tagonists, including Castro's Cuba, Mu'ammar Qaddafi's Libya, Houari Bou-médiène's Algeria, and Michael Manley's People's National Party Jamaica, the high point of globally configured Third Worldism would be reached with the 1974 campaign for a New International Economic Order.[105]

The All-African People's Conference and Unity Moves

As independence leader and, later, Ghana's first president, Kwame Nkrumah straddled both generations, becoming Africa's preeminent Third Worldist. His international politics, if not his domestic authoritari-anism, connected the strategic and economic reorientations of the Third Worldist agenda to the realization of pan-Africanist integration.[106] George Padmore, a prominent attendee at Ghana's independence celebrations in March 1957 and then a permanent resident in its capital, Accra, shared Nkrumah's conviction that the work of decolonization had only just begun.[107] The measure of Ghana's achievement would lie not so much in carving a path to nationhood as in building an authentic African socialism grounded in pan-Africanist ideals and the practice of confederation.[108] As a first step, Padmore backed union between Ghana and Guinea, which, in July 1958, became the first territory in Francophone West Africa to break definitively with France.[109] But it was as organizers of the All-African People's Conference (AAPC) in Accra between December 5 and 13, 1958, that the Padmore–Nkrumah vision of black internationalism crystal-ized.[110] The AAPC combined the pan-Africanist aspirations of Manchester with consideration of practical support to decolonization struggles.[111] It was also a powerful statement: a warning to fellow Africans not to replace the politics of colonial difference with hierarchies of elitism, ethnicity, or class.[112] To be sure, the Accra Conference endorsed favored party political and insurgent clients. But the 'performed solidarity' on display obscured the diversity of opinion among civil society groups, student organizations, and others within the countries and communities ostensibly represented at the AAPC.[113]

The short-term political results of the Accra Conference were difficult to gauge, so historians have understandably fixed on the AAPC's longer-term cultural significance. This was substantial. A supranational African voice took institutional form in the OAU. Announced on May 25, 1963, the OAU Charter affirmed the connection between the independence of its member states and the rejection of external infringements—political, economic, or otherwise—on territorial sovereignty.[114] In a nod to Pad-more's pan-Africanist anticolonialism, the OAU also made the strategic support of African liberation movements its chief international priority.[115] A tearful, tub-thumping speech by Ahmed Ben Bella gave the OAU's foundational conference in Addis Ababa its pinnacle moment. The Algerian president lifted delegates' gaze from economic modernization, pleading for liberation movements in Portuguese Africa. In a vivid rhetorical flourish, Ben Bella framed his call for aid and military intervention to fellow freedom fighters as an African 'blood bank' to complement OAU enthusiasm for a development bank.[116]

Rhetoric was one thing, action another. The radical internationalism among some of decolonization's leading supporters conjured a more equitable international order but was not intrinsically transformative. At its outset, the appointment as OAU secretary-general of Guinean diplomat Diallo Telli, chair of the UN Committee against Apartheid, suggested the new organization would align its policy positions with its anticolonialist sympathies.[117] But neither the hierarchies of race and power within the international society the OAU was joining nor the infringements on member states' economic autonomy by foreign aid providers and multinational conglomerates convinced the organization to pursue federal integration as a defensive response.[118] The OAU's support for decolonization struggles was reflexive. But it was also calibrated. The organization's founding countries tied their defense of sovereign rights to whichever bounded, territorialized vision of the nation best represented the interests of member states' governing regimes.[119] Those nationalist politicians, eager to hold general elections, whether to confirm their claims to office, to fashion their local supporters into voting citizens, or to tie the nation to their ideological vision of its future, were almost bound to strengthen the identification of decolonization, legitimacy, and nationhood. However deep their enthusiasm for pan-Africanist integration, the challenges of binding together the colony-turned-nation favored particularity, expressed as an assertion of national sovereignty.[120]

Two consequences followed. One was the OAU's hostility to secessionist claims. This struck a heavy blow to Nkrumah's pan-Africanist vision of a federated Union of African States pooling their sovereignty.[121] Preoccupied by threats to domestic stability, Morocco, Nigeria, Ethiopia, Sudan, Kenya, and others rejected the proposition that ethnic minorities might secede, a decision confirmed by the OAU's Cairo summit declaration recognizing existing territorial boundaries in September 1964.[122] The longstanding permeability of colonial borders crisscrossed by migratory corridors was spurned in favor of frontier demarcations, new discriminations against minorities, and, in some cases, border wars.[123] It became clear that formal decolonization was not an end to state-making processes. Codifying who did or did not 'belong' was only beginning.[124] The OAU's rejection of secession and its intolerance toward the migratory movements of nomadic pastoralists were preludes to a stricter delimitation of national boundaries and citizenship qualifications. Passage of its July 1964 'Resolution on the Intangibility of Frontiers' set a marker, in historian Julie Macarthur's words, 'delegitimizing any future claims to alternative sovereignties as dissident acts'.[125]

Most OAU members opposed Katangese secession from the Congo in July 1960.[126] Zambia, the soon-to-be frontline state most affected by Katanga's bid for separation, led the charge. In the three years before Kenneth Kaunda's United National Independence Party (UNIP) took office in Lusaka at independence in October 1964, UNIP representatives asserted the legitimacy of Zambian nationhood while decrying Katanga's destructive balkanization of the Congo. Other Central and East African civil society groups, from the region's youth and student internationals to the London-based Committee of African Organisations founded by former Makerere University College student Abu Mayanja, decried Congolese independence as a sham.[127] In this reading, the Congo 'crisis' was an imperialist deception in which the victimization of the country's emblematic leader Patrice Lumumba confirmed the West's refusal to concede authentic freedom to Africa as a whole.[128] Moïse Tshombe's Katangan regime was easily derided as a neocolonial enterprise in hock to Belgian and other Western capitalist interests.[129] But few would endorse Biafra's attempted secession from Nigeria seven years later, despite Igbo claims of minority persecution and genocidal violence against them.[130] Colonies might become nations, but the OAU did not want to redraw Africa's geopolitical map in more fundamental ways.[131] Other participants were more sympathetic to Biafra and fearful of Nigerian regional dominance, such as the Francophone members of the Organisation commune africaine et malgache (OCAM), established in 1965 and headquartered in Bangui, capital of the Central African Republic. But their partiality was no less apparent than that of the OAU, whose efforts to broker an end to the Nigerian–Biafran war in 1967 and 1968 were doomed to fail.[132]

Changing Patterns of Alignment

Below the level of national and supranational politics, patterns of decolonization reconfigured the global cultures of those who supported the process as much as those same global networks influenced the forms that decolonization took. For some activists, personal encounter with conflict zones and communities living under colonialism was jarring. It shattered romanticized, 'radical orientalist' notions of revolutionary solidarity and gender equality. The readiness of decolonized nations from North Korea to Algeria to provide sanctuary, facilities, and high-level support to a spectrum of both peaceful and violent anticolonial social movements presented other dilemmas. Safe havens offering access to the powerful came with strings attached, threatening to compromise the integrity of the groups involved.[133]

The misdeeds of postindependence regimes, particularly those pursuing irredentist or imperialistic agendas of their own, also complicate the picture. Calling out Morocco's pro-Western monarchical regime for its colonialist repression of Western Sahara's *Polisario* front was easy enough. So too Syria's immersion in Lebanon's sectarian politics or apartheid South Africa's destabilization of the frontline states in its regional neighborhood. But what about the imperialist actions of the Indonesian Republic, host of Bandung and an animating spirit of nonalignment, in denying Papuan and Timorese claims to nationhood through protracted campaigns of military repression, forced resettlement, and mass killing?[134] Conversely, certain postcolonial regimes previously derided for breaking with radical nonalignment in the early 1960s used support for self-determination claims and unresolved liberation struggles to rehabilitate themselves as true heirs to the anticolonial fronts of old.[135] Such was the case with Léopold Senghor's Senegal, a relatively conservative regime at the heart of *Francafrique*. By the early 1970s Senegal hosted several 'guerrilla embassies', including Yasser Arafat's Palestine Liberation Organization (PLO) and Ben Tangghama's Revolutionary Provisional Government of West Papau. More proximately, it offered sanctuary and aid to Amílcar Cabral's African Party for the Liberation of Guinea and Cape Verde (PAIGC in its Portuguese acronym) in its armed struggle for the independence of neighboring (Portuguese) Guiné.[136]

With some of nonalignment's preeminent Asian and African nations either tainted or mutually antagonistic, radical Third Worldists turned to another continent—Latin America—for inspiration as the 1960s unfolded. There, the 'crimes' of Western imperialism were predominantly 'Yankee'. Cemented in the preceding decade, US support for rightist dictators, exploitative corporations, and landed elites was epitomized by the overthrow of their opponents and the subversion of democratic parties, trade unions, and peasants' movements through psychological warfare, covert military intervention, and CIA-sponsored assassination.[137] Defying such behavior, the revolutionary pioneer in America's Caribbean backyard became the emblematic Third Worldist regime. From its January 1959 inception, Fidel Castro's Cuba was a beacon for anticolonialism. Its promise of an alternate path to postcolonial modernization was especially alluring. Cuba's leaders lost no time in mobilizing cultural support domestically and internationally, their accent on popular engagement and revolutionary consciousness a powerful counterpoint to what they derided as the bourgeois capitalism of US modernization theory. Cuba's revolutionaries were multimedia communicators: youthful, photogenic, and loud. Pronouncements on gender equality, an end to racial discrimination, and uncompromising opposition to imperialism in all its forms excited support. Their internationalism was avowedly Third Worldist, triangulating national liberation and socialist modernization with authentically popular revolution.[138]

Havana, even more so than Algiers and Hanoi, attracted new left devotees making their pilgrimage to the cultural epicenter of radical anticolonialism. New leftist identification with the overthrow of capitalist imperialism implied a readiness to endorse the insurgent action needed to end empire, pushing anticolonialism toward the embrace of revolutionary violence elaborated most clearly by Fanon.[139] At the same time, nostalgia persisted for 'people power': the idea that multicultural voices united in a just cause might carry the day through moral persuasion.[140] A fine example was the January 1968 Havana Cultural Congress, which blended political discussion of freedom for the Third World with protest music, literary readings, and revolutionary art in what Britain's leading Marxist historian and Congress attendee Eric Hobsbawm described as 'endearing excursions into anti-materialist utopia'.[141]

Utopian perhaps, but Cuba's enduring pride of place as cultural hub of anticolonial globalism mattered. Two years earlier, in January 1966, Cuba's leaders inaugurated the Organization of Solidarity with the People of Africa, Asia, and Latin America (OSPAAL), better known as the Tricontinental.[142] With some five hundred attendees from eighty-two country delegations, the inaugural OSPAAL conference, held between January 3 and 15, 1966, at the Hotel Habana Libre (formerly the Havana Hilton) confirmed Third Worldist identification between anti-imperialist struggles throughout the three continents, pushing Bandung's anticolonialist agenda in new directions.[143] The Tricontinental was virulently anti-American in its pronouncements, singling out the Organization of American States as the 'Yankee Ministry of Colonies'.[144] More positively, the Tricontinental was globally focused in its internationalism, explicitly connecting socialist egalitarianism with support for national liberation.[145] Its striking iconography, in which women freedom fighters featured prominently, lent visual substance to the conference's equation among anticolonialism, antiracism, and socialism.[146]

Still, the OSPAAL could be read in more instrumental terms as a strategic gambit catalyzed by rifts within the Communist bloc. OSPAAL's Cuban sponsors, resentful of Moscow's overbearing economic influence and patronizing diktats, seized an opportunity to supplant Communist China's leading role as the ideological inspiration for Third Worldism.[147] Determined to foreground Latin America's anti-imperialist struggles, Castro's regime overcame Soviet pressure for OSPAAL's headquarters to be in Cairo rather than Havana, but could not convince the Chinese to concede that OSPAAL and its forerunner, the Afro-Asian People's Solidarity Organization (AAPSO), should be fused.[148] The contested paternity of radical internationalism, a marker of the Sino–Soviet split, boiled over as the delegates gathered in Havana. Mao's regime laid stronger claim to a directive role in south–south relations. Foreign Minister Zhou Enlai's 'Eight Principles of Foreign and Technical Aid' wisely differentiated between China's commitment to fortifying decolonizing nations through low-cost grassroots support and the top-heavy, strings-attached development on offer from the Soviet Union's centralized civilian and military bureaucracies and their East European satellites.[149] To the more skeptical observer, Sino-Soviet friction, and the Cuban regime's determination to transcend it, mocked the Tricontinental's vision for a unified revolutionary anticolonial front. It also had material consequences, hardening otherwise incipient divisions within and between those national liberation movements most dependent on Communist bloc support.[150]

Intercommunist rivalries, though, are only part of the story. Backroom squabbling between rival communist patrons was only too familiar, but, as an idea and as a social movement, the Tricontinental was strikingly different: its anti-imperialism originated among global South actors determined to drive its long-term agenda by tying the anticolonialism of the Afro-Asian bloc to the anticapitalist and antiracism campaigns more familiar in the Americas.[151] Outlined by Che Guevara and others in 1961, its details were elaborated by a working group of African, Asian, and Latin American representatives convened in Ghana in 1965 and chaired by Morocco's leading leftist dissident, Mehdi Ben Barka.[152]

A procession of insurgent leaders came to Havana seeking material aid, knowing they would encounter a Cuban regime eager to help.[153] The friendship between Fidel Castro and Ahmed Ben Bella personified this revolutionary internationalism.[154] Defying American protests, on October 16, 1962, the Algerian president ended his first formal discussions with the Kennedy administration not by traveling home but by flying directly from New York to Havana. There were both realpolitik calculations and showmanship in this, but, as Piero Gleijeses discerns, the mutual admiration and sense of revolutionary possibility were genuine.[155] If the Algerian FLN were the pathbreakers in their exploitation of transnational connection and the mobilization of sympathetic international opinion for their cause, others, from Vietnam's National Liberation Front (NLF, widely known as the Viet Cong) and Amílcar Cabral's PAIGC to Palestine's Fatah, would carry the torch of globalized anti-imperialist insurgency forward into the late 1960s and '70s.[156]

The NLF's North Vietnamese regime patrons were also accomplished transnational propagandists, sponsoring high-profile visits to Hanoi by antiwar campaigners and supporting the 1966–1967 International War Crimes Tribunal instigated by British philosopher Bertrand Russell and fellow anti–Vietnam War activists in Stockholm to highlight the devastating human costs of US conflict escalation in Vietnam.[157] The revolutionary cosmopolitanism of the Vietnamese, Palestinians, Cubans, and others upended what historian Paul Thomas Chamberlin describes as the 'imagined geography of the Cold War order', rejecting East–West binaries to assert the greater revolutionary potential of Third Worldist anticolonialism.[158] Vietnam, in particular, cemented the bond, as much romantic and imagined as practical and real, between anti-imperial struggle and new global solidarities.[159]

Ironically, the Tricontinental provided less material support to other Latin American radicals.[160] Some bridled at Castro's eagerness to play the role of 'revolutionary pope'. Few were convinced by Che Guevara's unrealistic insistence on armed revolution, their reservations vindicated by Che's October 1967 capture and killing in Bolivia.[161] Most, though, faced murderous domestic repression as one regime after another fell to rightist

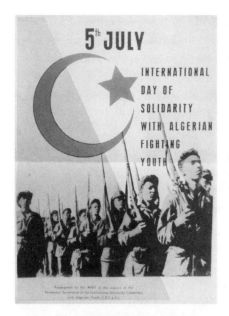

FIGURE 14.3. Images of Third Worldist struggle: (*top left*) International Day of Solidarity with Algerian Fighting Youth, July 5, 1962; (*top right*) 'For the Victory of the Vietnamese People, Freedom, Independence and Peace,' 1968; (*bottom*) 'MPLA Is the People,' no date. Source: IISH, WFDY archive, ARCH01665, General Affairs, 1965–85.

military control and US investment strengthened the apparatus of Latin American counterinsurgency.[162] In Africa, by contrast, both the Tricontinental's ideological inspiration and Cuban military and social interventionism were pivotal.[163] Cabral, leader of the PAIGC, figured strongly. His invocation of the insurgent movements' moral authority to fight colonialist regimes that denied basic dignity to their subjects resonated, not just with fellow attendees but with the OAU, the Arab League, and the UN Special Committee on Decolonization, which later pushed for certain national liberation movements, among them the PLO and South Africa's ANC, to be granted observer status at the United Nations.[164] Marking a heightened combativeness in global anticolonialism and an affirmation of Cuba's leading role within it, the Tricontinental gave Third Worldism strategic bite. Cuban military support to the People's Movement for the Liberation of Angola (MPLA) was vital, first in bringing the movement to power, then in keeping it there, a huge commitment that became integral to Cuban revolutionary identity.[165] Whether in its cultural pronouncements or its armed interventionism, the Tricontinental sponsored 'new transnational communities of gender, class, and racial parity'.[166]

In October 1968 the Palestinian National Liberation Movement, better known as Fatah, made the most of the new atmosphere. Invoking the UN Charter and the Universal Declaration of Human Rights, Fatah spokesmen pushed for recognition of the Palestinian struggle as a popular resistance movement fighting for self-determination against decades of colonialist oppression.[167] In geopolitical terms, Palestinian movements cemented their place alongside South Africa's ANC, Castro's Cuba, and the Hanoi regime as emblematic figures in the Third Worldist struggle against a Western colonialism exemplified by Israeli occupation, apartheid racism, and American imperialism.[168] Significantly, Europe's imperial states did not figure alongside this trio that Third Worldist propagandists identified as the worst of 1960s colonialism. Others, though, had longer memories. In conceptual terms, Tricontinental thinking would find clearest expression in the writings of the Guyanese scholar-activist Walter Rodney.[169]

Rodney initially worked from a black Atlantic perspective, then, after spells in Jamaican, British, and Tanzanian universities, from an international Marxist one. His capstone work, *How Europe Underdeveloped Africa*, first published in 1972, cut to the heart of Tricontinental philosophy.[170] Western colonialism, from its early iteration in the Atlantic slave economy to its late-twentieth-century exercises in developmental modernization, rested on two pillars. One was the exploitation of non-European peoples, Africans and black diaspora populations foremost. The other was a racialized extractive capitalism that enriched 'the West' and impoverished 'the rest'.[171] A defining statement of dependency theory, Rodney's wider insights were scathingly simple: just as anticolonialism without anticapitalism was half-baked, so Marxist internationalism without recognition of the global entanglement between capitalist accumulation and racial hierarchy was nonsensical.[172] Alongside the imperialists in his sights, Rodney took aim at the local elites within colonized societies who transitioned from imperialism's administrative auxiliaries to seizing the reins of power as postindependence autocrats. Authentic freedom meant sweeping away these comprador 'sell outs'.[173]

Oppositionists and Social Rankings

The task Rodney identified would be a difficult one. From Indonesia to India, from Morocco to Mozambique, the leadership cadres and the rank and file of proto-nationalist parties, social movements, and insurgent groups drew their members in large number from intermediary or 'middle classes'. Members of these leadership elites were part of decolonization's conference cultures but often spent years overseas, immersed in the cosmopolitan networks of political exiles and activist communities of major cities and ports.[174] Predominantly young and male, some studied at foreign universities or military academies before leading an itinerant existence, whether as insurgent fighters or politicians seeking support from sympathetic donor governments, security agencies, and client groups.[175] Many such exiles worked at the offices established by liberation movements in friendly countries or within frontline states across the border from their homelands.[176] Some put their education to use as publicists, working with journalists, affiliate parties, and protest groups to disseminate information connecting local fights for decolonization with the global anti-imperialist cause.

If this conjures an image of cross-cultural solidarity, it bears emphasizing that the transnational networks of which such exile activists were a part could be fractious. Often, money was tight. Access to local powerbrokers might be withheld, offices shut down, and visas withdrawn. Life within exile communities in emblematic anticolonial capitals like Algiers, Accra, and Dar es Salaam was rarely unproblematic. Host governments, such as Julius Nyerere's Tanzanian regime, welcomed liberation movement representatives but also constrained them. Conscious of how incendiary the presence of insurgent leaders would be, Nyerere's lieutenants monitored the exiles' activities and Tanzanian Army liaison officers supervised the transshipment of weapons and other supplies from Communist bloc providers to Southern African liberation movements.[177] In Dar es Salaam, as elsewhere, relationships between liberation movement representatives could become stifling and factionalized. Personal rivalries, interethnic tensions, and the envy of rank-and-file members toward privileged leadership cadres could escalate into murderous competition.[178] Tensions festered during long periods confined in foreign capitals or sanctuary bases, complicating propagandist narratives of internationalist solidarity. The connection between protracted exile and internecine violence was, for instance, apparent in the struggle between exile factions of Algeria's FLN after 1957. It also explains the 1969 murder in Dar es Salaam of Eduardo Mondlane, leader of FRELIMO, whose intellectualism and foreign connections sealed his fate at the hands of rivals wedded to a narrowly sectarian Marxism.[179]

Not all political activists, insurgent organizers, anticolonial writers, and intelligence-gatherers were outsiders. Some were to be found within colonial administrations, typically working in highly gendered 'white collar' clerical positions. Their working life and public persona were defined as much by their performative aspects—the cultural practices and ethical values they embodied—as by nature of the work done and the social status it conferred.[180] Some of empire's most audacious opponents on the transnational stage were models of bourgeois propriety at home. Tellingly, members of these subaltern elites were the primary targets of the Eisenhower administration's 1950s cultural assistance programs. Funded by grants to universities and charitable foundations, these schemes offered advanced education in an effort to cultivate pro-Western leaders capable of building the administrative capacity needed to assure stability after independence.[181] The Americans were not alone in recognizing the strategic return on such investments. Cultural assistance, its educational dimensions especially, became a focal point not just of Cold War competition, but of rivalry among imperial powers, UN agencies, and other supranational bodies. Each offered 'preparatory' training to local elites who later figured in government.[182]

Talk of class and social rankings risks transposing essentially Western categories onto very different colonial societies.[183] Eschewing the rigidities of class labeling, Su Sin Lewis, in her study of a trio of interwar Southeast Asian port cities, describes a 'history from the middle', of multiethnic urban professionals whose cosmopolitanism was nurtured by interaction with other ethnicities and social groups.[184] The term 'middle class' may be colonially problematic, but the double bind intrinsic to it was replicated, even amplified, within dependent societies.[185] From postal workers and policemen to office 'boys' and customs officials, certain colonial employments offered new possibilities: a suit or a uniform, a more varied diet, a better education for one's children, a bank account, and the ability to save money. If this looked like the embrace of Western-style modernity and, with it, the

copycat quality of acculturation to colonialist norms that Partha Chatterjee characterized as a 'derivative discourse', it was also something more: an
affirmation that literate colonial 'elites' could advance so far but no further
within societies defined by racially unequal relations of power.[186] Local
staffers of the Indian Civil Service, Egyptian and Sudanese *effendiyya*, or
Gold Coast 'verandah boys' did empire's office work, but they would never
run the show.[187] Not for them the boardrooms, the whites-only hotel suites,
and the drinks before dinner that underlined colonialism's racial divides.[188]
This was the double bind. And this was what ensured that many at the fore-
front of decolonization's conference cultures were members of what has
been recently identified as a 'global bourgeoisie'.[189]

Conclusion

Scholar of postcolonialism Robert J. C. Young puts it succinctly: 'The
struggle against imperialism involved national campaigns that took
international forms and were always conditioned by international contexts'.[190] The process Young identifies also worked transnationally. Shared
opposition to foreign occupation among anticolonial networks sustained
the process, driving campaigns forward. We should, though, tread cautiously before representing these networks as a unified global movement
for decolonization. That smacks too much of grand narrative and risks
concealing the local variations and inconvenient exceptions that defy such
generalization. As historian Rebecca Herman reminds us in the context
of 1940s working practices in the Panama Canal Zone, those facing racial
discrimination and colonialist capitalism might also uphold distinct racial
hierarchies of their own. Faced with racism, not all became antiracist.[191]

What can be said is that anticolonialism accrued power thanks to its
resonances across empires and among communities aware of the commonalities of discrimination and their shared roots in political repression
and cultural denigration. Colonialism was, in this sense, self-destructive.
Local curbs on freedom to organize and speak out built new solidarities against them. The longer empires clung on, the less persuasive their
arguments became for doing so. By contrast, anticolonialist claims were
articulated in more imaginative forms ideologically, strategically, and
organizationally. Third World conference cultures exemplified this evolution. Their forms and content shaped and refracted a global decolonization process that by the mid-1960s was manifestly incomplete despite the
contraction of formal empire.

CHAPTER FIFTEEN

Endgames? Decolonization's Third-World Wars

MOZAMBIQUE, OCTOBER 1964. GUERRILLA units of Dr. Eduardo Mondlane's FRELIMO and Adelino Gwambe's Comité Revolucionário de Moçambique (COREMO) spearheaded the first large-scale attacks on Portuguese colonial security forces in what would be an eleven-year decolonization war. At its start, small bands of insurgents exploited their ability to operate from camps across Mozambique's frontiers in newly independent Tanzania and Zambia.[1] Sanctuary bases offered more than refuge, as we have seen. They provided platforms for the launch of transnational propaganda and the cultivation of guerrilla diplomacy with friendly regimes throughout the global South.[2] Safe havens also facilitated resupply with munitions from the Eastern Bloc and, later, with land mines and machine guns from China and with medicines and health care from Cuba.[3] Assured arms supplies helped to overcome the military imbalance between insurgent forces and the Portuguese military. Most salient was the connection between more destructive weaponry and the proximity of key economic targets, including hydroelectric dams and other power installations, in Mozambique's border regions of Nyassa, Cabo Delgado, and Tete.[4] Sabotage of these targets became the vernacular index of conflict escalation.

For their part, by 1966 Portuguese dictator Dr. António de Oliveira Salazar's lieutenants justified heightened military spending in Mozambique by exaggerating the threat of British intervention against Ian Smith's breakaway 'UDI' government in neighboring Rhodesia.[5] The willingness of Kenneth Kaunda's Zambian government and that of his Malawian counterpart, Hastings Banda, to tolerate the presence of foreign fighters and consequent border insecurity depended, in turn, on the depth of

Portuguese support for Smith's Rhodesian regime, including incursions into Zambia by 'pseudo-gangs' run by the PIDE secret police.[6] Combatants and proxies were, in other words, adept at manipulating the regional insecurity their own actions created to secure strategic advantage in Mozambique's war of decolonization. Each felt compelled to do so because neither side could achieve a decisive breakthrough. Portuguese security forces were overstretched, despite the thousands of conscripts shipped to Southern Africa year after year. Knowing they could not move enough soldiers to win the war, colonial commanders moved civilians instead. The forcible relocation of rural populations into purpose-built *aldeamentos* villages was as coercive in Mozambique as it was in Angola.[7] The aldeamentos program, the centerpiece of Portuguese counterinsurgency, was framed in a rhetoric of modernist development. Yet it was emblematic of worsening rights abuses as rural populations became the critical resource to be denied to the insurgents.[8]

I started this chapter with this brief outline because the way insurgent rebellion and counterinsurgent repression unfolded in 1960s Mozambique illustrates many of the issues arising from empires' violent endgames. Portugal's Salazarist dictatorship, still fascistic but increasingly geriatric, fought three intractable African colonial wars simultaneously, in Angola beginning in 1961, in Portuguese Guinea (Guiné-Bissau) beginning in 1963 and in Mozambique beginning in 1964. As with Fourth Republic France and the Algerian conflict, Portugal's colonial wars brought the metropolitan regime to collapse after a revolt by its colonial army. So Portuguese Africa will provide the principal examples discussed below alongside other internationalized Third World wars of the 1960s and 1970s.[9]

Colonialism remained a living reality for millions as the 'global 1960s' unfolded.[10] Legacies of discrimination in nominally decolonized societies were still being revealed, comprehended, and combated. Elsewhere, colonial governors and white settler regimes clung to power. The decade began with a mixture of hope and despair. The anticipation of multiple decolonizations in the 'year of Africa' was, within months, besmirched by the murder of Congolese independence leader Patrice Lumumba, one of several acts that commingled Cold War realpolitik with regional competition for postcolonial influence. Together, these turned independence for the Belgian Congo into the calamitous Congo crisis, a shorthand term covering foreign interventionism, army mutiny, the July 1960 secession of the Congo's mineral-rich southern province Katanga, and civil war.[11] 'Lessons' drawn from the Congo's decolonization hardened the opposing ideological positions of those involved. US Central Intelligence Agency

(CIA) backing for Belgian governmental, commercial, and mercenary efforts, first to derail Lumumba's Mouvement National Congolais, then to support Colonel Joseph-Desiré Mobutu's military takeover, were matched by Washington's longer-term manipulation of UN peacekeeping to secure its favored political outcome in the Congo.[12] The itinerant UN secretary-general Dag Hammarskjöld, keen to work with the UN General Assembly's Afro-Asian block but no fan of Lumumba's vision for the Congo, found himself marginalized by Washington's hard-liners.[13]

Western toleration of Katangan separatism suggested not that former imperial powers understood the aspirations of the region's Lunda majority for ethnic self-determination but, rather, that money still talked between governments and corporations when high-value multinational investments came under threat.[14] Strikingly, many of the Congo's Belgian settlers, like their counterparts in Algeria and across Southern Africa, seemed unrepentantly colonialist. Few accepted that decolonization was inexorable. Many found inventive self-justifications either to hold onto power and privilege or to cry foul when they were challenged with violence.[15] At the opposing end of the ideological spectrum, the lessons seemed starker still. Lumumba's death and the 1962 overthrow of the leftist regime established by his deputy, Antoine Gizenga, in eastern Congo's Orientale province underlined the limits of Soviet influence and Chinese power projection in the face of concerted Western interventionism and the conflicting demands of the Congo's neighbor states.[16] Anticolonial solidarity was made to look febrile next to mounting evidence that hostile foreign interests would use all means to prevent African socialists like Lumumba or his successor Gizenga from taking power.[17]

The decolonization denied of the Congo crisis was a leitmotif: even viewed conventionally in terms of territories living under colonial flags, for hundreds of millions of people across large areas of the global South imperial rule persisted or even intensified at the supposed 'high point' of empire collapse in the early 1960s. This very late colonialism had distinct regional configurations. Strategically located emirates spanning the Persian and Oman Gulfs, plus Kuwait to the north and Yemen to the south, saw British 'protection' turn to intervention, regime overthrow, and counterinsurgency when local leaders or social movements chose independence or revolution over neocolonialism and imperial clientage.[18] Here, as elsewhere in the Arab world as well as south of the Sahara, what Abdel Razzaq Takriti characterizes as 'coups as containment' were fomented, sponsored, or engineered to perpetuate Western imperial influence despite gathering anticolonial pressure from below.[19]

More diverse than the coastal emirates of the Gulf were the island dependencies scattered across the Pacific, Indian, and Atlantic Oceans. From exoticized tourist destinations to penal colonies, strategic outposts to mining settlements, most were shaped by violent histories of colonization that ran from slavery and indenture through carceral settlements to the foundation of military bases and airfields through community expulsion and environmental clearance.[20] Some island territories embraced decolonization, others rejected it, but the history and demography of each were marked by some combination of colonial settlement (including the interethnic frictions arising from the permanent relocation of indentured laborers), foreign interference, and external control.[21] Class divisions and racial tensions hampered nationalist parties in the Anglophone Caribbean, whose southernmost territory of British Guiana witnessed bitter rivalry between an Afro-Guyanese community wedded to Garveyism and Indo-Guyanese supporters of Cheddi Jagan's socialist-inspired Progressive People's Party.[22] British policy exploited this segmentation first to delay decolonization, then to manipulate its political complexion. Presumptive connections among ethnicity, social rank, and political affiliation ossified in numerous Caribbean postcolonies.[23] Similar tensions and parallel outcomes were evident in Fiji, whose demography reflected the impact of colonial capitalism and the oceanic patterns of indenture that supported it.[24] Indigenous peoples in Pacific Island communities fared especially badly, their cultures trampled by waves of immigration and land seizure, their claims obscured by base rights diplomacy and UN preoccupation with formal transfers of power.[25]

In two massive archipelagic territories of Southeast Asia—New Guinea (Irian Jaya) and Borneo—the former colonial rulers, the Netherlands and Britain, became embroiled in armed campaigns to halt what they decried as Indonesian expansionism, what Sukarno's Jakarta regime claimed was justifiable irredentism. In the Dutch-administered territory of West Papua, Indonesian security force incursions in 1961–1962, the likely prelude to full-scale invasion, instead catalyzed negotiations in the summer and fall of 1962 over a Dutch withdrawal, interim UN administration, and a plebiscite on West New Guinea's attachment to Indonesia.[26] In May of the following year Western Papua New Guinea was formally 'transferred' to Indonesian administration.[27] This was not decolonization but a new imperialism facilitated by UN acquiescence in Indonesian expansion.[28] In Borneo, meanwhile, between 1963 and 1966 British military backing for Malaysian forces in their *Konfrontasi* with Indonesia blurred the lines between what could be viewed as either 'late colonial' or 'postcolonial' counterinsurgency in defense of a preferred regional client.[29] British Army support for its Malaysian ally was limited, but its use of sinister propaganda to demonize Sukarno's Indonesian regime as a communistic snake in the grass prefigured the elimination—some might say, the policide—of Indonesian communists, workers' groups, and leftist students by General Suharto's military regime, which set about the 'De-Sukarnoization' of Indonesian society after their September 1965 coup in Jakarta.[30]

More familiar were the African decolonizations still unfolding. From Namibia and Portuguese Angola on Africa's Southern Atlantic shore through South Africa and Southern Rhodesia/Zimbabwe to Portuguese Mozambique on Africa's Indian Ocean coast, white-minority rule traced an arc across the continent's south.[31] The Portuguese-ruled territories were notionally integrated into a wider lusotropical empire whose authoritarian rulers claimed to have transcended racist colonialism.[32] Salazar's dictatorship went further, tying its conception of Portuguese national identity to the country's integrationist imperial tradition. Angola and Mozambique figured largest in regime thinking, but even in the tiny West African colony of Guiné-Bissau official rhetoric maintained that talk of colonial exploitation and racial inequality made no sense.[33] Coined by Brazilian sociologist Gilberto Freyre, 'lusotropicalism' was adapted to the Salazarist message that colonialist inequalities were secondary to a shared imperial identity. Despite abundant evidence of discrimination, whether legal, educational, economic, or political, the administration depicted Guiné as part of a united Lusophone 'community of peoples'.[34]

Apartheid South Africa and UDI Rhodesia, in different ways, also insisted they represented authentic white African nations; each conflated minority rule with settler identity and the survival of white cultures of global settlerism.[35] National Party South Africa was defiantly independent, having left a hostile Commonwealth in 1961. So was UDI Rhodesia, which came into being in November 1965.[36] The international sanctions imposed against it compounded the Rhodesian Front (RF) regime's determination to exercise what historian Luise White tellingly identifies as an 'unpopular sovereignty'.[37] The Secretary for Internal Affairs in the Salisbury government captured the messianic spirit of UDI:

> Many important dates are recorded in the history of Rhodesia, but the 11th November, 1965, transcends them all and will go down in history to mark not only the birth of a proud nation, but also the first significant step taken to halt the march of communism which has steadily been blowing down Africa in the wake of the 'winds of change'. . . . The

spirit of our forefathers who, as 'Pioneers', faced and overcame extreme
adversity to implant civilization in this part of Africa only 75 years ago,
is surely manifested in the courage that has enabled the small Rhodesian nation to expose to the world the intrigues of international finance
and other tools of communism which are causing the lights to flicker
down Africa.[38]

Strategic cooperation between these white-minority regimes increased
in tandem with their international isolation and mounting global derision
for colonial settler privilege.[39] As historian Michael Evans discerns, Rhodesian Front politics inverted the Fanonian logic of cultural emancipation
of the oppressed through revolutionary violence. Ian Smith's RF supporters
dug in against decolonization. They lambasted Britain for going soft and
defended white-minority rule as an ideological struggle against leftist Third
Worldism. Militarily, theirs was an unapologetic doctrine of 'maximum
force' to protect their embattled cultural identity and, more instrumentally,
to keep what they held.[40]

Settlers may be identifiable with racial dominance, but most in Lusophone Africa were poorer and more politically marginal than their Eng-
lish- and Afrikaans-speaking counterparts. In its largest African territory, the Lisbon regime sold a dream of Portuguese rurality transposed
to Angola's interior.[41] But the influx of white colonists to Angola, whose
settler population rose from approximately 40,000 in 1940 to 290,000 in
1970, diluted neither the countryside dominance of the wealthiest 'coffee
barons' and cattle ranchers nor the industrial supremacy of the colony's oil
and mining conglomerates.[42] There may be substance in identifying common settler interests in a racially configured social order, but it is misleading to imagine that white settler populations were homogeneous or united
in defense of the status quo. As the grip of distant imperial governments
loosened, the cracks in Southern Africa's settler politics opened wider.[43]

Moving elsewhere, decolonization was intrinsic to the three most devastating bloodlettings of the mid-1960s and early 1970s.

As mentioned just now, the Konfrontasi over Borneo between Indonesia and their British-backed Malaysian opponents was a prelude to Sukarno's overthrow by the 30th September movement (Gerakan September Tiga
Puluh), a putsch against Sukarno loyalists swiftly put down by other units
of the Indonesian Army and blamed on the country's communist party, the
PKI. As a military junta under General Suharto consolidated its grip on
national power in October 1965, the new regime pursued a program of mass
killing, which targeted communists and other opponents of military rule,

as well as ethnic minorities and regionalist coalitions accused of disloyalty to Jakarta.[44] The death toll remains bitterly disputed, with estimates ranging from fewer than 80,000 to over a million.[45] Dutch involvement was marginal next to loud American support for Suharto's takeover, but the consequences of PKI marginalization from the fruits of independence after 1949 were integral to the claims and counterclaims of all involved in the violence of 1965–1966.[46]

Changing our focus from Southeast Asia to West Africa, Nigeria's Biafra War triggered the worst violence in any of the continent's formally decolonized states. It pitched former coimperialists, Britain and France, against one another as proxy supporters of the opposing combatants.

For decolonization skeptics, the 1967–1970 war between Nigeria's federal government and the secessionist Biafra Republic in the Igbo heartland of the country's southeast distilled every nightmarish outcome of national projects gone wrong. Coups and countercoups in the Nigerian capital catalyzed, first, a turn to authoritarianism, then secessionism and ethnically charged civil war. The United Nations appeared impotent as foreign powers poured weapons into the country. Ethnic cleansing and widespread rights abuses proceeded unchecked as Nigerian federal forces and Biafran troops roamed back and forth across the country's southeast. With no decisive military breakthrough, Lieutenant-Colonel Yakubu Gowon's Lagos government blockaded the breakaway republic, the prelude to humanitarian disaster.[47] Nigeria's civil war escalated markedly in 1968 as federal troops finally moved deeper into Biafran territory. Their occupation of Asaba, a Niger riverside town bordering the Biafra Republic, the previous October was grimly portentous. Army killings of over 1,000 civilians and the systematic rape of women and girls pointed to a war of terror.[48]

Gowon's federal government tightened its economic stranglehold on Biafra as its forces advanced, producing chronic malnutrition and child starvation.[49] Transnational commerce and extensive local food production meant that Southeastern Nigeria was almost self-sustaining before the war began, but, in addition to the federal blockade, the Biafran authorities' refusal to permit relief corridors or federally supervised aid flights worsened food shortages.[50] Calorific intake declined in absolute terms, but chronic shortages of essential foodstuffs, salt and other minerals in particular, increased the death toll among children, the elderly, and the infirm.[51] Worsening local conditions amplified the Biafran case for self-determination as a moral imperative.[52] Federal denial of human security and democratic rights to the people of Southeastern Nigeria made Biafra's case for self-rule.[53] As the war unfolded, to these human rights arguments were added humanitarian ones, Biafran suffering in the face of siege, massacre, and famine conjuring images less of civil war than of genocide.[54] The American Committee to Keep Biafra Alive (ACKBA), the largest US civil society movement supporting the breakaway republic, got the point. ACKBA activists claimed that rights withheld were the counterpoint to the deliberate starvation of Biafra's people. Both were acts of erasure: one political, the other biological.[55] Self-determination was the only sure way to prevent either one.

On October 2, 1968, President de Gaulle's administration, the most prominent Western supporter of the Biafran cause, reiterated these ethical claims. The Élysée presidential office equated blockade-induced famine and unrestrained military violence with the worst of Nazi occupation. France's NATO partners and African client states were unconvinced, either by French arguments or their sincerity.[56] Gaullist moralizing was plainly self-serving, triggered by the same imperialistic reflex that nourished Jacques Foccart's infamous networks of covert support for African regimes willing to bargain base rights, privileged economic access, and oil company concessions for French money and guns.[57] The prominence of French mercenaries, many of them former supporters of the Organisation de l'Armée Secrète, in Katanga's secession, their defeat of a February 1964 coup attempt against Gabonese President Léon M'Ba and the decisive contributions of Foccart's network and the French intelligence agency SDECE's African Service in advancing French strategic initiatives in black Africa underscored the instrumentality of de Gaulle's humanitarianism. The speed with which Georges Pompidou's government mended fences with Lagos after Nigeria's final victory in 1970 confirmed it.[58] From a more global perspective, Biafra highlighted the limits of transnational activism. Intense media attention, sustained NGO involvement, and public outrage could not alone prevent millions from dying in what the Biafran government insisted was the attempted elimination of the Igbo.[59] Biafra's propaganda directorate lambasted foreign governments that tolerated and even connived in the destruction of a people committed to nationhood.[60]

Conflicting international responses gave extra ammunition to those most cynical about decolonization. That apartheid South Africa, Salazarist Portugal, and Gaullist France would lend support to Biafran resistance to weaken West Africa's strongest country, or that China would follow suit to undermine Soviet military backing for the Lagos regime, indicated that realpolitik calculation trumped humanitarian concern. Most telling was the reaction of Africa's foremost supranational organization. Anxious not to give encouragement to separatists within their own states, OAU members endorsed the federal government's right to restore internal order through repression, a sorry echo of the arguments advanced only years earlier by the rulers of empire fighting the anticolonial movements the OAU claimed to represent.[61] But recollections of the Congo crisis figured larger than past controversies over national liberation. The OAU response was more understandable in light of the connections its members discerned between Western complicity in the January 1961 murder of Patrice Lumumba, the Katanga secession, and the Congolese civil war that followed. Admittedly, Biafra was no Katanga. Chukwuemeka Odumegwu Ojukwu's arguments for independence built on accusations against the federal regime that Biafra's Igbos were victims of discrimination, stolen resource wealth, and state persecution.[62] For all that, insofar as the Biafran cause necessitated the breakup of West Africa's largest independent country, it was antithetical to African state-building projects.[63]

Others disagreed. For Biafra's supporters, including Julius Nyerere's Tanzania, the image of an African military regime employing violence and mass starvation to coerce dissentient subjects into submission suggested that more important lessons of the fight against imperialism—about popular will and state legitimacy—had been forgotten. Nor was Biafra easily dismissed, either as politically unrepresentative or as the cat's-paw of foreign capitalist interest. In some fields Ojukwu's regime was boldly innovative. The guiding principles of Biafra's legal system, for instance, were laid out in the Ahiara Declaration, a statement of constitutional intent that identified the breakaway republic with a civic nationalism at odds with the civil war's reductive logic of opposing ethnicities. As Biafran-controlled territory shrank and the rival combatants used ethnicity to demonize one another, the original precepts of Biafran lawmaking became clouded. Biafran political identity was increasingly identifiable with being Igbo. In the war's opening stages, though, Biafra's state-making was ambitious and inclusive, its ideals enshrined in new law courts and the judges who presided over them.[64] Court proceedings were transparent, although sessions sometimes convened as Special Tribunals working as adjuncts to the military's 1967 Law and Order (Maintenance) Edict. Court rulings and judges' pronouncements were didactic: lessons in ideas of Biafran citizenship. They became integral to the efforts of Biafra's elite opinion-makers to codify what a state should be and the duties its citizens owed it. In this sense, Biafra's law courts were decolonizers and state-builders at the same time. They rejected the artificiality of colonial 'customary law' but embraced the identification between political belonging and place of origin.[65]

None of this was to last. A decisive federal offensive led by Colonel (and later President) Olusegun Obasango in late December 1969 broke through Biafran defenses. Ojukwu left for exile in Ivory Coast on January 7, 1970, the prelude to the surrender and dissolution of the breakaway republic. In its place, the enduring image of Biafra in the global sphere was of avoidable famine and the world's collective failure to stop it.[66]

A year after the demise of the Biafran Republic in 1970, Bangladesh's war of secession signaled the largest territorial change on the Indian subcontinent since 1947 and another devastatingly violent South Asian partition combining policide, civil war, and mass rape.[67] The contest to secure an independent, Bengali-run state of Bangladesh was also a decolonization of sorts. Its characteristics owed much to the legacy of geographical division, political frictions, economic disparities, and cultural tensions left by the earlier partition of 1947. West Pakistan's military governments had not helped matters, seeing East Pakistan more as territory to be exploited than a partner in national creation.[68] Discriminatory treatment exacerbated the income inequalities, limited economic opportunities, and cultural prejudice facing Bengali-speakers, leaving East Pakistan 'a marginalized province of a developing state'.[69]

The resulting groundswell of opposition could not be stifled. Sheikh Mujibur Rahman's pro-independence Awami League, its popularity affirmed by national elections in December 1970, left Yahia Khan's Islamabad government with little political room for maneuver. Talks with Awami League leaders continued, but no postelection National Assembly convened. Instead, West Pakistani troops prepared for a crackdown, focused initially on East Pakistan's capital, Dhaka, and its hinterland. Beginning on March 25, 1971, Operation Searchlight's killings of Awami League supporters, government employees, East Pakistani soldiers, university students, and civil society intellectuals left no way back. The repression triggered a Bangladesh declaration of independence a day later. Thousands, then millions of refugees struggled to find sanctuary from a multidimensional civil conflict involving militias, self-defense groups, and other violence actors from each of the territory's ethnoreligious groups.[70]

Some of these paramilitaries were sponsored and armed by West Pakistani security forces, others by India. The Bangladesh civil war reveals a complex picture of layered violence, whose microdynamics illustrate how individual agency was asserted or denied. Its intensity and performance, deliberate and slow in some places, devastatingly fast in others, mirrored levels of local insecurity and the instrumentalization of violence, not just to achieve political or economic ends but to convey particular cultural

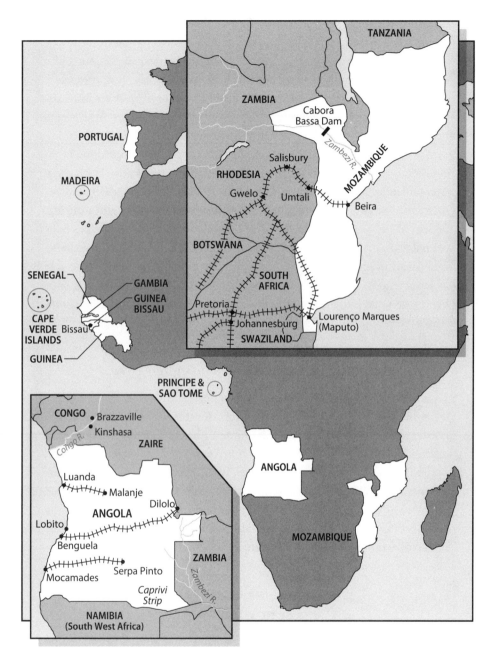

MAP 15.1. Portuguese Africa.

meanings.[71] Some villages were effaced, their inhabitants massacred; others were spared. Acts of compassion and a determination to speak out about the killings persisted alongside cycles of retributive violence, the silencing of victims, and crass generalizations about their experience.[72] The legacies of maltreatment, trauma, and loss endure.[73] But the immediate geopolitical consequence was an Indian military invasion on December 3, 1971, which forced a Pakistani surrender a fortnight later.[74]

Dwelling on Indonesia, Biafra, and Bangladesh, three quasi-colonial conflict zones, is not even to mention perhaps better known last-stage decolonizations that were also Third World wars: deepening US involvement in Vietnam and the fights for independence in Portuguese Africa, which, in the cases of Angola and Mozambique, descended into decades of civil war and foreign intervention lasting into the 1990s.[75] The coercive mobilization intrinsic to Vietnam's fight for independence, its civil war aspects, and its global salience as scion of Third World resistance have been discussed in earlier chapters. Each found their echo in Portuguese Africa, the subject of the section below.

Violent Decolonization in Portuguese Africa

Four concerns drove changes in Portuguese counterinsurgency strategies in their Southern African conflicts. First was the matter of cross-border infiltration and sanctuary bases described in this chapter's opening example. Second was the awkward marriage between social policy and psychological warfare that so often characterized late colonial counterinsurgency. Third were the foreign connections and claims to statehood of the insurgent movements fighting Portuguese rule. And last was the decisive importance of forced population removal to the outcome of some of decolonization's longest Third World wars. Let's look at these in turn.

CROSS-BORDER INFILTRATION
AND SANCTUARY BASES

In the third week of July 1968 nine ANC fighters entered Mozambique heading for South Africa's Transvaal. The group relied on local guides supplied by Paulo Gumane's COREMO guerrillas, at the time the main oppositional force cross-border raiding into Mozambique's Tete district from neighboring Zambia. Agents of the colony's International and State Security Police (Polícia Internacional e de Defesa do Estado—PIDE) discovered the incursion, so the nine ANC men were pursued across central

Mozambique by Portuguese troops. The fighters split up in an attempt to evade capture. One group was intercepted and wiped out, but the other ambushed the PIDE agents sent to arrest them, killing the three police officers involved.[76] The partial interdiction of the ANC fighters and the bloodshed that followed illustrated several broader trends evident in Portuguese Mozambique by the fall of 1968: the importance of foreign involvement and regional ideological attachments between the warring parties; the escalation in lethal violence as larger rebel bands began operating more widely and Portuguese security forces in turn stepped up their efforts to destroy guerrilla encampments; and the worsening insecurity across a larger span of Mozambique's northern and central districts.[77]

Similar patterns were traceable in Angola. There, fighters of Holden Roberto's Union of Angolan Peoples (UPA) infiltrated Angola's northern Uige and Zaire districts from neighboring Congo-Zaire.[78] UPA pamphlets spread the word of rebellion to rural communities across northern Angola, their dissemination tracked obsessively by the Portuguese secret police.[79] The Angolan rebellion had begun with coordinated UPA attacks mounted from Congolese bases against Portuguese-run coffee plantations and administrative centers, heralding what settlers termed 'the great fear' of 1961.[80] In later years, the far south and east of the country lay open to similar cross-border raiding into the vast Cuanda Cubango and Moxico districts by rival People's Movement for the Liberation of Angola (MPLA) and União Nacional para a Independência Total de Angola (UNITA) guerrillas operating from Zambia and Namibia.[81] The use of sanctuary bases and the consequent thrust of insurgent operations mapped closely onto the region's ethnic geography as well as the ideological solidarities among Angola's neighbor states.[82] Marrying local concerns with bolder claims to statehood, effective governance, and strong foreign connections was pivotal to the contests for civilian support between rival UPA, MPLA, and UNITA guerrillas.[83] These local competitions for influence were critical to the movements involved, but they were endlessly frustrating for the insurgents' foreign backers. For the mid-level Soviet bureaucrats and military liaison officers charged with forging a 'common front' among Angola's anticolonial forces after 1961, internecine divisions retarded Moscow's plans for Angolan revolution.[84] The backing of frontline neighbors also had its limits, particularly for Angola. Joseph Mobutu's Zaire and Kenneth Kuanda's landlocked Zambia opposed unrestricted UPA and MPLA activities, afraid that the sabotage of Angola's rail system would disrupt essential transcontinental trade.

Returning to Mozambique, the configuration of international support looked different. Aside from COREMO's Zambian sanctuaries, FRELIMO fighters were by 1967 embedded in forward bases along Mozambique's borders with southern Tanzania and Malawi. Soviet and, more especially, Chinese weapons were transported the short distance from the Tanzanian port of Mtwara to FRELIMO bases at Nashinguea and Mahuta. From there, guerrillas split into mobile units to reprovision bases in Cabo Delgado and Niassa districts. Smaller numbers of FRELIMO guerrillas traversed Lake Malawi or infiltrated from their main supply base outside Malawi's Fort Johnson through the forested hills further south.[85] Once within Niassa district, these Malawi-based fighters threatened arterial communications linking north and south. Increasing insurgent activity in central and southern Mozambique, areas minimally touched by FRELIMO operations between 1966 and 1969, compelled the Portuguese command to garrison troops across Mozambique's central belt, a major drain on the resources of a 40,000-strong expeditionary force.[86] FRELIMO attacks on the vital Cahora Bassa Dam, still in the early stages of construction, held unique symbolism. Sabotaging Cahora Bassa struck a blow at not just Portuguese governance but the regime's capitalist modernization agenda and the South African financing behind it, something that European leftists and trade unions condemned.[87] FRELIMO's sanctuary bases made all this possible. Strategically, cross-border havens determined Portuguese deployments, not just in the most insecure regions but in areas far removed from the rebellious frontier districts as well.[88]

Insurgents moving across borders illustrated how these Southern African conflicts' transnational and international dimensions converged. External support was critical to all the warring parties, but the insurgents' ability to secure foreign governmental backing was contingent on the extent to which guerrilla units could connect their support structures within Mozambique to their supply networks in neighboring states. FRELIMO and the MPLA were notably successful in this regard. Despite praising Malawian premier Hastings Banda's 'Bourguiban' preference for pragmatic accommodation with the West, the Portuguese regime had few illusions that any African front line states, from Guinea in West Africa, to Zaire, Zambia, Malawi, and Tanzania in central southern Africa, would abandon their insurgent clients.[89]

FRELIMO stepped up their attacks beginning in February 1968. These consisted not just of cross-border raids, but of sustained activity by larger bands of over one hundred fighters rather than the smaller groups of ten to fifteen more familiar to Portuguese security forces. The plentiful supply of reliable, easy-assembly Chinese rifles enabled FRELIMO fighters to engage army patrols on more even terms.[90] FRELIMO units also used

Chinese antipersonnel mines (APMs) to make farming prohibitively dangerous for peasant families. Part of the plastics revolution that allowed manufacturers to saturate war zones with millions of cheap APMs, these weapons transformed the nature of rural insurgency, causing devastation among human and animal populations.[91]

Settlements that raised a self-defense militia were especially vulnerable. Designed to maim rather than kill, the tens of thousands of APMs deployed between 1969 and 1974 were laid with ruthless efficiency down access roads, along irrigation dykes, and around watering holes and latrines, disrupting the rural economy and coercing community compliance.[92] Civilians fared worse, children and field laborers worst of all, but mine-blast injuries to ground patrols also influenced the Portuguese army's shift in Mozambique and, to a lesser extent, Angola toward helicopter missions. Between 1967 and 1972 airborne operations targeted insurgent supply bases close to sensitive border areas.[93] In Mozambique the northern districts of Tete, Niassa, and Cabo Delgado bore the brunt.[94] Most significantly in this insurgency arms race, by mid-1972 some FRELIMO units fielded shoulder-borne Soviet Grad-P rocket launchers. Serving as rudimentary surface-to-air missiles, something mobile assault troops had never faced in British Kenya or French Algeria for instance, these weapons helped turn the tide against the insurgents' pursuers.[95]

In Angola, too, frontier districts witnessed intense military activity: Uige and Cabinda in the north and the Cuando-Cabango pocket in the southeast. Unlike Mozambique, however, insurgency also disrupted Angola's political and commercial heartland. MPLA units sustained a presence in key urban centers and in the central highlands east of the capital, Luanda.[96] The combination of escalating UPA attacks in Cabinda, the MPLA sabotage of road and rail links in the Upper Zambesi Valley and the prospect of a new southern front in Cuanda Cubango forced the resignation of Angola's governor, Colonel Silvino Silvério Marques, in September 1966.[97]

SOCIAL POLICY AND PSYCHOLOGICAL WARFARE

Angola's loss of a governor committed to the 'social recuperation' welfarism of the civilian-led 'psycho-social action service' prefigured a major escalation in these Southern African wars. Mass detentions, PIDE torturers, and the use of napalm in retaliatory bombing raids exposed civilian populations in rebel zones and the poorest urban districts to worsening abuses.[98] As the rhythm of cross-border incursions quickened in Mozambique and Angola, arguments intensified among regime commanders about the severity of their response.[99] Having established self-defense militias in eastern Mozambique and among Makau communities further south along the Zambesi River valley, army units fixed their attention on the rebellion's epicenters in Mozambique's poorer northern and western frontier districts. Sending troops into villages and setting up militias was designed to compel FRELIMO fighters among Makonde communities either to leave their families and withdraw northward toward the Muede plateau or, faced with this alternative, to renounce their involvement in insurgency. As an added inducement, farmland in territories brought under government control would be redistributed to loyalist villagers and militia leaders.

Psychological warfare initiatives like those being rolled out in Mozambique also gathered pace in Angola after 1967. The new governor, Camilo Rebocha Vaz, shared the social policy concerns of his predecessor and extended the powers of civilian action teams in providing basic welfare services, elementary schooling, and microfinancing to supposedly 'rallied' communities. Rebocha Vaz insisted that meaningful security was impossible without the assurance of economic stability.[100] Retaliatory strikes designed to exploit intelligence, destroy guerrilla bases, and disrupt the insurgents' transnational networks did not alter the war's strategic direction. They merely antagonized the civilian populations caught in the crossfire.[101] Community coercion of this type also added to the vilification heaped on the Portuguese regime by African frontline states, the Organization of African Unity, and the UN General Assembly.[102] Countervailing Portuguese efforts to highlight improving living standards in supposed 'loyalist' districts were undermined by reportage indicating that such measures were highly selective and locally coercive, a colonial reflection of *Estado Novo* autocracy.[103]

STATEHOOD AND FOREIGN CONNECTIONS

Insurgent groups in Mozambique and Angola shared their regime opponents' preoccupation with social control, using it to assert their claims to statehood with foreign audiences, both governmental and nongovernmental.[104] In the year before FRELIMO leader Eduardo Mondlane's assassination in February 1969, the cross-border raiders infiltrating Niassa and Tete districts signaled a change in the movement's strategy, approved by the movement's Central Committee based in Dar es Salaam. Assigning larger numbers of fighters to remain in place indefinitely, the aim was to demarcate 'sovereign zones', beginning with the rebellion's heartland on the Makonde plateau. From there FRELIMO consolidated local administrative control. The creation of a safe zone linking Mozambique's border districts with sanctuary bases in Tanzania ensured the uninterrupted flow of Chinese war material. With it came Chinese advisers. Mondlane was a southerner, a cosmopolitan intellectual reluctant to sever all contacts with the west.[105] His replacement by a collective leadership, an 'Action Committee' with Maoist leanings, put implementing peasant communism in northern Mozambique first.[106]

With Mozambique's far northeast becoming the conflict's military and ideological proving ground, during the spring of 1969 General Kaulza de Arriaga's army command responded in kind. Makonde community leaders in and around Cabo Delgado were cajoled into changing sides by relentless propaganda, material incentives, and a stronger army presence. The regime redoubled support for the Malawi-based Union Nationale Africaine de Rumbézie, advocates of a negotiated settlement. But the personal animosity between new FRELIMO chief Uria Simango and Makonde leader Lazaro Kavandame was more decisive. Once Kavandame was expelled from FRELIMO's Central Committee in January 1969, the Portuguese military rallied his twelve Makonde guerrilla units, some three hundred fighters in total.[107] After this symbolic success the previous trickle of monthly declarations of loyalty became a flood, spurring the creation of self-defense militias in Mozambique's northerly districts where Portugal's administrative presence was weakest.[108]

In Angola, meanwhile, former governor Silvino Marques's criticism of Lisbon's centralized direction of the war coalesced around the issue of national consciousness. Contrary to regime insistence that lusotropicalism represented the integration of Portugal's European and African 'provinces', Marques stressed that aggressive counterinsurgency hardened the obvious ethnic divides between metropole and colony. Subject populations in the areas worst affected by raids, forced population removal, and the disruption of agriculture shared a sense of national belonging derived from common experiences of discrimination, security force violence, and loss of access to land. Added to this was a growing awareness that Angola's natural resources were politically determinant, a source of wealth whose benefits had yet to be distributed locally.[109]

POPULATION REMOVAL AND THE LONG HAUL

In the central years of their Southern African wars between the military stalemates of 1966–1967 and the decisive insurgent breakthroughs in 1971, Portuguese army analyses were peppered with the rhetoric of what French observers termed the *longue durée*: the 'long haul'.[110] A mantra pivotal to counterinsurgency thinking, the assertion that victory required not years but decades of social engineering seems farcical. This is not a hindsight judgment but one shared by Angolan and Mozambican communities wracked by insecurity, by a Portuguese population exasperated by the Estado Novo and by the army conscripts sent to fight seemingly unwinnable wars.

By October 1971 the Portuguese military was in retreat. In conflicts of such duration, this was more of a psychological shock than a strategic watershed. Mozambique exemplified the shift. It was FRELIMO that had the stomach for the long haul. And, as ever, control of Tete district was pivotal. Jutting northwest, the region conferred access to Cahora Bassa and the rich farmland of the Angónia plateau. Tete was also the crossroads to Malawi and Rhodesia. Fighters evaded Portuguese pursuit operations by criss-crossing Tete's borders, defying the hostility of the Rhodesian and Malawian governments.[111] Regime sponsorship of Portuguese agricultural colonization of Mozambique's northern districts was left in tatters. Promised expenditure on settlements and irrigation projects was abandoned.[112]

As the extent and scale of FRELIMO insurgency intensified in 1971–1972, it became even more apparent that Mozambique's population was the principal resource at issue in the struggle. Local readings of the war's direction or, in FRELIMO's terms, Mozambican political consciousness, mattered most.[113] FRELIMO now took the initiative in psychological warfare, creating pervasive insecurity among loyalist communities and rural settlements whose inhabitants were desperate to avoid involvement in the war. FRELIMO's greater capacity to affect rural life choices and thus impose social control increased over time, adding to pressure on the Portuguese authorities to halt the slide or leave.[114] There would be no such reversal. Instead, FRELIMO turned the screw further, targeting loyalist militias, assassinating 'collaborationist' tribal chiefs and local administration officials, and kidnapping villagers accused of doubting 'the cause'.[115] In the last week of January 1972 alone, within Tete district FRELIMO conducted three assassinations, six kidnappings, and four attacks against village settlements. In the same district, during the first ten months of 1971, eleven assassinations, thirty-two seizures of tribal chiefs, twenty-eight killings, and 128 kidnappings of local people took place.[116] FRELIMO violence was lethal but measured: killing and kidnappings were less common than social coercion practiced through nighttime raids on villages and thousands of APMs strung around problem settlements and regime-built aldeamentos.[117] Long signposted, the speed of travel toward decolonization was quickening.

Violent decolonization in Angola and Mozambique could be viewed through a Cold War prism but, for participants and their supporters world-wide, local fights for nationhood were also part of a transnational freedom struggle, a singular Third World War against imperialist interference.[118]

Revolution in Portuguese Guinea

The tiny size of Portugal's other African colonial cluster—the colony of Guiné-Bissau on the mainland plus the Cabo Verde islands offshore—and the impressive strength of the anticolonial movement within it made for greater unity of anticolonial purpose. With a small population, short supply lines, and friendly states across Guiné's border, the task of the Partido Africano para a Independência da Guiné e Cabo Verde (PAIGC) in attracting recruits, launching raids, and evading the Portuguese security forces was less daunting than that of its insurgent counterparts in the larger, more ethnically complex territories of Angola and Mozambique.[119] PAIGC guerrillas began attacks on Portuguese security forces in January 1963. Quickly, they extended their grip over Guiné's southwesternmost province, Tombali, from which Czechoslovakian weapons could be shipped in along the Atlantic coast from Morocco to the north and Guinea to the south.[120] These early gains notwithstanding, not until a decisive February 1964 party congress at Cassaca did PAIGC leader Amílcar Cabral impose his ideological vision and strategic priorities over the movement. Local commanders accused of mistreating the local population were purged. Provision of basic health and educational services within liberated areas was systematized. And guerrilla bands were reorganized into 'People's Revolutionary Forces' with first Czech and, from 1965, Soviet instructors directing their operational training.[121]

Cassaca was a breakthrough. Thereafter, Cabral's PAIGC, despite occasional military reverses, made the political weather internally, internationally, and transnationally. During the late 1960s PAIGC activists, a high proportion of them *mestiço* (mixed race) Cabo Verdeans educated in Lisbon, consolidated a functioning insurgent state within what remained nominally Portuguese Guinea. For Cabral's lieutenants, the overthrow of colonialism prefigured a deeper social revolution that pitched secular modernization, statist planning, and gender equality against the cultural conventions, economic practices, and patriarchal hierarchies of indigenous agricultural society. This egalitarian struggle against 'two colonialisms'—foreign occupation and gender discrimination—was at odds with the predominance of high-status men from Cabo Verde within the PAIGC leadership but became integral to party ideology even so.[122] Cabral's insistence that authentic freedom demanded respect for individual agency, or 'personhood', resonated with the PAIGC's women's section, the Democratic Union of Guinean and Cape Verdean Women. It also drove party activists such as social policy specialist Carmen Pereira, who promoted welfare programs in the cause of rural women's emancipation from the life cycle of early marriage, field labor, political invisibility, and minimal property rights.[123]

Cabral did not live to see these aspirations realized. He survived an assassination attempt in November 1970 when the Portuguese security service, the Direção-Geral de Segurança (DGS), tried to kill him at the PAIGC's headquarters in the Guinean capital Conakry. A bungled assault flagrantly conducted in a sovereign state, the attack provoked UN Security Council condemnation. It also smothered any possibility of direct negotiations between Lisbon and the PAIGC executive. Attention then shifted to Senegalese premier Léopold Senghor's longstanding offer to act as an intermediary. Like his more radical French-speaking rival, Guinea's Ahmed Sékou Touré, Senghor saw an opportunity to make political capital out of Portugal's mounting crisis in Guiné. He also wanted to stabilize a dangerous situation along Senegal's frontier with the embattled colony. This time it was the PAIGC that spoiled things, correctly calculating that Senghor's peace plan would only propose autonomy, not full independence. Guerrilla attacks in border areas intensified, their purpose being to provoke Portuguese reprisals and renewed UN criticism of army abuses.[124]

Cabral's luck ran out on January 20, 1973. He was murdered during a failed kidnap attempt in Conakry. The Guinean capital had long been the PAIGC's primary sanctuary, the country's shared frontier essential to insurgent incursion, evacuation, and resupply. But Cabral's relationship with Sékou Touré's authoritarian regime remained tense. The killing was carried out by two Guinean-Bissauans, Inocêncio Kani and Mamadou Ndjai, perhaps jealous at the dominance of Cape Verdeans within the PAIGC executive, but the plot was orchestrated by the Portuguese secret police, which had 'turned' a number of captured PAIGC commanders during their detention. Despite his charismatic leadership, Cabral's death did not throw Portuguese Guinea's decolonization off course. Knowing that party rivals had fired the lethal shots at the party's foreign headquarters, Cabral's successor, his half-brother Luis, unleashed a bloody purge of senior PAIGC cadres. The Soviet Union, meanwhile, increased the quantity and type of weapons supplied to the movement to prevent any loss of strategic impetus in the wake of Cabral's assassination.[125] International revulsion at Amílcar Cabral's murder ensured wider UN backing for his successor's demands for immediate independence. Alongside these diplomatic weapons came real ones. Within weeks the PAIGC's 7,000 guerrilla fighters took delivery of a first consignment of Soviet surface-to-air Strela-2 missiles. Faced with being shot down, Portuguese aircraft cut short their bombing of PAIGC 'liberated zones'.[126]

Neither last-ditch Portuguese efforts to exploit PAIGC factionalism nor the infighting between the movement's primary external sponsors, Sékou Touré's Guinea and Léopold Senghor's Senegal, slowed the PAIGC's final march to independence.[127] Elections were organized with UN oversight in the 'liberated zones', the prelude to resounding PAIGC victory and the unilateral declaration of an independent Guiné Republic in September 1973.[128] Like their FLN antecedents in Algeria, the PAIGC had won the political battle for international recognition before the colonial power finally withdrew. The supposed indivisibility of the Portuguese Empire was over.

International developments also played a role in Portugal's final pullout from Africa. One side of the Cold War's geopolitical equation in Africa saw US and UN pressure on Lisbon intensify as part of wider efforts to clear obstacles to East–West détente. Another, more ideological side of the equation saw Angola and Mozambique edging closer to postcolonial civil war as their Marxist state-makers, the MPLA and FRELIMO, reinvigorated with Cuban and Chinese support, confronted their Western-backed opponents, UNITA and RENAMO (Resistência Nacional Moçambicana).[129] Military hardware lent muscle to the ideological ties between insurgents and their sponsors. For MPLA cadres in particular, guerrilla warfare training in Communist bloc bases, such as the Simferopol training camp on the Crimean Peninsula and the 'Northern Training Center' in Moscow, cemented lasting connections between politics and military practice.[130] In the Zimbabwean struggle against the white-minority Rhodesian regime, meanwhile, guerrillas' use of the AK-47 automatic rifle came to symbolize affective ties of ideology and transnational anticolonialism while nodding to Soviet and Maoist techniques of revolutionary warfare.[131] Escalation of the anticolonial Bush War in white-ruled Rhodesia also registered in changing patterns of violence along the territory's leaky frontier with Mozambique. Warring parties in both countries crisscrossed the border, chasing down opponents and terrorizing civilians in their demands for refuge and recruits.[132]

The endgames of decolonization in Rhodesia and Portuguese Africa left civilians chronically exposed to the depredations of all sides. Amid a torrent of retaliatory violence between guerrillas and colonial paramilitaries, in one of the most shocking of such episodes, on December 15, 1972, a company of locally recruited parachute commandos decimated the Wiriyamu Triangle, a cluster of over forty villages in northern Mozambique's Tete region.[133] The commandos' handlers, secret police officers of the DGS, suspected the Triangle's inhabitants of aiding FRELIMO guerrillas.[134] Actually less suspected than condemned: their guilt was already presumed. A FRELIMO logistics route ran through the Triangle. Villagers and their chiefs were reluctant to relocate to an aldeamento resettlement village as previously instructed. And a local DGS informant, Chico Cachavi, with an axe to grind against a community that shunned him, provided damning 'intelligence' that he knew was a death warrant.[135] Most villagers were unaware of any of this as the first commandos descended from helicopters just before noon on the 16th. By day and into the following night the soldiers killed residents in five of these settlements: Wiriyamu, Djemusse, Riachu, Juawa, and Chaworha.[136] Hundreds of people of all ages were massacred: 385 verifiably named as victims of gunshots, hand grenades, burnings, stabbings, and beatings, the fate of others unknown.[137] To its very end, Portuguese actions in Africa left some of the most socially devastating legacies of colonial violence.

Other Colonialisms

In other regions, colonialism persisted in an invidious but less obvious form. Colonial counterinsurgency campaigns in Asia and Africa exemplified decolonization's asymmetric 'dirty wars' between 1945 and 1965 but, from radical Third Worldists to hawkish Cold Warriors, attention shifted thereafter to America's expanding ground war in Vietnam and Israel's military occupation of Palestinian territory in the West Bank and Gaza Strip following its lightning victory in June 1967.[138] Algeria's triumph against colonial odds remained exemplary, and the ANC's unending struggle against apartheid galvanized global antiracist sympathies, but by the late 1960s violent decolonization's most active volcanoes were elsewhere.[139] Within months of the Six-Day War, the political stakes, geographic locales, and ideological contexts of liberation struggle all changed. The audacious Vietnamese Tet assault on American-held Saigon in February 1968 confirmed that the Hanoi regime and its NLF ally represented one regional wing of a global guerrilla offensive.[140] The fierce resistance by fighters of Palestine's Fatah movement to the March 1968 Israeli Defense Force raid on Jordan's al-Karama refugee camp underlined that thousands of stateless Palestinians represented the other.[141]

The unresolved fate of Palestine and the wider Arab–Israeli conflict were problems defined by older colonial divisions and their legacies: a refugee diaspora, pan-Arabist solidarities warped by the Cold War into a pervasive anti-Westernism, and the relentless settlement pressure at the expanding margins of the Israeli state.[142] The Six-Day War of June 1967 might be framed within this larger picture of postimperial fallout. It becomes harder to map subsequent Middle East conflicts onto the contours of decolonization following Gamal Abdel Nasser's death on September 28, 1970, and the Damascus coup that saw Air Force General Hafez al-Assad seize power two months later in the wake of Syria's failed military intervention in Jordan. Instead, the Arab coalition's disastrous effort to recover lost ground with their Yom Kippur offensive in 1973 was primarily an interstate conflict for local supremacy.

These confrontations signified deeper changes in the nature of contested decolonization: at once generational, ideological, and geopolitical. To the colonial subjects facing imperial repression as Europe's empires withered away in the 1960s and 1970s were added the millions confronting imperialist intervention by other Cold War actors, as well as the settler colonialism of an expanding Israeli state. The death throes of European empire looked different in this light. What had been clearly distinguishable wars of decolonization were increasingly conceptualized by those who lived through them and others still having to fight them as part of something even bigger: demands among peoples of the global South, not just for sovereignty and nationhood, but for basic rights long withheld.[143] As if to confirm this tilt toward the shared anticolonialism of the world's newer nations, beginning in 1969 the United Nations' Special Committee on Decolonization, better known as the Committee of 24, pushed the General Assembly to endorse guerrilla movements fighting the last bastions of white imperial power in Africa and to recognize the legitimacy of liberation movements contesting all forms of 'colonialist and racialist oppression'. In the short term, this pressure culminated in passage of UN Resolution 2908 on November 2, 1972, which lamented that millions still lived under colonialism twelve years after the UN's December 1960 Declaration 1514 on the Granting of Independence to Colonial Countries and Peoples.[144]

It was in this more radical atmosphere that Third World and Communist bloc delegates to the 1968 UN Human Rights Conference in Tehran took aim at imperialist violence and international law's apparent blindness to it. They redoubled ICRC concentration on the issue but, otherwise, secured no immediate result.[145] Still, the change in tone mattered. Stung by the criticisms voiced at Tehran and painfully aware of its limited impact on contemporary conflicts in Vietnam, the Middle East, and Nigeria–Biafra, the ICRC initiated a series of meetings on revisions to international humanitarian law in armed conflicts.[146] These diplomatic wheels turned, but slowly. It was not until the early 1970s diplomatic conferences preparatory to the signing of the 1977 Protocols Additional to the earlier Geneva Conventions that the suffering of civilians and the combatant rights of anticolonial insurgents were firmly embedded within international laws on the conduct of war.[147]

International partnerships and transnational pressures from the global South converged to do so. Delegates from countries recently decolonized, as well as anticolonialists fighting for national liberation or the advancement of particular ethnic interests in Southeast Asia and Southern Africa, were pivotal to this reconceptualization of international law. These actors mapped the language of anti-imperialism and collective rights to self-determination onto the arguments of just war theory to highlight the limitations of existing humanitarian laws regulating the conduct of war, the protection of its victims, and the recognition of belligerent status. 'Just' war in this context was less an invocation of medieval thinking about the legitimate conduct of military violence than an adaptation to decolonization conflicts of earlier Leninist and Maoist support for partisan resistance to oppressive occupation.[148] The ideological objective was clearly anticolonial, in Jessica Whyte's telling phrase, to pit 'the realities of a decolonizing present against the legal norms of a colonial past'.[149]

The ICRC, although reluctant to identify with this radical agenda, could still endorse it as a worthwhile effort to extend the scope of humanitarian oversight to minimize suffering.[150] This congruence assured, the core success of the 1977 Additional Protocols were the sentences written into Article 1, paragraph 4 of Additional Protocol I, which extended legal protections to cover 'armed conflicts in which people are fighting against colonial domination and alien occupation and against racist regimes in the exercise of their right to self-determination'.[151] To American consternation, wars of decolonization at last came within the purview of international laws regulating war between states. Anticolonial insurgents had argued for decades that international humanitarian law served imperial interests by denying those fighting for national liberation, other ethnically organized self-defense groups, and the surrounding civilian population the same protections as their armed occupiers.[152] By extending the scope of belligerent rights and civilian protections, the Protocols Additional acknowledged this to have been the case.

By making civilian populations in dependent territories and those who chose to fight against colonial rule visible in international law, passage of the Additional Protocols marked an important transition, if not an end point, in decolonization's advance. The final collapse of the Portuguese Empire in Africa in 1973–1975 meanwhile saw the last of the large agglomerations of European overseas colonies dissolved. Elsewhere, though, decolonization remained unfinished.

Epilogue

The 1980s saw interethnic tensions and local fury at the human and environmental costs of French nuclear testing turn to violence in New Caledonia, where indigenous Kanak claims of colonial discrimination and French neglect escalated into protests, clashes, and clampdowns. New Caledonia's experience of conflict, and the centrality of indigenous rights to it, was a powerful reminder of other still-unresolved decolonizations in Pacific and Indian Ocean territories where the slow violence of colonial-era environmental spoliation has melded with existential threats of climate change.[153]

The fall of the Berlin Wall in 1989 heralded a different decolonization of sorts, as well as an eclipse of the Second World–Third World connections so crucial to anticolonialists in earlier decades. The demise of the Soviet Empire and its preceding humiliation in Afghanistan put an end to Eastern bloc immersion in decolonization conflicts.[154] But the breakup of the Soviet Union only increased Moscow's readiness to back favored proxies militarily or to crush dissident republics—and, in 2022, a sovereign neighbor state—seeking to escape Russia's strategic orbit. The eclipse of Cold War bipolarity changed the ideological complexion of interstate competition for influence and commercial gain across the global South but did not lessen its vigor. If 1989 signified an end to a particular form of geopolitical confrontation in Europe, in much of the global South the transition to a post–Cold War 1990s was marked by an intensification of violence and civil war.[155] Within less than a decade, Africa's Great Lakes region would witness not only the Rwandan genocide of 1994 but the outbreak of Africa's largest conflict since 1945: Laurent-Désirée Kabila's 1998 overthrow of the Mobutu regime triggered conflict in the Democratic Republic of Congo that was internationalized into the 'Great African War' by the involvement of numerous limitrophe states. From Algeria to Kuwait, the late 1980s and early 1990s also heralded crippling political violence and continuing international conflict in the Arab world. For countries

shaped by decolonization—by the political transitions, state-building projects, debt crises, and resource and frontier disputes induced by the end
of European imperial domination—1989 did not herald any reduction in
political violence within or between them.[156]

At its hardest edge, foreign involvement in wars and civil conflicts
during the 1990s and beyond has, if anything, become more complex and
diffuse. Civil conflicts in West Africa spawned ongoing arguments about
'greed versus grievance' dynamics and the distinctiveness or otherwise of
postcolonial 'new wars'.[157] The eclipse of apartheid as South Africa transitioned to majority rule in 1994 was rightly celebrated as a signal political
victory. But South Africa's subsequent experience highlighted the difficulties of dismantling the economic structures and cultural legacies of
colonial discrimination, let alone the challenges of healing the invisible
scars of institutionalized racism and political violence. The 1997 expiry of
Britain's Hong Kong 'lease' and its replacement with China's 'one country,
two systems' formula has been supplanted by something more authoritarian: Beijing's enforcement of one country, one system. For all these
unfinished decolonizations, controversies over empire have changed focus
again over the past twenty years or so. The apparent relentlessness of
globalization at the dawn of the twenty-first century, for some, framed
understandings of American and Western coalition involvement in foreign
wars not as counterterrorism writ large, but as a new imperialism, even
a return to empire. More recently still, it is decolonization itself that has
garnered most attention. As both concept and objective it remains a rallying cry, but one less to do with ending foreign occupation and claiming
sovereignty than with confronting racism and social exclusion in all their
manifestations.

A World Remade by Decolonization?

DEFINING WHEN AND if empire ended is difficult. Integrating global factors that accelerated or slowed decolonization adds complexity.[1] Writing in 2005, at the height of arguments over a new American empire, political scientist Barry Gills suggested that globalizing processes, which brought humanity into closer 'physical and communicative proximity' were really aspects of what he labeled 'a clash of globalizations' between 'Empire' and 'Cosmopolis'. Empire represented the imposition of foreign imperial control. Cosmopolis rested on shared recognition of a single global humanity, an aspiration to greater partnership and diminishing inequality. In this characterization, it is tempting to read decolonization as steps away from empire and toward Cosmopolis. Yet, while he mused on the possibilities of globalization, Gills treated decolonization as something done, a transition from empire to independence.[2] This book has suggested otherwise. Decolonization was messier and less absolute, a multivalent process, varied in form, extent, and finality.

There's not much epistemological or ontological precision to help us navigate through all of this. The meaning of decolonization is contested because disagreement persists about its essential qualities. The word 'decolonization' did not have common currency before the Second World War. Nor was the term widely used at the height of the process it describes in the 1950s and 1960s. Rather, decolonization was a process of several moving parts: the withdrawal of European rule, the takeover of governmental apparatus by anticolonial nationalists, the pressures of Cold War rivalries, and the efforts by minority groups in decolonizing states to assert separate claims to nationhood.[3]

Locating those processes historically invites global perspectives and a stress on contingency. Some colonial demands for change were articulated in a language of reform, not revolution. Paying attention to gradualist reformers is fundamental to historicizing decolonization not as something inexorable and long foreseen but as an outcome neither anticipated nor desired by local politicians, trade unionists, and civil society actors trying to dismantle colonial discrimination through empire rather than against it. Anticolonialism makes sense as a unifying abstraction, an expression of opposition to something ethically indefensible, rather than as unswerving support for a particular national form.[4] The idea that, one after another, colonies would become nations ignores the multiplicity of viewpoints and the alternatives in play. Imperial and nationalist conceptions of bounded sovereignty jarred with the pluralistic arrangements and local improvisations that had enabled empires to survive despite the weakness of their structures and the porousness of their borderlands.[5] Transnational connections, cosmopolitan influences, and differing layers of attachment to kin, community, faith, and locality were everywhere different, yet always the same in exposing the myth of nationalism triumphant.

Decolonization's interactions with capitalist globalization or its antonym in socialist internationalism also suggest that bilateral 'transfers of power' between a single ruling authority and a dominant local movement were never total.[6] The strands of economic connectivity, capital movement, communications links, and migratory flows integral to globalization defied the ideological attachments of 'red globalism', nonalignment, and other south–south visions of a postcolonial world, tying former colonies into new international coalitions and economic blocs. Mention of globalization reminds us that the substance of western European and American colonialism was capitalistic. From investment capital and foreign-owned banking networks to hierarchically ordered workplaces, coercive labor practices, and the prioritization of export-oriented production, the economic life of empires reflected forms of racial capitalism that reinforced inequalities in the distribution of power and protections. Decolonization promised an end to such practices but, for many, failed to deliver as much economically and socially as it did politically or constitutionally. Taking Africa as their case study, leading economic historians reject the idea that colonialism and capitalism were somehow coeval. They suggest instead that levels of inequality across a decolonized continent were, in some cases, only little affected by decolonization but in others, and notably in those territories reshaped by settler colonialism, deeply marked by it.[7] Sovereignty changes, in other words, were insufficient in themselves to stop capitalist globalization in its tracks. Anticolonial modernizers pursued various strategies of development, infrastructure building, education provision, and cultural and linguistic renewal designed to make independence 'real'. Few did so unilaterally. Foreign sponsors, technocratic 'expertise', and loan capital created political economies of influence and obligation that jarred with assertions of sovereignty.

For many of those living under colonialism, as well as the writers and political activists who challenged it, the violence inherent to imperialist practices was self-evident. Some described this violence in structural terms. From the Atlantic world capitalism made possible by the slave trade, the devastation of indigenous populations in the Americas and elsewhere after contact with conquistadors and their pathogens, to the neocolonialism, economic dependency, and indebtedness that blighted decolonizing nations, colonialism has been indicted as the root of the worst contemporary evils.[8] Slavery was fundamental to the colonial capitalism of plantation agriculture, as insatiable in its demand for transported labor as it was destructive of tropical environments. This combination of human commodification and ecological degradation was sufficiently pervasive by the early nineteenth century to be labeled by scholars a 'plantationocene', devastating to communities and environments in the Americas, the Caribbean, Africa, and South Asia.[9] The colonialism challenged by twentieth-century decolonization was less blatantly rapacious but was still racially configured, socially stratified, and environmentally transformative.[10]

The peace settlement to emerge from that century's first world war was a case in point. Colonial territories were systematically excluded from the liberal order that Europe's imperial powers tried to impose.[11] Imperialism was not somehow less colonialist after the conflict than before it. The victors' empires left in place the administrative regulations, economic practices, and cultural discriminations that underpinned the everyday violence of colonialism. New ideas of sovereignty and self-determination meanwhile set Europe apart from the wider world over which its leading state actors claimed dominion. The liberal internationalism of the interwar period distilled the imperialist mindset to its hypocritical essence.[12]

The colonial continuities embedded within the First World War peace settlement also suggest that it makes little sense to analyze the interwar years either as choke-points in the otherwise onward march of globalization or as the watershed cleaving empire growth from irreversible empire decline. The aspirations of black radicalism would be disappointed in the short term, but other opponents of empire were closer to meeting their goals. By 1919, from Central Europe to Eastern Asia, internal oppositionists and external challengers stood at the threshold of bringing down empires that were centuries in the making. Eventually, these challenges proved decisive only for the landmass empires of Eurasia—the Austro-Hungarian, the Ottoman, and the Imperial Russian—but not for the oceanic empires of Britain, France, and the United States or for the imperial holdings of Belgium, the Netherlands, and Portugal.[13] African, Asian, and Caribbean anticolonialism was held in check. The claims made by the early proponents of non-Western models of freedom, citizenship, and statehood would end in frustration for most, detention for many, and, in the short term at least, imperial rejection of their demands for self-rule.

The 1920s and 1930s did witness decisive colonial changes—in governance and repressive violence, in ideas about collective and individual rights, in economies and trade patterns reshaped by protracted depression, in print culture and urban cosmopolitanism, in transnational consolidation of oppositional networks—but these are better understood as 'globalizing': global in impact and reach but not a part of some unstoppable globalization steamroller.

The Second World War catalyzed deeper changes. Fighting total war encouraged bigger government and, with it, information collection about the governed as imperial states intruded deeper into the lives of metropolitan citizens and colonial subjects, demanding increased effort and resources. But the pressures of global war sometimes severed links between metropolitan governments and colonial dependencies entirely, most obviously for defeated imperial states, France, the Netherlands, and Belgium. The British Empire also suffered total humiliation in the first phase of war against Japan.[14] In this and other interimperial contests the violence of war tore administrative and economic fabrics apart, leaving the poorest and weakest in colonial societies chronically insecure. The revisionist empire-building of Japan's Co-Prosperity Sphere professed a martial pan-Asianism but was more significant in the stimulus it provided to Southeast Asian resistance movements. Admittedly, when disaggregated to the micro-level of individual encounters, the kaleidoscope of militias, militaries, and guerrilla movements from Indonesia through Vietnam to Malaya and Burma pursued various local economic interests, ethnic claims, and wider political objectives that do not map neatly onto macro-level narratives of violent decolonization. Whatever their inspiration, colonial acts of group violence, plus less visible but more prevalent civilian noncompliance with reoccupation ordinances, fiscal demands, and labor requirements, undermined the claims of returning European administrators that Western empires could be rebuilt. The Second World War's colonial famines in India, Indonesia, and Vietnam, meanwhile, registered the largest loss of civilian lives in modern colonialism—a cumulative total of more than five million people either starved or afflicted by epidemic illnesses their bodies were too malnourished to resist.

By 1945, the architecture of Bretton Woods with dollar supremacy at its foundation, the prioritization of European relief, and the supranationalism of the United Nations and its affiliate agencies rendered the dynamics of north–south inequality more transparent than ever. Colonialist presumptions were harder for international actors to reconcile with building a new global order, whatever their attachments in the emerging Cold War. International law, which at the start of the twentieth century had presupposed a racially configured world, was, after 1945, edging toward the repudiation of colonialism. Neither the UN Charter nor the wave of human rights protections of the late 1940s did so unequivocally, but their globalism put Europe's imperial powers on the defensive.[15] Still, empire was far from done. Even after 'civilizational' claims became patently ludicrous in the face of a second interimperial World War and were excised from official statements justifying empire after 1945, imperialist thinking shaped ideas about how sovereign statehood should be constituted and when independent nations should be recognized. Its traces were evident in everything from the constitutional plans of late colonial reformists and the calamities of partition to the developmental projects and human rights discourses promoted by supranational agencies and NGOs in the 1960s and beyond.[16] The decolonizing world was assigned junior status within this global political geography, its elevation to full integration dependent on foreign-led modernization, capital investment, and technology transfer.[17]

Developmental economics, much like Western immigration policies and Cold War security strategies, still rested on racial tenets, which divided rich world from poor.[18] Western Europe's imperial technocrats, US modernization theorists, and Communist bloc 'advisers' shared similar presumptions of superior knowledge and expertise to guide former colonies to either capitalist or socialist modernity. They were challenged by local claims to rights equality and cultural respect. But these were articulated in different registers. In some regions, such as French black Africa, civil protest, strike actions and rights claims prefigured wider citizenship, increased representation, and sustained reformist dialogue. In others, opposition expressed itself through violence. The late 1940s wave of Asian decolonization conflicts pitched nationalist republics in

Indonesia and Vietnam and leftist insurgents in Malaya into years of war. In South Asia and Palestine, intercommunal violence and administrative breakdown prefigured territorial partition, displacement, refugee crises, and loss of life on such calamitous scale that the decolonization behind them was obscured by its human costs. Elsewhere, though, reformism and developmental interventions held sway, spurred by local demands, postwar expectations, and new codifications of individual rights and collective entitlements.

Whatever the original UN Charter's inclusions and omissions, and no matter how limited the General Assembly's power to pass enforceable resolutions, the organization's credibility in the global South rested squarely on its rejection of colonialism and an embrace of the collective right to self-determination.[19] On the matter of inalienable individual rights, the voices of anticolonialists outside the United Nations and the tone of sympathetic General Assembly delegations inside it were more dissonant. To be sure, trade unionists and lawyers representing what we'd now describe as political prisoners—those detained in colonial prisons, often for peaceful oppositional activity—invoked both the December 1948 Universal Declaration of Human Rights and the later European Convention on Human Rights to highlight abuses.[20] India, as an original UN member and a soon-to-be-independent state, was keen to establish itself as a powerful international actor and a leader of global anticolonialism.[21] Led by Vijay Lakshmi Pandit, Nehru's sister, and Hans Mehta, a compelling advocate within the Human Rights Commission, India's UN delegation strenuously opposed imperial powers' insistence that colonial affairs were matters of internal sovereign jurisdiction. Anxious to support the millions of Indians living and working outside the subcontinent, India's delegates also led calls for stronger protections for diaspora communities facing discrimination and rights denial as immigrants.[22]

For other leading anticolonial nationalists, individual rights were secondary to collective freedom and the material benefits of enhanced social rights. Some went further still, dismissing the prioritization of the rights of the person over the needs of the group as a Western invention and an imperialistic one at that.[23] In this strand of thinking, decolonization as an expression of inalienable rights was first and foremost a quest for nationhood. The broader point, though, is that decolonization politics was in some measure rights politics. Historian Roland Burke is surely right that, by the late 1940s, organized anticolonialism was increasingly articulated in a language of rights. As he and others have stressed, the more difficult question to answer is rights of which type: those inhering in the individual

or those owed to communities denied opportunities to express their collective aspirations?[24] The two were not mutually exclusive; the issue was,
rather, which was the more locally urgent before independence and which
held political priority after it.[25] Time would tell. With notable exceptions,
India included, across Asia and Africa, the governments of former dependencies were as resistant as their former colonial rulers had been to international oversight of their performance in upholding rights protections.[26]

Clearly, the invocation of human rights to serve both wider political
objectives and personal demands for restitution did not end once formal
decolonization was achieved. Rather, as the editors of a recent specialist
volume indicate, across the chronological divides separating late colonial
contestation from the construction of independent states and societies,
'Human rights became a perennial aspect of anti-imperial and postcolonial phraseology not for its conceptual clarity, but for its versatility as
a language with all-purpose emancipatory potential'.[27] Writing human
rights declarations or international laws with enforcement procedures
sufficiently robust to give such rights tangible substance was difficult. In
adversarial politics, human rights, it seemed, could be invoked by any and
everyone; not just by anticolonialists, but by imperial authorities and the
sternest authoritarians claiming they had people's best interests at heart.[28]
Repressive regimes eager to conceal systemic rights abuses, from the
Shah's Iran to apartheid South Africa, stressed their comparatively high
development spending when compared with regional neighbors.[29]

Where do these contests over rights and competing claims to oversee
improvements in living standards within late colonial societies leave us in
assessing how the end of empires came about? Tempting though it might
be to imagine an irresistible groundswell of popular support for decolonization, with one imperial domino after another falling before local
demands for self-determination, the end of empires was less visible and
more negotiable than this image implies. For one thing, colonial politics
after 1945 was never reducible to a binary choice for or against national
sovereignty. Often, talk of independence was closer to a murmur than a
scream. For another thing, anticolonialism was never monolithic. Its ideological ingredients varied, as did the actions of its supporters. So, too,
did debates over the means to achieve more equitable societies. Historian
Gregory Mann, describing the situation in postwar French black Africa,
captures the flux intrinsic to anticolonialism's evolution:

In the 1940s, it meant contesting the dual authority of French administrators and canton chiefs in the countryside, demanding equal pay for

equal work in the formal sector, and struggling to give content to the promise of colonial citizenship held out by the Fourth Republic and its French Union. By 1960, it meant asserting autonomy from France in three key sectors preserved for Paris in the constitution of the Fifth Republic: diplomacy, defense, and foreign policy.[30]

Third Worldist attachments and hostility to foreign economic interference typically featured as well, confirming that anticolonialism was at once locally constituted and globally connected. In some places, India for one, such discussions could be characterized as a kind of national dialogue. For the most part, though, anticolonial activism was either an elite affair or the work of dedicated cadres operating outside the mainstream of workaday life.[31]

The notion of a unity of anticolonial purpose and intercultural solidarity, effusively described by Richard Wright's 1956 account of the Bandung spirit, elided the multiple perspectives on what the previous year's Bandung Conference meant and the disagreements over how to fulfill its promise. As we saw in chapter 14, Bandung's transformative power was more evident in its potential than its concrete results. But it mattered. What has been characterized as a communitas or 'community of feeling' took shape at Bandung, one that guided global South interaction in a collective effort to make decolonization real.[32] Aside from drawing clearer outlines for the institutional framework of a nonaligned coalition of states and social movements, Bandung solidified the image of decolonization as a moral struggle for freedoms and dignity denied. In the diversity of its delegations, the range of global audiences it addressed and the way it spoke to them, it changed the style and the substance of decolonization geopolitics. After Bandung, it was impossible to make a convincing ethical case for colonial oversight.

Bandung and the spread of guerrilla diplomacy were also responses to the efforts by imperial powers to hold on to empire militarily. In the mythmaking of its protagonists, the colonial counterinsurgency characteristic of decolonization conflicts was proportionate and restrained. Claims of minimum force, targeted violence, *longue durée* population control, and an abiding concern with social welfare were as stereotypical as they were self-serving. Their supposed achievements were wildly inflated and, in most cases, inaccurate. The violence of decolonization's wars hit colonial subjects hardest, their status as vulnerable civilians unrecognized politically or legally. Artillery shelling, assault helicopters, and long-range bombers were indiscriminate killers, but the low technology practice of infantry searches, village clearances, and the removal of populations also caused civilian deaths through malnourishment, increased infant mortality, and epidemic outbreaks among the displaced.

With international law doing little to restrain them, in decolonization conflicts spanning thirty years from the Vietnamese Revolution of August 1945 to Portugal's African withdrawal after the 1974 Carnation Revolution in Lisbon, aerial bombing and napalm jelly incinerated people, reprisal killings and degrading treatment remained widespread, detainees were tortured, and security force 'sweeps' and free-fire zones put residents in the firing line.[33] Collective punishments saw villages destroyed (generic); farmland, work routes and tracks to water sources mined (in North and Southern African and Southeast Asian conflicts); ecosystems degraded (generic); and millions incarcerated in resettlement camps and 'new villages' (prevalent in Vietnam, Madagascar, Malaya, Kenya, Algeria, Angola, and Mozambique).[34]

To dwell on perhaps the best-known colonial example, the wealth of evidence provided about systematic coercion bursts the myth of British 'minimum force' restraint when confronted with colonial rebellion. In Cyprus, Aden, and Northern Ireland, as beforehand in Malaya and Kenya, civilians faced collective punishments, curfews, and eviction from their homes, while captured insurgents and other detainees were assaulted, degraded, sometimes even killed, all actions defended at the time as core components of effective counterinsurgency.[35] Equally striking is the imperial complacency—whether British, French, Dutch, Portuguese, or otherwise—about acts of retributive violence by security force personnel. Time and again, legitimate efforts to protect soldiers and police personnel facing bullets, brickbats, and threats to their families slipped into indulgence for acts of indiscipline that ranged from beatings and property destruction to torture and summary executions.[36] The disturbing intersections among colonialism, racism, and rights violations were starkest in decolonization conflicts whose collapsing ethical boundaries typified a continuing twentieth-century civilianization of war.

More than anything else, civilian victimization brought decolonization's hidden wars under global scrutiny. Deploying evidence of rights abuses lent moral authority to anticolonial claims of legitimacy. Building foreign networks of support was vital for armed oppositionists as well.[37] Sympathetic foreign governments defended these violent nonstate actors in international forums. They offered sanctuary, weapons, and material aid. Whether operating inside colonial territory or from 'sanctuary bases' and through 'governments in exile' located within other friendly states, insurgent movements used transnational connections to embed alternate governance structures.[38] And recognition by friendly governments validated the guerrilla diplomacy of insurgent movements fighting imperialist rule.[39] Decolonization required more than evicting colonial rulers; it meant governing in their place. So the impulse among anticolonial movements to act as a presumptive state was commensurately strong.[40] The geopolitical theaters and ideational spaces in which these contests to win over states and publics took place expanded markedly after the Second World War. Increasing global connectivity, new media, and consequent growth in the opportunity to spread one's message, whether in person, in print, or over the airwaves, helped make such guerrilla diplomacy not just an international phenomenon but a transnational one as well. Breaking the grip of established state actors over the instruments of formal diplomacy by asserting the rights and claims of colonized peoples became an essential part of global decolonization.

Evidence from late-stage decolonizations of the 1960s and 1970s indicates that the international politics of proxy confrontation and the political economies of foreign investment in independent states merged with the contests between insurgent movements and their opponents over three issues: sanctuary bases and supply routes; the domination of local populations, whether by imposing security or disrupting it; and the use of external partners to stake local and global claims to political legitimacy and nationalist authenticity.[41] The growth of supranational organizations from the 1940s onward provided additional focal points for anticolonial movements. From the United Nations to the OAU, supranational agencies nourished transnational lobby groups and anti-imperial provisional governments working to establish themselves in a postcolonial world.

Doing politics or business with insurgent partners both reflected the transregional alignments of decolonization and contributed to them. A willingness to sustain political dialogue alongside the promise of privileged economic access and trade deals after independence became levers used to extract strategic concessions and international recognition. All of this meant that, by the 1960s, guerrilla diplomacy was a normative standard, not some contingent facet of insurgencies but part of the stuff of international politics in the global South.[42]

In some places, the incumbent regime was so blatantly racist that opposition to it was hardly a matter of choice.[43] Apartheid South Africa was the archetype here. Antiapartheid solidarity movements were a global phenomenon but developed especially rapidly in the Anglophone West Indies and among Afro-Caribbean communities in Britain. The 1951 murder of Barbadian seaman Milton King at the hands of Cape Town police triggered widespread protests across the West Indies, drawing on a longer tradition of transatlantic solidarity against colonialist racism.[44] In March 1958 African students in Britain organized a Committee of African Organizations (CAO) to coordinate support for a 'boycott South Africa' campaign that lasted for decades.[45] Metropolitan imperial governments rarely understood the visceral antiracist quality of such anticolonialism, but European politicians who encountered the lived experience of black South Africans immediately grasped what apartheid meant. Granted access to ANC detainees in January 1958, Barbara Castle struggled to unravel the precise legal implications of its multiple laws and restrictions. As she recorded in her diary, it took a visit to Johannesburg's O/K Department Store to make her realize what apartheid looked like:

> 1st went to haberdashery counter. 3 black women waiting diffidently to be served. 'Go up and she will serve you first', said Peter. White assistant first took tape measure and money black girl holding out, then turned to me. 'This lady is next' I said indicating African woman next to me. The white assistant snarled: 'I can't tell who's next' and flounced off down the counter to a white woman at the far end. 'You see?' said Peter and we walked away.[46]

Castle's recollections, with which this book also began, testify to empire's indefensibility and decolonization's incompleteness.

In the political realm, quasi-colonial relationships subsist with numerous island territories and other relatively small dependencies in oceanic 'peripheries'. Big and small, some postcolonial nations have remained aligned with their former imperial rulers.[47] Local protests have been conducted since 2019 against the West African and Central African CFA franc, monetary unions pegged to the euro but established by France, rehearsing accusations of European neocolonialism, and a form of French 'colonial tax'.[48] West Africa's monetary disputes remind us that singular focus on the major, cataclysmic ends of empire left more complex networks of connection and dependency unaddressed.[49] There are important exceptions to this trend, and they have become more apparent as global history's work in de-provincializing colonial history has gathered momentum.[50] It remains difficult, even so, to account for territories that, in the words of one scholar, 'seek imperialism's embrace' rather than struggling to be free of it.[51]

The world remade by decolonization is, though, different from the world of empires that preceded it. Numerous former dependencies across a broad Asian arc stretching from Korea to Israel and including India,

Pakistan, and Indonesia have become powerful global actors. For others, their sovereign independence remains compromised by problems of debt and dependency, instability and foreign interventionism.[52] Sometimes dismissed as 'failed states', a more accurate measure of their sovereignty is whether their governments remain the primary instrument through which political decisions and economic activities are mediated.[53]

Crucial here was how well the newly independent states managed what political economists term 'structural dependence', namely the danger for developing countries that inward investment might come with political strings attached. For supporters of globalization, the answer lay not in rejecting such foreign investment but in embracing multiple providers. Diversifying the number and type of investors offered better protection than anything else. In this reading, a virtuous circle might result in which investors promoted open labor markets and democratic accountability, knowing that capital was safer in countries with good standards of governance. The contrary argument, popularized by dependency theorists, suggested the opposite outcome: that investors tolerated coercive labor practices and authoritarian government to keep wages low, populations compliant, and profits high.[54]

Trade, understood as an exchange of goods and services, is now dwarfed by the monetary value of global capital markets. Decolonized nations are not somehow immune to this shift even if their currency reserves may be small and worldwide movements of capital tend to cluster in areas of dense industrial activity.[55] Several possess lucrative resources, presenting high-gain opportunities for foreign investment and environmental degradation.[56] The point is significant because capital flows are more responsive to risk than longer-term patterns of trade. Globalization, in other words, may draw decolonized states, especially those that are resource-rich, into international capital markets, increasing the interdependence between countries while reducing the likelihood of conflict between them.[57] At the same time, risk-sensitive investors are liable to withdraw their money from unstable places, meaning that poorer countries beset with structural problems may lose out. Unsurprisingly, the incidence of political violence also affects levels of foreign direct investment.[58] Differently put, globalization works in both integrative and discriminatory fashion, tending to benefit rich-world countries more than poor ones.

Aside from capital flows, patterns of investment, and the treatment of workers, land redistribution provides another index of decolonization's political economies. Decolonization did not, for the most part, revolutionize systems of landholding in newly independent states, the majority of

which remained predominantly agricultural. Land reforms were enacted
in some of decolonization's emblematic national cases in Asia, among
them China, India, and Vietnam, although with very different results.[59]
But land redistribution in a decolonizing Africa was rare. It was started
but then halted in Algeria to the north, and it entrenched the power of a
ruling party elite in Zimbabwe to the south. For the most part, though,
the socialization of land, as pursued in Julius Nyerere's Tanzania, did not
transform rural living standards.[60] In numerous sub-Saharan territories,
land reforms either fell short as redistributive measures or were not implemented at all. More common was the continuation of some sort of mixed
economy in which a minority, often those with administrative or political
connections, acquired additional land and power as a rentier class.[61] For
the rural majority, as well as those confined to squatter residencies in urban
shantytowns, secure property ownership remained impossible.[62] In Sudan
and Kenya, the Great Lakes region, and the Democratic Republic of the
Congo, land inequalities have been identified as central in political violence and armed conflict from the 1970s onward.[63] Understood as a more
equitable and sustainable ownership of farmland, land reform cannot be
counted a postcolonial success.[64]

Decolonization as a global cause peaked somewhere between 1959 and
1974. The long 1960s that opened with the Cuban revolution of 1959, that
continued with successive African decolonizations, and that sustained its
radical intensity through the Third Worldism of the 1966 Tricontinental
and transnational opposition to South African, Biafran, Palestinian and
Vietnamese suffering, ended with the post–oil shock failure of the New
International Economic Order (NIEO) in 1974.[65] Admittedly, as with any
attenuated definition of a transformative period, one risks attaching too
much cultural baggage to the idea of a 'global Sixties'. As historian Salar
Mohandesi warns, the concept has become chaotically diffuse, its symbols
including everything from 'the Beatles, the Shah's modernization programs, Twiggy, the Sino–Soviet split, the refrigerator, Sputnik, oil prices,
Vatican II, the Algerian War, pornography, the coup in Brazil, Afrobeat,
the Six-Day War' to 'Star Trek, the Munich Olympics . . . the moon landing, the Montgomery bus boycott' and 'LSD'.[66] But surely one thing that
set these years apart was an ideational change, a new theory space, in
which leading actors in the decolonization story recognized that political
independence was not enough. Meaningful self-determination for new
nations, decolonizing communities, and individuals also demanded economic sovereignty and the capacity to sustain human security through
enhanced economic and social rights.[67] Among Adom Getachew's many

insights is her recognition that well-known political contests and military struggles between imperial powers and their anticolonial opponents over state-making were not the culmination of decolonization but a step toward it. Numerous newly independent countries of the global South found their sovereignty compromised by an international economic order, enshrined at Bretton Woods and hardened by Cold War rivalries, which condemned Third World states to subservience to the rich world's economic demands.

If this looks like dependency theory warmed up, or a return to Nkrumah's warnings against neocolonialism, it is persuasive nonetheless. What makes it so is Getachew's analysis of the institutional mechanisms and political-economic thinking of the Third Worldist advocates of global redistribution. Working through the supranational forums of UNCTAD, the G77, and, latterly, the NIEO, the preoccupation among these opponents of neocolonial dependency was that global financial and trading systems were so stacked against them that political decolonization was undermined.[68] The oil crisis was pivotal. It forced rich-world countries to face uncomfortable truths about their reliance on vital commodities, which were slipping from their control.[69] Ultimately, though, it did not reorder the world.

So why did the NIEO falter? For one thing, it never represented a sustainable coalition. Its member states ranged from the socialist experimenters of West and East Africa to the ultra-capitalist oil producers of the Middle East. Persecution of domestic opponents and sharp inequalities within some G77 countries jarred with their claims against an unjust international system.[70] Even so, their call for a rebalancing of economic power between the industrial consumers of the global North and the commodity producers of the global South marked the biggest ideational challenge to the capitalist world order since the Chinese Revolution of 1949.[71]

Moving from economic contests to political ones, in the early 1990s historical sociologist Charles Tilly singled out decolonizing states as highly militaristic, their regimes often authoritarian and prone to violent overthrow. From 1960 to 1987, aggregate defense expenditure among former colonies was relatively high when compared with their rich-world counterparts, the burden of financing military costs falling hardest on low-income societies.[72] Tilly's arguments resonate with those who insist that violence was both integral to decolonization and constitutive of postcolonial state power. Here, too, there is powerful evidence of an enduring imperial hangover. It is easy to lament the spread of authoritarian, often military rule across the global South. But arms control treaties and other global 'rules' ostensibly designed to limit the violence capability of states whose standards of governance and rights protections fall short of United Nations criteria tend to benefit the rule-makers within a Western-led international order.[73] Little wonder that China and Putin's Russia figure large among the countries that reject any equivalence between democratic governance, international oversight, and the 'right' to support or supply client states, many of which escaped empire through violence. Political scientist Tarak Barkawi puts it bluntly: 'War making, much of it by Asian and African peasants, played more of a role in ending colonial empires than western peacemaking or law-making. The AK-47 was more significant than the pen'.[74]

Perhaps so, but by the mid-1970s among decolonization's 'victor powers', from Algeria and Angola to Indonesia and Vietnam, the hard realities of statist one-party regimes took the tarnish off some of decolonization's pioneers. Where imperial states once tried to hide the scale and methods of colonial repression, postimperial governments now struggle to acknowledge the messy incompleteness of decolonization. On November 22, 2019, the UK Foreign and Commonwealth Office (FCO) issued a terse dismissal at the expiry of a six-month United Nations deadline to end British colonial rule over the Chagos Islands. Still a 'British Indian Ocean Territory', this island archipelago rises from the center of the Indian Ocean halfway between Africa and Indonesia. Its isolated position confers an enormous strategic advantage to Britain and its friends, allowing long-range aircraft to reach continental landmasses to the north, south, east, and west. Indeed, the Chagos are perhaps better known for the US airbase at Diego Garcia than for the 1,500 or so islanders who were deported from their homeland between Mauritian independence in 1968 and the definitive lease of the airbase to US authorities in 1973.[75] The majority of these Chagossians are descendants of slaves and indentured laborers, people transported to the islands during Britain's colonial rule.[76] Aware that the UN vote was nonbinding, the FCO insisted that Mauritius had no lawful claim on the Chagos, which had been under continuous British sovereignty since 1814. In the midst of a general election campaign, Labour Party leader Jeremy Corbyn disagreed. A supporter of the islanders' right of return, he reaffirmed his determination to 'right one of the wrongs of history' by putting an end to British colonialism should Labour win the election.[77] His claim proved overly bold on all counts, but it marked an admission of unaddressed injustice. Arguments over the Chagos Islands also point to something broader.

By focusing on paths of colonial destruction, this book has argued that empires have ended without, I hope, suggesting that decolonization is somehow done. The difficulty, of course, is that the unequal relations of power characteristic of colonialism persist in places long since formally decolonized. If the political task is to find ways to address such inequalities, the analytical challenge is to reach a judgment about whether or not the ostensible end of empires signified a genuine decolonization. For some scholars, particularly in the field of postcolonial studies, colonialism endures in patterns of thought, speech, and behavior. Those working in international political economy reach similar conclusions but do so using data on exchange rates, commodity pricing, and unfair trade terms between developing countries and rich-world importers.[78]

If the socioeconomic markers of twenty-first-century colonialism may be registered in discrepancies of life expectancy, poverty, and life chances between rich world and poor, for those more interested in cultural markers, the greater salience of colonialism lies in the casual racism of the everyday.[79] At stake in these arguments are the dominant self-image of particular nations, their professed values, and their occlusion of a 'difficult' imperial past.[80] People marginalized by ethnicity, religious affiliation, or income from the narratives of rich-world politics underline that the unmaking of empire did not mean the end of colonialism.[81] We still have some way to go.

NOTES

Introduction: Ending Empire and Remaking the World

1. Barbara Castle papers, BLO, MS Castle 16: Diary/notebook of visit to Kenya and independence celebrations, Dec. 1963, fo. 3.

2. Castle papers, notebook of visit to Kenya and independence celebrations, fos. 5–7.

3. Castle papers, notebook of visit to Kenya and independence celebrations, fo. 7.

4. Castle papers, notebook of visit to Kenya and independence celebrations, fos. 8–13.

5. Daniel Branch, "The Enemy Within: Loyalists and the War against Mau Mau in Kenya," *Journal of African History* 48, no. 2 (2007): 295–99, 314–15; Justin Willis, Gabrielle Lynch, and Nic Cheeseman, "Voting, Nationhood, and Citizenship in Late-Colonial Africa," *Historical Journal* 61, no. 4 (2018): 1116–17, 1126–32.

6. A. G. Hopkins, "Rethinking Decolonization," *Past & Present* 200 (August 2008): 211–12.

7. David Armitage, *The Declaration of Independence: A Global History* (Cambridge, MA: Harvard University Press, 2007), especially chapters 2–3.

8. Krishan Kumar, "Empires and Nations, Convergence or Divergence," in *Empire and Sociology: The Imperial Entanglements of a Discipline*, ed. George Steinmetz (Durham, NC: Duke University Press, 2013), 283–95; Barry Buzan and Amitav Archarya, *Re-Imagining International Relations: World Orders in the Thought and Practice of Indian, Chinese and Islamic Civilisations* (Cambridge, UK: Cambridge University Press, 2021).

9. James R. Brennan, "Lowering the Sultan's Flag: Sovereignty and Decolonization in Coastal Kenya," *Comparative Studies in Society and History* 50, no. 4 (2008): 831–38.

10. Su Sin Lewis, *Cities in Motion: Urban Life and Cosmopolitanism in Southeast Asia, 1920–1940* (Cambridge, UK: Cambridge University Press, 2016), 1–5, 71, 92–94.

11. For discussion of connections among empire, colonialism and contemporary constructions of race and global justice, see Duncan Bell, "Introduction: Empire, Race, and Global Justice," in *Empire, Race, and Global Justice*, ed. Duncan Bell (Cambridge, UK: Cambridge University Press, 2019), 1–11.

12. Itay Lotem, *The Memory of Colonialism in Britain and France: The Sins of Silence* (Cham: Palgrave Macmillan, 2021), 191–227.

13. Samir Puri, *The Great Imperial Hangover: How Empires Have Shaped the World* (London: Atlantic Books, 2020).

14. For evaluation of these macro forces, see Jason C. Parker, "Decolonization, the Cold War, and the Post-Columbian Era," in *The Cold War in the Third World*, ed. Robert J. McMahon (Oxford: Oxford University Press, 2013), 124–38, at 124–25; and, in a continental setting, Frank Gerits, *The Ideological Scramble for Africa: How the Pursuit of Anticolonial Modernity Shaped a Postcolonial Order, 1945–1966* (Ithaca, NY: Cornell University Press, 2023).

15. Gyan Prakash and Jeremy Adelman, "Introduction: Imagining the Third World: Genealogies of Alternative Global Histories," in *Inventing the Third World: In Search of Freedom for the Postwar Global South*, ed. Gyan Prakash and Jeremy Adelman (London: Bloomsbury Academic, 2023), 9–24. For distinct spaces of Second–Third World encounter, from schools and hospitals to military training camps, see the chapter contributions in Kristin Roth-Ey, ed., *Socialist Internationalism and the Gritty Politics of the Particular: Second-Third World Spaces in the Cold War* (London: Bloomsbury Academic, 2023).

16. James Tully, "Lineages of Contemporary Imperialism," in *Lineages of Empire: The Historical Roots of British Imperial Thought*, ed. Duncan Kelly (Oxford: Oxford University Press, 2009), 7–10, 27–29; also cited in Bell, "Introduction: Empire," 6–7.

17. For contemporary, twenty-first-century conflict: Tarak Barkawi, "War and Decolonization in Ukraine," *New Perspectives* 30, no. 4 (2022): 317–22.

18. Globalization–decolonization connections, most thoroughly examined by Anthony Hopkins, are also explored in his analysis of American empire: see Hopkins, "Rethinking Decolonization," 211–47, and "Globalisation and Decolonisation," *Journal of Imperial & Commonwealth History* 45, no. 5 (2017): 729–45; idem, *American Empire: A Global History* (Princeton, NJ: Princeton University Press, 2018). See also Martin Thomas and Andrew Thompson, "Rethinking Decolonization: A New Research Agenda for the Twenty-First Century," in *The Oxford Handbook of the Ends of Empire*, ed. Thomas and Thompson (Oxford: Oxford University Press, 2018), 1–4.

19. Exponents of this view include Frederick Cooper, *Citizenship between Empire and Nation: Rethinking France and French Africa, 1945–1960* (Princeton, NJ: Princeton University Press, 2014); Todd Shepard, *The Invention of Decolonization: The Algerian War and the Remaking of France* (Ithaca, NY: Cornell University Press, 2006); Gary Wilder, *Freedom Time: Negritude, Decolonization, and the Future of the World* (Durham, NC: Duke University Press, 2015); Michael Collins, "Decolonisation and the 'Federal Moment,'" *Diplomacy & Statecraft* 24, no. 1 (2013): 21–40; and Meredith Terretta, "From Below and to the Left? Human Rights and Liberation Politics in Africa's Postcolonial Age," *Journal of World History* 24 (June 2015): 389–416.

20. Heather J. Sharkey, "African Colonial States," in *The Oxford Handbook of Modern African History*, ed. John Parker and Richard Reid (Oxford: Oxford University Press, 2013), 155–66.

21. Marc Matera, "Metropolitan Cultures of Empire and the Long Moment of Decolonization," *American Historical Review* 121, no. 5 (2016): 1435.

22. Richard Reid, "State of Anxiety: History and Nation in Modern Africa," *Past & Present* 229, no. 1 (2015): 242–48, 251–2.

23. Angela Zimmerman, *Alabama in Africa: Booker T. Washington, the German Empire, and the Globalization of the New South* (Princeton, NJ: Princeton University Press, 2010), 1, also cited in Michelle Moyd, "Color Lines, Front Lines: The First World War from the South," *Radical History Review* 131 (May 2018): 15, n.18. For general analysis of the phenomenon and its analytical implications, see Marilyn Lake and Henry Reynolds, *Drawing the Global Colour Line: White Men's Countries and the International Challenge of Racial Equality* (Cambridge, UK: Cambridge University Press, 2008); Alexander Anievas, Nivi Manchanda, and Robbie Shilliam, eds., *Race and Racism in International Relations: Confronting the Global Colour Line* (London: Routledge, 2014).

24. This and the subsequent paragraphs draw on Thomas and Thompson, "Rethinking Decolonization," 1–26.

25. Bronwen Manby, *Citizenship in Africa: The Law of Belonging* (London: Bloomsbury/Hart Publishing, 2018), 6–18, 47–59, 61–70.

26. For examples of the physical and cultural barriers faced by a distinct transnational constituency—African university students—see Ismay Milford, *African Activists in a Decolonising World: The Making of an Anticolonial Culture, 1952–1966* (Cambridge, UK: Cambridge University Press, 2023), 5–15; Małgorzata Mazurek, "The University: The Decolonization of Knowledge? The Making of the African University, the Power of the Imperial Legacy, and Eastern European Influence," in Roth-Ey, *Socialist Internationalism*, 119–38.

27. Jean Allman and Antoinette Burton, "Destination Globalization? Women, Gender and Comparative Colonial Histories in the New Millennium," *Journal of Colonialism and Colonial History* 4, no. 1 (2003), published online.

Chapter One: Decolonization and the End of Empires

1. Raewyn Connell, "Understanding Empire," in *Empire and Sociology: The Imperial Entanglements of a Discipline*, ed. George Steinmetz (Durham, NC: Duke University Press, 2013), 489.

2. David Strang, "Global Patterns of Decolonization, 1500–1987," *International Studies Quarterly* 35, no. 4 (1991): 429.

3. Jan C. Jansen and Jürgen Osterhammel, *Decolonization: A Short History* (Princeton, NJ: Princeton University Press, 2017), 9–10; Raphaëlle Khan, "Between Ambitions and Caution: India, Human Rights, and Self-Determination at the United Nations," in *Decolonization, Self-Determination, and the Rise of Global Human Rights Politics*, ed. A. Dirk Moses, Marco Duranti, and Roland Burke (Cambridge, UK: Cambridge University Press, 2020), 235.

4. Jean Allman, "Between the Present and History: African Nationalism and Decolonization," in *The Oxford Handbook of Modern African History*, ed. John Parker and Richard Reid (Oxford: Oxford University Press, 2013), 224–40.

5. Emanuel Kreike, *Scorched Earth: Environmental Warfare as a Crime against Humanity and Nature* (Princeton, NJ: Princeton University Press, 2021), 360–4.

6. Tracey Banivanua Mar, *Decolonisation and the Pacific: Indigenous Globalisation and the Ends of Empire* (Cambridge, UK: Cambridge University Press, 2016), 217–24.

7. Mar, *Decolonisation and the Pacific*, 225.

8. Frederick Cooper has consistently warned against a linear, teleological view of decolonization, most recently in "Decolonizations, Colonizations, and More Decolonizations: The End of Empire in Time and Space," *Journal of World History* 33, no. 3 (2022): 491–526.

9. Guy Fiti Sinclair, *To Reform the World: International Organizations and the Making of Modern State*s (Oxford: Oxford University Press, 2017), 142. The list of 1955's new UN members highlights the combination of decolonization pressures, Cold War rivalries, and the relaxation of the bar on fascist regimes that shaped which states secured admission: Albania, Austria, Bulgaria, Cambodia, Ceylon (Sri Lanka), Finland, Hungary, Ireland, Italy, Jordan, Laos, Libya, Nepal, Portugal, Romania, Spain.

10. African member states contributed over a third of seventy-six UN General Assembly votes supporting China's admission, a sign of the PRC's support for national liberation movements in southern Africa after the abandonment of disastrous Cultural Revolution initiatives that antagonized insurgent movements and independent regimes; see Ian Taylor, "Mao Zedong's China and Africa," *Twentieth Century Communism* 15 (Fall 2018): 53–55.

11. Taylor, "Mao Zedong's China and Africa," 49–53. Ironically, Nkrumah's February 1966 overthrow by Ghana's "National Liberation Council" occurred during his official visit to China.

12. See https://www.un.org/en/about-us/growth-in-un-membership. Accessed on February 10, 2020.

13. Erez Manela, "International Society as a Historical Subject," *Diplomatic History* 44, no. 2 (2020): 185–86, 200; David Lake, Lisa L. Martin, and Thomas Risse, "Challenges to the Liberal Order: Reflections on International Organization," *International Organization* 75 (Spring 2021): 247–49.

14. Mark Mazower, *No Enchanted Palace: The End of Empire and the Ideological Origins of the United Nations* (Princeton, NJ: Princeton University Press, 2009).

15. Anna Stilz, "The Value of Self-Determination," *Oxford Studies in Political Philosophy* 2, no. 2 (2016): 98–127; Adom Getachew, "Securing Postcolonial Independence: Kwame Nkrumah and the Federal Idea in the Age of Decolonization," *Ab Imperio* 3 (2018): 90.

16. James Mayall, "International Society, State Sovereignty, and National Self-Determination," in *The Oxford Handbook of the History of Nationalism*, ed. John Breuilly (Oxford: Oxford University Press, 2013), online publication, 1–6.

17. Bernhard Struck, Kate Ferris, and Jacques Revel, "Introduction: Space and Scale in Transnational History," *International History Review*, 33, no. 4 (2011): 574–75.

18. Jean L. Cohen, *Globalization and Sovereignty: Rethinking Legality, Legitimacy, and Constitutionalism* (New York: Cambridge University Press, 2012), and idem, "Whose Sovereignty? Empire and International Law," *Ethics & International Affairs* 18, no. 3 (2004): 1–5.

19. Kimberley Hutchings, "Cosmopolitan Just War and Coloniality," in *Empire, Race, and Global Justice*, ed. Duncan Bell (Cambridge, UK: Cambridge University Press, 2019), 211–27; Cohen, "Whose Sovereignty?" 5–19; Michelle Moyd, "What's Wrong with Doing Good? Reflections on Africa, Humanitarianism, and the Challenge of the Global," *Africa Today* 63, no. 2 (2016): 92–96.

20. Rob Nixon, *Slow Violence and the Environmentalism of the Poor* (Cambridge, MA: Harvard University Press, 2011), 13–14; Kreike, *Scorched Earth*, 2–7, 360–93; David Zierler, "Going Global after Vietnam: the End of Agent Orange and the Rise of an International Environmental Regime," in *Nation-States and the Global Environment: New Approaches to International Environmental History*, ed. Erika Marie Bsumek, David Kinkela, and Mark Atwood Lawrence (Oxford: Oxford University Press, 2013), 97–101. Mention of deforestation must be accompanied by recognition that colonial forestry services and their successors within supranational organizations and postindependence governments tried to protect forested areas: Gregory A. Barton, "Environmentalism, Development and British Policy in the Middle East, 1945–65," *Journal of Imperial & Commonwealth History* 38 (2010): 619–39.

21. Greg Grandin, "Facing South: How Latin America Socialized United States Diplomacy," Emmanuelle Saada, "The Absent Empire: The Colonies in French Constitutions," Joya Chatterji, "From Subjecthood to Citizenship in South Asia: Migration, Nationality, and the Post-Imperial Global Order," all in *Endless Empire: Spain's Retreat, Europe's Eclipse, America's Decline,* ed. Alfred W. McCoy, Josep M. Fradera, and Stephen Jacobson (Madison: University of Wisconsin Press, 2012), 107–21, 205–15, and 306–17; Todd Shepard, "Excluding the *Harkis* from Repatriate Status, Excluding Muslim Algerians from French Identity," in *Transnational Spaces and Identities in the Francophone World,* ed. Hafid Gafaïti, Patricia M. E. Lorcin, and David G. Troyansky (Lincoln: University of Nebraska Press, 2009), 94–110; Bronwen Manby, "Trends in Citizenship Law and Politics in Africa since the Colonial Era," in *Routledge Handbook of Global Citizenship Studies,* ed. Engin F. Isin and Peter Nyers (London: Routledge, 2014), 174–81.

22. Summarizing key arguments in a British and South African context, see Katie Donington, "Relics of Empire? Colonialism and the Culture Wars," and Saul Dubow, "Rhodes Must Fall, Brexit, and Circuits of Knowledge and Influence," both in *Embers of Empire in Brexit Britain,* ed. Stuart Ward and Astrid Rasch (London: Bloomsbury, 2019), 121–31 and 111–20; Corinna Fowler, *Green Unpleasant Land: Creative Responses to Rural England's Colonial Connections* (Leeds: Peepal Tree Press, 2020); "Only a Fifth of UK Universities Say They Are 'Decolonising' Curriculum," *The Guardian,* June 12, 2020, online edition: https://www.theguardian.com/us-news/2020/jun/11/only-fifth-of-uk-universities-have-said-they-will-decolonise-curriculum; Gurminder K. Bhambra, Dalia Gebrial, and Kerem Nişancıoğlu, "Introduction: Decolonising the University?" in *Decolonising the University,* ed. idem (London: Pluto Press, 2018), 1–16; Maura Reilly, *Curatorial Activism: Towards an Ethics of Curating* (London: Thames & Hudson 2018); Mark Sealy, *Decolonising the Camera: Photography in Racial Time* (London: Lawrence & Wishart, 2019).

23. For discussion of these causal connections as perceived by antiracist theorists W. E. B. Du Bois and Alan Locke, see Errol A. Henderson, "The Revolution Will Not Be Theorised: Du Bois, Locke, and the Howard School's Challenge to White Supremacist IR Theory," *Millennium: Journal of International Studies* 45, no. 3 (2017): 492–510, quote at 493.

24. A 2021 exhibition on Dutch colonial enslavement at the Amsterdam Rijksmuseum tackled these issues: "Dutch Colonial Rule: Return of the Repressed," *The Economist,* June 5, 2021, 79–80.

25. Stephen Howe, "Falling Rhodes, Building Bridges, Finding Paths: Decoloniality from Cape Town to Oxford and Back," in *The Break-Up of Greater Britain,* ed. Christian D. Pedersen and Stuart Ward (Manchester, UK: Manchester University Press, 2021), 294–310.

26. Walter D. Mignolo and Catherine E. Walsh, *On Decoloniality: Concepts, Analytics, Praxis* (Durham, NC: Duke University Press, 2018).

27. Boaventura De Sousa Santos, *Epistemologies of the South: Justice against Epistemicide* (London: Routledge, 2014), 24–27; Sabelo J. Ndlovu-Gatsheni, *Decolonization, Development and Knowledge in Africa: Turning over a New Leaf* (London: Routledge, 2020), 17–40.

28. Naeem Inayatullah and David L. Blaney, "Race and Global Inequality," in *Race, Gender and Culture in International Relations: Postcolonial Perspectives,* ed. Randolph B. Persaud and Alena Sajed (London: Routledge, 2018), 116–30; for a powerful

statement of this view, see Kris Manjapra, *Colonialism in Global Perspective* (Cambridge, UK: Cambridge University Press, 2020).

29. Arne de Boever, "Prologue: The Future of Sovereignty," in *Plastic Sovereignties: Agamben and the Politics of Aesthetics*, ed. Arne de Boever, Peg Birmingham, and Dimitris Vardoulakis (Edinburgh: Edinburgh University Press, 2016), 7–16.

30. Prasenjit Duara, "Modern Imperialism," in *The Oxford Handbook of World History*, ed. Jerry H. Bentley (Oxford: Oxford University Press, 2011), 379–80.

31. For discussion of empires' spatial dynamics, see Gavin Murray-Miller, *Empire Unbound: France and the Muslim Mediterranean, 1880–1918* (Oxford: Oxford University Press, 2022), and Cyrus Schayegh, *The Middle East and the Making of the Modern World* (Cambridge, UK: Harvard University Press, 2017).

32. Jock McCulloch, "Empire and Violence, 1900–1939," in *Gender and Empire*, ed. Philippa Levine (Oxford: Oxford University Press, 2004), 221–22, 225–26.

33. Sebastian Conrad, *What Is Global History?* (Princeton, NJ: Princeton University Press, 2016), 3–4; Durba Ghosh, "AHR Forum: Another Set of Imperial Turns?" *American Historical Review* 117, no. 3 (June 2012): 778–93.

34. Jansen and Osterhammel, *Decolonization*, 1.

35. The importance of decolonization–IR intersections is amplified by foundational IR scholars who were also political actors involved in constructing a liberal internationalist imperial order after 1919; see Jan Stöckmann, *The Architects of International Relations: Building a Discipline, Designing the World, 1914–1940* (Cambridge, UK: Cambridge University Press, 2022), 2–4, 14–19.

36. Nicolas Guilhot, "Imperial Realism: Post-War IR Theory and Decolonisation," *International History Review* 36, no. 4 (2014): 698–720, quote at 699; Branwen Gruffydd Jones, ed., *Decolonizing International Relations* (Lanham, MD: Rowman & Littlefield, 2006); John Hobson, *The Eurocentric Conception of World Politics: Western International Theory, 1760–2010* (Cambridge, UK: Cambridge University Press, 2010); Alexander Anievas, Nivi Manchanda, and Robbie Shilliam, eds., *Race and Racism in International Relations: Confronting the Global Colour Line* (London: Routledge, 2014); Tim Dunne and Christian Reus-Smit, eds., *The Globalization of International Society* (Oxford: Oxford University Press, 2017).

37. Ian Hall, "The Revolt against the West: Decolonisation and Its Repercussions in British International Thought, 1945–75," *International History Review* 33, no. 1 (2011): 48–5; idem, "The 'Revolt against the West' Revisited," in Dunne and Reus-Smit, *Globalization of International Society*, 349–51.

38. Hall, "Revolt against the West," 48–51; Hedley Bull, "The Revolt against the West," in *The Expansion of International Society*, ed. Adam Watson and Hedley Bull (Oxford: Clarendon Press, 1984), 217–28.

39. Thomas Bottelier and Jan Stöckmann, "Instruments of International Order Internationalism and Diplomacy from 1900 to 1950," in *Instruments of International Order: Internationalism and Diplomacy from 1900 to 1950*, ed. idem (Manchester, UK: Manchester University Press, 2023); Patricia Owens et al., *Women's International Thought: Towards a New Canon* (Cambridge, UK: Cambridge University Press, 2022), 1–6, 9–16.

40. Robert Vitalis, "The Graceful and Generous Liberal Gesture: Making Racism Invisible in American International Relations," *Millennium* 29, no. 2 (2000): 331–56,

also cited in Duncan Bell, "Before the Democratic Peace: Racial Utopianism, Empire, and the Abolition of War," *European Journal of International Relations* 20, no. 3 (2014): 649. For a skeptical take on IR's conceptual splits: Lucian M. Ashworth, "Did the Realist–Idealist Great Debate Really Happen? A Revisionist History of International Relations," *International Relations* 16, no. 1 (2002): 33–51.

41. See the contributions in Dunne and Reus-Smit, *Globalization of International Society*, especially Jennifer M. Welsh, "Empire and Fragmentation," 145–64; Jacinta O'Hagan, "The Role of Civilization in the Globalization of International Society," 185–203; and Barry Buzan, "Universal Sovereignty," 227–47. See also Barry Buzan and George Lawson, *The Global Transformation: History, Modernity and the Making of International Relations* (Cambridge, UK: Cambridge University Press, 2015), 273–78; and Alena Sajed and Randolph Persaud, eds., *Race, Gender and Culture in International Relations: Postcolonial Perspectives* (London: Routledge, 2018), authors' introduction, 1–14. For ideas of global IR in general and the ways that decolonizing societies asserted their agency in international politics, see Amitav Acharya, *Rethinking Power, Institutions and Ideas in World Politics: Whose IR?* (Abingdon, UK: Routledge, 2013); idem, "Global International Relations (IR) and Regional Worlds: A New Agenda for International Studies," *International Studies Quarterly* 58, no. 4 (2014): 647–59; idem, "Norm Subsidiarity and Regional Orders: Sovereignty, Regionalism, and Rule-Making in the Third World," *International Studies Quarterly* 55, no. 1 (2011): 95–123; Zeynep Gulsah, "Decolonising International Relations?" *Third World Quarterly* 38, no. 1 (2017): 1–15; Manela, "International Society," 184–209.

42. Alina Sajed, "The Post Always Rings Twice? The Algerian War, Poststructuralism and the Postcolonial in IR Theory," *Review of International Studies* 38, no. 1 (2011): 142–47, 152–56; Tarak Barkawi, "Decolonising War," *European Journal of International Security* 1, no. 2 (2016), 200–2.

43. Tarak Barkawi and Mark Laffey, "Retrieving the Imperial: Empire and International Relations," *Millennium: Journal of International Relations* 31, no. 1 (2002): 109–12.

44. Martti Koskenniemi, *The Gentle Civilizer of Nations: The Rise and Fall of International Law, 1870–1960* (Cambridge, UK: Cambridge University Press, 2010), 492.

45. Joseph Anthony Maiolo, "Systems and Boundaries in International History," *International History Review* 40, no. 3 (2018): 579–82. Petra Goedde makes a similar point: "Power is about difference, and difference can only be measured when one investigates the interactions between the powerful and the powerless." Goedde, "Power, Culture, and the Rise of Transnational History in the United States," *International History Review* 40, no. 3 (2018): 592–608, at 601.

46. I borrow this idea of an alternative "global architecture" from Robbie Shilliam, "Colonial Architecture or Relatable Hinterlands? Locke, Nandy, Fanon, and the Bandung Spirit," *Constellations* 23, no. 3 (2016): 425–35.

47. Amitav Acharya, "Studying the Bandung Conference from a Global IR Perspective," *Australian Journal of International Affairs* 70, no. 4 (2016): 344; idem, "Who Are the Norm Makers? The Asian–African Conference in Bandung and the Evolution of Norms," *Global Governance* 20 (2014): 405–7. Historian Penny Von Eschen uses the term 'anticolonial counterpublics' to describe transnational contacts between

antiracist opponents of empire in North America, Africa, and Europe: see her "From London 1948 to Dakar 1966: Crises in Anticolonial Counterpublics," in *Inventing the Third World: In Search of Freedom for the Postwar Global South*, ed. Gyan Prakash and Jeremy Adelman (London: Bloomsbury Academic, 2023), 137–40.

48. Brian C. Schmidt, "Internalism versus Externalism in the Disciplinary History of International Relations," in *Historiographical Investigations in International Relations*, ed. Brian C. Schmidt and Nicolas Guilhot (Basingstoke, UK: Palgrave Macmillan, 2019), 127–48, at 129–31.

49. John M. Hobson, "What's at Stake in Doing (Critical) IR/IPE Historiography? The Imperative of Critical Historiography," in Schmidt and Guilhot, *Historiographical Investigations*, 151–60.

50. Nicolas Guilhot, "Introduction," in Schmidt and Guilhot, *Historiographical Investigations*, 3–4.

51. Robert Vitalis has gone furthest in criticizing the narrowness and racism of such an approach: Robert Vitalis, *White World Order, Black Power Politics: The Birth of American International Relations* (New York: Columbia University Press, 2016).

52. For a critique of modernization theory's operating principles, see Anne Phillips, "Global Justice: Just Another Modernisation Theory?" in *Empire, Race, and Global Justice*, ed. Duncan Bell (Cambridge, UK: Cambridge University Press, 2019), 149–51.

53. Guilhot, "Imperial Realism," 703–7. On the impact of modernization theory, particularly in Southeast Asia, see Michael E. Latham, *Modernization as Ideology: American Social Science and "Nation Building" in the Kennedy Era* (Chapel Hill: University of North Carolina Press, 2000); Mark T. Berger, "Decolonisation, Modernisation and Nation-Building: Political Development Theory and the Appeal of Communism in Southeast Asia, 1945–1975," *Journal of Southeast Asian Studies* 34, no. 3 (2003): 421–48; Giuliano Garavini, *After Empires: European Integration, Decolonization, and the Challenge from the Global South 1957–1986* (Oxford: Oxford University Press, 2012), 27–30.

54. For exceptions among African-American sociologists of the mid-twentieth century, see Sam Klug, "Social Science in Black and White: Rethinking the Disciplines in the Jim Crow Empire," *Modern Intellectual History* 15, no. 3 (2018): 917–18. Klug is here reviewing Robert Vitalis's *White World Order, Black Power Politics*.

55. Hobson, "What's at Stake," 159–64.

56. Guilhot, "Imperial Realism," 714–15.

57. Federico Romero, "Cold War Historiography at the Crossroads," *Cold War History* 14, no. 4 (2014): 693. Matthew Connelly challenged this approach in "Taking off the Cold War Lens: Visions of North–South Conflict during the Algerian War for Independence," *American Historical Review* 105, no. 3 (2000): 739–69, and idem, *A Diplomatic Revolution: Algeria's Fight for Independence and the Origins of the Post–Cold War Era* (New York: Oxford University Press, 2002).

58. Talbot Imlay, *The Practice of Socialist Internationalism: European Socialists and International Politics, 1914–1960* (Oxford: Oxford University Press, 2017), 409–11. As Imlay suggests, an irony of the United Nations' expansion is that new nation-states resisted supranational infringements on their sovereignty, notably regarding the rights of minorities exposed to new forms of discrimination after national independence was achieved.

59. Anthony Hopkins uses Iraq's unending experiences of foreign occupation as introduction and epilogue to his defining work on decolonization: A. G. Hopkins, *American Empire: A Global History* (Princeton, NJ: Princeton University Press, 2018), 1–9, 730–38.

60. TNA, Air Ministry (AIR) files: AIR 9/19, "Report on Middle East Conference Held in Cairo and Jerusalem, March 12 to 30, 191: Section II: Mesopotamia"; AIR 23/562, AIR HQ Iraq, "Transport of Troops by Air," September 11, 1924; R. M. Douglas, "Did Britain Use Chemical Weapons in Mandatory Iraq?" *Journal of Modern History* 81 (December 2009): 859–87.

61. Robert Blyth, *The Empire of the Raj: India, Eastern Africa and the Middle East, 1858–1947* (London: Palgrave, 2003), 165–66; and John Fisher, *British Imperialism in the Middle East, 1916–19* (London: Frank Cass, 1999), 128–29.

62. TNA Colonial Office (CO) files: CO 935/1/1, "Report on Middle East Conference Held in Cairo and Jerusalem," n.d. [1921].

63. TNA, CO 730/13, Middle East Interdepartmental Committee report, para. 44: "Advisors and Political Officers—Mesopotamia," January 31, 1921; AIR 23/453, AIR 23/454, and AIR 23/568: SSO intelligence reports, Hillah, Ramadi, and Sulaimaniyah, 1923–1924.

64. Saad Eskander, "Britain's Policy in Southern Kurdistan: The Formation and the Termination of the First Kurdish Government, 1918–1919," *British Journal of Middle Eastern Studies* 27, no. 2 (2000): 139–63; idem, "Southern Kurdistan under Britain's Mesopotamian Mandate: From Separation to Incorporation, 1920–23," *Middle Eastern Studies* 37, no. 2 (2001): 153–80; IOA, L/PS/11/193, no. P7701, Sir Arthur Hirtzel, "Kurdistan—India Office Recommendations," December 20, 1919.

65. IOR, L/PS/10/782, tel. 302, Admiral de Robeck (Constantinople) to Foreign Office, March 29, 1920; TNA, Foreign Office (FO) correspondence: FO 371/5230, E12339/2719/44, "Mesopotamia: Preliminary Report on Causes of Unrest," September 14, 1920; FO 371/5230, E12038/2719/14, Captain B. S. Thomas, Nasariyah, to Baghdad Civil Commissioner, July 31, 1920; Amal Vinogradov, "The 1920 Revolt in Iraq Reconsidered: The Role of the Tribes in National Politics," *International Journal of Middle East Studies* 3, no. 1 (1972): 126–37.

66. TNA, CO 835/1/11, "Report of the High Commission on the Development of Iraq, 1920–1925," Baghdad Residency, August 6, 1925.

67. Jonathan Wyrtzen, *Worldmaking in the Long Great War: How Local and Colonial Struggles Shaped the Modern Middle East* (New York: Columbia University Press, 2022), 2–3, 173–86.

68. Keith Watenpaugh, *Being Modern in the Middle East: Revolution, Nationalism, Colonialism, and the Arab Middle Class* (Princeton, NJ: Princeton University Press, 2006); James L. Gelvin, *Divided Loyalties: Nationalism and Mass Politics in Syria at the Close of Empire* (Berkeley: University of California Press, 1999).

69. Marian Kent, *Oil and Empire: British Policy and Mesopotamian Oil, 1900–1920* (New York: Barnes & Noble, 1976); Fiona Venn, "Oleaginous Diplomacy: Oil, Anglo-American Relations and the Lausanne Conference, 1922–23," *Diplomacy and Statecraft* 20, no. 3 (2009): 414–33. For eventual Iraqi assertion of raw material sovereignty: Christopher R. W. Dietrich, "'Arab Oil Belongs to the Arabs': Raw Material Sovereignty, Cold War Boundaries, and the Nationalisation of the Iraq

Petroleum Company, 1967–1973," *Diplomacy and Statecraft* 22, no. 3 (2011): 450–79.

70. Susan Pedersen, "Getting out of Iraq—in 1932: The League of Nations and the Road to Normative Statehood," *American Historical Review* 115, no. 4 (2010): 975–1000.

71. TNA, Ramsay MacDonald papers, PRO 30/69/338: Middle East, 1929–1935, "Note on Major General Ja'far Pasha al-Askari, CMG."

72. Cyrus Schayegh, "1958 Reconsidered: State Formation and the Cold War in the Early Postcolonial Arab Middle East," *International Journal of Middle East Studies* 45, no. 3 (2013): 421–43.

73. Kerry Rittich, "Occupied Iraq: Imperial Convergences?" *Leiden Journal of International Law* 31, no. 3 (2018): 485–91.

74. For the "imperial formations" concept, see Ann Laura Stoler, "On Degrees of Imperial Sovereignty," *Public Culture* 18, no. 1 (2006): 125–46; Ann Laura Stoler, Carole McGranahan, and Peter C. Perdue, eds., *Imperial Formations* (Santa Fe: SAR Press, 2007), 3–42.

75. Ronald Robinson, "Non-European Foundations of European Imperialism: Sketch for a Theory of Collaboration," in *Studies in the Theory of Imperialism*, ed. Roger Owen and Bob Sutcliffe (London: Longman, 1972), 117–42, at 137.

76. Ann Laura Stoler, *Along the Archival Grain: Epistemic Anxieties and Colonial Common Sense* (Princeton, NJ: Princeton University Press, 2009), cited in Todd Shepard, "'History Is Past Politics'? Archives, 'Tainted Evidence,' and the Return of the State," *American Historical Review* 115, no. 2 (April 2010): 483.

77. Jordanna Bailkin, "AHR Roundtable: Where Did the Empire Go? Archives and Decolonization in Britain," *American Historical Review* 120, no. 3 (June 2015): 887–88. Bailkin cites numerous examples of British officials destroying colonial archives before formal independence, including three Land Rovers full of Ugandan administrative records dumped into Lake Victoria.

78. Mandy Banton, "Destroy? 'Migrate'? Conceal? British Strategies for the Disposal of Sensitive Records of Colonial Administrations at Independence," *Journal of Imperial & Commonwealth History* 40, no. 2 (2012): 321–35, at 328: In July 1947 British administrators in New Delhi drew unwanted Indian attention to a bonfire of administrative archives. A decade or so later, British colonial officials in Kuala Lumpur were more surreptitious. Before leaving Malaysia for good they employed British expatriates and Chinese laborers to load sensitive archives onto army lorries bound for the Singapore naval base. There, the records were quietly destroyed.

79. Lydia Walker, "Decolonization in the 1960s: On Legitimate and Illegitimate Nationalist Claims-Making," *Past & Present* 242 (February 2019): 233.

80. Karl Hack, "Unfinished Decolonisation and Globalisation," *Journal of Imperial & Commonwealth History* 47, no. 5 (2019): 832.

81. Banivanua Mar, *Decolonisation and the Pacific*, 217–24, quote at 224.

82. United Nations General Assembly, *Declaration on the Granting of Independence to Colonial Countries and Peoples*, 14 December 1960, A/RES/1514 (XV); Jacinta O'Hagen, "The Role of Civilization in the Globalization of International Society," in Dunne and Reus-Smit, *Globalization of International Society*, 196.

83. Eric D. Weitz, "Self-Determination: How a German Enlightenment Idea Became the Slogan of National Liberation and a Human Right," *American Historical Review* 20, no. 2 (2015): 492–94.

84. Oliver Turner, "'Finishing the Job': The UN Special Committee on Decolonization (SCD) and the Politics of Self-Governance," *Third World Quarterly* 34, no. 7 (2013): 1195–96. In 1962 an additional seven national representatives joined the committee's initial membership of seventeen, after which the SCD became known as "the Committee of 24". The committee worked alongside the Decolonization Unit of the United Nations' Department of Political Affairs.

85. Wm. Roger Louis, "Public Enemy Number One: The British Empire in the Dock at the United Nations, 1957–1971," in *The British Empire in the 1950s: Retreat or Revival?*, ed. Martin Lynn (Basingstoke, UK: Palgrave Macmillan, 2006), 196–206. Members of Britain's UN delegation, led initially by former Cyprus Governor Sir Hugh Foot, tried limited engagement with the Committee of 24 but gave up entirely in 1971.

86. Turner, "'Finishing the Job,'" 1198–200; Alicia Campos, "The Decolonization of Equatorial Guinea: The Relevance of the International Factor," *Journal of African History* 44, no. 1 (2003): 106–7.

87. Sarah Teitt, "Sovereignty as Responsibility," in Dunne and Reus-Smit, *Globalization of International Society*, 325, citing Robert H. Jackson, *Quasi-States: Sovereignty, International Relations and the Third World* (Cambridge, UK: Cambridge University Press, 1990), 2.

88. Eileen M. Ford, "Insurgent Citizenships: Armed Rebellions and Everyday Acts of Resistance in the Global South," in *World Histories from Below: Disruption and Dissent, 1750 to the Present*, 2nd ed., ed. Antoinette Burton and Tony Ballantyne (London: Bloomsbury, 2022), 88–90, 98–101.

89. Afro-Asian Networks Research Collective Manifesto, "Networks of Decolonization in Asia and Africa," *Radical History Review* 131 (May 2018): 176–78; for the tensions within and differences between early nonalignment and later radical Third Worldism, see Jeffrey James Byrne, "Beyond Continents, Colours, and the Cold War: Yugoslavia, Algeria, and the Struggle for Non-Alignment," *International History Review* 37, no. 5 (2015): 912–32.

90. Lorenz M. Lüthi, "The Non-Aligned Movement and the Cold War, 1961–1973," *Journal of Cold War Studies* 18, no. 4 (2016): 127–44.

91. A point made by Anthony Hopkins: "Instead of fitting decolonisation into the Cold War," still a predominant historical approach, "the Cold War needs to be fitted into decolonisation, which in turn needs to be placed in the even wider context of the global transformation of power, interests, and values in the post-war era." A. G. Hopkins, "Is Globalisation Yesterday's News?" *Itinerario* 41, no. 1 (2017): 120–24, quote at 120.

92. Elizabeth Kolsky, "The Colonial Rule of Law and the Legal Regime of Exception: 'Frontier Fanaticism' and State Violence in British India," *American Historical Review* 120, no. 4 (2015); Gregory Mann, "What Was the *Indigénat*? The 'Empire of Law' in French West Africa," *Journal of African History* 50, no. 2 (2009): 331–53.

93. Kristie Dotson, "Tracking Epistemic Violence, Tracking Practices of Silencing," *Hypatia* 26, no. 2 (2011): 236–38, 242–45.

94. Deborah Posel, "Getting Inside the Skin of the Consumer: Race, Market Research, and the Consumerist Project in Apartheid South Africa," *Itinerario* 42, no. 1 (2018): 124–34.

95. For discussion of approaches: Nancy Scheper-Hughes and Philippe Bourgois, eds., *Violence in War and Peace: An Anthology* (Oxford: Blackwell, 2004), part I; Philippe Bourgois, "Recognizing Invisible Violence: A Thirty Year Ethnographic Perspective," in *Global Health in Times of Violence*, ed. Barbara Rylko-Bauer, Linda Whiteford, and Paul Farmer (Santa Fe, NM: SAR Books, 2009), 17–40; Marnia Lazreg, *Torture and the Twilight of Empire: From Algiers to Baghdad* (Princeton, NJ: Princeton University Press, 2008); Efrat Ben Ze'ev, Ruth Ginio, and Jay Winter, eds., *Shadows of War: A Social History of Silence in the Twentieth Century* (Cambridge, UK: Cambridge University Press, 2010); Deana Heath, *Colonial Terror: Torture and State Violence in Colonial India* (Oxford: Oxford University Press, 2021); Elizabeth Frazer and Kimberley Hutchings, "The Politics Violence Frontier," *Journal of Political Ideologies* 25, no. 3 (2020): 229–47.

96. Ian Tyrrell, "Resource Use, Conservation, and the Environmental Limits of Anti-Imperialism, c. 1880–1930," in *Empire's Twin: U.S. Anti-Imperialism from the Founding Era to the Age of Terrorism*, ed. Ian Tyrrell and Jay Sexton (Ithaca, NY: Cornell University Press, 2015), 168, citing the arguments of Richard Tucker, *Insatiable Appetite: The United States and the Ecological Degradation of the Tropical World* (Berkeley: University of California Press, 2000).

97. Richard Drayton highlights this difference of perspective in his review of Frederick Cooper's *Between Empire and Nation*: Drayton, "Federal Utopias and the Realities of Imperial Power," *Comparative Studies of South Asia, Africa and the Middle East* 37, no. 2 (August 2017): 401–6, at 404.

98. Stuart Ward, "The European Provenance of Decolonization," *Past and Present* 230 (February 2016): 227–60.

99. Jamie Martin, *The Meddlers: Sovereignty, Empire, and the Birth of Global Economic Governance* (Cambridge, MA: Harvard University Press, 2022), 3–5, 10–20, 65–69, 99–126.

100. Hideki Kan, "Informal Empire and the Cold War," *Journal of Imperial & Commonwealth History* 49, no. 3 (2021): 581–83; Martin, *Meddlers*, 79–88.

101. Quinn Slobodian, *The Globalists: The End of Empire and the Birth of Neoliberalism* (Cambridge, MA: Harvard University Press, 2018), 97–98.

102. Ward, "European Provenance," 248, citing Henri Labouret, *Colonisation, colonialisme, décolonisation* (Paris: Larose, 1952), 19.

103. Todd Shepard, *The Invention of Decolonization: The Algerian War and the Remaking of France* (Ithaca, NY: Cornell University Press, 2006); Ward, "The European Provenance," 258–59.

104. Shepard, "'History Is Past Politics'?" 474–83.

105. Ward, "European Provenance," 254–55.

106. Duncan Bell, *Reordering the World: Essays on Liberalism and Empire* (Princeton, NJ: Princeton University Press, 2016), 114.

107. Penny von Eschen, *Race against Empire: Black Americans and Anticolonialism, 1937–1957* (Ithaca, NY: Cornell University Press, 1997); Brenda Gayle Plummer, *In Search of Power: African Americans in the Era of Decolonization, 1956–1974*

(Cambridge, UK: Cambridge University Press, 2013); Carol Anderson, *Bourgeois Radicals: The NAACP and the Struggle for Colonial Liberation, 1941–1960* (New York: Cambridge University Press, 2015).

108. John Munro, *The Anticolonial Front: The African-American Freedom Struggle and Global Decolonisation, 1945–1960* (Cambridge, UK: Cambridge University Press, 2017), 4. Munro (16–19) describes how W. E. B. Du Bois elucidated these connections in his 1935 book *Black Reconstruction in America, 1860–1880.* For a succinct explanation of the racial differentiation intrinsic to modern capitalism, see Manjapra, *Colonialism in Global Perspective,* 8–11.

Chapter Two: Decolonization and Globalization

1. H. H. Henson, "The Ethics of Empire," Ninth Earl Grey Memorial Lecture. February 17, 1927, 6.

2. Brett Bennett and Gregory Barton, "Generalizations in Global History: Dealing with Diversity without Losing the Big Picture," *Itinerario* 41, no. 1 (2017): 15–20; A. G. Hopkins, "Is Globalisation Yesterday's News?" *Itinerario* 41, no. 1 (2017): 112, 116–17.

3. Maria Paula Diogo and Dirk van Laak, *Europeans Globalizing: Mapping, Exploiting, Exchanging* (London: Palgrave Macmillan, 2016), 9–16.

4. Clare Anderson, "Global Modalities," in *World Histories from Below: Disruption and Dissent, 1750 to the Present,* 2nd ed., ed. Antoinette Burton and Tony Ballantyne (London: Bloomsbury, 2022), 169–70, 180–84; and, in the same collection, Heather Streets-Salter, "International and Global Anti-Colonial Movements," 47–48. As Clare Anderson notes (169), the irony is that the mass movement of people within and between empires did not represent genuine freedom of movement insofar as slavery, indenture and other forms of unfree labor predominated, often beyond the scrutiny of international law. See also Ashutosh Kumar, "Legal Discourse on 'Coolies'' Migration from India to the Sugar Colonies, 1837–1922," in *South Asian Migrations in Global History: Labor, Law, and Wayward Lives,* ed. Neilesh Bose (London: Bloomsbury, 2021), 85–111. For the European shift to legislative oversight of labor migration after World War I, see Christoph Rass, "Temporary Labour Migration and State-Run Recruitment of Foreign Workers in Europe, 1919–1975: A New Migration Regime?" *International Review of Social History* 57 special issue (2012): 191–224. On globality, described as "an interregional reproduction of power . . . networked worldwide": Michael Lang, "Globalization: Its History," *Journal of Modern History* 78 (December 2006): 901 and quote at 929; Daniel Gorman, *International Cooperation in the Early Twentieth Century* (London: Bloomsbury, 2017), 9–10.

5. Ethan A. Nadelmann, "Global Prohibition Regimes: The Evolution of Norms in International Society," *International Organization* 44 (1990): 479–526; Magaly Rodrìguez García, "The League of Nations and the Moral Recruitment of Women," *International Review of Social History* 57 (2012): 98–105.

6. Steffen Rimner, *Opium's Long Shadow: From Asian Revolution to Global Drugs Control* (Cambridge, MA: Harvard University Press, 2018), chapters 6–8; Diana S. Kim, *Empire of Vice: The Rise of Opium Prohibition across Southeast Asia* (Princeton, NJ: Princeton University Press, 2020). For gender dimensions, see García, "League of Nations," 107–10.

7. Robert Kubicek, "British Expansion, Empire and Technological Change," in *The Oxford History of the British Empire*, vol. 3: *The Nineteenth Century*, ed. Andrew Porter (Oxford: Oxford University Press, 1999), 247–70; Gary B. Magee and Andrew S. Thompson, *Empire and Globalisation: Networks of People, Goods and Capital in the British World, c. 1850–1914* (Cambridge, UK: Cambridge University Press, 2010), 67. For case studies of China's lighthouse infrastructure and the nationalization of telecommunications networks in the late British Empire, see R. A. Bickers, "Infrastructural Globalisation: Lighting the China Coast, 1860s–1930s," *Historical Journal 56*, no. 2 (2013): 431–58; Richard Collins, "The Reith Mission, Global Telecommunications and the Decline of the British Empire," *Historical Journal of Film, Radio and Television 32*, no. 2 (2012): 167–85.

8. A. G. Hopkins, *American Empire: A Global History* (Princeton, NJ: Princeton University Press, 2018), 29–30.

9. Simone M. Müller, *Wiring the World: The Social and Cultural Creation of Global Telegraph Networks* (New York: Columbia University Press, 2016), especially chapter 6.

10. Arthur Asseraf, *Electric News in Colonial Algeria* (Oxford: Oxford University Press, 2019), 75–84, 97.

11. Corey Ross, *Ecology and Power in the Age of Empire: Europe and the Transformation of the Tropical World* (Oxford: Oxford University Press, 2019), 5, 8; Alison Bashford, "'The Age of Universal Contagion': History, Disease and Globalization," in *Medicine at the Border: Disease, Globalization and Security, 1850 to the Present*, ed. Alison Bashford (Basingstoke, UK: Palgrave Macmillan, 2006), 1–16; Jari Eloranta and Mark Harrison, "War and Disintegration, 1914–1950," in *The Economics of Coercion and Conflict*, ed. Mark Harrison (Singapore: World Scientific Publishing, 2015), 41–46; Hannah Whittaker, "Frontier Security in North East Africa: Conflict and Colonial Development on the Margins, c. 1930–60," *Journal of African History 58*, no. 3 (2017): 381–83.

12. Robert Schütze, "International Governance: Theory and Practice," in *Globalisation and Governance: International Problems, European Solutions*, ed. Robert Schütze (Cambridge, UK: Cambridge University Press, 2018), 1; Amber Huff and Lyla Mehta, "Untangling Scarcity," in *Scarcity in the Modern World: History, Politics, Society and Sustainability, 1800–2075*, ed. Fredrik Albritton Jonsson (London: Bloomsbury, 2019), 27–33.

13. Mark Duffield, *Global Governance and the New Wars: The Merging of Development and Security* (London: Zed Books, 2001, 2nd edition 2014), 44–47.

14. Gorman, *International Cooperation*, 11; Giordano Nanni, *The Colonisation of Time: Ritual, Routine and Resistance in the British Empire* (Manchester, UK: Manchester University Press, 2012); Kaletso E. Atkins, "'Kafir Time': Preindustrial Temporal Concepts and Labour Discipline in Nineteenth-Century Colonial Natal," *Journal of African History 29*, no. 2 (1988): 229–44.

15. Charles S. Maier, "Consigning the Twentieth Century to History: Alternative Narratives for the Modern Era," *American Historical Review 105*, no. 3 (2000): 816.

16. For nineteenth-century French "investment colonization," see David Todd, *A Velvet Empire: French Informal Imperialism in the Nineteenth Century* (Princeton University Press, 2021), 179–218.

17. Karoline Postel-Vinay, "European Power and the Mapping of Global Order," in *Echoes of Empire: Memory, Identity and Colonial Legacies*, ed. Kalypso Nicolaïdis, Berny Sèbe, and Gabrielle Maas (London: I. B. Tauris, 2015), 327–28, 333.

18. Using the numerical indicator of dependent populations, the United States entered World War II as the world's fifth-largest colonial power: Daniel Immerwahr, "The Greater United States: Territory and Empire in U.S. History," *Diplomatic History* 40, no. 3 (2016): 373–83; Hideki Kan, "Informal Empire and the Cold War," *Journal of Imperial & Commonwealth History* 49, no. 3 (2021): 585–94.

19. Quinn Slobodian, *The Globalists: The End of Empire and the Birth of Neoliberalism* (Cambridge, MA: Harvard University Press, 2018), 20. For presumptive connections among twentieth-century globalization, free-market capitalism and the hegemony of an informal "American empire", see Neil Smith, *American Empire: Roosevelt's Geographer and the Prelude to Globalization* (Berkeley: University of California Press, 2004).

20. A now-classic account of the process is Barry Eichengreen, *Golden Fetters: The Gold Standard and the Great Depression, 1919–1939* (Oxford: Oxford University Press, 1992).

21. Merve Fejzula, "The Cosmopolitan Historiography of Twentieth-Century Federalism," *Historical Journal* 63, no. 1 (2020): 17.

22. Slobodian, *Globalists*, 20–22, 56.

23. Jane Burbank and Frederick Cooper, "Empires after 1919: Old, New, Transformed," *International Affairs* 95, no. 1 (2019): 81, 85–89; Hopkins, *American Empire*, 459–61; Martin, *Meddlers*, 6–7.

24. Jayeeta Sharma, "Food and Empire," in *The Oxford Handbook of Food History*, ed. Jeffrey M. Pilcher (Oxford: Oxford University Press, 2012), online publication, 2.

25. Reto Hofmann, "The Fascist New-Old Order," *Journal of Global History* 12, no. 1 (2017): 173–77. I am drawn to Hofmann's idea of an "imperial deficit" and his reconceptualization of the relationship among imperialism, nation and capital. I am less persuaded that fascist empire-building was derivative of older liberal imperialism. For the Japanese case, see Louise Young, "When Fascism Met Empire in Japanese-Occupied Manchuria," *Journal of Global History* 12, no. 2 (2017): 274–96; more broadly: Cemil Aydin, *The Politics of Anti-Westernism in Asia: Visions of World Order in Pan-Islamic and Pan-Asian Thought* (New York: Columbia University Press, 2007), 161–84.

26. Louise Young, "Early-Twentieth-Century Japan in a Global Context: Introduction: Japan's New International History," *American Historical Review* 119, no. 4 (2014): 1117–28, at 1121, citing Frederick R. Dickinson, "Toward a Global Perspective of the Great War: Japan and the Foundations of a Twentieth-Century World," *American Historical Review* 119, no. 4 (2014): 1154–83.

27. Roberta Pergher, *Mussolini's Nation-Empire: Sovereignty and Settlement in Italy's Borderlands, 1922–1943* (Cambridge, UK: Cambridge University Press, 2018); Hofmann, "Fascist New-Old Order," 166–68, 173–81; Michael R. Ebner, "Fascist Violence and the 'Ethnic Reconstruction' of Cyrenaica (Libya), 1922–1934," in *Violence, Colonialism, and Empire in the Modern World*, ed. Philip Dwyer and Amanda Nettelbeck (Basingstoke, UK: Palgrave Macmillan, 2018), 197–201; Francis Nicosia, *Nazi Germany and the Arab World* (Cambridge, UK: Cambridge University Press, 2015), 104–27.

28. Young, "Early-Twentieth-Century Japan," 1121. Here, as she acknowledges, she echoes Akira Iriye's *After Imperialism: The Search for a New Order in the Far East, 1921–1931* (Cambridge, MA: Harvard University Press, 1965).

29. A point nicely proven by Márcia Gonçalves's study of Portuguese regime fears in the 1930s that Britain and France would sell them out, offering Lusophone territories to the fascist powers in exchange for peace in Europe. See her "The Scramble for Africa Reloaded? Portugal, European Colonial Claims and the Distribution of Colonies in the 1930s," *Contemporary European History* 29 (June 2020): 1–14.

30. Prasenjit Duara, "The Cold War as a Historical Period: An Interpretative Essay," *Journal of Global History* 6 (2011): 460. Duara terms the imperial expansionism of these interwar revisionists the 'imperialism of nation-states'; Madeleine Herren, "Fascist Internationalism," in *Internationalisms: A Twentieth Century History*, ed. Glenda Sluga and Patricia Clavin (Cambridge, UK: Cambridge University Press, 2016), 192–95. Using the fascist powers as her example, Herren questions the presumption that internationalism need necessarily be either liberal or pacific in intent.

31. Jessica Reinisch, "Introduction: Agents of Internationalism," *Contemporary European History* 25 (2016): 198; Kelly A. Hammond, "Managing Muslims: Imperial Japan, Islamic Policy, and Axis Connections during the Second World War," *Journal of Global History* 12 (2017): 251–53, 261–67.

32. Lang, "Globalization," 908–10; Eloranta and Harrison, "War and Disintegration," 39–41; more generally, Harold James, *International Monetary Cooperation since Bretton Woods* (New York: Oxford University Press, 1996), especially chapters 3–4; Harold James, "The Multiple Contexts of Bretton Woods," *Past & Present* 210, Supplement 6 (2011): 300–8.

33. Daniel Sargent, "Globalization's Paradox: Economic Interdependence and Global Governance," in *Outside In: The Transnational Circuitry of US History*, ed. Andrew Preston and Doug Rossinow (New York: Oxford University Press, 2017), 38–39; James, "Multiple Contexts," 294–300.

34. Matthew Hilton, "Consumers and the State since the Second World War," *Annals of the American Academy of Political and Social Science* 611 (2007): 66–81, at 66, also cited in Andrea Westermann, "When Consumer Citizens Spoke Up: West Germany's Early Dealings with Plastic Waste," *Contemporary European History* 22, no. 3 (2013): 477–98, at 481–83.

35. Hopkins, "Is Globalisation Yesterday's News?" 111–12; Gregory Mann, *From Empires to NGOs in the West African Sahel: The Road to Nongovernmentality* (Cambridge, UK: Cambridge University Press), 2–8.

36. Miles Larmer, "Nation-Making at the Border: Zambian Diplomacy in the Democratic Republic of Congo," *Comparative Studies in Society and History* 61, no. 1 (2019): 146–48. On citizenship recalibrated by decolonization: Emma Hunter, "Dutiful Subjects, Patriotic Citizens and the Concept of 'Good Citizenship' in Twentieth-Century Tanzania," *Historical Journal* 56, no. 1 (2013): 257–77; idem, *Political Thought and the Public Sphere in Tanzania: Freedom, Democracy and Citizenship in the Era of Decolonisation* (Cambridge, UK: Cambridge University Press, 2015), 187–209.

37. This is central to Niall Ferguson's *Empire: The Rise and Demise of the British World Order and the Lessons for Global Power* (New York: Basic Books, 2003). As historian Dane Kennedy observes, the presumption that empires promoted globalization

by sustaining a stable world order also underlies Deepak Lal's *In Praise of Empires: Globalization and Order* (New York: Basic, 2004). Both works cited in Dane Kennedy, "Essay and Reflection: On the American Empire from a British Imperial Perspective," *International History Review* 29, no. 1 (2007): 86–87.

38. John Darwin, *Unlocking the World: Port Cities and Globalization in the Age of Steam, 1830–1930* (London: Allen Lane, 2020), chapters 5–7 passim.

39. David Northrup, *Indentured Labour in the Age of Imperialism, 1834–1922* (Cambridge, UK: Cambridge University Press, 1995); Walton Look Lai, *Indentured Labor, Caribbean Sugar: Chinese and Indian Migrants to the British West Indies, 1838–1918* (Baltimore: Johns Hopkins University Press, 1993); Catherine Ash, "Forced Labour in Colonial West Africa," *History Compass* 4, no. 3 (2006): 402–6; Rana P. Behal, "Coolie Drivers or Benevolent Paternalists? British Tea Planters in Assam and the Indenture Labour System," *Modern Asian Studies* 44, no. 1 (2010): 29–51; Wiseman Chijere Chirwa, "Child and Youth Labour on the Nyasaland Plantations, 1890–1953," *Journal of Southern African Studies* 19, no. 4 (1993): 662–80; Allen Isaacman, "Coercion, Paternalism and the Process: The Mozambican Cotton Regime, 1938–1961," *Journal of Southern African Studies* 18, no. 3 (1992): 487–526; Daniel Maul, "The International Labour Organization and the Struggle against Forced Labour from 1919 to the Present," *Labour History* 48 (2007): 477–500; Bridget O'Laughlin, "Proletarianisation, Agency and Changing Rural Livelihoods: Forced Labour and Resistance in Colonial Mozambique," *Journal of Southern African Studies* 28, no. 3 (2002): 511–30; Gregory Mann, "What Was the *Indigénat*? The 'Empire of Law' in French West Africa," *Journal of African History* 50, no. 2 (2009): 331–53.

40. Dipesh Chakrabarty cited in Uday Singh Mehta, "The Dream Machine," in *Reordering the World: Essays on Liberalism and Empire*, ed. Duncan Bell (Princeton, NJ: Princeton University Press, 2016), 27.

41. Roland Paris, "International Peacebuilding and the '*Mission Civilisatrice*,'" *Review of International Studies* 28, no. 4 (2002): 637–38, 641–44.

42. Heonik Kwon, *After the Korean War: An Intimate History* (Cambridge, UK: Cambridge University Press, 2020), 117, and building on Dipesh Chakrabarty, *Provincializing Europe: Postcolonial Thought and Historical Difference* (Princeton, NJ: Princeton University Press, 2000), new edition, 2008, especially chapter 6: "Nation and Imagination."

43. Paul Adler, *No Globalization without Representation: U.S. Activists and World Inequality* (Philadelphia: University of Pennsylvania Press, 2021), 1–6, 21–23, 49–55.

44. Andrew S. Sartori, "The British Empire and Its Liberal Mission," *Journal of Modern History* 78, no. 3 (2006): 641–42.

45. Ross, *Ecology and Power*, 416, 421.

46. Ross, *Ecology and Power*, 417; Sharma, "Food and Empire."

47. Barry Buzan and George Lawson, *The Global Transformation: History, Modernity and the Making of International Relations* (Cambridge, UK: Cambridge University Press, 2015), 273–78, 22–32.

48. Political scientist John Nagl highlights the blindness in this advocacy of 'capitalist peace' toward internal conflicts within postcolonial nations: "Nostrum or Palliative: Contesting the Capitalist Peace in Violently Divided Societies," *Civil Wars* 12, no. 3 (2010): 218–36, 219–33.

49. Lang, "Globalization," 906. For the differing globalization paths traced by North and Southeast Asia, see Mark Beeson, *Regionalism and Globalisation in East Asia: Politics, Security and Economic Development*, 2nd edition (London: Bloomsbury, 2014), chapters 2–3.

50. Barbara Castle papers, BLO, MS Castle 2: notebook of visit to the Middle East, Jan. 1953, fos. 9–13: dinner with Jordanian premier, Amman, January 5, 1953.

51. Castle papers, MS Castle 2, fos. 21–35: Brigadier Sheshekly (al-Shishakli) meeting, January 7, 1953.

52. Castle papers, MS Castle 2, fos. 40–62: Baghdad meeting with oppositionists Mohammed Haded Jamil of National Democratic Party and former premier Muzahim Pachachi, January 12, 1953.

53. Frederick Cooper, "Gatekeeping Practices, Gatekeeper States and Beyond," *Third World Thematics* 3, no. 3 (2018): 455–68; Justin Willis, "Chieftaincy," in *The Oxford Handbook of Modern African History*, ed. John Parker and Richard Reid (Oxford: Oxford University Press, 2013), 216–17.

54. Justin Willis, Gabrielle Lynch, and Nic Cheeseman, "Voting, Nationhood, and Citizenship in Late-Colonial Africa," *Historical Journal* 61, no. 4 (2018): 1113–35.

55. Natalya Vince, *The Algerian War, the Algerian Revolution* (London: Bloomsbury, 2020), 157–61, 169–70.

56. Natalya Vince, *Our Fighting Sisters: Nation, Memory and Gender in Algeria, 1954–2012* (Manchester, UK: Manchester University Press, 2015), 202–51; for more recent parallels: Karen Kampwirth, *Feminism and the Legacy of Revolution: Nicaragua, El Salvador, Chiapas* (Athens: Ohio University Press, 2004).

57. Jeffrey James Byrne, "Africa's Cold War," in *The Cold War in the Third World*, ed. Robert J. McMahon (Oxford: Oxford University Press, 2013), 102; Wael Hallaq, *The Impossible State: Islam, Politics, and Modernity's Moral Predicament* (New York: Columbia University Press, 2012), 140–46.

58. Stuart Ward, *Untied Kingdom: A Global History of the End of Britain* (Cambridge, UK: Cambridge University Press, 2023), 7.

59. A. G. Hopkins, "Rethinking Decolonization," *Past & Present* 200 (August 2008): 215–17, 230; idem, "Is Globalisation Yesterday's News?" 109–28.

60. Wm. Roger Louis and Ronald Robinson, "The Imperialism of Decolonization," *Journal of Imperial & Commonwealth History* 22, no. 3 (1994): 462–511; Gregory A. Barton, *Informal Empire and the Rise of One World Culture* (Basingstoke, UK: Palgrave Macmillan, 2014), 168–75, 179–84.

61. Marc Levinson, *The Box: How the Shipping Container Made the World Smaller and the World Economy Bigger* (Princeton, NJ: Princeton University Press, 2006).

62. Nicholas J. White, "Thinking Outside 'the Box': Decolonization and Containerization," in *Shipping and Globalization in the Post-War Era*, ed. Niels P. Petersson, Stig Tenold, and Nicholas J. White (Basingstoke, UK: Palgrave Macmillan, 2019), 67–99, at 68–73.

63. White, "Thinking Outside," 73–76.

64. Drawing on the work of Ephraim Kleiman, White describes this as the breakdown of colonialism's 'enforced bilateralism': White, "Thinking Outside," 76, citing Ephraim Kleiman, "Trade and the Decline of Colonialism," *Economic Journal* 86 (1976): 459–480, at 462. On Soviet backing for UNCTAD, see James Mark and Yakov

Feygin, "The Soviet Union, Eastern Europe, and Alternative Visions of a Global Economy, 1950s–1980s," in *Alternative Globalizations: Eastern Europe and the Postcolonial World*, ed. James Mark, Artemy M. Kalinovsky, and Steffi Marung (Bloomington: Indiana University Press, 2020), 36–42.

65. White, "Thinking Outside," 77–78.

66. Lang, "Globalization," 899–900 and 908–10.

67. Bernhard Struck, Kate Ferris, and Jacques Revel, "Introduction: Space and Scale in Transnational History," *International History Review* 33, no. 4 (2011): 574–78.

68. Matthias Middell and Katya Naumann, "Global History and the Spatial Turn: From the Impact of Area Studies to the Study of Critical Junctures of Globalization," *Journal of Global History* 5, no. 1 (2010): 155.

69. M. J. Maynes and Ann Waltner, "Modern Political Revolutions: Connecting Grassroots Political Dissent and Global Historical Transformations," in Burton and Ballantyne, *World Histories*, 11–19, 28–36; Durba Ghosh, "AHR Forum: Another Set of Imperial Turns?" *American Historical Review* 117, no. 3 (June 2012): 779, 793; Petra Goedde, "Power, Culture, and the Rise of Transnational History in the United States," *International History Review* 40, no. 3 (2018): 601; Gorman, *International Cooperation*, 3–9; Mann, *From Empires to NGOs*, 5–8, 110–19.

70. Richard Drayton and David Motadel, "Discussion: The Futures of Global History," *Journal of Global History* 13 (2018): 1–21, at 4 and 13; Márcia Gonçalves, "Of Peasants and Settlers: Ideals of Portugueseness, Imperial Nationalism and European Settlement in Africa, c. 1930–c.1945," *European Review of History* 25, no. 1 (2018): 166–77.

71. Middell and Naumann, "Global History and the Spatial Turn," 160–61.

72. A clear summary of connections between global history and the study of globalization and empire is Jürgen Ostehammel, "Globalizations," in *The Oxford Handbook of World History*, ed. Jerry H. Bentley (Oxford: Oxford University Press, 2011), 89–104.

73. Samuel Moyn, "Fantasies of Federalism," *Dissent* 62, no. 1 (2015): 148–49.

74. Byrne, "Africa's Cold War," 102–4.

75. Michael Collins, "Decolonisation and the 'Federal Moment,'" *Diplomacy & Statecraft* 24, no. 1 (2013): 22–24; Frederick Cooper, *Citizenship between Empire and Nation: Rethinking France and French Africa, 1945–1960* (Princeton, NJ: Princeton University Press, 2014), 216–19, 237–46; Adom Getachew, "Securing Postcolonial Independence: Kwame Nkrumah and the Federal Idea in the Age of Decolonization," *Ab Imperio* 3 (2018): 95–105.

76. Collins, "Decolonisation and the 'Federal Moment,'" 36.

77. Gyan Prakash, "Anxious Constitution-Making," in *The Postcolonial Moment in South and Southeast Asia*, ed. Gyan Prakash, Michael Laffan, and Nikhil Menon (London: Bloomsbury, 2018), 145–46.

78. Mandy Sadan, "Contested Meanings of Postcolonialism and Independence in Burma," in Prakash, Laffan, and Menon, *Postcolonial Moment*, 56–60.

79. Collins, "Decolonisation and the 'Federal Moment,'" 34–35.

80. Castle papers, MS Castle 243, ANC/2/4, Letter from H. M. Nkumbula, President-general, ANC Northern Rhodesia, and Kenneth Kaunda, Secretary-general

to Governor of Northern Rhodesia, January 24, 1958. See also fo. 152: copy of letters from Kenneth Kaunda to Commander T. S. L. Fox-Pitt and James Callaghan, March 20, 1959.

81. Collins, "Decolonisation and the 'Federal Moment,'" 21–40. Examples of federal schema within the British Empire include the Central African Federation, 1953–1963; the East African High Commission, 1948–1961; the West Indies Federation, 1958–1962; the Malay Federation, 1948–1963, and the Federation of South Arabia, 1962–1967.

82. This is central to Wael Hallaq's arguments about the incompatibility of Muslim attachment to supreme religious authority and imperialist imposition of secular institutional structures, laws, and constructions of citizenship: Hallaq, *Impossible State*, 1–4, 20–24, 44–48.

83. Aydin cites African-American journalist Richard Wright, who singled out the prime importance for Bandung delegates of the 'Color Curtain' over and above the Cold War's 'Iron Curtain'; see *Politics of Anti-Westernism in Asia*, 200. Guiliano Garavini also stresses the geopolitical factors and the risk of Sino-American confrontation in Asia in motivating the conference. Bandung, in other words, helped foreclose US pressure for additional anti-Communist pacts, akin to 1954's Southeast Asia Treaty Organization. See Giuliano Garavini, *After Empires: European Integration, Decolonization, and the Challenge from the Global South 1957–1986* (Oxford: Oxford University Press, 2012), 12.

84. Cemil Aydin cites secular Turkish republicanism in the 1920s as an example of the triumph of nationalism as a unifier over and above either pan-Islamic or pan-Asianist alternatives; see his *Politics of Anti-Westernism in Asia*, 128–41.

85. Partha Chatterjee, *Nationalist Thought and the Colonial World: A Derivative Discourse*, 2nd edition (Minneapolis: University of Minnesota Press, 1993).

86. Jennifer M. Welsh, "Empire and Fragmentation," in *The Globalization of International Society*, ed. Tim Dunne and Christian Reus-Smit (Oxford: Oxford University Press, 2017), 157.

87. Frantz Fanon, *The Wretched of the Earth* (London: Penguin Modern Classics, 2001), 55, also cited in Tarak Barkawi, "From Law to History: The Politics of War and Empire," *Global Constitutionalism* 7, no. 3 (2018): 315.

88. Brooke Coe, "Sovereignty Regimes and the Norm of Noninterference in the Global South: Regional and Temporal Variation," *Global Governance* 21 (2015): 275–98, at 280–82.

89. Gregory Mann makes similar points about the dismantling of chieftaincy and the Africanization of bureaucracy by Mamadou Madeira Keita's Union-Soudanaise-Rassemblement Démocratique Africain regime in the Mali Federation; see Mann, *From Empires to NGOs*, 21, 36–37, 62–77.

90. On the most ambitious of those political-economic efforts, typified by the formation of UNCTAD in 1964 and the launch of the New International Economic Order a decade later, see Adom Getachew, *Worldmaking after Empire: The Rise and Fall of Self-Determination* (Princeton, NJ: Princeton University Press, 2019); idem, "Securing Postcolonial Independence"; Giuliano Garavini, "Completing Decolonization: The 1973 'Oil Shock' and the Struggle for Economic Rights," *International History Review* 33, no. 3 (2011): 473–87; Vanessa Ogle, "State Rights against Private Capital: the 'New International Economic Order' and the Struggle over Aid, Trade, and Foreign Investment,

1962–1981," *Humanity* 5, no. 2 (2014): 211–34; Johanna Bockman, "Socialist Globalization against Capitalist Neocolonialism: The Economic Ideas behind the New International Economic Order," *Humanity* 6, no. 1 (2015): 109–28.

91. Koskenniemi, *Gentle Civilizer of Nations*, 175.

92. Frederick Cooper, "What Is the Concept of Globalization Good for? An African Historian's Perspective," *African Affairs* 100, no. 399 (2001): 205–6.

93. Cooper, "What Is the Concept," 205–6.

94. Frederick Cooper, "Decolonizations, Colonizations, and More Decolonizations: The End of Empire in Time and Space," *Journal of World History* 33, no. 3 (2022): 510–18.

95. Drayton and Motadel, "Discussion: The Futures of Global History," 1–15.

96. Todd Shepard, "'History Is Past Politics'? Archives, 'Tainted Evidence,' and the Return of the State," *American Historical Review* 115, no. 2 (April 2010): 474–83, at 480–81.

97. Cyrus Schayegh, *The Middle East and the Making of the Modern World* (Cambridge, MA: Harvard University Press, 2017), especially chapters 2–4.

98. Schayegh, *Middle East*, 164–78. By the same token, and as Schayegh demonstrates, Aleppo, formerly the hub connecting northern Syria with trade and livestock markets in Ottoman Anatolia and Iraq, suffered especially badly from the new territorialization, the economic barriers erected between Mandate Syria and Republican Turkey in particular.

99. Schayegh, *Middle East*, 2–18, 137–39. Keith Watenpaugh reaches similar conclusions about the significance of cross-border connection in his study of Syria's northern commercial hub, Aleppo: Watenpaugh, *Being Modern in the Middle East: Revolution, Nationalism, Colonialism, and the Arab Middle Class* (Princeton, NJ: Princeton University Press, 2006).

100. A point powerfully made by Tarak Barkawi and Mark Laffey, "The Imperial Peace: Democracy, Force, and Globalization," *European Journal of International Relations* 5, no. 4 (1999): 403–34.

101. Saphia Arezki, *De l'ALN à l'ANP, la construction de l'armée algérienne, 1954–1991* (Paris: Éditions de la Sorbonne, 2022), 244–57; Jeffrey James Byrne, *Mecca of Revolution: Algeria, Decolonization, & the Third World Order* (Oxford: Oxford University Press, 2019), 144–47, 158–67; Max Trecker, *Red Money for the Global South: East-South Economic Relations in the Cold War* (London: Routledge, 2020), especially chapter 6.

102. Tarak Barkawi, "Political Military Legacies of Empire in World Politics," in *Legacies of Empire: Imperial Roots of the Contemporary Global Order*, ed. Sandra Halperin and Ronen Palan (Cambridge, UK: Cambridge University Press, 2015), 27–45.

103. As in the case of American access, first to British, then to other allies' bases from the Caribbean to Oceania: Hopkins, *American Empire*, 469, 474, 659, 670.

104. Alexander Cooley, "Foreign Bases, Sovereignty and Nation Building after Empire: The United States in Comparative Perspective," in Halperin and Palan, *Legacies of Empire*, 173–96.

105. Coe, "Sovereignty Regimes," 282–87; Paris, "International Peacebuilding," 637–56.

106. Schütze, "International Governance," 2–3.

107. Coe, "Sovereignty Regimes," 278–88.

108. Coe, "Sovereignty Regimes," 293–94.

109. Sundha Pahuja, *Decolonising International Law: Development, Economic Growth and the Politics of Universality* (Cambridge, UK: Cambridge University Press, 2013), 45.

110. Jessica Lynn Pearson, "Defending Empire at the United Nations: The Politics of International Colonial Oversight in the Era of Decolonisation," *Journal of Imperial & Commonwealth History* 45, no. 3 (2017): 541.

111. Wm. Roger Louis, "Public Enemy Number One: The British Empire in the Dock at the United Nations, 1957–1971," in *The British Empire in the 1950s: Retreat or Revival?* ed. Martin Lynn (Basingstoke, UK: Palgrave Macmillan, 2006), 188–89.

112. Rose Ndengue, "Social Imaginaries in Tension? The Women of Cameroon's Battle for Equal Rights under French Rule at the Turn of the 1940s–50s," in *Black French Women and the Struggle for Equality, 1848–2016*, ed. Félix Germain and Silvane Larcher (Lincoln: University of Nebraska Press, 2018), 237–51.

113. Terretta, "From Below," 393–95.

114. Terretta, "From Below," 411–14; for the wider history of the UPC campaign and the violence of French counterinsurgency against it, see Meredith Terretta, *Nation of Outlaws, State of Violence: Nationalism, Grassfields Tradition, and State Building in Cameroon* (Athens: University of Ohio Press, 2014); idem, "Cameroonian Nationalists Go Global: From Forest Maquis to a Pan-African Accra," *Journal of African History* 52, no. 2 (2010): 189–212.

115. Hopkins, *American Empire*, 26–27.

116. Barton, *Informal Empire*, 2–10, 26–28.

117. Lorenzo Veracini, *The World Turned Inside Out: Settler Colonialism as a Political Idea* (London: Verso, 2021), chapters 2–3; Edward Cavanagh and Lorenzo Veracini, eds., *The Routledge Handbook of the History of Settler Colonialism* (Abingdon, UK: Routledge, 2016), 1–8; James Belich, *Replenishing the Earth: The Settler Revolution and the Rise of the Angloworld, 1783–1939* (Oxford: Oxford University Press, 2009); Magee and Thompson, *Empire and Globalisation*; Alan Lester, "British Settler Discourse and the Circuits of Empire," *History Workshop Journal* 54, no. 1 (2002): 24–48; Carl Bridge and Kent Fedorowich, "Mapping the British World," *Journal of Imperial & Commonwealth History* 31, no. 2 (2003): 1–11; Todd, *Velvet Empire*; John Griffiths, "Were There Municipal Networks in the British World, 1890–1939?" *Journal of Imperial & Commonwealth History* 37, no. 4 (2009): 575–97.

118. James Mark et al., *Socialism Goes Global: The Soviet Union and Eastern Europe in the Age of Decolonization* (Oxford: Oxford University Press, 2022).

119. Postel-Vinay, "European Power," 323–36, at 324.

120. The landmark statement of this decentered view remains C. A. Bayly, *The Birth of the Modern World, 1780–1914: Global Connections and Comparisons* (Oxford: Oxford University Press, 2004). That for empire's 'afterlife' is Jordanna Bailkin, *The Afterlife of Empire* (Berkeley: University of California Press, 2012). For detailed examples: Inés Valdez, "Association, Reciprocity, and Emancipation: A Transnational Account of the Politics of Global Justice," in *Empire, Race, and Global Justice*, ed. Duncan Bell (Cambridge, UK: Cambridge University Press, 2019), 123–25; Sven Beckert, *Empire of*

Cotton: A Global History (New York: Knopf, 2014); Christina Lubinski, "Global Trade and Indian Politics: The German Dye Business in India before 1947," *Business History Review* 89 (Fall 2015): 503–8; Sunil Amrith, *Crossing the Bay of Bengal: The Furies of Nature and the Fortunes of Migrants* (Cambridge, MA: Harvard University Press, 2013); Su Sin Lewis, *Cities in Motion: Urban Life and Cosmopolitanism in Southeast Asia, 1920–1940* (Cambridge, UK: Cambridge University Press, 2016); Mann, *From Empires to NGOs*, 110–19; and, for a worldwide picture, Adam McKeown, "Global Migration, 1846–1940," *Journal of World History* 15, no. 2 (2004): 155–89.

Chapter Three: Decolonization and Its Alternatives

1. Samuel Fury Childs Daly, "A Nation on Paper: Making a State in the Republic of Biafra," *Comparative Studies in Society & History* 62, no. 4 (2020): 892–93, citing Gary Wilder, *Freedom Time: Negritude, Decolonization, and the Future of the World* (Durham, NC: Duke University Press, 2015), 4.

2. Julie MacArthur, "Decolonizing Sovereignty: States of Exception along the Kenya–Somali Frontier," *American Historical Review* 124, no. 1 (2019): 109–17; Arne de Boever, "Prologue: The Future of Sovereignty," in *Plastic Sovereignties: Agamben and the Politics of Aesthetics*, ed. Arne de Boever, Peg Birmingham, and Dimitris Vardoulakis (Edinburgh: Edinburgh University Press, 2016), 4–16.

3. The literature is extensive. For contrasting Arab world examples: Joel Beinen and Zachary Lockman, *Workers on the Nile: Nationalism, Communism, Islam and the Egyptian Working Class, 1882–1954* (Cairo: American University in Cairo Press, 1998); Rana Barakat, "Reading Palestinian Agency in Mandate History: The Narrative of the Buraq Revolt as Anti-Relational," *Contemporary Levant* 4, no. 1 (2019): 28–38; Kamel Bouguessa, *Aux sources du nationalisme algérien. Les pioniers du populisme révolutionnaire en marche* (Algiers: Éditions Casbah, 2000); James Jankowski and Israel Gershoni, eds., *Rethinking Nationalism in the Arab Middle East* (New York: Columbia University Press, 1997); Gilles Lafuente, *La Politique berbère de la France et le nationalisme marocain* (Paris: l'Harmattan, 1999); Charles-Robert Ageron, "L'Association des étudiants musulmans nord-africains en France durant l'entre-deux-guerres. Contribution à l'étude des nationalismes maghrébins," *Revue Française d'Histoire d'Outre-Mer* 70, no. 258 (1983): 25–56; Michael Eppel, "The Elite, the *Effendiyya*, and the Growth of Nationalism and Pan-Arabism in Hashemite Iraq, 1921–1958," *International Journal of Middle East Studies* 30 (1998): 411–34; James L. Gelvin, "The Social Origins of Popular Nationalism in Syria: Evidence for a New Framework," *International Journal of Middle East Studies* 26 (1994): 645–61; Israel Gershoni, "The Emergence of Pan-Nationalism in Egypt: Pan-Islamism and Pan-Arabism in the 1930s," *Asian and African Affairs* 16, no. 1 (1982): 59–94.

4. Christopher E. Goscha, *Vietnam: A New History* (New York: Basic, 2016), 98–105.

5. Philippe Peycam, *The Birth of Vietnamese Political Journalism: Saigon, 1916–1930* (New York: Columbia University Press, 2015); David G. Marr, *Vietnamese Tradition on Trial, 1920–1945* (Berkeley: University of California Press, 1981); Shawn McHale, *Print and Power: Confucianism, Communism, and Buddhism in the Making of Modern Vietnam* (Honolulu: University of Hawai'i Press, 2004).

6. M. Kathryn Edwards, "An Indochinese Dominion: *L'Effort Indochinois* and Autonomy in a Global Context, 1936–1939," *French Politics, Culture and Society* 38, no. 2 (2020): 9–34. And for similar tensions in Korean nationalism, see Michael Edson Robinson, *Cultural Nationalism in Colonial Korea, 1920–1925* (Seattle: University of Washington Press, 1988), 158–68.

7. Micheline Lessard, "More than Half the Sky: Vietnamese Women and Anti-French Political Activism, 1858–1945," in *Vietnam and the West: New Approaches*, ed. Wynn Wilcox (Ithaca, NY: Cornell University Press, 2010), 91–92; David E. F. Henley, "Ethnogeographic Integration and Exclusion in Anticolonial Nationalism: Indonesia and Indochina," *Comparative Studies in Society and History* 37, no. 2 (1995): 286–324.

8. Micheline Lessard, "'We Know . . . the Duties We Must Fulfill': Modern 'Mothers and Fathers' of the Vietnamese Nation," *French Colonial History* 3, no. 1 (2003): 119–41.

9. Connections forensically analyzed in Su Sin Lewis, *Cities in Motion: Urban Life and Cosmopolitanism in Southeast Asia, 1920–1940* (Cambridge, UK: Cambridge University Press, 2016), especially chapters 3–5.

10. Heather Marie Stur, *Saigon at War: South Vietnam and the Global Sixties* (Cambridge, UK: Cambridge University Press, 2020), 77–98, 109–11. For the diversity of student opinion in South Vietnam's civil society, see Van Nguyen-Marshall, "Student Activism in a Time of War: Youth in the Republic of Vietnam, 1960s–1970s," *Journal of Vietnamese Studies* 10, no. 2 (2015): 45–47, 53–64.

11. On the exceptions: Meredith Terretta, "'In the Colonies, Black Lives Don't Matter': Legalism and Rights Claims across the French Empire," *Journal of Contemporary History* 53, no. 1 (2018): 12–37.

12. Jansen and Osterhammel, *Decolonization*, 46–48.

13. These themes are explored by contributors to *The Postcolonial Moment in South and Southeast Asia*, ed. Gyan Prakash, Michael Laffan, and Nikhil Menon (London: Bloomsbury, 2018). For the Algerian case, see J. N. C. Hill, "Remembering the War of Liberation: Legitimacy and Conflict in Contemporary Algeria," *Small Wars & Insurgencies* 23, no. 1 (2012): 12–14.

14. Martti Koskenniemi, *The Gentle Civilizer of Nations: The Rise and Fall of International Law, 1870–1960* (Cambridge, UK: Cambridge University Press, 2010), 98.

15. Mark Lewis, *The Birth of the New Justice: The Internationalization of Crime and Punishment, 1919–1950* (Oxford: Oxford University Press, 2014), 29–33. Increasingly precise as instruments of justice, these international laws retreated from utopian *fin-de siècle* visions of global government and an end to war; see Stephen Wertheim, "The League of Nations: Retreat from International Law?" *Journal of Global History* 7, no. 2 (2012): 210–32, also cited in Duncan Bell, "Race, Utopia, Perpetual Peace," in *American Foreign Policy*, ed. Jean-François Drolet and James Dunkerley (Manchester, UK: Manchester University Press, 2017), chapter 2.

16. Lewis, *Birth of the New Justice*, 65, 291; Jonathan E. Gumz, *The Resurrection and Collapse of Empire in Habsburg Serbia, 1914–1918* (Cambridge, UK: Cambridge University Press, 2009); Michael A. Reynolds, *Shattering Empires: The Clash and Collapse of the Ottoman and Russian Empires, 1908–1918* (Cambridge, UK:

Cambridge University Press, 2011); Laura Robson, *States of Separation: Transfer, Partition, and the Making of the Modern Middle East* (Berkeley: University of California Press, 2017). For longer-term background: Dominik Geppert, William Mulligan, and Andreas Rose, eds., *The Wars before the Great War: Conflict and International Politics before the Outbreak of the First World War* (Cambridge, UK: Cambridge University Press, 2015); Eric D. Weitz, "Germany and the Ottoman Borderlands: The Entwining of Imperial Aspirations, Revolution, and Ethnic Violence," in *Shatterzone of Empire: Coexistence and Violence in the German, Habsburg, Russian and Ottoman Borderlands*, ed. Omer Bartov and Eric D. Weitz (Bloomington: Indiana University Press, 2013), chapter 8. For a Russian case study, see Alexander Morrison, Cloé Drieu, and Aminat Chokobaeva, eds., *The Central Asian Revolt of 1916: A Collapsing Empire in the Age of War and Revolution* (Manchester, UK: Manchester University Press, 2019).

17. Robert Gerwarth and John Horne, eds., *War in Peace: Paramilitary Violence in Europe after the Great War* (Oxford: Oxford University Press, 2013). For the wartime roots of this violence on the Ottoman 'home front', Yiğit Akın, *When the War Came Home: The Ottomans' Great War and the Devastation of an Empire* (Stanford, CA: Stanford University Press, 2018), especially chapter 4.

18. Peter Gatrell, *The Making of the Modern Refugee* (Oxford: Oxford University Press, 2013), 18–19, 53–59; Michelle Tusan, "'Crimes against Humanity': Human Rights, the British Empire, and the Origins of the Response to the Armenian Genocide," *Journal of American History* 119, no. 1 (2014): 62–69; Keith David Watenpaugh, "The League of Nations' Rescue of Armenian Genocide Survivors and the Making of Modern Humanitarianism, 1920–1927," *American Historical Review* 115, no. 5 (2010): 1315–39; Tehila Sasson, "From Empire to Humanity: The Russian Famine and the Imperial Origins of International Humanitarianism," *Journal of British Studies* 55 (2016): 519–37.

19. Lewis, *Birth of the New Justice*, 290.

20. For critical analysis of the limited enforcement mechanisms of international law within the peace settlement, see Wertheim, "League of Nations," 210–32, at 228.

21. Lauren Benton, "Made in Empire: Finding the Origins of International Law in Imperial Locations," *Leiden Journal of International Law* 31, no. 3 (2018): 473–77; Adam Guerin, "Racial Myth, Colonial Policy, and the Invention of Customary Law in Morocco, 1912–1930," *Journal of North African Studies* 16, no. 3 (2011): 361–80.

22. Mary Dewhurst Lewis, *Divided Rule: Sovereignty and Empire in French Tunisia, 1881–1938* (Berkeley: University of California Press, 2014), especially chapters 3 and 5.

23. Martin Thomas, *Violence and Colonial Order: Police, Workers, and Protest in the European Colonial Empires, 1918–1940* (Cambridge, UK: Cambridge University Press, 2012), 64–86.

24. J. P. Daughton, "ILO Expertise and Colonial Violence in the Interwar Years," in *Globalizing Social Rights*, ed. Sandrine Kott and Joëlle Droux (Basingstoke, UK: Palgrave Macmillan, 2013), 85–97, at 86.

25. TNA, CO 323/1170/5: Forced Labour Convention, Arthur Wauchope, High Commissioner for Transjordan, Jerusalem, to Colonial Secretary Sir Philip Cunliffe-Lister, 3 December 1932. Section 8 of the Organic Law applying the Convention concerning Forced or Compulsory Labour stated that compulsory labor 'may be exacted

for public purposes only and shall invariably be labour of an exceptional character, shall always require adequate remuneration, and shall not involve the removal of labourers from their usual place of residence.' See also Marie Rodet, "Forced Labor, Resistance, and Masculinities in Kayes, French Sudan, 1919–1946," *International Labor and Working-Class History* 86, no. 1 (2014): 107–23. There are parallels here with the legislative regulation and medical oversight of colonial prostitution, particularly in interwar ports around the Mediterranean, as analyzed by Liat Kozma, *Global Women, Colonial Ports: Prostitution in the Interwar Middle East* (Albany: SUNY Press, 2017).

26. Frederick Cooper, "Afterword: Social Rights and Human Rights in the Time of Decolonization," *Humanity* 3, no. 3 (2012): 481. As Cooper points out, while the League and the ILO imposed a simple binary between forced and free labor without taking closer interest in the social rights of workers, the Forced Labour Convention of 1930 did at least provide a new juridical framework against which colonial working practices could be judged.

27. Florian Wagner, *Colonial Internationalism and the Governmentality of Empire, 1893–1982* (Cambridge, UK: Cambridge University Press, 2022), 210, 220, 236–38.

28. Cooper, "Afterword," 480–81.

29. Sacha Hepburn and April Jackson, "Colonial Exceptions: The International Labour Organization and Child Labour in British Africa, c.1919–1940," *Journal of Contemporary History* 57, no. 2 (2022): 230–34.

30. IOR, Mss EUR F174: India Tea Association papers, file 628a: *Detailed Report of the General Committee of the Indian Tea Association for the Year 1937* (Calcutta, 1938), 30–31.

31. Sugata Bose, *Peasant Labour and Colonial Capital: Rural Bengal since 1770* (Cambridge, UK: Cambridge University Press, 1993), 161–48; Margo Groenewoud, "Towards the Abolition of Penal Sanctions in Dutch Colonial Labour Legislation: An International Perspective," *Itinerario* 19, no. 2 (1995): 72–90.

32. Marilyn Lake and Henry Reynolds, *Drawing the Global Colour Line: White Men's Countries and the International Challenge of Racial Equality* (Cambridge, UK: Cambridge University Press, 2008), 23; Gary B. Magee and Andrew S. Thompson, *Empire and Globalisation: Networks of People, Goods and Capital in the British World, c. 1850–1914* (Cambridge, UK: Cambridge University Press, 2010), 66.

33. For the French Empire case, see: ANOM, Marius Moutet papers, 28PA/carton 3, "La législation française et le travail forcé," "L'Organisation internationale du Travail et le travail indigène," "Argument de la compétence," none dated, but all likely 1930. For the high mortality and morbidity rates among indentured laborers in late nineteenth and early twentieth-century colonies from southeast Asia to the islands of the Pacific and Indian Oceans, see David Northrup, *Indentured Labour in the Age of Imperialism, 1834–1922* (Cambridge, UK: Cambridge University Press, 1995); Sunil S. Amrith, "Tamil Diasporas across the Bay of Bengal," *American Historical Review* 114, no. 3 (2009): 563–69; Andreas Steen, "Germany and the Chinese Coolie: Labor, Resistance, and the Struggle for Equality, 1884–1914," in *German Colonialism Revisited: African, Asian, and Oceanic Experiences*, ed. Nina Berman, Klaus Mühlhahn, and Patrice Nganang (Ann Arbor: University of Michigan Press, 2014), 147–49; Eric

Allina, "'No Real Freedom for the Natives': The Men in the Middle and Critiques of Colonial Labor in Central Mozambique," *Humanity* 3, no. 3 (2012): 337–59.

34. Stanley L. Engerman, "Contract Labor, Sugar, and Technology in the Nineteenth Century," *Journal of Economic History* 43, no. 3 (1983): 635–39; Alec Gordon, "The Agrarian Question and Colonial Capitalism: Coercion and Java's Colonial Sugar Plantation System, 1870–1941," *Journal of Peasant Studies* 27, no. 1 (1999): 1–34.

35. Corinna R. Unger, *International Development: A Postwar History* (London: Bloomsbury, 2018), 31–33, 37–39; idem, "The Decolonization of Development: Rural Development in India before and after 1947," in *Internationalism, Imperialism and the Formation of the Contemporary World: The Pasts of the Present*, ed. Miguel Bandeira Jerónimo and José Pedro Monteiro (Basingstoke, UK: Palgrave Macmillan, 2018), 253–78.

36. Thomas, *Violence and Colonial Order*, 166, 188–92.

37. Jamie Martin, *The Meddlers: Sovereignty, Empire, and the Birth of Global Economic Governance* (Cambridge, MA: Harvard University Press, 2022), 185–205.

38. TNA, CO 717/73/22, Report on the working of the Federation of Malay States Labour Department, 1929, 9. The 1929 figures for complaints by coolies registered sixty-four allegations of assaults by managers and 221 by clerks or *kanganis*. None were taken up by labor controllers or the police. TNA CO 717/91/3, despatch 302, enclosure 3: "Note by Controller of Labour, Malaya, on Work and Wages during the Year 1931," May 12, 1932; Guildhall Library, London, Rubber Growers' Association (RGA) papers, Council minute books, MS24863/34, Report of the Netherlands Indies Committee, April 25, 1932; Alexander Keese, "Between Violence, Racism and Reform: São Tomé e Príncipe in the Great Depression Years (1930–1937)," *Journal of Contemporary History* 56, no. 2 (2021): 255–65.

39. Belgian Foreign Ministry archives, Brussels, Archives Africaines, Archives du Fonds des Affaires Indigènes (AI), File AI/1403, dossier: Impôt indigène: tax receipts for Belgian Congo, 1931–33. Private consortia, such as the Lever Brothers' network of Congolese palm oil factories, broadly followed suit; see Reuben Loffman and Benoît Henriet, "'We Are Left with Barely Anything': Colonial Rule, Dependency, and the Lever Brothers in the Belgian Congo, 1911–1960," *Journal of Imperial & Commonwealth History* 48, no. 1 (2020): 83–87.

40. Victor Fernández Soriano, "'*Travail et progrès*': Obligatory 'Educational' Labour in the Belgian Congo," *Journal of Contemporary History* 53, no. 2 (2018): 293, 297–302; for the wider persistence of disguised forced labor practices in sub-Saharan Africa, see Alexander Keese, "The Slow Abolition within the Colonial Mind: British and French Debates about 'Vagrancy,' 'African Laziness,' and Forced Labour in West Central and South Central Africa, 1945–1965," *International Review of Social History* 59, no. 3 (2014): 377–407.

41. ANOM, Marius Moutet papers, Carton 5: colonial governors' conference, 1937/dossier 149bis, Ministry of Colonies, Cabinet du Ministre, to Governor General of AEF, June 17, 1936. The administrator responsible for enforcing this policy was accused of 'terrorizing' village headmen.

42. TNA, FO 371/21605, C916/141/17, Consul D. Helm-Smith (Antananarivo) to FO, January 7, 1938, Inspection du Travail, "Textes portant réglementation du travail indigene à Madagascar et dependences, (décret du 7 avril 1938)." The depression also

drove the Madagascar government to lobby successfully for the return of some Malagasy plantation laborers from Réunion and a ban on the most skilled from migrating there; see Hildebert Isnard, *La Réunion: Problèmes démographiques, économiques et sociaux*, undated pamphlet.

43. TNA, FO 371/21605, C10769/141/17, Imprimerie Officielle pamphlet, Tananarive, 1938, sent by Antananarivo consul to Foreign Office, August 26, 1938.

44. Amanda Kay McVety, "Wealth and Nations: The Origins of International Development Assistance," in *The Development Century*, ed. Stephen J. Macekura and Erez Manela (Cambridge, UK: Cambridge University Press, 2018), 26–29.

45. Valeska Huber, "Introduction: Global Histories of Social Planning," *Journal of Contemporary History* 52, no. 1 (2017): 6–10; Christopher Bonneuil, "Development as Experiment: Science and State-Building in Late Colonial and Postcolonial Africa, 1930–1970," *Osiris* 15 (2000): 258–81; Eric Worby, "'Discipline without Oppression': Sequence, Timing, and Marginality in Southern Rhodesia's Post-War Development Scheme," *Journal of African History* 41, no. 1 (2000): 102–4; Samuël Coghe, "Reordering Colonial Society: Model Villages and Social Planning in Rural Angola, 1920–45," *Journal of Contemporary History* 52, no. 1 (2017): 28–30, 34–37.

46. The Forced Labour Convention's definition of forced labor as 'all work or service, which is exacted from any person under the menace of any penalty and for which the said person has not offered himself voluntarily' served the ILO well. It was general enough to cover everything from slavery and debt bondage to *corvée* practices and, potentially, the sexual exploitation of women and children: Sandrine Kott and Joel Golb, "The Forced Labor Issue between Human and Social Rights, 1947–1957," *Humanity* 3, no. 3 (2012): 321–23.

47. Miguel Bandeira Jerónimo and José Pedro Monteiro, "The Inventors of Human Rights in Africa: Portugal, Late Colonialism, and the UN Human Rights Regime," in *Decolonization, Self Determination, and the Rise of Global Human Rights Politics*, ed. A. Dirk Moses, Marco Duranti, and Roland Burke (Cambridge, UK: Cambridge University Press, 2020), 294–96.

48. Kott and Golb, "Forced Labor Issue," 328–30; Daughton, "ILO Expertise," 85–97.

49. Meredith Terretta and Benjamin N. Lawrance, "'Sons of the Soil,' Cause Lawyers, the Togo-Cameroun Mandates, and the Origins of Decolonization," *American Historical Review* 124, no. 5 (2019): 1709–14; Achille Mbembe, *La naissance du maquis dans le Sud-Cameroun (1920–1960)* (Paris: Karthala, 1996), 226–28.

50. Joseph McQuade, "Beyond an Imperial Foreign Policy? India at the League of Nations, 1919–1946," *Journal of Imperial & Commonwealth History* 48, no. 2 (2020): 272, 276.

51. McQuade, "Beyond an Imperial," 282–86.

52. Daughton, "ILO Expertise," 93–95.

53. Barbara M. Cooper, *Marriage in Maradi: Gender and Culture in a Hausa Society in Niger, 1900–1989* (Oxford: James Currey, 1997), 176–77; for longer-term context: Durba Ghosh, "Gender and Colonialism: Expansion or Marginalization?" *Historical Journal* 47, no. 3 (September 2004): 737–55.

54. Rose Ndengue, "Social Imaginaries in Tension? The Women of Cameroon's Battle for Equal Rights under French Rule at the Turn of the 1940s–50s," in *Black*

French Women and the Struggle for Equality, 1848-2016, ed. Félix Germain and Silvane Larcher (Lincoln: University of Nebraska Press, 2018), 237-54.

55. Cooper, "Afterword," 482; Guy Fiti Sinclair, *To Reform the World: International Organizations and the Making of Modern States* (Oxford: Oxford University Press, 2017), 97-102.

56. Eileen Boris, *Making the Woman Worker: Precarious Labor and the Fight for Global Standards, 1919-2019* (New York: Oxford University Press, 2019), 78-79, 90-94.

57. Cooper, "Afterword," 473-92, at 477; Kott and Golb, "Forced Labor Issue," 322-29; Ndengue, "Social Imaginaries in Tension?" 240-48.

58. Nicholas J. White, "Thinking Outside 'the Box': Decolonization and Containerization," in *Shipping and Globalization in the Post-War Era*, ed. Niels P. Petersson, Stig Tenold, and Nicholas J. White (Basingstoke, UK: Palgrave Macmillan, 2019), 80; Frederick Cooper, *Decolonization and African Society: The Labor Question in French and British Africa* (Cambridge, UK: Cambridge University Press, 1996), 280-92, 324-36.

59. Gerard McCann, "Possibility and Peril: Trade Unionism, African Cold War, and the Global Strands of Kenyan Decolonization," *Journal of Social History* 53, no. 2 (2019): 351-52, 356-63. The ICFTU emerged in 1949 following its split from the WFTU, which had been established four years earlier at the end of World War II. A trade unionist and future president, Guinea's Sékou Touré organized UGTAN over the winter of 1956-1957.

60. Leslie James, "'Essential Things such as Typewriters': Development Discourse, Trade Union Expertise, and the Dialogues of Decolonization between the Caribbean and West Africa," *Journal of Social History* 53, no. 2 (2019): 382-89.

61. Cooper, *Decolonization and African Society*, 336-48.

62. Barbara Castle papers, BLO, MS Castle 8: Diary/notebook of visit to Southern Rhodesia and Nyasaland, Jan.-Feb. 1958, fo. 12: "ANC 21/1/58"; MS Castle 9: Diary/notebook of visit to Northern Rhodesia and Nyasaland, Jan.-Feb. 1958, fos. 2-4.

63. Castle papers, MS Castle 9, Jan.-Feb. 1958, fos. 21-22.

64. L. J. Butler, *Copper Empire: Mining and the Colonial State in Northern Rhodesia, c. 1930-1964* (Basingstoke, UK: Palgrave Macmillan, 2007), 260-73; Miles Larmer, "Unrealistic Expectations? Zambia's Mineworkers from Independence to the One-Party State, 1964-1972," *Journal of Historical Sociology* 18, no. 4 (2005): 318-23.

65. Sharon Stichter, *Migrant Labour in Kenya: Capitalism and African Response, 1895-1975* (London: Longman, 1982), 27-28, cited in Andreas Eckert, "Regulating the Social: Social Security, Social Welfare and the State in Late Colonial Tanzania," *Journal of African History* 45, no. 3 (2004): 473.

66. Eckert, "Regulating the Social," 472.

67. Jack Lord, "Child Labour in the Gold Coast: The Economics of Work, Education, and the Family in Late-Colonial African Childhoods, c. 1940-57," *Journal of the History of Childhood and Youth* 4, no. 1 (2011): 88-115.

68. The League's information-gathering was conducted in the shadow of its efforts to establish global prohibitions against human trafficking for prostitution: Magaly Rodrìguez García, "The League of Nations and the Moral Recruitment of Women," *International Review of Social History* 57 (2012): 97-128; Barbara Metzger, "Towards

an International Human Rights Regime during the Inter-War Years: The League of Nations Combat of Traffic in Women and Children," in *Beyond Sovereignty: Britain, Empire and Transnationalism, c.1880–1950*, ed. Kevin Grant, Philippa Levine, and Frank Trentmann (Basingstoke, UK: Palgrave Macmillan: 2007), 54–79.

69. Rhian Keyse, "Imperial, International, and Local Responses to Early and Forced Marriage in British Colonial Africa, c. 1920–1962," University of Exeter PhD, 2019, 52–53, 83, 267.

70. Keyse, "Imperial, International," 115–16.

71. Keyse, "Imperial, International," 200–3; idem, "'Hidden Motives'? African Women, Forced Marriage and Knowledge Production at the United Nations, 1950–1962," *Journal of Contemporary History* 57, no. 2 (2022): 268–92.

72. Sarah C. Dunstan, "'Une Negre de drame': Jane Vialle and the Politics of Representation in Colonial Reform, 1945–1953," *Journal of Contemporary History* 55, no. 3 (2020): 645–65.

73. Eckert, "Regulating the Social," 473–75; Cooper, *Decolonization and African Society*, 323–30.

74. Miguel Bandeira Jerónimo and José Pedro Monteiro, "Colonial Labour Internationalized: Portugal and the Decolonization Momentum (1945–1975)," *International History Review*, 42, no. 3 (2020): 485–90.

75. Tunisia's leading trade union, the Union Générale des Travailleurs Tunisiens (UGTT), and its FLN-supporting Algerian cousin, the Union Générale des Travailleurs Algériens (UGTA), exemplified the trend. Each worked with rival communist and noncommunist international trade union confederations, manipulating them to serve their North African decolonization struggles: see Mathilde von Bülow, "Beyond the Cold War: American Labor, Algeria's Independence Struggle, and the Rise of the Third World (1954–62)," *Journal of Social History* 53, no. 2 (2019): 356–75.

76. British NGOs figured prominently here: Matthew Hilton, "International Aid and Development NGOs in Britain and Human Rights since 1945," *Humanity* 3, no. 3 (2012): 451, 459–62.

77. Bandeira Jerónimo and Monteiro, "Colonial Labour Internationalized," 485–504.

78. Bandeira Jerónimo and Monteiro, "Colonial Labour Internationalized," 485–504.

79. Aharon de Grassi, "Rethinking the 1961 Baixa de Kassanje Revolt: Towards a Relational Geo-History of Angola," *Mulemba: Revista Angolana de Ciências Sociais* (2015): 58–62, 68–73; João Sicato Kandjo, "A influência da Baixa de Kasanji na independência de Angola," *Mulemba; Revista Angolana de Ciências* 2, no. 1 (2020): 148–66; Inge Brinkman, "'The Time of the Leaflet': Pamphlets and Political Communication in the UPA (Northern Angola around 1961)," *Africa* 85, no. 2 (2015): 221–25.

80. Kristen Stromberg Childers, "The Evolution of the Welfare State: Social Rights and the Nationalization of Welfare in France, 1880–1947," *French Politics, Culture, and Society* 24, no. 2 (2006): 131–35, and for the longer-term impact of the two World Wars: Paul V. Dutton, *Origins of the French Welfare State: The Struggle for Social Reform in France, 1914–1947* (Cambridge, UK: Cambridge University Press, 2002).

81. Alex Marshall, "Imperial Nostalgia, the Liberal Lie, and the Perils of Postmodern Counterinsurgency," *Small Wars & Insurgencies* 21, no. 2 (2010): 244–46; Jane

Burbank and Frederick Cooper, *Empires in World History: Power and the Politics of Difference* (Princeton, NJ: Princeton University Press, 2010), 413. As Burbank and Cooper put it, 'The colonialism that collapsed in Africa and Asia in the 1950s and 1960s was not the conservative variant of the interwar decades but a colonialism that was interventionist, reformist, and accordingly open to challenge.'

82. Roland Burke, "Some Rights Are More Equal than Others: The Third World and the Transformation of Economic and Social Rights," *Humanity* 3, no. 3 (2012): 427–30.

83. Burbank and Cooper, *Empires in World History*, 420.

84. Patricia Owens, *Economy of Force: Counterinsurgency and the Historical Rise of the Social* (Cambridge, UK: Cambridge University Press, 2015).

85. Frederick Cooper, *Citizenship between Empire and Nation: Rethinking France and French Africa, 1945–1960* (Princeton, NJ: Princeton University Press, 2014), 52–53, 178–86.

86. Alison Bashford, *Global Population: History, Geopolitics, and Life on Earth* (New York: Columbia University Press, 2014), 319–21, 330–34.

87. Rebekah Lee, *Health, Healing and Illness in African History* (London: Bloomsbury, 2021), 57–66.

88. Miguel Bandeira Jerónimo and António Costa Pinto, eds., *The Ends of European Empires: Cases and Comparisons* (Basingstoke, UK: Palgrave Macmillan, 2017), Part I: "Competing Developments: The Idioms of Reform and Resistance."

89. Subir Sinha, "Lineages of the Developmental State: Transnationality and Village India, 1900–1965," *Comparative Studies in Society and History* 50, no. 1 (2008): 60–71.

90. Sundha Pahuja, *Decolonising International Law: Development, Economic Growth and the Politics of Universality* (Cambridge, UK: Cambridge University Press, 2013), 45–46, 67–83; Balakrishnan Rajagopal, "Counter-Hegemonic International Law: Rethinking Human Rights and Development as a Third World Strategy," *Third World Quarterly* 27, no. 5 (2006): 767–83.

91. Justin Willis, Gabrielle Lynch, and Nic Cheeseman, "Voting, Nationhood, and Citizenship in Late-Colonial Africa," *Historical Journal* 61, no. 4 (2018): 1134.

92. Bridget L. Coggins, "Rebel Diplomacy: Theorizing Violent Non-State Actors' Use of Talk," in *Rebel Governance in Civil War*, ed. Ana Arjona, Nelson Kasfir, and Zachariah Mampilly (Cambridge, UK: Cambridge University Press, 2015), 103–4.

93. Burke, "Some Rights," 428.

94. Boris, *Making the Woman Worker*, 96–101.

95. Jan Eckel, "Human Rights and Decolonization: New Perspectives and Open Questions," *Humanity* 1, no. 1 (Fall 2010): 113, 119, 129; Burke, "Some Rights," 436–37; Huw Bennett, *Fighting the Mau Mau: The British Army and Counter-Insurgency in the Kenya Emergency* (Cambridge, UK: Cambridge University Press, 2012), 61–65.

96. Mark Philip Bradley, *The World Reimagined: Americans and Human Rights in the Twentieth Century* (New York: Cambridge University Press, 2016), 3–8.

97. New legislative instruments included the 1946 Nuremberg Principles, the 1948 Convention on the prevention and punishment of the crime of genocide, the 1949 Fourth Geneva Convention relating to the protection of civilian persons in time of war, the 1951 Refugee Convention, and the 1954 Convention relating to the status of

stateless persons. Articles within the 1945 UN Charter also stipulated rights obligations for member states domestically and internationally.

98. Allida Black, "Are Women 'Human'? The UN and the Struggle to Recognize Women's Rights as Human Rights," in *The Human Rights Revolution: An International History*, ed. Akira Iriye, Petra Goedde, and William D. Hitchcock (New York: Oxford University Press, 2012), 133–55; Bradley, *World Reimagined*, 62–63, 82–88; Imaobong D. Umoren, *Race Women Internationalists: Activist Intellectuals and Global Freedom Struggles* (Berkeley: University of California Press, 2018), 82–83.

99. Tara Zahra, *The Lost Children: Reconstructing Europe's Families after World War II* (Cambridge, MA: Harvard University Press, 2011), 118–19; Bronwen Manby, "Trends in Citizenship Law and Politics in Africa since the Colonial Era," in *Routledge Handbook of Global Citizenship Studies*, ed. Engin F. Isin and Peter Nyers (London: Routledge, 2014), 173.

100. Tara Zahra, "'The Psychological Marshall Plan': Displacement, Gender, and Human Rights after World War II," *Central European History* 44, no. 1 (2011): 37–40.

101. Emily Baughan, *Saving the Children: Humanitarianism, Internationalism, and Empire* (Berkeley: University of California Press, 2022), 140–44, 153–55, 160–62; Jennifer Johnson, "The Limits of Humanitarianism: Decolonization, the French Red Cross, and the Algerian War," in *Decolonization, Self Determination, and the Rise of Global Human Rights Politics*, ed. A. Dirk Moses, Marco Duranti, and Roland Burke (Cambridge, UK: Cambridge University Press, 2020), 99–108.

102. Stuart Ward, *Untied Kingdom: A Global History of the End of Britain* (Cambridge, UK: Cambridge University Press, 2023), 202–6, for thoughtful analysis of these contradictions.

103. Lydia Walker, "Decolonization in the 1960s: On Legitimate and Illegitimate Nationalist Claims-Making," *Past & Present* 242 (February 2019): 237–40; Brad Simpson, "The Biafran Secession and the Limits of Self-Determination," *Journal of Genocide Research* 16, no. 2–3 (2014): 338–40.

104. Bradley, *World Reimagined*, 6–8, 62–67, 86. Chapter XI of the UN Charter, which stipulated terms for the international supervision of non-self-governing territories, caused similar controversy: Sinclair, *To Reform the World*, 125–28.

105. Brooke Coe, "Sovereignty Regimes and the Norm of Noninterference in the Global South: Regional and Temporal Variation," *Global Governance* 21 (2015): 275–98.

106. Cooper, "Afterword," 478.

107. Bradley, *World Reimagined*, 114; Ward, *Untied Kingdom*, 208–10; TNA, DO 35/3753, UNGA 1947, 2nd session, Dominions Office notes: "Question of Treatment of Indians by South Africa, 1947–8." The matter would also be raised at subsequent UN General Assembly sessions of the 1950s; see DO 35/6972–6974.

108. Bradley, *World Reimagined*, 54–5.

109. TNA, FO 371/63567, F10493/8800/85, High Commissioner, New Delhi, to Cabinet Office, July 30, 1947. The Indian Government also intimated to its British counterpart that the path to financial cooperation between them might be eased if Britain endorsed India's opposition to a continuing Dutch presence in Indonesia: FO 371/63568, Board of Trade memo, "India and Indonesia," September 1, 1947.

110. Sunil Amrith, "Reconstructing the 'Plural Society': Asian Migration between Empire and Nation, 1940–1948," *Past & Present* 210, Supplement 6 (2011): 254–56.

111. TNA, FO 371/63568, F12253/8800/85, Saigon High Commission to FO, August 18, 1947, F12356/8800/85, Hanoi Consular report, August 18, 1947, F12254/8800/85, Batavia Consulate to FO, August 26, 1947, F12258/8800/85, Beira Consulate to FO, August 18, 1947. An estimated thousand visitors attended celebrations of Pakistan and Indian independence in Saigon's principal mosques and Hindu temples. In East Sumatra, separate celebrations of Indian and Pakistan independence were organized by the island's South Asian expatriate communities. South Asian religious 'clubs' in the Mozambican port of Beira held similar celebrations.

112. Christy Thornton, "A Mexican International Economic Order? Tracing the Hidden Roots of the Charter of Economic Rights and Duties of States," *Humanity* 9, no. 3 (2018): 392–98; idem, *Revolution in Development: Mexico and the Governance of the Global Economy* (Berkeley: University of California Press, 2021), 18–24.

113. Marc Opper, *People's Wars in China, Malaya, and Vietnam* (Ann Arbor: University of Michigan Press, 2020), 174–77. It is important to note that the Nine Point program did not last long. Identified with former MCP leader (and British double-agent) Lai Teck, the program was repudiated by the new MCP leadership under Chin Peng, which called for revolutionary war in their defining March 1948 statement on 'The Present Situation and the Party's Political Line'.

114. Bonny Ibhawoh, "Seeking the Political Kingdom: Universal Human Rights and the Anti-Colonial Movement in Africa," in *Decolonization, Self Determination, and the Rise of Global Human Rights Politics*, ed. A. Dirk Moses, Marco Duranti, and Roland Burke (Cambridge, UK: Cambridge University Press, 2020), 37.

115. Eckel, "Human Rights and Decolonization," 111–35, at 125–27.

116. Burke, "Some Rights," 428.

117. Jeremy Kuzmarov, "Modernizing Repression: Police Training, Political Violence, and Nation-Building in the 'American Century,'" *Diplomatic History* 33, no. 2 (2009): 195–204, 211–14; Alfred W. McCoy, "Torture in the Crucible of Counterinsurgency," in *Iraq and the Lessons of Vietnam: Or, How Not to Learn from the Past*, ed. Lloyd C. Gardner and Marilyn B. Young (New York: New Press, 2007), 232–41, 244–51.

118. For typologies of such coups, from the neocolonial to the anticolonial, see Abdel Razzaq Takriti, "Colonial Coups and the War on Popular Sovereignty," *American Historical Review* 124, no. 3 (2019): 880–83.

119. Roland Burke, "From Individual Rights to National Development: The First UN International Conference on Human Rights, Tehran, 1968," *Journal of World History* 19, no. 3 (2008): 275–83.

120. Boris, *Making the Woman Worker*, 94, 118–19; Burke, "From Individual Rights," 284–87, 294–96.

121. Samuel Moyn, "The Political Origins of Global Justice," in *The Worlds of American Intellectual History*, ed. Joel Isaac et al. (Oxford: Oxford University Press, 2016), 134–40.

122. Burke, "Some Rights," 427–28.

123. An issue addressed by political theorist Annelien de Dijn, *Freedom: An Unruly History* (Cambridge, MA: Harvard University Press, 2020), especially part III.

124. Simpson, "Biafran Secession," 337–38.

125. The reservation of certain socioeconomic rights to ethnic Malays within the 1957 Malayan constitution reveals the pitfalls: Joseph M. Fernando, "Special Rights in the Malaysian Constitution and the Framers' Dilemma, 1956–57," *Journal of Imperial & Commonwealth History* 43, no. 3 (2015): 535–56.

126. M. Rafiqul Islam, "Secessionist Self-Determination: Some Lessons from Katanga, Biafra and Bangladesh," *Journal of Peace Research* 22, no. 3 (1985): 211–13.

127. Simpson, "Biafran Secession," 339, 347.

Chapter Four: Greater War and Decolonization's First Global Wave

1. TNA, FO 141/511/14086, Egyptian Society telegram, January 3, 1922. The message was one of several sent by Egyptian students, émigrés and expatriate merchants to Safiya Zaghloul over the winter of 1921–1922.

2. TNA, FO 141/511/14086, First Secretary, Cairo, to Tahar el Lozy Bey, December 27, 1921. Safiya Zaghloul's threatening potential was enhanced by her familial connections. She was the daughter of a revered public official, Mustafa Pasha Fahmy.

3. TNA, FO 141/511/14086, "The Appeal of the Leader's Wife," February 4, 1922.

4. TNA, FO 141/511/14086, Safiya Zaghloul letter to her husband, February 3, 1922.

5. Beth Baron has argued that in post-war Egypt women came to symbolize an embattled nation that was itself conceptualized in gendered terms as a woman despoiled by European dominance, see her "The Construction of National Honour in Egypt," *Gender and History* 5, no. 2 (1993): 245.

6. TNA, FO 608/214 British Delegation to Paris Peace Congress, 1919, Africa files: Egypt 1919. no. 14069, Intelligence GHQ to Colonel C. E. Dansey, IG734, June 30, 1919; FO 141/511/14086, Cairo tel. 284, A. Mackintosh (for Director-General of Public Security) letter to Foreign Office, October 8, 1922. Safiya Zaghloul returned to Egypt in late July 1923, crowds of Wafd supporters turning out to greet her on disembarkation at Alexandria and, later, after her train journey to Cairo. See TNA, FO 141/511/14086, Lord Lloyd to Foreign Secretary, Sir Austen Chamberlain, July 23, 1923.

7. Lanver Mak, *The British in Egypt: Community, Crime and Crises, 1882–1922* (London: I. B. Tauris, 2012), 214–19; Ellis Goldberg, "Peasants in Revolt—Egypt 1919," *International Journal of Middle East Studies* 24 (1992): 261–80; James Kitchen, "Violence in Defence of Empire: The British Army and the 1919 Egyptian Revolution," *Journal of Modern European History* 13, no. 2 (2015): 249–67.

8. Heather Streets-Salter, "International and Global Anti-Colonial Movements," in *World Histories from Below: Disruption and Dissent, 1750 to the Present*, 2nd ed., ed. Antoinette Burton and Tony Ballantyne (London: Bloomsbury, 2022), 47–65. Focusing on the efforts made by German Orientalists to stimulate Indian revolution before and during World War I, Kris Manjapra makes clear that these deeper transnational connections did not imply genuine sympathy for Indian anticolonialism; see Kris K. Manjapra, "The Illusions of Encounter: Muslim 'Minds' and Hindu Revolutionaries in First World War Germany and After," *Journal of Global History* 1, no. 3 (2006): 363–82, at 364.

9. MAE, série K: Afrique 1918–40, sous-série: Affaires Musulmanes vol. 2, dossier général: Questions réligieuses/panislamisme 1920–2, tel. 3, Henri Gaillard, Ministre de France en Egypte to Georges Leygues, PM and Foreign Minister, January 10, 1921: "Agitation islamique et propagande étrangère". For a longer-term perspective on Cairo universities' transnational connections, see Valeska Huber, "Educational Mobility and Globalisation: Universities in Cairo between Competition and Standardisation, 1900–1950," in *A Global Middle East: Mobility, Materiality and Culture in the Modern Age, 1880–1940*, ed. Cyrus Schayegh, Avner Wishnitzer, and Liat Kozma (London: Bloomsbury, 2014), 81–108.

10. Elizabeth Thompson, *Justice Interrupted: The Struggle for Constitutional Government in the Middle East* (Cambridge, MA: Harvard University Press, 2013), 154–57, for the 1919 revolution's formative influence on Hasan al-Banna's Muslim Brotherhood, Egypt's foremost exponent of political Islam.

11. Eric D. Weitz, "From the Vienna to the Paris System: International Politics and the Entangled Histories of Human Rights, Forced Deportations, and Civilizing Missions," *American Historical Review* 113, no. 5 (2008): 1326–33.

12. Historians of humanitarianism highlight liberal internationalism's racial and global blindspots: Matthew Hilton, Emily Baughan, Eleanor Davey, Bronwen Everill, Kevin O'Sullivan, and Tahila Sasson, "History and Humanitarianism: A Conversation," *Past and Present* 241, no. 1 (2018): 1–12; Robert D. Venosa, "Liberal Internationalism, Decolonization, and International Accountability at the United Nations: The British Dilemma," *Journal of Contemporary History* 57, no. 2 (2022): 242–57.

13. Martin Thomas, *Violence and Colonial Order: Police, Workers, and Protest in the European Colonial Empires, 1918–1940* (Cambridge, UK: Cambridge University Press, 2012), chapters 1–2; Michelle Gordon, *Extreme Violence and the "British Way": Colonial Warfare in Perak, Sierra Leone and Sudan* (London: Bloomsbury, 2020).

14. Maartje Abbenhuis, *An Age of Neutrals: Great Power Politics, 1815–1914* (Cambridge, UK: Cambridge University Press, 2014), 239–42; T. G. Otte, "Introduction: British World Power and the White Queen's Memory," in *British World Policy and the Projection of Global Power, c. 1830–1960*, ed. T. G. Otte (Cambridge, UK: Cambridge University Press, 2019), 1–7.

15. Michelle Moyd, "Centring a Sideshow: Local Experiences of the First World War in Africa," *First World War Studies* 7, no. 2 (2016): 111–15.

16. As evidenced in the chapter contributions to Andrew Tait Jarboe and Robert S. Fogarty, eds., *Empires in World War I: Shifting Frontiers and Imperial Dynamics in a Global Conflict* (London: Bloomsbury, 2020). The exception here is Belgium, which, even prior to occupation, chose not to recruit large numbers of Congolese to fight or work in Europe for fear of potential destabilization in the Belgian Congo: Matthew G. Stanard, "Digging-in: The Great War and the Roots of Belgian Empire," in Jarboe and Fogarty, *Empires in World War I*, 26.

17. Over the longer term, from the 1800s to the 1920s, the largest regional movement of colonial migrants remained that of South Asian laborers across the Bay of Bengal, principally to Malaya, Ceylon, and Burma; see Sunil Amrith, *Crossing the Bay of Bengal: The Furies of Nature and the Fortunes of Migrants* (Cambridge, MA: Harvard University Press, 2013). Domestic labor shortages caused by the war also

triggered huge internal migrations of nonwhite workers, perhaps most notably so in the 'Great Migration' of over 400,000 African-Americans from southern states to industrial centers in the northern United States between 1916 and 1918: Michael A. Gomez, *Reversing Sail: A History of the African Diaspora*, 2nd edition (Cambridge, UK: Cambridge University Press, 2020), 190.

18. Rebekah Lee, *Health, Healing and Illness in African History* (London: Bloomsbury, 2021), 66–67.

19. David Stevenson, *Armaments and the Coming of War: Europe, 1904–1914* (Oxford: Oxford University Press, 1996), reprint 2004, 409; Prasenjit Duara, "The Discourse of Civilization and Pan-Asianism," *Journal of World History* 12 (2001): 99–130, also cited in Carolien Stolte and Harald Fischer-Tiné, "Imagining Asia in India: Nationalism and Internationalism (ca. 1905–1940)," *Comparative Studies in Society & History* 54, no. 1 (2012): 65–92, at 66–67; see the essays in parts I and II of Santanu Das, ed., *Race, Empire, and First World War Writing* (Cambridge, UK: Cambridge University Press, 2011) and the chapter contributions in parts II and III of Jarboe and Fogarty, *Empires in World War I*.

20. Dónal Hassett, "Colonialism and Contested Cultures of Victory in the French Empire of the 1920s," *Journal of Contemporary History* 54, no. 4 (2019): 769–74.

21. Tyler Stovall, "The Color Line behind the Lines: Racial Violence in France during the First World War," *American Historical Review* 103, no. 3 (1998): 739–69; Michelle Moyd, "Color Lines, Front Lines: The First World War from the South," *Radical History Review* 131 (May 2018): 13–35, at 14–16. Moyd notes that some 2,350,000 African troops and laborers were mobilized, while India supplied 1.4 million soldiers and workers and China a further 140,000 laborers. On the largest cohort of colonial troops—Indian Army soldiers—see Gajendra Singh, *The Testimonies of Indian Soldiers and the Two World Wars: Between Self and Sepoy* (London: Bloomsbury, 2014), especially chapter 2; Santanu Das, *India, Empire, and First World War Culture: Writing, Images, and Songs* (Cambridge, UK: Cambridge University Press, 2018), parts I and II. Focused on their destabilizing potential, these global movements of colonized people fed obsessive concern with communist influence, particularly among colonial workers, troops and, later, university students in both the French and British interwar empires; see MAE, PA-AP 216, Augustin Bernard papers, file 15, Procès-verbaux des séances du Commission interministérielle des affaires musulmanes (CIAM), 1929–36, CIAM, 178th Meeting, procès-verbal, October 30, 1934 and annex "Rapport du Lieutenant-Colonel de Goislard de Monsabert sur la propagande révolutionnaire dans les Unités Nord-Africaines stationnées en France"; CIAM sub-committee paper, "Les conditions du séjour à Paris des étudiants musulmans nord-africains," n.d. February 1935; Clifford Rosenberg, *Policing Paris: The Origins of Modern Immigration Control between the Wars* (Ithaca, NY: Cornell University Press, 2006); TNA, MI5 papers, KV 3/32, Report of the International Colonial Conference, June 11 and 12, 1925; John Fisher, "The Interdepartmental Committee on Eastern Unrest and British Responses to Bolshevik and Other Intrigues against the Empire during the 1920s," *Journal of Asian History* 34, no. 1 (2000): 1–34.

22. Tyler Stovall, "Colour-Blind France? Colonial Workers during the First World War," *Race and Class* 35, no. 2 (1993): 35–55; idem, "Love, Labor, and Race: Colonial Men and White Women in France during the Great War," in *French Civilization and*

Its Discontents: Orientalism, Colonialism, Race, ed. Tyler Stovall and Georges van den Abbeele (Lanham, MD: Lexington, 2003), 297–314.

23. For an overview, see the essays in Jonathan Krause, ed., *The Greater War: Other Combatants and Other Fronts, 1914–1918* (Basingstoke, UK: Palgrave Macmillan, 2014). Revealing case studies are Gilbert Meynier, "Algerians in the French Army, 1914–1918: From Military Integration to the Dawn of Algerian Patriotism," and Salavat M. Iskhalov, "Turkic Muslims in the Russian Army: From the Beginning of the First World War to the Revolution of 1917," both in *Combatants of Muslim Origin in European Armies in the Twentieth Century,* ed. Xavier Bougarel, Raphaëlle Branche, and Cloé Drieu (London: Bloomsbury, 2018).

24. Andrew Tait Jarboe and Robert S. Fogarty, "Introduction: An Imperial Turn in First World War Studies," in Jarboe and Fogarty, *Empires in World War I*, clauses quoted from 1 and 8.

25. Carl Strikwerda, "World War I in the History of Globalization," *Historical Reflections* 42, no. 3 (Winter 2016): 116–20. On the fiscal consequences, and borrowing especially, see Martin Horn, *Britain, France, and the Financing of the First World War* (Montreal: McGill-Queen's University Press, 2002), 79–92, 101–4.

26. Jayeeta Sharma, "Food and Empire," in *The Oxford Handbook of Food History,* ed. Jeffrey M. Pilcher (Oxford: Oxford University Press, 2012), online publication.

27. Jonathan Krause, "Islam and Anticolonial Rebellion in North and West Africa, 1914–1918," *Historical Journal* 64, no. 3 (2020): 674–95.

28. Jane Burbank and Frederick Cooper, "Empires after 1919: Old, New, Transformed," *International Affairs* 95, no. 1 (2019): 71, 85.

29. Richard S. Fogarty, "Gender and Race," in *Gender and the Great War,* ed. Susan R. Grayzel and Tammy M. Proctor (Oxford: Oxford University Press, 2017), 67–73. Emma Hanna captures these polyglot colonial encounters in "Musical Entertainment and the British Empire, 1914–1918," in *The Great War and the British Empire: Culture and Society,* ed. Michael Walsh and Andrekos Varnava (Abingdon, UK: Routledge, 2017), 74.

30. A nod to British Foreign Secretary Lord Curzon's inelegant phrase: L. V. Smith, *Sovereignty at the Paris Peace Conference of 1919* (Oxford: Oxford University Press, 2018), 143, 165.

31. B. Venkat Mani, "Anti-Colonial Nationalism and Cosmopolitan 'Standard Time': Lala Har Dayal's *Forty-Four Months in Germany and Turkey* (1920)," in *German Colonialism Revisited: African, Asian, and Oceanic Experiences,* ed. Nina Berman, Klaus Mühlhahn, and Patrice Nganang (Ann Arbor: University of Michigan Press, 2014), 203–5; Jennifer Jenkins, Heike Liebau, and Larissa Schmid, "Transnationalism and Insurrection: Independence Committees, Anti-Colonial Networks, and Germany's Global War," *Journal of Global History* 15, no. 1 (2020): 61–79; Manjapra, "Illusions of Encounter," 363–82; Ku Daeyeol, *Korea, 1905–1945: From Japanese Colonialism to Liberation and Independence* (Amsterdam: Amsterdam University Press, 2022), 107–10.

32. Melanie Tanielian, "Politics of Wartime Relief in Ottoman Beirut (1914–1918)," *First World War Studies* 5, no. 1 (2014): 69–82. The Ottoman-governed provinces of Greater Syria suffered particularly high mortality and morbidity rates during the war. Elizabeth Thompson cites estimates ranging between a low of 12 per cent wartime

deaths in a population of between three and four million and a high of 18 per cent: Elizabeth Thompson, *Colonial Citizens: Republican Rights, Paternal Privilege, and Gender in French Syria and Lebanon* (New York: Columbia University Press, 1999), 23; Laura Robson also draws on these figures in her *States of Separation: Transfer, Partition, and the Making of the Modern Middle East* (Berkeley: University of California Press, 2017), 35 n.2. For hardship on Ottoman 'home fronts' more generally, see Yiğit Akın, *When the War Came Home: The Ottomans' Great War and the Devastation of an Empire* (Stanford, CA: Stanford University Press, 2018).

33. G. John Ikenberry, "The End of Liberal International Order?" *International Affairs* 94, no. 1 (2018): 11–12. For a thoughtful reassessment of liberal internationalism's imperial characteristics, see Ali Parchami, "Imperial Projections and Crisis: The Liberal International Order as a Pseudo-Empire," *Journal of Imperial & Commonwealth History* 47, no. 5 (2019): 1044–61.

34. Dominic Sachsenaiser, "Alternative Visions of World Order in the Aftermath of World War I: Global Perspectives on Chinese Approaches," in *Competing Visions of World Order: Global Moments and Movements, 1880s–1930s*, ed. Sebastien Conrad and Dominic Sachsenmaier (Basingstoke, UK: Palgrave Macmillan, 2007), 157–69; Francis Nicosia, *Nazi Germany and the Arab World* (Cambridge, UK: Cambridge University Press, 2015), 46–54, 72–81; Georgi M. Derluguian, "Mozambique in the 1980s: Periphery Goes Postmodern," in *The War Within: New Perspectives on the Civil War in Mozambique, 1976–1992*, ed. Eric Morier-Genoud, Michel Cahen, and Domingos M. do Rosário (Woodbridge, UK: James Currey, 2018), 208.

35. Quinn Slobodian, *The Globalists: The End of Empire and the Birth of Neoliberalism* (Cambridge, MA: Harvard University Press, 2018), 27–28.

36. Robert Gerwarth and Erez Manela, "The Great War as a Global War: Imperial Conflict and the Reconfiguration of World Order, 1911–1923," *Diplomatic History* 38, no. 4 (2014): 798–800.

37. Jonathan Wyrtzen, *Worldmaking in the Long Great War: How Local and Colonial Struggles Shaped the Modern Middle East* (New York: Columbia University Press, 2022), 1–26. My thanks to Jonathan for sharing his ideas with me before the publication of this book.

38. Donald Bloxham, *The Great Game of Genocide: Imperialism, Nationalism, and the Destruction of the Ottoman Armenians* (Oxford: Oxford University Press, 2005), especially part I; Robson, *States of Separation*, 35–63; G. T. Mavrogrdatis, *Stillborn Republic: Social Coalitions and Party Strategies in Greece, 1922–36* (Berkeley: University of California Press, 1922), chapter 1; Peter Gatrell, *The Making of the Modern Refugee* (Oxford: Oxford University Press, 2013), 62–67; Eric D. Weitz, "Self-Determination: How a German Enlightenment Idea Became the Slogan of National Liberation and a Human Right," *American Historical Review* 20, no. 2 (2015): 487.

39. Erez Manela, *The Wilsonian Moment: Self Determination and the International Origins of Anticolonial Nationalism* (New York: Oxford University Press, 2007); Erez Manela, "Dawn of a New Era: The 'Wilsonian Moment' in Colonial Contexts and the Transformation of World Order, 1917–1920," in Conrad and Sachsenmaier, *Competing Visions of World Order*, 121–49; Andrew Arsan, "The Patriarch, the Amir and the Patriots: Civilization and Self-Determination at the Paris Peace

Conference," in *The First World War and Its Aftermath: The Shaping of the Modern Middle East*, ed. T. G. Fraser (London: Gingko Library, 2015), 127–46.

40. Manela, "Dawn of a New Era," 140–42, quote at 123.

41. Erez Manela, "Global Anti-Imperialism in the Age of Wilson," in *Empire's Twin: U.S. Anti-Imperialism from the Founding Era to the Age of Terrorism*, ed. Ian Tyrrell and Jay Sexton (Ithaca, NY: Cornell University Press, 2015), 142–51; Smith, *Sovereignty at the Paris Peace Conference*, 5–6, 35; for the racialized and gendered dimensions of Wilsonian thought, see Lloyd E. Ambrosius, *Woodrow Wilson and American Internationalism* (Cambridge, UK: Cambridge University Press, 2017), 56–61, 107–12; Neil Smith, *American Empire: Roosevelt's Geographer and the Prelude to Globalization* (Berkeley: University of California Press, 2004), 140–42, 176–78.

42. Erez Manela, "Averting Anarchy: Rethinking the Logic of Wilsonianism," paper at University of Glasgow conference *Visions of Global Order, 1919: Peace, Law and Security after the First World War*, May 29, 2019; idem, "Dawn of a New Era," 126–29.

43. For the divisions between communist and noncommunist francophone pan-Africanists after these Paris meetings, see Gary Wilder, "Panafricanism and the Republican Political Sphere," in *The Color of Liberty: Histories of Race in France*, ed. Sue Peabody and Tyler Stovall (Durham, NC: Duke University Press, 2003), 240–42.

44. MAE, série K: Afrique 1918–40, sous-série: Affaires Musulmanes, vol. 23: Agitateurs musulmans—propagande bolsheviste, mo. 413, Sous Direction d'Afrique, Maurice Herbette, Brussels Ambassador to Aristide Briand, April 4, 1927; for background and legacies, see Fredrik Petersson, *Willi Münzenberg, the League against Imperialism, and the Comintern, 1925–1933* (New York: Edwin Mellen, 2014).

45. Michele Louro, *Comrades against Imperialism: Nehru, India, and Interwar Internationalism* (Cambridge, UK: Cambridge University Press, 2018), 19–20.

46. Christy Thornton, "A Mexican International Economic Order? Tracing the Hidden Roots of the Charter of Economic Rights and Duties of States," *Humanity* 9, no. 3 (2018): 392, 395.

47. Stolte and Fischer Tiné, "Imagining Asia in India," 74.

48. Louro, *Comrades against Imperialism*, 27–28.

49. Sarah C. Dunstan, "Conflicts of Interest: The 1919 Pan-Africanist Congress and the Wilsonian Moment," *Callaloo* 39, no. 1 (2016): 134–42.

50. Dunstan, "Conflicts of Interest," 143–46.

51. Alan McPherson, "World War I and US Empire in the Americas," in Jarboe and Fogarty, *Empires in World War I*, 336–43.

52. Alan McPherson, *The Invaded: How Latin Americans and Their Allies Fought and Ended U.S. Occupations* (New York: Oxford University Press, 2014), 159–71, 194–204. The Dominicans enjoyed the greatest success in this regard. American occupiers withdrew from the Dominican Republic in July 1924, from Nicaragua in January 1933, and from Haiti in August 1934.

53. Christopher J. Lee, "The Rise of Third World Diplomacy: Success and Its Meanings at the 1955 Asian–African Conference in Bandung, Indonesia," in *Foreign Policy Breakthroughs: Cases in Successful Diplomacy*, ed. Robert Hutchings and Jeremi Suri (New York: Oxford University Press, 2015), 53.

54. McPherson, *Invaded*, 172–80. In November 1920 the US Navy Department conducted a limited court of inquiry into allegations of numerous killings perpetrated by American marines in Dominica. A larger congressional inquiry into the US occupation of Haiti, headed by Senator Medill McCormick and conducted both in Washington and in situ, between August 1921 and June 1922, gathered damning testimonies about the nature of the occupation. To the fury of NAACP cofounder W. E. B. Du Bois, the McCormick inquiry came out against US withdrawal, claiming that Haiti would succumb to 'brigandage and revolution' were the marines to go home.

55. McPherson, *Invaded*, 159–74.

56. Bernard Bate, "'To Persuade Them into Speech and Action': Oratory and the Tamil Political, Madras, 1905–1919," *Comparative Studies in Society & History* 55, no. 1 (2013): 145–60.

57. Baik Youngseo, "1919 in Dynamic East Asia: March First and May Fourth as a Starting Point for Revolution," *Chinese Studies in History* 52, no. 3–4 (2019): 278–85.

58. Richard Devine, "Japanese Rule in Korea after the March First Uprising: Governor General Hasegawa's Recommendations," *Monumenta Nipponica* 52, no. 4 (1997): 523–27.

59. Gi-Wook Shin and Rennie Moon, "1919 in Korea: National Resistance and Contending Legacies," *Journal of Asian Studies* 78, no. 2 (2019): 399–402; Seungyop Shin, "Living with the Enemies: Japanese Imperialism, Protestant Christianity, and Marxist Socialism in Colonial Korea, 1919–1945," *Religions* 13, no. 9 (2022): 3–8; for British complaints at Japanese maltreatment of Korean demonstrators, the use of flogging especially: Ku Daeyeol, *Korea, 1905–1945*, 117–18.

60. Cemil Aydin uses the examples of the Indian pan-Asianist Rabindranath Tagore and the Japanese pan-Asianist Ôkawa Shûmei to illustrate this point; see his *The Politics of Anti-Westernism in Asia: Visions of World Order in Pan-Islamic and Pan-Asian Thought* (New York: Columbia University Press, 2007), 23–28, 195–96. See also Stolte and Fischer Tiné, "Imagining Asia in India," 69–80, 84–91. For a longer-term perspective, see Selçuk Esenbel, "Japan's Global Claim to Asia and the World of Islam: Transnational Nationalism and World Power, 1900–1945," *American Historical Review* 109, no. 4 (2004): 1140–70.

61. Joseph McQuade, "Beyond an Imperial Foreign Policy? India at the League of Nations, 1919–1946," *Journal of Imperial & Commonwealth History* 48, no. 2 (2020): 270–71.

62. Maryanne A. Rhett, "Race and Imperial Ambition: The Case of Japan and India after World War I," in Jarboe and Fogarty, *Empires in World War I*, 50–59; Antony Best, *British Engagement with Japan, 1854–1922: The Origins and Course of an Unlikely Alliance* (Abingdon, UK: Routledge, 2020), 180–84.

63. Mithi Mukherjee, "Transcending Identity: Gandhi, Nonviolence, and the Pursuit of a 'Different' Freedom in India," *American Historical Review* 115, no. 2 (2010): 467–72; Durba Ghosh, *Gentlemanly Terrorists: Political Violence and the Colonial State in India, 1919–1947* (Cambridge, UK: Cambridge University Press, 2017), 60–72; Streets-Salter, "International and Global," 49–58.

64. Liang Pan, "National Internationalism in Japan and China," in *Internationalisms: A Twentieth Century History*, ed. Glenda Sluga and Patricia Clavin (Cambridge, UK: Cambridge University Press, 2016), 170–77.

65. Aydin, *Politics of Anti-Westernism*, 197; Jeremy A. Yellen, *The Greater East Asia Co-Prosperity Sphere: When Total Empire Met Total War* (Ithaca, NY: Cornell University Press, 2019), 76–102; Shin, "Living with the Enemies," 12–13. For Japanese ethnographic and propagandist portrayals of Korean backwardness: E. Taylor Atkins, *Primitive Selves: Koreana in the Japanese Colonial Gaze, 1910–1945* (Berkeley: University of California Press, 2010), 78–93; Hakjoon Kim, "A Devil Appears in a Different Dress: Imperial Japan's Deceptive Propaganda and Rationalization for Making Korea Its Colony," in *International Impact of Colonial Rule in Korea, 1910–1945*, ed. Yong-Chool Ha (Seattle: University of Washington Press, 2019), 32–42.

66. It bears emphasizing that others—most notably the Bolsheviks—who rejected the liberal international order espoused by Wilson and Smuts had been using a similar language of rights to self-determination since at least 1917. See Borislav Chernev, "The Brest-Litovsk Moment: Self-Determination Discourse in Eastern Europe before Wilsonianism," *Diplomacy & Statecraft* 22, no. 3 (2011): 369–87. For British idealist advocates of a gradual extension of social rights to colonial peoples, see Nazli Pinar Kaymaz, "From Imperialism to Internationalism: British Idealism and Human Rights," *International History Review* 41, no. 6 (2019): 1245–49.

67. Christian Guelen, "The Common Grounds of Conflict: Racial Visions of World Order, 1880–1940," in Conrad and Sachsenmaier, *Competing Visions of World Order*, 69–71, 88–89.

68. Trygve Throntveit, "The Fable of the Fourteen Points: Woodrow Wilson and National Self-Determination," *Diplomatic History* 35 (June 2011): 447–73, quote at 469. Revisiting Wilson's famous Fourteen Points, Throntveit highlights the wording of Point V, which called for 'free, open-minded, and absolutely impartial adjustment of all colonial claims', affirming that 'the interests of the populations concerned must have equal weight with the equitable claims of the government whose title is to be determined.'

69. Robson, *States of Separation*, 9–11, 20–23.

70. Martin Thomas, "France and the Ethiopian Crisis, 1935–1936: Security Dilemmas and Adjustable Interests," in *Collision of Empires: Italy's Invasion of Ethiopia and Its International Impact*, ed. G. Bruce Strang (London: Routledge, 2013), 109–34; John Munro, "'Ethiopia Stretches Forth across the Atlantic': African American Anticolonialism during the Interwar Period," *Left History* 13, no. 2 (2008): 37–63.

71. Adom Getachew, *Worldmaking after Empire: The Rise and Fall of Self-Determination* (Princeton, NJ: Princeton University Press, 2019), 37–62, quote at 52.

72. Eric D. Weitz, *A World Divided: The Global Struggle for Human Rights in the Age of Nation-States* (Princeton, NJ: Princeton University Press, 2019), 178–79.

73. Weitz, *World Divided*, 183–95.

74. Guillaume Mouralis and Annette Weinke, "Justice," in *Europe's Postwar Periods—1989, 1945, 1918: Writing History Backwards*, ed. Martin Conway, Pieter Lagrou, and Henry Rousso (London: Bloomsbury, 2019), 68–70.

75. Mark Lewis, *The Birth of the New Justice: The Internationalization of Crime and Punishment, 1919–1950* (Oxford: Oxford University Press, 2014), 27–28.

76. Michelle Tusan, "'Crimes against Humanity': Human Rights, the British Empire, and the Origins of the Response to the Armenian Genocide," *Journal of American History* 119, no. 1 (2014): 62–69.

77. Julia F. Irwin, "Taming Total War: Great War–Era American Humanitarianism and Its Legacies," *Diplomatic History* 38, no. 4 (2014): 771–73; Frank Ninkovich, *The Global Republic: America's Inadvertent Rise to World Power* (Chicago: University of Chicago Press, 2014), 100.

78. Lewis, *Birth of the New Justice*, 3–4: Lewis suggests that the drive among Allied nations and Balkan successor states to codify international laws to punish acts of national or imperial aggression, criminalize ethnic cleansing and other forms of 'denationalization' and restrict violence against civilians in wartime represented a 'new justice'.

79. MAE, 29PAAP32: Léon Bourgeois papers: SDN/Mandats généralités, Foreign Ministry Service français de la Société des Nations, "Note au sujet des Mandats A," February 2, 1921.

80. Erez Manela, "Imagining Woodrow Wilson in Asia: Dreams of East–West Harmony and the Revolt against Empire in 1919," *American Historical Review* 111, no. 5 (2006): 1327–31.

81. Carole Fink, *Defending the Rights of Others: The Great Powers, the Jews, and International Minority Protection, 1878–1938* (Cambridge, UK: Cambridge University Press, 2004), parts II and III; Volker Prott, *The Politics of Self-Determination: Remaking Territories and National Identities in Europe, 1917–1923* (Oxford: Oxford University Press, 2016), 212–33. For the system's shortcomings in eastern Europe, see Stefan Dyroff, "*Avant-Garde* or Supplement? Advisory Bodies of Transnational Associations as Alternatives to the League's Protection System, 1919–1939," *Diplomacy & Statecraft* 24, no. 2 (2013): 192–208. For the absence of protections for a 'minority' on the wrong side of the war's outcome—the ethnic Germans of French Lorraine—see Carolyn Grohmann, "From Lothringen to Lorraine: Expulsion and Voluntary Repatriation," *Diplomacy & Statecraft* 16, no. 3 (2005): 571–87.

82. James Mark et al., *Socialism Goes Global: The Soviet Union and Eastern Europe in the Age of Decolonization* (Oxford: Oxford University Press, 2022).

83. Dyroff, "*Avant-Garde* or Supplement?" 192–203. As Dyroff points out, to maximize their influence, these lobby groups had to work within the rules and limits set by the League's MPS rather than in defiance of them.

84. Mira L. Siegelberg, "Neither Right nor Left: Interwar Internationalism between Justice and Order," *Humanity* 6, no. 3 (2015): 466.

85. Sunil Amrith and Patricia Clavin, "Feeding the World: Connecting Europe and Asia, 1930–1945," *Past & Present*, Supplement 8 (2013): 29–50. Countering this view, and focusing on tuberculosis vaccination, Aro Velmet argues that the League of Nations Health Organization provoked 'epistemological anarchy' by disrupting national practices: Velmet, *Pasteur's Empire: Bacteriology and Politics in France, Its Colonies, and the World* (Oxford: Oxford University Press, 2020), 142–43.

86. Andrew Arsan, "'This Is the Age of Associations': Committees, Petitions, and the Roots of Interwar Middle Eastern Internationalism," *Journal of Global History* 7 (2012): 166–88; Natasha Wheatley, "Mandatory Interpretation: Legal Hermeneutics and the New International Order in Arab and Jewish Petitions to the League of Nations," *Past & Present* 27 (May 2015): 206–48; Mark Philip Bradley, *The World Reimagined: Americans and Human Rights in the Twentieth Century* (New York:

Cambridge University Press, 2016), 59–60. Petitioning was already commonplace among colonial elites and local ex-servicemen and public servants whose careers conferred citizenship or other social rights. See MAE, PA-AP 65, private papers of Edmond Doutte, Commission interministérielle des affaires musulmanes (CIAM), file 2: "Représentations des indigènes d'Algérie au Parlement, 1919–1923." The interdepartmental commission on Muslim affairs, which handled such petitions from French North Africa, convened 143 sessions in the decade between the end of World War I and the start of 1929; see MAE, PA-AP 65, Edmond Doutte papers, file 1, "Compterendus des réunions du CIAM, 1922–1924"; PA-AP 216, Augustin Bernard papers, file 15, "Procès-verbaux des séances du CIAM, 1929–1936." Augustin Bernard was a Sorbonne professor and secretary-general of the CIAM, whose sessions took place in the French Foreign Ministry. Membership included former colonial governors, specialist academics (particularly jurists) and Colonial and War Ministry representatives. See, for instance, MAE, PA-AP 216, Augustin Bernard papers, file 15, "CIAM Procès verbal de la réunion du 31 Mai 1929," 146th Meeting held to discuss anomalies in Muslim voting rights between French African territories under civilian and military administration.

87. Robson, *States of Separation*, 25–26, 32–33.

88. Liberal internationalists such as the Labour Party's Leonard Woolf saw value in the Mandate system because of its character as a form of trusteeship; see Luke Reader, "'An Alternative to Imperialism': Leonard Woolf, the Labour Party and Imperial Internationalism, 1915–1922," *International History Review* 41, no. 1 (2019): 162–65.

89. For petitions submitted regarding the mentally ill, see Chris Wilson, "Petitions and Pathways to the Asylum in British Mandate Palestine, 1930–1948," *Historical Journal* 62, no. 2 (2019): 451–71.

90. Natasha Wheatley, "New Subjects in International Law and Order," in Sluga and Clavin, *Internationalisms*, 265–81. Aside from petitioning over rights infringements, the cloudiness of international law was evident in asymmetric conflicts over which the League of Nations was asked to reach a judgment. In such cases throughout the interwar years the organization never resolved matters to the benefit of the weaker military actor; see Mathias Schulz, "Cultures of Peace and Security from the Vienna Congress to the Twenty-First Century: Characteristics and Dilemmas," in *Securing Europe after Napoleon: 1815 and the New European Security Culture*, ed. Beatrice de Graaf, Ido de Haan, and Brian Vick (Cambridge, UK: Cambridge University Press, 2019), 30–33.

91. Véronique Dimier, "On Good Colonial Government: Lessons from the League of Nations," *Global Society* 18, no. 3 (2004): 282–85; Florian Wagner, *Colonial Internationalism and the Governmentality of Empire, 1893–1982* (Cambridge, UK: Cambridge University Press, 2022), 209–11, 219–26.

92. Susan Pedersen, *The Guardians: The League of Nations and the Crisis of Empire* (Oxford: Oxford University Press, 2015); Cyrus Schayegh, *The Middle East and the Making of the Modern World* (Cambridge, MA: Harvard University Press, 2017), 132–64; Simon Jackson, *Mandatory Development: French Colonial Empire, Global Capitalism, and the Politics of the Economy after World War One* (Ithaca, NY: Cornell University Press, forthcoming), chapters 1 and 2. Véronique Dimier suggests

that French colonial officials were less well placed than their British counterparts to manipulate the PMC and were slower to recognize the implications of its scrutiny; see her "On Good Colonial Government," 282–93.

93. Sherene Seikaly uses a striking phrase, the 'temporality of deferral', to capture the sense of sovereign rights postponed for those living within the Mandates. See her "The Matter of Time," *American Historical Review* 124, no. 5 (2019): 1681–88, quote at 1683.

94. Smith, *Sovereignty at the Paris Peace Conference*, 49.

95. Susan Pedersen, "An International Regime in an Age of Empire," *American Historical Review* 124, no. 5 (2019): 1678.

96. Meredith Terretta and Benjamin N. Lawrance, "'Sons of the Soil,' Cause Lawyers, the Togo-Cameroun Mandates, and the Origins of Decolonization," *American Historical Review* 124, no. 5 (2019): 1709–14.

97. Smith, *Sovereignty at the Paris Peace Conference*, 47–49.

98. Leonard V. Smith, "Drawing Borders in the Middle East after the Great War: Political Geography and 'Subject Peoples,'" *First World War Studies* 7, no. 1 (2016): 5–7. For the opposing Ottoman view that their empire had treated its 'subject peoples' more equitably next to the colonial racism of the Allied imperial powers, see Lerna Ekmekçioglu, "'Republic of Paradox': The League of Nations Minority Protection Regime and New Turkey's Step-Citizens," *International Journal of Middle East Studies* 46, no. 4 (2016): 667–68.

99. Martti Koskenniemi, *The Gentle Civilizer of Nations: The Rise and Fall of International Law, 1870–1960* (Cambridge, UK: Cambridge University Press, 2010), 98–103, 171–74.

100. British Library, MS49752, Papers of Sir Arthur Balfour, Papers relating to the Paris Peace Conference, Balfour memo. "Syria, Palestine, Mesopotamia," August 11, 1919.

101. Boris N. Mamlyuk, "Decolonization as a Cold War Imperative: Bandung and the Soviets," in *Bandung, Global History, and International Law*, ed. Luis Eslava, Michael Fakhri, and Vasuki Nesiah (Cambridge, UK: Cambridge University Press, 2017), 199–206. Both prolific writers, Pashukanis rose to a leading position in the Soviet Academy of Sciences, while Korovin became secretary to the Russian branch of the ICRC.

102. MAE, série K: Afrique 1918–40, sous-série: Congo Belge, vol. 8: Rapports annuels du Ministre Belge des Colonies sur l'administration du Congo, 1919–28, Governor General Lippens, "Rapport sur l'administration belge du Ruanda-Urundi pendant l'année 1928 présenté aux Chambres par le Premier Ministre, Ministre des Colonies, Henri Jaspar," 10.

103. MAE, série K: Afrique 1918–40, sous-série: Congo Belge, vol. 8, "Rapport sur l'administration belge du Ruanda-Urundi pendant l'année 1928 présenté aux Chambres par le Premier Ministre, Ministre des Colonies, Henri Jaspar." Famine conditions were also blamed for the shelving of plans to indigenize Rwanda's provincial administration.

104. Hoover Institution archive, Stanford University, Louis Loucheur papers, box 2, folder 8, "La Pacification du Maroc et les opérations militaires en 1921–1922," *L'Illustration*, no. 4125, March 25, 1922; Caroline Campbell, "The Battle of El Herri in Morocco: Colonial Narratives of Conquest during World War I," *Historical Reflections* 46, no. 3 (2020): 9–30.

105. Adam Guerin, "'Not a Drop for the Settlers': Reimagining Popular Protest and Anti-Colonial Nationalism in the Moroccan Protectorate," *Journal of North African Studies* 20, no. 2 (2015): 229.

106. MAE, PA-AP 258: Léopold Benazet papers, file 1: Western Sahara, Moroccan students, protectorate organization, "Rapport sur les travaux de la Commission chargée d'étudier l'emploi des Marocains dans les administrations du Protectorat," June 23, 1934. Following the commission report a government recruitment campaign, with posters in Arabic and French, was launched.

107. In 1921 Marshal Louis-Hubert Lyautey, founding father of the Moroccan protectorate system, identified its first principle as regulatory control as distinct from direct governance; see MAE, PA-AP 258: Léopold Benazet papers, file 1: no. 355GL, Lyautey memo, "Politique indigène," May 14, 1921.

108. MAE, série K: Afrique 1918–40, sous-série: Affaires Musulmanes, vol. 25: Nationalisme tunisien et maghrebin, 1927–8, no 2025, Théodore Steeg, Rabat Residency, to Foreign Ministry, December 27, 1927: "La Communisme et les Comités Pan-islamiques au Maroc."

109. MAE, PA-AP 258: Léopold Benazet papers, file 1, Direction des Affaires indigènes, Benazet, "Note confidentielle sur la réorganisation des Services Chérifiens. Propositions de M. Zeys [Inspecteur des Juridictions Chérifiens]," n.d. 1932; Benazet "Note sur sujet du Dahir Berbère," September 29, 1933; note sur le Makhzen central, Rabat, January 25, 1934; Délégué à la Residence Générale, Rabat, to Foreign Ministry, Section Afrique Levant, "A/S des événements du 10 Mai 1934 à Fès et de leurs conséquences," May 21, 1934. Its passage delayed by the Rif War in 1925, the Berber dahir came into force on May 16, 1930. It created new legal tribunals to administer Berber-majority districts and extended French legal jurisdiction for crimes committed within those regions, whosoever committed the alleged offence. Protests against the measure culminated in riots in Fez on May 19, 1934, which definitively aligned the sultan with the nationalist "Action bloc".

110. Churchill held the posts of Secretary of State for War and Air, then of Colonial Secretary, between 1919 and 1922. R. M. Douglas, "Did Britain Use Chemical Weapons in Mandatory Iraq?" *Journal of Modern History* 81 (December 2009): 859–87, at 872 and 882. On British interwar debates on the use of chemical weapons against colonial protestors, see Simeon Shoul, "British Tear Gas Doctrine between the World Wars," *War in History* 15, no. 2 (2008): 168–90. And for the largest sustained use of chemical warfare agents within a territory, see Edwin A. Martini, "Hearts, Minds, and Herbicides: The Politics of the Chemical War in Vietnam," *Diplomatic History* 37, no. 1 (2013): 58–84.

111. For British governmental security planning in Iraq, see TNA, War Office (WO) files: WO 32/5234, Report of the Committee on Mesopotamia appointed by the Secretary of State for War, January 21, 1921.

112. Keith Shear, "Chiefs or Modern Bureaucrats: Black Police in Early Twentieth-Century South Africa," *Comparative Studies in Society and History* 54, no. 2 (2012): 265–69.

113. For the nineteenth-century origins of such practices in the world's largest colony, British India, see Deana Heath, *Colonial Terror: Torture and State Violence in Colonial India* (Oxford: Oxford University Press, 2021), 73–82, 113–32.

114. For detailed, empire-wide description, see TNA, CO 774/835: British Empire, riots and disturbances, 1915–1919. For specific regional examples: Shereen Ilahi, *Imperial Violence and the Path to Independence: India, Ireland and the Crisis of Empire* (London: I. B. Tauris, 2016); William J. Berridge, "Object Lessons in Violence: The Rationalities and Irrationalities of Urban Struggle during the Egyptian Revolution of 1919," *Journal of Colonialism and Colonial History* 12, no. 3 (2011): published online; Wadie Jwaideh, *The Kurdish National Movement: Its Origins and Development* (Syracuse: Syracuse University Press, 2006), 173–79; Lyndall Ryan, "Martial Law in the British Empire," in *Violence, Colonialism, and Empire in the Modern World*, ed. Philip Dwyer and Amanda Nettelbeck (Basingstoke, UK: Palgrave Macmillan, 2018), 93–109; John Horne, "End of a Paradigm? The Cultural History of the Great War," *Past & Present* 242 (February 2019): 155–92, at 174–77. For background to such punitive legislation and the British pathologization of anticolonial religious violence behind it, see Mark Condos, "License to Kill: The Murderous Outrages Act and the Rule of Law in Colonial India, 1867–1925," *Modern Asian Studies* 50, no. 2 (2016): 479–517; idem, "'Fanaticism' and the Politics of Resistance along the North-West Frontier of British India," *Comparative Studies in Society and History* 58, no. 3 (2016): 717–45, at 727–31.

115. Ghosh, *Gentlemanly Terrorists*, 27–34, 38–45; Joshua Ehrlich, "Anxiety, Chaos, and the Raj," *Historical Journal* 63, no. 3 (2020): 785; David M. Anderson, "Master and Servant in Colonial Kenya, 1895–1930," *Journal of African History* 41, no. 3 (2000): 473–83; Matthew Hughes, *Britain's Pacification of Palestine: The British Army, the Colonial State, and the Arab Revolt, 1936–1939* (Cambridge, UK: Cambridge University Press, 2019), 215–49.

116. Jonathan Saha, *Law, Disorder and the Colonial State: Corruption in Burma c.1900* (Basingstoke, UK: Palgrave Macmillan, 2013), 97–125; idem, "Whiteness, Masculinity and the Ambivalent Embodiment of 'British Justice' in Colonial Burma," *Cultural and Social History*, 14, no. 4 (2017): 527–42.

117. Albert Sarraut papers, 12J280, "Discours d'Albert Sarraut sur la situation en Indochine devant la Chambre des Députés," draft, no date 1919.

118. MAE, série K: Afrique 1918–40, sous-série: Congo Belge, vol. 8: Rapports annuels du Ministre Belge des Colonies sur l'administration du Congo, 1919–28, Governor General E. Henry, "Rapport sur l'administration du Congo belge pendant l'année 1919," submitted to Brussels Chamber of Representatives on October 7, 1920.

119. Leigh Gardner, "Fiscal Policy in the Belgian Congo in Comparative Perspective," in *Colonial Exploitation and Economic Development: The Belgian Congo and the Netherlands Indies Compared*, ed. Ewout Frankema and Frans Buelens (Abingdon, UK: Routledge, 2013), 138–43, and, in the same collection, Anne Booth, "Varieties of Exploitation in Colonial Settings: Dutch and Belgian Policies in Indonesia and the Congo and Their Legacies," 70–71.

120. NA, AIR 75/27, Official papers of MRAF Sir John Slessor, "Air Control—The Other Point of View," May 1931, and Air Staff memo., "What Air Control Means in War and Peace; What It Has Achieved," June 20, 1930; David Omissi, *Air Power and Colonial Control: The Royal Air Force, 1919–1939* (Manchester, UK: Manchester University Press, 1990); Priya Satia, "The Defense of Inhumanity: Air Control and the British Idea of Arabia," *American Historical Review* 111, no. 1 (2006): 26–32; Jafna L. Cox,

"A Splendid Training Ground: The Importance to the Royal Air Force of Its Role in Iraq, 1919–32," *Journal of Imperial & Commonwealth History* 13, no. 2 (1985): 157–84; Michael Paris, "Air Power and Imperial Defence," *Journal of Contemporary History* 24, no. 2 (1989): 209–25; Charles Townshend, "Civilisation and 'Frightfulness': Air Control in the Middle East between the Wars," in *Warfare, Diplomacy and Politics*, ed. C. Wrigley (London: Hamish Hamilton, 1986), 142–62.

121. MAE, série K: Afrique 1918–40, sous-série: Affaires Musulmanes, vol. 25, no. 400, Urbain Blanc, Rabat Residency to Sous-Direction d'Afrique, February 29, 1928: "Propagande antimilitariste et communiste"; Hughes, *Britain's Pacification*, 281–88.

122. Roberta Pergher, *Mussolini's Nation-Empire: Sovereignty and Settlement in Italy's Borderlands, 1922–1943* (Cambridge, UK: Cambridge University Press, 2018), 15–16, also citing Matthew H. Ellis, "Over the Borderline? Rethinking Territoriality at the Margins of Empire and Nation in the Modern Middle East (Part I and II)," *History Compass* 13, no. 8 (2015): 411–22 and 423–34.

123. Pergher, *Mussolini's Nation-Empire*, 16, citing Pekka Hämäläinen and Samuel Truett, "On Borderlands," *Journal of American History* 98, no. 2 (September 2011): 338–61.

124. Michael Provence, "Ottoman Modernity, Colonialism, and Insurgency in the Interwar Arab East," *International Journal of Middle East Studies* 43 (2011): 205–8, 215–18; Daniel Neep, *Occupying Syria under the French Mandate: Insurgency, Space and State Formation* (Cambridge, UK: Cambridge University Press, 2012).

125. TNA, MI5 papers, KV 6/18, "Down with French Imperialism! Long Live the People of Syria," May 11, 1924. Executive Committee of the Communist International, three-page press release.

126. Carol Hakim, "The French Mandate in Lebanon," *American Historical Review* 124, no. 5 (2019): 1689–91; Philip S. Khoury, "The Tribal Shaykh, French Tribal Policy, and the Nationalist Movement in Syria between Two World Wars," *Middle Eastern Studies* 18, no. 2 (1982): 183–86.

127. Stacy D. Fahrenthold, *Between the Ottomans and the Entente: The First World War in the Syrian and Lebanese Diaspora, 1908–1925* (New York: Oxford University Press, 2019).

128. Benjamin Thomas White, "Refugees and the Definition of Syria, 1920–1939," *Past and Present* 235 (May 2017): 141–44, 147–51.

129. For eloquent summaries of these processes, see Schayegh, *The Middle East*, 181–88; Laura Robson, *The Politics of Mass Violence in the Middle East* (Oxford: Oxford University Press, 2020), 35–39.

130. Dominic Lieven, *Empire: The Russian Empire and Its Rivals* (New Haven, CT: Yale University Press, 2001), xiii, also cited in Alan Mikhail and Christine M. Philliou, "The Ottoman Empire and the Imperial Turn," *Comparative Studies in Society and History* 54, no. 4 (2012): 737–38.

131. Manela, *Wilsonian Moment*; James Mayall, "International Society, State Sovereignty, and National Self-Determination," in *The Oxford Handbook of the History of Nationalism*, ed. John Breuilly (Oxford: Oxford University Press, 2013), online publication, 3; Gerwarth and Manela, "Great War as a Global War," 786–800; Weitz, "From the Vienna to the Paris System," 1313–21.

132. Pedersen, *Guardians*; McQuade, "Beyond an Imperial," 282–86.

133. Brad Simpson, "The United States and the Curious History of Self-Determination," *Diplomatic History* 36, no. 4 (2012): 676–79.

134. Weitz, *A World Divided*, 331–34; Wheatley, "Mandatory Interpretation," 206–35; Arsan, "'This Is the Age of Associations,'" 166–88; Susan Pedersen, "The Impact of League Oversight on British Policy in Palestine," in *Britain, Palestine, and Empire: The Mandate Years*, ed. Rory Miller (Farnham, UK: Ashgate, 2010), 39–64.

135. A recent history that ends by invoking this postwar crisis of empire is John Connor, *Someone Else's War: Fighting for the British Empire in World War I* (London: I. B. Tauris, 2019), 241–47.

136. For a clear-sighted summary of these trends, see William Mulligan, *The Great War for Peace* (New Haven, CT: Yale University Press, 2014), 302–38; Robson, *Politics of Mass Violence*, 54–83.

137. Weitz, "Self-Determination," 483–85.

138. Schayegh, *The Middle East*, 132–64. A similar point about the absence of geographical or political fixity in early mandate Syria is made by Benjamin Thomas White, "Refugees and the Definition of Syria, 1920–1939," 141–57. See also Jackson, *Mandatory Development*, chapters 1 and 2; Ekmekçioglu, "'Republic of Paradox,'" 657–79.

139. Pedersen, *Guardians*; Pedersen, "Empires, States and the League of Nations," in Sluga and Clavin, *Internationalisms*, 113–38; Leonard V. Smith, *Sovereignty at the Paris Peace Conference*; Wheatley, "Mandatory Interpretation," 206–35; idem, "Spectral Legal Personality in Interwar International Law: On New Ways of Not Being a State," *Law And History Review* 35, no. 3 (2017): 753–87; Arsan, "'This Is the Age of Associations,'" 166–88.

140. On the nature and persistence of often nonlethal political violence in 1920s Ireland, see Anne Dolan, "Killing in 'the Good Old Irish Fashion'? Irish Revolutionary Violence in Context," *Irish Historical Studies* 44, no. 165 (2020): 11–24. Grievances among Irishwomen faced initially with conscription, then with the abrupt loss of employment opportunities postwar, are also revealing: see Fionnuala Walsh, *Irish Women and the Great War* (Cambridge, UK: Cambridge University Press, 2020), 183–88, 197–206.

141. Sudan is a useful example here, British-ruled, but in nominal—often antagonistic—partnership with the Egyptian authorities and, in practice, scarcely administered outside its urban centers, beyond which violent dissent remained endemic; see TNA, AIR 20/680, Report on Operations, South East Sudan, 1920–1, RAF Operations Communiqué No. 2: "Operations of H Unit RAF, South East Sudan, January to June 1920," Air Ministry, DO1, June 1921; WO 32/5588, E10510/10086/16, FO Egyptian Section, "Covering Memo. on Sir Lee Stack's memorandum of October 11th 1923"; WO 33/999 Sudan Monthly Intelligence Reports, 1922–5, especially reports 359–70 covering the breakdown of Anglo-Egyptian cooperation in Khartoum in 1924; WO 33/2764: War Office, General Staff, "Military Report on the Sudan 1927."

142. Kimberly Jensen, "Gender and Citizenship," in *Gender and the Great War*, ed. Susan R. Grayzel and Tammy M. Proctor (Oxford: Oxford University Press, 2017), 10–11, 18–19.

143. Michael Joseph, "First World War Veterans and the State in the French and British Caribbean, 1919–1939," *First World War Studies* 10, no. 1 (2019): 31–48. Joseph brings out the divergence between the interwar welfarism and assimilationist

promises made to French Caribbean servicemen and the neglect of their equivalents in British-ruled Jamaica and Barbados.

144. Glenda Sluga, "Remembering 1919: International Organizations and the Future of International Order," *International Affairs* 95, no. 1 (2019): 33. On early claims-making by Muslim women subjects in French Algeria, see Sara Rahnama, "Hijabs and Hats in Interwar Algeria," *Gender & History* 32, no. 2 (2020): 429–46; Avner Ofrath, *The Unmaking of Citizenship: Republican France and Algeria, 1848–1958* (London: Bloomsbury, 2021), chapter 2.

145. Sacha Hepburn and April Jackson, "Colonial Exceptions: The International Labour Organization and Child Labour in British Africa, c.1919–1940," *Journal of Contemporary History* 57, no. 2 (2022): 222–40.

146. The arguments produced in defense of a particularly egregious use of such repressive means—air power—are analyzed by Priya Satia, "The Defense of Inhumanity," 16–51; see also J. P. Daughton, "Behind the Imperial Curtain: International Humanitarian Efforts and the Critique of French Colonialism in the Interwar Years," *French Historical Studies* 34, no. 3 (2011): 527–28.

147. There is a wealth of outstanding recent work in this field, among it: Keith David Watenpaugh, *Bread from Stones: The Middle East and the Making of Modern Humanitarianism* (Berkeley: University of California Press, 2015); idem, "The League of Nations' Rescue of Armenian Genocide Survivors and the Making of Modern Humanitarianism, 1920–1927," *American Historical Review* 115, no. 5 (December 2010): 1315–39; Davide Rodogno, *Against Massacre: Humanitarian Interventions in the Ottoman Empire, 1815–1914* (Princeton, NJ: Princeton University Press, 2015); idem, "The American Red Cross and the International Committee of the Red Cross' Humanitarian Politics and Policies in Asia Minor and Greece (1922–1923)," *First World War Studies* 5, no. 1 (2014): 82–99; Michelle Tusan, *Smyrna's Ashes: Humanitarianism, Genocide, and the Birth of the Middle East* (Berkeley: University of California Press, 2012); idem, "'Crimes against Humanity,'" 47–77; Weitz, "From the Vienna to the Paris System," 1313–43. See also Simon Jackson's important intervention: *Mandatory Development*.

148. Manela, *Wilsonian Moment*; Michael Provence, *The Great Syrian Revolt and the Rise of Arab Nationalism* (Austin: University of Texas Press, 2005), 57–64.

149. Laura Robson, "Refugees and the Case for International Authority in the Middle East: The League of Nations and the United Nations Relief and Works Agency for Palestinian Refugees in the Near East Compared," *International Journal of Middle East Studies* 49 (2017): 627–33; Robson, *States of Separation*, 37–51.

150. White, "Refugees and the Definition of Syria," 140–44; Lauren Banko, "Refugees, Displaced Migrants, and Territorialization in Mandate Palestine," *Mashriq & Mahjar* 5, no. 2 (2018): 27–28.

151. White, "Refugees and the Definition of Syria," 152–67.

Chapter Five: The Economic Side of Empire Decline

1. For discussions of these factors in different colonial regions, see Ali Abdullatif Ahmida, *Forgotten Voices: Power and Agency in Colonial and Postcolonial Libya* (Abingdon, UK: Routledge, 2005), 1–10; Christian Lentz, *Contested Territory: Điện Biên Phu and the Making of Northwest Vietnam* (New Haven, CT: Yale University Press, 2019), 4–7, 26–48.

2. Recent studies of settler colonialism's political-economic impacts in mandate Palestine provide a crucial exception: Jacob Norris, *Land of Progress: Palestine in the Age of Colonial Development, 1905–1948* (Oxford: Oxford University Press, 2013); Sherene Seikaly, *Men of Capital: Scarcity and Economy in Mandate Palestine* (Stanford, CA: Stanford University Press, 2015); Rana Barakat, "Reading Palestinian Agency in Mandate History: The Narrative of the Buraq Revolt as Anti-Relational," *Contemporary Levant* 4, no. 1 (2019): 28–38.

3. For war victims more generally: Bruno Cabanes, *The Great War and the Origins of Humanitarianism, 1918–1924* (Cambridge, UK: Cambridge University Press, 2014), chapters 2–4.

4. David Arnold, "Looting, Grain Riots and Government Policy in South India, 1918," *Past & Present* 84 (August 1979): 111–14, 133–41; Suranjan Das, *Communal Riots in Bengal, 1905–1947* (Delhi: Oxford University Press, 1991); Linda Schatkowski-Schilcher, "The Famine of 1915–1918 in Greater Syria," in *Problems of the Modern Middle East in Historical Perspective: Essays in Honour of Albert Hourani*, ed. John P. Spagnolo (Reading: Ithaca, 1992), 229–58; Melanie Schulze Tanielian, "Feeding the City: The Beirut Municipality and the Politics of Food during World War I," *International Journal of Middle East Studies* 46, no. 4 (2014): 737–58.

5. Steven Serels, "Starving for Someone Else's Fight: The First World War and Food Insecurity in the African Red Sea Region," in *Environmental Histories of the First World War*, ed. Richard P. Tucker, Tait Keller, J. R. McNeill, and Martin Schmid (Cambridge, UK: Cambridge University Press, 2018), 208–30.

6. Alison Bashford, "Global Biopolitics and the History of World Health," *History of the Human Sciences* 19 (2006): 67–88; Karl Ittmann, *A Problem of Great Importance: Population, Race, and Power in the British Empire, 1919–1973* (Berkeley: University of California Press, 2013), 48–55.

7. M. Foucault, "The Birth of Biopolitics," in *Ethics, Subjectivity, and Truth*, ed. P. Rabinow and J. D. Faubion (New York: New Press, 1997); T. Lemke, *Biopolitics: An Advanced Introduction* (New York: New York University Press, 2011); Daniel Neep, *Occupying Syria under the French Mandate: Insurgency, Space and State Formation* (Cambridge, UK: Cambridge University Press, 2012), 14–15.

8. Patrick Bernhard, "Borrowing from Mussolini: Nazi Germany's Colonial Aspirations in the Shadow of Italian Expansionism," *Journal of Imperial & Commonwealth History* 41 (2013): 619–20; idem, "Hitler's Africa in the East: Italian Colonialism as a Model for German Planning in Eastern Europe," *Journal of Contemporary History* 51, no. 1 (2016): 61–90.

9. Alison Bashford, *Global Population: History, Geopolitics, and Life on Earth* (New York: Columbia University Press, 2016), parts II and III; idem, "Global Biopolitics," 67–88; idem, "Nation, Empire, Globe: The Spaces of Population Debate in the Interwar Years," *Comparative Studies in Society and History* 49, no. 1 (2007): 170–201; idem, "Population Planning for a Global Middle Class," in *The Global Bourgeoisie: The Rise of the Middle Classes in the Age of Empire*, ed. Christof Dejung, David Motadel, and Jürgen Osterhammel (Princeton, NJ: Princeton University Press, 2019), 85–101, at 90–95.

10. Bashford, "Nation, Empire, Globe," 193–97.

11. Bashford, "Nation, Empire, Globe," 177–80, 199.

12. Bashford, "Nation, Empire, Globe," 188–91. Bashford's insights resonate with Michel Foucault's definition of governmentality as a 'science of populations': Benoît de l'Estoile, Federico Neiberg, and Lygia Sigaud, "Anthropology and the Government of 'Natives': A Comparative Approach," in *Empires, Nations, and Natives: Anthropology and State-Making*, ed. idem (Durham, NC: Duke University Press, 2005), 12–14.

13. Matthew Connelly, "Seeing beyond the State: The Population Control Movement and the Problem of Sovereignty," *Past and Present* 193 (November 2006): 197–233; idem, "Population Control Is History: New Perspectives on the International Campaign to Limit Population Growth," *Comparative Studies in Society and History* 45, no. 1 (2003): 122–47.

14. Connelly, "Seeing beyond the State," 198–202. For the longer-term origins of these racist constructions and their changing enunciation over time, see Matthew Connelly, "To Inherit the Earth: Imagining World Population, from the Yellow Peril to the Population Bomb," *Journal of Global History* 1, no. 3 (2006): 299–319.

15. MAE, série K: Afrique 1918–40, sous-série: Questions générales africaines, vol. 31: *Emploi de la main d'oeuvre indigène, 1921–1925*, Direction du Contrôle et de la Comptabilité 1ᵉ Bureau to Poincaré, June 23, 1922. 'Repatriement de travailleurs coloniaux.'

16. MAE, série K: Afrique 1918–40, sous-série: Questions générales africaines, vol. 31: *Emploi de la main d'oeuvre indigène, 1921–1925*, no. 1479, Ministère du Travail, Service de la Main-d'Oeuvre étrangère to Premier Poincaré, June 17, 1922; no. 3552, Office du Protectorat de la République Française au Maroc (Paris) to Foreign Ministry, July 22, 1922.

17. MAE, série K: Afrique 1918–40, sous-série: Questions générales africaines, vol. 125: Dossier divers—"Protection des races indigènes, 1921–1927"; vol. 31, Direction des Affaires Algériennes 1ᵉ Bureau to Foreign Ministry, November 27, 1924; Direction des Affaires Algériennes 1ᵉ Bureau to Foreign Ministry, "Surveillance et protection des travailleurs indigènes nord-africains dans la région Parisienne," July 28, 1925.

18. Clifford Rosenberg, *Policing Paris: The Origins of Modern Immigration Control between the Wars* (Ithaca, NY: Cornell University Press, 2006), 135–41, 155–62. Experiences of discrimination catalyzed the integral Algerian nationalism of Messali Hadj's *Etoile nord-africaine* (ENA—North African Star), founded in 1926: Rabah Aissaoui, *Immigration and National Identity: North African Political Movements in Colonial and Postcolonial France* (London: I. B. Tauris, 2009), 14–24, 41–56.

19. MAE, série K: Afrique 1918–40, sous-série: Affaires Musulmanes, vol. 25: Nationalisme tunisien et maghrebin, 1927–8, no 2025, Théodore Steeg, Rabat Residency, to Foreign Ministry, "La Communisme et les Comités Panislamiques au Maroc," December 27, 1927.

20. On the British colonial case, see Sunil Amrith, "Struggles for Citizenship around the Bay of Bengal," in *The Postcolonial Moment in South and Southeast Asia*, ed. Gyan Prakash, Michael Laffan, and Nikhil Menon (London: Bloomsbury, 2018), 110–13. For evidence from the French Empire, see Elisa Camiscioli, "Race Making and Race Mixing in the Early Twentieth-Century Immigration Debate," in *Transnational Spaces and Identities in the Francophone World*, ed. Hafid Gafaïti, Patricia M. E. Lorcin, and David G. Troyansky (Lincoln: University of Nebraska Press, 2009), 53–67.

21. MAE, série K: Afrique 1918–40, sous-série: Questions générales africaines, vol. 31: Emploi de la main d'oeuvre indigène, 1921–5, no. 1479, Ministère du Travail, Service de la Main-d'Oeuvre étrangère to Foreign Minister and Premier Poincaré, June 17, 1922; Ministère de l'Intérieur Direction des Affaires Algériennes 1e Bureau to Foreign Ministry, "Exode des indigènes 'Nord Africains' dans la Métropole," January 14, 1924.

22. Matthew Connelly describes the resulting population control measures as a form of 'public-private partnership', for the greater part transnational in origin rather than state-led: Connelly, "Seeing beyond the State," 226–33, quote at 226.

23. Leslie James, "'Essential Things such as Typewriters': Development Discourse, Trade Union Expertise, and the Dialogues of Decolonization between the Caribbean and West Africa," *Journal of Social History* 53, no. 2 (2019): 379, citing *Modernization as Spectacle in Africa*, ed. Peter J. Bloom, Stephan F. Miescher, and Takyiwaa Manuh (Bloomington: Indiana University Press, 2014).

24. Seikaly, *Men of Capital*, 86–90, 94–99.

25. Nick Cullather, "The Foreign Policy of the Calorie," *American Historical Review* 112, no. 2 (April 2007): 342, 346. As Cullather remarks, new tools of measurement discredited older theories about differing food needs between ethnicities.

26. David Engerman, "American Knowledge and Global Power," *Diplomatic History* 31, no. 4 (2007): 612.

27. Sunil Amrith and Patricia Clavin, "Feeding the World: Connecting Europe and Asia, 1930–1945," *Past & Present*, Supplement 8 (2013): 34–39.

28. Amrith and Clavin, "Feeding the World," 39–44.

29. Michael Worboys, "The Discovery of Colonial Malnutrition between the Wars," in *Imperial Medicine and Indigenous Societies*, ed. David Arnold (Manchester, UK: Manchester University Press, 1988), 210–16; Vincent Bonnecase, "Avoir faim en Afrique Occidentale Française (1920–1960): investigations et représentations coloniales," *Revue d'Histoire des Sciences Humaines* 21 (2009): 151–59, both also cited in Samuël Coghe, "Reordering Colonial Society: Model Villages and Social Planning in Rural Angola, 1920–45," *Journal of Contemporary History* 52, no. 1 (2017): 27–28.

30. Cullather, "Foreign Policy of the Calorie," 355–59.

31. Samantha Iyer, "Colonial Population and the Idea of Development," *Comparative Studies in Society and History* 55, no. 1 (2013): 76–7; Amrith and Clavin, "Feeding the World," 39, 43–44. Mahatma Gandhi paid close attention to the League's research into nutritional science, integrating it into his vision of an equitable, self-sufficient India with a clear moral economy of food provision. An example of the distorting effects of an imperial market is the introduction of Vietnamese rice to French Senegal. Easy to cook, it supplanted locally available sources of carbohydrate like sorghum and millet whose production French administrators discouraged in their efforts to expand the cultivation of groundnuts, the principal source of colonial export revenue from the Senegambian basin. See Jayeeta Sharma, "Food and Empire," in *The Oxford Handbook of Food History*, ed. Jeffrey M. Pilcher (Oxford: Oxford University Press, 2012), online publication.

32. Sharma, "Food and Empire," 350, 355–56. Quinn Slobodian highlights a bitter irony here insofar as governments and supranational agencies developed greater statistical sophistication only to turn away from global economic and political solutions with the worldwide turn to protectionism in the depression years of the 1930s. As he

puts it in reference to the neoliberal thinkers at the heart of his work, 'For liberals it was a painful irony that the world economy came into focus as a totality in statistics at the very moment it seemed to vanish in real life.' See Quinn Slobodian, *The Globalists: The End of Empire and the Birth of Neoliberalism* (Cambridge, MA: Harvard University Press, 2018), 56.

33. Coghe, "Reordering Colonial Society," 19–22. Ironically, imperial administrative concern at the destabilizing political consequences of high rates of colonial population growth also informed these early developmental ideas; see Iyer, "Colonial Population," 82–88.

34. Gregory A. Barton, "Environmentalism, Development and British Policy in the Middle East, 1945–65," *Journal of Imperial & Commonwealth History* 38 (2010): 620.

35. Cullather, "Foreign Policy of the Calorie," 337–39, quote at 337.

36. Tehila Sasson, "Milking the Third World? Humanitarianism, Capitalism, and the Moral Economy of the Nestlé Boycott," *American Historical Review* 121, no. 4 (2016): 1200–1, also citing Nancy Rose Hunt, "'Le bébé en brousse': European Women, African Birth Spacing and Colonial Intervention in Breast Feeding in the Belgian Congo," *International Journal of African Historical Studies* 21, no. 3 (1988): 401–32; Bonnie McElhinny, "'Kissing a Baby Is Not at All Good for Him': Infant Mortality, Medicine, and Colonial Modernity in the U.S.-Occupied Philippines," *Peace Research Abstracts Journal* 42, no. 6 (2005): 183–94.

37. Cullather, "Foreign Policy of the Calorie," 337–39, quote at 337. For official efforts to measure food policy outcomes in a particular imperial territory, see Sherene Seikaly, "A Nutritional Economy: The Calorie, Development and War in Mandate Palestine," in *Home Fronts: Britain and the Empire at War, 1939–45,* ed. Mark J. Crowley and Sandra Trudgen Dawson (Woodbridge, UK: Boydell Press, 2017), 37–58.

38. Susan Pedersen, "Empires, States and the League of Nations," in *Internationalisms: A Twentieth Century History,* ed. Glenda Sluga and Patricia Clavin (Cambridge, UK: Cambridge University Press, 2016), 116, 122, quote at 116.

39. Aro Velmet, *Pasteur's Empire: Bacteriology and Politics in France, Its Colonies, and the World* (Oxford: Oxford University Press, 2020), 152–59.

40. Sunil S. Amrith, "Internationalising Health in the Twentieth Century," in Sluga and Clavin, *Internationalisms,* 252–53; Velmet, *Pasteur's Empire,* 160–68.

41. Corinna R. Unger, *International Development: A Postwar History* (London: Bloomsbury, 2018), 18; Amalia Ribi Forclaz, "A New Target for International Social Reform: The International Labour Organisation and Working and Living Conditions in Agriculture in the Interwar Years," *Journal of Contemporary History* 20, no. 3 (2011): 315–21.

42. Unger, *International Development,* 16–17, 34–43; Luis Eslava, "The Moving Location of Empire: Indirect Rule, International Law, and the *Bantu Educational Kinema Project,*" *Leiden Journal of International Law* 31, no. 3 (2018): 544–54.

43. Anne Deighton, "Entente Neo-Coloniale?: Ernest Bevin and the Proposals for an Anglo-French Third World Power, 1945-1949," *Diplomacy & Statecraft* 17, no. 4 (2006): 837.

44. Nicholas J. White, "Reconstructing Europe through Rejuvenating Empire: The British, French, and Dutch Experiences Compared," *Past & Present* 210, Supplement 6 (2011): 220–26.

45. Emily Lynn Osborn, "Containers, Energy and the Anthropocene in West Africa," in *Economic Development and Environmental History in the Anthropocene: Perspectives on Asia and Africa*, ed. Gareth Austin (London: Bloomsbury, 2017), 89–90.

46. Austin, *Economic Development and Environmental History*, 1–6.

47. Coghe, "Reordering Colonial Society," 24–31. For the dawning awareness among British colonial agronomists and social anthropologists that rural modernization strategies could be wrongheaded and environmentally damaging, see Helen Tilley, *Africa as a Living Laboratory: Empire, Development, and the Problem of Scientific Knowledge, 1870–1950* (Chicago: University of Chicago Press, 2011), 117–20, 123–24, 134–38.

48. Adam Guerin, "Disaster Ecologies: Land, Peoples and the Colonial Modern in the Gharb, Morocco, 1911–1936," *Journal of the Economic and Social History of the Orient* 59 (2016): 334–39; Edmund Burke III, *The Ethnographic State: France and the Invention of Moroccan Islam* (Berkeley: University of California Press, 2014), 78.

49. Guerin, "Disaster Ecologies," 340–59; idem, "'Not a Drop for the Settlers': Reimagining Popular Protest and Anti-Colonial Nationalism in the Moroccan Protectorate," *Journal of North African Studies* 20, no. 2 (2015): 225–27, 230–31; idem, "Racial Myth, Colonial Policy, and the Invention of Customary Law in Morocco, 1912–1930," *Journal of North African Studies* 16, no. 3 (2011): 361–80.

50. Sunil Amrith, "Reconstructing the 'Plural Society': Asian Migration between Empire and Nation, 1940–1948," *Past & Present* 210, Supplement 6 (2011): 239–40.

51. Amrith, "Reconstructing the 'Plural Society,'" 244–45.

52. Colonial governments struggled to get reliable economic data from colonial smallholders, meaning that basic information about income, output, livestock, and crop losses was approximate at best. Instead of deriving such information from local sources, French officials relied on export tonnage statistics from the principal colonial ports from which extrapolations were made about improving or declining revenues and conditions. See: AN, F^{60} 1426, Conseil National Économique, "Rapport présenté par M. Chappaz, Inspecteur Général de l'Agriculture, L'organisation du marché des fruits et légumes," May 10, 1937.

53. Barry Eichengreen, *Golden Fetters: The Gold Standard and the Great Depression, 1919–1939* (Oxford: Oxford University Press, 1992), 221–32; Oscar Sanchez-Sibony, *Red Globalization: The Political Economy of the Soviet Cold War from Stalin to Khrushchev* (Cambridge, UK: Cambridge University Press, 2014), 28–29, 43–44, 50–54. As exporters of primary products, colonial experiences mirrored those of the Soviet economy to a remarkable extent. In the USSR, as in much of the decolonizing world, import substitution strategies to diminish reliance on rich world trading partners were designed to nurture support among local elites.

54. ANOM, Papiers Marius Moutet, 28PA/carton 3, dossier 113, "Note sur la politique sociale aux colonies: Note sur la fiscalité colonial," no date, but July or August 1936.

55. Useful here are the series of reports on colonial social conditions and economic hardship compiled by former French North African governor Théodore Steeg's Popular Front–appointed Inquiry Commission between 1936 and 1938: AN, F^{60} 763, Commission d'enquête dans les territoires de la France d'Outre-Mer, 1936–38.

56. Slobodian, *Globalists*, 56.

57. Owen White, *The Blood of the Colony: Wine and the Rise and Fall of French Algeria* (Cambridge, MA: Harvard University Press, 2021), 6, 120–22.

58. White, *Blood of the Colony*, 92–102, 125–38, 151–52. It bears emphasizing that, while the French authorities took some steps to safeguard Algeria's smaller wine producers, many organized into cooperatives, the beneficiaries were overwhelmingly European settlers, not Algerians.

59. MAE, série K: Afrique 1918–40, sous-série: Questions générales, vol. 65: Conférences Nord Africaines 1930–1, 7th Conference Nord-Africaine, Tunis, June 1, 1931.

60. MAE, série K: Afrique 1918–40, sous-série: Questions générales, vol. 65, K1631, Minister of Interior to Direction des affaires politiques, January 29, 1930: "Résolutions adoptées par la 6ème Conférence Nord-Africaine."

61. TNA, FO 371/19874, C375/375/17, "Annual Report on France for 1935," January 3, 1936, FO 371/21589, C14755/1/17, "France, Annual Report, Economic (B)," November 26, 1938.

62. Pedersen, "Empires, States and the League of Nations," 131; Slobodian, *Globalists*, 94.

63. Cyrus Schayegh, *The Middle East and the Making of the Modern World* (Cambridge, MA: Harvard University Press, 2017), 201–7, 222–26.

64. Schayegh, *Middle East*, 9, 157–64, 226–30.

65. Schayegh, *Middle East*, 10.

66. Schayegh, *Middle East*, 222–30, 242–55. *Qawmiyya* connotes commitment to unity of the Arab nation.

67. Hyoung-kyu Chey, "International Political Economy Thought in Pre-Modern and Colonial Korea," *International Trade, Politics, and Development* 3, no. 1 (2019), 22–23.

68. Pierre Brocheux and Daniel Hémery, *Indochina: An Ambiguous Colonization, 1858–1954* (Berkeley: University of California Press, 2009), 255–59.

69. Shawn F. McHale, *The First Vietnam War: Violence, Sovereignty, and the Fracture of the South, 1945–1956* (Cambridge, UK: Cambridge University Press, 2021), 34–35.

70. Brocheux and Hémery, *Indochina*, 262–73.

71. TNA, FO 371/21589, C1582/8/17, Consul General W. W. Coultas (Saigon) to FO, "Report on Conditions and Events in Indochina, January 1938," February 5, 1938.

72. Catherine Coquery-Vidrovitch, "Mutation de l'impérialisme colonial français dans les années trente," *African Economic History* 4 (1977): 117.

73. AN, F60 713, Note pour M. le Secrétaire Général, Présidence du Conseil, "Sécheresse et famine en Afrique du Nord," July 1, 1937.

74. White, *Blood of the Colony*, 140.

75. AN, F60 713, Note pour M. le Secrétaire Général, Présidence du Conseil, "Sécheresse et famine en Afrique du Nord," July 1, 1937.

76. Pablo La Porte, "Colonial Dreams and Nightmares: British and French Perceptions of Republican Policies in Spanish Morocco (1931–1936)," *International History Review* 41, no. 4 (2019): 821–44; for French Moroccan monitoring of the situation in the neighboring Spanish zone under the Second Republic, see MAE, série M MAROC 1917–40, vol. 85: Politique générale marocaine, dossier général 1935–6.

77. MAE, PA-AP 258: Léopold Benazet papers, file 1, Direction des Affaires Indigènes, "Note au sujet de l'état d'esprit des indigènes au Maroc en Décembre 1934." In North Africa's major cities, tradesmen and skilled workers suffered acutely in the depression. Fez was typical, registering 4,000 unemployed tradesmen by December 1934. On urban growth in French North Africa, see Jim House, "Colonial Containment? Repression of Pro-Independence Street Demonstrations in Algiers, Casablanca and Paris, 1945–1962," *War in History* 25, no. 2 (2018): 172–201, at 177–78.

78. MAE, PA-AP 258: Léopold Benazet papers, file 2: Archives personnelles concernant le Maroc, 1934–7, file 2, Directeur des Affaires Indigènes Benazet, "Note au sujet du refoulement des Marocains indigents sur leur tribu d'origine," March 27, 1935.

79. MAE, PA-AP 258: Léopold Benazet papers, file 2, Directeur des Affaires Indigènes Benazet, "Note au sujet du refoulement des Marocains indigents sur leur tribu d'origine," March 27, 1935.

80. MAE, PA-AP 258: Léopold Benazet papers, file 2, 1934–7, Direction des Affaires Indigènes, "Note sur les moyens mis en oeuvre pour diminuer les charges supportées par les indigènes et leur venir en aide," November 22, 1935.

81. Guerin, "Disaster Ecologies," 358–61. For the narrative of inexorable environmental degradation prevalent among French agronomists and forestry specialists in depression-era French Morocco, see Diana K. Davis, *Resurrecting the Granary of Rome: Environmental History and French Colonial Expansion in North Africa* (Athens: Ohio University Press, 2007), 150–61; and for its colonial prehistory: Diana K. Davis, "Desert 'Wastes' of the Maghreb: Desertification Narratives in French Colonial Environmental History of North Africa," *Cultural Geographies* 11 (2004): 364–68, 376–80. For parallels in British colonial Africa during the Depression years, see David M. Anderson, "Depression, Dust Bowl, Demography, and Drought: The Colonial State and Soil Conservation in East Africa during the 1930s," *African Affairs* 83, no. 332 (1984): 322–43.

82. Davis, *Resurrecting the Granary of Rome*, 161–63; Guerin, "'Not a Drop for the Settlers,'" 230–35. As Adam Guerin notes, difficult weather conditions, harvest failures and livestock pressure all exacerbated the situation in the mid-1930s. But the changing structure and ecological complexion of Moroccan agriculture as French business and settlers moved in were more decisive, prompting anti-settler protests in Meknès in early September 1937.

83. MAE, PA-AP 258: Léopold Benazet papers, file 1, Direction des Affaires Indigènes, "Note au sujet de l'état d'esprit des indigènes au Maroc en Décembre 1934." An estimated 30,000 Moroccans from the Rif Mountains of the north to the Tafilalet oasis in the pre-Sahara traveled to Algeria in search of seasonal employment in the fall and winter of 1934. Even before the depression hit, rates of infant mortality in France's other North African protectorate, Tunisia, remained high and were shockingly disproportionate between Tunisia's three main ethnoreligious communities of Europeans, Jews and Muslims. Aggregate recorded rates between 1909 and 1928 for deaths of infants under one year old were 117 per 1,000 for Europeans, 175 per 1,000 for Jews, and 236 per 1,000 for Muslims: Richard C. Parks, *Medical Imperialism in French North Africa: Regenerating the Jewish Community of Colonial Tunis* (Lincoln: University of Nebraska Press, 2017), 129, 132.

84. MAE, PA-AP 258: Léopold Benazet papers, file 2, Directeur des Affaires Indigènes, "Note au sujet de la situation des populations indigènes (misère)," February 15, 1937.

85. AN, F⁶⁰ 713, no. 928, General Noguès, Resident General to Yvon Delbos, Sous-Direction Afrique-Levant, "Situation économique au Maroc: Sécheresse et famine," April 30, 1937.

86. AN, F⁶⁰ 713, Report by Théodore Steeg, former Moroccan Resident General, sent to PM's Office, June 21, 1937, and unsigned letter from Prime Minister Camille Chautemps' office to Steeg, November 5, 1937. The Finance Ministry authorized the relief spend but subdivided it into two tranches, payable over 1937 and 1938, the second of which was never fully paid. In 1937, 167.5 million francs was paid out: 80 million to Morocco, 61.5 million to Algeria, 28 million to Tunisia.

87. Roger Richardot, "Le Crédit Agricole chez les indigènes d'Algérie," *Outre-Mer* 8, no. 1 (1936): 20–32.

88. AN, F⁶⁰ 1426: Dossiers de Camille Chautemps, "Plan d'équipement social indigène et économique, 1938–39"; AN, F⁶⁰ 733, dossier: Budgets de l'Algérie 1937-9, questions financières. Lines of credit to peasant farmers to help them buy seeds, fertilizer, and basic agricultural equipment were an early priority of Popular Front colonial reform: ANOM, Papiers Marius Moutet, 28PA/carton 3, dossier 116, Président du Comité d'Action Colonisatrice et de Paysannat Indigène, to Minister of Colonies, "Aménagement du Crédit agricole aux colonies," July 7, 1936.

89. In each case, the local currency—the Indochinese paistre, the Moroccan franc, and the Syro-Lebanese franc—was tied to the value of the French franc (at parity in the Moroccan case). For a particular case, see AN, F⁶⁰ 733, dossier: Questions financiers, no. 8714, Ministère des Finances Direction du Mouvement Général des Fonds/BI Service Extérieur, June 14, 1938: "Reévaluation de l'encaisse or de la Banque de l'Algérie."

90. Assemblée Générale des Actionnaires de la Banque de France du 28 janvier 1938, *Compte Rendu au nom du Conseil Général de la Banque et rapport de MM. Les Censeurs* (Paris: Imprimerie Paul Dupont, 1938); TNA, FO 371/20695, Dakar Consulate, "Two-Monthly Report on Economic Conditions in French West Africa," n.d. January 1937.

91. ANOM, ALGÉRIE, Gouvernement-Général, Cabinet du Gouverneur Général Jules Carde, 1930–5, Carton GGA/2cab/3, No. 7/2 bis Brigade d'Aïn-Fakroun, Rapport du maréchal-des-logis chef Pernoud sur les agissements du Docteur Bendjelloul, Aïn-Fakroun, September 16, 1932. Bendjelloul founded the *Fédération des Élus Musulmans d'Algérie* in 1930.

92. ANOM, Carton GGA/3cab/41, Cabinet du Gouverneur Général de l'Algérie, Direction des Affaires Indigènes report, "Situation politique et économique des indigènes de l'Algérie," December 1935, 45–46.

93. Institut d'Histoire sociale, Nanterre, Charles Dumas papers, "Note pour M. Marx Dormoy (Interior Minister) sur Mohamed Ben Hamida Ben Salem," August 19, 1937.

94. Ewout Frankema, "Raising Revenue in the British Empire, 1870–1940: How 'Extractive' Were Colonial Taxes?" *Journal of Global History* 5 (2010): 447–49, 462, 468.

95. AN, F⁶⁰ 733, dossier: questions financières, no. 1789/SP, Algiers Governor-General Georges Le Beau to Camille Chautemps, May 3, 1939.

96. Patricia M. E. Lorcin, *Historicizing Colonial Nostalgia: European Women's Narratives of Algeria and Kenya, 1900–Present* (New York: Palgrave Macmillan, 2012), introduction.

97. The complicity between the Algiers colonial administration and settler opponents of what they characterized as leftist colonial reform was nicely illustrated by a 1937 ban imposed on a Socialist Party initiative to organize charity collections in Algiers for homeless Algerian children: Institut d'Histoire sociale, Nanterre, Charles Dumas papers, box 1, Parti Socialiste, SFIO, Fédération d'Alger, Secretary P. Cremadez to Interior Minister Marx Dormoy, December 5, 1937.

98. Dónal Hassett, *Mobilizing Memory: The Great War and the Language of Politics in Colonial Algeria, 1918–1939* (Oxford: Oxford University Press, 2019), 44–45, 59–67. The project granted property-owning Muslim males employed in Algerian public service the right to vote with male settlers for the electoral college from which the colony's national representatives were chosen.

99. AN, F⁶⁰ 728, Sous-dossier: Commission d'enquête, Algérie, "Rapport présenté à la Commission de l'Algérie, des Colonies et Pays de Protectorat sur les résultats des investigations de la Sous-Commission relativement aux divers moyens préconisés pour étendre les droits politiques des indigènes algeriens," presented by Joseph Lagrossillière, November 15, 1937. For the extreme-right in 1930s Algeria, see Samuel Kalman, *French Colonial Fascism: The Extreme Right in Algeria, 1919–1939* (Basingstoke, UK: Palgrave, 2013), chapters 3–4.

100. AN, F⁶⁰ 730, "Le Gouverneur général fait d'importantes déclarations," Echo d'Alger, January 5, 1937; Jacques Doriot, "L'application du projet Viollette marquerait la fin de l'Algérie française," February 17, 1938; "Contre le projet Viollette," *Dépêche Algérienne*, March 9, 1938.

101. TNA, FO 371/21601, Algiers Consulate quarterly report no. 6, June 30, 1938. Ironically, Algeria, France's foremost settler colony, was excluded from the largest such prewar survey, which the Guernat commission appointed in 1936 to explore the structural causes of colonial poverty. See AN, Parliamentary Commission files: Assemblée Nationale XVIème Législature, C15150, Commission de l'Algérie, des Colonies et des Protectorats, Séance du 12 Août 1936.

102. SHD, FM, C223/D122, SEA report, "Note sur les conditions psychologiques d'une mobilisation générale en Algérie (Mai 1935)"; AN, F⁶⁰ 733, dossier: questions financières, no. 1789/SP, Algiers Governor-General Georges Le Beau to Camille Chautemps, May 3, 1939.

103. Institut d'Histoire Sociale, Nanterre, Archives Charles Dumas, Box 4: Années 30, Gaston Doumergue to Interior Minister Marx Dormoy, February 24, 1937.

104. Ingrid de Zwarte, *The Hunger Winter: Fighting Famine in the Occupied Netherlands, 1944–1945* (Cambridge, UK: Cambridge University Press, 2020), 43–59, 257–60.

105. Bryan L. McDonald, *Food Power: The Rise and Fall of the Postwar American Food System* (New York: Oxford University Press, 2017), 28–39.

106. McDonald, *Food Power*, 24.

107. Ian Duncan, "The Politics of Liberalisation in Early Post-Independence India: Food Deregulation in 1947," *Journal of Commonwealth and Comparative Politics* 33, no. 1 (1995): 28–34. Tighter regulation of India's internal food market followed—rather

than anticipated—Japan's advance into Southeast Asia. And Gandhi's hostility to food controls amid continued rationing in postwar India was pivotal to the deregulation of prices and foodstuff markets in December 1947, a decision reversed in 1948.

108. Taylor C. Sherman, "From 'Grow More Food' to 'Miss a Meal': Hunger, Development, and the Limits of Post-Colonial Nationalism in India, 1947–1957," *South Asia* 36, no. 4 (2013): 572–83; Duncan, "Politics of Liberalisation," 30–43; Mark B. Tauger, "Entitlement, Shortage and the 1943 Bengal Famine: Another Look," *Journal of Peasant Studies* 31, no. 1 (2003): 45–72.

109. Anwesha Roy, *Making Peace, Making Riots: Communalism and Communal Violence, Bengal, 1940–1947* (Cambridge, UK: Cambridge University Press, 2018), 69–80.

110. A searing narrative of the famine is Janam Mukherjee, *Hungry Bengal: War, Famine and the End of Empire* (London: Hurst, 2015), especially chapters 3–4; on British governmental and civil society responses, see Joanna Simonow, "The Great Bengal Famine in Britain: Metropolitan Campaigning for Food Relief and the End of Empire, 1943–44," *Journal of Imperial & Commonwealth History* 48, no. 1 (2020): 175–83.

111. Urvi Khaitan, "Women beneath the Surface: Coal and the Colonial State in India during the Second World War," *War & Society* 39, no. 3 (2020): 174–75. Legislation passed in 1842 prohibited women from underground mine labour in Britain.

112. Khaitan, "Women beneath the Surface," 184–85.

113. Khaitan, "Women beneath the Surface," 177–80.

114. Numbers of female and child victims seem to have been underestimated, because neither were liable to pay head tax; see Bùi Minh Dũng, "Japan's Role in the Vietnamese Starvation of 1944–45," *Modern Asian Studies* 29, no. 3 (1995): 574–76; Stein Tønnesson, *The Vietnamese Revolution of 1945: Roosevelt, Ho Chi Minh and de Gaulle in a World at War* (London: Sage, 1991), 293–302.

115. Bùi Minh Dũng, "Japan's Role," 586–98.

116. Bùi Minh Dũng, "Japan's Role," 602–18.

117. McDonald, *Food Power*, 2–12; Seikaly, *Men of Capital*, 94–102, 160–69.

118. McDonald, *Food Power*, 31.

119. Duncan, "Politics of Liberalisation," 28–30.

120. Gyan Prakash, "Anxious Constitution-Making," in *The Postcolonial Moment in South and Southeast Asia*, ed. Gyan Prakash, Michael Laffan, and Nikhil Menon (London: Bloomsbury, 2018) 147–49, 157.

121. Bernhard, "Borrowing from Mussolini," 619–20.

122. Roberta Pergher, *Mussolini's Nation-Empire: Sovereignty and Settlement in Italy's Borderlands, 1922–1943* (Cambridge, UK: Cambridge University Press, 2018), 7–11; Eileen Ryan, "Violence and the Politics of Prestige: The Fascist Turn in Colonial Libya," *Modern Italy* 20, no. 2 (April 2015): 123–35; Michael R. Ebner, "Fascist Violence and the 'Ethnic Reconstruction' of Cyrenaica (Libya), 1922–1934," in *Violence, Colonialism, and Empire in the Modern World*, ed. Philip Dwyer and Amanda Nettelbeck (Basingstoke, UK: Palgrave Macmillan, 2018), 204–15; Rania Maktabi, "The Lebanese Census of 1932 Revisited: Who Are the Lebanese?" *British Journal of Middle Eastern Studies* 26, no. 2 (1999): 219–41; Martin Thomas, "Economic Conditions and the Limits to Mobilization in the French Empire, 1936–1939," *Historical Journal* 48, no. 2 (2005): 471–98.

123. Leigh Gardner, "Fiscal Policy in the Belgian Congo in Comparative Perspective," in *Colonial Exploitation and Economic Development: The Belgian Congo and the Netherlands Indies Compared*, ed. Ewout Frankema and Frans Buelens (Abingdon, UK: Routledge, 2013), 145.

124. ANOM, Marius Moutet papers, 28/PA/5, dossier 131, Note for Moutet, "Crédit local et accession à la petite propriété," n.d. 1937.

125. High levels of long-term debt among North African smallholders featured prominently in the early discussion of colonial reform priorities under the Popular Front; see AN, Parliamentary Commission files: Assemblée Nationale XVIème Législature (June 1, 1936–May 31, 1942), C15150, Commission de l'Algérie, des Colonies et des Protectorats, Séance du 6 Août 1936.

126. Márcia Gonçalves, "Of Peasants and Settlers: Ideals of Portugueseness, Imperial Nationalism and European Settlement in Africa, c. 1930–c.1945," *European Review of History* 25, no. 1 (2018): 167–72. The angolar replaced the escudo in Angola, remaining in circulation until 1958.

127. Slobodian, *Globalists*, 93.

128. Joseph Bohling, "Colonial or Continental Power? The Debate over Economic Expansion in Interwar France, 1925–1932," *Contemporary European History* 26, no. 2 (2017): 235–39.

129. French Indochina, the largest colonial federation outside the gold standard system in the late 1920s, was effectively bolted onto the French-led 'gold bloc' in April 1930. At that point, the Indochinese piastre, previously a currency valued against silver, had lost some 20 per cent of its tradable value. Living costs in Hanoi were estimated to have increased by 10 per cent over the winter of 1929–30: MAE, série E: Asie 1918–40, sous-série: Indochine Française, vol. 45: Situation économique 1930–40, no. 195, Comte Damien de Martel, French Ambassador to China, to Aristide Briand, April 30, 1930. See also Carl Strikwerda, "World War I in the History of Globalization," *Historical Reflections* 42, no. 3 (Winter 2016): 123; Matthew Stubbings, "Free Trade Empire to Commonwealth of Nations: India, Britain and Imperial Preference, 1903–1932," *International History Review* 41, no. 2 (2019): 335–37.

130. Strikwerda, "World War I in the History of Globalization," 112–32.

131. Patricia Clavin and Madeleine Dungy, "Trade, Law, and the Global Order of 1919," *Diplomatic History* 44, no. 4 (2020): 561, 571–7; Slobodian, *Globalists*, 56, 95; Amrith, "Struggles for Citizenship," 112–13.

132. Christy Thornton, *Revolution in Development: Mexico and the Governance of the Global Economy* (Berkeley: University of California Press, 2021), 42–47; idem, "A Mexican International Economic Order? Tracing the Hidden Roots of the Charter of Economic Rights and Duties of States," *Humanity* 9, no. 3 (2018): 397–98.

Chapter Six: Making Decolonization's Global Cultures

1. Christoph Kalter, *The Discovery of the Third World: Decolonization and the Rise of the New Left in France c. 1950–1976* (Cambridge, UK: Cambridge University Press, 2016), 419; Sarah C. Dunstan, "*La Langue de nos maîtres*: Linguistic Hierarchies, Dialect, and Canon Decolonization during and after the *Présence Africaine* Congress of 1956," *Journal of Modern History* 93, no. 1 (2021): 861–95.

2. As an example: Sönke Kunkel, "Global Media, Emotions, and the 'Kennedy Narrative': Kennedy as Seen from the 'Global South,'" in *Globalizing the U.S. Presidency: Postcolonial Views of John F. Kennedy*, ed. Cyrus Schayegh (London: Bloomsbury, 2021), 100–14.

3. Black Panther Party organizers and the broad coalition of US anti–Vietnam War activists studied by Judy Tzu-Chun Wu exemplify these trends; see her *Radicals on the Road: Internationalism, Orientalism, and Feminism during the Vietnam Era* (Ithaca, NY: Cornell University Press, 2013).

4. Deborah Thomas, *Exceptional Violence: Embodied Citizenship in Transnational Jamaica* (Durham, NC: Duke University Press, 2011), 199–205. Myles Osborne, "'Mau Mau Are Angels . . . Sent by Haile Selassie': A Kenyan War in Jamaica," *Comparative Studies in Society and History* 62, no. 4 (2020): 714–29. Focusing on support for Mau Mau among, respectively, Jamaica's Rastafarian community and the island's urban poor, Thomas and Osborne identify a 'black internationalism' less elitist than the pan-Africanism of organized anticolonial movements in the Anglophone Caribbean and the United States.

5. A good example are interwar non-European women's movements such as the All-Asian Women's Conference and the All-India Women's Conference that helped decenter women's rights away from European feminism and toward local manifestations of colonial discrimination; see Marie Sandell, "Regional versus International: Women's Activism and Organisational Spaces in the Inter-War Period," *International History Review* 33, no. 4 (2011): 607–16. For differing strategies of colonial protest, see Adam Branch and Zachariah Mampilly, *Africa Uprising: Popular Protest and Political Change* (London: Bloomsbury, 2015), 14–39.

6. Daniel Laqua, "Student Activists and International Cooperation in a Changing World, 1919–1960," in *Internationalists in European History: Rethinking the Twentieth Century*, ed. David Brydan and Jessica Reinisch (London: Bloomsbury Academic, 2022), 170–81.

7. Ismay Milford highlights the political frustrations and legal restrictions experienced by East African anticolonial activists, former students of Uganda's Makerere University College, despite their widening transnational connections in the 1950s, see his *African Activists in a Decolonising World: The Making of an Anticolonial Culture, 1952–1966* (Cambridge, UK: Cambridge University Press, 2023), 5, 10–15, 26–27.

8. Martin Thomas, *Empires of Intelligence: Security Services and Colonial Disorder after 1914* (Berkeley: University of California Press, 2008), chapters 1 and 3.

9. Useful, although not colonially focused, is Antje Dietze and Katja Naumann, "Revisiting Transnational Actors from a Spatial Perspective," *European Review of History: Revue Européenne d'histoire* 25, no. 3–4 (2018): 415–30. Also essential is Milford, *African Activists in a Decolonising World*, 33–45, 98–113.

10. For a case study of such transnational linkage, focused on British expulsion from India of the American communist John Wilson Johnstone, following his discussions with All-India Trades Union Congress in late 1928, see Michele Louro, "The Johnstone Affair and Anti-Communism in Interwar India," *Journal of Contemporary History* 53, no. 1 (2018): 38–60.

11. Tzu-Chun Wu, *Radicals on the Road*, 3–4, 26–27, 94–95; Robert J. Bookmiller, "The Algerian War of Words: Broadcasting and Revolution, 1954–1962," *Maghreb*

Review 14, no. 3–4 (1989): 196–213; Elidor Mëhilli, "Radio and Revolution: Tirana via Bari, from Moscow to Beijing," in Brydan and Reinisch, *Internationalists*, 80–83.

12. Ismay Milford, Gerard McCann, Emma Hunter and Daniel Branch. "Another World? East Africa, Decolonisation, and the Global History of the Mid-Twentieth Century" *Journal of African History* 62, no. 3 (2021): 394–410; Daniel Branch, "Political Traffic: Kenyan Students in Eastern and Central Europe, 1958–1969," *Journal of Contemporary History* 53, no. 4 (2018): 811–31.

13. Katharine McGregor, "Opposing Colonialism: The Women's International Democratic Federation and Decolonisation Struggles in Vietnam and Algeria, 1945–1965," *Women's History Review* 25, no. 6 (2016): 925–32, 936–38.

14. MAE, série Afrique-Levant, sous-série: Généralités, 1944–52, file 65, no. 53/AS, J. Royère, Consul general, Shanghai, to Foreign Ministry/Direction Asie-Océanie, March 9, 1950. "A.S. Lettre de la Fédération Chinoise des Femmes Démocrates à la section féminine du RDA."

15. Su Sin Lewis and Carolien Stolte, "Other Bandungs: Afro-Asian Internationalisms in the Early Cold War," *Journal of World History* 30, no. 1–2 (2019): 2–5, 9–17.

16. Patricia A. Schechter, "Feminist Historiography, Anti-Imperialism, and the Decolonial," in *Empire's Twin: U.S. Anti-Imperialism from the Founding Era to the Age of Terrorism*, ed. Ian Tyrrell and Jay Sexton (Ithaca, NY: Cornell University Press, 2015), 154–66.

17. Nico Slate, *Colored Cosmopolitanism: The Shared Struggle for Freedom in the United States and India* (Cambridge, MA: Harvard University Press, 2012), 65–67.

18. Gerard McCann uses trade unionist and Kenyan African National Union activist Tom Mboya to illustrate the connection, beginning his analysis with Mboya's April 18, 1959, speech to a 20,000-strong *Youth March for Integrated Schools* in Washington DC, which was also addressed by Martin Luther King Jr. Gerard McCann, "Possibility and Peril: Trade Unionism, African Cold War, and the Global Strands of Kenyan Decolonization," *Journal of Social History* 53, no. 2 (2019): 348–49.

19. Imaobong D. Umoren, *Race Women Internationalists: Activist Intellectuals and Global Freedom Struggles* (Berkeley: University of California Press, 2018), 1–3, 9; Sarah Dunstan, "Imperialism," in Patricia Owens et al., *Women's International Thought: Towards a New Canon* (Cambridge, UK: Cambridge University Press, 2022), 131–34, 138–41, 143–51.

20. Leslie James, "'Essential Things such as Typewriters': Development Discourse, Trade Union Expertise, and the Dialogues of Decolonization between the Caribbean and West Africa," *Journal of Social History* 53, no. 2 (2019): 381–85; Sunil Amrith, "Reconstructing the 'Plural Society': Asian Migration between Empire and Nation, 1940–1948," *Past & Present* 210, Supplement 6 (2011): 237–57; Sunil Amrith, *Crossing the Bay of Bengal: The Furies of Nature and the Fortunes of Migrants* (Cambridge, MA: Harvard University Press, 2013), especially chapters 6 and 7; Tracey Banivanua Mar, *Decolonisation and the Pacific: Indigenous Globalisation and the Ends of Empire* (Cambridge, UK: Cambridge University Press, 2016).

21. Michael A. Gomez, *Reversing Sail: A History of the African Diaspora*, 2nd edition (Cambridge, UK: Cambridge University Press, 2020), 201–2.

22. Paul Thomas Chamberlin, *The Global Offensive: The United States, the Palestine Liberation Organization, and the Making of the Post–Cold War Order* (Oxford:

Oxford University Press, 2012). For African-American conceptualization of 'internal colonialism' in the United States, see Sam Klug, "First New Nation or Internal Colony? Modernization Theorists, Black Intellectuals, and the Politics of Colonial Comparison in the Kennedy Years," in Schayegh, *Globalizing the U.S.*, 21–29, and, more generally, Penny von Eschen, *Race against Empire: Black Americans and Anticolonialism, 1937–1957* (Ithaca, NY: Cornell University Press, 1997); Brenda Gayle Plummer, *In Search of Power: African Americans in the Era of Decolonization, 1956–1974* (Cambridge, UK: Cambridge University Press, 2013); Van Nguyen-Marshall, "Student Activism in a Time of War: Youth in the Republic of Vietnam, 1960s–1970s," *Journal of Vietnamese Studies* 10, no. 2 (2015): 43–81; Heather Marie Stur, *Saigon at War: South Vietnam and the Global Sixties* (Cambridge, UK: Cambridge University Press, 2020), 112–18, 125–26; Constantin Katsakioris, "Students from Portuguese Africa in the Soviet Union, 1960–74: Anti-Colonialism, Education, and the Socialist Alliance," *Journal of Contemporary History* 56, no. 1 (2021): 142–65; James Mark and Péter Apor, "Socialism Goes Global: Decolonization and the Making of a New Culture of Internationalism in Socialist Hungary, 1956–1989," *Journal of Modern History* 87 (December 2015): 857–62.

23. MAE, série Europe 1949–55, sous-série Grande-Bretagne, vol. 104: Afrique Noire, no. 131/AL M. O. Renner, Consulat de France, Accra, to Foreign Ministry: Visite en Gold Coast d'agents du Department of State, July 24, 1949; Carol Anderson, "The Histories of African-Americans' Anticolonialism during the Cold War," in *The Cold War in the Third World*, ed. Robert J. McMahon (Oxford: Oxford University Press, 2013), 178–80.

24. Francis Njubi Nesbitt, *Race for Sanctions: African Americans against Apartheid, 1946–1994* (Bloomington: Indiana University Press, 2004); Nicholas Grant, "The Global Antiapartheid Movement and the Racial Politics of the Cold War," *Radical History Review* 119 (2014): 72–93; Rob Skinner, "Humanitaranism and Human Rights in Global Apartheid," in *A Global History of Anti-Apartheid: "Forward to Freedom" in South Africa*, ed. Anna Konieczna and Rob Skinner (Cham: Palgrave Macmillan, 2019), 36–55.

25. Paul A. Kramer, "Shades of Sovereignty: Racialized Power, the United States and the World," in *Explaining the History of American Foreign Relations*, ed. Frank Costigliola and Michael J. Hogan (Cambridge, UK: Cambridge University Press, 2016), 245–46, 256–64.

26. Robert Trent Vinson, "Up from Slavery and Down with Apartheid! African-Americans and Black South Africans against the Global Color Line," *Journal of American Studies* 52, no. 2 (2018): 302–17.

27. John Munro, *The Anticolonial Front: The African-American Freedom Struggle and Global Decolonisation, 1945–1960* (Cambridge, UK: Cambridge University Press, 2017).

28. Bridget L. Coggins, "Rebel Diplomacy: Theorizing Violent Non-State Actors' Use of Talk," in *Rebel Governance in Civil War*, ed. Ana Arjona, Nelson Kasfir, and Zachariah Mampilly (Cambridge, UK: Cambridge University Press, 2015), 100.

29. Daniel Edmonds, Evan Smith, and Oleksa Drachewych, "Editorial: Transnational Communism and Anti-Colonialism," *Twentieth Century Communism* 18 (Spring 2020): 5–13. As Su Sin Lewis points out, similar transnational networks

connected socialist internationalists in Asia; see Lewis, "Asian Socialism and the For-gotten Architects of Post-Colonial Freedom, 1952–1956," *Journal of World History* 30, no. 1 (2019): 55–88.

30. Heather Streets-Salter and Trevor R. Getz provide insights into anticolonial perspectives, methods and connections: *Empires and Colonies in the Modern World: A Global Perspective* (New York: Oxford University Press, 2015), chapter 15: "Unravel-ing Colonialism".

31. TNA, MI5 papers, KV 3/32, Report of the International Colonial Conference, June 11 and 12, 1925.

32. Sara Salem, *Anticolonial Afterlives in Egypt: The Politics of Hegemony* (Cam-bridge, UK: Cambridge University Press, 2020), 6: Minkah Makalani, *In the Cause of Freedom: Radical Black Internationalism from Harlem to London, 1917–1919* (Chapel Hill: University of North Carolina Press, 2011), 75–102, 174–93; Sophie Quinn-Judge, *Ho Chi Minh: The Missing Years, 1919–1941* (London: Hurst, 2003); Walter Rodney, *How Europe Underdeveloped Africa* (London: Bogle-L'Ouverture Publications, 1972); on the particular influence on Rodney of Tanzania's ujamaa socialist project, see Immanuel R. Harisch, "Facets of Walter Rodney's Pan-African Intellectual Activism during his Dar es Salaam Years, 1966–1974," *Vienna Journal of African Studies* 20, no. 38 (2020): 104–8, 111–12.

33. For French, Algerian and other seditionist networks monitored by Alge-rian colonial authorities in the late 1920s, see ANOM, Archives départementales d'Alger, série F: police et maintien d'ordre, carton F408: Communisme, syndicalisme, Croix de Feu, groupements divers, 1929–39; for communist ideological inspiration and organizational models, see Joachim C. Häberlin, "Between Global Aspirations and Local Realities: The Global Dimensions of Interwar Communism," *Journal of Global His-tory* 7, no. 3 (2012): 415–37; Thomas Beaumont, *Fellow Travellers: Communist Trade Unionism and Industrial Relations on the French Railways, 1914–1939* (Liverpool: Liverpool University Press, 2019), 137–49; Heather Streets-Salter, "International and Global Anti-Colonial Movements," in *World Histories from Below: Disruption and Dissent, 1750 to the Present,* 2nd ed., ed. Antoinette Burton and Tony Ballantyne (Lon-don: Bloomsbury, 2022), 64–66.

34. An example being the Profintern-affiliated International Trade Union Com-mittee of Negro Workers analyzed by Hakim Adi, *Pan-Africanism and Communism: The Communist International, Africa and the Diaspora, 1919–1939* (Trenton, NJ: Africa World Press, 2013). And for an Indonesian case study: John T. Sidel, *Republi-canism, Communism, Islam: Cosmopolitan Origins of Revolution in Southeast Asia* (Ithaca, NY: Cornell University Press, 2021), 6–14, 121.

35. MAE, série K: Afrique, sous-série: Affaires Musulmanes, vol. 15, Direction Asie-Océanie intercepted transcript of Soviet military attaché note, "Instructions for the enlistment of secret co-workers in foreign general consulates (British, American, Japanese)," April 4, 1927.

36. Kasper Breskén, "'Whether Black or White—United in the Fight!' Connecting the Resistance against Colonialism, Racism, and Fascism in the European Metropo-les, 1926–1936," *Twentieth Century Communism* 18 (2020): 127–44.

37. Oleksa Drachewych, "Great Disappointment, Shifting Opportunities: A Glimpse into the Comintern, Western European Parties and Their Colonial Work

in the Third Period," *Twentieth Century Communism* 18 (Spring 2020): 150–73. On Münzenberg's efforts to strengthen international ties, see Fredrik Petersson, *Willi Münzenberg, the League against Imperialism, and the Comintern, 1925–1933* (New York: Edwin Mellen, 2014), especially chapters 5–7.

38. Daniel Edmonds, "Shapurji Saklatvala, the Workers' Welfare League of India, and Transnational Anti-Colonial Labour Organising in the Inter-War Period," *Twentieth Century Communism* 18 (Spring 2020): 14–23; Michele Louro, *Comrades against Imperialism: Nehru, India, and Interwar Internationalism* (Cambridge, UK: Cambridge University Press, 2018), 152–7.

39. Edmonds, "Shapurji Saklatvala," 26–28.

40. Claire Lowrie, *Masters and Servants: Cultures of Empire in the Tropics* (Manchester, UK: Manchester University Press, 2016), 145; the associational links among Southeast Asian oppositionists, exiles, travelers and literary figures are nicely described in John Sidel's analysis of Indonesia's Sarekat Islam movement: Sidel, *Republicanism*, 21, 123–29, 143–45, and in Kris Alexanderson's discussion of 'global communist liaisons' facilitated by merchant shipping between Asian and other ports: Kris Alexanderson, *Subversive Seas: Anticolonial Networks across the Twentieth-Century Dutch Empire* (Cambridge, UK: Cambridge University Press, 2019), 170–82.

41. MAE, série K: Afrique 1918–40, sous-série: Questions générales, vol.: 125: Protection des races indigènes, 1921–7, no. 593, Marshal Lyautey to Direction es Affaires Politiques et Commerciales Afrique-Levant, "A/S Surveillance à Paris des indigènes de l'Afrique du Nord," April 2, 1924; Foreign Ministry, Service Français de la Société des Nations, "Note pour la Sous-Direction d'Afrique," February 28, 1924.

42. Michael Goebel, *Anti-Imperial Metropolis: Interwar Paris and the Seeds of Third World Nationalism* (Cambridge, UK: Cambridge University Press, 2015), 2.

43. For insights into these women's works, see Umoren, *Race Women Internationalists*, 11–22; Jacqueline Couti, "Am I My Sister's Keeper? The Politics of Propriety and the Fight for Equality in the Works of French Antillean Women Writers, 1920s–1940s," in *Black French Women and the Struggle for Equality, 1848–2016*, ed. Félix Germain and Silvane Larcher (Lincoln: University of Nebraska Press, 2018), 129–47; Claire Oberon Garcia, "Remapping the Metropolis: Theorizing Black Women's Subjectivities in Interwar Paris," in Germain and Larcher, *Black French Women*, 215–36.

44. Goebel, *Anti-Imperial Metropolis*.

45. Trinidadian writer-activist C. L. R. James, who worked on his defining work *The Black Jacobins* during several extended interwar stays in Paris, personified this combination of activism, itinerancy, and anticolonialism; see Christian Høgsbjerg, "Globalising the Haitian Revolution in Black Paris: C.L.R. James, Metropolitan Anti-Imperialism in Interwar France and the Writing of *The Black Jacobins*," *Journal of Imperial & Commonwealth History* 48, no. 3 (2020): 493–9, 506–8.

46. Su Sin Lewis, *Cities in Motion: Urban Life and Cosmopolitanism in Southeast Asia, 1920–1940* (Cambridge, UK: Cambridge University Press, 2016), 207–11.

47. Umoren, *Race Women Internationalists*, 13–17; Gary Wilder, *Freedom Time: Negritude, Decolonization, and the Future of the World* (Durham, NC: Duke University Press, 2015), 21–24, 50–53. Most comprehensive is Jennifer Anne Boittin, *Colonial Metropolis: The Urban Grounds of Anti-Imperialism and Feminism in Interwar Paris* (Lincoln: University of Nebraska Press, 2015).

48. For Cold War–era anticolonial networks in Paris, see Munro, *Anticolonial Front*, 219–30; Tyler Stovall, "The Fire This Time: Black American Expatriates and the Algerian War," *Yale French Studies* 98 (2000): 182–200; James Campbell, *Exiled in Paris: Richard Wright, James Baldwin, Samuel Beckett, and Others on the Left Bank* (Berkeley, University of California Press, 2003).

49. Marc Matera, *Black London: The Imperial Metropolis and Decolonization in the Twentieth Century* (Berkeley: University of California Press, 2015); Makalani, *In the Cause of Freedom*, especially chapters 3–5; Umoren, *Race Women Internationalists*, 22–35. On Russian, then Soviet, oil-town Baku as another center of early anticolonial cosmopolitanism, see Sidel, *Republicanism*, 72–81.

50. For Geneva and Berlin examples: William S. Cleveland, *Islam against the West: Shakib Arslan and the Campaign for Islamic Nationalism* (London: Al Saqi Books, 1985); B. Venkat Mani, "Anti-Colonial Nationalism and Cosmopolitan 'Standard Time': Lala Har Dayal's *Forty-Four Months in Germany and Turkey* (1920)," in *German Colonialism Revisited: African, Asian, and Oceanic Experiences*, ed. Nina Berman, Klaus Mühlhahn, and Patrice Nganang (Ann Arbor: University of Michigan Press, 2014), 203–9; on the contacts between Indian nationalists, including Jawaharlal Nehru, in Weimar Berlin, see Louro, *Comrades against Imperialism*, 29–33. For Arab contacts with the Nazi regime, especially during the Palestine Revolt of 1936–1939, see Francis Nicosia, *Nazi Germany and the Arab World* (Cambridge, UK: Cambridge University Press, 2015), especially 70–89.

51. MAE, série K: Afrique, sous-série: Affaires Musulmanes, vol. 15, Sûreté note on anticolonial groups in the capital, March 13, 1936.

52. Makalani, *In the Cause of Freedom*, 134–48.

53. Robbie Aitken, "From Cameroon to Germany and Back via Moscow and Paris: The Political Career of Joseph Bilé (1892–1959), Performer, '*Negerarbeiter*' and Comintern Activist," *Journal of Contemporary History* 43, no. 4 (2008): 597–610.

54. Adi, "Pan-Africanism and Communism," 237–54.

55. MAE, série K: Afrique, sous-série: Affaires Musulmanes, vol. 15: Étudiants nord-africains 1932–8, Pozzo du Borgo, "Note relative au IIIème Congrès des Étudiants Nord-Africains," January 15, 1934; "Note: l'Association des Étudiants Nord-Africains," n.d. 1934, fos. 110–14; Scott McConnell, *Leftward Journey: The Education of Vietnamese Students in France, 1919–1939* (Abingdon, UK: Routledge, 1989), especially chapters 2–5; Clifford Rosenberg, *Policing Paris: The Origins of Modern Immigration Control between the Wars* (Ithaca, NY: Cornell University Press, 2006), 149–50; Charles-Robert Ageron, "L'Association des étudiants musulmans nord-africains en France durant l'entre-deux-guerres. Contribution à l'étude des nationalismes maghrébins," *Revue Française d'Histoire d'Outre-Mer* 70, no. 258 (1983): 25–56.

56. Tyler Stovall, *The Rise of the Paris Red Belt* (Berkeley: University of California Press, 1992); for a British parallel, see Matera, *Black London*.

57. Stovall, *Rise of the Paris Red Belt*; idem, *Paris Noir: African Americans in the City of Light* (New York: Houghton Mifflin, 1996). For details of the role of Nguyen Ai Quoc, the future Ho chi Minh, in this communist anticolonialism, see ANOM, online archive, Service de l'Indochine, Minister of Colonies letter to President's Secretary, "Revendications Annamites," et Paris Prefect of Police to Ministry of Colonies Service

de l'Indochine, August 9, 1919; idem, file: Documents rédigés par Nguyen Ai Quoc et saisis par la police, 1919-31, "Copies de notes relevées sur le carnet de Nugyen Ai Quôc." Ho's correspondence, seized from his Paris flat by French police in 1919, suggests that he was already committed to Communist internationalism and less drawn to Wilsonian ideas of self-determination.

58. TNA, MI5 papers, KV 6/18, "Down with French Imperialism! Long Live the People of Syria," May 11, 1924. Executive Committee of the Communist International, three-page press release designated for *Workers' Weekly*.

59. Archives Départementales de l'Aude, Albert Sarraut papers, 12J43, "Meeting organisé par le Comité d'Action de la Région Parisienne du Parti Communiste, Luna Park," May 16, 1925; David H. Slavin, "The French Left and the Rif War, 1924-25: Racism and the Limits of Internationalism," *Journal of Contemporary History* 26, no. 1 (1991): 5-18.

60. Burak Sayim, "Communist Anti-Militarism in France and Anti-Colonial Wars in Morocco and Syria," *Twentieth Century Communism* 24 (2023): 25-30.

61. Organized by Willi Münzenberg, the chair of the Communist Internationale Arbeiter-Hilfe (Workers' International Relief), the LAI conference not only debated colonial interference in China, but also US imperialism in Latin America and the colonial roots of racial discrimination. French authorities charged Léopold Senghor, future president of Senegal, with treason in response to his speech at the conference: MAE, série K: Afrique 1918-40, sous-série: Affaires Musulmanes, vol. 23: Agitateurs musulmans—propagande bolsheviste, no. 413, Sous Direction d'Afrique, Brussels Ambassador Maurice Herbette to Aristide Briand, April 4, 1927.

62. Louro, *Comrades against Imperialism*, 36-37.

63. Louro, *Comrades against Imperialism*, 37-39.

64. Louro, *Comrades against Imperialism*, 42-44.

65. Adi, *Pan-Africanism*, 107-12; Richard Overy, *Blood and Ruins: The Great Imperial War 1931-1945* (London: Allen Lane, 2021), 48-50.

66. Imaobong D. Umoren, "Anti-Fascism and the Development of Global Race Women, 1928-1945," *Callaloo* 39, no. 1 (2016): 157-60; idem, *Race Women Internationalists*, 37-45; Gary Wilder, "Panafricanism and the Republican Political Sphere," in *The Color of Liberty: Histories of Race in France*, ed. Sue Peabody and Tyler Stovall (Durham, NC: Duke University Press, 2003), 248-50; John Munro, "'Ethiopia Stretches Forth across the Atlantic': African American Anticolonialism during the Interwar Period," *Left History* 13, no. 2 (2008): 38-50.

67. Alison Donnell, "Una Marson: Feminism, Anti-Colonialism and a Forgotten Fight for Freedom," in *West Indian Intellectuals in Britain*, ed. Bill Schwarz (Manchester, UK: Manchester University Press, 2003), 117-18; Robin D. G. Kelley, "'But a Local Phase of a World Problem': Black History's Global Vision, 1883-1950," *Journal of American History* 86, no. 3 (1999): 1069-72; Umoren, *Race Women Internationalists*, chapters 3-4. For the Indian dimension and Jawaharlal Nehru's centrality to these internationalist networks, see Louro, *Comrades against Imperialism*, 23-24, 33-41. An attendee of the Brussels Conference but skeptical of the League against Imperialism's Soviet-inspired Marxism, Nehru was suspended from the organization in 1932; see Vineet Thakur, "An Asian Drama: The Asian Relations Conference, 1947," *International History Review* 41, no. 3 (2019): 677.

68. Andrew Ivaska, "Liberation in Transit: Eduardo Mondlane and Che Guevara in Dar es Salaam," in *The Routledge Handbook of the Global Sixties: Between Protest and Nation-Building*, ed. Chen Jian et al. (London: Routledge, 2008), 27, 30–31.

69. Eric Burton, "Hubs of Decolonization: African Liberation Movements and 'Eastern' Connections in Cairo, Accra, and Dar es Salaam," in *Southern African Liberation Movements and the Global Cold War 'East': Transnational Activism 1960–1990*, ed. Lena Dallywater, Chris Saunders, and Helder Adegar Fonseca (Oldenbourg: De Gruyter, 2019), 25–30.

70. Introduction, *The Internationalist Moment: South Asia, Worlds, World Views 1917–1939*, ed. Ali Raza, Franzisca Roy, and Benjamin Zachariah (New Delhi: Sage, 2015).

71. Benoît de l'Estoile, Federico Neiberg, and Lygia Sigaud, "Anthropology and the Government of 'Natives': A Comparative Approach," in *Empires, Nations, and Natives: Anthropology and State-Making*, ed. idem (Durham, NC: Duke University Press, 2005), 19; Amit Prakash, *Empire on the Seine: The Policing of North Africans in Paris, 1925–1975* (Oxford: Oxford University Press, 2022), 26–32.

72. ANOM, Archives départementales d'Alger, série F, Carton F408: Communisme, syndicalisme, Croix de Feu, groupements divers, 1929–39, no. 1243, Chef de la Sûreté départementale to Algiers Prefect, April 16, 1929, and no. 92C, "Ordre particulier pour le 1er Mai 1929."

73. ANOM, Archives départementales d'Alger, série F, Carton F408, no. 1079, Sûreté départementale "Rapport A/S Parti Populaire Français," to Algiers Prefect, February 25, 1937; for background, see Samuel Kalman, *French Colonial Fascism: The Extreme Right in Algeria, 1919–1939* (Basingstoke, UK: Palgrave, 2013).

74. An illustration of this interwar specificity are Constantine's riots and race killings in the summer of 1934: see Joshua Cole, *Lethal Provocation: The Constantine Murders and the Politics of French Algeria* (Ithaca, NY: Cornell University Press, 2020).

75. Erez Manela, *The Wilsonian Moment: Self-Determination and the International Origins of Anticolonial Nationalism* (New York: Oxford University Press, 2007), part III.

76. Manu Goswami, "Imaginary Futures and Colonial Internationalisms," *American Historical Review* 117, no. 5 (2012): 1463–64.

77. Goswami, "Imaginary Futures," 1467–68, 1477–78.

78. Robbie Shilliam, "What about Marcus Garvey? Race and the Transformation of Sovereignty Debate," *Review of International Studies* 32 (2006): 379–80. Some estimates suggest two million UNIA members: Adi, *Pan-Africanism*, 30.

79. Manu Karuka, "Black and Native Visions of Self-Determination," *Critical Ethnic Studies* 3, no. 2 (2017): 82–83.

80. The crucial work here is Paul Gilroy's *The Black Atlantic: Modernity and Double Consciousness* (London: Verso, 1993), especially chapters 1 and 2; for more consideration of the black Altantic's African and Brazilian dynamics, see Andreas Eckert, "Bringing the 'Black Atlantic' into Global History: The Project of Pan-Africanism," in *Competing Visions of World Order: Global Moments and Movements, 1880s–1930s*, ed. Sebastien Conrad and Dominic Sachsenmaier (Basingstoke, UK: Palgrave Macmillan, 2007), 237–38.

81. Eckert, "Bringing the 'Black Atlantic,'" 247–50; Shilliam, "What about Marcus Garvey?" 391–92, 396–97; Randolph B. Persaud, "The Racial Dynamic in International Relations: Some Thoughts on the Pan-African Antecedents of Bandung," in *Meanings of Bandung: Postcolonial Orders and Decolonial Visions*, ed. Quynh N. Pham and R. Shilliam (London: Rowman & Littlefield, 2016), 139–40.

82. Alan McPherson, "Anti-Imperialist Racial Solidarity before the Cold War: Success and Failure," in *Latin America and the Global Cold War*, ed. Thomas C. Field, Stella Krepp, and Vanni Pettinà (Chapel Hill: University of North Carolina Press, 2020), 206–19.

83. Shilliam, "What about Marcus Garvey?" 397–99.

84. Owens et al., *Women's International Thought*, 11, citing Ula Yvette Taylor, *The Veiled Garvey: The Life and Times of Amy Jacques Garvey* (Durham, NC: University of North Carolina Press, 2002).

85. Munro, *Anticolonial Front*, 16–20; Marilyn Lake and Henry Reynolds, *Drawing the Global Colour Line: White Men's Countries and the International Challenge of Racial Equality* (Cambridge, UK: Cambridge University Press, 2008), 2–4; Daniel Gorman, *International Cooperation in the Early Twentieth Century* (London: Bloomsbury, 2017), 29–33. For the distinctiveness of Du Bois's thinking, particularly in regard to pan-Africanism and the dangers of a more limiting anticolonial nationalism, see Brandon Kendhammer, "DuBois the Pan-Africanist and the Development of African Nationalism," *Ethnic and Racial Studies* 30, no. 1 (2007): 54–67. For Du Bois's distinctive sociological ideas, see Sam Klug, "Social Science in Black and White: Rethinking the Disciplines in the Jim Crow Empire," *Modern Intellectual History* 15, no. 3 (2018): 910–15. On Du Bois's rivalry with Garvey, see Gomez, *Reversing Sail*, 203–4.

86. Charisse Burden-Stelly, "W.E.B. Du Bois in the Tradition of Radical Blackness: Radicalism, Repression, and Mutual Comradeship, 1930–1960," *Socialism and Democracy* 32, no. 3 (2018): 193–206.

87. Seneca Vaught, "Du Bois as Diplomat: Race Diplomacy in *Foreign Affairs*, 1926–1945," *Journal of Race and Global Social Change* 1, no. 1 (2014): 11–20.

88. Eric Helleiner, *The Contested World Economy: The Deep and Global Roots of International Political Economy* (Cambridge, UK: Cambridge University Press, 2023), 197–99.

89. Makalani, *In the Cause of Freedom*, 173–94; Bill Schwarz, "George Padmore," in *West Indian Intellectual*, 135–36. A more longstanding communist, another Trinidadian, journalist Claudia Jones, shared Padmore's black internationalist outlook, as propagated in *The West Indian Gazette*, the newspaper she founded in London in 1958: Monique Bedasse, Kim D. Butler, Carlos Fernandes, Dennis Laumann, Tejasvi Nagaraja, Benjamin Talton, Kira Thurman, "AHR Conversation: Black Internationalism," *American Historical Review* 125, no. 5 (2020): 1721.

90. Leslie James, *George Padmore and Decolonization from Below: Africanism, the Cold War, and the End of Empire* (Basingstoke, UK: Palgrave Macmillan, 2015), 2–5, 8–12.

91. Joanna Simonow, "The Great Bengal Famine in Britain: Metropolitan Campaigning for Food Relief and the End of Empire, 1943–44," *Journal of Imperial & Commonwealth History* 48, no. 1 (2020): 178–80; Christopher Goscha, "The Hunger

General: Economic Warfare during the Indochina War," in *The Oxford Handbook of Late Colonial Insurgencies & Counter-Insurgencies*, ed. Martin Thomas and Gareth Curless (Oxford: Oxford University Press, 2023), 622–35.

92. David Motadel, "The Global Authoritarian Moment and the Revolt against Empire," *American Historical Review* 124, no. 3 (2019): 843–48. Michael Ortiz's analysis of India's Radical Democratic Party leader M. N. Roy's hostility to Gandhian nonviolence fits the same pattern: Michael Ortiz, "'Disown Gandhi or Be Damned': M. N. Roy, Gandhi, and Fascism," *Journal of Colonialism and Colonial History* 21, no. 3 (2020), online publication.

93. Ortiz, "'Disown Gandhi,'" 843–77.

94. Rana Mitter, "Nationalism, Decolonization, Geopolitics and the Asian Post-War," in *The Cambridge History of the Second World War*, vol. 3: *Total War: Economy, Society and Culture*, ed. Michael Geyer and Adam Tooze (Cambridge, UK: Cambridge University Press, 2015), 606.

95. Eric D. Weitz, *A World Divided: The Global Struggle for Human Rights in the Age of Nation-States* (Princeton, NJ: Princeton University Press, 2019), 404. Inspired by the Atlantic Charter, Nelson Mandela and the ANC devised their own, calling for black African freedom, land rights, and an end to discrimination.

96. For analysis of the black–nonblack color line, white supremacism, and other racial divides in the wartime US military, see Thomas A. Guglielmo, *Divisions: A New History of Racism and Resistance in America's World War II Military* (New York: Oxford University Press, 2021).

97. Munro, *Anticolonial Front*, 44–52. Munro stresses the importance in preparing the intellectual agenda of the Manchester Congress of the April 1945 conference organized by the Council on African Affairs at Harlem's Schomberg Library. Munro and Ula Yvette Taylor also highlight the input from several activists, including Jamaican Amy Jacques Garvey and Martinican writer Paulette Nardal, who were unable to attend the Manchester Congress in person; see Taylor, *Veiled Garvey*, 165–93.

98. Adi, *Pan-Africanism*, 124–26.

99. Munro, *Anticolonial Front*, 48–54, 62–67. Ras T. Makonnen was born George T. N. Griffith but, in solidarity with Ethiopia's struggle against Italian fascism, took his new name after Ras Mäkonnen Wäldä-Mika'él, former governor, aide to Emperor Menelik II, and father of Tafari Mäkonnen, the Emperor Haile Selassie. On The Cosmopolitan's connective role, see John McLeod, "A Night at 'The Cosmopolitan': Axes of Transnational Encounter in the 1930s and 1940s," *Interventions* 4, no. 1 (2002): 54–67.

100. Elizabeth M. Williams, *The Politics of Race in Britain and South Africa: Black British Solidarity and the Anti-Apartheid Struggle* (London: I. B. Tauris, 2017), 20–23.

101. Munro, *Anticolonial Front*, 73–74.

102. Munro, *Anticolonial Front*, 221–31; Salar Mohandesi, *Red Internationalism: Anti-Imperialism and Human Rights in the Global Sixties and Seventies* (Cambridge, UK: Cambridge University Press, 2023), 63–64, 73.

103. Gary Wilder, *The French Imperial Nation-State: Negritude and Colonial Humanism between the Two World Wars* (Chicago: University of Chicago Press, 2005), 150–61; idem, *Freedom Time*, 5–7.

104. Adam B. Lerner, "Collective Trauma and the Evolution of Nehru's Worldview: Uncovering the Roots of Nehruvian Non-Alignment," *International History Review*

41, no. 6 (2019): 1278, 1284–86, 1291–93. Lerner stresses that Nehru's commitment to nonalignment had yet to crystalize but connects Nehru's interwar internationalism, his lengthy spells in prison, and his ruminations about World War II and the feasibility of a pacifist isolationism after independence.

105. Thakur, "Asian Drama," 674–81; Itty Abraham, "From Bandung to NAM: Non-Alignment and Indian Foreign Policy, 1947–65," *Commonwealth and Comparative Politics* 46 (2008): 197–203.

106. Eileen Boris, *Making the Woman Worker: Precarious Labor and the Fight for Global Standards, 1919–2019* (New York: Oxford University Press, 2019), 95, 98–99.

107. Sunil Amrith, "Struggles for Citizenship around the Bay of Bengal," in *The Postcolonial Moment in South and Southeast Asia*, ed. Gyan Prakash, Michael Laffan, and Nikhil Menon (London: Bloomsbury, 2018), 107, 114–15.

108. Cindy Ewing, "The Third World before Afro-Asia," in *Inventing the Third World: In Search of Freedom for the Postwar Global South*, ed. Gyan Prakash and Jeremy Adelman (London: Bloomsbury Academic, 2023), 30–36.

109. Young-Sun Hong, *Cold War Germany, the Third World, and the Global Humanitarian Regime* (Cambridge, UK: Cambridge University Press, 2017), 32–33.

110. Carolien Stolte and Harald Fischer-Tiné, "Imagining Asia in India: Nationalism and Internationalism (ca. 1905–1940)," *Comparative Studies in Society & History* 54, no. 1 (2012): 84–91.

111. Sinderpal Singh, "From Delhi to Bandung: Nehru, 'Indian-ness' and 'Pan-Asian-ness,'" *South Asia: Journal of South Asian Studies* 34 (2011): 55–59.

112. Thakur, "Asian Drama," 673. As Thakur suggests, Shone was probably repeating usage of the term by conference delegates. With its Asian focus, this first use of the term 'third world' differed from its better-known successor, which encompassed what is now commonly described as the global South.

Chapter Seven: Decolonization in the Greater Second World War

1. ANOM, GGA/3Cab/3, no. 1390, Commissaire de Police, Aumale, to Algiers Prefect, May 26, 1940.

2. ANOM, Cabinet du Gouverneur Général de l'Algérie, Georges Le Beau, GGA/3Cab/3, CIE Algiers, "Note A/S recrutement des travailleurs destinés aux unités paramilitaires," February 24, 1940.

3. ANOM, GGA/3Cab/3, no. 1390, Commissaire de Police, Aumale, to Algiers Prefect, May 26, 1940.

4. Annie-Rey Goldzeiger, *Aux origines de la guerre d'Algérie, 1940–1945: de Mers el-Kébir aux massacres nord-constantinois* (Paris: Éditions la découverte, 2002), 294–304; Jean-Pierre Peyroulou, *Guelma, 1945; Une subversion française dans l'Algérie colonial* (Paris: Éditions la découverte, 2009).

5. Martin Thomas, "Colonial Violence in Algeria and the Distorted Logic of State Retribution: The Setif Uprising of 1945," *Journal of Military History* 75, no. 1 (2011): 125–57.

6. Peter Krause, *Rebel Power: Why National Movements Compete, Fight, and Win* (Ithaca, NY: Cornell University Press, 2017), 106.

7. AN, Ministère de l'intérieur, F/1a/3298: dossier A1, Procureur Général près la Cour d'Appel d'Alger to Monsieur le Garde des Sceaux, June 4, 1945; Algiers Governor Yves Chataigneau to Adrien Tixier, June 20, 1945: "Rapport relatif aux événements du département de Constantine."

8. Andrew Buchanan makes a similar argument in "Globalizing the Second World War," *Past & Present* 258, no. 1 (2023): 246–81. His call is to reframe 'World War II as a long war whose central paroxysm (1942–1945) emerged out of and then bled back into a series of regional wars (1931–1953)'. My thanks to Andrew for sharing his ideas with me.

9. I borrow the term from Peter Gatrell, "Trajectories of Population Displacement in the Aftermath of Two World Wars," in *The Disentanglement of Populations: Migration, Expulsion and Displacement in Postwar Europe, 1944–49*, ed. Jessica Reinisch and Elizabeth White (Basingstoke, UK: Palgrave Macmillan, 2011), 3–6, quote at 5; for Asian parallels, see Christopher E. Goscha, "Bringing Asia into Focus: Civilians and Combatants in the Line of Fire in China and Indochina," *War & Society* 31, no. 2 (2012): 87–105.

10. Robert Gerwarth and John Horne, "Paramilitarism in Europe after the Great War: An Introduction," in their *War in Peace: Paramilitary Violence in Europe after the Great War* (Oxford: Oxford University Press, 2012), 1–18.

11. The idea of 'transwar' is more accurate: Reto Hofmann and Max Ward, "The Long Transwar Asia," in *Transwar Asia: Ideology, Practices, and Institutions, 1920–1960*, ed. Reto Hofmann and Max Ward (London: Bloomsbury, 2022). For discussion of the concept in relation to pan-Asianist thinking, see Ethan Mark, "'Asia's' Transwar Lineage: Nationalism, Marxism, and 'Greater Asia' in an Indonesian Inflection," *Journal of Asian Studies* 65, no. 3 (2006): 461–68, 487–89.

12. Sunil Amrith, "Reconstructing the 'Plural Society': Asian Migration between Empire and Nation, 1940–1948," *Past & Present* 210, Supplement 6 (2011): 245–53.

13. Ina Zweiniger-Barqielowska, *Austerity in Britain: Rationing, Controls, and Consumption, 1939–1955* (Oxford: Oxford University Press, 2002); Jessica Reinisch, "Internationalism in Relief: The Birth (and Death) of UNRRA," *Past & Present* 210, Supplement 6 (2011): 258–89; Lizzie Collingham, *A Taste for War: World War II and the Battle for Food* (London: Allen Lane, 2012), chapters 5 and 15.

14. Martin Thomas, "European Crisis, Colonial Crisis: Signs of Fracture in the French Empire from Munich to the Outbreak of War," *International History Review* 32, no. 3 (2010): 393–96, 406.

15. Eric Jennings, *Free French Africa in World War II: The African Resistance* (Cambridge, UK: Cambridge University Press, 2014), 175–78, 188–97, 217–28; Urvi Khaitan, "Women beneath the Surface: Coal and the Colonial State in India during the Second World War," *War & Society* 39, no. 3 (2020): 171–88.

16. Frederick Cooper, "Reconstructing Empire in British and French Africa," *Past & Present* 210, Suppl. 6 (2011): 196–210; idem, "'Our Strike': Equality, Anticolonial Politics and the 1947–48 Railway Strike in French West Africa," *Journal of African History* 37, no. 1 (1996): 81–118.

17. Adam Hanieh, "Petrochemical Empire: The Geo-Politics of Fossil-Fuelled Production," *New Left Review* 130 (July–August 2021): 25–51.

18. Corey Ross, *Ecology and Power in the Age of Empire: Europe and the Transformation of the Tropical World* (Oxford: Oxford University Press, 2019), 231–33.

19. Daniel Hedinger, "The Imperial Nexus: The Second World War and the Axis in Global Perspective," *Journal of Global History* 12 (2017): 188–95, 200–3.

20. Anticipating the Japanese takeover, the defending European imperialists destroyed their oil hubs and local stockpiles, causing major environmental damage. The Dutch opened the tank valves and ignited the contents of their Sumatran oilfields in February–March 1942. The British did the same to their facilities in Burma. The Japanese then repeated the process as they neared defeat in the summer of 1945. See Ross, *Ecology and Power*, 235–36.

21. Jeremy A. Yellen, *The Greater East Asia Co-Prosperity Sphere: When Total Empire Met Total War* (Ithaca, NY: Cornell University Press, 2019), 141–51, 200–1.

22. Yellen, *Greater East Asia*, 144–45.

23. Yellen, *Greater East Asia*, 19–20.

24. Yellen, *Greater East Asia*, 56–58, 72.

25. On Japanese efforts to secure larger slices of Indonesian trade and resources from the 1930s, see Kris Alexanderson, *Subversive Seas: Anticolonial Networks across the Twentieth-Century Dutch Empire* (Cambridge, UK: Cambridge University Press, 2019), 212–20, 228.

26. David E. F. Henley, "Ethnogeographic Integration and Exclusion in Anticolonial Nationalism: Indonesia and Indochina," *Comparative Studies in Society and History* 37, no. 2 (1995): 286–324.

27. Yellen, *Greater East Asia*, 86–88.

28. Taomo Zhou, *Migration in the Time of Revolution: China, Indonesia, and the Cold War* (Ithaca, NY: Cornell University Press, 2019), 38–51; Richard Overy, *Blood and Ruins: The Great Imperial War 1931-1945* (London: Allen Lane, 2021), 186–98.

29. Louise Young, "Early-Twentieth-Century Japan in a Global Context: Introduction: Japan's New International History," *American Historical Review* 119, no. 4 (2014): 1123.

30. Kelly A. Hammond, *China's Muslims and Japan's Empire: Centering Islam in World War II* (Chapel Hill: University of North Carolina Press, 2020).

31. Ethan Mark, "The Perils of Co-Prosperity: Takeda Rintarō, Occupied Southeast Asia, and the Seductions of Postcolonial Empire," *American Historical Review*, 119, no. 4 (2014): 1198–1204.

32. See the contributions to George Akita and Brandon Palmer, eds., *The Japanese Colonial Legacy in Korea, 1910-1945: A New Perspective* (Honolulu: University of Hawai'i Press, 2015); Scott Simon, "Making Natives: Japan and the Creation of Indigenous Formosa," in *Japanese Taiwan: Colonial Rule and Its Contested Legacies*, ed. Andrew D. Morris (London: Bloomsbury, 2015), 85–92.

33. Sang Sook Jeon, "Establishing Japanese National Identity and the 'Chosŏn Issue,'" in *International Impact of Colonial Rule in Korea, 1910-1945*, ed. Yong-Chool Ha (Seattle: University of Washington Press, 2019), 58–68.

34. Hammond, *China's Muslims*, especially chapters 3–5.

35. On the Japanese promotion of different ideals of female beauty, whiteness, and gendered virtue, see L. Ayu Saraswati, *Seeing Beauty, Sensing Race in Transnational Indonesia* (Honolulu: University of Hawai'i Press, 2013), 53–58. There are parallels here with the racial hierarchies and gender stereotypes intrinsic to creole nationalism in Jamaica; see Rochelle Rowe, "'Glorifying the Jamaican Girl': The 'Ten

Types One People' Beauty Contest, Racialized Femininities, and Jamaican Nationalism," *Radical History Review* 103 (Winter 2009): 36–58.

36. Kelly A. Hammond, "Managing Muslims: Imperial Japan, Islamic Policy, and Axis Connections during the Second World War," *Journal of Global History* 12 (2017): 269–72.

37. For the role of maritime shipping and communications networks in disseminating pan-Asianist ideas, see Alexanderson, *Subversive Seas*, 224–27, 241–42.

38. Angus McIntyre, "The 'Greater Indonesia' Idea of Nationalism in Malaya and Indonesia," *Modern Asian Studies* 7, no. 1 (1973): 78–83.

39. Hugh Tinker, ed., *Burma. The Struggle for Independence, 1944–1948*, vol. 2: *From General Strike to Independence, 31 August 1946 to 4 January 1948* (London: HMSO: 1984), doc. 83, "AFPFL and Communists Part as Friends," *The Burman*, November 3, 1946.

40. Amrith, "Reconstructing the 'Plural Society,'" 240–43, 247–49. South Indian migrant laborers and traders in wartime Burma suffered especially badly. Perhaps 140,000 were forced out of the country as refugees, tens of thousands dying in a long march overland to North East India. An estimated 600,000–700,000 South Indians returned to postwar Burma even so, facing new insecurities over their status as 'residents', 'domiciles', or 'immigrants'.

41. IOR, Mss EUR MSS EUR F169/1: Sir Hubert Rance papers, file 33/GS47, "Prosecution of Aung San," Sir Reginald Dorman-Smith to Burma Office, London, June 4, 1946; Yellen, *Greater East Asia*, 105–40 passim; on the pro-Japanese Young Malay Union (Kesatuan Melayu Muda), see Cheah Boon Kheng, *Red Star over Malaya: Resistance and Social Conflict during and after the Japanese Occupation, 1941–1946* (Singapore: NUS Press, 2012), 102–9.

42. Walter C. Ladwig III, *The Forgotten Front: Patron–Client Relationships in Counterinsurgency* (Cambridge, UK: Cambridge University Press, 2017), 86–89.

43. Daniel Immerwahr, "The Greater United States: Territory and Empire in U.S. History," *Diplomatic History* 40, no. 3 (2016): 386–88.

44. A. G. Hopkins, *American Empire: A Global History* (Princeton, NJ: Princeton University Press, 2018), 653–56.

45. Ladwig, *Forgotten Front*, 91–99, 104–6, 110–13. For abuses conducted by the paramilitary police, the Philippine Constabulary, and the Constabulary's consequent incorporation into the army, see Walter C. Ladwig, "When the Police Are the Problem: The Philippine Constabulary and the Hukbalahap Rebellion," in *Policing Insurgencies: Cops as Counter-Insurgents*, ed. C. Christine Fair and Sumit Ganguly (Oxford: Oxford University Press, 2014), 21–34.

46. Ladwig, *Forgotten Front*, 118–25, 140–43. Ladwig praises the US decision to tie external aid to Philippine governmental changes, tax reforms, and military accountability but passes over its imperialistic dimensions.

47. Ladwig, *Forgotten Front*, 113–19. Magsaysay was killed in a March 1957 plane crash.

48. Hopkins, *American Empire*, 671–74.

49. Pieter Lagrou, "1945–1955: The Age of Total War," in *Histories of the Aftermath*, ed. Frank Biess and Robert Moeller (Oxford: Berghahn, 2010), 287–96.

50. Claude Liauzu, *Histoire de l'anticolonialisme en France. Du XVIe siècle à nos jours* (Paris: Armand Colin, 2007), 195–206; Alain Ruscio, "L'opinion publique et la guerre d'Indochine. Sondages et témoignages," *Vingtième Siècle* 1 (1991): 35–46; Stephen Howe, *Anticolonialism in British Politics: The Left and the End of Empire, 1918–1964* (Oxford: Clarendon, 1993), 176–88.

51. Barbara Castle papers, BLO, MS Castle 245, fos. 13–16: Barbara Castle article, "Justice in Kenya," *The New Statesman and Nation*, December 17, 1955; Howe, *Anticolonialism*, 173–81.

52. Erik Linstrum, "Facts about Atrocity: Reporting Colonial Violence in Postwar Britain," *History Workshop Journal* 84 (2017): 113–15, 117–18.

53. Linstrum, "Facts about Atrocity," 116–17.

54. Castle papers, MS Castle 245, fos. 153–5: Barbara Castle article, "Eleven Dead Men," *New Statesman*, May 16, 1959.

55. Robert Gildea, *Empires of the Mind: The Colonial Past and the Politics of the Present* (Cambridge, UK: Cambridge University Press, 2019), 79.

56. Ross, *Ecology and Power*, 365–66.

57. Mathilde von Bülow, "Exile, Safe Havens, and Rear Bases: External Sanctuaries and the Transnational Dimension of Late Colonial Insurgencies and Counter-Insurgencies," in *The Oxford Handbook of Late Colonial Insurgencies and Counter-Insurgencies*, ed. Martin Thomas and Gareth Curless (Oxford: Oxford University Press, 2023), 653–73.

58. For theoretical analysis of violent and nonviolent alternatives in settling disputed frontiers, see Toby J. Rider and Andrew P. Owsiak, *On Dangerous Ground: A Theory of Bargaining, Border Settlement, and Rivalry* (Cambridge, UK: Cambridge University Press, 2021), 4–13, 38–49.

59. Karl Ittmann, *A Problem of Great Importance: Population, Race, and Power in the British Empire, 1919–1973* (Berkeley: University of California Press, 2013), 93–95; Sarah Frank, "'Meet the New Empire, Same as the Old Empire': Visions and Realities of French Imperial Policy in 1944," in *Reading the Postwar Future: Textual Turning Points from 1944*, ed. Kirrily Freeman and John Munro (London: Bloomsbury, 2021), 79–95.

60. Steven Morewood, *The British Defence of Egypt, 1935–1940: Conflict and Crisis in the Eastern Mediterranean* (London: Frank Cass, 2005), 199–205; Heather J. Sharkey, *Living with Colonialism: Nationalism and Culture in the Anglo-Egyptian Sudan* (Berkeley: University of California Press, 2005), 95–119; Martin Thomas, "Resource War, Civil War, Rights War: Factoring Empire into French North Africa's Second World War," *War in History* 18, no. 2 (2011): 1–24.

61. Haile Larebo, "Empire-Building and Its Limitations: Ethiopia, 1935–1941," in *Italian Colonialism*, ed. Ruth Ben-Ghiat and Mia Fuller (Basingstoke, UK: Palgrave Macmillan, 2005), 83–94; Roberta Pergher, *Mussolini's Nation-Empire: Sovereignty and Settlement in Italy's Borderlands, 1922–1943* (Cambridge, UK: Cambridge University Press, 2018), 251–53.

62. Deborah Posel, *The Making of Apartheid, 1948–1961: Conflict and Compromise* (Oxford: Clarendon, 1991), 23–39, 45–50.

63. Jamie Martin, *The Meddlers: Sovereignty, Empire, and the Birth of Global Economic Governance* (Cambridge, MA: Harvard University Press, 2022), 25–27.

The force of Latin American opposition was diminished in the late 1940s by Brazil's alignment with US foreign and economic policy: Miguel Serra Coelho, "Brazil and India: A Brave New World, 1948–1961," in *Latin America and the Global Cold War*, ed. Thomas C. Field, Stella Krepp, and Vanni Pettinà (Chapel Hill: University of North Carolina Press, 2020), 18–20.

64. Kosmas Tsokhas, "Dedominionization: The Anglo-Australian Experience, 1939–1945," *Historical Journal* 37, no. 4 (1994): 861–83; Christopher Waters, *The Empire Fractures: Anglo-Australian Conflict in the 1940s* (Melbourne: Australian Scholarly Publishing, 1995).

65. Aviel Roshwald, *Estranged Bedfellows: Britain and France in the Middle East during the Second World War* (Oxford: Oxford University Press, 1990), chapter 8; TNA, CAB 122/810, Anthony Eden to Lord Halifax, November 14, 1943.

66. SHD, 4H360/D1, no. 1591/2S, Commandement Supérieur des Troupes du Levant memo., June 1, 1945; TNA, FO 371/45580, E5800/8/89, War Office Historical Record—Levant May 29–June 11, 1945. Contemporary estimates of Syrian fatalities range from 400 to 700.

67. Martin Thomas, "Divisive Decolonization: The Anglo-French Withdrawal from Syria and Lebanon, 1944–46," *Journal of Imperial & Commonwealth History* 28, no. 3 (2000): 89–91; Hoover Institution archive, General Henri Fernand Dentz, "Affaires de Syrie," Août 1945; on the French expeditionary force in Saigon, see Shawn F. McHale, *The First Vietnam War: Violence, Sovereignty, and the Fracture of the South, 1945–1956* (Cambridge, UK: Cambridge University Press, 2021), 69–74, 96–98, 136–38.

68. Each divided under occupation, Belgium and the Netherlands established governments-in-exile in London after their May 1940 defeat. In spite of its fascistic regime, Portugal maintained its centuries-old alliance with Britain and technically became a pro-Allied nonbelligerent after finalizing an Azores base agreement with the United States on November 28, 1944.

69. Wendy Webster, *Mixing It: Diversity in World War Two Britain* (Oxford: Oxford University Press, 2018), 6–19. Webster uses three vectors—speech and language, women's relationships with men, and uniforms and appearance—to gauge the impact of this cultural diversity in Britain.

70. Jeremy A. Crang, *Sisters in Arms: Women in the British Armed Forces during the Second World War* (Cambridge, UK: Cambridge University Press, 2020), 180–81; Imaobong D. Umoren, *Race Women Internationalists: Activist Intellectuals and Global Freedom Struggles* (Berkeley: University of California Press, 2018), 68–69.

71. Wendy Webster, "Maintaining Racial Boundaries: Greater Britain in the Second World War and Beyond," in *The Break-Up of Greater Britain*, ed. Christian D. Pedersen and Stuart Ward (Manchester, UK: Manchester University Press, 2021), 22–40.

72. Herrick Chapman, "The Liberation of France as a Moment of State-Making," in *Crisis and Renewal in France, 1918–1962*, ed. Martin S. Alexander and Kenneth E. Mouré (Oxford: Berghahn, 2002), 174–98; idem, *France's Long Reconstruction: In Search of the Modern Republic* (Cambridge, MA: Harvard University Press, 2018), 19–40.

73. AN, F/1a/3293: 1944–7 dossier VI-B-1: Problèmes Algériens actuels, CAB 6418/45, Adrien Tixier memo, May 19, 1945, "Rapport général sur les problèmes

actuels en Algérie"; MAE, Archives du Ministère des états associés, 1945–57, carton 73, DRV Under-secretary for foreign affairs, Hoang Minh Giam, January 9, 1947, "Les manœuvres colonialistes depuis le 6 mars 1946 et les origines de l'actuel conflit."

74. Christoph Kalter, *The Discovery of the Third World: Decolonization and the Rise of the New Left in France c. 1950–1976* (Cambridge, UK: Cambridge University Press, 2016), 85–89, 93–94.

75. Alice L. Conklin, *In the Museum of Man: Race, Anthropology, and Empire in France, 1850–1950* (Ithaca, NY: Cornell University Press, 2013), chapter 7, 327–31.

76. Florian Wagner, *Colonial Internationalism and the Governmentality of Empire, 1893–1982* (Cambridge, UK: Cambridge University Press, 2022), 315–18.

77. Marco Duranti, "Decolonizing the United Nations: Anti-Colonialism and Human Rights in the French Empire," in *Decolonization, Self Determination, and the Rise of Global Human Rights Politics*, ed. A. Dirk Moses, Marco Duranti, and Roland Burke (Cambridge, UK: Cambridge University Press, 2020), 54–66.

78. In his redemptive memoir published at the end of the Algerian War, Naegelen preferred to stress his efforts to keep the peace: *Mission en Algérie* (Paris: Flammarion, 1962).

79. Frederick Cooper, *Citizenship between Empire and Nation: Rethinking France and French Africa, 1945–1960* (Princeton, NJ: Princeton University Press, 2014), chapters 2–4; Kristen Stromberg Childers, "The Evolution of the Welfare State: Social Rights and the Nationalization of Welfare in France, 1880–1947," *French Politics, Culture, and Society* 24, no. 2 (2006): 129–38.

80. Gary Wilder, *Freedom Time: Negritude, Decolonization, and the Future of the World* (Durham, NC: Duke University Press, 2015), 107–12, 123–24; Annette K. Joseph-Gabriel, *Reimagining Liberation: How Black Women Transformed Citizenship in the French Empire* (Urbana: University of Illinois Press, 2020).

81. Martin Shipway, "Madagascar on the Eve of Insurrection, 1944–47: The Impasse of a Liberal Colonial Policy," *Journal of Imperial & Commonwealth History* 24, no. 1 (1996): 83–98; ANOM, 6(2)D161: Recensement par provinces des membres du MDRM, 1947–8.

82. ANOM, Madagascar, 6(2)D123: Notes de renseignements des services de police adressées au cabinet civil du GGM, 1947–Jan. 1948, sous dossier: Renseignements Sûreté Mars 1947, no. 2772/DISCF, R. Baron, Chef de la Sûreté Générale Tananarive "Renseignements," "Réunion des membres du MDRM de la section de Faravohitra du 24 Mars 1947."

83. ANOM, Madagascar, 3D32/Mission Demaille, Chef de Mission report, "Service de la Trésorerie Générale de Madagascar et Dépendances," Tananarive, June 11, 1948. The provincial tax burden in areas of intense rebel activity increased as local populations were required to meet the costs of military and police reinforcements.

84. These administrative problems were highlighted during the Ministry of Overseas France inspection mission of former rebel-held areas after the uprising ended: ANOM, 3D34, Mission Mérat, Inspection des Colonies, Mission 1948, "Rapport concernant l'organisation de la gendarmerie et de la garde indigène à Madagascar," Tananarive, May 1, 1949.

85. ANOM, Missions d'inspection, 3D355: opérations de police conduite par l'Inspection des affaires administratives, 1949: compte-rendus de patrouilles.

86. TNA, FO 371/67721, Z6417/3290/69/G, Maj.-Gen. Salisbury-Jones, WO Director of Military Intelligence, "Situation in Madagascar and Indo-China," July 2, 1947.

87. ANOM, Madagascar, 3D32/Mission Demaille, "Rapport concernant le rétablissement de la confiance franco-malgache," Tananarive, June 4, 1948.

88. Eric T. Jennings, *Perspectives on French Colonial Madagascar* (New York: Palgrave Macmillan, 2017), 131–36.

89. Adria Lawrence, "Driven to Arms? The Escalation to Violence in Nationalist Conflicts," in *Rethinking Violence: States and Non-State Actors in Conflict*, ed. Erica Chenoweth and Adria Lawrence (Cambridge, MA: MIT Press, 2010), 144–46.

90. Achille Mbembe makes a similar point, tracing from one chieftaincy authority to another what he calls the 'rural micro-procedures' behind local allegiance to Cameroon's anticolonial resistance movement, the Union des Populations du Cameroun (UPC); see Mbembe, *La naissance du maquis dans le Sud-Cameroun (1920–1960)* (Paris: Karthala, 1996), 238–52.

91. MAE, série Z: Europe 1944–9, sous-série Grande-Bretagne, vol. 40, No. 495-CD, High Commissioner Pierre de Chevigné to Minister of Overseas France, December 31, 1948.

92. ANOM, 4D48: Rapports d'ensemble sur le territoire de Madagascar, 1949–53; 6(2)D189, Amnistie, 1953–4.

93. MAE, série Afrique-Levant 1944–59, sous-série: Algérie 1944–52, vol. 6 Questions politiques, doc. 453/NA 3, Edmond Naegelen, Cabinet du Gouverneur Général Alger to Ministère de l'Intérieur Cabinet, February 28, 1949: "Manuscrit rédigé par un des dirigeants du PPA-MTLD."

94. MAE, série Afrique-Levant, sous-série: Généralités, 1944–52, file 65: Politique soviétique en Afrique/Communisme/PCF-RDA, 1949–52, Summary of Soviet press articles on Communism in Africa: World Federation of Democratic Youth, February 1950. IISH, World Federation of Democratic Youth (WFDY) archive (ref: ARCH01665), sub-file: WFDY 1950. The WFDY's decisive pivot to the Communist bloc came in January 1950 when its Executive Committee, meeting in Bucharest, married calls for an end to the armaments race and the threat of atomic bombing with the cessation of colonial military intervention against the peoples of Indonesia, Malaya, and Vietnam.

95. IISH, WFDY archive (ref: ARCH01665), file WFDY 1, 1945–55, press release no. 12, "World Youth Conference," London, November 1945. The WFDY's inaugural World Youth Conference was held at London's Seymour Hall from October 31 to November 10. Mimicking the United Nations' globalist working practices, proceedings were conducted in five official languages: English, French, Spanish, Russian, and Chinese. The BBC transmitted the opening conference pageant, convened for 5,000 invitees at the Royal Albert Hall on October 29, 1945. Messages of support were sent by Britain's King George VI, Prime Minister Clement Attlee, and Foreign Secretary Ernest Bevin, as well as US President Harry Truman and Secretary of State Edward Stettinius.

96. IISH, WFDY archive (ref: ARCH01665), "20 ans au service de la jeunesse: anniversaire de fédération mondiale de la jeunesse démocratique, 1945–1965." Admittedly, WFDY anticolonialism became more radical and Third Worldist during the

1960s. By mid-decade, WFDY propaganda affirmed solidarity with the youth of Vietnam, the Congo, Angola, Cyprus, Venezuela, Colombia, Guatemala, Algeria, Spain, and Cuba and others fighting for independence and peace.

97. Mark Edele, *Stalinism at War: The Soviet Union in World War II* (London: Bloomsbury, 2021), 152–73.

98. Araragi Shinzō, "The Collapse of the Japanese Empire and the Great Migrations: Repatriation, Assimilation, and Remaining behind," in *The Dismantling of Japan's Empire in East Asia: Deimperialization, Postwar Legitimation, and Imperial Afterlife*, ed. Barak Kushner and Sherzod Muminov (London: Routledge, 2017), 66–83.

99. Christopher Bayly and Tim Harper, *Forgotten Wars: Freedom and Revolution in Southeast Asia* (Cambridge: Belnap Press, 2007), 5.

100. On these processes, see Rana Mitter, *China's War with Japan, 1937–1945: The Struggle for Survival* (London: Allen Lane, 2013), part II; idem, *The Manchurian Myth: Nationalism, Resistance, and Collaboration in Modern China* (Berkeley: University of California Press, 2000), chapters 3–4.

101. Immerwahr, "Greater United States," 387.

102. The movements were the Viet Minh, the Malayan People's Anti-Japanese Army, and the Hukbalahap or *Hukbo ng Bayan Laban sa Hapon* (People's Army against the Japanese).

103. Bradley R. Simpson, "Southeast Asia in the Cold War," in *The Cold War in the Third World*, ed. Robert J. McMahon (Oxford: Oxford University Press, 2013), 50–51; Rana Mitter, *Bitter Revolution: China's Struggle with the Modern World* (Oxford: Oxford University Press, 2005), 153–94.

104. Graham Hutchings, *China, 1949: Year of Revolution* (London: Bloomsbury 2021), 55–75; Christopher Goscha, "A 'Total War' of Decolonization? Social Mobilization and State-Building in Communist Vietnam (1949–54)," *War and Society* 31, no. 2 (2012): 140–41.

105. Edele, *Stalinism at War*, 176–80; idem, "Soviet Liberations and Occupations, 1939–1949," in *The Cambridge History of the Second World War*, vol. 2: *Politics and Ideology*, ed. Richard Bosworth and Joe Maiolo (Cambridge, UK: Cambridge University Press, 2015), 497–500; Vladimir Pechatnov, "The Soviet Union and the World, 1944–1953," and Norman Naimark, "The Sovietization of Eastern Europe, 1944–1993," both in *The Cambridge History of the Cold War*, vol. I, ed. Melvyn P. Leffler and Odd Arne Westad (Cambridge, UK: Cambridge University Press, 2010), 90–111 and 175–97.

106. David P. Chandler, Robert Cribb, and Li Narangoa, eds., *End of Empire: 100 Days in 1945 that Changed Asia and the World* (Copenhagen: NIAS Press, 2016).

107. Bayly and Harper, *Forgotten Wars*, 7; also cited in Gyan Prakash, Michael Laffan, and Nikhil Menon, "Introduction: The Postcolonial Moment," in *The Postcolonial Moment in South and Southeast Asia*, ed. idem (London: Bloomsbury, 2018), 2.

108. McIntyre, "'Greater Indonesia' Idea," 75–83; Cheah Boon Kheng, "The Japanese Occupation of Malaya, 1941–45: Ibrahim Yaacob and the Struggle for Indonesia Raya," *Indonesia* 28 (October 1979): 84–120; Phạm Văn Thuỷ, *Beyond Political Skin: Colonial to National Economies in Indonesia and Vietnam (1910s–1960s)* (Singapore: Springer Nature, 2019); Ethan Mark, *Japan's Occupation of Java in the Second World War: A Transnational History* (London: Bloomsbury, 2019).

109. Zhou, *Migration in the Time of Revolution*, 38–44. Highlighting the role of Chinese Communist Party intellectual Ba Ren in wartime Sumatra, Taomo Zhou points to the organization of two youth-based movements, the Antifascist Alliance of the Chinese in Sumatra (*Sumendala huaqiao fanfanxisi tongmeng*) and the Chinese Association against Enemies (*Huaqiao kangdi xiehui*).

110. Robert Cribb, "Genocide in Indonesia, 1965–1966," *Journal of Genocide Research* 3, no. 2 (2001): 226–27.

Chapter Eight: Revolutionary Decolonization in Southeast Asia?

1. SHD, 10161, "Projet de l'occupation de l'Indochine française," August 26, 1945. Thanks to Pierre Asselin for sharing this material.

2. Shawn F. McHale, *The First Vietnam War: Violence, Sovereignty, and the Fracture of the South, 1945–1956* (Cambridge, UK: Cambridge University Press, 2021), 42–48.

3. TNA, WO 193/195, DMO note on JPS(45)339, "French Resistance in Indochina," March 18, 1945; Martin Thomas, "Free France, the British Government and the Future of French Indochina, 1940–45," *Journal of Southeast Asian Studies*, 28, no. 1 (1997): 155–59; R. B. Smith, "The Japanese Period in Indochina and the Coup of 9 March 1945," *Journal of Southeast Asian Studies*, 9, no. 2 (1978): 268–301.

4. Christian Lentz, *Contested Territory: Đien Biên Phu and the Making of Northwest Vietnam* (New Haven, CT: Yale University Press, 2019), 1–3, 9. Mùong Thanh is a Tai language place-name.

5. SHD, 1K306/D6, Troupes Françaises en Chine, Etat-Major: interview between General Allesandri and Marshal Ho Ying Ching, July 26, 1945.

6. Lentz, *Contested Territory*, 2.

7. TNA, CAB 122/495, J(45)207, Joint Planning Staff (JPS) report, "Liaison with European Allies," August 16, 1945; WO 203/4564, SEAC JPS memo., "Occupation of French Indochina," August 28, 1945; *FRUS*, 1945, vol. VI, US Embassy, Paris, to James Byrnes, August 11, 1945; Smith, "Japanese Period in Indochina," 268–301 William J. Duiker, *The Communist Road to Power in Vietnam* 2nd edition (Boulder, CO: Westview Press, 1996), 95–104.

8. McHale, *First Vietnam War*, 37–39.

9. David G. Marr, *Vietnam, 1945: The Quest for Power* (Berkeley: University of California Press, 1995), 97–104; Stein Tønnesson, *Vietnam 1946: How the War Began* (Berkeley: University of California Press, 2010), 117–21; on Mekong Delta rice production and devastation of the regional economy: McHale, *First Vietnam War*, 34–36.

10. Young-Sun Hong, *Cold War Germany, the Third World, and the Global Humanitarian Regime* (Cambridge, UK: Cambridge University Press, 2017), 112–13. Hanoi's one substantial medical facility, the Phu Doan Hospital, came under Viet Minh control during the August 1945 revolution, too late to offer remedial help to famine victims.

11. Gregg Huff, "Causes and Consequences of the Great Vietnam Famine, 1944–5," *Economic History Review* 72, no. 1 (2019): 290–95, 303–7. Huff's even-handed assessment is that French and Japanese administrators' efforts to alleviate the famine were hampered by local hoarding, disruption to transportation networks, and food shortages on Japan's home islands. But he acknowledges the wider failure of colonial governance involved.

12. Excellent surveys include Christopher Goscha and Benoît de Tréglodé, eds., *Naissance d'un État-Parti: le Viêt Nam depuis 1945* (Paris: Indes savants, 2004); Mark Atwood Lawrence, *Assuming the Burden: Europe and the American Commitment to War in Vietnam* (Berkeley: University of California Press, 2005); Christopher Goscha, *Vietnam: un État né de la guerre, 1945-1954* (Paris: Armand Colin, 2011); and McHale, *First Vietnam War*, who emphasizes the sectarian divisions within this civil war, particularly in Saigon and the Mekong Delta.

13. TNA, WO 208/3042, War Office Military Intelligence report, "Summary of Changes to the Japanese Forces in Indochina," no date, June 1945; WO 208/4927, Directorate of Military Intelligence, "Report on North Indochina," January 12, 1946.

14. Brocheux and Hémery, *Indochina*, 351-2.

15. McHale, *First Vietnam War*, 48-50.

16. SHD, 10161, "Projet de l'occupation de l'Indochine française," August 26, 1945, 1-2. Thanks to Pierre Asselin for sharing this document with me.

17. SHD, 10161, "Projet de l'occupation de l'Indochine française," August 26, 1945.

18. McHale, *First Vietnam War*, 87-93, 95-101; idem, "Understanding the Fanatic Mind? The Viêt Minh and Race Hatred in the First Indochina War (1945-1954)," *Journal of Vietnamese Studies*, 4, no. 3 (2009): 109-17.

19. McHale, *First Vietnam War*, 75-87; Christopher Goscha, "A 'Popular' Side of the Vietnamese Army: General Nguyễn Binh and the Early War in the South (1910-1951)," in Goscha and de Tréglodé, *Naissance d'un État-Parti*, 350-52.

20. Quoting political scientist Stathis Kalyvas, Shawn McHale describes the kaleidoscope of violence actors and violent acts in the Mekong Delta as 'locally segmented monopolies of violence': McHale, *First Vietnam War*, 54-60, 132-34, 143-47, quote at 134; idem, "Understanding the Fanatic Mind?" 98-99, 118-23.

21. Richard Overy, *Blood and Ruins: The Great Imperial War 1931-1945* (London: Allen Lane, 2021), 818.

22. For a French treatment of one such sectarian group, the *Dai Viet*, see François Guillemot, *Dai Viet: indépendance et révolution au Viêt-Nam: l'échec de la troisième voie, 1938-1955* (Paris: les Indes Savantes, 2012).

23. McHale, *First Vietnam War*, 101-4; for longer-term sources of Khmer-Vietnamese antagonism but also the fluidity of ethnic identities, see Shawn F. McHale, "Ethnicity, Violence, and Khmer-Vietnamese Relations: The Significance of the Lower Mekong Delta, 1757-1954," *Journal of Asian Studies*, 72, no. 2 (2013): 369-80.

24. General Nguyen Binh, selected in part because he was not a communist, orchestrated killings of Hòa Hảo, Cao Dài and Binh Xuyen militia leaders, which, by 1948, drove these movements to accommodation with the French; see Jessica M. Chapman, *Cauldron of Resistance: Ngo Dinh Diem, the United States, and 1950s Southern Vietnam* (Ithaca, NY: Cornell University Press, 2013), 32-38.

25. Christopher Goscha, "A 'Total War' of Decolonization? Social Mobilization and State-Building in Communist Vietnam (1949-54)," *War and Society* 31, no. 2 (2012): 140-48, 152-55.

26. Lentz, *Contested Territory*, 25-48; François Guillemot, "Au cœur de la fracture vietnamienne: l'élimination de l'opposition nationaliste et anticolonialiste dans le Nord Viet Nam (1945-1946)" in Goscha and de Tréglodé, *Naissance d'un État-Parti*, 175-216.

27. Lentz, *Contested Territory*, 30.

28. Archives Nationales, Paris, Marcel-Edmond Naegelen Papers: 518AP/5/ Dossier: Gouverneur-Général de l'Algérie, Juin 1948–Avril 1951, Federal Commissioner Jean Bourgoin, Saigon letter to Governor General Marcel-Edmond Naegelen, April 13, 1948; McHale, *First Vietnam War*, 1–17.

29. Robert Buzzanco, "Ruling-Class Anti-Imperialism in the Era of the Vietnam War," in *Empire's Twin: U.S. Anti-Imperialism from the Founding Era to the Age of Terrorism*, ed. Ian Tyrrell and Jay Sexton (Ithaca, NY: Cornell University Press, 2015), 204–5. Discussing the Joint Chiefs' hostility to involvement in Vietnam, Buzzanco cites their policy paper JCS 1992/4 of July 1949, which rejected intervention, warning that the 'rise of militant nationalism among the subject people [of Vietnam] cannot be reversed.'

30. Peter Dennis, *Troubled Days of Peace: Mountbatten and South East Asia Command, 1945–6* (Manchester, UK: Manchester University Press, 1990).

31. T. O. Smith, *Britain and the Origins of the Vietnam War: UK Policy in Indo-China, 1943–50* (Basingstoke, UK: Palgrave Macmillan, 2007), 38–52; idem, "Major-General Sir Douglas Gracey: Peacekeeper or Peace Enforcer?" *Diplomacy & Statecraft*, 21, no. 2 (2010): 226–39.

32. Christopher Goscha, *Vietnam: un État né de la guerre*, 26–27; McHale, *First Vietnam War*, 56–59. Shawn McHale calculates 135 kidnappings and disappearances during the massacre between September 23 and 25 in Saigon and Cholon.

33. Pierre Asselin and Henk Schulte Nordholt, "Cracking Down on Revolutionary Zeal and Violence: Local Dynamics and Early Colonial Responses to the Independence Struggle in Indochina and the Indonesian Archipelago, 1945–1947," in *Empire's Violent End: Comparing Dutch, British, and French Wars of Decolonization, 1945–1962*, ed. Thijs Brocades Zaalberg and Bart Luttikhuis (Ithaca, NY: Cornell University Press, 2022), 133–39.

34. Rana Mitter, "Nationalism, Decolonization, Geopolitics and the Asian Post-War," in *The Cambridge History of the Second World War*, vol. 3: *Total War: Economy, Society and Culture*, ed. Michael Geyer and Adam Tooze (Cambridge, UK: Cambridge University Press, 2015), 599–602.

35. Qiang Zhai, "Transplanting the Chinese Model: Chinese Military Advisers and the First Vietnam War, 1950–1954," *Journal of Military History* 57, no. 4 (1993): 689–715. For Chinese aid in developing DRV health care, see Young-Sun Hong, *Cold War Germany*, 119–20.

36. CWIO, OCI 1002/62, ESAU XVIII-62, CIA Office of Current Intelligence, Staff Study memorandum, "North Vietnam and Sino–Soviet Relations," March 4, 1962.

37. In 1948, at a regional conference in Calcutta of Communist parties convened to disseminate the new line of armed insurrection in Asia, the Chinese Communist representative staked a claim to leadership over the national liberation movement in Southeast Asia. Weeks after the establishment of the Chinese People's Republic in October 1949, Liu Shao-chi elaborated this claim in a speech before a Conference of Asian and Australasian Trade Unions in Beijing, proclaiming the 'road of Mao Tse-tung' as the revolutionary model for other Asian Communist parties to follow. Two

years later, on the occasion of the thirtieth anniversary of the Chinese Communist Party, this claim was reiterated in speeches hailing the Chinese revolution as 'the classic type of revolution in colonial and semi-colonial countries': CWIO, OCI 1002/62, ESAU XVIII-62, CIA Office of Current Intelligence, "North Vietnam and Sino–Soviet Relations," March 4, 1962.

38. Charles Kraus, "A Border Region 'Exuded with Militant Friendship': Provincial Narratives of China's Participation in the First Indochina War, 1949–1954," *Cold War History* 12, no. 3 (2012), 495–514; Jiayi Gao, "Fighting Side by Side: Cross-Border Military Exchanges and Cooperation between the Chinese Communist Party and the Viet Minh, 1945–1949," *China Review* 19, no. 3 (2019): 123–48.

39. Heather Goodall, *Beyond Borders: Indians, Australians and the Indonesian Revolution, 1939 to 1950* (Amsterdam: Amsterdam University Press, 2018), 209–14, 226–31; Richard McMillan, *The British Occupation of Indonesia, 1945–1946: Britain, the Netherlands and the Indonesian Revolution* (Abingdon, UK: Routledge, 2005), 31–58.

40. On Indian opposition to the use of Indian colonial troops in other Southeast Asian imperial territories, see TNA, Ernest Bevin Private Office papers, FO 800/470, tel. 427, Esler Dening to Bevin, September 1, 1945. Congress leader Nehru did not, however, push strongly for recognition of Vietnam's independence. Perhaps mindful of the need to negotiate over the remaining French colonial enclaves in India, in November 1946 Nehru blocked efforts to form a 'Vietnam Brigade' to support the embattled Hanoi Republic. Vineet Thakur, "An Asian Drama: The Asian Relations Conference, 1947," *International History Review* 41, no. 3 (2019): 679–80; Christopher E. Goscha, *Thailand and the Southeast Asian Networks of the Vietnamese Revolution, 1885–1954* (Abingdon, UK: Routledge, 1999), 249–50.

41. Christopher Bayly and Tim Harper, *Forgotten Wars: Freedom and Revolution in Southeast Asia* (Cambridge: Belnap Press, 2007), chapter 4; McMillan, *British Occupation*, 85–88, 165–68.

42. Robert Cribb, "The Brief Genocide of the Eurasians in Indonesia, 1945/1946," in *Empire, Colony, Genocide: Conquest, Occupation, and Subaltern Resistance in World History*, ed. A. Dirk Moses (Oxford: Berghahn, 2008), 424–39; Roel Frakking, "Beyond Sticks and Carrots: Local Agency in Counterinsurgency," *Humanity* 5, no. 3 (2014): 391–415.

43. Gregg Huff, "The Great Second World War Vietnam and Java Famines," *Modern Asian Studies* 54, no. 2 (2020): 634–7.

44. Huff, "Great Second World War," 640–3.

45. McMillan, *British Occupation*, chapters 1–2.

46. The most exhaustive account of that violence is Rémy Limpach, *De brandende kampongs van Generaal Spoor* (Amsterdam: Boom, 2016).

47. McMillan, *British Occupation*, 99–112; Bart Luttikhuis and A. Dirk Moses, "Mass Violence and the End of the Dutch Colonial Empire in Indonesia," *Journal of Genocide Research* 14, no. 3–4 (2012): 257–76.

48. Memorandum by C. J. Jeffries, "A Plan for the Colonial Office," no date, November 1942, *British Documents on the End of Empire*, Series A, Volume 1: *Imperial Policy and Colonial Practice, 1925–1945*, ed. S. R. Ashton and S. E. Stockwell (London: HMSO, 1996), doc. 4.

49. T. N. Harper, "The Politics of Disease and Disorder in Post-War Malaya," *Journal of Southeast Asian Studies* 21, no. 1 (1990): 90–102, 109–13; A. J. Stockwell, "Colonial Planning during World War Two: The Case of Malaya," *Journal of Imperial & Commonwealth History* 2, no. 3 (1974): 333–51.

50. Sunil Amrith, "Reconstructing the 'Plural Society': Asian Migration between Empire and Nation, 1940–1948," *Past & Present* 210, Supplement 6 (2011): 250–54, quotation at 246.

51. T. N. Harper, *The End of Empire and the Making of Malaya* (Cambridge, UK: Cambridge University Press, 1999), 55–93 passim; Wen-Qing Ngoei, *Arc of Containment: Britain, the United States, and Anticommunism in Southeast Asia* (Ithaca, NY: Cornell University Press, 2019), 59–80.

52. The legal treatment of domestic violence cases among the plantation workforce offers a good example of the cultural and gender stereotyping of Malaya's Indian community by British officials and their Indian nationalist critics; see Arunima Datta, "'Immorality,' Nationalism and the Colonial State in British Malaya: Indian Coolie Women's Intimate Lives as Ideological Battleground," *Women's History Review* 25, no. 4 (2016): 584–601.

53. Wen-Qing Ngoei, *Arc of Containment*, 59–80; A. J. Stockwell, "The Formation and First Years of the United Malays National Organization (U.M.N.O.)," *Modern Asian Studies* 11, no. 4 (1977): 481–83; Anna Belogurova, "The Malayan Communist Party and the Malayan Chinese Association: Internationalism and Nationalism in Chinese Overseas Political Participation, c. 1920–1960," in *Decolonization and the Cold War: Negotiating Independence*, ed. Leslie James and Elisabeth Leake (London: Bloomsbury, 2015), 133–36.

54. Gareth Curless, "'The People Need Civil Liberties': Trade Unions and Contested Decolonisation in Singapore," *Labour History* 57, no. 1 (2016): 55.

55. Kumar Ramakrishna, *Emergency Propaganda: The Winning of Malayan Hearts and Minds, 1948–1958* (Richmond: Curzon, 2002), 28–30.

56. Cheah Boon Kheng, *Red Star over Malaya: Resistance and Social Conflict during and after the Japanese Occupation, 1941–1946* (Singapore: NUS Press, 2012), 57–74.

57. Roger Arditti and Philip H. J. Davies, "Rethinking the Rise and Fall of the Malayan Security Service, 1946–48," *Journal of Imperial & Commonwealth History* 43, no. 2 (2015): 293–99.

58. Arditti and Davies, "Rethinking," 299–304.

59. Arditti and Davies, "Rethinking," 304–11. MSS intelligence work was divided between Malayan and Singapore police Special Branches, but the shortage of Chinese-speaking personnel persisted.

60. Huw Bennett, "'A Very Salutary Effect': The Counter-Terror Strategy in the Early Malayan Emergency, June 1948 to December 1949," *Journal of Strategic Studies* 32, no. 3 (2009): 417–19, 427–31; Karl Hack, "Detention, Deportation and Resettlement: British Counterinsurgency and Malaya's Rural Chinese, 1948–60," *Journal of Imperial & Commonwealth History* 43, no. 4 (2015): 611–40; Benjamin Grob-Fitzgibbon, *Imperial Endgame: Britain's Dirty Wars and the End of Empire* (Basingstoke, UK: Palgrave Macmillan, 2011), 117–20.

61. Hugh Tinker, ed., *Burma. The Struggle for Independence, 1944–1948*, vol. 2: *From General Strike to Independence, 31 August 1946 to 4 January 1948* (London:

HMSO: 1984), doc. 105 encl.: Sir Raibeart MacDougall, "Memo. on the Need to Accelerate the Programme of Constitutional Advance for Burma Set out in the White Papers of May 1945."

62. TNA, CAB 66/65/25, WP(45)275, "Policy in Burma," India Committee report, May 1, 1945.

63. TNA, CO 537/3362, Burma Office memo., no date March 1947; IOR, Mss EUR, F169/5, Rance papers, file 23/GS47: GOC Burma Command, "Situation in the Immediate Future," March 28, 1947.

64. TNA, CO 537/3362, F/4795/1371/79, "Burma—Communist-Inspired Strikes," April 1, 1948.

65. TNA, CAB 121/684, tels. 691 and 760, reports on army mutinies, August 10 and 21, 1948.

66. TNA, CAB 195/4/86, CM(107)46, Cabinet minutes, item 2: Burma, December 19, 1946.

67. TNA, CAB 129/32/25, CP(49)25, annexes 1 and 2: conversations with Indian High Commissioner, February 3, 1949, and Pakistan High Commissioner, February 5, 1949.

68. TNA, CAB 129/32/22, CP(49)22, Foreign Secretary memo., "Indonesia," February 4, 1949.

69. Rachel Leow, *Taming Babel: Language in the Making of Malaysia* (Cambridge, UK: Cambridge University Press, 2016), 148–49.

70. Ramakrishna, *Emergency*, 36–47.

71. Leow, *Taming Babel*, 159–65, 173–74.

72. Leow, *Taming Babel*, 143–9, 152–56.

73. Bennett, "'A Very Salutary Effect,'" 427–31; Karl Hack, "Everyone Lived in Fear: Malaya and the British Way of Counter-Insurgency," *Small Wars & Insurgencies* 23, no. 4/5 (2012): 671–99.

74. Christopher Hale, "Batang Kali: Britain's My Lai?" *History Today* 62, no. 7 (2012): 3–4; Karl Hack, "'Devils that Suck the Blood of the People': The Case for Post-Revisionist Analysis of Counter-Insurgency Violence," *War in History* 25, no. 2 (2018): 203–4, 209–17, 223–24.

75. Grob-Fitzgibbon, *Imperial Endgame*, 136–38, 155–57.

76. TNA, CAB 134/497, Mal.C(50)2nd and 3rd meetings, April 24, and May 1, 1950. Malaya Committee members acknowledged that mass deportations were impossible in the short term but remained wedded to enforcing them in the longer term. Aware that deportations to Communist China were difficult, committee members favored using Christmas Island, a dependency leased to Australia and New Zealand, as an offshore detention center. On pejorative labeling, see Philip Deery, "The Terminology of Terrorism: Malaya, 1948–52," *Journal of Southeast Asian Studies* 34, no. 2 (2003): 236–47, and CAB 134/497, Mal.C(50)4th meeting, May 8, 1950, 1–2.

77. TNA, CAB 134/497, Mal.C(50)1st meeting, April 19, 1950.

78. TNA, DO 133/19,CRO to Delhi High Commission, October 29, 1949, tel. 920 Singapore to FO, November 4, 1949; DO 133/20, tel. 454 INTEL to overseas missions, December 13, 1949, circular 44 to Commonwealth Governments, January 11, 1950. Deportation became easier once the British government recognized the PRC regime in January 1950.

79. TNA, CAB 134/497, Mal.C(50)1st meeting, April 19, 1950, 3–4.

80. TNA, CAB 134/497, Mal.C(50)9th meeting, September 25, 1950.

81. TNA, CAB 134/497, Mal.C(50)10th meeting, October 17, 1950.

82. Good guides are Karl Hack, "The Malayan Emergency as Counter-Insurgency Paradigm," *Journal of Strategic Studies* 32, no. 3 (2009): 383–414; Hack, "Everyone Lived in Fear," 671–99; Frakking, "Beyond Sticks and Carrots," 394–407; Wen-Qing Ngoei, *Arc of Containment*, 84–90.

83. Corey Ross, *Ecology and Power in the Age of Empire: Europe and the Transformation of the Tropical World* (Oxford: Oxford University Press, 2019), 365; T. N. Harper, "The Politics of the Forest in Colonial Malaya," *Modern Asian Studies* 31, no. 1 (1997): 13–25.

84. David French, *The British Way in Counter-Insurgency, 1945–1957* (Oxford: Oxford University Press, 2011), 116–26; Ramakrishna, *Emergency*, 104–19.

85. TNA, WO 291/1773, ORS(PW) Memorandum 11/53, P. B. Humphrey, "A Study of the Reasons for Entering the Jungle among Chinese Communist Terrorists in Malaya," November 1953. Thanks to Roel Frakking for sharing this source with me.

86. TNA, WO 291/1773, ORS(PW) Memorandum 11/53, 3 and 6–7.

87. Erik Linstrum, *Ruling Minds: Psychology in the British Empire* (Cambridge, MA: Harvard University Press, 2015), 155–57, 176–78.

88. TNA, WO 291/1773, ORS(PW) Memorandum 11/53, 9–12; these findings are echoed in Kumar Ramakrishna's insight that numerous SEPs surrendered because of bullying by MCP leaders: Ramakrishna, *Emergency*, 38–39.

89. TNA, FO 371/101271, Federation of Malaya, paper no. 3, "Report of the Committee Appointed by the High Commissioner to Investigate the Squatter Problem," January 10, 1949, 1–3.

90. TNA, FO 371/101271, Federation of Malaya, paper no. 3, 3.

91. TNA, FO 371/101271, Federation of Malaya, paper no. 3, 4–5.

92. The Federal Executive Council considered the committee's report on January 27, Malaya's state and settlement administrations following suit a day later. The detention measures were, by then, in full swing; see TNA, FO 371/101271, Federation of Malaya paper no. 14, "The Squatter Problem in the Federation of Malaya in 1950," 3.

93. Hack, "'Devils that Suck the Blood of the People,'" 219–23.

94. TNA, FO 371/101271, Federation of Malaya paper no. 14, "The Squatter Problem in the Federation of Malaya in 1950," 1–2, 4–5. In the first round-up, 6,343 men, women and children were detained. A further 117 babies were born to detention camp families by March 20, 1950.

95. Matthew Hughes, *Britain's Pacification of Palestine: The British Army, the Colonial State, and the Arab Revolt, 1936–1939* (Cambridge, UK: Cambridge University Press, 2019), 35, 51–54; TNA, FO 371/101271, Federation of Malaya paper no. 14, appendix B, undated, "Measures in the States and Settlements for the Administrative Control of Squatters," 8–13.

96. TNA, FO 371/101271, Federation of Malaya paper no. 14, 5.

97. Karl Hack, "'Screwing down the People': The Malayan Emergency, Decolonisation, and Ethnicity," in *Imperial Policy and Southeast Asian Nationalism*, ed. Hans Antlöv, Hans, and Stein Tønnesson (London: Curzon Press, 1995), 83–109.

98. Jacob Darwin Hamblin, *Arming Mother Nature: The Birth of Catastrophic Environmentalism* (Oxford: Oxford University Press, 2013), 63–65; Owens, *Economy of Force*, 175–78.

99. Heng Pek Koon, "The Social and Ideological Origins of the Malayan Chinese Association, 1948–1957," *Journal of Southeast Asian History* 14, no. 2 (1983): 306–11; Ramakrishna, *Emergency*, 179–201.

100. Owens, *Economy of Force*, 186–88.

101. Alain Ruscio, "French Public Opinion and the War in Indochina, 1945–1954," in *War and Society in Twentieth Century France*, ed. Mike Scriven and Peter Wagstaff (Oxford: Berg, 1991), 117–29; M. Kathryn Edwards, *Contesting Indochina: French Remembrance between Decolonization and the Cold War* (Berkeley: University of California Press, 2016), 22–23.

102. Mark Atwood Lawrence, "Transnational Coalition-Building and the Making of the Cold War, 1947–1949," *Diplomatic History* 26, no. 3 (2002): 460–65. In early 1947 dockworkers in Indian, Ceylonese and Malayan ports refused to handle British shipments of war material destined for Vietnam, a sensitive issue for Attlee's government as withdrawal from the Indian subcontinent heightened British determination to conserve the economic benefits of control over Malaya.

103. Jacques Valette, "Les opérations de 1947 en Haut-Tonkin: les incertitudes d'une stratégie," *Guerres Mondiales et Conflits Contemporains* 240, no. 4 (2010): 63–79.

104. MAE, 217PAAP1: Henri Bonnet papers, correspondance 1947–53. (M/film P/6813), Alexandre Parodi, Note on the Indochina situation, February 10, 1950.

105. McHale, *First Vietnam War*, 164–67.

106. Chapman, *Cauldron*, 44–7.

107. McHale, *First Vietnam War*, 153–5, 159–63.

108. Brett Reilly, "The Sovereign States of Vietnam, 1945–1955," *Journal of Vietnamese Studies* 11, no. 3/4 (2016): 121–27.

109. Kevin Li coins the term 'outlaw partisan' in his study of Bình Xuyên paramilitaries, most of whom rallied to the French-Bao Dai alliance over the summer of 1948: Kevin Li, "Partisan to Sovereign: the Making of the Bình Xuyên in Southern Vietnam, 1945–1948," *Journal of Vietnamese Studies* 11, no. 3/4 (2016): 143–47, 168–73.

110. McHale, *First Vietnam War*, 167–70, 174–78. Shawn McHale describes how French jurists and diplomats circumscribed South Vietnam's autonomy in international and supranational forums but were hidebound by the mounting evidence of a functioning South Vietnamese state.

111. Reilly, "Sovereign States," 105.

112. McHale, *First Vietnam War*, 267.

113. Reilly, "Sovereign States," 127–28, 131–33; Chapman, *Cauldron*, 48–49, 61–62.

114. Lawrence, "Transnational Coalition-Building," 473–80; idem, *Assuming the Burden*.

115. Jean-Marc Le Page, *Les services secrets en Indochine* (Paris: Nouveau Monde, 2014), 33–43.

116. Frédéric Turpin, "Cao Bang, autumne 1950: autopsie d'un désastre," *Revue Historique des Armées* 3 (2000): 25–34; Alexander Zervoudakis, "'Nihil mirare, nihil contemptare, omnia intelligere': Franco-Vietnamese Intelligence in Indochina, 1950–1954," *Intelligence and National Security* 13, no. 1 (1998): 195–229.

117. Le Page, *Les services secrets*, 133–53; Alec Holcombe, *Mass Mobilization in the Democratic Republic of Vietnam, 1945–1960* (Honolulu: University of Hawai'i Press, 2020), 93–96.

118. Marc Michel, "De Lattre et les débuts de l'américanisation de la guerre d'Indochine," *Revue Française d'Histoire d'Outre-Mer* 77 (1985): 321–34; NARA, Policy Planning Staff records, RG 59/250/D/12/01, Box 15, Washington discussions with General de Lattre, September 7, 1951.

119. McHale, *First Vietnam War*, 221–34.

120. François Guillemot, "'Be Men!': Fighting and Dying for the State of Vietnam (1951–54)," *War & Society* 31, no. 2 (2012): 184–89; Le Page, *Les services secrets*, 401–3, 415–21.

121. Chi-Kwan Mark, "Lack of Means or Loss of Will? The United Kingdom and the Decolonization of Hong Kong, 1957–1967," *International History Review* 31, no. 1 (2009): 45–71, at 56–57. The Chinese regime, it appears, was reconciled to waiting for the 1997 expiry of the British colonial lease in Hong Kong, aware that the British could not defend the territory but conscious that the United States might take a firmer stand over it.

122. CWIO, OCI 1002/62, ESAU XVIII-62, CIA Staff Study memorandum, "North Vietnam and Sino–Soviet Relations," March 4, 1962; Goscha, "A 'Total War,'" 147–52.

123. Edward C. O'Dowd, "Ho Chi Minh and the Origins of the Vietnamese Doctrine of Guerrilla Tactics," *Small Wars & Insurgencies* 24, no. 3 (2013): 564–65 and 567–87: appendix: Guerrilla Tactics (*Cach Danh Du Kich*).

124. Goscha, "A 'Total War,'" 155–61; Holcombe, *Mass Mobilization*, 87–92.

125. Lentz, *Contested Territory*, 7–9, 136–41.

126. Stacey Hynd, "'Uncircumcised Boys' and 'Girl Spartans': Youth, Gender and Generation in Colonial Insurgencies and Counter-Insurgency, c.1954–9," *Gender & History* 33, no. 2 (2021): 536–56.

127. Harper, *End of Empire*, 149; Stacey Hynd, "Small Warriors? Children and Youth in Colonial Insurgencies and Counterinsurgency, ca. 1945–1960," *Comparative Studies in Society and History* 62, no. 4 (2020): 697–98.

128. Francois Guillemot, "Death and Suffering at First Hand: Youth Shock Brigades during the Vietnam War," *Journal of Vietnamese Studies* 4, no. 3 (2009): 17–60; also cited in Hynd, "Small Warriors?" 698.

129. Goscha, "A 'Total War,'" 155–56.

130. Goscha, "A 'Total War,'" 158–61.

131. Goscha, "A 'Total War,'" 140–43, 146–47; Lentz, *Contested Territory*, 16, 98–115.

132. Young-Sun Hong, *Cold War Germany*, 120.

133. CWIO, OCI 1002/62, ESAU XVIII-62, CIA Staff Study memorandum, "North Vietnam and Sino–Soviet Relations," March 4, 1962.

134. Yves Godard papers, Hoover Institution, Stanford University, box 2, Forces Terrestres du Laos, "Opération 'Drome', rapport du Lt.-Colonel Godard," December 23, 1953.

135. Lentz, *Contested Territory*, 137–59.

136. Chris Pearson, *Mobilizing Nature: The Environmental History of War and Militarization in Modern France* (Manchester, UK: Manchester University Press, 2012), 214; Goscha, "A 'Total War,'" 139–40.

137. Lentz, *Contested Territory*, 161, 164–65. The PAVN Supply Department target was 7,730 tons of rice. Its eventual tripling underlines the scale of the supply effort and the battle's duration.

138. Lentz, *Contested Territory*, 142–44, 155–56, 161. Vietnamese and French official estimates of PAVN military losses range from 4,000 to 8,000 but are likely underestimates. Tallying civilian losses is harder still. Christian Lentz's 'conservative estimate' of total Vietnamese participants, soldiers and civilians combined, is 314,000 (*Contested Territory*, 170).

139. Fredrik Logevall, *Embers of War: The Fall of an Empire and the Making of America's Vietnam* (New York: Random House, 2012), 510–46; Kathryn Edwards, *Contesting Indochina*, 20–21, 25–26; Lentz, *Contested Territory*, 161. As the PAVN advanced, some parachute drops fell into their hands. Adding to the poignancy, members of the defending garrison had originally parachuted into Dien Biên Phu as part of the original reinforcement program on November 20, 1953.

140. "Indochina: The fall of Dien Bien Phu," *Time*, May 17, 1954; Yves Godard papers, Hoover Institution, Stanford University, box 2, Condor/Albatros (8 Avril–24 Mai 1954), "Compte rendu d'opération du groupement mobile nord."

141. Malika Rahal, "Empires," in *Europe's Postwar Periods—1989, 1945, 1918: Writing History Backwards*, ed. Martin Conway, Pieter Lagrou, and Henry Rousso (London: Bloomsbury, 2019), 141–44; Owen White, *The Blood of the Colony: Wine and the Rise and Fall of French Algeria* (Cambridge, MA: Harvard University Press, 2021), 179.

142. Useful here are parallel debates on the growing use of firearms in criminal violence within European imperial states transitioning from war to peace in the 1940s; see Pieter Lagrou, "Regaining the Monopoly of Force: Agents of the State Shooting Fugitives in and around Belgium, 1940–1950," *Past & Present* 210, Supplement 6 (2011): 177–95; Marco Maria Aterrano, "Civilian Disarmament: Public Order and the Restoration of State Authority in Italy's Postwar Transition, 1944–6," *Journal of Contemporary History* 56, no. 2 (2020): 1–25.

143. Lagrou, "Regaining the Monopoly of Force," 177–81.

144. Robert Gerwarth is the pioneer here; see his *The Vanquished: Why the First World War Failed to End, 1917–1923* (London: Penguin, 2017), as well as the chapter contributions in his earlier coedited collection with John Horne, *War in Peace: Paramilitary Violence in Europe after the Great War* (Oxford: Oxford University Press, 2013).

Chapter Nine: Partitions Dissected

1. Arie M. Dubnov and Laura Robson, "Drawing the Line, Writing beyond It: Toward a Transnational History of Partitions," in *Partitions: A Transnational History of Twentieth-Century Territorial Separatism* (Stanford, CA: Stanford University Press, 2019), 3, 25–27; Ian Talbot, "The End of the European Colonial Empires and Forced Migration: Some Comparative Case Studies," in *Refugees and the End of Empire: Imperial Collapse and Forced Migration in the Twentieth Century*, ed. Panikos Panayi and Pippa Virdee (Basingstoke, UK: Palgrave Macmillan, 2011), 28–41.

2. Mark Levene, "The Tragedy of the Rimlands: Nation-State Formation and the Destruction of Imperial Peoples, 1912–1948," in Panayi and Virdee, *Refugees and*

the End of Empire, 60–70; Eric D. Weitz, *A World Divided: The Global Struggle for Human Rights in the Age of Nation-States* (Princeton, NJ: Princeton University Press, 2019), 320, 333.

3. Laura Robson, *States of Separation: Transfer, Partition, and the Making of the Modern Middle East* (Berkeley: University of California Press, 2017), 169–71.

4. Natasha Wheatley, "Mandatory Interpretation: Legal Hermeneutics and the New International Order in Arab and Jewish Petitions to the League of Nations," *Past & Present* 27 (May 2015): 245–46.

5. Kate O'Malley, "'Indian Ulsterisation'—Ireland, India, and Partition: The Infection of Example?" in Dubnov and Robson, *Partitions*, 119–21, 123–26.

6. Md. Mahbubar Rahman and Willem Van Schendel, "'I Am Not a Refugee': Rethinking Partition Migration," *Modern Asian Studies* 37, no. 3 (2003): 551–53.

7. Dirk Moses summarizes this viewpoint: 'Wherever culturally, religiously, or nationally motivated intergroup violence is thought to be endemic and intractable, partition of territory and populations looms as a possible solution.' A. Dirk Moses, "Partitions, Hostages, Transfer: Retributive Violence and National Security," in Dubnov and Robson, *Partitions*, 257. For comparisons: Robert Holland, Carl Bridge, and H. V. Brasted, "Counsels of Despair or Withdrawals with Honour? Partitioning in Ireland, India, Palestine and Cyprus 1920–1960," *Round Table* 86, no. 342 (1997): 257–68.

8. Hayat Alvi-Aziz, "The (Non)Governance of Divided Territories: A Comparative Study of Bangladesh, Pakistan, and Palestine," *Comparative Studies of South Asia, Africa, and the Middle East* 28, no. 3 (2008): 461–72.

9. Ellen Jenny Ravndal, "Exit Britain: British Withdrawal from the Palestine Mandate in the Early Cold War, 1947–1948," *Diplomacy & Statecraft* 21, no. 3 (2010): 418.

10. IISH, COLL00201, Algeria, social and political developments collection, folder 3, GPRA Evian conference delegation, "Texte de la conférence de Presse de M. Belkacam KRIM," Vice-President GPRA, head of delegation, no date, May 1961.

11. Dubnov and Robson, "Drawing the Line," 1–27, especially 16–25.

12. Moses, "Partitions, Hostages, Transfer," 259–61; Alexios Alecou, "Safeguarding through Stability: British Constitutional Proposals in Post-War Cyprus," *Journal of Human Rights in the Commonwealth* 2, no. 2 (2016): 52–56.

13. Dubnov and Robson, "Drawing the Line," 1–2.

14. Dubnov and Robson, "Drawing the Line," 2.

15. Joya Chatterji, *The Spoils of Partition: Bengal and India, 1947–1967* (Cambridge, UK: Cambridge University Press, 2007), 19–33; idem, "The Fashioning of a Frontier: The Radcliffe Line and Bengal's Border Landscape, 1947–52," *Modern Asian Studies* 33, no. 1 (1999): 199–213; Lucy P. Chester, *Boundaries and Conflict in South Asia: The Radcliffe Boundary Commission and the Partition of Punjab* (Manchester, UK: Manchester University Press, 2009); David Gilmartin, "Partition, Pakistan, and South Asian History: In Search of a Narrative," *Journal of Asian Studies* 57, no. 4 (1998): 1081–89; Moses, "Partitions, Hostages, Transfer," 271–78.

16. Sarah Ansari and William Gould, *Boundaries of Belonging: Localities, Citizenship and Rights in India and Pakistan* (Cambridge, UK: Cambridge University Press, 2019), 67–82.

17. Taylor C. Sherman, "Moral Economies of Violence in Hyderabad State, 1948," *Deccan Studies* 8, no. 2 (2010): 65–90, cited in Moses, "Partitions, Hostages, Transfer," 265.

18. India Office Private Office papers, Mss Eur F164: Sir Francis Mudie papers, F164/10: Papers on the constitutional situation following the failure of the Simla Conference, 1945–7, R. F. Mudie note to Sir Evan Jenkins, Viceroy's House, New Delhi, July 16, 1945.

19. Victor Kattan and Amit Ranjan, "Introduction: Connecting the Partitions of India and Palestine: Institutions, Policies, Laws and People," in *The Breakup of India and Palestine: The Causes and Legacies of Partition*, ed. Victor Kattan and Amit Ranjan (Manchester, UK: Manchester University Press, 2023), 1–10.

20. For European and colonial perspectives, see Panayi and Virdee, *Refugees*, 3–27, 28–50.

21. Dubnov and Robson, "Drawing the Line," 8.

22. Jan Eckel, "Human Rights and Decolonization: New Perspectives and Open Questions," *Humanity* 1, no. 1 (Fall 2010): 113–17.

23. The Delhi correspondent of *The Times* emphasized a month after independence that levels of partition displacement and mass violence outweighed any contemporary European experience; "Indian Communal War: The Present Fever of Violence Diagnosed," *The Times*, September 18, 1947.

24. Official figures released at Government House in Delhi recorded a total of 323,000 Muslims and 838,000 non-Muslims as having crossed the 'principal frontier posts between Pakistan and India.' Enumerating only those refugees who were officially registered at the major crossing points, these figures, although unreliably low, give some indication of the size of the process; see TNA, FO 371/63568, F15446/8800/85, High Commission tel., "Refugees," September 17, 1947.

25. Sir Francis Mudie papers, F164/20B, Note prepared by the Chief Liaison Officer, West Punjab, no date, but likely September 1947.

26. Rahman and Schendel, "'I Am Not a Refugee,'" 562–70.

27. Joya Chatterji, "Partition Studies: Prospects and Pitfalls," *Journal of Asian Studies* 73, no. 2 (2014): 310–11.

28. This was a point conceded with rare frankness by Lord Ismay, chief of staff to Viceroy Mountbatten, one of the few top officials prepared to admit both that collective violence was predictable and that the British, along with the Indian and Pakistan governments, overestimated their ability to control events; see TNA, FO 371/63570, F13771/8800/85, "India and Pakistan, Statement by Lord Ismay," no date, September 1947.

29. TNA, FO 371/63565, Viceroy to Secretary of State for India, June 27, 1947.

30. TNA, FO 371/63565, IB(47)37th meeting, June 30, 1947, and Annex II: interim government.

31. TNA, FO 371/63565, F9247/8800/85, "The Future Status of India," May 1, 1947; K. Santhanam, "False Alarms," *Hindustan Times*, June 22, 1947; Secretary, Constituent Assembly committee to British Cabinet Mission, Delhi, August 1, 1947.

32. TNA, FO 371/63567, F11235/8800/85, IB(47)146, "Hyderabad," July 25, 1947; FO 371/63568, F11837/8800/85, "Future Position of the Indian States," July 15, 1947; FO 371/63568, F12649/8800/85, Southeast Asia Department memo., "India and

Hyderabad," September 17, 1947; FO 371/63669, F13715/8800/85, "Status of Kashmir," October 8, 1947. Hyderabad's state government protested to London about the loss of autonomous status and the repudiation of preexisting treaty arrangements between Britain and the princely state. Frictions over Kashmir were illustrated, meanwhile, by a rumor circulating in early October after engine trouble forced a senior adviser to Kashmir's maharajah into an unscheduled stop at Pakistan's Lahore airport. The rumor had it that a secret search of his belongings revealed details of a secret treaty in which the Delhi authorities promised new communications links in return for Kashmir's accession to India: see FO 371/63570, F13715/8800/85, Pakistan High Commission tel., "The Status of Kashmir," October 8, 1947. More reliable were reported incursions by Muslim paramilitaries and Indian Army troops, the prelude to armed confrontations in late October 1947; see CRO tel. to High Commissions, October 26, 1947; F14419/8800/85, CRO memo., "Situation in Kashmir," October 27, 1947.

33. Ahmad Safeer Bhat, "Jammu and Kashmir on the Eve of Partition: A Study of Political Conditions," *South Asian Studies* 32, no. 2 (2017): 285–95; Kavita Saraswathi Datla, "Sovereignty and the End of Empire: The Transition to Independence in Colonial Hyderabad," *Ab Imperio* 3 (2018): 73, 79–86.

34. Ilyas Chattha, "Escape from Violence: The 1947 Partition of India and the Migration of Kashmiri Muslim Refugees," in Panayi and Virdee, *Refugees*, 197–211. Chattha estimates deaths in Jammu and Kashmir's partition violence at 250,000 to 300,000 and displacement at 1 million.

35. Drawing on the work of Paula A. Michaels and Christina Twomey, I use the terms 'trauma' and 'traumatized' in reference to a sudden, catastrophic occurrence that exceeds a person's psychological or physiological capacity to cope with it; see Paula A. Michaels and Christina Twomey, eds., *Gender and Trauma since 1900* (London: Bloomsbury, 2021), 3–4.

36. Gyan Prakash, "Anxious Constitution-Making," in *The Postcolonial Moment in South and Southeast Asia*, ed. Gyan Prakash, Michael Laffan, and Nikhil Menon (London: Bloomsbury, 2018), 148.

37. Joya Chatterji, "South Asian Histories of Citizenship, 1946–70," *Historical Journal* 55, no. 4 (2012): 1049–71; Taylor C. Sherman, "Migration, Citizenship and Belonging in Hyderabad (Deccan), 1945–1956," *Modern Asian Studies* 45, no. 1 (2011): 81–107, cited in Sunil Amrith, "Struggles for Citizenship around the Bay of Bengal," in *The Postcolonial Moment in South and Southeast Asia*, ed. Gyan Prakash, Michael Laffan, and Nikhil Menon (London: Bloomsbury, 2018), 113.

38. TNA, FO 371/63570, F13771/8800/85, IB(47)176, CRO memo., "India-Pakistan Dispute," October 3, 1947.

39. Joya Chatterji, "Fashioning of a Frontier," 185–87.

40. Even British official reportage trying to convey the human consequences of partition dealt in numbers so large that they defied disaggregation or comprehension as lives lost or forever transformed: TNA, FO 371/63568, F11884/8800/85, Summary of High Commission telegrams, "Communal Situation in Punjab," August 21, 1947. For the final months of colonial administration and frontier delimitation in Punjab: Tahir Kamran, "The Unfolding Crisis in Punjab, March–August 1947: Key Turning Points and British Responses," *Journal of Punjab Studies* 14 (2007): 194–205.

41. Ian Copland, "The Further Shores of Partition: Ethnic Cleansing in Rajasthan, 1947," *Past & Present* 160 (1998): 215–35. Unknown thousands of Muslims were killed in Rajasthan's urban centers, Alwar and Bharatpur above all.

42. Chatterji, "South Asian Histories of Citizenship," 1057–59. Admitting the likelihood that their military forces would not remain neutral, the MEO was organized along communal lines, its units comprised of Indian and Pakistan regiments assigned to protect their coreligionists.

43. For Sindh and its largest city, Karachi: Sarah Ansari, *Life after Partition: Migration, Community and Strife in Sindh, 1947–1962* (Oxford: Oxford University Press, 2005).

44. TNA, FO 371/63568, F11883/8800/85, High Commissioner to CRO, August 21, 1947, Shone to Commonwealth Relations Office (CRO), August 21, 1947.

45. TNA, FO 371/63568, F11883/8800/85, High Commissioner to CRO, August 21, 1947.

46. Sir Francis Mudie papers, F164/20B, Statement dated October 6, 1947, of Major Mirza Daud Ahmed, 15 Punjab Regiment; "Report on the Situation in the West Punjab for the Period Ending 31-8-47 from Chief Secretary, West Punjab Government"; Pippa Virdee, "'No Home but in Memory': The Legacies of Colonial Rule in the Punjab," in Panayi and Virdee, *Refugees*, 179–83.

47. Ian Talbot, "The August 1947 Violence in Sheikhupura City," in *The Independence of India and Pakistan: New Approaches and Reflections*, ed. Ian Talbot (Oxford: Oxford University Press, 2013), 90–120.

48. Sir Francis Mudie papers, F164/16: Correspondence file of incidents occurring during the exchange of evacuees between East and West Punjab, August 1947–February 1948, West Punjab government instruction to police inspector generals, September 16, 1947.

49. For the challenges in recovering histories of women's experiences of partition, see Urvashi Butalia, *The Other Side of Silence: Voices from the Partition of India* (Durham, NC: Duke University Press, 2000); Gyanendra Pandey, *Remembering Partition: Violence, Nationalism and History in India* (Cambridge, UK: Cambridge University Press, 2001).

50. Sir Francis Mudie papers, F164/20C: "Disturbances in East Punjab and Contiguous Areas during and after August 1947. Part II Selected Official Statements and Reports"; FO 371/63568, F15446/8800/85, High Commission tel., September 17, 1947.

51. TNA, FO 371/63668, F11884/8800/85, Shone tel. to CRO, August 23, 1947.

52. Sir Francis Mudie papers, F164/16, Gopichand Bhargva, Prime Minister East Punjab, telegram to Khan of Mamdot, Prime Minister of Lahore, no date, September 1947.

53. Sir Francis Mudie papers, F164/16, Advanced HQ/ME Pakistan, Amritsar, "Report on East Punjab Situation," September 24, 1947.

54. TNA, FO 371/63568, tels. 658, 666, 667, Punjab situation reports, August 23, 27 and 30, 1947.

55. TNA, FO 371/63568, tel. 682, "Punjab," August 30, 1947.

56. TNA, FO 371/63570, F13771/8800/85, IB(47)176, CRO memo., "India-Pakistan Dispute," October 3, 1947.

57. Sir Francis Mudie papers, F164/16, Advanced HQ/ME Pakistan, Amritsar, "Report on East Punjab Situation," September 24, 1947.

58. Sir Francis Mudie papers, F164/20A: "Disturbances in East Punjab and Contiguous Areas during and after August 1947," Governor-General's Press, Karachi, 1948; F164/20B: "Disturbances in East Punjab and Contiguous Areas during and after August 1947. Part II: Selected Official Statements and Reports." Although partial, the case-by-case nature of these compilations allows some trend analysis.

59. Sir Francis Mudie papers, F164/16, Advanced HQ/ME Pakistan, Amritsar, "Report on East Punjab Situation," September 24, 1947.

60. Punjab correspondence reports: TNA, FO 371/63568.

61. Chester, *Boundaries*, 41–43; Chatterji, "Fashioning of a Frontier," 193–97.

62. Lucy P. Chester, "Boundary Commissions as Tools to Safeguard British Interests at the End of Empire," *Journal of Historical Geography* 34, no. 3 (2008): 507–10.

63. Chatterji, "Fashioning of a Frontier," 185–87; Chester, *Boundaries*, 51–70, 83–88.

64. Joya Chatterji, "Dispositions and Destinations: Refugee Agency and 'Mobility Capital' in the Bengal Diaspora, 1947–2007," *Comparative Studies in Society and History* 55, no. 2 (2013): 273–74, 292–96; idem, "South Asian Histories of Citizenship," 1060–63.

65. Haimanti Roy, *Partitioned Lives: Migrants, Refugees, Citizens in India and Pakistan, 1947–1965* (New Delhi: Oxford University Press, 2012), 164–69.

66. Roy, *Partitioned Lives*, 149–57; Urvashi Butalia, "Legacies of Departure: Decolonizaton, Nation-Making, and Gender," in *Gender and Empire*, ed. Philippa Levine (Oxford: Oxford University Press, 2004), 204–18. Urvashi Butalia estimates that 100,000 women were subjected to rape and abduction during partition. Most never returned to their families, despite the efforts of police and government social workers. Legislation to assist the process also objectified the women as victims rather than citizens with the legal autonomy to determine their own preferences.

67. According to British intelligence, at least 10 million refugees fled East Pakistan for India after General Yahya Khan's Pakistan government began its failed repression of the Bangladeshi independence movement; see Angela Debnath, "British Perceptions of the East Pakistan Crisis 1971: 'Hideous Atrocities on Both Sides'?" *Journal of Genocide Research* 13, no. 4 (2011): 421–22.

68. India Office Private Office papers, L/PO/12/12: Corrrespondence with Sir Terence Shone, British High Commissioner to India, March 12, 1947–May 11, 1948, "Note of a Discussion with Mr Jinnah, in the Presence of Lord Ismay, Government House, Lahore, 1st November 1947 from 2 o'clock to 5.30pm."

69. India Office Private Office papers, L/PO/12/12: "History of Attempt to Bring Pandit Nehru and Mr Jinnah together: 28th October–1st November 1947."

70. TNA, FO 371/63570, F14516/8800/85, Auchinleck tel. 1114, October 28, 1947.

71. TNA, FO 371/63568/8800/85, IB(47)163, "Situation in the Punjab," and attached memo., September 3, 1947. Not until October 3 did the Cabinet Committee receive details on the spread of mass violence with receipt of a CRO report prepared for the UK delegation to the United Nations in anticipation of an Indo-Pakistan war over Kashmir: TNA, FO 371/63570, F13771/8800/85, IB(47)176, CRO memo., "India-Pakistan Dispute," October 3, 1947.

72. TNA, FO 371/63568, F12631/8800/85, Minute by Peter Murray, September 19, 1947.

73. Such language pervades exchanges between officials of the Foreign and Commonwealth Relations Offices, as evidenced in the principal Foreign Office record group, FO 371. Sometimes derided by historians as articulating unalloyed colonialism, these Foreign Office records, if read against the grain, are particularly revealing for that reason.

74. TNA, FO 371/63570, CA(47)6, Auchinleck memo. for Commonwealth Affairs Committee, "Situation in India and Pakistan," September 28, 1947, plus annexes I and II: "Terms of Reference of Armed Forces Reconstitution Committee/Partition of the Armed Forces." A day later Foreign Secretary Ernest Bevin penned a note to Attlee, offering to send Foreign Office personnel to help staff the new British High Commissions in Delhi and Karachi. As matters stood, neither had the people or the equipment to communicate daily with London. To send encrypted correspondence from Karachi, High Commissioner Grafftey-Smith relied entirely on two 'cypher girls,' one of whom had just contracted dysentery; see TNA, Ernest Bevin Private Office papers, FO 800/470, PM/47/135, Bevin letter to Prime Minister, September 29, 1947.

75. Nicholas Owen, *The British Left and India: Metropolitan Anti-Imperialism, 1885–1947* (Oxford: Oxford University Press, 2007), 272–73, 293–96.

76. Ian Talbot, "The Mountbatten Viceroyalty Reconsidered: Personality, Prestige and Strategic Vision in the Partition of India," in Kattan and Ranjan, *The Breakup of India and Palestine*, 37–46.

77. TNA, FO 371/63570, F14120/8800/85, Cabinet Office note, October 13, 1947.

78. Efrat Ben-Ze'ev, *Remembering Palestine in 1948: Beyond National Narratives* (Cambridge, UK: Cambridge University Press, 2011), chapter 6: "Underground Memories, Collecting Traces of the Palestinian Past," 101–24. Created in 1941, Palmach military units took the leading role in fighting for the creation of the state of Israel in 1948.

79. Nur Masalha, "Indigenous versus Colonial-Settler Toponymy and the Struggle over the Cultural and Political Geography of Palestine: The Appropriation of Palestinian Place Names by the Israeli State," in *Decolonizing the Study of Palestine: Indigenous Perspectives and Settler Colonialism after Elia Zureik*, ed. Ahmad H. Sa'di and Nur Masalha (London: I. B. Tauris, 2023), 47–48.

80. The strongest assertion of ethnic cleansing is Ilan Pappé's *The Ethnic Cleansing of Palestine* (Oxford: Oneworld, 2006); for opposing views in the resulting controversy, see Benny Morris, "The Liar as Hero," *The New Republic*, March 17, 2011; Jeremy R. Hammond, *Benny Morris's Untenable Denial of the Ethnic Cleansing of Palestine* (Cross Village, MI: Worldview, 2016). On the Indian experience: Peter Gatrell, *The Making of the Modern Refugee* (Oxford: Oxford University Press, 2013), 85–88, 149, 168–69. In the six years after the Indian government passed an Abducted Persons Recovery Act in 1949, some 22,000 Muslim women were 'recovered' to Pakistan, while at least 8,000 Sikh and Hindu women were returned from Pakistan to India. These figures likely conceal thousands more who were either coerced into conversion and marriage or otherwise hidden from official view.

81. Weitz, *A World Divided*, 356–59.

82. Abdel Razzaq Takriti, *Monsoon Revolution: Republicans, Sultans, and Empires in Oman, 1965–1976* (Oxford: Oxford University Press, 2013), 49–53, 56–58.

83. Norman Rose, *A Senseless, Squalid War: Voices from Palestine 1945–1948* (London: Bodley Head, 2009), 215, cited in Gabriel Warburg, "'A Senseless, Squalid War': Voices from Palestine 1945–1948," *Middle Eastern Studies* 46, no. 4 (2010): 619; Rashid Khalidi, "The Palestinians and 1948: The Underlying Causes of Failure," in *The War for Palestine: Rewriting the History of 1948*, ed. Eugene L. Rogan and Avi Schlaim (Cambridge, UK: Cambridge University Press, 2001), 21–29.

84. Ravndal, "Exit Britain," 424–25. Germany's Allied occupiers oscillated between sympathy and frustration toward what fast became an uncontrollable flow of Jewish Displaced Persons. For the French case: Laure Humbert, *Reinventing French Aid: The Politics of Humanitarian Relief in French-Occupied Germany, 1945–1952* (Cambridge, UK: Cambridge University Press, 2021), 94–95; Julia Maspero, "French Policy on Postwar Migration of Eastern European Jews through France and French Occupation Zones in Germany and Austria," *Jewish History Quarterly* 2 (2013): 319–39.

85. Weitz, *A World Divided*, 349; Michael J. Cohen, "The Zionist Perspective," and Walid Khalidi, "The Arab Perspective," both in *The End of the Palestine Mandate*, ed. Wm. Roger Louis and Robert W. Stookey (London: I. B. Tauris, 1986), 83–85 and 109–10. Division between the Arab League and the Palestinian Higher Arab Committee weakened their case: Haim Levenberg, *Military Preparations of the Arab Community in Palestine, 1945–1948* (London: Frank Cass, 1993), 9–17, 43–45.

86. Zvi Elpeleg, *The Grand Mufti Haj Amin al-Hussaini, Founder of the Palestinian National Movement* (London: Frank Cass, 1993); Rana Barakat, "Reading Palestinian Agency in Mandate History: The Narrative of the Buraq Revolt as Anti-Relational," *Contemporary Levant* 4, no. 1 (2019): 28–29, 36–37; Hillel Cohen, *Army of Shadows: Palestinian Collaboration with Zionism, 1917–1948* (Berkeley: University of California Press, 2008), 84; Matthew Hughes, *Britain's Pacification of Palestine: The British Army, the Colonial State, and the Arab Revolt, 1936–1939* (Cambridge, UK: Cambridge University Press, 2019), 101–4, 155–57.

87. Hughes, *Britain's Pacification*, 28, 246–47. Matthew Hughes estimates that over 10 per cent of Palestinians were detained by British security forces during the Arab Revolt of 1936–1939.

88. Cohen, *Army of Shadows*, 202–13.

89. Ben-Ze'ev, *Remembering Palestine*, 26–28, 33–34.

90. Hughes, *Britain's Pacification*, 28, 346–38; Avi Schlaim, "Israel and the Arab Coalition in 1948," in Rogan and Schlaim, *War for Palestine*, 79–80.

91. Maurice M. Labelle Jr., "A New Age of Empire? Arab 'Anti-Americanism,' US Intervention, and the Lebanese Civil War of 1958," *International History Review* 35, no. 1 (2013): 44–45.

92. Penny Sinanoglou, "British Plans for the Partition of Palestine, 1929–1938," *Historical Journal* 52, no. 1 (2009): 131–52.

93. Jacob Metzer, *The Divided Economy of Mandate Palestine* (Cambridge, UK: Cambridge University Press, 1998), 91–108, 200–6; Martin Kolinsky, *Law, Order and Riots in Mandatory Palestine, 1928–1935* (Basingstoke, UK: Palgrave Macmillan, 1993), 220–27.

94. For the analogies and precedents, see Lucy Chester, "'Close Parallels'? Interrelated Discussions of Partition in South Asia and the Palestine Mandate (1936–1948)," in Dubnov and Robson, *Partitions*, 132–36, 146–53. Irish precedents were more frequently invoked in the case of India's partition, as Kate O'Malley shows in the same edited collection: "'Indian Ulsterisation,'" 113–20.

95. Gershon Shafir, "Theorizing Zionist Settler Colonialism in Palestine," and Arnon Degani, "From Republic to Empire: Israel and the Palestinians after 1948," both in *The Routledge Handbook of the History of Settler Colonialism*, ed. Edward Cavanagh and Lorenzo Veracini (Abingdon, UK: Routledge, 2016), 339–50 and 353–54.

96. Jørgen Jensehaugen, Marte Heian-Engdal, and Hilde Henriksen Waage, "Securing the State: From Zionist Ideology to Israeli Statehood," *Diplomacy & Statecraft* 23, no. 2 (2012): 282–85.

97. Zachary Lockman, *Comrades and Enemies: Arab and Jewish Workers in Palestine, 1906–1948* (Berkeley: University of California Press, 1996), 313–14; Wm. Roger Louis, "British Imperialism and the End of the Palestine Mandate," in Louis and Stookey, *End of the Palestinian Mandate*, 19.

98. David Ceserani, "The British Security Forces and the Jews in Palestine, 1945–48," in *Rethinking History, Dictatorship and War: New Approaches and Interpretations*, ed. Claus-Christian W. Szejnmann (London: Continuum, 2009), 193–94, 200; David A. Charters, *The British Army and Jewish Insurgency in Palestine, 1945–47* (Basingstoke, UK: Macmillan, 1989).

99. Levenberg, *Military Preparations*, 85–90.

100. Calder Walton, "British Intelligence and the Mandate of Palestine: Threats to British National Security Immediately after the Second World War," *Intelligence & National Security* 23, no. 4 (2008): 435–62; David Cesarini, "Remember Cable Street? Wrong Battle, Mate," *History and Policy*, online journal paper available at https://www.historyandpolicy.org/policy-papers/papers/remember-cable-street -wrong-battle-mate.

101. James Barr, *A Line in the Sand: Britain, France and the Struggle that Shaped the Middle East* (London: Simon & Schuster, 2012), 320–25; Walton, "British Intelligence," 439–41. Stern Gang bomb-maker Yaacov Levstein assembled the Colonial Office device, working with the French security service Bureau Noir, and David Knout, a Russian Jewish émigré who founded the French resistance network the Armée Juive. Knout's daughter, Betty, planted the bomb. Belgian customs officials arrested Levstein and Betty Knout later in 1947 during a letter-bombing campaign targeting British politicians.

102. For the evolution of partition thinking and the part played by leading Zionist agencies and the president of the World Zionist Organization, Dr. Chaim Weizmann, in particular, see Motti Golani, "'The Meat and the Bones': Reassessing the Origins of the Partition of Mandate Palestine," in Dubnov and Robson, *Partitions*, 85–97, 107–8.

103. Weitz, *A World Divided*, 342–48.

104. Laura Robson, "Partition and the Question of International Governance: The 1947 United Nations Special Committee on Palestine," in Kattan and Ranjan, *Breakup of India and Palestine*, 79–85.

105. Wm. Roger Louis, *The British Empire in the Middle East: Arab Nationalism, the United States, and Postwar Imperialism, 1945–1951* (Oxford: Oxford University Press, 1984), 464–77.

106. Weitz, *A World Divided*, 350–53; Jensehaugen, Heian-Engdal, and Waage, "Securing the State," 285–93. The authors also underline the importance of the Jewish Agency's diplomacy and anti-Palestinian propaganda, its lobbying of potential backers at the UN especially.

107. Jensehaugen, Heian-Engdal, and Waage, "Securing the State," 294–95.

108. CWIO, ORE 55, CIA intelligence estimate, "The Consequences of the Partition of Palestine," November 28, 1947. Anticipation of imminent war was equally evident among Jewish and Arab military personnel who deserted British security forces to fight for their respective communities: Christopher Caden and Nir Arielli, "British Army and Palestine Police Deserters and the Arab–Israeli War of 1948," *War in History* 28, no. 1 (2021): 200–21.

109. TNA, FO 492/2, E7247/1078/31, Washington Embassy review, "Palestine: United States Policy," May 24, 1948.

110. TNA, CAB 128/12/12, CM(48)12, Cabinet minutes, item 1: Palestine, February 5, 1948.

111. TNA, FO 492/2, E5497/4/G, FO memo., "Situation in Palestine—Attitude of Neighbouring States," April 29, 1948.

112. TNA, FO 492/2, E4834//8/31, "Palestine—Termination of British Mandate and Withdrawal of High Commissioner," May 29, 1948; E7835/1/31, "Jerusalem—Capture of Jewish Quarter of Old City," May 30, 1948.

113. TNA, FO 492/2, E3673/14/80, A. S. Kirkbride, Amman, "Anglo-Transjordan Treaty of Alliance," March 15, 1948; CAB 195/6/56, CM 71(48), Cabinet minutes, item 1, November 12, 1948. Hence the government's reluctance to provide arms and logistic support to their principal local ally, Transjordan, despite the fact that Jordan's Arab Legion remained under British direction.

114. TNA, FO 492/2, E13348/375/31, "Recognition of the Gaza Government of Palestine," October 13, 1948; E13498/4/G, "Transjordan's Suggestions for a Solution to the Palestine Problem," October 15, 1948; E13849/27/93, Baghdad Embassy report, "Arab Position in Palestine," December 6, 1948; Eugene L. Rogan, "Jordan and 1948: The Persistence of an Official History," in Rogan and Schlaim, *War for Palestine*, 104–5, 109–13.

115. Ghazi Falah, "The 1948 Israeli-Palestinian War and Its Aftermath: The Transformation and De-Signification of Palestine's Cultural Landscape," *Annals of the Association of American Geographers* 86, no. 2 (1996): 256–85; Walid Khalidi, *All That Remains: The Palestinian Villages Occupied and Depopulated by Israel in 1948* (Washington, DC: Institute for Palestine Studies, 1992).

116. On the role of IDF troops during Operation *Hiram* in the Galilee and subsequent village massacres, see Benny Morris, "Revisiting the Palestinian Exodus of 1948," in Rogan and Schlaim, *War for Palestine*, 48–56.

117. Gatrell, *Making of the Modern Refugee*, 124–7; Laura Robson, *The Politics of Mass Violence in the Middle East* (Oxford: Oxford University Press, 2020), 107. For arguments over the extent of these massacres, see Benny Morris, "Operation *Dani* and the Palestinian Exodus from Lydda and Ramle in 1948," *Middle East Journal* 40,

no. 1 (1986): 82–109; Alon Kadish and Avraham Sela, "Myths and Historiography of the 1948 Palestine War Revisited: The Case of Lydda," *Middle East Journal* 59, no. 4 (2005): 617–34.

118. Through interviews with former Palmach fighters, Efrat Ben-Ze'ev's remarkable anthropological study gets beyond the collective silence about these events; see his *Remembering Palestine*, 33–34, 128–29.

119. Gatrell, *Making of the Modern Refugee*, 130–31, 136. According to Gatrell, after Palestinian refugee numbers increased following the second Arab–Israeli War in 1956, the US State Department, UNRWA's primary funder, conceded that the expenditure contained the refugee problem rather than solving it. Underlining the connection between decolonization and displacement in the Middle East, Palestinian refugees, denied Lebanese nationality lest they disrupt the country's intercommunal balance, were housed in seventeen UNRWA refugee camps formerly occupied by Armenian refugees.

120. Ilana Feddman, "Difficult Distinctions: Refugee Law, Humanitarian Practice and Political Identification in Gaza," *Cultural Anthropology* 22, no. 1 (2007): 129–69, at 135, also cited in Gatrell, *Making of the Modern Refugee*, 135.

121. Jagmohan Meher, "Dynamics of Pakistan's Disintegration: The Case of East Pakistan, 1947–1971," *India Quarterly* 71, no. 4 (2015): 300–17, argues that East Pakistan was always untenable.

122. Gatrell, *Making of the Modern Refugee*, 148, 170–71; Wardatul Akmam, "Atrocities against Humanity during the Liberation War in Bangladesh: A Case of Genocide," *Journal of Genocide Research* 4, no. 4 (2002): 549–51; Sarmila Bose, "Anatomy of Violence: Analysis of Civil War in East Pakistan in 1971," *Economic and Political Weekly* 40, no. 41 (2005): 4463–71; idem, "History on the Line: Fragments of Memories: Researching Violence in the 1971 Bangladesh War," *History Workshop Journal* 73, no. 1 (2012): 285–95.

123. For early evidence of UN inability to take action over Kashmir, despite the presentation in November 1950 of a petition with 1 million signatures, see TNA, DO 134/13, Press release M/689, "Kashmir 'liberation pledge'" presented to Secretary-General, November 16, 1950; "State of Disgrace, India's Courts and Kashmir," *The Economist*, October 5, 2019, 59–60.

124. Vazira Fazila-Yacoobali Zamindar, *The Long Partition and the Making of Modern South Asia: Refugees, Boundaries, Histories* (New York: Columbia University Press, 2007), chapters 2–3; for the legal incorporation of partition refugees as 'minority citizens', see Chatterji, "South Asian Histories of Citizenship," 1060–71.

125. Mangeet K. Ramgotra, "Post-Colonial Republicanism and the Revival of a Paradigm," *The Good Society* 26, no. 1 (2018): 41, 45–48.

126. Ansari and Gould, *Boundaries of Belonging*, 137–44, 148–53.

127. Ornit Shani, "Making Universal Franchise and Democratic Citizenship in the Postcolonial Moment," in *The Postcolonial Moment in South and Southeast Asia*, ed. Gyan Prakash, Michael Laffan, and Nikhil Menon (London: Bloomsbury, 2018), 162–75.

128. The status of mixed-race 'Anglo-Indians' in India and Pakistan, as well as the millions of South Asian emigrants living overseas, were issues of particular concern; see Sarah Ansari, "Subjects or Citizens? India, Pakistan and the 1948 British

Nationality Act," *Journal of Imperial & Commonwealth History* 41, no. 2 (2013): 288–93, 299–305.

129. Prakash, "Anxious Constitution-Making," 149–57.

130. Ansari and Gould, *Boundaries of Belonging*, 223–24, 239–47.

131. Kalathmika Natarajan, "Entangled Citizens: The Afterlives of Empire in the Indian Citizenship Act, 1947–1955," in *The Break-Up of Greater Britain*, ed. Christian D. Pedersen and Stuart Ward (Manchester, UK: Manchester University Press, 2021), 63–83.

132. Ansari and Gould, *Boundaries of Belonging*, 225, 230–32; Rohit De, "Evacuee Property and the Management of Economic Life in Postcolonial India," in Prakash, Laffan, and Menon, *Postcolonial Moment*, 88–96. In Pakistan, from which more 'evacuations' had occurred than in India, the scale of the problem was staggering, Government of Pakistan figures recording 313,132 urban houses, 131,084 shops, 75,857 homes under construction, 3,189 small businesses, and 849 larger industrial concerns left behind (De, "Evacuee Property," 90).

133. Uditi Sen, "The Myths Refugees Live By: Memory and History in the Making of Bengali Refugee Identity," *Modern Asian Studies* 48, no. 1 (2014): 39–44.

134. Chatterji, *Spoils of Partition*, part II: "The Bengal Diaspora," 105–208; idem, "Dispositions and Destinations," 273–83. As Joya Chatterji points out, the 'mobility capital' that encouraged refugees toward cities and towns often included preexisting knowledge of government bureaucracy, red tape, and how to 'work' the system to secure the licenses and permissions needed to settle legally or to set up small businesses.

135. Chatterji, "Dispositions and Destinations," 288–91, quote at 277.

136. O'Malley, "'Indian Ulsterisation,'" 115. Kate O'Malley cites Arthur Balfour, for many the original sinner of British imperial policy in Palestine, who defined democratic coexistence as the ability of a people 'to bicker' but nonviolently. Uditi Sen's analysis of East Bengali refugee marginalization within Indian West Bengal is telling: Sen, "Myths Refugees Live By," 45–57.

137. MAE, série Y: Internationale sous-série: 1944–9, vol. 655, Direction des Affaires Politiques note, "L'Amerique et les colonies," March 12, 1945.

138. *DDF*, January–June 1946, doc. 23, Jacques Soustelle to AOF Governor, January 9, 1946; Frederick Cooper, *Citizenship between Empire and Nation: Rethinking France and French Africa, 1945–1960* (Princeton, NJ: Princeton University Press, 2014), 52–53, 178–84, 202–4; Lisa A. Lindsay, "Domesticity and Difference: Male Breadwinners, Working Women, and Colonial Citizenship in the 1945 Nigerian General Strike," *American Historical Review* 104, no. 3 (1999): 783–812.

139. MAE, série Z: Europe 1944–9, sous-série Grande-Bretagne, vol. 40, Direction Afrique memo., "Memorandum des conversations Franco-Anglo-Belges des 20–22 Mai 1947." Robert Delavignette, Laurentie's successor as Colonial Ministry head of political affairs, led the French delegation to the May 1947 talks.

140. Naïma Maggetti, "La Grande-Bretagne à l'ONU dans les années 1940 et 1950: sa défense d'un colonialisme 'liberal et éclairé,'" *Relations Internationales* 177, no. 1 (2019): 35–44.

141. Mary Ann Heiss, "National Prerogatives versus International Supervision: Britain's Evolving Policy toward the Campaign for Equivalency of United Nations' Handling of Dependent Territories, 1945–1963," in *The United Nations and*

Decolonization, ed. Nicole Eggers, Jessica Lynne-Pearson, and Aurora Almada e Santos (Abingdon, UK: Routledge, 2020), 23–27.

142. Jessica Lynne Pearson, *The Colonial Politics of Global Health: France and the United Nations in Postwar Africa* (Cambridge, MA: Harvard University Press, 2018), 54–59.

143. Jessica Lynn Pearson, "Defending Empire at the United Nations: The Politics of International Colonial Oversight in the Era of Decolonisation," *Journal of Imperial & Commonwealth History* 45, no. 3 (2017) 528–33; idem, *Colonial Politics*, 45–53. The UN special committee was first convened in September 1948.

144. Pearson, "Defending Empire," 526–28, 534–36.

145. Something the Portuguese and Spanish dictatorships found to their cost, as Article 73e was used against them from the 1950s: Alicia Campos, "The Decolonization of Equatorial Guinea: The Relevance of the International Factor," *Journal of African History* 44, no. 1 (2003): 97–103.

146. Pearson, *Colonial Politics*, 61–66; Maggetti, "La Grande-Bretagne à l'ONU," 39–44; Miguel Bandeira Jerónimo and José Pedro Monteiro, "The Inventors of Human Rights in Africa: Portugal, Late Colonialism, and the UN Human Rights Regime," in *Decolonization, Self Determination, and the Rise of Global Human Rights Politics*, ed. A. Dirk Moses, Marco Duranti, and Roland Burke (Cambridge, UK: Cambridge University Press, 2020), 288–90.

147. Pearson, *Colonial Politics*, 142–43.

148. MAE, série Z: Europe 1944–9, sous-série Grande-Bretagne, vol. 40, Association Nationale d'Expansion économique, "Note sur l'Association pour l'union économique de la France et de la Grande-Bretagne et pour les rapports avec leurs territoires d'Outre-Mer," November 19, 1947; Peo Hansen and Stefan Jonsson, "Building Eurafrica: Reviving Colonialism through European Integration, 1920–1960," in *Echoes of Empire: Memory, Identity and Colonial Legacies*, ed. Kalypso Nicolaïdis, Berny Sèbe, and Gabrielle Maas (London: I. B. Tauris, 2015), 213–21.

149. MAE, série Z: Europe 1944–9, sous-série Grande-Bretagne, vol. 40, JL/MT, "Coopération franco-britannique en matière politique dans les territoires africains," June 24, 1948.

150. MAE, série Z: Europe 1944–9, sous-série Grande-Bretagne, vol. 40, Foreign Ministry note, "Extension de la coopération franco-britannique sur le plan politique," n.d. June 1948.

151. Richard Rathbone, "The Transfer of Power and Colonial Civil Servants in Ghana," *Journal of Imperial & Commonwealth History* 28, no. 2 (2000): 68–77.

152. MAE, série Z: Europe 1944–9, sous-série Grande-Bretagne, vol. 40, no. 127, 3ᵉ Bur., "Note: Conférence Africaine, Londres, 29 Septembre–9 Octobre 1948."

153. MAE, série Z: Europe 1944–9, sous-série Grande-Bretagne, vol. 40, Secrétariat général memo. (probably signed off by Jean Chauvel), February 17, 1949.

154. Meir Zamir, "'Bid' for *Altalena*: France's Covert Action in the 1948 War in Palestine," *Middle Eastern Studies* 46, no. 1 (2010): 17–58.

155. MAE, série Z: Europe 1944–9, sous-série Grande-Bretagne, vol. 40, Secrétariat général memo., February 17, 1949.

156. Elizabeth Thompson, *Justice Interrupted: The Struggle for Constitutional Government in the Middle East* (Cambridge, MA: Harvard University Press, 2013), 169–73.

Hasan al-Banna, who also called for nationalization of the Suez Canal, was assassinated on February 12, 1949, by which point the Muslim Brotherhood was already banned.

157. Jacob Darwin Hamblin, *Arming Mother Nature: The Birth of Catastrophic Environmentalism* (Oxford: Oxford University Press, 2013), 21–22.

158. Sunil S. Amrith, "Internationalising Health in the Twentieth Century," in *Internationalisms: A Twentieth Century History*, ed. Glenda Sluga and Patricia Clavin (Cambridge, UK: Cambridge University Press, 2016), 247; Valeska Huber, "International Bodies: The Pilgrimage to Mecca and International Health Regulations," in *The Hajj: Pilgrimage in Islam*, ed. Eric Tagliacozzo and Shawkat M. Toorawa (Cambridge, UK: Cambridge University Press, 2016), 175–95; on cooperation over cholera prevention: Valeska Huber, "The Unification of the Globe by Disease? The International Sanitary Conferences on Cholera, 1851–1894," *Historical Journal*, 49, no. 2 (2006): 452–76.

159. Amrith, "Internationalising Health," 245–64, at 251–52.

160. Amrith, "Internationalising Health," 252.

161. TNA, FO 492/2, J373/68/16, "Wafd's Condemnation of 'Imperialistic' Policy in Palestine," January 12, 1948.

162. Barbara Castle papers, BLO, MS Castle 2: Diary/notebook of visit to the Middle East, Jan. 1953, fos. 21–35: Damascus, January 7, 1953, Conversation with Adib Shishakli.

163. Castle papers, MS Castle 2: Diary/notebook of visit to the Middle East, fos. 40–62: Iraq: January 12, 1953: Baghdad. Castle also met former premier Muzahim Pachachi in Baghdad. A bitter opponent of the state of Israel, Pachachi echoed Shishakli's view that the Palestinian question was the acid test by which Western actions in the region would, in future, be measured.

164. Butalia, "Legacies of Departure," 208–18.

165. British newsreel footage, much of it filmed by Indian brothers Ved and Mohan Parkash, which included shots of massacred refugees, was overshadowed by the editorial emphasis on an orderly 'transfer of power' benevolently overseen by the last Viceroy couple, a ubiquitous Lord and Lady Mountbatten; see Philip Woods, "Business as Usual? British Newsreel Coverage of Indian Independence and Partition, 1947–1948," in *Media and the British Empire*, ed. Chandrika Kaul (Basingstoke, UK: Palgrave Macmillan, 2006), 145–56.

166. Differences in the quantity and quality of evidential data between centrally ruled provinces and the princely states add to the problem; see Copland, "Further Shores of Partition," 212–16.

167. Jansen and Osterhammel, *Decolonization*, 49–50.

Chapter Ten: Hiding Wars

1. Jason C. Parker, "Decolonization, the Cold War, and the Post-Columbian Era," in *The Cold War in the Third World*, ed. Robert J. McMahon (Oxford: Oxford University Press, 2013), 128–31.

2. John Kent suggests the British government pushed for trusteeship over Libya to compensate for withdrawal from Palestine and its weakening grip on Egypt: John Kent, *British Imperial Strategy and the Origins of the Cold War, 1944–49* (Leicester: Leicester University Press, 1993), 104.

3. David M. Anderson and Daniel Branch, "Allies at the End of Empire: Loyalists, Nationalists and the Cold War, 1945–1976," *International History Review* 39, no. 1 (2016): 1–13.

4. David M. Anderson, "Making the Loyalist Bargain: Surrender, Amnesty and Impunity in Kenya's Decolonization, 1952–63," *International History Review* 39, no. 1 (2016): 48–70; Roel Frakking, "'Collaboration Is a Delicate Concept': Alliance-Formation and the Colonial Defense of Indonesia and Malaysia, 1945–1957," PhD Thesis, European University Institute, Florence, 2017.

5. Huw Bennett, *Fighting the Mau Mau: The British Army and Counter-Insurgency in the Kenya Emergency* (Cambridge, UK: Cambridge University Press, 2012), 16–17, 216–19, 250–53.

6. Daniel Branch, "The Enemy Within: Loyalists and the War against Mau Mau in Kenya," *Journal of African History* 48, no. 2 (2007): 291–315; Douglas Wheeler, "African Elements in Portugal's Armies in Africa (1961–1974)," *Armed Forces and Society* 2, no. 2 (1976): 233–50; Roel Frakking, "'Who Wants to Cover Everything Covers Nothing': The Organization of Indigenous Security Forces in Indonesia, 1945–50," in *Colonial Counterinsurgency and Mass Violence: The Dutch Empire in Indonesia*, ed. Bart Luttikhuis and A. Dirk Moses (Abingdon, UK: Routledge, 2014), 111–27.

7. Barry R. Posen, "The Security Dilemma and Ethnic Conflict," *Survival* 35, no. 1 (1993): 27–47.

8. For one such example: Lennart Bolliger, "Apartheid's Transnational Soldiers: The Case of Black Namibian Soldiers in South Africa's Former Security Forces," *Journal of Southern African Studies* 43, no. 1 (2017): 195–214; Frakking, "'Collaboration,'" 185–250 passim.

9. John Lonsdale, "Ornamental Constitutionalism in Africa: Kenyatta and the Two Queens," *Journal of Imperial & Commonwealth History* 34, no. 1 (2006): 89, 97–98.

10. John Lonsdale, "KAU's Cultures: Imaginations of Community and Constructions of Leadership in Kenya after the Second World War," *Journal of African Cultural Studies* 13, no. 1 (2000): 107–24.

11. Lonsdale, "Ornamental Constitutionalism," 91. John Lonsdale explains the 'civic virtue' pivotal to this moral economy of labor, generational deference, and ultimate reward in "The Moral Economy of Mau Mau: Wealth Poverty, and Civic Virtue in Kikuyu Political Thought," in *Unhappy Valley: Conflict in Kenya and Africa II: Violence and Ethnicity*, ed. Bruce Berman and John Lonsdale (Oxford: James Currey, 1992), 315–504.

12. For African parallels in the context of attitudes to disability, see Oche Anazi, *An African Path to Disability Justice: Community, Relationships and Obligations* (Cham: Springer, 2019).

13. Daniel Branch, "Enemy Within," 292–96.

14. John Lonsdale, "Authority, Gender, and Violence: The War within Mau Mau's Fight for Land and Freedom," in *Mau Mau and Nationhood*, ed. E. S. Atieno Odhambo and John Lonsdale (Oxford: James Currey, 2003), 48–55.

15. Stacey Hynd, "Pickpockets, Pilot Boys and Prostitutes: The Construction of Juvenile Delinquency in the Gold Coast, c.1929–57," *Journal of West African History* 4, no. 2 (2018): 48–74.

16. Emily Baughan, *Saving the Children: Humanitarianism, Internationalism, and Empire* (Berkeley: University of California Press, 2022), 148, 160–61.

17. Emily Baughan, "Rehabilitating an Empire: Humanitarian Collusion with the Colonial State during the Kenyan Emergency, ca. 1954–1960," *Journal of British Studies* 59 (January 2020): 57–58, 61–68; idem, *Saving the Children*, 161–68.

18. Branch, "Enemy Within," 300–14.

19. Lonsdale, "KAU's Cultures," 109–22; Paul Kelemen, "Modernising Colonialism: The British Labour Movement and Africa," *Journal of Imperial & Commonwealth History* 34, no. 2 (2006): 229–30; Bruce Berman, *Control and Crisis in Colonial Kenya: The Dialectic of Domination* (Oxford: James Currey, 1990), 322–25.

20. John Lonsdale, "Mau Maus of the Mind: Making Mau Mau and Remaking Kenya," *Journal of African History* 31, no. 3 (1990): 393–421.

21. Daniel Branch, *Defeating Mau Mau, Creating Kenya: Counterinsurgency, Civil War, and Decolonization* (Cambridge, UK: Cambridge University Press, 2009), 36–39.

22. David M. Anderson, *Histories of the Hanged: The Dirty War in Kenya and the End of Empire* (New York: Norton, 2005), 11–12, 28–30, 39–43.

23. Ronald Hyam, *Britain's Declining Empire: The Road to Decolonisation, 1918–1968* (Cambridge, UK: Cambridge University Press, 2006), 189–90.

24. Caroline Elkins, "The Struggle for Mau Mau Rehabilitation in Late Colonial Kenya," *International Journal of African Historical Studies* 33, no. 1 (2000): 25–27. Other colonial states attributed alleged psychosis to a crisis of transition to modernity: Theodore Jun Yoo, *It's Madness: The Politics of Mental Health in Colonial Korea* (Berkeley: University of California Press, 2016), 116–36.

25. Branch, *Defeating Mau Mau*, 2–3, 24, 40–52; Dane Kennedy, "Constructing the Colonial Myth of Mau Mau," *International Journal of African Historical Studies* 25, no. 2 (1992): 248–56. Kennedy stresses the liberal paternalism behind colonial constructions of Mau Mau and remedial measures proposed.

26. Erik Linstrum, *Ruling Minds: Psychology in the British Empire* (Cambridge, MA: Harvard University Press, 2015), 157.

27. Owens, *Economy of Force*, 191; Anderson, *Histories of the Hanged*, 205.

28. Linstrum, *Ruling Minds*, 180–84.

29. Elkins, "Struggle for Mau Mau," 30–40, 44–50.

30. Frank Furedi, *The Mau Mau War in Perspective* (Oxford: James Currey, 1989), 22–28, 40–50.

31. Corey Ross, *Ecology and Power in the Age of Empire: Europe and the Transformation of the Tropical World* (Oxford: Oxford University Press, 2019), 374.

32. Anderson, *Histories of the Hanged*, 62–63.

33. Moritz Feichtinger, "'A Great Reformatory': Social Planning and Strategic Resettlement in Late Colonial Kenya and Algeria, 1952–63," *Journal of Contemporary History* 52, no. 1 (2017): 52.

34. Sloan Mahone, "East African Psychiatry and the Practical Problems of Empire," in *Psychiatry and Empire*, ed. Sloan Mahone and Megan Vaughan (Basingstoke, UK: Palgrave Macmillan, 2007), 51–54.

35. Ross, *Ecology and Power*, 374–75.

36. Feichtinger, "'A Great Reformatory,'" 54, citing Joseph Hodge, "British Colonial Expertise, Postcolonial Careering and the Early History of International Development," *Journal of Modern European History* 8, no. 1 (2010): 24–46.

37. Ross, *Ecology and Power*, 376.

38. Will Jackson, "Settler Colonialism in Kenya, 1880–1963," in *The Routledge Handbook of the History of Settler Colonialism*, ed. Edward Cavanagh and Lorenzo Veracini (Abingdon, UK: Routledge, 2016), 240–41.

39. Caroline Elkins, "Detention, Rehabilitation and the Destruction of Kikuyu Society," in Odhambo and Lonsdale, *Mau Mau and Nationhood*, 191–93.

40. David M. Anderson, "Surrogates of the State: Collaboration and Atrocity in Kenya's Mau Mau War," in *The Barbarisation of Warfare*, ed. George Kassimeris (London: Hurst, 2006), 172–73.

41. Katherine Bruce-Lockhart, "Reconsidering Women's Roles in the Mau Mau Rebellion in Kenya, 1952–1960," in *Decolonization and Conflict: Colonial Comparisons and Legacies*, ed. Gareth Curless and Martin Thomas (London: Bloomsbury, 2017), 164–68; Katherine Bruce-Lockhart and Bethany Ribesz, "Discourses of Development and Practices of Punishment: Britain's Gendered Counter-Insurgency Strategy in Colonial Kenya," in *The Oxford Handbook of Late Colonial Insurgencies and Counter-Insurgencies*, ed. Martin Thomas and Gareth Curless (Oxford: Oxford University Press, 2023), 486–504.

42. Megan Vaughan, "Suicide in Late Colonial Africa: The Evidence of Inquests from Nyasaland," *American Historical Review* 115, no. 2 (2010): 387.

43. Alice B. Conklin, "The New 'Ethnology' and 'La Situation Coloniale' in Interwar France," *French Politics, Culture, and Society* 20, no. 2 (2002): 29–46.

44. Benoît de l'Estoile, "Rationalizing Colonial Domination? Anthropology and Native Policy in French-Ruled Africa," in *Empires, Nations, and Natives: Anthropology and State-Making*, ed. Benoît de l'Estoile, Federico Neiburg, and Lygia Sigaud (Durham, NC: Duke University Press, 2005), 49–54.

45. Helen Tilley and Robert J. Gordon, eds., *Ordering Africa: Anthropology, European Imperialism, and the Politics of Knowledge* (Manchester, UK: Manchester University Press, 2007), 6–9.

46. Frederick Cooper, *Colonialism in Question: Theory, Knowledge, History* (Berkeley: University of California Press, 2005), 144.

47. Alice L. Conklin, "'Democracy Rediscovered': Civilization through Association in French West Africa (1914–1930)," *Cahiers d'Etudes Africaines* 145, no. 37 (1997): 59–60.

48. MAE, file 3: Kenya, French Ambassador, London, February 26, 1955, "A.S. pendaisons au Kenya."

49. TNA, CO 323/1525/7, Colonial Secretary memo, "Developments in Native Administration," draft, March 1937.

50. MAE, série Afrique-Levant, sous-série: Nord-Est Africain britannique, 1953–9, file 3: Kenya, Administration de la colonie, répression du mouvement Mau Mau, 1953–9, no. 97/AL, A. G. Morand, Consul-General Nairobi, to Foreign Ministry, March 31, 1953, "A/S Situation au Kenya."

51. MAE, file 3: Kenya: no. 132/AL, A. G. Morand, Consul-General Nairobi, "A.S. la situation au Kenya pendant le mois d'Avril 1953."

52. MAE, file 3: Kenya, no. 154/AL, A. G. Morand, Nairobi, to Direction Afrique-Levant, May 19, 1953, "A.S. de la situation au Kenya au cours de la première quinzaine de mai."

53. MAE, série: EUROPE 1949–55, sous-série: Grande-Bretagne, vol. 104, no. 44/AL, A. G. Morand, French Consul Nairobi to Direction Afrique-Levant, January 28, 1955, "La situation au Kenya." Morand highlighted the figures given to him by the British Army command, which recorded 8,602 Mau Mau killed during 1953–1954, of whom 991 were executed.

54. Joanna Lewis, "Daddy Wouldn't Buy Me a Mau Mau: The British Popular Press and the Demoralisation of Empire," in Odhambo and Lonsdale, *Mau Mau and Nationhood*, 241–46; Barbara Castle papers, MS Castle 245, fos. 153–55, "Eleven Dead Men," *New Statesman*, May 16, 1959. Castle lambasted policy in Kenya in the parliamentary debate on the massacre.

55. On the Conservative Party's split over speedier reforms in British Africa, see Philip Murphy, *Party Politics and Decolonization: The Conservative Party and British Colonial Policy in Tropical Africa, 1951–1964* (Oxford: Oxford University Press, 1995), 173–82.

56. Richard Toye, "Arguing about Hola Camp: The Rhetorical Consequences of a Colonial Massacre," in *Rhetorics of Empire: Languages of Colonial Conflict after 1900*, ed. Martin Thomas and Richard Toye (Manchester, UK: Manchester University Press, 2017), 189–98; Andrew Cohen, *The Politics and Economics of Decolonization: The Failed Experiment of the Central African Federation* (London: I. B. Tauris, 2017), 82–85.

57. Branch, "Enemy Within," 306–9.

58. British Online Archives, Colonial Rule in Kenya, J. L. Husband, Acting Labour Commissioner, Government of Kenya Labour Department Annual Report for the Year 1959, 15, 22–24.

59. Husband, Annual Report for the Year 1959, 67.

60. Lewis, "Daddy Wouldn't Buy Me," 230–42; Stephen Howe, "When (if Ever) Did Empire End? 'Internal Decolonisation' in British Culture since the 1950s," in *The British Empire in the 1950s: Retreat or Revival?* ed. Martin Lynn (Basingstoke, UK: Palgrave Macmillan, 2006), 214–34.

61. Ismay Milford, *African Activists in a Decolonising World: The Making of an Anticolonial Culture, 1952–1966* (Cambridge, UK: Cambridge University Press, 2023), 136–46.

62. Cohen, *Politics and Economics*, 95–99.

63. 'Small storms' in Stephen Howe's coruscating depiction of British 1950s provincialism: Howe, "When (if Ever) Did Empire End?" 225.

64. For the long-term background to legal impunity and institutional racism: Jordanna Bailkin, "The Boot and the Spleen: When Was Murder Possible in British India?" *Comparative Studies of Society and History* 48, no. 2 (2006): 462–94; idem, *The Afterlife of Empire* (Berkeley: University of California Press, 2012), chapters 5 and 6.

65. Cohen, *Politics and Economics*, 180–82; Donal Lowry, "Rhodesia 1890–1980: 'The Lost Dominion,'" in *Settlers and Expatriates: Britons over the Seas*, ed. Robert Bickers (Oxford: Oxford University Press, 2010), 112–14; Christian D. Pedersen,

"The Birth of 'White' Republics and the Demise of Greater Britain: The Republican Referendums in South Africa and Rhodesia," in *The Break-Up of Greater Britain*, ed. Christian D. Pedersen and Stuart Ward (Manchester, UK: Manchester University Press, 2021), 125–46.

66. Joshua Brownell, *The Collapse of Rhodesia: Population Demographics and the Politics of Race* (London: Bloomsbury, 2020), 14–20, quote at 16.

67. Josiah Brownell, "The Hole in Rhodesia's Bucket: White Emigration and the End of Settler Rule," *Journal of South African Studies* 34, no. 3 (2008): 591–610.

68. Alice Ritscherle, "Disturbing the People's Peace: Patriotism and 'Respectable' Racism in British Responses to Rhodesian Independence," in *Gender, Labour, War and Empire: Essays on Modern Britain*, ed. Philippa Levine and Susan R. Grayzel (London: Palgrave Macmillan, 2008), 197–202; Luise White, *Unpopular Sovereignty: Rhodesian Independence and African Decolonization* (Chicago: University of Chicago Press, 2015), 105–6, 109–13; for Northern Irish Loyalist links, see Donal Lowry, "'King's Men,' 'Queen's Rebels' and 'Last Outposts': Ulster and Rhodesia in an Age of Imperial Retreat," in Pedersen and Ward, *Break-Up of Greater Britain*, 147–71, at 159–62.

69. Luise White, *Fighting and Writing: The Rhodesian Army at War and Postwar* (Durham, NC: Duke University Press, 2021), 13–17; idem, "Civic Virtue, Young Men, and the Family: Conscription in Rhodesia, 1974–1980," *International Journal of African Historical Studies* 37, no. 1 (2004): 103–21.

70. Rob Skinner, *The Foundations of Anti-Apartheid: Liberal Humanitarians and Transnational Activists in Britain and the United States, c. 1919–64* (Basingstoke, UK: Palgrave, 2010), 129–51.

71. Skinner, *Foundations of Anti-Apartheid*, 156–58, 165–66, 188–89.

72. Rob Skinner, "The Moral Foundations of British Anti-Apartheid Activism, 1946–1960," *Journal of Southern African Studies* 35, no. 2 (2009): 399–416; and, looking forward to the 1980s, Gavin Brown and Helen Yaffe, *Youth Activism and Solidarity: The Non-Stop Picket against Apartheid* (London: Routledge, 2017).

73. Rob Skinner, "Humanitaranism and Human Rights in Global Apartheid," in *A Global History of Anti-Apartheid: "Forward to Freedom" in South Africa*, ed. Anna Konieczna and Rob Skinner (Cham: Palgrave Macmillan, 2019), 35–41.

74. Philip Murphy, "'An Intricate and Distasteful Subject': British Planning for the Use of Force against the European Settlers of Central Africa, 1952–65," *English Historical Review* 121, no. 492 (2006): 750–54.

75. Cohen, *Politics and Economics*, 40–9.

76. Barbara Castle papers, MS Castle 243: Northern Rhodesia, July 1954–April 1958, MS Castle 243, ANC/2/4, letter from H. M. Nkumbula, President-General, ANC Northern Rhodesia, and Kenneth Kaunda, Secretary-General, to Northern Rhodesia Governor, Lusaka, January 24, 1958.

77. Michael Collins, "Decolonisation and the 'Federal Moment,'" *Diplomacy & Statecraft* 24, no. 1 (2013): 35.

78. Philip Murphy, "'Government by Blackmail': The Origins of the Central African Federation Reconsidered," in Lynn, *British Empire in the 1950s*, 60–73.

79. Merve Fejzula, "The Cosmopolitan Historiography of Twentieth-Century Federalism," *Historical Journal* 63, no. 1 (2020): 13–14.

80. Fejzula, "Cosmopolitan Historiography," 13; for an official South Rhodesian view of the CAF breakup, see "Report of the Secretary for Internal Affairs for the Year 1963," and, within it, "Annual Report of the Native Councils Board for the Year 1963," 83–86, both in British Online Archives, "Zimbabwe under Colonial Rule," Internal Affairs, 1947–73.

81. Tinashe Nyamunda, "'More a Cause than a Country': Historiography, UDI and the Crisis of Decolonisation in Rhodesia," *Journal of Southern African Studies* 42, no. 5 (2016): 107–11; Tinashe Nyamunda, "Money, Banking and Rhodesia's Unilateral Declaration of Independence," *Journal of Imperial & Commonwealth History* 45, no. 5 (2017): 756–68.

82. Luise White, "What Does It Take to Be a State? Sovereignty and Sanctions in Rhodesia, 1965–1980," in *The State of Sovereignty: Territories, Laws, Populations*, ed. Douglas Howland and Luise White (Bloomington: Indiana University Press, 2009), 150–56.

83. White, *Unpopular Sovereignty*, 103–4, 115–16; Lowry, "Rhodesia 1890–1980," 116–22. At the decade's end, Rhodesia's settlers numbered 228,296 among a black population of five million.

84. Richard Coggins, "Wilson and Rhodesia: UDI and British Policy towards Africa," *Contemporary British History* 20, no. 3 (2006): 363–70.

85. Carl Watts, "Britain, the Old Commonwealth, and the Problem of Rhodesian Independence, 1964–65," *Journal of Imperial & Commonwealth History* 36, no. 1 (2008): 77–80, 83–90.

86. Carl Watts, "Killing Kith and Kin: The Viability of British Military Intervention in Rhodesia, 1964–5," *Twentieth Century British History*, 16 (2005): 382–415; Murphy, "'Intricate and Distasteful,'" 763–66.

87. White, *Unpopular Sovereignty*, 117, 119–22; Joshua Brownell, "'A Sordid Tussle of the Strand': Rhodesia House During the UDI Rebellion, 1965–80," *Journal of Imperial & Commonwealth History* 38, no. 3 (2010): 471–99.

88. White, *Fighting*, 5–9.

89. Joseph Mtisi, Munyaradzi Nyakudya, and Teresa Barnes, "War in Rhodesia, 1965–1980," in *Becoming Zimbabwe: A History from the Pre-Colonial Period to 2008*, ed. Brian Raftopoulos and A. S. Mlambo (Harare: Weaver Press, 2009), 141–45, 151–58.

90. Eddie Michel, "'This Outcome Gives Me No Pleasure, It Is Extremely Painful to Me to Be the Instrument of Their Fate': White House Policy on Rhodesia during the UDI Era (1965–1979)," *South African Historical Journal* 71, no. 3 (2019): 450–53.

91. John W. Young, *The Labour Governments, 1964–1970*, vol. 2: *International Policy* (Manchester, UK: Manchester University Press, 2003), 173–78; Mark Stuart, "A Party in Three Pieces: The Conservative Split over Rhodesian Oil Sanctions, 1965," *Contemporary British History* 16, no. 1 (2002): 51–88.

92. Andrew Cohen, "Lonrho and Oil Sanctions against Rhodesia in the 1960s," *Journal of Southern African Studies* 37, no. 4 (2011): 715–30.

93. White, *Unpopular Sovereignty*, 128–29, 138–44; Joanna Warson, "A Transnational Decolonisation: Britain, France and the Rhodesian Problem, 1965–1969," in *Francophone Africa at Fifty*, ed. Tony Chafer and Alexander Keese (Manchester, UK: Manchester University Press, 2013), 171–86.

94. Nyamunda, "Money, Banking," 765–68.

95. Ian Phimister and Victor Gwande, "Secondary Industry and Settler Colonialism: Southern Rhodesia before and after the UDI," *African Economic History* 45, no. 2 (2017): 95–103. Sanctions literature is summarized in White, *Unpopular Sovereignty*, 126–36.

96. White, *Unpopular Sovereignty*, 129–30.

97. SHD, Indochina files, 10H2897, no. 697/3, Forces Terrestres du Nord Vietnam, Lieutenant-Colonel Huot to M. le Chef de Province de Vinh Phúc, May 18, 1954. The *motif* of superficial daytime control in a hostile colonial environment is familiar in numerous decolonization wars. But it features alongside a narrative of stoic but doomed and politically bankrupt military endeavor in French cinematic and media depiction of the Indochina War: M. Kathryn Edwards, *Contesting Indochina: French Remembrance between Decolonization and the Cold War* (Berkeley: University of California Press, 2016), 169–88.

98. SHD, 10H2897, Sous-dossier: Chrono—*départ*, June–July 1954.

99. SHA, 10H160, Sous-dossier: *Pacific*, no. 108/CAB-CE/DC/TS, Commandant en Chef des Forces en Indochine, "Note relative au but et au fonctionnement du Comité de Guerre," October 11, 1953.

100. Laurent Cesari, "The Declining Value of Indochina: France and the Economics of Empire," in *The First Vietnam War: Colonial Conflict and Cold War Crisis*, ed. Mark Atwood Lawrence and Fredrik Logevall (Cambridge, MA: Harvard University Press, 2007), 183–89.

101. Jessica M. Chapman, *Cauldron of Resistance: Ngo Dinh Diem, the United States, and 1950s Southern Vietnam* (Ithaca, NY: Cornell University Press, 2013), 51–60.

102. SHA, 10H160, *Pacific*, Haut Comité de Guerre, Conduite des Opérations, August 5, 1953.

103. Sophie Quinn-Judge, "Giving Peace a Chance: National Reconciliation and a Neutral South Vietnam, 1954–1964," *Peace and Change* 38, no. 4 (2013): 385–97; Jessica Elkind, "'The Virgin Mary Is Going South': Refugee Resettlement in South Vietnam, 1954–1956," *Diplomatic History* 38, no. 5 (2014): 987–1016; Philip E. Catton, "'It Would Be a Terrible Thing if We Handed These People over to the Communists': The Eisenhower Administration, Article 14(d), and the Origins of the Refugee Exodus from North Vietnam," *Diplomatic History* 39, no. 2 (2015): 331–58.

104. SHD, 10H2897, no. 697/3, Forces Terrestres du Nord Vietnam, Lieutenant-Colonel Huot to M. le Chef de Province de Vinh Phúc, May 18, 1954.

105. Letter from Adrian Pelt (Geneva) to Dag Hammarskjöld, May 7, 1954, Cordier Papers, catalogued correspondence, box 2, Columbia University, New York: cited in Per-Axel Frielingsdorf, "'*Machiavelli of Peace*': Dag Hammarskjöld and the Political Role of the Secretary-General of the United Nations," London School of Economics and Political Science PhD, 2016, 56.

106. Jock McCulloch, *Colonial Psychiatry and "the African Mind"* (Cambridge, UK: Cambridge University Press, 1995), 99–104; Jacques Tronchon, *L'insurrection malgache de 1947* (Paris: Karthala, 1986), 74–79. For a similar ethnographic portrayal of a supposedly backward society, colonial Korea, in need of foreign (Japanese) guidance to modernity, see E. Taylor Atkins, *Primitive Selves: Koreana*

in the Japanese Colonial Gaze, 1910–1945 (Berkeley: University of California Press, 2010), chapter 2.

107. Alice Bullard, "Sympathy and Denial: A Post-Colonial Re-Reading of Emotions, Race, and Hierarchy," *Historical Reflections* 34, no. 1 (2008): 124–28.

108. SHD, 1H1379/D1, EMA1, "Fiche relative au rappel des disponibles," no date, April 1956.

109. SHD, 1H1463, no. 6283/EMA/2/EG, Chef du 2e Bureau de l'EMA, "Synthèse de renseignements sur les activités subversives en Afrique du Nord, semaine du 23 au 30 mars 1956," 1–3.

110. SHD, 1H1374/D2, ex 7/20, "Situation des effectifs en AFN au 1er avril 1956"; Nicolas Bancel, Pascal Blanchard, and Françoise Vergès, *La République coloniale: essai sur une utopie* (Paris: Albin Michel, 2003), 120–21.

111. SHD, 1H1463: Synthèses hebdomadaires de renseignements sur les activités subversives et sur la situation en Afrique francaise du Nord, no. 6283/EMA/2/EG, Colonel Dalstein, Chef du 2e Bureau de l'EMA, "Synthèse de renseignements sur les activités subversives en Afrique du Nord, semaine du 23 au 30 mars 1956," 2.

112. SHD, 1H1463, no. 9787/EMA/2/EG, Dalstein, "Synthèse de renseignements sur les activités subversives en Afrique du Nord, semaine du 11 au 18 Mai 1956."

113. Saphia Arezki, *De l'ALN à l'ANP, la construction de l'armée algérienne, 1954–1991* (Paris: Éditions de la Sorbonne, 2022), 109–14.

114. Neil MacMaster, *War in the Mountains: Peasant Society and Counterinsurgency in Algeria, 1918–1958* (Oxford: Oxford University Press, 2020), 304–5, 331–35.

115. Peter Krause, *Rebel Power: Why National Movements Compete, Fight, and Win* (Ithaca, NY: Cornell University Press, 2017), 113–26.

116. Gilbert Meynier, *Histoire Intérieure du FLN* (Paris: Fayard, 2002), 446–47; Rabah Aissaoui, *Immigration and National Identity: North African Political Movements in Colonial and Postcolonial France* (London: I. B. Tauris, 2009), 139–49.

117. Muriam Haleh Davis, "Restaging *Mise en Valeur*: 'Postwar Imperialism' and the Plan de Constantine," *Review of Middle Eastern Studies* 44, no. 2 (2010): 176–86.

118. Amelia H. Lyons, *The Civilizing Mission in the Metropole: Algerian Families and the French Welfare State during Decolonization* (Stanford, CA: Stanford University Press, 2013), 143, 153.

119. Hoover Institution Archive, Stanford, Robert Delavignette Papers, box I, Paul Chauvin, Conseiller Economique, President of Algiers chamber of agriculture, letter to Robert Delavignette, June 11, 1955: "La situation économique et sociale en Algérie," May 26, 1955.

120. Lyons, *Civilizing Mission*, 157–58.

121. Feichtinger, "'A Great Reformatory,'" 62–63.

122. MAE, série Afrique-Levant, sous-série: Algérie 1953–9, file 15, Questions militaires, annex II, Goussault memo., "L'action psychologique dans la guerre révolutionnaire d'Algérie."

123. On Galula's influence on counterinsurgency strategists in the United States, Latin America, and elsewhere, Jacques Frémeaux, "The French Experience in Algeria:

Doctrine, Violence and Lessons Learnt," *Civil Wars* 14, no. 1 (2012): 49–62; Alexander Grenoble and William Rose, "David Galula's Counterinsurgency: Occam's Razor and Colombia," *Civil Wars* 13, no. 3 (2011): 282–86.

124. Alex Marshall, "Imperial Nostalgia, the Liberal Lie, and the Perils of Postmodern Counterinsurgency," *Small Wars & Insurgencies* 21, no. 2 (2010): 243–49.

125. Muriam Haleh Davis, "'The Transformation of Man' in French Algeria: Economic Planning and the Postwar Social Sciences, 1958–62," *Journal of Contemporary History* 52, no. 1 (2017): 74–85.

126. The literature on 'Suez' is enormous. Excellent guides are: Mohamed H. Heikal, *Cutting the Lion's Tail: Suez through Egyptian Eyes* (London: Andre Deutsch, 1986); W. Scott Lucas, *Divided We Stand: Britain, the US and the Suez Crisis* (London: Hodder & Stoughton, 1991); Simon C. Smith, ed., *Reassessing Suez 1956: New Perspectives on the Crisis and its Aftermath* (Aldershot: Ashgate, 2008).

127. Todd Shepard, "'History Is Past Politics'? Archives, 'Tainted Evidence,' and the Return of the State," *American Historical Review* 115, no. 2 (April 2010): 481.

128. MAE, Archives du Ministère des états associés, 1945–57, carton 73, DRV Under-Secretary, Hoang Minh Giam, January 9, 1947, "Note sur le conflit franco-vietnamien: ce que veut le Viet-Nam"; Foreign Ministry, "Réponse au mémorandum vietnamien "Sur les manœuvres colonialistes depuis le 6 mars 1946"; ANOM, Madagascar, carton 6(2)D189: Rébellion de 1947.

129. AN, F/1a/3293: 1944–47, dossier VI-B-1, Renseignements généraux, "L'affaiblissement politique de la France en Islam et les dangereuses atteintes à la souveraineté française en Afrique du Nord," March 22, 1945.

130. AN, Marcel-Edmond Naegelen Papers: 518AP/5/Dossier: Gouverneur-Général de l'Algérie, Juin 1948–Avril 1951, "Note pour Monsieur, Gouverneur Général de l'Algérie," n.d. November 1950. In the National Assembly's October 20, 1950, session, parliamentarians, including communist deputy Alice Sportisse, criticized ministers for ignoring the Algerian Statute and failing to increase Algerian representation in local government. Two years earlier, Governor Marcel-Edmond Naegelen had rigged Algeria's first national elections since 1945, decried by critics as 'an electoral Sétif'; see, same file, SFIO section de Batna proclamation, n.d. February 1949.

131. Frederick Cooper, *Citizenship between Empire and Nation: Rethinking France and French Africa, 1945–1960* (Princeton, NJ: Princeton University Press, 2014), 186–202; Gary Wilder, *Freedom Time: Negritude, Decolonization, and the Future of the World* (Durham, NC: Duke University Press, 2015), 139–52.

132. Jean-Pierre Rioux, *The Fourth Republic* (Cambridge, UK: Cambridge University Press, 1987), part III.

133. Rioux, *Fourth Republic*, 219, 237–8, 287–92.

134. Irwin M. Wall, *France, the United States, and the Algerian War* (Berkeley: University of California Press, 2001), 134–56.

135. Rioux, *Fourth Republic*, 254–84; Matthew Connelly, "Taking off the Cold War Lens: Visions of North–South Conflict during the Algerian War for Independence," *American Historical Review* 105, no. 3 (2000): 743–47.

136. Jim House, "Shantytowns and Rehousing in Late Colonial Algiers and Casablanca," in *France's Modernising Mission: Citizenship, Welfare and the Ends of Empire*, ed. Ed Naylor (London: Palgrave Macmillan, 2018), 147–50.

137. MAE, série Afrique-Levant, sous-série: Algérie 1953–9, file 15, no. 3238, Hervé Alphand to Christian Pineau, November 5, 1956. "Calm Mayor of Violent Algiers," *New York Times*, October 28, 1956.

138. Sheila Crane, "Housing as Battleground: Targeting the City in the Battles of Algiers," *City and Society* 29, no. 1 (2017): 192, 194–202. Public authority was represented, on the one hand, by the Social Centres established on the initiative of governor Jacques Soustelle and his sociologist adviser Germaine Tillion and, on the other hand, by the army's emergency powers.

139. Crane, "Housing as Battleground," 190–94; Jennifer Johnson, *The Battle for Algeria: Sovereignty, Health Care, and Humanitarianism* (Philadelphia: University of Pennsylvania Press, 2016), 48–55.

140. ANOM, Carton 11cab/51: Cabinet Soustelle 1955, "Opinion de Germaine Tillion sur le 'palabre' de l'Aurès," March 31, 1955.

141. Emma Kuby, *Political Survivors: The Resistance, the Cold War, and the Fight against Concentration Camps after 1945* (Ithaca, NY: Cornell University Press, 2019), 200–1, 217–19; Lyons, *Civilizing Mission*, 151–53.

142. IISH, COLL00201, Algeria, social and political developments collection, folder 4: GPRA, The Algerian Office, 150 East 56th Street, New York, commentary on Germaine Tillion BBC broadcast, "The Unresolved Problem of Algeria," no date March 1960. Tillion was also despised by the FLN's principal rival, the Mouvement National Algérien. Its leader, Messali Hadj, sued her for libel in April 1961. In her book on Algeria's internecine party warfare, *Les Ennemis complémentaires*, Tillion incorrectly suggested that Messali followed the advice of French fascist leader Colonel Jean de la Rocque in creating the Algerian People's Party. See IISH, COLL00201, Algeria, folder 2, Secrétariat du président Messali Hadj, Manoir de Toutevoie, Oise, April 17, 1961.

143. MAE, série Afrique-Levant, sous-série: Algérie 1953–9, file 15, "Les Missions de l'Armée Française dans la guerre révolutionnaire d'Algérie," conférence donnée à S.H.A.P.E. par le Général de Corps d'Armée Allard commandant le Corps d'Armée d'Alger, le 15 novembre 1957.

144. Christopher Griffin, "Major Combat Operations and Counterinsurgency Warfare: Plan Challe in Algeria, 1959–1960," *Security Studies* 19 (2010): 555–89.

145. Feichtinger, "'A Great Reformatory,'" 55–56.

146. Johnson, *Battle for Algeria*, 4, 40–5, 75–6.

147. Mohamed Harbi, *Les Archives de la révolution algérienne* (Paris: Jeune Afrique, 1981), docs. 39, 40, 44; MacMaster, *War in the Mountains*, 19–20.

148. Neil MacMaster, "The Roots of Insurrection: The Role of the Algerian Village Assembly (Djemâa) in Peasant Resistance, 1863–1962," *Comparative Studies in Society & History* 52, no. 2 (2013): 429–32.

149. Feichtinger, "'A Great Reformatory,'" 56, 69.

150. Feichtinger, "'A Great Reformatory,'" 66–69; on the fate of the *harkis* and other Algerians in the French security forces: Martin Evans, "Reprisal Violence and the Harkis in French Algeria, 1962," *International History Review* 39, no. 1 (2017): 89–106.

151. Young-Sun Hong, *Cold War Germany, the Third World, and the Global Humanitarian Regime* (Cambridge, UK: Cambridge University Press, 2017), 134–37. The FLN capitalized on this French hypocrisy, establishing an Algerian Red Crescent Society in 1956 to relay humanitarian assistance from nonaligned and socialist bloc countries to Algerian refugees.

152. Johnson, *Battle for Algeria*, 50–63.

153. Hoover Institution Archive, Yves Godard papers, box 3, 10e Région Militaire, EM-Bureau psychologique, General Salan to M. le Ministre de l'Algérie, no date, 1957.

154. James McDougall, "The Impossible Republic: The Reconquest of Algeria and the Decolonization of France, 1945–62," *Journal of Modern History* 89, no. 4 (2017): 777–78; Miguel Bandeira Jerónimo and José Pedro Monteiro, "The Inventors of Human Rights in Africa: Portugal, Late Colonialism, and the UN Human Rights Regime," in *Decolonization, Self Determination, and the Rise of Global Human Rights Politics*, ed. A. Dirk Moses, Marco Duranti, and Roland Burke (Cambridge, UK: Cambridge University Press, 2020), 296–300.

155. Véronique Dimier, "Bringing the Neo-Patrimonial State back to Europe: French Decolonization and the Making of the European Development Aid Policy," *Archiv für Sozialgeschichte* 48 (2008): 433–57.

156. Jean-Charles Jauffret, *Soldats en Algérie, 1954–1962: expériences constrastées des hommes du contingent* (Paris: Autrement, 2000).

157. Rémy Foucault, "Que racontent les hebdomadaires locaux de l'entrée et de la sortie de guerre," in *La France en guerre 1954–1962: Expériences métropolitaines de la guerre d'indépendance algérienne*, ed. Raphaëlle Branche and Sylvie Thénault (Paris: Autrement, 2008), 40–47.

158. Marc Martin, "'Radio Algérie': un acteur méconnu de mai 1958," *Vingtième Siècle* 19 (July 1988): 97–99.

159. Robert J. Bookmiller, "The Algerian War of Words: Broadcasting and Revolution, 1954–1962," *Maghreb Review* 14, no. 3–4 (1989): 196–213; Rebecca P. Scales, "Subversive Sound: Transnational Radio, Arabic Recordings, the Danger of Listening in French Colonial Algeria, 1934–39," *Comparative Studies in Society and History* 52, no. 2 (2010): 414–17; Young-Sun Hong, *Cold War Germany*, 148–49; Hoover Institution Archive, Yves Godard papers, box 3, 10e Région Militaire, EM-Bureau psychologique, General Salan to M. le Ministre de l'Algérie, n.d. 1957.

160. Arthur Asseraf, *Electric News in Colonial Algeria* (Oxford: Oxford University Press, 2019), 184–86.

161. Ideas identified with 'Algerianist' writers, and Albert Camus especially: Peter Dunwoodie, *Writing French Algeria* (Oxford: Oxford University Press, 1998), 246–74.

162. Harbi, *Les archives de la Révolution algérienne*, doc. 19: "Intégration des 'Combattants de la liberation' à l'ALN," July 1, 1956.

163. MAE, série Afrique-Levant, Algérie 1953-9, file 24, Procès de Djamila Bouhired: protestations à l'étranger, Mars–Avril 1958, "Note rélative à la condamnation de Djamila Bouhired."

164. Neil MacMaster, *Burning the Veil: The Algerian War and the "Emancipation" of Muslim Women, 1954–1962* (Manchester, UK: Manchester University Press, 2009), 99, 317–23. Djamila Bouhired went furthest in defending FLN violence; see James D.

Le Sueur, *Uncivil War: Intellectuals and Identity Politics during the Decolonization of Algeria* (Philadelphia: University of Pennsylvania Press, 2001), 288 n.81.

165. Natalya Vince, *Our Fighting Sisters: Nation, Memory and Gender in Algeria, 1954–2012* (Manchester, UK: Manchester University Press, 2015), 82–83.

166. IISH, COLL00201, Algeria, social and political developments collection, folder 4, GPRA office, New York, "French Justice in Algeria," June 13, 1960; "For Djamila Boupacha" published in *Le Monde* by Simone de Beauvoir on June 2, 1960.

167. Natalya Vince, *The Algerian War, the Algerian Revolution* (London: Bloomsbury, 2020), 95.

168. Young-Sun Hong, *Cold War Germany*, 151.

169. Vince, *Our Fighting Sisters*, 84–85; MacMaster, *Burning the Veil*, 318; for divisions among French lawyers, see Sylvie Thénault, *Une drôle de justice: les magistrats dans la guerre d'Algérie* (Paris: La Découverte, 2001), chapter 5.

170. Le Sueur, *Uncivil War*, 204–5.

171. "French Justice in Algeria," June 13, 1960. Jean Bireaud, commander of the mobile security group which arrested the three members of the Boupacha family, was put before a Bordeaux military tribunal in 1960, accused of causing the death of another detainee, Sergeant Madani Said, who died under questioning after his lung was punctured by a kicked-in rib. Lacking enough evidence to proceed, the tribunal gave Bireaud the 'benefit of the doubt' and dropped the case.

172. Jauffret, *Soldats en Algérie*; Marnia Lazreg, *Torture and the Twilight of Empire: From Algiers to Baghdad* (Princeton, NJ: Princeton University Press, 2008), 159–60, 297 n.75; "For Djamila Boupacha." As historians Judith Surkis and Natalya Vince note, Simone de Beauvoir emphasized Boupacha's virginal victimhood: Judith Surkis, "Ethics and Violence: Simone de Beauvoir, Djamila Boupacha and the Algerian War," *French Politics, Culture, and Society* 28, no. 2 (2010): 45; also cited in Vince, *Our Fighting Sisters*, 85.

173. "French Justice in Algeria," June 13, 1960, GPRA, Algerian Office, New York.

174. Anne Renoult, "*Indochine SOS*: Andrée Viollis et la Question coloniale (1931–1950)," in *Nouvelle histoire des colonisations européennes (xIXe–XXe siècles): Sociétés, Cultures, Politiques*, ed. Amaury Lorin and Christelle Taraud (Paris: Presses Universitaires de France, 2013), 144–46.

175. Martin Thomas, "Fighting 'Communist Banditry' in French Vietnam: The Rhetoric of Repression after the Yen Bay Uprising, 1930–1932," *French Historical Studies* 34, no. 4 (2011): 611–48; Peter Zinoman, *The Colonial Bastille: A History of Imprisonment in Vietnam 1862–1940* (Berkeley: University of California Press, 2001), 204–15.

176. Renoult, "*Indochine SOS*," 147–52.

177. Kuby, *Political Survivors*, 1–9.

178. Kuby, *Political Survivors*, 193–209.

179. Kuby, *Political Survivors*, 209–220. As Kuby notes, the CICRC's compromised position was foreshadowed in its equivocation over the detention of Tunisian trade unionists, politicians, lawyers, and other nationalist opponents of the French in Tunis during 1952–1953: idem, 168–71.

180. IISH, Pierre Avot-Meyers papers (ARCH03107), file 12: "Un an dans les Aurès," testimony of Jacques Pucheu. Ten-page typescript detailing executions,

torture and other rights abuses while serving on army operational patrols in the Aurès and Constantine, April 1956 to April 1957.

181. Picked up by the Algerian Provisional Government, an International Commission of Jurists pointed out in December 1960 that France could not have it both ways in Algeria. If the territory was an integral part of France, its people should enjoy the same constitutional protections as French citizens. There was no legal basis to support what was actually happening: the prosecution of a war disguised as an operation to restore order to place it outside the purview of international law. See IISH, COLL00201, Algeria, social and political developments collection, folder 4: "The Algerian Conflict and the Rule of Law," *Bulletin of the International Commission of Jurists*, December 1960. Circulated in January 1961 by GPRA New York Office.

182. Raphaëlle Branche, *La torture et l'armée pendant la guerre d'Algérie* (Paris: Gallimard, 2001), especially chapter 14; idem, "Des viols pendant la guerre d'Algérie," *Vingtième Siècle* 75 (July–September 2002), 123–32; Lazreg, *Torture*, 5–7, 154–60.

183. "French Justice in Algeria," June 13, 1960, GPRA, New York. Seven months after the lawyers' revelations, on April 12, 1959, a report by thirty-five Roman Catholic priests serving with the army in Algeria and sent to bishops in France noted: 'Arbitrary arrests and detentions are numerous. Interrogations are all too frequently conducted by methods that we must call torture.'

184. IISH, COLL00201, Algeria, folder 3, GPRA Delegation to UN, "The Algerian Question: The FLN Carries the War to France," no date, September 1958.

185. IISH, COLL00201, folder 3, GPRA delegation to UN, no date, September 1958.

186. IISH, COLL00201, "The Algerian Question: The FLN Carries the War to France," September 1958.

187. Yves Godard papers, Hoover Institution, box 3, douzième conférence: Capitaine Michel Lesourd du Corps des Officiers des affaires militaires musulmanes, "Immigration en métropole."

188. Françoise de Barros, "Protests against Shantytowns in the 1950s and 1960s: Class Logics, Clientist Relations and 'Colonial Redeployments,'" in Naylor, *France's Modernising Mission*, 199–208.

189. Emmanuel Blanchard, "Contrôler, enfermer, éloigner. La répression policière et administrative des algériens de métropole (1946–1962)," in Branche and Thénault, *La France en guerre*, 318–31; idem, *La Police Parisienne et les Algériens (1944-1962)* (Paris: Nouveau Monde éditions, 2011).

190. Jim House, "Colonial Containment? Repression of Pro-Independence Street Demonstrations in Algiers, Casablanca and Paris, 1945–1962," *War in History* 25, no. 2 (2018): 172–201.

191. House, "Colonial Containment?" 177–85.

192. Grégor Mathias, "La fin d'une rumeur: l'organisation des manifestations de décembre 1960 à Alger par les officiers des SAU d'Alger," in *Des hommes et des femmes en guerre d'Algérie*, ed. Jean-Charles Jauffret (Paris: Autrement, 2003), 510–21.

193. House, "Colonial Containment?" 195–98. It bears emphasizing that other elements of the security forces did fire, causing at least ninety deaths.

194. Nadia Sariahmed Belhadj, "The December 1960 Demonstrations in Algiers: Spontaneity and Organisation of Mass Action," *Journal of North African Studies* (2020): 1–39; Crane, "Housing," 187–89, 205–8.

195. Interviewed about the Algiers protests on Moroccan radio on December 13, 1960, Dr. Mostefai Chawki, head of the GPRA mission in Rabat, accepted that the demonstrations were locally organized. He accused the colonial authorities of complicity in the decision to fire on the crowd in the Place du Gouvernement: MAE, série Afrique-Levant, sous-série MAROC, 1956–68, vol. 87, Rabat embassy tel. 6312, December 14, 1960; Mathias, "La fin d'une rumeur," 221–24.

196. House, "Colonial Containment?" 191, 195–98.

197. Belhadj, "December 1960 Demonstrations," 29–36.

198. IISH, COLL00201, Algeria, folder 4, "Text of a Declaration Issued by the Ministry of Information of the GPRA, Tunis," September 13, 1961. Vigilante violence was severest in ethnically mixed urban districts such as Bab el-Oued in Algiers. There, Muslims' homes and businesses were targeted and street attacks were frequent. On September 11, 1961, for instance, at least seven Algerians were murdered in Bab el-Oued following a settler funeral.

199. IISH, COLL00201, Algeria, file 1, *El Moudjahid*, no. 93, June 27, 1962, 7: "Les activités de l'Union des femmes algériennes."

200. Connelly, "Taking off the Cold War Lens," 756–69.

201. MAE, 217PAAP1: Henri Bonnet papers: correspondance 1947–53. (M/film P/6813), Jean Chauvel to Bonnet, February 14, 1950.

Chapter Eleven: Decolonization and the Civilianization of Violence

1. Matthew Hughes, *Britain's Pacification of Palestine: The British Army, the Colonial State, and the Arab Revolt, 1936–1939* (Cambridge, UK: Cambridge University Press, 2019); Martin Thomas, *Violence and Colonial Order: Police, Workers, and Protest in the European Colonial Empires, 1918–1940* (Cambridge, UK: Cambridge University Press, 2012); Martha Crenshaw Hutchinson, *Revolutionary Terrorism: The FLN in Algeria, 1954–1962* (Stanford, CA: Hoover Institution Press, 1978).

2. Stathis Kalyvas, "The Paradox of Terrorism in Civil War," *Journal of Ethics* 8 (2004): 108–10, 113–15.

3. Luise White, *Fighting and Writing: The Rhodesian Army at War and Postwar* (Durham, NC: Duke University Press, 2021), 24–27. White's thoughtful analysis of white Rhodesian soldiers fighting the Bush War of the 1960s and 1970s stresses the centrality of the local environment, its dangers, and its mastery as contributors to the forms of violence enacted.

4. Maja Zehfuss, "Killing Civilians: Thinking the Practice of War," *British Journal of Politics and International Relations* 14, no. 3 (2012): 423–40; Helen M. Kinsella, "Superfluous Injury and Unnecessary Suffering: National Liberation and the Laws of War," *Political Power and Social Theory* 32 (2017): 205–31; Alexander B. Downes, "Draining the Sea by Filling the Graves: Investigating the Effectiveness of Indiscriminate Violence as a Counterinsurgency Strategy," *Civil Wars* 9, no. 4 (2007): 420–44; Alex J. Bellamy, "Supreme Emergencies and the Protection of Non-Combatants in War," *International Affairs* 80, no. 5 (2004): 829–50.

5. Benjamin Valentino, Paul Huth, and Dylan Balch-Lindsay, "'Draining the Sea': Mass Killing and Guerrilla Warfare," *International Organisation* 58, no. 2 (2004): 375-407; Uğur Ümit Üngör, *Paramilitarism: Mass Violence in the Shadow of the State* (Oxford: Oxford University Press, 2020), 43-47. A thoughtful survey, Üngör's study says little about paramilitaries in decolonization conflicts.

6. Laura Robson, *The Politics of Mass Violence in the Middle East* (Oxford: Oxford University Press, 2020), 5-9, 85-66.

7. For a grassroots perspective on what this meant, see Christian Lentz's study of the Black River region in Northern Vietnam during the Indochina War: *Contested Territory: Ðien Biên Phu and the Making of Northwest Vietnam* (New Haven, CT: Yale University Press, 2019).

8. I use the terms 'civilian', 'unarmed colonial subject', and 'noncombatant' interchangeably, following social scientific writing on just war theory and military violence against noncombatants. Good introductions are Alexander B. Downes, "Desperate Times, Desperate Measures: The Causes of Civilian Victimisation in War," *International Security* 30, no. 4 (2006): 152-95; Seth Lazar, "Necessity and Non-Combatant Immunity," *Review of International Studies* 40, no. 1 (2014): 53-76.

9. Charles W. Anderson, "When Palestinians Became Human Shields: Counterinsurgency, Racialization, and the Great Revolt (1936-1939)," *Comparative Studies in Society and History* 63, no. 3 (2021): 634-42. Only Palestinian males appear to have been used as 'human shields' to protect British army units during the Great Revolt in mandate Palestine.

10. The 'elderly' are defined here as those beyond locally understood working age.

11. Miranda Alison, "Women as Agents of Political Violence: Gendering Security," *Security Dialogue* 35, no. 4 (2004): 447-48, and, more generally, Alexis Leanna Henshaw, "Where Women Rebel: Patterns of Women's Participation in Armed Rebel Groups, 1990-2008," *International Feminist Journal of Politics* 18, no. 1 (2016): 39-60. The tendency to analyze war and collective violence as male activities is evident in political sociology as well. For a critique, see Siniša Malešević, *The Sociology of War and Violence* (Cambridge, UK: Cambridge University Press, 2010), 288-306.

12. Harry G. West, "Girls with Guns: Narrating the Experience of War of Frelimo's 'Female Detachment,'" *Anthropological Quarterly* 73, no. 4 (2000): 180-94; Miranda Alison, "Cogs in the Wheel? Women in the Liberation Tigers of Tamil Eelam," *Civil Wars* 6, no. 4 (2003): 37-54.

13. "Guerre de libération nationale. Un témoignage d'Anissa Barkat, née Derrar," Centre national d'études historiques, 1977, Centre El Biar, Algiers; Natalya Vince, *Our Fighting Sisters: Nation, Memory and Gender in Algeria, 1954-2012* (Manchester, UK: Manchester University Press, 2015), 144-46, 197-201; Joseph Mtisi, Munyaradzi Nyakudya, and Teresa Barnes, "War in Rhodesia, 1965-1980," in *Becoming Zimbabwe: A History from the Pre-Colonial Period to 2008*, ed. Brian Raftopoulos and A. S. Mlambo (Harare: Weaver Press, 2009), 141-58: giving figures of some 2,000 Zimbabwe People's Revolutionary Army (ZIPRA) women guerrillas and between 1,000 and 2,000 in the Zimbabwe National Liberation Army (ZANLA); Inês Galvão and Catarina Laranjeiro, "Gender Struggle in Guinea-Bissau: Women's Participation on and off the Liberation Record," in Domingos, Bandeira Jerónimo, and Roque, *Resistance*

and Colonialism," 103–6. Although PAIGC leader Amílcar Cabral condemned it, some women fighters in the PAIGC faced abuse by male commanders and risked alienation from their extended kin networks.

14. Diane Sambron, "La politique d'émancipation du gouvernement français à l'égard des femmes algériennes pendant la guerre d'Algérie," in *Des hommes et des femmes en guerre d'Algérie*, ed. Jean-Charles Jauffret (Paris: Autrement, 2003), 239.

15. Benjamin Twagira, "Embodied, Psychological and Gendered Trauma in Militarized Kampala (Uganda)," in *Gender and Trauma since 1900*, ed. Paula A. Michaels and Christina Twomey (London: Bloomsbury, 2021), 163–72; Emily Bridger, "Gender, Mobilisation, and Insurgency in South Africa: Young Comrades in the 1980s Township Uprisings," in *The Oxford Handbook of Late-Colonial Insurgencies and Counter-Insurgencies*, ed. Martin Thomas and Gareth Curless (Oxford: Oxford University Press, 2023), 369–85.

16. Janet I. Lewis, *How Insurgency Begins: Rebel Group Formation in Uganda and Beyond* (Cambridge, UK: Cambridge University Press, 2020), 7–10, 38–45.

17. Lewis, *How Insurgency Begins*, 14–15, 46–54, 126–28.

18. James Raymond Vreeland, "The Effect of Political Regime on Civil War: Unpacking Anocracy," *Journal of Conflict Resolution* 52, no. 3 (June 2008): 401–25; White, *Fighting and Writing*, 19–25.

19. Richard Overy, *Blood and Ruins: The Great Imperial War 1931–1945* (London: Allen Lane, 2021), 766–90, 793–816.

20. Mark Edele and Robert Gerwarth, "The Limits of Demobilization: Global Perspectives on the Aftermath of the Great War," *Journal of Contemporary History* 50, no. 1 (2015): 3–14; Mark Edele and Filip Slaveski, "Violence from Below: Explaining Crimes against Civilians across Soviet Space, 1943–1947," *Europe–Asia Studies* 68, no. 6 (2016): 1020–35; Alexander Statiev, "Soviet Partisan Violence against Soviet Civilians: Targeting Their Own," *Europe–Asia Studies* 66, no. 9 (2014): 1525–55; and idem, *The Soviet Counterinsurgency in the Western Borderlands* (Cambridge, UK: Cambridge University Press, 2010), especially chapters 9 and 11. For the comparatively low levels of demobilization-related violence in European empires after World War I, see Richard S. Fogarty and David Killingray, "Demobilization in British and French Africa at the End of the First World War," *Journal of Contemporary History* 50, no. 1 (2015): 100–23. On violent peacetime: Peter Gatrell, "Trajectories of Population Displacement in the Aftermath of Two World Wars," in *The Disentanglement of Populations: Migration, Expulsion and Displacement in Postwar Europe, 1944–49*, ed. Jessica Reinisch and Elizabeth White (Basingstoke, UK: Palgrave Macmillan, 2011), 5.

21. Eileen Boris, *Making the Woman Worker: Precarious Labor and the Fight for Global Standards, 1919–2019* (New York: Oxford University Press, 2019), 98–102, 106–8.

22. Moritz Feichtinger, "'A Great Reformatory': Social Planning and Strategic Resettlement in Late Colonial Kenya and Algeria, 1952–63," *Journal of Contemporary History* 52, no. 1 (2017): 64–67; Katherine Bruce-Lockhart and Bethany Ribesz, "Discourses of Development and Practices of Punishment: Britain's Gendered Counter-Insurgency Strategy in Colonial Kenya," in *The Oxford Handbook of Late Colonial Insurgencies and Counter-Insurgencies*, ed. Martin Thomas and Gareth Curless (Oxford: Oxford University Press, 2023), 486–504.

23. Administrative practice within and between colonies and empires varied, but the centrality of indigenous auxiliaries stands out even so. For useful comparisons, see Justin Willis, "Chieftaincy," in *The Oxford Handbook of Modern African History*, ed. John Parker and Richard Reid (Oxford: Oxford University Press, 2013), 208–23.

24. Skeptical treatments of the extractive nature of colonial governance include Ewout Frankema, "Raising Revenue in the British Empire, 1870–1940: How 'Extractive' Were Colonial Taxes?" *Journal of Global History* 5, no. 3 (2010): 447–77; Ewout Frankema and Frans Buelens, eds., *Colonial Exploitation and Economic Development: The Belgian Congo and the Netherlands Indies Compared* (Abingdon, UK: Routledge, 2013); and, for interactions between local and imperial officials: Benjamin N. Lawrance, Emily Lynn Osborn, and Richard L. Roberts, eds., *Intermediaries, Interpreters, and Clerks: African Employees in the Making of Colonial Africa* (Madison: University of Wisconsin Press, 2006); Christopher Prior, *Exporting Empire: Africa, Colonial Officials and the Construction of the Imperial State, c. 1900–1939* (Manchester, UK: Manchester University Press, 2013).

25. Mahmood Mamdani, *Citizen and Subject: Contemporary Africa and the Legacy of Late Colonialism* (Princeton, NJ: Princeton University Press, 1996), 48; also cited in Anne Phillips, "Global Justice: Just Another Modernisation Theory?" in *Empire, Race, and Global Justice*, ed. Duncan Bell (Cambridge, UK: Cambridge University Press, 2019), 148, 155.

26. Alan McPherson, *The Invaded: How Latin Americans and Their Allies Fought and Ended U.S. Occupations* (New York: Oxford University Press, 2014), 140–41.

27. Justin Willis, "Tribal Gatherings: Colonial Spectacle, Native Administration and Local Government in Condominium Sudan," *Past & Present* 211 (May 2011): 245.

28. Willis, "Tribal Gatherings," 256, 266–67.

29. Anderson, "When Palestinians Became Human Shields," 625–27.

30. Stathis Kalyvas, *The Logic of Violence in Civil Wars* (Cambridge, UK: Cambridge University Press, 2006), 58–61, 141–4; Neil MacMaster, *War in the Mountains: Peasant Society and Counterinsurgency in Algeria, 1918–1958* (Oxford: Oxford University Press, 2020), 164–72; Roel Frakking, "Beyond Sticks and Carrots: Local Agency in Counterinsurgency," *Humanity* 5, no. 3 (2014): 391–415.

31. McPherson, *Invaded*, 142–48, 264.

32. André Nouschi, *L'Algérie amère 1914–1994* (Paris: Sciences de l'homme, 1995), 20–26.

33. Hoover Institution Archive, Robert Delavignette Papers, box I, Paul Chauvin, President of Algiers Chamber of Agriculture, letter to Robert Delavignette, June 11, 1955: "La situation économique et sociale en Algérie." May 26, 1955.

34. Neil MacMaster, "From Tent to Village *Regroupement*: The Colonial State and Social Engineering of Rural Space, 1843–1962," in *France's Modernising Mission: Citizenship, Welfare and the Ends of Empire*, ed. Ed Naylor (London: Palgrave Macmillan, 2018), 120–25; Feichtinger, "'A Great Reformatory,'" 51.

35. Owen White, *The Blood of the Colony: Wine and the Rise and Fall of French Algeria* (Cambridge, MA: Harvard University Press, 2021), 193–96.

36. White, *Blood of the Colony*, 196–203.

37. These strategies are explored in the cases of the Chinese and Malayan Communist Parties and the Vietnamese National Liberation Front in Marc Opper, *People's Wars in China, Malaya, and Vietnam* (Ann Arbor: University of Michigan Press, 2020), especially 235–46.

38. Ana Arjona, "Civilian Resistance to Rebel Governance," in *Rebel Governance in Civil War*, ed. Ana Arjona, Nelson Kasfir, and Zachariah Mampilly (Cambridge, UK: Cambridge University Press, 2015), 180–84.

39. Charles W. Anderson, "State Formation from Below and the Great Revolt in Palestine," *Journal of Palestine Studies* 47, no. 1 (2017): 41–48.

40. Arjona, "Civilian Resistance," 185–87.

41. Vanda Felbab-Brown, Harold Trinkunas, and Shadi Hamid, *Militants, Criminals, and Warlords: The Challenge of Local Governance in an Age of Disorder* (Washington, DC: Brookings Institution Press, 2018), 6–7, 17–20.

42. Roel Frakking and Martin Thomas, "Windows onto the Microdynamics of Insurgent and Counterinsurgent Violence: Evidence from Late Colonial Southeast Asia and Africa Compared," in *Empire's Violent End: Comparing Dutch, British, and French Wars of Decolonization, 1945–1962*, ed. Thijs Brocades Zaalberg and Bart Luttikhuis (Ithaca, NY: Cornell University Press, 2022), 78–126; Roel Frakking, "'Gathered on the Point of a Bayonet': The Negara Pasundan and the Colonial Defence of Indonesia, 1946–50," *International History Review* 39, no. 1 (2017): 30–47; Huw Bennett, *Fighting the Mau Mau: The British Army and Counter-Insurgency in the Kenya Emergency* (Cambridge, UK: Cambridge University Press, 2012), 216–19. For militia violence against civilians, see Laia Balcells, *Rivalry and Revenge: The Politics of Violence during Civil War* (Cambridge, UK: Cambridge University Press, 2017), 5–10, 21–29.

43. For Indonesia: Frakking, "'Gathered,'" 30–44; for Kenya: Daniel Branch, "Loyalists, Mau Mau and Elections in Kenya: The First Triumph of the System, 1957–58," *Africa Today* 53 (2006): 27–50; for Bangladesh: Sarmila Bose, "Anatomy of Violence: Analysis of Civil War in East Pakistan in 1971," *Economic and Political Weekly* 40, no. 41 (2005): 4464–69.

44. Benjamin C. Brower, "Partisans and Populations: The Place of Civilians in War, Algeria (1954–62)," *History and Theory* 3 (September 2017): 394–97.

45. Paul Staniland, "Counter-Insurgency and Violence Management," in *The New Counter-Insurgency Era in Critical Perspective*, ed. David Martin Jones, Celeste Ward Gventer, and M. L. R. Smith (Basingstoke, UK: Palgrave Macmillan, 2014), 150.

46. David M. Anderson and Daniel Branch, "Allies at the End of Empire: Loyalists, Nationalists and the Cold War, 1945–1976," *International History Review* 39, no. 1 (2016): 3, 6–8. For contemporary parallels: Paul Staniland, *Networks of Rebellion: Explaining Insurgent Cohesion and Collapse* (Ithaca, NY: Cornell University Press, 2014), chapter 8.

47. Kumar Ramakhrishna, "Content, Credibility and Context: Propaganda, Government Surrender Policy and the Malayan Communist Mass Surrender of 1958," *Intelligence & National Security* 14, no. 4 (1999): 242–66; idem, *Emergency Propaganda: The Winning of Malayan Hearts and Minds, 1948–1958* (Richmond: Curzon, 2002); Charles-Robert Ageron, "Une troisième force combattante pendant la guerre d'Algérie. L'armée nationale du peuple algérien en son chef le "général" Bellounis.

Mai 1957–juillet 1958," *Outre-Mers* 321 (1998): 65–76; Milos Popovic, "Fragile Proxies: Explaining Rebel Defection against their State Sponsors," *Terrorism and Political Violence* 29, no. 6 (2017): 922–30.

48. Staniland, "Counter-Insurgency and Violence Management," 144–52.

49. Mark Harrison, ed., *The Economics of Coercion and Conflict* (Singapore: World Scientific Publishing, 2015), 1–6; Stephen Broadberry and Mark Harrison, eds., *The Economics of World War II* (Cambridge, UK: Cambridge University Press, 1998), 1–27.

50. Harrison, *Economics of Coercion*, 1–6.

51. As was the case in South Vietnam's Mekong Delta after 1945: McHale, *First Vietnam War*, 180–94. See also Ross, *Ecology and Power*, 365; Edwin A. Martini, "Even We Can't Prevent Forests: The Chemical War in Vietnam and the Illusion of Control," *War and Society* 31, no. 3 (2012): 264–79.

52. Karl Hack, "'Screwing Down the People': The Malayan Emergency, Decolonisation, and Ethnicity," in *Imperial Policy and Southeast Asian Nationalism*, ed. Hans Antlöv and Stein Tønnesson (London: Curzon Press, 1995), 83–109.

53. Rob Nixon, *Slow Violence and the Environmentalism of the Poor* (Cambridge, MA: Harvard University Press, 2011), 19.

54. Here I am applying what Emanuel Kreike defines as 'the loss of proprietary resources': Emanuel Kreike, *Scorched Earth: Environmental Warfare as a Crime against Humanity and Nature* (Princeton, NJ: Princeton University Press, 2021), 2–7, 9–17, quote at 15.

55. David French, "The British Empire and the Meaning of 'Minimum Force Necessary' in British Counter-Insurgencies Operations c. 1857–1967," in *British World Policy and the Projection of Global Power, c. 1830–1960*, ed. T. G. Otte (Cambridge, UK: Cambridge University Press, 2019), 47–56; Benjamin C. Brower, *A Desert Named Peace: The Violence of France's Empire in the Algerian Sahara, 1844–1902* (New York: Columbia University Press, 2009).

56. Keith Shear, "Chiefs or Modern Bureaucrats: Black Police in Early Twentieth-Century South Africa," *Comparative Studies in Society and History* 54, no. 2 (2012): 255–58, 265–69, 273–74; Martin Thomas, "The Gendarmerie, Information Collection, and Violence in French North Africa between the Wars" *Historical Reflections* 36, no. 2 (2010): 79–83.

57. Kim Wagner, "Savage Warfare, Violence and the Rule of Colonial Difference in Early British Counterinsurgency," *History Workshop Journal* 85 (Spring 2018): 217–37, at 221.

58. Wagner, "Savage Warfare," 223.

59. Algeria's provisional FLN government made these connections repeatedly: IISH, COLL00201, Algeria, social and political developments collection, folder 4, GPRA pamphlet *Le napalme en Algérie*, published in August 1960.

60. Huw Bennett, "'Words Are Cheaper than Bullets': Britain's Psychological Warfare in the Middle East, 1945–60," *Intelligence and National Security* 34, no. 7 (2019): 931–32.

61. The laws involved sought to limit civilian freedom of movement as a strategic objective. For the colonial production of these legal precepts, see Lazar, "Necessity and Non-Combatant Immunity," 53–57; Nasser Hussain, *The Jurisprudence of*

Emergency: Colonialism and the Rule of Law (Ann Arbor: University of Michigan Press, 2003), 101–13.

62. David French, *The British Way in Counter-Insurgency, 1945-1957* (Oxford: Oxford University Press, 2011), 74–82; Karl Hack, "Everyone Lived in Fear: Malaya and the British Way of Counter-Insurgency," *Small Wars & Insurgencies* 23, no. 4/5 (2012): 671–99; John Reynolds, *Empire, Emergency and International Law* (Cambridge, UK: Cambridge University Press, 2017), 68–93.

63. IISH, COLL00201, Algeria, social and political developments collection, folder 1, GPRA pamphlet, *Génocide en Algérie: Les Camps de regroupement,* October 1960.

64. Benjamin C. Brower, "Regroupment Camps and Shantytowns in Late-Colonial Algeria," *L'Année du Maghreb* 20 (2019): 99–101; Amelia H. Lyons, *The Civilizing Mission in the Metropole: Algerian Families and the French Welfare State during Decolonization* (Stanford, CA: Stanford University Press, 2013), 159–60.

65. Feichtinger, "'A Great Reformatory,'" 45–72; Miguel Bandeira Jerónimo, "A Robust Operation: Resettling, Security, and Development in Late Colonial Angola (1960s–1970s)," *Itinerario* 44, no. 1 (2020): 1–25.

66. Giorgio Agamben, "The Sovereign Police," in *The Politics of Everyday Fear,* ed. Brian Massumi (Minneapolis: University of Minnesota Press, 1993), 61–63.

67. AN, Ministry of Justice files, BB/18/3613: Ministère de la Justice, 1er Bureau Criminel: Algérie, no. 4679/CDP, Governor-General to Prefects of Oran, Alger and Constantine, August 28, 1947: "A/S de la répression des 'propos anti-française.'"

68. Sylvie Thénault, "L'état d'urgence (1955–2005). De l' Algérie coloniale à la France contemporaine: destin d'une loi," *Le Mouvement Social* 218, no. 1 (2007): 63–78.

69. Sylvie Thénault, *Violence ordinaire dans l'Algérie coloniale: camps, internements, assignations à résidence* (Paris: Odile Jacob, 2012), chapter 12.

70. ANOM, carton 11cab/51: Cabinet Soustelle 1955, HP Eydoux, "Zone d'urgence du Constantinois," May 16, 1955; carton 11cab/89, HP Eydoux "Note," August 29, 1955.

71. Valentino, Huth, and Balch-Lindsay, "'Draining the Sea,'" 375–407; Downes, "Draining the Sea," 420–44.

72. Frederick Cooper, *Colonialism in Question: Theory, Knowledge, History* (Berkeley: University of California Press, 2005), 154–57.

73. Lentz, *Contested Territory,* 41–46, 96–102; Christopher Goscha, *Vietnam: un État né de la guerre, 1945-1954* (Paris: Armand Colin, 2011), 423–33.

74. Lentz, *Contested Territory,* 115–27; Christopher Goscha, "A 'Total War' of Decolonization? Social Mobilization and State-Building in Communist Vietnam (1949–54)," *War and Society* 31, no. 2 (2012): 140–48, 152–55.

75. The fullest discussion of this rebel governance phenomenon is within the comparative politics literature on civil wars, the exemplary work being Ana Arjona, Nelson Kasfir, and Zachariah Mampilly, eds., *Rebel Governance in Civil War* (Cambridge, UK: Cambridge University Press, 2015).

76. Heonik Kwon, *After the Korean War: An Intimate History* (Cambridge, UK: Cambridge University Press, 2020), 5–6, citing Steven Hugh Lee, *The Korean War* (New York: Longman, 2001).

77. Kwon, *After the Korean War,* 3–4.

78. Dong Choon Kim, "Forgotten War, Forgotten Massacres: The Korean War (1950–1953) as Licensed Mass Killings," *Journal of Genocide Research* 6, no. 4 (2004): 526–29. For the colonial origins of Korean-on-Korean violence during the initial wave of social protest in 1946, see Jin-Yeon Kang, "Colonial Legacies and the Struggle for Social Membership in a National Community: The 1946 People's Uprisings in Korea," *Journal of Historical Sociology* 24, no. 3 (2011): 329–49.

79. Dong Choon Kim, "Forgotten War, Forgotten Massacres," 537–39.

80. Those living in frontier districts and other remote areas often fared worse; see Heike I. Schmidt, *Colonialism and Violence in Zimbabwe: A History of Suffering* (Woodbridge, UK: James Currey, 2013), 134–46, 157–63; Luise White, "'Heading for the Gun': Skills and Sophistication in an African Guerrilla War," *Comparative Studies in Society & History* 51, no. 2 (2009): 236–59.

81. Kwon, *After the Korean War*, 90–98.

82. Eric D. Weitz, "Self-Determination: How a German Enlightenment Idea Became the Slogan of National Liberation and a Human Right," *American Historical Review* 20, no. 2 (2015): 489–92.

83. Michael Bryant, *A World History of War Crimes: From Antiquity to the Present*, 2nd edition (London: Bloomsbury, 2021), 263–65; David M. Crowe, *War Crimes, Genocide, and Justice: A Global History* (Basingstoke, UK: Palgrave Macmillan, 2014), 308–14; Young-Sun Hong, *Cold War Germany, the Third World, and the Global Humanitarian Regime* (Cambridge, UK: Cambridge University Press, 2017), 19.

84. TNA, CO 936/391: International Red Cross Geneva Conventions for the Protection of War Victims, applicability in colonial disturbances, 1954–1956.

85. Bryant, *A World History of War Crimes*, 265–66; Crowe, *War Crimes*, 315–16.

86. Fabian Klose, "Human Rights for and against Empire, Legal and Public Discourses in the Age of Decolonisation," *Journal of the History of International Law* 18 (2016): 320–27.

87. Alex Marshall, "Imperial Nostalgia, the Liberal Lie, and the Perils of Postmodern Counterinsurgency," *Small Wars & Insurgencies* 21, no. 2 (2010): 233–58, at 241; on British obstructionism: Bennett, *Fighting the Mau Mau*, 65–68.

88. The fullest treatment is Boyd van Dijk, *Preparing for War: The Making of the 1949 Geneva Conventions* (Oxford: Oxford University Press, 2022), 99–104, 113–44.

89. Marshall, "Imperial Nostalgia," 233–58, at 241.

90. Frédéric Mégret, "From 'Savages' to 'Unlawful Combatants': A Postcolonial Look at International Law's 'Other,'" in *International Law and Its "Others,"* ed. Anne Orford (Cambridge, UK: Cambridge University Press, 2006), 1–17, also cited in Anna Chotzen, "Beyond Bounds: Morocco's Rif War and the Limits of International Law," *Humanity* 5, no. 1 (2014): 33–34.

91. van Dijk, *Preparing for War*, 176–77, 188.

92. Amanda Alexander, "International Humanitarian Law: Postcolonialism and the 1977 *Geneva Protocol I*," *Melbourne Journal of International Law* 17, no. 1 (2016): 19–22; also cited in Jessica Whyte, "The 'Dangerous Concept of the Just War': Decolonization, Wars of National Liberation, and the Additional Protocols to the Geneva Conventions," *Humanity* 9, no. 3 (2018): 335 n.45; and for FLN use of French POWs to advance the case for legal recognition: Raphaëlle Branche, *Prisonniers du FLN* (Paris: Payot, 2014), 80–95.

93. For Vietnam: Peter Zinoman, *The Colonial Bastille: A History of Impris-onment in Vietnam 1862–1940* (Berkeley: University of California Press, 2001), chapters 5–7; for Northern Ireland: Tony Craig, "Internment, Imprisonment, Interrogation and Resistance in Low Intensity Conflict: Carceral Warfare and Republican Paramilitaries in Northern Ireland 1968–c1988," in *The Oxford Hand-book of Late Colonial Insurgencies and Counter-Insurgencies*, ed. Martin Thomas and Gareth Curless (Oxford: Oxford University Press, 2023), 254–75. For the hun-ger strike by members of the FLN's French Federation imprisoned in France: IISH, COLL00201, Algeria, social and political developments collection, folder 4, 'Back-ground Document on the Situation of the Thousands of Algerian Political Prisoners in France and Algeria,' text of communiqué issued by FLN French Federation on November 5, 1961. The hunger strike began on November 2, 1961. After refusing food for between two and three weeks, 420 prisoners in the Baumettes prison at Marseilles and 100 imprisoned in the eastern city of Metz prison were dispersed in groups of twenty to other prisons in France.

94. Young-Sun Hong, *Cold War Germany*, 136–40.

95. MAE, série Afrique-Levant, sous-série MAROC, 1956–68, vol. 87, PD/EA, Note sur les réfugiés algériens au Maroc, May 14, 1958. For discussion of refugee expo-sure to civil conflict, see Idean Salehyan, "Refugees and the Study of Civil War," *Civil Wars* 9, no. 2 (2007): 127–35.

96. For colonialist practices in metropolitan refugee camps in Britain and France, see Jordanna Bailkin, *Unsettled: Refugee Camps and the Making of Multicultural Britain* (Oxford: Oxford University Press, 2018); Jean-Philippe Marcy, "L'Aide aux internes: la CIMADE au camp du Larzac (1959–1961)," in *La France en guerre 1954–1962: Expériences métropolitaines de la guerre d'indépendance algérienne*, ed. Raphaëlle Branche and Sylvie Thénault (Paris: Autrement, 2008), 380–89.

97. MAE, série Afrique-Levant, sous-série MAROC, 1956–68, vol. 87: Réfugiés algériens/affaires algériennes, 1958–60, no. 0003/L, Alexandre Parodi, French Ambassador to Morocco, to Foreign Minister Christian Pineau, January 2, 1958. "A/S: réfugiés musulmans algériens au Maroc."

98. MAE, série Afrique-Levant, sous-série MAROC, 1956–68, vol. 87: no. 0003/L, Parodi to Pineau, January 2, 1958.

99. MAE, série Afrique-Levant, sous-série MAROC, 1956–68, vol. 87, no. 303/CGO, H. de Bourdeille, French Consul, Oujda, to Alexandre Parodi, February 12, 1958, "Nombre de réfugiés dans l'Oriental." Swiss Red Cross officials, who distributed aid sent from Egypt's Red Crescent, complained that local FLN organizers diverted the support provided to their frontline fighters at refugees' expense. See MAE, sous-série MAROC, 1956–68, vol. 87, tel. 5345, Langlais, Foreign Ministry, to Algiers and Rabat, November 17, 1958; no. 3752/L, Jean Le Roy, Rabat Chargé d'Affaires, "A/S Secours aux 'réfugiés' algériens musulmans au Maroc," November 27, 1958.

100. MAE, sous-série MAROC, 1956–68, vol. 87, no. 3665, Rabat Ambassador Alexandre Parodi, to Foreign Ministry Sous-Direction du Maroc, "A/S trafic d'armes au profit du FLN," August 8, 1958: tableau III: Envois d'armes annoncés dont l'arrivée n'a pas été signalée. Evidence mounted in 1959 that the USSR, Yugoslavia, and others funneled arms and supplies to ALN insurgents in Algeria through consignments of aid to Algerian refugees in eastern Morocco; see MAE, série Afrique-Levant,

sous-série MAROC, 1956–68, vol. 87, tel. 2046, Le Grandville, Moscow Embassy, to Foreign Ministry, May 30, 1959.

101. It was agreed at the 19th International Conference of the Red Cross in Delhi that Morocco's Red Crescent would coordinate relief efforts for Algerian refugees on behalf of all national Red Cross and Red Crescent agencies: MAE, série Afrique-Levant, sous-série MAROC, 1956–68, vol. 87, no. 0236/SG/AS1, Parodi, Rabat, to Christian Pineau, January 25, 1958.

102. MAE, série Afrique-Levant, sous-série MAROC, 1956–68, vol. 87, Presse étrangère: *Mediterranean Courier*, April 10, 1959, "Du blé américain pour les réfugiés algériens."

103. MAE, sous-série MAROC, 1956–68, vol. 87, "Question orale sans débat no. 1058 posée, le 18 mars 1958, par Michel Debré, Senateur—éléments pour un projet de réponse."

104. Jennifer Johnson, "The Limits of Humanitarianism: Decolonization, the French Red Cross, and the Algerian War," in *Decolonization, Self Determination, and the Rise of Global Human Rights Politics*, ed. A. Dirk Moses, Marco Duranti, and Roland Burke (Cambridge, UK: Cambridge University Press, 2020), 99–102.

105. MAE, série Afrique-Levant, sous-série MAROC, 1956–68, vol. 83, MLA, Foreign Ministry to French Ambassador, Rabat, December 9, 1959.

106. Johnson, "Limits of Humanitarianism," 79–108.

107. Young-Sun Hong, *Cold War Germany*, 134, 137–38.

108. Fabian Klose, *Human Rights in the Shadow of Colonial Violence: The Wars of Independence in Kenya and Algeria* (Philadelphia: University of Pennsylvania Press, 2013).

109. In Brian Drohan's words, 'Activism linked the metaphorical battlefield of law, diplomacy, propaganda, and public opinion with the physical battlefield of ambushes, house searches, arrests, and interrogations.' Brian Drohan, *Brutality in an Age of Human Rights: Activism and Counterinsurgency at the End of the British Empire* (Ithaca, NY: Cornell University Press, 2017), 15.

110. Drohan, *Brutality*, 6–7, 134–40, 188–89.

111. Drohan, *Brutality*, 17, 29–34; 134–40.

112. Mandy Banton, "Destroy? 'Migrate'? Conceal? British Strategies for the Disposal of Sensitive Records of Colonial Administrations at Independence," *Journal of Imperial & Commonwealth History* 40, no. 2 (2012): 323–37; *The Guardian* online, "Files Reveal Brutal Treatment Meted out by British Forces in 1950s Cyprus," July 27, 2012: https://www.theguardian.com/uk/2012/jul/27/brutality-british-forces-1950s-cyprus.

113. Bennett, "'Words Are Cheaper,'" 337–38. The Special Investigations Group (SIG) looked into 191 incidents during its nine-month term in Cyprus in 1958–1959. The majority seem to have been examined thoroughly but, as Huw Bennett points out, the SIG was part of a security apparatus designed to counteract the demoralizing effect of EOKA propaganda on British troops.

114. Drohan, *Brutality*, 47–56, 161–66. In 1956 and 1957 the Greek government petitioned the European Court of Human Rights citing forty-nine cases of torture in Cyprus.

115. Drohan, *Brutality*, 123–26.

116. David French, "Toads and Informers: How the British Treated Their Collaborators during the Cyprus Emergency, 1955–9," *International History Review* 39, no. 1 (2017): 72–78.

117. Drohan, *Brutality*, 23, 31–32.

118. Nicole L. Immler and Stef Scagliola, "Seeking Justice for the Mass Execution in Rawagede: Probing the Concept of Entangled History in a Colonial Setting," *Rethinking History: The Journal of Theory and Practice* 24, no. 1 (2020): 1–9. The most wide-ranging analysis is Rémy Limpach, *De brandende kampongs van Generaal Spoor* (Amsterdam: Boom, 2016).

119. Rémy Limpach, "'Information Costs Lives': The Intelligence War for Indonesia, 1945–1949," in *Beyond the Pale: Dutch Extreme Violence in the Indonesian War of Independence, 1945–1949*, ed. Gert Oostindie, Ben Schoenmaker, and Frank van Tree (Amsterdam: Amsterdam University Press, 2022), 207–37.

120. Christiaan Harinck, "Late Colonial Counterinsurgency as an Intellectual Challenge: The Development of Dutch Tactical Doctrine during the Indonesian War, 1945–1949," in Thomas and Curless, *Oxford Handbook of Late Colonial Insurgencies and Counter-Insurgencies*, 179–97.

121. Drohan, *Brutality*, 23, 31–32, 86–89, quote at 88.

122. Drohan, *Brutality*, 112–13.

123. Drohan, *Brutality*, 157–59.

124. Mark McGovern, "State Violence and the Colonial Roots of Collusion in Northern Ireland," *Race & Class* 57, no. 2 (2015): 5–6, 10–11; Bennett, *Fighting the Mau Mau*, 84–90.

125. Bennett, *Fighting the Mau Mau*, 265–68, quote at 265.

126. Samantha Newbery, *Interrogation, Intelligence and Security: Controversial British Techniques* (Manchester, UK: Manchester University Press, 2015), 14–17; Andrew Mumford, "Minimum Force Meets Brutality: Detention, Interrogation and Torture in British Counter-Insurgency Campaigns," *Journal of Military Ethics* 11, no. 1 (2012): 17–19. The 'five techniques' of interrogation were being forced to stand in a stress position, being hooded to restrict vision, exposure to continuous noise, limited access to food and water, and sleep deprivation. British security forces used all these techniques against detainees in 1960s Aden, before applying them in 1970s Northern Ireland.

127. Drohan, *Brutality*, 159–61; Newbery, *Interrogation*, 62–113; idem, "Terrorism, Torture and Intelligence," *International Politics* 50, no. 4 (2013): 512–31.

128. Drohan, *Brutality*, 162–86.

129. Kinsella, "Superfluous Injury," 214; Whyte, "The 'Dangerous Concept,'" 316.

130. Boyd Van Dijk, "'The Great Humanitarian': The Soviet Union, the International Committee of the Red Cross, and the Geneva Conventions of 1949," *Law and History Review* 37, no. 1 (2019): 209–35, at 225–29, 234.

131. Drohan, *Brutality*, 11, 99–101, 191.

132. Drohan, *Brutality*, 11–12; Weitz, *A World Divided*, 423; Todd Shepard, "'History Is Past Politics'? Archives, 'Tainted Evidence,' and the Return of the State," *American Historical Review* 115, no. 2 (April 2010): 474–83.

133. Julia F. Irwin, "Taming Total War: Great War–Era American Humanitarianism and Its Legacies," *Diplomatic History* 38 no. 4 (2014): 774–75; Tarak Barkawi, "Decolonising War," *European Journal of International Security* 1, no. 2 (2016): 211–13.

134. Stathis Kalyvas, *The Logic of Violence in Civil Wars* (Cambridge, UK: Cambridge University Press, 2006); Daniel Branch, *Defeating Mau Mau, Creating Kenya: Counterinsurgency, Civil War, and Decolonization* (Cambridge, UK: Cambridge University Press, 2009). For comparison: Pierre Asselin and Martin Thomas, "French Decolonisation and Civil War: The Dynamics of Violence in the Early Phases of Anti-Colonial War in Vietnam and Algeria, 1940–56," *Journal of Modern European History* 20, no. 4 (2022): 513–35.

135. For extended coverage: MAE, série Afrique Levant, sous-série: Algérie 1953–9, 31QO, files 28–38: La question algérienne aux Nations Unies, 1953–59; Matthew Connelly, *Diplomatic Revolution: Algeria's Fight for Independence and the Origins of the Post-Cold War Era* (New York: Oxford University Press, 2002); Jennifer Johnson, *The Battle for Algeria: Sovereignty, Health Care, and Humanitarianism* (Philadelphia: University of Pennsylvania Press, 2016), 157–91; Klose, "Human Rights for and against Empire," 327–31.

136. This issue came to a head in Algeria over the May 1957 massacre of over 300 civilians in five hamlets in the Melouza district of highland Kabylia, accused of supporting MNA-linked militias. The FLN initially denied involvement, triggering the dissemination of highly emotive French evidence to the contrary: MAE, série Afrique Levant, sous-série: Algérie 1953–9, 31QO *File 24: Affaire du massacre de Melouza* telegram 1119, "Conférence de Presse de Mohammed Yazid, New York," June 11, 1957; FLN delegation New York, pamphlet *War in Algeria: The "Massacre" of Melouza*; Service de Presse booklet: *Melouza & Wagram accusent . . .* The Algerian Red Crescent, meanwhile, produced evidence of French Army killings, torture of civilians, and forced population removals: Johnson, *Battle for Algeria*, 118–20.

137. Drohan, *Brutality*; David M. Anderson, "British Abuse and Torture in Kenya's Counter-Insurgency, 1952–1960," *Small Wars & Insurgencies* 23, no. 4/5 (2012): 700–19; and, in the same journal issue, David French, "Nasty Not Nice: British Counter-Insurgency Doctrine and Practice," 744–61.

138. TNA, CO 936/391, Colonial Office minutes on ICRC conventions for the protection of war victims: applicability in colonial disturbances, various dates, January 1957.

Chapter Twelve: Political Economies of Decolonization and Development

1. Miguel Bandeira Jerónimo and José Pedro Monteiro, "Colonial Labour Internationalized: Portugal and the Decolonization Momentum (1945–1975)," *International History Review*, 42, no. 3 (2020): 489; Andreas Stucki, *Violence and Gender in Africa's Iberian Colonies: Feminizing the Portuguese and Spanish Empire, 1950s–1970s* (Basingstoke, UK: Palgrave Macmillan, 2019), 4–9.

2. Frederick Cooper, "Empire Multiplied: A Review Essay," *Comparative Studies in Society and History* 46, no. 2 (2004): 270.

3. Karl Ittmann, *A Problem of Great Importance: Population, Race, and Power in the British Empire, 1919–1973* (Berkeley: University of California Press, 2013), 83–87.

4. Patricia Clavin, "What's in a Living Standard? Bringing Society and Economy together in the ILO and the League of Nations Depression Delegation, 1938–1945,"

in *Globalizing Social Rights*, ed. Sandrine Kott and Joëlle Droux (Basingstoke, UK: Palgrave Macmillan, 2013), 234–38.

5. Clavin, "What's in a Living Standard?" 240–42; Dane Kennedy, "Essay and Reflection: On the American Empire from a British Imperial Perspective," *International History Review* 29, no. 1 (2007): 102–3.

6. Clavin, "What's in a Living Standard?" 243.

7. Stephen Wertheim, "The League of Nations: Retreat from International Law?" *Journal of Global History* 7, no. 2 (2012): 231.

8. Jamie Martin, *The Meddlers: Sovereignty, Empire, and the Birth of Global Economic Governance* (Cambridge, MA: Harvard University Press, 2022), 135, 175–76.

9. D. K. Fieldhouse, *The West and the Third World: Trade, Colonialism, Dependence and Development* (Oxford: Blackwell, 1999), 71–90; Jane Burbank and Frederick Cooper, *Empires in World History: Power and the Politics of Difference* (Princeton, NJ: Princeton University Press, 2010), 413.

10. Andrew Dilley, "Business, the Commonwealth and the Rhetoric of Development: The Federation of Commonwealth Chambers of Commerce and Africa, 1945–1974," in *The Business of Development in Post-Colonial Africa*, ed. Véronique Dimier and Sarah Stockwell (Basingstoke, UK: Palgrave Macmillan, 2020), 42–52.

11. Ittmann, *Problem of Great Importance*, 108–13.

12. Michael Collins, "Decolonisation and the 'Federal Moment,'" *Diplomacy & Statecraft* 24, no. 1 (2013): 26–27; Andrew Shennan, *Rethinking France: Plans for Renewal* (Oxford: Clarendon, 1989), chapter 7.

13. Erik Linstrum, *Ruling Minds: Psychology in the British Empire* (Cambridge, MA: Harvard University Press, 2015), 161–67, 171–74.

14. Corey Ross, *Ecology and Power in the Age of Empire: Europe and the Transformation of the Tropical World* (Oxford: Oxford University Press, 2019), 352–53; for the primacy of reconstruction and humanitarian relief within Europe, see Ben Shephard, "'Becoming Planning Minded': The Theory and Practice of Relief, 1940–1945," *Journal of Contemporary History* 43, no. 3 (2008): 411–19; Jessica Reinisch, "Introduction: Agents of Internationalism," *Contemporary European History* 25 (2016): 379–89; idem, "Internationalism in Relief: The Birth (and Death) of UNRRA," *Past & Present* 210, Supplement 6 (2011): 258–89.

15. For Britain's national (rather than imperial) reconstruction priorities, see David Edgerton, "War, Reconstruction and the Nationalization of Post-War Britain, 1945–1951," *Past & Present* 210, Supplement 6 (2011): 34–35, 41–43.

16. Giuliano Garavini, *After Empires: European Integration, Decolonization, and the Challenge from the Global South 1957–1986* (Oxford: Oxford University Press, 2012), 21–23.

17. John Darwin, "Was There a Fourth British Empire?" in *The British Empire in the 1950s: Retreat or Revival?* ed. Martin Lynn (Basingstoke, UK: Palgrave Macmillan, 2006), 23–25.

18. Reuben Loffman and Benoît Henriet, "'We Are Left with Barely Anything': Colonial Rule, Dependency, and the Lever Brothers in the Belgian Congo, 1911–1960," *Journal of Imperial & Commonwealth History* 48, no. 1 (2020): 88–91.

19. Nicholas J. White, "Decolonisation in the 1950s: The Version According to British Business," in Lynn, *British Empire in the 1950s*, 102. The Anglo-Iranian Oil

Company, forerunner to British Petroleum, resisted Iran's nationalization in 1951 and bought a 50 per cent stake in the Kuwait Oil Company.

20. Ross, *Ecology and Power*, 354–55. For the local impact of such policies, see Peder Anker, *Imperial Ecology: Environmental Order in the British Empire, 1895–1945* (Cambridge, MA: Harvard University Press, 2002).

21. Tara Zahra, "'The Psychological Marshall Plan': Displacement, Gender, and Human Rights after World War II," *Central European History* 44, no. 1 (2011): 37–52, 61–62; Tehyun Ma, "'The Common Aim of the Allied Powers': Social Policy and International Legitimacy in Wartime China, 1940–47," *Journal of Global History* 9, no. 2 (2014): 254–75.

22. Paul Kelemen, "Modernising Colonialism: The British Labour Movement and Africa," *Journal of Imperial & Commonwealth History* 34, no. 2 (2006): 229–32.

23. Rachel Leow, "Asian Lessons in the Cold War Classroom: Trade Union Networks and the Multidirectional Pedagogies of the Cold War in Asia," *Journal of Social History* 53, no. 2 (2019): 431–42.

24. Paulo Capuzzo, "Markets," in *Europe's Postwar Periods—1989, 1945, 1918: Writing History Backwards*, ed. Martin Conway, Pieter Lagrou, and Henry Rousso (London: Bloomsbury, 2019), 166.

25. Eric Helleiner, *Forgotten Foundations of Bretton Woods: International Development and the Making of the Postwar Order* (Ithaca, NY: Cornell University Press, 2014), 221, 225–26.

26. Helleiner, *Forgotten Foundations*, 211–13. During the war, as Helleiner points out, British business consortia, including the Federation of British Industries and the London Chamber of Commerce, acknowledged the link more explicitly than did their political leaders.

27. Helleiner, *Forgotten Foundations*, 227–31.

28. Charlotte Lydia Riley, "'Tropical Allsorts': The Transnational Flavor of British Development Policies in Africa," *Journal of World History* 26, no. 4 (2015): 839–64, at 846–52.

29. TNA, Board of Trade records, BT 11/4973: UN Economic Commission for Asia and Far East, 2nd Trade Promotion Conference, Manila, 1952–3, UN Delegation to UN, "ECAFE," July 26, 1952.

30. Marc L. J. Dierikx, "Policy versus Practice. Behind the Scenes in Dutch Development Aid, 1949–1989," *International History Review* 39, no. 4 (2017): 639–41.

31. Keith Tribe, "The Colonial Office and British Development Economics, 1940–60," *History of Political Economy* 50, annual supplement (2018): 97–98.

32. Burbank and Cooper, *Empires in World History*, 420.

33. Gregory A. Barton, "Environmentalism, Development and British Policy in the Middle East, 1945–65," *Journal of Imperial & Commonwealth History* 38 (2010): 621.

34. The same point could be made about other European imperial powers facing similar deficits and dollar shortages; see Nicholas J. White, "Reconstructing Europe through Rejuvenating Empire: The British, French, and Dutch Experiences Compared," *Past & Present* 210, Supplement 6 (2011): 214.

35. Vanessa Ogle, "Archipelago Capitalism: Tax Havens, Offshore Money, and the State, 1950s–1970s," *American Historical Review* 122, no. 5 (2017): 1439–41.

36. Joseph M. Hodge and Gerald Hödl, "Introduction," in *Developing Africa*, ed. Joseph M. Hodge, Gerald Hödl, and Martina Kopf (Manchester, UK: Manchester University Press, 2014), 1–5, 16, at 3.

37. Moritz Feichtinger and Stephan Malinowski, "Transformative Invasions: Western Post-9/11 Counterinsurgency and the Lessons of Colonialism," *Humanity* 3, no. 1 (2012): 35–63.

38. For punchy critiques, see: Editors' Introduction in Stephen J. Macekura and Erez Manela, eds., *The Development Century* (Cambridge, UK: Cambridge University Press, 2018), 1–13; David Engerman, "American Knowledge and Global Power," *Diplomatic History* 31, no. 4 (2007): 618–21.

39. Randall Packard, "Visions of Postwar Health and Development and Their Impact on Public Health Interventions in the Developing World," in *International Development and the Social Sciences: Essays on the History and Politics of Knowledge*, ed. Frederick Cooper and Randall M. Packard (Berkeley: University of California Press, 1998), 93–95.

40. Max Trecker, *Red Money for the Global South: East-South Economic Relations in the Cold War* (London: Routledge, 2020), chapter 2; James Mark et al., *Socialism Goes Global: The Soviet Union and Eastern Europe in the Age of Decolonization* (Oxford: Oxford University Press, 2022).

41. Randall Packard, "Malaria Dreams: Postwar Visions of Health and Development in the Third World," *Medical Anthropology* 17 (1997): 287–9.

42. Mark Cleary, "Land Codes and the State in French Cochinchina c. 1900–1940," *Journal of Historical Geography* 29, no. 3 (2003): 362–68; McHale, *First Vietnam War*, 33.

43. Edward Miller, "Development, Space, and Counterinsurgency in South Vietnam's Ben Tre Province, 1954–1960," in Macekura and Manela, *Development Century*, 151–52.

44. Hoover Institution Archive, Robert Delavignette Papers, box I, Paul Chauvin, President of Algiers Chamber of Agriculture, letter to Robert Delavignette, June 11, 1955: "La situation économique et sociale en Algérie." May 26, 1955.

45. Diana K. Davis, *Resurrecting the Granary of Rome: Environmental History and French Colonial Expansion in North Africa* (Athens: Ohio University Press, 2007), 166–69.

46. Corinna R. Unger, *International Development: A Postwar History* (London: Bloomsbury, 2018), 49–61, 79–84.

47. Dorothy L. Hodgson, "Taking Stock: State Control, Ethnic Identity and Pastoralist Development in Tanganyika, 1949–58," *Journal of African History* 41, no. 1 (2000): 55–78, quote at 64.

48. Øystein H. Rolandsen and Cherry Leonardi, "Discourses of Violence in the Transition from Colonialism to Independence in Southern Sudan, 1955–1960," *Journal of East African Studies* 8, no. 4 (2014): 609–22.

49. Alden Young, *Transforming Sudan: Decolonization, Economic Development, and State Formation* (Cambridge, UK: Cambridge University Press, 2017), 1–6, 11–13, 85–89. Begun in the early twentieth century, the Gezira Scheme centered on a vast cotton irrigation network in the Sudanese state of Al-Jazirah (anglicized to 'Gezira') bordering the Blue Nile.

50. For exemplary cases from Portuguese Africa, see Allen F. Isaacman and Barbara S. Isaacman, *Dams, Displacement, and the Delusion of Development: Cahora Bassa and Its Legacies in Mozambique, 1965–2007* (Athens: Ohio University Press, 2013) and Todd Cleveland, "Feeding the Aversion: Agriculture and Mining Technology on Angola's Colonial-Era Diamond Mines, 1917–1975," *Agricultural History* 92, no. 3 (2018): 328–50.

51. Hoover Institution archive, folder: Africa, General, "Note sur les recherches de pétrole en Afrique Equatoriale," n.d. September 1936.

52. Rob Nixon, *Slow Violence and the Environmentalism of the Poor* (Cambridge, MA: Harvard University Press, 2011), 16–18.

53. William Beinart, "Soil Erosion, Conservationism, and Ideas about Development: A Southern African Exploration, 1900–1960," *Journal of Southern African Studies* 11, no. 1 (1984): 61–79; David M. Anderson, "Depression, Dust Bowl, Demography, and Drought: The Colonial State and Soil Conservation in East Africa during the 1930s," *African Affairs* 83, no. 332 (1984): 333–43; James Fairhead and Melissa Leach, "Desiccation and Domination: Science and Struggles over Environment and Development in Colonial Guinea," *Journal of African History* 41, no. 1 (2000): 43–52.

54. Gareth Austin, "Africa and the Anthropocene," in *Economic Development and Environmental History in the Anthropocene: Perspectives on Asia and Africa*, ed. Gareth Austin (London: Bloomsbury, 2017), 97–107.

55. 'Land extensive' agriculture prioritized returns on labor over yields per unit area, which, as Gareth Austin summarizes it, 'was logical in a region where it was usually the supply of labour, not land, which constrained the expansion of output. It was often a response to environmental constraints such as thin topsoil, which—along with animal sleeping sickness in much of the subcontinent—usually meant reliance on the hoe rather than the plough': Austin, "Introduction," in *Economic Development*, 14.

56. Jennifer Johnson, "The Contradictions of Sovereignty: Development, Family Planning and the Struggle for Population Control in Postcolonial Morocco," *Humanity* 11, no. 3 (Winter 2020): 259–79, drawing from Ellen Amster, *Medicine and the Saints: Science, Islam, and the Colonial Encounter in Morocco, 1877–1956* (Austin: University of Texas Press, 2013).

57. For colonial preoccupation with soil degradation and consequent efforts to regulate the cultivation of upland areas, particularly through terracing, see Ross, *Ecology and Power*, 370–72.

58. Eric Worby, "'Discipline without Oppression': Sequence, Timing, and Marginality in Southern Rhodesia's Post-War Development Scheme," *Journal of African History* 41, no. 1 (2000): 119–22.

59. Hodge and Hödl, "Introduction," 15–21; Ross, *Ecology and Power*, 354–63.

60. Philip J. Havik, "Public Health and Tropical Modernity: The Combat against Sleeping Sickness in Portuguese Guinea, 1945–74," *História, Ciências, Saúde: Manguinhos* 21, no. 2 (2014): 641–66.

61. Taylor C. Sherman, "From 'Grow More Food' to 'Miss a Meal': Hunger, Development, and the Limits of Post-Colonial Nationalism in India, 1947–1957," *South Asia* 36, no. 4 (2013): 571–72, 581–88; Unger, *International Development*, 10–11, 39–43, 51–55.

62. Muriam Haleh Davis, "'The Transformation of Man' in French Algeria: Economic Planning and the Postwar Social Sciences, 1958–62," *Journal of Contemporary History* 52, no. 1 (2017): 73 n.3; Jeffrey James Byrne, "Our Own Special Brand of Socialism: Algeria and the Contest of Modernities in the 1960s," *Diplomatic History* 33, no. 3 (2009): 429–30.

63. Byrne, "Our Own Special," 431–32, 443–44.

64. Michael Jennings, "'A Very Real War': Popular Participation in Development in Tanzania during the 1950s and 1960s," *International Journal of African Historical Studies* 40, no. 1 (2007): 71–84. Tanzania is frequently cited as the archetypal African developmental state, thanks to its nationwide network of Village Development Committees set up in 1962 and, more particularly, to President Julius Nyerere's identification of the country's brand of socialist modernization, or *ujamaa*, with participatory, but increasingly authoritarian rural development schemes.

65. Michael Jennings, "'We Must Run While Others Walk,': Popular Participation and Development Crisis in Tanzania, 1961–9," *Journal of Modern African Studies* 41, no. 3 (2003): 163–78; Benjamin Siegel, "Modernizing Peasants and 'Master Farmers': Progressive Agriculture in Early Independent India," *Comparative Studies of South Asia, Africa and the Middle East* 37, no. 1 (2017): 64–85.

66. Frances Stewart, "Changing Approaches to Development since 1950: Drawing on Polanyi," *History of Political Economy* 50: annual supplement (2018): 24–25.

67. Burke, "Some Rights," 428; Byrne, "Our Own Special," 433–39.

68. Jennings, "'We Must Run,'" 179–86.

69. Véronique Dimier, "Constructing Conditionality: The Bureaucratization of EC Development Aid," *European Foreign Affairs Review* 11 (2006): 266–67; idem, "Bringing the Neo-Patrimonial State back to Europe: French Decolonization and the Making of the European Development Aid Policy," *Archiv für Sozialgeschichte* 48 (2008): 433–57. For a pithy summary of the widening scope of development histories: Manela, "International Society," 200–4.

70. Dimier, "Constructing Conditionality," 267–69; idem, "L'institutionnalisation de la Commission Européenne (DG Développement): du role des leaders dans la construction d'une administration multinationale, 1958–1975," *Etudes internationales* 34 (2003): 401–28.

71. Dimier, "Constructing Conditionality," 274–77. With the UK's admission to the European Economic Community in 1975, association arrangements with former colonial dependencies were rethought. Development aid was tied to the performance of recipient governments under the terms of revised agreements (the Lomé Conventions) renegotiated at five-year intervals.

72. Beinart, "Soil Erosion," 52; Anderson, "Depression, Dust Bowl," 322–26.

73. Ian Tyrrell, "Resource Use, Conservation, and the Environmental Limits of Anti-Imperialism, c. 1880–1930," in *Empire's Twin: U.S. Anti-Imperialism from the Founding Era to the Age of Terrorism*, ed. Ian Tyrrell and Jay Sexton (Ithaca, NY: Cornell University Press, 2015), 168–74.

74. Hannah Whittaker, "Frontier Security in North East Africa: Conflict and Colonial Development on the Margins, c. 1930–60," *Journal of African History* 58, no. 3 (2017): 384–85, 388–93.

75. Mobutu's Zaire is perhaps the preeminent example. The former Belgian Congo shifted from being an export-driven economy to bare subsistence in its first postindependence decades: Jan-Frederik Abbeloos, "Mobutu, Suharto, and the Challenges of Nation-Building and Economic Development, 1965–97," in *Colonial Exploitation and Economic Development: The Belgian Congo and the Netherlands Indies Compared*, ed. Ewout Frankema and Frans Buelens (Abingdon, UK: Routledge, 2013), 251–69.

76. Paul Kelemen, "Planning for Africa: The British Labour Party's Colonial Development Policy, 1920–1964," *Journal of Agrarian Change* 1, no. 7 (2007): 76–98; Herrick Chapman, *France's Long Reconstruction: In Search of the Modern Republic* (Cambridge, MA: Harvard University Press, 2018), chapters 5–7.

77. Editors' introduction to Michel Christian, Sandrine Kott, and Ondřej Matějka, eds., *Planning in Cold War Europe: Competition, Cooperation, Circulations (1950s–1970s)* (Berlin: de Gruyter, 2018), 1–3; Valeska Huber, "Introduction: Global Histories of Social Planning," *Journal of Contemporary History* 52, no. 1 (2017): 9–11.

78. Barton, "Environmentalism," 622–23.

79. Barton, "Environmentalism," 624–33.

80. John Kent, *British Imperial Strategy and the Origins of the Cold War, 1944–49* (Leicester: Leicester University Press, 1993).

81. Duncan Bell, *Reordering the World: Essays on Liberalism and Empire* (Princeton, NJ: Princeton University Press, 2016), 258. As Bell concludes, 'The idea was that over time, and often with the explicit intervention of imperial powers, the uncivilized could reach the level of development necessary for reclassification.'

82. On Soviet aid after the 1949 launch of its Council of Mutual Economic Assistance, see Trecker, *Red Money*, chapters 3 and 6; Alessandro Iandolo, "The Rise and Fall of the 'Soviet Model of Development' in West Africa, 1957–1964," *Cold War History* 12, no. 4 (2012): 684–85, 691–92.

83. G. John Ikenberry, "The End of Liberal International Order?" *International Affairs* 94, no. 1 (2018): 13–17; and for Bretton Woods' longer-term origins: Martin, *Meddlers*, 211–31.

84. Amy L. S. Staples, *The Birth of Development: How the World Bank, Food and Agriculture Organization, and World Health Organization Have Changed the World* (Kent, OH: Kent State University Press, 2006), chapter 3; Odd Arne Westad, *The Global Cold War: Third World Interventions and the Making of Our Times* (Cambridge, UK: Cambridge University Press, 2005), 153; Unger, *International Development*, 63.

85. TNA, BT 11/3975, A. L. Burgess, Board of Trade memo., "Special Exchange Agreements," October 19, 1948.

86. TNA, BT 11/3590, Board of Trade note, "Compensation Trading in Relation to the International Trade Charter and General Agreement on Tariffs and Trade," no date, November 1947; BT 11/4222, G. Bowen, Board of Trade, to L. Jasper, March 25, 1949.

87. Martin, *Meddlers*, 238.

88. Garavini, *After Empires*, 20–23.

89. Garavini, *After Empires*, 22.

90. Quinn Slobodian, *The Globalists: The End of Empire and the Birth of Neoliberalism* (Cambridge: Harvard University Press, 2018), 119; Thomas McCarthy,

Race, Empire, and the Idea of Human Development (Cambridge, UK: Cambridge University Press, 2009), 194–5.

91. Mats Ingulstad, "The Interdependent Hegemon: The United States and the Quest for Strategic Raw Materials during the Early Cold War," *International History Review* 37, no. 1 (2015): 59–79, at 61.

92. Ingulstad, "Interdependent Hegemon," 65–71. To illustrate the economic stakes involved, Ingulstad points out that, by late 1949, US$600 million in commodity exports from European colonies almost matched the total value of western European exports.

93. Kris Manjapra, *Colonialism in Global Perspective* (Cambridge, UK: Cambridge University Press, 2020), 162–63, 176–78.

94. Martin, *Meddlers*, 250–55.

95. Yannis Dafermos, Daniela Gabor, and Jo Michell, "The Wall Street Consensus in Pandemic Times: What Does It Mean for Climate-Aligned Development?" *Canadian Journal of Development Studies* 42, no. 1–2 (2021): 240–41.

96. Oscar Sanchez-Sibony, *Red Globalization: The Political Economy of the Soviet Cold War from Stalin to Khrushchev* (Cambridge, UK: Cambridge University Press, 2014), 58–62.

97. Harold James, "The Multiple Contexts of Bretton Woods," *Past & Present* 210, Supplement 6 (2011): 291, 296.

98. Sanchez-Sibony, *Red Globalization*, 70–72.

99. Oscar Sanchez-Sibony, "The Cold War in the Margins of Capital: The Soviet Union's Introduction to the Decolonized World, 1955–1961," in *Alternative Globalizations: Eastern Europe and the Postcolonial World*, ed. James Mark, Artemy M. Kalinovsky, and Steffi Marung (Bloomington: Indiana University Press, 2020), 60–67.

100. Sanchez-Sibony, *Red Globalization*, 77–79, 127.

101. Sanchez-Sibony, *Red Globalization*, 129–34.

102. Slobodian, *Globalists*, 10, 118–22.

103. James, "Multiple Contexts," 301.

104. TNA, FO 371/97358, 1081/1, R. Cecil memo., "Problems of Nationalism— Latin America," May 15, 1952; Martin, *Meddlers*, 232, 244.

105. This is the core argument of Christy Thornton, *Revolution in Development: Mexico and the Governance of the Global Economy* (Berkeley: University of California Press, 2021), which traces Mexican initiatives for a more equitable multilateral economic order.

106. Slobodian, *Globalists*, 125–33; Ingulstad, "Interdependent Hegemon," 62.

107. Slobodian, *Globalists*, 17.

108. Thornton, *Revolution in Development*, 88–94.

109. Oscar Sanchez-Sibony, "Capitalism's Fellow Traveler: The Soviet Union, Bretton Woods, and the Cold War, 1944–1958," *Comparative Studies in Society and History* 56, no. 2 (2014): 293–301.

110. James, "Multiple Contexts," 293–95, 300; Helleiner, *Forgotten Foundations*, 4–13.

111. For background to the Bretton Woods–dependency connection, see Barry Eichengreen, *Globalizing Capital: A History of the International Monetary System*, 2nd edition (Princeton, NJ: Princeton University Press, 2008), 107–33, and Arturo

Escobar, *Encountering Development: The Making and Unmaking of the Third World*, 2nd edition (Princeton, NJ: Princeton University Press, 2011), especially chapter 3.

112. Eric Helleiner, *The Contested World Economy: The Deep and Global Roots of International Political Economy* (Cambridge, UK: Cambridge University Press, 2023), 77–78, 211–13.

113. Eric Helleiner, "Sun Yat-sen as a Pioneer of International Development," *History of Political Economy* 50, no. 1 (2018): 76–93; idem, *Forgotten Foundations*, 189–96; Amanda Kay McVety, "Wealth and Nations: The Origins of International Development Assistance," in *The Development Century*, ed. Stephen J. Macekura and Erez Manela (Cambridge, UK: Cambridge University Press, 2018), 21–23; Mexico's contribution to the refinement of development thinking is emphasized in Thornton, *Revolution in Development*.

114. Helleiner, *Forgotten Foundations*, 22, 221, 250–51.

115. Beverley Loke, "Conceptualising the Role and Responsibility of Great Power: China's Participation in Negotiations toward a Post–Second World War Order," *Diplomacy & Statecraft* 24, no. 2 (2013): 217–20.

116. Sanchez-Sibony, *Red Globalization*, 122, 125; Giuliano Garavini, "Completing Decolonization: The 1973 'Oil Shock' and the Struggle for Economic Rights," *International History Review* 33, no. 3 (2011): 473–87.

117. Alessandro Iandolo, *Arrested Development: The Soviet Union in Ghana, Guinea, and Mali, 1955–1968* (Ithaca, NY: Cornell University Press, 2022), 93–129.

118. Sanchez-Sibony, "Capitalism's Fellow Traveler," 305.

119. Sanchez-Sibony, *Red Globalization*, 130–34, 142–49; Guy Fiti Sinclair, *To Reform the World: International Organizations and the Making of Modern States* (Oxford: Oxford University Press, 2017), 221–26; David C. Engerman, *The Price of Aid: The Economic Cold War in India* (Cambridge, MA: Harvard University Press, 2018), especially chapter 2.

120. Young-Sun Hong, *Cold War Germany, the Third World, and the Global Humanitarian Regime* (Cambridge, UK: Cambridge University Press, 2017), 37–43.

121. Iandolo, "Rise and Fall," 684–86.

122. Constantin Katsakioris, "Soviet Lessons for Arab Modernization: Soviet Educational Aid to Arab Countries after 1956," *Journal of Modern European History* 8, no. 1 (2010): 85–105; Young-Sun Hong, *Cold War Germany*, 46–47; Iandolo, *Arrested Development*, 140–43.

123. Sanchez-Sibony, *Red Globalization*, 152–54.

124. Abou B. Bamba, "Displacing the French? Ivorian Development and the Question of Economic Decolonisation, 1946–1975," in Dimier and Stockwell, *Business of Development*, 275–300.

125. Young-Sun Hong, *Cold War Germany*, 40.

126. Iandolo, "Rise and Fall," 686–95; for the brief federation between Ghana and Guinea, see Adom Getachew, "Securing Postcolonial Independence: Kwame Nkrumah and the Federal Idea in the Age of Decolonization," *Ab Imperio* 3 (2018): 98–104.

127. Iandolo, "Rise and Fall," 699–701.

128. Natalia Telepneva, *Cold War Liberation: The Soviet Union and the Collapse of the Portuguese Empire in Africa, 1961–1975* (Chapel Hill: University of North Carolina Press, 2021), 88–89.

129. Sanchez-Sibony, "Cold War in the Margins of Capital," 59–79.

130. Gerold Krozewski, *Money and the End of Empire: British International Economic Policy and the Colonies, 1947–58* (Basingstoke, UK: Palgrave Macmillan, 2001), 171–86; idem, "Finance and Empire: The Dilemma Facing Great Britain in the 1950s," *International History Review* 18, no. 1 (1996): 48–69; David Howarth and Joachim Schild, "France and European Macroeconomic Policy Coordination: From the Treaty of Rome to the Euro Area Sovereign Debt Crisis," *Modern & Contemporary France* 25, no. 2 (2017): 171–74.

131. TNA, BT 11/2557, Board of Trade minute, "Article VIII of Monetary Fund," April 6, 1945; CAB 75/23/53, Financial Secretary to the Treasury memo, "Bretton Woods," November 2, 1945; T 160/238, Treasury Economic Advisory Section file: "Interpretation of the Bretton Woods Conference, 1944–5"; Michael D. Bordo, Dominique Simard, and Eugene White, "France and the Bretton Woods International Monetary System, 1960 to 1968," NBER Working Paper 4642, 1–6.

132. Guy Martin, "The Franc Zone: Underdevelopment and Dependency in Francophone Africa," *Third World Quarterly* 8, no. 1 (1986): 207–9, 220–22; Paul R. Mason and Catherine Pattillo, *The Monetary Geography of Africa* (New York: Brookings Institution Press, 2005), 15.

133. Steve Marsh, "The United States, Iran and Operation 'Ajax': Inverting Interpretative Orthodoxy," *Middle Eastern Studies* 39, no. 3 (2003): 1–38; Andreas Etges, "All that Glitters Is Not Gold: The 1953 Coup against Mohammed Mossadegh in Iran," *Intelligence & National Security* 26, no. 4 (2011): 495–508.

134. Stein Tønnesson, *Vietnam 1946: How the War Began* (Berkeley: University of California Press, 2010), 116–25.

135. Talbot Imlay, *The Practice of Socialist Internationalism: European Socialists and International Politics, 1914–1960* (Oxford: Oxford University Press, 2017), 410–22.

136. Frederick Cooper, *Citizenship between Empire and Nation: Rethinking France and French Africa, 1945–1960* (Princeton, NJ: Princeton University Press, 2014), 9–12, 294–306.

137. Sarah C. Dunstan, "'Une Negre de drame': Jane Vialle and the Politics of Representation in Colonial Reform, 1945–1953," *Journal of Contemporary History* 55, no. 3 (2020): 645–65; Jan C. Jansen and Jürgen Osterhammel, *Decolonization: A Short History* (Princeton, NJ: Princeton University Press, 2017), 104–5.

138. Early consideration of a regional bloc of sub-Saharan African territories tied into commercial and strategic partnership with the countries of Northwest Europe had included Britain. But as Britain distanced itself from the foundational arrangements of the EEC, ideas of *Eurafrique* assumed a more exclusively francophone character: Anne Deighton, "Entente Neo-Coloniale?: Ernest Bevin and the Proposals for an Anglo-French Third World Power, 1945–1949," *Diplomacy & Statecraft* 17, no. 4 (2006): 835–52; John Kent, *The Internationalization of Colonialism: Britain, France, and Black Africa, 1939–1956* (Oxford: Clarendon Press, 1992), chapters 7–8.

139. Cooper, *Citizenship between Empire and Nation*.

140. Stuart Ward, *Untied Kingdom: A Global History of the End of Britain* (Cambridge, UK: Cambridge University Press, 2023), 481–82.

141. Ronald Hyam, *Britain's Declining Empire: The Road to Decolonisation, 1918–1968* (Cambridge, UK: Cambridge University Press, 2006), 115–22.

142. Ian Brown, "The Economics of Decolonization in Burma," in *Africa, Empire, and Globalization: Essays in Honor of A. G. Hopkins*, ed. Toyin Falola and Emily Brownell (Durham, NC: Carolina Academic Press, 2011), 433–45; Hugh Tinker, "Burma's Struggle for Independence: The Transfer of Power Thesis Re-Examined," *Modern Asian Studies* 20, no. 3 (1986): 470–81.

143. Daniel Haines, "A 'Commonwealth Moment' in South Asian Decolonization," in *Decolonization and the Cold War: Negotiating Independence*, ed. Leslie James and Elisabeth Leake (London: Bloomsbury, 2015), 191–96.

144. TNA, FO 371/62419, UE170/170/53, FO Minute by Hall-Patch for Kenneth Anderson, India Office, "Economic Effects of Loss of India and Burma," January 1, 1947; John Darwin, *The Empire Project: The Rise and Fall of the British World-System, 1830–1970* (Cambridge, UK: Cambridge University Press, 2009), 539–40, 543–44, 553–54, 561; Marcelo de Paiva Abreu, "Britain as a Debtor: Indian Sterling Balances, 1940–53," *Economic History Review* 70, no. 2 (2017), 593–600. More remarkable as the Government of India was gearing up for war with Pakistan over Kashmir while, at the same time, struggling to avoid any repetition of the Bengal famine, a threat made more likely by a succession of weather-induced harvest failures as well as the disruption of South Asian food supply chains caused by partition; see Sherman, "From 'Grow More Food,'" 576–78, 583–84.

145. Abreu, "Britain as a Debtor," 591.

146. For officials' fears of a harder Indian government line, see India Office Private Office papers, L/PO/12/12: Correspondence with Sir Terence Shone, British High Commissioner to India, March 1947–May 1948, Shone letter to D. T. Monteath, India Office, May 13, 1947. On the Bengal famine and British responses, see Janam Mukherjee, *Hungry Bengal: War, Famine and the End of Empire* (London: Hurst, 2015), 11–16, 181–208; Joanna Simonow, "The Great Bengal Famine in Britain: Metropolitan Campaigning for Food Relief and the End of Empire, 1943–44," *Journal of Imperial & Commonwealth History* 48, no. 1 (2020): 168–85.

147. Abreu, "Britain as a Debtor," 592–94.

148. Kennetta Hammond Perry, *London Is the Place for Me: Black Britons, Citizenship and the Politics of Race* (Oxford: Oxford University Press, 2015), 48–51, 57–60; Sarah Ansari, "Subjects or Citizens? India, Pakistan and the 1948 British Nationality Act," *Journal of Imperial & Commonwealth History* 41, no. 2 (2013): 286–99.

149. Ward, *Untied Kingdom*, 164, and, for the precedent set by Canada's 1946 Citizenship Act: 175.

150. Jordanna Bailkin, *The Afterlife of Empire* (Berkeley: University of California Press, 2012), 164–201; Christian Ydesen and Kevin Myers, "The Imperial Welfare State? Decolonisation, Education, and Professional Interventions on Immigrant Children in Birmingham, 1948–1971," *Paedagogica Historica* 52, no. 5 (2016): 456–66.

151. Wendy Webster, *Mixing It: Diversity in World War Two Britain* (Oxford: Oxford University Press, 2018), 118–19, 233–34, 239–44.

152. Elizabeth Buettner, "Toxic Comfort Blanket: Imperial Delusion in Modern Britain," *Times Literary Supplement*, September 28, 2018, 13.

153. Su Sin Lewis, "Asian Socialism and the Forgotten Architects of Post-Colonial Freedom, 1952–1956," *Journal of World History* 30, no. 1 (2019): 60–69.

154. First enunciated in 1953, the ASC argument that national liberation was the necessary prelude to leftist internationalism won acceptance among Western Europe's socialist parties as war in Algeria intensified after 1955: Imlay, *Practice of Socialist Internationalism*, 435–44; Lewis, "Asian Socialism," 74–78.

155. Imlay, *Practice of Socialist Internationalism*, 421–28.

156. Imlay, *Practice of Socialist Internationalism*, 429–32, 435.

157. Imlay, *Practice of Socialist Internationalism*, 413–18.

158. Imlay, *Practice of Socialist Internationalism*, 427–29.

159. TNA, FO 371/84524, F2108/1, "British Policy in Asia," speech by Minister of State Kenneth Younger at Foreign Policy Association lunch, New York, December 2, 1950.

160. Imlay, *Practice of Socialist Internationalism*, 418–21.

161. Imlay, *Practice of Socialist Internationalism*, 419.

162. Jessica Lynne Pearson, *The Colonial Politics of Global Health: France and the United Nations in Postwar Africa* (Cambridge, MA: Harvard University Press, 2018), 23–30, 34–36; Jennifer Johnson, *The Battle for Algeria: Sovereignty, Health Care, and Humanitarianism* (Philadelphia: University of Pennsylvania Press, 2016), 40–42, 48–61.

163. Pearson, *Colonial Politics*, 34.

164. Pearson, *Colonial Politics*, 38–42. This was a lesson learned by members of the French Army's psychological warfare division, which insisted that modernization risked antagonizing its Muslim subjects, women especially. See Yves Godard papers, Hoover Institution, box 3, "Septième Conférence: Corps des Officiers des affaires militaires musulmanes, La femme musulmane."

165. Anne Phillips, "Global Justice: Just Another Modernisation Theory?" in *Empire, Race, and Global Justice*, ed. Duncan Bell (Cambridge, UK: Cambridge University Press, 2019), 149; Sherman, "From 'Grow More Food,'" 577–82; Jennings, "'A Very Real War,'" 75–80, 86–88.

166. Packard, "Malaria Dreams," 281, 283, 287–91.

167. Young-Sun Hong, *Cold War Germany*, 30–47.

168. A brilliant analysis of competition between 'First' and 'Second' World development providers to the Third World is Young-Sun Hong, *Cold War Germany*.

169. Packard, "Malaria Dreams," 291–97; Packard, "Visions of Postwar Health," 96–108.

170. Sunil S. Amrith, "Internationalising Health in the Twentieth Century," in *Internationalisms: A Twentieth Century History*, ed. Glenda Sluga and Patricia Clavin (Cambridge, UK: Cambridge University Press, 2016), 255–59. Somalia witnessed the final epidemic of smallpox in 1977. The Western backlash against DDT, strongly associated with the 1962 publication of Rachel Carson's *Silent Spring*, was already gathering momentum within societies directly affected by spraying programs; see Jacob Darwin Hamblin, *Arming Mother Nature: The Birth of Catastrophic Environmentalism* (Oxford: Oxford University Press, 2013), 72, 164–65.

171. Packard, "Malaria Dreams," 291. Young-Sun Hong makes a similar point about the assumptions behind epidemiological campaigns in the global South in *Cold War Germany*, 19–23.

172. Amrith, "Internationalising Health," 255–59, quote at 255; Young-Sun Hong, *Cold War Germany*, 25–28.

173. Although, as Matthew Connelly points out, in the early 1950s the WHO's directorate shied away from promoting prophylactic birth control, fearful of antagonizing Catholic member states; see Matthew Connelly, "Seeing beyond the State: The Population Control Movement and the Problem of Sovereignty," *Past and Present* 193 (November 2006): 218–19.

174. Roger Jeffery, *The Politics of Health in India* (Berkeley: University of California Press, 1988), 189–217.

175. Marcos Cueto, Theodore M. Brown, and Elizabeth Fee, *The World Health Organization: A History* (Cambridge, UK: Cambridge University Press, 2019), 86–145.

176. Ana Antic, *Non-Aligned Psychiatry in the Cold War: Revolution, Emancipation and Re-Imagining the Human Psyche* (Basingstoke: Palgrave Macmillan, 2022), chapters 3–5; Hans Pols, *Nurturing Indonesia: Medicine and Decolonisation in the Dutch East Indies* (Cambridge, UK: Cambridge University Press, 2018), 204–28.

177. Sung Lee, "WHO and the Developing World: The Contest for Ideology," in *Western Medicine as Contested Knowledge*, ed. Andrew Cunningham and Bridie Andrews (Manchester, UK: Manchester University Press, 1997), 24–45.

178. Mark T. Berger, "Decolonisation, Modernisation and Nation-Building: Political Development Theory and the Appeal of Communism in Southeast Asia, 1945-1975," *Journal of Southeast Asian Studies* 34, no. 3 (2003): 421–48; Nathan J. Citino, *Envisioning the Arab Future: Modernization in U.S.-Arab Relations, 1945-1967* (Cambridge, UK: Cambridge University Press, 2017), 6–8, 65–84.

179. Debra Thompson, "Through, against, and beyond the Racial State: The Transnational Stratum of Race," in *Race and Racism: Confronting the Global Colour Line*, ed. Alexander Anievas, Nivi Manchanda, and Robbie Shilliam (London: Routledge, 2014), 52.

180. John M. Hobson, "Re-Embedding the Global Colour Line within Post-1945 International Theory," in Anievas, Manchanda and Shilliam, *Race and Racism*, 81–97, at 83.

Chapter Thirteen: Political Economies of Decolonization II: The 1950s and 1960s

1. Roland Burke, "The Internationalism of Human Rights," in *Internationalisms: A Twentieth Century History*, ed. Glenda Sluga and Patricia Clavin (Cambridge, UK: Cambridge University Press, 2016), 287–90, quote at 287.

2. Burke, "Internationalism of Human Rights," 294–95.

3. Roland Burke, *Decolonization and the Evolution of International Human Rights* (Philadelphia: University of Pennsylvania Press, 2010), 116–21; idem, "'A World Made Safe for Diversity': Apartheid and the Language of Human Rights, Progress, and Pluralism," in *Decolonization, Self Determination, and the Rise of Global Human Rights Politics*, ed. A. Dirk Moses, Marco Duranti, and Roland Burke (Cambridge, UK: Cambridge University Press, 2020), 320–21.

4. Eric D. Weitz, "Self-Determination: How a German Enlightenment Idea Became the Slogan of National Liberation and a Human Right," *American Historical Review* 20, no. 2 (2015): 489–92.

5. Brad Simpson, "The United States and the Curious History of Self-Determination," *Diplomatic History* 36, no. 4 (2012): 677–82.

6. Burke, "Internationalism of Human Rights," 301–2.

7. P. K. MacDonald and J. M. Parent, "Graceful Decline? The Surprising Success of Great Power Retrenchment," *International Security* 35, no. 4 (2011): 7–44.

8. George C. Peden, "Recognising and Responding to Relative Decline: The Case of Post-War Britain," *Diplomacy & Statecraft* 24, no. 1 (2013): 65–72; Frederick Cooper, *Decolonization and African Society: The Labor Question in French and British Africa* (Cambridge, UK: Cambridge University Press, 1996), 392–400; A. G. Hopkins, *American Empire: A Global History* (Princeton, NJ: Princeton University Press, 2018), 484–85.

9. Exceptions for the British Empire are Krozewski, *Money and the End of Empire: British International Economic Policy and the Colonies, 1947–58* (Basingstoke, UK: Palgrave Macmillan, 2001); idem, "Finance and Empire: The Dilemma Facing Great Britain in the 1950s," *International History Review* 18, no. 1 (1996): 48–69; and Steven G. Galpern, *Money, Oil and Empire in the Middle East: Sterling and Postwar Imperialism, 1944–1971* (Cambridge, Cambridge University Press, 2009).

10. David French, "Duncan Sandys and the Projection of British Power after Suez," *Diplomacy & Statecraft* 24, no. 1 (2013): 41–52. Britain mounted three such expeditionary operations between 1958 and 1964, the first to bolster Jordan's King Hussein in July 1958, a second to Kuwait three years later to deter an Iraqi invasion, and a third to East Africa in January 1964 to support the governments of Kenya, Uganda, and Tanzania against potential army coups.

11. Peden, "Recognising," 60–61.

12. Catherine R. Schenk, "The Origins of the Eurodollar Market in London, 1955–63," *Explorations in Economic History* 35, no. 2 (1998): 221–38.

13. Vanessa Ogle, "Archipelago Capitalism: Tax Havens, Offshore Money, and the State, 1950s–1970s," *American Historical Review* 122, no. 5 (2017): 1437–38, 1445–47.

14. Nicholas J. White, "Reconstructing Europe through Rejuvenating Empire: The British, French, and Dutch Experiences Compared," *Past & Present* 210, Supplement 6 (2011): 214–16.

15. Ogle, "Archipelago Capitalism," 1438–45; idem, " 'Funk Money': The End of Empires, the Expansion of Tax Havens, and Decolonization as an Economic and Financial Event," 249, no. 1 (2020): 216–17, 226–32. Ogle ranks Malta, Bahrain, Singapore, the Channel Islands, and the New Hebrides among the most significant British-linked tax havens developed from the 1950s onward, alongside their more familiar counterparts in various Caribbean Island territories.

16. Sarah Stockwell makes the argument succinctly, identifying the 1950s as the critical decade in Britain's economic decolonization. See her "Trade, Empire, and the Fiscal Context of Imperial Business during Decolonization," *Economic History Review* 57, no. 1 (2004): 142–60, at 143–44.

17. Anthony Hopkins, "Macmillan's Audit of Empire, 1957," in *Understanding Decline: Perceptions and Realities of British Economic Performance*, ed. Peter Clarke and Clive Trebilcock (Cambridge, UK: Cambridge University Press, 1997), 234–60.

18. Peden, "Recognising," 65.

19. Hopkins, "Macmillan's Audit," 241–42, 246–48.

20. Hopkins, "Macmillan's Audit," 234–60.

21. Nicholas J. White, *Business, Government, and the End of Empire: Malaya, 1942–1957* (Kuala Lumpur: Oxford University Press, 1996), 36–38; idem, "The Business and the Politics of Decolonization: The British Experience in the Twentieth Century," *Economic History Review*, 53, no. 3 (2000): 545–46.

22. Nicholas J. White, "Decolonisation in the 1950s: The Version According to British Business," in *The British Empire in the 1950s: Retreat or Revival?* ed. Martin Lynn (Basingstoke, UK: Palgrave Macmillan, 2006), 100.

23. White, *Business, Government*, 120; also cited in Stockwell, "Trade, Empire, and the Fiscal Context," 146; for anxieties within Britain's colonial business communities in the 1950s about being 'sold out' by their metropolitan government: White, "Business and the Politics," 554–57.

24. Sarah Stockwell, "The 'Know-How of the World Is Mainly with Private Companies': The Commonwealth Development Corporation and British Business in Post-Colonial Africa," in *The Business of Development in Post-Colonial Africa*, ed. Véronique Dimier and Sarah Stockwell (Basingstoke, UK: Palgrave Macmillan, 2020), 189–200.

25. White, "Decolonisation in the 1950s," 103, 105–11.

26. Stockwell, "Trade, Empire, and the Fiscal Context," 150–59.

27. Matthew Connelly, *Diplomatic Revolution: Algeria's Fight for Independence and the Origins of the Post–Cold War Era* (New York: Oxford University Press, 2002), parts III and IV; Todd Shepard, *The Invention of Decolonization: The Algerian War and the Remaking of France* (Ithaca, NY: Cornell University Press, 2006), 60–61.

28. Ogle, "'Funk Money,'" 219–25, 246–47.

29. Ogle, "'Funk Money,'" 228–31, 236–37.

30. David M. Anderson and Daniel Branch, "Allies at the End of Empire: Loyalists, Nationalists and the Cold War, 1945–1976," *International History Review* 39, no. 1 (2016): 1–13.

31. Shepard, *Invention of Decolonization*, 114–15, 140–42.

32. Cooper, *Citizenship between Empire and Nation*, 326–49.

33. François Pacquement, "Decolonising Finance, Africanising Banking," in Dimier and Stockwell, *Business of Development*, 213–28.

34. Achille Mbembe, *La naissance du maquis dans le Sud-Cameroun (1920–1960)* (Paris: Karthala, 1996), 349–57.

35. Stuart Ward "'No Nation Could Be Broker': The Satire Boom and the Demise of Britain's World Role," in *British Culture and the End of Empire*, ed. Stuart Ward (Manchester, UK: Manchester University Press, 2001), 91–99.

36. Peden, "Recognising," 72.

37. Saki Dockrill, *Britain's Retreat from East of Suez: The Choice between Europe and the World?* (Basingstoke, UK: Palgrave Macmillan, 2002), 105–19, 186–88; Rolf Steininger, "'The Americans Are in a Hopeless Position': Britain and the War in Vietnam, 1964–65," *Diplomacy & Statecraft* 8, no. 3 (1997): 237–48, 252–54.

38. Richard Coggins, "Wilson and Rhodesia: UDI and British Policy towards Africa," *Contemporary British History* 20, no. 3 (2006): 363–70; Carl Watts, "Britain, the Old Commonwealth, and the Problem of Rhodesian Independence, 1964–65,"

Journal of Imperial & Commonwealth History 36, no. 1 (2008): 83–90; Dockrill, *Britain's Retreat*, 178–85; Jeffrey Pickering, *Britain's Withdrawal from East of Suez: The Politics of Retrenchment* (Basingstoke, UK: Palgrave Macmillan, 1998), 32–34, 150–74.

39. Martin Farr, "Swinging Imperialism: Days in the Life of the Commonwealth Office, 1966–1968," in *The MacKenzie Moment and Imperial History: Essays in Honour of John M. MacKenzie*, ed. Stephanie L. Barczewski and Martin Farr (Cham: Palgrave Macmillan, 2019), chapter 5.

40. Daniel Sargent, "Lyndon Johnson and the Challenges of Economic Globalization," in *Beyond the Cold War: Lyndon Johnson and the New Global Challenges of the 1960s*, ed. Francis J. Gavin and Mark Atwood Lawrence (Oxford: Oxford University Press, 2014), 24–28, 32–36.

41. Ronen Palan, "The Second British Empire and the Re-Emergence of Global Finance," in *Legacies of Empire: Imperial Roots of the Contemporary Global Order*, ed. Sandra Halperin and Ronen Palan (Cambridge, UK: Cambridge University Press, 2015), 46–47.

42. Schenk, "Origins of the Eurodollar Market," 221–23. As Schenk points out, British banks had a longer history of accumulating hard currency deposits stretching back to the interwar years. But the lifting of postwar exchange controls, plus greater sterling convertibility after December 1958 differentiated the Eurodollar market in scale. Meanwhile, the use made of the Euromarket's dollar deposits to finance third party loans set it apart in activity, making it the principal source of global lending capital by the early 1960s.

43. Schenk, "The Origins of the Eurodollar Market," 224–29. Schenk acknowledges the relevance of these restrictions but traces the Eurodollar market to innovative measures by Britain's Midland Bank in 1955–1956 to attract foreign capital for short-term lending and interest rate arbitrage.

44. Palan, "Second British Empire," 53–56.

45. Schenk, "Origins of the Eurodollar Market," 233–37.

46. Oscar Sanchez-Sibony, *Red Globalization: The Political Economy of the Soviet Cold War from Stalin to Khrushchev* (Cambridge, UK: Cambridge University Press, 2014), 73.

47. An exponent of this view is Palan, "Second British Empire," 46–68.

48. Thomas McCarthy, *Race, Empire, and the Idea of Human Development* (Cambridge, UK: Cambridge University Press, 2009), 194–97, 203–7.

49. Mark T. Berger, "Decolonisation, Modernisation and Nation-Building: Political Development Theory and the Appeal of Communism in Southeast Asia, 1945–1975," *Journal of Southeast Asian Studies* 34, no. 3 (2003): 422. *Guerrilla Communism in Malaya: Its Social and Political Meaning*, a 1956 book by Lucian W. Pye, a founding member of an early academic forum for modernization theorists, the Committee on Comparative Politics, drew interest from the Eisenhower administration. In his own work, an Indonesia specialist, Clifford Geertz, addressed a challenge of modernization theory—how to overcome ethnic attachments in pursuit of new nation-building efforts. Walt Whitman Rostow, a former member of the Office of Strategic Services and the leading modernization theorist among a large team at MIT, would head the State Department's policy planning staff under President Kennedy, later

serving as Lyndon Johnson's national security adviser; see Berger, "Decolonisation," 432–38.

50. Prasenjit Duara, "The Cold War as a Historical Period: An Interpretative Essay," *Journal of Global History* 6 (2011): 473–75.

51. Berger, "Decolonisation," 425–26; Tom Robertson, "'Thinking Globally': American Foreign Aid, Paul Ehrlich, and the Emergence of Environmentalism in the 1960s," in *Beyond the Cold War*, ed. Francis J. Gavin and Mark Atwood Lawrence (Oxford: Oxford University Press, 2014), 186–96; Michael E. Latham, *Modernization as Ideology: American Social Science and "Nation Building" in the Kennedy Era* (Chapel Hill: University of North Carolina Press, 2000); Philip E. Muehlenbeck, *Betting on the Africans: John F. Kennedy's Courting of African Nationalist Leaders* (New York, Oxford University Press, 2012).

52. Duara, "Cold War as a Historical Period," 463–64.

53. Berger, "Decolonisation," 439–40; Simon Toner, "'The Life and Death of Our Republic': Modernization, Agricultural Development and the Peasantry in the Mekong Delta in the Long 1970s," in *Decolonization and the Cold War: Negotiating Independence*, ed. Leslie James and Elisabeth Leake (London: Bloomsbury, 2015), 43–52; Bradley R. Simpson, *Economists with Guns: Authoritarian Development and U.S.-Indonesian Relations, 1960–1968* (Stanford, CA: Stanford University Press, 2010). For the technocratic ideas undergirding these policy prescriptions, see Michael Adas, *Dominance by Design: Technological Imperatives and America's Civilizing Mission* (Cambridge, MA: Harvard University Press, 2006).

54. Wm. Roger Louis and Ronald Robinson, "The Imperialism of Decolonization," *Journal of Imperial & Commonwealth History* 22, no. 3 (1994): 462–511.

55. Robert McMahon, *Colonialism and Cold War: The United States and the Struggle for Indonesian Independence, 1945–49* (Ithaca, NY: Cornell University Press, 1981); Kathryn C. Statler, *Replacing France: The Origins of American Intervention in Vietnam* (Lexington: University Press of Kentucky, 2007), part III; David Stenner, *Globalizing Morocco: Transnational Activism and the Postcolonial State* (Stanford, CA: Stanford University Press, 2019), 2–9, 195–96; Irwin M. Wall, *France, the United States, and the Algerian War* (Berkeley: University of California Press, 2001), 99–156.

56. Latham, *Modernization as Ideology*, chapters 2 and 5; David C. Engerman et al., eds., *Staging Growth: Modernization, Development, and the Global Cold War* (Amherst: University of Massachusetts Press, 2003).

57. Alfred W. McCoy, "Torture in the Crucible of Counterinsurgency," in *Iraq and the Lessons of Vietnam: Or, How Not to Learn from the Past*, ed. Lloyd C. Gardner and Marilyn B. Young (New York: New Press, 2007); Jeremy Kuzmarov, "Modernizing Repression: Police Training, Political Violence, and Nation-Building in the 'American Century,'" *Diplomatic History* 33, no. 2 (2009): 201–7; idem, *Modernizing Repression: Police Training and Nation-Building in the American Century* (Amherst: University of Massachusetts Press, 2012), parts II and III.

58. Wen-Qing Ngoei, *Arc of Containment: Britain, the United States, and Anticommunism in Southeast Asia* (Ithaca, NY: Cornell University Press, 2019), 93–96.

59. Wen-Qing Ngoei, *Arc of Containment*, 104–7.

60. Bryan L. McDonald, *Food Power: The Rise and Fall of the Postwar American Food System* (New York: Oxford University Press, 2017), 145–54.

61. Nick Cullather, "LBJ's Third War: The War on Hunger," in Gavin and Lawrence, *Beyond the Cold War*, 123. The Johnson administration also applied a 'short leash' strategy toward population control, pushing India into a larger sterilization program: see Matthew Connelly, "LBJ and World Population: Planning the Greater Society One Family at a Time," in *Beyond the Cold War*, 150–55.

62. Adom Getachew, "Securing Postcolonial Independence: Kwame Nkrumah and the Federal Idea in the Age of Decolonization," *Ab Imperio* 3 (2018): 93–99; Kwame Nkrumah, *Neo-Colonialism: The Last Stage of Imperialism* (London: Thames Nelson, 1965).

63. Young-Sun Hong, *Cold War Germany, the Third World, and the Global Humanitarian Regime* (Cambridge, UK: Cambridge University Press, 2017), 295–99, 305–7; Emma Hunter, *Political Thought and the Public Sphere in Tanzania: Freedom, Democracy and Citizenship in the Era of Decolonisation* (Cambridge, UK: Cambridge University Press, 2015), 210–30.

64. Getachew, "Securing Postcolonial Independence," 98–104.

65. Adom Getachew, *Worldmaking after Empire: The Rise and Fall of Self-Determination* (Princeton, NJ: Princeton University Press, 2019), 108.

66. Amber Huff and Lyla Mehta, "Untangling Scarcity," in *Scarcity in the Modern World: History, Politics, Society and Sustainability, 1800–2075*, ed. Fredrik Albritton Jonsson (London: Bloomsbury, 2019), 33–35, 38–41.

67. Christy Thornton, "A Mexican International Economic Order? Tracing the Hidden Roots of the Charter of Economic Rights and Duties of States," *Humanity* 9, no. 3 (2018): 389–96.

68. Giuliano Garavini, *After Empires: European Integration, Decolonization, and the Challenge from the Global South 1957–1986* (Oxford: Oxford University Press, 2012), 25–27.

69. Garavini, *After Empires*, 35–42; Christoph Kalter, *The Discovery of the Third World: Decolonization and the Rise of the New Left in France c. 1950–1976* (Cambridge, UK: Cambridge University Press, 2016), 48–50; Getachew, *Worldmaking*, 151–60.

70. Stephen G. Rabe, *The Killing Zone: The United States Wages Cold War in Latin America* (Oxford: Oxford University Press, 2012), 86–97. As laid out at an August 1961 inter-American conference in the Uraguayan resort of Punta del Este, the Alliance for Progress promised $20 billion in US investment to Latin America over ten years. Issued as loan capital, the program delivered $15 billion to favored client states. Tilted toward anticommunist authoritarian regimes, the Alliance for Progress also failed to keep pace with Latin America's rapid population growth.

71. D. K. Fieldhouse, *Merchant Capital and Economic Decolonization: The United Africa Company 1929–1987* (Oxford: Clarendon Press, 1994); Catherine Coquery-Vidrovitch, "L'Impact des intérêts coloniaux: S.C.O.A. et C.F.A.O. dans l'Ouest Africain, 1910–1965," *Journal of African History* 16, no. 4 (1975): 595–621.

72. As Phia Steyn shows, as early as 1904 the Conservative Party government decided to reserve future oil concessions in Britain's empire to British-owned companies. Eight years later Winston Churchill, serving as First Lord of the Admiralty, committed the Royal Navy to oil, rejecting arguments in favor of coal-fired warships. For all that, until the First World War Westminster remained remarkably *laissez-faire*

about the development of the British Empire as a global oil producer. It was left to private investors, initially small oil exploration companies, later the two British-controlled majors, Royal Dutch/Shell and British Petroleum, to take the lead. Phia Steyn, "Oil Exploration in Colonial Nigeria, c. 1903–58," *Journal of Imperial & Commonwealth History* 37, no. 2 (2009): 249–72, at 251–57. See also Edward Peter Fitzgerald, "The Power of the Weak and the Weakness of the Strong: Explaining Corporate Behavior in Middle Eastern Oil after the Second World War," *Business and Economic History Review* 23, no. 2 (1994): 108–28.

73. In British Africa, for instance, only after another World War and desperately short of dollar earnings did British ministers, Colonial Office planners, and the local colonial administration back oil exploration in Southeastern Nigeria. Initially operating secretively and in the teeth of local opposition coordinated by Dr. Nnamdi Azikiwe's National Council for Nigeria and the Cameroons (NCNC), it would be more than a decade before commercially viable oil deposits came on stream in Nigeria. By the time the first Nigerian oil shipments sailed for Rotterdam in 1958, the colonial administration had agreed to a local profit-sharing scheme with Royal Dutch/Shell that diluted nationalist opposition to what originally seemed like classic colonial extraction; see Steyn, "Oil Exploration," 261–65. On the 'Red Line Agreement' between British, US and French oil companies governing oil exploitation in Iraq between 1928 and 1947, see Anand Toprani, "The French Connection: A New Perspective on the End of the Red Line Agreement, 1945–1948," *Diplomatic History* 36, no. 2 (2012): 261–64.

74. As host of the Third Session of the United Nations Conference on Trade and Development (UNCTAD) in Santiago, Chile's Salvador Allende made this connection in his opening address on April 13, 1972. See Sundhya Pahuja, "Corporations, Universalism and the Domestication of Race in International Law," in *Empire, Race, and Global Justice*, ed. Duncan Bell (Cambridge, UK: Cambridge University Press, 2019), 79–80.

75. John Kent, *America, the UN and Decolonisation: Cold War Conflict in the Congo* (London: Routledge, 2011), 87–89, 100–3; David N. Gibbs, *The Political Economy of Third World Intervention: Mines, Money, and U.S. Policy in the Congo Crisis* (Chicago: University of Chicago Press, 1991).

76. Charlotte Strick, "Belgian Firms, Development Plans and the Independence of the Belgian Congo," in Dimier and Stockwell, *Business of Development*, 99–120.

77. Garavini, *After Empires*, 32–35.

78. Heloise Weber and Poppy Winanti, "The 'Bandung Spirit' and Solidarist Internationalism," *Australian Journal of International Affairs* 70, no. 4 (2016): 401–2. Completed in 1971, the best-known statement of this view remains Walter Rodney, *How Europe Underdeveloped Africa* (London: Bogle-L'Ouverture Publications, 1972).

79. IISH, COLL00201, Algeria, folder 4, *El Moudjahid* study, "The Requirements of National Development," published December 21, 1961, circulated by GPRA, New York.

80. IISH, African Labour History archive (ARCH02615), file 60: 1969–87, North and North Eastern Africa, Hugh Roberts, "The Sociology of Algerian State Capitalism," 42–106.

81. J. N. C. Hill, "Challenging the Failed State Thesis: IMF and World Bank Intervention and the Algerian Civil War," *Civil Wars* 11, no. 1 (2009): 46–50; David Sogge,

"Angola: Reinventing Pasts and Futures," *Review of African Political Economy* 38, no. 127 (2011): 85–91; Werner Biermann and Jumanne Wagoo, "The Quest for Adjustment: Tanzania and the IMF, 1980–1986," *African Studies Review* 29, no. 4 (1986): 89–96; D. A. Dunkley, "Hegemony in Post-Independence Jamaica," *Caribbean Quarterly* 57, no. 2 (2011): 1–4, 10–12; Odd Arne Westad, *The Global Cold War: Third World Interventions and the Making of Our Times* (Cambridge, UK: Cambridge University Press, 2005), 359–62; Giuliano Garavini, "Completing Decolonization: The 1973 'Oil Shock' and the Struggle for Economic Rights," *International History Review* 33, no. 3 (2011): 484.

82. Getachew, *Worldmaking*, 160–68.

83. Gregory Mann, *From Empires to NGOs in the West African Sahel: The Road to Nongovernmentality* (Cambridge, UK: Cambridge University Press), 75–78.

84. Gareth Curless, "Violence and (Dis)Order in the Caribbean Post-Colony," in *The Oxford Handbook of Late Colonial Insurgencies and Counter-Insurgencies*, ed. Martin Thomas and Gareth Curless (Oxford: Oxford University Press, 2023), 726–48.

85. Getachew, "Securing Postcolonial Independence," 104–11.

86. Garavini, "Completing Decolonization," 475–79.

87. Jennifer Bair, "Corporations at the United Nations: Echoes of the New International Economic Order," *Humanity:* 6, no. 1 (2015): 159–60.

88. Garavini, "Completing Decolonization," 473–75.

89. Getachew, *Worldmaking*, 142–46, 151–60, quote at 168.

90. Pahuja, "Corporations," 81–83; Bair, "Corporations at the United Nations," 159–71.

91. The argument that capitalist intrusion and Western financial control of global commodity markets were root causes of structural inequality and poverty in the global South was elaborated by Argentine economist and head of the United Nations' Economic Commission for Latin America Raúl Prebisch in a 1950 report on the Commission on Latin America's development challenges. The ideas of Prebisch and other dependency theorists were adopted by the Non-Aligned Movement in the early 1960s, becoming the guiding philosophy of the Group of 77 (G77) and its UN arm, the United Nations Conference for Trade and Development (UNCTAD); see Garavini, *After Empires*, 25–27, 35–42; Kalter, *Discovery of the Third World*, 48–50.

92. Garavini, *After Empires*, 178; Getachew, *Worldmaking*, 166–69.

93. Garavini, *After Empires*, 175–77; Jeffrey James Byrne, *Mecca of Revolution: Algeria, Decolonization, & the Third World Order* (Oxford: Oxford University Press, 2019), 295.

94. Johanna Bockman, "Socialist Globalization against Capitalist Neocolonialism: The Economic Ideas behind the New International Economic Order," *Humanity* 6, no. 1 (2015): 109–28.

95. Thornton, "Mexican New International," 302–8, 318–26; Christy Thornton, *Revolution in Development: Mexico and the Governance of the Global Economy* (Berkeley: University of California Press, 2021), 166–72; Garavini, *After Empires*, 182.

96. Thornton, *Revolution in Development*, 173–88, 190–91. Defying the United Nations' December 12, 1974, adoption of the Charter as UNGA resolution 3281, the US government voted against it.

97. Daniel J. Sargent, *A Superpower Transformed: The Remaking of American Foreign Relations in the 1970s* (Oxford: Oxford University Press, 2015), 177–82.

98. Getachew, *Worldmaking*, 160–71. As writers on human rights have suggested, the NIEO's advocates also derided western supporters of human rights as servants of neocolonialism: Roland Burke, Marco Duranti, and A. Dirk Moses, "Introduction: Human Rights, Empire, and after," in *Decolonization, Self Determination, and the Rise of Global Human Rights Politics*, ed. A. Dirk Moses, Marco Duranti, and Roland Burke (Cambridge, UK: Cambridge University Press, 2020), 18.

99. Pahuja, "Corporations," 90.

100. Bair, "Corporations at the United Nations," 161–69. Pursuant to UN Resolution 3201, establishing the NIEO, a subsequent UN Resolution (1913 of December 1974) created both the Intergovernmental Commission and an Information and Research Center on Transnational Corporations under the umbrella of the UN Economic and Social Council. Their focus remained on the operations of multinational companies, but in their initial activities the Commission and Information and Research Center lent weight to attempts by NIEO-supporting states to secure debt adjustments, technology transfer and sovereign control over economic resources. As it became clearer that these goals would not be realized, the Commission shifted its attention to questions of corporate responsibility for human rights protections.

101. Pahuja, "Corporations," 88–92; Bair, "Corporations at the United Nations," 162.

102. Richard L. Bernal, "The IMF and Class Struggle in Jamaica, 1977–1980," *Latin American Perspectives* 11, no. 3 (Summer 1984): 53–58, 61–70; Getachew, *Worldmaking*, 172–73.

103. For contemporary parallels in the so-called Wall Street consensus on private lending to global South nations, see Yannis Dafermos, Daniela Gabor, and Jo Michell, "The Wall Street Consensus in Pandemic Times: What Does It Mean for Climate-Aligned Development?" *Canadian Journal of Development Studies* 42, no. 1–2 (2021): 241–47; Jason Hickel, Dylan Hickel, and Huzaifa Zoomkawala, "Plunder in the Post-Colonial Era: Quantifying Drain from the Global South through Unequal Exchange, 1960–2018," *New Political Economy* 26, no. 6 (2021): 1030–47.

104. Hicke, Hickel, and Zoomkawala, "Plunder," 1031–38.

105. Genevieve Lebaron and Alison Y. Ayers, "The Rise of a 'New Slavery'? Understanding African Unfree Labour through Neoliberalism," *Third World Quarterly* 34, no. 5 (2013): 879–83.

106. Jeffrey James Byrne, "Africa's Cold War," in *The Cold War in the Third World*, ed. Robert J. McMahon (Oxford: Oxford University Press, 2013), 103, 111–17.

107. John Walton and David Seddon, *Free Markets and Food Riots: The Politics of Global Adjustment* (Oxford: Blackwell, 1994), 10–22, 137–46, 171–91.

Chapter Fourteen: Conference Cultures and Third-World Decolonization

1. For the 'Third World' construction, see Christoph Kalter, "A Shared Space of Imagination, Communication, and Action: Perspectives on the History of the 'Third World,'" in *The Third World and the Global 1960s*, ed. Samantha Christiansen and Zachary A. Scarlett (Oxford: Berghahn, 2013), 23–34.

2. Odd Arne Westad, *The Global Cold War: Third World Interventions and the Making of Our Times* (Cambridge, UK: Cambridge University Press, 2005); Philip E. Muehlenbeck and Natalia Telepneva, "Introduction," in *Warsaw Pact Intervention in the Third World: Aid and Influence in the Cold War*, ed. idem (London: I. B. Tauris, 2018), 1–10; Greg Grandin, *The Last Colonial Massacre: Latin America in the Cold War* (Chicago: University of Chicago Press, 2004); Greg Grandin and Gilbert M. Joseph, eds., *A Century of Revolution: Insurgent and Counterinsurgent Violence during Latin America's Long Cold War* (Durham, NC: Duke University Press, 2010).

3. Joseph Hodge, "Writing the History of Development (Part 2: Longer, Deeper, Wider)," *Humanity:* 7, no. 1 (2016), 125–74; *Staging Growth: Modernization, Development, and the Global Cold War*, ed. David C. Engerman et al. (Amherst: University of Massachusetts Press, 2003); Jeffrey James Byrne, *Mecca of Revolution: Algeria, Decolonization, & the Third World Order* (Oxford: Oxford University Press, 2019), 70–73, 115–16.

4. MAE, série Afrique-Levant, sous-série: Généralités, 1944–52, file 65: Politique soviétique en Afrique, 1949–52, no. 300/AL, Yves Chataigneau to Robert Schuman, "De l'Afrique en particulier, 'des colonies et pays dépendants' en général," March 21, 1950.

5. Jordan Baev, "Bulgarian Military and Humanitarian Aid to Third World Countries, 1955–75," in Muehlenbeck and Telepneva, *Warsaw Pact*, 299; Ana Antic, "Imagining Africa in Eastern Europe: Transcultural Psychiatry and Psychoanalysis in Cold War Yugoslavia," *Contemporary European History* 28, no. 2 (2019): 234–45, 249–51.

6. Iris Borowy, "Medicine, Economics and Foreign Policy: East German Medical Academics in the Global South during the 1950s and 1960s," in Muehlenbeck and Telepneva, *Warsaw Pact*, 178–89; John M. Kirk, "Cuban Medical Internationalism and Its Role in Cuban Foreign Policy," *Diplomacy & Statecraft* 20, no. 2 (2009): 275–78; Piero Gleijeses, *Conflicting Missions: Havana, Washington and Africa, 1959–1976* (Chapel Hill: University of North Carolina Press, 2003), 166–69, 199–203.

7. Mangeet K. Ramgotra, "Post-Colonial Republicanism and the Revival of a Paradigm," *The Good Society* 26, no. 1 (2018): 42–43.

8. Rachel Leow, "A Missing Peace: The Asia-Pacific Peace Conference in Beijing, 1952 and the Emotional Making of Third World Internationalism," *Journal of World History* 30, no. 1–2 (2019): 21–34.

9. Patrick Iber, "From Peace to National Liberation: Mexico and the Tricontinental," in Prakash and Adelman, *Inventing the Third World: In Search of Freedom for the Postwar Global South*, 47–48.

10. Carolien Stolte, "'The People's Bandung': Local Anti-Imperialists on an Afro-Asian Stage," *Journal of World History* 30, no. 1–2 (2019): 140–2.

11. Stolte, "'People's Bandung,'" 133–40. Several organizers of CRIT, including Ramashwari Nehru, had participated in the 1947 Asian Relations Conference and viewed the 1955 meeting as a bridge between this earlier iteration of Afro-Asianism and the Bandung Conference to come.

12. Global historians are skeptical of the hagiographic literature on Bandung, what Rachel Leow describes as 'a fantasy of Third World agency formed out of easy metonymy: Bandung the place, Bandung the spirit, Bandung the moment, Bandung

the History.' See her "Asian Lessons in the Cold War Classroom: Trade Union Networks and the Multidirectional Pedagogies of the Cold War in Asia," *Journal of Social History* 53, no. 2 (2019): 430. I share this wariness about the shorthand term 'Bandung', but the fact remains that the conference location was used evocatively for years afterward to symbolize anticolonialist aspirations.

13. Chen Yifeng, "Bandung, China, and the Making of World Order in East Asia," in *Bandung, Global History, and International Law*, ed. Luis Eslava, Michael Fakhri, and Vasuki Nesiah (Cambridge, UK: Cambridge University Press, 2017), 179–82.

14. Matthew Jones, "A 'Segregated' Asia?: Race, the Bandung Conference, and Pan-Asianist Fears in American Thought and Policy, 1954–1955," *Diplomatic History* 29, no. 5 (2005): 852.

15. Cindy Ewing, "The Colombo Powers: Crafting Diplomacy in the Third World and Launching Afro-Asia at Bandung," *Cold War History*, 19, no. 1 (2019): 6 and 15.

16. For a multilateral account of Colombo Powers diplomacy and a skeptical assessment of 'the Bandung spirit', see Ewing, "The Colombo Powers," 1–19.

17. Jones, "'Segregated' Asia?" 847–52.

18. Christopher J. Lee, "Between a Moment and an Era: The Origins and Afterlives of Bandung," in *Making a World after Empire: The Bandung Moment and Its Political Afterlives*, ed. Christopher J. Lee (Athens: Ohio University Press, 2010), 17–19, 26–28. For discussion of competing views of Bandung, from narratives of failure to romanticized idealism, see Michael Fakhri and Kelly Reynolds, "The Bandung Conference," in *Oxford Bibliographies in International Law*, ed. Anthony Carty (Oxford: Oxford University Press, 2017), available online at https://www.oxfordbibliographies.com/.

19. Young-Sun Hong, *Cold War Germany, the Third World, and the Global Humanitarian Regime* (Cambridge, UK: Cambridge University Press, 2017), 33.

20. Cited in Sabelo J. Ndlovu-Gatsheni, *Decolonization, Development and Knowledge in Africa: Turning over a New Leaf* (London: Routledge, 2020), 47.

21. Naoko Shimazu, "Diplomacy as Theatre: Staging the Bandung Conference of 1955," *Modern Asian Studies* 48, no. 1 (2014): 231–34. Zhou led a large Chinese conference delegation, which included Vice-Premier Chen Yi and fifteen journalists. As important, Zhou's conciliatory attitude allayed fears among fellow Asian attendees, first about the split loyalties of the twelve million or so expatriate Chinese living in Southeast Asia, second about the PRC's approach to border disputes: see: Yifeng, "Bandung, China," 183, 189–91.

22. Shimazu, "Diplomacy as Theatre," 235–51, emphasizes the Indonesian attention within the conference and in the city of Bandung to matters of urban renewal, public engagement and staging, most notably the delegates' city walkabouts en route to the Freedom Building conference venue. Aside from venue hosts Sukarno and Vice-President Hatta, each of whom had an eye on Indonesia's first national elections, scheduled for September 1955, Zhou Enlai, Nasser, and Nehru pulled in particularly large crowds.

23. Luis Eslava, Michael Fakhri and Vasuki Nesiah describe the conference's 'utopian, forward-looking dimension' as delegates reimagined a future global order: "The Spirit of Bandung," in Eslava, Fakhri, and Nesiah, *Bandung, Global History*, 3–4. Unusually, several attendees wrote extensively about its transformative potential, including conference secretary-general Roeslan Abdulgani [*The Bandung Spirit*

(Jakarta: Prapantja Publishing, 1964)], Indian commentator Angadipuram Appadorai [*The Bandung Conference* (New Delhi: Indian Council of World Affairs, 1955)], Cornell University researcher George McTurnan Kahin [*The Asian-African Conference: Bandung, Indonesia, April 1955* (London: Kennikat, 1956)], Philippines delegate Carlos P. Romolo [*The Meaning of Bandung* (Chapel Hill: University of North Carolina Press, 1956)], and, most influentially, African-American writer and activist Richard Wright [*The Color Curtain: A Report of the Bandung Conference* (Cleveland, OH: World Publishing, 1956)]. See Shimazu, "Diplomacy as Theatre," 227–29; Amitav Acharya, *Whose Ideas Matter? Agency and Power in Asian Regionalism* (Ithaca, NY: Cornell University Press, 2009), chapters 3 and 4; Su Sin Lewis and Carolien Stolte, "Other Bandungs: Afro-Asian Internationalisms in the Early Cold War," *Journal of World History* 30, no. 1–2 (2019): 2–3. For all the outward harmony, there were tensions behind the scenes, notably regarding the arrogance of Nehru and his adviser V. K. Krishna Menon: Sally Percival Wood, "Retrieving the Bandung Conference . . . Moment by Moment," *Journal of Southeast Asian Studies* 43, no. 3 (2012): 525–26.

24. Frank Gerits situates this tendency within a rhetoric of Asian-led development predicated on the idea that India, Indonesia, and others might supplant the imperial powers and Cold War giants as providers of external expertise; see his "Bandung as the Call for a Better Development Project: US, British, French and Gold Coast Perceptions of the Afro-Asian Conference (1955)," *Cold War History* 16, no. 3 (2016): 258, 261–62, 270.

25. The organizers were Indonesia, India, Pakistan, Ceylon/Sri Lanka, and Burma. Also attending were national delegations from Afghanistan, Cambodia, China, Egypt, Ethiopia, Gold Coast, Iran, Iraq, Japan, Jordan, Laos, Lebanon, Liberia, Libya, Nepal, the Philippines, Saudi Arabia, Sudan, Syria, Thailand, Turkey, the Democratic Republic of Vietnam (Hanoi regime), the State of Vietnam (Saigon regime), and Yemen: Amitav Acharya, "Studying the Bandung Conference from a Global IR Perspective," *Australian Journal of International Affairs* 70, no. 4 (2016): 342–57, at 343.

26. B. S. Chimni, "Anti-Imperialism: Then and Now," in Eslava, Fakhri, and Nesiah, *Bandung, Global History*, 35; Petra Goedde, *The Politics of Peace: A Global Cold War History* (New York: Oxford University Press, 2019), 34–36.

27. Heloise Weber and Poppy Winanti, "The 'Bandung Spirit' and Solidarist Internationalism," *Australian Journal of International Affairs* 70, no. 4 (2016): 394–98; Gerits, "Bandung," 255–62.

28. Heloise Weber, "The Political Significance of Bandung for Development: Challenges, Contradictions and Struggles for Justice," *Meanings of Bandung: Postcolonial Orders and Decolonial Visions*, ed. Quynh N. Pham and R. Shilliam (London: Rowman & Littlefield, 2016), 155–57.

29. Robbie Shilliam, "Colonial Architecture or Relatable Hinterlands? Locke, Nandy, Fanon, and the Bandung Spirit," *Constellations* 23, no. 3 (2016): 426.

30. Vijay Prashad, *The Poorer Nations: A Possible History of the Global South* (London: Verso, 2013), 1–3.

31. Yifeng, "Bandung, China," 184–86.

32. Ian Taylor, "Mao Zedong's China and Africa," *Twentieth Century Communism* 15 (Fall 2018): 48–49.

33. Jeffrey James Byrne, "Beyond Continents, Colours, and the Cold War: Yugoslavia, Algeria, and the Struggle for Non-Alignment," *International History Review* 37, no. 5 (2015): 913–15; Aldo Marchesi, *Latin America's Radical Left: Rebellion and Cold War in the Global 1960s* (Cambridge, UK: Cambridge University Press, 2017), 69–70.

34. Eric Gettig, "Cuba, the United States, and the Uses of the Third World Project, 1959–1967," in *Latin America and the Global Cold War*, ed. Thomas C. Field, Stella Krepp, and Vanni Pettinà (Chapel Hill: University of North Carolina Press, 2020), 252–62; Cynthia A. Young, *Soul Power: Culture, Radicalism, and the Making of a U.S. Third World Left* (Durham, NC: Duke University Press, 2006), 18–25.

35. Iber, "From Peace to National Liberation," 51–53.

36. Iber, "From Peace to National Liberation," 53–56.

37. Stella Krepp, "Brazil and Non-Alignment: Latin America's Role in the Global Order, 1961–1964," in Field, Krepp, and Pettinà, *Latin America and the Global Cold War*, 101–18; Gettig, "Cuba, the United States," 242, 246–50.

38. Acharya, "Studying the Bandung Conference," 347–49.

39. Acharya, "Studying the Bandung Conference," 345–47. Having tried to organize a wider boycott, the British pressed delegates from the Central African Federation and Singapore to stay away.

40. For differences in Franco-British responses, see Gerits, "Bandung," 264–69.

41. François Bédarida and Jean-Pierre Rioux, eds., *Pierre Mendès France et le mendésisme: L'expérience gouvernementale et sa postérité (1954–1955)* (Paris: Fayard, 1985); René Girault et al., eds., *Pierre Mendès France et le rôle de la France dans le monde* (Grenoble: Presses Universitaires de Grenoble, 1991).

42. Byrne, "Beyond Continents," 915–18.

43. Sarah C. Dunstan, "*La Langue de nos maîtres*: Linguistic Hierarchies, Dialect, and Canon Decolonization during and after the *Présence Africaine* Congress of 1956," *Journal of Modern History* 93, no. 1 (2021): 861–63, 874–75.

44. Dunstan, "*La Langue*," 865–73; John Munro, *The Anticolonial Front: The African-American Freedom Struggle and Global Decolonisation, 1945–1960* (Cambridge, UK: Cambridge University Press, 2017), 230–31.

45. Munro, *Anticolonial Front*, 206–9; Westad, *Global Cold War*, 99; Vijay Prashad, *The Darker Nations: A People's History of the Third World* (New York: New Press, 2007), 45.

46. IISH, Pierre Avot-Meyers papers, ARCH03107, file 12, Front de Libération nationale, Fédération de France, Bulletin intérieur d'information, December 1958–January 1959.

47. Ismay Milford, *African Activists in a Decolonising World: The Making of an Anticolonial Culture, 1952–1966* (Cambridge, UK: Cambridge University Press, 2023), 97–98.

48. Eslava, Fakhri, and Nesiah, "Spirit of Bandung," 4–6, 13; Anne Garland Mahler, *From the Tricontinental to the Global South: Race, Radicalism, and Transnational Solidarity* (Durham, NC: Duke University Press, 2018), 69–70.

49. Eslava, Fakhri, and Nesiah, "Spirit of Bandung," 10–11, 23–24.

50. Eslava, Fakhri, and Nesiah, "Spirit of Bandung," 9, 16–19. Boris Mamlyuk discusses Bandung's echoes of the early Soviet challenge to international law and the

imperialist hypocrisy of the supranational bodies that upheld it; see Boris N. Mamlyuk, "Decolonization as a Cold War Imperative: Bandung and the Soviets," in Eslava, Fakhri, and Nesiah, *Bandung, Global History*, 197–207.

51. Goedde, *Politics of Peace*, 34; Amitav Acharya, "Who Are the Norm Makers? The Asian–African Conference in Bandung and the Evolution of Norms," *Global Governance* 20 (2014): 410–12.

52. Opening statement by Honorable Carlos P. Romolo, from *Selected Documents of the Bandung Conference: Texts of Selected Speeches and Final Communiqué of the Asian-African Conference* (New York: Institute of Pacific Relations, 1955), 17, cited in Goedde, *Politics of Peace*, 35. Romulo had worked at the UN from its inception and, like fellow conference attendee Charles Malik, sat on the working group that drafted the Universal Declaration of Human Rights in 1948.

53. Roland Burke, *Decolonization and the Evolution of International Human Rights* (Philadelphia: University of Pennsylvania Press, 2010), 45–46.

54. Yifeng, "Bandung, China," 187–89.

55. Goedde, *Politics of Peace*, 34; Odd Arne Westad notes that delegates were reluctant to focus attention on the absence of democratic freedoms and rights protections within their own countries: *Global Cold War*, 102. For an assessment of Malik's role and a critique of the wider conference, see Roland Burke, "Afro-Asian Alignment: Charles Malik and the Cold War at Bandung," in *Bandung 1955: Little Histories*, ed. Antonia Finnane and Derek McDougall (Caulfield, Australia: Monash University Press, 2010), 27–41.

56. Frederick Cooper, "Afterword: Social Rights and Human Rights in the Time of Decolonization," *Humanity* 3, no. 3 (2012): 478.

57. Roland Burke, "'The Compelling Dialogue of Freedom': Human Rights at the Bandung Conference," *Human Rights Quarterly* 28, no. 4 (2006): 947–65.

58. Westad, *Global Cold War*, 102–4.

59. Lee, "Between a Moment and an Era," 1–42.

60. Munro, *Anticolonial Front*, 208–9; James Mark, Tobias Rupprecht, and Ljubica Spaskovska, *1989: Eastern Europe in Global Perspective* (Cambridge, UK: Cambridge University Press, 2019), 149–52; Goedde, *Politics of Peace*, 162–64.

61. IISH, ARCH01665, World Federation of Democratic Youth (WFDY) archive, World Youth Supplement no. 2/1958, "The Afro-Asian People's Solidarity Conference," no date [January 1958]: Egyptian Delegation report, "Imperialism in the Throes of Death"; WFDY resolution, "Organise Solidarity for Algeria."

62. Eric Burton, "Hubs of Decolonization: African Liberation Movements and 'Eastern' Connections in Cairo, Accra, and Dar es Salaam," in *Southern African Liberation Movements and the Global Cold War 'East': Transnational Activism 1960–1990*, ed. Lena Dallywater, Chris Saunders, and Helder Adegar Fonseca (Oldenbourg: De Gruyter, 2019), 31–38.

63. Katherine McGregor and Vannessa Hearman, "Challenging the Lifeline of Imperialism: Reassessing Afro-Asian Solidarity and Related Activism in the Decade 1955–1965," in Eslava, Fakhri, and Nesiah, *Bandung, Global History*, 165–69.

64. Young-Sun Hong, *Cold War Germany*, 233–35.

65. MAE, série Afrique-Levant, sous-série: Généralités, 1944–52, file 65: Politique soviétique en Afrique, 1949–52: WFDY "Day of Struggle against Colonialism,"

no date [February 1950]. Elizabeth Schmidt highlights the vindictiveness of de Gaulle's government in pushing Guinea toward Eastern bloc partners after Guineans voted against membership of the French Community in September 1958: Elizabeth Schmidt, *Cold War and Decolonization in Guinea, 1946–1958* (Athens: Ohio University Press, 2007), 168–76.

66. IISH ARCH01665, file WFDY 1, "What Is the WFDY?" printed in Budapest, 1952; sub-file, WFDY 1954 "Special Newspaper for International Day of Struggle against Colonialism and Solidarity with the Youth of Colonial Countries," February 24, 1954; James Mark and Péter Apor, "Socialism Goes Global: Decolonization and the Making of a New Culture of Internationalism in Socialist Hungary, 1956–1989," *Journal of Modern History* 87 (December 2015): 856–62, 870–78.

67. Sara Pugach, "Eleven Nigerian Students in Cold War East Germany: Visions, of Science, Modernity, and Decolonization," *Journal of Contemporary History* 54, no. 3 (2019): 551–72.

68. Daniel Branch, "Political Traffic: Kenyan Students in Eastern and Central Europe, 1958–69," *Journal of Contemporary History* 53, no. 4 (2018): 812–27.

69. Helder Adegar Fonseca, "The Military Training of Angolan Guerrillas in Socialist Countries: A Prosopographical Approach, 1961–1974," in Dallywater, Saunders, and Fonseca, *Southern African Liberation Movements*, 107–27.

70. Milford, *African Activists*, 186–95.

71. TNA, WO 208/4908, Quarterly MI reports, May 1961, "The Arabian Peninsula in British Strategy," abridged from article by D. C. Watt in *Military Review*, February 1961, 45. It bears emphasizing that in 1960 there were over 12,000 African university students in Britain alone.

72. Watt abridgment, 46–47; on East Germany's preoccupation with recognition by African states, see George Roberts, "Press, Propaganda and the German Democratic Republic's Search for Recognition in Tanzania, 1964–72," in Muehlenbeck and Telepneva, *Warsaw Pact*, 148–58.

73. TNA, WO 208/4908, Quarterly MI reports, May 1961, "The Arabian Peninsula," 47–48; Robert Mortimer, "Algeria, Vietnam and Afro-Asian Solidarity," *The Maghreb Review* 28, no. 1 (2003): 60–66; Salar Mohandesi, *Red Internationalism: Anti-Imperialism and Human Rights in the Global Sixties and Seventies* (Cambridge, UK: Cambridge University Press, 2023), 51.

74. Byrne, *Mecca of Revolution*, 284–85.

75. McGregor and Hearman, "Challenging," 164, 172–75; David Stenner, *Globalizing Morocco: Transnational Activism and the Postcolonial State* (Stanford, CA: Stanford University Press, 2019), 198–202.

76. Natalia Telepneva, *Cold War Liberation: The Soviet Union and the Collapse of the Portuguese Empire in Africa, 1961–1975* (Chapel Hill: University of North Carolina Press, 2021), 101–4. Fearing this 'coup contagion', Leonid Brezhnev's government cultivated stronger ties with African militaries and insurgent commanders as a result.

77. Randolph B. Persaud, "The Racial Dynamic in International Relations: Some Thoughts on the Pan-African Antecedents of Bandung," in *Meanings of Bandung: Postcolonial Orders and Decolonial Visions*, ed. Quynh N. Pham and R. Shilliam (London: Rowman & Littlefield, 2016), 136–41.

78. Stolte, "'People's Bandung,'" 149–53.

79. Ahmad Rozky Mardhatillah Umar, "Rethinking the Legacies of the Bandung Conference: Global Decolonization and the Making of Modern International Order," *Asian Politics and Policy* 11, no. 3 (2019): 467–68, 470–71. Umar points out that Japan's East Asia Co-Prosperity Sphere should also be acknowledged as a spur to pan-Asianism, although it jarred with the respect for racial equality that underpinned Bandung's internationalism.

80. For tensions at Bandung between the constraints of the international order and the quest to replace it, see Andrew Phillips, "Beyond Bandung: The 1955 Asian–African Conference and Its Legacies for International Order," *Australian Journal of International Affairs* 70, no. 4 (2016): 329–41.

81. Robert J. C. Young, "Postcolonialism: From Bandung to the Tricontinental," *Historein* 5 (2006): 11–21. Rachel Leow pinpoints the elitist dimension to Bandung, highlighting the fixation on a nonalignment origin story 'saturated with Nehrus, Nassers, Sukarnos, and Zhou Enlais.' Rachel Leow, "Asian Lessons," 429–53, quote at 431.

82. Mark, Rupprecht, and Spaskovska, *1989*, 149–50.

83. Giuliano Garavini, *After Empires: European Integration, Decolonization, and the Challenge from the Global South 1957–1986* (Oxford: Oxford University Press, 2012), 13–15.

84. Vanni Pettinà, "Global Horizons: Mexico, the Third World, and the Non-Aligned Movement at the Time of the 1961 Belgrade Conference," *International History Review* 38, no. 4 (2016): 748–58.

85. Byrne, "Beyond Continents," 919–23.

86. IISH, COLL00201, Algeria, folder 4, GPRA memorandum, "The Belgrade Conference of Non-Aligned Countries," September 1–5, 1961. Article 3 of the Belgrade Conference Declaration affirmed that 'The participating countries consider the struggle of the people of Algeria for freedom, self-determination and independence, and for the integrity of its national territory including the Sahara, to be just and necessary and are, therefore, determined to extend to the people of Algeria all the possible support and aid.'

87. IISH, COLL00201, Algeria, folder 4, "Statement by Mr Benyoussef Benkhedda, Premier of the PGAR, at the Belgrade Conference of Non-Aligned Countries, Belgrade, September 4, 1961, Circulated by GPRA, New York."

88. Friendly ties between Chilean leftists and the FLN exemplify the transnational connections involved; see Eugenia Palieraki, "Chile, Algeria, and the Third World in the 1960s and 1970s: Revolutions Entangled," in Field, Krepp, and Pettinà, *Latin America and the Global Cold War*, 278–85.

89. Christoph Kalter, *The Discovery of the Third World: Decolonization and the Rise of the New Left in France c. 1950–1976* (Cambridge, UK: Cambridge University Press, 2016), 35–36; Claude Liauzu, "Le tiersmondisme des intellectuels en accusation: Le sens d'une trajectoire," *Vingtième Siècle* 12 (October 1986): 73–80; Young, *Soul Power*, 19–25, 29–34; Mohandesi, *Red Internationalism*, 106–10.

90. Piero Gleijeses, "Cuba's First Venture in Africa: Algeria, 1961–1965," *Journal of Latin American Studies* 28, no. 1 (1996): 164–70. A first consignment of Cuban military supplies was shipped to Casablanca for onward delivery to Algeria in December 1961, but the initial fifty-five-person medical team, accompanied by Cuba's health minister, arrived by plane in May 1963. Sixty-one additional medical staff flew in the following year: Young-Sun Hong, *Cold War Germany*, 156–57.

91. By 2006 over 130,000 Cuban doctors had served overseas since the Algerian deployment in 1963. Significantly, the Cuban soldier who, in 1967, executed Che Guevara in Bolivia had his cataracts removed forty years later as part of 'Operation Miracle,' a Cuban international program to combat sight loss; see Kirk, "Cuban Medical Internationalism," 276–77, 280–84.

92. For discussion of these Third Worldist orientations, plus criticism of continuing use of 'Third World' as ahistorical and Eurocentric, see Arif Dirlik, "Spectres of the Third World: Global Modernity and the End of the Three Worlds," *Third World Quarterly* 25, no. 1 (2004): 131–41.

93. Kalter, *Discovery of the Third World*, 42–44. As we saw earlier, the term had arisen at the Asian Relations Conference in 1947 but did not register the same impact: see Vineet Thakur, "An Asian Drama: The Asian Relations Conference, 1947," *International History Review* 41, no. 3 (2019): 673–74; Cindy Ewing, "The Third World before Afro-Asia," in *Inventing the Third World: In Search of Freedom for the Postwar Global South*, ed. Gyan Prakash and Jeremy Adelman (London: Bloomsbury Academic, 2023), 31–32.

94. Léon Sabah, "Alfred Sauvy: Statistician, Economist, Demographer and Iconoclast (1898–1990)," *Population Studies* 45 (1991): 353–7.

95. It was this socioeconomic dimension, with its accent on underdevelopment, that predominated in *Le Tiers Monde: Sous-développement et développement*, a 1956 collection of essays dedicated to Sauvy and edited by the sociologist Georges Balandier; see Marcin Wojciech Solarz, "'Third World': The 60th Anniversary of a Concept that Changed History," *Third World Quarterly* 33, no. 9 (2012): 1564; Kalter, *Discovery of the Third World*, 44–46.

96. Solarz, "'Third World,'" 1561–71; Young-Sun Hong, *Cold War Germany*, 16–17; Martin Evans, "Whatever Happened to the Non-Aligned Movement?" *History Today*, December 2007, 49; Kalter, *Discovery of the Third World*, 42–43. These authors stress Sauvy's play on words in invoking a *tiers monde* (rather than a numerical *troisième monde*), the intention being to draw a parallel with the 'third estate' (*tiers état*), identified in January 1789 by clergyman and pamphleteer Emmanuel Sieyès as the poor majority in prerevolutionary France who later overthrew the *Ancien Régime*.

97. Marchesi, *Latin America's Radical Left*, 1–5, 12–14.

98. Samantha Christiansen and Zachary A. Scarlett, "Introduction," *The Third World and the Global 1960s*, ed. idem (Oxford: Berghahn, 2013), 1–4.

99. Taomo Zhou, "Global Reporting from the Third World: The Afro-Asian Journalists' Association, 1963–1974," *Critical Asian Studies* 51, no. 2 (2019): 166–67

100. Mark T. Berger, "After the Third World? History, Destiny and the Fate of the Third World," *Third World Quarterly* 25, no. 1 (2004): 9–39, at 10–14; Vedi R. Hadiz, "The Rise of Neo-Third Worldism? The Indonesian Trajectory and the Consolidation of Illiberal Democracy," *Third World Quarterly* 25, no. 1 (2004): 55–71.

101. Zhou, "Global Reporting," 179–93.

102. Young-Sun Hong, *Cold War Germany*, 170–71.

103. Thomas C. Field, Stella Krepp, and Vanni Pettinà, "Between Nationalism and Internationalism: Latin America and the Third World," in Field, Krepp, and Pettinà, *Latin America and the Global Cold War*, 1–7.

104. Kalter, "Shared Space," 28–29.

105. Berger, "After the Third World?" 19–24; Robert Malley, *The Call from Algeria: Third Worldism, Revolution, and the Turn to Islam* (Berkeley: University of California Press, 1996), 89–93; Getachew, *Worldmaking*, 153–57; D. A. Dunkley, "Hegemony in Post-Independence Jamaica," *Caribbean Quarterly* 57, no. 2 (2011): 7–17. For analysis of Manley's 1989 return to office in more moderate guise, see Anthony Payne, "The 'New' Manley and the New Political Economy of Jamaica," *Third World Quarterly* 13, no. 3 (1992): 463–73.

106. Berger, "After the Third World?" 18; Jeffrey S. Ahlman, "The Algerian Question in Nkrumah's Ghana, 1958–1960: Debating 'Violence' and 'Non-Violence' in African Decolonization," *Africa Today* 57, no. 2 (2010): 67–84; Frank Gerits, "'When the Bull Elephants Fight': Kwame Nkrumah, Non-Alignment, and Pan-Africanism as an Interventionist Ideology in the Global Cold War (1957–66)," *International History Review* 37, no. 5 (2015): 951–69; Adom Getachew, "Securing Postcolonial Independence: Kwame Nkrumah and the Federal Idea in the Age of Decolonization," *Ab Imperio* 3 (2018): 89–113.

107. Views he expressed in his last book: George Padmore, *Pan-Africanism or Communism? The Coming Struggle for Africa* (London: Dobson, 1956); Leslie James, *George Padmore and Decolonization from Below: Africanism, the Cold War, and the End of Empire* (Basingstoke, UK: Palgrave Macmillan, 2015), 137–45; Munro, *Anticolonial Front*, 252–54. Padmore advised Nkrumah until his death in September 1959.

108. Michael Gomez singles out Ghana's independence struggle as one of five African decolonizations to stir the greatest transnational interest among the continent's diaspora communities, the others being Kenya's Mau Mau War, the Congo crisis, the Algerian conflict, and the antiapartheid struggle; see Michael A. Gomez, *Reversing Sail: A History of the African Diaspora*, 2nd edition (Cambridge, UK: Cambridge University Press, 2020), 230.

109. James, *George Padmore*, 163–73; Elizabeth Schmidt, "Top down or Bottom up? Nationalist Mobilization Reconsidered with Special Reference to Guinea (French West Africa)," *American Historical Review* 110, no. 4 (2005): 975–1014.

110. James, *George Padmore*, 179–83.

111. IISH, Pierre Avot-Meyers papers (ARCH03107), file 12, Front de Libération nationale, Fédération de France, Bulletin intérieur d'information, December 1958–January 1959; Burton, "Hubs of Decolonization," 40–43.

112. Munro, *Anticolonial Front*, 257–59; Imaobong D. Umoren, *Race Women Internationalists: Activist Intellectuals and Global Freedom Struggles* (Berkeley: University of California Press, 2018), 111.

113. Milford, *African Activists*, 98–100, 103–6, 111–18, 133–35. The term 'performed solidarity' is at p. 100.

114. Charles G. Thomas and Toyin Falola, *Secession and Separatist Conflicts in Postcolonial Africa* (Calgary: University of Calgary Press, 2020), 63.

115. James, *George Padmore*, 194.

116. Gleijeses, "Cuba's First Venture," 170.

117. Anna Konieczna, "'We the People of the United Nations': The UN and the Global Campaigns against Apartheid," in *A Global History of Anti-Apartheid: "Forward to Freedom" in South Africa*, ed. Anna Konieczna and Rob Skinner (Cham: Palgrave Macmillan, 2019), 72–73, 77–78, 82. Supported by another Guinean, Achkar

Marof, Diallo's successor as OAU secretary-general, the OAU continued to coordinate cooperation between sympathetic states and national antiapartheid movements in Africa and Europe especially.

118. Getachew, "Securing Postcolonial Independence," 93, 105–11.

119. Julie MacArthur, "Decolonizing Sovereignty: States of Exception along the Kenya–Somali Frontier," *American Historical Review* 124, no. 1 (2019): 108–9, 138–42.

120. Justin Willis, Gabrielle Lynch, and Nic Cheeseman, "Voting, Nationhood, and Citizenship in Late-Colonial Africa," *Historical Journal* 61, no. 4 (2018): 1113–35, at 1130.

121. Merve Fejzula, "The Cosmopolitan Historiography of Twentieth-Century Federalism," *Historical Journal* 63, no. 1 (2020): 18; Miles Larmer, "Nation-Making at the Border: Zambian Diplomacy in the Democratic Republic of Congo," *Comparative Studies in Society and History* 61, no. 1 (2019): 146–49.

122. Bronwen Manby, "Trends in Citizenship Law and Politics in Africa since the Colonial Era," in *Routledge Handbook of Global Citizenship Studies*, ed. Engin F. Isin and Peter Nyers (London: Routledge, 2014), 172, 182.

123. Ana Torres-García, "US Diplomacy and the North African 'War of the Sands' (1963)," *Journal of North African Studies* 18, no. 2 (2013): 328–30; Sarah Vaughan, "Ethiopia, Somalia, and the Ogaden: Still a Running Sore at the Heart of the Horn of Africa," in *Secessionism in African Politics: Aspiration, Grievance, Performance, Disenchantment*, ed. Lotje de Vries, Pierre Englebert, and Mareike Schomerus (Cham: Palgrave Macmillan, 2019), 100–3; Øystein H. Rolandsen and Cherry Leonardi, "Discourses of Violence in the Transition from Colonialism to Independence in Southern Sudan, 1955–1960," *Journal of East African Studies* 8, no. 4 (2014): 609–10, 617–25; Hannah Whittaker, "Legacies of Empire: State Violence and Collective Punishment in Kenya's North Eastern Province, c. 1963–Present," *Journal of Imperial & Commonwealth History* 43, no. 4 (2015): 641–57; Jeremy Prestholdt, "Politics of the Soil: Separatism, Autochthony, and Decolonization at the Kenyan Coast," *Journal of African History* 55, no. 2 (2014): 260–70; James D. Fearon and David D. Laitin, "Sons of the Soil, Migrants, and Civil War," *World Development* 39, no. 2 (2010): 199–211.

124. Richard Reid, "State of Anxiety: History and Nation in Modern Africa," *Past & Present* 229, no. 1 (2015): 255–56.

125. MacArthur, "Decolonizing Sovereignty," 140.

126. Thomas and Falola, *Secession*, 63–64.

127. Milford, *African Activists*, 10–11, 118–21, 173–76.

128. Milford, *African Activists*, 173–95.

129. Larmer, "Nation-Making at the Border," 146–47, 157–64. Zambia joined the OAU three months after independence on December 16, 1964.

130. Brad Simpson, "The Biafran Secession and the Limits of Self-Determination," *Journal of Genocide Research* 16, no. 2–3 (2014): 339–41; Lasse Heerten and A. Dirk Moses, "The Nigeria–Biafra War: Postcolonial Conflict and the Question of Genocide," *Journal of Genocide Research* 16, no. 2–3 (2014): 174–76. Julius Nyerere's Tanzania broke ranks in recognizing Biafra in April 1968, followed some months later by Gabon, Ivory Coast, and Zambia.

131. James Mayall, "International Society, State Sovereignty, and National Self-Determination," in *The Oxford Handbook of the History of Nationalism*, ed. John Breuilly (Oxford: Oxford University Press, 2013), online publication, 8–10.

132. Thomas and Falola, *Secession*, 91–93.

133. Judy Tzu-Chun Wu, *Radicals on the Road: Internationalism, Orientalism, and Feminism during the Vietnam Era* (Ithaca, NY: Cornell University Press, 2013), 116–22.

134. Quito Swan, "Blinded by Bandung: Illumining West Papua, Senegal, and the Black Pacific," *Radical History Review* 131 (May 2018): 58–81.

135. On disunity and decline in the NAM, see Mark Atwood Lawrence, "The Rise and Fall of Nonalignment," in *The Cold War in the Third World*, ed. Robert J. McMahon (Oxford: Oxford University Press, 2013), 148–52.

136. Swan, "Blinded by Bandung," 65–67, 69–72; Norrie MacQueen, "Portugal's First Domino: 'Pluricontinentalism' and Colonial War in Guiné-Bissau, 1963–1974," *Contemporary European History* 8, no. 2 (1999): 217–20. For background to Senegal's tilt toward the PAIGC: Telepneva, *Cold War Liberation*, 89–90.

137. Powerful introductions to this history are Stephen G. Rabe, *The Killing Zone: The United States Wages Cold War in Latin America* (Oxford: Oxford University Press, 2012); Greg Grandin, *Empire's Workshop: Latin America, the United States, and the Rise of the New Imperialism* (New York: Henry Holt, 2006); for the violence and suffering involved: Grandin and Joseph, *A Century of Revolution*; and, for the extent of CIA involvement in its first Cold War overthrow of a Latin American regime: Nick Cullather, *Secret History: The CIA's Classified Account of Its Operations in Guatemala, 1952–1954* (Stanford, CA: Stanford University Press, 2006).

138. John A. Gronbeck-Tedesco, *Cuba, the United States, and Cultures of the Transnational Left, 1930–1975* (Cambridge, UK: Cambridge University Press, 2015), 171–80 and, on the distinctiveness of Cuban revolutionary feminism, 256–63; Michelle Getchell, "Cuba, the USSR, and the Non-Aligned Movement: Negotiating Non-Alignment," in Field, Krepp, and Pettinà, *Latin America and the Global Cold War*, 157–66.

139. Young, *Soul Power*, 19–34, 50–52.

140. Goedde, *Politics of Peace*, 162–66, 183–87; Kalter, "Shared Space," 32–33.

141. Quoted in Gronbeck-Tedesco, *Cuba*, 180–82, at 181.

142. For a vivid narrative: Roger Faligot, *Tricontinental: Quand Che Guevara, Ben Barka, Cabral, Castro et Hô Chi Minh préparaient La Révolution mondiale (1964–1968)* (Paris: La Découverte, 2013), parts II and III.

143. R. Joseph Parrott, "Tricontinentalism and the Anti-Imperial Project," in *The Tricontinental Revolution: Third World Radicalism and the Cold War*, ed. R. Joseph Parrott and Mark Atwood Lawrence (Cambridge, UK: Cambridge University Press, 2022), 1–35; Marchesi, *Latin America's Radical Left*, 70–3, 94–5.

144. Getchell, "Cuba, the USSR," 157; Manuel Barcia, "'Locking Horns with the Northern Empire': Anti-American Imperialism at the Tricontinental Conference of 1966 in Havana," *Journal of Transatlantic Studies* 7, no. 3 (2009): 2010–14.

145. Mahler, *From the Tricontinental*, 22–25, 71–77; Prashad, *Darker Nations*, 107–18; Getchell, "Cuba, the USSR," 155–58.

146. Leni Hanna, "Tricontinental's International Solidarity: Emotion in OSPAAL as Tactic to Catalyze Support of Revolution," *Radical History Review* 136 (January 2020): 169–84, at 169–71. As Anne Garland Mahler defines it, tricontinentalism 'reflected a deterritorialized vision of imperial power and a recognition of imperialism

and racial oppression as interlinked': Mahler, *From the Tricontinental*, 22. The dual representation of colonized women as heroic resisters and victims of security force violence was equally apparent in *Women of the Whole World*, the monthly publication of the largest Communist-affiliated women's anticolonial movement, the Women's International Democratic Federation; see Katharine McGregor, "Opposing Colonialism: The Women's International Democratic Federation and Decolonisation Struggles in Vietnam and Algeria, 1945–1965," *Women's History Review* 25, no. 6 (2016): 931–35.

147. Gleijeses, *Conflicting Missions*, 217–18; Rabe, *Killing Zone*, 67. On Cuban regime efforts to leverage strategic links with Soviet Russia, see Getchell, "Cuba, the USSR," 149, 159–67.

148. Mahler, *From the Tricontinental*, 76–77; Rafael M. Hernández and Jennifer Ruth Hosek, "Tricontinentalism: The Construction of Global Alliances," in Parrott and Lawrence, *Tricontinental Revolution*, 71–82.

149. Jeremy Friedman, "Reddest Place North of Havana: The Tricontinental and the Struggle to Lead the 'Third World,'" in Parrott and Lawrence, *Tricontinental Revolution*, 208–15; Telepneva, *Cold War Liberation*, 2–3, 6–7, 105–6; Young-Sun Hong, *Cold War Germany*, 288.

150. Telepneva, *Cold War Liberation*, 74–87.

151. Mahler, *From the Tricontinental*, 71–81; Monique Bedasse et al., "AHR Conversation: Black Internationalism," *American Historical Review* 125, no. 5 (2020): 1714.

152. Kalter, *Discovery of the Third World*, 266–8, 422.

153. Gronbeck-Tedesco, *Cuba*, 209–12; John A. Gronbeck-Tedesco, "The Left in Transition: The Cuban Revolution in US Third World Politics," *Journal of Latin American Studies* 40, no. 4 (2008): 653–55, 659–61; Prashad, *Darker Nations*, 107–18; Barcia, "'Locking Horns,'" 208–13. Barcia stresses Ben Barka's organizational role. A founder of Morocco's leading nationalist party, the Istiqlal, Ben Barka broke with his former colleagues in 1959 over independent Morocco's pro-Western international policies and monarchist conservatism at home. The leader of Morocco's National Union of Popular Forces, but living in exile, he was murdered in Paris in October 1965, probably by agents of the Rabat regime. Among the insurgent leaders to request support were Amílcar Cabral, who directed Guiné-Bissau's fight against Portugal, Guatemala's rebel commander, Luis Turcios Lima, and two Vietnamese delegates: Nguyen Van Tien, representing South Vietnam's National Liberation Front, and Trần Danh Tuyên, representing the Hanoi regime.

154. Jeffery James Byrne, "The Romance of Revolutionary Transatlanticism: Cuban-Algerian Relations and the Diverging Trends within Third World Internationalism," in Parrott and Lawrence, *Tricontinental Revolution*, 163–90.

155. Gleijeses, "Cuba's First Venture," 162–64, 190. As Gleijeses notes, the Cuban people made substantial sacrifices in support of the Algerian revolution. Castro also spoke out against Ben Bella's June 1965 overthrow by his former Defense Minister, Houari Boumédiène.

156. Robert K. Brigham, *Guerrilla Diplomacy: The NLF's Foreign Relations and the Viet Nam War* (Ithaca, NY: Cornell University Press, 1999), 19–39, 58–74; Mohandesi, *Red Internationalism*, 118–40; Paul Thomas Chamberlin, *The Global*

Offensive: The United States, the Palestine Liberation Organization, and the Making of the Post–Cold War Order (Oxford: Oxford University Press, 2012), 4–7, 19–22; Chamberlin, "The PLO and the Limits of Secular Revolution, 1975–1982," in Parrott and Lawrence, *Tricontinental Revolution*, 93–109.

157. My thanks to Pierre Asselin for letting me read an advance draft of his article "Welcoming American Friends to Defeat American Enemies: Hanoi's Visitor Diplomacy in the Vietnam War." See also Harish C. Mehta, "North Vietnam's Informal Diplomacy with Bertrand Russell: Peace Activism and the International War Crimes Tribunal," *Peace & Change* 37, no. 1 (2012): 64–87.

158. Chamberlin, *Global Offensive*, quote at 21, and for Algerian support for their Palestinian 'protégé': 52–53.

159. Mohandesi, *Red Internationalism*, 80–101.

160. Patrick Iber, "From Peace to National Liberation: Mexico and the Tricontinental," in *Inventing the Third World: In Search of Freedom for the Postwar Global South*, ed. Gyan Prakash and Jeremy Adelman (London: Bloomsbury, 2022), 45–63.

161. On Bolivia and reactions to Che's death: Marchesi, *Latin America's Radical Left*, 86–93.

162. Rabe, *Killing Zone*, 65–66, 80–84; and for the ideological path trodden by Venezuela's 1960s leftists: Stephen G. Rabe, "The Caribbean Triangle: Betancourt, Castro, and Trujillo and U.S. Foreign Policy, 1958–1963," *Diplomatic History* 20, no. 1 (1996): 55–78.

163. Gleijeses, *Conflicting Missions*, 168–69, 197–208, 227–28.

164. R. Joseph Parrott, "Brother and a Comrade: Amílcar Cabral as Global Revolutionary," in Parrott and Lawrence, *Tricontinental Revolution*, 247–61; Helen M. Kinsella, "Superfluous Injury and Unnecessary Suffering: National Liberation and the Laws of War," *Political Power and Social Theory* 32 (2017): 216–17; Konieczna, "'We the People of the United Nations,'" 69–79.

165. Christabelle Peters, *Cuban Identity and the Angolan Experience* (Basingstoke, UK: Palgrave Macmillan, 2012), parts II and III.

166. Gronbeck-Tedesco, *Cuba*, 10.

167. Chamberlin, *Global Offensive*, 24–25.

168. Chamberlin, *Global Offensive*, 19–27, 37–42, 101–2; Olivia C. Harrison, ed., *Transcolonial Maghreb: Imagining Palestine in the Era of Decolonization* (Stanford, CA: Stanford University Press, 2015), part I; Adrien Delmas, "Cuba and Apartheid," in Konieczna and Skinner, *Global History of Anti-Apartheid*, 134–36.

169. Andreas Eckert, "Radical Scholarship and Political Activism: Walter Rodney as Third World Intellectual and Historian of the Third World," in Adelman and Prakash, *Inventing the Third World*, 118–24.

170. Walter Rodney, *How Europe Underdeveloped Africa* (London: Bogle-L'Ouverture Publications, 1972), part VI: "Colonialism as a System for Underdeveloping Africa"; on Rodney's 1968 expulsion from Jamaica and his involvement in the island's political culture, see James Bardford, "Brother Wally and De Burnin' of Babylon: Walter Rodney's Impact on the Reawakening of Black Power, the Birth of Reggae, and Resistance to Global Imperialism," in Christiansen and Scarlett, *The Third World and the Global 1960s*, 143–46.

171. On academic reception of Rodney's work, which criticized its polemicism but acknowledged its significance, see Eckert, "Radical Scholarship," 125.

172. Immanuel R. Harisch, "Facets of Walter Rodney's Pan-African Intellectual Activism during his Dar es Salaam Years, 1966–1974," *Vienna Journal of African Studies* 20, no. 38 (2020): 108–9; Iandolo, *Arrested Development*, 21–23.

173. Harisch, "Facets," 109–12.

174. Su Sin Lewis, *Cities in Motion: Urban Life and Cosmopolitanism in Southeast Asia, 1920–1940* (Cambridge, UK: Cambridge University Press, 2016), 9–11.

175. Daniel Kaiser, "'Makers of Bonds and Ties': Transnational Socialisation and National Liberation in Mozambique," in *Transnational Histories of Southern Africa's Liberation Movements*, ed. Jocelyn Alexander, Joann McGregor, and Blessing-Miles Tendi (Abingdon, UK: Routledge, 2020), 33–43.

176. Christian A. Williams, "Education in Exile: International Scholarships, Cold War Politics, and Conflicts among SWAPO Members in Tanzania, 1961–1968," in Alexander, McGregor, and Tendi, *Transnational Histories*, 123–39.

177. Burton, "Hubs of Decolonization," 47–55.

178. George Roberts, "The Assassination of Eduardo Mondlane: FRELIMO, Tanzania, and the Politics of Exile in Dar es Salaam," *Cold War History* 17, no. 1 (2017): 1–19.

179. Saphia Arezki, *De l'ALN à l'ANP, la construction de l'armée algérienne, 1954–1991* (Paris: Éditions de la Sorbonne, 2022); Andrew Ivaska, "Liberation in Transit: Eduardo Mondlane and Che Guevara in Dar es Salaam," in *The Routledge Handbook of the Global Sixties: Between Protest and Nation-Building*, ed. Chen Jian et al. (London: Routledge, 2008), 27–38.

180. Christof Dejung, David Motadel, and Jürgen Osterhammel, "Worlds of the Bourgeoisie," in *The Global Bourgeoisie: The Rise of the Middle Classes in the Age of Empire*, ed. idem (Princeton, NJ: Princeton University Press, 2019), 2, 5–6, 25.

181. Frank Gerits, "Hungry Minds: Eisenhower's Cultural Assistance to Sub-Saharan Africa, 1953–1961," *Diplomatic History* 41, no. 3 (2017): 603–10.

182. Emma Hunter, "Modernity, Print Media, and the Middle Class in Colonial East Africa," in Dejung, Motadel, and Osterhammel, *Global Bourgeoisie*, 108.

183. For analysis, see Partha Chatterjee, *The Nation and Its Fragments: Colonial and Postcolonial Histories* (Princeton, NJ: Princeton University Press, 1993), 33–75.

184. Lewis, *Cities in Motion*, 15–16, 96–99, 121–30.

185. For analysis of the analytical pitfalls and potentialities, see Richard Drayton, "Race, Culture, and Class: European Hegemony and Global Class Formation, circa 1800–1950," in Dejung, Motadel, and Osterhammel, *Global Bourgeoisie*, 341–48.

186. Partha Chatterjee, *Nationalist Thought and the Colonial World: A Derivative Discourse*, 2nd edition (Minneapolis: University of Minnesota Press, 1993), also cited in Dejung, Motadel, and Osterhammel, *Global Bourgeoisie*, 16.

187. This is not to deny the agency of those in clerical positions, who became adept at manipulating conflicting regulations and their understanding of local languages; see Benjamin N. Lawrance, Emily Lynn Osborn, and Richard L. Roberts, eds., *Intermediaries, Interpreters, and Clerks: African Employees in the Making of Colonial Africa* (Madison: University of Wisconsin Press, 2006).

188. John Flint, "Scandal at the Bristol Hotel: Some Thoughts on Racial Discrimination in Britain and West Africa and Its Relationship to the Planning of

Decolonisation, 1939–1947," *Journal of Imperial & Commonwealth History* 12, no. 1 (1983): 74–93.

189. Dejung, Motadel, and Osterhammel, *Global Bourgeoisie*. For discussion of the phenomenon from the late twentieth century, see Hagen Koo, "The Global Middle Class: How Is It Made, What Does It Represent?" *Globalizations* 13, no. 4 (2016): 440–53.

190. Robert J. C. Young, "From the Anti-Colonial Movements to the New Social Movements," in *Echoes of Empire: Memory, Identity and Colonial Legacies*, ed. Kalypso Nicolaïdis, Berny Sèbe, and Gabrielle Maas (London: I. B. Tauris, 2015), 374–76, quote at 374.

191. Rebecca Herman, "The Global Politics of Anti-Racism: A View from the Canal Zone," *American Historical Review* 125, no. 2 (2020): 463–64, 469–71.

Chapter Fifteen: Endgames?
Decolonization's Third-World Wars

1. John A. Marcum, *Conceiving Mozambique* (Cham: Palgrave Macmillan, 2018), 45–47, 58–60; Norrie MacQueen, *The Decolonization of Portuguese Africa: Metropolitan Revolution and the Dissolution of Empire* (London: Longman, 1997), 32–34.

2. A term coined regarding Vietnam's National Liberation Front: Robert K. Brigham, *Guerrilla Diplomacy: The NLF's Foreign Relations and the Viet Nam War* (Ithaca, NY: Cornell University Press, 1999).

3. Justin Pearce, "Global Ideologies, Local Politics: The Cold War as Seen from Central Angola," *Journal of Southern African Studies* 43, no. 1 (2017): 17–23.

4. MAE, série Afrique-Levant, sous-série Mozambique 1960–72, 59QO29: "A/S Rébellion au Mozambique," June 18, 1966.

5. MAE, sous-série Mozambique 1960–72, 59QO29: Action rebelle et défense portugais, May 1966–December 1972, no. 198/AL, Jacques Honoré, Lourenço Marques Consul, to French Ambassador, Lisbon, "A.S. des mesures de défense prises au Mozambique," May 26, 1966.

6. Priya Lal, "Decolonization and the Gendered Politics of Developmental Labor in Southeastern Africa," in *The Development Century*, ed. Stephen J. Macekura and Erez Manela (Cambridge, UK: Cambridge University Press, 2018), 183–84; Filipe Ribeiro de Meneses and Robert McNamara, "Parallel Diplomacy, Parallel War: The PIDE/DGC's Dealings with Rhodesia and South Africa, 1961–1974," *Journal of Contemporary History* 49, no. 2 (2014): 371–72, 377–88.

7. MAE, sous-série Mozambique 1960–72, 59QO30: Action rebelle et défense portugais, no. 122, Raymond Pierre, Lourenço Marques Consul, "A/S: De la réaction du FRELIMO contre les 'aldeamentos,'" July 28, 1972; Miguel Bandeira Jerónimo, "A Robust Operation: Resettling, Security, and Development in Late Colonial Angola (1960s–1970s)," *Itinerario* 44, no. 1 (2020): 1–25.

8. MAE, 59QO30, no. 143, Consulat-Général, Lourenço Marques to French Ambassador, Lisbon, "A/S: Arrestations en masse ou la répression préventive," August 23, 1972.

9. Odd Arne Westad, "The Third World Revolutions," in *Revolutionary World: Global Upheaval in the Modern Age*, ed. David Motadel (Cambridge, UK: Cambridge University Press, 2021), 186–91.

10. Editors' "Introduction," in *The Third World and the Global 1960s*, ed. Samantha Christiansen and Zachary A. Scarlett (Oxford: Berghahn, 2013), 3–5.

11. On the authenticity of Congo's sovereign independence before and after Katanga's secession, see Ryan M. Irwin, "Sovereignty in the Congo Crisis," in *Decolonization and the Cold War: Negotiating Independence*, ed. Leslie James and Elisabeth Leake (London: Bloomsbury, 2015), 203–14; Miles Larmer, "Nation-Making at the Border: Zambian Diplomacy in the Democratic Republic of Congo," *Comparative Studies in Society and History* 61, no. 1 (2019): 148–62.

12. Alanna O'Malley, *The Diplomacy of Decolonisation, America, Britain and the United Nations during the Congo Crisis 1960–64* (Manchester, UK: Manchester University Press, 2018), chapters 5–6.

13. John Kent, *America, the UN and Decolonisation: Cold War Conflict in the Congo* (London: Routledge, 2011), chapters 1–2; David N. Gibbs, "The United Nations, International Peacekeeping and the Question of 'Impartiality': Revisiting the Congo Operation of 1960," *Journal of Modern African Studies* 38, no. 3 (2000): 359–82. For Hammarskjöld's work with Afro-Asian UNGA members: O'Malley, *Diplomacy of Decolonisation*, 38–42. Hammarskjöld died an air crash while shuttling between rival Congolese delegations in September 1961.

14. Miles Larmer and Eric Kennes, "Rethinking the Katangese Secession," *Journal of Imperial & Commonwealth History* 42 (2014): 741–51; Olivier Boehme, "The Involvement of the Belgian Central Bank in the Katanga Secession, 1960–1963," *African Economic History* 33 (2005): 1–13.

15. Florence Gillet, "Les anciens coloniaux belges face à l'indépendance du Congo: entre discours et réalité," and Alexander Keese, "La décolonisation bloquée: négociations, évolutions et l'ombre du travail forcé en Angola sous l'État colonial tardif (1955–1974)," both in *Démontage d'empires*, ed. Jean Fremigacci, Daniel Lefeuvre, and Marc Michel (Paris: Riveneuve editions, 2012), 94–98 and 102–24; Jamie Miller, *An African Volk: The Apartheid Regime and Its Search for Survival* (Oxford: Oxford University Press, 2016), chapters 2–3.

16. *Foreign Relations of the United States* (FRUS) 1961–3, vol. 20: Congo Crisis (Washington DC: US Government Printing Office, 1994), doc. 7, "Briefing Paper Prepared in the Department of State," n.d. 1961; Gibbs, *The Political Economy*, 126–34.

17. Odd Arne Westad, *The Global Cold War: Third World Interventions and the Making of Our Times* (Cambridge, UK: Cambridge University Press, 2005), 137–39. Matthew Hughes, "Fighting for White Rule in Africa: The Central African Federation, Katanga, and the Congo Crisis, 1958–1965," *International History Review* 25 (2003): 592–613.

18. For an exemplary case, plus analysis of the dynamics of such neocolonial coups, see Abdel Razzaq Takriti, *Monsoon Revolution: Republicans, Sultans, and Empires in Oman, 1965–1976* (Oxford: Oxford University Press, 2013); idem, "Colonial Coups and the War on Popular Sovereignty," *American Historical Review* 124, no. 3 (2019): 880–903. For the Yemeni case: Asher Orkaby, *Beyond the Arab Cold War: The International History of the Yemen Civil War, 1962–68* (New York: Oxford University Press, 2017), 161–68; Clive Jones, *Britain and the Yemen Civil War, 1962–1965: Ministers, Mercenaries and Mandarins* (Brighton: Sussex Academic Press, 2004); Aaron Edwards, "A Triumph of Realism? Britain, Aden and the End of Empire," in *Britain*

and State Formation in Arabia, 1962–1971, ed. Clive Jones (Abingdon, UK: Routledge, 2018), 5–17.

19. Takriti, "Colonial Coups," 907–9.

20. From the 1930s, the global proliferation of the United States' 'empire of bases' figured especially large: see Chalmers Johnson, *The Sorrows of Empire: Militarism, Secrecy, and the End of the Republic* (New York: Metropolitan, 2004), chapter 6, plus the contributions to Catherine Lutz, ed., *The Bases of Empire: The Global Struggle against U.S. Military Posts* (New York: NYU Press, 2009), part 2: "Global Resistance."

21. John Connell and Robert Aldrich, *The Ends of Empire: The Last Colonies Revisited* (Basingstoke, UK: Palgrave Macmillan, 2020), 417–50.

22. Colin A. Palmer, *Cheddi Jagan and the Politics of Power: British Guiana's Struggle for Independence* (Chapel Hill: University of North Carolina Press, 2010), chapters 6–7; and for the Cold War dimension: Stephen G. Rabe, *U.S. Intervention in British Guiana: A Cold War Story* (Chapel Hill: University of North Carolina Press, 2005).

23. Anton L. Allahar, "Situating Ethnic Nationalism in the Caribbean," in *Ethnicity, Class, and Nationalism: Caribbean and Extra-Caribbean Dimensions*, ed. Anton L. Allahar (Lanham, MD: Lexington Books, 2005), 1–22; Aaron Kamugisha, *Beyond Coloniality: Citizenship and Freedom in the Caribbean Intellectual Tradition* (Bloomington: Indiana University Press, 2019).

24. Robert Norton, "Accommodating Indigenous Privilege: Britain's Dilemma in Decolonizing Fiji," *Journal of Pacific History* 37, no. 2 (2002): 133–46; Gregory Rawlings, "Lost Files, Forgotten Papers and Colonial Disclosures: The 'Migrated Archives' and the Pacific, 1963–2013," *Journal of Pacific History* 50, no. 2 (2015): 200–3.

25. Tracey Banivanua Mar, *Decolonisation and the Pacific: Indigenous Globalisation and the Ends of Empire* (Cambridge, UK: Cambridge University Press, 2016), 133–41, 151–59.

26. Matthew Jones, *Conflict and Confrontation in South East Asia, 1961–1965* (Cambridge, UK: Cambridge University Press, 2002), 40–53.

27. Jones, *Conflict and Confrontation*, 53–54. A referendum, the so-called Act of Free Choice, was held in Western Papua New Guinea in July–August 1969. For many, Indonesian military pressure during the referendum delegitimized its result: confirmation of the territory's attachment to Indonesia.

28. As Margot Tudor demonstrates, UN peacekeeping forces deployed to West Papua silenced oppositional Papuan voices; see her "Gatekeepers to Decolonisation: Recentring the UN Peacekeepers on the Frontline of West Papua's Recolonisation, 1962–3," *Journal of Contemporary History* 57, no. 2 (2022): 293–316.

29. Jones, *Conflict*, 126–28, 268–77.

30. "Slaughter in Indonesia: Britain's Secret Propaganda War," *The Observer*, October 17, 2021. The British propaganda offensive was coordinated by the secretive Foreign Office Cold War propaganda arm, the Information Research Department. Estimates of the death toll in Indonesia's DeSukarnoization vary, but, according to one estimate, at least half a million people lost their lives and over a million more were detained: Geoffrey B. Robinson, *The Killing Season: A History of the Indonesian Massacres, 1965–66* (Princeton, NJ: Princeton University Press, 2018), 1–3,

7–10, and, on British propaganda, 188–93. For connections between propaganda and torture of Indonesia's leftists, see John Roosa, *Buried Histories: The Anticommunist Massacres of 1965–1966 in Indonesia* (Madison: University of Wisconsin Press, 2020), 87–106.

31. James Jacobs, "Namibia: Effective Strategic Buffer Zone or Draining Foreign Adventure?" in *In Different Times: The War for Southern Africa, 1966–1989*, ed. Ian van der Waag and Albert Grundlingh (Stellenbosch: African Sun Media, 2019), 93–99; for South Africa's covert assistance to Rhodesia's UDI: Sue Onslow, "A Question of Timing: South Africa and Rhodesia's Unilateral Declaration of Independence, 1964–65," *Cold War History* 5, no. 2 (2005): 129–59; for Portuguese-Rhodesian economic cooperation following a 1964 trade agreement: Tinashe Nyamunda, "In Defence of White Rule in Southern Africa: Portuguese–Rhodesian Economic Relations to 1974," *South African Historical Journal* 71, no. 3 (2019): 394–416.

32. Omar Ribeiro Thomaz, "'The Good-Hearted Portuguese People': Anthropology of Nation, Anthropology of Empire," in *Empires, Nations, and Natives: Anthropology and State-Making*, ed. Benoît de l'Estoile, Federico Neiburg, and Lygia Sigaud (Durham, NC: Duke University Press, 2005), 58–69.

33. Antoinette Errante, "White Skin, Many Masks: Colonial Schooling, Race, and National Consciousness among White Settler Children in Mozambique, 1934–1974," *International Journal of African Historical Studies* 36, no. 1 (2003): 7–33.

34. Peter Karibe Mendy, "Portugal's Civilizing Mission in Colonial Guinea-Bissau: Rhetoric and Reality," *International Journal of African Historical Studies* 36, no. 1 (2003): 35–8.

35. Miller, *African Volk*, 32–51; Josiah Brownell, "Out of Time: Global Settlerism, Nostalgia, and the Selling of the Rhodesian Rebellion Overseas," *Journal of Southern African Studies* 43, no. 4 (2017): 805–24.

36. Luise White, "What Does It Take to Be a State? Sovereignty and Sanctions in Rhodesia, 1965–1980," in *The State of Sovereignty: Territories, Laws, Populations*, ed. Douglas Howland and Luise White (Bloomington: Indiana University Press, 2009), 148–56.

37. Luise White, *Unpopular Sovereignty: Rhodesian Independence and African Decolonization* (Chicago: University of Chicago Press, 2015).

38. British Archives online, "Zimbabwe under Colonial Rule," Internal Affairs, 1947–73, "Report of the Secretary of Internal Affairs for the Year 1965," 1, deposited April 7, 1966.

39. Reflecting this resentment, Salazar's Portugal was one of two regimes, along with Communist China, that did not send condolences to Washington at John F. Kennedy's assassination: Philip E. Muehlenbeck, "John F. Kennedy as Viewed by Africans," in *Globalizing the U.S. Presidency: Postcolonial Views of John F. Kennedy*, ed. Cyrus Schayegh (London: Bloomsbury, 2021), 37–38.

40. Michael Evans, "The Wretched of the Empire: Politics, Ideology and Counterinsurgency in Rhodesia, 1965–80," *Small Wars & Insurgencies* 18, no. 2 (2007): 175–95, at 179–80. The diversity of opinion and the generational conflict behind supposedly monolithic settlerism is nicely described in Luise White, "Civic Virtue, Young Men, and the Family: Conscription in Rhodesia, 1974–1980," *International Journal of African Historical Studies* 37, no. 1 (2004): 103–21.

41. Cláudia Castelo, "Reproducing Portuguese Villages in Africa: Agricultural Science, Ideology and Empire," *Journal of Southern African Studies* 42, no. 2 (2016): 271–77.

42. Fernando Tavares Pimenta, "White Settler Politics and Euro-African Nationalism in Angola, 1945–1975," in *The Routledge Handbook of the History of Settler Colonialism*, ed. Edward Cavanagh and Lorenzo Veracini (Abingdon, UK: Routledge, 2016), 278–83.

43. For brief summaries, see the following contributions in Cavanagh and Veracini, *Routledge Handbook of the History of Settler Colonialism*: Enocent Msindo, "Settler Rule in Southern Rhodesia, 1890–1979," 257–59; Pimenta, "White Settler Politics," 280–86; Edward Cavanagh, "Settler Colonialism in South Africa: Land, Labour and Transformation, 1880–2015," 292–99.

44. John Roosa, *Pretext for Mass Murder: The September 30th Movement and Suharto's Coup d'état in Indonesia* (Madison: University of Wisconsin Press, 2006): 34–60.

45. Robert Cribb, "Genocide in Indonesia, 1965–1966," *Journal of Genocide Research* 3, no. 2 (2001): 219–39; Douglas Kammen and Katharine McGregor, eds., *The Contours of Mass Violence in Indonesia, 1965–1968* (Singapore: NIAS Press, 2012).

46. Robinson, *The Killing Season*, chapters 2–3; Roosa, *Pretext for Mass Murder*, 176–98; Taomo Zhou, "China and the Thirtieth of September Movement," *Indonesia* 98 (October 2014): 29–58; Mark Atwood Lawrence, *The End of Ambition: The United States and the Third World in the Vietnam Era* (Princeton, NJ: Princeton University Press, 2021), 213–16, 231–49.

47. Douglas Anthony, "'Ours Is a War of Survival': Biafra, Nigeria and Arguments about Genocide, 1966–70," *Journal of Genocide Research* 16, no. 2–3 (2014): 205–25, at 205–11. A military coup in January 1966 saw a predominantly Igbo group of military officers overthrow a regime dominated by northern Nigerians. Three waves of northern violence and ethnic cleansing of Igbos living outside their home region followed over the summer of 1966, during which General J. T. U. Aguiyi-Ironsi, the head of state installed in the January coup, was murdered along with more than 200 fellow Igbos in various army positions. Civilian deaths, although untallied, were certainly higher, stoking Igbo claims that the new federal regime led by Lieutenant-Colonel Yakubu Gowon was determined not just to suppress regional autonomy but to pursue a genocidal campaign against the Biafran Republic, which declared its independence on May 30, 1967.

48. S. Elizabeth Bird and Fraser Ottanelli, "The Asaba Massacre and the Nigerian Civil War: Reclaiming Hidden History," *Journal of Genocide Research* 16, no. 2–3 (2014): 379–99.

49. On child mortality, the evacuation of some 4,000 Biafran children to Gabon, Côte d'Ivoire and São Tomé and the consequent Africanization of the UNHCR, see Bonny Obhawoh, "Refugees, Evacuees, and Repatriates: Biafran Children, UNHCR, and the Politics of International Humanitarianism in the Nigerian Civil War," *African Studies Review* 63, no. 3 (2020): 569–76.

50. Taiwo Bello, "Ojukwu's Biafra: Relief Corridor, Arms Smuggling, and Broken Diplomacy in the Nigerian Civil War," *War & Society* 40, no. 3 (2021): 211–24.

51. Obhawoh, "Refugees, Evacuees," 572–76.

52. Lasse Heerten, *The Biafran War and Postcolonial Humanitarianism: Spectacles of Suffering* (Cambridge, UK: Cambridge University Press, 2017), 55–68.

53. Brad Simpson, "The Biafran Secession and the Limits of Self-Determination," *Journal of Genocide Research* 16, no. 2–3 (2014): 341.

54. Simpson, "Biafran Secession," 350; for background: Bertrand Taithe, "Biafra, Humanitarian Intervention and History," *Journal of Humanitarian Affairs* 3, no. 1 (2021): 68–78.

55. Brian McNeil, "'And Starvation Is the Grim Reaper': The American Committee to Keep Biafra Alive and the Genocide Question during the Nigerian Civil War, 1968–70," *Journal of Genocide Research* 16, no. 2–3 (2014): 317–28.

56. Christopher Griffin, "French Military Policy in the Nigerian Civil War, 1967–1970," *Small Wars & Insurgencies* 26, no. 1 (2015): 114, 122–25. Its covert support notwithstanding, the French government stopped short of granting official recognition to the Biafra Republic. Beginning in 1968 the French overseas intelligence agency, the SDECE African Service headed by Colonel Maurice Robert, also instructed its operatives to promote accusations of genocide.

57. Bruno Charbonneau and Tony Chafer, "Introduction: Peace Operations and Francophone Spaces," *International Peacekeeping* 19, no. 3 (2012): 276. Foccart's 'Africa cell' inside the Élysée administration cultivated connections with African regimes built on defense cooperation and security assistance, the prelude to some thirty-five French military interventions in Africa between 1960 and 1995.

58. Griffin, "French Military Policy," 115–21, 129; Jean-Pierre Batt, *Le syndrome Foccart: la politique française en Afrique de 1959 à nos jours* (Paris: Gallimard, 2012), 198–202, 220–41.

59. Kevin O'Sullivan, *The NGO Moment: The Globalisation of Compassion from Biafra to Live Aid* (Cambridge, UK: Cambridge University Press, 2021), 19–33; Lasse Heerten and A. Dirk Moses, "The Nigeria–Biafra War: Postcolonial Conflict and the Question of Genocide," *Journal of Genocide Research* 16, no. 2–3 (2014): 169–73.

60. Roy Doron, "Marketing Genocide: Biafran Propaganda Strategies during the Nigerian Civil War, 1967–70," *Journal of Genocide Research* 16, no. 2–3 (2013): 230–35, 241–43.

61. Heerten and Moses, "Nigeria–Biafra War," 174–76.

62. Simpson, "Biafran Secession," 341.

63. Simpson, "Biafran Secession," 339–40; Heerten, *Biafran War*, 72–75.

64. Samuel Fury Childs Daly, "A Nation on Paper: Making a State in the Republic of Biafra," *Comparative Studies in Society and History* 62, no. 4 (2020): 868–94. For a parallel case of the territorialization of political identity, see Julie MacArthur, "Decolonizing Sovereignty: States of Exception along the Kenya–Somali Frontier," *American Historical Review* 124, no. 1 (2019): 108–43.

65. Daly, "Nation on Paper," 874–77, 885–86.

66. Heerten, *The Biafran War*, part 2.

67. Wardatul Akmam, "Atrocities against Humanity during the Liberation War in Bangladesh: A Case of Genocide," *Journal of Genocide Research* 4, no. 4 (2002): 549–58; Yasmin Saikia, "Beyond the Archive of Silence: Narratives of Violence of the 1971 Liberation War of Bangladesh," *History Workshop Journal* 58, no. 1 (2004): 275–87; Sarmila Bose, "The Question of Genocide and the Quest for Justice in the 1971 War,"

Journal of Genocide Research 13, no. 4 (2011): 393–411; Nayanika Mookherjee, "The Absent Piece of Skin: Gendered, Racialized, and Territorial Inscriptions of Sexual Violence during the Bangladesh War," *Modern Asian Studies* 46, no. 6 (2012): 1575–601. Nayanika Mookherjee also analyses killings and rapes of men based on their identification as uncircumcised and, therefore, non-Muslim.

68. Jagmohan Meher, "Dynamics of Pakistan's Disintegration: The Case of East Pakistan, 1947–1971," *India Quarterly* 71, no. 4 (2015): 301–10.

69. Amber Abbas, review of Sarmila Bose, *"Dead Reckoning": Memories of the 1971 Bangladesh War*, H-Memory, March 20, 2012, 2. On Pakistan's imposition of Urdu-based language policy on Bengali speakers, see Philip Oldenburg, "'A Place Insufficiently Imagined': Language, Belief and the Pakistan Crisis of 1971," *Journal of Asian Studies* 44, no. 4 (1985): 718–27. Bengali speakers were, of course, neither homogeneous nor the only ethnolinguistic group adversely affected by coercive state-building. The indigenous communities of the Chittagong Hill Tracts in Southeastern Bangladesh offer a counterpoint: Bhumitra Chakma, "The Post-Colonial State and Minorities: Ethnocide in the Chittagong Hill Tracts, Bangladesh," *Commonwealth & Comparative Politics* 48, no. 3 (2010): 281–300, at 285–90.

70. Perhaps the best-known account of Searchlight's opening stages came from US Consul Archer Blood. On March 28 he telegrammed Washington thus, 'SUBJECT: Selective Genocide. Here in Dacca we are mute and horrified witnesses to a reign of terror by the Pak. Military.' He went on to describe Awami League activists, student leaders and academics 'marked for extinction' alongside house-by-house killings of non-Muslim Bengalis. *FRUS*, e7, doc. 125, Blood tel. to State, March 28, 1971. As is well known, the Nixon White House was unsympathetic, hostile to Indira Gandhi's India and preoccupied with its tilt to China, a Pakistan ally: Gary J. Bass, *The Blood Telegram: Nixon, Kissinger, and a Forgotten Genocide* (New York: Knopf, 2013); Geoffrey Warner, "Nixon, Kissinger and the Breakup of Pakistan, 1971," *International Affairs* 81, no. 5 (2005): 1102–4. For Congressional hostility to Nixon administration policy and Capitol Hill pressure for an arms embargo and humanitarian assistance: P. V. Rao, "The US Congress and the 1971 Crisis in East Pakistan," *International Affairs* 43, no. 1 (2006): 73–91.

71. The use of violence as a cultural weapon is evident in wartime rape and killings of uncircumcised males: Nayanika Mookherjee, "The Raped Woman as a Horrific Sublime and the Bangladesh War of 1971," *Journal of Material Culture* 20, no. 4 (2015): 280–86; idem, "'Absent Piece of Skin,'" 1578–93.

72. Yasmin Saikia, "Insāniyat for Peace: Survivors' Narrative of the 1971 War of Bangladesh," *Journal of Genocide Research* 13, no. 4 (2011): 484–96; Sarmila Bose, "Losing the Victims: Problems of Using Women as Weapons in Recounting the Bangladesh War," *Economic and Political Weekly* 42, no. 38 (2007): 3864–71.

73. Nayanika Mookherjee, "'Remembering to Forget': Public Secrecy and Memory of Sexual Violence in the Bangladesh War of 1971," *Journal of the Royal Anthropological Institute* 12 (2006): 433–50, especially 438–42.

74. Sonia Cordera, "India's Response to the 1971 East Pakistan Crisis: Hidden and Open Reasons for Intervention," *Journal of Genocide Research* 17, no. 1 (2015): 46–47, 51–56; Onkar Marwah, "India's Military Intervention in East Pakistan, 1971–1972," *Modern Asian Studies* 13, no. 4 (1979): 551–55, 564–74.

75. Antonio Costa Pinto, "La fin de l'Empire portugais," in *L'Europe face à son passé colonial*, ed. Olivier Dard and Daniel Lefeuvre (Paris: Riveneuve editions, 2008), 205–13; Salar Mohandesi, *Red Internationalism: Anti-Imperialism and Human Rights in the Global Sixties and Seventies* (Cambridge, UK: Cambridge University Press, 2023), 51–58, 72–79.

76. MAE, vol. 59QO29, no. 88/AL, Jacques Honoré, Lourenço Marques, to Lisbon Embassy, "A.S. infiltration à travers le Mozambique des guerrilleros du Pan Africanist Congress," July 22, 1968.

77. Portugal's Southern African territories were subdivided into districts, Angola and Mozambique being designated 'overseas provinces' of Portugal. Only after independence were interior districts administratively classified as provinces.

78. Inge Brinkman, "'The Time of the Leaflet': Pamphlets and Political Communication in the UPA (Northern Angola around 1961)," *Africa* 85, no. 2 (2015): 225–26.

79. Brinkman, "'Time of the Leaflet,'" 229–41.

80. MAE, 37QO26, no. 70/AL, Bruno Radius, Luanda, to Direction d'Afrique-Levant, "Plan de réforme de l'administration de l'Outre-Mer," March 3, 1969.

81. Justin Pearce, *Political Identity and Conflict in Central Angola, 1975–2002* (Cambridge, UK: Cambridge University Press, 2015), 47–53, 61–64, 94–98, 103–6.

82. MAE, 37QO26, no. 4/AL, Robert Marsan, Luanda, to Lisbon Embassy, "Action psychologique et promotion sociale," March 24, 1972.

83. Pearce, "Global Ideologies, Local Politics," 15–22.

84. Natalia Telepneva, *Cold War Liberation: The Soviet Union and the Collapse of the Portuguese Empire in Africa, 1961–1975* (Chapel Hill: University of North Carolina Press, 2021), 75–81. Initial Soviet plans hinged on uninterrupted cross-border supply to Angolan fighters through Congo-Zaire.

85. MAE, vol. 59QO29, no. 56/AL, Jacques Honoré to French Ambassador, Lisbon, "A.S. de la situation d'ensemble (un nouveau chapitre plus complexe s'annonce.)," May 1, 1968: three Mozambican townships on the Malawi frontier, Madimba, Novo Freixo and Milange, were judged crucial to FRELIMO's capacity to infiltrate into the more densely populated Zambesi district, the strategic pivot linking the north and south of the country. On weapons supply: Telepneva, *Cold War Liberation*, 101–2.

86. MAE, vol. 59QO29, no. 44, Honoré memo., "A.S. de certaines informations," April 4, 1967. The reference is to Tunisia's nationalist leader and first president, Habib Bourguiba; MacQueen, *Decolonization of Portuguese Africa*, 46–47.

87. Konrad J. Kuhn, "Liberation Struggle and Humanitarian Aid: International Solidarity Movements and the 'Third World' in the 1960s," in Christiansen and Scarlett, *Third World and the Global 1960s*, 75–78.

88. MAE, vol. 59QO29, MD 5–5, "Mozambique: assassinat du Dr Mondlane," February 19, 1969. French intelligence analysis confirmed that when former FRELIMO Deputy-President Uria Simango seized power following Eduardo Mondlane's assassination on February 2, 1969, the movement began pressing for Banda's overthrow, fearful that its sanctuary bases in Malawi might be shut down; see MAE, vol. 59QO29, no. 10451/DN, Colonel Bourgogne, Chef du Centre d'exploitation du renseignement, "Evolution de la situation au Mozambique," May 5, 1969.

89. MAE, vol. 59QO29, no. 55/AL, Jacques Honoré to Lisbon Embassy, "A.S. de trente ans de confrontation au Mozambique," April 15, 1967.

90. MAE, vol. 59QO29, no. 23/AL, Jacques Honoré to Lisbon Embassy, "A.S. de la situation militaire," February 28, 1968.

91. Neil Andersson, Cesar Palha Da Souza, and Sergio Paredes, "Social Cost of Land Mines in Four Countries: Afghanistan, Bosnia, Cambodia and Mozambique," *British Medical Journal* 311, no. 7007 (1995): 718–21; Alberto Ascherio and Robin Beillik, "Deaths and Injuries Caused by Land Mines in Mozambique," *The Lancet* 346, no. 8977 (1995): 721; Jean-Louis Arcand et al., "The Impact of Land Mines on Child Health: Evidence from Angola," *Economic Development and Social Change* 63, no. 2 (2015): 249–79.

92. MAE, vol. 59QO29, no. 175/AL, Raymond Pierre to Lisbon Embassy, "La lutte pour le contrôle de la population," December 16, 1971.

93. An army communiqué issued in Beira on November 10 claimed, for instance, that ninety-seven 'terrorists' were killed during security force operations in October 1968 in northern Mozambique, during which an improbably large figure of 132 rebel camps, most in the vicinity of the Zambian frontier, were allegedly destroyed; see MAE, vol. 59QO29, no. 6739, "Les opérations des forces portugaises au nord du Mozambique," November 12, 1968.

94. MAE, vol. 59QO29, Lourenço Marques consulate, translation of Portuguese army command communiqué for April 1967 (released on May 9, 1967): "Intense activité des forces armées au Nord de la Province"; Consulate LM, note d'information, no. 182, "A.S. nouveau succès portugais dans le Cabo Delgado," December 29, 1971.

95. Telepneva, *Cold War Liberation*, 152–55. FRELIMO later received Soviet deliveries of the more advanced Strela-2 rocket-launcher, although the weapons were not deployed before 1974, too late according to Telepneva, to make a major impact on the war.

96. Pearce, *Political Identity*, 55–56, 66–76.

97. MAE, vol. 37QO26: Situation intérieure, 1966–72, no. 256/AL, Robert Massé, Luanda, to Direction d'Afrique-Levant, "A.S. départ du Gouverneur Général de l'Angola," September 27, 1966.

98. MAE, vol. 37QO26, no. 274/AL, Robert Massé to Direction d'Afrique-Levant, "Situation politique en Angola après le départ du Gouverneur Général," October 18, 1966.

99. MAE, vol. 59QO29, no. 44, Jacques Honoré, "A.S. de certaines informations," April 4, 1967.

100. MAE, vol. 37QO26, no. 70/AL, Bruno Radius, Luanda, to Direction d'Afrique-Levant, "Plan de réforme de l'administration de l'Outre-Mer," March 3, 1969, no. 312/AL, Bruno Radius to Direction d'Afrique-Levant, "Gouverneur Général de l'Angola," October 23, 1970.

101. MAE, vol. 37QO26, no. 39/AL, Robert Marsan, Luanda, to Direction d'Afrique-Levant, "ANGOLA 72, sur les airs de fado," February 6, 1972.

102. Helen M. Kinsella, "Superfluous Injury and Unnecessary Suffering: National Liberation and the Laws of War," *Political Power and Social Theory* 32 (2017): 215–17.

103. MAE, vol. 59QO29, no. 66/AL, Jacques Honoré, "Renversement de la situation politico-militaire au Nord," April 9, 1969; Miguel Bandeira Jerónimo and José

Pedro Monteiro, "The Labours of (In)security in Portuguese Late Colonialism," in *The Oxford Handbook of Late Colonial Insurgencies and Counter-Insurgencies*, ed. Martin Thomas and Gareth Curless (Oxford: Oxford University Press, 2023), 505–25.

104. This state-building preoccupation persisted into the Angolan civil war after 1975: Pearce, *Political Identity*, 65–79.

105. For an observer's view of Mondlane's vulnerability to FRELIMO rivals, see Marcum, *Conceiving Mozambique*, 11–27, 40–48, 60–69, 85–98, 129–48. For the Soviet perspective: Telepneva, *Cold War Liberation*, 127–31.

106. MAE, vol. 59QO29, no. 10450/DN, Centre d'exploitation du renseignement memo., "Evolution de la situation au Mozambique," May 2, 1969; on the dynamics of FRELIMO politics in Dar es Salaam, see Roberts, "Assassination of Eduardo Mondlane," 1–19; Telepneva, *Cold War Liberation*, 131–35.

107. MAE, vol. 59QO29, no. 10450/DN, Centre d'exploitation du renseignement memo.: "Evolution de la situation au Mozambique," May 2, 1969.

108. MAE, vol. 59QO29, no. 10450/DN, Centre d'exploitation du renseignement memo.: "Evolution de la situation au Mozambique," May 2, 1969.

109. MAE, vol. 37QO26, no. 70/AL, Bruno Radius to Direction d'Afrique-Levant, "Plan de réforme de l'administration de l'Outre-Mer," March 3, 1969.

110. MAE, vol. 59QO29, Lourenço Marques consulate translation of speech by Governor-General to Mozambique legislative council, final session, April 1967.

111. MAE, vol. 59QO29, no. 163/AL, Raymond Pierre to Lisbon Embassy, "A.S. de la situation militaire dans le district de Tete," November 26, 1971.

112. MAE, vol. 59QO29, n. 151/AL, Raymond Pierre to Lisbon Embassy, "Difficultés de la colonisation dans le district de Cabo Delgado," November 18, 1971.

113. MAE, vol. 59QO30, no. 47, Consulat-Général L. M. memo, "Evolution de la lutte contre la subversion," March 8, 1972.

114. MAE, vol. 59QO30, no. 47, Consulat-Général L. M. memo, "Evolution de la lutte contre la subversion," March 8, 1972.

115. MAE, vol. 59QO30, no. 16, Consulat-Général L. M. memo, "Opérations portugaises près de lac Niassa," February 3, 1972.

116. MAE, vol. 59QO30, no. 25 Consulat-Général L. M. memo, "A.S: la terrorisme sélectif dans le district de Tete," February 14, 1972.

117. MAE, vol. 59QO30, no. 47, Consulat-Général L. M. memo, "Evolution de la lutte contre la subversion," March 8, 1972.

118. Paul Thomas Chamberlin, *The Global Offensive: The United States, the Palestine Liberation Organization, and the Making of the Post–Cold War Order* (Oxford: Oxford University Press, 2012), 92–95.

119. Patrick Chabal, *Amílcar Cabral: Revolutionary Leadership and People's War* (London: Hurst, 1983), 205.

120. Telepneva, *Cold War Liberation*, 106–9.

121. Telepneva, *Cold War Liberation*, 109–17.

122. Inês Galvão and Catarina Laranjeiro, "Gender Struggle in Guinea-Bissau: Women's Participation on and off the Liberation Record," in *Resistance and Colonialism*, ed. Nuno Domingos, Miguel Bandeira Jerónimo, and Ricardo Roque (Basingstoke, UK: Palgrave Macmillan 2019), 91–98.

123. Galvão and Laranjeiro, "Gender Struggle," 98–100, 103–5.

124. Norrie MacQueen, "Portugal's First Domino: 'Pluricontinentalism' and Colonial War in Guiné-Bissau, 1963–1974," *Contemporary European History* 8, no. 2 (1999): 216–21.

125. Telepneva, *Cold War Liberation*, 159–62

126. Westad, *Global Cold War*, 212–24; Telepneva, *Cold War Liberation*, 162–64.

127. MacQueen, "Portugal's First Domino," 216–29; Richard Robinson, "The Influence of Overseas Issues in Portugal's Transition to Democracy," in *The Last Empire: Thirty Years of Portuguese Decolonization*, ed. Stewart Lloyd-Jones and António Costa Pinto (Bristol: Intellect, 2003), 6–9.

128. Westad, *Global Cold War*, 226–29.

129. For analysis of the internecine warfare in Angola and Mozambique, see MacQueen, *Decolonization of Portuguese Africa*, chapters 5 and 6. While these civil wars had unique local dynamics, proxy interventions prolonged them; see Linda M. Heywood, "Towards an Understanding of Modern Political Ideology in Africa: The Case of the Ovimbundu in Angola," *Journal of Modern African Studies* 36, no. 1 (1998): 149–65; Margaret Hall, "The Mozambican National Resistance Movement (Renamo): A Study in the Destruction of an African Country," *Africa* 60, no. 1 (1990): 39–68; JoAnn McGregor, "Violence and Social Change in a Border Economy: War in the Maputo Hinterland, 1984–1992," *Journal of Southern African Studies* 24, no. 1 (1998): 37–60; Pearce, *Political Identity*, 53–64 and chapters 5 and 7. For the Cubans, see Gleijeses, *Conflicting Missions*; for the Soviets and Chinese: Thomas H. Henriksen, "Angola, Mozambique and Soviet Intervention: Liberation and the Quest for Influence," in *Soviet and Chinese Aid to African Nations*, ed. Warren Weinstein and Thomas H. Henriksen (New York: Praeger, 1980); Steven F. Jackson, "China's Third World Foreign Policy: The Case of Angola and Mozambique, 1961–1993," *China Quarterly* 142 (1995): 388–422; and for the US and South Africans: Witney W. Schneidman, *Engaging Africa: Washington and the Fall of Portugal's Colonial Empire* (Dallas: University Press of America, 2004); Robert Scott Jaster, *The Defence of White Power: South African Foreign Policy under Pressure* (London: Macmillan, 1988).

130. Helder Adegar Fonseca, "The Military Training of Angolan Guerrillas in Socialist Countries: A Prosopographical Approach, 1961–1974," in Dallywater, Saunders, and Fonseca, *Southern African Liberation Movements*, 114–17.

131. Luise White, "'Heading for the Gun': Skills and Sophistication in an African Guerrilla War," *Comparative Studies in Society & History* 51, no. 2 (2009): 242–50, 253–59.

132. Heike I. Schmidt, *Colonialism and Violence in Zimbabwe: A History of Suffering* (Woodbridge, UK: James Currey, 2013), 42–44, 142–45. For South African regime reaction, see Jamie Miller, "Things Fall Apart: South Africa and the Collapse of the Portuguese Empire, 1973–74," *Cold War History* 12, no. 2 (2012): 183–204.

133. IISH, Africa Labour History, ARCH02615, file 38, International Defence and Aid Fund, London, Special Report no. 2, "Terror in Tete, a Documentary Report of Portuguese Atrocities in Tete District, Mozambique, 1971–1972."

134. MacQueen, *Decolonization of Portuguese Africa*, 48–49; Mustafah Dhada, *The Portuguese Massacre of Wiriyamu in Colonial Mozambique, 1964–2013* (London: Bloomsbury, 2016), 51, 56; K. B. Wilson, "On Truths about Truth in Mozambique's Liberation Struggle," *Journal of Southern African Studies* 43, no. 4 (2017): 846–48, at 847. Renamed in 1969, the DGS was the successor to the PIDE.

135. Dhada, *Portuguese Massacre*, 154–57, 163.

136. Dhada, *Portuguese Massacre*, 140–43; Wilson, "On Truths," 847.

137. Dhada, *Portuguese Massacre*, 112–17, 159–72, 190–94: tables 8–12. Mustafah Dhada's fieldwork makes plain that the 385 figure refers *solely* to the named dead and is likely an underestimate. Chico Cachavi was later assassinated by a FRELIMO female detachment.

138. Chamberlin, *Global Offensive*, 5–7.

139. MAE, 29QO/16, JMD/MD, "Note pour M. de Laboulaye, A/S La coopération franco-algérienne," October 20, 1966; Namari Burki, "From the Theory to the Practice of Liberation: Fanon, May '68 and the Black Consciousness Movement in South Africa," in *A Global History of Anti-Apartheid: "Forward to Freedom" in South Africa*, ed. Anna Konieczna and Rob Skinner (Cham: Palgrave Macmillan, 2019), 105–30; Heather Marie Stur, *Saigon at War: South Vietnam and the Global Sixties* (Cambridge, UK: Cambridge University Press, 2020); Robert Trent Vinson, "Up from Slavery and down with Apartheid! African-Americans and Black South Africans against the Global Color Line," *Journal of American Studies* 52, no. 2 (2018): 297–329; Brenda Gayle Plummer, *In Search of Power: African Americans in the Era of Decolonization, 1956–1974* (Cambridge, UK: Cambridge University Press, 2013), 210–14, 270–77.

140. For assessment of Tet: Lien-Hang T. Nguyen, *Hanoi's War: An International History of the War for Peace in Vietnam* (Chapel Hill: University of North Carolina Press, 2012), 115–29.

141. Chamberlin, *Global Offensive*, 43–49. The Israeli government's justification of the al-Karama raid as a retaliatory police action only added to the impression that it signified colonial-style warfare and colonialist behavior.

142. The confluence between these elements emerged during Nasser's only face-to-face meeting with President Eisenhower during a September 1960 UN session in New York: Salim Yaqub, *Containing Arab Nationalism: The Eisenhower Doctrine and the Middle East* (Chapel Hill: University of North Carolina Press, 2004), 265–66.

143. Chamberlin, *Global Offensive*, 19–22, 52–61; Mohandesi, *Red Internationalism*, 118–40.

144. Mohandesi, *Red Internationalism*, 104–5.

145. Jessica Whyte, "The 'Dangerous Concept of the Just War': Decolonization, Wars of National Liberation, and the Additional Protocols to the Geneva Conventions," *Humanity* 9, no. 3 (2018): 316–17; Roland Burke, *Decolonization and the Evolution of International Human Rights* (Philadelphia: University of Pennsylvania Press, 2010), 93–95, 106–11.

146. Eleanor Davey, "Decolonizing the Geneva Conventions: National Liberation and the Development of Humanitarian Law," in *Decolonization, Self Determination,*

and the Rise of Global Human Rights Politics, ed. A. Dirk Moses, Marco Duranti, and Roland Burke (Cambridge, UK: Cambridge University Press, 2020), 375–96. ICRC experiences in the Biafra conflict were especially influential; see Marie-Luce Desgrandchamps, "'Organising the Unpredictable': The Nigeria–Biafra War and Its Impact on the ICRC," *International Review of the Red Cross* 94, no. 888 (2012): 1413–32.

147. Kinsella, "Superfluous Injury," 218–24.

148. Whyte, "'Dangerous Concept,'" 323–28.

149. Whyte, "'Dangerous Concept,'" 315.

150. Davey, "Decolonizing the Geneva Conventions," 381–84, 388. Davey stressed the pivotal roles of, first, Mouloud Belaoune, former FLN doctor and president of the Algerian Red Crescent between 1967 and 1994, then of the OAU's Coordinating Committee for the Liberation of Africa as liaisons between anticolonial insurgents and the ICRC.

151. Cited in Whyte, "'Dangerous Concept,'" 329.

152. Davey, "Decolonizing the Geneva Conventions," 390–91, 394–96. For the varieties of combatant groups, their transnational complexion, and the inadequacy of a 'national liberation' descriptor, see Luise White and Miles Larmer, "Mobile Soldiers and the Un-National Liberation of Southern Africa," *Journal of Southern African Studies* 40, no. 6 (2014): 1271–4.

153. Benoît Trépied, "Decolonization without Independence? Breaking with the Colonial in New Caledonia (1946–1975)," in *France's Modernising Mission: Citizenship, Welfare and the Ends of Empire*, ed. Ed Naylor (London: Palgrave Macmillan, 2018), 68–76; Margaret Jolly, "Horizons and Rifts in Conversations about Climate Change in Oceania," in *Pacific Futures: Past and Present*, ed. Warwick Anderson, Miranda Johnson, and Barbara Brookes (Honolulu: University of Hawai'i Press, 2018), 23–40.

154. James Mark, Tobias Rupprecht, and Ljubica Spaskovska, *1989: Eastern Europe in Global Perspective* (Cambridge, UK: Cambridge University Press, 2019), 36–37.

155. Mark, Rupprecht, and Spaskovska, *1989*, 20.

156. Malika Rahal, "Empires," in *Europe's Postwar Periods—1989, 1945, 1918: Writing History Backwards*, ed. Martin Conway, Pieter Lagrou, and Henry Rousso (London: Bloomsbury, 2019), 140–41.

157. As foundational work in a now-vast literature: Mary Kaldor, *New and Old Wars: Organized Violence in a Global Era*, 3rd edition (London: Polity, 2012); Paul Collier and Anke Hoeffler, "Greed and Grievance in Civil War," *Oxford Economic Papers* 56 (2004): 563–95; M. Berdal and D. Malone, eds., *Greed and Grievance: Economic Agendas in Civil Wars* (Boulder, CO: Lynne Rienner, 2000); C. Allen, "Warfare, Endemic Violence and State Collapse," *Review of African Political Economy* 81 (1999): 367–84.

Conclusion: A World Remade by Decolonization?

1. Michael Lang, "Globalization: Its History," *Journal of Modern History* 78 (December 2006): 926.

2. Barry K. Gills, "'Empire' versus 'Cosmopolis': The Clash of Globalizations," *Globalizations* 2, no. 1 (2005): 5–13.

3. Lydia Walker, "Decolonization in the 1960s: On Legitimate and Illegitimate Nationalist Claims-Making," *Past & Present* 242 (February 2019): 231.

4. Frederick Cooper, "Decolonizations, Colonizations, and More Decolonizations: The End of Empire in Time and Space," *Journal of World History* 33, no. 3 (2022): 514–26.

5. For a transregional example of these processes, see Christopher Vaughan, "Violence and Regulation in the Darfur–Chad Borderland, c. 1909–1956," *Journal of African History* 54, no. 2 (2013): 177–98; more broadly: Robert S. G. Fletcher, *British Imperialism and the "Tribal Question": Desert Administration and Nomadic Societies in the Middle East, 1919–1936* (Oxford: Oxford University Press, 2015).

6. A. G. Hopkins, *American Empire: A Global History* (Princeton, NJ: Princeton University Press, 2018), 18; James Mark et al., *Socialism Goes Global: The Soviet Union and Eastern Europe in the Age of Decolonization* (Oxford: Oxford University Press, 2022).

7. Ewout Frankema, Michiel de Haas, and Marlous van Waijenburg, "Inequality Regimes in Africa from Pre-Colonial Times to the Present," *African Affairs* 122, no. 486 (2023): 57–71.

8. Defining examples include Alfred Crosby, *Ecological Imperialism: The Biological Expansion of Europe, 900–1900*, 2nd edition (Cambridge, UK: Cambridge University Press, 2015); John R. McNeill, *Mosquito Empires: Ecology and War in the Greater Caribbean, 1620–1914* (Cambridge, UK: Cambridge University Press, 2010); Mike Davis, *Late Victorian Holocausts: El Niño Famines and the Making of the Third World* (London: Verso reprint, 2017).

9. Robert M. Pouphail, "The Anthropocene's 'Belows': Nature and Power in Global History," in *World Histories from Below: Disruption and Dissent, 1750 to the Present*, 2nd ed., ed. Antoinette Burton and Tony Ballantyne (London: Bloomsbury, 2022), 257–65.

10. As Corey Ross puts it, late colonial politics was strongly ecological in its emphasis on the management of land and natural resources: Corey Ross, *Ecology and Power in the Age of Empire: Europe and the Transformation of the Tropical World* (Oxford: Oxford University Press, 2019), 378.

11. Eric D. Weitz, "From the Vienna to the Paris System: International Politics and the Entangled Histories of Human Rights, Forced Deportations, and Civilizing Missions," *American Historical Review* 113, no. 5 (2008): 1326–33.

12. Michael Ortiz, *Anti-Colonialism and the Crises of Inter-War Fascism* (London: Bloomsbury, 2023), forthcoming.

13. Joshua A. Sanborn, *Imperial Apocalypse: The Great War and the Destruction of the Russian Empire* (Oxford: Oxford University Press, 2014), 211–37; Eugene Rogan, *The Fall of the Ottomans: The Great War in the Middle East, 1914–1920* (New York: Basic Books, 2015), 385–406.

14. John Darwin, *The Empire Project: The Rise and Fall of the British World-System, 1830–1970* (Cambridge, UK: Cambridge University Press, 2009), 512–13; Stuart Ward, *Untied Kingdom: A Global History of the End of Britain* (Cambridge, UK: Cambridge University Press, 2023), 97–99, 483.

15. Boyd Van Dijk, *Preparing for War: The Making of the 1949 Geneva Conventions* (Oxford: Oxford University Press, 2022), 113–27.

16. Arie M. Dubnov, "Civil War, Total War or a War of Partition? Reassessing the 1948 War in Palestine from a Global Perspective," in *The Breakup of India and Palestine: The Causes and Legacies of Partition*, ed. Victor Kattan and Amit Ranjan (Manchester, UK: Manchester University Press, 2023), 222–35, 246–50; Subir Sinha, "Lineages of the Developmental State: Transnationality and Village India, 1900–1965," *Comparative Studies in Society and History* 50, no. 1 (2008): 72–73; Michael E. Latham, *The Right Kind of Revolution: Modernization, Development, and U.S. Foreign Policy from the Cold War to the Present* (Ithaca, NY: Cornell University Press, 2011); Bradley R. Simpson, *Economists with Guns: Authoritarian Development and U.S.-Indonesian Relations, 1960–1968* (Stanford, CA: Stanford University Press, 2010).

17. Taylor C. Sherman, "From 'Grow More Food' to 'Miss a Meal': Hunger, Development, and the Limits of Post-Colonial Nationalism in India, 1947–1957," *South Asia* 36, no. 4 (2013): 571.

18. Debra Thompson, "Through, against, and beyond the Racial State: The Transnational Stratum of Race," in *Race and Racism: Confronting the Global Colour Line*, ed. Alexander Anievas, Nivi Manchanda, and Robbie Shilliam (London: Routledge, 2014), 44; Karl Ittmann, *A Problem of Great Importance: Population, Race, and Power in the British Empire, 1919–1973* (Berkeley: University of California Press, 2013), 89–93, 119–21; Young-Sun Hong, *Cold War Germany, the Third World, and the Global Humanitarian Regime* (Cambridge, UK: Cambridge University Press, 2017), 20–25.

19. James Mayall, "International Society, State Sovereignty, and National Self-Determination," in *The Oxford Handbook of the History of Nationalism*, ed. John Breuilly (Oxford: Oxford University Press, 2013), online publication, 6–7; Wm. Roger Louis, "Public Enemy Number One: The British Empire in the Dock at the United Nations, 1957–1971," in *The British Empire in the 1950s: Retreat or Revival?* ed. Martin Lynn (Basingstoke, UK: Palgrave Macmillan, 2006), 192–96; Young-Sun Hong, *Cold War Germany*, 18.

20. Bonny Ibhawoh, "Testing the Atlantic Charter: Linking Anticolonialism, Self-Determination, and Universal Human Rights," *International Journal of Human Rights* 18, no. 7–8 (2014): 1–19; Duranti, "Decolonizing the United Nations," 64, 66–73. The Council of Europe adopted the European Convention on Human Rights in November 1950.

21. Raphaëlle Khan, "Between Ambitions and Caution: India, Human Rights, and Self-Determination at the United Nations," in *Decolonization, Self Determination, and the Rise of Global Human Rights Politics*, ed. A. Dirk Moses, Marco Duranti, and Roland Burke (Cambridge, UK: Cambridge University Press, 2020), 209–11, 218.

22. Khan, "Between Ambitions and Caution," 208–9, 213–22, 224–26. As Khan makes clear, racial discrimination against the large Indian community in South Africa was a source of particular concern. For the turn among Asian nations away from the free circulation of migrants and toward tighter immigration restrictions, see Sunil Amrith, "Struggles for Citizenship around the Bay of Bengal," in *The Postcolonial Moment in South and Southeast Asia*, ed. Gyan Prakash, Michael Laffan, and Nikhil Menon (London: Bloomsbury, 2018), 107–18.

23. Bonny Ibhawoh, "Seeking the Political Kingdom: Universal Human Rights and the Anti-Colonial Movement in Africa," in Moses, Duranti, and Burke, *Decolonization, Self Determination*, 35–37.

24. Roland Burke, "The Internationalism of Human Rights," in *Internationalisms: A Twentieth Century History*, ed. Glenda Sluga and Patricia Clavin (Cambridge, UK: Cambridge University Press, 2016), 287–314; introduction to Moses, Duranti, and Burke, *Decolonization, Self Determination*, 35–37.

25. Salar Mohandesi, *Red Internationalism: Anti-Imperialism and Human Rights in the Global Sixties and Seventies* (Cambridge, UK: Cambridge University Press, 2023), 245–49.

26. Meredith Terretta, "From Below and to the Left? Human Rights and Liberation Politics in Africa's Postcolonial Age," *Journal of World History* 24 (June 2015): 398–408; on India: Khan, "Between Ambitions and Caution," 234–35.

27. Burke, Duranti, and Moses, "Introduction," 6.

28. Burke, Duranti, and Moses, "Introduction," 8–11; more generally, see Michael Barnett, *Empire of Humanity: A History of Humanitarianism* (Ithaca, NY: Cornell University Press, 2011), and, for a telling example: Alice L. Conklin, "Colonialism and Human Rights, a Contradiction in Terms? The Case of France and West Africa, 1895–1914," *American Historical Review* 103, no. 2 (1998): 419–42.

29. Roland Burke, "'A World Made Safe for Diversity': Apartheid and the Language of Human Rights, Progress, and Pluralism," in Moses, Duranti, and Burke, *Decolonization, Self Determination*, 331.

30. Gregory Mann, "Anti-Colonialism and Social Science: Georges Balandier, Madeira Keita and 'the Colonial Situation' in French Africa," *Comparative Studies in Society and History* 55, no. 1 (2013): 101. See also Annette K. Joseph-Gabriel, *Reimagining Liberation: How Black Women Transformed Citizenship in the French Empire* (Urbana: University of Illinois Press, 2020).

31. Ismay Milford, *African Activists in a Decolonising World: The Making of an Anticolonial Culture, 1952–1966* (Cambridge, UK: Cambridge University Press, 2023).

32. Daniel Byrne, review of Christopher J. Lee, ed., *Making a World after Empire: The Bandung Moment and Its Political Afterlives* (Athens: Ohio University Press, 2010), H-Diplo, H-Net reviews, May 2012, URL: http://www.h-net.org.uoelibrary.idm.oclc.org/reviews/showrev.php?id=35411.

33. "Guerre de libération nationale. Un témoignage d'Anissa Barkat, née Derrar," Centre national d'études historiques, 1977, Centre El Biar, Algiers, 1, 12. Member of an ALN nursing team in Algeria's wilaya V, Anissa Barkat was wounded by rocket fire from two French attack helicopters on May 3, 1959. My thanks to Natalya Vince for this reference.

34. Miguel Bandeira Jerónimo, "A Robust Operation: Resettling, Security, and Development in Late Colonial Angola (1960s–1970s)," *Itinerario* 44, no. 1 (2020): 1–25; David M. Anderson, *Histories of the Hanged: The Dirty War in Kenya and the End of Empire* (New York: Norton, 2005), 96–98; Moritz Feichtinger, "'A Great Reformatory': Social Planning and Strategic Resettlement in Late Colonial Kenya and Algeria, 1952–63," *Journal of Contemporary History* 52, no. 1 (2017): 52–57; Raphaëlle Branche, "Fighters for Independence and Rural Society in Colonial Algeria," in *Resistance and Colonialism*, ed. Nuno Dominos, Miguel Bandeira Jerónimo, and Ricardo Roque (Basingstoke, UK: Palgrave Macmillan, 2019), 72–78; Patricia Owens, *Economy of Force: Counterinsurgency and the Historical Rise of the Social* (Cambridge, UK: Cambridge University Press, 2015), 177–78, 197–207.

35. Karl Hack, "Detention, Deportation and Resettlement: British Counterinsurgency and Malaya's Rural Chinese, 1948–60," *Journal of Imperial & Commonwealth History* 43, no. 4 (2015): 611–40; Huw Bennett and Andrew Mumford, "Policing in Kenya during the Mau Mau Emergency, 1952–60," in *Policing Insurgencies: Cops as Counter-Insurgents*, ed. C. Christine Fair and Sumit Ganguly (Oxford: Oxford University Press, 2014), 89–94.

36. Matthew Hughes, *Britain's Pacification of Palestine: The British Army, the Colonial State, and the Arab Revolt, 1936–1939* (Cambridge, UK: Cambridge University Press, 2019), 318–19, 332, 337–40; Brian Drohan, *Brutality in an Age of Human Rights: Activism and Counterinsurgency at the End of the British Empire* (Ithaca, NY: Cornell University Press, 2017), 66–74.

37. Idean Salehyan, *Rebels without Borders: Transnational Insurgencies in World Politics* (Ithaca, NY: Cornell University Press, 2009), 32–40, 62–64.

38. Salehyan, *Rebels without Borders*, 40–46; Jeffrey T. Checkel, ed., *Transnational Dynamics of Civil War* (Cambridge, UK: Cambridge University Press, 2013), 3–20.

39. Bridget L. Coggins, "Rebel Diplomacy: Theorizing Violent Non-State Actors' Use of Talk," in *Rebel Governance in Civil War*, ed. Ana Arjona, Nelson Kasfir, and Zachariah Mampilly (Cambridge, UK: Cambridge University Press, 2015), 98–118.

40. Bridget Coggins makes this point in relation to civil war rebels, but it is equally applicable to decolonization conflicts: "Rebel Diplomacy," 105.

41. Salehyan, *Rebels without Borders*, 32–40, 62–64.

42. Chris Saunders, Helder Adegar Fonseca, and Lena Dallywater, "Southern African Liberation Movements and the Global Cold War 'East': Transnational Activism, 1960–1990," in *Southern African Liberation Movements and the Global Cold War 'East': Transnational Activism 1960–1990*, ed. Lena Dallywater, Chris Saunders, and Helder Adegar Fonseca (Oldenbourg: De Gruyter, 2019), 5–10, 14–17.

43. Nicholas Grant, "The Global Antiapartheid Movement and the Racial Politics of the Cold War," *Radical History Review* 119 (2014): 72–93.

44. Elizabeth M. Williams, *The Politics of Race in Britain and South Africa: Black British Solidarity and the Anti-Apartheid Struggle* (London: I. B. Tauris, 2017), 12–14.

45. Williams, *Politics of Race*, 25; Milford, *African Activists*, 118–19. CAO founders included members of student associations from South Africa, West Africa, Ghana, Uganda, Kenya, Tanganyika, and Sierra Leone.

46. BLO, MS Castle 7: Diary/notebook of visit to South Africa, January 1958, fo. 18; MS Castle 239, fo. 357: "Visiting M.P. Finds Union Tenser than Russia," *The Star*, January 13, 1958.

47. Jennifer M. Welsh, "Empire and Fragmentation," in *The Globalization of International Society*, ed. Tim Dunne and Christian Reus-Smit (Oxford: Oxford University Press, 2017), 161.

48. Paul Melly, "Why France Faces So Much Anger in West Africa," *BBC World*, December 5, 2021: https://www.bbc.co.uk/news/world-africa-59517501.

49. "The End of the CFA—Francly Speaking," *The Economist*, January 4, 2020, 35–36.

50. Sarah J. Wood, "How Empires Make Peripheries: Overseas France in Contemporary History," *Contemporary European History* 28 (2019), 434–45.

51. Kristen Stromberg Childers, *Seeking Imperialism's Embrace: National Identity, Decolonization, and Assimilation in the French Caribbean* (Oxford: Oxford University Press, 2016).

52. Robert H. Jackson analyzed this compromised sovereignty in his *Quasi-States: Sovereignty, International Relations and the Third World* (Cambridge, UK: Cambridge University Press, 1990).

53. Charles T. Call, "The Fallacy of the 'Failed State,'" *Third World Quarterly* 29, no. 8 (2008): 1491–507, at 1502.

54. Jason Sorens and William Ruger, "Globalisation and Intrastate Conflict: An Empirical Analysis," *Civil Wars* 16, no. 4 (2014): 381–401, at 383–84.

55. Erik Gartzke and Quan Li, "War, Peace, and the Invisible Hand: Positive Political Externalities of Economic Globalization," *International Studies Quarterly* 47 (2003): 561–86, at 561–63.

56. Iva Peša, "Between Waste and Profit: Environmental Values on the Central African Copperbelt," *The Extractive Industries and Society* 8, no. 4 (2021): 1–8; idem, "Decarbonization, Democracy and Climate Justice: The Connections between African Mining and European Politics," *Journal of Modern European History* 20, no. 3 (2022): 299–303.

57. Erik Gartzke, Quan Li, and Charles Boehmer, "Investing in the Peace: Economic Interdependence and International Conflict," *International Organization* 55, no. 2 (2001): 391–93, 397–402.

58. Quan Li, "Foreign Direct Investment and Interstate Military Conflict," *Journal of International Affairs* 62, no. 1 (2008), 54–59.

59. Brian Demare, *Land Wars: The Story of China's Agrarian Revolution* (Stanford, CA: Stanford University Press, 2019); Trung Dinh Dang, "Post-1975 Land Reform in Southern Vietnam: How Local Actions and Responses Affected National Land Policy," *Journal of Vietnamese Studies* 5, no. 3 (2010): 72–98; Susie Jacobs, "*Doi Moi* and Its Discontents: Gender, Liberalisation, and Decollectivisation in Rural Vietnam," *Journal of Workplace Rights* 13, no. 1 (2008): 18–32; Benjamin Siegel, "'The World Has Changed': Development, Land Reform, and the Ethical Work of India's Independence," in *The Postcolonial Moment in South and Southeast Asia*, ed. Gyan Prakash, Michael Laffan, and Nikhil Menon (London: Bloomsbury, 2018), 205–14; Christopher Goscha, "A 'Total War' of Decolonization? Social Mobilization and State-Building in Communist Vietnam (1949–54)," *War and Society* 31, no. 2 (2012): 153. Christopher Goscha notes that the Hanoi regime pursued land reform in 1953 to maximize peasant support for the mobilization required to defeat the French in the coming year. An abandonment of previous 'united front' policies, Vietnamese land reform took aim at landowners big and small, including smallholders whose ability to produce surplus foodstuffs had been critical to the country's internal food security.

60. Hannah Marcus, "Julius Nyerere: At the Crossroads of Postcolonial Tanzania's Reconstructed Socioeconomic and Political Reality," *International Journal of African Historical Studies* 53, no. 3 (2020): 413–16; John Saul, "Tanzania Fifty Years On (1961–2011): Rethinking *Ujamaa*, Nyerere and Socialism in Africa," *Review of African Political Economy* 39, no. 131 (2012): 118–22. For reflection on why Tanzania's 'socialism from below' did not materialize, see John S. Saul, "Poverty Alleviation and

the Revolutionary-Socialist Imperative: Learning from Nyerere's Tanzania," *International Journal* 57, no. 2 (2002): 193–207.

61. Beth S. Rabinowitz, *Coups, Rivals, and the Modern State: Why Rural Coalitions Matter in Sub-Saharan Africa* (Cambridge, UK: Cambridge University Press, 2018), 19–22, 33–40.

62. "Property Rights: Parcels, Plots and Power," *The Economist*, September 12, 2020, 37–40.

63. Petros Sekeris, "Land Inequality and Conflict in Sub-Saharan Africa," *Journal of Peace Economics, Peace Science and Public Policy* 16, no. 2 (2020): 3–5, 9–13.

64. B. S. Chimni, "Anti-Imperialism: Then and Now," in *Bandung, Global History, and International Law: Critical Pasts and Pending Futures*, ed. Luis Eslava, Michael Fakhri, and Vasuki Nesiah (Cambridge, UK: Cambridge University Press, 2017), 41–47.

65. Christoph Kalter, *The Discovery of the Third World: Decolonization and the Rise of the New Left in France c. 1950–1976* (Cambridge, UK: Cambridge University Press, 2016); John Munro, *The Anticolonial Front: The African-American Freedom Struggle and Global Decolonisation, 1945–1960* (Cambridge, UK: Cambridge University Press, 2017); Anna Konieczna and Rob Skinner, *A Global History of Anti-Apartheid: "Forward to Freedom" in South Africa* (Cham: Palgrave Macmillan, 2019); Paul Thomas Chamberlin, *The Global Offensive: The United States, the Palestine Liberation Organization, and the Making of the Post–Cold War Order* (Oxford: Oxford University Press, 2012); Jeremy Adelman, "International Finance and Political Legitimacy: A Latin American View of the Global Shock," in *The Shock of the Global: The 1970s in Perspective*, ed. Niall Ferguson, Charles S. Maier, Erez Manela, and Daniel Sargent (Cambridge, MA: Belknap, 2010), 113–23.

66. Salar Mohandesi, "Thinking the Global Sixties," *The Global Sixties* 15, no. 1–2 (2022): 5.

67. Adom Getachew, *Worldmaking after Empire: The Rise and Fall of Self-Determination* (Princeton, NJ: Princeton University Press, 2019), 13–20, 24–30.

68. Getachew, *Worldmaking*, 151–71.

69. Giuliano Garavini, *After Empires: European Integration, Decolonization, and the Challenge from the Global South 1957–1986* (Oxford: Oxford University Press, 2012), 169.

70. Cooper, "Decolonizations, Colonizations," 523.

71. Getachew, *Worldmaking*, 169–72.

72. Charles Tilly, *Coercion, Capital and European States, AD 990–1992* (Oxford: Blackwell, 1992), 209, 221, cited in Prasenjit Duara, "The Cold War as a Historical Period: An Interpretative Essay," *Journal of Global History* 6 (2011): 470.

73. Anna Stavrianakis, "Controlling weapons Circulation in a Postcolonial Militarised World," *Review of International Studies* 45, no. 1 (2019): 63–66.

74. Tarak Barkawi, "From Law to History: The Politics of War and Empire," *Global Constitutionalism* 7, no. 3 (2018): 317.

75. "MPs Make Secretive Visit to Diego Garcia and Chagos Islands," *The Guardian*, September 11, 2019, UK online edition: https://www.theguardian.com/world/2019/sep/11/mps-make-secretive-visit-to-diego-garcia-and-chagos-islands. Most of the expellees settled in three locations: Mauritius, the Seychelles, and the UK, where, for many, their rights of citizenship and residency remain unresolved.

76. Oliver Turner, "'Finishing the Job': The UN Special Committee on Decolonization (SCD) and the Politics of Self-Governance," *Third World Quarterly* 34, no. 7 (2013): 1200.

77. "Labour Would Return Chagos Islands, Says Jeremy Corbyn," *The Guardian*, November, 22, 2019, UK online edition: https://www.theguardian.com/world/2019/nov/22/uk-set-to-defy-un-deadline-to-return-chagos-islands.

78. Jason Hickel, Dylan Hickel, and Huzaifa Zoomkawala, "Plunder in the Post-Colonial Era: Quantifying Drain from the Global South through Unequal Exchange, 1960–2018," *New Political Economy* 26, no. 6 (2021): 1031–38.

79. "The Tale of Algeria's Stolen Cannon and France's Cockerel," *BBC Africa News*, December 29, 2020, https://www.bbc.co.uk/news/world-africa-54432571.

80. For the French Empire case, see: Daniel Lefeuvre, "La France face à son passé colonial: un double enjeu," in *L'Europe face à son passé colonial*, ed. Olivier Dard and Daniel Lefeuvre (Paris: Riveneuve Editions, 2008), 365–78. Contributors to this collection also reflect on contested memories of the Portuguese, Italian, Dutch, Belgian, and Japanese Empires.

81. Turner, "'Finishing the Job,'" 1198–204.

Archives Consulted

Archives Africaines, Belgian Foreign Ministry archives, Brussels (AA)
Archives Nationales, France (AN)
Archives Nationales d'Outre-Mer, Aix-en-Provence, France (ANOM)
Bodleian Library, Oxford (BLO)
India Office Records, British Library, London (IOR)
International Institute of Social History, Amsterdam (IISH)
Middle East Centre, St Antony's College, Oxford (MEC)
Ministère des Affaires Etrangères, Paris (MAE)
The National Archives, London (TNA)
Rhodes House Library, Oxford (RHL)
Service Historique de la Défense, Vincennes (SHD)
United States National Archives, College Park, MD (USNA)

Published Documents

BDEEP British Documents on the End of Empire Project
DDF   Documents Diplomatiques Français
FRUS   Foreign Relations of the United States (Washington, DC: US Government
       Printing Office, various dates)
CWIO   Cold War Intelligence Online, ed. Matthew M. Aid, Brill Online Primary
       Sources. Accessed via http://0-primarysources.brillonline.com.lib.exeter.ac
       .uk/browse/cold-war-intelligence/

Books, Articles, and Book Chapters

Abou-El-Fadl, Reem. "Neutralism Made Positive: Egyptian Anti-Colonialism on the Road to Bandung." *British Journal of Middle Eastern Studies* 42, no. 2 (2015): 219–40.

Abraham, Itty. "From Bandung to NAM: Non-Alignment and Indian Foreign Policy, 1947–65." *Commonwealth and Comparative Politics* 46 (2008): 195–219.

Accornero, Guya. *The Revolution before the Revolution: Late Authoritarianism and Student Protest in Portugal.* Oxford: Berghahn, 2016.

Acharya, Amitav. "Global International Relations (IR) and Regional Worlds: A New Agenda for International Studies." *International Studies Quarterly* 58, no. 4 (2014): 647–59.

———. "Norm Subsidiarity and Regional Orders: Sovereignty, Regionalism, and Rule-Making in the Third World." *International Studies Quarterly* 55, no. 1 (2011): 95–123.

Acharya, Amitav. *Rethinking Power, Institutions and Ideas in World Politics: Whose IR?* Abingdon, UK: Routledge, 2013.

———. "Studying the Bandung Conference from a Global IR Perspective." *Australian Journal of International Affairs* 70, no. 4 (2016): 342–57.

———. "Who Are the Norm Makers? The Asian–African Conference in Bandung and the Evolution of Norms." *Global Governance* 20 (2014): 405–17.

———. *Whose Ideas Matter? Agency and Power in Asian Regionalism.* Ithaca, NY: Cornell University Press, 2009.

Adams, Melinda. "Colonial Policies and Women's Participation in Public Life: The Case of British Southern Cameroons." *African Studies Quarterly* 8, no. 3 (2006): 1–22.

Adas, Michael. *Dominance by Design: Technological Imperatives and America's Civilizing Mission.* Cambridge, MA: Harvard University Press, 2006.

———. *Machines as the Measure of Men: Science, Technology, and Ideologies of Western Dominance.* Ithaca, NY: Cornell University Press, 2015.

Adelman, Jeremy. "An Age of Imperial Revolutions." *American Historical Review* 113, no. 2 (2008): 319–40.

———. *Empire and the Social Sciences: Global Histories of Knowledge.* London: Bloomsbury, 2019.

———. "International Finance and Political Legitimacy: A Latin American View of the Global Shock." In Ferguson et al., *Shock of the Global*, 113–27.

Adelman, Jeremy, and Gyan Prakash, eds. *Inventing the Third World: In Search of Freedom for the Postwar Global South.* London: Bloomsbury, 2022.

Adi, Hakim. *Pan-Africanism: A History.* London: Bloomsbury, 2018.

———. "Pan-Africanism and Communism: The Comintern, the "Negro Question" and the First International Conference of Negro Workers, Hamburg 1930." *African and Black Diaspora: An International Journal* 1, no. 2 (2008): 237–54.

———. *Pan-Africanism and Communism: The Communist International, Africa and the Diaspora, 1919–1939.* Trenton, NJ: Africa World Press, 2013.

Adler, Paul. *No Globalization without Representation: U.S. Activists and World Inequality.* Philadelphia: University of Pennsylvania Press, 2021.

Afro-Asian Networks Research Collective Manifesto. "Networks of Decolonization in Asia and Africa." *Radical History Review* 131 (May 2018): 176–82.

———. Special Issue: "Other Bandungs: Afro-Asian Networks in the Early Cold War." *Journal of World History* 29, no. 4 (Winter 2018/19).

———. Special Issue: "Trade Union Networks and the Politics of Expertise in an Age of Afro-Asian Solidarity." *Journal of Social History* 53, no. 2 (December 2019).

Agamben, Giorgio. "The Sovereign Police." In *The Politics of Everyday Fear*, edited by Brian Massumi, 61–63. Minneapolis: University of Minnesota Press, 1993.

Ageron, Charles-Robert. "L'Association des étudiants musulmans nord-africains en France durant l'entre-deux-guerres. Contribution à l'étude des nationalismes maghrébins." *Revue Française d'Histoire d'Outre-Mer* 70, no. 258 (1983): 25–56.

———. "Une troisième force combattante pendant la guerre d'Algérie. L'armée nationale du peuple algérien en son chef le 'général' Bellounis. Mai 1957–juillet 1958." *Outre-Mers* 321 (1998): 65–76.

Ahlman, Jeffrey. "The Algerian Question in Nkrumah's Ghana, 1958–1960: Debating 'Violence' and 'Non-Violence' in African Decolonization." *Africa Today* 57, no. 2 (2010): 67–84.

——. *Living with Nkrumahism: Nation, State, and Pan-Africanism in Ghana*. Athens: Ohio University Press, 2017.

Ahmida, Ali Abdullatif. *Forgotten Voices: Power and Agency in Colonial and Postcolonial Libya*. Abingdon, UK: Routledge, 2005.

——. *Genocide in Libya: Shar, a Hidden Colonial History*. Abingdon, UK: Routledge, 2021.

Aires, Oliveira Pedro. "Saved by the Civil War: African 'Loyalists' in the Portuguese Armed Forces and Angola's Transition to Independence." *International History Review* 39, no. 1 (2017): 126–42.

Aissaoui, Rabah. *Immigration and National Identity: North African Political Movements in Colonial and Postcolonial France*. London: I. B. Tauris, 2009.

Aitken, Robbie. "From Cameroon to Germany and Back via Moscow and Paris: The Political Career of Joseph Bilé (1892–1959), Performer, 'Negerarbeiter' and Comintern Activist." *Journal of Contemporary History* 43, no. 4 (2008): 597–616.

Akın, Yiğit. *When the War Came Home: The Ottomans' Great War and the Devastation of an Empire*. Stanford, CA: Stanford University Press, 2018.

Akita, George, and Brandon Palmer, eds. *The Japanese Colonial Legacy in Korea, 1910–1945: A New Perspective*. Honolulu: University of Hawai'i Press, 2015.

Akmam, Wardatul. "Atrocities against Humanity during the Liberation War in Bangladesh: A Case of Genocide." *Journal of Genocide Research* 4, no. 4 (2002): 543–59.

Alecou, Alexios. "Safeguarding through Stability: British Constitutional Proposals in Post-War Cyprus." *Journal of Human Rights in the Commonwealth* 2, no. 2 (2016): 50–56.

Alexander, Amanda. "International Humanitarian Law: Postcolonialism and the 1977 *Geneva Protocol I*." *Melbourne Journal of International Law* 17, no. 1 (2016): 15–50.

Alexander, Jocelyn. "Dissident Perspectives on Zimbabwe's Post-Independence War." *Africa* 68, no. 2 (1998): 151–82.

——. "The Political Imaginaries and Social Lives of Political Prisoners in Post-2000 Zimbabwe." *Journal of Southern African Studies* 36, no. 2 (2010): 483–503.

——. "The Productivity of Political Imprisonment: Stories from Rhodesia." *Journal of Imperial & Commonwealth History* 47, no. 2 (2019): 300–24.

——. "State Writing, Subversion and Citizenship in Southern Rhodesia's State of Emergency, 1959–1960." *Canadian Journal of African Studies* 52, no. 3 (2018): 289–309.

Alexander, Jocelyn, Joann McGregor, and Blessing-Miles Tendi, eds. *Transnational Histories of Southern Africa's Liberation Movements*. Abingdon, UK: Routledge, 2020.

Alexanderson, Kris. *Subversive Seas: Anticolonial Networks across the Twentieth-Century Dutch Empire*. Cambridge, UK: Cambridge University Press, 2019.

Alison, Miranda. "Cogs in the Wheel? Women in the Liberation Tigers of Tamil Eelam." *Civil Wars* 6, no. 4 (2003): 37–54.

Allahar, Anton L., ed. *Ethnicity, Class, and Nationalism: Caribbean and Extra-Caribbean Dimensions*. Lanham, MD: Lexington Books, 2005.

Allain, Jean. "Slavery and the League of Nations: Ethiopia as a Civilized Nation." *Journal of the History of International Law* 8 (November 2006): 213–44.

Allen, C. "Warfare, Endemic Violence and State Collapse." *Review of African Political Economy* 81 (1999): 367–84.

Allen, T., and D. Styan. "A Right to Interfere? Bernard Kouchner and the New Humanitarianism." *Journal of International Development* 12 (2000): 825–42.

Allina, Eric. "'No Real Freedom for the Natives': The Men in the Middle and Critiques of Colonial Labor in Central Mozambique." *Humanity: An International Journal of Human Rights, Humanitarianism, and Development* (cited hereafter as *Humanity*) 3, no. 3 (2012): 337–59.

Allman, Jean. "Between the Present and History: African Nationalism and Decolonization." In Parker and Reid, *Oxford Handbook of Modern African History*, 224–40.

———. "Nuclear Imperialism and the Pan-African Struggle for Peace and Freedom: Ghana, 1959–1962." *Souls: A Critical Journal of Black Politics, Culture and Society* 10 (June 2008): 83–102.

Alvi-Aziz, Hayat. "The (Non)Governance of Divided Territories: A Comparative Study of Bangladesh, Pakistan, and Palestine." *Comparative Studies of South Asia, Africa, and the Middle East* 28, no. 3 (2008): 461–72.

Ambaras, David. "Social Knowledge, Cultural Capital, and the New Middle Class in Japan, 1895–1912." *Journal of Japanese Studies* 24, no. 1 (1998): 1–33.

Ambrosius, Lloyd E. *Woodrow Wilson and American Internationalism*. Cambridge, UK: Cambridge University Press, 2017.

Amrith, Sunil. *Crossing the Bay of Bengal: The Furies of Nature and the Fortunes of Migrants*. Cambridge, MA: Harvard University Press, 2013.

———. "Reconstructing the 'Plural Society': Asian Migration between Empire and Nation, 1940–1948." *Past & Present* 210, Supplement 6 (2011): 237–57.

———. "Tamil Diasporas across the Bay of Bengal." *American Historical Review* 114, no. 3 (2009): 547–72.

Amrith, Sunil, and Patricia Clavin. "Feeding the World: Connecting Europe and Asia, 1930–1945." *Past & Present* Supplement 8 (2013): 29–50.

Anazi, Oche. *An African Path to Disability Justice: Community, Relationships and Obligations*. Cham, Switzerland: Springer, 2019.

Anderson, Carol. *Bourgeois Radicals: The NAACP and the Struggle for Colonial Liberation, 1941–1960*. New York: Cambridge University Press, 2015.

Anderson, Charles W. "State Formation from Below and the Great Revolt in Palestine." *Journal of Palestine Studies* 47, no. 1 (2017): 39–55.

———. "When Palestinians Became Human Shields: Counterinsurgency, Racialization, and the Great Revolt (1936–1939)." *Comparative Studies in Society and History* 63, no. 3 (2021): 625–54.

Anderson, David M. "British Abuse and Torture in Kenya's Counter-Insurgency, 1952–1960." *Small Wars & Insurgencies* 23, no. 4/5 (2012): 700–19.

———. "Depression, Dust Bowl, Demography, and Drought: The Colonial State and Soil Conservation in East Africa during the 1930s." *African Affairs* 83, no. 332 (1984): 321–43.

———. "Guilty Secrets: Deceit, Denial, and the Discovery of Kenya's 'Migrated Archive.'" *History Workshop Journal* 80, no. 1 (2015): 142–60.

———. "Making the Loyalist Bargain: Surrender, Amnesty and Impunity in Kenya's Decolonization, 1952–63." *International History Review* 39, no. 1 (2017): 48–70.

———. "Master and Servant in Colonial Kenya, 1895–1930." *Journal of African History* 41, no. 3 (2000): 459–85.

———. "Mau Mau in the High Court and the 'Lost' British Empire Archives: Colonial Conspiracy or Bureaucratic Bungle?" *Journal of Imperial & Commonwealth History* 39, no. 5 (2011): 699–716.

———. "Surrogates of the State: Collaboration and Atrocity in Kenya's Mau Mau War." In *The Barbarisation of Warfare*, edited by George Kassimeris, 172–88. London: Hurst, 2006.

Anderson, David M., and Daniel Branch. "Allies at the End of Empire: Loyalists, Nationalists and the Cold War, 1945–1976." *International History Review* 39, no. 1 (2017): 1–13.

Anderson, David M., and Øystein H. Rolandsen. "Violence as Politics in Eastern Africa, 1940–1990: Legacy, Agency, Contingency." *Journal of Eastern African Studies* 8, no. 4 (2014): 539–57.

Anderson, David M., and Juliane Weis. "The Prosecution of Rape in Wartime: Evidence from the Mau Mau Rebellion, Kenya 1952–60." *Law & History Review* 36, no. 2 (2018): 267–94.

Anderson, Warwick, Ricardo Roque, and Ricardo Ventura Santos, eds. *Luso-Tropicalism and Its Discontents: The Making and Unmaking of Racial Exceptionalism*. Oxford: Berghahn, 2019.

Anghie, Antony. *Imperialism, Sovereignty, and the Making of International Law*. Cambridge, UK: Cambridge University Press, 2005.

———. "Legal Aspects of the New International Economic Order." *Humanity* 6 (Spring 2015): 145–58.

———. "Whose Utopia? Human Rights, Development, and the Third World." *Qui Parle: Critical Humanities and Social Sciences* 22 (Fall/Winter 2013): 63–80.

Anievas, Alexander, Nivi Manchanda, and Robbie Shilliam. *Race and Racism in International Relations: Confronting the Global Colour Line*. London: Routledge, 2014.

Ankit, Rakesh. "Britain and Kashmir, 1948: 'The Arena of the UN.'" *Diplomacy & Statecraft* 24, no. 2 (2013): 273–90.

Ansari, Sarah. *Life after Partition: Migration, Community and Strife in Sindh, 1947–1962*. Oxford: Oxford University Press, 2005.

———. "Subjects or Citizens? India, Pakistan and the 1948 British Nationality Act." *Journal of Imperial & Commonwealth History* 41, no. 2 (2013): 285–312.

Ansari, Sarah, and William Gould. *Boundaries of Belonging: Localities, Citizenship and Rights in India and Pakistan*. Cambridge, UK: Cambridge University Press, 2019.

Anthony, Douglas. "'Ours Is a War of Survival': Biafra, Nigeria and Arguments about Genocide, 1966–70." *Journal of Genocide Research* 16, no. 2–3 (2014): 205–25.

———. "Resourceful and Progressive Blackmen: Modernity and Race in Biafra, 1967–1970." *Journal of African History* 51, no. 1 (2010): 41–61.

Antic, Ana. "Imagining Africa in Eastern Europe: Transcultural Psychiatry and Psychoanalysis in Cold War Yugoslavia." *Contemporary European History* 28, no. 2 (2019): 234–51.

———. *Non-Aligned Psychiatry in the Cold War: Revolution, Emancipation and Re-Imagining the Human Psyche*. Basingstoke: Palgrave-Macmillan, 2022.

Arditti, Roger, and Philip H. J. Davies. "Rethinking the Rise and Fall of the Malayan Security Service, 1946–48." *Journal of Imperial & Commonwealth History* 43, no. 2 (2015): 292–316.

Arezki, Saphia. *De l'ALN à l'ANP, la construction de l'armée algérienne, 1954–1991.* Paris: Éditions de la Sorbonne, 2022.

Arielli, Nir, and Bruce Collins, eds. *Transnational Soldiers: Foreign Military Enlistment in the Modern Era.* New York: Palgrave Macmillan, 2013.

Arjona, Ana. "Civilian Resistance to Rebel Governance." In Arjona, Kasfir, and Mampilly, *Rebel Governance in Civil War,* 180–202.

Arjona, Ana, Nelson Kasfir, and Zachariah Mampilly, eds. *Rebel Governance in Civil War.* Cambridge, UK: Cambridge University Press, 2015.

Armitage, David. *The Declaration of Independence: A Global History.* Cambridge, MA: Harvard University Press, 2007.

Armstrong, Elizabeth. "Before Bandung: The Anti-Imperialist Women's Movement in Asia and the Women's International Democratic Federation." *Signs* 41, no. 2 (2015): 305–31.

Arnold, David. "Looting, Grain Riots and Government Policy in South India, 1918." *Past & Present* 84 (August 1979): 111–45.

Arsan, Andrew. *Interlopers of Empire: The Lebanese Diaspora in Colonial West Africa.* Oxford: Oxford University Press, 2014.

——. "'This Is the Age of Associations': Committees, Petitions, and the Roots of Interwar Middle Eastern Internationalism." *Journal of Global History* 7 (2012): 166–88.

Ash, Catherine. "Forced Labour in Colonial West Africa." *History Compass* 4, no. 3 (2006): 402–6.

Ashworth, Lucian M. "Did the Realist–Idealist Great Debate Really Happen? A Revisionist History of International Relations." *International Relations* 16, no. 1 (2002): 33–51.

——. "Realism and the Spirit of 1919: Halford Mackinder, Geopolitics, and the Reality of the League of Nations." *European Journal of International Relations* 17, no. 2 (2010): 279–301.

Asselin, Pierre, and Martin Thomas. "French Decolonisation and Civil War: The Dynamics of Violence in the Early Phases of Anti-Colonial War in Vietnam and Algeria, 1940–56." *Journal of Modern European History* 20, no. 4 (2022): 513–35.

Asseraf, Arthur. *Electric News in Colonial Algeria.* Oxford: Oxford University Press, 2019.

Aterrano, Marco Maria. "Civilian Disarmament: Public Order and the Restoration of State Authority in Italy's Postwar Transition, 1944–6." *Journal of Contemporary History* 56, no. 2 (2020): 1–25.

Atieno Odhambo, E. S., and John Lonsdale, eds. *Mau Mau and Nationhood.* Oxford: James Currey, 2003.

Atkins, E. Taylor. *Primitive Selves: Koreana in the Japanese Colonial Gaze, 1910–1945.* Berkeley: University of California Press, 2010.

Atkins, Kaletso E. "'Kafir Time': Preindustrial Temporal Concepts and Labour Discipline in Nineteenth-Century Colonial Natal." *Journal of African History* 29, no. 2 (1988): 229–44.

Austin, Gareth. "Africa and the Anthropocene." In Austin, *Economic Development*, 95–118.

——, ed. *Economic Development and Environmental History in the Anthropocene: Perspectives on Asia and Africa.* London: Bloomsbury, 2017.

——. *Labour, Land and Capital in Ghana: From Slavery to Free Labour in Asante, 1807–1956.* Rochester, NY: University of Rochester Press, 2005.

——. "Mode of Production or Mode of Cultivation: Explaining the Failure of European Cocoa Planters in Competition with African Farmers in Colonial Ghana." In *Cocoa Pioneer Fronts since 1800: The Role of Smallholders, Planters and Merchants*, edited by William G. Clarence-Smith, 154–75. Basingstoke, UK: Macmillan, 1996.

——. "Resources, Techniques and Strategies South of the Sahara: Revising the Factor Endowments Perspective on African Economic Development, 1500–2000." *Economic History Review* 61, no. 3 (2008): 587–624.

Awenengo D'Alberto, Séverine. "Hidden Debates over the Status of the Casamance during the Decolonization Process in Senegal: Regionalism, Territorialism, and Federalism at a Crossroads, 1946–62." *Journal of African History* 61, no. 1 (2020): 67–88.

Ax, Christina Folke, Neils Brimnes, Niklas T. Jensen, and Karen Oslund, eds. *Cultivating the Colonies: Colonial States and Their Environmental Legacies.* Athens: Ohio University Press, 2014.

Aydin, Cemil. *The Politics of Anti-Westernism in Asia: Visions of World Order in Pan-Islamic and Pan-Asian Thought.* New York: Columbia University Press, 2007.

Ayers, A. J. "Sudan's Uncivil War: The Global-Historical Constitution of Political Violence." *Review of African Political Economy* 37, no. 124 (2010): 153–71.

Azam, Jean-Paul, and Anke Hoeffler. "Violence against Civilians in Civil Wars: Looting or Terror?" *Journal of Peace Research* 39, no. 4 (2002): 461–85.

Baev, Jordan. "Bulgarian Military and Humanitarian Aid to Third World Countries, 1955–75." In Muehlenbeck and Telepneva, *Warsaw Pact*, 298–325.

Bailkin, Jordanna. *The Afterlife of Empire.* Berkeley: University of California Press, 2012.

——. "AHR Roundtable: Where Did the Empire Go? Archives and Decolonization in Britain." *American Historical Review* 120, no. 3 (2015): 884–99.

——. "The Boot and the Spleen: When Was Murder Possible in British India?" *Comparative Studies of Society and History* 48, no. 2 (2006): 462–94.

——. *Unsettled: Refugee Camps and the Making of Multicultural Britain.* Oxford: Oxford University Press, 2018.

Bair, Jennifer. "Corporations at the United Nations: Echoes of the New International Economic Order." *Humanity* 6, no. 1 (2015): 159–71.

Balcells, Laia. *Rivalry and Revenge: The Politics of Violence during Civil War.* Cambridge, UK: Cambridge University Press, 2017.

Bamba, Abou B. "At the Edge of the Modern? Diplomacy, Public Relations, and Media Practices during Houphouët-Boigny's 1962 Visit to the United States." *Diplomacy & Statecraft* 22, no. 2 (2011): 219–38.

——. "Displacing the French? Ivorian Development and the Question of Economic Decolonisation, 1946–1975." In Dimier and Stockwell, *Business of Development*, 275–303.

Bancel, Nicolas, Pascal Blanchard, and Françoise Vergès. *La République coloniale: essai sur une utopie.* Paris: Albin Michel, 2003.

Bandeira Jerónimo, Miguel. "A Robust Operation: Resettling, Security, and Development in Late Colonial Angola (1960s–1970s)." *Itinerario* 44, no. 1 (2020): 1–25.

Bandeira Jerónimo, Miguel, and José Pedro Monteiro. "Colonial Labour Internationalized: Portugal and the Decolonization Momentum (1945–1975)." *International History Review* 42, no. 3 (2020): 485–504.

———, eds. *Internationalism, Imperialism and the Formation of the Contemporary World: The Pasts of the Present.* Basingstoke, UK: Palgrave Macmillan, 2018.

———. "The Inventors of Human Rights in Africa: Portugal, Late Colonialism, and the UN Human Rights Regime." In Moses, Duranti, and Burke, *Decolonization, Self Determination*, 285–315.

Banko, Lauren. "Claiming Identities in Palestine: Migration and Nationality under the Mandate." *Journal of Palestine Studies* 46, no. 1 (2017): 26–43.

———. "Keeping out the 'Undesirable Elements': The Treatment of Communists, Transients, Criminals and the Ill in Mandate Palestine." *Journal of Imperial & Commonwealth History* 47, no. 6 (2019): 1153–80.

———. "Refugees, Displaced Migrants, and Territorialization in Mandate Palestine." *Mashriq & Mahjar* 5, no. 2 (2018): 19–49.

Banton, Mandy. "Destroy? 'Migrate'? Conceal? British Strategies for the Disposal of Sensitive Records of Colonial Administrations at Independence." *Journal of Imperial & Commonwealth History* 40, no. 2 (2012): 323–37.

Barakat, Rana. "Reading Palestinian Agency in Mandate History: The Narrative of the Buraq Revolt as Anti-Relational." *Contemporary Levant* 4, no. 1 (2019): 28–38.

Barcia, Manuel. "'Locking Horns with the Northern Empire': Anti-American Imperialism at the Tricontinental Conference of 1966 in Havana." *Journal of Transatlantic Studies* 7, no. 3 (2009): 208–17.

Barkawi, Tarak. "Decolonising War." *European Journal of International Security* 1, no. 2 (2016): 199–214.

———. "War and Decolonization in Ukraine." *New Perspectives* 30, no. 4 (2022): 317–22.

Barkawi, Tarak, and Mark Laffey. "The Imperial Peace: Democracy, Force, and Globalization." *European Journal of International Relations* 5, no. 4 (1999): 403–34.

Barker, Joshua. "Beyond Bandung: Developmental Nationalism and (Multi)cultural Nationalism in Indonesia." *Third World Quarterly* 29, no. 3 (2008): 521–40.

Baron, Beth. "The Construction of National Honour in Egypt." *Gender and History* 5, no. 2 (1993): 244–55.

Barr, James. *A Line in the Sand: Britain, France and the Struggle That Shaped the Middle East.* London: Simon & Schuster, 2012.

Barrera, Giulia. "Mussolini's Colonial Race Laws and State–Settler Relations in Africa Orientale Italiana (1935–41)." *Journal of Modern Italian Studies* 8, no. 3 (2003): 425–43.

Barros, Françoise de. "Protests against Shantytowns in the 1950s and 1960s: Class Logics, Clientist Relations and 'Colonial Redeployments.'" In Naylor, *France's Modernising Mission*, 199–224.

Barroso, Luís. "The Origins of Exercise ALCORA: South Africa and the Portuguese Counterinsurgency Strategy in Southern Angola." *South African Historical Journal* 69, no. 3 (2017): 468–85.

Barton, Gregory A. "Environmentalism, Development and British Policy in the Middle East, 1945–65." *Journal of Imperial & Commonwealth History* 38 (2010): 619–39.

———. *Informal Empire and the Rise of One World Culture.* Basingstoke, UK: Palgrave Macmillan, 2014.

Barton, Gregory A., and Brett M. Bennett. "Decolonizing Informal Empire: The Loss of the British Teak Trade in Thailand, 1941–1958." *Pacific Historical Review* 90, no. 2 (2021): 211–32.

Bashford, Alison. *Global Population: History, Geopolitics, and Life on Earth.* New York: Columbia University Press, 2014.

———, ed. *Medicine at the Border: Disease, Globalization and Security, 1850 to the Present.* Basingstoke, UK: Palgrave Macmillan, 2006.

Bass, Gary J. *The Blood Telegram: Nixon, Kissinger, and a Forgotten Genocide.* New York: Knopf, 2013.

Batt, Jean-Pierre. *Le syndrome Foccart: La politique française en Afrique de 1959 à nos jours.* Paris: Gallimard, 2012.

Baughan, Emily. "Rehabilitating an Empire: Humanitarian Collusion with the Colonial State during the Kenyan Emergency, ca. 1954–1960." *Journal of British Studies* 59 (January 2020): 57–79.

———. *Saving the Children: Humanitarianism, Internationalism, and Empire.* Berkeley: University of California Press, 2022.

Bayly, C. A. *The Birth of the Modern World, 1780–1914: Global Connections and Comparisons.* Oxford: Oxford University Press, 2004.

Bayly, Susan. "French Anthropology and the Durkheimians in Colonial Indochina." *Modern Asian Studies* 34, no. 3 (2000): 581–622.

Beaumont, Thomas. *Fellow Travellers: Communist Trade Unionism and Industrial Relations on the French Railways, 1914–1939.* Liverpool: Liverpool University Press, 2019.

Becker, Jean-Jacques, and Serge Berstein. *Histoire de l'Anti-Communisme.* Paris: Olivier Orban, 1987.

Beckert, Sven. *Empire of Cotton: A Global History.* New York: Knopf, 2014.

Bédarida, François, and Jean-Pierre Rioux, eds. *Pierre Mendès France et le mendésisme: L'expérience gouvernementale et sa postérité (1954–1955).* Paris: Fayard, 1985.

Bedasse, Monique. *Jah Kingdom: Rastafarians, Tanzania, and Pan-Africanism in the Age of Decolonization.* Chapel Hill: University of North Carolina Press, 2017.

Bedasse, Monique, Kim D. Butler, Carlos Fernandes, Dennis Laumann, Tejasvi Nagaraja, Benjamin Talton, and Kira Thurman. "AHR Conversation: Black Internationalism." *American Historical Review* 125, no. 5 (2020): 1699–739.

Beeson, Mark. *Regionalism and Globalisation in East Asia: Politics, Security and Economic Development.* 2nd edition. London: Bloomsbury, 2014.

Behal, Rana P. "Coolie Drivers or Benevolent Paternalists? British Tea Planters in Assam and the Indenture Labour System." *Modern Asian Studies* 44, no. 1 (2010): 29–51.

Beinart, William. "Soil Erosion, Conservationism and Ideas about Development: A Southern African Exploration, 1900–1960." *Journal of Southern African Studies* 11, no. 1 (1984): 52–83.

Beinen, Joel, and Zachary Lockman. *Workers on the Nile: Nationalism, Communism, Islam and the Egyptian Working Class, 1882–1954.* Cairo: American University in Cairo Press, 1998.

Belhadj, Nadia Sariahmed. "The December 1960 Demonstrations in Algiers: Spontaneity and Organisation of Mass Action." *Journal of North African Studies* 27, no. 1 (2020): 1–39.

Belich, James. *Replenishing the Earth: The Settler Revolution and the Rise of the Angloworld, 1783–1939*. Oxford: Oxford University Press, 2009.

Bell, Duncan. "Before the Democratic Peace: Racial Utopianism, Empire, and the Abolition of War." *European Journal of International Relations* 20, no. 3 (2014): 647–70.

———, ed. *Empire, Race, and Global Justice*. Cambridge, UK: Cambridge University Press, 2019.

———. "Writing the World: Disciplinary History and Beyond." *International Affairs* 85, no. 1 (2009): 3–22.

———. "Writing the World (Remix)." In Schmidt and Guilhot, *Historiographical Investigations*, 15–40.

Bello, Taiwo. "Ojukwu's Biafra: Relief Corridor, Arms Smuggling, and Broken Diplomacy in the Nigerian Civil War." *War & Society* 40, no. 3 (2021): 206–24.

Bellucci, Stefano, and Holger Weiss, eds. *The Internationalisation of the Labour Question: Ideological Antagonism, Workers' Movements and the ILO since 1919*. Basingstoke, UK: Palgrave Macmillan, 2020.

Belogurova, Anna. "The Malayan Communist Party and the Malayan Chinese Association: Internationalism and Nationalism in Chinese Overseas Political Participation, c. 1920–1960." In James and Leake, *Decolonization and the Cold War*, 125–44.

Ben-Ze'ev, Efrat. *Remembering Palestine in 1948: Beyond National Narratives*. Cambridge, UK: Cambridge University Press, 2011.

Ben-Ze'ev, Efrat, Ruth Ginio, and Jay Winter, eds. *Shadows of War: A Social History of Silence in the Twentieth Century*. Cambridge, UK: Cambridge University Press, 2010.

Bennett, Brett, and Gregory Barton. "Generalizations in Global History: Dealing with Diversity without Losing the Big Picture." *Itinerario* 41, no. 1 (2017): 15–25.

Bennett, Huw. *Fighting the Mau Mau: The British Army and Counter-Insurgency in the Kenya Emergency*. Cambridge, UK: Cambridge University Press, 2012.

———. "'A Very Salutary Effect': The Counter-Terror Strategy in the Early Malayan Emergency, June 1948 to December 1949." *Journal of Strategic Studies* 32, no. 3 (2009): 415–44.

———. "'Words Are Cheaper than Bullets': Britain's Psychological Warfare in the Middle East, 1945–60." *Intelligence and National Security* 34, no. 7 (2019): 925–44.

Bennett, Huw, and Andrew Mumford. "Policing in Kenya during the Mau Mau Emergency, 1952–60." In Fair and Ganguly, *Policing Insurgencies*, 83–106.

Benton, Lauren. "From International Law to Imperial Constitutions: The Problem of Quasi-Sovereignty, 1870–1900." *Law and History Review* 26, no. 3 (2008): 595–619.

———. *Law and Colonial Cultures: Legal Regimes in World History, 1400–1900*. Cambridge, UK: Cambridge University Press, 2002.

———. "Made in Empire: Finding the Origins of International Law in Imperial Locations." *Leiden Journal of International Law* 31, no. 3 (2018): 473–78.

Benvenuti, Andrea. "The British Are 'Taking to the Boat': Australian Attempts to Forestall Britain's Military Disengagement from Southeast Asia, 1965–1966." *Diplomacy & Statecraft* 20, no. 1 (2009): 86–106.

Berdal, Mats, and David Malone, eds. *Greed and Grievance: Economic Agendas in Civil Wars.* Boulder, CO: Lynne Rienner, 2000.

Berger, Mark T. "After the Third World? History, Destiny and the Fate of the Third World." *Third World Quarterly* 25, no. 1 (2004): 9–39.

———. "Decolonisation, Modernisation and Nation-Building: Political Development Theory and the Appeal of Communism in Southeast Asia, 1945-1975." *Journal of Southeast Asian Studies* 34, no. 3 (2003): 421–48.

Berman, Bruce, and John Lonsdale, eds. *Unhappy Valley: Conflict in Kenya and Africa II: Violence and Ethnicity.* Oxford: James Currey, 1992.

Berman, Nina, Klaus Mühlhahn, and Patrice Nganang, eds. *German Colonialism Revisited: African, Asian, and Oceanic Experiences.* Ann Arbor: University of Michigan Press, 2014.

Bernal, Richard L. "The IMF and Class Struggle in Jamaica, 1977–1980." *Latin American Perspectives* 11, no. 3 (Summer 1984): 53–83.

Bernal, Victoria. "Colonial Moral Economy and the Discipline of Development: The Geriza Scheme and 'Modern' Sudan." *Cultural Anthropology* 12, no. 4 (1997): 447–79.

Berridge, William J. "Object Lessons in Violence: The Rationalities and Irrationalities of Urban Struggle during the Egyptian Revolution of 1919." *Journal of Colonialism and Colonial History* 12, no. 3 (2011), published online.

Best, Antony. *British Engagement with Japan, 1854-1922: The Origins and Course of an Unlikely Alliance.* Abingdon, UK: Routledge, 2020.

———. "The 'Ghost' of the Anglo-Japanese Alliance: An Examination into Historical Myth-Making." *Historical Journal* 49, no. 3 (2006): 811–31.

———. "The Leith-Ross Mission and British Policy towards East Asia, 1934-7." *International History Review* 35, no. 4 (2013): 681–701.

Bhambra, Gurminder K., Dalia Gebrial, and Kerem Nişancıoğlu. "Decolonising the University?" In *Decolonising the University*, edited by Gurminder K. Bhambra, Dalia Gebrial, and Kerem Nişancıoğlu. London: Pluto Press, 2018.

Bhat, Ahmad Safeer. "Jammu and Kashmir on the Eve of Partition: A Study of Political Conditions." *South Asian Studies* 32, no. 2 (2017): 285–95.

Bickers, Robert. "Infrastructural Globalisation: Lighting the China Coast, 1860s–1930s." *Historical Journal* 56, no. 2 (2013): 431–58.

Biermann, Werner, and Jumanne Wagoo. "The Quest for Adjustment: Tanzania and the IMF, 1980–1986." *African Studies Review* 29, no. 4 (1986): 89–103.

Biggs, David. "Managing a Rebel Landscape: Conservation, Pioneers, and the Revolutionary Past in the U Minh Forest, Vietnam." *Environmental History* 10, no. 3 (2005): 448–76.

Biltoft, Carolyn N. *A Violent Peace: Media, Truth, and Power at the League of Nations.* Chicago: University of Chicago Press, 2021.

Bini, Elisabetta, Giuliano Garavini, and Federico Romero, eds. *Oil Shock: The 1973 Crisis and Its Economic Legacy.* London: I. B. Tauris, 2016.

Bird, S. Elizabeth, and Fraser Ottanelli. "The Asaba Massacre and the Nigerian Civil War: Reclaiming Hidden History." *Journal of Genocide Research* 16, no. 2–3 (2014): 379–99.

Black, Allida. "Are Women 'Human'? The UN and the Struggle to Recognize Women's Rights as Human Rights." In *The Human Rights Revolution: An International*

History, edited by Akira Iriye, Petra Goedde, and William D. Hitchcock, 133–55. New York: Oxford University Press, 2012.

Blanchard, Emmanuel. "Contrôler, enfermer, éloigner: La répression policière et administrative des algériens de métropole (1946–1962)." In Branche and Thénault, *La France en guerre*, 318–31.

———. *La Police Parisienne et les Algériens (1944–1962)*. Paris: Nouveau Monde éditions, 2011.

Blaney, David L., and Arlene B. Tickner. "Worlding, Ontological Politics and the Possibility of a Decolonial IR." *Millennium: Journal of International Studies* 45, no. 3 (2017): 293–311.

Blyth, Robert. *The Empire of the Raj: India, Eastern Africa and the Middle East, 1858–1947*. London: Palgrave, 2003.

Bockman, Johanna. "Socialist Globalization against Capitalist Neocolonialism: The Economic Ideas behind the New International Economic Order." *Humanity* 6, no. 1 (2015): 109–28.

Boehme, Olivier. "The Involvement of the Belgian Central Bank in the Katanga Secession, 1960–1963." *African Economic History* 33 (2005): 1–29.

Bohling, Joseph. "Colonial or Continental Power? The Debate over Economic Expansion in Interwar France, 1925–1932." *Contemporary European History* 26, no. 2 (2017): 217–41.

Boittin, Jennifer Anne, Christina Firpo, and Emily Musil Church. "Hierarchies of Race and Gender in the French Colonial Empire, 1914–1946." *Historical Reflections* 37, no. 1 (2011): 60–90.

Bonnecase, Vincent. "Avoir faim en Afrique Occidentale Française (1920–1960): Investigations et représentations coloniales." *Revue d'Histoire des Sciences Humaines* 21 (2009): 151–74.

Bonneuil, Christopher. "Development as Experiment: Science and State-Building in Late Colonial and Postcolonial Africa, 1930–1970." *Osiris* 15 (2000): 258–81.

Bookmiller, Robert J. "The Algerian War of Words: Broadcasting and Revolution, 1954–1962." *Maghreb Review* 14, no. 3–4 (1989): 196–213.

Boomgaard, Peter. "The Welfare Services in Indonesia, 1900–1942." *Itinerario* 10, no. 1 (1986): 57–82.

Booth, Anne. "Government and Welfare in the New Republic: Indonesia in the 1950s." *Itinerario*, 34, no. 1 (2010): 57–76.

———. "Towards a Modern Fiscal State in Southeast Asia, c. 1900–1960." In Frankema and Booth, *Fiscal Capacity*, 36–76.

Boris, Eileen. *Making the Woman Worker: Precarious Labor and the Fight for Global Standards, 1919–2019*. New York: Oxford University Press, 2019.

Borowy, Iris. "Medicine, Economics and Foreign Policy: East German Medical Academics in the Global South during the 1950s and 1960s." In Muehlenbeck and Telepneva, *Warsaw Pact*, 173–96.

Bose, Sarmila. "Anatomy of Violence: Analysis of Civil War in East Pakistan in 1971." *Economic and Political Weekly* 40, no. 41 (2005): 4463–71.

———. "History on the Line: Fragments of Memories: Researching Violence in the 1971 Bangladesh War." *History Workshop Journal* 73 (2012): 285–95.

———. "Losing the Victims: Problems of Using Women as Weapons in Recounting the Bangladesh War." *Economic and Political Weekly* 42, no. 38 (2007): 3864–71.

Bose, Sugata. *Peasant Labour and Colonial Capital: Rural Bengal since 1770*. Cambridge, UK: Cambridge University Press, 1993.

Bose, Sugata, and Kris Manjapra. *Cosmopolitan Thought Zones: South Asia and the Global Circulation of Ideas*. Basingstoke, UK: Palgrave Macmillan, 2010.

Bosworth, Richard, and Joe Maiolo, eds. *The Cambridge History of the Second World War*. Vol. 2: *Politics and Ideology*. Cambridge, UK: Cambridge University Press, 2015.

Bott, Sandra, Marco Wyss, Jussi M. Hanhimaki, and Janick Schaufelbuehl, eds. *Neutrality and Neutralism in the Global Cold War: Between or within the Blocs?* London: Routledge, 2016.

Bougarel, Xavier, Raphaëlle Branche, and Cloé Drieu, eds. *Combatants of Muslim Origin in European Armies in the Twentieth Century*. London: Bloomsbury, 2018.

Bouguessa, Kamel. *Aux sources du nationalisme algérien: Les pioniers du populisme révolutionnaire en marche*. Algiers: Éditions Casbah, 2000.

Bourgois, Philippe. "Recognizing Invisible Violence: A Thirty-Year Ethnographic Perspective." In *Global Health in Times of Violence*, edited by Barbara Rylko-Bauer, Linda Whiteford, and Paul Farmer, 17–40. Santa Fe, NM: SAR Books, 2009.

Boyce, Robert. *The Great Interwar Crisis and the Collapse of Globalization*. Basingstoke, UK: Palgrave Macmillan, 2009.

Bradley, Mark Philip. *The World Reimagined: Americans and Human Rights in the Twentieth Century*. Cambridge, UK: Cambridge University Press, 2016.

Branch, Adam, and Zachariah Mampilly. *Africa Uprising: Popular Protest and Political Change*. London: Bloomsbury, 2015.

Branch, Daniel. *Defeating Mau Mau, Creating Kenya: Counterinsurgency, Civil War, and Decolonization*. Cambridge, UK: Cambridge University Press, 2009.

———. "The Enemy Within: Loyalists and the War against Mau Mau in Kenya." *Journal of African History* 48, no. 2 (2007): 291–315.

———. "Imprisonment and Colonialism in Kenya, c. 1930–1952: Escaping the Carceral Archipelago." *International Journal of African Historical Studies* 38, no. 2 (2005): 239–65.

———. "Political Traffic: Kenyan Students in Eastern and Central Europe, 1958–69." *Journal of Contemporary History* 53, no. 4 (2018): 811–31.

Branche, Raphaëlle. "Fighters for Independence and Rural Society in Colonial Algeria." In Domingos, Bandeira Jerónimo, and Roque, *Resistance and Colonialism*, 63–84.

———. *La guerre d'Algérie. Une histoire apaisée?* Paris: Seuil, 2005.

———. "The Martyr's Torch: Memory and Power in Algeria." *Journal of North African Studies* 16, no. 3 (2011): 431–43.

———. *Prisonniers du FLN*. Paris: Payot, 2014.

———. *La torture et l'armée pendant la guerre d'Algérie*. Paris: Gallimard, 2001.

———. "Des viols pendant la guerre d'Algérie." *Vingtième Siècle* 75 (July–September 2002): 123–32.

Branche, Raphaëlle, and Sylvie Thénault, eds. *La France en guerre 1954–1962: Expériences métropolitaines de la guerre d'indépendance algérienne*. Paris: Autrement, 2008.

Brands, Hal. "Wartime Recruiting Practices, Martial Identity and Post–World War II Demobilization in Colonial Kenya." *Journal of African History* 46 (2005): 103–25.

Brennan, James R. "Lowering the Sultan's Flag: Sovereignty and Decolonization in Coastal Kenya." *Comparative Studies in Society and History* 50, no. 4 (2008): 831–61.

Breskén, Kasper. "'Whether Black or White—United in the Fight!': Connecting the Resistance against Colonialism, Racism, and Fascism in the European Metropoles, 1926-1936." *Twentieth Century Communism* 18 (2020): 126–49.

Bridge, Carl, and Kent Fedorowich, eds. *The British World: Diaspora, Culture and Identity*. Abingdon, UK: Routledge, 2003.

Bridger, Emily. *Young Women against Apartheid: Gender, Youth and South Africa's Liberation Struggle*. Oxford: James Currey, 2021.

Brigham, Robert K. *Guerrilla Diplomacy: The NLF's Foreign Relations and the Viet Nam War*. Ithaca, NY: Cornell University Press, 1999.

Brinkman, Inge. "'The Time of the Leaflet': Pamphlets and Political Communication in the UPA (Northern Angola around 1961)." *Africa* 85, no. 2 (2015): 221–44.

Broadberry, Stephen, and Mark Harrison, eds. *The Economics of World War Two*. Cambridge, UK: Cambridge University Press, 2000.

Brocheux, Pierre, and Daniel Hémery. *Indochina: An Ambiguous Colonization, 1858-1954*. Berkeley: University of California Press, 2009.

Brower, Benjamin C. *A Desert Named Peace: The Violence of France's Empire in the Algerian Sahara, 1844-1902*. New York: Columbia University Press, 2009.

———. "Partisans and Populations: The Place of Civilians in War, Algeria (1954-62)." *History and Theory* 3 (September 2017): 389–97.

———. "Regroupment Camps and Shantytowns in Late-Colonial Algeria." *L'Année du Maghreb* 20 (2019): 93–106.

Brownell, Josiah. *The Collapse of Rhodesia: Population Demographics and the Politics of Race*. London: Bloomsbury, 2020.

———. "Out of Time: Global Settlerism, Nostalgia, and the Selling of the Rhodesian Rebellion Overseas." *Journal of Southern African Studies* 43, no. 4 (2017): 805–24.

———. "'A Sordid Tussle of the Strand': Rhodesia House during the UDI Rebellion, 1965-80." *Journal of Imperial & Commonwealth History* 38, no. 3 (2010): 471–99.

Brown, Ian. "The Economics of Decolonization in Burma." In *Africa, Empire, and Globalization: Essays in Honor of A. G. Hopkins*, edited by Toyin Falola and Emily Brownell, 433–45. Durham, NC: Carolina Academic Press, 2011.

Bruchhausen, Walter. "From Precondition to Goal of Development: Health and Medicine in the Planning and Politics of British Tanganyika." In Hodge, Hödl, and Kopf, *Developing Africa*, 207–21.

Bryant, Michael. *A World History of War Crimes: From Antiquity to the Present*. 2nd edition. London: Bloomsbury, 2021.

Brydan, David, and Jessica Reinisch, eds. *Internationalists in European History: Rethinking the Twentieth Century*. London: Bloomsbury Academic, 2022.

Buchanan, Andrew. "Globalizing the Second World War." *Past and Present* 258, no. 1 (2023): 246–81.

Buettner, Elizabeth. *Europe after Empire: Decolonization, Society, and Culture*. Cambridge, UK: Cambridge University Press, 2016.

———. "Extended Families or Bodily Composition: Biological Metaphors in the Age of European Decolonization." In *Rhetorics of Empire: Languages of Colonial Conflict after 1900*, edited by Martin Thomas and Richard Toye, 208–27. Manchester, UK: Manchester University Press, 2017.

———. "'Going for an Indian': South Asian Restaurants and the Limits of Multiculturalism in Britain." *Journal of Modern History* 80 (December 2008): 865–901.

Bührer, Tanja, Flavio Eichmann, Stig Förster, and Benedikt Stuchtey, eds. *Cooperation and Empire: Local Realities of Global Processes*. New York: Berghahn, 2017.

Bullard, Alice. "Sympathy and Denial: A Post-Colonial Re-Reading of Emotions, Race, and Hierarchy." *Historical Reflections* 34, no. 1 (2008): 122–42.

Bull, Hedley, and Adam Watson, eds. *The Expansion of International Society*. Oxford: Oxford University Press, 2020.

Bunch, Charlotte. "Women's Rights as Human Rights: Toward a Re-Vision of Human Rights." *Human Rights Quarterly* 12 (1990): 486–98.

Burden-Stelly, Charisse. "W. E. B. Du Bois in the Tradition of Radical Blackness: Radicalism, Repression, and Mutual Comradeship, 1930–1960." *Socialism and Democracy* 32, no. 3 (2018): 181–206.

Burke, Edmund III. *The Ethnographic State: France and the Invention of Moroccan Islam*. Berkeley: University of California Press, 2014.

Burke, Roland. "Afro-Asian Alignment: Charles Malik and the Cold War at Bandung." In *Bandung 1955: Little Histories*, edited by Antonia Finnane and Derek McDougall, 27–41. Caulfield, Australia: Monash University Press, 2010.

———. "'The Compelling Dialogue of Freedom': Human Rights at the Bandung Conference." *Human Rights Quarterly* 28, no. 4 (2006): 947–65.

———. *Decolonization and the Evolution of International Human Rights*. Philadelphia: University of Pennsylvania Press, 2010

———. "From Individual Rights to National Development: The First UN International Conference on Human Rights, Tehran, 1968." *Journal of World History* 19, no. 3 (2008): 275–96.

———. "'How Time Flies': Celebrating the Universal Declaration of Human Rights in the 1960s." *International History Review* 38, no. 2 (2016): 394–420.

———. "The Internationalism of Human Rights." In Sluga and Clavin, *Internationalisms*, 287–314.

———. "'A World Made Safe for Diversity': Apartheid and the Language of Human Rights, Progress, and Pluralism." In Moses, Duranti, and Burke, *Decolonization, Self Determination*, 316–39.

Burki, Namari. "From the Theory to the Practice of Liberation: Fanon, May '68 and the Black Consciousness Movement in South Africa." In Konieczna and Skinner, *Global History of Anti-Apartheid*, 105–30.

Burk, Kathleen. "Financial and Commercial Networks between Britain and Latin America during the Long Nineteenth Century." In Otte, *British World Policy and the Projection of Global Power*, 111–28.

Burton, Antoinette. "Not Even Remotely Global? Method and Scale in World History." *History Workshop Journal* 64, no. 1 (2007): 323–28.

Burton, Antoinette, and Tony Ballantyne, eds. *World Histories from Below: Disruption and Dissent, 1750 to the Present*. 2nd edition. London: Bloomsbury, 2022.

Burton, Eric. "Hubs of Decolonization. African Liberation Movements and 'Eastern' Connections in Cairo, Accra, and Dar es Salaam." In Dallywater, Saunders, and Fonseca, *Southern African Liberation Movements*, 25–56.

Bush, Barbara. "Feminising Empire? Britain's Women's Activist Networks in Defending and Challenging Empire from 1918 to Decolonization." *Women's History Review* 25, no. 4 (2016): 499–519.

———. "Motherhood, Morality, and Social Order: Gender and Development Discourse and Practice in Late Colonial Africa." In Hodge, Hödl, and Kopf, *Developing Africa*, 270–92.

Bussmann, Margit, Gerard Schneider, and Nina Weisehomeier. "Foreign Economic Liberalization and Peace: The Case of Sub-Saharan Africa." *European Journal of International Relations* 11, no. 4 (2005): 551–79.

Butalia, Urvashi. *The Other Side of Silence: Voices from the Partition of India*. Durham, NC: Duke University Press, 2000.

Butler, L. J. *Copper Empire: Mining and the Colonial State in Northern Rhodesia, c. 1930–1964*. Basingstoke, UK: Palgrave Macmillan, 2007.

Buzan, Barry, and Amitav Archarya. *Re-Imagining International Relations: World Orders in the Thought and Practice of Indian, Chinese and Islamic Civilisations*. Cambridge, UK: Cambridge University Press, 2021.

Buzan, Barry, and George Lawson. *The Global Transformation: History, Modernity and the Making of International Relations*. Cambridge, UK: Cambridge University Press, 2015.

Byrne, Jeffrey James. "Beyond Continents, Colours, and the Cold War: Yugoslavia, Algeria, and the Struggle for Non-Alignment." *International History Review* 37, no. 5 (2015): 912–32.

———. *Mecca of Revolution: Algeria, Decolonization, & the Third World Order*. Oxford: Oxford University Press, 2019.

———. "Our Own Special Brand of Socialism: Algeria and the Contest of Modernities in the 1960s." *Diplomatic History* 33, no. 3 (2009): 427–47.

———. "The Romance of Revolutionary Transatlanticism: Cuban-Algerian Relations and the Diverging Trends within Third World Internationalism." In Parrott and Lawrence, *Tricontinental Revolution*, 163–90.

Cabanes, Bruno. *The Great War and the Origins of Humanitarianism, 1918–1924*. Cambridge, UK: Cambridge University Press, 2014.

Caden, Christopher, and Nir Arielli. "British Army and Palestine Police Deserters and the Arab–Israeli War of 1948." *War in History* 28, no. 1 (2021): 200–22.

Cain, Frank. "Exporting the Cold War: British Responses to the USA's Establishment of COCOM, 1947–51." *Journal of Contemporary History* 29, no. 3 (1994): 501–22.

Call, Charles T. "The Fallacy of the 'Failed State.'" *Third World Quarterly* 29, no. 8 (2008): 1491–507.

Camiscioli, Elisa. "Race Making and Race Mixing in the Early Twentieth-Century Immigration Debate." In Gafaïti, Lorcin, and Troyansky, *Transnational Spaces*, 53–67.

Campbell, Caroline. "The Battle of El Herri in Morocco: Colonial Narratives of Conquest during World War I." *Historical Reflections* 46, no. 3 (2020): 9–30.

Campbell, James. *Exiled in Paris: Richard Wright, James Baldwin, Samuel Beckett, and Others on the Left Bank*. Berkeley: University of California Press, 2003.

Campos, Alicia. "The Decolonization of Equatorial Guinea: The Relevance of the International Factor." *Journal of African History* 44, no. 1 (2003): 95–116.

Capuzzo, Paulo. "Markets." In Conway, Lagrou, and Rousso, *Europe's Postwar Periods*, 155–77.

Castelo, Cláudia. "Reproducing Portuguese Villages in Africa: Agricultural Science, Ideology and Empire." *Journal of Southern African Studies* 42, no. 2 (2016): 267–81.

Castro, Alfonso Peter, and Kreg Ettenger. "Counterinsurgency and Socioeconomic Change: The Mau Mau War in Kirinyaga, Kenya." *Research in Economic Anthropology* 15 (1994): 63–101.

Catton, Philip E. "'It Would Be a Terrible Thing if We Handed These People over to the Communists': The Eisenhower Administration, Article 14(d), and the Origins of the Refugee Exodus from North Vietnam." *Diplomatic History* 39, no. 2 (2015): 331–58.

Cavanagh, Edward. "Settler Colonialism in South Africa: Land, Labour and Transformation, 1880–2015." In Cavanagh and Veracini, *Routledge Handbook of the History of Settler Colonialism*, 291–309.

Cavanagh, Edward, and Lorenzo Veracini, eds. *The Routledge Handbook of the History of Settler Colonialism*. Abingdon, UK: Routledge, 2016.

Cerny, Philip G. "Neomedievalism, Civil War and the New Security Dilemma: Globalisation as Durable Disorder." *Civil Wars* 1, no. 1 (1998): 36–64.

Ceserani, David. "The British Security Forces and the Jews in Palestine, 1945–48." In *Rethinking History, Dictatorship and War: New Approaches and Interpretations*, edited by Claus-Christian W. Szejnmann, 191–210. London: Continuum, 2009.

Chabal, Patrick. *Amilcar Cabral: Revolutionary Leadership and People's War*. London: Hurst, 1983.

Chafer, Tony, and Amanda Sackur, eds. *French Colonial Empire and the Popular Front: Hope and Disillusion*. Basingstoke, UK: Macmillan, 1999.

Chakma, Bhumitra. "The Post-Colonial State and Minorities: Ethnocide in the Chittagong Hill Tracts, Bangladesh." *Commonwealth & Comparative Politics* 48, no. 3 (2010): 281–300.

Chakrabarty, Dipesh. *Provincializing Europe: Postcolonial Thought and Historical Difference*. Princeton, NJ: Princeton University Press, 2008.

Chamberlin, Paul Thomas. *The Global Offensive: The United States, the Palestine Liberation Organization, and the Making of the Post–Cold War Order*. Oxford: Oxford University Press, 2012.

———. "The PLO and the Limits of Secular Revolution, 1975–1982." In Parrott and Lawrence, *Tricontinental Revolution*, 93–109.

Chandler, David P., Robert Cribb, and Li Narangoa, eds. *End of Empire: 100 Days in 1945 That Changed Asia and the World*. Copenhagen: NIAS Press, 2016.

Chapman, Herrick. *France's Long Reconstruction: In Search of the Modern Republic*. Cambridge, MA: Harvard University Press, 2018.

———. "The Liberation of France as a Moment of State-Making." In *Crisis and Renewal in France, 1918–1962*, edited by Martin S. Alexander and Kenneth E. Mouré, 174–98. Oxford: Berghahn, 2002.

Chapman, Jessica M. *Cauldron of Resistance: Ngo Dinh Diem, the United States, and 1950s Southern Vietnam*. Ithaca, NY: Cornell University Press, 2013.

Charbonneau, Bruno. *France and the New Imperialism: Security Policy in Sub-Saharan Africa*. Aldershot, UK: Ashgate, 2008.

Charters, David A. *The British Army and Jewish Insurgency in Palestine, 1945–47*. Basingstoke, UK: Macmillan, 1989.

Chatterjee, Partha. *Nationalist Thought and the Colonial World: A Derivative Discourse*. 2nd edition. Minneapolis: University of Minnesota Press, 1993.

———. *The Nation and Its Fragments: Colonial and Postcolonial Histories*. Princeton, NJ: Princeton University Press, 1993.

———. *The Politics of the Governed: Reflections on Popular Politics in Most of the World*. New York: Columbia University Press, 2004.

Chatterji, Joya. "Dispositions and Destinations: Refugee Agency and 'Mobility Capital' in the Bengal Diaspora, 1947–2007." *Comparative Studies in Society and History* 55, no. 2 (2013): 273–304.

———. "The Fashioning of a Frontier: The Radcliffe Line and Bengal's Border Landscape, 1947–52." *Modern Asian Studies* 33, no. 1 (1999): 185–242.

———. "From Subjecthood to Citizenship in South Asia: Migration, Nationality, and the Post-Imperial Global Order." In McCoy, Fradera, and Jacobson, *Endless Empire*, 306–17.

———. *Partition's Legacies*. New York: SUNY Press, 2021.

———. "Partition Studies: Prospects and Pitfalls." *Journal of Asian Studies* 73, no. 2 (2014): 309–12.

———. "South Asian Histories of Citizenship, 1946–70." *Historical Journal* 55, no. 4 (2012): 1049–71.

———. *The Spoils of Partition: Bengal and India 1947–1967*. Cambridge, UK: Cambridge University Press, 2007.

Checkel, Jeffrey T., ed. *Transnational Dynamics of Civil War*. Cambridge, UK: Cambridge University Press, 2013.

Cheeseman, Nic, and Jonathan Fisher. *Authoritarian Africa: Repression, Resistance, and the Power of Ideas*. Oxford: Oxford University Press, 2021.

Chen, Martha Alter. "Engendering World Conferences: The International Women's Movement and the United Nations." *Third World Quarterly* 16, no. 3 (1995): 477–94.

Chernev, Borislav. "The Brest-Litovsk Moment: Self-Determination Discourse in Eastern Europe before Wilsonianism." *Diplomacy & Statecraft* 22, no. 3 (2011): 369–87.

Chester, Lucy P. "Boundary Commissions as Tools to Safeguard British Interests at the End of Empire." *Journal of Historical Geography* 34, no. 3 (2008): 507–10.

Chey, Hyoung-kyu. "International Political Economy Thought in Pre-Modern and Colonial Korea." *International Trade, Politics, and Development* 3, no. 1 (2019): 11–29.

Childers, Kristen Stromberg. "The Evolution of the Welfare State: Social Rights and the Nationalization of Welfare in France, 1880–1947." *French Politics, Culture, and Society* 24, no. 2 (2006): 129–38.

———. *Seeking Imperialism's Embrace: National Identity, Decolonization, and Assimilation in the French Caribbean*. Oxford: Oxford University Press, 2016.

Chimni, B. S. "Anti-Imperialism: Then and Now." In Eslava, Fakhri, and Nesiah, *Bandung, Global History, and International Law*, 35–48.

Chirwa, Wiseman Chijere. "Child and Youth Labour on the Nyasaland Plantations, 1890–1953." *Journal of Southern African Studies* 19, no. 4 (1993): 662–80.

Choi, Sung-Eun. *Decolonization and the French of Algeria.* Basingstoke, UK: Palgrave Macmillan, 2016.

Chotzen, Anna. "Beyond Bounds: Morocco's Rif War and the Limits of International Law." *Humanity* 5, no. 1 (2014): 33–54.

Christian, Michel, Sandrine Kott, and Ondřej Matějka, eds. *Planning in Cold War Europe: Competition, Cooperation, Circulations (1950s–1970s).* Berlin: de Gruyter, 2018.

Christiansen, Samantha, and Zachary A. Scarlett, eds. *The Third World and the Global 1960s.* Oxford: Berghahn, 2013.

Citino, Nathan J. *Envisioning the Arab Future: Modernization in U.S.–Arab Relations, 1945–1967.* Cambridge, UK: Cambridge University Press, 2017.

——. "Nasser, Hammarskjöld, and Middle East Development in Different Scales of Space and Time." In Macekura and Manela, *Development Century*, 283–304.

Clare, Horatio. *Down to the Sea in Ships: Of Ageless Oceans and Modern Men.* London: Chatto and Windus, 2014.

Clarke, Colin. *Decolonizing the Colonial City: Urbanization and Stratification in Kingston, Jamaica.* Oxford: Oxford University Press, 2006.

Clarke, Sabine. "A Technocratic Imperial State? The Colonial Office and Scientific Research, 1940–1960." *Twentieth Century British History* 18, no. 4 (2007): 453–80.

Clavin, Patricia. *Securing the World Economy: The Reinvention of the League of Nations, 1920–1946.* Oxford: Oxford University Press, 2013.

Clavin, Patricia, and Madeleine Dungy. "Trade, Law, and the Global Order of 1919." *Diplomatic History* 44, no. 4 (2020): 554–79.

Cleary, Mark. "Land Codes and the State in French Cochinchina c. 1900–1940." *Journal of Historical Geography* 29, no. 3 (2003): 356–75.

——. "Managing the Forest in Colonial Indochina c. 1900–1940." *Modern Asian Studies* 39, no. 2 (2005): 257–83.

Cleveland, Todd. "Feeding the Aversion: Agriculture and Mining Technology on Angola's Colonial-Era Diamond Mines, 1917–1975,"*Agricultural History* 92, no. 3 (2018): 328–50.

Cleveland, William S. *Islam against the West: Shakib Arslan and the Campaign for Islamic Nationalism.* London: Al Saqi Books, 1985.

Coates, Oliver. "New Perspectives on West Africa and World War Two." *Journal of African Military History* 4, no. 1–2 (2020): 5–39.

Cochrane, Martin. "Security Force Collusion in Northern Ireland 1969–1999: Substance or Symbolism?" *Studies in Conflict and Terrorism* 36, no. 1 (2013): 77–97.

Cockburn, Cynthia. "The Continuum of Violence: A Gender Perspective on War and Peace." In *Sites of Violence: Gender and Conflict Zones*, edited by Wenona Giles and Jennifer Hyndman, 24–44. Berkeley: University of California Press, 2004.

Coe, Brooke. "Sovereignty Regimes and the Norm of Noninterference in the Global South: Regional and Temporal Variation." *Global Governance* 21, no. 2 (2015): 275–98.

Coelho, Miguel Serra. "Brazil and India: A Brave New World, 1948–1961." In Field, Krepp, and Pettinà, *Latin America and the Global Cold War*, 17–43.

Coggins, Bridget L. "Rebel Diplomacy: Theorizing Violent Non-State Actors' Use of Talk." In Arjona, Kasfir, and Mampilly, *Rebel Governance in Civil War*, 98–118.

Coggins, Richard. "Wilson and Rhodesia: UDI and British Policy towards Africa." *Contemporary British History* 20, no. 3 (2006): 363–81.

Coghe, Samuël. "Reordering Colonial Society: Model Villages and Social Planning in Rural Angola, 1920–45." *Journal of Contemporary History* 52, no. 1 (2017): 16–44.

Cohen, Andrew. "Lonrho and Oil Sanctions against Rhodesia in the 1960s." *Journal of Southern African Studies* 37, no. 4 (2011): 715–30.

———. *The Politics and Economics of Decolonization: The Failed Experiment of the Central African Federation.* London: I. B. Tauris, 2017.

Cohen, Hillel. *Army of Shadows: Palestinian Collaboration with Zionism, 1917–1948.* Berkeley: University of California Press, 2008.

Cohen, Jean L. *Globalization and Sovereignty: Rethinking Legality, Legitimacy, and Constitutionalism.* New York: Cambridge University Press, 2012.

———. "Whose Sovereignty? Empire and International Law." *Ethics & International Affairs* 18, no. 3 (2004): 1–24.

Cohen, Stuart. "Imperial Policing against Illegal Immigration: The Royal Navy and Palestine, 1945–48." *Journal of Imperial & Commonwealth History* 22, no. 2 (1994): 275–93.

Cohen, William B. "The Algerian War, the French State and Official Memory." *Historical Reflections/Réflexions Historiques* 28, no. 2 (2002): 219–39.

Cole, Joshua. *Lethal Provocation: The Constantine Murders and the Politics of French Algeria.* Ithaca, NY: Cornell University Press, 2020.

———. "Massacres and Their Historians: Recent Histories of State Violence in France and Algeria in the Twentieth Century." *French Politics, Culture, and Society* 28, no. 1 (2010): 106–26.

Collier, Paul, and Anke Hoeffler. "Greed and Grievance in Civil War." *Oxford Economic Papers* 56, no. 4 (2004): 563–95.

Collingham, Lizzie. *A Taste for War: World War II and the Battle for Food.* London: Allen Lane, 2012.

Collins, Michael. "Decolonisation and the 'Federal Moment.'" *Diplomacy & Statecraft* 24, no. 1 (2013): 21–40.

Collins, Richard. "The Reith Mission, Global Telecommunications and the Decline of the British Empire." *Historical Journal of Film, Radio and Television* 32, no. 2 (2012): 167–85.

Condos, Mark. "'Fanaticism' and the Politics of Resistance along the North-West Frontier of British India." *Comparative Studies in Society and History* 58, no. 3 (2016): 717–45.

———. "The Indian 'Alsatia': Sovereignty, Extradition, and the Limits of Franco-British Colonial Policing." *Journal of Imperial & Commonwealth History* 48, no. 1 (2020): 101–26.

———. "License to Kill: The Murderous Outrages Act and the Rule of Law in Colonial India, 1867–1925." *Modern Asian Studies* 50, no. 2 (2016): 479–517.

Condos, Mark, and Gavin Rand. "Coercion and Conciliation at the Edge of Empire: State-Building and Its Limits in Waziristan." *Historical Journal*, published online October 8, 2017: 1–27.

Conklin, Alice L. "Colonialism and Human Rights, a Contradiction in Terms? The Case of France and West Africa, 1895–1914." *American Historical Review* 103, no. 2 (1998): 419–42.

———. *In the Museum of Man: Race, Anthropology, and Empire in France, 1850–1950*. Ithaca, NY: Cornell University Press, 2013.

———. *A Mission to Civilize: The Republican Idea of Empire in France and West Africa, 1895–1930*. Stanford, CA: Stanford University Press, 1997.

———. "The New 'Ethnology' and 'La Situation Coloniale' in Interwar France." *French Politics, Culture, and Society*, 20, no. 2 (2002): 29–46.

Connelly, Matthew. *A Diplomatic Revolution: Algeria's Fight for Independence and the Origins of the Post–Cold War Era*. New York: Oxford University Press, 2002.

———. "Population Control Is History: New Perspectives on the International Campaign to Limit Population Growth." *Comparative Studies in Society and History* 45, no. 1 (2003): 122–47.

———. "Seeing Beyond the State: The Population Control Movement and the Problem of Sovereignty." *Past and Present* 193 (November 2006): 197–233.

———. "Taking off the Cold War Lens: Visions of North–South Conflict during the Algerian War for Independence." *American Historical Review* 105, no. 3 (2000): 739–69.

———. "To Inherit the Earth: Imagining World Population, from the Yellow Peril to the Population Bomb." *Journal of Global History* 1, no. 3 (2006): 299–319.

Connor, John. *Someone Else's War: Fighting for the British Empire in World War I*. London: I. B. Tauris, 2019.

Conrad, Sebastien, and Dominic Sachsenmaier, eds. *Competing Visions of World Order: Global Moments and Movements, 1880s–1930s*. Basingstoke, UK: Palgrave Macmillan, 2007.

Conway, Martin, Pieter Lagrou, and Henry Rousso, eds. *Europe's Postwar Periods—1989, 1945, 1918: Writing History Backwards*. London: Bloomsbury, 2019.

Coombs, Catherine. "Partition Narratives: Displaced Trauma and Culpability among British Civil Servants in 1940s Punjab." *Modern Asian Studies*, 45, no. 1 (2011): 201–24.

Cooper, Barbara M. *Marriage in Maradi: Gender and Culture in a Hausa Society in Niger, 1900–1989*. Oxford: James Currey, 1997.

Cooper, Frederick. "African History/Empire History." *Ab Imperio* 4 (2019): 159–66.

———. "Afterword: Social Rights and Human Rights in the Time of Decolonization." *Humanity* 3, no. 3 (2012): 473–92.

———. *Citizenship between Empire and Nation: Rethinking France and French Africa, 1945–1960*. Princeton, NJ: Princeton University Press, 2014.

———. *Colonialism in Question: Theory, Knowledge, History*. Berkeley: University of California Press, 1991.

———. *Decolonization and African Society: The Labor Question in French and British Africa*. Cambridge, UK: Cambridge University Press, 1996.

Cooper, Frederick. "Decolonizations, Colonizations, and More Decolonizations: The End of Empire in Time and Space." *Journal of World History* 33, no. 3 (2022): 491–526.

——. "Decolonizing Situations: The Rise, Fall, and Rise of Colonial Studies, 1951–2001." *French Politics, Culture, and Society* 20, no. 2 (2002): 47–76.

——. "Empire Multiplied: A Review Essay." *Comparative Studies in Society and History* 46, no. 2 (2004): 247–72.

——. "Gatekeeping Practices, Gatekeeper States and Beyond." *Third World Thematics* 3, no. 3 (2018): 455–68.

——. "'Our Strike': Equality, Anticolonial Politics and the 1947–48 Railway Strike in French West Africa." *Journal of African History* 37, no. 1 (1996): 81–118.

——. "Reconstructing Empire in British and French Africa." *Past & Present* 210, Supplement 6 (2011): 196–210.

Cooper, Frederick, and Jane Burbank. *Empires in World History: Power and the Politics of Difference*. Princeton, NJ: Princeton University Press, 2011.

Cooper, Frederick, and Randall M. Packard, eds. *International Development and the Social Sciences: Essays on the History and Politics of Knowledge*. Berkeley: University of California Press, 1998.

Cooper, Frederick, and Ann Laura Stoler, eds. *Tensions of Empire: Colonial Cultures in a Bourgeois World*. Berkeley: University of California Press, 1997.

Copland, Ian. "The Further Shores of Partition: Ethnic Cleansing in Rajasthan, 1947." *Past & Present* 160 (1998): 203–39.

Coquery-Vidrovitch, Catherine. "L'Impact des intérêts coloniaux: S.C.O.A. et C.F.A.O. dans l'Ouest Africain, 1910–1965." *Journal of African History* 16, no. 4 (1975): 595–621.

——. "Mutation de l'impérialisme colonial français dans les années trente." *African Economic History* 4 (1977): 103–52.

Cordera, Sonia. "India's Response to the 1971 East Pakistan Crisis: Hidden and Open Reasons for Intervention." *Journal of Genocide Research* 17, no. 1 (2015): 45–62.

Costa Pinto, Antonio. "La fin de l'Empire portugais." In Dard and Lefeuvre, *L'Europe face à son passé colonial*, 197–218.

Couti, Jacqueline. "Am I My Sister's Keeper? The Politics of Propriety and the Fight for Equality in the Works of French Antillean Women Writers, 1920s–1940s." In Germain and Larcher, *Black French Women*, 129–47.

Crane, Sheila. "Housing as Battleground: Targeting the City in the Battles of Algiers." *City and Society* 29, no. 1 (2017): 187–212.

Crang, Jeremy A. *Sisters in Arms: Women in the British Armed Forces during the Second World War*. Cambridge, UK: Cambridge University Press, 2020.

Cribb, Robert. "The Brief Genocide of the Eurasians in Indonesia, 1945/1946." In Moses, *Empire, Colony, Genocide*, 424–39.

——. "Genocide in Indonesia, 1965–1966." *Journal of Genocide Research* 3, no. 2 (2001): 219–39.

Crosby, Alfred. *Ecological Imperialism: The Biological Expansion of Europe, 900–1900*. 2nd edition. Cambridge, UK: Cambridge University Press, 2015.

Crowe, David M. *War Crimes, Genocide, and Justice: A Global History*. Basingstoke, UK: Palgrave Macmillan, 2014.

Cueto, Marcos, Theodore M. Brown, and Elizabeth Fee. *The World Health Organization: A History*. Cambridge, UK: Cambridge University Press, 2019.

Cullather, Nick. "The Foreign Policy of the Calorie." *American Historical Review*, 112, no. 2 (April 2007): 337–64.

———. "Fuel for the Good Dragon: The United States and Industrial Policy in Taiwan, 1950–1965." *Diplomatic History* 20, no. 1 (1996): 1–26.

———. *Secret History: The CIA's Classified Account of Its Operations in Guatemala, 1952–1954*. Stanford, CA: Stanford University Press, 2006.

Cullen, Poppy. *Kenya and Britain after Independence: Beyond Neocolonialism*. Basingstoke, UK: Palgrave, 2017.

———. "'Playing Cold War Politics': The Cold War in Anglo-Kenyan Relations in the 1960s." *Cold War History* 18, no. 1 (2018): 37–54.

Cunningham, Andrew, and Bridie Andrews, eds. *Western Medicine as Contested Knowledge*. Manchester, UK: Manchester University Press, 1997.

Curless, Gareth. "'The People Need Civil Liberties': Trade Unions and Contested Decolonisation in Singapore." *Labour History* 57, no. 1 (2016): 53–70.

———. "Violence and (Dis)Order in the Caribbean Post-Colony." In Thomas and Curless, *Oxford Handbook of Late Colonial Insurgencies*, 726–52.

Daeyeol, Ku. *Korea, 1905–1945: From Japanese Colonialism to Liberation and Independence*. Amsterdam: Amsterdam University Press, 2022.

Dafermos, Yannis, Daniela Gabor, and Jo Michell. "The Wall Street Consensus in Pandemic Times: What Does It Mean for Climate-Aligned Development?" *Canadian Journal of Development Studies* 42, no. 1–2 (2021): 238–51.

Daily, Andrew. "Race, Citizenship, and Antillean Student Activism in Postwar France, 1946–1968." *French Historical Studies* 37, no. 2 (2014): 331–57.

Dallywater, Lena, Chris Saunders, and Helder Adegar Fonseca, eds. *Southern African Liberation Movements and the Global Cold War 'East': Transnational Activism 1960–1990*. Oldenbourg: De Gruyter, 2019.

Daly, Samuel Fury Childs. *A History of the Republic of Biafra: Law, Crime, and the Nigerian Civil War*. Cambridge, UK: Cambridge University Press, 2020.

———. "A Nation on Paper: Making a State in the Republic of Biafra." *Comparative Studies in Society and History* 62, no. 4 (2020): 868–94.

Damousi, Joy, Trevor Burnard, and Alan Lester, eds. *Humanitarianism, Empire, and Transnationalism, 1760–1995: Selective Humanity in the Anglophone World*. Manchester, UK: Manchester University Press, 2022.

Dang, Trung Dinh. "Post-1975 Land Reform in Southern Vietnam: How Local Actions and Responses Affected National Land Policy." *Journal of Vietnamese Studies* 5, no. 3 (2010): 72–105.

Dard, Olivier, and Daniel Lefeuvre, eds. *L'Europe face à son passé colonial*. Paris: Riveneuve, 2008.

Darwin, John. *Unlocking the World: Port Cities and Globalization in the Age of Steam, 1830–1930*. London: Allen Lane, 2020.

Das, Santanu. *India, Empire, and First World War Culture: Writing, Images, and Songs*. Cambridge, UK: Cambridge University Press, 2018.

Das, Suranjan. *Communal Riots in Bengal, 1905–1947*. New York: Oxford University Press, 1991.

Datla, Kavita Saraswathi. "Sovereignty and the End of Empire: The Transition to Independence in Colonial Hyderabad." *Ab Imperio* 3 (2018): 63–88.

Datta, Arunima. "'Immorality,' Nationalism and the Colonial State in British Malaya: Indian Coolie Women's Intimate Lives as Ideological Battleground." *Women's History Review* 25, no. 4 (2016): 584–601.

Daughton, J. P. "Behind the Imperial Curtain: International Humanitarian Efforts and the Critique of French Colonialism in the Interwar Years." *French Historical Studies* 34, no. 3 (2011): 503–28.

———. "ILO Expertise and Colonial Violence in the Interwar Years." In Kott and Droux, *Globalizing Social Rights*, 85–97.

Davey, Eleanor. "Decolonizing the Geneva Conventions: National Liberation and the Development of Humanitarian Law." In Moses, Duranti, and Burke, *Decolonization, Self Determination*, 375–96.

Davey, Gregor. "Conflicting Worldviews, Mutual Incomprehension: The Production of Intelligence across Whitehall and the Management of Subversion during Decolonisation, 1944–1966." *Small Wars & Insurgencies* 25, no. 3 (2014): 539–59.

Davis, Diana K. "Desert 'Wastes' of the Maghreb: Desertification Narratives in French Colonial Environmental History of North Africa." *Cultural Geographies* 11 (2004): 359–87.

———. *Resurrecting the Granary of Rome: Environmental History and French Colonial Expansion in North Africa*. Athens: Ohio University Press, 2007.

Davis, Diana K., and Edmund Burke III, eds. *Environmental Imaginaries of the Middle East and North Africa*. Athens: Ohio University Press, 2011.

Davis, Diane E., and Anthony W. Pereira, eds. *Irregular Armed Forces and Their Role in Politics and State Formation*. Cambridge, UK: Cambridge University Press, 2003.

Davis, Mike. *Late Victorian Holocausts: El Niño Famines and the Making of the Third World*. London: Verso, 2017.

Davis, Muriam Haleh. "Restaging *Mise en Valeur*: 'Postwar Imperialism' and the Plan de Constantine." *Review of Middle Eastern Studies* 44, no. 2 (2010): 176–86.

———. "'The Transformation of Man' in French Algeria: Economic Planning and the Postwar Social Sciences, 1958–62." *Journal of Contemporary History* 52, no. 1 (2017): 73–94.

Day, Christopher R., and William S. Reno. "In Harm's Way: African Counter-Insurgency and Patronage Politics." *Civil Wars* 16, no. 2 (2014): 105–126.

Debnath, Angela. "British Perceptions of the East Pakistan Crisis 1971: 'Hideous Atrocities on Both Sides'?" *Journal of Genocide Research* 13, no. 4 (2011): 421–50.

de Boever, Arne, Peg Birmingham, and Dimitris Vardoulakis, eds. *Plastic Sovereignties: Agamben and the Politics of Aesthetics*. Edinburgh: Edinburgh University Press, 2016.

Decker, Stephanie. "Corporate Legitimacy and Advertising: British Companies and the Rhetoric of Development in West Africa, 1950–1970." *Business History Review* 81, no. 1 (2007): 59–86.

Deery, Philip. "The Terminology of Terrorism: Malaya, 1948–52." *Journal of Southeast Asian Studies* 34, no. 2 (2003): 236–47.

Degani, Arnon. "From Republic to Empire: Israel and the Palestinians after 1948." In Cavanagh and Veracini, *Routledge Handbook of the History of Settler Colonialism*, 353–67.

De Grassi, Aharon. "Rethinking the 1961 Baixa de Kassanje Revolt: Towards a Relational Geo-History of Angola." *Mulemba: Revista Angolana de Ciências Sociais* (2015): 53–133.

Deighton, Anne. "Entente Neo-Coloniale? Ernest Bevin and the Proposals for an Anglo-French Third World Power, 1945–1949." *Diplomacy & Statecraft*, 17, no. 4 (2006): 835–52.

Dejung, Christof, David Motadel, and Jürgen Osterhammel, eds. *The Global Bourgeoisie: The Rise of the Middle Classes in the Age of Empire*. Princeton, NJ: Princeton University Press, 2019.

Demare, Brian. *Land Wars: The Story of China's Agrarian Revolution*. Stanford, CA: Stanford University Press, 2019.

Desgrandchamps, Marie-Luce. "'Organising the Unpredictable': The Nigeria–Biafra War and Its Impact on the ICRC." *International Review of the Red Cross* 94, no. 888 (2012): 1409–32.

Devine, Richard. "Japanese Rule in Korea after the March First Uprising: Governor General Hasegawa's Recommendations." *Monumenta Nipponica* 52, no. 4 (1997): 523–40.

Dhada, Mustafah. *The Portuguese Massacre of Wiriyamu in Colonial Mozambique, 1964–2013*. London: Bloomsbury, 2016.

Dharmasena, K. "The Entry of Developing Countries into World Shipping." *International Journal of Maritime History* 1 (1989): 85–112.

Di Donato, Michele, and Mathieu Fulla, eds. *Leftist Internationalisms: A Transnational Political History*. London: Bloomsbury Academic, 2023.

Dierikx, Marc L. J. "Policy versus Practice: Behind the Scenes in Dutch Development Aid, 1949–1989." *International History Review* 39, no. 4 (2017): 638–53.

Dietrich, Christopher. "'Arab Oil Belongs to the Arabs': Raw Material Sovereignty, Cold War Boundaries, and the Nationalisation of the Iraq Petroleum Company, 1967–1973." *Diplomacy & Statecraft* 22, no. 3 (2011): 450–79.

———. "'A Climate of Collaboration': The Rhodesian Oil Embargo and Portuguese Diplomacy in Southern Africa, 1965–1967." *Itinerario* 35, no. 1 (2011): 97–120.

———. *Oil Revolution: Anticolonial Elites, Sovereign Rights, and the Economic Culture of Decolonization*. Cambridge, UK: Cambridge University Press, 2017.

Dietze, Antje, and Katja Naumann. "Revisiting Transnational Actors from a Spatial Perspective." *European Review of History: Revue Européenne d'histoire* 25, no. 3–4 (2018): 415–30.

Dijn, Annelien de. *Freedom: An Unruly History*. Cambridge, MA: Harvard University Press, 2020.

Di John, Jonathan. "Oil Abundance and Violent Political Conflict: A Critical Reassessment." *Journal of Development Studies* 43, no. 6 (2007): 961–86.

Dimier, Véronique. "Bringing the Neo-Patrimonial State back to Europe: French Decolonization and the Making of the European Development Aid Policy." *Archiv für Sozialgeschichte* 48 (2008): 433–57.

———. "Constructing Conditionality: The Bureaucratization of EC Development Aid." *European Foreign Affairs Review* 11 (2006): 263–80.

———. "L'institutionnalisation de la Commission Européenne (DG Développement): du rôle des leaders dans la construction d'une administration multinationale, 1958–1975." *Etudes internationales* 34 (2003): 401–28.

Dimier, Veronique. "On Good Colonial Government: Lessons from the League of Nations." *Global Society* 18, no. 3 (2004): 279–99.

Dimier, Véronique, and Sarah Stockwell, eds. *The Business of Development in Post-Colonial Africa.* Basingstoke, UK: Palgrave Macmillan, 2020.

Dimitrakis, Panagiotis. "British Intelligence and the Cyprus Insurgency, 1955–1959." *International Journal of Intelligence and Counterintelligence* 21, no. 2 (2008): 375–94.

Diogo, Maria Paula, and Dirk van Laak. *Europeans Globalizing: Mapping, Exploiting, Exchanging.* London: Palgrave Macmillan, 2016.

Dirlik, Arif. "Global South: Predicament and Promise." *The Global South* 1, no. 1–2 (2007): 12–23.

———. "Spectres of the Third World: Global Modernity and the End of the Three Worlds." *Third World Quarterly* 25, no. 1 (2004): 131–48.

Dixon, Paul. "Britain's 'Vietnam Syndrome'? Public Opinion and British Military Intervention from Palestine to Yugoslavia." *Review of International Studies* 26, no. 1 (2000): 99–121.

Dockrill, Saki. *Britain's Retreat from East of Suez: The Choice between Europe and the World?* Basingstoke, UK: Palgrave Macmillan, 2002.

Dolan, Anne. "Killing in 'the Good Old Irish Fashion'? Irish Revolutionary Violence in Context." *Irish Historical Studies* 44, no. 165 (2020): 11–24.

Domingos, Nuno, Miguel Bandeira Jerónimo, and Ricardo Roque, eds. *Resistance and Colonialism: Insurgent Peoples in World History.* Basingstoke, UK: Palgrave, 2019, 85–122.

Doron, Roy. "Marketing Genocide: Biafran Propaganda Strategies during the Nigerian Civil War, 1967–70." *Journal of Genocide Research* 16, no. 2–3 (2013): 227–46.

Dotson, Kristie. "Tracking Epistemic Violence, Tracking Practices of Silencing." *Hypatia* 26, no. 2 (2011): 236–57.

Douglas, R. M. "Did Britain Use Chemical Weapons in Mandatory Iraq?" *Journal of Modern History* 81 (December 2009): 859–87.

Downes, Alexander B. "Desperate Times, Desperate Measures: The Causes of Civilian Victimisation in War." *International Security* 30, no. 4 (2006): 152–95.

———. "Draining the Sea by Filling the Graves: Investigating the Effectiveness of Indiscriminate Violence as a Counterinsurgency Strategy." *Civil Wars* 9, no. 4 (2007): 420–44.

Drachewych, Oleksa. "Great Disappointment, Shifting Opportunities: A Glimpse into the Comintern, Western European Parties and Their Colonial Work in the Third Period." *Twentieth Century Communism* 18 (Spring 2020): 150–73.

Drayton, Richard. "Federal Utopias and the Realities of Imperial Power." *Comparative Studies of South Asia, Africa and the Middle East* 37, no. 2 (August 2017): 401–6.

———. *Nature's Government: Science, Imperial Britain, and the "Improvement" of the World.* New Haven, CT: Yale University Press, 2000.

Drohan, Brian. *Brutality in an Age of Human Rights: Activism and Counterinsurgency at the End of the British Empire.* Ithaca, NY: Cornell University Press, 2017.

Duara, Prasenjit. "The Discourse of Civilization and Pan-Asianism." *Journal of World History* 12, no. 1 (2001): 99–130.

———. *Sovereignty and Authenticity: Manchukuo and the East Asian Modern.* Lanham, MD: Rowman & Littlefield, 2003.

Dubnov, Arie M. "Civil War, Total War or a War of Partition? Reassessing the 1948 War in Palestine from a Global Perspective." In Kattan and Ranjan, *Breakup of India and Palestine*, 222–58.

Dubnov, Arie M., and Laura Robson, eds. *Partitions: A Transnational History of Twentieth-Century Territorial Separatism.* Stanford, CA: Stanford University Press, 2019.

Duffield, Mark. *Global Governance and the New Wars: The Merging of Development and Security.* London: Zed Books, 2001. 2nd edition 2014.

Duiker, William J. *The Communist Road to Power in Vietnam.* 2nd edition. Boulder, CO: Westview Press, 1996.

Duncan, Ian. "The Politics of Liberalisation in Early Post-Independence India: Food Deregulation in 1947." *Journal of Commonwealth and Comparative Politics* 33, no. 1 (1995): 25–45.

Dũng, Bùi Minh. "Japan's Role in the Vietnamese Starvation of 1944–45." *Modern Asian Studies* 29, no. 3 (1995): 573–618.

Dunkley, D. A. "Hegemony in Post-Independence Jamaica." *Caribbean Quarterly* 57, no. 2 (2011): 1–23.

Dunne, Tim, and Christian Reus-Smit, eds. *The Globalization of International Society.* Oxford: Oxford University Press, 2017.

Dunstan, Sarah C. "Conflicts of Interest: The 1919 Pan-Africanist Congress and the Wilsonian Moment." *Callaloo* 39, no. 1 (2016): 133–50.

———. "*La Langue de nos maîtres*: Linguistic Hierarchies, Dialect, and Canon Decolonization during and after the *Présence Africaine* Congress of 1956." *Journal of Modern History* 93, no. 4 (2021): 861–95.

———. "'Une Negre de drame': Jane Vialle and the Politics of Representation in Colonial Reform, 1945–1953." *Journal of Contemporary History* 55, no. 3 (2020): 645–65.

———. *Race, Rights and Reform: Black Activism in the French Empire and the United States from World War I to the Cold War.* Cambridge, UK: Cambridge University Press, 2021.

Dunwoodie, Peter. *Writing French Algeria.* Oxford: Oxford University Press, 1998.

Duranti, Marco. "Decolonizing the United Nations: Anti-Colonialism and Human Rights in the French Empire." In Moses, Duranti, and Burke, *Decolonization, Self Determination*, 54–78.

Dutton, Paul V. *Origins of the French Welfare State: The Struggle for Social Reform in France, 1914–1947.* Cambridge, UK: Cambridge University Press, 2002.

Duyvesteyn, Isabelle, and Bart Schuurman. "The Paradoxes of Negotiating with Terrorist and Insurgent Organisations." *The Journal of Imperial & Commonwealth History* 39, no. 4 (2011): 677–92.

Dwyer, Philip, and Amanda Nettelbeck, eds. *Violence, Colonialism, and Empire in the Modern World.* Basingstoke, UK: Palgrave Macmillan, 2018.

Dyroff, Stefan. "Avant-Garde or Supplement? Advisory Bodies of Transnational Associations as Alternatives to the League's Minority Protection System, 1919–1939." *Diplomacy & Statecraft* 24, no. 2 (2013): 192–208.

Dyson, Tom. "Convergence and Divergence in Post–Cold War British, French, and German Military Reforms." *Security Studies* 17, no. 4 (2008): 725–74.

Dzanic, David. "Between Fanaticism and Loyalty: Algerian Prisoners within the French Mediterranean Empire." *Journal of North African Studies* 22, no. 2 (2016): 204–24.

Eckel, Jan. "Human Rights and Decolonization: New Perspectives and Open Questions." *Humanity* 1, no. 1 (2010): 124–48.

Eckel, Jan, and Samuel Moyn, eds. *The Breakthrough: Human Rights in the 1970s.* Philadelphia: University of Pennsylvania Press, 2014.

Eckert, Andreas. "Radical Scholarship and Political Activism: Walter Rodney as Third World Intellectual and Historian of the Third World." In Prakash and Adelman, *Inventing the Third World*, 117–36.

———. "Regulating the Social: Social Security, Social Welfare and the State in Late Colonial Tanzania." *Journal of African History* 45, no. 3 (2004): 467–89.

Eckes, Alfred E. Jr., and Thomas Zeiler. *Globalization and the American Century.* New York: Oxford University Press, 2003.

Edele, Mark. *Stalinism at War: The Soviet Union in World War II.* London: Bloomsbury, 2021.

Edele, Mark, and Robert Gerwarth. "The Limits of Demobilization: Global Perspectives on the Aftermath of the Great War." *Journal of Contemporary History* 50, no. 1 (2015): 3–14.

Edele, Mark, and Filip Slaveski. "Violence from Below: Explaining Crimes against Civilians across Soviet Space, 1943–1947." *Europe-Asia Studies* 68, no. 6 (2016): 1020–35.

Edgerton, David. "The Decline of Declinism." *Business History Review* 71, no. 2 (1997): 201–6.

———. "War, Reconstruction and the Nationalization of Post-War Britain, 1945–1951." *Past & Present* 210, Supplement 6 (2011): 29–56.

Edington, Claire E. *Beyond the Asylum: Mental Illness in French Colonial Vietnam.* Ithaca, NY: Cornell University Press, 2019.

———. "Going in and Getting out of the Colonial Asylum: Families and Psychiatric Care in French Indochina." *Comparative Studies in Society and History* 55 (2013): 725–55.

Edmonds, Daniel. "Shapurji Saklatvala, the Workers' Welfare League of India, and Transnational Anti-Colonial Labour Organising in the Inter-War Period." *Twentieth Century Communism* 18 (Spring 2020): 14–38.

Edmonds, Daniel, Evan Smith, and Oleksa Drachewych. "Editorial: Transnational Communism and Anti-Colonialism." *Twentieth Century Communism* 18 (Spring 2020): 5–13.

Edwards, Aaron. "A Triumph of Realism? Britain, Aden and the End of Empire." In Jones, *Britain and State Formation in Arabia*, 5–17.

Edwards, M. Kathryn. *Contesting Indochina: French Remembrance between Decolonization and Cold War.* Berkeley: University of California Press, 2016.

———. "An Indochinese Dominion: *L'Effort Indochinois* and Autonomy in a Global Context, 1936–1939." *French Politics, Culture and Society* 38, no. 2 (2020): 9–34.

Eggers, Nicole, Jessica Lynne Pearson, and Aurora Almada e Santos, eds. *The United Nations and Decolonization*. Abingdon, UK: Routledge, 2020.

Ehrlich, Joshua. "Anxiety, Chaos, and the Raj." *Historical Journal* 63, no. 3 (2020): 777–87.

Eichengreen, Barry. *Globalizing Capital: A History of the International Monetary System*. 2nd edition. Princeton, NJ: Princeton University Press, 2008.

———. *Golden Fetters: The Gold Standard and the Great Depression, 1919–1939*. Oxford: Oxford University Press, 1992.

Eisner, Manuel. "The Uses of Violence: An Examination of Some Cross-Cutting Issues." *International Journal of Conflict and Violence* 3, no. 1 (2009): 40–59.

Ekmekçioglu, Lerner. "'Republic of Paradox': The League of Nations Minority Protection Regime and New Turkey's Step-Citizens." *International Journal of Middle East Studies* 46, no. 4 (2016): 657–79.

Eley, Geoff. "Historicizing the Global, Politicizing Capital: Giving the Present a Name." *History Workshop Journal* 63, no. 1 (2007): 154–88.

Elkind, Jessica. "'The Virgin Mary Is Going South': Refugee Resettlement in South Vietnam, 1954–1956." *Diplomatic History* 38, no. 5 (2014): 987–1016.

Elkins, Caroline. "The Struggle for Mau Mau Rehabilitation in Late Colonial Kenya." *International Journal of African Historical Studies* 33, no. 1 (2000): 25–57.

Eloranta, Jari, and Mark Harrison. "War and Disintegration, 1914–1950." In *The Economics of Coercion and Conflict*, edited by Mark Harrison, 39–66. Singapore: World Scientific Publishing, 2015.

Engerman, David, and Corinna Unger. "Towards a Global History of Modernization." *Diplomatic History* 33, no. 3 (2009): 375–85.

Engerman, David C. "American Knowledge and Global Power." *Diplomatic History* 31, no. 4 (2007): 599–622.

———. *Modernization from the Other Shore: American Intellectuals and the Romance of Russian Development*. Cambridge, MA: Harvard University Press, 2004.

———. *The Price of Aid: The Economic Cold War in India*. Cambridge, MA: Harvard University Press, 2018.

Engerman, David C., Nils Gilman, Michael E. Latham, and Mark H. Hacfelc, eds. *Staging Growth: Modernization, Development, and the Global Cold War*. Amherst: University of Massachusetts Press, 2003.

Engerman, Stanley L. "Contract Labor, Sugar, and Technology in the Nineteenth Century." *Journal of Economic History* 43, no. 3 (1983): 635–59.

Eppel, Michael. "The Elite, the Effendiyya, and the Growth of Nationalism and Pan-Arabism in Hashemite Iraq, 1921–1958." *International Journal of Middle East Studies* 30 (1998): 411–34.

Erickson, Edward J., ed. *A Global History of Relocation in Counterinsurgency Warfare*. London: Bloomsbury, 2020.

Errante, Antoinette. "White Skin, Many Masks: Colonial Schooling, Race, and National Consciousness among White Settler Children in Mozambique, 1934–1974." *International Journal of African Historical Studies* 36, no. 1 (2003): 7–33.

Ertola, Emanuele. "The Italian Fascist Settler Empire in Ethiopia, 1936–1941." In Cavanagh and Veracini, *Routledge Handbook of the History of Settler Colonialism*, 263–76.

Eschen, Penny M. Von. "From London 1948 to Dakar 1966: Crises in Anticolonial Counterpublics." In Prakash and Adelman, *Inventing the Third World*, 137–54.

——. *Race against Empire: Black Americans and Anticolonialism, 1937–1957*. Ithaca, NY: Cornell University Press, 1997.

Escobar, Arturo. *Encountering Development: The Making and Unmaking of the Third World*. 2nd edition. Princeton, NJ: Princeton University Press, 2011.

Esenbel, Selçuk. "Japan's Global Claims to Asia and the World of Islam: Transnational Nationalism and World Power, 1900–1945." *American Historical Review* 109, no. 4 (2004): 1140–70.

Eskander, Saad. "Britain's Policy in Southern Kurdistan: The Formation and the Termination of the First Kurdish Government, 1918–1919." *British Journal of Middle Eastern Studies* 27, no. 2 (2000): 139–63.

——. "Southern Kurdistan under Britain's Mesopotamian Mandate: From Separation to Incorporation, 1920–23." *Middle Eastern Studies* 37, no. 2 (2001): 153–80.

Eslava, Luis. "The Moving Location of Empire: Indirect Rule, International Law, and the *Bantu Educational Kinema Project*." *Leiden Journal of International Law* 31, no. 3 (2018): 539–67.

Eslava, Luis, Michael Fakhri, and Vasuki Nesiah, eds. *Bandung, Global History, and International Law: Critical Pasts and Pending Futures*. Cambridge, UK: Cambridge University Press, 2017.

——. "The Spirit of Bandung." In Eslava, Fakhri, and Nesiah, *Bandung, Global History, and International Law*, 3–32.

Estoile, Benoît de l'. "Rationalizing Colonial Domination? Anthropology and Native Policy in French-Ruled Africa." In *Empires, Nations, and Natives: Anthropology and State-Making*, edited by Benoît de l'Estoile, Federico Neiburg, and Lygia Sigaud, 30–57. Durham, NC: Duke University Press, 2005.

Etges, Andreas. "All that Glitters Is Not Gold: The 1953 Coup against Mohammed Mossadegh in Iran." *Intelligence and National Security* 26, no. 4 (2011): 495–508.

Evans, Harold. "Studies in Wartime Organisation (2): The Resident Ministry in West Africa." *African Affairs* 43, no. 173 (1944): 152–58.

Evans, Martin. "Reprisal Violence and the Harkis in French Algeria, 1962." *International History Review* 39, no. 1 (2017): 89–106.

Evans, Michael. "The Wretched of the Empire: Politics, Ideology and Counterinsurgency in Rhodesia, 1965–80." *Small Wars & Insurgencies* 18, no. 2 (2007): 175–95.

Evenden, Matthew. "Aluminium, Commodity Chains, and the Environmental History of the Second World War." *Environmental History* 16 (2011): 69–93.

Ewing, Cindy. "The Colombo Powers: Crafting Diplomacy in the Third World and Launching Afro-Asia at Bandung." *Cold War History* 19, no. 1 (2019): 1–19.

Fahrenthold, Stacy D. *Between the Ottomans and the Entente: The First World War in the Syrian and Lebanese Diaspora, 1908–1925*. New York: Oxford University Press, 2019.

Fair, C. Christine, and Sumit Ganguly, eds. *Policing Insurgencies: Cops as Counter-Insurgents*. Oxford: Oxford University Press, 2014.

Fairhead, James, and Melissa Leach. "Desiccation and Domination: Science and Struggles over Environment and Development in Colonial Guinea." *Journal of African History* 41, no. 1 (2000): 35–54.

Fakhri, Michael, and Kelly Reynolds. "The Bandung Conference." In *Oxford Bibliographies in International Law*, edited by Anthony Carty. Oxford: Oxford University Press, 2017, available online at https://www.oxfordbibliographies.com.

Falah, Ghazi. "The 1948 Israeli-Palestinian War and Its Aftermath: The Transformation and De-Signification of Palestine's Cultural Landscape." *Annals of the Association of American Geographers* 86, no. 2 (1996): 256–85.

Faligot, Roger. *Tricontinental: Quand Che Guevara, Ben Barka, Cabral, Castro et Hô Chi Minh préparaient La Révolution mondiale (1964–1968)*. Paris: La Découverte, 2013.

Falola, Toyin, and Hetty Ter Haar, eds. *Narrating War and Peace in Africa*. Rochester: University of Rochester Press, 2010.

Fearon, James D., and David D. Laitin. "Sons of the Soil, Migrants, and Civil War." *World Development* 39, no. 2 (2010): 199–211.

Fedman, David. *Seeds of Control: Japan's Empire of Forestry in Colonial Korea*. Seattle: University of Washington Press, 2020.

Feichtinger, Moritz. "'A Great Reformatory': Social Planning and Strategic Resettlement in Late Colonial Kenya and Algeria, 1952–63." *Journal of Contemporary History* 52, no. 1 (2017): 45–72.

Feichtinger, Moritz, and Stephan Malinowski. "Transformative Invasions: Western Post-9/11 Counterinsurgency and the Lessons of Colonialism." *Humanity* 3, no. 1 (2012): 35–63.

Fejzula, Merve. "The Cosmopolitan Historiography of Twentieth-Century Federalism." *Historical Journal* 63, no. 1 (2020): 1–24.

Felbab-Brown, Vanda, Harold Trinkunas, and Shadi Hamid. *Militants, Criminals, and Warlords: The Challenge of Local Governance in an Age of Disorder*. Washington, DC: Brookings Institution Press, 2018.

Ferguson, Niall, Charles S. Maier, Erez Manela, and Daniel Sargent, eds. *The Shock of the Global: The 1970s in Perspective*. Cambridge, MA: Belknap, 2010.

Fernando, Joseph M. "Special Rights in the Malaysian Constitution and the Framers' Dilemma, 1956–57." *Journal of Imperial & Commonwealth History* 43, no. 3 (2015): 535–56.

Fessin, Didier. *Humanitarian Reason: A Moral History of the Present*. Berkeley: University of California Press, 2012.

Fichter, James R., ed. *British and French Colonialism in Africa, Asia and the Middle East: Connected Empires across the Eighteenth to Twentieth Centuries*. Cham: Palgrave Macmillan, 2019.

Fieldhouse, D. K. *Merchant Capital and Economic Decolonization: The United Africa Company 1929–1987*. Oxford: Clarendon Press, 1994.

———. *The West and the Third World: Trade, Colonialism, Dependence and Development*. Oxford: Blackwell, 1999.

Field, Thomas C., Stella Krepp, and Vanni Pettinà, eds. *Latin America and the Global Cold War*. Chapel Hill: University of North Carolina Press, 2020, 1–14.

Fink, Carole. *Defending the Rights of Others: The Great Powers, the Jews, and International Minority Protection, 1878–1938*. Cambridge, UK: Cambridge University Press, 2004.

Finnemore, Martha. *The Purpose of Intervention: Changing Beliefs about the Use of Force*. Ithaca, NY: Cornell University Press, 2003.

Firpo, Christina. *Black Market Business: Selling Sex in Northern Vietnam, 1920–1945.* Ithaca, NY: Cornell University Press, 2020.

Firpo, Christina, and Margaret Jacobs. "Taking Children, Ruling Colonies: Child Removal and Colonial Subjugation in Australia, Canada, French Indochina, and the United States, 1870s–1950s." *Journal of World History* 29, no. 4 (2018): 529–62.

Fisher, John. *British Imperialism in the Middle East, 1916–19.* London: Frank Cass, 1999.

——. "The Interdepartmental Committee on Eastern Unrest and British Responses to Bolshevik and Other Intrigues against the Empire during the 1920s." *Journal of Asian History* 34, no. 1 (2000): 1–34.

Fitzgerald, Edward Peter. "France's Middle Eastern Ambitions, the Sykes-Picot Negotiations, and the Oil Fields of Mosul, 1915–1918." *Journal of Modern History* 66, no. 4 (1994): 697–725.

——. "The Power of the Weak and the Weakness of the Strong: Explaining Corporate Behavior in Middle Eastern Oil after the Second World War." *Business and Economic History Review* 23, no. 2 (1994): 108–28.

Flint, John. "Scandal at the Bristol Hotel: Some Thoughts on Racial Discrimination in Britain and West Africa and Its Relationship to the Planning of Decolonisation, 1939–1947." *Journal of Imperial & Commonwealth History* 12, no. 1 (1983): 74–93.

Fogarty, Richard S., and David Killingray. "Demobilization in British and French Africa at the End of the First World War." *Journal of Contemporary History* 50, no. 1 (2015): 100–23.

Fonseca, Helder Adegar. "The Military Training of Angolan Guerrillas in Socialist Countries: A Prosopographical Approach, 1961–1974." In Dallywater, Saunders, and Fonseca, *Southern African Liberation Movements*, 103–28.

Forclaz, Amalia Ribi. "From Reconstruction to Development: The Early Years of the Food and Agriculture Organization (FAO) and the Conceptualization of Rural Welfare, 1945–1955." *International History Review* 41, no. 2 (2019): 351–71.

——. "A New Target for International Social Reform: The International Labour Organisation and Working and Living Conditions in Agriculture in the Interwar Years." *Journal of Contemporary History* 20, no. 3 (2011): 307–29.

Førland, T. Egil. "'Economic Warfare' and 'Strategic Goods': A Conceptual Framework for Analyzing COCOM." *Journal of Peace Research* 28, no. 2 (1991): 191–204.

Fourchard, Laurent. "Lagos and the Invention of Juvenile Delinquency in Nigeria, 1920–60." *Journal of African History* 47, no. 1 (2006): 115–37.

Fowler, Corinna. *Green Unpleasant Land: Creative Responses to Rural England's Colonial Connections.* Leeds: Peepal Tree Press, 2020.

Frakking, Roel. "Beyond Sticks and Carrots: Local Agency in Counterinsurgency." *Humanity* 5, no. 3 (2014): 391–415.

——. "'Gathered on the Point of a Bayonet': The Negara Pasundan and the Colonial Defence of Indonesia, 1946–50." *International History Review* 39, no. 1 (2017): 30–47.

Frakking, Roel, and Martin Thomas. "Windows onto the Microdynamics of Insurgent and Counterinsurgent Violence: Evidence from Late Colonial Southeast Asia and Africa Compared." In Zaalberg and Luttikhuis, *Empire's Violent End*, 78–126.

Frankema, Ewout. "Raising Revenue in the British Empire, 1870–1940: How 'Extractive' Were Colonial Taxes?" *Journal of Global History* 5, no. 3 (2010): 447–77.

Frankema, Ewout, and Anne Booth, eds. *Fiscal Capacity and the Colonial State in Africa and Asia, c. 1850–1960*. Cambridge, UK: Cambridge University Press, 2019.

Frankema, Ewout, and Frans Buelens, eds. *Colonial Exploitation and Economic Development: The Belgian Congo and the Netherlands Indies Compared*. Abingdon, UK: Routledge, 2013.

Frankema, Ewout, Michiel de Haas, and Marlous van Waijenburg. "Inequality Regimes in Africa from Pre-Colonial Times to the Present." *African Affairs* 122, no. 486 (2023): 57–94.

Fraser, Arvonne. "Becoming Human: The Origins and Development of Women's Human Rights." *Human Rights Quarterly* 21, no. 4 (1999): 853–906.

Frazer, Elizabeth, and Kimberley Hutchings. "The Politics Violence Frontier." *Journal of Political Ideologies* 25, no. 3 (2020): 229–47.

Frémeaux, Jacques. "The French Experience in Algeria: Doctrine, Violence and Lessons Learnt." *Civil Wars* 14, no. 1 (2012): 49–62.

Fremigacci, Jean, Daniel Lefeuvre, and Marc Michel, eds. *Démontage d'empires*. Paris: Riveneuve editions, 2012.

French, David. "The British Empire and the Meaning of 'Minimum Force Necessary' in British Counter-Insurgencies Operations c. 1857–1967." In T. G. Otte, *British World Policy and the Projection of Global Power, c. 1830–1960*, 46–66. Cambridge, UK: Cambridge University Press, 2019.

———. *The British Way in Counter-Insurgency, 1945–1957*. Oxford: Oxford University Press, 2011.

———. "Duncan Sandys and the Projection of British Power after Suez." *Diplomacy & Statecraft* 24, no. 1 (2013): 41–58.

———. *Fighting EOKA: The British Counter-Insurgency Campaign on Cyprus, 1955–1959*. Oxford: Oxford University Press, 2015.

———. "Nasty Not Nice: British Counter-Insurgency Doctrine and Practice." *Small Wars & Insurgencies* 23, no. 4/5 (2012): 744–61.

———. "Toads and Informers: How the British Treated Their Collaborators during the Cyprus Emergency, 1955–9." *International History Review* 39, no. 1 (2017): 71–88.

Frey, Marc, Sönke Kunkel, and Corinna Unger, eds. *International Organizations and Development, 1945–1990*. Basingstoke, UK: Palgrave Macmillan, 2014.

Friedman, Jeremy. "Reddest Place North of Havana: The Tricontinental and the Struggle to Lead the 'Third World.'" In Parrott and Lawrence, *Tricontinental Revolution*, 193–215.

———. *Shadow Cold War: The Sino-Soviet Competition for the Third World*. Chapel Hill: University of North Carolina Press, 2015.

Furedi, Frank. *The Mau Mau War in Perspective*. Oxford: James Currey, 1989.

Gafaïti, Hafid, Patricia M. E. Lorcin, and David G. Troyansky, eds. *Transnational Spaces and Identities in the Francophone World*. Lincoln: University of Nebraska Press, 2009.

Galpern, Steven G. *Money, Oil and Empire in the Middle East: Sterling and Postwar Imperialism, 1944–1971*. Cambridge, UK: Cambridge University Press, 2009.

Galvao, Inês, and Catarina Laranjeiro. "Gender Struggle in Guiné-Bissau: Women's Participation on and off the Liberation Record." In Domingos, Bandeira Jerónimo, and Roque, *Resistance and Colonialism*, 85–122.

Gao Jiayi. "Fighting Side by Side: Cross-Border Military Exchanges and Cooperation between the Chinese Communist Party and the Viet Minh, 1945–1949." *China
Review* 19, no. 3 (2019): 123–48.

Garavini, Giuliano. *After Empires: European Integration, Decolonization, and the
Challenge from the Global South 1957–1986.* Oxford: Oxford University Press, 2012.

———. "Completing Decolonization: The 1973 'Oil Shock' and the Struggle for Economic Rights." *International History Review* 33, no. 3 (2011): 473–87.

Garcia, Claire Oberon. "Remapping the Metropolis: Theorizing Black Women's Subjectivities in Interwar Paris." In Germain and Larcher, *Black French Women*,
215–36.

García, Magaly Rodríguez. "The League of Nations and the Moral Recruitment of
Women." *International Review of Social History* 57 (2012): 97–128.

Gardner, Leigh. "New Colonies, Old Tools: Building Fiscal Systems in East and Central
Africa." In Frankema and Booth, *Fiscal Capacity and the Colonial State*, 193–229.

Gartzke, Erik, and Quan Li. "War, Peace, and the Invisible Hand: Positive Political
Externalities of Economic Globalization." *International Studies Quarterly* 47
(2003): 561–86.

Gartzke, Erik, Quan Li, and Charles Boehmer. "Investing in the Peace: Economic
Interdependence and International Conflict." *International Organization* 55, no. 2
(2001): 391–438.

Gates, Scott. "Recruitment and Allegiance: The Microfoundations of Rebellion." *Journal of Conflict Resolution* 46, no. 1 (2002): 111–30.

Gatrell, Peter. *The Making of the Modern Refugee.* Oxford: Oxford University Press,
2013.

———. "Trajectories of Population Displacement in the Aftermath of Two World Wars."
In *The Disentanglement of Populations: Migration, Expulsion and Displacement
in Postwar Europe, 1944–49*, edited by Jessica Reinisch and Elizabeth White. Basingstoke, UK: Palgrave Macmillan, 2011, 3–6.

Gavin, Francis J., and Mark Atwood Lawrence, eds. *Beyond the Cold War: Lyndon
Johnson and the New Global Challenges of the 1960s.* Oxford: Oxford University
Press, 2014.

Gelvin, James L. *Divided Loyalties: Nationalism and Mass Politics in Syria at the
Close of Empire.* Berkeley: University of California Press, 1999.

———. "The Social Origins of Popular Nationalism in Syria: Evidence for a New Framework." *International Journal of Middle East Studies* 26 (1994): 645–61.

Gendry, Thaïs. "Le cannibale et la justice: de l'obsession coloniale à la mort pénale
(Côte d'Ivoire et Guinée Française, années 1920)." *Vingtième Siècle, Revue d'Histoire*
140, no. 4 (2018): 55–68.

George, Rose. *Deep Sea and Foreign Going: Inside Shipping, the Invisible Industry
That Brings You 90% of Everything.* London: Portobello, 2013.

Geppert, Dominik, William Mulligan, and Andreas Rose, eds. *The Wars before the Great
War: Conflict and International Politics before the Outbreak of the First World War.*
Cambridge, UK: Cambridge University Press, 2015.

Gerits, Frank. "Bandung as the Call for a Better Development Project: US, British,
French and Gold Coast Perceptions of the Afro-Asian Conference (1955)." *Cold
War History* 16, no. 3 (2016): 255–72.

——. "'Défendre l'oeuvre que nous réalisons en Afrique': Belgian Public Diplomacy and the Global Cold War (1945–1966)." *Dutch Crossing* 40, no. 1 (2016): 68–80.

——. "Hungry Minds: Eisenhower's Cultural Assistance to Sub-Saharan Africa, 1953–1961." *Diplomatic History* 41, no. 3 (2017): 594–619.

——. *The Ideological Scramble for Africa: How the Pursuit of Anticolonial Modernity Shaped a Postcolonial Order, 1945–1966.* Ithaca, NY: Cornell University Press, 2023.

——. "The Postcolonial Cultural Transaction: Rethinking the Guinea Crisis within the French Cultural Strategy for Africa, 1958–60." *Cold War History* 19, no. 4 (2019): 493–509.

——. "'When the Bull Elephants Fight': Kwame Nkrumah, Non-Alignment, and Pan-Africanism as an Interventionist Ideology in the Global Cold War (1957–66)." *International History Review* 37, no. 5 (2015): 951–69.

Gerlach, Christian. *Extremely Violent Societies: Mass Violence in the Twentieth Century World.* Cambridge, UK: Cambridge University Press, 2010.

Germain, Félix, and Silvane Larcher, eds. *Black French Women and the Struggle for Equality, 1848–2016.* Lincoln: University of Nebraska Press, 2018.

Gershoni, Israel. "The Emergence of Pan-Nationalism in Egypt: Pan-Islamism and Pan-Arabism in the 1930s." *Asian and African Affairs* 16, no. 1 (1982): 59–94.

Gershoni, Israel, and James Jankowski, eds. *Rethinking Nationalism in the Arab Middle East.* New York: Columbia University Press, 1997.

Gerwarth, Robert. *The Vanquished: Why the First World War Failed to End, 1917–1923.* London: Penguin, 2017.

Gerwarth, Robert, and John Horne, eds. *War in Peace: Paramilitary Violence in Europe after the Great War.* Oxford: Oxford University Press, 2013.

Getachew, Adom. "The Plantation in Comparative Perspective: Toward a Theory of Colonial Modernity." In Jenco, Idris, and Thomas, *Oxford Handbook of Comparative Political Theory,* 41–60.

——. "Securing Postcolonial Independence: Kwame Nkrumah and the Federal Idea in the Age of Decolonization." *Ab Imperio* 3 (2018): 89–113.

——. *Worldmaking after Empire: The Rise and Fall of Self-Determination.* Princeton, NJ: Princeton University Press, 2019.

Getchell, Michelle. "Cuba, the USSR, and the Non-Aligned Movement: Negotiating Non-Alignment." In Field, Krepp, and Pettinà, *Latin America and the Global Cold War,* 148–73.

Gettig, Eric. "Cuba, the United States, and the Uses of the Third World Project, 1959–1967." In Field, Krepp, and Pettinà, *Latin America and the Global Cold War,* 241–73.

Geyer, Michael, and Adam Tooze, eds. *The Cambridge History of the Second World War.* Vol. 3: *Total War: Economy, Society and Culture.* Cambridge, UK: Cambridge University Press, 2015.

Ghettas, Mohammed Lakhdar. *Algeria and the Cold War: International Relations and the Struggle for Autonomy.* London: Bloomsbury, 2019.

Ghosh, Durba. "AHR Forum: Another Set of Imperial Turns?" *American Historical Review* 117, no. 3 (2012): 772–93.

——. "Gender and Colonialism: Expansion or Marginalization?" *Historical Journal* 47, no. 3 (2004): 737–55.

Ghosh, Durba. *Gentlemanly Terrorists: Political Violence and the Colonial State in India, 1919–1947*. Cambridge, UK: Cambridge University Press, 2017.

Gibbs, David N. *The Political Economy of Third World Intervention: Mines, Money, and U.S. Policy in the Congo Crisis*. Chicago: University of Chicago Press, 1991.

Gildea, Robert. *Empires of the Mind: The Colonial Past and the Politics of the Present*. Cambridge, UK: Cambridge University Press, 2019.

Gills, Barry K. "'Empire' versus 'Cosmopolis': the Clash of Globalizations." *Globalizations* 2, no. 1 (2005): 5–13.

Girault, René, et al., eds. *Pierre Mendès France et le rôle de la France dans le monde*. Grenoble: Presses Universitaires de Grenoble, 1991.

Girvan, Norman, et al., "The Third World and the IMF: The Case of Jamaica, 1974–1980." *Development Dialogue* 2 (1980): 113–65.

Glasman, Joël. *Humanitarianism and the Quantification of Human Needs: Minimal Humanity*. Abingdon, UK: Routledge, 2019.

Gleijeses, Piero. *Conflicting Missions: Havana, Washington and Africa, 1959–1976*. Chapel Hill: University of North Carolina Press, 2003.

———. "Cuba's First Venture in Africa: Algeria, 1961–1965." *Journal of Latin American Studies* 28, no. 1 (1996): 159–95.

———. "Moscow's Proxy? Cuba and Africa 1975–1988." *Journal of Cold War Studies* 8, no. 2 (2006): 3–51.

Goebel, Michael. *Anti-Imperial Metropolis: Interwar Paris and the Seeds of Third World Nationalism*. Cambridge, UK: Cambridge University Press, 2015.

Goedde, Petra. *The Politics of Peace: A Global Cold War History*. New York: Oxford University Press, 2019.

———. "Power, Culture, and the Rise of Transnational History in the United States." *International History Review* 40, no. 3 (2018): 592–608.

Go, Julian. *Patterns of Empire: The British and American Empires, 1688 to Present*. Cambridge, UK: Cambridge University Press, 2011.

Goldberg, Ellis. "Peasants in Revolt—Egypt 1919." *International Journal of Middle East Studies* 24 (1992): 261–80.

Goldzeiger, Annie-Rey. *Aux origines de la guerre d'Algérie, 1940–1945: de Mers el-Kébir aux massacres nord-constantinois*. Paris: Éditions la découverte, 2002.

Gomez, Michael A. *Reversing Sail: A History of the African Diaspora*. 2nd edition. Cambridge, UK: Cambridge University Press, 2020.

Gonçalves, Márcia. "Of Peasants and Settlers: Ideals of Portugueseness, Imperial Nationalism and European Settlement in Africa, c. 1930–c.1945." *European Review of History* 25, no. 1 (2018): 166–86.

———. "The Scramble for Africa Reloaded? Portugal, European Colonial Claims and the Distribution of Colonies in the 1930s." *Contemporary European History* 29 (June 2020): 1–14.

Goodall, Heather. *Beyond Borders: Indians, Australians and the Indonesian Revolution, 1939 to 1950*. Amsterdam: Amsterdam University Press, 2018.

Gordon, Alec. "The Agrarian Question and Colonial Capitalism: Coercion and Java's Colonial Sugar Plantation System, 1870–1941." *Journal of Peasant Studies* 27, no. 1 (1999): 1–34.

Gorman, Daniel. *International Cooperation in the Early Twentieth Century*. London: Bloomsbury, 2017.

Goscha, Christopher E. "Bringing Asia into Focus: Civilians and Combatants in the Line of Fire in China and Indochina." *War & Society* 31, no. 2 (2012): 87–105.

———. "The Hunger General: Economic Warfare during the Indochina War." In Martin Thomas and Gareth Curless, *The Oxford Handbook of Late-Colonial Insurgencies & Counter-Insurgencies*, Oxford: Oxford University Press, 2023, 622–35.

———. "A 'Total War' of Decolonization? Social Mobilization and State-Building in Communist Vietnam (1949–54)." *War & Society* 31, no. 2 (2012): 136–62.

———. *Vietnam: A New History*. New York: Basic, 2016.

———. *Vietnam: un État né de la guerre, 1945–1954*. Paris: Armand Colin, 2011.

Gosnell, Jonathan. *The Politics of Frenchness in Colonial Algeria, 1930–1954*. Rochester: University of Rochester Press, 2002.

Goswami, Manu. "Imaginary Futures and Colonial Internationalisms." *American Historical Review* 117, no. 5 (2012): 1461–85.

———. *Producing India: From Colonial Economy to National Space*. Chicago: University of Chicago Press, 2004.

Gould, Eliga H. "Zones of Law, Zones of Violence: The Legal Geography of the British Atlantic, circa 1771." *William and Mary Quarterly* 60, no. 3 (2003): 471–510.

Graaf, Beatrice de, Ido de Haan, and Brian Vick, eds. *Securing Europe after Napoleon: 1815 and the New European Security Culture*. Cambridge, UK: Cambridge University Press, 2019.

Grandin, Greg. *Empire's Workshop: Latin America, the United States, and the Rise of the New Imperialism*. New York: Henry Holt, 2006.

———. "Facing South: How Latin America Socialized United States Diplomacy." In McCoy, Fradera, and Jacobson, *Endless Empire*, 107–21.

———. *The Last Colonial Massacre: Latin America in the Cold War*. Chicago: University of Chicago Press, 2004.

Grandin, Greg, and Gilbert M. Joseph, eds. *A Century of Revolution: Insurgent and Counterinsurgent Violence during Latin America's Long Cold War*. Durham, NC: Duke University Press, 2010.

Grant, Nicholas. "The Global Antiapartheid Movement and the Racial Politics of the Cold War." *Radical History Review* 119 (2014): 72–93.

Grenoble, Alexander, and William Rose. "David Galula's Counterinsurgency: Occam's Razor and Colombia." *Civil Wars* 13, no. 3 (2011): 280–311.

Griffin, Christopher. "French Military Policy in the Nigerian Civil War, 1967–1970." *Small Wars & Insurgencies* 26, no. 1 (2015): 114–35.

———. "Major Combat Operations and Counterinsurgency Warfare: Plan Challe in Algeria, 1959–1960." *Security Studies* 19 (2010): 555–89.

Griffiths, John. "Were There Municipal Networks in the British World, c. 1890–1939?" *Journal of Imperial & Commonwealth History* 37, no. 4 (2009): 575–97.

Grilli, Matteo. *Nkrumaism and African Nationalism: Ghana's Pan-African Foreign Policy in the Age of Decolonization*. Basingstoke, UK: Palgrave Macmillan, 2018.

Grob-Fitzgibbon, Benjamin. *Imperial Endgame: Britain's Dirty Wars and the End of Empire*. Basingstoke, UK: Palgrave Macmillan, 2011.

Groenewoud, Margo. "Towards the Abolition of Penal Sanctions in Dutch Colonial Labour Legislation: An International Perspective." *Itinerario* 19, no. 2 (1995): 72–90.

Gronbeck-Tedesco, John A. *Cuba, the United States, and Cultures of the Transnational Left, 1930–1975.* Cambridge, UK: Cambridge University Press, 2015.

———. "The Left in Transition: The Cuban Revolution in US Third World Politics." *Journal of Latin American Studies* 40, no. 4 (2008): 651–73.

Gross, Michael L. *The Ethics of Insurgency: A Critical Guide to Just Guerrilla Warfare.* Cambridge, UK: Cambridge University Press, 2015.

Gruhn, Isebill V. "The Lomé Convention: Inching towards Interdependence." *International Organization* 30, no. 2 (1976): 241–62.

Guelton, Frédéric. "The French Army 'Centre for Training and Preparation in Counter-Guerilla Warfare' (CIPCG) at Arzew." *Journal of Strategic Studies* 25, no. 2 (2002): 35–53.

Guerin, Adam. "Disaster Ecologies: Land, Peoples and the Colonial Modern in the Gharb, Morocco, 1911–1936." *Journal of the Economic and Social History of the Orient* 59 (2016): 333–65.

———. "'Not a Drop for the Settlers': Reimagining Popular Protest and Anti-Colonial Nationalism in the Moroccan Protectorate." *Journal of North African Studies* 20, no. 2 (2015): 225–46.

———. "Racial Myth, Colonial Reform, and the Invention of Customary Law in Morocco, 1912–1930." *Journal of North African Studies* 16, no. 3 (2011): 361–80.

Guglielmo, Thomas A. *Divisions: A New History of Racism and Resistance in America's World War II Military.* New York: Oxford University Press, 2021.

Guilhot, Nicolas. "Imperial Realism: Post-War IR Theory and Decolonisation." *International History Review* 36, no. 4 (2014): 698–720.

Guillemot, François. "'Be men!': Fighting and Dying for the State of Vietnam (1951–54)." *War & Society* 31, no. 2 (2012): 184–210.

———. *Dai Viet: indépendance et révolution au Viêt-Nam: l'échec de la troisième voie, 1938–1955.* Paris: Les Indes Savantes, 2012.

Gulsah, Zeynep. "Decolonising International Relations?" *Third World Quarterly* 38, no. 1 (2017): 1–15.

Gumz, Jonathan E. *The Resurrection and Collapse of Empire in Habsburg Serbia, 1914–1918.* Cambridge, UK: Cambridge University Press, 2009.

Guyot-Réchard, Bérénice. "The Fear of Being Compared: State-Shadowing in the Himalayas, 1910–1962." *Political Geography* 75 (2019), published online.

Gventer, Celeste Ward, David Martin Jones, and M. L. R. Smith, eds. *The New Counter-Insurgency Era in Critical Perspective.* Basingstoke, UK: Palgrave Macmillan, 2014.

Häberlin, Joachim C. "Between Global Aspirations and Local Realities: The Global Dimensions of Interwar Communism." *Journal of Global History* 7, no. 3 (2012): 415–37.

Hack, Karl. "Between Terror and Talking, the Place of 'Negotiation' in Colonial Conflict." *Journal of Imperial & Commonwealth History* 39, no. 4 (2011): 539–49.

———. "Detention, Deportation and Resettlement: British Counterinsurgency and Malaya's Rural Chinese, 1948–60." *Journal of Imperial & Commonwealth History* 43, no. 4 (2015): 611–40.

———. "'Devils That Suck the Blood of the People': The Case for Post-Revisionist Analysis of Counter-Insurgency Violence." *War in History* 25, no. 2 (2018): 202–26.

———. "Everyone Lived in Fear: Malaya and the British Way of Counter Insurgency." *Small Wars & Insurgencies* 23, no. 4/5 (2012): 671–99.

———. "The Malayan Emergency as Counter-Insurgency Paradigm." *Journal of Strategic Studies* 32, no. 3 (2009): 383–414.

———. "Negotiating with the Malayan Communist Party, 1948–89." *Journal of Imperial & Commonwealth History* 39, no. 4 (2011): 607–32.

———. "'Screwing down the People' The Malayan Emergency, Decolonisation, and Ethnicity." In *Imperial Policy and Southeast Asian Nationalism*, edited by Hans Antlöv and Stein Tønnesson, 83–109. London: Curzon Press, 1995.

———. "Unfinished Decolonisation and Globalisation." *Journal of Imperial & Commonwealth History* 47, no. 5 (2019): 818–50.

Hadiz, Vedi R. "The Rise of Neo-Third Worldism? The Indonesian Trajectory and the Consolidation of Illiberal Democracy." *Third World Quarterly* 25, no. 1 (2004): 55–71.

Hadjiathanasiou, Maria. *Propaganda and the Cyprus Revolt: Rebellion, Counter-Insurgency and the Media, 1955–59*. London: I. B. Tauris, 2020.

Haines, Daniel. "A 'Commonwealth Moment' in South Asian Decolonization." In James and Leake, *Decolonization and the Cold War*, 185–202.

Hajjat, Abdellali. "Colonial Legacies: Housing Policy and Riot Prevention Strategies in the Minguettes District of Vénissieux." In Naylor, *France's Modernising Mission*, 225–50.

Hakim, Carol. "The French Mandate in Lebanon." *American Historical Review* 124, no. 5 (2019): 1689–93.

Hall, Anthony J. *Earth into Property: Colonization, Decolonization, and Capitalism*. Montreal: McGill-Queens University Press, 2010.

Hallaq, Wael. *The Impossible State: Islam, Politics, and Modernity's Moral Predicament*. New York: Columbia University Press, 2012.

Hall, Ian. "The Revolt against the West: Decolonisation and Its Repercussions in British International Thought, 1945–75." *International History Review* 33, no. 1 (2011): 43–64.

Hall, Margaret. "The Mozambican National Resistance Movement (Renamo): A Study in the Destruction of an African Country." *Africa* 60, no. 1 (1990): 39–68.

Halperin, Sandra, and Ronen Palan, eds. *Legacies of Empire: Imperial Roots of the Contemporary Global Order*. Cambridge, UK: Cambridge University Press, 2015.

Halvorson, Dan. "From Commonwealth Responsibility to the National Interest: Australia and Post-War Decolonisation in South-East Asia." *International History Review* 40, no. 4 (2018): 870–92.

Hamblin, Jacob Darwin. *Arming Mother Nature: The Birth of Catastrophic Environmentalism*. Oxford: Oxford University Press, 2013.

———. "The Vulnerability of Nations: Food Security in the Aftermath of World War II." *Global Environment* 10 (2012): 42–65.

Hammond, Kelly A. *China's Muslims and Japan's Empire: Centering Islam in World War II*. Chapel Hill: University of North Carolina Press, 2020.

———. "Managing Muslims: Imperial Japan, Islamic Policy, and Axis Connections during the Second World War." *Journal of Global History* 12 (2017): 251–73.

Hammond Perry, Kennatta. *London Is the Place for Me: Black Britons, Citizenship and the Politics of Race*. Oxford: Oxford University Press, 2015.

Hanieh, Adam. *Lineages of Revolt: Issues of Contemporary Capitalism in the Middle East*. London: Haymarket Books, 2013.

Hanna, Leni. "Tricontinental's International Solidarity: Emotion in OSPAAL as Tactic to Catalyze Support of Revolution." *Radical History Review* 136 (2020): 169–84.

Hänni, Adrian. "Secret Bedfellows: The KGB, Carlos the Jackal and Cold War Psychological Warfare." *Studies in Conflict & Terrorism* 43, no. 1 (2020): 69–87.

Hansen Peo, and Stefan Jonsson. *Eurafrica: The Untold History of European Integration and Colonialism*. London: Bloomsbury, 2014.

Harbi, Mohamed. *Les Archives de la révolution algérienne*. Paris: Jeune Afrique, 1981.

Harisch, Immanuel R. "Facets of Walter Rodney's Pan-African Intellectual Activism during his Dar es Salaam Years, 1966–1974." *Vienna Journal of African Studies* 20, no. 38 (2020): 101–29.

Harper, T. N. *The End of Empire and the Making of Malaya*. Cambridge, UK: Cambridge University Press, 1999.

——. "The Politics of Disease and Disorder in Post-War Malaya." *Journal of Southeast Asian Studies* 21, no. 1 (1990): 88–113.

——. "The Politics of the Forest in Colonial Malaya." *Modern Asian Studies* 31, no. 1 (1997): 1–29.

——. *Underground Asia: Global Revolutionaries and the Assault on Empire*. London: Allen Lane, 2020.

Harrison, Mark, and Inge Zaksauskiene. "Counter-Intelligence in a Command Economy." *Economic History Review* 69, no. 1 (2016): 131–58.

Harrison. Olivia C., ed. *Transcolonial Maghreb: Imagining Palestine in the Era of Decolonization*. Stanford, CA: Stanford University Press, 2015.

Hassett, Dónal. "Colonialism and Contested Cultures of Victory in the French Empire of the 1920s." *Journal of Contemporary History* 54, no. 4 (2019): 759–79.

——. *Mobilizing Memory: The Great War and the Language of Politics in Colonial Algeria, 1918–1939*. Oxford: Oxford University Press, 2019.

Havik, Philip J. "Public Health and Tropical Modernity: The Combat against Sleeping Sickness in Portuguese Guinea, 1945–74." *História, Ciências, Saúde: Manguinhos* 21, no. 2 (2014): 641–66.

Heath, Deana. *Colonial Terror: Torture and State Violence in Colonial India*. Oxford: Oxford University Press, 2021.

Hecht, Gabrielle, ed. *Entangled Geographies: Empire and Technopolitics in the Global Cold War*. Cambridge, MA: MIT Press, 2011.

Hedinger, Daniel. "The Imperial Nexus: The Second World War and the Axis in Global Perspective." *Journal of Global History* 12 (2017): 184–205.

Heerten, Lasse. *The Biafran War and Postcolonial Humanitarianism: Spectacles of Suffering*. Cambridge, UK: Cambridge University Press, 2017.

Heerten, Lasse, and A. Dirk Moses. "The Nigeria–Biafra War: Postcolonial Conflict and the Question of Genocide." *Journal of Genocide Research* 16, no. 2–3 (2014): 169–203.

Heikal, Mohamed H. *Cutting the Lion's Tail: Suez through Egyptian Eyes*. London: Andre Deutsch, 1986.

Heimann, Gadi. "A Case of Diplomatic Symbiosis: France, Israel and the Former French Colonies, 1958–1962." *Journal of Contemporary History* 51, no. 1 (2016): 145–64.

———. "From Friendship to Patronage: France–Israel Relations, 1958–1967." *Diplomacy & Statecraft* 21, no. 2 (2010): 240–58.

Heiss, Mary Ann. "National Prerogatives versus International Supervision: Britain's Evolving Policy toward the Campaign for Equivalency of United Nations' Handling of Dependent Territories, 1945–1963." In Eggers, Pearson, and Almada e Santos, *United Nations and Decolonization*, 23–39.

Heitmeyer, William, Heinz-Gerhard Haupt, Andrea Kirschner, and Gerhard Malthaner, eds. *Control of Violence: Historical and International Perspectives on Violence in Modern Societies*. New York: Springer, 2011.

Helleiner, Eric. *The Contested World Economy: The Deep and Global Roots of International Political Economy*. Cambridge, UK: Cambridge University Press, 2023.

———. *Forgotten Foundations of Bretton Woods: International Development and the Making of the Postwar Order*. Ithaca, NY: Cornell University Press, 2014.

———. "Sun Yat-sen as a Pioneer of International Development." *History of Political Economy* 50, no. 1 (2018): 76–93.

Henderson, Errol A. "The Revolution Will Not Be Theorised: Du Bois, Locke, and the Howard School's Challenge to White Supremacist IR Theory." *Millennium: Journal of International Studies* 45, no. 3 (2017): 492–510.

Henderson, Errol A., and J. David Singer. "Civil War in the Post-Colonial World, 1946–92." *Journal of Peace Research*, 37, no. 3 (2000): 275–99.

Hendrickson, Burleigh. *Decolonizing 1968: Transnational Student Activism in Tunis, Paris, and Dakar*. Ithaca, NY: Cornell University Press, 2022.

Henley, David E. F. "Ethnogeographic Integration and Exclusion in Anticolonial Nationalism: Indonesia and Indochina." *Comparative Studies in Society and History* 37, no. 2 (1995): 286–324.

Henriet, Benoît. "Anxieux ethnographes: pratiques quotidiennes du pouvoir au Congo belge, 1930–1940." *Vingtième Siècle* 4, no. 140 (2018): 41–64.

Henriksen, Thomas H. "Angola, Mozambique and Soviet Intervention: Liberation and the Quest for Influence." In *Soviet and Chinese Aid to African Nations*, edited by Warren Weinstein and Thomas H. Henriksen, 56–75. New York: Praeger, 1980.

Henriot, Christian. "Beyond Glory: Civilians, Combatants, and Society during the Battle of Shanghai." *War & Society* 31, no. 2 (2012): 106–35.

Henshaw, Alexis Leanna. "Where Women Rebel: Patterns of Women's Participation in Armed Rebel Groups, 1990–2008." *International Feminist Journal of Politics* 18, no. 1 (2016): 39–60.

Hepburn, Sacha, and April Jackson. "Colonial Exceptions: The International Labour Organization and Child Labour in British Africa, c.1919–1940." *Journal of Contemporary History* 57, no. 2 (2022): 218–41.

Herbst, Jeffrey. *States and Power in Africa: Comparative Lessons in Authority and Control*. Princeton, NJ: Princeton University Press, 2000.

———. "Theories of International Cooperation: The Case of the Lomé Convention." *Polity* 19, no. 4 (Summer 1987): 637–59.

Herman, Rebecca. "The Global Politics of Anti-Racism: A View from the Canal Zone." *American Historical Review* 125, no. 2 (2020): 460–86.

Hernández, Rafael M., and Jennifer Ruth Hosek. "Tricontinentalism: The Construction of Global Alliances." In Parrott and Lawrence, *Tricontinental Revolution*, 69–92.

Heuser, Beatrice. "Exploring the Jungle of Terminology." *Small Wars & Insurgencies* 25, no. 4 (2014): 741–53.

Heuser, Beatrice, and Eitan Shamir, eds. *Insurgencies and Counterinsurgencies*. Cambridge, UK: Cambridge University Press, 2017.

Hevia, James. *The Imperial Security State: British Colonial Knowledge and Empire-Building in Asia*. Cambridge, UK: Cambridge University Press, 2012.

Heywood, Linda M. "Towards an Understanding of Modern Political Ideology in Africa: The Case of the Ovimbundu in Angola." *Journal of Modern African Studies* 36, no. 1 (1998): 149–65.

Hickel, Jason, Dylan Hickel, and Huzaifa Zoomkawala. "Plunder in the Post-Colonial Era: Quantifying Drain from the Global South through Unequal Exchange, 1960–2018." *New Political Economy* 26, no. 6 (2021): 1030–47.

Hillbom, Ellen, and Erik Green. *An Economic History of Development in Sub-Saharan Africa: Economic Transformations and Political Changes*. Basingstoke: Palgrave Macmillan, 2019.

Hill, J. N. C. "Challenging the Failed State Thesis: IMF and World Bank Intervention and the Algerian Civil War." *Civil Wars* 11, no. 1 (2009): 39–56.

——. "Remembering the War of Liberation: Legitimacy and Conflict in Contemporary Algeria." *Small Wars & Insurgencies* 23, no. 1 (2012): 4–31.

Hill, Peter. "Ottoman Despotism and Islamic Constitutionalism in Mehmed Ali's Egypt." *Past & Present* 237, no. 1 (November 2017).

Hilton, Matthew. "Consumers and the State since the Second World War." *Annals of the American Academy of Political and Social Science* 611 (2007): 66–81.

——. "International Aid and Development NGOs in Britain and Human Rights since 1945." *Humanity* 3, no. 3 (2012): 449–72.

Hilton, Matthew, Emily Baughan, Eleanor Davey, Bronwen Everill, Kevin O'Sullivan, and Tahila Sasson. "History and Humanitarianism: A Conversation." *Past & Present* 241, no. 1 (2018): 1–38.

Hobson, John. *The Eurocentric Conception of World Politics: Western International Theory, 1760–2010*. Cambridge, UK: Cambridge University Press, 2012.

——. "What's at Stake in Doing (Critical) IR/IPE Historiography? The Imperative of Critical Historiography." In Schmidt and Guilhot, *Historiographical Investigations*, 149–70.

Hodge, Joseph M. "British Colonial Expertise, Postcolonial Careering and the Early History of International Development." *Journal of Modern European History* 8, no. 1 (2010): 24–46.

——. "Colonial Foresters versus Agriculturalists: The Debate over Climate Change and Cocoa Production in the Gold Coast." *Agricultural History* 83, no. 2 (2009): 201–20.

——. *Triumph of the Expert: Agrarian Doctrines of Development and the Legacies of British Colonialism*. Athens: Ohio University Press, 2007.

——. "Writing the History of Development (Part 1: The First Wave)." *Humanity* 6, no. 3 (2015): 429–63.

———. "Writing the History of Development (Part 2: Longer, Deeper, Wider)." *Humanity* 7, no. 1 (2016): 125–74.

Hodge, Joseph M., Gerald Hödl, and Martina Kopf, eds. *Developing Africa: Concepts and Practices in Twentieth-Century Colonialism*. Manchester, UK: Manchester University Press, 2014.

Hodgson, Dorothy L. "Taking Stock: State Control, Ethnic Identity and Pastoralist Development in Tanganyika, 1948–1958." *Journal of African History* 41 (2000): 58–78.

———. "Women's Rights as Human Rights: Women in Law and Development in Africa (WiLDAF)." *Africa Today* 49, no. 2 (2002): 3–26.

Ho, Engseng. "Empire through Diasporic Eyes: A View from the Other Boat." *Comparative Studies of Society and History* 46, no. 2 (2004): 210–46.

Hoffman, Stefan-Ludwig. "Human Rights and History." *Past & Present* 232 (2016): 272–322.

Hofmann, Reto, and Max Ward, eds. *Transwar Asia: Ideology, Practices, and Institutions, 1920–1960*. London: Bloomsbury, 2022.

Høgsbjerg, Christian. "Globalising the Haitian Revolution in Black Paris: C. L. R. James, Metropolitan Anti-Imperialism in Interwar France and the Writing of *The Black Jacobins*." *Journal of Imperial & Commonwealth History* 48, no. 3 (2020): 491–519.

Holá, Barbora, Holly Nyseth Nzitatira, and Maartje Weerdesteijn, eds. *The Oxford Handbook on Atrocity Crimes*. Oxford: Oxford University Press, 2022.

Holcombe, Alex. *Mass Mobilization in the Democratic Republic of Vietnam, 1945–1960*. Honolulu: University of Hawai'i Press, 2020.

Holland, Robert. *Britain and the Revolt in Cyprus, 1954–1959*. Oxford: Clarendon Press, 1998.

Hong, Young-Sun. *Cold War Germany, the Third World, and the Global Humanitarian Regime*. Cambridge, UK: Cambridge University Press, 2015.

Hoogvelt, A. M. *Globalization and the Postcolonial World: The New Political Economy of Development*. Basingstoke, UK: Macmillan, 1997.

Hopkins, Anthony G. *American Empire: A Global History*. Princeton, NJ: Princeton University Press, 2018.

———. "Globalisation and Decolonisation." *Journal of Imperial & Commonwealth History* 45, no. 5 (2017): 729–45.

———. "Is Globalisation Yesterday's News?" *Itinerario* 41, no. 1 (2017): 109–28.

———. "Macmillan's Audit of Empire, 1957." In *Understanding Decline: Perceptions and Realities of British Economic Performance*, edited by Peter Clarke and C. Trebilcock, 234–60. Cambridge, UK: Cambridge University Press, 1997.

———. "Rethinking Decolonization." *Past and Present* 200 (August 2008): 211–47.

Horne, Gerald. *Mau Mau in Harlem: The US and the Liberation of Kenya*. Basingstoke, UK: Palgrave Macmillan, 2009.

Horne, Janet R. "'To Spread the French Language Is to Extend the Patrie': The Colonial Mission of the Alliance Française." *French Historical Studies* 40, no. 1 (2017): 95–127.

Horne, John. "End of a Paradigm? The Cultural History of the Great War." *Past & Present* 242 (February 2019): 255–92.

Horn, Martin. *Britain, France, and the Financing of the First World War*. Montreal: McGill-Queen's University Press, 2002.

House, Jim. "Colonial Containment? Repression of Pro-Independence Street Demonstrations in Algiers, Casablanca and Paris, 1945–1962." *War in History* 25, no. 2 (2018): 172–201.

———. "Shantytowns and Rehousing in Late Colonial Algiers and Casablanca." In Naylor, *France's Modernising Mission*, 133–63.

Howard, Lise Morjé, and Alexandra Stark. "How Civil Wars End: The International System, Norms, and the Role of External Actors." *International Security* 42, no. 3 (2017): 127–71.

Howarth, David, and Joachim Schild. "France and European Macroeconomic Policy Coordination: From the Treaty of Rome to the Euro Area Sovereign Debt Crisis." *Modern & Contemporary France* 25, no. 2 (2017): 171–90.

Howe, Stephen. *Anticolonialism in British Politics: The Left and the End of Empire, 1918–1964*. Oxford: Clarendon, 1993.

———. "Falling Rhodes, Building Bridges, Finding Paths: Decoloniality from Cape Town to Oxford and Back." In Pedersen and Ward, *Break-Up of Greater Britain*, 294–310.

———. "When—If Ever—Did Empire End? Recent Studies of Imperialism and Decolonization." *Journal of Contemporary History* 40, no. 3 (2005): 585–99.

Howland, Douglas, and Luise White, eds. *The State of Sovereignty: Territories, Laws, Populations*. Bloomington: Indiana University Press, 2009.

Huber, Valeska. "Educational Mobility and Globalisation: Universities in Cairo between Competition and Standardisation, 1900–1950." In *A Global Middle East: Mobility, Materiality and Culture in the Modern Age, 1880–1940*, edited by Cyrus Schayegh, Avner Wishnitzer, and Liat Kozma, 81–108. London: Bloomsbury, 2014.

———. "Introduction: Global Histories of Social Planning." *Journal of Contemporary History* 52, no. 1 (2017): 3–15.

———. "The Unification of the Globe by Disease? The International Sanitary Conferences on Cholera, 1851–1894." *Historical Journal* 49, no. 2 (2006): 452–76.

Huff, Amber, and Lyla Mehta. "Untangling Scarcity." In Jonsson et al., *Scarcity in the Modern World*, 27–45.

Huff, Gregg. "Causes and Consequences of the Great Vietnam Famine, 1944–5." *Economic History Review* 72, no. 1 (2019): 286–316.

———. "The Great Second World War Vietnam and Java Famines." *Modern Asian Studies* 54, no. 2 (2020): 618–53.

Hughes, Matthew. "The Banality of Brutality: British Armed Forces and the Repression of the Arab Revolt in Palestine, 1936–39." *English Historical Review* 124, no. 507 (April 2009): 313–54.

———. *Britain's Pacification of Palestine: The British Army, the Colonial State, and the Arab Revolt, 1936–1939*. Cambridge, UK: Cambridge University Press, 2019.

———. "Fighting for White Rule in Africa: The Central African Federation, Katanga, and the Congo Crisis, 1958–1965." *International History Review* 25 (2003): 592–613.

———. "A History of Violence: The Shooting of British Assistant Superintendent Alan Sigrist, 12 June 1936." *Journal of Contemporary History* 45, no. 4 (2010): 725–43.

———. "The Practice and Theory of British Counterinsurgency: The Histories of the Atrocities at the Palestinian Villages of al-Bassa and Halhul, 1938–1939." *Small Wars & Insurgencies* 20, no. 3–4 (2009): 528–50.

———. "Terror in Galilee: British-Jewish Collaboration and the Special Night Squads in Palestine during the Arab Revolt, 1938–39." *Journal of Imperial & Commonwealth History* 43, no. 4 (2015): 590–610.

Humbert, Laure. *Reinventing French Aid: The Politics of Humanitarian Relief in French-Occupied Germany, 1945–1952*. Cambridge, UK: Cambridge University Press, 2021.

Hunter, Emma. "Dutiful Subjects, Patriotic Citizens and the Concept of 'Good Citizenship' in Twentieth-Century Tanzania." *The Historical Journal* 56, no. 1 (2013): 257–77.

———. "Languages of Freedom in Decolonising Africa." *Transactions of the Royal Historical Society* 27 (2017): 253–69.

———. *Political Thought and the Public Sphere in Tanzania: Freedom, Democracy and Citizenship in the Era of Decolonisation*. Cambridge, UK: Cambridge University Press, 2015.

Hunt, Lynn. "The Long and the Short of the History of Human Rights." *Past & Present* 233 (2016): 323–31.

Hunt, Nancy Rose. "'Le bébé en brousse': European Women, African Birth Spacing and Colonial Intervention in Breast Feeding in the Belgian Congo." *International Journal of African Historical Studies* 21, no. 3 (1988): 401–32.

Hurrell, Andrew, and Nguire Woods, eds. *Inequality, Globalization, and World Politics*. Oxford: Oxford University Press, 1999.

Hussain, Nasser. *The Jurisprudence of Emergency: Colonialism and the Rule of Law*. Ann Arbor: University of Michigan Press, 2003.

Hutchings, Graham. *China, 1949: Year of Revolution*. London: Bloomsbury, 2021.

Hutchings, Kimberley. "Cosmopolitan Just War and Coloniality." In Bell, *Empire, Race, and Global Justice*, 211–27.

Hutchinson, Martha Crenshaw. *Revolutionary Terrorism: The FLN in Algeria, 1954–1962*. Stanford, CA: Hoover Institution Press, 1978.

Hynd, Stacey. "Small Warriors? Children and Youth in Colonial Insurgencies and Counterinsurgency, ca. 1945–1960." *Comparative Studies in Society and History* 62, no. 4 (2020): 684–713.

———. "'Uncircumcised Boys' and 'Girl Spartans': Youth, Gender and Generation in Colonial Insurgencies and Counter-Insurgency, c.1954–9." *Gender & History* 33, no. 2 (2021): 536–56.

Hyslop, Jonathan. "Steamship Empire: Asian, African and British Sailors in the Merchant Marine, c. 1880–1945." *Journal of Asian and African Studies* 44, no. 1 (2009): 49–67.

Iandolo, Alessandro. *Arrested Development: The Soviet Union in Ghana, Guinea, and Mali, 1955–1968*. Ithaca, NY: Cornell University Press, 2022.

———. "De-Stalinizing Growth: Decolonization and the Development of Development Economics in the Soviet Union." In Macekura and Manela, *Development Century*, 197–219.

———. "The Rise and Fall of the 'Soviet Model of Development' in West Africa, 1957–1964." *Cold War History* 12, no. 4 (2012): 683–704.

Iber, Patrick. "From Peace to National Liberation: Mexico and the Tricontinental." In Prakash and Adelman, *Inventing the Third World*, 45–63.

Ibhawoh, Bonny. *Imperialism and Human Rights: Colonial Discourses of Rights and Liberties in African History* Albany: SUNY Press, 2007.

Ibhawoh, Bonny. "Refugees, Evacuees, and Repatriates: Biafran Children, UNHCR, and the Politics of International Humanitarianism in the Nigerian Civil War." *African Studies Review* 63, no. 3 (2020): 568–92.

——. "Seeking the Political Kingdom: Universal Human Rights and the Anti-Colonial Movement in Africa." In Moses, Duranti, and Burke, *Decolonization, Self Determination,* 35–53.

Ikenberry, G. John. "The End of Liberal International Order?" *International Affairs* 94, no. 1 (2018), 7–23.

——. *Liberal Leviathan: The Origins, Crisis, and Transformation of the American World Order.* Princeton, NJ: Princeton University Press, 2011.

Ilahi, Shereen. *Imperial Violence and the Path to Independence: India, Ireland and the Crisis of Empire.* London: I. B. Tauris, 2016.

Imlay, Talbot C. "Clarence Streit, Federalist Frameworks, and Wartime American Internationalism." *Diplomatic History* 44, no. 5 (2020): 808–33.

——. "Exploring What Might Have Been: Parallel History, International History, and Post-War Socialist Internationalism." *International History Review* 31, no. 3 (2009): 521–57.

——. "International Socialism and Decolonization during the 1950s: Competing Rights and the Postcolonial Order." *American Historical Review* 118, no. 4 (2013): 1105–32.

——. *The Practice of Socialist Internationalism: European Socialists and International Politics, 1914–1960.* Oxford: Oxford University Press, 2017.

Immler, Nicole L., and Stef Scagliola. "Seeking Justice for the Mass Execution in Rawagede/Probing the Concept of Entangled History in a Colonial Setting." *Rethinking History: The Journal of Theory and Practice* 24, no. 1 (2020): 1–28.

Inayatullah, Naeem, and David L. Blaney. "Race and Global Inequality." In *Race, Gender and Culture in International Relations: Postcolonial Perspectives,* edited by Randolph B. Persaud and Alena Sajed, 116–30. London: Routledge, 2018.

Ingulstad, Mats. "The Interdependent Hegemon: The United States and the Quest for Strategic Raw Materials during the Early Cold War." *International History Review* 37, no. 1 (2015): 59–79.

Ireland, Benjamin Hiramatsu. "The Japanese in New Caledonia: Histories of Citizenship, Incarceration, and Nippo-Kanak Identity." *French Historical Studies* 43, no. 4 (2020): 667–703.

Iriye, Akira. *Global Community: The Role of International Organizations in the Making of the Contemporary World.* Berkeley: University of California Press, 2002.

——, ed. *Global Interdependence: The World after 1945.* Cambridge, MA: Harvard University Press, 2014.

Irwin, Julia F. "The 'Development' of Humanitarian Relief: US Disaster Assistance Operations in the Caribbean Basin, 1917–1931." In Macekura and Manela, *Development Century,* 40–60.

——. "Taming Total War: Great War–Era American Humanitarianism and Its Legacies." *Diplomatic History* 38, no. 4 (2014): 763–75.

Irwin, Ryan M. "Apartheid on Trial: South West Africa and the International Court of Justice, 1960–66." *International History Review* 32, no. 4 (2010): 619–42.

——. "Sovereignty in the Congo Crisis." In James and Leake, *Decolonization and the Cold War*, 203–18.

——. "A Wind of Change? White Redoubt and the Postcolonial Moment, 1960–1963." *Diplomatic History* 33, no. 5 (2009): 897–925.

Isaac, Joel, James T. Kloppenberg, Michael O'Brien, and Jennifer Ratner-Rosenhagen, eds. *The Worlds of American Intellectual History*. New York: Oxford University Press, 2017.

Isaacman, Allen F. "Coercion, Paternalism and the Process: The Mozambican Cotton Regime, 1938–1961." *Journal of Southern African Studies* 18, no. 3 (1992): 487–526.

——. *Cotton Is the Mother of Poverty: Peasants, Work, and Rural Struggle in Colonial Mozambique, 1938–1961*. Portsmouth, NH: Heinemann, 1996.

Isaacman, Allen F., and Barbara S. Isaacman. *Dams, Displacement, and the Delusion of Development: Cahora Bassa and Its Legacies in Mozambique, 1965–2007*. Athens: Ohio University Press, 2013.

Isaacman, Allen, and Chris Sneddon. "Toward a Social and Environmental History of the Building of the Cahora Bassa Dam." *Journal of Southern African Studies* 26 (2000): 597–632.

Islam, M. Rafiqul. "Secessionist Self-Determination: Some Lessons from Katanga, Biafra and Bangladesh." *Journal of Peace Research* 22, no. 3 (1985): 211–21.

Ittmann, Karl. "The Colonial Office and the Population Question in the British Empire, 1918–62." *Journal of Imperial & Commonwealth History* 27, no. 3 (1999): 55–81.

——. *A Problem of Great Importance: Population, Race, and Power in the British Empire, 1919–1973*. Berkeley: University of California Press, 2013.

Ittmann, Karl, Dennis D. Cordell, and Gregory H. Maddox, eds. *The Demographics of Empire: The Colonial Order and the Creation of Knowledge*. Athens: Ohio University Press, 2010.

Ivaska, Andrew. "Liberation in Transit: Eduardo Mondlane and Che Guevara in Dar es Salaam." In *The Routledge Handbook of the Global Sixties: Between Protest and Nation-Building*, edited by Chen Jian, Martin Klimke, Masha Kirasirova, Mary Nolan, Marilyn Young, and Joanna Waley-Cohen, 27–38. London: Routledge, 2018.

Iyer, Samantha. "Colonial Population and the Idea of Development." *Comparative Studies in Society and History* 55, no. 1 (2013): 65–91.

Jackson, Peter. "Great Britain in French Policy Conceptions at the Paris Peace Conference, 1919." *Diplomacy & Statecraft* 30, no. 2 (2019): 358–97.

Jackson, Peter, William Mulligan, and Glenda Sluga, eds. *Peacemaking and International Order after the First World War*. Cambridge, UK: Cambridge University Press, 2023.

Jackson, Robert H. *Quasi-States: Sovereignty, International Relations and the Third World*. Cambridge, UK: Cambridge University Press, 1990.

Jackson, Simon, and Alanna O'Malley, eds. *The Institution of International Order: From the League of Nations to the United Nations*. London: Routledge, 2018.

Jackson, Steven F. "China's Third World Foreign Policy: The Case of Angola and Mozambique, 1961–1993." *China Quarterly* 142 (1995): 388–422.

Jackson, Will. "The Private Lives of Empire: Emotion, Intimacy, and Colonial Rule." *Itinerario* 42, no. 1 (2018): 1–15.

Jacobs, Susie. "*Doi Moi* and Its Discontents: Gender, Liberalisation, and Decollectivisation in Rural Vietnam." *Journal of Workplace Rights* 13, no. 1 (2008): 17–39.

James, Harold. *International Monetary Cooperation since Bretton Woods*. New York: Oxford University Press, 1996.

———. "The Multiple Contexts of Bretton Woods." *Past & Present* 210, Supplement 6 (2011): 290–308.

James, Leslie. "'Essential Things such as Typewriters': Development Discourse, Trade Union Expertise, and the Dialogues of Decolonization between the Caribbean and West Africa." *Journal of Social History* 53, no. 2 (2019): 378–401.

———. *George Padmore and Decolonization from Below: Pan-Africanism, the Cold War, and the End of Empire*. Basingstoke, UK: Palgrave Macmillan, 2015.

———. "'Playing the Russian Game': Black Radicalism, the Press, and Colonial Office Attempts to Control Anti-Colonialism in the Early Cold War, 1946–1950." *Journal of Imperial & Commonwealth History* 43, no. 3 (2015): 509–34.

James, Leslie, and Elisabeth Leake, eds. *Decolonization and the Cold War: Negotiating Independence*. London: Bloomsbury, 2015.

Jansen, Jan C., and Jürgen Osterhammel. *Decolonization: A Short History*. Princeton, NJ: Princeton University Press, 2017.

Jarboe, Andrew Tait, and Richard S. Fogarty, eds. *Empires in World War I: Shifting Frontiers and Imperial Dynamics in a Global Conflict*. London: Bloomsbury, 2020.

Jauffret, Jean-Charles, ed. *Des hommes et des femmes en guerre d'Algérie*. Paris: Autrement, 2003.

———. *Soldats en Algérie, 1954–1962: expériences contrastées des hommes du contingent*. Paris: Autrement, 2000.

Jeffery, Keith. "The Road to Asia, and the Grafton Hotel, Dublin: Ireland in the 'British World.'" *Irish Historical Studies* 142 (November 2008): 243–56.

Jeffery, Roger. *The Politics of Health in India*. Berkeley: University of California Press, 1988.

Jenco, Leigh K., Murad Idris, and Magan C. Thomas, eds. *The Oxford Handbook of Comparative Political Theory*. Oxford: Oxford University Press, 2020.

Jenkins, Jennifer, Heike Liebau, and Larissa Schmid. "Transnationalism and Insurrection: Independence Committees, Anti-Colonial Networks, and Germany's Global War." *Journal of Global History* 15, no. 1 (2020): 61–79.

Jennings, Eric. *Free French Africa in World War II: The African Resistance*. Cambridge, UK: Cambridge University Press, 2014.

Jennings, Michael. "Building Better People: Modernity and Utopia in Late Colonial Tanganyika." *Journal of East African Studies* 3, no. 1 (2009): 94–111.

———. "'A Very Real War': Popular Participation in Development in Tanzania during the 1950s and 1960s." *International Journal of African Historical Studies* 40, no. 1 (2007): 71–95.

———. "'We Must Run While Others Walk': Popular Participation and Development Crisis in Tanzania, 1961–9." *Journal of Modern African Studies* 41, no. 3 (2003): 163–87.

Jensehaugen, Jørgen, Marte Heian-Engdal, and Hilde Henriksen Waage. "Securing the State: From Zionist Ideology to Israeli Statehood." *Diplomacy & Statecraft* 23, no. 2 (2012): 280–303.

Jensen, Steven L. B. *The Making of International Human Rights: The 1960s, Decolonization and the Reconstruction of Global Values.* Cambridge, UK: Cambridge University Press, 2017.

Jeon, Sang Sook. "Establishing Japanese National Identity and the 'Chosŏn Issue.'" In *International Impact of Colonial Rule in Korea, 1910–1945*, edited by Yong-Chool Ha, 49–72. Seattle: University of Washington Press, 2019.

Johnson, Chalmers. *The Sorrows of Empire: Militarism, Secrecy, and the End of the Republic.* New York: Metropolitan, 2004.

Johnson, Jennifer. *The Battle for Algeria: Sovereignty, Health Care, and Humanitarianism.* Philadelphia: University of Pennsylvania Press, 2016.

———. "The Contradictions of Sovereignty: Development, Family Planning and the Struggle for Population Control in Postcolonial Morocco." *Humanity* 11, no. 3 (Winter 2020): 259–79.

Jolly, Margaret. "Horizons and Rifts in Conversations about Climate Change in Oceania." In *Pacific Futures: Past and Present*, edited by Warwick Anderson, Miranda Johnson, and Barbara Brookes, 17–48. Honolulu: University of Hawai'i Press, 2018.

Jones, Branwen Gruffydd. "African Anticolonialism in International Relations: Against the Time of Forgetting." In *Recentering Africa in International Relations: Beyond Lack, Peripherality, and Failure*, edited by M. Iñiguez de Heredia and Z. Wai, 187–223. New York: Palgrave Macmillan, 2018.

Jones, Clive. *Britain and State Formation in Arabia, 1962–1971.* Abingdon, UK: Routledge, 2018.

———. *Britain and the Yemen Civil War, 1962–1965: Ministers, Mercenaries and Mandarins.* Brighton: Sussex Academic Press, 2004.

Jones, Matthew. *Conflict and Confrontation in South East Asia, 1961–1965.* Cambridge, UK: Cambridge University Press, 2002.

———. "A 'Segregated' Asia?: Race, the Bandung Conference, and Pan-Asianist Fears in American Thought and Policy, 1954–1955." *Diplomatic History* 29, no. 5 (2005): 841–68.

Jones, Seth G. *Waging Insurgent Warfare: Lessons from the Vietcong to the Islamic State.* Oxford: Oxford University Press, 2017.

Jonsson, Fredrik Albritton, John Brewer, Neil Fromer, and Frank Trentmann, eds. *Scarcity in the Modern World: History, Politics, Society and Sustainability, 1800–2075.* London: Bloomsbury, 2019.

Joseph-Gabriel, Annette K. *Reimagining Liberation: How Black Women Transformed Citizenship in the French Empire.* Urbana: University of Illinois Press, 2020.

Joseph, Michael. "First World War Veterans and the State in the French and British Caribbean, 1919–1939." *First World War Studies* 10, no. 1 (2019): 31–48.

Jundanian, Brendan F. "Resettlement Programs: Counterinsurgency in Mozambique." *Comparative Politics*, 6, no. 4 (1974): 519–40.

Just, Daniel. *Literature, Ethics and Decolonization in Postwar France.* Cambridge, UK: Cambridge University Press, 2017.

Kadish, Alon, and Avraham Sela. "Myths and Historiography of the 1948 Palestine War Revisited: The Case of Lydda." *Middle East Journal* 59, no. 4 (2005): 617–34.

Kaempf, Sebastian. *Saving Soldiers or Civilians: Casualty Aversion versus Civilian Protection in Asymmetric Conflicts*. Cambridge, UK: Cambridge University Press, 2018.

———. "Violence and Victory: Guerrilla Warfare, 'Authentic Self-Affirmation' and the Overthrow of the Colonial State." *Third World Quarterly* 30, no. 1 (2009): 129–46.

Kaiser, David. "'Makers of Bonds and Ties': Transnational Socialisation and National Liberation in Mozambique." In Alexander, McGregor, and Tendi, *Transnational Histories*, 28–47.

Kaldor, Mary. *New and Old Wars: Organized Violence in a Global Era*. 3rd edition. London: Polity, 2012.

Kalinovsky, Artemy M. "Writing the Soviet South into the History of the Cold War and Decolonization." In Mark, Kalinovsky, and Marung, *Alternative Globalizations*, 189–208.

Kalman, Samuel. *French Colonial Fascism: The Extreme Right in Algeria, 1919–1939*. Basingstoke, UK: Palgrave Macmillan, 2013.

Kalter, Christoph. *The Discovery of the Third World: Decolonization and the Rise of the New Left in France c. 1950–1976*. Cambridge, UK: Cambridge University Press, 2016.

———. "From Global to Local and Back: The Third World Concept and the New Radical Left in France." *Journal of Global History* 12, no. 1 (2017): 115–36.

Kalyvas, Stathis N. "'New' and 'Old' Civil Wars: A Valid Distinction?" *World Politics* 54, no. 1 (2001): 99–118.

———. "The Paradox of Terrorism in Civil War." *Journal of Ethics* 8 (2004): 101–15.

Kammen, Douglas, and Katharine McGregor, eds. *The Contours of Mass Violence in Indonesia, 1965–1968*. Singapore: NIAS Press, 2012.

Kampwirth, Karen. *Feminism and the Legacy of Revolution: Nicaragua, El Salvador, Chiapas*. Athens: Ohio University Press, 2004.

Kamran, Tahir. "The Unfolding Crisis in Punjab, March–August 1947: Key Turning Points and British Responses." *Journal of Punjab Studies* 14 (2007): 187–210.

Kamugisha, Aaron. *Beyond Coloniality: Citizenship and Freedom in the Caribbean Intellectual Tradition*. Bloomington: Indiana University Press, 2019.

Kandjo, João Sicato. "A influência da Baixa de Kasanji na independência de Angola." *Mulemba: Revista Angolana de Ciências* 2, no. 1 (2020): 148–66.

Kang, Jin-Yeon. "Colonial Legacies and the Struggle for Social Membership in a National Community: The 1946 People's Uprisings in Korea." *Journal of Historical Sociology* 24, no. 3 (2011): 321–54.

Kan, Hideki. "Informal Empire and the Cold War." *Journal of Imperial & Commonwealth History* 49, no. 3 (2021): 576–606.

Kapoor, Ilan. "Capitalism, Culture, Agency: Dependency versus Postcolonial Theory." *Third World Quarterly* 23, no. 4 (2002): 647–64.

Karuka, Manu. "Black and Native Visions of Self-Determination." *Critical Ethnic Studies* 3, no. 2 (2017): 77–98.

Katsakioris, Constantin. "Soviet Lessons for Arab Modernization: Soviet Educational Aid to Arab Countries after 1956." *Journal of Modern European History* 8, no. 1 (2010): 85–105.

———. "Students from Portuguese Africa in the Soviet Union, 1960–74: Anti-Colonialism, Education, and the Socialist Alliance." *Journal of Contemporary History* 56, no. 1 (2021): 142–65.

Kattan, Victor, and Amit Ranjan, eds. *The Breakup of India and Palestine: The Causes and Legacies of Partition.* Manchester, UK: Manchester University Press, 2023.

Kaul, Chandrika, ed. *Media and the British Empire.* Basingstoke, UK: Palgrave Macmillan, 2006.

Kayaoğlu, Turan. *Legal Imperialism: Sovereignty and Extraterritoriality in Japan, the Ottoman Empire and China.* Cambridge, UK: Cambridge University Press, 2010.

Kaymaz, Nazli Pinar. "From Imperialism to Internationalism: British Idealism and Human Rights." *International History Review* 41, no. 6 (2019): 1235–55.

Keese, Alexander. "Between Violence, Racism and Reform: São Tomé e Príncipe in the Great Depression Years (1930–1937)." *Journal of Contemporary History* 56, no. 2 (2021): 243–67.

———. "Developmentalist Attitudes and Old Habits: Portuguese Labour Policies, South African Rivalry, and Flight in Southern Angola, 1945–1974." *Journal of Southern African Studies* 41, no. 2 (2015): 237–53.

———. "The Slow Abolition within the Colonial Mind: British and French Debates about 'Vagrancy,' 'African Laziness,' and Forced Labour in West Central and South Central Africa, 1945–1965." *International Review of Social History* 59, no. 3 (2014): 377–407.

Kelemen, Paul. "Modernising Colonialism: The British Labour Movement and Africa." *Journal of Imperial & Commonwealth History* 34, no. 2 (2006): 223–44.

———. "Planning for Africa: The British Labour Party's Colonial Development Policy, 1920–1964." *Journal of Agrarian Change* 7, no. 1 (2007): 76–98.

Kelley, Robin D. G. "'But a Local Phase of a World Problem': Black History's Global Vision, 1883–1950." *Journal of American History* 86, no. 3 (1999): 1045–77.

Kelly, Catriona. "Defending Children's Rights, 'In Defence of Peace': Children and Soviet Cultural Diplomacy." *Kritika: Explorations in Russian and Eurasian History* 9, no. 4 (2008): 711–46.

Kelly, John D., and Martha Kaplan. "Legal Fictions after Empire." In Howland and White, *State of Sovereignty*, 169–95.

Kelly, Patrick William. "The 1973 Chilean Coup and the Origins of Transnational Human Rights Activism." *Journal of Global History* 8, no. 1 (2013): 165–86.

Kendhammer, Brandon. "DuBois the Pan-Africanist and the Development of African Nationalism." *Ethnic and Racial Studies* 30, no. 1 (2007): 51–71.

Kennedy, Dane. "Constructing the Colonial Myth of Mau Mau." *International Journal of African Historical Studies* 25, no. 2 (1992): 241–60.

———. "Essay and Reflection: On the American Empire from a British Imperial Perspective." *International History Review* 29, no. 1 (2007): 83–108.

———. "Imperial History and Postcolonial Theory." *Journal of Imperial & Commonwealth History* 24, no. 3 (1996): 345–63.

———. *The Imperial History Wars: Debating the British Empire.* London: Bloomsbury, 2018.

Kenrick, David W. *Decolonisation, Identity and Nation in Rhodesia, 1964–1979: A Race against Time.* Basingstoke, UK: Palgrave Macmillan, 2019.

Kent, John. *America, the UN and Decolonisation: Cold War Conflict in the Congo.* London: Routledge, 2011.

——. *British Imperial Strategy and the Origins of the Cold War, 1944–49.* Leicester: Leicester University Press, 1993.

——. *The Internationalization of Colonialism: Britain, France, and Black Africa, 1939–1956.* Oxford: Clarendon Press, 1992.

Kent, Marian. *Oil and Empire: British Policy and Mesopotamian Oil, 1900–1920.* New York: Barnes & Noble, 1976.

Keohane, Robert O., and Joseph S. Nye. "Globalization: What's New? What's Not? (and So What?)." *Foreign Policy* 118 (2000): 104–19.

Keyse, Rhian Elinor. "'Hidden Motives'? African Women, Forced Marriage and Knowledge Production at the United Nations, 1950–1962." *Journal of Contemporary History* 57, no. 2 (2022): 268–92.

Khaitan, Urvi. "Women beneath the Surface: Coal and the Colonial State in India during the Second World War." *War & Society* 39, no. 3 (2020): 171–88.

Khalidi, Walid. *All That Remains: The Palestinian Villages Occupied and Depopulated by Israel in 1948.* Washington, DC: Institute for Palestine Studies, 1992.

Khalili, Laleh. "Gendered Practices of Counterinsurgency." *Review of International Studies* 37, no. 4 (2011): 1471–91.

——. "The Location of Palestine in Global Counterinsurgencies." *International Journal of Middle East Studies* 42, no. 3 (2010): 413–33.

——. *Time in the Shadows: Confinement in Counterinsurgencies.* Stanford, CA: Stanford University Press, 2013.

Kheng, Cheah Boon. "The Japanese Occupation of Malaya, 1941–45: Ibrahim Yaacob and the Struggle for Indonesia Raya." *Indonesia* 28 (October 1979): 84–120.

——. *Red Star over Malaya: Resistance and Social Conflict during and after the Japanese Occupation, 1941–1946.* Singapore: NUS Press, 2012.

Khoo, Nicholas. "Breaking the Ring of Encirclement: The Sino–Soviet Rift and Chinese Policy toward Vietnam, 1964–1968." *Journal of Cold War Studies* 12, no. 1 (2010): 3–42.

Khoury, Philip S. "The Tribal Shaykh, French Tribal Policy, and the Nationalist Movement in Syria between Two World Wars." *Middle Eastern Studies* 18, no. 2 (1982): 180–93.

Kilcullen, David. "Globalisation and the Development of Indonesian Counterinsurgency Tactics." *Small Wars & Insurgencies* 17, no. 1 (2006): 44–46.

Kim, Diana S. *Empires of Vice: The Rise of Opium Prohibition across Southeast Asia.* Princeton, NJ: Princeton University Press, 2020.

Kim, Dong Choon. "Forgotten War, Forgotten Massacres: The Korean War (1950–1953) as Licensed Mass Killings." *Journal of Genocide Research* 6, no. 4 (2004): 523–44.

Kim, Hakjoon. "A Devil Appears in a Different Dress: Imperial Japan's Deceptive Propaganda and Rationalization for Making Korea Its Colony." In *International Impact of Colonial Rule in Korea, 1910–1945,* edited by Yong-Chool Ha, 19–48. Seattle: University of Washington Press, 2019.

Kim, Marie Seong-Hak. "Customary Law and Colonial Jurisprudence in Korea." *American Journal of Comparative Law* 57, no. 1 (2009): 205–48.

Kinsella, Helen M. *The Image before the Weapon: A Critical History of the Distinction between Combatant and Civilian*. Ithaca, NY: Cornell University Press, 2011.

———. "Superfluous Injury and Unnecessary Suffering: National Liberation and the Laws of War." *Political Power and Social Theory* 32 (2017): 205–31.

Kirk, John M. "Cuban Medical Internationalism and Its Role in Cuban Foreign Policy." *Diplomacy & Statecraft* 20, no. 2 (2009): 275–90.

Kitchen, James E. "Violence in Defence of Empire: The British Army and the 1919 Egyptian Revolution." *Journal of Modern European History* 13, no. 2 (2015): 249–67.

Klinger, Janeen. "A Sympathetic Appraisal of Cold War Modernization Theory." *International History Review* 39, no. 4 (2017): 691–712.

Klose, Fabian. "Human Rights for and against Empire, Legal and Public Discourses in the Age of Decolonisation." *Journal of the History of International Law* 18 (2016): 316–38.

———. *Human Rights in the Shadow of Colonial Violence: The Wars of Independence in Kenya and Algeria*. Philadelphia: University of Pennsylvania Press, 2013.

———. "'Source of Embarrassment': Human Rights, State of Emergency, and the Wars of Decolonization." In *Human Rights in the Twentieth Century*, edited by Stefan-Ludwig Hoffman, 237–57. Cambridge, UK: Cambridge University Press, 2011.

Klug, Sam. "First New Nation or Internal Colony? Modernization Theorists, Black Intellectuals, and the Politics of Colonial Comparison in the Kennedy Years." In Schayegh, *Globalizing the U.S. Presidency*, 19–33.

———. "Social Science in Black and White: Rethinking the Disciplines in the Jim Crow Empire." *Modern Intellectual History* 15, no. 3 (2018): 909–21.

Kohn, Margaret, and Keally McBride. *Political Theories of Decolonization: Postcolonialism and the Problem of Foundations*. Oxford: Oxford University Press, 2011.

Kolinsky, Martin. *Law, Order and Riots in Mandatory Palestine, 1928–1935*. Basingstoke, UK: Palgrave Macmillan, 1993.

Kolsky, Elizabeth. "The Colonial Rule of Law and the Legal Regime of Exception: Frontier 'Fanaticism' and State Violence in British India." *American Historical Review* 120, no. 4 (2015): 1218–46.

Konieczna, Anna, and Rob Skinner, eds. *A Global History of Anti-Apartheid: "Forward to Freedom" in South Africa*. Cham: Palgrave Macmillan, 2019.

Koon, Heng Pek. "The Social and Ideological Origins of the Malayan Chinese Association, 1948–1957." *Journal of Southeast Asian History* 14, no. 2 (1983): 290–311.

Koskenniemi, Martti. "Conclusion: After Globalisation, Engaging the Backlash." In *Globalisation and Governance: International Problems, European Solutions*, edited by Robert Schütze, 453–64. Cambridge, UK: Cambridge University Press, 2018.

———. *The Gentle Civilizer of Nations: The Rise and Fall of International Law, 1870–1960*. Cambridge, UK: Cambridge University Press, 2010.

———. "A History of International Law Histories." In *The Oxford Handbook of the History of International Law*, edited by Bardo Fassbender and Ann Peters, 943–71. Oxford: Oxford University Press, 2012.

Kott, Sandrine, and Joélle Droux, eds. *Globalizing Social Rights: The International Labour Organization and Beyond*. Basingstoke, UK: Palgrave Macmillan, 2013.

Kott, Sandrine, and Joel Golb. "The Forced Labor Issue between Human and Social Rights, 1947–1957." *Humanity* 3, no. 3 (2012): 321–35.

Kozma, Liat. *Global Women, Colonial Ports: Prostitution in the Interwar Middle East.* Albany: SUNY Press, 2017.

Kramer, Martin. *Islam Assembled: The Advent of the Muslim Congresses.* New York: Columbia University Press, 1986.

Kramer, Paul A. "Empires, Exceptions, and Anglo-Saxons: Race and Rule between the British and United States Empires, 1880–1910." *Journal of American History* (2002): 1316–52.

——. "Shades of Sovereignty: Racialized Power, the United States and the World." In *Explaining the History of American Foreign Relations*, edited by Frank Costigliola and Michael J. Hogan, 245–70. Cambridge, UK: Cambridge University Press, 2016.

Kraus, Charles. "A Border Region 'Exuded with Militant Friendship': Provincial Narratives of China's Participation in the First Indochina War, 1949–1954." *Cold War History* 12, no. 3 (2012): 495–514.

——. "'The Danger is Two-Fold': Decolonisation and Cold War in Anti-Communist Asia, 1955–7." *International History Review* 39, no. 2 (2017): 256–73.

Krause, Jonathan, ed. *The Greater War: Other Combatants and Other Fronts, 1914–1918.* Basingstoke, UK: Palgrave Macmillan, 2014.

——. "Islam and Anticolonial Rebellion in North and West Africa, 1914–1918." *Historical Journal* 64, no. 3 (2020): 674–95.

Krause, Peter. *Rebel Power: Why National Movements Compete, Fight, and Win.* Ithaca, NY: Cornell University Press, 2017.

Kreike, Emanuel. *Scorched Earth: Environmental Warfare as a Crime against Humanity and Nature.* Princeton, NJ: Princeton University Press, 2021.

Krepp, Stella. "Brazil and Non-Alignment: Latin America's Role in the Global Order, 1961–1964." In Field, Krepp, and Pettinà, *Latin America and the Global Cold War,* 100–22.

Krozewski, Gerold. "Finance and Empire: The Dilemma Facing Great Britain in the 1950s." *International History Review* 18, no. 1 (1996): 48–69.

——. *Money and the End of Empire: British International Economic Policy and the Colonies, 1947–58.* Basingstoke, UK: Palgrave Macmillan, 2001.

Kubicek, Robert. "British Expansion, Empire and Technological Change." In *The Oxford History of the British Empire*. Vol. 3: *The Nineteenth Century*, edited by Andrew Porter, 247–70. Oxford: Oxford University Press, 1999.

Kuby, Emma. *Political Survivors: The Resistance, the Cold War, and the Fight against Concentration Camps after 1945.* Ithaca, NY: Cornell University Press, 2019.

Kunkel, Sönke. "Global Media, Emotions, and the 'Kennedy Narrative': Kennedy as Seen from the 'Global South.'" In Schayegh, *Globalizing the U.S. Presidency,* 100–14.

Kushner, Barak, and Sherzod Muminov, eds. *The Dismantling of Japan's Empire in East Asia: Deimperialization, Postwar Legitimation, and Imperial Afterlife.* London: Routledge, 2017.

Kuzmarov, Jeremy. *Modernizing Repression: Police Training and Nation-Building in the "American Century."* Amherst: University of Massachusetts Press, 2012.

——. "Modernizing Repression: Police Training, Political Violence, and Nation-Building in the 'American Century.'" *Diplomatic History* 33, no. 2 (2009): 191–222.

Kwon, Heonik. *After the Korean War: An Intimate History*. Cambridge, UK: Cambridge University Press, 2020.

———. *The Other Cold War*. New York: Columbia University Press, 2010.

Laakkonen, Simo, Richard P. Tucker, and Timo Vuorisalo, eds. *The Long Shadows: A Global Environmental History of the Second World War*. Corvallis: Oregon State University Press, 2017.

Labelle Jr., Maurice M. "A New Age of Empire? Arab 'Anti-Americanism,' US Intervention, and the Lebanese Civil War of 1958." *International History Review* 35, no. 1 (2013): 42–69.

———. "Tensions of Decolonization: Lebanon, West Africans, and a Color Line within the Global Color Line, May 1945." *Radical History Review* 131 (May 2018): 36–57.

Laderman, Scott. "Waves of Segregation: Surfing and the Global Antiapartheid Movement." *Radical History Review* 119 (Spring 2014): 94–121.

Ladwig, Walter C. III *The Forgotten Front: Patron–Client Relationships in Counterinsurgency*. Cambridge, UK: Cambridge University Press, 2017.

———. "When the Police Are the Problem: The Philippine Constabulary and the Hukbalahap Rebellion." In Fair and Ganguly, *Policing Insurgencies*, 19–45.

Lafuente, Gilles. *La Politique berbère de la France et le nationalisme marocain*. Paris: l'Harmattan, 1999.

Lagrou, Pieter. "1945–1955: The Age of Total War." In *Histories of the Aftermath*, edited by Frank Biess and Robert Moeller, 287–96. Oxford: Berghahn, 2010.

———. "Regaining the Monopoly of Force: Agents of the State Shooting Fugitives in and around Belgium, 1940–1950." *Past & Present* 210, Supplement 6 (2011): 177–95.

Lake, David, Lisa L. Martin, and Thomas Risse. "Challenges to the Liberal Order: Reflections on International Organization." *International Organization* 75 (Spring 2021): 225–57.

Lake, Marilyn. "From Self-Determination via Protection to Equality via Non-Discrimination: Defining Women's Rights at the League of Nations and the United Nations." In *Women's Rights and Human Rights: International Historical Perspectives*, edited by Patricia Grimshaw, Katie Holmes, and Marilyn Lake, 254–71. Basingstoke, UK: Palgrave Macmillan, 2001.

Lake, Marilyn, and Henry Reynolds. *Drawing the Global Colour Line: White Men's Countries and the International Challenge of Racial Equality*. Cambridge, UK: Cambridge University Press, 2008.

Lang, Michael. "Globalization and Global History in Toynbee." *Journal of World History* 22, no. 4 (2011): 747–83.

———. "Globalization and Its History." *Journal of Modern History* 78 (December 2006): 899–931.

Larebo, Haile. "Empire-Building and Its Limitations: Ethiopia, 1935–1941." In *Italian Colonialism*, edited by Ruth Ben-Ghiat and Mia Fuller, 83–94. Basingstoke, UK: Palgrave Macmillan, 2005.

Larmer, Miles. *Mineworkers in Africa: Labour and Political Change in Post-Colonial Africa*. London: Bloomsbury, 2020.

———. "Nation-Making at the Border: Zambian Diplomacy in the Democratic Republic of Congo." *Comparative Studies in Society and History* 61, no. 1 (2019): 145–75.

Larmer, Miles. "Unrealistic Expectations? Zambia's Mineworkers from Independence to the One-Party State, 1964–1972." *Journal of Historical Sociology* 18, no. 4 (2005): 318–23.

Larmer, Miles, and Eric Kennes. "Rethinking the Katangese Secession." *Journal of Imperial & Commonwealth History* 42 (2014): 741–61.

Laron, Guy. "Semi-Peripheral Countries and the Invention of the 'Third World,' 1955–65." *Third World Quarterly* 35, no. 9 (2014): 1547–65.

Laskier, Michael M. "Israel and Algeria amid French Colonialism and the Arab–Israeli Conflict, 1954–1978." *Israel Studies* 6, no. 2 (2001): 1–32.

Latham, Michael E. *Modernization as Ideology: American Social Science and "Nation-Building" in the Kennedy Era*. Chapel Hill: University of North Carolina Press, 2000.

———. *The Right Kind of Revolution: Modernization, Development, and U.S. Foreign Policy from the Cold War to the Present*. Ithaca, NY: Cornell University Press, 2011.

Lauro, Amandine. "Maintenir l'ordre dans la colonie-modèle: note sur les désordres urbains et la police des frontières raciales au Congo belge." *Crime, Histoire & Sociétés* 15, no. 2 (2011): 97–121.

Lawrance, Benjamin N., Emily Lynn Osborn, and Richard L. Roberts, eds. *Intermediaries, Interpreters, and Clerks: African Employees in the Making of Colonial Africa*. Madison: University of Wisconsin Press, 2006.

Lawrence, Adria K. *Imperial Rule and the Politics of Nationalism: Anti-Colonial Protest in the French Empire*. Cambridge, UK: Cambridge University Press, 2013.

———. "Triggering Nationalist Violence: Competition and Conflict in Uprisings against Colonial Rule." *International Security* 35, no. 2 (2010): 88–122.

Lawrence, Jon. "Forging a Peaceable Kingdom: War, Violence and the Fear of Brutalization in Post–First World War Britain." *Journal of Modern History* 75, no. 3 (2003): 557–89.

———. "Social Science Encounters and the Negotiation of Difference in Early 1960s England." *History Workshop Journal* 77 (2014): 215–39.

Lawrence, Mark Atwood. *Assuming the Burden: Europe and the American Commitment to War in Vietnam*. Berkeley: University of California Press, 2005.

———. *The End of Ambition: The United States and the Third World in the Vietnam Era*. Princeton, NJ: Princeton University Press, 2021.

———. "Transnational Coalition-Building and the Making of the Cold War, 1947–1949." *Diplomatic History* 26, no. 3 (2002): 453–80.

———. "Universal Claims, Local Uses: Reconceptualizing the Vietnam Conflict, 1945–60." In *Global History: Interactions between the Universal and the Local*, edited by A. G. Hopkins, 229–56. Basingstoke, UK: Palgrave Macmillan, 2006.

Lawrence, Mark Atwood, and Fredrik Logevall, eds. *The First Vietnam War: Colonial Conflict and Cold War Crisis*. Cambridge, MA: Harvard University Press, 2007.

Lazar, Seth. "Necessity and Non-Combatant Immunity." *Review of International Studies* 40, no. 1 (2014): 53–76.

Lazreg, Marnia. "The Colonial in the Global: Where Does the Third World Fit In?" *Journal of Third World Studies* 26, no. 1 (2009): 17–30.

———. *Torture and the Twilight of Empire: From Algiers to Baghdad*. Princeton, NJ: Princeton University Press, 2008.

Leake, Elisabeth. "The Great Game Anew: US Cold-War Policy and Pakistan's North-West Frontier, 1947–65." *International History Review* 35, no. 1 (2013): 1–24.

Lebaron, Genevieve, and Alison Y. Ayers. "The Rise of a 'New Slavery'? Understanding African Unfree Labour through Neoliberalism." *Third World Quarterly* 34, no. 5 (2013): 873–92.

Le Billon, Philippe. "Geographies of War: Perspectives on 'Resource Wars.'" *Geography Compass* 1, no. 2 (2007): 163–82.

———. "The Geopolitical Economy of 'Resource Wars.'" In *The Geopolitics of Resource Wars: Resource Dependence, Governance and Violence*, edited by Philippe Le Billon, 1–28. London: Frank Cass, 2005.

———. "The Political Ecology of War: Natural Resources and Armed Conflicts." *Political Geography* 20 (2001): 561–84.

Le Billon, Philippe, and Rosaleen V. Duffy. "Conflict Ecologies: Connecting Political Ecology and Peace and Conflict Studies." *Journal of Political Ecology* 25, no. 1 (2018): 239–60.

Lebovics, Herman. *Bringing the Empire Back Home: France in the Global Age*. Durham, NC: Duke University Press, 2004.

Lee, Christopher J., ed. *Making a World after Empire: The Bandung Moment and Its Political Afterlives*. 2nd edition. Athens: Ohio University Press, 2019.

Lee, Rebekah. *Health, Healing and Illness in African History*. London: Bloomsbury, 2021.

Lefebvre, Camille. "We Have Tailored Africa: French Colonialism and the 'Artificiality' of Africa's Borders in the Interwar Period." *Journal of Historical Geography* 37 (2011): 191–202.

Lefeuvre, Daniel. "La France face à son passé colonial: un double enjeu." In Dard and Lefeuvre, *L'Europe face à son passé colonial*, 365–78.

Leffler, Melvyn P., and Odd Arne Westad, eds. *The Cambridge History of the Cold War*. Cambridge, UK: Cambridge University Press, 2010.

Lentz, Carola. "African Middle Classes: Lessons from Transnational Studies and a Research Agenda." In *The Rise of Africa's Middle Class*, edited by Henning Melber, 17–53. London: Zed Books, 2016.

Lentz, Christian. *Contested Territory: Đien Biên Phu and the Making of Northwest Vietnam*. New Haven, CT: Yale University Press, 2019.

———. "The King Yields to the Village? A Micropolitics of Statemaking in Northwest Vietnam." *Political Geography* 39, no. 1 (2014): 1–10.

Leonard, Douglas W. *Anthropology, Colonial Policy and the Decline of the French Empire in Africa*. London: Bloomsbury, 2020.

Leow, Rachel. "Asian Lessons in the Cold War Classroom: Trade Union Networks and the Multidirectional Pedagogies of the Cold War in Asia." *Journal of Social History* 53, no. 2 (2019): 429–53.

———. "A Missing Peace: The Asia-Pacific Peace Conference in Beijing, 1952 and the Emotional Making of Third World Internationalism." *Journal of World History* 30, no. 1–2 (2019): 21–53.

———. *Taming Babel: Language in the Making of Malaysia*. Cambridge, UK: Cambridge University Press, 2016.

Le Page, Jean-Marc. *Les services secrets en Indochine*. Paris: Nouveau Monde, 2014.

Lerner, Adam B. "Collective Trauma and the Evolution of Nehru's Worldview: Uncovering the Roots of Nehruvian Non-Alignment." *International History Review* 41, no. 6 (2019): 1276–1300.

Lerner, Mitch. "Climbing off the Back Burner: Lyndon Johnson's Soft Power Approach to Africa." *Diplomacy & Statecraft* 22, no. 4 (2011): 578–607.

Lessard, Micheline. "'Organisons Nous!' Racial Antagonism and Vietnamese Economic Nationalism in the Early Twentieth Century." *French Colonial History* 8, no. 1 (2007): 171–201.

———. "'We Know . . . the Duties We Must Fulfill': Modern 'Mothers and Fathers' of the Vietnamese Nation." *French Colonial History* 3, no. 1 (2003): 119–43.

Lester, Alan. "British Settler Discourse and the Circuits of Empire." *History Workshop Journal* 54, no. 1 (2002): 24–48.

Le Sueur, James D. *Uncivil War: Intellectuals and Identity Politics during the Decolonization of Algeria*. Philadelphia: University of Pennsylvania Press, 2001.

Levene, Mark. "Empire, Native Peoples, and Genocide." In Moses, *Empire, Colony, Genocide*, 183–204.

Levinson, Marc. *The Box: How the Shipping Container Made the World Smaller and the World Economy Bigger*. Princeton, NJ: Princeton University Press, 2006.

Levite, Ariel, Bruce W. Jentleson, and Larry Berman. *Foreign Military Intervention: The Dynamics of Protracted Conflict*. New York: Columbia University Press, 1992.

Lewis, Janet I. "How Does Ethnic Rebellion Start?" *Comparative Political Studies* 50, no. 10 (2017): 1420–50.

———. *How Insurgency Begins: Rebel Group Formation in Uganda and Beyond*. Cambridge, UK: Cambridge University Press, 2020.

Lewis, Joanna. "Daddy Wouldn't Buy Me a Mau Mau: The British Popular Press and the Demoralisation of Empire." In Odhambo and Lonsdale, *Mau Mau and Nationhood*, 227–50.

———. *Empire of Sentiment: The Death of Livingstone and the Myth of Victorian Imperialism*. Cambridge, UK: Cambridge University Press, 2018.

———. *Empire State-Building: War and Welfare in Kenya, 1925–1952*. Oxford: James Currey, 2000.

———. "Tropical East Ends and the Second World War: Contradictions in Colonial Office Welfare Initiatives." *Journal of Imperial & Commonwealth History* 28, no. 2 (2000): 42–66.

Lewis, Mark. *The Birth of the New Justice: The Internationalization of Crime and Punishment, 1919–1950*. Oxford: Oxford University Press, 2014.

Lewis, Mary Dewhurst. *Divided Rule: Sovereignty and Empire in French Tunisia, 1881–1938*. Berkeley: University of California Press, 2014.

Lewis, Su Sin. "Asian Socialism and the Forgotten Architects of Post-Colonial Freedom, 1952–1956." *Journal of World History* 30, no. 1–2 (2019): 55–88.

———. *Cities in Motion: Urban Life and Cosmopolitanism in Southeast Asia, 1920–1940*. Cambridge, UK: Cambridge University Press, 2016.

Lewis, Su Sin, and Carolien Stolte. "Other Bandungs: Afro-Asian Internationalisms in the Early Cold War." *Journal of World History* 30, no. 1–2 (2019): 1–19.

Liauzu, Claude. *Histoire de l'anticolonialisme en France. Du XVIe siècle à nos jours*. Paris: Armand Colin, 2007.

———. "Le tiersmondisme des intellectuels en accusation: Le sens d'une trajectoire." *Vingtième Siècle* 12 (October 1986): 73–80.

Li, Kevin. "Partisan to Sovereign: The Making of the Bình Xuyên in Southern Vietnam, 1945–1948." *Journal of Vietnamese Studies* 11, no. 3/4 (2016): 140–87.

Li, Lifeng. "Rural Mobilization in the Chinese Communist Revolution: From the Anti-Japanese War to the Chinese Civil War." *Journal of Modern Chinese History* 9 (2015): 95–116.

Limpach, Rémy. *De brandende kampongs van Generaal Spoor*. Amsterdam: Boom, 2016.

———. "'Information Costs Lives': The Intelligence War for Indonesia, 1945–1949." In Oostindie, Schoenmaker, and van Tree, *Beyond the Pale*, 203–39.

Lindblad, J. Thomas. "Economic Growth and Decolonisation in Indonesia." *Itinerario* 34, no. 1 (2010): 97–112.

Lindner, Ulrike. "The Transfer of European Social Policy Concepts to Tropical Africa, 1900–50: The Example of Maternal and Child Welfare." *Journal of Global History* 9, no. 2 (2014): 208–31.

Lindsay, Lisa A. "Domesticity and Difference: Male Breadwinners, Working Women, and Colonial Citizenship in the 1945 Nigerian General Strike." *American Historical Review* 104, no. 3 (1999): 783–812.

Linstrum, Erik. "Facts about Atrocity: Reporting Colonial Violence in Postwar Britain." *History Workshop Journal* 84 (2017): 109–23.

———. *Ruling Minds: Psychology in the British Empire*. Cambridge, MA: Harvard University Press, 2015.

Li, Quan. "Foreign Direct Investment and Interstate Military Conflict." *Journal of International Affairs* 62, no. 1 (2008): 53–66.

Litonjua, M. D. "Third World/Global South: From Development to Globalization to Imperial Project." *Journal of Third World Studies* 27, no. 1 (2010): 107–32.

Lockman, Zachary. *Comrades and Enemies: Arab and Jewish Workers in Palestine, 1906–1948*. Berkeley: University of California Press, 1996.

Lodge, Tom. "Conflict Resolution in Nigeria after the 1967–1970 Civil War." *African Studies* 77, no. 1 (2018): 1–22.

Loffman, Reuben, and Benoît Henriet. "'We Are Left with Barely Anything': Colonial Rule, Dependency, and the Lever Brothers in the Belgian Congo, 1911–1960." *Journal of Imperial & Commonwealth History* 48, no. 1 (2020): 71–100.

Logevall, Fredrik. *Embers of War: The Fall of an Empire and the Making of America's Vietnam*. New York: Random House, 2012.

Loke, Beverley. "Conceptualising the Role and Responsibility of Great Power: China's Participation in Negotiations toward a Post–Second World War Order." *Diplomacy & Statecraft* 24, no. 2 (2013): 209–26.

Lonsdale, John. "KAU's Cultures: Imaginations of Community and Constructions of Leadership in Kenya after the Second World War." *Journal of African Cultural Studies* 13, no. 1 (2000): 107–24.

———. "Mau Maus of the Mind: Making Mau Mau and Remaking Kenya." *Journal of African History* 31, no. 3 (1990): 393–421.

———. "Ornamental Constitutionalism in Africa: Kenyatta and the Two Queens." *Journal of Imperial & Commonwealth History* 34, no. 1 (2006): 87–103.

Look Lai, Walton. *Indentured Labor, Caribbean Sugar: Chinese and Indian Migrants to the British West Indies, 1838–1918.* Baltimore: Johns Hopkins University Press, 1993.

Lorcin, Patricia M. E. *Historicizing Colonial Nostalgia: European Women's Narratives of Algeria and Kenya, 1900–Present.* New York: Palgrave Macmillan, 2012.

———. *Imperial Identities: Stereotyping, Prejudice and Race in Colonial Algeria.* London: I. B. Tauris, 1995.

Lord, Jack. "Child Labour in the Gold Coast: The Economics of Work, Education, and the Family in Late-Colonial African Childhoods, c. 1940–57." *Journal of the History of Childhood and Youth* 4, no. 1 (2011): 88–115.

Loris, Marius. *Désobéir en guerre d'Algérie. Une histoire des réfractaires et des déviants, 1954–1964.* Paris: Seuil, 2021.

Lotem, Itay. *The Memory of Colonialism in Britain and France: The Sins of Silence.* Cham: Palgrave Macmillan, 2021.

Louis, William Roger, and Ronald Robinson. "The Imperialism of Decolonization." *Journal of Imperial & Commonwealth History* 22, no. 3 (1994): 462–511.

Louis, Wm. Roger. *The British Empire in the Middle East: Arab Nationalism, the United States, and Postwar Imperialism, 1945–1951.* Oxford: Oxford University Press, 1984.

———. "British Imperialism and the End of the Palestine Mandate." In *The End of the Palestine Mandate*, edited by Wm. Roger Louis and Robert W. Stookey, 1–31. Austin: University of Texas Press, 1986.

Louro, Michele. *Comrades against Imperialism: Nehru, India, and Interwar Internationalism.* Cambridge, UK: Cambridge University Press, 2018.

———. "The Johnstone Affair and Anti-Communism in Interwar India." *Journal of Contemporary History* 53, no. 1 (2018): 38–60.

Louro, Michele, Carolien Stolte, and Heather Streets-Salter, eds. *The League against Imperialism: Lives and Afterlives.* Leiden: Leiden University Press, 2020.

Lowry, Donal. "'King's Men,' 'Queen's Rebels' and 'Last Outposts': Ulster and Rhodesia in an Age of Imperial Retreat." In Pedersen and Ward, *Break-Up of Greater Britain*, 147–71.

Lubinski, Christina. "Global Trade and Indian Politics: The German Dye Business in India before 1947." *Business History Review* 89 (Fall 2015): 503–30.

Lucas, W. Scott. *Divided We Stand: Britain, the US and the Suez Crisis.* London: Hodder & Stoughton, 1991.

Lüthi, Lorenz M. *Cold Wars: Asia, the Middle East, Europe.* Cambridge, UK: Cambridge University Press, 2020.

———. "The Non-Aligned Movement and the Cold War, 1961–1973." *Journal of Cold War Studies* 18, no. 4 (2016): 98–147.

———. "Non-Alignment, 1946–1965: Its Establishment and Struggle against Afro-Asianism." *Humanity* 7, no. 2 (2016): 201–23.

Luttikhuis, Bart, and A. Dirk Moses. "Mass Violence and the End of the Dutch Colonial Empire in Indonesia." *Journal of Genocide Research* 14, no. 3–4 (2012): 257–76.

Lutz, Catherine, ed. *The Bases of Empire: The Global Struggle against U.S. Military Posts.* New York: NYU Press, 2009.

Lynn, Martin, ed. *The British Empire in the 1950s: Retreat or Revival?* Basingstoke, UK: Palgrave Macmillan, 2006.

Lyons, Amelia H. *The Civilizing Mission in the Metropole: Algerian Families and the French Welfare State during Decolonization*. Stanford, CA: Stanford University Press, 2013.

——. "French or Foreign? The Algerian Migrants' Status at the End of Empire (1962–1968)." *Journal of Modern European History* 12, no. 1 (2014): 126–44.

——. "Social Welfare, French Muslims and Decolonization in France: The Case of the *Fonds d'action sociale*." *Patterns of Prejudice* 43, no. 1 (2009): 65–89.

Maat, Harro, and Sandip Hazareesingh, eds. *Local Subversions of Colonial Cultures: Commodities and Anti-Commodities in Global History*. Basingstoke, UK: Palgrave Macmillan, 2016.

MacArthur, Julie. "Decolonizing Sovereignty: States of Exception along the Kenya–Somali Frontier." *American Historical Review* 124, no. 1 (2019): 108–43.

MacDonald, P. K., and J. M. Parent. "Graceful Decline? The Surprising Success of Great Power Retrenchment." *International Security* 35, no. 4 (2011): 7–44.

Macekura, Stephen J. *Of Limits and Growth: The Rise of Global Sustainable Development in the Twentieth Century*. Cambridge, UK: Cambridge University Press, 2016.

Macekura, Stephen J., and Erez Manela, eds. *The Development Century: A Global History*. Cambridge, UK: Cambridge University Press, 2018.

MacMaster, Neil. *Burning the Veil: The Algerian War and the "Emancipation" of Muslim Women, 1954–1962*. Manchester, UK: Manchester University Press, 2009.

——. "From Tent to Village *Regroupement*: The Colonial State and Social Engineering of Rural Space, 1843–1962." In Naylor, *France's Modernising Mission*, 109–31.

——. "The Roots of Insurrection: The Role of the Algerian Village Assembly (Djemâa) in Peasant Resistance, 1863–1962." *Comparative Studies in Society and History* 52, no. 2 (2013): 419–47.

——. *War in the Mountains: Peasant Society and Counterinsurgency in Algeria, 1918–1958*. Oxford: Oxford University Press, 2020.

MacQueen, Norrie. "Belated Decolonization and UN Politics against the Backdrop of the Cold War Portugal, Britain, and Guinea-Bissau's Proclamation of Independence, 1973–1974." *Journal of Cold War Studies* 8, no. 4 (2006): 29–56.

——. *The Decolonization of Portuguese Africa: Metropolitan Revolution and the Dissolution of Empire*. London: Longman, 1997.

——. "Peacekeeping by Attrition: The United Nations in Angola." *Journal of Modern African Studies* 36, no. 3 (1998): 399–422.

——. "Portugal's First Domino: 'Pluricontinentalism' and Colonial War in Guiné-Bissau, 1963–1974." *Contemporary European History* 8, no. 2 (1999): 209–30.

Maekawa, Ichiro. "Neo-Colonialism Reconsidered: A Case Study of East Africa in the 1960s and 1970s." *Journal of Imperial & Commonwealth History* 43, no. 2 (2015): 317–41.

Magee, Gary B., and Andrew S. Thompson. *Empire and Globalisation: Networks of People, Goods and Capital in the British World, c. 1850–1914*. Cambridge, UK: Cambridge University Press, 2010.

Maggetti, Naïma. "La Grande-Bretagne à l'ONU dans les années 1940 et 1950: sa défense d'un colonialisme 'liberal et éclairé.'" *Relations Internationales* 177, no. 1 (2019): 31–44.

Mahler, Anne Garland. *From the Tricontinental to the Global South: Race, Radicalism, and Transnational Solidarity.* Durham, NC: Duke University Press, 2018.

Mahler, Vincent A. "The Lomé Convention: Assessing a North–South Institutional Relationship." *Review of International Political Economy* 1, no. 2 (1994): 233–56.

Mahoney, Michael. "Estado Novo, Homem Novo (New State, New Man): Colonial and Anti-Colonial Development Ideologies in Mozambique, 1930–1977." In Engerman et al., *Staging Growth*, 165–97.

Maier, Charles S. *Among Empires: American Ascendancy and Its Predecessors.* Cambridge, MA: Harvard University Press, 2006.

———. "Consigning the Twentieth Century to History: Alternative Narratives for the Modern Era." *American Historical Review* 105, no. 3 (2000): 807–31.

———. *Once within Borders: Territories of Power, Wealth, and Belonging since 1500.* Cambridge, MA: Harvard University Press, 2016.

Maiolo, Joseph M. "Systems and Boundaries in International History." *International History Review* 40, no. 3 (2018): 576–91.

Makalani, Minkah. *In the Cause of Freedom: Radical Black Internationalism from Harlem to London, 1917–1919.* Chapel Hill: University of North Carolina Press, 2011.

Makko, Aryo. "Arbitrator in a World of Wars: The League of Nations and the Mosul Dispute, 1924–1925." *Diplomacy & Statecraft* 21, no. 4 (2010): 631–49.

Mak, Lanver. *The British in Egypt: Community, Crime and Crises, 1882–1922.* London: I. B. Tauris, 2012.

Mälksoo, Maria. "The Normative Threat of Subtle Subversion: The Return of 'Eastern Europe' as an Ontological Insecurity Trope." *Cambridge Review of International Affairs* 32, no. 3 (2019): 365–83.

———. *The Politics of Becoming European: A Study of Polish and Baltic Post-Cold War Security Imaginaries.* London: Routledge, 2009.

Malley, Robert. *The Call from Algeria: Third Worldism, Revolution, and the Turn to Islam.* Berkeley: University of California Press, 1996.

Mamdani, Mahmood. *Citizen and Subject: Contemporary Africa and the Legacy of Late Colonialism.* Princeton, NJ: Princeton University Press, 1996.

Mamlyuk, Boris N. "Decolonization as a Cold War Imperative: Bandung and the Soviets." In Eslava, Fakhri, and Nesiah, *Bandung, Global History, and International Law*, 196–214.

Manby, Bronwen. *Citizenship in Africa: The Law of Belonging.* London: Bloomsbury, 2018.

———. *Struggles for Citizenship in Africa.* London: Bloomsbury, 2009.

———. "Trends in Citizenship Law and Politics in Africa since the Colonial Era." In *Routledge Handbook of Global Citizenship Studies*, edited by Engin F. Isin and Peter Nyers, 172–85. London: Routledge, 2014.

Manela, Erez. "International Society as a Historical Subject." *Diplomatic History* 44, no. 2 (2020): 184–209.

———. "A Pox on Your Narrative: Writing Disease Control into Cold War History." *Diplomatic History* 34, no. 2 (2010): 299–323.

———. "Smallpox and the Globalization of Development." In Macekura and Manela, *Development Century*, 83–103.

——. *The Wilsonian Moment: Self-Determination and the International Origins of Anticolonial Nationalism*. Oxford: Oxford University Press, 2007.

Mani, B. Venkat. "Anti-Colonial Nationalism and Cosmopolitan 'Standard Time': Lala Har Dayal's *Forty-Four Months in Germany and Turkey* (1920)." In Berman, Mühlhahn, and Nganang, *German Colonialism Revisited*, 195–211.

Manjapra, Kris. "Asian Plantation Histories at the Frontiers of Nation and Globalization." *Modern Asian Studies* 52, no. 6 (2018): 2137–58.

——. *Colonialism in Global Perspective*. Cambridge, UK: Cambridge University Press, 2020.

——. "The Illusions of Encounter: 'Muslim' Minds and Hindu Revolutionaries in First World War Germany and After." *Journal of Global History* 1, no. 3 (2006): 363–82.

Mann, Gregory. "Anti-Colonialism and Social Science: Georges Balandier, Madeira Keita and 'the Colonial Situation' in French Africa." *Comparative Studies in Society and History* 55, no. 1 (2013): 92–119.

——. *From Empires to NGOs in the West African Sahel: The Road to Nongovernmentality*. Cambridge, UK: Cambridge University Press, 2015.

——. "What Was the *Indigénat*? The 'Empire of Law' in French West Africa." *Journal of African History* 50, no. 2 (2009): 331–53.

Mantena, Karuna. "Another Realism: The Politics of Gandhian Nonviolence." *American Political Science Review* 106, no. 2 (2012): 455–70.

——. "On Gandhi's Critique of the State: Sources, Contexts, Conjunctures." *Modern Intellectual History* 9, no. 3 (2012): 535–63.

——. "Popular Sovereignty and Anti-Colonialism." In *Popular Sovereignty in Historical Perspective*, edited by Richard Bourke and Quentin Skinner, 297–319. New York: Cambridge University Press, 2016.

Mantena, Rama Sundari. "Anticolonialism and Federation in Colonial India." *Ab Imperio* 3 (2018): 36–62.

Mantilla, Giovanni. *Lawmaking under Pressure: International Humanitarian Law and Internal Armed Conflict*. Ithaca, NY: Cornell University Press, 2020.

Marchesi, Aldo. *Latin America's Radical Left: Rebellion and Cold War in the Global 1960s* Cambridge, UK: Cambridge University Press, 2017.

Marcum, John A. *Conceiving Mozambique*. Cham: Palgrave Macmillan, 2018.

Marcus, Hannah. "Julius Nyerere: At the Crossroads of Postcolonial Tanzania's Reconstructed Socioeconomic and Political Reality." *International Journal of African Historical Studies* 53, no. 3 (2020): 413–20.

Mark, Chi-Kwan. "Lack of Means or Loss of Will? The United Kingdom and the Decolonization of Hong Kong, 1957–1967." *International History Review* 31, no. 1 (2009): 45–71.

Marker, Emily. *Black France, White Europe: Youth, Race, and Belonging in the Postwar Era*. Ithaca, NY: Cornell University Press, 2022.

Mark, Ethan. "'Asia's' Transwar Lineage: Nationalism, Marxism, and 'Greater Asia' in an Indonesian Inflection." *Journal of Asian Studies* 65, no. 3 (2006): 461–93.

——. *Japan's Occupation of Java in the Second World War: A Transnational History*. London: Bloomsbury, 2019.

Mark, Ethan. "The Perils of Co-Prosperity: Takeda Rintarō, Occupied Southeast Asia, and the Seductions of Postcolonial Empire." *American Historical Review* 119, no. 4 (2014): 1184–206.

Mark, James, and Péter Apor. "Socialism Goes Global: Decolonization and the Making of a New Culture of Internationalism in Socialist Hungary, 1956–1989." *Journal of Modern History* 87 (December 2015): 852–91.

Mark, James, Paul Betts, Alena Alamgir, Péter Apor, Eric Burton, Bogdan C. Iacob, Steffi Marung, and Radina Vučetić. *Socialism Goes Global: The Soviet Union and Eastern Europe in the Age of Decolonization.* Oxford: Oxford University Press, 2022.

Mark, James, and Yakov Feygin. "The Soviet Union, Eastern Europe, and Alternative Visions of a Global Economy, 1950s–1980s." In Mark, Kalinovsky, and Marung, *Alternative Globalizations,* 35–58.

Mark, James, Artemy M. Kalinovsky, and Steffi Marung, eds. *Alternative Globalizations: Eastern Europe and the Postcolonial World.* Bloomington: Indiana University Press, 2020.

Mark, James, Tobias Rupprecht, and Ljubica Spaskovska. *1989: Eastern Europe in Global Perspective.* Cambridge, UK: Cambridge University Press, 2019.

Marquis, Jefferson. "The Other Warriors: American Social Science and Nation-Building in Vietnam." *Diplomatic History* 24, no. 1 (2000): 79–105.

Marr, David G. *Vietnamese Tradition on Trial, 1920–1945.* Berkeley: University of California Press, 1981.

———. *Vietnam, 1945: The Quest for Power.* Berkeley: University of California Press, 1995.

Marshall, Alex. "Imperial Nostalgia, the Liberal Lie, and the Perils of Postmodern Counterinsurgency." *Small Wars & Insurgencies* 21, no. 2 (2010): 233–58.

Marshall, Dominique. "The Rise of Coordinated Action for Children in War and Peace: Experts at the League of Nations, 1924–1945." In Rodogno, Struck, and Vogel, *Shaping the Transnational Sphere,* 82–107.

Marsh, Steve. "The United States, Iran and Operation 'Ajax': Inverting Interpretative Orthodoxy." *Middle Eastern Studies* 39, no. 3 (2003): 1–38.

Marten, Kimberly Zisk. *Enforcing the Peace: Learning from the Imperial Past.* New York: Columbia University Press, 2004.

Martin, Garrett. "Playing the China Card? Revisiting France's Recognition of Communist China, 1963–1964." *Journal of Cold War Studies* 10, no. 1 (2008): 52–80.

Martin, Guy. "The Franc Zone: Underdevelopment and Dependency in Francophone Africa." *Third World Quarterly* 8, no. 1 (1986): 205–35.

Martini, Edwin A. "Even We Can't Prevent Forests: The Chemical War in Vietnam and the Illusion of Control." *War & Society* 31, no. 3 (2012): 264–79.

———. "Hearts, Minds, and Herbicides: The Politics of the Chemical War in Vietnam." *Diplomatic History* 37, no. 1 (2013): 58–84.

———. *Proving Grounds: Militarized Landscapes, Weapons Testing, and the Environmental Impact of U.S. Bases.* Seattle: University of Washington Press, 2015.

Martin, Jamie. *The Meddlers: Sovereignty, Empire, and the Birth of Global Economic Governance.* Cambridge, MA: Harvard University Press, 2022.

Martin, Marc. "'Radio Algérie': un acteur méconnu de mai 1958." *Vingtième Siècle* 19 (July 1988): 97–99.

Mar, Tracey Banivanua. *Decolonisation and the Pacific: Indigenous Globalisation and the Ends of Empire*. Cambridge, UK: Cambridge University Press, 2016.

Marwah, Onkar. "India's Military Intervention in East Pakistan, 1971–1972." *Modern Asian Studies* 13, no. 4 (1979): 549–80.

Masalha, Nur. "Indigenous versus Colonial-Settler Toponymy and the Struggle over the Cultural and Political Geography of Palestine: The Appropriation of Palestinian Place Names by the Israeli State." In Sa'di and Masalha, *Decolonizing the Study of Palestine*, 37–71.

Mason, Paul R., and Catherine Pattillo. *The Monetary Geography of Africa*. New York: Brookings Institution Press, 2005.

Maspero, Julia. "French Policy on Postwar Migration of Eastern European Jews through France and French Occupation Zones in Germany and Austria." *Jewish History Quarterly* 2 (2013): 319–39.

Ma, Tehyun. "'The Common Aim of the Allied Powers': Social Policy and International Legitimacy in Wartime China, 1940–1947." *Journal of Global History* 9, no. 2 (2014): 254–75.

Matera, Marc. "Colonial Subjects: Black Intellectuals and the Development of Colonial Studies in Britain." *Journal of British Studies* 49, no. 2 (2010): 388–418.

——. "Metropolitan Cultures of Empire and the Long Moment of Decolonization." *American Historical Review* 121, no. 5 (2016): 1435–43.

Maul, Daniel. "'Help Them Move the ILO Way': The International Labor Organization and the Modernization Discourse in the Era of Decolonization and the Cold War." *Diplomatic History* 33, no. 3 (2009): 387–404.

——. *Human Rights, Development, and Decolonization: The International Labour Organization, 1940–70*. Basingstoke, UK: Palgrave Macmillan, 2012.

——. "The International Labour Organization and the Struggle against Forced Labour from 1919 to the Present." *Labour History* 48 (2007): 477–500.

Mawby, Spencer. *The End of Empire in Uganda: Decolonization and Institutional Conflict, 1945–79*. London: Bloomsbury, 2020.

Maxon, Robert M. *Struggle for Kenya: The Loss and Reassertion of Imperial Initiative, 1912–1923*. Rutherford, NJ: Fairleigh Dickinson University Press, 1993.

Mayall, James. "International Society, State Sovereignty, and National Self-Determination." In *The Oxford Handbook of the History of Nationalism*, edited by John Breuilly. Oxford: Oxford University Press, 2013, online publication.

Mazower, Mark. *No Enchanted Palace: The End of Empire and the Ideological Origins of the United Nations*. Princeton, NJ: Princeton University Press, 2010.

——. "Reconstruction: The Historiographical Issues." *Past & Present* 210, Supplement 6 (2011): 17–28.

Mazurek, Małgorzata. "The University: The Decolonization of Knowledge? The Making of the African University, the Power of the Imperial Legacy, and Eastern European Influence." In Roth-Ey, *Socialist Internationalism*, 119–38.

Mbembe, Achille. *La naissance du maquis dans le Sud-Cameroun (1920–1960)*. Paris: Karthala, 1996.

——. "Necropolitics." *Public Culture* 15, no. 1 (2003): 11–40.

McAlister, Melanie. *Epic Encounters: Culture, Media, and U.S. Interests in the Middle East since 1945*. Berkeley: University of California Press, 2001.

McCann, Gerard. "Possibility and Peril: Trade Unionism, African Cold War, and the Global Strands of Kenyan Decolonization." *Journal of Social History* 53, no. 2 (2019): 348–77.

McCarthy, Thomas. *Race, Empire, and the Idea of Human Development*. Cambridge, UK: Cambridge University Press, 2009.

McConnell, Scott. *Leftward Journey: The Education of Vietnamese Students in France, 1919–1939*. Abingdon, UK: Routledge, 1989.

McCourt, David M. "What Was Britain's 'East of Suez Role'? Reassessing the Withdrawal, 1964–1968." *Diplomacy & Statecraft* 20, no. 3 (2009): 453–72.

McCoy, Alfred W. *In the Shadows of the American Century: The Rise and Decline of US Global Power*. London: Oneworld, 2018.

———. "Torture in the Crucible of Counterinsurgency." In *Iraq and the Lessons of Vietnam: Or, How Not to Learn from the Past*, edited by Marilyn B. Young and Lloyd C. Gardner, 230–62. New York: New Press, 2007.

McCoy, Alfred W., Josep M. Fradera, and Stephen Jacobson, eds. *Endless Empire: Spain's Retreat, Europe's Eclipse, America's Decline*. Madison: University of Wisconsin Press, 2012.

McCracken, John. "In the Shadow of Mau Mau: Detainees and Detention Camps during Nyasaland's State of Emergency." *Journal of Southern African Studies* 37, no. 3 (2011): 535–50.

McDonald, Bryan L. *Food Power: The Rise and Fall of the Postwar American Food System*. New York: Oxford University Press, 2017.

McDougall, James. "The Impossible Republic: The Reconquest of Algeria and the Decolonization of France, 1945–62." *Journal of Modern History* 89, no. 4 (December 2017): 782–811.

———. "Rule of Experts? Governing Modernisation in Late Colonial French Africa." In Naylor, *France's Modernising Mission*, 87–108.

———. "The Secular State's Islamic Empire: Muslim Spaces and Subjects of Jurisdiction in Paris and Algiers, 1905–1957." *Comparative Studies in Society and History* 52, no. 3 (2010): 553–80.

McElhinny, Bonnie. "'Kissing a Baby Is Not at All Good for Him': Infant Mortality, Medicine, and Colonial Modernity in the U.S.-Occupied Philippines." *Peace Research Abstracts Journal* 42, no. 6 (2005): 183–94.

McGregor, JoAnn. "Violence and Social Change in a Border Economy: War in the Maputo Hinterland, 1984–1992." *Journal of Southern African Studies* 24, no. 1 (1998): 37–60.

McGregor, Katharine. "Opposing Colonialism: The Women's International Democratic Federation and Decolonisation Struggles in Vietnam and Algeria, 1945–1965." *Women's History Review* 25, no. 6 (2016): 925–44.

McGregor, Katharine, and Vannessa Hearman. "Challenging the Lifeline of Imperialism: Reassessing Afro-Asian Solidarity and Related Activism in the Decade 1955–1965." In Eslava, Fakhri, and Nesiah, *Bandung, Global History, and International Law*, 161–76.

McGuinness, Margaret E. "Peace v. Justice: The Universal Declaration of Human Rights and the Modern Origins of the Debate." *Diplomatic History* 35, no. 5 (2011): 749–68.

McHale, Shawn F. "Ethnicity, Violence, and Khmer-Vietnamese Relations: The Significance of the Lower Mekong Delta, 1757–1954." *Journal of Asian Studies* 72, no. 2 (2013): 367–90.

——. *The First Vietnam War: Violence, Sovereignty, and the Fracture of the South, 1945–1956*. Cambridge, UK: Cambridge University Press, 2021.

——. "Understanding the Fanatic Mind? The Viêt Minh and Race Hatred in the First Indochina War (1945–1954)." *Journal of Vietnamese Studies* 4, no. 3 (2009): 98–138.

McIntyre, Angus. "The 'Greater Indonesia' Idea of Nationalism in Malaya and Indonesia." *Modern Asian Studies* 7, no. 1 (1973): 75–83.

McKeown, Adam. "Global Migration, 1846–1940." *Journal of World History* 15, no. 2 (2004): 155–89.

McLeod, John. "A Night at 'The Cosmopolitan': Axes of Transnational Encounter in the 1930s and 1940s." *Interventions* 4, no. 1 (2002): 54–67.

McMahon, Robert J., ed. *The Cold War in the Third World*. Oxford: Oxford University Press, 2013.

McMillan, Richard. *The British Occupation of Indonesia, 1945–1946: Britain, the Netherlands and the Indonesian Revolution*. Abingdon, UK: Routledge, 2005.

McNeil, Brian. "'And Starvation is the Grim Reaper': The American Committee to Keep Biafra Alive and the Genocide Question during the Nigerian Civil War, 1968–70." *Journal of Genocide Research* 16, no. 2–3 (2014): 317–36.

McNeill, John R. *Mosquito Empires: Ecology and War in the Greater Caribbean, 1620–1914*. Cambridge, UK: Cambridge University Press, 2010.

——. *Something New under the Sun: An Environmental History of the Twentieth Century*. London: Allen Lane, 2000.

McPherson, Alan. "Anti-Imperialist Racial Solidarity before the Cold War: Success and Failure." In Field, Krepp, and Pettinà, *Latin America and the Global Cold War*, 201–20.

——. *The Invaded: How Latin Americans and Their Allies Fought and Ended U.S. Occupations*. Oxford: Oxford University Press, 2014.

——. "The Irony of Legal Pluralism in U.S. Occupations." *American Historical Review* 117, no. 4 (October 2012): 1149–72.

McQuade, Joseph. "Beyond an Imperial Foreign Policy? India at the League of Nations, 1919–1946." *Journal of Imperial & Commonwealth History* 48, no. 2 (2020): 263–95.

McVety, Amanda Kay. "Wealth and Nations: The Origins of International Development Assistance." In Macekura and Manela, *Development Century*, 21–39.

Meher, Jagmohan. "Dynamics of Pakistan's Disintegration: The Case of East Pakistan, 1947–1971." *India Quarterly* 71, no. 4 (2015): 300–17.

Mehta, Harish C. "North Vietnam's Informal Diplomacy with Bertrand Russell: Peace Activism and the International War Crimes Tribunal." *Peace & Change* 37, no. 1 (2012): 64–94.

Mendy, Peter Karibe. "Portugal's Civilizing Mission in Colonial Guinea-Bissau: Rhetoric and Reality." *International Journal of African Historical Studies* 36, no. 1 (2003): 35–58.

Meneses, Filipe Ribeiro de, and Robert McNamara. "The Last Throw of the Dice: Portugal, Rhodesia and South Africa, 1970–74." *Portuguese Studies* 28, no. 2 (2012): 201–15.

Meneses, Filipe Ribeiro de, and Robert McNamara. "Parallel Diplomacy, Parallel War: The PIDE/DGC's Dealings with Rhodesia and South Africa, 1961–1974." *Journal of Contemporary History* 49, no. 2 (2014): 366–89.

———. *The White Redoubt, the Great Powers and the Struggle for Southern Africa, 1960–1980*. Basingstoke, UK: Palgrave, 2018.

Menzel, Jörg. "Justice Delayed or Too Late for Justice? The Khmer Rouge Tribunal and the Cambodian 'Genocide' 1975–79." *Journal of Genocide Research* 9, no. 2 (2007): 215–33.

Metzer, Jacob. *The Divided Economy of Mandate Palestine*. Cambridge, UK: Cambridge University Press, 1998.

Metzger, Barbara. "Towards an International Human Rights Regime during the Inter-War Years: The League of Nations Combat of Traffic in Women and Children." In *Beyond Sovereignty: Britain, Empire and Transnationalism, c.1880–1950*, edited by Kevin Grant, Philippa Levine, and Frank Trentmann, 54–79. Basingstoke, UK: Palgrave Macmillan: 2007.

Meynier, Gilbert. *Histoire intérieure du FLN 1954–1962*. Paris: Fayard, 2002.

Michel, Eddie. "'This Outcome Gives Me No Pleasure, It Is Extremely Painful to Me to Be the Instrument of Their Fate': White House Policy on Rhodesia during the UDI Era (1965–1979)." *South African Historical Journal* 71, no. 3 (2019): 442–65.

Middell, Matthias, and Katya Naumann. "Global History and the Spatial Turn: From the Impact of Area Studies to the Study of Critical Junctures of Globalization." *Journal of Global History* 5, no. 1 (2010): 149–70.

Mignolo, Walter D., and Catherine E. Walsh. *On Decoloniality: Concepts, Analytics, Praxis*. Durham, NC: Duke University Press, 2018.

Milford, Ismay. *African Activists in a Decolonising World: The Making of an Anti-colonial Culture, 1952–1966*. Cambridge, UK: Cambridge University Press, 2023.

Milford, Ismay, Gerard McCann, Emma Hunter, and Daniel Branch. "Another World? East Africa, Decolonisation, and the Global History of the Mid-Twentieth Century." *Journal of African History* 62, no. 3 (2021): 394–410.

Miller, Edward, and Tuong Vu. "The Vietnam War as a Vietnamese War: Agency and Society in the Study of the Second Indochina War." *Journal of Vietnamese Studies* 4, no. 3 (2009): 1–16.

Miller, Jamie. *An African Volk: The Apartheid Regime and Its Search for Survival*. Oxford: Oxford University Press, 2016.

———. "Things Fall Apart: South Africa and the Collapse of the Portuguese Empire, 1973–74." *Cold War History* 12, no. 2 (2012): 183–204.

Mitchell, Timothy. *Rule of Experts: Egypt, Techno-Politics, Modernity*. Berkeley: University of California Press, 2002.

Mitter, Rana. *China's War with Japan, 1937–1945: The Struggle for Survival*. London: Allen Lane, 2013.

———. *The Manchurian Myth: Nationalism, Resistance, and Collaboration in Modern China*. Berkeley: University of California Press, 2000.

———. "Nationalism, Decolonization, Geopolitics and the Asian Post-War." In Geyer and Tooze, *Cambridge History* Vol. 3, 599–622.

Mitter, Rana, and Matthew Hilton, eds. *Transnational History in a Globalised World*. Oxford: Oxford University Press, 2012.

Mitton, Kieran. "The Natural Environment and Atrocity Crimes." In Holá, Nzitatira, and Weerdesteijn, *Oxford Handbook on Atrocity Crimes*, 159–86.

Mkandawire, Thandika. "The Terrible Toll of Post-Colonial 'Rebel Movements' in Africa: Towards an Explanation of the Violence against the Peasantry." *Journal of Modern African Studies* 40, no. 2 (2002): 181–215.

Mlambo, A. S. "'We Have Blood Relations over the Border': South Africa and Rhodesian Sanctions, 1965–1975." *African Historical Review* 40, no. 1 (2008): 1–29.

Mohandesi, Salar. *Red Internationalism: Anti-Imperialism and Human Rights in the Global Sixties and Seventies*. Cambridge, UK: Cambridge University Press, 2023.

——. "Thinking the Global Sixties." *The Global Sixties* 15, no. 1–2 (2022): 1–20.

Money, Daniel, and Danelle van Zyl-Hermann, eds. *Rethinking White Societies in Southern Africa, 1930s–1990s*. London: Routledge, 2020.

Monteiro, José Pedro. "The International Dimensions of Resistance: Portuguese Colonial Labour Policies and Its Critics Abroad (1944–1962)." In Domingos, Bandeira Jerónimo, and Roque, *Resistance and Colonialism*, 313–38.

Mookherjee, Nayanika. "The Absent Piece of Skin: Gendered, Racialized, and Territorial Inscriptions of Sexual Violence during the Bangladesh War." *Modern Asian Studies* 46, no. 6 (2012): 1572–601.

——. "The Raped Woman as a Horrific Sublime and the Bangladesh War of 1971." *Journal of Material Culture* 20, no. 4 (2015): 379–95.

——. "'Remembering to Forget': Public Secrecy and Memory of Sexual Violence in the Bangladesh War of 1971." *Journal of the Royal Anthropological Institute* 12 (2006): 433–50.

Moravcsik, Andrew. "De Gaulle between Grain and Grandeur: The Political Economy of French EC Policy, 1958–1970 (Part 1)." *Journal of Cold War Studies* 2, no. 2 (2000): 3–43.

Morefield, Jeanne. "Challenging Liberal Belief: Edward Said and the Critical Practice of History." In Bell, *Empire, Race, and Global Justice*, 184–210.

——. *Covenants without Swords: Idealist Liberalism and the Spirit of Empire*. Princeton, NJ: Princeton University Press, 2005.

——. *Empires without Imperialism: Anglo-American Decline and the Politics of Deflection*. Oxford: Oxford University Press, 2014.

Morrison, Alexander. "Sufism, Pan-Islamism and Information Panic: Nil Sergeevich Lykoshin and the Aftermath of the Andijan Uprising." *Past and Present* 214 (February 2012): 255–304.

Morrison, Alexander, Cloé Drieu, and Aminat Chokobaeva, eds. *The Central Asian Revolt of 1916: A Collapsing Empire in the Age of War and Revolution*. Manchester, UK: Manchester University Press, 2019.

Mortimer, Robert. "Algeria, Vietnam and Afro-Asian Solidarity." *Maghreb Review* 28, no. 1 (2003): 60–67.

Moses, A. Dirk, ed. *Empire, Colony, Genocide: Conquest, Occupation, and Subaltern Resistance in World History*. Oxford: Berghahn, 2008.

——. *Genocide and Settler Society: Frontier Violence and Stolen Indigenous Children in Australian History*. Oxford: Berghahn, 2004.

Moses, A. Dirk. "*Das römische Gespräch* in a New Key: Hannah Arendt, Genocide, and the Defense of Republican Civilization." *Journal of Modern History* 85, no. 4 (2013): 867–913.

Moses, A. Dirk, Marco Duranti, and Roland Burke, eds. *Decolonization, Self Determination, and the Rise of Global Human Rights Politics.* Cambridge, UK: Cambridge University Press, 2020.

Motadel, David, ed. "The Global Authoritarian Moment and the Revolt against Empire." *American Historical Review* 124, no. 3 (2019): 843–77.

——. *Revolutionary World: Global Upheaval in the Modern Age.* Cambridge, UK: Cambridge University Press, 2021.

Mouralis, Guillaume, and Annette Weinke. "Justice." In Conway, Lagrou, and Rousso, *Europe's Postwar Periods*, 55–80.

Moyd, Michelle. "Centring a Sideshow: Local Experiences of the First World War in Africa." *First World War Studies* 7, no. 2 (2016): 111–30.

——. "Color Lines, Front Lines: The First World War from the South." *Radical History Review* 131 (May 2018): 13–35.

——. "What's Wrong with Doing Good?: Reflections on Africa, Humanitarianism, and the Challenge of the Global." *Africa Today* 63, no. 2 (2016): 92–96.

Moyn, Samuel. "The End of Human Rights History." *Past and Present* 233 (2016): 307–22.

——. "Fantasies of Federalism." *Dissent* 62, no. 1 (2015): 145–51.

——. *The Last Utopia: Human Rights in History.* Cambridge, MA: Harvard University Press, 2010.

——. "The Political Origins of Global Justice." In Isaac et al., *Worlds of American Intellectual History*, 133–53.

Msindo, Enocent. "Settler Rule in Southern Rhodesia, 1890–1979." In Cavanagh and Veracini, *Routledge Handbook of the History of Settler Colonialism*, 247–62.

Muehlenbeck, Philip E. *Betting on the Africans: John F. Kennedy's Courting of African Nationalist Leaders.* New York, Oxford University Press, 2012.

——. "John F. Kennedy as Viewed by Africans." In Schayegh, *Globalizing the U.S. Presidency*, 34–47.

Muehlenbeck, Philip E., and Natalia Telepneva, eds. *Warsaw Pact Intervention in the Third World: Aid and Influence in the Cold War.* London: I. B. Tauris, 2018.

Mukherjee, Janam. *Hungry Bengal: War, Famine and the End of Empire.* London: Hurst, 2015.

Mukherjee, Mithi. "Transcending Identity: Gandhi, Nonviolence, and the Pursuit of a 'Different' Freedom in India." *American Historical Review* 115, no. 2 (2010): 453–73.

Müller, Simone M. *Wiring the World: The Social and Cultural Creation of Global Telegraph Networks.* New York: Columbia University Press, 2016.

Mulligan, William. *The Great War for Peace.* New Haven, CT: Yale University Press, 2014.

Mumford, Andrew. "Minimum Force Meets Brutality: Detention, Interrogation and Torture in British Counter-Insurgency Campaigns." *Journal of Military Ethics* 11, no. 1 (2012): 10–25.

Munochiveyi, Munyaradzi. "Suffering and Protest in Rhodesian Prisons during the Zimbabwean Liberation Struggle." *Journal of Southern African Studies* 41, no. 1 (2015): 47–61.

Munro, John. *The Anticolonial Front: The African-American Freedom Struggle and Global Decolonization, 1945–1960*. Cambridge, UK: Cambridge University Press, 2017.

———. "'Ethiopia Stretches Forth Across the Atlantic': African American Anticolonialism during the Interwar Period." *Left History* 13, no. 2 (2008): 37–63.

Murphy, Philip. "'An Intricate and Distasteful Subject': British Planning for the Use of Force against the European Settlers of Central Africa, 1952–65." *English Historical Review* 121, no. 492 (2006): 746–77.

———. *Monarchy and the End of Empire: The House of Windsor, the British Government, and the Postwar Commonwealth*. Oxford: Oxford University Press, 2013.

———. *Party Politics and Decolonization: The Conservative Party and British Colonial Policy in Tropical Africa, 1951–1964*. Oxford: Oxford University Press, 1995.

Murray-Miller, Gavin. "Civilization, Modernity and Europe: The Making and Unmaking of a Conceptual Unity." *History* 103, no. 356 (2018): 418–33.

———. "Empire and Trans-Imperial Subjects in the Muslim Mediterranean." *Historical Journal* 63, no. 4 (2020): 958–79.

———. *Empire Unbound: France and the Muslim Mediterranean, 1880–1918*. Oxford: Oxford University Press, 2022.

Muschik, Eva-Maria. "Managing the World: The United Nations, Decolonization, and the Strange Triumph of State Sovereignty in the 1950s and 1960s." *Journal of Global History* 13, no. 1 (2018): 121–44.

Naegelen, Marcel-Edmond. *Mission en Algérie*. Paris: Flammarion, 1962.

Nagl, John. "Nostrum or Palliative: Contesting the Capitalist Peace in Violently Divided Societies." *Civil Wars* 12, no. 3 (2010): 218–36.

Namikas, Lise. *Battleground Africa: Cold War in the Congo, 1960–1965*. Stanford, CA: Stanford University Press, 2013.

Nandjui, Pierre. *Houphouët-Boigny: L'homme de la France en Afrique*. Paris: Éditions L'Harmattan, 1995.

Nanni, Giordano. *The Colonisation of Time: Ritual, Routine and Resistance in the British Empire*. Manchester, UK: Manchester University Press, 2012.

Natarajan, Kalathmika. "Entangled Citizens: The Afterlives of Empire in the Indian Citizenship Act, 1947–1955." In Pedersen and Ward, *Break-Up of Greater Britain*, 63–83.

———. "The Privilege of the Indian Passport (1947–1967): Caste, Class, and the Afterlives of Indenture in Indian Diplomacy." *Modern Asian Studies*, online (2022): 1–30.

Naylor, Ed, ed. *France's Modernising Mission: Citizenship, Welfare and the Ends of Empire*. London: Palgrave Macmillan, 2018.

Nayoung, Aimee Kwon. *Intimate Empire: Collaboration and Colonial Modernity in Korea and Japan*. Durham, NC: Duke University Press, 2015.

Ndengue, Rose. "Social Imaginaries in Tension? The Women of Cameroon's Battle for Equal Rights under French Rule at the Turn of the 1940s–50s." In Germain and Larcher, *Black French Women*, 237–54.

Ndlovu-Gatsheni, Sabelo J. *Decolonization, Development and Knowledge in Africa: Turning over a New Leaf*. London: Routledge, 2020.

Neep, Daniel. *Occupying Syria under the French Mandate: Insurgency, Space and State Formation*. Cambridge, UK: Cambridge University Press, 2012.

Neill, Deborah J. *Networks in Tropical Medicine: Internationalism, Colonialism, and the Rise of a Medical Specialty, 1890–1930*. Stanford, CA: Stanford University Press, 2012.

Nesbitt, Nick. "Departmentalization and the Logic of Decolonization." *L'Esprit Créateur* 47, no. 1 (2007): 32–43.

Neumann, R. P. "The Postwar Conservation Boom in British Colonial Africa." *Environmental History* 7 (2002): 22–47.

Newbery, Samantha. *Interrogation, Intelligence and Security: Controversial British Techniques*. Manchester, UK: Manchester University Press, 2015.

Newman, E. "Failed States and International Order: Constructing a Post-Westphalian World." *Contemporary Security Policy* 30, no. 3 (2009): 421–43.

Ngoei, Wen-Qing. *Arc of Containment: Britain, the United States, and Anticommunism in Southeast Asia*. Ithaca, NY: Cornell University Press, 2019.

Nguyen-Marshall, Van. "Student Activism in a Time of War: Youth in the Republic of Vietnam, 1960s–1970s." *Journal of Vietnamese Studies* 10, no. 2 (2015): 43–81.

Nicolaïdis, Kalypso, Berny Sèbe, and Gabrielle Maas, eds. *Echoes of Empire: Memory, Identity and Colonial Legacies*. London: I. B. Tauris, 2015.

Nicosia, Francis. *Nazi Germany and the Arab World*. Cambridge, UK: Cambridge University Press, 2015.

Ninkovich, Frank. *The Global Republic: America's Inadvertent Rise to World Power*. Chicago: University of Chicago Press, 2014.

Nixon, Rob. *Slow Violence and the Environmentalism of the Poor*. Cambridge, MA: Harvard University Press, 2011.

Nkrumah, Kwame. *Neo-Colonialism: The Last Stage of Imperialism*. London: Thames Nelson, 1965.

Nolan, Mary. *The Transatlantic Century: Europe and America, 1890–2010*. Cambridge, UK: Cambridge University Press, 2012.

Norris, Jacob. *Land of Progress: Palestine in the Age of Colonial Development, 1905–1948*. Oxford: Oxford University Press, 2013.

Northrup, David. *Indentured Labour in the Age of Imperialism, 1834–1922*. Cambridge, UK: Cambridge University Press, 1995.

Norton, Robert. "Accommodating Indigenous Privilege: Britain's Dilemma in Decolonizing Fiji." *Journal of Pacific History* 37, no. 2 (2002), 133–56.

Nouschi, André. *L'Algérie amère 1914–1994*. Paris: Sciences de l'homme, 1995.

Novo, Andrew R. *The EOKA Cause: Nationalism and the Failure of Cypriot Enosis*. London: Bloomsbury, 2021.

———. "Friend or Foe? The Cyprus Police Force and the EOKA Insurgency." *Small Wars & Insurgencies* 23, no. 3 (2012): 414–31.

———. "The God Dilemma: Faith, the Church and Political Violence in Cyprus." *Journal of Modern Greek Studies* 31 (2013): 193–216.

———. "An Insoluble Problem: The Harding-Makarios Negotiations, Turkey, and the Cause of Cypriot *Enosis*." *Journal of Mediterranean Studies* 24, no. 1 (2015): 89–105.

Nyamunda, Tinashe. "In Defence of White Rule in Southern Africa: Portuguese-Rhodesian Economic Relations to 1974." *South African Historical Journal* 71, no. 3 (2019): 394–422.

———. "Money, Banking and Rhodesia's Unilateral Declaration of Independence." *Journal of Imperial & Commonwealth History* 45, no. 5 (2017): 746–76.

——. "'More a Cause than a Country': Historiography, UDI and the Crisis of Decoloni-sation in Rhodesia." *Journal of Southern African Studies* 42, no. 5 (2016): 1005–19.

Ocobock, Paul. "'Joy Rides for Juveniles': Vagrant Youth and Colonial Control in Nai-robi, Kenya, 1901–52." *Social History* 31, no. 1 (2006): 39–59.

O'Dowd, Edward C. "Ho Chi Minh and the Origins of the Vietnamese Doctrine of Guerrilla Tactics." *Small Wars & Insurgencies* 24, no. 3 (2013): 561–87.

Ogle, Vanessa. "Archipelago Capitalism: Tax Havens, Offshore Money, and the State, 1950s–1970s." *American Historical Review* 122, no. 5 (2017): 1431–58.

——. "'Funk Money': The End of Empires, the Expansion of Tax Havens, and Decolo-nization as an Economic and Financial Event." *Past and Present* 249, no. 1 (2020): 213–49.

——. "State Rights against Private Capital: The 'New International Economic Order' and the Struggle over Aid, Trade, and Foreign Investment, 1962–1981." *Humanity* 5, no. 2 (2014): 211–34.

Okia, Opolot. *Labor in Colonial Kenya after the Forced Labor Convention, 1930–1963*. Basingstoke, UK: Palgrave Macmillan, 2019.

O'Laughlin, Bridget. "Proletarianisation, Agency and Changing Rural Livelihoods: Forced Labour and Resistance in Colonial Mozambique." *Journal of Southern African Studies* 28, no. 3 (2002): 511–30.

Oldenburg, Philip. "'A Place Insufficiently Imagined': Language, Belief and the Paki-stan Crisis of 1971." *Journal of Asian Studies* 44, no. 4 (1985): 711–33.

Oliveira, Pedro Aires. "Saved by the Civil War: African 'Loyalists' in the Portuguese Armed Forces and Angola's Transition to Independence." *International History Review* 39, no. 1 (2017): 126–42.

O'Malley, Alanna. *The Diplomacy of Decolonisation, America, Britain and the United Nations during the Congo Crisis 1960–64*. Manchester, UK: Manchester University Press, 2018.

——. "Ghana, India, and the Transnational Dynamics of the Congo Crisis at the United Nations, 1960–1." *International History Review* 37, no. 5 (2015): 970–90.

O'Malley, Kate. *Ireland, India and Empire: Indo-Irish Radical Connections, 1919–64*. Manchester, UK: Manchester University Press, 2008.

Omar, Hussein. "Arabic Thought in the Liberal Cage." In *Islam after Liberalism*, edited by Faisal Devji and Zaheer Kasmi, 17–46. London: Hurst, 2017.

Onslow, Sue. "'Battlelines for Suez': The Abadan Crisis of 1951 and the Formation of the Suez Group." *Contemporary British History* 17, no. 2 (2003): 1–28.

——. "A Question of Timing: South Africa and Rhodesia's Unilateral Declaration of Independence, 1964–65." *Cold War History* 5, no. 2 (2005): 129–59.

Oostindie, Gert, Ben Schoenmaker, and Frank van Tree, eds. *Beyond the Pale: Dutch Extreme Violence in the Indonesian War of Independence, 1945–1949*. Amsterdam: Amsterdam University Press, 2022.

Opper, Marc. *People's Wars in China, Malaya, and Vietnam*. Ann Arbor: University of Michigan Press, 2020.

Orford, Anne, ed. *International Law and Its "Others."* Cambridge, UK: Cambridge University Press, 2006.

Orkaby, Asher. *Beyond the Arab Cold War: The International History of the Yemen Civil War, 1962-68*. New York: Oxford University Press, 2017.

Ortiz, Michael. "'Disown Gandhi or Be Damned': M. N. Roy, Gandhi, and Fascism." *Journal of Colonialism and Colonial History* 21, no. 3 (2020), online publication.

———. "Spain! Why?: Jawaharlal Nehru, Non-Intervention, and the Spanish Civil War." *European History Quarterly* 49, no. 3 (2019): 445–66.

Osborn, Emily Lynn. "Containers, Energy and the Anthropocene in West Africa." In Austin, *Economic Development*, 69–94.

Osborne, Myles. "'Mau Mau Are Angels . . . Sent by Haile Selassie': A Kenyan War in Jamaica." *Comparative Studies in Society and History* 62, no. 4 (2020): 714–44.

———. "'The Rooting Out of Mau Mau from the Minds of the Kikuyu is a Formidable Task': Propaganda and the Mau Mau War." *Journal of African History* 56, no. 1 (2015): 77–97.

Osterhammel, Jürgen. "Globalizations." In *Oxford Handbook of World History*, edited by Jerry H. Bentley, 89–104. Oxford: Oxford University Press, 2011.

O'Sullivan, Kevin. "Biafra's Legacy: NGO Humanitarianism and the Nigerian Civil War." In *Learning from the Past to Shape the Future: Lessons from the History of Humanitarian Action in Africa*, edited by Christina Bennett, Matthew Foley, and Hanna B. Krebs, 5–14. London: ODI, 2016.

———. *The NGO Moment: The Globalisation of Compassion from Biafra to Live Aid*. Cambridge, UK: Cambridge University Press, 2021.

Otte, T. G., ed. *British World Policy and the Projection of Global Power, c. 1830–1960*. Cambridge, UK: Cambridge University Press, 2019.

———. "British World Power and the White Queen's Memory." In Otte, *British World Policy*, 1–23.

Ottmann, Martin. "Rebel Constituencies and Rebel Violence against Civilians in Civil Conflicts." *Conflict Management and Peace Science* 34, no. 1 (2017): 27–51.

Overy, Richard. *Blood and Ruins: The Great Imperial War, 1931–1945*. London: Allen Lane, 2021.

Owen, Nicholas. *The British Left and India: Metropolitan Anti-Imperialism, 1885–1947*. Oxford Historical Monographs. Oxford: Oxford University Press, 2007.

Owens, Patricia. *Economy of Force: Counterinsurgency and the Historical Rise of the Social*. Cambridge, UK: Cambridge University Press, 2015.

Owens, Patricia, Katherina Rietzler, Kimberley Hutchings, and Sarah C. Dunstan. *Women's International Thought: Towards a New Canon*. Cambridge, UK: Cambridge University Press, 2022.

Packard, Randall. "Malaria Dreams: Postwar Visions of Health and Development in the Third World." *Medical Anthropology* 17 (1997): 279–96.

Padmore, George. *Pan-Africanism or Communism? The Coming Struggle for Africa*. London: Dobson, 1956.

Pahuja, Sundha. "Corporations, Universalism and the Domestication of Race in International Law." In Bell, *Empire, Race, and Global Justice*, 74–93.

———. *Decolonising International Law: Development, Economic Growth and the Politics of Universality*. Cambridge, UK: Cambridge University Press, 2013.

Paiva Abreu, Marcelo de. "Britain as a Debtor: Indian Sterling Balances, 1940–53." *Economic History Review* 70, no. 2 (2017): 586–617.

Palen, Marc-William. *The Conspiracy of Free Trade: The Anglo-American Struggle over Empire and Economic Globalisation, 1846–1896*. Cambridge, UK: Cambridge University Press, 2016.

Palieraki, Eugenia. "Chile, Algeria, and the Third World in the 1960s and 1970s: Revolutions Entangled." In Field, Krepp, and Pettinà, *Latin America and the Global Cold War*, 274–300.

Palmer, Colin A. *Cheddi Jagan and the Politics of Power: British Guiana's Struggle for Independence*. Chapel Hill: University of North Carolina Press, 2010.

Panayi, Panikos, and Pippa Virdee, eds. *Refugees and the End of Empire: Imperial Collapse and Forced Migration in the Twentieth Century*. Basingstoke, UK: Palgrave Macmillan, 2011.

Pandey, Gyanendra. *Remembering Partition: Violence, Nationalism and History in India* Cambridge, UK: Cambridge University Press, 2001.

Parchami, Ali. "Imperial Projections and Crisis: The Liberal International Order as a Pseudo-Empire." *Journal of Imperial & Commonwealth History* 47, no. 5 (2019): 1043–69.

Paris, Roland. *At War's End: Building Peace after Civil Conflict*. Cambridge, UK: Cambridge University Press, 2004.

———. "The 'Responsibility to Protect' and the Structural Problems of Preventive Humanitarian Intervention." *International Peacekeeping* 21, no. 5 (2014): 569–603.

Paris, Roland, and Timothy D. Sisk, eds. *The Dilemmas of Statebuilding: Confronting the Contradictions of Postwar Peace Operations*. London: Routledge, 2008.

Parker, Jason C. "Cold War II: The Eisenhower Administration, the Bandung Conference, and the Reperiodization of the Postwar Era." *Diplomatic History* 30, no. 5 (2005): 867–91.

———. *Hearts, Minds, Voices: U.S. Cold War Public Diplomacy and the Formation of the Third World*. Oxford: Oxford University Press, 2016.

———. "'Made-in-America Revolutions'? The 'Black University' and the American Role in the Decolonization of the Black Atlantic." *Journal of American History* 96, no. 3 (2009): 727–50.

Parker, John, and Richard Reid, eds. *The Oxford Handbook of Modern African History*. Oxford: Oxford University Press, 2013.

Parks, Richard C. *Medical Imperialism in French North Africa: Regenerating the Jewish Community of Colonial Tunis*. Lincoln: University of Nebraska Press, 2017.

Parrott, R. Joseph. "Brother and a Comrade: Amílcar Cabral as Global Revolutionary." In Parrott and Lawrence, *Tricontinental Revolution*, 245–75.

Parrott, R. Joseph, and Mark Atwood Lawrence, eds. *The Tricontinental Revolution: Third World Radicalism and the Cold War*. Cambridge, UK: Cambridge University Press, 2022.

Parsons, Laila. *The Commander: Fawzi al-Qawuqji and the Fight for Arab Independence 1914–1948*. London: Saqi, 2016.

Patil, Vrushali. "Contending Masculinities: The Gendered (Re)Negotiation of Colonial Hierarchy in the United Nations Debates on Decolonization." *Theory and Society* 38, no. 2 (2009): 195–215.

Paulmann, Johannes. "Conjunctures in the History of Humanitarian Aid during the Twentieth Century." *Humanity* 4, no. 2 (2013): 215–38.

Payne, Anthony. "The 'New' Manley and the New Political Economy of Jamaica." *Third World Quarterly* 13, no. 3 (1992): 463–73.

Pearce, Jenny. "Policy Failure and Petroleum Predation: The Economics of Civil War Debate Viewed 'from the War-Zone.'" *Government and Opposition* 40, no. 2 (2005): 152–80.

Pearce, Justin. "Global Ideologies, Local Politics: The Cold War as Seen from Central Angola." *Journal of Southern African Studies* 43, no. 1 (2017): 13–27.

——. *Political Identity and Conflict in Central Angola, 1975–2002*. Cambridge, UK: Cambridge University Press, 2015.

Pearson, Jessica Lynne. *The Colonial Politics of Global Health: France and the United Nations in Postwar Africa*. Cambridge, MA: Harvard University Press, 2018.

——. "Defending Empire at the United Nations: The Politics of International Colonial Oversight in the Era of Decolonisation." *Journal of Imperial & Commonwealth History* 45, no. 3 (2017): 525–49.

Peden, George C. "Recognising and Responding to Relative Decline: The Case of Post-War Britain." *Diplomacy & Statecraft* 24, no. 1 (2013): 59–76.

——. "Suez and Britain's Decline as a World Power." *Historical Journal* 55, no. 4 (2012): 1073–96.

Pedersen, Christian D. "The Birth of 'White' Republics and the Demise of Greater Britain: The Republican Referendums in South Africa and Rhodesia." In Pedersen and Ward, *Break-Up of Greater Britain*, 125–46.

Pedersen, Christian D., and Stuart Ward, eds. *The Break-Up of Greater Britain*. Manchester, UK: Manchester University Press, 2021.

Pedersen, Susan. "Empires, States and the League of Nations." In Sluga and Clavin, *Internationalisms*, 113–38.

——. "Getting out of Iraq—in 1932: The League of Nations and the Road to Normative Statehood." *American Historical Review* 115, no. 4 (2010): 975–1000.

——. *The Guardians: The League of Nations and the Crisis of Empire*. Oxford: Oxford University Press, 2015.

——. "An International Regime in an Age of Empire." *American Historical Review* 124, no. 5 (2019): 1676–80.

——. "Metaphors of the Schoolroom: Women Working the Mandates System of the League of Nations." *History Workshop Journal* 66 (2008): 188–207.

——. "National Bodies, Unspeakable Acts: The Sexual Politics of Colonial Policy-Making." *Journal of Modern History* 63, no. 4 (1991): 647–80.

Pella, J. A. "International Relations in Africa before the Europeans." *International History Review* 37, no. 1 (2015): 99–118.

Pergher, Roberta. *Mussolini's Nation-Empire: Sovereignty and Settlement in Italy's Borderlands, 1922–1943*. Cambridge, UK: Cambridge University Press, 2018.

Pernet, Corinne A., and Amalia Ribi Forclaz. "Revisiting the Food and Agriculture Organization (FAO): International Histories of Agriculture, Nutrition, and Development." *International History Review* 41, no. 2 (2019): 345–50.

Pero, Mario De. "Which Chile, Allende? Henry Kissinger and the Portuguese Revolution." *Cold War History* 11, no. 4 (2011): 625–57.

Perret, Françoise, and François Bugnion. "Between Insurgents and Government: The International Committee of the Red Cross's Action in the Algerian War (1954–1962)." *International Review of the Red Cross* 93, no. 883 (2011): 707–42.

Persaud, Randolph B. "The Racial Dynamic in International Relations: Some Thoughts on the Pan-African Antecedents of Bandung." In Pham and Shilliam, *Meanings of Bandung*, 133–42.

Peša, Iva. "Between Waste and Profit: Environmental Values on the Central African Copperbelt." *The Extractive Industries and Society* 8, no. 4 (2021): 1–8.

———. "Decarbonization, Democracy and Climate Justice: The Connections between African Mining and European Politics." *Journal of Modern European History* 20, no. 3 (2022): 299–303.

Pessis, Céline. "The Tractor as a Tool of Development? The Mythologies and Legacies of Mechanised Tropical Agriculture in French Africa, 1944–56." In Hodge, Hödl, and Kopf, *Developing Africa*, 179–203.

Peters, Christabelle. *Cuban Identity and the Angolan Experience*. Basingstoke, UK: Palgrave Macmillan, 2012.

Petersson, Fredrik. *Willi Münzenberg, the League against Imperialism, and the Comintern, 1925–1933*. New York: Edwin Mellen, 2014.

Petersson, Niels P., Stig Tenold, and Nicholas J. White, eds. *Shipping and Globalization in the Post-War Era*. Basingstoke, UK: Palgrave Macmillan, 2019.

Pettinà, Vanni. "Global Horizons: Mexico, the Third World, and the Non-Aligned Movement at the Time of the 1961 Belgrade Conference." *International History Review* 38, no. 4 (2016): 741–64.

Peyroulou, Jean-Pierre. *Guelma, 1945: Une subversion française dans l'Algérie colonial*. Paris: Éditions la découverte, 2009.

Pfingst, Annie. "Militarised Violence in the Service of State-Imposed Emergencies over Palestine and Kenya." *Cosmopolitan Civil Societies Journal* 6, no. 3 (2014): 6–37.

Pham, Quynh N., and R. Shilliam, eds. *Meanings of Bandung: Postcolonial Orders and Decolonial Visions*. London: Rowman & Littlefield, 2016.

Phillips, Andrew. "Beyond Bandung: The 1955 Asian–African Conference and its Legacies for International Order." *Australian Journal of International Affairs* 70, no. 4 (2016): 329–41.

———. "Saving Civilization from Empire: Belligerency, Pacifism and the Two Faces of Civilization during the Second Opium War." *European Journal of International Relations* 18, no. 1 (2011): 5–27.

———. *War, Religion and Empire: The Transformation of International Orders*. Cambridge, UK: Cambridge University Press, 2011.

Phillips, Anne. "Global Justice: Just Another Modernisation Theory?" in Bell, *Empire, Race, and Global Justice*, 145–62.

Phimister, Ian, and Victor Gwande. "Secondary Industry and Settler Colonialism: Southern Rhodesia before and after the Unilateral Declaration of Independence." *African Economic History* 45, no. 2 (2017): 85–112.

Pholsena, Vatthana. "The (Transformative) Impacts of the Vietnam War and the Communist Revolution in a Border Region in Southeastern Laos." *War & Society* 31, no. 2 (2012): 163–83.

Pickering, Jeffrey. *Britain's Withdrawal from East of Suez: The Politics of Retrench-ment*. Basingstoke, UK: Palgrave Macmillan, 1998.

Pieris, Anoma, and Lynne Horiuchi. *Intersectional Sovereignties: Carceral Architec-tures of the Pacific War*. Cambridge, UK: Cambridge University Press, 2021.

Pimenta, Fernando Tavares. "White Settler Politics and Euro-African Nationalism in Angola, 1945–1975." In Cavanagh and Veracini, *Routledge Handbook of the History of Settler Colonialism*, 277–89.

Pinto da Cruz, Bernardo. "The Penal Origins of Colonial Model Villages: From Aborted Concentration Camps to Forced Resettlement in Angola (1930–1969)." *Journal of Imperial & Commonwealth History* 47, no. 2 (2019): 343–71.

Pitts, Jennifer. *Boundaries of the International: Law and Empire*. Cambridge, MA: Harvard University Press, 2018.

———. "The Critical History of International Law." *Political Theory* 43 (2015): 541–52.

Plummer, Brenda Gayle. *In Search of Power: African Americans in the Era of Decolo-nization, 1956–1974*. Cambridge, UK: Cambridge University Press, 2013.

Polónia, Amélia, and Jorge M. Pacheco. "Environmental Impacts of Colonial Dynam-ics, 1400–1800: The First Global Age and the Anthropocene." In Austin, *Economic Development*, 23–49.

Pols, Hans. *Nurturing Indonesia: Medicine and Decolonisation in the Dutch East Indies*. Cambridge, UK: Cambridge University Press, 2018.

Popovic, Milos. "Fragile Proxies: Explaining Rebel Defection against their State Spon-sors." *Terrorism and Political Violence* 29, no. 6 (2017): 922–42.

Porte, Pablo La. "Colonial Dreams and Nightmares: British and French Perceptions of Republican Policies in Spanish Morocco (1931–1936)." *International History Review* 41, no. 4 (2019): 821–44.

Posel, Deborah. "Getting Inside the Skin of the Consumer: Race, Market Research, and the Consumerist Project in Apartheid South Africa." *Itinerario* 42, no. 1 (2018): 120–38.

———. *The Making of Apartheid, 1948–1961: Conflict and Compromise*. Oxford: Clar-endon, 1991.

Powell, Julie M. "About-Face: Gender, Disfigurement and the Politics of French Recon-struction, 1918–24." *Gender & History* 28, no. 3 (2016): 604–22.

Powell, Nathaniel K. "Battling Instability? The Recurring Logic of French Military Interventions in Africa." *African Security* 10, no. 1 (2017): 47–72.

———. "The 'Cuba of the West'? France's Cold War in Zaire, 1977–1978." *Journal of Cold War Studies* 18, no. 2 (2016): 64–96.

———. "'Experts in Decolonization'?: French Statebuilding and Counterinsurgency in Chad, 1969–1972." *International History Review* 42, no. 2 (2020): 318–35.

Prakash, Amit. *Empire on the Seine: The Policing of North Africans in Paris, 1925–1975*. Oxford: Oxford University Press, 2022.

Prakash, Gyan, and Jeremy Adelman, eds. *Inventing the Third World: In Search of Freedom for the Postwar Global South*. London: Bloomsbury Academic, 2023.

Prakash, Gyan, Michael Laffan, and Nikhil Menon, eds. *The Postcolonial Moment in South and Southeast Asia*. London: Bloomsbury, 2018.

Prashad, Vijay. *The Darker Nations: A People's History of the Third World*. New York: New Press, 2007.

———. *The Poorer Nations: A Possible History of the Global South*. London: Verso, 2013.

Presley, Cora Ann. "The Mau Mau Rebellion, Kikuyu Women, and Social Change." *Canadian Journal of African Studies* 22, no. 3 (1988): 502–27.

Prestholdt, Jeremy. "Politics of the Soil: Separatism, Autochthony, and Decolonization at the Kenyan Coast." *Journal of African History* 55, no. 2 (2014): 249–70.

Preston, Andrew, and Doug Rossinow, eds. *Outside In: The Transnational Circuitry of US History*. New York: Oxford University Press, 2017.

Price, Richard. "One Big Thing: Britain, Its Empire, and Their Imperial Culture." *Journal of British Studies* 45 (July 2006): 602–27.

Pringle, Yolanda. *Psychiatry and Decolonisation in Uganda*. Basingstoke, UK: Palgrave Macmillan, 2019.

Prochaska, David. "Making Algeria French and Unmaking French Algeria." *Journal of Historical Sociology* 3, no. 4 (1990): 305–28.

Profant, Tomáš. "French Geopolitics in Africa: From Neocolonialism to Identity." *Review of International Affairs* 18, no. 1 (2010): 41–62.

Prott, Volker. *The Politics of Self-Determination: Remaking Territories and National Identities in Europe, 1917–1923*. Oxford: Oxford University Press, 2016.

Provence, Michael. *The Great Syrian Revolt and the Rise of Arab Nationalism*. Austin: University of Texas Press, 2005.

———. "Ottoman Modernity, Colonialism, and Insurgency in the Interwar Arab East." *International Journal of Middle East Studies* 43 (2011): 205–25.

Pugach, Sara. "Eleven Nigerian Students in Cold War East Germany: Visions of Science, Modernity, and Decolonization." *Journal of Contemporary History* 54, no. 3 (2019): 551–72.

Puri, Samir. *The Great Imperial Hangover: How Empires Have Shaped the World*. London: Atlantic Books, 2020.

Quinn-Judge, Sophie. *Ho Chi Minh: The Missing Years, 1919–1941*. London: Hurst, 2003.

Rabe, Stephen G. "The Caribbean Triangle: Betancourt, Castro, and Trujillo and U.S. Foreign Policy, 1958–1963." *Diplomatic History* 20, no. 1 (1996): 55–78.

———. *The Killing Zone: The United States Wages Cold War in Latin America*. Oxford: Oxford University Press, 2012.

———. *U.S. Intervention in British Guiana: A Cold War Story*. Chapel Hill: University of North Carolina Press, 2005.

Rabinowitz, Beth S. *Coups, Rivals, and the Modern State: Why Rural Coalitions Matter in Sub-Saharan Africa*. Cambridge, UK: Cambridge University Press, 2018.

Rafael, Vincente L. "Welcoming What Comes: Sovereignty and Revolution in the Colonial Philippines." *Comparative Studies in Society & History* 52, no. 1 (2010): 157–79.

Raftopoulos, Brian, and A. S. Mlambo, eds. *Becoming Zimbabwe: A History from the Pre-Colonial Period to 2008*. Harare: Weaver Press, 2009.

Raghavan, Pallavi. "Partition: An International History." *International History Review* 42, no. 5 (2020): 1029–47.

Raghaven, Srinath. *1971: A Global History of the Creation of Bangladesh*. Cambridge, MA: Harvard University Press, 2013.

Rahal, Malika. "Empires." In Conway, Lagrou, and Rousso, *Europe's Postwar Periods*, 137–54.

——. "Fused Together and Torn Apart: Stories and Violence in Contemporary Algeria." *History and Memory* 24, no. 1 (2012): 118–51.

——. "A Local Approach to the UDMA: Local-Level Politics during the Decade of Political Parties, 1946–56." *Journal of North African Studies* 18, no. 5 (2013): 703–24.

Rahman, Md. Mahbubar, and Willem Van Schendel. "'I Am Not a Refugee': Rethinking Partition Migration." *Modern Asian Studies* 37, no. 3 (2003): 551–84.

Rajagopal, Balakrishnan. "Counter-Hegemonic International Law: Rethinking Human Rights and Development as a Third World Strategy." *Third World Quarterly* 27, no. 5 (2006): 767–83.

Ramakrishna, Kumar. "Content, Credibility and Context: Propaganda, Government Surrender Policy and the Malayan Communist Mass Surrender of 1958." *Intelligence & National Security* 14, no. 4 (1999): 242–66.

——. *Emergency Propaganda: The Winning of Malayan Hearts and Minds, 1948–1958.* Richmond: Curzon, 2002.

Ramgotra, Mangeet K. "India's Republican Moment: Freedom in Nehru's Political Thought." In *The Indian Constituent Assembly: Deliberations on Democracy*, edited by Udit Bhatia, 196–221. New Delhi: Routledge India, 2017.

——. "Post-Colonial Republicanism and the Revival of a Paradigm." *The Good Society* 26, no. 1 (2018): 34–54.

Randall, Vicky. "Using and Abusing the Concept of the Third World: Geopolitics and the Comparative Political Study of Development and Underdevelopment." *Third World Quarterly* 25, no. 1 (2004): 41–53.

Rao, P. V. "The US Congress and the 1971 Crisis in East Pakistan." *International Affairs* 43, no. 1 (2006): 73–91.

Rass, Christoph. "Temporary Labour Migration and State-Run Recruitment of Foreign Workers in Europe, 1919–1975: A New Migration Regime?" *International Review of Social History* 57 (2012): 191–224.

Rathbone, Richard. "The Transfer of Power and Colonial Civil Servants in Ghana." *Journal of Imperial & Commonwealth History* 28, no. 2 (2000): 67–84.

Ravndal, Ellen Jenny. "Colonies, Semi-Sovereigns, and Great Powers: IGO Membership Debates and the Transition of the International System." *Review of International Studies* 46, no. 2 (2019): 278–98.

——. "Exit Britain: British Withdrawal from the Palestine Mandate in the Early Cold War, 1947–1948." *Diplomacy & Statecraft* 21, no. 3 (2010): 416–33.

——. "'The First Major Test': The UN Secretary-General and the Palestine Problem, 1947–49." *International History Review* 38, no. 1 (2016): 196–213.

Rawlings, Gregory. "Lost Files, Forgotten Papers and Colonial Disclosures: The 'Migrated Archives' and the Pacific, 1963–2013." *Journal of Pacific History* 50, no. 2 (2015): 189–212.

Raza, Ali, Franzisca Roy, and Benjamin Zachariah, eds. *The Internationalist Moment: South Asia, Worlds, World Views 1917–1939.* New Delhi: Sage, 2015.

Reader, Luke. "'An Alternative to Imperialism': Leonard Woolf, the Labour Party and Imperial Internationalism, 1915–1922." *International History Review* 41, no. 1 (2019): 157–77.

Regan-Lefebvre, Jennifer. *Cosmopolitan Nationalism in the Victorian Empire: Ireland, India and the Politics of Alfred Webb*. Basingstoke, UK: Palgrave Macmillan, 2009.

Regan, Patrick M. *Civil Wars and Foreign Powers: Outside Intervention in Intrastate Conflict*. Ann Arbor: University of Michigan Press, 2000.

Reid, Richard. "State of Anxiety: History and Nation in Modern Africa." *Past & Present* 229, no. 1 (2015): 239–69.

Reilly, Brett. "The Sovereign States of Vietnam, 1945–1955." *Journal of Vietnamese Studies* 11, no. 3–4 (2016): 103–39.

Reilly, Maura. *Curatorial Activism: Towards an Ethics of Curating*. London: Thames & Hudson, 2018.

Reinisch, Jessica. "Internationalism in Relief: The Birth (and Death) of UNRRA." *Past & Present* 210, Supplement 6 (2011): 258–89.

———. "Introduction: Agents of Internationalism." *Contemporary European History* 25 (2016): 195–205.

———. "Introduction: Relief in the Aftermath of War." *Journal of Contemporary History* 43, no. 3 (2008): 371–404.

———. *The Perils of Peace: The Public Health Crisis in Occupied Germany*. Oxford: Oxford University Press, 2013.

Reis, Bruno Cardoso. "The Myth of British Minimum Force in Counterinsurgency Campaigns During Decolonisation, 1945–1970." *Journal of Strategic Studies* 34, no. 2 (2011): 245–79.

———. "Portugal and the UN: A Rogue State Resisting the Norm of Decolonization (1956–1974)." *Portuguese Studies* 29, no. 2 (2013): 251–76.

Renda, Mary A. *Taking Haiti: Military Occupation and the Culture of U.S. Imperialism, 1915–1940*. Chapel Hill: University of North Carolina Press, 2001.

Renoult, Anne. "*Indochine SOS*: Andrée Viollis et la Question coloniale (1931–1950)." In *Nouvelle histoire des colonisations européennes (XIXe–XXe siècles): Sociétés, Cultures, Politiques*, edited by Amaury Lorin and Christelle Taraud, 141–56. Paris: Presses Universitaires de France, 2013.

Renou, Xavier. "A New French Policy for Africa?" *Journal of Contemporary African Studies* 20, no. 1 (2002): 5–27.

Reus-Smit, Christian. "Human Rights and the Social Construction of Sovereignty." *Review of International Studies* 27, no. 4 (2001): 519–38.

Reynolds, Henry. *Truth-Telling: History, Sovereignty and the Uluru Statement*. Kensington, NSW: New South Publishing, 2021.

Reynolds, John. *Empire, Emergency and International Law*. Cambridge, UK: Cambridge University Press, 2017.

Reynolds, Michael A. *Shattering Empires: The Clash and Collapse of the Ottoman and Russian Empires, 1908–1918*. Cambridge, UK: Cambridge University Press, 2011.

Rider, Toby J., and Andrew P. Owsiak. *On Dangerous Ground: A Theory of Bargaining, Border Settlement, and Rivalry*. Cambridge, UK: Cambridge University Press, 2021.

Rid, Thomas. "The Nineteenth Century Origins of Counterinsurgency Doctrine." *Journal of Strategic Studies* 33, no. 5 (2010): 727–58.

Riley, Charlotte Lydia. "'Tropical Allsorts': The Transnational Flavour of British Development Policies in Africa." *Journal of World History* 26, no. 4 (2015): 839–64.

Rimner, Steffen. *Opium's Long Shadow: From Asian Revolution to Global Drugs Control*. Cambridge, MA: Harvard University Press, 2018.

Rioux, Jean-Pierre. *The Fourth Republic*. Cambridge, UK: Cambridge University Press, 1987.

Rist, Gilbert. *The History of Development: From Western Origins to Global Faith*. Translated by Patrick Camiller. London: Zed, 1997.

Rittich, Kerry. "Occupied Iraq: Imperial Convergences?" *Leiden Journal of International Law* 31, no. 3 (2018): 479–501.

Roberts, George. "The Assassination of Eduardo Mondlane: FRELIMO, Tanzania, and the Politics of Exile in Dar es Salaam." *Cold War History* 17, no. 1 (2017): 1–19.

——. "Press, Propaganda and the German Democratic Republic's Search for Recognition in Tanzania, 1964–72." In Muehlenbeck and Telepneva, *Warsaw Pact*, 148–72.

Robertson, Tom. "'Thinking Globally': American Foreign Aid, Paul Ehrlich, and the Emergence of Environmentalism in the 1960s." In Gavin and Lawrence, *Beyond the Cold War*, 185–205.

Robinson, David. *Paths of Accommodation: Muslim Societies and French Colonial Authorities in Senegal and Mauritania, 1880–1920*. Athens: Ohio University Press, 2000.

Robinson, Geoffrey B. *The Killing Season: A History of the Indonesian Massacres, 1965–66*. Princeton, NJ: Princeton University Press, 2018.

Robinson, Michael Edson. *Cultural Nationalism in Colonial Korea, 1920–1925*. Seattle: University of Washington Press, 1988.

Robinson, Richard. "The Influence of Overseas Issues in Portugal's Transition to Democracy." In *The Last Empire: Thirty Years of Portuguese Decolonization*, edited by Stewart Lloyd-Jones and António Costa Pinto. Bristol: Intellect, 2003.

Robson, Laura. "Partition and the Question of International Governance: The 1947 United Nations Special Committee on Palestine." In Kattan and Ranjan, *Breakup of India and Palestine*, 75–90.

——. *The Politics of Mass Violence in the Middle East*. Oxford: Oxford University Press, 2020.

——. "Refugees and the Case for International Authority in the Middle East: The League of Nations and the United Nations Relief and Works Agency for Palestinian Refugees in the Near East Compared." *International Journal of Middle East Studies* 49 (2017): 625–44.

——. *States of Separation: Transfer, Partition, and the Making of the Modern Middle East*. Berkeley: University of California Press, 2017.

Rodet, Marie. "Forced Labor, Resistance, and Masculinities in Kayes, French Sudan, 1919–1946." *International Labor and Working-Class History* 86, no. 1 (2014): 107–23.

Rodet, Marie, and Brandon County. "Old Homes and New Homelands: Imagining the Nation and Remembering Expulsion in the Wake of the Mali Federation's Collapse." *Africa: Journal of the International Africa Institute* 88, no. 3 (2018): 469–91.

Rodney, Walter. *How Europe Underdeveloped Africa*. London: Bogle-L'Ouverture Publications, 1972, reprint, Black Classic Press, 2012.

Rodogno, Davide, Bernhard Struck, and Jacob Vogel, eds. *Shaping the Transnational Sphere: Transnational Networks of Experts and Organizations (c. 1850–1930)*. New York: Berghahn, 2014.

Rogan, Eugene L. *The Fall of the Ottomans: The Great War in the Middle East, 1914-1920*. New York: Basic Books, 2015.

Rogan, Eugene L., and Avi Schlaim, eds. *The War for Palestine: Rewriting the History of 1948*. Cambridge, UK: Cambridge University Press, 2001.

Rolandsen, Øystein H., and Cherry Leonardi. "Discourses of Violence in the Transition from Colonialism to Independence in Southern Sudan, 1955-1960." *Journal of East African Studies* 8, no. 4 (2014): 609-25.

Romero, Federico. "Cold War Historiography at the Crossroads." *Cold War History* 14, no. 4 (2014): 685-703.

Rönnbäck, Klas, and Oskar Broberg. *Capital and Colonialism: The Return on British Investments in Africa, 1869-1969*. Basingstoke, UK: Palgrave Macmillan, 2019.

Roosa, John. *Buried Histories: The Anticommunist Massacres of 1965-1966 in Indonesia*. Madison: University of Wisconsin Press, 2020.

———. *Pretext for Mass Murder: The September 30th Movement and Suharto's Coup d'Etat in Indonesia*. Madison: University of Wisconsin Press, 2006.

Rosenberg, Clifford. *Policing Paris: The Origins of Modern Immigration Control between the Wars*. Ithaca, NY: Cornell University Press, 2006.

Ross, Corey. "Developing the Rain Forest: Rubber, Environment and Economy in Southeast Asia." In Austin, *Economic Development*, 199-218.

———. *Ecology and Power in the Age of Empire: Europe and the Transformation of the Tropical World*. Oxford: Oxford University Press, 2017.

———. "The Plantation Paradigm: Colonial Agronomy, African Farmers, and the Global Cocoa Boom, 1870s-1940s." *Journal of Global History* 9, no. 1 (2014): 49-71.

Roth-Ey, Kristin. "How Do You Listen to Radio Moscow? Moscow's Broadcasters, 'Third World' Listeners, and the Space of the Airwaves in the Cold War." *Slavonic and East European Review* 98, no. 4 (2020): 712-41.

———, ed. *Socialist Internationalism and the Gritty Politics of the Particular: Second-Third World Spaces in the Cold War*. London: Bloomsbury Academic, 2023.

Rotter, Andrew J. *Empires of the Senses: Bodily Encounters in Imperial India and the Philippines*. Oxford: Oxford University Press, 2019.

———. "Empires of the Senses: How Seeing, Hearing, Smelling, Tasting, and Touching Shaped Imperial Encounters." *Diplomatic History* 35, no. 1 (2011): 3-19.

Rowe, Rochelle. "'Glorifying the Jamaican Girl': The 'Ten Types One People' Beauty Contest, Racialized Femininities, and Jamaican Nationalism." *Radical History Review* 103 (Winter 2009): 36-58.

Roy, Anwesha. *Making Peace, Making Riots: Communalism and Communal Violence, Bengal, 1940-1947*. Cambridge, UK: Cambridge University Press, 2018.

Roy, Haimanti. *Partitioned Lives: Migrants, Refugees, Citizens in India and Pakistan, 1947-1965*. Oxford: Oxford University Press, 2012.

Ruscio, Alain. *Nostalgérie: l'interminable histoire de l'OAS* Paris: La Découverte, 2015.

———. "L'opinion publique et la guerre d'Indochine. Sondages et témoignages." *Vingtième Siècle* 1 (1991): 35-46.

Russo, Guisi. "Contested Practices, Human Rights, and Colonial Bodies in Pain: The UN's Gender Politics in Africa, 1940s-1960s." *Gender and History* 30, no. 1 (2018): 196-213.

———. "The UN and the Colonial World: New Questions and New Directions." *Journal of Contemporary History*, 57, no. 2 (2022): 212-17.

Ryan, Eileen. *Religion as Resistance: Negotiating Authority in Italian Libya*. Oxford: Oxford University Press, 2018.

Saada, Emmanuelle. "The Absent Empire: The Colonies in French Constitutions." In McCoy, Fradera, and Jacobson, *Endless Empire*, 205–15.

Sackley, Nicole. "The Village as Cold War Site: Experts, Development and the History of Social Reconstruction." *Journal of Global History* 6 (2011): 481–504.

Sacriste, Fabien. *Les camps de regroupement en Algérie. Une histoire des déplacements forcés (1954–1962)*. Paris: Presses de Sciences Po., 2022.

Sa'di, Ahmad H., and Nur Masalha, eds. *Decolonizing the Study of Palestine: Indigenous Perspectives and Settler Colonialism after Elia Zureik*. London: I. B. Tauris, 2023.

Saha, Jonathan. *Law, Disorder and the Colonial State: Corruption in Burma c.1900*. Basingstoke, UK: Palgrave Macmillan, 2013.

——. "Madness and the Making of a Colonial Order in Burma." *Modern Asian Studies* 47, no. 2 (2013): 406–35.

——. "A Mockery of Justice? Colonial Law, the Everyday State, and Village Politics in the Burma Delta, c.1890–1910." *Past & Present* 217 (2012): 187–212.

——. "Whiteness, Masculinity and the Ambivalent Embodiment of 'British Justice' in Colonial Burma." *Cultural and Social History* 14, no. 4 (2017): 527–42.

Saikia, Yasmin. "Beyond the Archive of Silence: Narratives of Violence of the 1971 Liberation War of Bangladesh." *History Workshop Journal* 58, no. 1 (2004): 275–87.

——. "Insāniyat for Peace: Survivors' Narrative of the 1971 War of Bangladesh." *Journal of Genocide Research* 13, no. 4 (2011): 475–501.

Sajed, Alina. "The Post Always Rings Twice? The Algerian War, Poststructuralism and the Postcolonial in IR Theory." *Review of International Studies* 38, no. 1 (2011): 141–63.

Salehyan, Idean. *Rebels without Borders: Transnational Insurgencies in World Politics*. Ithaca, NY: Cornell University Press, 2009.

——. "Refugees and the Study of Civil War." *Civil Wars* 9, no. 2 (2007): 127–41.

Salem, Sara. *Anticolonial Afterlives in Egypt: The Politics of Hegemony*. Cambridge, UK: Cambridge University Press, 2020.

Sanborn, Joshua A. *Imperial Apocalypse: The Great War and the Destruction of the Russian Empire*. Oxford: Oxford University Press, 2014.

Sanchez-Sibony, Oscar. "Capitalism's Fellow Traveler: The Soviet Union, Bretton Woods, and the Cold War." *Comparative Studies in Society and History* 56, no. 2 (2014): 290–319.

——. "The Cold War in the Margins of Capital: The Soviet Union's Introduction to the Decolonized World, 1955–1961." In Mark, Kalinovsky, and Marung, *Alternative Globalizations*, 59–79.

——. *Red Globalization: The Political Economy of the Soviet Cold War from Stalin to Khrushchev*. Cambridge, UK: Cambridge University Press, 2014.

Sandell, Marie. "Regional versus International: Women's Activism and Organisational Spaces in the Inter-War Period." *International History Review* 33, no. 4 (2011): 607–25.

Santoru, Marina. "The Colonial Idea of Women and Direct Intervention: The Mau Mau Case." *African Affairs*, 95, no. 379 (1996): 253–67.

Santos, Boaventura De Sousa. *Epistemologies of the South: Justice against Epistemicide*. London: Routledge, 2014.

Saraswati, L. Ayu. *Seeing Beauty, Sensing Race in Transnational Indonesia*. Honolulu: University of Hawai'i Press, 2013.

Sargent, Daniel J. "The Cold War and the International Political Economy in the 1970s." *Cold War History* 13, no. 3 (2013): 393–425.

———. "North/South: The United States Responds to the New International Economic Order." *Humanity* 6 (Spring 2015): 201–16.

———. *A Superpower Transformed: The Remaking of American Foreign Relations in the 1970s*. Oxford: Oxford University Press, 2015.

Sartori, Andrew S. "The British Empire and Its Liberal Mission." *Journal of Modern History* 78, no. 3 (2006): 623–42.

———. *Liberalism in Empire: An Alternative History*. Berkeley: University of California Press, 2014.

Sasson, Tehila. "From Empire to Humanity: The Russian Famine and the Imperial Origins of International Humanitarianism." *Journal of British Studies* 55 (2016): 519–37.

———. "Milking the Third World? Humanitarianism, Capitalism, and the Moral Economy of the Nestlé Boycott." *American Historical Review* 121, no. 4 (2016): 1196–2224.

Saul, John S. "Poverty Alleviation and the Revolutionary-Socialist Imperative: Learning from Nyerere's Tanzania." *International Journal* 57, no. 2 (2002): 193–207.

———. "Tanzania Fifty Years On (1961–2011): Rethinking *Ujamaa,* Nyerere and Socialism in Africa." *Review of African Political Economy* 39, no. 131 (2012): 117–25.

Saull, Richard. "Locating the Global South in the Theorization of the Cold War: Capitalist Development, Social Revolution and Geopolitical Conflict." *Third World Quarterly* 26, no. 2 (2005): 253–80.

Saul, Samir. "Milieux d'affaires de l'Outre-Mer français et Grande Dépression des années 1930." *French Colonial History* 10 (2009): 209–43.

———. "Les pouvoirs publics métropolitains face à la Dépression: La Conférence économique de la France métropolitaine et d'Outre-Mer (1934–1935)." *French Colonial History* 12 (2011): 167–91.

Savage, Jesse Dillon. *Political Violence and Sovereignty in International Relations*. Cambridge, UK: Cambridge University Press, 2020.

Savarese, Éric. *L'ordre colonial et sa légitimation en France métropolitaine. Oublier l'autre*. Paris: L'Harmattan, 1998.

Sayim, Burak. "Communist Anti-Militarism in France and Anti-Colonial Wars in Morocco and Syria." *Twentieth Century Communism* 24 (2023): 17–42.

Scagliola, Stef. "Cleo's 'Unfinished Business': Coming to Terms with Dutch War Crimes in Indonesia's War of Independence." *Journal of Genocide Research* 14, no. 3–4 (2012): 419–39.

Scales, Rebecca P. *Radio and the Politics of Sound in Interwar France, 1921–1939*. Cambridge, UK: Cambridge University Press, 2018.

———. "Subversive Sound: Transnational Radio, Arabic Recordings, the Danger of Listening in French Colonial Algeria, 1934–39." *Comparative Studies in Society and History* 52, no. 2 (2010): 384–417.

Schatkowski-Schilcher, Linda. "The Famine of 1915–1918 in Greater Syria." In *Problems of the Modern Middle East in Historical Perspective: Essays in Honour of Albert Hourani*, edited by John P. Spagnolo, 229–58. Reading: Ithaca, 1992.

Schayegh, Cyrus, ed. *Globalizing the U.S. Presidency: Postcolonial Views of John F. Kennedy*. London: Bloomsbury, 2021.

———. *The Middle East and the Making of the Modern World*. Cambridge, MA: Harvard University Press, 2017.

———. "1958 Reconsidered: State Formation and the Cold War in the Early Postcolonial Arab Middle East." *International Journal of Middle East Studies* 45, no. 3 (2013): 421–43.

Scheele, Judith. "A Taste for Law: Rule-Making in Kabylia (Algeria)." *Comparative Studies in Society and History* 50, no. 4 (2008): 895–919.

Scheipers, Sibylle. "Counterinsurgency or Irregular Warfare? Historiography and the Study of 'Small Wars.'" *Small Wars & Insurgencies* 25, no. 5–6 (2014): 879–99.

———. "The Use of Camps in Colonial Warfare." *Journal of Imperial & Commonwealth History* 43, no. 4 (2015): 678–98.

Schenk, Catherine R. "The Origins of the Eurodollar Market in London, 1955–63." *Explorations in Economic History* 35, no. 2 (1998): 221–38.

Scheper-Hughes, Nancy, and Philippe Bourgois, eds. *Violence in War and Peace: An Anthology*. Oxford: Blackwell, 2004.

Schlichte, Klause. *In the Shadow of Violence: The Politics of Armed Groups*. Frankfurt: Campus, 2009.

Schmidt, Brian C. "Lessons from the Past: Reassessing the Interwar Disciplinary History of International Relations." *International Studies Quarterly* 42, no. 3 (1998): 433–59.

Schmidt, Brian C., and Nicolas Guilhot, eds. *Historiographical Investigations in International Relations*. Basingstoke, UK: Palgrave Macmillan, 2019.

———. "Internalism versus Externalism in the Disciplinary History of International Relations." In Schmidt and Guilhot, *Historiographical Investigations*, 127–48.

Schmidt, Elizabeth. *Cold War and Decolonization in Guinea, 1946–1958*. Athens: Ohio University Press, 2007.

———. "Cold War in Guinea: The Rassemblement Démocratique Africain and the Struggle over Communism, 1950–1958." *Journal of African History* 48, no.1 (2007): 95–121.

———. "Top down or Bottom up? Nationalist Mobilization Reconsidered, with Special Reference to Guinea (French West Africa)." *American Historical Review* 110, no. 4 (2005): 975–1014.

Schmidt, Heike I. *Colonialism and Violence in Zimbabwe: A History of Suffering*. Woodbridge: James Currey, 2013.

Schneidman, Witney W. *Engaging Africa: Washington and the Fall of Portugal's Colonial Empire*. Dallas: University Press of America, 2004.

Schofield, Camilla. *Enoch Powell and the Making of Postcolonial Britain*. Cambridge, UK: Cambridge University Press, 2013.

Schütze, Robert. "International Governance: Theory and Practice." In *Globalisation and Governance: International Problems, European Solutions*, edited by Robert Schütze, 1–8. Cambridge, UK: Cambridge University Press, 2018.

Schwarz, Bill. "An Unsentimental Education: John Darwin's Empire." *Journal of Imperial & Commonwealth History* 43, no. 1 (2015): 125–44.

——, ed. *West Indian Intellectuals in Britain*. Manchester, UK: Manchester University Press, 2003.

Scott, Catherine. *State Failure in Sub-Saharan Africa: The Crisis of Post-Colonial Order*. London: I. B. Tauris, 2019.

Scott, James C. *Seeing like a State: How Certain Schemes to Improve the Human Condition Have Failed*. New Haven, CT: Yale University, Press, 1998.

Sealy, Mark. *Decolonising the Camera: Photography in Racial Time*. London: Lawrence & Wishart, 2019.

Sèbe, Berny, and Matthew G. Stanard, eds. *Decolonising Europe: Popular Responses to the End of Empire*. London: Routledge, 2020.

Segalla, Spencer D. *Empire and Catastrophe: Decolonization and Environmental Disaster in North Africa and Mediterranean France since 1954*. Lincoln: University of Nebraska Press, 2021.

——. "Georges Hardy and Educational Ethnology in French Morocco, 1920–26." *French Colonial History* 4 (2003): 171–90.

Seikaly, Sherene. "The Matter of Time." *American Historical Review* 124, no. 5 (2019): 1681–88.

——. *Men of Capital: Scarcity and Economy in Mandate Palestine*. Stanford, CA: Stanford University Press, 2015.

——. "A Nutritional Economy: The Calorie, Development and War in Mandate Palestine." In *Home Fronts: Britain and the Empire at War, 1939–45*, edited by Mark J. Crowley and Sandra Trudgen Dawson, 37–58. London: Boydell and Brewer, 2017.

Sekeris, Petros. "Land Inequality and Conflict in Sub-Saharan Africa." *Journal of Peace Economics, Peace Science and Public Policy* 16, no. 2 (2020): 1–18.

Sen, Uditi. "The Myths Refugees Live By: Memory and History in the Making of Bengali Refugee Identity." *Modern Asian Studies* 48, no. 1 (2014): 37–76.

Serels, Steven. "Starving for Someone Else's Fight: The First World War and Food Insecurity in the African Red Sea Region." In Tucker et al., *Environmental Histories of the First World War*, 208–30.

Shafir, Gershon. "Theorizing Zionist Settler Colonialism in Palestine." In Cavanagh and Veracini, *Routledge Handbook of the History of Settler Colonialism*, 339–52.

Sharkey, Heather J. "African Colonial States." In Parker and Reid, *Oxford Handbook of Modern African History*, 151–70.

——. *Living with Colonialism: Nationalism and Culture in the Anglo-Egyptian Sudan* Berkeley: University of California Press, 2005.

Sharma, Jayeeta. "Food and Empire." In *The Oxford Handbook of Food History*, edited by Jeffrey M. Pilcher. Oxford: Oxford University Press, 2012, online publication.

Sharma, Patrick A. "Between North and South: The World Bank and the New International Economic Order." *Humanity* 6, no. 1 (2015): 189–200.

——. "The United States, the World Bank, and the Transformation of Development in the 1970s." *Diplomatic History* 37, no. 3 (2013): 572–604.

Shear, Keith. "Chiefs or Modern Bureaucrats: Black Police in Early Twentieth-Century South Africa." *Comparative Studies in Society and History* 54, no. 2 (2012): 251–74.

Sheffy, Yigal. "Chemical Warfare and the Palestine Campaign." *Journal of Military History* 73 (July 2009): 803–44.

Shennan, Andrew. *Rethinking France: Plans for Renewal, 1940–46*. Oxford: Clarendon, 1989.

Shepard, Todd. "Algerian Nationalism, Zionism, and French *Laïcité*: A History of Ethnoreligious Nationalisms and Decolonization." *International Journal of Middle East Studies* 45, no. 3 (2013): 445–67.

———. "Excluding the *Harkis* from Repatriate Status, Excluding Muslim Algerians from French Identity." In Gafaïti, Lorcin, and Troyansky, *Transnational Spaces*, 94–110.

———. "'History Is Past Politics'? Archives, 'Tainted Evidence,' and the Return of the State." *American Historical Review* 115, no. 2 (2010): 474–83.

———. *The Invention of Decolonization: The Algerian War and the Remaking of France*. Ithaca, NY: Cornell University Press, 2006.

———. "'Something Notably Erotic': Politics, 'Arab Men,' and Sexual Revolution in Postdecolonization France, 1962–1974." *Journal of Modern History* 84, no. 1 (2012): 80–115.

Shephard, Ben. "'Becoming Planning Minded': The Theory and Practice of Relief, 1940–1945." *Journal of Contemporary History* 43, no. 3 (2008): 405–19.

Sherman, Taylor C. "From 'Grow More Food' to 'Miss a Meal': Hunger, Development, and the Limits of Post-Colonial Nationalism in India, 1947–1957." *South Asia* 36, no. 4 (2013): 571–88.

———. "Migration, Citizenship and Belonging in Hyderabad (Deccan), 1945–1956." *Modern Asian Studies* 45, no. 1 (2011): 81–107.

Sherman, Taylor C., William Gould, and Sarah Ansari, eds. *From Subjects to Citizens*. Cambridge, UK: Cambridge University Press, 2011.

Shilliam, Robbie. "Colonial Architecture or Relatable Hinterlands? Locke, Nandy, Fanon, and the Bandung Spirit." *Constellations* 23, no. 3 (2016): 425–35.

———. "What about Marcus Garvey? Race and the Transformation of Sovereignty Debate." *Review of International Studies* 32 (2006): 379–400.

Shimazu, Naoko. "Diplomacy as Theatre: Staging the Bandung Conference of 1955." *Modern Asian Studies* 48, no. 1 (2014): 225–52.

Shin, Gi-Wook, and Rennie Moon. "1919 in Korea: National Resistance and Contending Legacies." *Journal of Asian Studies* 78, no. 2 (2019): 399–408.

Shin, Seungyop. "Living with the Enemies: Japanese Imperialism, Protestant Christianity, and Marxist Socialism in Colonial Korea, 1919–1945." *Religions* 13, no. 9 (2022): 1–17.

Shipway, Martin. *Decolonization and Its Impact: A Comparative Approach to the End of the European Empires*. Oxford: Wiley, 2007.

———. "Madagascar on the Eve of Insurrection, 1944–47: The Impasse of a Liberal Colonial Policy." *Journal of Imperial & Commonwealth History* 24, no. 1 (1996): 72–100.

Shiroyama, Tomoko. *China during the Great Depression: Market, State, and the World Economy, 1929–1937*. Cambridge, MA: Harvard University Press, 2008.

Sidel, John T. *Republicanism, Communism, Islam: Cosmopolitan Origins of Revolution in Southeast Asia*. Ithaca, NY: Cornell University Press, 2021.

Siegel, Benjamin. "Modernizing Peasants and 'Master Farmers': Progressive Agriculture in Early Independent India." *Comparative Studies of South Asia, Africa and the Middle East* 37, no. 1 (2017): 64–85.

Silvestri, Michael. *Policing 'Bengali Terrorism' in India and the World.* Basingstoke, UK: Palgrave Macmillan, 2019.

Simonow, Joanna. "The Great Bengal Famine in Britain: Metropolitan Campaigning for Food Relief and the End of Empire, 1943–44." *Journal of Imperial & Commonwealth History* 48, no. 1 (2020): 168–97.

Simon, Scott. "Making Natives: Japan and the Creation of Indigenous Formosa." In *Japanese Taiwan: Colonial Rule and Its Contested Legacies,* edited by Andrew D. Morris, 75–92. London: Bloomsbury, 2015.

Simpson, Brad. "The Biafran Secession and the Limits of Self-Determination." *Journal of Genocide Research* 16, no. 2–3 (2014): 337–54.

———. "Self-Determination, Human Rights, and the End of Empire in the 1970s." *Humanity* 4, no. 2 (2013): 239–60.

———. "The United States and the Curious History of Self-Determination." *Diplomatic History* 36, no. 4 (2012): 675–94.

Simpson, Bradley R. *Economists with Guns: Authoritarian Development and U.S.-Indonesian Relations, 1960–1968.* Stanford, CA: Stanford University Press, 2010.

———. "Indonesia's 'Accelerated Modernization' and the Global Discourse of Development, 1960–1975." *Diplomatic History* 33, no. 3 (2009): 467–83.

———. "The United States, Indonesia, and the Ranking of Human Rights by the Carter Administration, 1976–1980." *International History Review* 31, no. 4 (2009): 798–826.

Sinanoglou, Penny. "British Plans for the Partition of Palestine, 1929–1938." *Historical Journal* 52, no. 1 (2009): 131–52.

Sinclair, Guy Fiti. *To Reform the World: International Organizations and the Making of Modern States.* Oxford: Oxford University Press, 2017.

Singh, Gajendra. *The Testimonies of Indian Soldiers and the Two World Wars: Between Self and Sepoy.* London: Bloomsbury, 2014.

Singh, Sinderpal. "From Delhi to Bandung: Nehru, 'Indian-ness' and 'Pan-Asian-ness.'" *South Asia: Journal of South Asian Studies* 34 (2011): 51–64.

Sinha, Mrinalina. *Specters of Mother India: The Global Restructuring of Empire.* Durham, NC: Duke University Press, 2006.

Sinha, Subir. "Lineages of the Developmental State: Transnationality and Village India, 1900–1965." *Comparative Studies in Society and History* 50, no. 1 (2008): 57–90.

Sisson, Richard, and Leo Rose. *War and Secession: Pakistan, India, and the Creation of Bangladesh.* Berkeley: University of California Press, 1990.

Skinner, Rob. *The Foundations of Anti-Apartheid: Liberal Humanitarians and Transnational Activists in Britain and the United States, c. 1919–64.* Basingstoke, UK: Palgrave Macmillan, 2010.

———. "Humanitarianism and Human Rights in Global Apartheid." In Konieczna and Skinner, *Global History of Anti-Apartheid,* 33–65.

———. "The Moral Foundations of British Anti-Apartheid Activism, 1946–1960." *Journal of Southern African Studies* 35, no. 2 (2009): 399–416.

Skocpol, Theda. *States and Social Revolutions: A Comparative Analysis of France, Russia, and China*. Cambridge, UK: Cambridge University Press, 2015.

Slate, Nico. *Colored Cosmopolitanism: The Shared Struggle for Freedom in the United States and India*. Cambridge, MA: Harvard University Press, 2012.

———. "'We the People of Color': Colored Cosmopolitanism and the Borders of Race." In Isaac et al., *Worlds of American Intellectual History*, 57–75.

Slavin, David H. "The French Left and the Rif War, 1924–25: Racism and the Limits of Internationalism." *Journal of Contemporary History* 26, no. 1 (1991): 5–32.

Slight, John. *The British Empire and the Hajj, 1865–1956*. Cambridge, MA: Harvard University Press, 2015.

Slobodian, Quinn. *Globalists: The End of Empire and the Birth of Neoliberalism*. Cambridge, MA: Harvard University Press, 2018.

Sluga, Glenda. *Internationalism in the Age of Nationalism*. Philadelphia: University of Pennsylvania Press, 2013.

———. "Remembering 1919: International Organizations and the Future of International Order." *International Affairs* 95, no. 1 (2019): 25–43.

Sluga, Glenda, and Patricia Clavin, eds. *Internationalisms: A Twentieth Century History*. Cambridge, UK: Cambridge University Press, 2016.

Smiley, Will. "Lawless Wars of Empire? The International Law of War in the Philippines, 1898–1903." *Law and History Review* 36, no. 3 (2018): 1–40.

Smith, Andrew. "African Dawn: Keïta Fodéba and the Imagining of National Culture in Guinea." *Historical Reflections/Réflexions Historiques* 43, no. 3 (2017): 102–21.

———. "Of Colonial Futures and an Administrative Alamo: Rethinking the Loi-Cadre (1956) in French West Africa." *French History* 28, no. 1 (2014): 92–113.

Smith, Leonard V. "Drawing Borders in the Middle East after the Great War: Political Geography and 'Subject Peoples.'" *First World War Studies* 7, no. 1 (2016): 5–21.

———. *Sovereignty at the Paris Peace Conference of 1919*. Oxford: Oxford University Press, 2018.

Smith, Neil. *American Empire: Roosevelt's Geographer and the Prelude to Globalization*. Berkeley: University of California Press, 2004.

Smith, R. B. "The Japanese Period in Indochina and the Coup of 9 March 1945." *Journal of Southeast Asian Studies* 9, no. 2 (1978): 268–301.

Smith, Simon C., ed. *Reassessing Suez 1956: New Perspectives on the Crisis and Its Aftermath*. Aldershot: Ashgate, 2008.

Smith, Timothy. "Major-General Sir Douglas Gracey: Peacekeeper or Peace Enforcer?" *Diplomacy & Statecraft* 21, no. 2 (2010): 226–39.

Snyder, Sarah B. "Bringing the Transnational in: Writing Human Rights into the International History of the Cold War." *Diplomacy & Statecraft* 24, no. 1 (2013): 100–16.

Sogge, David. "Angola: Reinventing Pasts and Futures." *Review of African Political Economy* 38, no. 127 (2011): 85–92.

Solarz, Marcin Wojciech. "'Third World': The 60th Anniversary of a Concept That Changed History." *Third World Quarterly* 33, no. 9 (2012): 1561–73.

Sorens, Jason, and William Ruger. "Globalisation and Intrastate Conflict: An Empirical Analysis." *Civil Wars* 16, no. 4 (2014): 381–401.

Soriano, Victor Fernández. "'*Travail et progrès*': Obligatory 'Educational' Labour in the Belgian Congo." *Journal of Contemporary History* 53, no. 2 (2018): 212–314.

Speek, Sven. "Ecological Concepts of Development? The Case of Colonial Zambia." In Hodge, Hödl, and Kopf, *Developing Africa*, 133–54.

Speich, Daniel. "The Kenyan Style of 'African Socialism': Developmental Knowledge Claims and the Explanatory Limits of the Cold War." *Diplomatic History* 33, no. 3 (2009): 449–63.

Spelling, Alex. "'Driven to Tears': Britain, CS Tear Gas, and the Geneva Protocol, 1969–1975." *Diplomacy & Statecraft* 27, no. 4 (2016): 701–25.

Srivastava, Neelam. *Italian Colonialism and Resistances to Empire, 1930–1970*. Basingstoke, UK: Palgrave Macmillan, 2018.

Stanard, Matthew G. *Selling the Congo: A History of European Pro-Empire Propaganda and the Making of Belgian Imperialism*. Lincoln: University of Nebraska Press, 2011.

Staniland, Paul. "Militia, Ideology, and the State." *Journal of Conflict Resolution* 59, no. 5 (2015): 770–93.

———. *Networks of Rebellion: Explaining Insurgent Cohesion and Collapse*. Ithaca, NY: Cornell University Press, 2014.

———. "States, Insurgents, and Wartime Political Orders." *Perspectives on Politics* 10, no. 2 (2012): 243–64.

Stanton, Jessica A. "Regulating Militias: Governments, Militias, and Civilian Targeting in Civil War." *Journal of Conflict Resolution* 59, no. 5 (2015): 899–923.

Staples, Amy L. S. *The Birth of Development: How the World Bank, Food and Agriculture Organization, and World Health Organization Have Changed the World*. Kent, OH: Kent State University Press, 2006.

———. "Seeing Diplomacy through Bankers' Eyes: The World Bank, the Anglo-Iranian Oil Crisis, and the Aswan High Dam." *Diplomatic History* 26, no. 3 (2002): 397–418.

Statiev, Alexander. *The Soviet Counterinsurgency in the Western Borderlands*. Cambridge, UK: Cambridge University Press, 2010.

———. "Soviet Partisan Violence against Soviet Civilians: Targeting Their Own." *Europe-Asia Studies* 66, no. 9 (2014): 1525–55.

Statler, Kathryn C. *Replacing France: The Origins of American Intervention in Vietnam*. Lexington: University Press of Kentucky, 2007.

Stavrianakis, Anna. "Controlling weapons Circulation in a Postcolonial Militarised World." *Review of International Studies* 45, no. 1 (2019): 57–76.

Steininger, Rolf. "'The Americans Are in a Hopeless Position': Britain and the War in Vietnam, 1964–65." *Diplomacy & Statecraft* 8, no. 3 (1997): 237–85.

Steinmetz, George, ed. *Sociology and Empire: The Imperial Entanglements of a Discipline*. Durham, NC: Duke University Press, 2013.

Stenner, David. "'Bitterness towards Egypt': The Moroccan Nationalist Movement, Revolutionary Cairo and the Limits of Anti-Colonial Solidarity." *Cold War History* 16, no. 2 (2016): 159–75.

———. "Centering the Periphery: Northern Morocco as a Hub of Transnational Anti-Colonial Activism, 1930–1943." *Journal of Global History* 11 (2016): 430–50.

———. *Globalizing Morocco: Transnational Activism and the Postcolonial State*. Stanford, CA: Stanford University Press, 2019.

Stewart, Frances. "Changing Approaches to Development since 1950: Drawing on Polanyi." *History of Political Economy* 50 (2018) annual supplement: 17–38.

Stewart, Geoffrey C. "Hearts, Minds and Cong Dan Vu: The Special Commissariat for Civic Action and Nation-Building in Ngo Dinh Diem's Vietnam, 1955–1957." *Journal of Vietnamese Studies* 6, no. 3 (2011): 44–100.

Steyn, Phia. "Oil Exploration in Colonial Nigeria c. 1903–58." *Journal of Imperial & Commonwealth History* 37 (2009): 249–74.

Stilz, Anna. "Decolonization and Self-Determination." *Social Philosophy and Policy* 32 (October 2015): 1–24.

———. "Settlement and the Right to Exclude." In *The Oxford Handbook of Global Justice*, edited by Thom Brooks, 429–49. Oxford: Oxford University Press, 2020.

———. *Territorial Sovereignty: A Philosophical Exploration*. Oxford: Oxford University Press, 2019.

———. "The Value of Self-Determination." *Oxford Studies in Political Philosophy* 2, no. 2 (2016): 98–127.

Stöckmann, Jan. *The Architects of International Relations: Building a Discipline, Designing the World, 1914–1940*. Cambridge, UK: Cambridge University Press, 2022.

———. "The First World War and the Democratic Control of Foreign Policy." *Past & Present* 249, no. 1 (2020): 121–66.

Stockwell, A. J. "Colonial Planning during World War Two: The Case of Malaya." *Journal of Imperial & Commonwealth History* 2, no. 3 (1974): 333–51.

———. "The Formation and First Years of the United Malays National Organization (U.M.N.O.)." *Modern Asian Studies* 11, no. 4 (1977): 481–513.

Stockwell, Sarah. *The British End of the British Empire*. Cambridge, UK: Cambridge University Press, 2018.

———. "Trade, Empire, and the Fiscal Context of Imperial Business during Decolonization." *Economic History Review* 57, no. 1 (2004): 142–60.

Stoler, Ann Laura. *Along the Archival Grain: Epistemic Anxieties and Colonial Common Sense*. Princeton, NJ: Princeton University Press, 2009.

———. *Duress: Imperial Durabilities in Our Times*. Durham, NC: Duke University Press, 2016.

———. "On Degrees of Imperial Sovereignty." *Public Culture* 18, no. 1 (2006): 125–46.

Stoler, Ann Laura, Carole McGranahan, and Peter C. Perdue, eds. *Imperial Formations*. Santa Fe: SAR Press, 2007.

Stolte, Carolien. "'Enough of the Great Napoleons!': Raj Mahendra Pratap's Pan-Asianist Projects (1929–1939)." *Modern Asian Studies* 46, no. 2 (2012): 402–23.

———. "'The People's Bandung': Local Anti-Imperialists on an Afro-Asian Stage." *Journal of World History* 30, no. 1–2 (2019): 125–56.

———. "Trade Union Networks and the Politics of Expertise in an Age of Afro-Asian Solidarity." *Journal of Social History* 53, no. 2 (2019): 331–47.

Stolte, Carolien, and Harald Fischer Tiné. "Imagining Asia in India: Nationalism and Internationalism (ca. 1905–1940)." *Comparative Studies in Society and History* 54, no. 1 (2012): 65–92.

Stovall, Tyler. "The Color Line behind the Lines: Racial Violence in France during the First World War." *American Historical Review* 103, no. 3 (1998): 739–69.

———. "Colour-Blind France? Colonial Workers during the First World War." *Race and Class* 35, no. 2 (1993): 35–55.

———. "The Fire This Time: Black American Expatriates and the Algerian War." *Yale French Studies* 98 (2000): 182–200.

——. *Paris Noir: African Americans in the City of Light*. New York: Houghton Mifflin, 1996.

——. *The Rise of the Paris Red Belt*. Berkeley: University of California Press, 1992.

Stovall, Tyler, and Georges van den Abbeele, eds. *French Civilization and Its Discontents: Orientalism, Colonialism, Race*. Lanham, MD: Lexington, 2003.

Strang, David. "From Dependency to Sovereignty: An Event History Analysis of Decolonization 1870–1987." *American Sociological Review* 55, no. 6 (1990): 846–60.

——. "Global Patterns of Decolonization, 1500–1987." *International Studies Quarterly* 35, no. 4 (1991): 429–54.

Strang, G. Bruce, ed. *Collision of Empires: Italy's Invasion of Ethiopia and Its International Impact*. London: Routledge, 2013.

Streets-Salter, Heather. *World War I in Southeast Asia: Colonialism and Anticolonialism in an Era of Global Conflict*. Cambridge, UK: Cambridge University Press, 2017.

Streets-Salter, Heather, and Trevor R. Getz. *Empires and Colonies in the Modern World: A Global Perspective*. New York: Oxford University Press, 2015.

Strick, Charlotte. "Belgian Firms, Development Plans and the Independence of the Belgian Congo." In Dimier and Stockwell, *Business of Development*, 99–126.

Strikwerda, Carl. "World War I in the History of Globalization." *Historical Reflections* 42, no. 3 (Winter 2016): 112–32.

Struck, Bernhard, Kate Ferris, and Jacques Revel. "Introduction: Space and Scale in Transnational History." *International History Review* 33, no. 4 (2011): 573–84.

Stuart, Mark. "A Party in Three Pieces: The Conservative Split over Rhodesian Oil Sanctions, 1965." *Contemporary British History* 16, no. 1 (2002): 51–88.

Stubbings, Matthew. "Free Trade Empire to Commonwealth of Nations: India, Britain and Imperial Preference, 1903–1932." *International History Review* 41, no. 2 (2019): 323–44.

Stubbs, Jonathan. "Making Headlines in a State of Emergency: The Case of the *Times of Cyprus*, 1955–1960." *Journal of Imperial & Commonwealth History* 45, no. 1 (2017): 70–92.

Stucki, Andreas. "'Frequent Deaths': The Colonial Development of Concentration Camps Reconsidered, 1868–1974." *Journal of Genocide Research* 20, no. 3 (2018): 305–26.

——. *Violence and Gender in Africa's Iberian Colonies: Feminizing the Portuguese and Spanish Empire, 1950s–1970s*. Basingstoke, UK: Palgrave Macmillan, 2019.

——. "Violence, Migration, and Gender in the Portuguese- and Spanish-Speaking World, 1945–2019." *Itinerario* 44, no. 1 (2020): 18–32.

Stur, Heather Marie. *Saigon at War: South Vietnam and the Global Sixties*. Cambridge, UK: Cambridge University Press, 2020.

Sun, Degang, and Yahia Zoubir. "Sentry Box in the Backyard: Analysis of French Military Bases in Africa." *Journal of Middle Eastern and Islamic Studies (in Asia)* 5 (2011): 82–104.

Sung Hee Ru, "Historical Geographies of Korea's Incorporation: The Rise of Underdeveloped and Modernized Colonial Port Cities." *Journal of Historical Geography* 17 (April 2022): 42–55.

Suri, Jeremy. *Power and Protest: Global Revolution and the Rise of Détente*. Cambridge, MA: Harvard University Press, 2003.

Surkis, Judith. "Ethics and Violence: Simone de Beauvoir, Djamila Boupacha and the Algerian War." *French Politics, Culture, and Society* 28, no. 2 (2010): 38–55.

Surun, Isabelle. "Une souveraineté à l'encre sympathetique? Souveraineté autochtone et appropriations territoriales dans les traités franco-africains au XIXe siècle." *Annales* 69, no. 2 (2014) 313–48.

Swan, Quito. "Blinded by Bandung: Illumining West Papua, Senegal, and the Black Pacific." *Radical History Review* 131 (May 2018): 58–81.

Swedenburg, Ted. *Memories of Revolt: The 1936–1939 Rebellion and the Palestinian National Past*. Fayetteville: University of Arkansas Press, 2003.

Szalontai, Balázs. "The 'Sole Legal Government of Vietnam': The Bao Dai Factor and Soviet Attitudes toward Vietnam 1947–1950." *Journal of Cold War Studies* 20 (2018): 3–56.

Taithe, Bertrand. "Biafra, Humanitarian Intervention and History." *Journal of Humanitarian Affairs* 3, no. 1 (2021): 68–78.

Takriti, Abdel Razzaq. "Colonial Coups and the War on Popular Sovereignty." *American Historical Review* 124, no. 3 (2019): 878–909.

———. *Monsoon Revolution: Republicans, Sultans, and Empires in Oman, 1965–1976*. Oxford: Oxford University Press, 2013.

Talbot, Ian, ed. *The Independence of India and Pakistan: New Approaches and Reflections*. Oxford: Oxford University Press, 2013.

———. "The Mountbatten Viceroyalty Reconsidered: Personality, Prestige and Strategic Vision in the Partition of India." In Kattan and Ranjan, *Breakup of India and Palestine*, 35–56.

Tanaka, Yuki, and Marilyn B. Young, eds. *Bombing Civilians: A Twentieth-Century History*. New York: New Press, 2009.

Tanielian, Melanie S. "Feeding the City: The Beirut Municipality and the Politics of Food during World War I." *International Journal of Middle East Studies* 46, no. 4 (2014): 737–58.

Tan, See Seng, and Amitav Acharya, eds. *Bandung Revisited: The Legacy of the 1955 Asian-African Conference for International Order*. Singapore: NUS Press, 2008.

Tauger, Mark B. "Entitlement, Shortage and the 1943 Bengal Famine: Another Look." *Journal of Peasant Studies* 31, no. 1 (2003): 45–72.

Taylor, Ian. "Mao Zedong's China and Africa." *Twentieth Century Communism* 15 (Fall 2018): 48–72.

Taylor, Ula Yvette. *The Veiled Garvey: The Life and Times of Amy Jacques Garvey*. Chapel Hill: University of North Carolina Press, 2002.

Telepneva, Natalia. *Cold War Liberation: The Soviet Union and the Collapse of the Portuguese Empire in Africa, 1961–1975*. Chapel Hill: University of North Carolina Press, 2021.

———. "The Military Training Camp: Co-Constructed Spaces—Experiences of PAIGC Guerrillas in Soviet Training Camps, 1961–1974." In Roth-Ey, *Socialist Internationalism*, 159–76.

———. "Saving Ghana's Revolution: The Demise of Kwame Nkrumah and the Evolution of Soviet Policy in Africa, 1966–1972." *Journal of Cold War Studies* 20, no. 4 (2019): 4–25.

Terretta, Meredith. "Cameroonian Nationalists Go Global: From Forest Maquis to a Pan-African Accra." *Journal of African History* 52, no. 2 (2010): 189–212.

———. "From Below and to the Left? Human Rights and Liberation Politics in Africa's Postcolonial Age." *Journal of World History* 24 (June 2015): 389–416.

———. "'In the Colonies, Black Lives Don't Matter': Legalism and Rights Claims across the French Empire." *Journal of Contemporary History* 53, no. 1 (2018): 12–37.

———. *Nation of Outlaws, State of Violence: Nationalism, Grassfields Tradition, and State Building in Cameroon*. Athens: University of Ohio Press, 2014.

Terretta, Meredith, and Benjamin N. Lawrance. "'Sons of the Soil,' Cause Lawyers, the Togo-Cameroun Mandates, and the Origins of Decolonization." *American Historical Review* 124, no. 5 (2019): 1709–14.

Thackeray, David. "Selling the Empire? Marketing and the Demise of the British World, c.1920–1960." *Journal of Imperial & Commonwealth History* 48, no. 4 (2020): 679–705.

Thakur, Vineet. "An Asian Drama: The Asian Relations Conference, 1947." *International History Review* 41, no. 3 (2019): 673–95.

Thaler, Kai M. "Ideology and Violence in Civil Wars: Theory and Evidence from Mozambique and Angola." *Civil Wars* 14, no. 4 (2012): 546–67.

Thénault, Sylvie. *Une drôle de justice. Les Magistrats dans la Guerre d'Algérie*. Paris: La Découverte, 2001.

———. "L'état d'urgence (1955–2005). De l'Algérie coloniale à la France contemporaine: destin d'une loi." *Le Mouvement Social* 218, no. 1 (2007): 63–78.

———. *Violence ordinaire dans l'Algérie coloniale. Camps, internements, assignations à résidence*. Paris: Odile Jacob, 2011.

Thomas, Charles G., and Toyin Falola. *Secession and Separatist Conflicts in Postcolonial Africa*. Calgary: University of Calgary Press, 2020.

Thomas, Deborah. *Exceptional Violence: Embodied Citizenship in Transnational Jamaica*. Durham, NC: Duke University Press, 2011.

Thomas, Lynn M. "Historicising Agency." *Gender & History* 28, no. 2 (2016): 324–39.

———. "Imperial Concerns and 'Women's Affairs': State Efforts to Regulate Clitoridectomy and Eradicate Abortion in Mero, Kenya, c. 1910–1950." *Journal of African History* 39, no. 1 (1998): 121–45.

Thomas, Martin. "Colonial Violence in Algeria and the Distorted Logic of State Retribution: The Setif Uprising of 1945." *Journal of Military History* 75, no. 1 (2011): 125–57.

———. *Empires of Intelligence: Security Services and Colonial Disorder after 1914*. Berkeley: University of California Press, 2008.

———. "The Gendarmerie, Information Collection, and Violence in French North Africa between the Wars." *Historical Reflections* 36, no. 2 (2010): 76–96.

———. "Resource War, Civil War, Rights War: Factoring Empire into French North Africa's Second World War." *War in History* 18, no. 2 (2011): 1–24.

———. *Violence and Colonial Order: Police, Workers, and Protest in the European Colonial Empires, 1918–1940*. Cambridge, UK: Cambridge University Press, 2012.

Thomas, Martin, and Gareth Curless, eds. *Decolonization and Conflict: Colonial Comparisons and Legacies*. London: Bloomsbury, 2017.

Thomas, Martin, and Gareth Curless, eds. *The Oxford Handbook of Late Colonial Insurgencies and Counter-Insurgencies*. Oxford: Oxford University Press, 2023.

Thomas, Martin, and Andrew S. Thompson, eds. *The Oxford Handbook of the Ends of Empire*. Oxford: Oxford University Press, 2018.

Thompson, Andrew S., ed. *Britain's Experience of Empire in the Twentieth Century*. Oxford: Oxford University Press, 2011.

———. "Humanitarian Principles Put to the Test: Challenges to Humanitarian Action during Decolonization." *International Review of the Red Cross* 97 (2016): 45–76.

———, ed. *Writing Imperial Histories*. Manchester, UK: Manchester University Press, 2013.

Thompson, Elizabeth. *Colonial Citizens: Republican Rights, Paternal Privilege, and Gender in French Syria and Lebanon*. New York: Columbia University Press, 1999.

———. *Justice Interrupted: The Struggle for Constitutional Government in the Middle East*. Cambridge, MA: Harvard University Press, 2013.

Thornton, Christy. "A Mexican International Economic Order? Tracing the Hidden Roots of the Charter of Economic Rights and Duties of States." *Humanity: International Journal of Human Rights, Humanitarianism, and Development* 9, no. 3 (2018): 389–421.

———. *Revolution in Development: Mexico and the Governance of the Global Economy*. Berkeley: University of California Press, 2021.

Throntveit, Trygve. "The Fable of the Fourteen Points: Woodrow Wilson and National Self-Determination." *Diplomatic History* 35 (June 2011): 445–81.

Thurber, Ches. *Between Mao and Gandhi: The Social Roots of Civil Resistance*. Cambridge, UK: Cambridge University Press, 2021.

Tilley, Helen, and Robert J. Gordon, eds. *Ordering Africa: Anthropology, European Imperialism and the Politics of Knowledge*. Manchester, UK: Manchester University Press, 2007.

Tinker, Hugh, ed. "Burma's Struggle for Independence: The Transfer of Power Thesis Re-Examined." *Modern Asian Studies* 20, no. 3 (1986): 461–81.

———. *Burma: The Struggle for Independence, 1944–1948*. Vol. 2: *From General Strike to Independence, 31 August 1946 to 4 January 1948*. London: HMSO, 1984.

Tischler, Julia. "Cementing Uneven Development: The Central African Federation and the Kariba Dam Scheme." *Journal of Southern African Studies* 40, no. 5 (2014): 1047–64.

Todd, David. *A Velvet Empire: French Informal Imperialism in the Nineteenth Century*. Princeton, NJ: Princeton University Press, 2021.

Tomlinson, B. R. "What Was the Third World?" *Journal of Contemporary History* 38, no. 2 (2003): 307–21.

Tomlinson, Jim. "The Commonwealth, the Balance of Payments and the Politics of International Poverty: British Aid Policy, 1958–1971." *Contemporary European History* 12, no. 4 (2003): 413–29.

Toner, Simon. "Imagining Taiwan: The Nixon Administration, the Developmental States, and South Vietnam's Search for Economic Viability, 1969–1975." *Diplomatic History* 41, no. 4 (2017): 772–98.

———. "'The Life and Death of Our Republic': Modernization, Agricultural Development and the Peasantry in the Mekong Delta in the Long 1970s." In James and Leake, *Decolonization and the Cold War*, 43–61.

Tønnesson, Stein. *The Vietnamese Revolution of 1945: Roosevelt, Ho Chi Minh and de Gaulle in a World at War*. London: Sage, 1991.

———. *Vietnam 1946: How the War Began*. Berkeley: University of California Press, 2010.

Toprani, Anand. "The French Connection: A New Perspective on the End of the Red Line Agreement, 1945–1948." *Diplomatic History* 36, no. 2 (2012): 261–99.

Torres-García, Ana. "US Diplomacy and the North African 'War of the Sands' (1963)." *Journal of North African Studies* 18, no. 2 (2013): 324–48.

Townshend, Charles. "The Defence of Palestine: Insurrection and Public Security, 1936–1939." *English Historical Review* 103 (1988): 919–49.

———. "Martial Law: Civil and Administrative Problems of Civil Emergency in Britain and the Empire, 1800–1940." *Historical Journal* 25, no. 1 (1982): 167–95.

Toye, Richard. "Developing Multilateralism: The Havana Charter and the Fight for the International Trade Organization, 1947–1948." *International History Review* 25, no. 2 (2003): 282–305.

Trecker, Max. *Red Money for the Global South: East-South Economic Relations in the Cold War*. London: Routledge, 2020.

Trentmann, Frank. *Empire of Things: How We Became a World of Consumers from the Fifteenth Century to the Twenty-First*. London: Allen Lane, 2016.

Trépied, Benoît. "Decolonization without Independence? Breaking with the Colonial in New Caledonia (1946–1975)." In Naylor, *France's Modernising Mission*, 59–84.

Tribe, Keith. "The Colonial Office and British Development Economics, 1940–60." *History of Political Economy* 50, annual supplement (2018): 97–113.

Trovão, Susana, and Sandra Araújo. "Ambivalent Relationships: The Portuguese State and the Indian Nationals in Mozambique in the Aftermath of the Goa Crisis, 1961–1971." *Itinerario* 44, no. 1 (April 2020): 106–39.

Tsokhas, Kosmas. "Dedominionization: The Anglo-Australian Experience, 1939–1945." *Historical Journal* 7, no. 4 (1994): 861–83.

Tsutsui, William M., and Timo Vuorisalo. "Japanese Imperialism and Marine Resources." In Laakkonen, Tucker, and Vuorisalo, *Long Shadows*, 251–74.

Tucker, David. "Colonial Sovereignty in Manchuria and Manchukuo." In Howland and White, *State of Sovereignty*, 75–93.

Tucker, Richard P. "Environmental Scars in Northeast India and Burma." In Laakkonen, Tucker, and Vuorisalo, *Long Shadows*, 117–34.

Tucker, Richard P., Tait Keller, J. R. McNeill, and Martin Schmid, eds. *Environmental Histories of the First World War*. Cambridge, UK: Cambridge University Press, 2018.

Tudor, Margot. "Gatekeepers to Decolonisation: Recentring the UN Peacekeepers on the Frontline of West Papua's Recolonisation, 1962–3." *Journal of Contemporary History* 57, no. 2 (2022): 293–316.

Tully, James. "Lineages of Contemporary Imperialism." In *Lineages of Empire: The Historical Roots of British Imperial Thought*, edited by Duncan Kelly. Oxford: Oxford University Press, 2009, published online.

Turner, Oliver. "'Finishing the Job': The UN Special Committee on Decolonization and the Politics of Self-Governance." *Third World Quarterly* 34, no. 7 (2013): 1193–1208.

Turpin, Frédéric. *De Gaulle, Pompidou et l'Afrique: Décoloniser et coopérer (1958–1974)*. Paris: Les Indes savantes, 2010.

Tusan, Michelle. *The British Empire and the Armenian Genocide: Humanitarianism and Imperial Politics from Gladstone to Churchill.* London: I. B. Tauris, 2017.

——. "'Crimes against Humanity': Human Rights, the British Empire, and the Origins of the Response to the Armenian Genocide." *Journal of American History* 119, no. 1 (2014): 47–77.

Twagira, Benjamin. "Embodied, Psychological and Gendered Trauma in Militarized Kampala (Uganda)." In *Gender and Trauma since 1900*, edited by Paula A. Michaels and Christina Twomey, 163–84. London: Bloomsbury, 2021.

Tyrrell, Ian, and Jay Sexton, eds. *Empire's Twin: U.S. Anti-Imperialism from the Founding Era to the Age of Terrorism.* Ithaca, NY: Cornell University Press, 2015.

Umar, Ahmad Rozky Mardhatillah. "Rethinking the Legacies of Bandung Conference: Global Decolonization and the Making of Modern International Order." *Asian Politics and Policy* 11, no. 3 (2019): 461–78.

Umoren, Imaobong D. "Anti-Fascism and the Development of Global Race Women, 1928-1945." *Callaloo* 39, no. 1 (2016): 151–65.

——. *Race Women Internationalists: Activist Intellectuals and Global Freedom Struggles.* Berkeley: University of California Press, 2018.

Unger, Corinna R. *International Development: A Postwar History.* London: Bloomsbury, 2018.

——. "Postwar European Development Aid: Defined by Decolonization, the Cold War, and European Integration?" In Macekura and Manela, *Development Century*, 240–60.

Üngör, Uğur Ümit. *Paramilitarism: Mass Violence in the Shadow of the State.* Oxford: Oxford University Press, 2020.

Valdez, Inés. "Association, Reciprocity, and Emancipation: A Transnational Account of the Politics of Global Justice." In Bell, *Empire, Race, and Global Justice*, 120–44.

Valentino, Benjamin, Paul Huth, and Dylan Balch-Lindsay. "'Draining the Sea': Mass Killing and Guerrilla Warfare." *International Organisation* 58, no. 2 (2004): 375–407.

Valette, Jacques. "Les opérations de l'automne 1947 en Haut-Tonkin: les incertitudes d'une stratégie." *Guerres Mondiales et Conflits Contemporains* 240, no. 4 (2010): 63–79.

van Beusekom, Monica M. *Negotiating Development: African Farmers and Colonial Experts at the Office du Niger, 1920-1960.* Oxford: Oxford University Press, 2002.

van Beusekom, Monica M., and Dorothy L. Hodgson. "Lessons Learned? Development Experiences in the Late Colonial Period." *Journal of African History* 41, no. 1 (2000): 29–33.

Van der Waag, Ian, and Albert Grundlingh, eds. *In Different Times: The War for Southern Africa, 1966-1989.* Stellenbosch: African Sun Media, 2019.

Van Dijk, Boyd. "'The Great Humanitarian': The Soviet Union, the International Committee of the Red Cross, and the Geneva Conventions of 1949." *Law and History Review* 37, no. 1 (2019): 209–35.

——. *Preparing for War: The Making of the 1949 Geneva Conventions.* Oxford: Oxford University Press, 2022.

Văn, Thuỷ Phạm. *Beyond Political Skin: Colonial to National Economies in Indonesia and Vietnam (1910s-1960s).* Singapore: Springer Nature, 2019.

Vargaftig, Nadia. "L'Empire des dictateurs: la propaganda coloniale sous Salazar et Mussolini (1922-1940)." In *Nouvelle histoire des colonisations européennes*

(XIXe–XXe siècles): Sociétés, Cultures, Politiques, edited by Amaury Lorin and Christelle Taraud, 65–76. Paris: Presses Universitaires de France, 2013.

Vaughan, Christopher. "The Politics of Regionalism and Federation in East Africa, 1958–1964." *Historical Journal* 62, no. 2 (2018): 519–40.

———. "Violence and Regulation in the Darfur–Chad Borderland, c. 1909–1956." *Journal of African History* 54, no. 2 (2013): 177–98.

Vaughan, Sarah. "Ethiopia, Somalia, and the Ogaden: Still a Running Sore at the Heart of the Horn of Africa." In *Secessionism in African Politics: Aspiration, Grievance, Performance, Disenchantment*, edited by Lotje de Vries, Pierre Englebert, and Mareike Schomerus, 91–123. Cham: Palgrave Macmillan, 2019.

Vaught, Seneca. "Du Bois as Diplomat: Race Diplomacy in *Foreign Affairs*, 1926–1945." *Journal of Race and Global Social Change* 1, no. 1 (2014): 4–29.

Velmet, Aro. *Pasteur's Empire: Bacteriology and Politics in France, Its Colonies, and the World*. Oxford: Oxford University Press, 2020.

Venn, Fiona. "Oleaginous Diplomacy: Oil, Anglo-American Relations and the Lausanne Conference, 1922–23." *Diplomacy & Statecraft* 20, no. 3 (2009): 414–33.

Venosa, Robert D. "Liberal Internationalism, Decolonization, and International Accountability at the United Nations: The British Dilemma." *Journal of Contemporary History* 57, no. 2 (2022): 242–67.

Veracini, Lorenzo. "Introduction: Settler Colonialism as a Distinct Mode of Domination." In Cavanagh and Veracini, *Routledge Handbook of the History of Settler Colonialism*, 1–8.

———. *The World Turned Inside Out: Settler Colonialism as a Political Idea*. London: Verso, 2021.

Vince, Natalya. *The Algerian War, the Algerian Revolution*. London: Bloomsbury, 2020.

———. *Our Fighting Sisters: Nation, Memory and Gender in Algeria, 1954–2012*. Manchester, UK: Manchester University Press, 2015.

Vinson, Robert Trent. "Up from Slavery and down with Apartheid! African-Americans and Black South Africans against the Global Color Line." *Journal of American Studies* 52, no. 2 (2018): 297–329.

Vitalis, Robert. "The Graceful and Generous Liberal Gesture: Making Racism Invisible in American International Relations." *Millennium* 29, no. 2 (2000): 331–56.

———. "The Midnight Ride of Kwame Nkrumah and Other Fables of Bandung (Bandoong)." *Humanity* 4, no. 2 (2013): 261–88.

———. *White World Order, Black Power Politics: The Birth of American International Relations*. Ithaca, NY: Cornell University Press, 2015.

Viterna, Jocelyn. "Pulled, Pushed, and Persuaded: Explaining Women's Mobilization into the Salvadorian Guerrilla Army." *American Journal of Sociology* 112, no. 1 (2006): 1–45.

von Bülow, Mathilde. "Beyond the Cold War: American Labor, Algeria's Independence Struggle, and the Rise of the Third World (1954–62)." *Journal of Social History* 53, no. 2 (2019): 354–86.

Wagner, Florian. *Colonial Internationalism and the Governmentality of Empire, 1893–1982*. Cambridge, UK: Cambridge University Press, 2022.

Wagner, Kim A. "Savage Warfare, Violence and the Rule of Colonial Difference in Early British Counterinsurgency." *History Workshop Journal* 85 (Spring 2018): 217–37.

Wagner, Kim A. "'Treading upon Fires': The 'Mutiny'-Motif and Colonial Anxieties in British India." *Past & Present* 218, no. 1 (2013): 159–97.

Walker, Lydia. "Decolonization in the 1960s: On Legitimate and Illegitimate Nationalist Claims-Making." *Past & Present* 242 (February 2019): 227–64.

Waller, Richard. "Rebellious Youth in Colonial Africa." *Journal of African History* 47, no. 1 (2006): 77–92.

Wall, Irwin M. *France, the United States, and the Algerian War*. Berkeley: University of California Press, 2001.

Walsh, Fionnuala. *Irish Women and the Great War*. Cambridge, UK: Cambridge University Press, 2020.

Walton, Calder. "British Intelligence and the Mandate of Palestine: Threats to British National Security Immediately after the Second World War." *Intelligence & National Security* 23, no. 4 (2008): 435–62.

Ward, Stuart, ed. *British Culture and the End of Empire*. Manchester, UK: Manchester University Press, 2001.

———. "The European Provenance of Decolonization." *Past and Present* 230 (February 2016): 227–60.

———. *Untied Kingdom: A Global History of the End of Britain*. Cambridge, UK: Cambridge University Press, 2023.

Ward, Stuart, and Astrid Rasch, eds. *Embers of Empire in Brexit Britain*. London: Bloomsbury, 2019.

Warner, Geoffrey. "Nixon, Kissinger and the Breakup of Pakistan, 1971." *International Affairs* 81, no. 5 (2005): 1097–118.

Warson, Joanna. "A Transnational Decolonisation: Britain, France and the Rhodesian Problem, 1965–1969." In *Francophone Africa at Fifty*, edited by Tony Chafer and Alexander Keese, 171–86. Manchester, UK: Manchester University Press, 2013.

Watenpaugh, Keith David. *Being Modern in the Middle East: Revolution, Nationalism, Colonialism, and the Arab Middle Class*. Princeton, NJ: Princeton University Press, 2006.

———. *Bread from Stones: The Middle East and the Making of Modern Humanitarianism*. Berkeley: University of California Press, 2015.

———. "The League of Nations' Rescue of Armenian Genocide Survivors and the Making of Modern Humanitarianism, 1920–1927." *American Historical Review* 115, no. 5 (2010): 1315–39.

Watts, Carl. "Britain, the Old Commonwealth, and the Problem of Rhodesian Independence, 1964–65." *Journal of Imperial & Commonwealth History* 36, no. 1 (2008): 75–99.

———. "Killing Kith and Kin: The Viability of British Military Intervention in Rhodesia, 1964–5." *Twentieth Century British History* 16 (2005): 382–415.

Weber, Heloise. "The Political Significance of Bandung for Development: Challenges, Contradictions and Struggles for Justice." In Pham and Shilliam, *Meanings of Bandung*, 153–64.

Weber, Heloise, and Poppy Winanti. "The 'Bandung Spirit' and Solidarist Internationalism." *Australian Journal of International Affairs* 70, no. 4 (2016): 391–406.

Webster, Wendy. "Maintaining Racial Boundaries: Greater Britain in the Second World War and Beyond." In Pedersen and Ward, *Break-Up of Greater Britain*, 22–40.

——. *Mixing It: Diversity in World War II Britain.* Oxford: Oxford University Press, 2018.

Weisbrode, Kenneth. "International Administration between the Wars: A Reappraisal." *Diplomacy & Statecraft*, 20, no. 1 (2009): 30–49.

Weitz, Eric D. "From the Vienna to the Paris System: International Politics and the Entangled Histories of Human Rights, Forced Deportations, and Civilizing Missions." *American Historical Review* 113, no. 5 (2008): 1313–43.

——. "Self-Determination: How a German Enlightenment Idea Became the Slogan of National Liberation and a Human Right." *American Historical Review* 20, no. 2 (2015): 462–96.

——. *A World Divided: The Global Struggle for Human Rights in the Age of Nation-States.* Princeton, NJ: Princeton University Press, 2019.

Wenzlhuemer, Roland. *Doing Global History: An Introduction in Six Concepts.* London: Bloomsbury, 2020.

Wertheim, Stephen. "The League of Nations: Retreat from International Law?" *Journal of Global History* 7, no. 2 (2012): 210–32.

——. "The League That Wasn't: American Designs for a Legalist-Sanctionist League of Nations and the Intellectual Origins of International Organization, 1914–1920." *Diplomatic History* 35, no. 5 (2011): 797–836.

——. *Tomorrow the World: The Birth of US Global Supremacy.* Cambridge, MA: Belknap Press, 2020.

Westad, Odd Arne. *The Global Cold War: Third World Interventions and the Making of Our Times.* Cambridge, UK: Cambridge University Press, 2005.

——. "The Third World Revolutions." In Motadel, *Revolutionary World*, 175–91.

Westermann, Andrea. "When Consumer Citizens Spoke Up: West Germany's Early Dealings with Plastic Waste." *Contemporary European History* 22, no. 3 (2013): 477–98.

West, Harry G. "Girls with Guns: Narrating the Experience of War of Frelimo's 'Female Detachment.'" *Anthropological Quarterly* 73, no. 4 (2000): 180–94.

Wheatley, Natasha. "Mandatory Interpretation: Legal Hermeneutics and the New International Order in Arab and Jewish Petitions to the League of Nations." *Past & Present* 27 (May 2015): 206–35.

——. "Spectral Legal Personality in Interwar International Law: On New Ways of Not Being a State." *Law And History Review* 35, no. 3 (2017): 753–87.

Whipple, Amy. "Revisiting the 'Rivers of Blood' Controversy: Letters to Enoch Powell." *Journal of British Studies* 48, no. 3 (2009): 717–35.

White, Benjamin Thomas. "Refugees and the Definition of Syria, 1920–1939." *Past & Present* 235 (May 2017): 141–78.

White, Christine. "Peasant Mobilization and Anti-Colonial Struggle in Vietnam: The Rent Reduction Campaign of 1953." *Journal of Peasant Studies* 10, no. 4 (1983): 187–213.

Whitehead, Mark, Rhys Jones, Rachel Lilley, Jessica Pycett, and Rachel Howell. *Neuroliberalism: Behavioural Government in the Twenty-First Century.* London: Routledge, 2018.

White, Luise. "Civic Virtue, Young Men, and the Family: Conscription in Rhodesia, 1974–1980." *International Journal of African Historical Studies* 37, no. 1 (2004): 103–21.

White, Luise. *Fighting and Writing: The Rhodesian Army at War and Postwar*. Durham, NC: Duke University Press, 2021.

———. "'Heading for the Gun': Skills and Sophistication in an African Guerrilla War." *Comparative Studies in Society and History* 51, no. 2 (2009): 236–59.

———. *Unpopular Sovereignty: Rhodesian Independence and African Decolonization*. Chicago: University of Chicago Press, 2015.

———. "What Does It Take to Be a State? Sovereignty and Sanctions in Rhodesia, 1965–1980." In Howland and White, *State of Sovereignty*, 148–68.

White, Luise, and Miles Larmer. "Mobile Soldiers and the Un-National Liberation of Southern Africa." *Journal of Southern African Studies* 40, no. 6 (2014): 1271–74.

White, Nicholas J. "The Business and the Politics of Decolonization: The British Experience in the Twentieth Century." *Economic History Review* 53, no. 3 (2000): 544–64.

———. "Reconstructing Europe through Rejuvenating Empire: The British, French, and Dutch Experiences Compared." *Past & Present* 210 Supplement 6 (2011): 211–36.

———. "Thinking Outside 'the Box': Decolonization and Containerization." In Petersson, Tenold, and White, *Shipping and Globalization in the Post-War Era*. Basingstoke, UK: Palgrave Macmillan, 2019, 67–99.

White, Nicholas J., J. M. Barwise, and Shakila Yacob. "Economic Opportunity and Strategic Dilemma in Colonial Development: Britain, Japan and Malaya's Iron Ore, 1920s to 1950s." *International History Review* 42, no. 2 (2020): 424–46.

White, Owen. *The Blood of the Colony: Wine and the Rise and Fall of French Algeria*. Cambridge, MA: Harvard University Press, 2021.

Whittaker, Hannah. "Frontier Security in North East Africa: Conflict and Colonial Development on the Margins, c. 1930–60." *Journal of African History* 58, no. 3 (2017): 381–402.

———. "Legacies of Empire: State Violence and Collective Punishment in Kenya's North Eastern Province, c. 1963–Present." *Journal of Imperial & Commonwealth History* 43, no. 4 (2015): 641–57.

Whyte, Jessica. "The 'Dangerous Concept of the Just War': Decolonization, Wars of National Liberation, and the Additional Protocols to the Geneva Conventions." *Humanity* 9, no. 3 (2018): 313–41.

Wichhart, Stefanie. "The Formation of the Arab League and the United Nations, 1944–5." *Journal of Contemporary History* 54, no. 2 (2019): 328–46.

Wilder, Gary. *Freedom Time: Negritude, Decolonization, and the Future of the World*. Durham, NC: Duke University Press, 2015.

———. *The French Imperial Nation-State: Negritude and Colonial Humanism between the Two World Wars*. Chicago: University of Chicago Press, 2005.

———. "Panafricanism and the Republican Political Sphere." In *The Color of Liberty: Histories of Race in France*, edited by Sue Peabody and Tyler Stovall, 237–58. Durham, NC: Duke University Press, 2003.

Williams, Christian A. "Education in Exile: International Scholarships, Cold War Politics, and Conflicts among SWAPO Members in Tanzania, 1961–1968." In Alexander, McGregor, and Tendi, *Transnational Histories*, 123–39.

———. *National Liberation in Postcolonial Southern Africa: A Historical Ethnography of SWAPO's Exile Camps*. Cambridge, UK: Cambridge University Press, 2015.

Williams, Elizabeth M. *The Politics of Race in Britain and South Africa: Black British Solidarity and the Anti-Apartheid Struggle.* London: I. B. Tauris, 2017.

Willis, Justin. "Chieftaincy." In Parker and Reid, *Oxford Handbook of Modern African History,* 208–23.

———. "Tribal Gatherings: Colonial Spectacle, Native Administration and Local Government in Condominium Sudan." *Past & Present* 211 (May 2011): 243–68.

Willis, Justin, Gabrielle Lynch, and Nic Cheeseman. "Voting, Nationhood, and Citizenship in Late-Colonial Africa." *Historical Journal* 61, no. 4 (2018): 1113–35.

Wilmington, Martin W. "The Middle East Supply Centre: A Reappraisal." *Middle East Journal* 6, no. 2 (1952): 144–66.

Wilson, Chris. "Petitions and Pathways to the Asylum in British Mandate Palestine, 1930–1948." *Historical Journal* 62, no. 2 (2019): 451–71.

Wilson, K. B. "On Truths about Truth in Mozambique's Liberation Struggle." *Journal of Southern African Studies* 43, no. 4 (2017): 846–48.

Witte, Ludo De. "The Suppression of the Congo Rebellions and the Rise of Mobutu, 1963–5." *International History Review* 39, no. 1 (2017): 107–25.

Wixforth, Harald. "The Economic Consequences of the First World War." *Contemporary European History* 11, no. 3 (2002): 477–88.

Wolfe, Patrick. "Land, Labor, Difference: Elementary Structures of Race." *American Historical Review* 106, no. 3 (2001): 866–905.

———. "Settler Colonialism and the Elimination of the Native." *Journal of Genocide Research* 8, no. 4 (2006): 387–409.

Wood, Elisabeth J. "Variation in Sexual Violence during War." *Politics and Society* 34, no. 3 (2006): 307–41.

Wood, R. M. "From Loss to Looting? Battlefield Costs and Rebel Incentives for Violence." *International Organization* 68, no. 4 (2014): 979–99.

Wood, Sally Percival. "Retrieving the Bandung Conference . . . Moment by Moment." *Journal of Southeast Asian Studies* 43, no. 3 (2012): 523–30.

Wood, Sarah J. "How Empires Make Peripheries: Overseas France in Contemporary History." *Contemporary European History* 28 (2019): 434–45.

Worboys, Michael. "The Discovery of Colonial Malnutrition between the Wars." In *Imperial Medicine and Indigenous Societies,* edited by David Arnold, 208–25. Manchester, UK: Manchester University Press, 1988.

Worby, Eric. "'Discipline without Oppression': Sequence, Timing, and Marginality in Southern Rhodesia's Post-War Development Scheme." *Journal of African History* 41, no. 1 (2000): 101–25.

Wu, Jialin Christina. "Private Lives, Public Spheres: Contesting Child Marriage at the Age of Independence in British Malaya, 1950." *Gender and History* 29, no. 3 (2017): 658–74.

Wu, Judy Tzu-Chun. "Journeys for Peace and Liberation: Third World Internationalism and Radical Orientalism during the U.S. War in Vietnam." *Pacific Historical Review* 76, no. 4 (2007): 575–84.

———. *Radicals on the Road: Internationalism, Orientalism, and Feminism during the Vietnam Era.* Ithaca, NY: Cornell University Press, 2013.

Wyrtzen, Jonathan. *Making Morocco: Colonial Intervention and the Politics of Identity.* Ithaca, NY: Cornell University Press, 2018.

Wyrtzen, Jonathan. *Worldmaking in the Long Great War: How Local and Colonial Struggles Shaped the Modern Middle East*. New York: Columbia University Press, 2022.

Wyss, Marco. *Postcolonial Security: Britain, France, and West Africa's Cold War*. Oxford: Oxford University Press, 2021.

———. "The United States, Britain, and Cold War Military Assistance to Nigeria." *Historical Journal* 61, no. 4 (2018): 1065–87.

Yaqub, Salim. *Containing Arab Nationalism: The Eisenhower Doctrine and the Middle East*. Chapel Hill: University of North Carolina Press, 2004.

Ydesen, Christian, and Kevin Myers. "The Imperial Welfare State? Decolonisation, Education, and Professional Interventions on Immigrant Children in Birmingham, 1948–1971." *Paedagogica Historica* 52, no. 5 (2016): 453–66.

Yellen, Jeremy A. *The Greater East Asia Co-Prosperity Sphere: When Total Empire Met Total War*. Ithaca, NY: Cornell University Press, 2019.

Yeo, Andrew, and Stacie Pettyjohn. "Bases of Empire? The Logic of Overseas U.S. Military Base Expansion, 1870–2016." *Comparative Strategy* 40, no. 1 (2021): 18–35.

Yifeng, Chen. "Bandung, China, and the Making of World Order in East Asia." In Eslava, Fakhri, and Nesiah, *Bandung, Global History, and International Law*, 177–95.

Yoo, Theodore Jun. *It's Madness: The Politics of Mental Health in Colonial Korea*. Berkeley: University of California Press, 2016.

Young, Alden. *Transforming Sudan: Decolonization, Economic Development, and State Formation*. Cambridge, UK: Cambridge University Press, 2017.

Young, Cynthia A. *Soul Power: Culture, Radicalism, and the Making of a U.S. Third World Left*. Durham, NC: Duke University Press, 2006.

Young, Louise. "When Fascism Met Empire in Japanese-Occupied Manchuria." *Journal of Global History* 12, no. 2 (2017): 274–96.

Young, Robert J. C. "Postcolonialism: From Bandung to the Tricontinental." *Historein* 5 (2006): 11–21.

Youngseo, Baik. "1919 in Dynamic East Asia: March First and May Fourth as a Starting Point for Revolution." *Chinese Studies in History* 52, no. 3–4 (2019): 277–91.

Yuh, Leighanne, and Claudia Soddu. "The Nationalist Critique of Female Double Suicide in Korea." *International Journal of Korean History* 27, no. 2 (2022): 1–29.

Zaalberg, Thijs Brocades, and Bart Luttikhuis, eds. *Empire's Violent End: Comparing Dutch, British, and French Wars of Decolonization, 1945–1962*. Ithaca, NY: Cornell University Press, 2022.

Zaccaria, Massimo. "Italian Colonialism in Africa as a Connected System: Institutions, Men and Colonial Troops." *Journal of Imperial & Commonwealth History* 47, no. 4 (2019): 718–41.

Zahra, Tara. *The Lost Children: Reconstructing Europe's Families after World War II*. Cambridge, MA: Harvard University Press, 2011.

———. "'The Psychological Marshall Plan': Displacement, Gender, and Human Rights after World War II." *Central European History* 44, no. 1 (2011): 37–62.

Zamindar, Vazira Fazila-Yacoobali. *The Long Partition and the Making of Modern South Asia: Refugees, Boundaries, Histories*. New York: Columbia University Press, 2007.

Zamir, Meir. "'Bid' for *Altalena*: France's Covert Action in the 1948 War in Palestine." *Middle Eastern Studies* 46, no. 1 (2010): 17–58.

Zanasi, Margherita. "Exporting Development: The League of Nations and Republican China." *Comparative Studies in Society and History* 49, no. 1 (2006): 143–69.

Zehfuss, Maja. "Killing Civilians: Thinking the Practice of War." *British Journal of Politics and International Relations* 14, no. 3 (2012): 423–40.

Zhai, Qiang. "Transplanting the Chinese Model: Chinese Military Advisers and the First Vietnam War, 1950–1954." *Journal of Military History* 57, no. 4 (1993): 689–715.

Zhou, Taomo. "China and the Thirtieth of September Movement." *Indonesia* 98 (October 2014): 29–58.

——. "Global Reporting from the Third World: The Afro-Asian Journalists' Association, 1963–1974." *Critical Asian Studies* 51, no. 2 (2019): 166–97.

——. *Migration in the Time of Revolution: China, Indonesia, and the Cold War.* Ithaca, NY: Cornell University Press, 2019.

Zierler, David. "Going Global after Vietnam: The End of Agent Orange and the Rise of an International Environmental Regime." In Bsumek, Kinkela, and Lawrence, *Nation-States and the Global Environment*, 97–114.

Zimmerman, Angela. *Alabama in Africa: Booker T. Washington, the German Empire, and the Globalization of the New South.* Princeton, NJ: Princeton University Press, 2010.

Zinoman, Peter. *The Colonial Bastille: A History of Imprisonment in Vietnam, 1862–1940.* Berkeley: University of California Press, 2001.

Zwarte, Ingrid de. *The Hunger Winter: Fighting Famine in the Occupied Netherlands, 1944–1945.* Cambridge, UK: Cambridge University Press, 2020.

Zweiniger-Barqielowska, Ina. *Austerity in Britain: Rationing, Controls, and Consumption, 1939–1955.* Oxford: Oxford University Press, 2002.

A NOTE ON THE TYPE

THIS BOOK has been composed in Miller, a Scotch Roman typeface designed by Matthew Carter and first released by Font Bureau in 1997. It resembles Monticello, the typeface developed for The Papers of Thomas Jefferson in the 1940s by C. H. Griffith and P. J. Conkwright and reinterpreted in digital form by Carter in 2003.

Pleasant Jefferson ("P. J.") Conkwright (1905–1986) was Typographer at Princeton University Press from 1939 to 1970. He was an acclaimed book designer and AIGA Medalist.

The ornament used throughout this book was designed by Pierre Simon Fournier (1712–1768) and was a favorite of Conkwright's, used in his design of the *Princeton University Library Chronicle*.